enigma
books

Hitler and His Generals

Military Conferences 1942-1945

**The First Complete Stenographic Record
of the Military Situation Conferences,
from Stalingrad to Berlin**

English edition Introduction by
Gerhard L. Weinberg

Original edition Preface and Notes by
Helmut Heiber

Editorial Advisor English edition
David M. Glantz

Enigma Books
New York

Published in the United States by:

Enigma Books
580 Eighth Avenue, New York, NY 10018 www.enigmabooks.com

"Die Originalausgabe ist eine Veröffentlichung des Instituts für Zeitgeschichte in München und erschien unter dem Titel

HITLERS LAGEBESPRECHUNGEN
Die Protokollfragmente seiner militärischen Konferenzen 1942-1945

© 1962 by Deutsche Verlags-Anstalt GmbH, Stuttgart; 1984 by R. Oldenbourg Verlag GmbH, München"
©*Der Spiegel Verlag* 1966
©Enigma Books 2003
©Enigma Books 2004
Translated by Roland Winter, Krista Smith, and Mary Beth Friedrich
First English-language edition
ISBN 1-929631-28-6

Third Printing
Printed in the United States of America
Library of Congress Cataloging-in-Publication Data

[Hitlers Lagebesprechungen.]
Hitler and his generals : military conferences 1942-1945 / English edition introduction by Gerhard L. Weinberg ; original edition introduction and notes by Helmut Heiber; English edition edited by David M. Glantz; translated by Roland Winter, Krista Smith. — 1st English language ed.

p. ; cm.

Includes index.

ISBN: 1-929631-28-6

1. Hitler, Adolf, 1889-1945. 2. World War, 1939-1945—Sources. 3. World War, 1939-1945—Communications—Germany. I. Weinberg, Gerhard L. II. Heiber, Helmut, 1924- III. Glantz, David M. IV. Winter, Roland. V. Smith, Krista. VI. Title: Hitlers Lagebesprechungen.

D743.5 .H514 2002
940.53

Hitler and His Generals

The original edition (1962) is a publication of the
Institut für Zeitgeschichte, Munich, and was published as:

Hitlers Lagebesprechungen

Die Protokollfragmente seiner militärischen Konferenzen 1942-1945.
Herausgegeben von Helmut Heiber.

Translated by Roland Winter, Krista Smith, and Mary Beth Friedrich

TABLE OF CONTENTS

Introduction by Gerhard L. Weinberg i
Preface by Helmut Heiber xi
Maps xxxv

Conference Transcripts

1942 3
Evening Situation Report, December 1, 1942 4
Midday Situation Conference, December 12, 1942,
    in the Wolfsschanze 18

1943 56
Midday Situation Conference, February 1, 1943, at the
    Wolfsschanze 57
Evening Situation Report, March 4, 1943, at the Wehrwolf 71
Midday Situation Report, March 5, 1943, at the Wehrwolf 82
Mid-March to March 21, 1943 99
Fragment of an Evening Situation Conference, between
    March 12 and 15, 1943, probably at the Wolfsschanze ... 100
Midday Situation Report, March 21, 1943, at the Berghof ... 113
Meeting between the Führer and Field Marshal Keitel,
    May 19, 1943 119
Meeting between the Führer and Sonderführer
    v. Neurath, May 20, 1943 132
Midday Situation Report, May 20 or 21, 1943 144
Meeting of the Führer with Field Marshal Keitel and
    General Zeitzler, June 8, 1943, in the Berghof 155
Midday Situation Report, July 25, 1943 166
Evening Situation Report, July 25, 1943 198
Second Evening Situation Report, July 25, 1943 212
Midday Situation Report, July 26, 1943 218
Meeting of the Führer with Field Marshal von Kluge,
    July 26, 1943. 252
Excerpt from an Evening Situation Report, probably
    October 3, 1943 267
Midday Situation Report, October 4, 1943,
    at the Wolfsschanze 268
Evening Situation Report, October 26, 1943,
    at the Wolfsschanze 276

Midday Situation Report, November 19, 1943 285
Evening Situation Report, probably December 20, 1943 307
End of the Evening Situation Report, December 21, 1943 . . . 322
Midday Situation Report, December 22, 1943
    at the Wolfsschanze 322
Meeting of the Führer with General Zeitzler,
    December 27, 1943 332
Meeting of the Führer with General Jodl and, joining later,
    General Zeitzler, December 28, 1943 346
Meeting of the Führer with General Zeitzler,
    December 29, 1943 371
Meeting of the Führer with Field Marshal von Küchler,
    December 30, 1943 at the Wolfsschanze. 375

1944 385
Adolf Hitler and the National Socialist Commanding
    Officer (NSFO) 385
Meeting of the Führer with General Reinecke, January 7,
    1944, in the Wolfsschanze 387
Midday Situation Report, January 28, 1944 401
Telephone Conversation Between the Führer and
    General Zeitzler, January 28, 1944 416
Excerpt from a Situation Report, presumably
    from March 1944 418
Midday Situation Report, April 6, 1944 419
Evening Situation Report, May 18, 1944, at the Berghof 432
Evening Situation Report, June 18, 1944, at the Berghof 437
Meeting of the Führer with Colonel General Jodl,
    July 31, 1944, in the Wolfsschanze 444
Meeting of the Führer with Lieutenant General Westphal
    and Lieutenant General Krebs, August 31, 1944,
    at the Wolfsschanze 464
Midday Situation Conference, September 1, 1944,
    at the Wolfsschanze 469
Evening Situation Report, September 17, 1944,
    at the Wolfsschanze 492
Midday Situation Report, November 6, 1944 507
The Führer's Speech to Division Commanders,
    December 12, 1944, at Adlerhorst 533
Meeting of the Führer with Colonel General Blaskowitz,
    December 28, 1944, at Adlerhorst 543

The Führer's Speech to Division Commanders,
    December 28, 1944, at Adlerhorst 554
Meeting of the Führer with Major General Thomale,
    December 29, 1944, at Adlerhorst 568

1945 585
Concluding Portion of a Midday Situation Report,
    presumably, January 9, 1945 585
Evening Situation Report, January 9, 1945, in Adlerhorst . . . 591
Midday Situation Report, January 10, 1945, at Adlerhorst . . . 596
Midday Situation Report, January 27, 1945, in Berlin 618
Evening Situation Report, February 24, 1945, in Berlin 667
Fragment of a Midday Situation Report, presumably
    March 1, 1945 675
Fragment of a Midday Situation Report, presumably
    March 2, 1945 677
Fragment of a Midday Situation Report, presumably
    on March 2, 1945 683
Final Part of the Midday Situation Report, March 2, 1945 . . . 685
Fragment of a Midday Situation Report, presumably
    March 10, 1945 694
Evening Situation Report, March 23, 1945, in the Führer's
    apartment in Berlin 697
Hitler's Situation Reports, April 23, 25, and 27 717
2nd Situation Report, April 23, 1945 718
3rd Situation Report, April 23, 1945 719
Wednesday, April 25, 1945 720
2nd Situation Report, April 25, 1945 725
Friday, April 27, 1945 726
2nd Situation Report, April 27, 1945 731
3rd Situation Report, April 27, 1945 733

List of Participants 739
Introduction to the Notes by Helmut Heiber 755
Notes 759
Bibliography 1128
Index 1140
Acknowledgements 1159

INTRODUCTION

by *Gerhard L. Weinberg*

I n the fall of 1942 a crisis of confidence developed in the German leadership. One of the results of that crisis was the creation of the source of which the known surviving remnants are published in this book. What was that crisis and why did it produce such an outcome?

The general long-term aim of the government Adolf Hitler hoped to establish in Germany and was enabled to create when appointed chancellor in 1933 was global conquest.[1] Such a project in his eyes required a dictatorially ruled one-party state at home, a people imbued with racial awareness, and a series of wars. From 1933 domestic requirements dominated German internal policies and politics; the expected wars framed the rearmament program. It was assumed that a preliminary war against Czechoslovakia would be easy and short. There would follow the war against France and Britain, a war that was expected to be very hard—that was where Germany had had problems in the war of 1914-18. The rearmament of the early and mid-1930s, therefore, was concentrated on weapons systems designed for the war in the West.

Victory over France and Britain was believed to be the necessary preliminary in securing the western border of Germany for the war in the East against the Soviet Union. That conflict, however, was always expected to be easy: the Germans had defeated Russia in the last war in spite of having to maintain enormous forces on the Western Front; and in the meantime Russia, by what Hitler considered a stroke of good fortune for Germany, had fallen under the control of the Bolsheviks, so that now the Slavic people he and most Germans believed to be inferior were also ruled by incompetents. No weapons systems needed to be developed for that war (and none would be until the Germans discovered in 1941 that they had miscalculated).

The quick conquest of the Soviet Union would provide not only vast lands for German agricultural settlements but also the raw materials, especially the oil, needed for the subsequent war against the United States, which, with its mixture of peoples, would be easy to defeat, but it was far away and had a large fleet. The weapons systems to overcome these practical handicaps would take time to create, and therefore once the weapons for war against Britain and France seemed to be coming along by 1937, the intercontinental bombers and the blue-water navy that would take care of these concerns were ordered.

At the last moment in 1938 Hitler drew back from the war against Czechoslovakia, a step he greatly regretted and was determined not to repeat in 1939. Since the Poles would not subordinate their newly regained independence to Germany, they were included into the war against the Western Powers. That war appeared to go just the way it was supposed to. Poland was defeated quickly in an alignment with a Soviet Union that was willing to help Germany start and wage war—since the Germans would crush the Soviet Union anyway, it made little difference to Berlin whether their army would subsequently have to go a few hundred kilometres more. Norway and Denmark were conquered quickly so that Germany could reach into the Atlantic, first against Britain and later against the United States. France was defeated and the British chased from the continent.

The immediate concerns of both Hitler and Germany's military leaders in the summer of 1940, as it seemed to them that the war in the West was over, were the next two wars: that against the Soviet Union and the one against the United States. While the attack on the Soviet Union was being discussed, with both Hitler and the army's chief of staff still hoping to launch it in the fall of that year, orders went out to immediately resume the construction of a navy needed for war with the United States. By the end of July, it had become clear that the idea of attacking the Soviet Union that September was impractical; reluctantly, the invasion toward the east was set for the early summer of 1941. Troops had to be moved from west to east, supplies built up near the border, allies recruited, and the transportation system improved. There was considerable military planning, but most attention, especially in the weeks before the attack, was concentrated on the exploitation of the lands confidently expected to be conquered easily, the killing of Jews and of substantial other portions of the population that would quickly come under German control—and the military operations in the

Middle East and northwest Africa that would follow the rapid defeat of the Soviet Union.

The attack on the Soviet Union in June 1941 produced the early victories the Germans had anticipated but not the collapse of the whole system that they had assumed would follow. Like Alexander I when Napoleon's army had taken Moscow, but unlike first the Czarist government of Nicholas II and then the Provisional Government of Alexander Kerensky, Stalin's regime maintained control of the *unoccupied* portions of the country and mobilized its human and material resources to fight the invaders. The horrendous conduct of the Germans made this much easier for a government that now looked benign by comparison—an extraordinary accomplishment. After thinking in July that they had won, the German leaders began to realize in August and September of 1941—some earlier, some later—that in fact they really had not yet won and that the fighting in the east would continue into 1942. And, furthermore, that they needed both bigger and better tanks to cope with those the Red Army had and that they also would have to send to the front in the East replacements for their own lost and damaged tanks from those held in reserve for the operations planned after what they had originally imagined would be a campaign lasting only a few weeks.

The defeats inflicted on the Germans by the Red Army in November and December 1941 only underscored the fact that the German hope of a quick victory had been unrealistic. The campaign in 1942 would therefore have to deliver the decisive blow. The losses Germany and its allies had already suffered, however, precluded a repetition in 1942 of the sort of simultaneous offensive on all segments of the front that they had carried out in 1941. The decision to strike in the southern portion of the front was conditioned by the need to seize the oilfields of the Caucasus for Germany's use and to deprive the Soviets of their main source of this vital supply. The German plan for the 1942 offensive, accordingly, had as its main focus a thrust toward the Caucasus, and, as a means of both supporting that thrust and protecting its northern flank, a push toward the Volga River, in particular its bend at Stalingrad.

While the first stages of the offensive appeared to go reasonably well for the Germans, problems soon appeared. Units of the Red Army were pulled back rather than allowing themselves to be surrounded as in 1941; the Germans simply did not have adequate forces for the double thrust into the Caucasus and toward the Volga; and Soviet resistance stiffened before both. It was in this context that the crisis in German headquarters developed. In the face of the German defeat before Moscow in December 1941, Hitler had reacted by taking over command of the German army himself; now it looked as if the operation designed to bring victory in 1942 was not going as planned. As he was being told that the German army was unable to punch through Red Army resistance in the western Caucasus on the road to Tuapse, while at the same time the German forces heading toward the main oilfields at Grozny and Baku, as well as those heading for Stalingrad, were making very slow progress—if any—Hitler blew up. He temporarily took over command of Army Group A in the Caucasus himself; he replaced the chief of staff of the German army; and he considered replacing his immediate assistants in the High Command of the Armed Forces [Oberkommando der Wehrmacht—OKW].

It was under these circumstances that Hitler, unwilling to recognize that, at his insistence, Germany had taken on a project far beyond its strength, preferred to shift the blame for the looming disaster to his military advisors. If he was infallible—as he was quite certain he was—failure must be the fault of those who had not carried out his brilliant plans in the way he dictated. So that he could make sure in the future that he was obeyed in all respects and that none could claim to have received other directives, Hitler instructed stenographers to record the military situation conferences, at which the detailed orders for future operations were issued. There are indications that he had contemplated such a procedure some months earlier; now he had it implemented.

For the remainder of World War II stenographers who once kept the record of debates in the German parliament—that had held its last meeting in April 1942—now kept shorthand records of the daily situation conferences and some related military conferences and then transcribed their notes. These notes and the transcriptions were collected at the same time, but were destroyed at the end of the war, ironically by order of General Walter Scherff, the man Hitler had designated to write a history of the war.

When American soldiers of the 101st Airborne Division arrived in the area where the destruction by fire of the notes had taken place, a member of an intelligence team, George R. Allen, had the captured stenographers reconstruct those fragments of the record that had not been burned completely or at all. A full account of that operation can be found in the preface by Helmut Heiber that follows this Introduction.[2] A few of the surviving conference texts were introduced as evidence at the Nuremberg trials, but the general public became aware of the existence of the transcripts through the publication by Felix Gilbert of a selection from them in 1950, under the title *Hitler Directs His War*.[3] Gilbert's selection, like the Heiber publication, was based on a set deposited by Allen, along with other materials, at the library of the University of Pennsylvania.[4] The following year George Fischer published the German text of an additional conference, that of June 8, 1943, which had originally been provided to another German agency, in the

Journal of Modern History.[5] He included an English translation in his book *Soviet Opposition to Stalin* in 1952.[6]

It was in 1962 that the Institute for Contemporary History in Munich published the complete collection of the surviving transcripts that provides the basis for most of the translations in this new edition.[7] Helmut Heiber as editor not only reconstructed the history of the documents but was careful to include all surviving readable transcripts and portions of transcripts. He also provided extremely useful notes and annotations, all of which are included here. He inserted at the appropriate chronological place the June 8, 1943 conference that Fischer had published. In addition, he included a further conference text, that of July 31, 1944, that had also been provided to another agency and hence survived the general destruction process. This conference is of special interest both because it reveals much about Hitler's reaction to the attempt on his life on July 20, 1944, and because it provides the first clear indications of his thinking on a future counter-offensive in the West, the operation that would eventually be known to the Germans as the Ardennes Offensive and to Americans as the Battle of the Bulge.

Still another conference transcript, that of January 7, 1944, had survived because a copy had been provided to the Nazi Party Chancellery; I published its German text in the Journal of the German Institute that had issued the Heiber volume.[8] This conference dealt with the introduction of political indoctrination officers into the German military. Subsequently it was learned that after most of the stenographers had left Hitler's bunker in Berlin in April 1945 at his direction, there had been some further conferences that Hitler ordered taken down. These records were published by the German magazine *Der Spiegel* in 1966.[9] Other than some military details about the final defense of Berlin, these transcripts are primarily of interest for Hitler's repeated and detailed explication of his reasons for remaining in Berlin rather than moving to South Germany, as many of his associates urged.

All of the known transcripts are included in this edition. Are there likely to be more? Just as several turned up after Heiber had expressed the opinion that this was most unlikely, one simply cannot exclude the possibility. If an extra copy was provided to some office or agency whose records were captured by the Red Army, were not turned over to the former German Democratic Republic, and have not been completely screened in their current depositories, the remote possibility does exist that one or another such item may yet surface. Until and unless that happens, this edition is the only complete one available.

Why is this record of Hitler's military conferences significant? Because it is here that both the general public and the specialist can see how decisions were actually reached at the highest level in World War II Germany. It is here that one can follow the role of key individuals in the German military and political hierarchy. It is here that one can observe how choices were made about weapons and units on the one hand, and broader strategic issues on the other. These documents, therefore, certainly provide additional details about the military history of the war, but a major interest lies elsewhere. Here we see Hitler in his dealings with the military and other leaders of the German war effort in full contemporary records. These are not subsequently edited minutes or reports. More important, they provide Hitler's side of issues that have been very largely and deliberately obscured by the endless flood of memoirs published by German military leaders after the war. There are, to be sure, other important sources for Hitler's views, such as his recorded table talk,[10] collections of his speeches,[11] and special reports, like the one of January 29, 1944, on his views about Germany's postwar birthrate;[12] but it is the military field where the distortions have been most extensive.

Anyone reading the memoirs of the German generals and field marshals might conclude not only that Stalin was able to arrange for it to snow and become freezing cold only on the German side of the front, while the Red Army enjoyed balmy weather, but also that any successes attained by Germany were due to the brilliance of the generals and all the defeats the result of Hitler's unwillingness to listen to their invariably wise advice. The possibility that when the Germans shortened their lines in order to facilitate the withdrawal of units into a reserve, it might also lead to a shortening of the lines of the Soviet forces facing them, never appears to have occurred to the self-proclaimed geniuses. Those who led more than ten million German soldiers under their command to death, crippling wounds and imprisonment were eager to shift the burden of responsibility to the shoulders of the man they had served with enthusiasm and from whom they had gladly received not only promotions but enormous secret bribes.[13] Since Hitler committed suicide, he was not around to correct them—and they knew it.

Especially because some of the most mendacious of military memoirs have become widely known, are frequently cited, and have in some instances been translated into English, the unvarnished contemporary record ought to be considered in any assessment of Germany's role in World War II. Serious scholars have, accordingly, made considerable use of the originals in the Heiber edition, but here the full surviving record is accessible in English.

None of this is to suggest that Hitler was the military genius he claimed to be and as so many Germans originally acclaimed him at the time. The record shows him as a mean and suspicious individual who made decisions on the basis of preposterous beliefs about such countries as the Soviet Union and the United States. He had a clear view of his aims, of broader strategic issues and their economic and political implications; in these matters he saw reality more clearly than the narrowly focused military professionals. He was also astonishingly familiar with a wide variety of technical details about weapons systems. What he lacked was an operational sense in the broad area between grand strategy and minute detail. And that could not be remedied by reminiscences of his experiences of the fighting in the trenches of the preceding conflict.

Since the arguments over Hitler's willingness or refusal to authorize substantial withdrawals play such a large role in the literature, it may be appropriate to call attention to a few major examples of this issue. When the German army group that had pushed into the Caucasus in 1942 was threatened with being cut off because of the Red Army's victory at Stalingrad, Hitler insisted that a small bridgehead across the Kerch Strait, separating the German-held Crimea from the northern Caucasus, be retained. This came to be called the Kuban bridgehead. Several German military leaders wanted the forces tied up there withdrawn to strengthen the southern portion of the front. Hitler insisted that the bridgehead be held because Germany would need the oil of the Caucasus to win the war, and it would be easier to resume the offensive in that direction if the Kerch straits had already been crossed. The bridgehead later had to be evacuated anyway—but that of course also released the Red Army units that had been tied down containing it up to that time. There is no evidence to suggest that an earlier shift of both sets of military units would have produced a different outcome at the southern end of the Eastern front.

In the fall of 1944 three German army groups in different theaters of war were threatened by the real possibility of being cut off, essentially simultaneously, by the Allies. The army group defending southwest France was about to be cut off by a meeting of the Allied forces breaking out of the Normandy beachhead with those that had landed on the Mediterranean coast. Hitler authorized a withdrawal, and most of the two German armies in southwest France were extricated. The German army group in southeast Europe was about to be cut off by the Red Army's occupation of Romania and Bulgaria, and then possibly joining Tito's forces, which by this time controlled substantial portions of Yugoslavia. Hitler authorized a withdrawal that then took place. The German army group at the northern segment of the Eastern Front was threatened by a Red Army thrust to the Baltic Sea. Once cut off, a corridor was reopened to it; but when the Red Army again reached the Baltic, Hitler allowed some of the units trapped in western Latvia to be evacuated by sea but insisted that what came to be called the Courland bridgehead be held by the divisions he ordered to remain there. It was over this issue that General Heinz Guderian was dismissed in March 1945 from his position as chief of the general staff of the German Army, a post he had held since July 1944.

Why did Hitler want to hold on to western Latvia as opposed to southwest France, Greece, and Albania? The answer has to be found in his hopes of winning the war by the employment of new types of submarines. As the Commander-in-Chief of the German Navy, Admiral Karl Dönitz assured him, holding Courland was essential for the control of the central Baltic, where the new submarines had to be run in before they could be sent into the Atlantic to turn the tide there once again, in Germany's favor, and deprive the American and British armies in the West of supplies and reinforcements. One is entitled to the opinion that these were the loony notions of the man who would succeed Hitler in 1945 and who maintained that he was Germany's legitimate ruler until his death in 1980; but there was at least some coherence between this concept and Hitler's simultaneous insistence on holding or destroying the ports on the French coast. As it was, the soldiers stranded in Courland, like those holding some of the French Atlantic ports until the surrender of May 1945, became prisoners of war rather than additional cannon fodder, as Guderian preferred.

The record shows that Hitler believed until very late in the war that Germany still had a chance to win or at least to profit from a division within the coalition he himself brought together against Germany. But in this he was not alone. Dönitz was one of many who still believed in achieving victory late in 1944. Albert Speer, whom some imagine to have been a clearsighted if deluded Nazi, believed in the possibility of a German victory or at least a satisfactory peace until late January 1945.[14] Guderian acquired a stolen estate in German-occupied Poland during the war and expected to keep it. Together with the senior officer on the rank list of the German army, Field Marshal Gerd von Rundstedt, he sat as judge on the court that threw out of the service those officers accused by the Gestapo of any connection with the effort to overthrow the Hitler regime in July 1944. At the time, both were secretly accepting bribes from their beloved Führer; while the accused were not allowed to appear before the court themselves or to be represented. This travesty was called a Court of Honor (*Ehrenhof*). It might well be suggested that Hitler and his generals deserved each other.

NOTES TO THE INTRODUCTION

1 The best study of this issue is by Jochen Thiess, *Architekt der Weltherrschaft: Die "Endziele" Hitlers* (Düsseldorf: Droste, 1976). A good description from 1927 may be found in Gerhard L. Weinberg, *Germany, Hitler, and World War II* New York: Cambridge University Press, 1995), chap. 2.

2 There is an additional recent account by George R. Allen, "World War II Documents: The Find of a Lifetime," *A. B. Bookman's Weekly*, 87 (6 May 1991), pp. 1838-50.

3 Felix Gilbert (ed. and trans.), *Hitler Directs His War: The Secret Records of His Daily Military Conferences* (New York: Oxford University Press, 1950). It should be noted that this edition contains less than a quarter of the surviving material.

4 There is a full listing in Gerhard L. Weinberg, "Supplement to the Guide to Captured German Documents" (Washington, D.C.: National Archives, 1959), pp. 67-68.

5 George Fischer, "Vlasov and Hitler," *Journal of Modern History* 23 (1951), 58-71.

6 George Fischer, *Soviet Opposition to Stalin: A Case Study in World War II* (Cambridge, MA: Harvard University Press, 1952), Appendix II.

7 Helmut Heiber (ed.), *Hitlers Lagebesprechungen: Die Protokollfragmente seiner militärischen Lagebesprechungen* (Stuttgart: Deutsche Verlags-Anstalt, 1962).

8 Gerhard L. Weinberg (ed.), "Adolf Hitler und der NS-Führungsoffizier," *Vierteljahrshefte fur Zeitgeschichte* (1964), 443-56.

9 "Zeitgeschichte: Hitler-Dokumente," *Der Spiegel*, January 10, 1966, pp. 30-46.

10 There are various editions of Hitler's table talk in German and in English, but there is as yet no complete critical publication in either language.

11 The most complete edition presently available for the war years is Max Domarus (ed.), *Hitler: Reden und Proklamationen 1932-1945*, Vol. II, *Untergang (1939-1945)* (Neustadt a.d. Aisch: Verlagsdruckerei Schmidt, 1963. The English language edition is in two volumes but only the first one has appeared: Max Domarus (ed.), *Hitler: Speeches and Proclamations 1932-1945,* Vol. III, *The Years 1939-1940* (Wauconda, IL: Bolchazy-Carducci Publishers, 1997). An important addition: Heinz-Heinrich Wilhelm (ed.), "Hitlers Ansprache vor Generalen und Offiziere am 26. Mai 1944," *Militärgeschichliche Mitteilungen* 1976 No. 2, pp. 123-70.

12 Oron J. Hale (ed.), "Adolf Hitler and the Post-War German Birthrate: An Unpublished Memorandum," *Journal of Central European Affairs* 17 (1957), 166-73.

[13] Norman J. W. Goda, "Black Marks: Hitler's Bribery of Senior Officers During World War II," *Journal of Modern History* 72 (2000), 413-52; Gerd R. Ueberschär and Winfried Vogel, *Dienen und Verdienen: Hitlers Geschenke an seine Eliten* (Frankfurt: S. Fischer, 1999).

[14] Alfred C. Mierzejewski, "When Did Albert Speer Give Up?" *The Historical Journal* 31 (1988), 391-97.

Preface

by Helmut Heiber[*]

I

T he Stenographic Service at Führer Headquarters began during those late summer weeks of 1942 when the most serious crises of confidence and trust were taking place between Hitler and his military aides. The German army's advance in the Caucasus, with the specific directive of taking the road to Tuapse, was the source of the disagreements. The root cause, though, lay in Hitler's profound exasperation and apprehension regarding the failure of Army Group A to bring the oil fields of the Caucasus under German control. The campaign had stalled because of the overextended front lines, insurmountable difficulties with reinforcements, and growing Soviet resistance. By mid-August the military advance had practically come to a halt between Kuban and Terek. The August 30 war diary entry for military headquarters contains the following notes:

---

[*] The representations given in the first five sections, unless otherwise noted, are taken from the following sources: 1. Oral and written communication between the editor and Heinz Buchholz, Hans Helling, Gerhard Herrgesell, Ludwig Krieger, Dr. Kurt Peschel and Dr. Ewald Reynitz. 2. Written records from Heinz Buchholz dated June 6, 1945, during his American assignment: "General Preliminary Remarks on the Fragments from the Stenographic Service in the FHQ." 3. George Allen: "Introduction to Hitler's 'Lagebesprechungen,'" Supplement to the LB copy of the library at the University of Pennsylvania; in modified form, "On the Dis-

> The Führer is very much dissatisfied with the development of the situation of Army Group A …His criticisms were not directed at the original organization of the forces, but at the fact that the Army Group had not changed the deployment when it became clear that no further advance was possible. The Führer sees little chance of success in taking the road to Tuapse. He opposed the idea of pulling out the XXXXIX Mountain Corps from the Suchumer [Sochi] road to reinforce the Tuapse effort[1]

Hitler's dissatisfaction affected not just the Commander-in-Chief of Army Group A, Field Marshal List, but also the Chief of the General Staff, General Halder, who warned about severe dangers to the southern Eastern Front, from the Don River to the Caucasus. Halder had sent General Jodl to inspect the situation in person, in order to lend additional strength and credibility to his point of view. Jodl was Chief of the Military Staff at the Armed Forces High Command and was fully aware of Halder's opinions on strategy and leadership in the Russian operation, but was not directly involved with Army Group A.

Jodl spoke with List at his headquarters in Stalino on September 7 and acknowledged after his return—on the basis of the conversation regarding the Field Marshal's opinion—that the XXXXIX Mountain Corps should be pulled out and placed in the vicinity of Maikop for a breakthrough to the coast, i.e., in the direction of Tuapse. The Armed Forces Headquarters staff war diary entry for September 8 noted:

> The Führer is very disgruntled about General Jodl's attitude, which is diametrically opposed to his own view. He ordered that all transcripts of orders relating to the Army Group A command since the crossing of the Don River be placed before him.[2]

Hitler was particularly angered to have to hear Jodl cite his own directions, and had to acknowledge that List had done nothing but follow and obey his—Hitler's—orders.[3] As a result of this confrontation with Jodl, the replacement of Keitel and Jodl by Kesselring and Paulus was left undecided until almost January 1943. This altercation must have already taken place on the evening of September 7 or in the early hours of the 8th, because not only were the communal meals at the Führer Headquarters stopped from this day until the end, but on that morning cables were already being sent from Vinnitsa to Munich, leading to the establishment of the Stenographic Services of the Führer Headquarters. The purpose of this service was to

---

covery and Preservation of the Record" as introduction to Felix Gilbert, *Hitler Directs His War*, New York 1950. 4. Statements from General Buhle and General Warlimont.

prevent such unjustified appeals, in Hitler's opinion, to his words in the future.

During the campaigns of the first two years of the war, Hitler had already ordered twice-daily front-line military situation reports on positions at the front—a task that was at that time primarily carried out by Commander Jodl, in the presence of Keitel. The Commander-in-Chief and Chief of General Staff of the Armed Forces branches were not regularly present at these meetings, but did attend on occasion to present reports or receive orders.[4] With the beginning of the Eastern campaign, these conferences—enhanced by the sprawling layout of the "Wolfsschanze" headquarters near Rastenburg in East Prussia—became more systematic. According to the daily routine ordered by Hitler, the first and more extensive meeting, the "midday conference," took place between noon and 3 p.m. and varied in length and number of participants, while the "evening conference," held in the early or late evening hours, was usually limited to the discussion of changes that had taken place that day at the front.

The scope of these situation conferences expanded again after Hitler took over the direct command of the army in December 1941. From then on, his Commander-in-Chief was regularly included, at least at the midday briefings, and a regular program for the meetings began to develop. Until the end of 1942, the midday conferences opened with a general overview by Jodl, sometimes supported by reports by a Luftwaffe meteorologist regarding weather conditions and forecasts. The weather conditions report was given for the first time on December 8, 1941, and was provided as needed until the end of the war—however, usually before and during a German offensive, major enemy attacks or in special cases; the weather maps were normally only presented at the Luftwaffe situation reports. If such introductions were not required (which was usually the case in the following texts), the appropriate general staff officers began with their individual situational reports. The Army Chief of the General Staff usually began reporting on the Eastern Front (for which, according to Hitler's peculiar system of dividing and overlapping areas of authority, the Army High Command alone was responsible). Then came the situation report by the Chief of the Armed Forces Operations Staff or his representative, discussing the rest of the land war theaters. Jodl's staff officers then presented the situation of their respective armed forces branches, both at sea and in the air. This sequence changed occasionally depending upon the current importance and activity level of each war theater. Hitler often concluded the proceedings—and also interrupted frequently during the meetings—by returning to the discussion of military activities that were important to him or arguing about political events. Contrary to what had become customary, political representatives were regularly present in later years. During the midday conferences, drafts of Armed Forces reports were presented for approval or modification, and at the end Hitler also frequently listened to foreign press reports, many of which were only loosely connected to military affairs. The conferences then became more casual and lost their original character, while the officers gradually began to withdraw.

Regular participants at the midday conferences—in addition to Hitler, his adjutants and the Chief of the Armed Forces High Command—included Chief of the Armed Forces Operations Staff and the Army Chief of the General Staff, along with a number of their staff members and adjutants, and representatives of the Commander-in-Chief of the Luftwaffe and of the Commander-in-Chief of the Navy, the Reichsführer SS, and also Hitler's war historian. Later, representatives of the Ministry of Foreign Affairs and the Reich Press Chief appeared frequently, as well as occasionally with an official from the Ministry of War Production. In the last months of the war an official from the party office was also present on some occasions. If the Commander-in-Chief of the Luftwaffe, the Commander-in-Chief of the Navy, the Reichsführer SS, the Chief of the General Staff of the Luftwaffe or the Chief of Naval Warfare happened to be at the Führer Headquarters, they also took part in the conferences—which was often in fact the basic reason for their visit. Along with the commanding officers from the front, who were ordered to attend, Hitler also invited the participation of interested department heads—primarily Ribbentrop, Dietrich and Speer—as well as foreign guests such as Mussolini or Marshal Antonescu.[5] The evening conferences, by contrast, had a much smaller circle of participants—often only Hitler, with one adjutant, and those officers with delegated responsibility for the Eastern Front situation report, the Armed Forces High Command war theaters, and the Luftwaffe.

Beginning with the third week of the Eastern Campaign, Hitler had had stenographic notes (in condensed form) taken during his "Table Talk." These notes cover the period from July 5, 1941, through September 7, 1942. After the confrontation with Jodl in the evening following September 7, Hitler ordered that the stenographic record of the situation reports be kept as well. This measure had obviously been under consideration for quite some time, however, since a representative of Martin Bormann had sounded out Ministry Director Kienast, the Reichstag director, in mid-July about sending stenographers to the Führer Headquarters, and in the same month the OT [Todt Organization] was instructed to build a stenographers' barracks at the Vinnitsa headquarters, then under construction. It is very likely that Hitler had truly contemplated this earlier. Therefore, in light of his behavior at the end of the war, credibility should be given to his many explicit statements that the stenographic records were only indirectly intended to protect him from inaccurate reports from subordinates and false interpretations of his orders. His first priority was to provide an accurate record for posterity and history, assigning responsibility for everything the German side did or did not do militarily during the war.[6]

II

On September 8 at 10:30 a.m., Hans Helling, Obergemeinschaftsleiter secretary and cryptographer at the Munich NSDAP head office, received orders to be ready to travel within the hour. He flew from Riem airport to Berlin, where he reported his arrival to Hitler's adjutant in the afternoon. The next day he flew via Warsaw to Zhitomir, in the same airplane as Senior Government Official[7] Dr. Kurt Haagen, a member of the Reichstag Stenographic Office. On the afternoon of September 9, both reported for duty to Bormann's adjutant, Heinrich Heim, in Vinnitsa and then to Bormann himself. Here they found out for the first time the details of their intended assignment. Bormann had thought that the two alone could produce the stenographic records of Hitler's military conferences, but the head of the party office was at first quite reluctant, since these requirements became clearly impossible to fulfill. It was a result of that discussion that, two days later, on September 11, two additional Reichstag stenographers, Dr. Kurt Peschel and Karl Thöt, arrived in the Ukraine.

The Reichstag Stenographic Office had had little work since 1933. A department rarely allows itself to die a natural death, however, and Reichstag president Göring found use for stenographers in his numerous other functions and occasionally also "loaned" them out, so the de facto disappearance of the Reichstag did not also mean the end of the stenographic organization. While parliamentary life had ended, the requirements of the bureaucracy in the ministries had grown. After 1933, Reichstag stenographers began to cover the proceedings of the Ministry of the Interior, the Ministry of Foreign Affairs, the Ministry of Transportation, etc. This had only been the case in limited form up to that point. They also assisted in various other areas: Gauleiter meetings, the Niemöller trial, the proceedings of the German Legal Academy (including its various technical committees), the Kristallnacht Conference of November 12, 1938, the proceedings of the Defense Council, and the trial of General Fritsch, and the proceedings of the War Court, as well as the Criminal Law Commission. Some stenographers were drafted into military service when the war began, and whereas some of them were pro forma soldiers and given assignments in their area of expertise (for example, recording the conferences with the general in charge of aviation production), most served in local defense units, propaganda companies, and Luftwaffe construction battalions.

When Bormann requested stenographers for the Führer Headquarters in September 1942, he told Ludwig Krieger, the head of the Stenographic Office, that the assignments meant a great deal of responsibility and that he therefore required highly qualified professionals who were also party members. But because there were very few individuals available who could fulfill both requirements, and military circumstances had to be taken into account as well, the political party affiliation requirement was dropped a few days later with the new batch of stenographers. The two gentlemen who arrived at Vinnitsa on September 11 confirmed Bormann's view that recording and editing daily meetings lasting two to six hours would require a much larger organization than was originally planned. In addition to recording the regular situation conferences, stenographic services would be required at Hitler's "Sonderbesprechungen" or "special conferences," which dealt with military engagements, operational plans, weapons issues, military-industrial questions, etc., with commanding officers or chiefs of staff from various units or army groups, with officers of the High Command or from the manpower and armaments production departments. Stenographers were also needed to listen in and record Hitler's telephone conversations. The military situation reports were first recorded on September 12, and four days later three additional Reichstag stenographers joined the group: Senior Government Officials Heinrich Berger, Dr. Hans Jonuschat and Dr. Ewald Reynitz, who began working two days later after being sworn in.

The scheduling of the two stenographic systems was based on three "tables," or stenographer pairs:

Table 1: Dr. Peschel/Dr. Jonuschat (Stolze-Schrey)
Table 2: Dr. Reynitz/Thöt (Gabelsberger)
Table 3: Berger/Dr. Haagen (Stolze-Schrey)

Each pair had to record all discussions in a 24-hour period, then dictate the notes during the following two days. During the next few months, however, it became obvious that this arrangement was still unsatisfactory. In December, when one stenographer became ill, it was decided to add another member of both systems to each group, allowing for a more flexible three-way rotation that would include rest days and take illness and vacation into account. So on December 24, 1942, two new arrivals from the Reichstag office joined the group at the Führer Headquarters (which had returned to East Prussia): Senior Government Officials Dr. Fritz Dörr (Gabelsberger) and Heinz Buchholz (Stolze-Schrey). However, Dr. Dörr found the emotional and physical strain of the Stalingrad campaign too taxing, and had to retire after little more than a month. Ludwig Krieger, director of the Reichstag Stenographic Office, replaced him on February 23, 1943. Krieger had been accompanying Göring on official trips for the past six months, but was now available. Dr. Peschel, who was familiar with the organization and its procedure, continued to act as head of the Stenographic Service at the Führer Headquarters.

This arrangement continued unchanged until the end of the war, with one exception. Senior Government Official Berger was one of the victims of the July 20, 1944, assassination attempt. Court Official Gerhard Herrgesell, who did not come from the Reichstag Office, but had served from 1928 to 1931 as parliament stenographer recording the proceedings of the provisional Reich Economic Council, replaced him. His Reichstag colleagues knew him from his activities during this period, and he used the required Stolze-Schrey system. After joining the Waffen SS in the artillery in 1940 due to a chance military transfer, Herrgesell had been recording government press conferences for the press office of the Reichsführung SS.

For the length of their tour of duty, the members of the Stenographic Service at the Führer Headquarters were under the supervision and a part of the staff of Reichsleiter Martin Bormann for military and administrative concerns. However, technical orders could not be issued by Bormann, because Hitler had reserved this prerogative for himself—along with the right to grant permission to view the transcripts. Each one of the stenographers was personally sworn in by Hitler before beginning work, and each had to sign a written statement promising to keep everything he saw and heard confidential, and agreeing not to take any notes for personal reasons or to make any copies of records or portions of records.

The members of the Stenographic Service wore field-gray officers' uniforms with the Government Official insignia on their sleeve and were assigned to a special barracks in Security District 1. Hitler's adjutancy informed the stenographers about requirements for the meetings. If the conferences were taking place at field headquarters with their own briefing rooms or at the Berghof hall, well known for its panoramic window, the stenographers gathered with the other meeting participants to wait for Hitler. But if, as was the case in the final months of the war, the meetings were held in his office in the Reich Chancellery[8] or, later, in the bunker, the stenographers were regularly called to the meeting table before the other participants. They were the only ones seated (only toward the end of the war did the weakened Führer join them at the table), either at both corners of the long sides or one at either of the short sides, with Hitler diagonally across and the other participants (at the midday meetings often 20 to 25 people) standing around the map-covered table. Both stenographers recorded the entire meeting.

Afterwards the transcripts were divided in half according to the noted time, and each stenographer dictated his half of the meeting notes, using the relevant section of his colleague's notes as a control.[9]

The recording of these conferences, often many hours long—the longest meeting lasted four hours—was extremely exhausting even for expert stenographers, which is why, from the beginning, it was customary to have double coverage for difficult assignments and parliament service.[10] The total length of the three regular daily meetings (two situation reports and one special conference) gradually increased as the war progressed. In 1942 the average number of transcript pages was 89; that number had grown to nearly 150 pages by 1945. Approximately 38 double-spaced pages corresponded to one hour of dictation time (the longest existing transcript, from the midday conference of January 27, 1945, reached 95½ pages). As a general rule, each spoken word had to be recorded. Only rarely did Hitler make a sign that some unimportant parenthetical comment need not be recorded. As is customary in stenographic practice, random peripheral remarks unrelated to the topic of discussion were not recorded—such as Hitler's occasional questions about the time (he never wore a watch), his comments about his German shepherd Blondi, or other similar remarks. Otherwise, everything was recorded until the (often vague) end of the meeting—as a rule, as long as a general was still present or until his adjutant gave a sign. The final transcript was followed; dictated with two carbon copies—both on equal weight original document paper. The now outdated and therefore expendable situation maps for the relevant day were available to the stenographers at that point, and sometimes also a brief written outline of the situation report. If a location name or context was still unclear after reviewing these documents, the stenographers—who were of course unable to interrupt during the meetings—could now ask officers in the adjutancy or the operations staff (usually Major Waizenegger) for clarification, although it was rarely necessary to do so.

All three copies together with the two sets of shorthand notes, were given to Helling, who directed the Stenographic Service together with a colleague by the name of Lutz. The Stenographic Service had seven women typists, brought in from the NSDAP Headquarters, available to take dictation from the stenographers. The designated "Führer copy" and the two sets of original shorthand notes were collected and, when a certain number had accumulated, periodically taken to Berlin by Helling or Lutz for storage in a vault in the Voss Strasse section of the Reich Chancellery. Helling and Lutz were allowed into this room only when accompanied by an officer of the security police. Before air strikes on German cities began Hitler had also ordered color slides (taken by Luftwaffe photographer

Frenz) of culturally and historically important church windows to be placed in this vault.

Of the two other copies, one was given to Hitler's military historian Scherff to be used in writing the history of the war. The other was kept as a working copy in a safe in Helling's office at the respective headquarters, available for reference in case of questions.[11] For this purpose, Helling created a handwritten index for each transcript, which was placed in front of the document, copied by typewriter, filed in a folder and entered by Lutz into the document catalog. Also besides Scherff, the military leadership at the Führer Headquarters often requested factual information from the transcripts, which could be easily located using the index. Earlier transcripts were also referenced about a dozen times to resolve arguments arising during situation conferences.

The collection of working documents was complete with the exception of special conference S 29/42, which was the transcript of a presentation by Field Marshal Rommel. This meeting took place at the end of November 1942, after El Alamein, and the stenographers were given specific orders not to make any copies. In the Scherff collection there were also several other transcripts missing, as in some cases orders were given to make only a single copy.

III

From the military perspective, claims have been made that these transcripts were no doubt falsified in Hitler's favor. Apart from the fact that this statement would not apply to the great majority of the existing documents anyway—at least not those where a second transcription of the original shorthand notes is available—such an allegation is, after a careful examination of the facts, clearly not the case in other situations either. Falsifying history—and ensuring that the falsification holds—is a laborious task requiring a great deal of diligence and care. It is unthinkable that Hitler himself would have taken the time to edit the documents. Witnesses have also attested that he never once reviewed the transcripts.[12] In fact, he was so sure of himself and his own infallibility (including militarily) that he would never have reviewed or corrected anything. Any of the other persons in question either had no access to the transcripts or lacked the specialized knowledge to evaluate military events.

None of the officers were allowed to view the records. Even Hitler's official military historian, General Scherff, could only have made corrections to his own copy, which would not be of interest in this context. In any case, it is inconceivable that Hitler would order a man like Scherff, who—as his writings show—was expected to function as military panegyrist and court historian,[13] to doctor material whose meaning and importance was not yet clear.

The stenographers or other Reichsleitung functionaries working at the Stenographic Service certainly did not possess the necessary authority. Because of the circumstances of their work, there was never really the opportunity or even the temptation. This was true also of Bormann himself, who, it is said, came to the office only once during a social evening. Because the Reichsleitung was not interested in the military situation conferences until 1945, and even then only occasionally sent a representative to participate, Bormann hardly concerned himself with the Stenographic Service at all. He had his adjutants review the operations of the service only once—soon after the institution was established, on October 10, 1942.

Revising the transcripts would have technically required the close cooperation of Scherff and Helling, which would have been nearly impossible considering that they worked in completely different divisions. And Hitler was, in his almost self-hypnotic manner, so convinced of the correctness of every single one of his decisions that a revision process of this sort would not even have been considered. On the contrary, he intended to use the transcripts to help catch (in supposed or actual mistakes) those generals who didn't heed his advice. Even when Hitler gave the war up for lost, *he* didn't order the transcripts destroyed—a low level officer made that decision. Hitler himself was much more concerned with specific arrangements for the last transcripts to be taken safely out of Berlin. He wanted to leave a complete record that would demonstrate his innocence to posterity after the war.

Errors, on the other hand, were naturally unavoidable. One of the two possible sources of mistakes (the other is addressed below) was in the recording of the meetings. Not just the length of the conferences but also the unfamiliar (at least initially) subject matter, chaotic discussion threads, and occasional individual conversations placed a great strain on the stenographers and made reliable hearing difficult. Frequent comings and goings,[14] telephone messages, noise outside the conference room, and other such distractions added to the difficulty, as did certain peculiarities of the meetings, which Senior Government Official Buchholz noted as follows for the Americans on July 6, 1945:

> The military situation presentations were always based on maps, and usually the individual sectors of the front were indicated with a vague "here" and a general indication toward the map. Many questions were answered by referring to written documents, which were then discussed without any clear explanation of their exact content. The Führer and other participants would fre-

quently refer to questions that had been raised earlier, without explaining the subject very precisely. With his interposed questions, interjections and random transitions, the Führer expected a high degree of familiarity with the question at hand. For critical remarks in particular, he liked to use ironic or sarcastic expressions that could really only be properly understood by experienced listeners. The words of the Führer sometimes contained a degree of ambiguity, especially when he addressed a question at length or discussed the same subject repeatedly. It was sometimes only clear to the specialized participants if he was giving an order, making a suggestion, a rhetorical statement, a spontaneous utterance, or criticizing something.

Aside from all these possibilities for random error, and excluding the circumstances of the second transcription discussed below, *intentional* changes to the situation report transcripts can be ruled out.

IV

By the second half of April 1945, when their work at Führer Headquarters was coming to an end, the stenographers had accumulated around 103,000 pages of single-sided text.[15] The night after Hitler's 56th birthday—when Göring, Himmler, Speer, and other prominent individuals, many airplanes, and a long column of trucks, left Berlin, by now threatened with being completely surrounded—six of the eight stenographers were also flown to Salzburg/Berchtesgaden. Drs. Haagen and Herrgesell, because of the rotation of stenographers, remained at the Führer's bunker in the Reich Chancellery to finish recording the last few meetings before the expected imminent shift of the Führer Headquarters to the "Alpenfestung" [the Alpine Redoubt]. In addition to the members of the Stenographic Service, the Ju [Junkers transport plane], which took off in the early morning hours of April 21 from Berlin's Schönefeld airport, also carried a number of boxes. These boxes contained the "Führer copies" and shorthand notes of the situation report transcripts, which Helling and Lutz had removed from the vault in the Reich Chancellery during the night. After a short stop in Prague, the airplane arrived at Salzburg without any difficulties. From there, Helling took his material by car to Obersalzberg in the early morning where he stored it in an air-raid shelter behind the Berghof. The tunnel was to serve as a document bunker. He gave the keys to Dr. Peschel for safekeeping; but others must have had access to the bunker as well, as subsequent events would indicate.

In Berlin, Haagen and Herrgesell recorded their last situation report on April 22, during which Hitler's faith in victory—if not for the first time, at least for the first time publicly—collapsed. He believed the war to be lost, and decided to remain in Berlin for good.[16] The two stenographers were released in order to take the records of the last 48 hours to their colleagues in Bavaria, so that—as Hitler expressly stated—the transcripts of those days would also be preserved for history. That same night Haagen and Herrgesell flew out of Gatow. Although their aircraft was somewhat damaged by Soviet anti-aircraft batteries, they reached their destination and arrived at Riem at 6 a.m. on April 23. The members were all in attendance when the Stenographic Service of the Führer Headquarters convened in a Berchtesgaden hotel the following day.

War historian General Scherff also relocated to Berchtesgaden, and his influence was probably significant to the destruction of the transcripts. Toward the end of April, he called the head of the Stenographic Service, Senior Government Official Dr. Peschel, to raise the question of what should be done with the transcripts in light of the impending defeat and occupation by American forces. Scherff made it plain that his opinion of Hitler as a general had changed, and he strongly criticized the military strategy of the last few years. Moreover, because he did not believe that any objective history would be written in the coming decades anyway, he thought it best to destroy everything. Peschel agreed and did not change his mind despite subsequent objections from his colleagues.[17]

Scherff was not authorized to dispose of the copies that were under the administration of the Stenographic Service, but as the only specialist on location, he was no doubt able to exercise considerable influence. The actual order to burn the material was given by Senate President Müller, Bormann's personal advisor. The execution of the order was carried out by a detail of the RSHA, probably part of the SD unit of SS Obersturmbannführer Dr. Frank, which was stationed on the mountain. The destruction occurred on one of the first days in May, shortly before the American occupation. Buchholz and Lutz were present from the Stenographic Service for identification purposes. They drove with SS personnel to an OT barracks or workshop in a wooded valley a few hundred meters beyond the Hintersee to the west of Berchtesgaden. The transcripts and shorthand notes had already been brought there (without the participation of the Stenographic Service), perhaps because of the April 25 RAF air attacks on Obersalzberg or perhaps simply in preparation for the burning. The selected boxes were pulled out from under everything else, carried to an open place, emptied into a ditch and set on fire.[18]

But what happened to the two remaining longhand copies? Before he committed suicide in May, Scherff is supposed to have destroyed his copies, which, considering his previously expressed opinions, is highly likely.[19] The other copies were stored with the Führer copies in the vault of the Reich

Chancellery when the Führer Headquarters were transferred to Berlin in January 1945. These working copies were supposedly burned in the furnace of the Reich Chancellery immediately after the stenographers, with their shorthand notes and Führer copies, traveled south during the night of April 21.[20]

V

American troops occupied Berchtesgaden on the afternoon of May 5. That evening they took over the Solekurbad Hotel where the stenographers and typists were staying, and asked them to leave with their private belongings and blankets to find different quarters—"if necessary to the church across the street." They found lodging in the guestrooms of the neighboring Café Grassl. Despite the civilian clothes they had brought with them, some of the staff were uneasy about their officers' dress uniforms and accompanying firearms, since the occupying troops could hardly be expected to understand the subtle differences between German uniforms. Those entrusted with the "objective preservation of the spoken word" would sooner or later have to explain their presence in Bavaria, now that they faced the threat of internment or a POW camp. In response to publicly announced orders, firearms were collected and turned over to the Americans. Opinions about what to do next, however, remained divided. On May 7, Herrgesell and Dr. Jonuschat reported to local American military administration offices, identified themselves and offered to share their knowledge. They were sent to the Bellevue Hotel, where the previous Sunday Sergeant George Allen of the 101st Airborne Division had opened a Military Intelligence Service (MIS) station and was now screening applicants for the local administrative positions which were almost completely vacant.

Allen was fascinated by the prospect of being one of the first persons to be confronted with revelations about the life of the mysterious German dictator. In order to get the whole group together, Allen instructed his two visitors to bring their colleagues the following day. This was an arbitrary act on Allen's part—and it is probably thanks to this decision that the transcript fragments of Hitler's situation reports were saved. According to regulations, he should have arrested the stenographers and sent them to one of the numerous internment camps, where they would have disappeared among the local informers. But because of Allen's call, on May 8—the day of Germany's surrender—the seven men from the Führer Headquarters could begin assisting the American MIS. Only one member of the group did not come along and would be interrogated later by the Americans: Dr. Haagen had separated himself from the others and had found private quarters in another part of town. He was working as an interpreter for the Berchtesgaden local administration.[21]

In the course of animated conversations between the stenographers and MIS personnel,[22] as well as the war correspondents from American news agencies, the conversation turned to (either on that day or the next) the documents brought to Berchtesgaden and the burning ceremony staged by the SS at the Hintersee. According to Allen's recollections it was around May 10 when he drove out to the Hintersee with Dr. Peschel, Buchholz, and Herrgesell. There they rummaged unsuccessfully through the garage and workshop, looking for parts of the collection that may have been overlooked during the last week, but finding only files from the party chancellery, military maps and art objects. Then they moved behind the building, between damaged Luftwaffe vehicles, to a ditch containing an ash heap more than half a meter high. With the help of the stenographers, Allen began to search carefully through the ashes to locate undamaged pieces. On that day and the two that followed (when he returned alone) Allen located record remnants from approximately 50 conferences.[23] Some records were completely or almost completely intact, while others consisted of only singed fragments or a few charcoaled pages. Some were typed transcripts, but most of them were shorthand notes—the latter in their protective envelopes, which is why in the respective cases *both* sets of shorthand notes, or parts of both sets, survived. The surviving documents were most likely on the edge or at the bottom of the pit, and were probably spared because of the obvious problems of burning large quantities of paper that had been packed in too tightly.

At the Bellevue Hotel, the stenographers were immediately put to work. The Stenographic Service operated in the same manner as at Führer Headquarters, but this time they were working for the Americans. Four of the former Reichsleitung typists, who were familiar with the material and the organization of the text, were available for transcription. The MIS provided typewriters, paper, and food from the former German military supply. Despite all the denazification decrees, Dr. Peschel was again appointed to supervise the stenographers—although there was admittedly not a great need for leadership, since each person busied himself with his own fragments.

The shorthand notes were again transferred to longhand, and the damaged portions were deciphered as much as possible. Generally, the same stenographer who had recorded and dictated the original notes worked on the same document once again. Only when it was clearly advisable to adjust the division of labor, or in the case of transcripts by Berger and Dr. Haagen, did a different colleague familiar with the relevant system fill in. Nevertheless, due to the length of time that had passed and the lack of supporting documents, mistakes were unavoidable in the second transcription; as is evidenced by the frequently misspelled or by now unidentifiable names of people and places. The other major cause of mistakes, and compared to the problems mentioned above, likely the greater of the two sources of errors, was that factual errors will have naturally slipped in—especially when there were gaps in the text—however, one can say that these mistakes were exceptions. For the most part, even the contents of the second transcription can be considered an accurate portrayal of the conference proceedings.

In order not to jeopardize the reliability of the second transcript, the stenographers rarely tried to fill in gaps from memory or rely on the context to supplement the existing text. All inferences from context, as well as words unclear due to fire damage, were placed in brackets. Indecipherable words and gaps due to fire damage were also indicated by punctuation. The fragments were numbered arbitrarily in the order in which they were processed, and taken by Senior Government Official Buchholz, who operated as head clerk for the team. He catalogued the finished pieces, and forwarded them to the Americans in six copies. One copy, along with the original fragments, was sent to the U.S. Seventh Army Document Center.[24] Three copies were given to the appropriate department of the War Crimes Commission, and two were retained by the MIS detachment of the 101st Airborne Division. Of these last two copies, one was designated for the division archives and the other remained with Allen, who later transferred the material to the University of Pennsylvania in his home city of Philadelphia. The Institut für Zeitgeschichte obtained a microfilm from the University of Pennsylvania in 1951.

By early June the most extensive of the document pieces had been processed (at least those posing the fewest problems), and on June 6 Buchholz signed the previously mentioned "General Preliminary Remarks," which would provide the Americans with a sort of user's guide. Altogether, the stenographers' work at the Bellevue Hotel in Berchtesgaden lasted about two months. The typists were released after the bulk of the transcription work was completed—when all that remained was the time-consuming and puzzling work of deciphering the most heavily damaged pages. After the final pieces were deciphered and forwarded to Wiesbaden, and the Stenographic Service at the Führer Headquarters (whose function Senior Government Official Krieger had already declared ended on May 4, before the Americans marched in) was finally disbanded.* In Wiesbaden, the War Crimes Commission selected three transcripts for use in the Nurem-

---

* The team remained together, however (with the two exceptions of Dr. Peschel and Herrgesell), and assisted the Americans in preparing for and conducting the Dachau trials.

berg Trials and entered them into the prosecution's list of exhibits: the evening conference of December 1, 1942 (1382-PS), the midday conference of December 12, 1942 (1383-PS), and the midday conference of January 27, 1945 (3786-PS). The transcript from June 8, 1943 (1384-PS), was also added from another source. Document 3786-PS, the transcript of the midday conference of January 27, 1945, was included in volume 33 of the "Blue Series" (the trial of major war criminals before the IMG, Nuremberg, 1949). In addition, Felix Gilbert, a professor at Bryn Mawr College in Philadelphia, published an English translation of selected transcripts—about one-sixth of the total—in 1950. This collection, entitled *Hitler Directs His War* (New York 1950), was, like the present work, based on the University of Pennsylvania documents. Gilbert also published the original German text of the February 1, 1943, midday conference in *Die Welt als Geschichte* in 1950 (vol. 10, pp. 226 ff.).

The texts that follow are printed according to the 1945 compilation, for the most part without omission or abbreviation. Aside from the reduction of passages, often up to one-half page long, which were left out by the stenographers, only single words without context were excluded. These sometimes remained intact, isolated at the beginning or at the end of lines throughout three-quarters of a whole page. If some sense could be made from the context the relevant passages were included, even at the expense of readability. Only obvious spelling errors were corrected, including, in clear-cut cases, names and units. Only two pieces were excluded:

a) Fragment 19b, which consists of five multiple-line but gap-filled pieces. Four of these originated with the deceased Berger and were therefore difficult to re-transcribe (one was a conference from the second half of July 1943, discussing measures against the expected defection of Italy).

b) Fragment 54, which does not belong in the Stenographic Service transcript collection. It is an insignificant eight-line piece, apparently the text or draft of one of Hitler's speeches. The date is unknown, and, as was typical practice in such cases, it was probably dictated by Hitler directly to a secretary (based on the format—"Führer typeface" and wide spacing).

The collection recovered from the Hintersee is supplemented here by transcripts of two additional special conferences, which were the only previously known transcripts from the series of conferences recorded by the Stenographic Service at Führer Headquarters. These were probably extra copies that on special instruction had been filed in another department. One of these transcripts covers the previously mentioned meeting between Hitler, Keitel and Zeitzler on June 8, 1943, and the other is the record of a meeting with Jodl on July 31, 1944. With the addition of these two, all currently known (and presumably all existing) verbatim transcripts and transcript fragments are accounted for in this edition.

To assist the reader, a general overview outlines the development of the military situation between the dates of the transcripts.

VI

Göring confided to Goebbels on March 1, 1943, that the working methods at the Führer Headquarters were thoroughly flawed, especially the new requirement that stenographers be present at situation conferences to record every word. "Eventually," Goebbels noted in his diary, "the Führer will be disadvantaged by this, as he never makes any secret of his opinions, while the generals always speak with the record in mind..."* Exactly the same criticism is made today by Hitler's conversation partners—but in reverse. Which of the two parties is correct? Hitler? The generals? Or both? Or neither of the two?

This problem is relevant in similar situations today, such as radio or television broadcasts of parliamentary sessions. The often-discussed danger arising from such a recording process is also present in the case of the situation reports: Hitler himself had, as already mentioned, indicated that the transcripts would play a role in the judgment of posterity, and the generals were no doubt aware of this. Nevertheless, it is unlikely that this fact could have had a decisive influence on the course of the discussions. One can certainly address future readers in contemplative diary entries, and for some time one can also—especially when questions of destiny are at stake—speak thoughtfully while gazing out the window instead of to a crowd. But it is impossible to deliberate on the future judgment of historians day after day for years, while not only speaking to future generations with every utterance but also making countless decisions that often dealt with matters of seemingly little importance and whose effects would not be immediately clear anyway.

Moreover, it does not appear readily explainable how this falsified "view of posterity" was supposed to have operated. If Hitler's opinion was that

---

* The sentence ends: "...Zeitzler, of course, excluded." (*Goebbels Diaries*, published by Louis P. Lochner, Doubleday 1948, p. 265). This expression of sympathy is insignificant here, as it no doubt goes back to the united stand that both had taken against Alfred Rosenberg that day—and which is why Goebbels had written in his diary 20 pages earlier that he had "found in Zeitzler a good friend." [NDT: *Goebbels Diaries*, p. 261, "I believe I have found a good friend in Zeitzler."]

Division X should be moved here or there, while General Y maintained that the units were needed more where they were and therefore argued against the transfer, then the two rivals would, of course, each be looking for the best possible outcome for the current situation. It is difficult to comprehend why either Hitler or General Y would have argued for a different solution than the one he actually thought best, simply because his position was being recorded on paper. If hasty statements or decisions could be avoided through such a procedure, so much the better.

But of course there was also the possibility—primarily on Hitler's part—of subsequently placing the blame on others when an operation failed because of poor decisions. For such an exercise a great deal of caution would be required, especially in view of the fragmented nature of this document collection. If a complete copy of the conference transcripts existed, there would be few unresolved problems regarding the evaluation of German military leadership, at least during the second half of World War II. It was not Hitler's will but an unfortunate chain of seemingly minor events and decisions during the turbulent days of Germany's collapse that prevented this. Nevertheless, the remains—perhaps one hundredth of the total collection—that were saved by chance, provide a historical record that is not to be underestimated. Here we have perhaps the only firsthand case where, in the postwar settling of accounts between the generals and Hitler, we can hear not only the accusers but also the accused. There are only a few other places, and unfortunately even here there are only a few single points, where is it possible to separate the decisions, interpretations, and opinions of Hitler from those of his generals and the generals from Hitler without relying on the words of just one of the parties.

Hitler and the generals—or, more broadly and euphemistically—Hitler and the Armed Forces! The preparation, execution, and breakdown of a marriage of convenience between two partners with little love for each other begins with the Freikorps and putsch episodes of the years after World War I and continues through the Ulm military trial and the fall of Röhm to the reintroduction of conscription, the Fritsch crisis, up until the ups and downs of the Second World War, and the July assassination attempt. There is a great deal of evidence of Hitler's increasing antipathy toward the generals. Goebbels noted on March 9, 1943, in his diary:

> The Führer's opinion about the generals was unfavorable. They cheated him, he said, wherever they could. Besides, they were uneducated and did not even understand their own profession of arms—the least one could expect of them. They could not be blamed for lacking culture, for that wasn't part of their upbringing, but the fact that they knew so little even about the purely material questions of war was absolutely against them. Their training had been

wrong for generations. We could now see the results of such education in our corps of higher officers. I was able to give him some examples from my own experience to confirm the Führer in his views. (*Goebbels Diaries*, p. 280.)

And the contrite renegade Hans Frank, in *Im Angesicht des Galgens*, recalled even stronger pronouncements, which presumably were also made before July 20, 1944 when Frank spoke to Hitler for the last time on February 6, 1944:

> If there was anything in the world that Hitler was inwardly hostile to in German history, it was that circle of the general staff which "Moltke and Schlieffen had long since betrayed, forgotten and sold," as he repeatedly said, and which had become a "special caste of particularly snobbish, pretentious airheads and destructive vermin to the nation, with no imagination, full of sterile fertility, cowardice and vanity." Another time he said, "Those gentlemen with their purple stripes on their trousers are sometimes more repugnant to me than the Jews, since the Jews at least fully acknowledge to themselves that they never want to be soldiers, while the generals claim that entitlement only for themselves." He was also the source of the often-quoted statement: "The general staff is the last order of Freemasonry that I have not yet done away with." (Dr. Hans Frank: *Im Angesicht des Galgens*, Müchen-Gräfelfing, 1953, p. 243.)

On the other hand, it is entirely understandable that military scholars and experts were also unable to muster much sympathy for Hitler—the self taught upstart who suddenly established himself as a petty and critical commander, and who sometimes made them stutter and stammer with his detailed knowledge of specific areas. Already the "old gentleman," Reich President and Field Marshal von Hindenburg—whom Hitler, with his typical theatricality, had suggested should depart to Valhalla—had made snide remarks to his friends von Ahr' and Halm about that "Bohemian soldier." Should others, when resentment is added to self-importance, be expected to be more magnanimous? These human motivations would be enough—irrespective of doubts and objections based on ethical, moral or other worthy reasons rooted in broad, established tradition—to oppose the rootless charlatan with his fatal readiness to assume criminal responsibility for everything he did.

It is therefore hardly surprising that one finds very few among Hitler's former military colleagues—with all self-evident reservations regarding the many other areas not to be discussed here—who do not view their commander-in-chief as an exclusively negative factor in the military strategy and conduct of the war. Aside from a few irrelevant exceptions and a handful of yes-men like Schmundt and Burgdorf, one can characterize the generals (at least those of the Army) as having serious reservations about Hitler's military leadership. Some of them were downright hostile. Some demonstrated their opposition openly—often at the risk of their lives—and the rest affirm it today quite plausibly in conversation and in an unending stream of memoirs.

For the most part, we have been able to see Hitler the military leader only through the eyes of these generals. Especially during the years of self-justification this often led to grotesque situations. It was easy to accuse the Commander-in-Chief, all things being equal, for having lost the war and the battles (since he held overall responsibility and was in any case dead), while the no-less-impressive military successes were—sometimes rightly, sometimes wrongly—attributed to others. Since then, this simplification has been revised. Not only foreign military writers but also German military experts who did not participate in (at least not influentially) key events at headquarters, have, in well-grounded analyses and demonstrations, debunked the view presented by the survivors, which had become the standard interpretation.

It is not true that—in simple black and white terms—the reasonable and promising ideas of Hitler's General Staff were regularly overridden by the stupid ignorance of a nonsense-planning and nonsense-demanding amateur, and that the war (the new sage was hard to ignore) need not have been lost if the confused ideas of the "commanding corporal" hadn't caused him to continually thwart, reverse and generally cancel the spectacular plans hatched by his assistants. It may suffice to refer to the two events which the revisionists used at that time, and which led to the most striking results: the French campaign of 1940 and the Russian winter of 1941-42. While it is not our purpose to write an outline of the history of World War II, we have attempted nevertheless—as an interim step—to provide at least a preliminary summary as far as the central figure of the situation reports is concerned.

On the plus-side, Hitler's vision and instinct for operational questions and opportunities can no more be denied than certain positive and, at least in clear-cut situations, successful leadership qualities: steadfastness and forward-driving energy. In addition, he had an almost phenomenal talent for memorizing technical military literature and for mastering theoretical military and historical information. He also had a good technical understanding and was therefore able to see potential applications for modern weapons. All of these capabilities astonished and confused the experts on more than one occasion. One can say without exaggeration that Hitler was one of the most knowledgeable and versatile technical military specialists of his time. And there is adequate evidence that his abilities went beyond simple rote memorization of instruction manuals, naval yearbooks, etc.

On the other hand, Hitler had no general staff training. And because he did not have it, he despised it. This attitude had a negative effect, especially when the retreat battles of the second half of the war placed demands on the military leadership that went beyond the "presuppositions of common sense" Moltke refers to. A general's craft of being able to defeat an aggressive adversary through mobile and flexible defense, was not among Hitler's qualities. Because of his doubts about the aggressive spirit and combative energy of his generals (valid in part, and groundless at other times—and later taking on pathological characteristics), every countervailing influence was increasingly resisted. Isolated encircled pockets dug themselves in, hoping vaguely for offensives to come, while weakened and irrelevant positions were held numbly and stubbornly, and imaginary flanking movements were ordered to close gaps that had long since been closed. These activities were hardly suited to stave off impending disaster. The only question still open is whether or not the flexible military strategy recommended so highly today by Hitler's adversaries would really have provided an alternative. In addition to his operational blunders, Hitler was interfering with increasing frequency in tactical movements on the battlefield, where he was often inspired by his experiences in the trenches of World War I. His interference clashed ominously with the traditional Prussian-German army chain of command, still deeply rooted despite some changes due to improved means of communication. In these collected transcripts, how Hitler, with his time as military commander running out, took increasing refuge in reminiscences from the World War I strike us as grotesque—as if the experiences of a private could somehow show him the way out of new strategic dilemmas.

Ultimately, however, the triumphant success in France in 1940 broadened Hitler's sense of mission (which until then had been focused primarily on the internal politics of the Third Reich) to include his military activities. In the successes achieved in the west despite frequent disagreements with his colleagues, Hitler—tending toward hubris and driven onward by a subservient environment—saw confirmation of the fact that the assignment Providence had given him also extended to the area of military leadership. From then on, his opinion could really only be imparted *ex cathedra*. With regard to fundamental questions there could be no further mistakes—only adverse circumstances, subordinates' failures and treacherous allies.

Nevertheless, one must grant that many of Hitler's military decisions until very near the end, were in the technical sense thoroughly reasonable—more reasonable, in any case, than the usual version of events would lead one to believe. In the published transcripts that follow there are a number of examples of Hitler's decisions that are usually thought of as insane, overly confident, or based on blind emotion at best, but which were actually rooted in considerations that at least at the time seemed plausible, even when in hindsight they cannot be judged as completely objective. And as already mentioned, there were also decisions that were fundamentally correct—even in hindsight—and which were successful or averted disaster. It would be difficult to reach a clear and unassailable judgment about whether or not Hitler's mistakes, all things considered, outweigh his intuitively correct decisions. But in any case, this is relevant only with regard to the progression of the war, not its outcome. Hitler, trusting in the guidance of Providence and in his military genius, had already taken fateful steps against the political outcome of the war, an area where he had in effect, already capitulated in 1941.

Whatever one credits or does not credit Hitler with as military leader, and whatever pieces of the mosaic are missing from this collection that would complete his portrait, one point should not be overlooked under any circumstances: the German Armed Forces were not defeated in World War II because Hitler led them poorly and continually handicapped his generals, nor because the clever instincts of the Führer were diluted or sabotaged by his generals, who were at the very least narrow-minded if not downright evil. However much his allies, secret agents, resistors or anyone else is to be blamed, whether or not there was betrayal or sabotage, and however disastrous Hitler's individual or even collective military strategy decisions were, *militarily* the war could not have been won *after* 1941, and it *wasn't* won *before* 1941, despite dazzling battlefield victories. The war itself and the constellation into which it had to be fed, were the result of Hitler's *politics*, and only *politically* might it still have been possible to attempt to get out the of the war with as little damage as possible. The decisions to pursue "total war," and "war until five minutes past midnight" were not military decisions but political ones. These and many others burdened Hitler the statesman, not the general. But here we are concerned only with the latter—not with Hitler the politician, not with the destroyer of Europe, the executioner of the Jews, or the man with racial delusions and fantasies of extermination. Though all of these characterizations come together into a single person, we can examine the individual parts one by one, as long as we remain aware of the grim complete picture. The negative hero cult, however, depicting Hitler as the demonic destroyer of gigantic proportions (in *all* areas, and often allowing one characteristic to take on undeserved importance), is still a hero cult. One must learn to understand that overall there are some facets that can make this man appear average or even moderately good.

VII

The following transcripts cover precisely the period when military fortunes were changing and the turning point toward military defeat was reached. The path covered here stretches from the Caucasus to the Oder, from Cirenaica to Bologna, from the Atlantic to the Rhine. With the exception of the amazingly stable Armed Forces High Command (OKW), we are missing a considerable number of names of the people who were involved in the fanfare of special communiqués. Regarding the Army, not only Brauchitsch but also Halder finally faded back into civilian life, and of his two successors, one embodied only to a limited degree (and the other not at all) the typical character and training of the Prussian-German general staff. Also Admiral Raeder fails to reappear, and we see the replacement of not less than four Chiefs of the General Staff at the head of the Luftwaffe.

However, even the Hitler of 1943 is no longer the Hitler of 1940. He no longer fights easily with good fortune at his side, but now does battle only doggedly against his fate. Once the war lost its seasonal character, he buried himself in his headquarters—in that "mixture of monastery and concentration camp," as Jodl described the Wolfsschanze at Nuremberg—and dedicated himself to military operations, relegating his position as Reich Chancellor to a mere sideline. The soldier who decided in 1918 to become a politician had now decided to become a soldier once again. Only occasionally did the Führer of the Greater German Reich come up to the surface from his lair inside the bunker—for a stay at Berchtesgaden, to meet with his Axis allies for one of the increasingly essential "hypnotic treatments" as he called them or, more rarely, and only at first, to participate in acts of state in Berlin. Besides those exceptions, Hitler returned to his capital, the center of political life of the Reich, only in the final months of the war, and then practically as a fugitive fleeing the advancing Red Army. The person to whom he wanted to speak was transported in his pseudo-reality to East Prussia or the Ukraine. Hitler was interested in one subject alone: compelling the gods of war—by the force of all his fanatical will—to favor him again. All other issues became meaningless. For the second time in his existence, he experienced war as his vital element.

In addition, in 1943 Hitler was, aside from his disputed psychosis, physically a sick, worn-out man. Only Dr. Morell's suspicious quack drugs, whose side effects were unknown, slowed his quickening decline. In the winter of 1942-43, after suffering from stomach pains and dizzy spells for a year, he was further afflicted by a trembling of the limbs on the left side of his body, which soon made public appearances impossible. Today his illness would be diagnosed as *paralysis agitans*, or Parkinson's disease. Parkinson's disease is a degenerative disease of the brain that causes serious nerve damage, but which also affects the patient's mental and emotional faculties, frequently leading to paranoid and delusional thoughts.

These elements, which carry weight on both sides, should not be forgotten when reading and attempting to draw conclusions from the transcripts. Once again, regardless of other reservations, momentous revelations should not be expected due to the fragmentary character of the collection. At best, the information should certainly be viewed as preliminary evidence; partial evidence of a Hitler who, in endless arrogant ranting, criticized only others and saw mistakes and failures only in others, a Hitler who interfered in tactical military operations to the point of deploying regimental groups and artillery battalions, who displayed a staggering ignorance in the evaluation of foreign peoples (for example the United States!), and who showed increasing symptoms of political wishful thinking, which led to unfounded hypotheses and a readiness to grasp at straws. This should also be seen as evidence of a Hitler who can captivate his audience through his amazing command of detail, a Hitler who for some decisions was capable of offering a *logical* rationale, and a Hitler who appears not to have been as isolated in his decisions opposing the rational rest of the world as we are often led to believe.

There is also evidence on the other hand favorable to those who were part of Hitler's military entourage—its emphatic representation of its own opinions, as well as its silence, agreement and compliance is also apparent. Reading even these comparatively few recovered pages is enough to create quite a clear picture of many of the people who were involved in military decisions—their content and their character. Before reaching the end, the attentive reader will know in each single case the role each person played and what kind of evaluation that person deserves. The reader will know that some challenged Hitler at considerable risk, but also that some willingly knew and accepted more, without resisting, than they would later be willing to admit.

This book offers an inside view of the German High Command and military leadership and the opportunity to get to know its personnel, a contribution to the portrait of Hitler, and some insight into the course of military history—more should not be expected from this collection of transcripts. But even considering the fragmentary nature of the compilation and all the reservations we have mentioned, this collection should be viewed as a unique historical document, because it would be hard to find another place where considerations and decisions at the highest military level were the subject of regular verbatim records.

MAPS

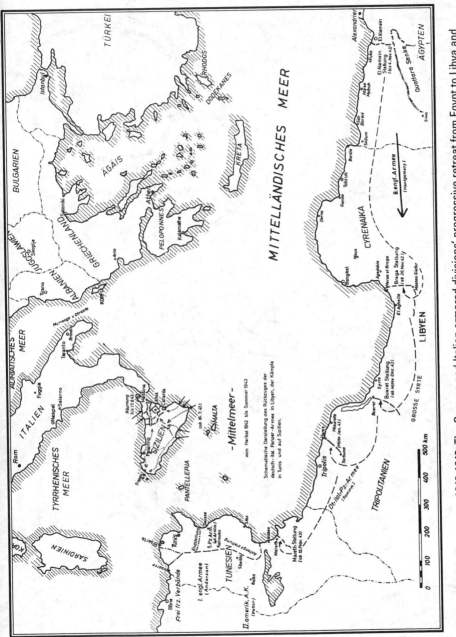

Map 1. The Mediterranean 1942-1943. The German and Italian armored divisions' progressive retreat from Egypt to Libya and Tunisia; the battles in Tunisia and Sicily.

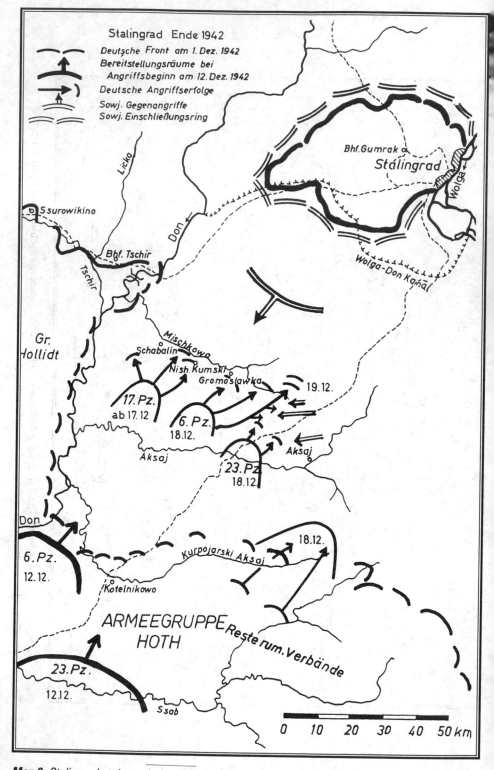

Map 2. Stalingrad at the end of 1942. German front lines on December 1 and December 12.

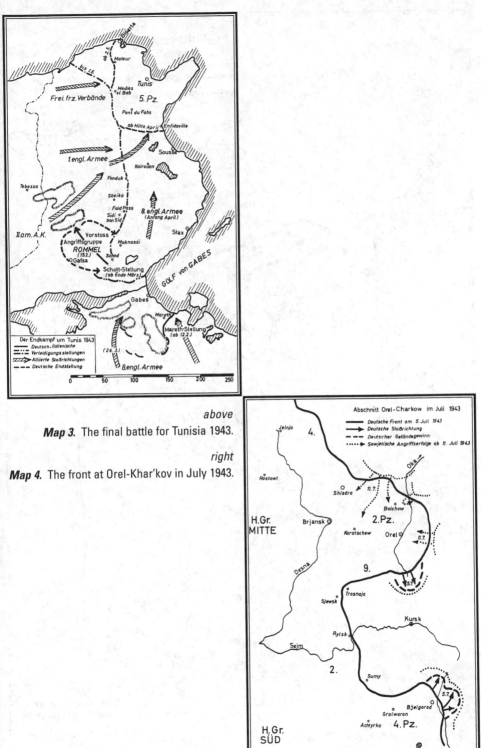

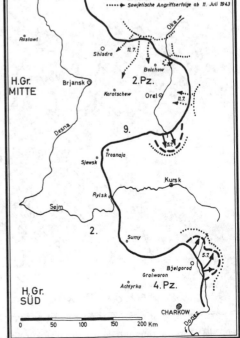

above

Map 3. The final battle for Tunisia 1943.

right

Map 4. The front at Orel-Khar'kov in July 1943.

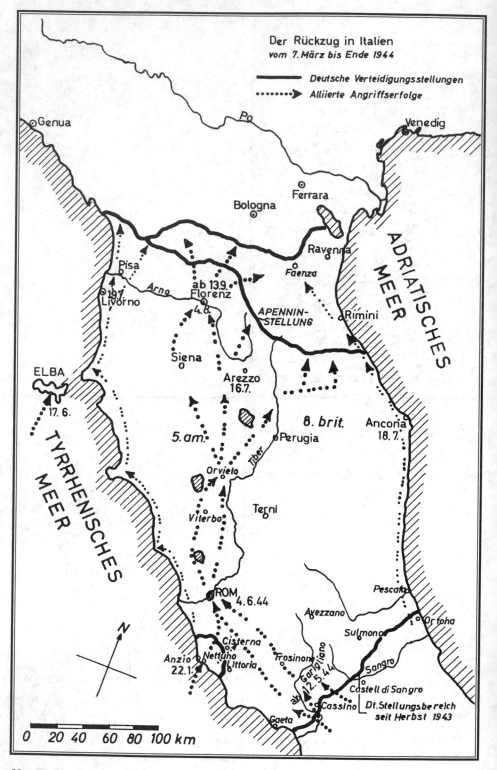

Map 5a. The fighting in Italy from March 7 to the end of 1944.

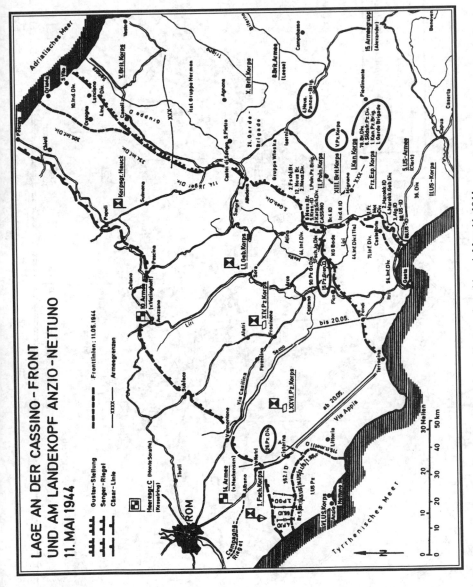

Map 5b. Italy: Monte Cassino and the Anzio-Nettuno beachhead, May 11, 1944

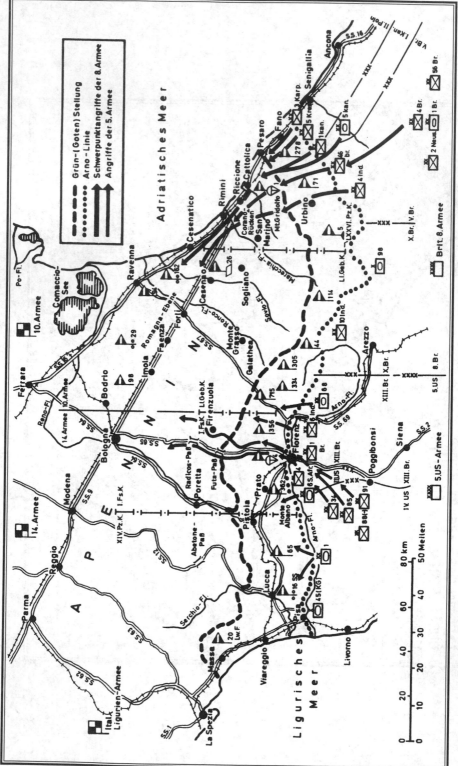

Map 5c. Italy: the Gothic Line, August 25, 1944.

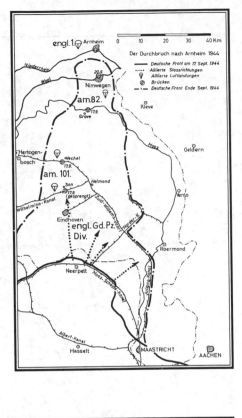

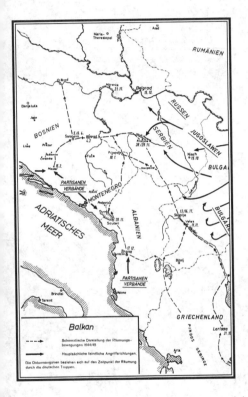

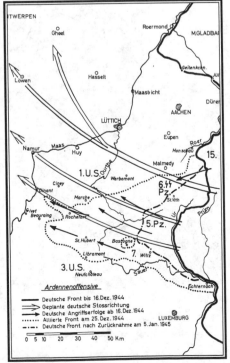

top, right
Map 6. The battle at Arnhem 1944.

above
Map 7. The Balkans 1944-1945.

right
Map 8. The Ardennes offensive
(the Battle of the Bulge), December 1944.

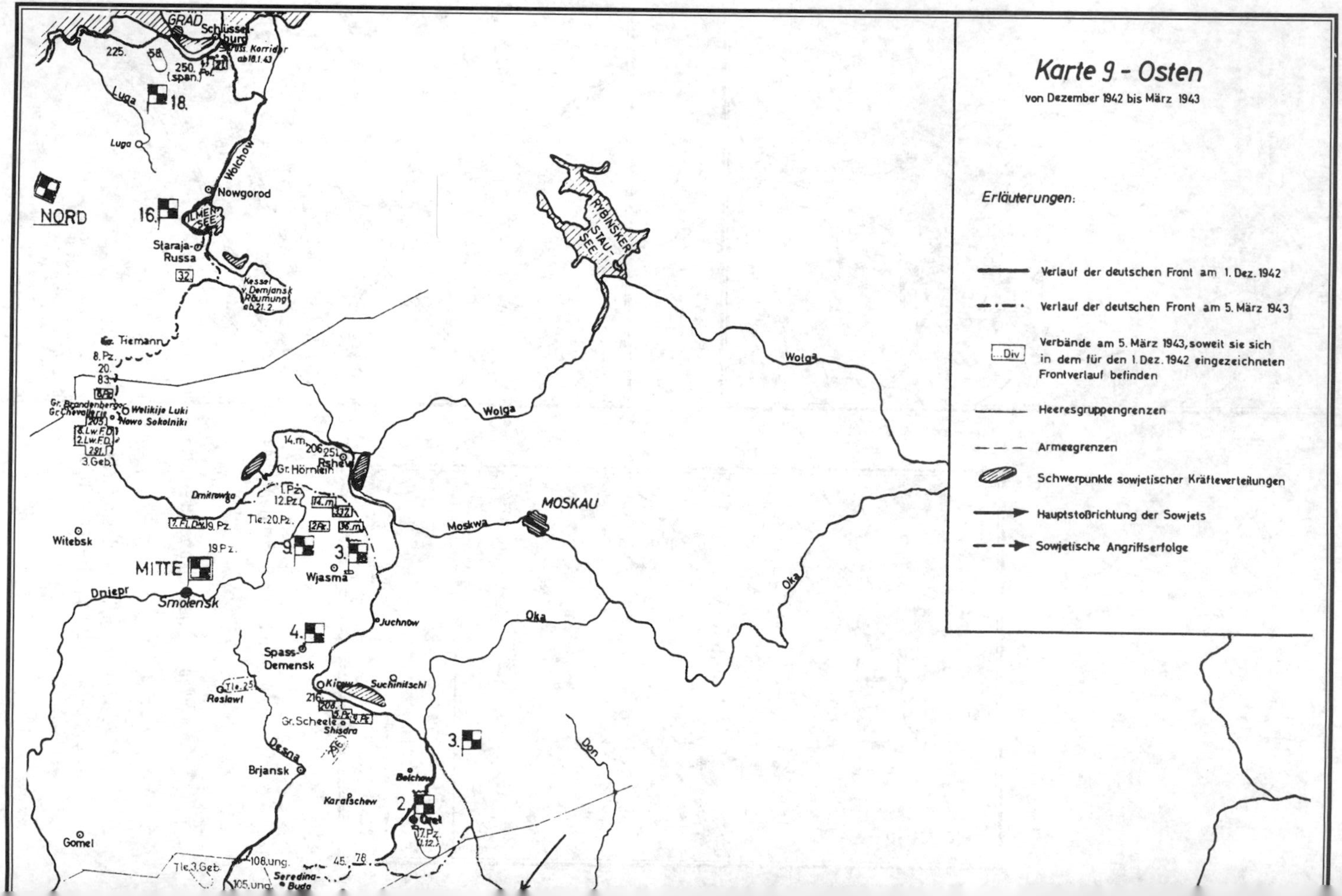

Karte 9 – Osten
von Dezember 1942 bis März 1943

Erläuterungen:

———— Verlauf der deutschen Front am 1. Dez. 1942

–·–·–· Verlauf der deutschen Front am 5. März 1943

Div. Verbände am 5. März 1943, soweit sie sich in dem für den 1. Dez. 1942 eingezeichneten Frontverlauf befinden

———— Heeresgruppengrenzen

–––––– Armeegrenzen

⬭ Schwerpunkte sowjetischer Kräfteverteilungen

⟶ Hauptstoßrichtung der Sowjets

⟶ Sowjetische Angriffserfolge

RYBINSKER STAU-SEE

Wolga

Oka

MOSKAU

Moskwa

Wolga

Oka

Don

Wolchow

Nowgorod

Staraja Russa

NORD

18.

16.

32.

Gr. Tiemann

8. Pz.
20.
83.

Gr. Brandenberger
Gr. Chevallerie

Wnikije Luki
Newe Sokolniki

3. Gb.

Welikije Luki
Nowo Sokolniki

[LFD]
[2.Lw.FD.]
[Lw.FD.]

Dnjepr

Witebsk

Smolensk

MITTE

V. FJ.
19 Pz.

Gomel

Gr. Hörnlein

12.Pz.
Tle 20.Pz.

25 Pz.

3.

Wjasma

9.

Spass
Demiensk

4.

Juchnow

Roslawl

Gr. Scheele
Ocssa

Brjansk

Sachinitsch

2.

Karatschew

Orel

3.

Saredino

Don

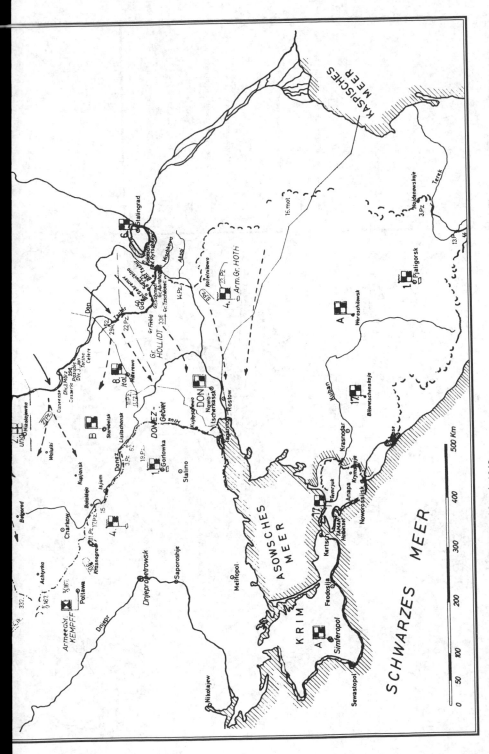

Map 9. The Eastern Front, December 1942 to March 1943.

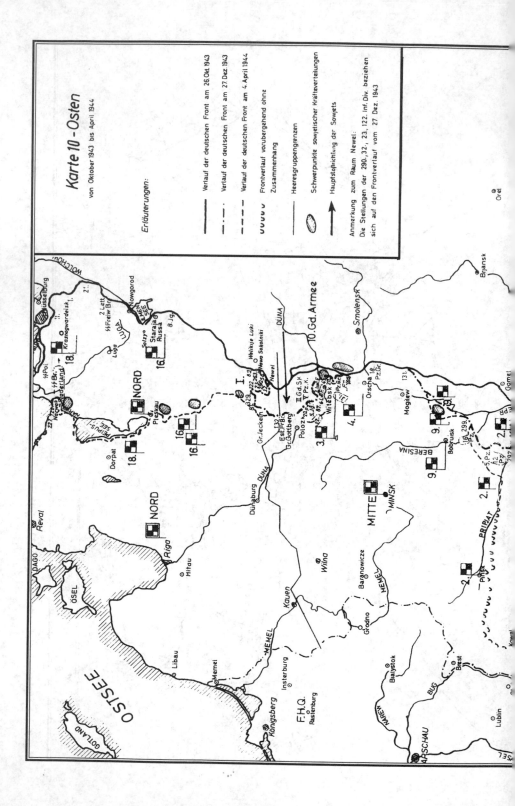

Karte 10 - Osten
von Oktober 1943 bis April 1944

Erläuterungen:

Verlauf der deutschen Front am 26.Okt.1943

Verlauf der deutschen Front am 27.Dez.1943

Verlauf der deutschen Front am 4.April 1944

Frontverlauf vorübergehend ohne Zusammenhang

Heeresgruppengrenzen

Schwerpunkte sowjetischer Kräfteverteilungen

Hauptstoßrichtung der Sowjets

Anmerkung zum Raum Newel:
Die Stellungen der 290.,32.,23.,122. Inf. Div. beziehen sich auf den Frontverlauf vom 27.Dez.1943

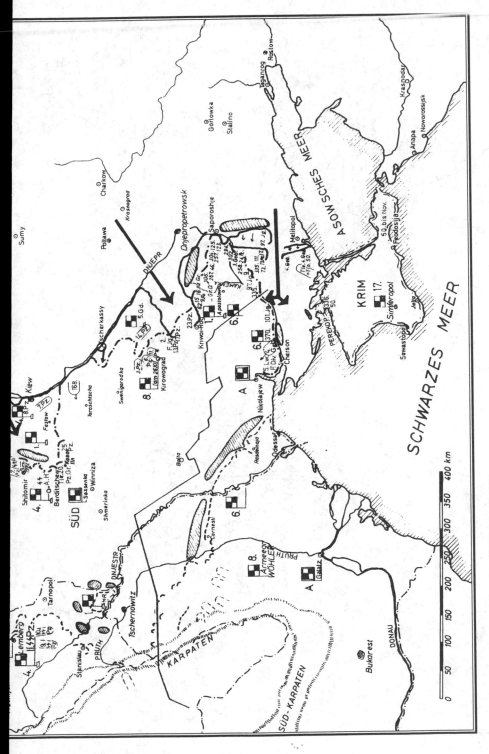

Map 10. The Eastern Front, October 1943 to April 1944.

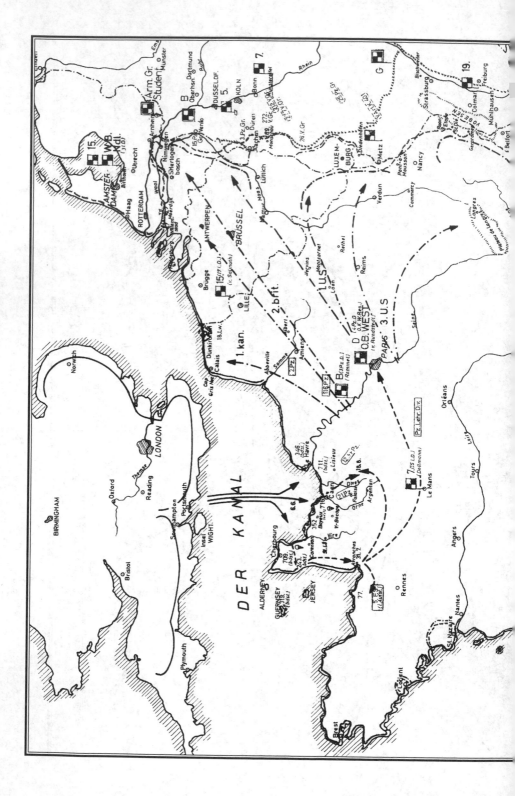

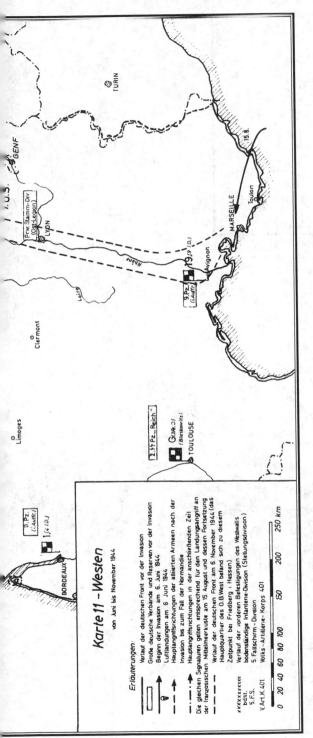

Map 11. The Western Front, June to November 1944.

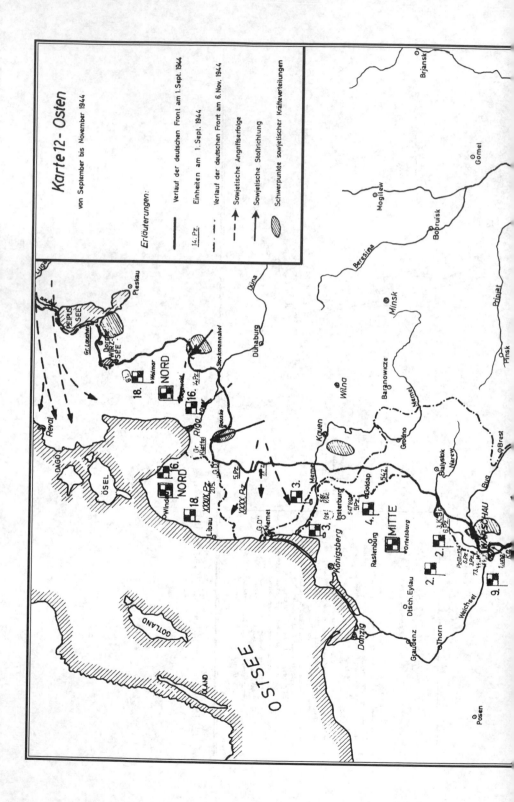

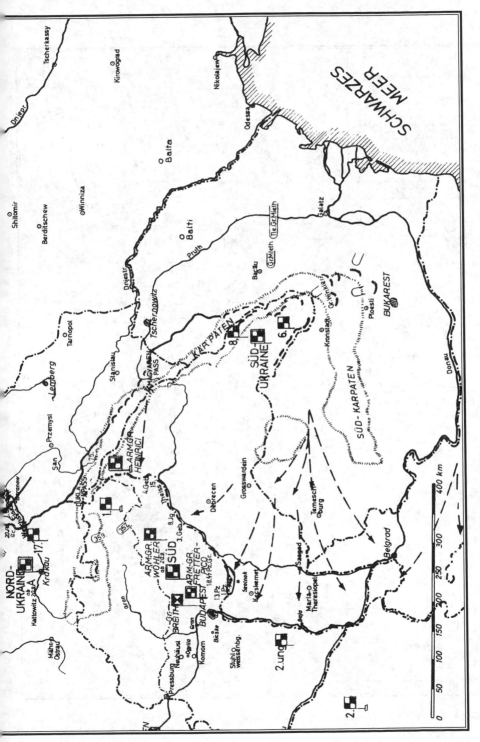

Map 12. The Eastern Front, September to November 1944.

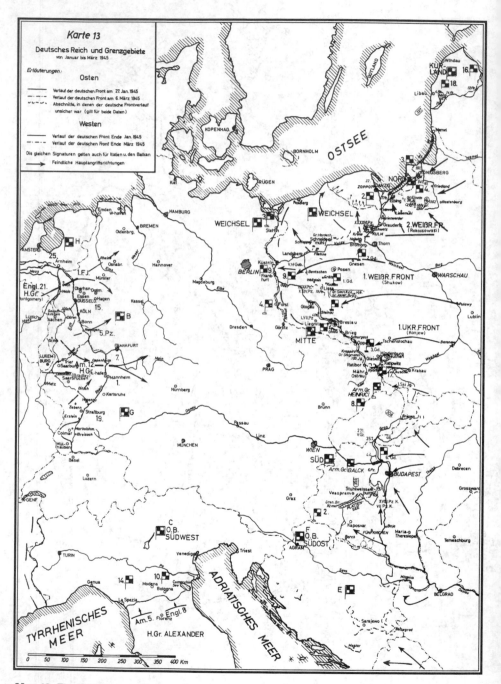

Map 13. The Western and Eastern Fronts, January to March 1945.

CONFERENCE TRANSCRIPTS

1942

* * * * *

During the preceding month of November, the military situation of Germany and its allies had fundamentally changed. Retreat had begun on all fronts. From now on resistance would be possible only at great sacrifice, and release from the pressure would be brief and affect only limited areas. There are three dates in that most eventful month which signal the change in the fortunes of war:

On November 4, Rommel was pushed back from the Egyptian position at El Alamein, 80 kilometers from Alexandria;

On November 8, the Americans entered the land war with Eisenhower's landing in Algiers and Morocco;

On November 19 and 20, the Russians broke through the overstretched lines of the [Axis] allies northwest and south of Stalingrad, and on the 22nd surrounded the German Sixth Army located there.

In Africa, in the meantime, Tobruk and Benghazi had fallen and Rommel's retreat was temporarily halted by the cautious and methodical leadership of Montgomery at the Mersa-el Brega position, between Benghazi and El Agheila on the southeastern shore of the Gulf of Sidra, and more than 1,000 kilometers from El Alamein. French North Africa is in the hands of the Anglo-Americans, apart from the eastern half of Tunisia—which was occupied by German troops as of November 10 and where they will still be able to hold the Gafsa-Faid-Fonduk-Tabarca line for months. Three days before, on November 28 while at the Führer's Headquarters, Rommel advised that Germany should retreat from Africa, because the problem of transporting supplies across the Mediterranean couldn't be solved. Hitler indignantly rebuked him.

At the southern end of the Eastern Front, two actions were successful: the establishment of a loose defense line along the Chir River and the defense of a bridgehead at the mouth of the Chir next to Verchne-Chirskii, barely 50 kilometers away from the Sixth Army's perimeter, which Hitler had forbidden them to break. However, south of Stalingrad, on the east bank of the river Don, the Russians had already advanced more than 100 kilometers to the south. And relief troops for Stalingrad could really only come from that direction, as the Don lies between the Chir front and the bend of the Volga.

In contrast to the dramatic events in the south, it is relatively quiet in the middle and northern parts of the Eastern Front, apart from a Soviet attack on the deep western flank of the German advance front of Rzhev in the area of Velikie Luki-Toropets-Belyi. Together with Demiansk, which has more or less been surrounded since February 8, this area is one of the remaining strongholds of a blocked Soviet breakthrough in the winter of 1941-42. (*Map 9*)

* * * * *

Eᴠᴇɴɪɴɢ Sɪᴛᴜᴀᴛɪᴏɴ Rᴇᴘᴏʀᴛ, Dᴇᴄᴇᴍʙᴇʀ 1, 1942[*]

Beginning: 8:20 p.m.

The East

THE FÜHRER: There was no attack at the Don?

JODL: Yes, the *Pasubio* Division[25] met a small advance at the Don. According to the statement of a prisoner, the Russians intend to attack the *Pasubio* from both sides tomorrow.

THE FÜHRER: Has the advance been finished off?

JODL: According to an Italian report, the enemy was driven back again. A cruiser and six small units have been observed here in the south. It seems as if the entire Russian fleet has sailed,[26] one unit to Bulgaria, the other to Romania and the third there.

THE FÜHRER: And the submarines?[27] In this case, one can't say that the Luftwaffe would be more suitable.

---

[*] Transcript No. 179/42—Fragment No. 29—fully preserved.

BODENSCHATZ: At the moment the clouds over the Black Sea are 400 meters high. It is nasty weather. The Russians chose to attack during this weather so that the Luftwaffe can't intervene.

THE FÜHRER: It doesn't matter to the motor torpedo boats and the submarines.

JODL: Otherwise heavy attacks against the 95th[28] [Infantry Division] have been driven back here. Today the enemy didn't attack here at all—or only very weakly. On the other hand, there is a prisoner's statement saying that the enemy wants to attack with the 2nd [Rifle] Corps, along with the 3rd Rifle, and 9th and 11th Guards [Rifle] Corps on December 2. After the failed attack yesterday, the enemy hasn't attacked again yet, only sought contact. But a weak attack is...

THE FÜHRER: We have to announce that tomorrow ... How did it go with the Italians?

JODL: Here, the 3rd Panzer Division pushed forward to Naidenovskoe and took 400 prisoners. It seems that the infantry has explored up to this line, and north of it the cavalry. The 3rd Panzer Division would like to push further forward, but at the moment it doesn't have any fuel; only a little bit that it can't use up completely.

THE FÜHRER: They must be supplied with some, or they will suddenly run out. Then they'll be immobile.

JODL: The 4th Guards [Rifle] Corps has made exploratory advances from here, but took only one village, which wasn't occupied. There were no major attacks along the entire Don front, not even against the Sixth Army.[29] Here the enemy tried to push forward but was driven back. Here the same thing happened. At the moment, an attack to the east of Kotel'nikovo against the village is in progress. The result is not yet known. Here, the enemy apparently only attacked fairly weakly. The exact report hasn't yet arrived. It seems as if the enemy is also worrying about being attacked now, and he seems to be filling in a bit more from that direction, since it was a bit livelier there. Here, where only cavalry were positioned, infantry can now also be found. The enemy attacked from the train station in Chir and was driven back again. There, where he was already positioned yesterday, he extended a little bit against the defenses, so he ought to be forced out by a group from the 336th [Infantry] Division tomorrow. Attacks against Surovikino were driven back. Combat continues at the train station of Sekretov. Attacks against ... were driven back. In those attacks, 120 were taken prisoner and 6 tanks were destroyed. Three tanks were destroyed here. The 40th Guards and the 321st [Rifle] Divisions should be here, but we have not been able to identify their location. In addition, the cavalry has pushed forward here and has apparently captured Kireev. The precise report hasn't arrived yet. It is quiet further north. With regard to the Italians there was the *Pasubio* attack.

According to prisoners' statements, there are two divisions located there, and a strong group here. The enemy would attack the *Pasubio* from two directions, from here and from here. Besides, according to the statement of a prisoner, there are 200 tanks there. Apart from the 298th [Infantry] Regiment, which is on the alert, a tank destroyer detachment and an engineer battalion were added. Today the Luftwaffe attacked this road southwest of Kalach.

THE FÜHRER: He must have used up most of it in these last few days.

JODL: On the Eastern Front, the situation of Army Group Center has continued to stabilize. All attacks were driven back today. Group[30] Schweitzer[31] wasn't attacked again at all. There was a penetration in the 88th [Infantry Division], which has been cleared out. The cavalry, which was west of Lozhki, was driven back and is getting out of the way to the west. It is on this road and will probably go over to the partisans, so that front is quite hopeless. Here, there is no other opposition. Up there, the enemy didn't attack, but brought in reinforcements against the front of the 251st [Infantry Division]. There, the artillery fired more energetically. The attacks against the 206th [Infantry Division] and against the boundary of the 206th [Infantry] and 14th [Motorized Divisions] were driven back. Here he made progress. At first, he attacked the western block of the Hörnlein[32] group and was driven back. But here he penetrated the first villages and captured Zhernasovo, a village which was defended by the regimental headquarters of an infantry regiment of the *Grossdeutschland* Division. The commander was killed in this action. The situation further south is not clear, but it is certain that Zhertushia is in our possession. Then the enemy took advantage of the gap and pushed forces forward at Korschevo, by advancing through the forest area. He didn't attack north against the road again, which was cleared out by the motorcycle infantry battalion *Grossdeutschland* yesterday, but he ordered more forces. He attacked the northern flank of the 1st Panzer Division and was driven back. He ordered more forces for further south. The 12th Panzer Division is attacking the group of forces standing to the north of this hill in the forest. The result is not yet final. Here are still several tanks, which are left from yesterday or the day before and which are now hanging around the train station in Dmitrovo, but they can't do much. They didn't cause a great deal of damage and will probably run out of fuel. Whereas here, the first thing that was lost was the military base. Then he penetrated this village from the rear, so that this base was also threatened from behind. He apparently didn't bother to attack further east. Here he sought further contact. Parts of the 19th Panzer [Division] have not yet been deployed. The majority of the 20th [Panzer Division] hasn't been used yet either.

THE FÜHRER: I don't think that this will be an operational breakthrough.

JODL: If one could bring things together, then this road would be very appropriate. What it offers is the 19th Panzer and these reserves, located here and waiting for the Russian attack, which I no longer think will come. At Group Chevallerie[33] it has definitely been successful in making contact with this base and linking up. This was possible because of a thrust by this regiment from the 3rd Mountain Division and this group from the 291st [Infantry Division]. It has established, if not a front, quite a contact. The enemy has been thrown out there. In addition, he broke away from this group further north. In any case, there are movements to be found there. At least he weakened himself. The attacks against Velikie Luki were weak. A bit stronger against the regiment of the 83rd [Infantry] Division, coming from the west. They were driven back. These two bases along the railroad are holding out; the enemy is sitting at one of the stations in between. Attacks from the southwest against Novosokol'niki were driven back. He is said to have come across the railway and the road in a western direction with one battalion. Then he attacked the Brandenberger[34] group more intensely, with Panzers from both sides of the road. The attacks were driven back. The left wing of the Brandenberger group was able to push further. Here the fighting was heavier; more casualties in the 8th Panzer Division were also reported here. The Tiemann[35] group reported that they had penetrated the lines here and captured the two villages Krischino and Semarkovo—and they were mainly hindered by the powerful mines, explosions and blockades which were laid out sequentially below.

THE FÜHRER: This will come to nothing.

JODL: This one won't work. Of course this is the result of an offensive in such weather. It is impossible to see what is going on. The people don't know what to do. All attacks to the south of Army Group North were driven back. All attacks to the north were also driven back. Another difficult area has come up, namely where the front turns the corner. There he attacked with 40 tanks and heavy infantry again, but 15 tanks were destroyed. Here is the front which was maybe extended a bit yesterday, but which is not entirely drawn in here. It goes along here and from there north.

THE FÜHRER: This is the next place where we will set something up, if we free these forces now. It will be more than 60 by December. The next place in the east is the road [—]

KEITEL: The Volga!

JODL: There has only been occasional long-range fire against the road behind the SS Police Division[36] and its own firing zone in the 57th [Infantry Division].

(*Long-distance call between the Führer and General Zeitzler.[37]*)

ZEITZLER: My Führer, may I report? First of all, general matters. At [Army Group] B everything is satisfactory. In the center, the northern front and the eastern front are satisfactory. The western front is not quite settled. Velikie Luki is satisfactory as well. In Army Group North the bottleneck,[38] is satisfactory in the southern direction. He expanded the northern point of penetration. I can report in detail the following, starting with the center. Everything is in order on the eastern front. Attacks were driven back. Attacks were also driven back on the northern front. Western front: first, General Hörnlein! He has a front toward the south. Today he penetrated this front at two points. This afternoon the army group requested to move this front back by approximately 10 kilometers—there, where there is a "Gr." for group on the map, cutting off about there. I said that I would present it to you, but basically I am against it. It is the same thing again—they want to give up the stronghold. Then he will basically have a big gap. He won't at all be able to fill it on his own. If it really does get penetrated a bit, we can always fill it.

THE FÜHRER: That's right!

ZEITZLER: May I decide this then?

THE FÜHRER: Yes!

ZEITZLER: Then I will prepare it. Otherwise the situation is not quite clear yet. The commander of the *Grossdeutschland* Infantry Regiment was killed in action at his command post. Further south at Belyi the situation has remained the same so far. I think the bad weather is the primary reason for it. Everything is incredibly slippery; neither group can move on. He pushed south in the gap and captured the village Nirovokovo—that is the northernmost small black spot that is drawn here. He merely put units in action against the 20th Panzer Division, which is pushing up from below. Further east, the 12th Panzer Division is doing battle with units that have broken through; there the enemy was behind parts of the 1st Panzer Division. The 12th Panzer Division couldn't get very far north. The enemy is still pushing to the east and the north. On the whole, the situation there is similar to what it was the day before, but probably even better. At Velikie Luki it was possible to advance with a battalion from General Jaschke's[39] lower group toward the next group of Colonel Klatt.[40] Klatt's group approached from the other side with a battalion and they met, so the connection has been established. Then he attacked here again with his entire 8th Panzer Division, so that the attack of the 8th Panzer Division couldn't win any ground. He attacked against Novosokol'niki and was driven back. The 8th Panzer Division wants to attack differently tomorrow—not from the furthest position toward the southeast, but more or less from the left wing down toward the south. They expect it to be better. They want to push down the road from approximately the point where Section 381 is located now, because the enemy opposite their actual front has become too strong. The Tiemann group has advanced 5 kilometers again today. It mainly has to contend with the terrain and the mines. [—] If I may now take a look at the south and remark on the following: reports arrived today from various sources regarding the Russian Black Sea fleet sailing again on the Black Sea—a few cruisers near Anapa and a few near the Crimea.

THE FÜHRER: If our motor torpedo boats don't discover them soon, the ones sailing around there [—]!

ZEITZLER: I asked them what they had done as a result of this. They have done nothing. Nevertheless I gave the order to alert the Crimean and coastal defenses and to send the reserves to the positions where they should be standing. It doesn't matter if it is not necessary; then they will have had a practice session. But I think that it is better to do so. [—] With the Seventeenth Army and the First Panzer Army nothing special has happened. The First Panzer Army deployed an infantry regiment with the 3rd Panzer Division at the Terek [River], against a threat that a cavalry is developing 20 to 25 kilometers to the north.

THE FÜHRER: I think we have to try to supply them with fuel[41] so that they will indeed be able to push north.

ZEITZLER: This morning I ordered two trains with fuel to come over here. I found out that they do have fuel for such a thrust down there and are able to do it. They are waiting a bit, though, since there is only enough for one thrust. But I think that in one or two days the fuel situation will have improved down there.[42]

THE FÜHRER: Good.

ZEITZLER: With the Manstein[43] group, at Kotel'nikovo, nothing special has happened. The Chir front was severely attacked today, from the train station in Chir where Colonel Tzschöckell[44] is located, past the Abraham[45] group and Schmidt group to the Fiebig[46] group. Everything was driven back by Colonel Tschücke from the entire front, 100 prisoners were taken. Yesterday a little penetration was reported at the next corner. This breakthrough was supposed to be attacked today, but the attack hasn't been able to advance because the enemy continued pushing against it. Several tanks were destroyed there. Tomorrow, parts of the 336th [Infantry Division] will be committed against it in order to push the enemy back. At the next corner... was attacked. Three tanks were destroyed. Everything held. Also on the next corner, by Colonel Schmidt, six tanks were destroyed. Near the Fiebig group there is a little village called Kireevo, where enemy cavalry with about 1,000 men entered. The following is interesting regarding this: prisoners were taken from the 40th Guards [Rifle] Division and the 321st [Rifle] Division. Both of these divisions were located at the northwest corner of the Sixth Army until now. The prisoners stated that they had been brought here during three nights on a quick march. From this we could conclude that he is weakening the front of the Sixth Army in order to destroy this point at the Chir. Further evidence of this is that the Sixth Army was only attacked weakly today. Approximately 100 tons were flown to the Sixth Army. The front further north! The 22nd Panzer Division and Group Hollidt[47] weren't attacked. But this afternoon he fired many shells at Hollidt, the rear connection and the headquarters. In this case, this always means a preparation for the days to come. Nothing in particular happened with the Italians. The *Pasubio* was attacked by reinforced assault troops—2 to 3 companies. Prisoners were taken, and they said he wanted to attack the *Pasubio* tomorrow and capture the entire bend—1 to 2 divisions and 200 tanks were ready. I ordered the army group to do something in response to this in any case. With the Romanians he also started with little things like this.[48] The army group put a tank destroyer company of the 298th [Infantry] Division along with an engineer battalion of the 298th [Infantry Division] into action with the *Pasubio*. One of the regiments—on the map it says "1/3 298"—was alerted and brought up behind the left wing of the *Pasubio*. In addition, the Luftwaffe provided an anti-aircraft unit, which also comes behind the *Pasubio*. At the moment, this is what we can do. [—] Five days ago I sent an anti-aircraft defense specialist to the Italians. He has found another depot: 9,000 rounds of hollow-cone shells. He brought these with the German engineer-training unit to the Italians, so they have small combat units of German engineers with heavy shells[49] and explosive shells. Nothing happened with the Hungarians. [—] Army Group Center didn't report anything. [—] In Army Group North, he attacked at the bottleneck from the south and was driven back. In the north he broke this little stronghold. He attacked there again today with heavy forces and was able to get close to the village of Rosino. This is not much, but hardly satisfying.

THE FÜHRER: That is not good to hear. Nothing can be lost up there.

ZEITZLER: Tomorrow the entire 58th [Infantry] Division will arrive, so we can hope that it will be supported to some extent. He seems to be systematically breaking out of one fence after the other. There is nothing further north. That would be all. (*End of the long-distance call.*)

THE FÜHRER: The Luftwaffe can settle this. Tomorrow the Luftwaffe units should also be alerted, and look out for the Italians. Under all circumstances we must use this one panzer unit, which is there, in particular [—]. If it really works like that with the "Tigers,"[50] then we will have to bring some down there. You are convinced that the program will go according to plans?

BUHLE: We can do it with the production from the second half of December, without any great effort. 50 tanks.

THE FÜHRER: 68 will be out then altogether.

BUHLE: Then we can use the production from the second half of December to protect a spot on the Eastern Front—a spot, in fact, where it is particularly necessary: at the bottleneck. The next one will then be established at Iukhnov. And later we will see where a few really dangerous places are located.

SPEER: You can't use any bridges.

THE FÜHRER: I told you that you have to build bridges that support more than 60 tons.

Tunis

BUHLE: I have received a message from Tunis. Thomale[51] is on his way. It seems as if there is some more... [—] but that is all [—] those should be warning shots.

THE FÜHRER: Has it finally been clarified?

JODL: It has been clarified.[52] We reported on November 27 that two ships arrived. On these ships there were 32 Panzer IIIs,[53] one Tiger [tank], and two tanks with long guns[54]—altogether 35 tanks and 28 patrol cars—not Italian Panzers, as the Reichsmarshal had heard. This group has now reached the front. They are the two companies that reported to us that had arrived there. They are at the front, and with them the force at the front has increased to 64 tanks that are ready to go.

BUHLE: 50 have actually been loaded.

JODL: 50 are loaded, of which the ... will arrive tomorrow.

THE FÜHRER: Then it will be 100.

BUHLE: There is another group. Then the tanks of the panzer division will be over there with the exception of a couple of Panzer IIs.

THE FÜHRER: They alone have 150.

BUHLE: 105 Panzer IIIs and 20 Panzer IVs, then a few more will be sent on later.

THE FÜHRER: Is there something new here?

JODL: No, only that our reconnaissance was able to establish quite good contact, as far as the area around Nudia.

THE FÜHRER: Air reconnaissance?

JODL: No, ground reconnaissance. In addition, they were pushed further on to Demiens and took 31 prisoners on the way. They came from these paratroopers here. It hasn't yet been confirmed if they are Americans or not. When they landed, they were reported to be Americans. Whereas, when they were taken prisoner [—]

THE FÜHRER: English people won't get caught so easily, they are tough dogs.

JODL: This group here doesn't seem to have had any major attacks yesterday. It seems to have turned more to the east. One gets the impression of smaller raids.

THE FÜHRER: When the French make something happen, then they will attack where there is clearly no danger, since they above all don't want any high-casualty raids.

JODL: Then they tried to attack the Witzig[55] group comprehensively. All these attacks were driven back. However, this reconnaissance effort proves that stronger forces are not ready yet. It was an attempt that wasn't particularly successful.

THE FÜHRER: Has something happened in the southeast?

JODL: No report from the panzer division.

Norway, Channel, Black Sea

Six steam engines were made available for the train to Narvik,[56] two of which were borrowed from Sweden.

THE FÜHRER: They will never get them back.

JODL: One heavy one, 2 medium-weight ones and 3 light ones.

THE FÜHRER: Narvik needs to have something now. If they cut off power there, the Narvik train will be finished.

KRANCKE: This is what they did back then with coal engines as well. Power was cut off, and we continued to run with steam engines as a reserve.

JODL: Then a report about the motor torpedo boat deployment in the Channel came in saying that a steamer of 3,000 tons was sunk and a security vessel was torpedoed.

THE FÜHRER: In the Channel it's working! Why isn't it working down there?[57]

KRANCKE: The Black Sea is bigger than the North Sea. Nothing can be done with motor torpedo boats if they don't know the exact location. They were in the wrong place and had the order to observe the traffic at Tuapse.

THE FÜHRER: The Russian fleet and our motor torpedo boats seem to me to be like two dogs that bark at each other through a fence and constantly run past the hole through which they could reach each other. They both get out of each other's way.

KRANCKE: We are not getting out of the way, but the sea area is too big.

THE FÜHRER: The room for operations is very small.

KRANCKE: Now they have gone out there and out to Constanza. Nobody was expecting that.

THE FÜHRER: Where are our submarines located? In the middle of the Black Sea?

KRANCKE: I believe they are located at Tuapse, where the supply lines are to be interrupted.

THE FÜHRER: But they have caught nothing there so far.[58] They have never seen anything. And the Russians go in and out constantly!

KRANCKE: They are looking and still need to get to know the waters.

JODL: Destroyers attacked some motor torpedo boats, but they immediately drove back the attack with their 4-cm guns.

THE FÜHRER: Motor torpedo boats don't have 4-cm guns.

JODL: It was reported: 4-cm guns.

THE FÜHRER: Then they must be bootleg weapons.

KRANCKE: Captured guns![59] We have a whole lot of 4-cm guns, which were sometimes used by the batteries as middle flak.

JODL: Apparently the entire Black Sea Fleet has put to sea except for the battleship. A group was in front of the mouth of the Danube, a second one was at Varna and a third one at Anapa. Four were in front of the Crimea.

THE FÜHRER: How active they are!

JODL: All of them were used again so that they don't rust. They fired some shots ashore and left again.

THE FÜHRER: That means a lot; and tomorrow they will report around the world again that they completely rule the Black Sea and go wherever they want there.

KRANCKE: We need to wait and see if they get home unscathed.

THE FÜHRER: Why should they not get home unscathed?

KRANCKE: I hope they will go where the submarines are based.

France

JODL: The Military Commander in France reports: Quite a quiet day yesterday. No recognizable change in the attitude of the population. No incidents with the demobilized French soldiers.[60] There was a robbery at a mayor's office in the district of Seine-et-Loire. The French police were able to arrest six armed offenders—all of them belonging to a terrorist group.

THE FÜHRER: Good! The police are good. We will rope them in and will only work with the police. Himmler knows his police. He proceeds with reprehensible means and is able to coerce the people. That will be an alliance with the police![61]

JODL: It makes the best impression.

THE FÜHRER: The police are hated more than anything else in the country, and they're looking for support from an even greater authority than their own state—that means us. The police will urge us not to leave the country.

JODL: Several days ago, the number of French workers working for the Reich exceeded 200,000.[62]

THE FÜHRER: That will increase as well. Above all, these people have nothing. And the other thing is, they say to themselves: At least there is no danger of war for us. They don't want a war. What for, anyway? They all have the feeling that whatever happens, the whole war was folly.

Tunis

JODL: Then I may mention the question of leadership in Africa. It is, of course, an organizational question. That's a "don't touch" issue for the Italians.[63] It won't take long before they say, "Of course we need to have the command of the war theater." But as far as this question is concerned, they haven't done anything yet.

THE FÜHRER: First of all, we are the ones who have made everything happen. Secondly, if there is any sort of major offensive advance, there won't be any Italians there anyway.

JODL: That's also the reason why they don't even mention us quietly leading the war theater. They have never said a word about it.

THE FÜHRER: They can't, either. There are at least four of our motorized divisions there—and another division is practically complete, if we add in the paratroopers, etc. Then it will be five divisions. Together with the two infantry divisions, that's seven divisions. With seven divisions, we are leading the war by ourselves anyway.[64] They aren't leading the war. As far as materiel is concerned, we also have to lead alone. They do, however, make the crossings. But after conquering the French, we also supported the sea region. And if we hadn't conquered the French, we wouldn't have the sea region either. When things up there are mopped up—

KRANCKE: —then we will be able to give them Tunis and we will take Algiers.

THE FÜHRER: Then they can take that into their administration completely.

BODENSCHATZ: We only have to handle the anti-aircraft artillery cover by ourselves.

KEITEL: The supply as well!

Draft of Official Regulations for the struggle against the partisans

I should remind everyone once again about this guerilla fighting.[65] Yesterday, in the middle of everything, there was a quick command regarding it.

THE FÜHRER: I think a certain preamble is necessary. Basically, in guerilla fighting, everything that leads to success is right—this has to be drummed into everybody. This is the first priority. If somebody does something which is not in accord with an order, but which can lead to a clear success, or if someone finds himself in an emergency situation that he can only confront with brute force, then every method that leads to success is correct.[66] The goal must be to destroy the guerillas and restore peace and order. Otherwise, we will end up in the same situation that we had once in our domestic affairs, with the so-called self-defense clause. This clause led to the situation that no policeman or soldier actually dared to use his gun in Germany.[67] This was such an elastic clause that the individual had to say to himself: If I unfortunately kill the other person, then I'm done for; if he kills me, then I'm also done for—but how do I make him unable to fight without injuring him, and without becoming unable to fight myself? That was the famous elastic clause in the self-defense law, which always trapped the person carrying the gun—regardless of whether they were in the police or army. This was exhibited at the incidents at Zabern the most crassly.[68] But it has been constantly repeated with the police. On the one hand, there was the order: You have to do this. But on the other hand, there was the danger of exceeding of the law of self-defense. So I think we have to include a preface: "Disregarding everything ... it is of the highest duty to destroy the gangs. Thus, everything will be regarded as right which helps destroy them, and, inversely, everything that doesn't help destroy the gangs will be regarded as wrong." That will give everyone freedom of action. What can they actually do in many cases? What should they do, if the pigs push women and children out in front? I went through that in Chemnitz, where the red pigs spit on us while holding their children in front of them. We were completely defenseless. God forbid, if we had touched those children! Fighting against the gangs is the same situation. If they push women and children out in front of them, then the officer or non-commissioned officer has to have the option of shooting them, regardless. The important thing is that he will fight his way through and destroy the gangs. The person carrying the gun has to be guaranteed complete cover from the rear. We can give him general orders, but we have to cover his back as well, so the poor devil doesn't have to say to himself, "Afterwards I will be held responsible." What should they do? The pigs barricade themselves into a house, and women and children are in there as well. Is the man allowed to set fire to the house or not? If he sets it on fire, the innocent will burn as well. [—] There should be no question about it! He has to set it on fire. One can't say, "The man wasn't allowed to do it; only an officer could do it." No! If the poor devil is standing there with six or seven men—what should he do then? That was the tragedy of the police—that it was only officers who could do this. When was an officer ever next to a policemen? The poor official was always completely on his own. That's why French policemen join the German police, because with us they get back-up for the first time. The French police have never experienced anything like that! When there were riots in Paris back then and shooting broke out, it cost the French policemen their necks. They were held accountable for it.[69] On the one hand, they had the order to protect the chamber and to take action against the demonstrators. How should they protect the chamber if the demonstrators were advancing? If they had marched forward and the officials hadn't protected the chamber, then they would have been punished for not doing anything about it. So they fired, and were punished for firing. One really has to be incredibly cautious with these things, for the sake of the little man. Also, one must always imagine the mentality of the fighter. We can say here at this green table, that common sense should be decisive: How could you be so foolish? [—] Haven't you thought about it? [—] The poor devil isn't able to think—he is fighting for his life, for his existence! And that little man precisely, the little non-commissioned officer, fights his way through the action, and shoots and kills so many women because he saw no other way to get through the village.

JODL: That is not an issue here. While fighting, they can do what they want. They can hang them, hang them upside down, or quarter them— nothing is mentioned about that in here.[70] The only restriction concerns reprisals after the fighting in areas where gangs had lived. That is an action that is cautiously (analyzed) by the Reichsführer himself, as he says: I have to be sure that by doing so I don't extend the areas of the gangs and don't (drive out) the entire male population.[71] The word would spread from village to village, and then 2,000 men will leave to go to the gang areas again. Otherwise, nothing is said about being allowed or not being allowed to do something. It is only the experience gained from reconnaissance and deployment.

THE FÜHRER: But, fundamentally, it must be written down in there that he is absolutely right if he thinks that he has to use the strongest means possible in order to carry out his duty, and that he will be covered for it afterward, whatever may happen.

JODL: This concerns the leadership above all, since the SS has more experience with it anyway.

THE FÜHRER: It has more experience. Listen to what is being said about the SS, because it has this experience! They are always saying that the SS acts brutally.

JODL: That is not true at all. They do everything quite cleverly—with a carrot and a stick, as it is done around the world!

THE FÜHRER: One excuses the carrot, but not the stick.

KEITEL: Not much is said about it in the partisan areas. We're glad that everyone is working together so well now. Everything is done together and under a unified command. All the actions that Bach-Zelewski[72] undertook were initiated by him alone, including the (police force) and the troops of the division located there.

THE FÜHRER: Bach-Zelewski is one of the (cleverest) people. Even in the party, I used to always use him for the most difficult things. If the Communist resistance couldn't be broken somewhere, I took him there and he smashed it!

France, technical questions

KEITEL: Then I must report only the following: I just informed Paris that we will confiscate everything and immediately claim it for the North African theater of operations. They[73] will be collected, and we will get a report from the Commander-in-Chief West [Oberbefehlshaber West—OB West].

BUHLE: They won't have produced them yet.

THE FÜHRER: They have received a certain percentage from us. They are new. They will be produced for us. They received a high percentage as well. They probably cheated us a bit. I'm convinced that they had a lot labeled "replacement parts" which they put together as new. That's also an issue that is not quite right. "So and so" also said that an entire Panzer is useless because of a single replacement part.

BUHLE: It has to be ensured in the (production). In aircraft production there is not a single airplane that isn't delivered with a second engine.[74]

THE FÜHRER: That is not possible at the moment. (We can't say:) It has to have two engines and transmissions ... If we start that, then we can't suddenly stop the entire new production (because of it)—then nothing will come out at all. Then every unit formation program will become unnecessary, and before long the troops won't help themselves any more. They'll say: Stop—we only need to make a phone call, and then we'll immediately get something new.

BUHLE: Zeitzler wanted to do something more, but I stopped it. Up there, we won't send any transmissions, but only the vehicles. Only to Africa, so they can help themselves.

THE FÜHRER: The case up there is slightly different. Maybe it is a case of sabotage. It was a type of oil that we don't use.

BUHLE: That is what the detachment commander said. Of course, he interpreted it differently.

THE FÜHRER: No, it is a completely different kind of oil. Usually it is used for totally different machines. Right from the beginning, this oil was so thick that it was bound to ruin it.

BUHLE: That is what the detachment commander said; ... put in with the old oil.

THE FÜHRER: They gave it to the SD, which is (now) looking into where it came from. I could only welcome it (if it were checked at) the factory. That is (indeed decisive). We can't let such a story get out. (If) sabotage cells ever develop (in a) factory and nothing is done, then it will gradually become a (threat). But if I (recognize) this danger in time and hang the people from the factory, then the problem will be solved once and for all.

BUHLE: I will handle this case that way.

THE FÜHRER: I have already done it! If a Panzer comes out of the factory without any brake fluid, it is the task of the approval commission to find that out. But if there is a different fluid in there instead of brake fluid—sulfuric acid, for example—then I can only call it sabotage.[75]

End: 9:15 p.m.

* * * * *

A few hours before the beginning of this conference, Army Group Hoth began operation "Wintergewitter"—relief for Stalingrad—from both sides of Kotel'nikovo, in the southern sector of the Eastern front. Otherwise, the situation in the East has changed very little, except that the Russians are now attacking the German salient of Rzhev from the south as well, between Rzhev and Gzhatsk.

In Libya, in the meantime, Montgomery has begun preparations for the attack against the Mersa-el Brega position. The situation in Tunis hasn't changed.

(*Maps 1, 2, 3, and 9*)

* * * * *

MIDDAY SITUATION CONFERENCE
DECEMBER 12, 1942, IN THE WOLFSSCHANZE[76]

Beginning: 12:45 p.m.

East

THE FÜHRER: Has something disastrous happened?

ZEITZLER: No, my Führer. Manstein has reached the sector[77] and controls one bridge. The only attacks are against the Italians. This one regiment, which had been alerted during the night, appeared at the command post at 10 a.m. That was good, because the Italians had already thrown in all their reserve battalions.

THE FÜHRER: I have more sleepless nights because of the action here than because of the South. We don't know what's happening.

BUHLE: They are unreliable.

ZEITZLER: Something has to be done as quickly as possible, just like yesterday evening. If the Russians had taken advantage of it, it could have turned into a catastrophe last night. The army group didn't want to send in the regiment until early morning. So we got it at exactly 10. In the Seventeenth Army area, there wasn't a lot going on. Agent reports are surfacing again regarding a landing in the Crimea[78]—they wanted to have really bad weather with snowstorms, etc.

THE FÜHRER: That's very likely. Is our Navy able to make use of such weather as well?

JODL: You can't land there.

THE FÜHRER: The Russians do it; they can get through. We would not land in snowstorms and the like. I admit that. But I believe the Russians would do it.

KRANCKE: If it isn't too bad. If there's frost and everything is icy, then it's bad. But if there's only snow and it's around freezing, then it will work.

THE FÜHRER: That works fine. That's like with fog—they land while there's fog.

ZEITZLER: Here[79] there were stronger attacks by battalions. For the first time, we have received from here reports of deaths caused by exhaustion—14 cases within 6 days. I asked them to give me the detailed documents on what this bend looks like, in case we have to decide to eliminate it. If we take it away, in my opinion, we could save most of a division. There's a huge number of battalions in there, because they're holding it pretty tightly. However, we can't attack down here within the next few weeks, and as to supplies, we can always get in the same situation again, so that we'll have just as hard a time as we're having right now.

THE FÜHRER: It depends on whether or not they get something final over there—and, secondly, they should build a final position.

ZEITZLER: If the weather was good and we drew this back, we would have a division. I worry a lot about the armored army[80] down there; we need to bring some additional forces in there. We could get these here free for a while. The other thing is that the mountain regiment can't be there before the 20th, and the Luftwaffe even later, so we don't have much available right now.

THE FÜHRER: I'm only afraid that if we draw back now, all the materiel will be lost. Then we won't have anything.

ZEITZLER: No, it will have to be well prepared, of course.

THE FÜHRER: The enemy will probably follow further, if they don't have a position here.

ZEITZLER: It's a huge waste of forces, if one looks at the whole battalion. It's awful.

JODL: All they have in there are mountain guns. Once they brought up one anti-aircraft battery and one heavy battery.

THE FÜHRER: We'll have to see what they have.

ZEITZLER: I think that in the winter the same situation could happen here again.

THE FÜHRER: It's not very nice here in the south.[81] They have to build a position.

ZEITZLER: They definitely have to work on it.

THE FÜHRER: Then we can always take it back again. What I wanted to say about this Georgian battalion or company[82]: I really don't know, to tell the truth; the Georgians are people who are not Muslims. So one can't call them a Turkish battalion. The Georgians don't belong to the Turkish peoples. The Georgians are a Caucasian tribe that has nothing to do with the Turkish peoples. I regard only the Muslims as safe. All the others I consider unsafe. That can happen to us anywhere, so we have to be incredibly cautious. For the time being, I regard building up battalions of these pure Caucasian nations as quite risky, whereas I don't see a danger in building up a unit consisting of only Muslims. They will always charge.

ZEITZLER: I have sent various questions down, in order to gather some experience. The Baltitz[83] asked a Russian general, who was quite open, about the Georgians. He answered, "We don't have any advantage or disadvantage because of the Georgians, but neither do you."

THE FÜHRER: I believe that. They only think of making themselves available to all sides. Secondly, they are, according to what we hear, quite unreliable to all sides. However, I can imagine that because Stalin himself is a Georgian, quite a lot of people are attracted to the Communists. They had a kind of autonomy. The real Turkish people are Muslims. The Georgians are not a Turkish people, rather a typical Caucasian tribe, probably even with some Nordic blood in them. Despite all explanations—either from Rosenberg or from the military side—I don't trust the Armenians, either. I consider the Armenian units to be just as unreliable and dangerous. The only ones I consider to be reliable are the pure Muslims, which means the real Turkish nations. Whether or not they are all militarily useful is a different question, which I can't assess. (*Presentation of the Armed Forces report.*[84])

ZEITZLER: He is getting a bit livelier down here near the First Panzer Army. He pushes forward a bit—on this front relatively little. But here there are bridge constructions in progress at seven locations, as if he has something special planned there. I already reported yesterday that the bunker and a company were destroyed here.

THE FÜHRER: Where is this position being built?

ZEITZLER: Here, my Führer. This position will save us some people. This position hardly saves us anything, actually; not a lot will be coming out of it. But this position saves people because of the mountains—according to my feeling, the entire 13th Panzer Division or the SS *Viking* [Panzer Grenadier Division],[85] depending on which of them we want to draw out. Strangely enough, during the night a request from the army and the army group arrived. They're worried because of this thing up here, and they want to pull this in, in order to draw out the 13th Panzer Division and the *Viking* [Division], and to pull them in a more mobile way to Army Group South.[86] I think we have to come to this decision. It's a pity to give it up, but we can take it again. We'll save an entire division if they prepare this. Up here there was a surprise, insofar as it was reported in writing that they had entered up to this point. I looked into that matter. It seems that it developed from the impression that the attack up there wasn't successful and had to retreat. The reasons are as follows: an armored group attacked here with an infantry regiment, and proceeded quite well. A Russian armored attack came from up there against the rear or the flank, so quite a few tanks were lost—18 were destroyed initially, and this morning another 16. Altogether 5 infantry [rifle] divisions, 6 cavalry brigades and 2 tank brigades are in opposition. It seems as if he drew everything together that was here—which I reported several days ago—and that there's an army of riders here that he's putting together. That is the bulk of it. He's relatively strong here. During the night, the order went out to hold this position to the very last man, and that it's forbidden to take a single step backward.

THE FÜHRER: Tell me one more thing. Where are the tanks that were eaten up by mice back then?[87]

ZEITZLER: They were up there with the 22nd Panzer Division. May I now give the order for these preparations?

THE FÜHRER: The decisive thing is that we take this road.

ZEITZLER: The roadblock doesn't do much, since there's a side road here. If we really block this army road, he can use this side road here. But including Schikola, so we have the whole thing.

THE FÜHRER: We have to remain over there, so that we have the road. That's an unpleasant thing.

ZEITZLER: We won't be able to do it. That frees up the only reserves. I have double-checked, and the mountain regiment won't arrive here before the 20th.

THE FÜHRER: Whether or not they'll finish the thing by the 20th is also a question. If they don't build themselves in, they'll retreat here.

ZEITZLER: I think, though, that it's naturally quite strong.

THE FÜHRER: Whenever they retreat, I always fear that they will leave the materiel behind.[88] Then we have troops but no materiel—leaving aside the issue of morale, because we can't do anything with it then.

ZEITZLER: The preparation has to be divided up over several days; then we'll get it back, because there is a position here with not much in it. The 16th Motorized Division has made quite a nice thrust—150 were taken prisoner and they went back with these.[89]

THE FÜHRER: They didn't conduct mobile warfare down there; they left the tanks behind and didn't do anything—position warfare.

ZEITZLER: We could have moved the flanks much further forward. Relatively little on this front. I've settled this thing with the retreat order. It will now be diluted a bit. He wanted to give the order to retreat. (*Presentation.*)

Thrust on Stalingrad

The situation here[90] has developed like this: this morning Field Marshal Manstein phoned me. He holds the bridge at this village. A little bit of pressure is already beginning against the 23rd Panzer Division. That's probably because of the troops that were brought in. The resistance here wasn't terribly strong. During the course of the day today, though, there was some quite heavy fighting. He took Rychkovskii. That's unfortunate because of the bridge. That was the connection we wanted to make over to this place. The attack has also spread out further to here, while on the whole, it has relaxed. We listened in on a radio message from the 8th Cavalry Corps and heard that they want to shift into defense posture. Up here it's still unclear what he's actually doing. One could regard it as a reaction to our radio operation, since it was especially high during the days before we lined up for the attack. But one could also see it as him wanting to do something. Attacks against the Sixth Army were mainly in this area here. Field Marshal Manstein called today about the coming of this attack,[91] and he put it down on paper as reiteration and sent it. (*Presentation.*[92])

THE FÜHRER: He has 80 kilometers as the crow flies.

ZEITZLER: He sent it as a written document. Perhaps you could read it. The 16th (likely referring to the 6th Panzer Division); is not up for discussion. If we pull the 16th out, the entire Romanian front will collapse, and we'll never get it right again. Maybe he thinks that because there is a gap, the panzer army can send something in there. Otherwise, I'm surprised that he actually came up with this suggestion.

THE FÜHRER: We'll have to wait and see what he has in the way of forces. After all, he has two strong divisions. One of them has 95, the other 138 tanks.

ZEITZLER: Of course, there's a risk, if two divisions are drawn out.

THE FÜHRER: I admit that—without doubt. However, he has Luftwaffe units there as well, and something has to come out here. When is the next infantry division coming?

ZEITZLER: It will be a long time—8 days—before we have them. We had hoped that the 11th Panzer Division would be able to go in there. That would be tolerable. If it can't go there, the two armored divisions[93] will be left behind. This 23rd [Panzer Division] is getting bitten into from the flank and will have to do it. The only one left is the 6th (Panzer). It's particularly difficult when the counterattacks come and the connection is supposed to be maintained. If we take away the 17th [Panzer] from up there, then a risk is created there, too. But the attack of two panzer divisions can wait, and it's possible that we'll be forced after 2 days to pull in the 17th [Panzer], and then maybe a day will have been lost.

THE FÜHRER: He wanted to put the 17th [Panzer Division] in here.

ZEITZLER: He wanted to pull this one in here and take this one over here.

THE FÜHRER: Actually, the 17th [Panzer Division] is of no value.

ZEITZLER: If any of them is, then it's the 11th [Panzer Division].

THE FÜHRER: It has only 45 tanks.

ZEITZLER: So far it had 49. Only a few have broken down. It has one detachment located up here, and we could add a regiment of the 306th [Infantry Division] as a temporary measure.

THE FÜHRER: When did the 11th [Panzer] lose so many tanks? It used to have 70 or 80 tanks up there.

ZEITZLER: As far as I know, it came down with 49 tanks.

THE FÜHRER: There are breakdowns again.

ZEITZLER: Of course, there are always short breakdowns, which last for a day. In such weather the number increases again the next day.

HEUSINGER: The 11th Panzer Division once had 57 down here.

THE FÜHRER: They left up there with 73 or 75.

ZEITZLER: I'll check it again. I don't know the number by heart. From my experience, in this kind of weather one generally has to count on 10 to 20 missing tanks.

THE FÜHRER: I want to hear the rest of the situation first. I will come back to this matter at the end.

Don front

ZEITZLER: On the whole, nothing else is going on here. With the Italians, it turned out yesterday that they had been in it after all, and dug a hole of 1,200 meters. Afterwards they marched here during the night, arrived at 10 a.m. and are now able to join in if something happens. The situation seems to be more or less under control. If attacks start here during the morning, it will be a good thing that the regiment is located here. He attacked again; yesterday he sought some contact here, and this morning here. Here he entered a bit. In reaction to this, the army group acted quickly and independently. They deployed a regiment of the 385th Infantry Division and gave the 385th the command in this small sector so that the "Cosseria" is free. I think this is right. There were only small thrusts there. He made a small advance west of Svoboda, came in a bit and left again. At the moment, one gets the impression that he is not really done here yet. It is also possible that this is only a holding action somehow. But with the Italians, one never knows what will come out of it. He can make a small tactical attack and be successful after all.

THE FÜHRER: Here they've been driven back everywhere?

ZEITZLER: Only at this spot. A regiment of the 385th [Infantry] Division is deployed here, and the 385th Division took over command.

THE FÜHRER: But there's a steep escarpment.

ZEITZLER: Yes, actually it was safe from tanks. He is not reported to have appeared with tanks.

THE FÜHRER: If we had had 14 days, these units would have been there. I wanted to give these tanks to the Italians. Actually, it is really a loss of 14 days. But on the other hand, to put three more German divisions in here, you know—until the railway functioned better, it would have been difficult to feed this.

ZEITZLER: The supply situation is already starting to get a bit tense. We already had a difficult supply situation back then. Now we have troop transports there. We actually have to juggle with the Quartermaster General every evening, whether to put those trains in there.

THE FÜHRER: Has this branch been completed?

ZEITZLER: The railway is done.

THE FÜHRER: Completely done?

ZEITZLER: Yes.

THE FÜHRER: Over the whole way?

ZEITZLER: Yes, it is already in use. It has some minor defects. It hasn't been completely graveled. Everything will be pressed out that can possibly be pressed out. I have set up supply trains instead of some troop transports. They will join this rail transport.

THE FÜHRER: If one looks at all the danger points, this front[94] is still the greatest danger. It's our weakest ally, and there's nothing behind it in places. The Schulte brigade is arriving now, and then our escort battalion.[95] The Schulte brigade will be pressed in somehow, in order to hold there, at least. That's a small block. But if they evade infantry attacks without tanks in a territory where they are quite good because of their colossal artillery power, then I have to be pessimistic. How is the *Cosseria*, actually?

ZEITZLER: As far as I know, 6 battalions.

JODL: A normal division, which has just arrived today. It hasn't been in action yet.

THE FÜHRER: And the *Cuneense?*

JODL: That is the Alpine [mountain troops] division.

HEUSINGER: There are three Alpine divisions.

THE FÜHRER: They will be better. [—] And the *Celere?*

JODL: *Celere, Torino,* and *Pasubio*[96] are the old ones. The *23 Marzo* division is the Fascists.

ZEITZLER: There is one *3 Gennaio* division and one *23 Marzo* division.

JODL: Those are the Fascist divisions.[97]

THE FÜHRER: Have they been taken out, or are they in there at the front?

JODL: They have them as reserves, and here they put the reserve battalion into action.

ZEITZLER: The 27th Panzer Division is not quite complete either. It's not doing a whole lot. It looks better on the map than it does in reality.

THE FÜHRER: I've been thinking about something. Here there is nothing more. If he starts here, then there's nothing left.

ZEITZLER: At most, we could put only a regiment of the 306th [Infantry] Division down there. That's the only way out of it. The army group suggested that they pull this one regiment group down to here. Then there would be something here tomorrow, and here we would have to pull in this regiment to here.

Thrust on Stalingrad, alternating with the Don front

THE FÜHRER: How many tanks does the 17th [Panzer] Division have?

ZEITZLER: They don't have very many either: 58—all with short guns.

THE FÜHRER: That's of no use here—not at all. At most they could only fire hollow shells.

ZEITZLER: The 11th [Panzer Division] has 30 tanks with long guns.

THE FÜHRER: It can only go against infantry and against T 34 [tanks], maybe with hollow-charge shells. How many does it have with short guns?

ZEITZLER: Altogether it has 19 IV [tanks] and 29 III [tanks], both with short guns.

THE FÜHRER: Of course, they can shoot with hollow-charge shells, but to attack here, only the 11th Panzer Division is of use.

ZEITZLER: Yes, indeed. And he thinks he won't be able to get that one free, so I was quite happy that the 11th is relatively free. We could take them across the bridge.

THE FÜHRER: Now he can't pull them over there at all. If the village is gone, then the bridge will be lost as well.[98]

ZEITZLER: One can't say how it will develop today. It's 3 to 4 kilometers. These are tanks from the 14th Panzer Division, there something was severed from the 14th Panzer Division, and that is this group here.

THE FÜHRER: When does the Schulte brigade actually arrive?

HEUSINGER: It's arriving now; the first train arrives today.

THE FÜHRER: Where will it go?

HEUSINGER: It will be moved up to Millerovo, and should be pulled up from here.

THE FÜHRER: And where do we put our Führer Escort Battalion?

ZEITZLER: It should join the 17th Panzer Division; it's part of the same movement.

HEUSINGER: If everything goes according to plan, the movement should start on the 18th.

THE FÜHRER: Then, of course, we don't have anything to put in here. Or should we possibly put this brigade together with this battalion?

JODL: To pull in with the 11th or 17th Panzer Division.

THE FÜHRER: In order to establish a mobile reserve here. Then we will have to think about it. This battalion has modern weapons, at any rate. There is also another possibility: We could add it to the 17th [Panzer Division] to strengthen it, since the 17th can't do much. Or, I thought that maybe we could leave the 17th here—or draw it here temporarily—and put this new reinforced brigade in this area. It has 21 tanks. It is somewhat mobile, at least, and could join in the action.

ZEITZLER: It looks as if there's no danger here at the moment, but it will come later.

THE FÜHRER: He comes like lightning. He will roll up suddenly, and we won't have anything here. Everything that's there is only a pretense. Of course, one can say that we could take a regiment of the 306th [Infantry] Division up here. We would have to do that anyway. That would be the minimum. But with only this one, we'll hardly be able to support it. If we put the 17th [Panzer Division] there in order to get the 11th [Panzer Division] out—how does the 11th Panzer Division look?

ZEITZLER: The 11th is good; it has fought quite well and has destroyed quite a few tanks. Altogether there are 5 battalions—one heavy and 4 medium-heavy battalions—29 medium anti-tank guns, 6 light batteries, 3 heavy batteries, 100% mobile. It has a consumption rate of about 3½.[99] Then it has 7 Panzer III [tanks] with short guns, 30 IIIs with long guns, 5 IVs with long guns—altogether 45 tanks, with a fighting value of 2.[100]

THE FÜHRER: We have to do something else now as well. That came to my mind because of the considerations from above. We have to distinguish two things when considering the fighting value: the fighting value of the unit itself and the condition of the unit. Condition and fighting value are two totally different concepts.

SCHMUNDT: Last time it was the condition.

THE FÜHRER: Otherwise, a very brave division may bleed itself to death and be characterized as a second-class division, only because it fought bravely, whereas another, which is located in one position, might be characterized as good because it is full. Condition and quality have to be distinguished.

ZEITZLER: In general, that is also what Küchler[101] reports. I had someone ask him how he came to that judgment because of the police division. He gives this in response. (*Presentation*)

THE FÜHRER: Assessment Center 4. One has to take the qualification that comes from the basic evaluation, the behavior of the group, and the leadership of the troops. Then one has an approximate picture. Leadership and behavior of the troops, inner character—and then the condition has to be added; otherwise one loses sight of reality. As an aside, I must say that I prefer a group whose condition is momentarily bad but which has a high character and which is commanded quite strictly, over a group whose condition is good but whose character is not. Look here. They're in good condition, but they have not fought at all yet.[102] But I would be damned happy if I had one of our worn-out divisions with good character instead of this one here, even if it does only make up 30% of them. That's the decisive thing; we have to aim for that. This one is quite good. Also we always have to consider that there's something here. Here, in any case, there are 3 divisions: the 297th [Infantry], the 29th [Motorized], and the 3rd [Motorized]. These three divisions also have to be considered in this matter.

ZEITZLER: For the next few days, I worry mostly about stopping, if he really gets up to here. He's coming toward us. Now something will come in here two or three days later.

THE FÜHRER: Now it will open up, of course. If it works at all, it will open up. But it's very clear that this whole thing has a potential crisis in it. However, there are also difficulties for the enemy, as he's pulling himself down far away from any railway.

ZEITZLER: He takes this railway to here. He still had locomotives for this end. I was also surprised that it was done so quickly.

THE FÜHRER: The Luftwaffe should destroy those few bridges that go across there. Christian, this railway absolutely must be destroyed, so he can't drive around on it. I have considered one thing, Zeitzler, looking at the big picture. We should under no circumstances give this[103] up. We won't get it back once it's lost. And we know what that means. I can't start any surprise operations, either. Unfortunately, it came too late this time as well. It would have been faster if we hadn't stayed at Voronezh for so long.[104] Maybe we could have slipped through in the first attempt. But to think that it would be possible to do it a second time, if we go back there and the materiel stays behind, is ridiculous. They can't take everything with them. The horses are tired, and they don't have any more strength to pull. I can't feed one horse with another. If they were Russians, I'd say, "One Russian eats up the other one." But I can't let one horse eat the other horse. That's of no use; everything is lost. One also can't say, "In two days it will be different, so give me a portion of oats." The horse won't get better in two days. Everything that one can't take out by vehicle will stay behind. There are so many heavy artillery howitzers in there; all that is lost.

ZEITZLER: We have a huge amount of Army artillery in there.

THE FÜHRER: We can't replace what we have in there. If we abandon it, we abandon the whole purpose for the campaign. To think that I will come back here next time is madness. Now, in the wintertime, we can build a blocking position with the forces. The enemy has the opportunity to transport forces in on his train. When the ice breaks, he can also use the Volga for transport. He knows how much depends on it. We won't come back here, so we can't leave. There has been too much bloodshed to do this. If I thought this was obvious, then I would say that I would only clear out the inner part when the floods come in spring, since they flood the whole area. The time will come—for many weeks—when the whole area will be completely flooded. Some of these floodplains are supposed to become 20 to 30 kilometers wide—down there even more, but also the individual islands. As you can see, there is no development near the town, only an island. Everything else is probably shrubs, and in spring it's under water.

KRANCKE: Especially when the ice breaks up.

THE FÜHRER: Then we can do the clearing up. Then the artillery will also be pushed out of the deep territory. He doesn't need to worry about it. However, the decisive thing is that we hold this thing. Of course, this matter has to be cleared up under all circumstances. If we can get our hands on this—and I imagine this pocket here, so I would like to compare it with Khar'kov. This is the pocket, which is now developing. The Khar'kov pocket went up almost to Krasnograd.[105]

HEUSINGER: It went down here, then it went here and then over to here.

THE FÜHRER: Maybe this is a bit bigger. But at least it is a similar situation. The only thing the other has as an advantage is the railway here. Also, this is a railway that goes over to the Italians here, but this part is under construction still, so it's irrelevant.

ZEITZLER: No, this one isn't. I wanted to bring a railway man and the quartermaster general with me tomorrow in order to discuss this question.

CHRISTIAN: What caused the biggest difficulty back then at Khar'kov was the fact that we had destroyed the bridges. He also built a lot of bridges this time. That's why the great traffic jam occurred.

THE FÜHRER: We can guess how the situation must have looked from the fact that it was initially believed that the thing couldn't be closed. Generally, I would put a German group here with the aim of pushing forward here in order to finish this action. The next important thrust would actually be this one. But we have to wait and see if it's possible or not. It's conceivable that it might not work, since he's probably expecting it. In that case, there's no other choice but to do the same old thrust with the main forces, then to stop here and wait and see what he is doing in the pocket. He will probably expect us to come around from both sides. The question is whether we'll be able to do it. In the end, it will be possible to transport units down here, assuming we can bring the train far enough to supply this. We'll be able to establish some armored groups here. I think the first thing is that we destroy this thing first and then do the old thrust. If we come any further in this direction, he'll have to pull out of the pocket. Then we would see if it's possible to advance up to here. I don't think we can do much more. But he'll expect a double action, of course. He'll expect us to advance here first. So I think it would be right to first make a thrust from the south to the north in order to break the whole thing down, and to open that in detail, and only then to continue with the thrust to the east. Of course, this is all in the future. First, we have to try to get forces free for it. It is very critical how things turn out today with the Italians. Under the circumstances, I really don't know if I can justify leaving here,[106] Jodl. I can cancel everything, of course.

JODL: On the other hand, there are so many problems that will remain unresolved because of this.

THE FÜHRER: I admit that. This thing could come together any time now. When do we get the connection from the train?

JODL: Generally there's a connection every two hours. It's quite rare that there's no connection for three hours—usually every two hours, sometimes more often.

BODENSCHATZ: The radiotelegraphic connection can also be maintained while it's sending messages.

THE FÜHRER: Is it possible to get a picture through radiotelegraph? Is it possible? And how long does it take? All that still has to be encoded. How long does it take to settle a small question?

JODL: It doesn't work.

HEWEL: One can only phone from the train station there.

THE FÜHRER: At every train station?

JODL: Not at the improvised train stations as well as at the ones that are prepared. But a connection is possible anyway.

THE FÜHRER: If I do this, then I would leave out Berlin. But we'll see today and tomorrow.

ZEITZLER: Very serious days are coming, with serious developments.

THE FÜHRER: I see quite a great danger here, since there's nothing there. If there were anything—OK, a regiment will come in. Here he pulled this one regiment down anyway. That means it's getting thin here. If we take the 17th Panzer Division away, there will be nothing left there. Here's the question: if the story ends, if we get the impression that the whole thing is not that big and the 27th Panzer Division forces are able to cope with whatever he brings up, then we could possibly go there and put the Schulte brigade and the Führer Escort Battalion together. Then it would be relatively strong. If we were able to transport it by train, then the 17th Panzer Division would be free. We could also leave the 17th Panzer Division here, since the major attack might not take place here, and pull this brigade down here—since it is of more value with its 21 modern tanks than the 17th Panzer Division with its old equipment. How does the 17th Panzer Division look, apart from that?

ZEITZLER: It has 5 strong battalions. [—] That's what Manstein wants.

THE FÜHRER: That's for sure.

ZEITZLER: The Schulte brigade hasn't been trained for attack yet. They can do defense. They have quite a few anti-tank guns—50.

THE FÜHRER: They could cope with the people who would be coming there. We could send the 17th Panzer Division over there and put the Schulte brigade in that area, if it is possible or if a crisis were to arise. For now, it's in the area of Millerovo. So nothing is lost here. We could, if necessary, take this over here. Or, if necessary, we could also take it up there.

JODL: Has a new unit been identified during this attack?

ZEITZLER: Nothing has been reported yet today.

THE FÜHRER: Jodl, you know how this appears. In three days there is suddenly something here. That dog manages it. He transports materiel there for two months, and during the last few days he brings in the forces. Suddenly he turns up with so many brigades. There is nothing behind those brigades—it's ridiculous—but many dogs will cause the rabbit's death. If I attack with 3 to 4 divisions, I will proceed up to there for sure, if there's nothing there. Where nothing is going on, nobody is there. When does he have to pull the 17th [Panzer Division] out?

ZEITZLER: The decision should actually be made today. We consciously take a risk here or there. We have to take a risk.

THE FÜHRER: Is he bringing them over here at all?

ZEITZLER: This morning the 23rd [Panzer Division] settled relatively quickly on this side here, so we have to believe that the 23rd will stop today and the 6th [Panzer Division] will move on. It would be good if we had something to follow.

THE FÜHRER: What's happening with the Luftwaffe units that are following?

ZEITZLER: He'll need those to cover something here, since it's fairly wide.

THE FÜHRER: What's happening here with the units that are being freed up?

ZEITZLER: There are only a few. He wants to take them over here for now.

THE FÜHRER: So he'll get 2 units here, of course, but also 3 units from here. Of these three units, only the 29th [Motorized Division] is still very strong. I think the 3rd Motorized Division is quite worn-out, and the 297th [Infantry Division]...

ZEITZLER: It's in relatively good condition. It still works.

THE FÜHRER: Only to provide cover, I mean.

ZEITZLER: The 297th [Infantry Division] was highly praised today. It's immaculate. There was a longer paragraph in the report. But I don't think the enemy will still attack here. He's pulled everything here. Everything depends on this attack—that we at least get the "tube" in here.

THE FÜHRER: If we open it, we'll get a sufficient width. And you think an infantry division can be there within 8 days?

ZEITZLER: Yes, the 306th [Infantry Division] will be there then. But this one regiment will be gone then. It has three regiments.

JODL: It's one hundred percent full, up to the very last man—9 battalions.

THE FÜHRER: Yes, one regiment is gone. It has nine 7.5-cm guns—on self-propelled mounts, right?

JODL: No, pulled.

THE FÜHRER: It has six, and the 22nd [Panzer Division] has 18 now.

ZEITZLER: Yes, it's gone up.

THE FÜHRER: That's also very weak: one 7.5-cm, two 7.6-cm. And he takes away one regiment of the 294th [Infantry] Division. With that the reserve will be gone here.

ZEITZLER: I think it's better, operationally.

THE FÜHRER: What does this mean here?

ZEITZLER: Movement and tanks—dug-in tanks.

THE FÜHRER: He always digs them in and then he drives out.

ZEITZLER: He drives out again. It could be protection from the cold.

HEUSINGER: The enemy has 16 rifle [infantry] divisions, 2 tank brigades and 4 cavalry divisions from here to here.

ZEITZLER: Of course, there can suddenly be something else. We don't know what else there is behind.

JODL: He won't be able to lead a full-scale attack along the entire front—against the Italians and here.

ZEITZLER: That's the only thing I'll say. He'll do something here and something there. But that's just a feeling.

THE FÜHRER: When does the decision have to be made?

ZEITZLER: The earlier the better.

THE FÜHRER: Is it OK if we make the decision today during the course of the day, so we can at least wait and see how the attacks turn out there? Because if they end well, if it holds at all, I would say that the Schulte brigade doesn't need to go up there. Instead, we could possibly make them available here. Then I would absolutely risk giving this away. When does it arrive?

HEUSINGER: The first train is supposed to arrive today, and the arrivals will continue until the 18th.

THE FÜHRER: Is the Schulte brigade entirely motorized?

BODENSCHATZ: Yes, indeed. 2 battalions, everything motorized.

THE FÜHRER: They could possibly come from Millerovo.

BUHLE: That's an enormous defense unit.

BODENSCHATZ: He has 3 companies with 12 anti-tank guns, 40 each.

THE FÜHRER: I acknowledge that. But what if I also give him our escort battalion—they're also trained in attacking. Their 21 tanks are not for defense; they have done counterthrusts everywhere.

BODENSCHATZ: There's also a mixed anti-aircraft detachment with three heavy batteries in there. It's an enormous defensive force.

JODL: 36 heavy anti-tank guns and three 8.8-cm batteries.

THE FÜHRER: If we had them there, I'd feel better. Then we could take everything away. Then we could put the 17th Panzer Division in here. We have to wait today anyway. He has to settle it first with the available forces. Otherwise, he won't be able to bring anything in behind, if he doesn't have the bridge.

ZEITZLER: Then he would have to go down around. There has been no report yet. The last report was from the Italians: individuals can cross.

THE FÜHRER: It's stupid to have a division here that hasn't been fighting at all. Has this one been involved in combat?

JODL: No, not yet. It's also a new division.

THE FÜHRER: These characters will bring shame on us. The Italians would be glad, anyway, if we took it away from them.

JODL: He won't be able to get there with one division.

ZEITZLER: He won't get there, and I fear that if we wait one day, it'll be even more difficult. Then he'll have settled himself. But if we attack immediately, then it'll go through.

THE FÜHRER: I think that's how it will be! Supposing the 23rd Panzer Division is stopped here, and he goes through here with the 6th [Panzer Division], then we will probably pull it in after the 6th. The 6th will always be the advance point. The greatest danger, in my eyes, is that the 23rd [Panzer Division] may not break through. I consider it impossible with those 95 tanks, but I'm convinced that the 23rd will reach this sector in any case. It will be able to handle anything that comes along now. According to yesterday's report, the enemy has altogether 85 tanks, and the 23rd by itself has 95. What kind of Panzers does the 23rd Panzer Division have?

ZEITZLER: 26 IV [tanks] with long guns and 26 IIIs with long guns—very good. I'm also afraid that it'll get stuck here.

THE FÜHRER: It may get stuck here. But at least the 6th [Panzer Division] will still go further over here, then the other one will push along after it. I assume that the other one will be there primarily to provide cover. The 6th will have to make the break-through, and the 3rd Motorized Division, the 29th [Motorized Division], and the 297th [Infantry Divisions] must work from the opposite direction here. The 3rd Motorized Division will have to try to open this up behind the sector, and the 297th [Infantry Division], too.

ZEITZLER: A wedge will come like this and like this, and from this wedge right now one side is missing.

THE FÜHRER: The 11th Panzer Division would be able to do it.

ZEITZLER: If it went along, we would have this wedge complete. But if the 11th doesn't go along, it would remain stuck to the wedge [?].

(... ?): We must have infantry for defense. The 11th has a relatively small sector. It has a relatively large number of infantry troops, but not many tanks. But for the defense, a certain part must be infantry.

THE FÜHRER: If the 17th [Panzer Division] moves in with its mass of infantry—it has fewer tanks than the 11th and is less valuable—then the action will turn out well.

ZEITZLER: Manstein is already taking out what he can. If he can get them free, he will do everything. But just now he is concerned internally that he will get stuck with both of them. It is understandable.

THE FÜHRER: How many tanks are there altogether?

HEUSINGER: He has about 130 tanks in total.

THE FÜHRER: That's not many. He must leave the tanks here as well. We have enough tanks. He will need them for his first push and then he can take them back immediately. But, of course, there is the possibility that the guy will take down everything here as fast as he can in order to throw it here.

ZEITZLER: To attack with one group from this side and with one group from this side.

THE FÜHRER: The panzer division would have to manage this here.

JODL: He will certainly manage all this. It's just that the territory is huge and there are few units—the enemy sneaks around behind.

THE FÜHRER: That's right. But if I open this up—we're standing up to here anyway. If they only take half of the front, they have almost the entire thing anyway. It can't get any worse than it is now. Just like they stopped here, they can stop here then, but with the difference that we then have a supply base. What he has here is less, because he's depending on a relatively difficult supply route.

ZEITZLER: Later, a panzer corps will push in here, which will establish a mobile defense, because we won't get a real front at first.

THE FÜHRER: If we have the connection, we can leave the 23rd [Panzer Division] and the 6th Panzer Division standing here. We can operate on both sides with that one, when necessary. We're clear about the fact that there are, of course, other situations that would be more desirable than this one. But it must be an uncompromising principle that we won't move away from here.

ZEITZLER: The push may not get stuck, because time is running short.

JODL: If we thought we had to keep something here, I would attack there as well. But only to leave something there in this situation.

THE FÜHRER: What happened there?

ZEITZLER: It was nothing special. There is a counterattack in progress by the local reserves.

THE FÜHRER: But they don't have anything there. They're such poor devils. There is nothing behind them. They are called "Guards," but they're only construction battalions.

ZEITZLER: There is also Luftwaffe there.

THE FÜHRER: I take back everything. [—] What is it?

ZEITZLER: These are the groups.

THE FÜHRER: That is very weak.

HEUSINGER: It's weak, but one division is moving around up above.

ZEITZLER: This here is the only thing that could be evaluated positively.

JODL: But leave only the 17th [Panzer Division] here, because the enemy may attack, but then he doesn't—I don't know.

THE FÜHRER: What is still coming from the 6th [Panzer Division]?

ZEITZLER: The second serial of the 6th Panzer Division. There are still 2 trains missing.

THE FÜHRER: Are there still tanks there?

ZEITZLER: No, they're the very last baggage trains, etc.

THE FÜHRER: According to the numerical values, the 23rd Panzer Division should absolutely be able to fight back and crush all that stuff, and, in fact, they should theoretically be able to enter this territory. The only problem is that we continue to follow this front afterward. If it crossed over as well, the connection would have to be able to be established then. Once the connection is made, it'll enlarge quickly, then the psychological moment will be gone, too; then they will say: the connection has been established. Let the first convoys come in,[107] and no matter how lousy they are, the world will look different again.

ZEITZLER: They're restless and want to be relieved. But that will change with one strike.

THE FÜHRER: The moment they know that they're free, it will be different. That was the old experience. Yes, I want to wait until 2 o'clock, until I have news about the situation. Or maybe we can ask again what kind of impression one has of the whole Italian front and also of the Hungarians. Because then I would say, "After the group comes to Millerovo anyway ... and we can push them to any side."

ZEITZLER: Then we take them as mobile group. At the moment it doesn't look threatening here. There are very large gaps

THE FÜHRER: But here there are better units already. What's the tank defense here like?

ZEITZLER: It's bad here; here it's gotten better.

THE FÜHRER: But it's said to be pretty good here. You see—the pig has crossed over here. Is there anything else further north?

ZEITZLER: No, nothing in particular further north.

THE FÜHRER: One thing can be excluded: the 16th Motorized Division can't be removed under any circumstances. Otherwise everything will collapse in the back.

ZEITZLER: There's no discussion about it. I don't understand why he wants to do that.

THE FÜHRER: It's not that fast anyway. It must be pulled together first. Days would go by before it really arrives. When does the 7th Panzer Division[108] come? It starts arriving here around the 28th or so?

ZEITZLER: The 26th is first. Right now it's one day late.

THE FÜHRER: So on the 27th?

ZEITZLER: It could be on the 27th.

THE FÜHRER: So that's another two weeks still. And it takes them how long?

ZEITZLER: The combat units will arrive within 6 days.

Rest of the Eastern Front

On this front in Army Group Center, we have sent out relatively few individual reconnaissance patrols. Not much has been reported about movements, either. Suddenly we have a picture from many radio messages that they repeatedly have to send ammunition over there; this happens repeatedly. First they had to give up some mortar ammunition. Then they were ordered back, then mortar ammunition was sent up. Now a unit has also moved up, so the whole thing seems to be loosening up. The 321st [Infantry Division] has just arrived, so we'll manage it. The movement of the 216th [Infantry Division] is in progress. Now some cavalry is sitting on the railway. They have probably gathered together and are starting to mess things up there. Yesterday there was a nice success here: 93 tanks destroyed. We are both in these districts now—the Russians and us—while this is being cleaned up. There were 30 tanks in the attack, and 13 of them were destroyed— quite a good number. Up above no change in the situation and few attacks. No changes there either. They are still sitting in the woods, and from us there is a kind of splitting up all around; they don't do anything either. Nothing special on this side. Small advances beaten back.

THE FÜHRER: Here my big concern is that this is going to become a partisan thing again.

ZEITZLER: We have ordered that they try to seal this off. But they don't have anything there at the moment. This pocket has shrunk significantly. 27 tanks destroyed. He attacked relatively strongly from here, but he hardly attacks at all in here anymore.

THE FÜHRER: And the southern pocket?

ZEITZLER: It's gone—blown up. I wanted to have the number of prisoners today, but they can't provide it yet.

THE FÜHRER: Did it fall apart?

ZEITZLER: I'm surprised by that as well. Normally, when a pocket goes, a message arrives right away with the number of prisoners and so on. It looks as if there wasn't much in there.

JODL: What about the regiment of the 328th [Infantry] Division? It's supposed to go to France. It's still waiting for an attack that isn't coming. That's the regiment where the division is in France. The division should be made ready. They are waiting for it to cross over.

ZEITZLER: Near Velikie Luki the situation isn't unfavorable. But I'm not satisfied, because there's been no change at all for two days. The resistance is not strong. We don't see him attacking somehow or advancing. That's why I sent out the message that they should report their intentions this afternoon— what and how they want to do it, as the picture has been generally the same for two days now. Earlier there was a radio message that Velikie Luki would be the target of a strong attack today. Maybe it's the reaction. I don't like the fact that they're acting so slowly. This here can be put under huge pressure. He does have a lot in here now. Yesterday heavy fog was reported, but that can't hold anyone up for days, though. In the north there's nothing really to report. The General Staff officer who was there is back now. He went to the front line and looked at everything himself and marked it afterward. It's the way we need it. The control went well. It was this little point. He brought back his personal impression that the troops are very exhausted. He said that mentally, the men are brilliant in every respect; that's impressive. But now they have to sit on this narrow front day and night, and they're on the alert all night and have to get out. An example: the men don't even take off their pants anymore; they just leave them on. They have become a little apathetic because of all those alarms. One has the impression that the combat was rather tough because he [the enemy] concentrated very much on single positions. That was very difficult for the troops concerned.

THE FÜHRER: He does it now in very narrow places. Our most serious mistake this year was the attack against Sukhinichi. That was an example with the headline: don't start an attack like this. They attacked wherever they could instead of concentrating everything and breaking through quickly with 5 tank divisions. We deployed about 500 tanks at Sukhinichi. But they managed to drive them off. That's a "glorious" act.[109]

ZEITZLER: They've reinforced the push in order to come in here. The order has been issued: as long as they have supplies, and whether it is necessary at all, they should stay the whole winter. Artillery fire here. Up here attacks with 2 companies. Weaker attacks here. He was fought back there. Here he came in a little bit. A counter-action is in progress there. Then here are some reports from individual officers, characterizing how tough it is at the front. (*Presentation*)

THE FÜHRER: I have to say one thing in all of these cases. I get too few suggestions from the Army for the Knight's Cross, and I get too few documents for the Oak Leaves—not only for generals, but also for officers, sergeants and whole units who distinguish themselves. That's also the case at the Luftwaffe; they get the Oak Leaves now, too. There's no relation there anymore today.[110]

ZEITZLER: Some time ago there was a request to clear this little point and move back behind it to save 6 km. I said back then: first, they must build this up; and second, because of our feint, we didn't want to go back. Now the mission is complete. They have set up a line behind the salient there. So we save 6 km for the one division. I think we can agree to that. Tactically it should be situated even better on the ground. [–] Nothing special on this front. Preparations for attack here, but with a question mark; above artillery fire. Then Field Marshal Küchler submitted a request to put the 225th [Infantry] Division in here. He sends a calculation up—he had so many losses. The 225th is so strong; it equals more or less zero then. But we can't actually do it.

THE FÜHRER: He wanted it here.

ZEITZLER: We wanted to put it here as a reserve, we said, for three cases: either for Staraia Russa or for Tim …or up here.

THE FÜHRER: Besides, he plucks that one first—a few battalions here and there—and in no time he will mess the whole thing up.

ZEITZLER: In Army Group Center, I ordered the 19th Panzer Division to prepare for transportation. I left it to them first, and they chose the 20th [Panzer Division], which is the worst one. So we chose the 19th Panzer Division. As for the West, the 1st Panzer Division will come down, and should hand in their equipment.

JODL: But we need four altogether.[111]

THE FÜHRER: We must set up at least 4 mobile units. There won't be anything left for the East in the spring. The 8 units that I wanted are messed up now because of the North Africa thing.[112]

ZEITZLER: The supply situation is starting to become a little tense for Army Group Center, too—first, because of the many transport trains, that is … the partisan activity has increased significantly again. The SS units have been taken away there. They seem to be starting more regularly. They don't do smaller blasts anymore; instead, they go to artificial structures and do things that take a little longer. Army Group Center, especially, needs many trains, and also has a big food allowance, so tensions are starting again there.

THE FÜHRER: On the other hand, if the Russians have to give up ammunition, the supply won't be that much either.

ZEITZLER: They pull it out from the troops. It was ordered directly: This detachment has to hand over ammunition to the rear.

THE FÜHRER: He has also lost many chemical factories.[113]

ZEITZLER: They have received the orders to save ammunition from Finland.

THE FÜHRER: With the tanks, too. If that damage continues, it will change over time.

BUHLE: Our people wouldn't sit in that T 34 as it was presented here.[114]

WARLIMONT: There is a new message about the fuel shortage. The last conservation order—the text is similar to ours—demands that if trucks are going in the same direction, one has to tow the other. We haven't even invented that yet.

THE FÜHRER: Here we didn't consider this story possible, but it is possible, of course. Towing a three-ton truck doesn't take any more fuel than being loaded with 3 tons.

ZEITZLER: 1,100 and 900, so altogether 2,100.

THE FÜHRER: Let's say, then, that there are still 1,500. But add at least 500 to that, for technical problems, and then we have 2,000. So, in fact, there are still at least 20, 25, or 30 brigades that have practically no tanks. One brigade might have 8 or 12 tanks. That is no longer a unit.

ZEITZLER: We've counted 4,800, according to agent reports, etc. Half of them would be gone. 4,800 is certainly quite high.[115]

THE FÜHRER: How strong are our tank numbers at the front right now?

ZEITZLER: I have a list, which I want to bring along. I carefully counted everything that's there at the moment, everything that's ready for deployment, and everything that's temporarily out of action.

BUHLE: It must be 1,000.

ZEITZLER: I had, I think, 1,300.

THE FÜHRER: So a ratio of one to two.

BUHLE: Altogether it will be around 1,800-2,000. But not all of them are ready to move.

THE FÜHRER: It is the same with the others. But I'm convinced that he has much worse maintenance companies than we have. He has one advantage, though. He produced for war earlier, and didn't bother at all about beauty. We're getting away from that, too, with our current production. I know the Radschlepper Ost [Wheeled Tractor East][116] looks great in a parade, of course.

BUHLE: They say they can't use it for heavy anti-tank guns. When the first Raupenschlepper Ost [Caterpillar Tractor East][117] came to the Viking brigade, they said it wouldn't pull it.

THE FÜHRER: It pulls a heavy field howitzer if necessary. It has 85 hp. How many would I have harnessed otherwise?

BUHLE: 4 or 6 horses.

THE FÜHRER: In the World War we transported the heaviest mortar attachments—up to the 42-cm mortar—with the 100-hp Daimler-Benz.

BUHLE: It doesn't go that fast.

THE FÜHRER: Of course not, but they don't drive that fast, either. If they drove that way, we would cover 300 km in one day. How much do they cover? This one division, if it's going well, covers 30, 40 or 45 km. If they drive for 8 hours, they cover 4-6 km each hour.

Southern Sector Again

HEUSINGER[118]: Nothing has happened with Army Group B along the front near the Italians. That means there haven't been any enemy attacks along the entire front from here up to here today. This town here, which he took yesterday, he evacuated today. Our forces advanced; today they stand on the heights south of this town. The Italian Commander-in-Chief reported that he didn't want to take the town itself, which lies in the lowlands, again, because it was totally destroyed and couldn't provide accommodation anyway. He said he controlled the town from above with fire. The regiment of the 298th [Infantry] Division is assembled here, ready to occupy the town itself if ordered. The army group itself also says, though, that it doesn't make sense to go into the town when it can be fully controlled from above. [—] There were no attacks here on this front. This penetration occurred, according to the army group, by enemy forces in regiment strength but without tanks. Now this regiment of the 385th [Infantry Division] is in position—after the division commander of the 385th took over the sector up to there—to throw the enemy out. The attack hadn't started yet; they had just arrived. [—] The Hungarian front is quiet, nothing happened. I haven't talked about down there. There's only one thing to be reported, and that is that unfortunately the Schulte brigade is a day and a half late, so it won't arrive until the day after tomorrow.

THE FÜHRER: And here?

HEUSINGER: I can call at the Don again.

THE FÜHRER: Call again. It might be possible that the guy has pulled everything together and isn't doing anything there anymore—that he can't attack such large fronts. That could be possible. If that were the case, I would say we should take the Schulte brigade down here. If worst comes to worst we can ... There are 2 battalions. ... They've all been trained for at least 6 months. They can attack for sure. No doubt they can attack! The battalions that Dietrich[119] gets out there are all trained like that. He chooses the people. Actually, he gets replacements. But he goes there and chooses the men. He has the right to choose every single man, and he keeps them in his replacement battalion for 6-8 months, because he says there's no use otherwise—those wonderful boys will only get shot up. And for 6 months he hasn't needed any replacements, since he hasn't had any losses—so he's completely covered.[120]

ZEITZLER: I spoke with Colonel Abraham, who was in here; he's severely ill, a kidney problem. He explained how this front developed. There was really nothing there. So some officers came, and then the emergency troops, which had never done such things in their life before—bakers, etc. It was very difficult to get the people into a position. Then came this panzer division with the remote-controlled ignition,[121] which we wanted to have. He left the tanks standing there and took over a new sector. The commander said it was really very hard, initially. When they left for a few hours at night, the people ran away because everything was new. The convoy guys didn't have the appropriate winter clothing either, since they had sat in the convoys as bakery convoys, etc. But it was similar to the Khar'kov mission.

THE FÜHRER: What does the Luftwaffe report?

CHRISTIAN: General Wöhler[122] from Army Group Center reports that the situation near Velikie Luki is getting critical. Tanks were deployed here—an armored attack, 100 tanks. Army Group Center has ordered the Chevallerie group to finish its preparations immediately and attack from the southwest tomorrow. But they repeat their request for the addition of the 11th Panzer [Division].

THE FÜHRER: I think we can risk that now.

ZEITZLER: They could have gotten further right away. Velikie Luki can come under intense pressure ...

THE FÜHRER: I'm just glad that Scherer[123] is in there.

ZEITZLER: He himself is not in there. The division is outside. Only the artillery commander is in there.

THE FÜHRER: When can this regiment be up there?

ZEITZLER: I can't tell for sure where it is, my Führer. It wasn't clearly reported how far it has gotten.

THE FÜHRER: That there is a solid unit here at least.

ZEITZLER: Yes, something has to come in. There are only outposts standing here.

THE FÜHRER: If we could at least get some support along this huge front—a solid unit. At the moment we have nothing there. If the action up there proves to be unnecessary—if nothing happens there, if the thing turns out like the Hornberg shooting—I would argue that we should bring all possible forces here: the Schulte brigade, the 7th Panzer Division right in here, also the 27th Panzer Division, the 17th [Panzer Division] here, and the 19th [Panzer Division] also, so we can quickly build up a unit that will allow us to make a push and grab it from behind. Because he has nothing here. If he breaks through there and attacks, I'm convinced that we can proceed here, because he has nothing in depth. In my opinion, this is the only possible operation. The question is whether we attack here or here. This would have the advantage that we wouldn't need to take over a large sector—it moves up, in general—while here we would need to cover several sectors. We did it that way back then, too.

ZEITZLER: It would be best to start where it has loosened up the most. The deeper we are the better, because as soon as we are through we can proceed easily.

THE FÜHRER: But a panzer force should be built up there, consisting—if he can get it there—of the 27th Panzer Division. Then, when everything has calmed down, we can pull out the 17th [Panzer Division]—if we can protect it enough—then these parts of ours: the 19th [Panzer Division] from above and the 7th [Panzer Division] from the West. Then we would have a panzer force here.

ZEITZLER: The XXX Corps performed extraordinarily in the action with the pocket. The commanding general is starting very sensibly. Manstein is also starting well.

THE FÜHRER: It's also valuable because if we advance here to cut these off here, then the entire lot is up in the air. If we manage to advance, the enemy can't stay in the tube either. He can't get supplies because he doesn't have a railway. We'll see. To be perfectly honest, it's an immense risk.

ZEITZLER: The other is a risk, too, if it gets stuck. So we'll just have to consciously accept one of them.

THE FÜHRER: What is there from the 336th [Infantry Division] that's still coming?

ZEITZLER: It can't be that much. I don't know if it's still a whole regiment. It's my feeling that everything in here are combat troops.

THE FÜHRER: We have to find out what it looks like here. Maybe we can ask in particular if the bridge is still in our possession. If not, where can he go to cross over?

ZEITZLER: Then we would have to take the lower bridge. We used that one already for the 6th Panzer Division

THE FÜHRER: It would be a huge detour, while it would be very simple if he could join here. If he takes the 17th [Panzer Division], I would immediately say to pull behind them here. Then he has the 11th [Panzer Division] here as cover.

ZEITZLER: Then there would be some reassurance, if the 11th [Panzer Division] stood here.

THE FÜHRER: He has enough good tanks here.

ZEITZLER: He has enough. It would actually be fine for him to take the 17th [Panzer Division] around down there. He has 5 strong battalions here. It looks pretty good.

THE FÜHRER: If the lot doesn't come over here, we're stuck. So I would say that it would almost be better—if the action can't be stopped—to block them off here and take the 17th right around here.

ZEITZLER: I would prefer that, too, because by the time they come, almost 24 hours will have passed. So they could be gone then.

THE FÜHRER: Then the 11th Panzer Division must come back again and go up here and around here after all. It can save itself all this distance.

ZEITZLER: I'm quite sure that he'll do that. But I'll talk to him later myself.

THE FÜHRER: The number of tanks doesn't really matter.

ZEITZLER: The 17th [Panzer Division] has 58 tanks.

THE FÜHRER: The other has 65.

ZEITZLER: The 17th [Panzer Division] has 19 Panzer IV [tanks] with short guns.

THE FÜHRER: The heavy tanks are up in Millerovo anyway. The other divisions have to do that in any case. How are they coming here? Are they coming by train?

ZEITZLER: No, they can't get through by train anymore. They're fully motorized.

THE FÜHRER: They will surely be able to get into this area. We can decide afterward whether to put them in here or here. It's basically the same distance.

ZEITZLER: It should be possible to pull something together so that the troop trains can go one after the other—so they don't trickle in—and then assemble at the other end.

HEUSINGER: I spoke with the general. The situation[124] is such that these forces are most likely about 6 km north of this sector[125] and the 23rd Panzer Division is now in combat in this area, against enemy tank forces which came from here—those are the forces that came here. The battle became more intense around noon, and Rychkovskii itself was lost. The enemy advanced to 1 km from the bridge, but the bridge itself isn't in enemy hands yet. I asked what they wanted to do if the bridge became unusable, and they said the Don was frozen. They thought the tanks could get across in places where the Don is quite shallow. But he couldn't confirm that. They were just considering that option in case they aren't able—which they still hope—to get the bridge free. The important thing is that they have the full 11th Panzer Division completely involved again. Parts of the division are mopping up this attack and parts are here.

THE FÜHRER: Wouldn't it be better to pull the 17th [Panzer Division] down here?

HEUSINGER: He said that if they were able to get the 17th free, they would consider possibly pulling it down here. Then he will get the 17th Panzer Division in here, although it won't help. It has 5 battalions—that's the good thing.

ZEITZLER: I think that's better. I'll speak to Manstein about it again afterward.

THE FÜHRER: It's a risky thing. It's questionable whether he can get the 11th [Panzer Division] out of there, and for the counterattack the 11th would be even better here.

ZEITZLER: It'll become very difficult in the next few days.

HEUSINGER: He added that there's nothing going on along this front. There were reconnaissance advances by the enemy, which returned again. On this front he had just spoken with the Hollidt group, and they said the picture was unclear—the enemy had dug in with tanks here. There were local movements here. But the people, who ... had come down ... Then he said this one division had pulled away. But they couldn't tell for sure whether it was an offensive or defensive action; it was unclear.

THE FÜHRER: Actually, they were ordered to build a line behind the salient.

ZEITZLER: That was ordered, and we received a sketch showing that they're building quite a neat thing with a small advanced position. I can bring the map tomorrow.

THE FÜHRER: So if worst comes to worst we could, if all else fails—but I believe we should move back immediately before a crisis comes. We could have to accept that. Then we could save some forces to strengthen the front itself.

ZEITZLER: Yes, Sir. We can save them.

THE FÜHRER: One division would always have to stay behind them. That's a third of the 262nd [Infantry Division].[126]

ZEITZLER: The 262nd and the 294th [Infantry Divisions]. There's also a regiment of the 262nd at the corner support.

THE FÜHRER: I would like to have a reconstruction.[127] When I'm traveling, I'll probably talk to Antonescu. If I remember correctly, the first message I received was that two attacks had been made here, but in general without artillery or tanks—and mostly by infantry, without major artillery preparation—and that the Romanians believe themselves capable of handling the situation.

ZEITZLER: That was the very first one.

THE FÜHRER: It started with that: the Romanians think they can handle this themselves. That might also explain why absolutely nothing was done in the first 24 hours.

ZEITZLER: For days there were these minor things, so they stopped believing that something big would happen, and thought the thing down there was an insignificant attack as well. That's the basic reason. The Russians managed that quite cleverly. Starting off so calmly like that lulls one into a false sense of security. One thinks it's only a minor action, and then all of a sudden a major attack starts in this area. The reserves actually fell for it. I can prepare some map sections for that.

THE FÜHRER: But if he[128] has the 11th [Panzer Division] in here anyway, the 11th is out of the question, because the problem is getting it over here. So in fact only the 17th [Panzer Division] can be considered. But then it's right to pull it over on the secure road right away. How is the 17th supplied with fuel?

ZEITZLER: It has 2½ to 3 consumption units now. He has to refuel down there.

THE FÜHRER: We have to do that.

HEUSINGER: 3 consumption units.

THE FÜHRER: One consumption unit lasts for 100 km.

ZEITZLER: In this weather, it should actually only last for 60 to 70 km.

HEUSINGER: But by then it will reach the railway.

ZEITZLER: So we can give it to him?

THE FÜHRER: Yes, it's the only one.[129] But the one regiment can come up here—but quick! I don't have a good feeling about this.

ZEITZLER: Maybe we can try to offer more transportation capacity to this one regiment, and let it stay with them so we can move them somewhere.

THE FÜHRER: To give them a tank destroyer company.

ZEITZLER: I'll point out again that he carries the responsibility for that, because it's his army group. He has to do something if it moves away.

THE FÜHRER: He must be sure of it. If it comes in here, we won't be able to cover it anymore. Then this will collapse as well. They will go around here immediately. Then the whole action will collapse. I go away with extremely mixed feelings, I must admit. We have to be concerned that he might some-how suddenly attack the Romanians.[130]

JODL: More is being done with the Romanians now.

THE FÜHRER: Have the Romanians improved their position at all?

JODL: I don't mean the position itself, but the bringing in of German forces.

THE FÜHRER: The Romanians complain about not having any construction material.

JODL: Yes, those troops were all in bad shape; although the Italians' supply was much better.

North Africa, Mediterranean

THE FÜHRER: I've received another message that he's moving back.[131]

JODL: Yes, he is. There's no doubt that the enemy started the first major attack, which he probably wanted to continue on the 13th. The air recon-naissance proves that his air force is finished, and he's pulled the base for-ward. He has his main fighter group with 130 single-engine and 120 twin-engine aircraft in the area north of Agedabia, and in the area between Sollum and (Marina) 100 single-engine and 40 twin-engine aircraft. All the radio communication reconnaissance also shows that he's ready—similar to be-fore the offensive against the El Alamein position—to move in here, so the Luftwaffe Air Commander Africa, also came to the conclusion that an Brit-ish offensive against Tripoli is imminent. Our forces, on the other hand, are weak—while the majority of the troops are in Sicily—and lie mostly behind the final position.[132]

THE FÜHRER: Who says this is final?

JODL: The Duce ordered it.

THE FÜHRER: The discussion that the Reichsmarshal had wasn't that clear.[133]

JODL: Rommel says the same in his telegram.

THE FÜHRER: What does he say?

JODL: He says: "The ones still in the area … will be led back into the final position." There's the word "final." So the general situation was such that he could count on that. Furthermore, he repelled the attacks yesterday, also those to the south, but says that the attacks will doubtless be continued today and that he can't allow all of the forces to wear themselves out here—particularly if the enemy advances also in the south, though with weak units, and he himself can't conduct an offensive and mobile combat due to the fuel shortage. The fuel situation actually forced him to retreat into that position. Again, he has to stay there until the 15th, so he can be mobile again. He can't get involved in anything. It's understandable if the fuel situation is like that; if he were freely mobile, he could drive around wherever he wants, and escape every encirclement.

THE FÜHRER: Actually, I have to say, though, that back then a huge army drove back here from the El Alamein position with fuel. They didn't drive with water. That whole time they hardly had any fuel. If they'd taken the fuel ahead instead of going back, they would have been able to operate out front. There's no doubt about that. Because it would have been easier to operate out front with a few divisions. In the end, though, it's only the tanks and some artillery. They covered 1,500 km with everything, even taking household effects and everything possible—that was there and what they could get. Fifty percent of the people we lost there no doubt got lost during the retreat, so the actual losses at the front were probably unusually low. There's no doubt that failing to break through in the first offensive,[134] under the impression of the sinking of the 4,000-ton steamer was wrong.[135] That's Kesselring's[136] opinion, and also Ramcke's.[137] He says: We don't understand why we didn't go further; the English were in utter flight and we just needed to keep pursuing and push in once more from any corner.[138] But I really believe we shouldn't leave a man with such heavy responsibility for a long time. That demoralizes him over time. There's a big difference, whether we withdraw a long way back. There we keep a clear head, of course. This wears the people down. We have to carry out the principle that we don't leave anyone in a theater of war for too long. It makes no sense. It's better to relieve him and let another come in, who wants to earn the laurels and is relatively fresh. So I've decided that we must relieve some of the generals now—who are in principle quite good—as soon as the first wave has passed. We must simply force them—also a field marshal—to take a few months' vacation, so that they are totally disengaged. We have to imagine the situation. He has to fight all the time with these miserable elements. No wonder he's so worn down gradually over the course of two years that he comes into a situation where he says, "I can't ..." Then things appear unbearable to him, which don't seem so monstrous looking back. We saw it last winter, where the people at the front were exhausted, just because of the effect of the weather catastrophes taking place before their eyes. They say: in retrospect they can talk easily; they aren't standing in this weather. That's correct, too. It must also be that each one is not continually exposed to the same effects. If I expose a higher staff to three weeks of the explosion of mines, I can't be surprised that their nerves are gone. That's why the commander's hill exists. Except for the final decision, where a general has to take the flag because it's a matter of life and death, he must be set off far away. Long term, it is impossible to lead the attack from the confusion of battle. Certainly—in this relatively narrow space one has to overlook almost the entire field. He also doesn't have access to news; instinct is needed here. But if he does that for two years, his nerves will suffer after some time. That's also the impression of the Reichsmarshal. He says that Rommel's[139] nerves are completely worn down.[140] And now there are those tragic side effects with the Italians—this steady uncertainty. We're experiencing it, too. I didn't sleep last night; that's the feeling of uncertainty. If I had a German front, it would also be possible that something could happen, but then we'd have the feeling that it would somehow be fixed again. In any case, an entire army doesn't collapse in a single day. The Russians said they took 94,000 prisoners, Axis forces; they took hardly any German prisoners, only Romanians.[141] The first air reports also said that huge gray convoys are crossing over there, probably all prisoners, and others are going back again; we don't know if those are Russians or also Romanians. Once a troop is in flight, if there is no iron discipline, the bonds of discipline and order vanish in a short time. It's a thousand times easier to charge forward with an army and win victories than to bring back a decent attitude after a setback or defeat. It may have been the greatest act of 1914 when they succeeded in bringing back the German army after the Marne imbecility, and got them to return to a certain line and got them in shape again. It may have been one of the greatest acts. You can only do that with excellent, disciplined troops.

JODL: It's been successful with the German troops here, too.

THE FÜHRER: It's been successful with the Germans, but it failed with the Italians, and it won't be successful anywhere else at all. That's why it's like that: if they break through there somewhere, it'll be a catastrophe. If a man has this continuous nervous pressure, he'll break under it in time.

JODL: Because with us[142] it's not just a small sector on the front, like with the Italian Eighth Army—the whole thing is his front.

THE FÜHRER: Maybe it would've been better to call him[143] back right away and put some other bull in there with the direct order: you must hold this here.

JODL: I don't think we can say anything against it here. It's like a man you're trying to keep alive with some milk and bread—you can't expect him to compete in the Olympics. He hasn't received anything for weeks. In the East they already complain loudly if they receive two trains less. He has the intention—and is forced by the materiel situation—to carry out the mission step by step, to gain time for the extension of this position.[144] There were still some parts of the XXI Corps here, which received the order today to come in here as well. He'll wait here until the British have built up again. They have to complete a reconstruction and push forward artillery. That'll take a few days.

THE FÜHRER: I hope so.

JODL: Certainly the English know that a large part of the forces have retreated back here. That may have given him reason to attack here a bit earlier.

THE FÜHRER: How much of this huge quantity of German supplies will he pull into this position? Will all that march toward Tripoli?

JODL: No, on the contrary. He reported 6 to 7 days ago that he had organized all the supplies, as far as possible, and placed them in the position.

THE FÜHRER: Because if 10-20,000 Germans are in such a position anyway, pushed in between the Italians, it's a small hold. It's impossible with the Italians alone.

JODL: He also reports that mines of all kinds, especially on the Via Balbia,[145] are and will be laid all over.

THE FÜHRER: The mining is very difficult, because we can only lay them behind us, and when we retreat, we don't have time and they see every mine in the road.

JODL: No, also in front of the position. He only needs an improvement in the fuel situation, because he doesn't have freedom of movement. If the enemy succeeds in making a strong advance from the south, the situation will be very difficult. But there's still the flat-bottomed craft traffic from the Sfax base, which is livelier than usual.[146] The individual flat-bottomed crafts aren't reported.

THE FÜHRER: So far they haven't moved.

JODL: Individual flat-bottomed craft have always gone here. At least Kesselring was quite relieved this morning, and claimed that since yesterday he had been released from a certain nightmare—regarding this whole supply situation.

THE FÜHRER: Those are the two greatest extremes. Rommel's has become the biggest pessimist and Kesselring an absolute optimist. That's endless progress.

KRANCKE: It can't be just flat-bottomed craft because we had 70 motor sailboats on the coast.

JODL: Of course, there are small ships going all the time. But they just didn't have anything for further transport so far. That only happened with the arrival of some forces in Sousse and Sfax. That's why the traffic moves on—and Kesselring points out all the time that the most important thing for him in this situation is the active traffic by small boats, flat-bottomed craft, and so on.

THE FÜHRER: I can only say that the ships in Marseille[147] and also in Toulon[148] must be used, and we might possibly also have to disregard all security regulations and just build ships. It doesn't matter. There weren't any security regulations before—no assignment of bulkheads or anything like that, and the ships went. I don't know what a kind of assignment of bulkheads they had 40, 50 years ago, when the first iron ships appeared. I want to see one of the old plans sometime. They traveled the seas all over the world. Now even a flat-bottomed craft has to have bulkheads. But if a torpedo hits it, it'll sink anyway, with or without bulkheads assigned to it. That's just the way it is.

KRANCKE: Yes, Sir.

THE FÜHRER: It uses up so much material. Now it's all about people getting life jackets. Life jackets are easier to produce than bulkheads. They have to jump into the water anyway. And they also take good four-barreled guns—those are the best bulkheads for a flat-bottomed craft.

JODL: The British report that action in the area of the Eighth Army is proceeding as planned. It seems as if the enemy is already putting some of his forces in motion toward the west and keeping some near El Agheila. But that's only speculation. No new reports from Tunis as of yesterday, except that there was a fairly weak attack here with several tanks. Other than that, there's generally nothing new. There are no major advance movements planned by the army right now, as it's still immobile. But the Fifth Panzer Army reports that German forces landed in Tunisia on December 9, 10, and 11 [—] (*Presentation*) The most positive thing might be the 186 trucks. Within a few days, we'll get the plan regarding which ships should sail in the next two weeks. Even right now, a lot of ships are sailing. One steamer is moving toward Tripoli. I might point out here that, long term, this passage to Tripoli can only be made by small boats. Because of its proximity to the front, Tripoli will be used less and less by the big steamers. One steamer is moving toward Sousse, 4 Navy flat-bottomed crafts are over here, and 2 big steamers are arriving late in Trapani due to an air attack. The escorts seem to be secured.

THE FÜHRER: This blockade—what does it mean?

JODL: It's been newly established by destroyers.[149]

KRANCKE: 6 destroyers laid out blockades. Of course, those are security escorts that set up the blockades when they aren't escorting.

JODL: That's why Kesselring urgently asks that those boats that are also suitable—the anti-U-Boat-fighters[150]—come down from Toulon.

KRANCKE: They have to be turned into anti-U-Boat-fighters first. They're fishing steamers. I can't just take any old fishing steamer. Weapons have to be brought on first.

JODL: They're waiting for any little ship that can be pulled out of somewhere.

KRANCKE: He will have 23 altogether.

THE FÜHRER: At the moment it's 400 men a day, so within 10 days 4,000 men and within 30 days 12,000 men. Then in mid-March the "Göring"[151] Division will come over. It can't be done that way. If it moves that slowly, it doesn't make sense to say, "I'll take the "Göring" Division over." Now, we can't eliminate Malta for certain. It's difficult from here, of course. When they're here, they'll be more likely to eliminate all this. They can come over from those airfields any day.

JODL: It's only possible to move here. But we can't go to Tripoli with big steamers anymore. That's why the smaller traffic is so important here.

THE FÜHRER: They were swarming around already instead of holding the position. Of course, the important thing is to clean this up first, then turn around. Those are all just big plans. To clean that up will take a year, and then to turn it around will take another year, and when the third year has passed the Italians will be gone, so Italy will be nothing more than a smoking heap of rubble. It's a weak theory. [—] What else is there?

JODL: Nothing else has happened. In contrast to this report, Kesselring is full of hope, after his meeting yesterday with the *Comando Supremo* [High Command], that the traffic really will start within the next two weeks. He'll report on that in greater detail.

THE FÜHRER: 16 steamers?[152]

JODL: Lying in the Bône harbor.

THE FÜHRER: We'll get four.

JODL: Not including a weak group. There's a late report that a submarine sank a destroyer on December 9.[153] And a strong group is on its way here—22 steamers, 2 transporters, and one tank transport—which has gathered near Gibraltar and is returning toward England.

THE FÜHRER: If we had our electronic locating equipment now, we could attack something like that at night, too.[154]

JODL: Then, the Duce [Benito Mussolini] ordered that the *Comando Supremo* be moved out of Rome, to take away the last military reason the English and Americans had for bombing Rome.

THE FÜHRER: Well—I want to speak with the Reichsmarshal anyway—we must build up the Berlin flak defense.[155] The moment will come, nevertheless, when the British must attack Berlin, and when they do so it'll be with non-stop attacks by high-altitude bombers.

CHRISTIAN: It's scheduled for January 30. It'll start at the end of December.

THE FÜHRER: I thought we would set up 100 batteries with 6 guns each, so we'd have those 600 guns that were intended for Berlin. During peacetime we had scheduled 150 batteries with 4 guns each for Berlin.[156]

CHRISTIAN: You did order that, my Führer—that 100 batteries would be there by January 30.

THE FÜHRER: Yes, with 4 barrels each.

CHRISTIAN: In Berlin they have 6.

JODL: The tank situation: there are still 100 tanks ready in southern Italy. 11 are on their way, and 64 are on their way from Germany to Italy—so 175 altogether are being supplied.

THE FÜHRER: What about the Tigers tanks? How many of those are over there?

BUHLE: Seven. One is on the way, three are in Italy, and nine are on their way to Italy.

THE FÜHRER: It's useless if they don't bring them over here.[157]

BUHLE: The next detachment will be ready within 8 to 10 days.

JODL: There's also news from an agent regarding possible British operations in the eastern Mediterranean.[158] He comes to the conclusion, then—he busies himself with rumors and all those messages circulating around—that the Allies will advance toward Crete and the Aegean islands, using Cyprus, Syria, or Egypt, and that he would make the following statements based on reports from his most reliable people. He says that an British mission against Crete in the spring of 1943 would be highly unlikely.

THE FÜHRER: No, I don't think so either, anymore.

JODL: He bases that on the shortage of larger transport ships and on the lack of smaller ships, which would all be needed for supply transfer for the English Eighth Army; on the unsuitability of Cyprus as a staging area and on the inadequate harbors of Cyprus with the lack of fighter protection, since there is no aircraft carrier available; and on unsuitable weather in the months of November and March.

THE FÜHRER: Until March or only November and March?

JODL: November until March. Seventh, on the temporary commitment of the Eighth Army in Cyrenaica. So that's why he concludes that the news about new upcoming actions is designed intentionally to pull German troops out of other theaters of war. He has documented that in detail. Maybe I can leave this here.

THE FÜHRER: I've thought about it constantly over the last few days. No matter where he lands, in the end there'll be a total number of men that have landed, facing a total number of men defending. If he divides up his landing—if we say he can land in 100 places—then he divides his landing strength, but he doesn't divide our defensive strength any more than he divides his landing strength. It's all the same. The decisive thing is: how many people can he land there at all, and in what time span can he do it? A landing of 60-70,000 men would be necessary to actually occupy the islands, and that would require a very large ship capacity. Significant capacity would be lost in a mission against Crete, with the occupation of Crete by fighter aircraft. Only, he can't come to Crete with only small ships; he can't do that. He can't afford that either. He has to go with big ships somehow, with that amount of materiel. We can see that in our case as well. The flat-bottomed craft don't work. If he wants to move 70,000 men there, and has to mobilize them and give them weapons, even only 50,000—

JODL: Then it will require a third of the ship capacity that was used against North Africa.

THE FÜHRER: So a huge amount will be lost. And it's not at all certain that he'll be able to hold here, if he's up here. He knows that we have a large number of German forces there. Therefore, I don't think that there'll be a landing on Crete. If there is, then it will most likely be in the Dodecanese, or rather in some place where he expects to be helped immediately by the inhabitants. But that's risky, too. He would have to enter the straits of Otranto, and would come close to our airfields, putting his ships in danger there. When we see with what cowardice he turns back and avoids our fighter planes, I don't think he'll move up to within 100 km of them. I find it hard to believe that. Instead, if he takes it back, I think he'll move the Eighth Army to Syria and will try to advance from there.

JODL: These reports give a very reasonable impression. He writes the following in conclusion: an operation is not expected before the spring of 1943. The mission will depend entirely on the development of the war situation, and a relocation of forces to Syria is more likely than to the Aegean islands ... Crete certainly suitable for preventive reasons. (*Reading aloud*)

THE FÜHRER: That is absolutely my opinion.

KRANCKE: Until spring, they will at most make larger- or smaller-scale raids.

France

JODL: The Military Commander in France reports: the number of French workers transported into the Reich since June 1 has now exceeded 220,000. About 110,000 skilled workers are in Berlin. [—] An agreement with the

French government regarding the transfer of a petroleum refinery of a half-million tons was successfully completed. Furthermore, the French government has agreed to make additional facilities available if necessary. (*Reading aloud*) There is nothing else to be reported from France. The transportation of the 121st and 304th [Infantry Divisions] went well—the one with more than 30 trains accomplished, the other with about 46 trains.

The Balkans

Down there in the Balkans the mopping-up action is in progress at Jace.[159] Where the enemy evaded us, he is being pursued here. The mountains here are quiet. Near ... advanced across the demarcation line[160] and threw the enemy back. Here he attacked at night, leaving behind 37 dead. People are being captured all the time in Belgrade. They say that around 15 to 30 Mihailovic followers[161] are shot every day. The pressure has become a little livelier up here, where the Italians are starting to retreat. There are assemblies here, and occasional railway destructions here—and also in this area, where the enemy pressure against those proposed Italian lines is becoming stronger. Down there another mopping-up action by the Italians is in progress.

Finland

There was complete quiet in Finland, even after those simulated attacks the day before yesterday.

Situation in the Air

CHRISTIAN: Yesterday the enemy carried out some major daytime attacks against France. With many of his fighter units he first played some kind of running game with our fighter units, then he flew in with 17[162] aircraft over Rouen to just south of Paris, under relatively low cloud cover. Consequently, he came out again with the majority of his aircraft. Fighters near Paris shot down 2 four-engine aircraft plus 3 Spitfires. Some damage occurred near Rouen—for example, a French orphanage was hit—but there was actually only damage to the civilian population.[163]

THE FÜHRER: Those are the honorable Allies; we can't help them.

JODL: We could bring that out in the French press.

CHRISTIAN: There were some nuisance attacks in this area at night, but only by single aircraft and without any damages reported—in most cases bombs weren't even dropped. One aircraft was shot down here. And there's a report later about an attack on Sunderland[164] ...

THE FÜHRER: The British report that 6 planes were in[165] the city. They report something like this so explicitly!

CHRISTIAN: 16 tactical aircraft at an altitude of between 700 and 2,000 m. Three SC-1000 bombs[166] were dropped ... 48 large high-explosive incendiary bombs and 840 incendiary bombs on the municipal area; three large fire sources in the area of the ... shipyard.

THE FÜHRER: Well, I believe that the English lie, but I can't imagine that they would just say there were only 6 aircraft, and almost no damage, when such a major attack occurs.

CHRISTIAN: 16 aircraft isn't that many.

THE FÜHRER: They claim it was only 6 planes.

JODL: It depends on whether they say it in the foreign press or in their own. They can't hide it as well in their own country.

THE FÜHRER: So far they haven't done it. They haven't denied the damage. One can't do it. It can't be risked anymore. It caused some bad blood here at the beginning of the war. But also later, a couple of times, based on Luftwaffe reports—very minor damage was reported when in fact very serious damage had occurred. I don't know what kind of local impression it made in the Rhineland when the Luftwaffe itself made such reports public. But now it's stopped. Only the precise reports are considered. It was especially tough in Cologne. The people there can take anything, but if it says in the official Armed Forces report that there was no damage or only minor, when in fact 9,000 houses were destroyed or damaged, that's really big.[167] The principle applies here as well: everything must be done to report the brutal truth. Because the most brutal truth, no matter how cruel it is, is easier to take than something good that doesn't exist at all.[168]

CHRISTIAN: The X Air Corps[169] has the order, per your command, my Führer, to attack the harbors and no other targets. The results: last night the harbor of Tobruk was attacked with 16 tactical aircraft. Detailed reports are not yet available. Today the harbor ... is supposed to be attacked. It was cloudy there, and it couldn't be done because of the weather conditions, so airfields were attacked instead. Individual aircraft of the Air Command Africa, mainly close-combat aircraft, attacked in advance of the front. Weather conditions weren't good in Tunis yesterday. Fighter-bombers were used, with good results: five tanks, one armored car, one tractor, and a number of other vehicles were destroyed. Individual tactical aircraft carried out armed reconnaissance here. There was an attack by 13 tactical aircraft against the Bône harbor during the night. Some flak positions were hit and a ship of 8,000 tons was set on fire.

THE FÜHRER: The ship of 8,000 tons is a loss; everything else is not.

CHRISTIAN: The fighters were deployed in large numbers again in the East yesterday, on the Terek, because there were good operational possibilities; they supported the battles here. The enemy has also been quite busy—yesterday primarily providing support for the advance of the two armored divisions in the direction of Stalingrad. Enemy convoys were fought here. Here there was support for defensive combat, especially near Rychkovskii and to the west. It was reported that a tank, an armored car, a multiple rocket launcher [*Katusha*], and a great number of vehicles were destroyed, and towns occupied by troops were set on fire, resulting in significant damage to weapons and equipment. Luftwaffe Don[170] flew sorties yesterday, primarily in front of the Italians, and worked with good numbers, although they had already given dive-bombers to the Fourth Air Fleet (Luftwaffe 4).[171] Otherwise, transfers are also now in progress. The railways could only be attacked here in the front, because the weather conditions in the rear were bad, with heavy fog and snowfall.

THE FÜHRER: So what's the situation now? Should we count on the possibility that sorties will take place in the future?

CHRISTIAN: It's good here; it's clear.

THE FÜHRER: And up here?

CHRISTIAN: Here there was fog, so no missions were possible yesterday—only individual dive-bombers went out. Up there an escort convoy was brought through. Two guns were destroyed.

THE FÜHRER: Let's say "silenced." What do you understand by "destroyed"? How can we confirm that?

CHRISTIAN: Hits directly on the guns. Those are dive-bombers. [—] Yesterday the Sixth Army was supplied with 50 tons of ammunition, 15 cubic meters of fuel and 8 tons of food. That wasn't much. Losses: 4 He 111s.

THE FÜHRER: That's terrible.[172]

CHRISTIAN: The weather situation in the Eastern combat theater in the area of Army Groups North and Center is variable. Mostly heavy clouds, with some precipitation, and temperatures hovering around the freezing point. In the next few days, increasing fog or high fog at the bend in the Don and the Volga; moderate frost. That's for the next few days.

THE FÜHRER: Moderate frost. If it would only stay frozen, but not too hard.

CHRISTIAN: The road conditions in [Army Groups'] North's and Center's sectors: less than 5 cm of snow, traffic mildly affected by slippery conditions. In the Southern sector, traffic ... with slippery conditions ... In the Donets area up to the bend in the Don, about 10 cm of snow. The roads are mostly free of snow, but many are iced over and extremely slippery. Traffic is hardly affected, though, as the roads have been sanded.

End: 3 p.m.

1943

* * * * *

February 1, 1943

The crushing Soviet penetrations along the Don [River]—through the lines of the Italian Eighth Army on December 18 and the Hungarian Second Army on January 14—threw the shattered front back to the Oskol and the Donets [Rivers], where the Russians achieved several encirclements.

Yesterday, on January 31, the rest of the Italian Alpine Corps and the XXIV Panzer Corps reached the German lines at Valuiki, with severe losses. Equally severe losses were suffered during these days as the surrounded Second Army broke out between Gorechnoe and Staryi Oskol. To the south, Army Group A has pulled out of the Caucasus and is withdrawing—the Seventeenth Army and parts of the First Panzer Army to the Kuban bridgehead, and the majority of the First Panzer Army to the lower Don, where Hoth's Fourth Panzer Army has been able to hold Rostov and the Don crossing until their arrival. A relief operation for the Sixth Army, which has been surrounded in Stalingrad since December 23, can no longer be considered. Yesterday, on January 31, Field Marshal Paulus surrendered. Only in the northern pocket is the remainder of the XI Army Corps still holding out.

In the northern and central sectors, the Russians have not achieved major changes. But Shlissel'burg did fall on January 18, which restored the Soviet land connection with Leningrad. In Africa, Rommel evaded in time the British attack against the Buerat position on January 18. On January 23, the

British occupied Tripoli, and the last remnant of the Italian colonial posses-
sions was lost. Only the eastern section, from Tunis up to the Mareth position, is now still in the hands of the Axis powers in Africa.
(*Maps 1, 3, and 9*)

* * * * *

MIDDAY SITUATION CONFERENCE,
FEBRUARY 1, 1943, AT THE WOLFSSCHANZE[173]

Beginning: 12:17 p.m.

The East

ZEITZLER: In general it appears that the encirclement along the Don is
now starting against the northern wing—a tank group with (numerous) tank
corps, up here in this area. Manstein is bringing up the 7th Panzer Division.
He is also taking the 3rd and the 11th Panzer Divisions over here. The 3rd
Panzer Division is marching toward Rostov. ... Of course, it could get very
difficult up there. This thing (with reference to the map): He's making a
mistake with a secondary action. It could, of course, be connected—like a
collapse. Which is why I came beforehand,[174] because I wanted to speak to
you again once more about this important issue.[175] In general, the situation
is now such that our offensive group in Khar'kov is being built up. One
division will soon be ready, (the other) on the 12th.[176] We formed it here in
order to push down here, to clear up this thing here and to (relieve) it. (It
may be that we now) have to take it up above, at least one division. That
would not be ideal. It totally depends: first, there's a huge amount of fuel
required here. ... Now, it depends: if we have to drive them up above, of
course, this salient (down below is endangered)...this salient, of course,
only temporarily. But then there is also an unpleasant situation up here.
(ZEITZLER): I always worried about that. With the 3rd Panzer Division he
has advanced quite well, and everything that's coming in is of extremely
high quality.
THE FÜHRER: How's it going now with the 13th [Panzer Division]?[177]
ZEITZLER: Down here it seems that all the movements are going very well
and are drawing near relatively quickly. The 3rd [Panzer] should now approach to here, and the 11th [Panzer] will follow. The ... arrives in this area
this evening and should come through in one push to this area up here.
THE FÜHRER: We want to make sure that we can still ... them
ZEITZLER: Yes! In any case, I consider it correct to attempt to put them in
up here.

THE FÜHRER: Is he going over here with the 7th Panzer Division?

ZEITZLER: Yes, he's going over there with the 7th Panzer Division.

THE FÜHRER: There are now 16 trains of the 335th [Infantry] Division there?

ZEITZLER: Yes! It was a little slower again, because of bomb damage along the way. [—] And now up here the question arises, ... to relieve...the cavalry corps. Then we would have something to provide cover below.

THE FÜHRER: The relief takes longer than the new arrivals.

ZEITZLER: ... But huge tension remains in any case, and I wanted to ask (For this reason,) that the economic program not be affected. [178]

THE FÜHRER: I'll think about that. But I can say one thing: then there would no longer be the possibility of ending the war through offensive action in the East. We have to bear that in mind.

(ZEITZLER: Yes!)

THE FÜHRER: Because I can't do it without the materiel. I can't do it with those people. Then I may have the people, but I have no materiel. The question is: what do we want now? We (now) have a width of 5 km,[179] but I can give the people guns and ammunition. Then I have only a 3 km width, but I have no more guns or ammunition. If you think we can fight at 3 km better without ammunition than at 5 km with ammunition, the calculation is correct.

ZEITZLER: Yes, that's a good question. At the moment it's not important, but it will be later.

THE FÜHRER: No, now as well as later! (At the same time) the whole defense production program becomes invalid. Our whole tank program that's made of electro steel then drops out immediately ... (Also) our gun program. Instead of 600 per month we could then produce only 150 guns. The large ammunition program is (eliminated) immediately as well. At that moment it drops swiftly. (It won't happen gradually); it'll happen rapidly. I wouldn't win anything with that. If I were to go back, I would lose the ..., there will be utter confusion, and the enemy would push in behind. We've also had those experiences while retreating.

ZEITZLER: That's quite clear to me. But if we hadn't conducted the retreat, it would have become even worse. They had to move back there and down here—here by the panzer army.

THE FÜHRER: I've said since the beginning—for me it was completely clear: if the action can't be undertaken here, then there are only the two bridgeheads. That's obvious. If (it had been done like that), as the good Manstein wanted, they would not have been able to withdraw and everything would have fallen to pieces. If I had given in to Manstein, they would (not have returned). ... (He would have) hadn't more panzer army nor would he have brought a Seventeenth Army back—everything would have collapsed. ... I've always been concerned that he might stay here too long[180] [—]

(ZEITZLER): And now I (thought) we might immediately bring the 337th [Infantry] Division up from France behind the 4th Panzer Division, with some of the 78th [Infantry] Division at the same time, in order to start forming a new block here. And now we have to see what happens with the advance of the SS units. If we take the "Reich" [SS Panzer Division][181] up there, they'll surely restore the situation. But that would take a long time. ... I'd like to think that we have no other choice but to put them in down there.

THE FÜHRER: We'll see. It depends on how it goes with the 4th Panzer Division. If the 4th Panzer Division gets off to a halfway good start [—]

ZEITZLER: There are 15 trains (on their way. Progress is slow) because they've destroyed everything with bombs; 7 trains should arrive today.

THE FÜHRER: When the 4th Panzer Division arrives (one unit will be there). Another unit will be there when the 337th [Infantry] Division comes behind it. And the 78th [Infantry Division] would come as well. With them, we'll have (a group of forces that might) permit us to take hold of (this thing). We have to wait and see. If we can grab it with that, it's [—] True to form, they surrendered themselves.[182] Because otherwise, you gather yourselves together, build an all-round defense, and shoot yourself with the last cartridge. If you imagine that a woman, after being insulted a few times, has so much pride that she goes out, locks herself in, and shoots herself dead immediately—then I have no respect for a soldier who (shrinks back from it and prefers) going into captivity. There I can only say: (I can understand it in a case) like General Giraud, where we come in, he gets out of the car, and is immediately captured.[183] But [—]

ZEITZLER: I can't understand it either. I still think that (it may not) be true—that he may be seriously wounded.

THE FÜHRER: No, it is true. The Russians will now ... immediately ... They will go to Moscow immediately, to the GRU [Military Intelligence Directorate], and they will give out orders that the northern pocket should surrender as well.[184] This Schmidt[185] will sign everything. A person who doesn't have courage at such a moment to take the step that everyone has to take once, won't have the strength to resist. He'll develop a martyr complex. (With us) the intellect is cultivated too much and strength of character not enough ...

ZEITZLER: One can't actually explain how.

THE FÜHRER: Don't say that! I had a letter [—] Below received the letter.[186] I can show it to you. There he said, "I reached the following judgment about those people"—and then it read: "Paulus[187]: Question mark; Seydlitz[188]: shoot him; Schmidt: shoot him."

ZEITZLER: I have also heard bad things of Seydlitz.

THE FÜHRER: And below them: "Hube[189]—*that* man!" Of course, (one could say that it might have been) better if Hube had stayed inside and the others had gone out. But because people are still important and because we need the men for the entire war, I'm really of the opinion that Hube will go out. In peacetime, 18,000 to 20,000 people chose suicide each year[190] in the German Reich, without being in any such situation. Here a man can see how 50,000 to 60,000 of his soldiers die and defend themselves bravely to the end—how can he then surrender to the Bolsheviks?! Oh, that is [—]!

ZEITZLER: It's something that we really can't understand at all.

THE FÜHRER: But the first (doubt had already arisen earlier). That was the moment when it was said that he asked what he should do now.[191] How can he even ask such a thing? So in the future, whenever a fortification is besieged and the commanding officer receives a demand to surrender, he's going to ask first, "What shall I do now?" [—][192] How easy he made it for himself![193] Or Becker[194]: he became confused when loading his weapon, made ... and later on he shoots himself.[195] How easy it is to do such a thing! The pistol—that's quite easy. What kind of cowardice it must be to flinch even from that! Ha! Better let yourself be buried alive! And in such a situation where he knows full well that his death is the requirement for holding the next pocket. Because if (he) gives (an example like that), you can't expect the men to continue fighting.

ZEITZLER: There's no excuse. Then he has to shoot himself before, if the nerves threaten to fail.

THE FÜHRER: If the nerves fail, there is nothing (left but to say:) I couldn't take it any longer—and shoot oneself. There you can also say: the man has to shoot himself, just like (in earlier times the generals) threw themselves onto their swords when they saw that all was lost. That's a matter of course. Even Varus ordered to the slaves: kill me now!

ZEITZLER: I still think that they might have done it, and (that the Russians only claim) they all gave themselves over into captivity.

THE FÜHRER: No!

ENGEL: The peculiar thing is—if I may say it—that they didn't announce (that Paulus was captured seriously wounded.) Then they could say tomorrow he died of his wounds.

THE FÜHRER: Do we have precise news about his wounds?[196] [—] The tragic thing has happened now. That might be a warning.

ENGEL: The names of the generals can't all be correct.

THE FÜHRER: During this war no one else will become a field marshal. That will all be done after the end of the war. One should not count ones chickens before they hatch.[197]

ZEITZLER: We were so strongly convinced about the end that we ... our last joy ...

THE FÜHRER: We had to assume it would end heroically.

ZEITZLER: One couldn't imagine anything else.

THE FÜHRER: And in this human environment, how could one act differently?! There I must say that every soldier is an idiot who risks his life, and risks his life again and again. If a little "pussy" is overwhelmed, I can still understand that.

ZEITZLER: The troop commander has it much easier. Everyone looks at him. For him it's simple to shoot himself. It's difficult for the ordinary man.

THE FÜHRER: If the little worm, on which everything is falling, says in such a situation, ... and lets himself be captured, then I can understand that. But I must say: how heroically have the ... One can't argue with that. Of course, also many Germans! [—] and that we don't achieve it with our intellectually superior command cadre, our high-quality soldiers and our weapons that are still in the end superior to the Russians'. Nevertheless, we were always superior, disregarding Stalingrad. When I heard it tonight, I had Puttkamer find out if the news was already out. If (it hadn't been announced) via radio broadcast, (I would have) stopped it immediately.[198] It hurts me so much because the heroism of so many soldiers is destroyed by a single spineless weakling—and the man is going to do that now. You have to imagine it: he comes to Moscow, and just imagine the "rat cage"![199] He'll sign everything there. He will make confessions and appeals. You'll see: they'll walk down the road completely disregarding any principle—to the deepest abyss. In this case one can also say: an evil deed generates new evil again and again.

ENGEL: One thing, tomorrow Major Zitzewitz[200] is scheduled to (speak about Stalingrad) to the domestic and foreign press. Should that be cancelled?

THE FÜHRER: No, ...

ENGEL: I come to that point because there, of course, questions will be asked, among others a question ...The best thing would be to ... only very generally [—]

(THE FÜHRER): ... If somebody knows something, we don't know about; it can't be determined exactly. But with soldiers, the primary thing is always the matter of principle, and if we can't cultivate that, if we breed only pure intellectual acrobats and intellectual athletes—mental athletes—then we never will get that species which alone can stand the heavy blows of fate. That's decisive.

ZEITZLER: Yes, also in the General Staff. For the first time, I gave the uniform to an officer[201] who hadn't gone through general staff officer training because his preparation for the withdrawal of the division was as brilliant as the General Staff does it. It also doesn't matter that he has been in the course only 8 weeks.[202] It had an immediate effect. I immediately said: as of today, you are a general staff officer.

THE FÜHRER: Yes, we have to take bold, courageous people who are also prepared (to risk their lives), just like every soldier risks his life. What does that mean, "Life"? Life ... people; the individual indeed has to die. What remains alive beyond the individual is the people. But how one can fear this moment—through which he (can free) himself from misery— (if) duty (doesn't) hold him back in this valley of suffering! Well! [—]

They also reported that Paulus was captured. I want to have it sorted out: captured and missing. If they break in and take it without a fight, everyone knows they've been captured. The others must be reported as missing. ...

ZEITZLER: ...The attacks didn't continue today. The report from (Kurzbach[203]) about the withdrawal is very reasonable—the order for it. He's also arranged it very sensibly. To be sure, he's sent a bit too much paper about how they are doing everything, but he did think about all those things. I don't know if it interests you. I can leave it here if it does. He has divided it into different stages. That's definitely good. And he also (planned) the immediate steps (correctly): that the thing here is thoroughly covered, and the ammunition goes in here, and also there—but first, that whatever comes from here, ... doesn't go in there under any circumstances. [—] Then I can leave it here.

THE FÜHRER: I don't know how to proceed in Paulus' case. (We must give the commander in the northern pocket an order that he must hold it under all circumstances. The pocket must be held until the end. [—])

(ZEITZLER: Then you agree) that I should do it this way?

THE FÜHRER: Yes! I'll come back to that thought again. The Romanian general Lascar fell with his men. I'm glad that I gave him the Oak Leaves. [204] How can such a thing happen? When I heard about that at 2:30 last night— I had gone to bed early—I had Puttkamer come right away in order to find out (if the radio report had gone out already. Because the Russians reported): Marshal Paulus captured with his entire staff. The whole staff surrendered. Now the Russians leave [—]

ZEITZLER: Just what I suspected! I thought they would misuse the dead Paulus ... And now it's even worse.

THE FÜHRER: He will soon speak via radio—you will see that.[205] Seydlitz and Schmidt will speak on the radio. They will lock them into rat cellars, and two days later they will have broken them, and then they'll speak immediately. A beautiful woman—who really was a first-rate beauty—is (insulted) with (a single word. She says afterward), because of some trifle: "Then I can go; I am superfluous." ... (replies:) "Then go!" Afterward, the woman leaves, writes farewell letters, (and shoots herself).[206] [—]

Did the wounding occur before Jaenecke's[207] departure or afterward?

ZEITZLER: I want to check on that. I'll phone Jaenecke, because he would know if it had happened beforehand.

THE FÜHRER: We have to confirm that! Then we have to take the position that the staff also fought to the last, and that they only gave in to the enemy's superior strength (and were taken into captivity) when they were wounded or overpowered.

ZEITZLER: That's surely what the majority of the staff did.

THE FÜHRER: We have to say that it wasn't a capitulation but an overpowering.

ZEITZLER: We can also write in: "The Russians will describe it differently"—that way the world press will get it from us first.

THE FÜHRER: (That they) hadn't received any supplies for months and that (therefore the Russians) succeeded in overwhelming some of them.

ZEITZLER: I agree that this direction is the right one.

THE FÜHRER: It's just the beginning. I would guess that in eight days at the latest [—]

(General Zeitzler excuses himself: 1:02 p.m.

Continuation of the conference at 1:05 p.m. with the usual circle of participants.)

THE FÜHRER: Can I get Below?

CHRISTIAN: I don't know if he drove to Leipzig today.

Mediterranean

JODL: *(Places a report on the table.)*

THE FÜHRER: I just read a report in the English press. There it's said that Cavallero[208] was removed because he was forming a kind of center for anti-Fascist elements. Is there also a description by Kesselring about the reasons?

JODL: Aside from what I presented yesterday, nothing. ... about an extraordinary additional distinction or honor for v. Papen.[209] [—] The British obviously haven't noticed Rommel's eastward withdrawal from the position. They ... didn't push their reconnaissance forward to the rear guard position until later in the day. Lively patrol action is reported to the south of the Mareth position. They assume (that the British are trying) to come (into the rear) of this position. [—] Further to the south the enemy attacked our[210] occupation of Sened. There he was thrown back. He occupied the town... It seems to be a significant success that we have occupied this high ground. Perhaps it happened already on Rommel's orders. That was the 21st Panzer Division. It's surprising how fast that division came. They gathered here and got Panzer Detachment 190 and lined up immediately.

THE FÜHRER: What does the panzer detachment consist of, Buhle?

BUHLE: Panzer Detachment 190 consists of three companies of 17 Panzer IIIs and one company with 10 Panzer IVs and a few Panzer IIs added to them.

THE FÜHRER: Very bad!

BUHLE: It's the same with the 10th Panzer Division, except for the assault gun detachment.

THE FÜHRER: Do they have Panzer IIIs?

JODL: There are only a few Panzer IIIs left in Italy.

THE FÜHRER: Do they have the short gun?

BUHLE: The 10th Panzer Division has …; the Tiger detachment has only short ones. At the moment there are 32 Panzer IVs in Italy.

THE FÜHRER: All those that went down also had the short …

JODL: The Tigers rolled off [—] it exploded later, after it caught fire. Maybe there was ammunition in it. During an attack on Bizerte, an Italian submarine chaser was torpedoed, a small floating dock was sunk, and a transport ship was hit by a bomb. A small steamer was outside of Sousse.[211]

THE FÜHRER: You can see how we can achieve the same if we attack the harbors again and again. Everything else becomes less significant in comparison.

JODL: Three ships are on their way from Naples to Sicily. Three of our motor torpedo boats laid a mine barrier outside of Bône, and made brief contact with enemy motor torpedo boats on the way back. But nothing seems to have happened. 105 ships arrived in Italy from France.[212] Busy traffic further to the west. As a result of the stronger concentration on Gibraltar, the Commander-in-Chief South expects lively action in the western Mediterranean. A large convoy of 16 ships may have (put to sea). The following are supposed to have arrived: 26 units, including 2 battleships, one carrier, 5 cruisers, and 10 destroyers.[213]

THE FÜHRER: When will that group there finally go down there?[214] Will it take months?

JODL: Kesselring told me that he's planning on February 10. [—]

JESCHONNEK: There were ten. They lost seven through suicide attacks and three were shot down.

THE FÜHRER: Well, fine—ten aircraft lost. But 2 battleships and 3 cruisers!![215]

Armed Forces Report

JODL: If we write "XI Corps" in the report, the German people will get the impression that all of what originally belonged to the XI Corps was in

Stalingrad. It would be better to write: "under the leadership of the commanding general of the XI Corps, Strecker."[216] We can write that, or just "under the leadership of General Strecker."

KEITEL: Yes, just "under the leadership of General Strecker."[217]

Mediterranean

JODL: Submarines have been identified south of the Otranto Straits, south of Taranto, in the Gulf of Naples, and two here.[218] In the eastern Mediterranean, no complete reconnaissance. In the northern Arctic, the Navy, based on radio reconnaissance, believes that 4 Russian submarines are present. It's also suspected that some Russian motor torpedo boats are stationed along the southern coast of the Fischer Peninsula. So the Naval Command expects stronger activity from the Russian fleet—if there is an improvement and calming in the weather situation during these first nights when there's a new moon.

THE FÜHRER: If the weather situation calms [—]

THE FÜHRER: In total they have around (150) trains. So that's actually as many trains as the Russians have—they brought 200 trains down to Toropets.

France

JODL: In France there were two railway accidents. Early on the 31st, a transport train carrying a local defense battalion derailed near Bourges; there were 10 dead, 20 severely wounded and 10 slightly wounded. Then the following night, in the area south of Dijon, a few cars of a freight train derailed, and was then hit shortly afterward by an oncoming freight train—so that stretch was blocked for two days. In both cases sabotage is suspected. Investigations are underway. [—]

Stalingrad

Concerning the Russian report, we are now checking carefully to see if there are any mistakes in it. Because a single mistake—a general who couldn't possibly have been there—would show that the whole thing was made up from a list that they captured somewhere and then published.

THE FÜHRER: (They report) that they captured Paulus, as well as Schmidt and Seydlitz.

JODL: I don't know about Seydlitz. They're not sure whether he's in the northern pocket. That's what will now be determined through a radio inquiry. Which generals exactly are in the northern pocket?

THE FÜHRER: He was surely with Paulus.[219] [—] I want to tell you something: I don't understand a man like (Paulus), who doesn't prefer death. The heroism of so many tens of thousands of men, officers and generals is wiped out (by a man like that,) who, when the moment comes, doesn't possess the character to do what a weak woman has done.

JODL: But I'm still not quite sure if that's right. [—]

(THE FÜHRER): ... The man and the woman were together there. Later the man died of his illness. Then I received a letter from that woman; she begged me to care for the children. It wasn't possible for her to continue living, despite her children. ... Then she shot herself. The woman did that; she found the strength—and soldiers don't find the strength! You'll see: It won't take eight days before Seydlitz and Schmidt and also Paulus speak on the radio.

JODL: I'm firmly convinced of that.

THE FÜHRER: They're now taken into the Lubyanka, and there rats will eat them. How can somebody be (so cowardly)? I don't understand it.

JODL: I still have doubts.

THE FÜHRER: I don't, unfortunately. Do you know—I also don't believe anymore in the wounds that (Paulus supposedly received). That doesn't seem to be true either. Because they still have to expect that they [—] What should we do then? Personally, it hurts me the most that I still did that—promoted him to field marshal. I wanted to give him the last (happiness). That's the last field marshal I will (make) during (this war). One should not praise the day until it's over. I don't understand that at all. If you see so many (men) die—I really must say how easy it was for our ...; he didn't consider anything. That is completely ridiculous. So many men have to die, and then a man like that goes out and besmirches the heroism of so many others at the last minute. (He could have) delivered (himself from every misery) and reached eternity and entered into the national immortality—but he preferred going to Moscow. How can (there even be a choice)? It's just crazy.

JODL: That's why I still have doubts [—]

(THE FÜHRER): ... just as if I were to say today: I'll give a fortification to General Förster. Then I know immediately that he'll be (the first one to) pull down the flag.[220] There are others who wouldn't do that. It's tragic that in such a moment heroism (is defiled) so terribly like that.

JESCHONNEK: I still consider it possible that the Russians (reported) that intentionally. Their work is very refined.

THE FÜHRER: They'll speak on the radio in eight days.

JESCHONNEK: The Russians will even manage to get (somebody else) to speak.

THE FÜHRER: No, they will speak personally over the radio. You will hear it right away. No, they will all speak personally on the radio! They will first order the men in the pocket to surrender, and will say the most awful things against the German Armed Forces. You have to bear in mind: (they come) to Moscow, to the Lubyanka, and are being "treated" there. If a person doesn't have the courage in such an hour [—] I also already told Zeitzler that he must give an order to Heitz, telling him to hold the northern pocket.

KEITEL: He was in the southern pocket, and Heitz wasn't mentioned (in the Russian report).[221]

THE FÜHRER: Then he must be dead if he wasn't mentioned.

JODL: Yes, and because of that we must also (inquire) and establish who is in the northern pocket now. If there are names in it[222] of people who are in the northern pocket, then it must be a list that they found somewhere and published. On the other hand, (it is already a fact) that they have not mentioned a man who certainly fell—Hartmann—who was in the southern pocket.

KEITEL: He was killed four days ago.[223]

JODL: Yes!

THE FÜHRER: If Heitz was in the southern pocket and wasn't mentioned ... I am convinced that the whole staff simply surrendered obediently [—]

Situation in the air

CHRISTIAN: Two daytime incursions yesterday in Norway, one as far as Oslo and the other to Stavanger—immediately shot down by fighters. There were three incursions along the northern French coast without attacks. We made a night fighter attack against towns along the (English) coast. In the Mediterranean area: no combat action reported over the eastern Mediterranean. Attacks against enemy convoys at ... Also support with stronger forces for the advance of the 21st Panzer Division and the ... Infantry Division against Sened. Two aircraft were shot down in aerial combat. Two aircraft were shot down during an (attack by) tactical aircraft and fighters against Gabes. The airfield ... was attacked. The remaining forces attacked enemy concentrations south of [—] Details about that haven't been reported. [—] Enemy air activity was very weak yesterday. Luftwaffe Command Don deployed 279 aircraft during the night—214 fighters in the area of the Tim front alone. During the night there was also armed reconnaissance in this area. In total, the following have been (reported) from these attacks: 197 aircraft of all kind destroyed, 98 trucks damaged, and three convoys (blown up). Transport aircraft supplied the troops that (are) marching back ... (are understood). Luftwaffe Command East[224] deployed 46 aircraft during the day. They fought bands in the rear area. Individual aircraft ..., because movements were also recognized there. The weather situation is bad, with some snowdrifts. [—]

(JESCHONNEK): ... transmitted the order that the Luftwaffe should be reinforced at Demiansk,[225] and transmitted the order that the dive-bomber group, which is now ... being replenished and should arrive in a few days, should be brought up here, and that the fighter protection will be strengthened as well. The fighter protection can be strengthened immediately with the help of three fighter squadrons that ... from the area ... in approximately two days—it is strictly a question of the weather conditions—can (be pulled further toward the front).

THE FÜHRER: Can they drop bombs at the same time?

JESCHONNEK: They're examining that. It depends on one thing: whether or not (there are) sufficient (bomb racks).

THE FÜHRER: Can't we produce them? Is that so difficult?[226] [—]

(JESCHONNEK): The group has 39 Stukas [dive bombers] ready for action.

THE FÜHRER: Then deploy the 3rd Fighter Squadron here!

JESCHONNEK: Yes, and the dive bombers will come in here anyway, so they should be sufficient in any case.

THE FÜHRER: Good, I agree. But make sure they (are equipped) to drop bombs.

JESCHONNEK: So we gain a whole dive-bomber group.

Miscellaneous

(*Presentation by Jodl: Organization of the* Hermann Göring *Division.*)

THE FÜHRER: The 17-cm guns ... Do we have a map of the Taman Peninsula? (*Presentation of the map.*) This is the 1:1,000,000 map. I'm of the opinion that we should (bring) some 17-cm guns over here and place them up here [—] In any case, the 17 cm—the one that's going over to Africa—must be placed in the ...position.

BUHLE: There's one of them down here.

THE FÜHRER: That's not enough. This one here is no doubt fixed, and that one can't be moved. A whole heavy artillery group must come here, to make sure nothing happens there [—]

(JESCHONNEK): ... That we—I want to say: bring in 70,000 men from the Luftwaffe, whom we need in order to keep the Luftwaffe field divisions.[227]

THE FÜHRER: We need to do that anyway!

JESCHONNEK: So the field divisions don't immediately all slide together!

THE FÜHRER: We've always said that that's obvious.

JESCHONNEK: Then the 2nd Parachute Division will come.

THE FÜHRER: We only need something in order to put it in the huge sack, into the Donets area. (If we lose that, we'll get no) more steel.[228]

JESCHONNEK: I'd like to take this opportunity to raise the question of the 7th Fighter Division [—]

Air armaments

(THE FÜHRER:) Although we don't train too many (tank drivers). I don't want it to become like in the Luftwaffe, where we say: the tanks exist—they're coming out now, but unfortunately we don't have drivers for them. That is indeed the problem (with the Luftwaffe), because we'll get enough aircraft this month.[229]

JESCHONNEK: But the fighter squadrons have been reporting that[230] for a year already.

THE FÜHRER: Yes, and I don't want that same thing to happen with the tanks—that there aren't enough crews ...

KEITEL: Thus the reorganization! [—]

(JESCHONNEK:) ... the reason given right now is that as soon the aircraft stand outside unprotected, moisture gets into the wiring and causes problems. The engines are overstrained as well.

THE FÜHRER: I have to say again and again: I consider the whole 177 Model a (mistake), because it was demonstrated already during the Great War that the problem of installing two engines on one shaft is extremely difficult to solve, and has led to constant difficulties.[231] The (results of) experience are nonsense, and only what the experts do is right! I received a report from Heinkel[232] that says the "FW" that we ... (should reach) a range of 8,200 km.[233] If they can make it reach 8,200 km, then (the range would suffice in order to) fly from Kirkenes to ....[234]

[—]

THE FÜHRER (*with the aid of a map*): Then we could push from here down to here. Then we might possibly have to make the approach over here in order to reach this area at dusk and then fly back in the dark via the shortest route. Sverdlovsk—here are the (armament factories). If we had 30 such aircraft, and every one (flew over) with 1,000 kg bombs, (we could) smash them. If we (fly in) from here from the back, I think they'll find it. There's nothing there.[235] ...and destroyed completely. There is also the aircraft factory. And we can't drop just one bomb, but 30 (1,000-kg bombs on one factory) and destroy it completely! [—] but two engines beside each other produce much more difficult conditions, and it was shown that the transfer to a ... and a central crank is always dangerous. If something goes wrong with one engine, the second is usually (finished) as well. That's

definitely a design failure. They also want to dive with the plane. But we haven't achieved anything with that. On June 22, 1941, (the first planes should have been ready for action). And they were to attack Moscow first. They were supposed to be ready back then. And what year do we have now? 1943!! [—] because the elements are the same. That's also the difficulty with heavy tanks when they have two engines. In theory it's wonderful. In practice, it's been shown that two engines in such heavy Panzers are dangerous. ... much heavier than one. It accumulates, of course. If I (have only one engine), I can brake much easier than if I have two. I can't say: ...; no, it accumulates and increases substantially. The technicians say that anyway, and we have to believe some of what they say. [—] (There are people who claim): it was different during the Great War. Those idiots! Because they didn't experience it! They only have to read up on it in a book. If they had read how during the Great War the Ruhr area and especially the Saar area was destroyed by night raids! But they (simply say that during the Great War flights took place only during the day. But the bombers did fly at night.[236] The fighters ... it ... No pig found the airfields at night, (but they did find the towns). These people weren't in the towns, but outside, and did (not notice anything. But the people) who had the misfortune to be inside the towns (know that.) But they simply say that No, (flights were only made during the daytime in the Great War.) [—] But the man didn't want to introduce flamethrowers. That was the General of the Engineers.[237] If it had been a cavalryman, (we could have said) "What does he know about hand grenades!" But no, it was an engineer by profession who said that to me. I first had to fight a huge battle to get the flamethrower introduced at all. [—] Here it's exactly the same [—]... *I can imagine.*
JESCHONNEK: The arguments are clear.
THE FÜHRER: I can imagine that everything will be torn to pieces now. But (before the) war I also always held the opinion that a fast bomber does (not) need (to be armed). Speed is its weapon and its offensive weapon is (the bomb). If we say they can only drop very small bombs—that's still enough (to) make (us) uneasy. The Reichsmarshal personally couldn't ... everything ... This impudent expression: "Mosquito," the thing is called! And it's made of wood![238] [—]
(*The meeting was interrupted by a short telephone conversation with the adjutant Colonel v. Below, regarding a letter sent to him by an officer from Stalingrad.*[239])

* * * * *

March 4-5, 1943

There have been no significant changes on the fronts of Army Groups North and Center, but the situation in the South and in Tunis has forced

Hitler to approve a straightening of the front in two places; on February 21 the evacuation of the Demiansk pocket began, which is essentially now complete, and on February 26 the evacuation of the Rzhev salient began.

In the southern sector, in the meantime, the front has been stabilized again. On the Black Sea, the Seventeenth Army pulled back to the Kuban bridgehead, where it is protecting access to the Crimea. Army Group South—formerly Don—threw the Russians back over the middle Donets [River] once again at the end of February, and is now holding the Mius [River]. A strong Russian combat group is encircled south of Khar'kov, after the city itself was lost as a result of the penetration of the Hungarian lines on February 18. To the north, after the breakthrough at Voronesh, the Soviets advanced far beyond Kursk, nearly to the Desna [River]. Hitler identified this area on March 5 as the theater for a German summer offensive, which was to smash the salients around Kursk concentrically in order to deny the enemy complete freedom of action. Otherwise, however, after the heavy and irreplaceable losses of the winter, he is forced to accept a strategic defense for 1943. The great decision in the East, which Hitler wanted to force first in 1941 and then again in 1942, can no longer be considered in the year of Stalingrad.

In Tunis the situation has changed little. In mid-February, Rommel led a push against the American concentration in the Faid-Gafsa area in order to eliminate the threat to the connection lines between the German-Italian army in the Mareth position and Tunis, 400 km away. He achieved a breakthrough—causing heavy enemy losses—and reached Kasserine Pass, but had to pull back again ten days later. But because the situation in Tunisia is hopeless unless one of the two hostile armies is defeated decisively, Rommel is now preparing for an attack against the British on the Mareth front, which will begin on March 6.

(*Maps 1, 3, 7, and 9*)

* * * * *

EVENING SITUATION REPORT,
MARCH 4, 1943, AT THE WEHRWOLF[240]

Beginning: 9:30 p.m.

Situation in the air

THE FÜHRER: The attack on London seems to have been successful, because otherwise they could (not) write that. We also couldn't write that the (attack on) Berlin was a complete failure.[241]

CHRISTIAN: According to the reports, 108.5 tons of demolition bombs and 16,000 incendiary bombs were dropped. The fighter-bomber raid was cancelled this afternoon. The cloud cover was gone, but there was less than 2 km visibility because of very strong haze. They want to do it early tomorrow.
THE FÜHRER: That should be a lesson to them, because the attack was nothing at all—it certainly failed.

Tunis, Mediterranean

JODL: The attack continues on the outer northern wing, and the Sedjenane station was taken, on the road leading west from Matear. The attack was also continued by the Djebel 464,. ... which was quite (exhausted) from the heavy fighting, (was relieved) by the 47th Regiment. (On the) road going west from Medjez el Bab, the (situation is unchanged). The enemy attacked with an armored group, but was unable to (take) the road because of the defensive fire. Further to the south there is only artillery fire, and, (in front of) this 10th Panzer Division sector, very strong to ..., so that we drew most of the troops back a little bit more here and left only strong points in front. Further to the south there was artillery fire and reinforcement by about two battalions in the direction of Pont du Fahs. The security line runs here, up to and including Gafsa. There was no particular combat action at the Mareth position[242] except artillery fire on both sides. The overall impression is that the enemy is approaching the Mareth position very strongly and is pushing in very close to the position itself, so we have to expect an attack against the position in the near future. The mobile combat group of the 10th and 21st Panzer Divisions is located north of Gabes.
CHRISTIAN: An overview of the deployment of the 8.8 cm anti-aircraft artillery 41[243]: (*Presentation.*) ... went in ...
THE FÜHRER: Why did they have only high-explosive shells?
CHRISTIAN: They had used everything else up.
(JODL:) There are 135 tanks at the moment.[244] Then an overall evaluation of the situation (arrived) from Rom(mel)—it is an inquiry that he had directed to the (*Comando*) *Supremo*,[245] with a comment by (Field Marshal) Kesselring. The numbers given here are the required strength. (*Presentation.*)
THE FÜHRER: This is a totally opposite evaluation from what he himself gave them before.[246]
JODL: He just wants a decision. That can't be done, of course. He did it from the point of view of his army.
THE FÜHRER: It's also an evasion by Kesselring, of course. First it was said that as soon as French ships come,[247] it will be fine. The French ships have come, and it's not fine. We can't talk our way out of it now based on the November shipbuilding program, because they won't be ready for that.

JODL: There should be enough ships. 112 or 113 ships have come across now.

THE FÜHRER: It (is) impossible for him to (pull) back on that now. It contradicts the statements that Kesselring made beforehand. We have to establish this (clearly for once). Kesselring (gave) assurances here, how things (would be arranged in a very short time). Now two months have passed, and during those (two months) it hasn't even come close to happening. But there (they can't) follow the program because the (program went ahead) anyway— and it didn't have anything to do with the two months that (are now) behind us, but with completely different things. Of course, if we carelessly let tank-ers be sunk[248] because the forces don't work together, then we can't be sur-prised if there are crises. A single tanker like that (would have) brought enough fuel to supply such operations. It would certainly have provided the 8 to 10 fuel consumption units. I don't know how high the consumption units will be here. I don't believe it'll be more. What daily consumption unit will they have? Surely not more than 500 cubic meters!

JODL: Less!

THE FÜHRER: So 14 daily units were lost through the carelessness of the Luftwaffe under Field Marshal Kesselring—that must be said—and through the sloppiness with which the Navy itself finally brings these small ships into action.

(JODL: That's) not even under consideration, of course, because ... can't be done.

THE FÜHRER: That's the end. Then the ... can be brought over.

JODL: Besides, then the whole connection ... is set. Then he can place the strong part(s of these) divisions here, which are indeed much strong(er and better). So that is not under consideration; instead, (he must) continually smash the attack preparation(s) in order to gain enough time to (bring) over additional forces here—so that in the end we bring all mobile units behind the front as reserves. Most of the *Hermann Göring* [Parachute Panzer] Divi-sion is available for this, with the (part) in France, the 999[249] Division and— I have asked for a report on the equipment—the special-purpose regiment, which belonged to Felmy[250] and which is still mostly together. It has no doubt lost men.

THE FUHRER: Where is the regiment?

JODL: It is still in the Mius [River] position.[251] The corps staff has been pulled out. If the situation calms down there anyway, through the weaken-ing of the Mius position, I think we should take out that regiment—because together with the African Legion, which is already there, it makes up a bri-gade. This regiment consists of 2 battalions, one assault gun company, one mortar detachment, one heavy anti-aircraft battery, one light anti-aircraft battery and one reconnaissance company.

THE FÜHRER: We must tell Rommel that (the evaluation) he is sending now (is) completely different (from the one) he sent before.

(JODL: I) can draw it up then. A (further) voluntarily retreat here would in any case mean giving up the bridgeheads.[252] If the (planned forces) were all there and the supply were to come over to here, (the) forces (should) be sufficient. He himself calculates 210,000 men. We have that many as well. We have 140,000 Germans (here) alone. But the English, of course, have much more materiel. Our materiel (is) in Italy. Of course, over (time) these small vessels will become more important. (So) I would like to request that we don't—through steel restrictions—let the production sink below the capacity of the shipyards. We have recently received numerous reports that the enemy will begin to take offensive action in the eastern Mediterranean, and—in number at least—the reports are greatly intensifying. But they come back again and again to the same point: They speak of huge concentrations on Cyprus that certainly don't exist.

HEWEL: On the other hand, they have a press directive that Sardinia should not be mentioned.

JODL: Yes, that seems very suspicious to me. On the other hand, the grouping together of the foreign (army) detachments shows (that of the) Briti(sh forces actually) situated in the (east)ern Mediterranean, none—or only a few—could be used (for such an) operation, because all of (the Indian) divisions and Polish divisions that are (there) would be out of the question for such an attack. The 9th Australian Infantry Division (is) still there, because (this here) has disappeared. But I don't believe that Australia would give permission for them to make an (attack) here again.[253] So in the end there remains a South African ... Division, the 8th British Armored Division and perhaps another (British) division that we don't know is there. (Everything) else that has been identified here couldn't be considered for an att(ack) against the Southeast. At the moment, I can't see any danger yet. I certainly consider it possible (that) attack preparations along this coast are being made, in so far as landing craft are being built so that,—when they have the Sicilian Straits in their possession—

THE FÜHRER: Are landing craft being built there?

JODL: Yes, informers report that landing craft are being built there, with special engines that use—it is an English invention—solid fuel.

THE FÜHRER: Solid fuel would be coal.

JODL: Yes, but there is no supply of coal down there either.

THE FÜHRER: What other kind of solid fuel could it be?

JODL: Something similar to methylated spirits.

THE FÜHRER: If they do something, they'll pull (the forces) together for it instantly.

The West

JODL: The picture in England itself has actually remained (unchanged). Also the distribution of landing craft is on … volumes on the southern coast of the Channel at all … equal everywhere, into all the bays. There are …33 divisions, 5 armored divisions, 5 independent brigades, 5 American divisions and— what … is … —two to three airborne divisions there, which could include (one) or more of the parachute divisions. Six divisions and two independent brigades weren't identified or remain unknown. In general the picture hasn't (changed). Six divisions have not appeared again. It could be that they have gone to the Far East.

Mediterranean

Field Marshal Kesselring then presented his final organization and the table of organization and equipment. I think it can now be approved. He integrated the entire operations section into the *Comando Supremo*. The headquarters are even physically close together. The Troop Movement Command and the Senior Quartermaster report to a general. He considers this necessary, because these staffs, too, are far away from him. Most importantly, the Troop Movement Command is located some 60 km away. For the ship cargoes and the constant changes, he has to be close to the Italian authorities. One ship … then there is another security … because everything is so far apart …together with him, he must have a general in his own office who represents … these matters. Then there is the intelligence chief, … as he is now called, the Chief Quartermaster (for the) entire region and a legal adviser. (*Report on evidence of strength is presented*)
THE FÜHRER: How many Tiger [tanks] are now operational?
JODL: Fifteen! There have been 4 total losses so far.

The Balkans

The Balkan operations are characterized by particular success by the Četniks. The SS division[254] is continuing to advance in columns. More detailed reports are not available. We know only that the Luftwaffe reported an amassing of the enemy near Rore, where the left column of the SS division is advancing. The enemy is retreating everywhere in that area. It has been confirmed that Livno was taken by the reconnaissance patrol of the 369th [Infantry] Division. There were no reports from the Italians, except that they don't face the enemy but have other difficulties. On the other hand, the Četniks not only took Cvrstnika, but moved up north through the Narenta valley and reoccupied Jablanica, where earlier ... were ... A reorganization takes place here, with the main (forces) ... being moved (to) the western hills in order to ... force the climb to the pass north of Prozor ... (The enemy) attacked here. The Luftwaffe has fought these ... in particular. We don't have a new report (from this) group. (In the end) it will probably be like this: the Italians stay put (and we) meet up with the Četniks who earlier threw the Communists back from the south. (The) order for the establishment of the assault brigade has been issued. (It is called) "Brigade 11."[255] It's comprised of a battalion, a battery, (an) infantry antitank company, an anti-aircraft unit (and) an assault gun company. The Italians very much approve of our intention to move such a brigade to Sardinia. Of course, it would have to be put under the command of the corps in Sardinia.

THE FÜHRER: We'll see. Let's establish it first.

JODL: It will be complete by around March 9. The instructions given by the Grand Admiral with regard to the blockade runners[256] are having the following effect, from a purely economic perspective, according to Admiral Groos[257]: (Presentation.) ... based on the proposition of the Grand Admiral ... an order is issued: (Presentation.) ...53 FW ... the report of a German industrialist (who) spoke (with) Laval. (Presentation.) (The attitude) of the Fourth Army is anything but confidence inspiring.[258] But this is clearly the fault of the officers.

Weapons for Italy

THE FÜHRER: I spoke to Schmundt to find out (whether we) have the people to do it. We'll give the Italians (weapons), and the weapons will find their way to people who will pass them on to the enemy, and before long we'll be attacked with them. It makes no difference whether these are weapons seized from the Russians or others—at any case, the weapons will soon be turned against us. I asked Schmundt whether we have the personnel to do something, if I could propose to the Duce—if I meet with him—to establish 6 Fascist divisions, which he would take out of the M-divisions[259] and we would establish, organize and train in Germany. They should consist of only tried and true Fascists. We could help them with the command and provide them with weapons. I'm thinking here of Italy, too, because to him two such divisions—one in Rome and the other (in northern Italy) are not less than ... God knows what ... Let's see, what the Duce ... thinks. We keep having to (supply) weapons anyway. There is no point in continuing like we have been. I can be quite frank (with the Duce), because he has ... told, that I'm going to tell him the whole truth about (the losses) in the East. I'll tell him: if you ... set up from scratch, you won't achieve anything. Of course, (you could) make up for it, provided you (had a) decent officer corps.

If you don't have that (and) if you don't start from scratch, the new formation will be doomed from the very beginning. In that case you would have to begin with (Adam and) Eve, otherwise the work would be useless. He has (good) people among them, of course, but they can't prevent the whole ... The M-battalions were included in the various divisions, but they're worn down there and don't have any value or impact. This will only change when he himself establishes 6 divisions to start with, and then 8, 10, or 12 divisions. If we have to supply weapons to them, then let's supply them for these units. They'll be excellently armed and give him support in his own country. As soon as he has four such divisions at his disposal, he'll be in a position to have his way and start disbanding the pathetic army divisions or integrate other officers ... in order to bring about a gradual improvement. (Without them) he can't do it. (This is) in our own interest. If there were Fascist (units) trained by us in North Africa, they'd be better than four such divisions, (who because of) their incapable commanders and their ... take off at the first gunshot. ... told me: one sees among the people many wonderful ...; but they didn't succeed in ... separating them. They just ... around everywhere ... and don't have any zeal. The officers have no sense of responsibility; their only thought is to go (to) the coffee shop.

Norway

JODL: We should implement the following changes in Norway: The 280th [Infantry] Division should move up from this area and take control of the northern sector, which could not be commanded from Bergen as it was completely separated. In exchange, the 214th [Infantry] Division should move in here, and the 710th [Security] Division, having been strengthened by adding another regiment, should take control of the entire southern coast where the danger is small. The majority of these changes have already been carried out. The 730th Infantry Regiment has been pulled out. It's to be relieved by a battalion. Three siege battalions have come in for that. The 280th [Infantry] Division has taken control of this sector. It's the least exposed, ... Sogne Fjord has, but no ... behind ... the 730th Regiment has been brought down here (and has) relieved the 367th [Regiment]. The 367th Regiment was moved to the Stavanger (area), which is, of course, very important. This area has been taken over by the 214th Division with two infantry regiments and 3 siege battalions ... for the most part carried out. (Because of the unsuitable weather conditions) we have seen relatively few air operations in Norway during the last week. 7,000 mines have been (laid). Due to snowdrifts, the road north of Fauske is completely impassable. That is unusual (because) this road can normally be kept open. But (at the moment) it's closed.

Situation in the air

CHRISTIAN: Last night, 5 mines and 19 high-explosive bombs were dropped on seven towns in the Rhenish-Westphalian industrial area, resulting in 11 dead and 69 wounded. During the air raid against Hamburg, a total of 22 mines, 360 high-explosive bombs and 40,600 incendiary bombs were dropped in 28 places. 2 mines and 31 high-explosive bombs were dropped on Hamburg alone, and 20 mines, 300 high-explosive bombs, 30 incendiary bombs and 21 phosphorus bombs on Wedel.[260]

THE FÜHRER: Were there not many more in Wesel?

CHRISTIAN: In Wedel[261] there were considerable losses: 20 dead, 150 wounded, 10 (missing). Out of the total of 700 homes, two-(thirds) are (either destroyed) or damaged. ... out of 8,000 inhabitants ... are (homeless). The station was heavily damaged. Traffic is ... maintained. An optics factory had some buildings damaged, resulting in a production loss of 20%. This factory produces 50% of the optical systems for Panzers (and) ... optical systems, of which 20% were lost. Last night's total losses in the Reich were ... dead, 295 wounded and 17 missing persons. (Today) from 10 to 11:05 a.m., bomber formations of initially 50 to 60 aircraft penetrated the territory of the (Reich), but the majority of them were driven away by fighters.[262] 20 to 25 aircraft then flew on to Hamm, where a total of 28 buildings, including the station post office, were destroyed. Direct hit on the wire industry. There are two factories there, one owned by United Steelworks, the other by Krupp. For the time being, 50% of the production facilities of the two factories are damaged. But production will be maintained by immediately relocating the factories. Only one track at the station was temporarily interrupted by a time bomb ... relatively few dead and injured people ... (but) one more report concerning this matter. It states that ... (a number of) people are still trapped in the works' air-raid shelters. (It's not yet clear) whether they will be rescued. If they can't be dug out (alive), the number of the dead would increase to ...

THE FÜHRER: How many were brought down?

CHRISTIAN: Ten! One of which is not yet confirmed. The fighters and the anti-aircraft artillery are still quarreling about it. Apart from that, nothing out of the ordinary is happening in the West. Today there are ... no reports about our action in the Mediterranean region. The enemy attacked Reggio and Tra(pani), but didn't cause any damage.

The East

ZEITZLER: Generally speaking, the large-scale attack from the north has been driven back. It wasn't conducted on a broad front. A major part of the heavy fire was of a diversionary nature. The temperature in the region of the Seventeenth Army is now minus two degrees. Rain has turned to snow, so they still have problems. There was no action along the entire front. Up here the enemy attacked, apparently in order to penetrate here and get this group out, as these ... not get through (anymore). But he was driven back ... suffered losses from the (flank) attack ... won and pushed them back ... was pressed in further, but they're ..., they put up very fierce resistance.

CHRISTIAN: The air transports improved today (because of) the frozen ground. Details (are not yet) available.

ZEITZLER: A minor scouting raid took place in this ... area of Army Group South. A single tank attacked here and was destroyed. This is the place were the lines were penetrated, but they don't wish to do anything about it because it's very difficult to bring the front back. (It's in) a deep gorge. Nothing out of the ordinary on this front. It's not been confirmed yet whether the motorized corps are ready. Up here, we again see a northward movement. All in all, the advance to the Donets was quite successful. The 62nd [Infantry] Division has advanced to this point, and the 19th [Panzer] Division has cleared out this curve. The 19th [Panzer] should be withdrawn and will stay behind the lines to provide emergency help if required. It has been relieved by the 62nd Division. The 3rd Panzer Division has also advanced to this point. They've also pushed forward to here. It's not quite clear yet how far they've advanced.

THE FÜHRER: Do they believe that they're in the position ... during muddy conditions, if the 19th Panzer Division ... ?

ZEITZLER: I think he intends to ... On this front, too, they (advanced) as far as the Donets. (The) ... division moved closer and moved into these ... They're supposed to clear out this curve and then stay up there. The 17th Panzer Division was attacked in the morning and launched a counterattack during (the afternoon). The result is (not yet quite) clear. (The advance) into this area was relatively unsuccessful. Part of the reason was that (the terrain) was still in poor condition. They advanced a little further along the road. Also, the bulk of forces were needed for the pocket. They moved in on the pocket [263] from all sides. According to the army group, quite a number of troops are in the pocket; this is quite possible. He's still radioing desperately from the pocket. Here are a few radio messages sent by one of the tank corps. The 18th Tank Corps reported, "We can't cross the Donets with our heavy equipment; we have to leave it over there." (Here it is) good enough that we can drive ... (to Stalino). These movements ... one can drive through this area. It's only ... into Stalino. This (route), too, will be passable soon. Here's one ... it will be OK on March 11. According to forecasts by inhabitants and meteorologists, there'll be frost until March 7, then temperatures will be around the freezing point ... and this is when the muddy period will begin.

CHRISTIAN: Today, there were difficulties here (because of) adverse weather.[264]

ZEITZLER: There was little action on this front, except for (a minor) attack here.

THE FÜHRER: Is the fellow encircled there?

ZEITZLER: Generally speaking, yes. Here there's only one small gap. Nothing unusual on this front. Just one attack here. The 167th [Infantry] Division is advancing up there, in order to get to that place.

CHRISTIAN: The Luftwaffe focused on this area, with the First and Fourth Panzer Armies and with the majority of the men in the encirclement. The action was interrupted by several snow showers caused by bad weather. Tonight's conditions are acceptable ... a very clear and good night, probably ... low temperatures, around minus 6 degrees ...

ZEITZLER. Everything went according to plan in the south. The sector is now completely occupied ... [the enemy] is retreating. The 332nd [Infantry] Division takes over (this sector), and the 4th Panzer Division will be placed at the flank. Little action was seen (on this) front. Only one attack near Sumy; (it was) driven back. ... The division is moving its last convoys. It came in very well. In the "hatch"[265] here in the center, the situation is still (unclear). Aerial reconnaissance reported a column in this area, but (there's still) a question mark. The Hungarian covering division[266] that was (in this circle) withdrew without an order. It's questionable whether the enemy has already advanced to this point. Up there, the enemy advanced to Seredina Buda and the next village. The part of the Hungarian covering division that is located in this area will probably pull out, too. But now parts of the 3rd Mountain Division have arrived—one regiment—and they'll be pushed forward to provide security themselves. Nothing much happened here, but more powerful attacks occurred in this area. Again, he attacked from all sides ... Strong ... had moved into the sector of the 707th [Security] Division. Field Marshal Kluge[267] ... is taking the (position) back. His final aim is ... will be massively flooded afterwards ... a muddy period following ... He mounted a major attack against the... division. (Fortunately,) the 78th [infantry] Division with its numerous assault guns is there. All attacks were driven back with very severe losses among the enemy. Nothing in particular on this front. (Here, too,) nothing's happened yet. However, we see downward movements from up there. Here, he didn't attack as fiercely as during the previous days. He (mainly) attacked the 208th [Infantry] Division and the 5th and 9th Panzer [Divisions] ... All attacks were driven back ... decided to (deploy) the 296th [Infantry] Division up there after all. It will arrive there tomorrow. He hadn't yet decided whether to deploy it here or there. But he knows that there's a considerable threat to this area up here. Regarding these movements, he followed where the three red arrows are. He then mounted a major attack against the 2nd Panzer Division and the 337th [Infantry] Division, but was driven back, suffering heavy losses. This is still the old position; there's still one piece of the old position in there. Up there, he just probed the area with reconnaissance parties. Tonight they'll move back to the broken green line, while this line will be held for one more day. ... there are still indications that any ... and that he moves ... somewhat closer.

THE FÜHRER: We should try to defend this position (as long as) possible, because if ... attacks, as soon as he gets to the old (position) ... he'll find it difficult. When will they occupy this line?

ZEITZLER: He gives one order at a time ... They won't move tonight. It (is not yet) clear whether he will do it tomorrow. It depends on the weather. (There are still) movements in this corner. That's why he transferred two heavy Army artillery units to the ... Luftwaffe field division.[268] In addition, if anything (should happen) here, while withdrawing he intends to move the 2nd Panzer Division to here and the 206th [Infantry] Division back to here, so as to release the 8th Panzer Division and move it gradually into that area. He would then have two mobile forces behind the front.

THE FÜHRER: He attacks here.

ZEITZLER: He may relieve them, but I would prefer to keep the 8th Panzer Division up here.

THE FÜHRER: If he attacks, he'll attack here. The only reason would be if he tried to get behind it. As soon as the route is open, he'll (reach around) and try to get to Smolensk from (the rear).

ZEITZLER: Maybe it's only a local (matter, and they) want to do something about the bands.

CHRISTIAN: The Luftwaffe operated (together with) the 78th Infantry Division. Details are not reported.

ZEITZLER: Down here there's only activity by reconnaissance patrols. (Apart from that,) nothing much happened. This is where this morning's attack took place, where the heavy shelling was reported. There was heavy gunfire along this entire front (all morning). Then the attack started, in precisely the way the captured officer had predicted: 4 to 5 divisions were brought together closely and moved against the left flank of the 32nd [Infantry] Division. The attack has been driven back everywhere. The 32nd Division now has many heavy weapons seized from the enemy, but no tanks. They report "heavy enemy losses." The attack along this front started at the same time. Again, it was driven back completely. The same applies to the entire north-

ern front up to Staraia Russa. He was driven back everywhere. Only here—
at this point of penetration, he advanced to the next village. But here again,
big losses are reported. It seems to have been his major operation ... when
they intend to take back ... take back behind the river section ...
CHRISTIAN: The entire Luftwaffe is (deployed) here.
ZEITZLER: Nothing unusual in the northern section of Lenin(grad ...).
End: 10:12 p.m.

* * * * *

MIDDAY SITUATION REPORT,
MARCH 5, 1943, AT THE WEHRWOLF[269]

Beginning: 12:38 p.m.

The East

ZEITZLER: No major developments, generally speaking, There are probably also infantry divisions in the "hatchway"[270] to the south of the two
panzer armies. But the "hatchway" is relatively narrow, and the first trains of
these three divisions are now starting to arrive. Then somehow a new Russian tank appeared.
THE FÜHRER: It was already reported at Stalingrad.
ZEITZLER: It's a very heavy tank. It wasn't seized by our men, but officers
crawled up to it and sketched it from a distance of 300 m. It weighs between
50 and 80 tons and has two turrets. A 7.5-cm shell would not have penetrated.[271] This is really the first time. I copied the company's combat report. It's actually quite interesting. But the tank was seen only in one place.
We can't generalize. (Maybe it) is a new tank. I don't believe it's an old American
(tank).
THE FÜHRER: That can be ruled out.
ZEITZLER: It has rounded contours all over.
THE FÜHRER: Then it must have been cast.
ZEITZLER: Regarding the Seventeenth Army, nothing out of the ordinary. Fewer troops crossed the river than on previous days, but still 1,300
horses [cavalry]. Nearly 12,000 horses have crossed. He's trying to bring in
reinforcements here ... large ships moved in yesterday. Gunfire forced
them to veer off. Parts of a mountain brigade have crossed. On this front,
they were only probing; a small attack was launched here. Yesterday's attack by one or two regiments took place here. More ground was won in
the counterattack. Here, too, he was driven back further. The temperature
was about 1 degree below zero, but that wasn't enough to make the roads

passable. On the other hand, the condition of the airfields today is said to have improved, so they think they'll be able to fly today. There are plans to evacuate 800 wounded by air today. Along this front we didn't see any loosening-up of the situation. It appeared that two corps had withdrawn, but we could not find out whether this was true. (Here) there was only strong artillery fire yesterday, and (breaches) in two places. He still has five crossing points here. These are small makeshift bridges, some of which are laid across the ice. An informer said that more troops are moving in. Here, 3 brigades are using the same route. These movements continue. The two tank corps can be tracked by radio, and we see that they're moving further up. Here in front was the one infantry column. It's very possible that he'll move around here. (A) prisoner said that the two headquarters have been deployed here for quite some time. We hadn't caught them before. Here there was a drive against a small bridgehead, which we control, with a bridge. Two tanks were destroyed. For the most part, we can say that the Donets [River] has been reached by the entire front. Only a few things are left. The 62nd [Infantry] Division has replaced the 19th Panzer Division as an emergency force. For the rest, reports are coming in from everywhere that he's moving troops in. They are probably the same troops we detected several days ago. This front is advancing. The 15th [Infantry] Division is forcing its way into this curve. He always (comes) out of Balaklaia to attack. This (here) is one of the major centers of the attack. (The) 11th Panzer Division is now free and will be (deployed) there. On the way, they're to finish off those who managed to get out of the pocket. Here, a small group has been taken care of already. The shape of the pocket is like this. They (think) they'll be able to finish it off today. There are still occasional attempts to break out. They move in on them from both sides. Yesterday they advanced relatively slowly. Because they were held up for 2 or 3 days, he was able to move in troops. They're considering the reorganization of forces for another push. 8 trains of the 106th [Infantry] Division will arrive today. There was a small raid up here, and substantial enemy forces are said to be hiding in this forest. Otherwise, nothing unusual from this whole front on up. The 46th [Infantry] Division, which liberated the area, will be rallied. Everything went according to plan down there for Army Group Center. The majority of the 4th Panzer Division retreated; it's supposed to move toward Glukhov, to this area up here. Parts of the 255th [Infantry] Division caught up and will be deployed here, so we'll have a long-term reinforcement in that area. Furthermore (compared to previous days), he stepped up his efforts to seek contact with the Second Army. There's movement here, and they're bringing up fresh troops, so we can expect major attacks during the next few days. The command structure in the "hatchway"[272] isn't quite clear, though. The 3rd Army was located, and it is clear that it'll advance in this direction. It's not known (whether) the 21st Army will move this way or that. Infantry [rifle] divisions (were) detected in the area of Seredina Buda (and) to the south. It's not yet known whether they're just providing cover for this thrust or whether this is the main advance. Probably they are just providing cover. But here, the security units of the covering regiment have already arrived, namely 2 battalions, one battalion of the mountain division as well as smaller units. Apart from them, two-thirds of the 45th [Infantry] Division has already arrived. The first train of the 72nd [Infantry] Division will arrive today; the same is true of the 251st [Infantry] Division, which withdrew on our order so that the situation could improve during the next few days. The attacks against the southern edge continued. They were particularly fierce at this flank and against the 78th [Infantry] Division, which is located up here. Supplies are also reported to be on the way. The 45th [Infantry] Division will now be brought in to strengthen it. Numerous small attacks, probably some kind of probing, occurred along this front for the first time. We presume (that the) large group that stopped here is preparing for a major attack, because the movements are still continuing. Up (there), near the 208th [Infantry] Division, he attacked along the entire front from the 208th Division to the ... the Division all day yesterday, but was always driven back. The 296th [Infantry] Division closed in very rapidly; one of its battalions is already in. The train transports as well as the makeshift solutions are working very (well), I must say. The 296th [infantry] Division was pulled out of here and is moving back, partly by rail and partly by truck.

THE FÜHRER: I wonder whether it's correct to withdraw them already—in case something might happen here.

ZEITZLER: Well, Field Marshal Kluge thinks that the situation up there[273] is absolutely dangerous. He says it's become a huge focal area. Yet, another division has joined the fighting, including many tanks. Yesterday they reported 1,000 dead. The enemy paid a high price in that attack. Yesterday's attack against this front involved 2 rifle divisions and 2 tank brigades, so it was a relatively strong attack. On the other front, they just pressed ahead. He took position today at the place marked by the arrow. Quite a number of troops will pass through Rzhev. Along the other front, he was driven back everywhere. They plan to retreat to the dotted line. This position has already been given up. (This) is not a proper position; actually, the last proper position was still located up here in this corner. Now the ... Division will be ... moved out by train. The 251st [Infantry] Division and the ... Division are already on the train ..., the latter on the first ...

THE FÜHRER: When does he think that'll be finished?

ZEITZLER: He hasn't specified the date; he evaluates the situation day-to-day. In view of the weather conditions, etc., he intends to stay another few days. The weather is good, down to (minus) ten degrees.

THE FÜHRER: When does he think he can finish it?

ZEITZLER: He'll need another ten days, if everything goes according to schedule.

THE FÜHRER: Where's the line now?

ZEITZLER: In front of this railway line. I'll have it marked tomorrow. We still hold this rail junction.

JODL: The army group will retreat then.

ZEITZLER: They haven't announced that yet. They'll probably go back to Minsk. We don't quite know what they plan to do in that area. What I mean is that partisan-related skirmishes and other little things. The bands tried to break through to the north. There's little radio traffic or patrol activity up there, so there might something be brewing. No major attacks have been reported so far today in the north. Down here, nothing much happened yesterday—just a few skirmishes and movements into assembly areas, which were destroyed by gunfire. Yesterday's attacks, which I reported last night, occurred mainly at this wing and involved heavy gunfire along the entire front, whereas the attack here was launched more by battalions or regiments against individual positions. Generally speaking, they were all pushed back. This is the only place where he advanced a little. Fighting hasn't yet started today.

THE FÜHRER: We'll have to smash this up someday with massive artillery.

ZEITZLER: Yes, they need this corner up here.

THE FÜHRER: If he were to move here, it would be less dangerous. This matter must be sorted out anyway.

ZEITZLER: Yes, once in a while he comes out from there. We're aware of that.

THE FÜHRER: We need to make a concerted effort.

ZEITZLER: Yes, Sir. I will speak to the army group. They'll retreat behind this line on March 10. Movements are starting again (here) in this area. Strange developments in radio traffic have been reported from this area up here. One army headquarters announced that radio traffic should be reduced, and the other one stopped radioing entirely. Then there was a major artillery duel at Shlissel'burg Station,[274] so there was no rail traffic all day yesterday. Nothing out of the ordinary on this front. Unless there are political considerations to prevent it, Field Marshal Küchler plans to deploy the Spaniards [the 250th Spanish Blue Division] here, where it's a bit quieter, a little south of the Volkhov front.[275]

THE FÜHRER: I hope it'll stay quiet there. They'll return to their old front. The Luftwaffe field division will be pulled out. Maybe it's possible to turn them around here and move them back to their old front.

ZEITZLER: There's no reason not to. His only concern is that something might happen up there.

THE FÜHRER: But the Spaniards are not too bad. The fact (that they) caved in doesn't prove anything. The troops here caved in too, in many places. There is a statement by a Russian prisoner who was involved up there. He said that they didn't attack the Spaniards (because) they are so fanatical.

ZEITZLER: I can discuss with him again what his reasons are.

Tunis

JODL: We have relatively little news from North Africa. The Bersaglieri[276] reconnaissance troops are advancing further, as they didn't detect strong enemy forces opposite the front. Very strong sustained gunfire here. There has been a partial reinforcement of enemy troops, as reported yesterday. Obviously, they called off the attack[277] without having announced it. The enemy then appeared east of Sheitla for the first time; he was detected by ground reconnaissance in the area of Sidi bou Zid. Several tanks and other movements. The southern area is now completely free. The 580th Reconnaissance Detachment moved forward to the mountain pass of Faid. The Africa Infantry Regiment, which was in the combat group, was pulled back behind the left wing of the Mareth position, as Rommel expects a possible attack in that area at any time—its conditions are most favorable for the enemy. Further to the south, the terrain is open to our own artillery. The losses that the Fifth Panzer Army[278] have reported so far are considerable. I have not yet received a detailed report. According to rumors, 19 Panzer IIIs … Panzer IVs and 7 Tigers were lost.

THE FÜHRER: The loss of the 7 Tigers can only be explained by problems with the gearshift that are only too well known to us, which caused the tanks to be abandoned.[279]

JODL: Rommel doesn't intend to go on leave right now, in spite of the recommendation of his doctor. He plans to stay until March 15 because he wants to launch the counterattack.[280]

THE FÜHRER: The only option we have is to move in more forces as quickly as possible.

JODL: This is the reply to the telegram. A number of ships arrived yesterday, with cargo as follows: 2,000 tons of ammunition, 1,000 tons of provisions, 600 tons of equipment, 180 vehicles, six 7.5-cm antitank guns, nine 5-cm antitank guns, one four-barreled gun, two 17-cm guns, one lightweight field howitzer, one heavy infantry gun, 21-cm mortars, launchers, listening equipment, searchlights and 2,200 German troops on the destroyers.[281]

Situation at sea

The Navy reported heavy artillery action in the Baltic Sea and intensive truck traffic to Seiskaari.[282] This may be due to the fact that they need to stock up on provisions before the ice breaks. At any rate, it's still possible to go there by truck. The escort vessels returning from the Arctic Ocean made contact with all submarines operating in that area, which, because of poor (visibility), fierce defense, and ice floes, weren't successful. Last night, the escort vessels were 110 nautical miles south-south(west) of Bear Island.[283] Seven boats checked the routes in the Arctic Ocean, and all sea lanes have been reopened.[284] Very intense but completely unsuccessful fire from the Fisherman's Peninsula toward a convoy headed to Petsamo.[285] In the Black Sea, no action outside of the Kerch Strait because of the weather. Even the planned departure of the naval ferries for Anapa also had to be cancelled because of weather conditions. There was a fairly heavy storm, strength 6, near the landing stage on the eastern side causing enough hindrance that 5 ferries were damaged by the waves.[286] It is still not possible to use Temriuk for loading—otherwise the successes would be even greater—because the route is almost completely blocked by ice, even though there are just a few ice floes in the harbor and at the mouth of the harbor. Yesterday 168 men, ... tons of supplies were ferried across to the Taman' Peninsula, while 1,839 men, ... horses, 434 vehicles (including 4 guns) were ferried back. Numerous mines were swept from the German Bay in the North Sea. The Elbe River had to be closed between Hamburg and Stade because of the risk of mines.[287] The March 4 air raid against Rotterdam caused damage to the shipyard and losses among Dutch shipyard workers. A coastal defense boat was damaged. Part of the escort route had to be stopped south of Boulogne because of mines. ... Last night, motor torpedo boat flotillas were deployed against a southbound convoy off the east coast of England.[288] One motor torpedo boat—the S 70—sank off the English coast after hitting a mine. No reports are in yet about the others. Another motor torpedo boat flotilla was deployed in the western Channel against an eastbound convoy. Again, no report as yet. At the Cape, a submarine operating 100 nautical miles south-southwest of Durban detected a convoy consisting of ten steamers on a southeasterly course.

V. PUTTKAMER: To Australia.

JODL: Of this convoy, the submarine sank 6 freighters and one tanker with a total of 48,000 tons. All ships were loaded to capacity.[289] Furthermore, the

British *California Star*, 8,300 tons, was sunk 600 nautical miles east-southeast of Newfoundland. It came from New Zealand and was bound for England. It was loaded to capacity with butter and meat.[290] Another submarine sank a … a fast steamer with a capacity of 9,000 tons and a speed of 16 nautical miles in the same area; the steamer had ammunition on board and exploded after it was hit.[291] [—]

The Mediterranean

The following vessels were moored in the port of Gibraltar on March 4: … battleships, one carrier, 14 destroyers, 26 corvettes, … escort vessels, 6 passenger ships, 8 tankers, 50 freighters. Consequently, after a sharp temporary dip, available cargo ship capacity in Gibraltar is back to the normal level.[292] West of the Straits of Gibraltar, intense enemy[293] air reconnaissance and sweeping for mines was detected. The assumption is that the enemy is expecting a convoy from the Atlantic Ocean and also feels threatened by our submarines. The following ships arrived in Tunis, at the port of Bizerte: the *Caterina Costa* with a capacity of 6,000 tons, the *Saluzzo* with a capacity of 3,740 tons, the *Pierre Claude* carrying 1,780 tons and 9 Navy ferries. Five destroyers carrying German troops came into the port of Tunis. They are already headed back to their home base. The convoy of ships that arrived in Bizerte during the night of March 4 had been attacked unsuccessfully with aerial torpedoes. The two war transports 13 and 14 returned to Palermo. Furthermore, a submarine west of Alexandria torpedoed a steamer of … tons that belonged to a travelling convoy of 5 steamers. They were unable to observe the sinking of the steamer. We received a report from the Aegean Sea that for the first time, a submarine was detected near Melos[294] again.

Norway

In Norway there was a short firefight 30 km southeast of Trondheim, between the SD and some Norwegian or other activists. One civilian is dead, another wounded. Details are not yet known.

France

In France, they're making further progress with the supplies … men of the 60th Motorized Division have arrived. Here the first train from one regiment arrived that is to be part of the 113th [Infantry] Division. The transportation of the first regiment of the 94th [Infantry] Division, which will be moved in here, has also started here. Then there are 3,200 men of the 24th Panzer Division also in place. The 106th [Infantry] Division left. 5 trains with parts of the 39th [infantry] Division have left, and 1,700 men of the 44th [Infantry] Division have arrived. A new rapid reaction unit is now in Holland.

THE FÜHRER: I talked to Zeitzler last night, and he shares my opinion, of course. We can deal with Leningrad in mid-June or early July at the earliest—an earlier date is out of the question. We must not waste time now. Zeitzler agreed with me that we should take advantage of the muddy period. We should try to reinforce these few panzer groups, (in particular) the SS Panzer Group and the two other panzer (groups) so that we can launch an attack with them as soon as the muddy period is over. For this purpose we would need more troops in that area. The question is what we do with the West. I think we should move to the West all those vehicles that are not quite in order yet.[295] They can do it as well there. It's only a sign of laziness when people say that these vehicles can't be sent there. So it would be best to transfer the Panthers and all free Tigers there, where they can be repaired and then returned to the East. The same applies to the assault guns. This is the production that moves the fastest. In particular, smaller units should be equipped with these assault guns, so that all of them get an assault gun company and we have emergency troops everywhere. The large tanks are better than anything else in the West anyway, because they were designed primarily to drive back attacks by enemy tanks and not to carry out independent strategic movements.[296] I must say that I prefer a Panther there to one in the East where I have to move it around. I'm not certain what I could do with it there. In the West, where roads are good, I could drive it to some place and, at the very worst, bury it like the Russians do and just use the long gun. The same is true for the Tigers. Buhle and Speer will come tomorrow. Then we'll find out about the condition of the individual vehicles. This would mean that, initially, the bulk of the Panzer IVs would be transferred to the East, plus some of the assault guns and motor vehicles. But I emphasize: it's absolutely necessary that we put the emergency units in order; including the Luftwaffe field division that is now at ...theim. We'll have a final discussion tomorrow, after we've been informed about the weapons output. One thing is quite clear: if the Russians deploy such huge tanks, our only option would be to attack them with dive bombers[297] because I'm currently unable to deploy heavy antitank weapons everywhere. There's certainly no defense available at the moment, when these huge tanks appear. Only hollow-charge projectiles would not ricochet. In the end, I wonder if the antitank units might not be equipped with a shorter 15-cm gun and hollow-charge projectiles.[298]

JODL: That will be the ultimate goal, because a gun as long as the 15-cm cannon is not suitable as an antitank gun.

THE FÜHRER: Yes, it all boils down to that, and even then (it isn't quite) certain that it won't ricochet.[299]

The Balkans

JODL: This affair in the Balkans is developing into something like the battle of Königsgrätz.[300] The enemy stops and avoids contact with us and apparently concentrates all (his) forces in this area. That's why the ... Division succeeded in forging ahead considerably in three columns.

THE FÜHRER: The battle of Königsgrätz wasn't bad either!

JODL: No. He sent a ... group after them on the road to Livno from Bos. Grajovo, and the reconnaissance detachment took the road leading west. We're not quite sure yet where they are at the moment. The enemy also evacuated this area—where, according to yesterday's report, a large force was positioned—so these columns gained a lot of ground. I can only imagine that he used up all his ammunition. But he must have major supplies near Prozor and the mountain pass, because he's attacking there with a large number of forces. New artillery and anti-aircraft guns were brought in, and he's launched fierce attacks against the 717th and 718th [Security] Divisions. And now another regiment—the 749th—that was covering the rear is now advancing. These forces will make their presence felt in the near future. The eastern group pushed through here as well. The resistance became weaker, and the Četniks, coming from the south, are moving both northward to this ridge and along the valley to the west. The Italians are the only ones missing on the battlefield. We don't have any reports about them. Here, though, the enemy seems to be prepared to fight with us, in spite of the threat from both flanks and from (the rear).

THE FÜHRER: Probably because he has his stores here, and besides, where else could he go? The region is controlled by the Četniks. So he'll probably take up a position there and we'll have to fight it through.

Japan

JODL: The military attaché from Tokyo will give you an overview of the distribution of Japanese forces.

THE FÜHRER: The Japanese have had bad luck with this big convoy, if the reports are true. The convoy seems to have been broken up.[301]

JODL: Regarding the overall strength, the military attaché reports the following figures: 63 divisions, 6 infantry brigades, 2 armored divisions, 4 motorized brigades and 18 reserve divisions of the reserve army at home. The Kwantung Army Group has apparently been weakened. At least we had earlier supposed their number to be greater. On the northeastern front there are 15 divisions and 2 armored divisions. There's another army, which includes the Manchurian divisions, further to the south: 2 infantry divisions, 2 infantry brigades, one cavalry division, one motorized brigade.

THE FÜHRER: And these three?

JODL: These three belong to Korea. Well, this ... the Korea Army and the Peking Army can be brought in.

THE FÜHRER: Then it adds up to 20 divisions after all.

JODL: Yes. We had assumed there would be more, namely ... divisions.

THE FÜHRER: What are the estimates?

JODL: According to estimates, there are 20 infantry divisions, 4 brigades ... cavalry divisions, 2 armored brigades and 3 motorized brigades.

THE FÜHRER: Those men are the best the Japanese have.

JODL: These are excellent divisions. There's the China Army Group and the Southern Group with 14 infantry divisions. Some of them are brigades. Then there's the Chinese National Army, which is included at a lower fighting value. Here there are 8 divisions and 2 infantry brigades deployed in the northern part. The Kwantung Army, with 4 infantry divisions and 2 infantry brigades, is also part of the China Army Group. The 1,500,000-man Chunking Force is deployed in the entire area. Next is the Southern Army Group with one army in Rangoon, which used to contain 5 divisions and has now been increased to 6. Then, behind the lines, the covering forces (and) 5 Thai divisions. One division with limited strength is stationed in Indochina, and another division is in Singapore. The forces on other islands are relatively weak. There are two divisions on Sumatra and more than one division of occupying forces on Java. Weak occupation forces on Borneo and Celebes. One army made up of two divisions is stationed in Manila. The new Southeast Army Group has now been established; it's comprised of two armies in Rabaul, which were recruited primarily from these forces and will now be transferred there. [—] The evacuation of Guadalcanal was obviously successful,[302] and a new Eastern Front is being established. To this end they're launching several attacks in order to bring the enemy down on New Guinea. The enemy has two American and two Australian divisions on New Guinea, plus 5 American divisions, one Marine division and a division from New Zealand on the eastern islands. Three American divisions and one from New Zealand are stationed in the New Hebrides.

THE FÜHRER: That makes 14 to 15 American divisions in all.

JODL: He deployed major forces on the Aleutian Islands as well. The Japanese limited themselves to keeping one reinforced regiment up there. But they don't have an airstrip. The number of aircraft reported for the enemy is not very large either. There are 8 British divisions and some 350 aircraft and 2 Chungking divisions in Burma, and there are some 250 aircraft on the Solomon Islands, 350 aircraft on New Guinea, 500 aircraft in Australia, 200 aircraft in … and 100 in the New Hebrides. The Japanese are convinced that the main action in 1943 will continue to take place in the European theater of operations.

THE FÜHRER: That doesn't please us greatly.

JODL: The evacuation of Guadalcanal was successful.

THE FÜHRER: We must not attach undue importance to what the Japanese say. I don't believe a word.

JODL: One can't believe them, for they're the only people who intentionally tell you a big lie with an expression of sincerity.

THE FÜHRER: They'll tell you a pack of lies—their reports and representations are calculated on something that proves to be deception later on.

HEWEL: The general public in America believes this to be the main theater of operations.

THE FÜHRER: I read a statement from Dieckhoff.[303] He disputes this. There isn't a bit of truth in it. If you want to win over the Americans, you only need to say the following: first, the war is being waged in America's interests; second, the British Empire will be liquidated; third, the Japanese are the main enemy. With these remarks you will get an overwhelming majority. The Jews are against it, but they[304] have the overwhelming majority. The English are now starting to complain (more and more) about the political developments, as they are afraid that things will turn against their empire.

HEWEL: It would be interesting to learn something about the condition of the American divisions in North Africa. Neurath[305] arrived from Tunis last night. He tells interesting stories. He questioned some American prisoners of war and (says) that they tell crazy stories. Most of them came over in order to earn money or for the excitement and adventure of it to see something different and be a part of it. No trace of political aims. They're just rowdies who will disappear quickly—they won't be able to get through a crisis.[306] He says he talked to hundreds of them. None of them had any political convictions or any great ideas.

THE FÜHRER: They will never become Rome. America will never be the Rome of the future. Rome was a peasants' state.

HEWEL: But the Americans have good human material somewhere.

JODL: That's only an outward appearance.

THE FÜHRER: Not as much as one might imagine. They live in the few regions where the Europeans are dominating. But on no account do they have the large … centers. The farmers are impoverished. I saw photographs.

Never before have I seen such pitiful and stunted farmers—nothing but uprooted beings wandering around.[307]

CHRISTIAN: No intellect, no inner (attitude).

JODL: Nothing like that.

HEWEL: You only have to look at the posters they use to publicize the war. They are impossible!

THE FÜHRER: There is no doubt that of all the Anglo-Saxons the English are the best.

JODL: With the English you have the feeling that they fight for their country and empire, but with the Americans, you don't have that feeling.

THE FÜHRER: That might explain why the English say that they can always handle the Americans.

HEWEL: That's a very thoughtless attitude. They can't "deal with" them, if only because they're economically and in every other respect dependent on them. But they consider themselves superior to the Americans both politically and militarily to such an extent that they say, "We will recapture the lost territory in 10 years." This is what the English are saying. Very thoughtless indeed.

THE FÜHRER: There's one thing, Jodl, that's also clear, when it comes to strength, it's not only the population that counts, but also the size of the territory. Just look at the Chinese empire. The fighting has been going on for five years and part of the country is occupied, but the whole block is still standing.

JODL: And, what's more, with hardly any weapons.

THE FÜHRER: This will definitely be the end, unless we can expand our space. Space is one of the most important military factors. You can only operate if you have space. The wars of the future will be won by those who have space. This is the bad luck of the French. During a single offensive last year we occupied more territory than during all of our Western offensives. So France was finished in 6 weeks, while we're enduring here in a huge territory. If we had experienced such a crisis along the old border on the Oder-Warthe bend, Germany would have been finished. But here in the East we can do something about it. We have a theater enabling us to operate.

JODL: Things have changed. Germany was an expanse during the Roman wars. In the Middle Ages, armies marched through Germany in all directions, and now, in the era of tanks and aircraft [—]

THE FÜHRER: It doesn't take more than an hour and a quarter to go from one end of the old Reich territory to the other in a fast plane.

JODL: But the Russian space is a space that is impossible even for aircraft, as illustrated by the industrial region in the Urals. You can't get there.

CHRISTIAN: It takes 2½ hours to fly from Cologne to Königsberg.

THE FÜHRER: If the aircraft has a speed of 600 km per hour, it takes 1¼ hour from Stettin to Munich. In the pre-war era, Germany was nothing more than Schleiz-Greiz,* etc., as far as the fragmentation of German territory was concerned. It was ridiculous compared with the rest of the world. Here we speak of entire continents: America, East Asia, or Russia. And Australia! Seven million people have an entire continent to themselves. This was one of the craziest proposals: the Prince of Windsor said back then that the Germans should settle in northern Australia.[308] He always was in favor of our getting that region. But then we would have settled there and one day the English would have taken it.

HEWEL: Australian agriculture is German! The German element has been the most creative one in Australia.[309]

THE FÜHRER: That's precisely why they want the Germans in that region. I told him that we don't attach much importance to it. Australia to the Australians! [—] I don't believe what the Japanese are saying.

JODL: The statements don't specify what they're doing there. On the other hand, they're saying that Vladivostok is unbearable in the long run. To avoid a fragmentation of forces, the Japanese won't attack the Soviet Far East right now, unless American bases were to be set up there or the Soviet Union collapses. In any case, the Japanese war economy is prepared for a long war. According to them, they don't think that 1943 would be the decisive year.

THE FÜHRER: If they're prepared for a long war, then they'll have to dig in there, because the Americans will certainly establish bases in that area.

HEWEL: They'll have to go to northern Australia.

THE FÜHRER: It is surprising that Stalin recently gave the Americans a slap in the face.[310]

HEWEL: I don't imagine that Churchill congratulated Stalin for it.

JODL: They must move in here.

HEWEL: Yes, this is the area from which they get their raw materials—their resources and their wealth—and as long as these resources last, they'll launch new attacks.

THE FÜHRER: Imagine how much the Japanese have accomplished in so short a period! It's ridiculous to believe that Japan is unable to put up more than 30 infantry divisions. Japan has a larger population than Germany in the territory of the old Reich. They should be able to establish 120 divisions. But we don't really know how many they have in reality. It stands to reason that they don't say how many they have, in order to be on the safe side. Then all of a sudden it turns out that they have not 15 but 30 infantry divisions up there.

---

* [NDT] Tiny principality in 18th Century Germany.

JODL: You never know with the Japanese.

HEWEL: If they operate in this area, it's not a fragmentation of their forces. The operations are quite independent.

THE FÜHRER: The only issue for them on which I can't give an opinion is the issue of tanks. Do they or don't they have a modern tank? What was Oshima's answer? I assume that this question was put to him.

HEWEL: He didn't tell me.

THE FÜHRER: I believe he said that they do have modern tanks.

CHRISTIAN: He's not properly informed[311] by his people. Their announcements on tanks are just as sparse as those regarding aircraft.

THE FÜHRER: They didn't say anything about ships, either, and then all of a sudden there they were with the heaviest ships on earth.[312] They didn't speak about aircraft carriers, and suddenly it turns out that they have the largest number of aircraft carriers.[313] However, after the war, they'll have to mothball their large battleships, because then only planes will be used. Even over there all talk centers on aircraft.

HEWEL: The Japanese have been bombed repeatedly; for instance, near the Midway Islands and down there.[314] They came too close.

THE FÜHRER: Nobody dares use such large ships anymore. What would be unpleasant for them would be if they couldn't get control of it quickly, i.e., that it might become a base for submarine warfare. I'm convinced that the Japanese will completely establish their base here before they start action. They'll probably not engage in maritime traffic, but might start with a blockade. One thing is certain. That's something we most certainly won't find out. These people send an ambassador and another ambassador to Washington to moan there and they themselves have no idea what they're talking about. I can imagine good old Kurusu waddling around there.[315] He has no idea what's going on and when he arrives at the White House, he's shouted at, "You're playing dirty tricks." The little Japanese was dumbfounded, as he had no idea that Pearl Harbor had been attacked. They don't say a word.[316] I don't say anything either.

HEWEL: Maybe they realized that it's necessary to build tanks first.

CHRISTIAN: Large tanks are of no use in the jungle.

THE FÜHRER: We don't drive around Yugoslavia in our heaviest tanks. Why should I take a Tiger to finish off a sniper? In view of the incredible Japanese secrecy and cleverness, in this regard, it's entirely conceivable that the Japanese have built heavy tanks, but don't use them for the time being so that the Russians don't notice anything. One day, they'll use them.[317] So we shouldn't be too concerned if they have two armored brigades and two armored divisions here because we can imagine what the Russians have there. They've been bled white three to five times already.

JODL: Whereas Japan has first-class troops.

THE FÜHRER: Yes, Russia has been bled white. If it were to start all of a sudden, one would assume it would crackle faster than elsewhere. Maybe they'll do it quite differently and will push in this direction. [318]

CHRISTIAN: They got a thrashing in their border conflicts with the Russians.

THE FÜHRER: Only once.[319] Stalin ... had ... They were encircled.

CHRISTIAN: Their air force also suffered.

THE FÜHRER. I don't know about that. They drove back ... all the attacks. There's only this single case, where they were ambushed. Stalin said, "I don't want to wage war against the Japanese, but if they raise a fight with us, they're mistaken, because we're also prepared."

CHRISTIAN: That was at the time of the old Russian Army of the Far East.

THE FÜHRER: That was still one of the best ones. The Japanese have usually defeated the Russians, and they'll continue to do so if they have nearly equivalent equipment. In this case, they waged war against the Chinese. The ship sent there was the *Itsomu*, launched in 1899—an old tub indeed.[320] That was the flagship. They only deployed very old ships and didn't attack a single ship. They saved their really good ones. We didn't fire on the Westerplatte with our most modern ships, either.[321]

JODL: He describes the armaments as follows: (*Text is read.*)

THE FÜHRER: If they plan something they'll never tell us. And if they draw our attention to the fact that they're planning an operation in the south, one could more likely expect something in the north instead. I told the foreign minister, "Dear Ribbentrop, do whatever you're able to do, and whatever you're able to do, do it. They'll take advantage of the time. They would be crazy if they didn't. As long as they notice that forces are being withdrawn, they say ... with Asian cunning. Let him bleed white. But the moment they realize that the situation could become stable here and reinforcements may be moved to the East, you'll see swift action on their part and they'll be there in time."

Situation in the air

CHRISTIAN: It was reported that a 13th aircraft was shot down during last night's raid against Hamburg. During the incursion to attack the station at Hamm, some aircraft, probably because of an emergency, dropped some of their bombs on Brielle in the Netherlands. 27 civilians are dead, mainly children.[322] In the Reich, the number of dead increased to 82 because two factory shelters were hit. The number of injured also increased to 161. A total of three air-raid shelters were hit, including the two factory shelters. During the night, 10 incursions were reported over the Reich territory (via Sealand), the area of Göteborg, the Swedish south coast, the Gulf of Danzig—then they returned via Elbing. They probably laid mines. There were also intrusions via the West Frisian Islands to Juist. They are also suspected of laying mines. 15 aircraft were observed in Nordhorn, west of Münster, south of Dortmund, Düsseldorf, Euskirchen, Trier. Thus far, there have been reports regarding the dropping of 15 high-explosive bombs and several incendiary bombs in various places. The production facilities of an industrial factory in Bochum were destroyed by 3 high-explosive bombs, but this won't cause major production losses.

THE FÜHRER: If we went to the "Felsennest"[323] again and stayed for only three days, Euskirchen and the surroundings would be destroyed, and that would be a great pity. We must not do it.

CHRISTIAN: Forty buildings are slightly damaged; the rest is damage to agricultural areas. Regarding our own raids, we received this report: the fighter-bomber attack could not be carried out this morning because of heavy fog and a sea like glass.

THE FÜHRER: Do the planes float?

CHRISTIAN: No, but they have to start at a low altitude and it's feared that the fighter-bombers may have problems in the fog. The weather won't change during the day. The fighter-bomber attack is scheduled for the day after tomorrow. Tomorrow the fighter-(bombers) will escort the 6 destroyers through the Channel. They're now in Cherbourg and all fighters will be assembled there.[324] Then we received an inquiry whether the 6th Bomber Wing, which took part in the raid on London, could be re-transferred to (south France) to continue its training.

THE FÜHRER: This is possible. But a new spirit has to be instilled in them. When will the Reichsmarshal come? [—] We can't go on like this; we'll never break the English if we act like this. We need another person there—another person must take over the command. It's not that we don't have the planes which would disturb him continuously and cause problems for him. We need another man there. I'm convinced that there's a tough guy somewhere in the East. I'm convinced that if (Droschel)[325] were given the order, he'd carry out the mission. With the present situation, it won't work.

CHRISTIAN: An enemy convoy west of Cape Finisterre was attacked by 3 fighters; the convoy consisted of 20 ships sailing north. A merchant ship of 8,000 tons was hit and began to list.[326] ... fighters attacked a southbound convoy of 50 ships. So there seems to be considerable traffic from England down to here, and pretty close to the coast. A fire broke out on a 7,000-ton merchant ship, which was listing badly; there were close-range hits of an 8,000-ton merchant ship, which caught fire as well. Apart from this, (nothing out of the ordinary) from this area. (Close-range) combat forces assembled in the Mediterranean area: 19 fighter-bombers, 28 dive-bombers, and 32 fighters. Another 18 fighter-bombers attacked the airstrip near Medenine and, while flying in front of the lines, destroyed one gun and a number of trucks, and strafed columns and dropped bombs on the remaining parts of the northern sector. 10 trucks were destroyed, and artillery positions were put out of action. All in all, 452 sorties were flown. Eighteen bombers were deployed during the night, 14 of which attacked ships in the port of Philippeville. Three merchant ships from 6,000 to 9,000 tons were damaged. Additional hits between the ships and on the harbor installations were observed.[327] Two airstrips in Tunisia were again raided by the enemy yesterday. There was no damage. Fifteen fighters raided one of our convoys in the sea territory east of Bizerte, but caused no damage. Air Force 4 attacked convoys and towns on the left wing of … with fighters and dive-bombers. As for the rest, the forces were mainly deployed north of the Don River, mostly in front of the First and Fourth Panzer Armies. Emphasis was placed on the destruction of the 3rd Tank Army. Details have not been reported. 40 fighters attacked the Valuiki-Kupiansk railroad line. The track and warehouses were hit. Three trains were damaged. Luftwaffe Command East attacked yesterday in the area of Dmitriev, mainly to assist in the defense of the 78th [Infantry] Division. Eighteen tanks and 60 vehicles of various types were destroyed, and numerous vehicles were damaged in this combat area. Columns were hit. More then 500 aircraft were in action. This is good, in view of the limited number of forces we have.

THE FÜHRER: Who's responsible?

CHRISTIAN: General Greim[328] is the commanding officer of Luftwaffe Command East. These are the detachments. I must admit, if the commander is not a tough guy, he can't order his subordinates to do such things.

THE FÜHRER: The major who came recently made an excellent impression on me.

CHRISTIAN: The one who was at Khar'kov? That was Pressler![329]

THE FÜHRER: An excellent impression. That is the man who flew (up to…) sorties with a dive-bomber formation.

CHRISTIAN: That's what they always do. At Luftwaffe Command East they have a combat formation and a dive-bomber formation, and they fly a lot of sorties—up to eight a day.

THE FÜHRER: There's no doubt that the battle against England is characterized by great laziness. The upshot of this sloppiness is that we rejected all warnings and recommendations as well. The command is to blame. This is unacceptable. The worst is the attitude of avoiding anything that could provoke the enemy. People like him should be transferred for a while to Cologne and Münster, to the Western region in general. Then they would quickly learn who's provoking whom.

CHRISTIAN: The leaders of the units are not to blame. [—] Air Force 1 attacked forest camps, assembly areas, positions and railroads close to the front.

THE FÜHRER: An English pilot wrote an article mentioning those damned searchlights. I sent it to the Reichsmarshal and Field Marshal Milch.[330]

CHRISTIAN: This is unbelievable. The British planes are still brightly painted and look like silver birds in the light of the searchlights. [—] The losses were as follows: 4 of our own and 12 enemy planes in the West, 4 of our aircraft and no enemy aircraft in the South, and ... of our own and 14 enemy aircraft in Russia.

THE FÜHRER: The figures are gradually starting to reflect the true situation.

CHRISTIAN: As far as the weather is concerned, a new disturbance, currently over Norway, is approaching. But this time it should affect only the front part of our combat area and then move eastward, toward Moscow. This means that the weather will improve. Good weather in the northern sector. In the central sector some snow, but winds at 40 to 50 km per hour and driving snow. Snow is blowing up. A few isolated snowfall areas in the south sector—several snow showers, but nothing significant. The sorties are in full swing, and the transports to the Taman Peninsula are also going well because of the frozen soil. The temperature was minus 6 degrees on the Taman Peninsula last night, minus 9 degrees in the Crimea, and minus 14 degrees in the Donets region. The temperature was measured at minus 9 degrees in the central sector. It was warmest in the north—minus 2 to minus 6 degrees. In view of the overall situation, the Fourth Air Fleet was ordered to maximize anti-aircraft artillery in the area.

(Order is read aloud.)

End: 1:50 p.m.

* * * * *

MID-MARCH TO MARCH 21, 1943

On March 6, Rommel advanced from the Mareth Line, but had to fall back that the same day. Two days later he left Africa to (unsuccessfully) obtain the order to evacuate Tunis. Hitler, who apparently was still dreaming of offensives reaching Casablanca, and who, out of consideration for Italy, was obliged to keep the "Tunis bridgehead" so as to protect the south flank of "Fortress Europe," sent the "Desert Fox" on vacation. After initial attacks had started on March 16, the British launched a frontal assault on the Mareth Line on the night of March 20, combined with a flanking movement by the New Zealand Corps.

While the situation in Africa became more critical, the Eastern Front consolidated further. Army Group Center successfully carried out the "Buffalo movement," i.e., the evacuation of the Rzhev-Iukhnov salient, reaching the new Spas-Demensk-Belyi line. In the south, the SS Panzer Corps recaptured Khar'kov in fierce street battles between March 12 and 15 and, under pressure from the German assault, the Russians retreated to behind the middle segment of the Donets River. The German southern front gained a continuous and straight defensive position from Taganrog to Belgorod, and along the Mius and Donets [Rivers]. This was essentially the same position from which Hitler, nine months earlier, had set out to the Don River, the Volga River and the Caucasus—an effort that had cost 75 divisions and huge amounts of materiel.
(*Maps 1, 3, 7 and 9*)

* * * * *

Fragment of an Evening Situation Conference,
between March 12 and 15, 1943, probably
at the Wolfsschanze [331]

The East

ZEITZLER: …was pushed into this region … *Grossdeutschland* [Panzer Grenadier Division] [332] is still covering the flank. The 206th [Infantry] Division, which was pulled out up there, launched an assault near …The right wing of the Second Army is advancing quite well. It's marked more clearly on the other map.

JODL: Is it still the plan to move the … infantry up there?

ZEITZLER: Not quite completely.

JODL: The 39th [Infantry Division], then the 6th [Infantry Division], and then the 38th [Infantry Division].

THE FÜHRER: The question is what they'll destroy in doing this. That's what it depends on.

ZEITZLER: It looks as if the group that's being brought in will be assigned exclusively to defense, so they probably aren't planning any major actions for the time being. The 106th [Infantry Division] will somehow … Then the 39th [Infantry Division] can arrive, and then we have to wait for the 38th [Infantry Division] [—] advanced well, generally speaking, between 12 and 15 km. The vanguard detachments are here. They said that their aim was this line. I don't think they can advance further. They won't be able to do it … *Grossdeutschland* should draw up an echelon… Manstein would like to see the entire Second Army advancing somewhat.

THE FÜHRER: That's not possible. It's much better to have forces at one's disposal and finish the business down there. That's much better ...

ZEITZLER: ... so many forces are ... available. Maybe, if we succeed, ...

THE FÜHRER: Say that again ...

ZEITZLER: Maybe something's brewing there.

THE FÜHRER: That we do it here and then there and then destroy a group again. That's a possibility.

ZEITZLER: The 4th Panzer Division has advanced up to that point. Army Group Center now intends to move the 88th and 82nd [Infantry Divisions] to the north, and the 4th Panzer to this area for now via ... We would then have somewhat less here. As a next step, they'll try to link up with ... Otherwise, the army group will try to advance further... in order to improve its position. Apart from this, there's nothing out of the ordinary along the entire front. He attacked various places up there near the "Buffalo Movement."[333] Here on the main road again, and here a few minor attacks. Tanks were involved up there. Today they're pulling back from the advanced position to the "B" position. It's between these two. We don't yet know the precise line. Up there they're pulling back to the green dotted line.

(THE FÜHRER): ... So we would move to that position anyway?

ZEITZLER: ... dotted line ...

THE FÜHRER: Oh, here it is.

ZEITZLER: It's a drawn-out line, at ... where they intended to retreat at one go. But we don't want them to do that. No reports are in yet from the left wing. Nothing out of the ordinary in the southern area controlled by Army Group North. Here there were attacks along the entire front. Here as well, at this breakthrough "hatchway." Generally speaking, everything's in order. Here he moved in further, with tanks and mounted infantry. That's only because they plan to retreat to ... position tonight ... if they give something ... They have a large mass in the position already. This is the inner group, with artillery and parts of the two light infantry divisions in this position. Barrages up there. I inquired about this matter here. They said they wanted to do it on the 18th. But then they had to throw the 30th into the battle. But they're firmly determined to sort this out. They know that this is serious. It must be sorted out. ... They brought in the smoke mortars[334] from the Leningrad Front so that they are available to the ... artillery and can handle everything with one division. Nothing here; successful defense here. These were very persistent attacks, apparently involving numerous heavy enemy tanks.

THE FÜHRER: Apparently there are many foreigners with the tanks. They're constantly moving in.

ZEITZLER: There were 20 motorized sleds on Lake Ilmen'. Eight were destroyed. Then here near Rovgorod ... it's possible to lay a pontoon. These stand-by troops were shelled.

THE FÜHRER: This is nothing but diversion; they only tie down our forces. It'll start up there!

ZEITZLER: We're seeing more active traffic again. Near Shlissel'burg, the railroad is constantly disturbed by artillery fire. That's why he moved the bulk of the traffic back to the road. The ice is still solid. There were stand-by troops there. Here, the army group fired several thousand volleys on a narrow assembly position and believes to have destroyed it. Generally speaking, there's nothing special here, just the usual traffic across this area.

THE FÜHRER: Here 6 assault guns and 3 tanks, and here 4 Tigers. How many do they have in that place? [—] 6 assault guns, another 6 assault guns here, and again here. [—] There is nothing left here.

ZEITZLER: We could transfer another 20 up there this month as replacements.

North Africa

JODL: This was a quiet day in Africa, mainly due to heavy rain; the whole area is quite muddy at the moment, ... so that along the entire front of the Fifth Panzer Army ... this will be a center of attack ... a very strong group here is very difficult. I don't think ... I think the focal point will remain in that area. There's no doubt, however, that this group is gradually being reinforced.

THE FÜHRER: The British are very skilled at preparing such a move carefully. They take their time.

Italian troops for the East

JODL: There's still the information from the *Comando Supremo* concerning the new establishment of ... a corps in the East. The Alpine troops won't stay in that area. But it could ... maybe we should suggest that they transfer a good Alpine division ... to Tunis.[335] That would be a gain in this mountainous area ... have long clamored for mountain troops anyway ...

THE FÜHRER: ... stopped their work [—]

JODL: In Turin.

THE FÜHRER: Yes, indeed. They demanded a pay rise.

JODL: Communist machinations.

THE FÜHRER: But that it's possible for workers of eight factories to stop working at the same time. That would be unthinkable for me. And now, they don't dare resort to drastic measures. Well, the strike failed, but they have not yet decided whether they should take rigorous action or not. I'm convinced if you show the slightest weakness in a case like this, you are lost. I've been saying this all the time. Unless the Duce transfers a division there, to be established by us, ... Just once I'd like to place at his disposal the resistance and fire power of, say, Hollidt's force. He needs to see the resistance of a German alarm company that was able to stop the Russians for a full two or even three weeks. He needs to see it and compare it to his own troops' defense and posture. I must point it out to him, especially in the presence of Ambrosio.[336] I'm of the opinion that it doesn't make sense to send the weapons away. I'll tell the Duce that it doesn't make sense. We bring in weapons, and it's nothing but a repetition of the self-deception to which we succumbed ... It's just the same ... and the result is a disaster. He attacks where the (Italians) ... They can't even be assigned so-called defensive tasks.[337] Why do we supply them with weapons? This year we can't meet all requests.

(BUHLE?): It's all a waste!

THE FÜHRER: We can't meet all requests this year; we can't allow ourselves to do this.

ZEITZLER: Otherwise German weapons would not be available for German units.

THE FÜHRER: That's clear. If we want to outfit our 21 divisions, we need the weapons ourselves.

JODL: They do have ... a few rifles and machine guns anyway. We can't do it at once anyway. We can't give away everything.

THE FÜHRER: It's impossible for us to equip another 700,000 men.[338] This is completely out of the question. We can't do it. That's ridiculous. We're short on weapons ourselves. First of all, there's the so-called Sixth Army in the East, the former Hollidt group[339]—it's only a phantom—not only with regard to the men (which can be corrected more easily), but also with regard to the weapons. It's ridiculous. They're not ready at all. Imagine what we have to do to put this right! And the same applies to the West. If what's-his-name says, "I'll throw in the available troops even if I have to equip them with sticks"—then it's absolutely correct and taken for granted. But ...

JODL: ...

THE FÜHRER: Yes, but if a major attack ... we can't discuss armaments today ... All calibers are ... introduced ... today. If something starts ... then only on condition that they don't shoot. But what are we to do if suddenly heavy fighting breaks out? We don't have the Russian guns yet. We don't have the ammunition for them either. Production must be launched. I can't say that we have the Russian guns, but the ammunition has yet to be produced. And the other weapons which we have at the moment ... machine guns and guns from all over the world. I can't regard this as fighting strength. But what's more important is that I get these units in order ... like the Romanians ... , for we don't know what they're doing. Nobody knows that. As far as the Romanians are concerned, it's necessary to relieve several units in the Crimea. Those who say that the Romanian Army is good for anything nowadays are dreamers. He's now recruiting between 600,000 and 700,000 men and we demand for the year ... if you believe that it'll be possible ... to train them. The Romanians are now starting to recruit. This will take all of March, April, through May, and then, in August, there'll be an "armed forces"! There will be nothing! Only our weapons will be gone by August. That's the only sure thing. At least for this year, we can't use these men in combat ...

(ZEITZLER?): ... need all this ourselves, my Führer.

THE FÜHRER: When we have increased our weapons production ... this is again a matter of labor. We base our deliberations on a factor—I'll talk to Sauckel[340] tomorrow—which is not quite certain yet, for on the one hand, between 800,000 and one million men are to be released[341]—this is absolutely necessary—and on the other hand production in all areas must now ... and in the next few months ... be tripled.[342] ... better if German weapons were exclusively used by us. If they say that it doesn't make sense until they have the same equipment as we do, I'll tell them that it's not a matter of equipment. I'll drive that message home to these people. Because the Italians arrived with weapons and equipment, which from the artillery point of view, was utterly ridiculous. If I look at the units ... after we ... had weeded them out in order to give them to others, and built up the resistance, then one must say ... The ammunition was also outrageous—ridiculous. The Russians themselves made a judgment: they killed them like rabbits. ... The Russians also say that the others just killed them. They probably killed all those invalids they didn't like ... only those who were good for something. Otherwise, they just ... As I said before, I'm absolutely against getting involved in anything ... I'll tell the Duce that it would be much better if he took all these units and got them in order on our territory. I'm very much in favor of doing that, but not in the way it's currently done. It makes no sense. The weapons are given away and no longer have any value; they're not used effectively. When you read ... today's alert reports you'll see that they're in conformity with ... He's afraid that these Communist ... He has Jews everywhere. He can't get rid of them, because the clerics are suddenly protecting the Jews.[343] ... just as it was during the revolution of 1918 in our country. The 1918 revolution would not have been possible without our dear clerics of the two denominations. To me, Erzberger is in any case more ... dangerous ... was just artificially built up by other members of the Center. At any rate, Erzberger was a subversive reality.[344]

JODL: What the Duce could do is to use his best people ... establish a first-class Alpine division and transfer it to Tunis, where everyone is clamoring for mountain troops.

THE FÜHRER: Either to Tunis or to Sardinia.

JODL: ...

THE FÜHRER: I would prefer the Balkans ... That would be better in any case. It would give us the opportunity to ... counter ... If we're able to settle this matter and help the Croats to establish their thing up there, there won't be any problems here. As I said, it doesn't make sense now to give the Italians weapons to help them build "an army" which will lay down arms at the first sight of any enemy. It doesn't make sense, either, to establish an army whose beliefs and convictions (are doubtful) ... to place, in a step-by-step process, two, four, six, eight divisions at the disposal of the Duce to ensure that domestic problems don't develop in Italy ... They're useless in the battles with foreign troops. I won't be deceived again! "Armaments!" It looks as if a hare or a sheep were dressed in the skin of a lion ... First the lion must ... it can more easily put up with a sheepskin than the other way round, don't you agree? Generally speaking, they have the required people; there's no doubt about it. They have to be selected and then pooled in a group with a firm Fascist ideology. But they themselves are ... I received (a letter) from Farinacci[345] and will be pleased to answer it. They're ... This is very difficult. It's like this: they came about at a time—maybe this is because we Germans are of the brooding type—which might not have been the right one, after all. The Duce once told me, "I myself didn't know how Fascism was going to win; I only knew that Italy would be lost unless Fascism prevailed." Now they've taken ... the basis. It is similar to the National Socialist Movement in Austria or in the Sudetenland—it never really became strong. The same happened in Italy. Only in Italy ... the personality of the Duce who bridged the gap, plus the courage of his own active Fascist fighting organization—there's no doubt about that. What they are lacking is a sound ideological basis and worldview. From the letters of ... I have ...

The Balkans

JODL: ... apparently the enemy vanished from this front, too. Only a few units seem to be hiding, scattered in these mountains so that the ... mountain division will be redeployed in order to comb through the area. At the 369th [Infantry Division]... sharply eastward in two columns. Here in front of the 217th [Infantry] Division's front ... still ... of the enemy. The 417th Division trail parties should stop here. Since the expected alignment of the enemy didn't take place, this group turned south and set out on this road.

These troops are confirmed. They are stopped ... by Četniks, who ... for the time being ...

THE FÜHRER: Yes, he can have ... We'll give him cavalry troops.

JODL: Then at least he'll have something, because the police ... personal guards are important. That is to say ... if anything should happen.

THE FÜHRER: Let's hope the guards don't hang him.

The East

(CHRISTIAN?): ...Troops are deployed in the usual form in the East, but there are no reports from the operational area yet. The only interesting report is from the Fourth Air Fleet. According to evidence given by a deserter—a member of the staff ... of the Russian 6th Guards Rifle Corps—the (losses) ... in the area of Losovaia are extremely high. ... The infantry division that's still in that theater ... is to ... the Russian Guards in the next few weeks ...

ZEITZLER: My Führer, I have checked this statement. There's an "Army High Command"-Line ... Dnieper [River], etc. This is ...

THE FÜHRER: I'm not aware of it.

ZEITZLER: I thought as much. They must be eliminated. It's likely that this wasn't submitted either.

THE FÜHRER: They never reported anything.

ZEITZLER: That is why it is called an "Army High Command"-Line. I was astonished, too, when I saw the map.

THE FÜHRER: They didn't report a single word!

ZEITZLER: This is the relevant order.

THE FÜHRER: Ask ... !

ZEITZLER: No, Heusinger also says that it wasn't reported. ... This is Melitopol', this ... everything within the line ... is included in the maps. In reality, there isn't anything in this area. I'll demand the destruction of this order.

THE FÜHRER: It doesn't exist.

ZEITZLER: The question, my Führer, is whether we should issue orders regarding this small corner up here. It could be that army groups ... might start doing something.

THE FÜHRER: An order for this small corner is possible.

ZEITZLER: They've done this right behind the front.

THE FÜHRER: The most decisive area is this corner. I don't think that civilian workers could do it.

ZEITZLER: So we'll issue an order for this corner and then move them closer to here.

THE FÜHRER: Yes, move them closer and concentrate the troops. Here as well, to the extent that they can actually build. It's possible here, ... They must stay here at all costs. I'm only concerned that if we make too many concessions—

ZEITZLER: I'll tell them: this is the only order that is valid for this area. It'll state that they must have a front ... behind ... one after the other ...

THE FÜHRER: They didn't report anything.

ZEITZLER: I was horrified when I read it. A major order.

THE FÜHRER: I can only say—

ZEITZLER: No, Heusinger himself said that he has a very bad conscience— he pulled it out and told me not to show it to anyone. One can see it at one glance by the army groups. I was astonished how ... to defend this large bridgehead. If they want to capture Novorossiisk, they would have to ... They would have reconnoitered ... German divisions and Romanian ... plus one at the Kerch Strait ... In the Crimea ... plus Romanians—nine all in all. That would free up just one division. That isn't acceptable in my opinion. But if we go ahead with this matter at the front and leave a total of ... in the Crimea, we will be able to do it as well. Besides, the Crimea looks OK right now ... and deploy a panzer division closely behind it—that would work for me. From the artillery point of view, quite a lot happens in the Crimea, as indicated by the figures. (*Presentation.*) If we really were to move three ... to the Crimea, ... that would make four, even six if the two on Taman were included. That would add up to ...

THE FÜHRER: I think we should move more to the Crimea.

ZEITZLER: ... In the Crimea, where they ... still being trained for six months, and another panzer division, that would be sufficient. If we do this at the front, then we need ... at least two divisions to stop ...

THE FÜHRER: On the other hand, to do it with just ... But the other can free up 20 divisions in this area.

ZEITZLER: If we free up ... here ... he should free up ... 16.

THE FÜHRER: He knows that we can't attack here any more. ... If he wants to back this, he can do it with a few divisions ... so as to disengage a few divisions.

ZEITZLER: Naturally, he'll also get something.

THE FÜHRER: Manstein has to understand that 16 divisions will probably...Perhaps you can give me the precise number of divisions by tomorrow ...

ZEITZLER: ...

THE FÜHRER: ... Manstein ... heavy troops away. We have to be aware of this.

ZEITZLER: My Führer, I studied very closely ... combed through during the three days of my stay here ... whatever we can do as far as replacement is concerned ... it'll be relatively acceptable, if we make everything available ... According to the order, we have 85% of the mobility and are lacking 6% of personnel.

THE FÜHRER: By April 15?

ZEITZLER: I've set the deadline of April 15. Manstein thought it would be later. But I'm in favor of finishing ... push it through. I took steps to have Wagner[346] and his repair shops ready. I'm confident they'll be able to fix quite a lot ...

THE FÜHRER: That's obvious, Zeitzler. But it doesn't match the ideal of what's-his-name.

ZEITZLER: Not at all, even if I wish it were so.

THE FÜHRER: Yes, indeed. But we must be uncompromising ... I can't allow this year to pass[347] ... and gets so much...materiel, which we don't ...

ZEITZLER: He'll wear us out before we're able to dismantle these things.

THE FÜHRER: He's in a condition now that we would be mad not to take advantage of it.

ZEITZLER: Absolutely! I met G...[348] and he asked for the future plans.

THE FÜHRER: We must have this on the side ...

ZEITZLER: We want to have do it on the side. It'll be possible in July/August. But today? ...

THE FÜHRER ... if Panthers, etc., return. Concerning the East, our position must be that we can't allow this matter to go on much longer. We simply can't allow this to happen—10 divisions!

ZEITZLER: ...which we removed from the center. If the 198th [Infantry Division] moves in, ... then we would have six good infantry divisions plus these six panzer divisions. That would result in an acceptable ... The following troops will come from the West: the 38th [Infantry Division] is scheduled to arrive on March 20, and the arrival of the other is planned for April 1. I don't know whether Jodl will really be able to have them ready. I would really like to have them. Then we would have ... to set this ... in order. ... what I can do with regard to smoke mortars and other equipment in order to strengthen this group. Three assault gun units are at least something. That is the most we can get out of this. They should be sufficient. Now, my Führer, a comment concerning the 1st Mountain Division. It's very difficult if the air division also ... from the Eastern front ... immediately ... It'll be difficult ... If we move the 1st Mountain Division to another theater of war, we will, of course, lose 10 days ... can't transport anything.

THE FÜHRER: Let me tell you something: Down there a catastrophe may happen at any time. You can see how weak the Italians are internally. As for the air division, it has to be removed at any rate—this doesn't mean that we give it away—so as to ...

ZEITZLER: ... so that we can get an idea of ...

THE FÜHRER: What I would like, of course, is for the air division to be moved back over to the corps, so that the entire corps would be on the other side. This here would naturally secure the division. As soon as the division arrives, this one can leave. They will certainly be moved out ... of course, as reserves ...

ZEITZLER: ...

THE FÜHRER: What Jodl said yesterday was correct ... we can't move them rapidly to somewhere ..., because from a certain point they will have to ... by planes ... If we have two such parachute divisions, they are, of course, elite troops that don't exist in any other force; I can assure you ... voluntarily reported, that he ... per month ... jumps from an altitude of 2,000 or 3,000 meters ...

ZEITZLER: My Führer, it would be ideal if we had five or six air divisions around Berlin.

THE FÜHRER: I would prefer to have them in France, no matter how they get there. It's just a difference of one day. They'll be moved there very rapidly.

ZEITZLER: ...

THE FÜHRER: That means that ...

ZEITZLER: Although I was given authority, I interfered as little as possible to avoid their whining. It is quite a lot. I can't get any more. The only thing about which ... will be sad is the 25% cut in the staff ... of the Panther troops.

THE FÜHRER: They're not available?

ZEITZLER: ... they agreed to the transfer of the tanks, my Führer, ... the motorized units over there... we'll not be able ... He'll have to accept the 25%. They'll get all the things listed in this document and part of the equipment listed here.

THE FÜHRER: Nothing can be done about that.

ZEITZLER: ... [The] *Hermann Göring* demands a lot ... vehicles. This is a painful decision. I kind of moved them there on the side... plus rear services.... If he gets 1,280, he should be ... satisfied.

THE FÜHRER: He'll be satisfied.

ZEITZLER: I would think so.

THE FÜHRER. I would ... the Estonian and Latvian SS [Divisions] ... with captured enemy materiel ...

ZEITZLER: Yes. They won't be ready in two months, either.

THE FÜHRER: They'll get the Russian things in exchange.

ZEITZELR: I'll speak to the Reichsführer himself.

THE FÜHRER: I'm sure he will agree to it.

ZEITZLER: I'd be pleased to help him. But one can ... the Germans ...

THE FÜHRER: ... will give him Russian infantry guns, so he has something right away. We will get the things together.

ZEITZLER: ... he will also come up with something ... the army troops, ... signal troops and all that materiel left behind ... This matter should be carried out ... My Führer, I'm actually pleased ... to the hill.

THE FÜHRER: Completely?

ZEITZLER: If he attacks from up there, he'd have a small spearhead of Panzers.

THE FÜHRER: He must get that.

ZEITZLER: Very well. I'll see to the 10th Motorized [Division], my Führer. I'd like to suggest that the 14th and 36th Motorized [Divisions], whose situation with regard to the vehicles is like this: (*Presentation*) Required strength: 3,000 ... They are operational and ready for combat ... so that we have partial motorized troops ... then a full body.

THE FÜHRER: He can make up for it later.

ZEITZLER: ... partially motorized ... to be enhanced later ...

THE FÜHRER: They will be proper panzer divisions anyway.

ZEITZLER: They will be proper panzer divisions.

THE FÜHRER: Only one thing is important: We must see if it's possible to put more assault guns at the disposal of what's-his-name up there.

ZEITZLER: ... more in South and Center ... I think North should be given some more. If the focus is on South and Center, I will get 160, 170 ... as replenishments. Those are assault troops. For Manstein's Donets front ... give to Manstein. We'll put them in down here.

THE FÜHRER: The Donets region is the most important one for us. He'll be attacked. It's most important that we don't lose anything there. That's why I asked Manstein for an overall chart indicating the areas down there that are suitable for attack by tanks.

ZEITZLER. ... as early as March ...

THE FÜHRER: ... out. I also spoke to Richthofen,[349] who also ... behind ... no surprise tank attacks. We'll be able to cope (with the) infantry.

ZEITZLER: I think so, too. Maybe we could give a little more to [the] North, if it's needed there, because it'll be very difficult to ...

THE FÜHRER: ... asked for a list of antitank guns available to him but, to be honest, all French 7.5-cm fire with hollow-charge projectiles ... are really antitank guns.

ZEITZLER: Yes, Sir. I'll ask for it again. ... I'll phase it out anyway. [—] If it goes like that, we'll have been quite successful ... (*Presentation*) As a next step, my Führer, I evaluated the experience from the withdrawal ... examined details ... since the situation calmed down a little. I discovered a great mess regarding clothing and other things. Here, for instance, a letter about clothing ... it's distressing to look into such a thing and to learn from letters ...

THE FÜHRER ...

ZEITZLER: ... a few more vehicles and everything ... However, we can't afford it ... tarpaulins are used as packaging material for wrapping weapons. That's a bad thing ... civilians wearing German coats ... military coats ... so that they're available for the auxiliary service draftees and any other ...

THE FÜHRER: I don't know ...

ZEITZLER: ...

THE FÜHRER: I have my doubts ...

ZEITZLER: All that....

THE FÜHRER: And if we took it away from them again?

ZEITZLER: Including the German ones they have stolen.

THE FÜHRER: We can't say whether they were stolen or not. Many worked in the Labor Service. In the winter they come ... boots ... free up ... They say they can't do it unless they are given boots, because they don't have any footwear ...

ZEITZLER: ... Well, you can interpret a lot into such a situation ... The officers, for instance, have so and so many hunting rifles ... etc. This shows that they take too much with them. I'd like to have a kind of ... drawn up, an order requiring the commanders in charge of division clear-out[350] ... to report ... so that they don't carry along so many things. This only fills ... as is indicated by the applications for compensation. Somebody is asking for 500, even 520 marks for a hunting rifle. Why does ... such a precious hunting rifle[351] ...? I also want to ... this cable ... a Krümperwagen.

THE FÜHRER: During the Great War, my unit had the following practice: whenever we left a position after a longer stay, a clear-out detail was set up; when we departed ... removed everything else. ... the division commander.

ZEITZLER: Everyone rides. Everyone has a sled for ... Naturally, one of the reasons is the long war—every soldier should have two sets of everything ... (*Presentation*) This starts with several interesting points. This here is actually the usual stuff back here. This is also very interesting. Many such small ..., my Führer, that, in part, are also tremendous ...

THE FÜHRER: ... What a mess! ... such a squad leader ... what can I do about it? I've been fighting for it for years. I issue orders to avoid these matters ... that one can't ... on the way ... endless court martial proceedings ...

ZEITZLER: Precisely in case of self-mutilation.[352]

THE FÜHRER: I absolutely agree that we have to change this practice.

ZEITZLER: Yes, Sir.

THE FÜHRER (*reading*): Another petition for clemency? ... This is a matter—I can tell this only to you—if the man sees that thousands of tons of materiel are lost, then he has no understanding of such a thing ... if guns are blown up, even light rifles are too much for them.

ZEITZLER: ... to travel from here and ... on site ... to save fuel and artillery ammunition ... maybe a final order should be issued after the business there is finished. Would you like me to prepare a draft? (*Presentation*) This was the order given to Army Group South. But the situation is such that we thought that [Army Groups] South and Center deserve some kind of recognition.

THE FÜHRER: I'll do that—I'll do it right away.

ZEITZLER: ... my Führer, I prepared ... to be taken down there[353] in case ... with the foreigners, and it is very short. I'd like to do it like that. (*Presentation*) This was the initial situation at ... after so many days it looked like that, so the development is very clear ... records ... with assessments of the troops.

THE FÜHRER: Yes!

ZEITZLER: This, for example, was written by an artillery commander. It is shocking to read ...

THE FÜHRER: ... these Hungarian ... always quite good.

ZEITZLER: Yes, always good.

THE FÜHRER: In contrast to the infantry.

ZEITZLER: This is unbelievable. I want to prepare a small map for every ally and give it to them, my Führer.

THE FÜHRER: Very good.

ZEITZLER: Next I want to ask you about the idea concerning the field training divisions, if maybe I could ... reinforce there ... I could take several such skeletons.[354]

THE FÜHRER: You must only get the people; I think the best would be if former SA and SS members were included, not members of ... spirit. .... So the question is ... to detail ... troops who can withstand ... The best thing to do would be to have the people, division commanders, etc., here one time to bring them together, and this would ... battalion commanders ... we should get them together and the spirit of the whole ... make clear, so ...

ZEITZLER: ...

THE FÜHRER: I don't know how long I'll be staying down there.[355] Maybe ... comeback up here anyway ... again right away ...

ZEITZLER: ... 100 general staff officers have just started.[356] I'd like to have them ... trained in the right spirit, the way I want it. I'll use the time when I go to Munich, I want to use one day to check whether the instructors are doing it properly. Do you agree?

THE FÜHRER: Yes! I, for my part, would just ask you to ...

ZEITZLER: How this came about is shown by these orders.

THE FÜHRER: ... "The Königsberg Line"...

ZEITZLER: This should be in the files. I'll find it. That's all, my Führer.

THE FÜHRER. ... not possible; we can't do it now. Right now is not the most favorable time. Nor may we say that this year we will fight minor battles, next year the major ones. Maybe the war will be decided this year.[357] I don't know. ... Now the other is also ...

ZEITZLER: If our units were to strike now, we could achieve great things.

THE FÜHRER: You must see to the SS ... getting the necessary personnel ...

ZEITZLER. I'll ... with the Reichsführer ...

THE FÜHRER: ... say that we will leave the recruits in the West and move the better-trained troops to the East. It's up to him, but this or a similar decision is required.

ZEITZLER: ... using a huge amount of fuel. We must check the calculations. The ideal is quite acceptable.

THE FÜHRER: ...

* * * * *

MIDDAY SITUATION REPORT, MARCH 21, 1943, AT THE BERGHOF[358]

Beginning: 12:16 p.m.

Situation at sea

JUNGE: During the night of March 20, the following vessels reached the port of Gibraltar from the Atlantic: three destroyers, two British auxiliary aircraft carriers with one destroyer, two corvettes and one ...

THE FÜHRER: Down in Sardinia. I'm afraid it'll start there, and that ...

JUNGE: Three U.S. destroyers left for the Atlantic. The following ships were in the port of Gibraltar on March 20, at 1 p.m.: *Malaya* in the harbor ... According to an Italian report, the heavy group was probably in the area of ... on March 20. Little convoy traffic off the Algerian coast. Around noon, a merchant ship headed west was sighted near Philippeville. No ... from the eastern Mediterranean [—] Tunis with German troops ... arrived in Trapani yesterday morning. Nothing out of the ordinary in the Aegean Sea. No damage caused by air raids on Petsamo on the 18th and 19th. 45 vessels were on their way in the Norwegian area. Motor torpedo boats weren't deployed in the Black Sea. The Kerch/Taman' traffic on March 20 ...

The West

JODL: ... I talked with the Commander-in-Chief West. Over there it's ... But it was completely quiet, with no signs of ... A slight increase. He plans to ... the distribution of forces [—] I had all commanding officers of fortified areas spoken to. ... was reported there. There are only a very few ... considered suitable for large-scale battle. Measures were taken to replace them.

THE FÜHRER: ... The best, most fanatical people must be deployed there ...[—]

JODL: ... Some of them are a bit older. Here ... Commander Schneider[359] is 61 years of age and well (suited) for large-scale battle on the strength of his personality and intellectual capacities.

The FÜHRER: It depends on the personality.

[—]

Situation in the air

THE FÜHRER: What about the air situation?

CHRISTIAN: ... a mixed unit of 15 aircraft (attacked) the railway repair works in Leeuwen, Belgium. ... Heavy damage was caused, but only a few dead ... at Antwerp and an army arsenal. [—] In the Mediterranean region, the air ... started yesterday afternoon ... tanks moving eastward ... columns west of Speiden. 3 planes were shot down. [—] Action with 595 tons on board—174 tons of fuel, 133 tons of supplies, the rest was equipment.[360] They brought back 257 injured, 297 soldiers, 207 tons of equipment. [—] Luftwaffe Command East committed 75 dive bombers against positions north of Zhizdra, 75 fighters and dive bombers against targets north of Spas-Demensk; planes flew raids of diversion against targets northwest of Seredina Buda and columns ... four were shot down in [—] the Fourth Air Fleet laid mines in the lakes near Gelendshik. Several railroad stations [—] He is reported to have major logistics problems. ... spoke with Field Marshal Richthofen about whether anything more could be done.

THE FÜHRER: Yes.

CHRISTIAN: He said he will try himself [—]

(The following is a telephone conversation between the Führer and General Zeitzler)

The East

ZEITZLER: ... along the eastern front and the old northern front, northeast of Khar'kov ... also the advance from Bjelgorod ...

THE FÜHRER: If, then, at Izium. I must always call attention back to the fact that if any advance is going to make sense, it will be an advance at Izium.

ZEITZLER: I ... with Field Marshal Manstein today. There's no point.[—]

THE FÜHRER: ... or as retaliation if the enemy does anything. In both cases, we have things ready. If the enemy really attacks, advances from Khar'kov to the (Southeast), ... him with this offensive completely in the back.

ZEITZLER: On the southern wing the Second Panzer Army is advancing well. Thirty minutes ago, we received a report that the 4th Panzer [Division] (linked up with the 10th [102nd Hungarian Division]).[361]

THE FÜHRER: Good!

ZEITZLER: That means that this corner is now closed. The enemy is still putting up considerable resistance. Today he ... Field Marshal Kluge holds the view ...[—] ... nothing out of the ordinary with regard to the Second Panzer Army, my Führer. In the sector held by Corps Group Scheele,[362] the attack of the ... and the 12th Panzer [Division] ... this bulge has become somewhat flatter near the 9th Panzer ... but then further north, in the area of the Fourth Army, very heavy attacks were launched north of ... in the same place he attacked yesterday. [—] The projecting bulge of this movement—the 36th Motorized [Division], 14th Motorized [Division], and 67th [Infantry Division]—has pulled back as planned. He will be up there in ... until the evening of the 21st ... The attacks of the 7th Air Division have by and large been driven back. He succeeded in ... including further north ... The entire Army Group North [—] ... reached of troops ... Further north, my Führer, we see signs of an attack being planned against this salient ... in the north, south of Shlissel'burg.

(*Telephone line is interrupted*)

THE FÜHRER: ... groups of destroyers moved down?

CHRISTIAN: Yes!

THE FÜHRER: ...

CHRISTIAN: ... hasn't yet been transferred, my Führer.

(*Telephone conversation with Zeitzler continues*)

ZEITZLER: My Führer, the line was interrupted.

THE FÜHRER: You were just getting ready to discuss the attack south of Shlissel'burg.

ZEITZLER: We see more and more evidence of an attack being prepared to gain control of the railroad ... a group containing the 21st and 223rd [Infantry] Divisions ... more penetrations... by us from the left wing of the 223rd ... [—] ... there a considerable, but very narrow indentation resulted from it. Our early-morning counterattack broke through it, so that ... there were heavy attacks again later in the morning … the penetrations is very narrow, though, so that they could … close it. [—]

THE FÜHRER: … It makes no sense for the Army Group South to continue its offensive in the direction of Kursk.[363]

ZEITZLER: Very well.

THE FÜHRER: Instead we should try to replace the units and build up the group in such a way that it … if possible … back against Izium …

ZEITZLER: Yes, that's what I told the Field Marshal this morning … and will again … [—]

ZEITZLER: The army group I talked to today is very grateful and will be pleased about it.

THE FÜHRER: Very good. [—] Thank you very much. Heil!

ZEITZLER: Heil, my Führer!

(*End of the telephone conversation*)

THE FÜHRER: … later bring up the 58th [Infantry Division]. This is nothing serious, just a bunch of diversionary activity.

[—]

THE FÜHRER: … attacks, so that he's worn down.

KEITEL: He's being worn down.

THE FÜHRER: When the right moment has come, we'll seize the element of action.

JODL: The unit that comes from the south [—]

THE FÜHRER: … if that happens, we'll have to be prepared for it. Up there, a major battle will be fought, no question about that. That's the only sure thing. We have to build up our own forces anyway. So it would be better to bring it up.

JODL: … to free up other units … is still valid?

THE FÜHRER: … They'll have to manage.

[—]

THE FÜHRER: As soon as he overcomes his psychosis (that these are) armies here, the matter will look quite different. Of course, I would have liked very much … to pull out the SS Panzer Corps …

[—]

THE FÜHRER: It was brought in with 23,000 [men].

(… ?): 23,000—that's more than the target.

THE FÜHRER: There were at least 18,000 to 19,000 troops.

(… ?): 18,000 troops, I should say.

[—]

THE FÜHRER: … our operation along the Dnieper River last year was really the first successful preliminary engagement …

KEITEL: If we …

THE FÜHRER: The same thing happened last year.

[—]

THE FÜHRER: ... it goes without saying that this accumulation of forces here ... it would be best to combine the three SS divisions.

JODL: He planned to substitute the 39th and 6th [Infantry Divisions] for the 11th Panzer [Division].

THE FÜHRER: ... and keep *Grossdeutschland* [Panzer Grenadier Division] here, so that we ... still have striking power with all those tanks [—] (... ?): ... This would be an important improvement. I would pull them out as well. Their movement down here seems to have been quite successful. And then the rear

[—]

(THE FÜHRER?): ... dealt him a blow that forced him once more to ... forces ... As soon as we are on the other side, we can do something, if he increases the pressure by interfering with the flank. The most important thing for us is to cross the Donets ... The Russians never had a great deployment in depth ... in contrast to us ... [—] There's no doubt: the more we succeed in realigning the front, the fewer forces we will need, and we could then interrupt his railroad line at Briansk. He himself ... the railroad again ...This would not result in an extension, but a shortening [—] An order should be issued now.

KEITEL: Zeitzler should be told.

THE FÜHRER: I'll speak again to Zeitzler.

KEITEL: The *Viking* [SS Panzer Division]!

JODL: The *Viking*, and the 17th Panzer [Division].

[—]

JODL: He doesn't have any more at the moment. Plus a fifth being replenished.

THE FÜHRER: ... in this short period of time to destroy them completely with the panzer divisions—it's ridiculous. I'm convinced; (the longer we) wait here, the more this character will consolidate his forces ... in order to do what can be done [—] I think the correct thing would actually have been to make a push in this direction and bring in the others, including the other units. The vermin there will be shown to be an "army" that is not backed by anything.

KEITEL: He doesn't have fresh forces. We can rule out that he has new, fresh forces up here. What we see broken up in this area is everything he has ... also proven by charging ahead ...

THE FÜHRER: One must imagine that they ... I don't know from where ... operations, it is OK ... [—] Just imagine that!

KEITEL: Not down here, outside Zaporozh'e.

THE FÜHRER: If he ever comes here, everything will be in disarray. He won't have anything left afterwards. This new line would help reduce the number of troops required, because he's now wasting his energy in uncoordinated efforts. ... not the Donets [River] either ... [—] (... ?): ... the most ideal line for the defense would be the one from Belgorod to Lisichansk via Kupiansk. The good thing about this line is that it gives us a number of important rail lines and (takes them away) from the enemy ... especially Kupiansk ... but the main advantage, that [—]

(THE FÜHRER): ... hides great risk of a later accumulation of attack forces ... In such as case, the army groups always reject beforehand ... But I (experienced) it myself at the Don River, where I always warned against the forests, where they always said [—] could be used for the production of timber. That's why I firmly believe that it is now necessary to, first, pull the SS Panzer Corps[364] out as soon as possible so that, if need be, the *Grossdeutschland* Division could be committed at the left wing of the army group ... as a mobile reserve behind it [—] toward Kupiansk. The advance toward Kupiansk is no more daring than the advance mounted by the *Grossdeutschland* Division from Akhtyrka towards Belgorod ... (Tomarovkaf) or the advance ... The Belgorod–Kupiansk–Lisichansk line would, firstly, reduce the threat to the Donets region, considerably, and secondly, ... result in a permanent position, which ... and finally ... perhaps ... the weather conditions [—] Otherwise the whole time would be wasted. I am of the opinion: if we were to ... a soft ... [—] save forces for the army group, shorten the division combat sectors, and the new front could be held by ... who are now ... or by the divisions ... [—] and thus result in a situation that is favorable in every respect so that, in my view, road and weather conditions permitting, such an operation could be imagined. It's not impossible that such an operation ... in 14 (days) [—] Moreover, the matter up there won't go away, while I'm convinced (that the situation here) will be a growing source of danger [—] was outside Zaporozh'e, then the elimination of the salient is not a greater ... than what was already [—] I read an opinion yesterday arguing that we can't count on a long (continuation of) the muddy period. He would need several days in any case [—] advance towards Kupiansk. That's no more daring that the advance to Belgorod [—] quite apart from the fact that I'm convinced that this character is so weak ... there are lots of "units" there, but [—] These forests are never dangerous if you face them, but in the event of a crisis—at the Donets, for instance—they can be dangerous. We experienced this several times ...

(*End is missing*)

* * * * *

May 19-21, 1943

The situation in the East hasn't changed; both sides are busy rehabilitating and replenishing units thinned during the winter campaigns. Hitler, who is resolved to develop a strategic defense, still plans (as part of an operation with a tactical goal) to attack the Kursk bulge of the Russian front. However, he hesitates and postpones the offensive several times—on the one hand, because of the situation in the Mediterranean region, and on the other, because he wants to be able to deploy the new "Panther" tanks. In the meantime, the battle on African soil ended on the Tunisian peninsula of Mauin on May 12. Once again, 250,000 troops—half of them Germans—were taken prisoner, and again immense quantities of war materiel were lost. Where will the Anglo-Americans turn now? Southern France? Corsica and Sardinia? Sicily? Greece?

The situation is worsened by the uncertainty of the Italian attitude. The Italians control all of the Mediterranean coasts with the exception of the Peloponnesian Peninsula. Within Italy, there are only remnants of German units that were unable to reach Tunis. Because of the planned offensive against Kursk, and also because of Mussolini's vanity, a stronger presence is not possible. New German units are now hastily being built up from march-battalions, and newly established full divisions are beginning to arrive. Preparations are discussed at Hitler's headquarters in order to be ready to help the Italians in the case of extreme danger with or without Mussolini's approval, but also—and above all—for the Germans to be able to organize the defense of the Italian-controlled regions should Italy suddenly collapse. (*Maps 1, 7, and 9*)

* * * * *

MEETING BETWEEN THE FÜHRER AND FIELD MARSHAL KEITEL, MAY 19, 1943[365]

Present:

The Führer,   *Field Marshal Keitel,*
Lieutenant General Buhle (joined later), *Lieutenant General Warlimont*

Mediterranean Panzer armaments

THE FÜHRER: During the last few days, and especially during the night last night, I reflected about what would happen if we were to lose the Balkans. There is no question that the consequences would be serious.[366]

KEITEL: Certainly much more serious than if we had to screen ourselves off somewhere along this Italian front. The question is very difficult to answer, because too many different people live in the Serbian, Romanian, and Hungarian areas.

THE FÜHRER: This would result in problems for our allies, and also in the loss of the Romanian oil fields and the bauxite and chrome mines.[367]

KEITEL: And copper.

THE FÜHRER: We would also lose the copper.[368] In view of this situation, I consider it necessary to take precautions against a possible attack on the Peloponnesian Peninsula. We are currently bringing in a division, the Luftwaffe field division,[369] but we don't have any panzer unit there.

WARLIMONT: The Luftwaffe field division is not stationed on the Peloponnesian Peninsula, but instead at the Isthmus of Corinth.

THE FÜHRER: It is stationed at the Isthmus of Corinth. But we don't have any panzer units there at all. That is why I think it is necessary to move one there. Too much depends on it, and in a critical situation it would take longer to move one there than to another place. It takes less time to transport a panzer unit from the West to the East than to move it there. So we have to move a panzer division there, whether we like it or not. The only question is where do we bring it from?

KEITEL: The only one ready to go in the West is the 24th [Panzer Division].

THE FÜHRER: Yes, that's the only one we could take from the West. And at the moment, I don't expect any problems in the West.

KEITEL: I would have to study the map closely and check the distribution of reserves.

THE FÜHRER: The 1st [Panzer Division] and the 24th [Panzer Division] have advanced the farthest.

WARLIMONT: The 26th [Panzer Division] as well.

KEITEL: Next is the 24th [Panzer Division], then the 16th [Panzer Division], which is now being moved to Italy, and then the 14th [Panzer Division].

WARLIMONT: In the near term, then, it's only the 24th [Panzer].

THE FÜHRER: What shape is the 1st [Panzer] in?

WARLIMONT: The 1st Panzer Division has some 50 operational tanks.

KEITEL: Several of them were previously transferred. This morning I discussed the shape of the individual divisions with Buhle, in case we move the 16th Panzer Division to Italy. Buhle is better informed than I am.

THE FÜHRER: Everything indicates that the situation down there is the most critical, because so many economic problems are connected with it and because our allies are so uncertain. In the past, we were lucky that we had arranged for a sufficiently large marshalling area in good time.

KEITEL: To be able to attack Yugoslavia then.

THE FÜHRER: The Italians can't be relied upon. On the other hand, I'm convinced that relatively few forces would be required if some sort of mess were to develop in Italy. Especially since the first combat troops will arrive within ten days anyway, according to Zeitzler's report.

KEITEL: If he starts now and the transportation goes according to plan, they would be on site in ten days.

THE FÜHRER: He says combat-ready units will arrive. He is dispatching 60 trains per day, which means that every two days a division will arrive.

WARLIMONT: Some of them will have to go to the Balkans, or we will be too late there. One-third of the Eastern trains will have to go to the Balkans. But according to our calculations, he will still have the bulk of the Gisela units[370] and the parachute corps for Italy.

THE FÜHRER: I would prefer to take the three SS divisions to Italy, because they are most familiar with Fascism.

WARLIMONT: They would have to be moved first.

THE FÜHRER: If only those in the West were already better!

KEITEL: It's been a long time since we did something for the benefit of the West.

THE FÜHRER: No, it's OK as is. As a precautionary measure, I will ask for a report on the current strength of the 9th and 10th SS Panzer Divisions in the West. They have young people, of course, who are inexperienced.

KEITEL: Cadre personnel and the 1925 age group.[371]

THE FÜHRER: They don't have the experience—including politically—or the agility of my old SS division members, who are propagandists. I'm convinced if we move in the three best SS divisions, they will be thick as thieves with Fascism after only a very short while.

KEITEL: Buhle says that 150 more of the Panzer IVs will be transferred to the East, and then we'll be on top of that. I asked him this morning, "When can we give something to the West?" He answered, "I think it will be possible to transfer 60 tanks to the 16th Panzer Division for Italy. That's the most we can do." I told him, "Then we have to give 15 to the Rhodes unit." He replied, "We'll have to see if that's possible. Whether they are transferred to Rhodes first depends on the time."

THE FÜHRER: This doesn't mean anything. Once the trained crew has arrived, we could assign them to the 26th [Panzer Division] just as well.

WARLIMONT: The 26th [Panzer] is complete.

THE FÜHRER: But it doesn't have any tanks.

WARLIMONT: It also has about 50 tanks.

THE FÜHRER: Equipment for another detachment could be sent later so that it could be moved to the Balkans—let's say the Athens region—in good time. Then they could be deployed in the Peloponnese.

KEITEL: In the area of Athens, south of Larissa.

THE FÜHRER: The risk is that they get a foothold on the Peloponnesian Peninsula.

WARLIMONT: If we want to be sure that they are available in the Peloponnese, they must be transferred to the peninsula itself because of the narrowness of the Isthmus of Corinth. So the question arises whether the 117th [Panzer Division] might not serve the same purpose.

THE FÜHRER: It is a bit too weak. If he lands in one place there, the only thing we could do would be to divide the 117th [Panzer] to shield the landing points and secure the airfields at least.

WARLIMONT: He will be joined by five fortress battalions, which will be available soon—in early June—but they are from the 999th [Infantry] Division. It was planned that way so that all of the 117th will be available again.

THE FÜHRER: That's only two divisions—that's no a lot. If something should happen down there, we don't have many units—and that should be clear to everyone. I have to be prepared for the worst case, which would mean problems nearby. Then we couldn't bring down the units from the Serbian sector.

WARLIMONT: Absolutely not.

THE FÜHRER: That is why units should be brought down there in any case.

WARLIMONT: We had planned to transfer the two panzer divisions to Greece, once they are on their way from the East?

KEITEL: Yes, we had this in mind. Considering the poor state of the railroad from Salonika, the transportation will take a long time, and 9½ trains will be required.

THE FÜHRER: Transports from the West would be the quickest. For a panzer division, we would need 15 days from the beginning of the operation. Allowing another seven days for preparation, the panzer division couldn't be down there in less than 3 weeks from now, at the earliest.

WARLIMONT: According to our calculations, it would take at least 30 days to drive a division from the East to the region of Bucharest, and then to march on from there.

THE FÜHRER: Now, we can't forget that we may not bring in the conditions of 1941 again. We can't because the conditions of 1941 are not comparable, as we had two huge bridges over the Danube back then. That's missing this time.

WARLIMONT: We can only cross on the bridge at Cernaroda and on the ferry at Giurgiu; it is set up for that.

KEITEL: Nevertheless, the ferry at Giurgiu provides a good deal of service, especially in the summer months, when the water conditions are favorable. A lot could be done in three days and three nights. If we pull out an armored division from the West, we should at least make a point of taking a unit that can be replenished. Even a skeleton unit that would have to be fleshed out with tanks—whether captured or training Panzers—would be better than nothing.

THE FÜHRER: Couldn't we set up a North African division in the West, by scraping together the available men into a division and moving it to the West?[372]

KEITEL: The mobile ones—one each from the Fifteenth, Twenty-First, and Tenth [Armies]—and set up a new one with the personnel.[373] I believe they have been transferred to the improvised units.

THE FÜHRER: To pull out a unit, a division X, says that more than 30 percent of the men from his panzer regiment alone are there. They could provide a base. It will probably not be possible to give them more tanks in the foreseeable future. The situation in the West will improve as soon as the two SS panzer detachments with the Panthers are operational.

KEITEL: Unless everything is again absorbed by the East.

THE FÜHRER: If it should become necessary, the two detachments could be assigned to one of the two panzer divisions—they would have to be divided up—or to the two SS divisions. If the two divisions have 100 Panthers, they will be in excellent condition and will be very efficient and effective divisions.

WARLIMONT: I'm thinking less about the requirements of the West and more about the needs that might come up in northern Italy if we can only get the first troops for this purpose from the West.

THE FÜHRER: In this case, the two panzer detachments could be used, provided we have a little more time. They are being trained now, and the tanks will arrive by the 15th of next month at the latest.

WARLIMONT: Yes.

THE FÜHRER: But for security reasons, I believe it is necessary to transfer a whole division there at once. In my view, it will take too long for them to arrive from the East, and we must not forget that in the East only—

(*Lieutenant General Buhle joins the meeting.*)

Buhle, after much reflection, and based on this document I received from the *Comando Supremo*,[374] I have come to the conclusion that the Balkans are almost an even greater threat to us than Italy—which, if worst comes to worst, we could seal off in some place. If a landing takes place in the Balkans, say on the Peloponnesian Peninsula, Crete will be lost soon, too. We have supplies there for six months.

KEITEL: Yes, average supplies for six months.

WARLIMONT: You speak of the average, but there are a few exceptions.

KEITEL: There are some exceptions. There was a certain delay in moving food supplies because of the billeting question. Ammunition is available, but not all types; scarce ammunition is in short supply. All in all, they have supplies for six months, but this doesn't apply to the Italians.

THE FÜHRER: If we lose the Peloponnesian Peninsula, further supplies will be blocked. We can't deceive ourselves about that. We won't be able to supply them any longer. So the control of the Peloponnese is a precondition of everything else. They are already starting to use their position finding planes for torpedo attacks. Right now several small German units are deployed on the Peloponnesian Peninsula, and a division, the 117th, is being moved there as well. Part of the Luftwaffe field division is stationed in Athens, another part at the Isthmus of Corinth, which means that it is not completely available. The next-nearest units are in action in Montenegro. If there are any problems, especially with the Italians, we can't count on those units at all, because we won't be able to get them out. We would need them to occupy the Montenegrin-Dalmatian coast and disarm the Italians. So I have decided to transfer a panzer division to the Peloponnese in any case—perhaps to the area of Athens, but the Peloponnesian Peninsula itself would be better. As things stand now, it can only be taken from the West. I want to draw on the East only as a last resort, of course—such as in the event of an Italian crisis. I don't wish to draw on the East only because of a landing operation. As long as the Italians stick with us, I don't want to interfere with the East. We should only draw on the East if there are signs of internal problems in Italy or if the Italians are starting to collapse. There are plans for the 16th Panzer Division to be transferred to Italy, but it is not yet equipped.

BUHLE: It needs to get tanks first. It has 8 Panzer IVs and 8 command tanks.[375]

THE FÜHRER: That's negligible—so the 16th [Panzer] is not armored.

BUHLE: It will get more at the end of the month. To reach the number for the East, another 40 tanks will have to be transferred to the SS corps. So many tanks have been shipped to the East. This month,[376] ten tanks will be shipped to the *Hermann Göring* [Parachute Panzer Division] and ten to Bulgaria.

THE FÜHRER: How many Panzer IVs does the *Hermann Göring* have?

BUHLE: Twenty. It will get another ten, which have just arrived in Italy. That makes thirty; another ten in May, which will make forty, plus 43 Panzer IIIs. Ten for Bulgaria, ten for the 25th Panzer Division, plus the ten for the *Hermann Göring*—all in all another thirty. They have just been shipped. We can now make plans for other panzer divisions.

KEITEL: They should reach the 16th [Panzer Division] in time, as it is not scheduled to move until early June. So the first June deliveries should go to the 16th Panzer Division.

THE FÜHRER: They should reach the others in time as well.

KEITEL: Yes, because it doesn't go any faster, is what I meant.

BUHLE: It depends on which division we choose.

THE FÜHRER. Which division do you personally regard as most suitable to be shipped to the Balkans right now?

BUHLE: The 1st Panzer Division.

THE FÜHRER: Isn't it already there?

KEITEL: The second was the 5th [Panzer Division].

WARLIMONT: In the cold light of day, the 1st Panzer Division is the only operational one.

BUHLE: It's by far the best. It has 60 Panzer IVs, 12 flame-thrower tanks,[377] and a dozen command tanks. A Panther detachment is being trained now. The personnel are available and the first vehicles are said to have arrived. This division has 60 Panzer IVs today.

KEITEL: What about the 26th [Panzer Division]?

THE FÜHRER: When will the Panther detachment be ready for the 1st [Panzer Division]?

BUHLE: Not before the end of June or middle of July, my Führer. It depends on when it gets the equipment. According to the current schedule, it will be the next in line after the two SS divisions.[378] If the two SS divisions have to be supplied first, the earliest possible date will be July.

THE FÜHRER: Why?

BUHLE: We will get 300 this month. That will be sufficient for two detachments and a weak SS detachment; twenty vehicles were shipped to the schools, so that all these men can be trained. We will need at least the total June output in order to build up the two SS divisions.

THE FÜHRER: This proves one thing: if we had attacked in the East[379] there would have been a gap of six weeks in our supply of tanks, which we couldn't have bridged. We would have been unable to catch up.

KEITEL: And what about the 26th [Panzer Division]?

BUHLE: The 26th Panzer Division has about 35 Panzer IIIs at the moment, half of them with 5-cm long guns, the other half with 7.5-cm short guns. In addition, they have three Panzer IVs with short guns. Those are the ones that were left behind. The others were taken away. Plus one makeshift armored vehicle[380] and a dozen flame-thrower tanks. They are lacking the 50 Panzer IVs that were taken away.

WARLIMONT: They are also lacking combat experience. Unlike the 1st Panzer Division, this one hasn't yet seen action.

BUHLE: This is a panzer division that hasn't yet been deployed.

KEITEL: The 24th [Panzer Division] is in even worse shape.

BUHLE: It hardly has anything.

THE FÜHRER: So the 1st Panzer Division is the only one worth considering.

BUHLE: If an operational panzer division is to be moved there, then it has to be the 1st Panzer Division.

KEITEL: What about the 3rd and 29th Motorized [Divisions]?

BUHLE: The 3rd and 29th [Divisions] are not usable—at least not for the time being. The 45 assault guns required for the 29th [Motorized] are on their way, and should arrive in two days. However, they don't yet have enough vehicles.

THE FÜHRER: Does the 1st Panzer Division have enough vehicles?

BUHLE: It's the best in this respect as well, because the 1st [Panzer Division] had been earmarked for action in the past.

THE FÜHRER: So how many panzer divisions will we have in the West, after the 16th and 1st [Panzer divisions] are taken out?

BUHLE: Disregarding the 16th and 1st [Panzer Divisions], we have the following there: the 24th, the 26th, and the 14th [Panzer Divisions], and three panzer grenadier divisions—the 3rd, the 29th and the 60th—plus the two SS divisions.

KEITEL: Then there are the two SS divisions mentioned earlier, plus the three—but they are extremely weak.

THE FÜHRER: ... their assault guns?

(... ?): ... in Brittany.

BUHLE: It will be pulled out this month. These are the first 100 it got.

THE FÜHRER: Two very strong Panther detachments will soon be available in the West.

KEITEL: With the SS Panzer Divisions.

THE FÜHRER: They will have Panthers. These will be delivered in time so that we have a high-class force in the West.

BUHLE: They will be ready in July.

THE FÜHRER: So they can be employed in July. Sepp Dietrich is very prudent and cautious. Before he accepted the tanks, he had his men in the factories for eight weeks to test drive them.

BUHLE: They won't get the tanks before mid-June.

THE FÜHRER: If there's a tough fight, he'll finish earlier. But he is extremely cautious, because he is an old tank hand. He doesn't believe in making promises he can't keep. But if worst comes to worst, they will be available. What is the situation in the West regarding the Tigers? Do we have any Tigers besides the ones made by Porsche?[381]

BUHLE: The first of the other Tigers are being shipped now. The 202nd Tiger Detachment, which was also earmarked for the Eastern front, will get 30.

THE FÜHRER: Will they be shipped to the East or the West?

BUHLE: To the West. That detachment was taken there in place of the 505th [Tiger Detachment], which was pulled out.

THE FÜHRER: It is not intended for the East?

BUHLE: It had been assigned to that operation originally. We discussed it here once, without reaching a final decision.

THE FÜHRER: It must be moved to the East. If I launch the operation in the East[382] I want to have everything ...

BUHLE: We can get 130 [tanks] for the Tiger detachments that were intended for the operation in the south ...

THE FÜHRER: Then we should assign one of the Tiger detachments to Army Group North in the event of a crisis.

BUHLE: The Leningrad [Tiger] Company has always been up with the Army Group North and, in principle, belongs to this detachment, which has just been established in the West but which was designated for the East.

KEITEL: If they are intended for this purpose, the situation is different. In this case only the two SS Panzer divisions would be available as the next reinforcements in the West. With the exception of the assault guns for the 3rd and 29th [Panzer Grenadier Divisions], it would cause considerable delay.

THE FÜHRER: How many Panzer IVs does the *Leibstandarte* [SS Panzer Grenadier Division][383] have?

BUHLE: As you ordered, the SS corps will be provided with another 75 Panzer IVs. I don't know the precise number for the corps, but I assume that the *Leibstandarte* will get at least 25, so it will have a total of 60 Panzer IVs. It will get 14 Tigers, and it currently has 32 assault guns, according to my records.

THE FÜHRER: No, 22.

BUHLE: Yesterday or the day before, 30 assault guns were dispatched to the SS Corps, so they will have those at least.

THE FÜHRER: It should have the required number of assault guns. Then it will have at least 90 to 95 heavy weapons. I don't know yet what the consequences of the disaster in the West will be.[384] I really don't know yet...

WARLIMONT: According to today's report it's not so bad.

THE FÜHRER: The consequences will be felt during the three summer months. If it's a dry year, it will be an outright disaster. But if the Ruhr gets sufficient water, we can manage.

BUHLE: After June the bulk of the tank output will be shipped to the West anyway—at least 120 Panzer IVs will be shipped to the West. Otherwise they never get anything. The maximum we can supply to the East in July will be 100.

THE FÜHRER: And how many assault guns?

BUHLE: Regarding the assault guns, the question of activating assault-gun detachments would have to be taken up with Zeitzler. In my view, it is absolutely impossible to organize three new assault-gun detachments each month until the end of December. We don't have the required number of vehicles.

THE FÜHRER: So let's organize tank destroyer companies.

BUHLE: It is not acceptable that Guderian commands the tank destroyer troops while the other assault gun detachments are commanded by Guderian and the General Staff.[385] Otherwise we would have to give Guderian another 80 assault guns, but require him to integrate them into the tank destroyer detachments of the infantry divisions.

THE FÜHRER: That doesn't make sense; the weapons are useless and we are building units at the same time.

KEITEL: Although the General Staff is opposing it and demanding an end to the build-up. They say that they will get everything that is required.

THE FÜHRER: Well, I will simply make the decision.

KEITEL: They have everything—field kitchens, the whole setup.

BUHLE: The 18th and 20th [Panzer Divisions] will go to the West.

KEITEL: That will delay everything. If only we had gotten them!

BUHLE: One should be moved to the Balkans right now.

KEITEL: If that had happened on May 3—I had arranged for it during my stay at Berchtesgaden—the 18th and 20th would have been pulled out and transferred to the West. The skeleton units were our trump card in the organization of the 15 divisions. In addition, we will get the three skeleton units from the three rudimentary divisions that are still involved in Operation "Zitadelle" [Citadel];[386] these will form the core of the new units. Everything will be postponed accordingly.

THE FÜHRER: That's why I don't believe in activation based on skeleton units, because they are never released. It's a shame. Everyone says it's more practical to rehabilitate them. Of course it's more practical. But it never happens, because no one will release them.[387]

BUHLE: If this doesn't happen, they have to be removed.

KEITEL: They have to be removed. Besides, they are just the rudiments and of no use to him.

BUHLE: The convalescents are all blocked for these core divisions; they're kept at home.

THE FÜHRER: That's why all these so-called ideal plans fail.

KEITEL: Everyone agreed to it completely back then. Everything was clear up to May 3. I was told that I could expect them after June 1, and now it won't be possible. We'll have to raise the matter with him[388] again because these formations are not combat-ready.

THE FÜHRER: But we don't need them now either ...

BUHLE: No, we don't need them until early July. Otherwise the 1st Panzer Division would be the only one. We could reinforce it by adding additional panzer detachments during the next three months.

THE FÜHRER: It has 60 Panzer IVs?

BUHLE: Yes, 60 Panzer IVs.

THE FÜHRER: Does it have assault guns as well?

BUHLE: No. It has 12 flame-thrower tanks and command tanks.

KEITEL: 72 combat vehicles.

BUHLE: The division personnel are being trained on Panthers.

KEITEL: They actually belong to the division.

BUHLE: Yes, the second detachment.

THE FÜHRER: Then they would have to be somewhat reinforced no matter what so that they can be moved there in any case. That way, we'll have a first-class panzer division in the Balkans.

KEITEL: Then we would certainly have the best one available.

BUHLE: As soon as we have replenished the 24th Panzer Division, we will have a first-class panzer division.

THE FÜHRER: The 24th doesn't have a Panther detachment at all?

BUHLE: No, not yet. They only have captured tanks and 14 flame-thrower tanks. None of the new formations have tanks so far, because until May everything was shipped to the East.

KEITEL: But now they will get equipment and be operational very soon. That should happen by June, provided the flow of supplies to the East slows down.

BUHLE: The 16th [Panzer Division] must get at least 50 or 60 Panzer IVs in early June.

THE FÜHRER: Yes, but without a panzer division we can't achieve anything in the Balkans.

BUHLE: The 18th and 25th [Panzer Divisions] have always been featured in the overall planning.

THE FÜHRER: In the event of a crisis, the forces currently deployed there will be useless—and we have to be prepared for a crisis. I can't leave it to chance that nothing will happen. I have to be prepared for the worst case. Just look at today's reports. Pirzio Biroli,[389] or whatever his name is, knew perfectly well where Mihailovic was hiding.

KEITEL: He's known it for months.

THE FÜHRER: We're trying to capture this character because he is in the service of the Entente, but he is aware of it and remains inactive.

KEITEL: Having begun quite well, it still looks as if the operation will be completed in eight to ten days.

WARLIMONT: I think the prospect is favorable, since the division arrived today in Ni...

KEITEL: I was always concerned that the tube would get squeezed out down there.

WARLIMONT: That is one of the main reasons for transferring the panzer division, because there is a shortage of trucks in the Balkans. If the division is there it can also be used for this purpose.

THE FÜHRER: Be that as it may, we need it in any case. I don't think the English will land in the West just now. Should anything happen right away, we still have something there until the Tiger detachment is moved out. It's being established now with 30 Tigers?

BUHLE: Yes, they are working on it.

THE FÜHRER: If we have another two or three weeks, at least the first supplies designated for the two SS divisions will be transferred to the Panther detachments.

KEITEL: But the first Panzer IVs, even in other divisions, may have to stay there

THE FÜHRER: Then this thing will take on a better picture. If we had the 16th Panzer Division brought to Italy, it would be good. I always ask myself a question. We have quite a few tanks in Sicily now. There are 17 Tigers there.

KEITEL: Seventeen Tigers and about 45 modern IVs with long guns.

BUHLE: Six or eight Panzer IIIs.

KEITEL: We have about 70 tanks there; 72 I think, with 17 Tigers that are in Sicily.

THE FÜHRER: How long will it be before the 16th Panzer Division leaves, anyway?

WARLIMONT: The Commander-in-Chief South will have to arrange that. Maybe he'll let the *Hermann Göring* [Parachute Panzer] Division leave first.

THE FÜHRER: Yes, I think it should leave first; the 16th [Panzer Division] should be second.

WARLIMONT: Even if the number of trains is not increased. This means that the 16th will arrive in mid-June at the earliest. If he can increase the number of trains, we could gain ten days.

THE FÜHRER: Today is the 19th. They will need at least ten days to get down there. So the 16th can't start in less than 10 days.

KEITEL: No, I didn't expect so.

THE FÜHRER: The picture will be clearer by then. I would still reconsider whether we can make do in Sicily without any additional troops, and keep the 16th in Italy and move others to Sardinia.[390] This requires careful consideration. Maybe we can get one thing or the other. I'm always afraid of having too much on my plate if I can't be one hundred percent certain that contact can be maintained.

KEITEL: I share your feelings. Down there we're like bees in a bag that someone is closing at the top. We really can't afford such a thing anymore. I am also of the opinion, my Führer, that we must consistently bring the units of the *Hermann Göring* together, so that it will finally be complete again. It is always fragmented: parts of it are deployed in Sicily, parts in Apulia, parts are being shipped, other parts are still in France. They need to be brought together.

THE FÜHRER: So we would at least have a division.

KEITEL: Conrath's[391] entire division staff down there is almost a reinforced division staff, considering the original strength of the division.

THE FÜHRER: How many tanks does it have besides the ones in Sicily that can't be included?

BUHLE: At the moment, the *Hermann Göring* has 48 Panzer IIIs and 20 Panzer IVs, several command vehicles and 22, or rather 20, assault guns, because two are to be transferred to Sardinia. They were sunk, but will be replaced. Ten Panzer IVs are on the way and another ten will arrive before the end of this month.

THE FÜHRER: 40 Panzer IVs, 40 Panzer IIIs and 20 assault guns—so 100 tanks all in all. Under these circumstances, we should prepare the 1st Panzer Division.

KEITEL: Yes, indeed—preparing them for transport to the Balkans.

THE FÜHRER: I'm absolutely convinced that nothing will happen in the West.

WARLIMONT: A pattern is emerging: they destroy supplies first and attack the front only later.

THE FÜHRER: It won't be possible in the West, where the defensive positions have been consolidated and improved. If they plan an attack, they will attack only in Italy and the Balkans, of course. The Balkans are dangerous. We have to take everything into consideration. If something happens in Turkey and we have to pull out forces from the East anyway, I will be left with only one reserve to fall back on there—the Bulgarians.

KEITEL: I have just examined the delivery lists for Bulgaria. No problems, really. We still have to give them tanks.

BUHLE: They will get ten this month. At the moment they have 15 tanks.

KEITEL: A total of 13 have arrived so far.

BUHLE: They will get 10 now and another ten next month, along with five assault guns.

KEITEL: Only 12 Panzer IIs are behind schedule; everything else, including ammunition and weapons, was shipped to Bulgaria. Yet I would suggest, for the third stage of the main shipment, to continue supplying them, because besides the Finns, the Bulgarians—provided they have arms[392]—are the best fighters we have. They were excellent in the Great War. They are brave, a peasant nation. If they get good weapons, we can count on their assistance.

WARLIMONT: If we have a problem in Italy, we would need at least five reliable Bulgarian divisions in the coastal zone, according to our calculations.

THE FÜHRER: It doesn't matter under these conditions, even if we bring in forces from the East. One division on the spot is more useful to me than three that are still on the way.

BUHLE: One was to be moved down there, according to our plans.

KEITEL: This is the most difficult transport route at the moment. No problem up to Salonika—9½ trains leave the city every day, and they have to live down there as well. It is a difficult task. If you have decided to bring one in down there, my Führer—

WARLIMONT: I submitted the order that General Fellgiebel[393] be installed there in the next few days.

BUHLE: I would see that 120 Panzer IVs will be made available in June, half of them for the 16th Panzer Division and half for the West. In addition, the West will get 100 assault guns so that every panzer division will get some.

THE FÜHRER: Yes, you should do that.

End: 3:28 p.m.

* * * * *

MEETING BETWEEN THE FÜHRER
AND SONDERFÜHRER V. NEURATH, MAY 20, 1943[394]

Present:

The Führer	*Ambassador Hewel*
Field Marshal Keitel	*Major General Schmundt*
Field Marshal Rommel	*Colonel Scherff*[397]
General Löhr[395]	*Lieutenant Colonel Langemann*[398]
Lieutenant General Breuer[396]	*Sonderführer v. Neurath*[399]
Lieutenant General Warlimont	*Hauptsturmführer Günsche*

Beginning: 1:19 p.m.

Italy

THE FÜHRER: You were in Sicily?

V. NEURATH: Yes, my Führer. I was there and spoke with Roatta,[400] whom I know very well from a long time ago because he was head of the group of attachés in Rome, where I met him. Among other things, he told me that he is not very optimistic about the possibility of defending Sicily. He claimed he was too weak and the equipment of his forces was inadequate. He complained that he had just one motorized division; all the others were ground troops. Day in, day out, the English attack the locomotives of the trains in Sicily, and he is aware of the fact that obtaining supplies and engine replacements will be very difficult or maybe even impossible now. In addition, when we crossed from Giovanni to Messina, my impression was that almost all traffic had ceased on this short route. Of the ferries that had previously operated there—I believe there were 6 of them—only one has survived. This ferry is "under museum protection," as they called it—they treat it as gently as possible and plan to preserve it for better purposes.

THE FÜHRER: What are "better purposes"?

V. NEURATH: Well, my Führer, the Italians often say, "When the war is over," and they also say "One never knows what the future will bring." At any rate, this ferry wasn't in operation. Maybe there was some technical problem. But the German gentlemen I met there said that there was no such problem. The German forces in Sicily have become relatively unpopular; there is no doubt about that. The situation is easy to explain; the Sicilians claim we brought war to their island, we ate—with more or less appetite— everything they owned, and now we're going to make the English land there as well. But on the whole—I noticed this again and again—the Sicilian peasants are not too sorry about this, because they assume that their suffering will soon be over. It's easy to understand, because the ordinary peasants don't see many other things and take the easiest goal as the next one. The war will be over when the English arrive—this opinion is shared by many people in southern Italy. They also believe that once the English have landed, the war will end sooner if the Germans have left than if they stay on and cause problems.

THE FÜHRER: What is the official Italian response to counter this opinion?

V. NEURATH: The prefects and the other authorities do little about it, as far as I can tell, my Führer. They see and hear it, but always say—I have pointed this out to the gentlemen on several occasions and told them, "If a German soldier is publicly abused in the street as a crook"—something one can frequently hear, particularly in Sicily—"what is done to counter this attitude? Because this is unacceptable in the long run." They answered, "What do you expect us to do? That's public opinion. The people see it that way— and they didn't make themselves popular with the people; they seized things and ate their chickens."—"We are not here as travelers, for our pleasure, but because of the war!" Because of this, a very difficult relationship exists. They answer, "We can't do anything about it. German soldiers insult Italian

soldiers too." In my opinion, more vigorous action should be taken by official authorities, to bring the most striking cases to account.

THE FÜHRER: They won't take vigorous action.

V. NEURATH: It's very difficult. They don't resort to drastic measures.
One reason might be the Sicilian temperament, which differs from the northern Italian one. By and large I can say that it is hard to accept how they let
matters slide. The threat from the air or the air superiority over Sicily is
tremendous; there is no question about that. This is certainly not news to
you. Palermo has been smashed up—large residential areas, including numerous beautiful old buildings, and, in particular, the harbor. The impression I gained in conversation with several gentlemen is that the English have
prepared the harbor in such a way that at least they won't be able to use it
themselves either. In contrast to this, the result of English raids against
Cagliari on Sardinia is said to be different. It was striking, I was told, that the
city and the warehouses were blown up, but all port installations and quays
were relatively well preserved.

THE FÜHRER: That is the report—

WARLIMONT: Admiral Ruge[401] said the same.

V. NEURATH: My Führer, the Italian Crown Prince is the supreme commander of the Italian forces—but I'm not well informed. Is he the supreme
commander of the Italian forces in Sardinia or in Sicily or in Sicily and
southern Italy or only in southern Italy?[402]

THE FÜHRER: When did you arrive?

V. NEURATH: I was in Berlin on Sunday.[403]

THE FÜHRER: And what's happening there?

V. NEURATH: It's striking that he is organizing many inspections and that
General Roatta devotes a lot of time to him and that General Roatta's staff
includes numerous officers—Italian staff officers—who are well-known
Anglophiles. Some of them have English wives or other relationships with
the English.

THE FÜHRER: What have I always said?!

V. NEURATH: Personally, the only thing I can say is that I wouldn't trust
him for a minute.

THE FÜHRER: No!

V. NEURATH: I always thought him very clever.

THE FÜHRER: Clever? He is the Fouché of the Fascist revolution, an
unprincipled spy. He is indeed a spy.[404]

V. NEURATH: He's a born spy—indeed the prototype of a spy. At any rate,
I'm convinced that he is playing a game. The German gentlemen confirmed
my impression; that it was striking how he increasingly used the Crown
Prince, how he tried to create a platform with him that would stand him in

good stead if the English attack on Sicily came. I can't tell whether he is able to do this; I have no knowledge of it, but I think it is safe to say that he is a dangerous gambler.

THE FÜHRER: I share your opinion!

V. NEURATH: There's no doubt that he is the absolute ruler in Sicily. He knows this. He is based in Enna where he has his headquarters. Everyone dances to his tune—I saw plenty of proof—and everyone says that nothing happens without General Roatta's approval.

THE FÜHRER: Did you discuss this matter with Kesselring?

V. NEURATH: I told General von Rintelen,[405] my Führer.

THE FÜHRER: We must be very cautious. Kesselring is a great optimist and we have to make sure that because of his optimism he doesn't miss the hour when optimism is no longer called for and drastic measures are required.[406]

V. NEURATH: The German Luftwaffe is certainly having a very hard time in Sicily at the moment. The air raids are fierce and I imagine the losses at the airstrips will be high. They may not even be able to take off from several of them.

WARLIMONT: Yesterday the situation was just the other way round: ... 27 planes attacked, 7 were shot down, no losses on our side.

THE FÜHRER: There are too few airstrips anyhow.

KEITEL: They are too concentrated.

V. NEURATH: They are indeed concentrated. Even the mood varies in Rome, my Führer. It is very unpleasant; the plutocratic clique, whose way of thinking we know—it toes the British line, of course—and the ordinary people now interpret the measures carried out resolutely by the Duce[407] as the beginning of a more equal sharing of the war burden. But on the other hand, I think it's already a bit late for these measures. I don't believe that it will be possible to stop the black marketeering that has taken hold of the people and spread like cancer. He won't make himself popular with this drive.

THE FÜHRER: How could one stop it in a country where the leading representatives of the armed forces and the state, etc.—where everyone is corrupt? Have you also been in northern Italy?

V. NEURATH: No, my Führer, I just passed through it.

THE FÜHRER: How long did you stay in Rome?

V. NEURATH: I was in Rome for only seven days.

THE FÜHRER: Seven days. What is the attitude of the man on the street toward the Germans?

V. NEURATH: It is such that there are no German soldiers to be seen in the streets. The German soldiers stay in uniform at the forward operations center or at the railroad station. Because of these arrangements, the details of which I don't know, the command centers were moved out of the city, in order to ... the military character of the city—[408]

WARLIMONT: This dates back to the time—

V. NEURATH: No, this is nothing new. I think it was a request by the Vatican. Otherwise the character of Rome is still—

THE FÜHRER: Peaceful?

V. NEURATH: Yes, peaceful; no one can doubt that. Arriving from Africa, the street scene always struck me as if nothing had happened for two years. The reason they give is that they are a poor nation; they don't have clothes and boots for their soldiers and therefore it is better to allow them to go for a walk in the streets.

THE FÜHRER: They should have given us workers; they could have worked at least.

ROMMEL: The plutocrats wouldn't like that. The workers would be "spoiled" by us.

V. NEURATH: Yes, as the Italians see it, the people would be "spoiled" by our progressive social measures.

THE FÜHRER: How many workers are now in Germany? Do you know, Hewel?

HEWEL: There were 230,000;[409] they were to be sent home starting in June.

THE FÜHRER: Starting in June?

HEWEL: I'm not entirely sure of it. I can find out.

THE FÜHRER: You can do that later.

KEITEL: Call Sauckel—he knows the exact figures.

THE FÜHRER: And Roatta himself?—I formed my opinion long ago: from the very beginning, a certain class in that country has consistently sabotaged the war. From the very beginning! Initially in 1939. Because of this sabotage, these people succeeded in preventing Italy from joining the war. That is to say: Italy didn't actually have to join the war. Because if Italy had issued a declaration of solidarity with Germany—as it was bound to do by the agreements—the war would not have started; the British and the French would not have started fighting. What happened was the following: two hours after the decision was made—it was immediately reported to London—that Italy would not take part, England signed the mutual assistance pact with Poland.[410] It hadn't been signed until then. Two hours after the end of this conversation the pact was signed. We saw this later. Every memorandum I sent to the Duce was immediately made known to the English. That is why I only included things I wanted the English to know. That was the best way to inform them without delay.

V. NEURATH: This fact still plays a great role in our dealings with England. The night before yesterday, when I was traveling by rail, the commanders of the submarines stationed in La Spezia said that they have first-class evidence that the battleship (*Ventroy*[411]) had radio communication with Malta from 8 to 10 a.m. every morning. A German counterintelligence officer who investigated it found this out and was then arrested by the Italian authorities for suspected spying when they realized that he had found out their tricks. There is no question about that.

THE FÜHRER: Is a representative of the Navy there? [—] But that isn't necessary. We have to make sure that the submarines in the Aegean Sea—

KEITEL: I've made a note of it already. We will include everything.[412] New ideas and points come up all the time.

THE FÜHRER: The vessels and all the other things, and above all the submarines.

KEITEL: All the auxiliary ships are already included in our notes.

WARLIMONT: On the southern coast of France—

THE FÜHRER: If they're on the southern coast of France, they may stay there, but not in Italian ports—in La Spezia, etc. [—] Günsche, measure the distance between England and Munich on the map and the distance as the crow flies between Munich and Corsica! Roatta is a spy after all!

V. NEURATH: It's no different as far as the *Göring* is concerned. The problem is that we won't get it out of Sicily unless the gentlemen help out.

THE FÜHRER: As I have said already, we must examine whether it makes sense at all to move the *Göring* Division. My view is that this should possibly not be done.[413]

KEITEL: My impression from the start is that it should be kept in southern Italy.

ROMMEL: It won't return. I don't share Field Marshal Kesselring's opinion that it will cross the straits under enemy pressure. Maybe a few individuals will succeed in returning, but not the bulk of the troops and the materiel— they will be lost.

KEITEL: Yes, all that will be lost.[414] My proposal was that parts of the *Göring* Division be moved to southern Italy so that we still have control of the division as such, and don't send any more of the *Hermann Göring* across. [—] Can this ferry be repaired?

V. NEURATH: Field Marshal, that should not be a problem.

THE FÜHRER: There you are!

V. NEURATH: It could even be done without such a ferry.

THE FÜHRER: Well, the point is this: the decisive element is not the ferry, but the will.

V. NEURATH: It's only the characteristic element!

THE FÜHRER: Where there is a will there is a ferry. Out of the 20 or 30 ferries operated by the Italians and by us, 60% of ours were operative and

10% of the Italian ones. They were constantly plagued with problems. Probably it was no different with tanks. I have seen the number of Italian tanks shrink very fast in each operation—after two or three days, there was hardly an Italian tank left. They were all being repaired. I'd say it's a problem of will.

SCHMUNDT: The distance from England to Munich is 1,000 km and 750 km from Corsica to Munich.

THE FÜHRER: Another point—write this down—is the following: the provision of ammunition for our anti-aircraft artillery down there must be carried out in such a way that the supply can be stopped at any time and that we don't have large stores there. There should be just enough!

WARLIMONT: Yes! For the anti-aircraft artillery we give to the Italians?

THE FÜHRER: All the anti-aircraft artillery.

ROMMEL: My Führer, wouldn't it be possible for the Italians to send more troops to Sicily and defend it instead of us?

THE FÜHRER: Everything is possible. The only question is whether they *want* to defend it. If they really want to defend, then anything could be done. What worries me is not the inability—for if one really wants to defend it, there is no doubt that it is possible, and we could bring in troops, too—no, what worries me is these people's lack of *desire*, and we do see this. The Duce can try as hard as he wants, but he is sabotaged. I read Bastianini's[415] speech. It was lazy, full of flimsy excuses—there's no doubt about that. The speech was—I don't know if you've read it—

KEITEL: No, I haven't read it. Just a short notice this morning stating that he had spoken.

THE FÜHRER: I received a dispatch; I have it over there. The tenor of the speech is this: Italy and Germany stand for justice, etc., the others for injustice, and the Italians would not accept an unconditional surrender and so on. Italy rallies around her king and will defend her army and king. When he spoke of the "king," certain senators applauded conspicuously. So there you are!

GÜNSCHE: My Führer, the distance from the northern tip of Corsica to Munich is 600 km and the distance from the southeast of England to Munich is 800 km.

(*Presentation by Ambassador Hewel.*[416])

THE FÜHRER: By way of introduction, Bastianini, the Under Secretary of State, pointed out that— (*Reading aloud.*) "Earlier it was different: 'Mare Nostrum,' ['Our Sea'—the Mediterranean] etc." (*Reading continues.*) "...to the goal." They would have ruled Croatia themselves, and I don't know what all else. They did have the "goal"—it's only the ability that was lacking. "Italy was the first in Europe..." (*Reading continues.*) "...in which we believe." "Divine commandments"! "On the Crimea!"

WARLIMONT: A historical survey.

THE FÜHRER: How many Italian soldiers fought on the Crimea in 1856?

LÖHR: One Italian division was there.

THE FÜHRER: But that took a long time. "This goal…" (*Reading aloud.*) "…to defend. Lively applause by the Senators. Shouts: 'Long live the King.'" "In view of the terrorist methods employed by our enemies…" (*Reading aloud.*) Well, that was a different kind of spirit. "There is no intention to destroy or humiliate France…" (*Reading aloud.*) "…but also to settle all matters that are still pending in her relationship with her conquerors." To say such a thing in public! The French deny having been defeated by the Italians. (*Reading continues.*) All in all a bad speech, a very bad speech. It only confirms my feeling that a crisis may erupt at any moment, in the way that we just discussed. Löhr, you will have to consider your objective and all the problems in this light,[417] namely—

KEITEL: The ideas that you discussed with him yesterday and the text that I showed you yesterday, my Führer, have all been discussed—he's aware of everything.

LÖHR: Yes!

THE FÜHRER: And you as well?

BREUER: Yes, Sir!

THE FÜHRER: We have to be on guard like a spider in its web. Thank God, I have a good nose for such things and can usually anticipate these developments beforehand.

KEITEL: Colonel General Löhr's staff talked again to our men yesterday, to discuss issues that might worry us as far as supplies are concerned. Today they saw the Quartermaster General about the shortage of ammunition, to find out the details. I discussed everything with them. We will then report everything that has been arranged. We have to use the time available now. The unfortunate thing is, as the Colonel General pointed out to me yesterday, that they're still working on improving the railroad, both the line to Salonika and from there to Athens. The work won't be completed before mid-June.

THE FÜHRER: And that would mean the ability to run more frequent trains?

LÖHR: From 15 … an increase from 12 to 18 on the track to Salonika, and from Salonika on [—]

THE FÜHRER: That's not so dangerous.

KEITEL: At the moment, it's even a problem for the railroad construction units, the track-laying units, etc.

THE FÜHRER: Nevertheless, we have to assume this risk now and see the matter through.

KEITEL: By all means! I also asked if we couldn't do something with the people, since we have a labor shortage. In addition, I wanted to take the Labor Service away from the Colonel General. It is supposed to join the Armed Forces on July 1. But since it concerns only one or two detachments, I would like to keep them there until the construction work is completed. I have to make a telephone call so that we can defer their entry into the service, if necessary, and put all our effort toward making the railroad operational, so that we can transport larger volumes.

THE FÜHRER: So far, every difficult situation has eventually resulted in an improvement for us.

KEITEL: I'm not worried about it either. But we have to help him—especially with regard to Crete, Rhodes, and the supplies for the south.

THE FÜHRER: It is extremely critical that we maintain control of the Balkans: copper, bauxite, and chromium.[418] And, above all, we have to make sure that there won't be an endless disaster there if the Italian problem starts.

LÖHR: The difficult thing is the time it will take before the 117th [Infantry] Division can be ready to intervene. It's not there yet, and also … not yet ready.

THE FÜHRER: Maybe we can move the 1st [Panzer Division] down there in the meantime.

LÖHR: If only we had a few tanks there!

THE FÜHRER: The 1st [Panzer] will leave in such a way that they [—]

KEITEL: The combat squadron! This time we fixed it according to the pattern that we also used in the East. [—] And then Colonel General Löhr just needs to be told that regarding the individual instructions for which no one is called to account, he must inform only those who really need to know about them. No one needs to know.

THE FÜHRER: No one needs to know the reasons; all orders that you give are based on your knowledge. Don't tell people more than they need to know to carry out their assignments. That is to say, if somebody asks about occupation, tell him it is not his concern. Every step has to be checked against this requirement. Our motive must always be to be careful, so that in the event of a collapse—which we have to expect—we can step in and help. This must be our leitmotif, right?

LÖHR: Yes, Sir!

THE FÜHRER: It could happen quite differently, of course. [—] Do you have anything else?

KEITEL: This morning the Duce paid a visit to the king and postponed the appointment with Rintelen.

THE FÜHRER: When will he see Rintelen?[419]

WARLIMONT: He promised to let us know as soon as he was allowed in. The last conversation I had with him was at 11:15.

THE FÜHRER: What is the time now?

WARLIMONT: 2 o'clock.

THE FÜHRER: When will Zeitzler arrive?

KEITEL: General Zeitzler will arrive at 3:30.

(*Presentation by Ambassador Hewel.*)

HEWEL: Just some of my ideas.

THE FÜHRER: These two worlds are nothing new. They have always existed, as early as the year ... of his Ethiopian offensive. If I had attacked Italy at that time, it would have collapsed immediately. I pointed it out to him back then, that he didn't ... I told him at the time, "I will never forget this."[420] And we will never forget it. Back then, on the occasion of the reception in Rome[421]—I still remember it—I noticed these two worlds quite acutely: on the one hand the Fascist warmth of the reception, etc., and on the other the chilly atmosphere surrounding the military and courtiers—people who are either insignificant or cowards anyway. In my opinion, all people who have assets of more than 250,000 marks generally become cowards, because they want to live off of their money and sit on their 250,000 marks. They lose all courage. If someone has 1 or 2 million, you can be reassured—those people won't start a revolution or anything else. That is why they oppose all wars, even if their compatriots are starving—they couldn't care less. So much for the ones who wear Russian leather [*Juchtenledernen*]. If everything were divided fairly in such a country—if everyone at least got his ration—even the English would have a certain predisposition to approve the possibility of imperial expansion. But this is not the case. These people live like lords; they can afford—and have—everything. Only the poor devils are doing badly. In Rome I saw how Fascism was. It couldn't prevail against the courtly world. A reception at court—which is a disgusting concept to us, and I would not even speak about it—but also by the Duce, and why? Because the courtly world is closely involved there. The same is true of Ciano.[422] I was to take Countess Edda Ciano to the table. But then suddenly Philip[423] and his Mafalda[424] burst in and the whole plan was wrecked. There was utter confusion, and I was given Mafalda as a dinner partner. How does Mafalda concern me at all? To me, Mafalda is the wife of a German senior president [Oberpräsident]—period. That's it. Besides, her intellectual qualities are not so outstanding that I could say she was captivating—and I'm only referring to the spiritual beauty, not the physical one, mind you. But this incident indicated again what the situation is like: the Quirinal is infiltrated with such scum. The separation was very clear when the Fascists and bodyguards were present. The court officials call them .... To me, the most important question is this: what is the state of the Duce's health?[425] That is critical for a man who has to make such difficult decisions. And secondly, what opportunities does he see for Italy in the event that the Fascist revolution or the royal house fades away? Those are the two problems. Either the royalty takes over from the Fascist revolution—and what opportunities does he see for his people in that case?—Or what does he expect if the royal house itself assumes power? And it is difficult to say. When he was at Klessheim, he made a comment over dinner. Suddenly he said, "My Führer,[426] I don't know; I don't have a successor in the Fascist revolution. A successor as a head of government can be found, but there is no successor to lead the revolution." That is, of course, tragic. His complaint began already in 1941, when we were down in the second headquarters—in the railway viaduct—during the Russian campaign.

KEITEL: Yes, indeed. Down there in Galicia, where the large tunnel was located.

THE FÜHRER: At night we spoke about the Russian commissars, and how it is impossible to have two powers,[427] etc. He became very pensive, and then I ate with him on the train. He suddenly told me, "What you said, Führer, is correct; there must not be two powers in one army. But what can one do, Führer, if one has officers who have … reservations about the regime and the conception of the state?" They say, because they are officers, that they have reservations. When one refers to the conception of the state or the reasons for the state, they say: "We are monarchists; we are subordinate to the king." That's the difference. So that was the problem already in 1941. It was even more acute on October 28, 1940, when I … returned—it was in 1940. He said suddenly, "You see, I trust the soldiers, but I don't trust my generals. I can't trust them at all."[428] This is what he told me on the day when the offensive against Greece or Albania was launched. If the Duce were 15 years younger, this wouldn't be a problem at all, but at age 60, it's a bit more difficult—so the question is, how is his health? But in my view, these two worlds have always existed. The one world wasn't eliminated; it has continued to spin its threads. I see it in all our people from down there. This evening—what's his name—will probably…

KEITEL: Djurisic![429]

THE FÜHRER: He will probably meet with the king today. Maybe it will turn out that this robber chief is a relative of the king.[430] Yes, a middle-class family would find it difficult to marry a daughter off when the father is a sheep thief and imprisoned x number of times. But in courtly life that is no scandal; rather, it's a great honor, and the princes scramble for the princesses. And good old Nikita[431] was nothing more than a rogue who escaped from Austria, practiced one blackmail scheme after the other, and always played Italy off against Austria. The guy even used the World Postal Union [*Weltpostverein*] to commit fraud—he cheated the Austrian state out of 1¾ million crowns. The Kaiser had to pay it from his private coffers.[432] What a scandal! But it's fine for aristocrats to do that.

KEITEL: I have another question, my Führer. Szombathelyi[433] sent me another telegram, requesting 250 submachine guns for the security brigades. I think he should get them.

THE FÜHRER: Immediately!

KEITEL: Initially, the General Staff recommended giving him 100 a month. But that doesn't make sense. I said he should be given the number required for three months—for both divisions at once. I request your approval.

THE FÜHRER: Yes.

KEITEL: My Führer, we have some additional thoughts—which are not fully developed yet—regarding the general instructions on which the deployment of Rommel's army could be based,[434] and the matter concerning Löhr, which I showed you last night. Löhr has been informed about our ideas. He knows, but he won't be given a document to take along.

THE FÜHRER: We have to be extremely careful with documents this time.

KEITEL: I know that that's what you want. Matters are added every day— for example, the submarine issue. (*Presentation.*) This is a general introduction that doesn't mean anything and doesn't commit anyone. But the important part afterward is the command, the forces, and precautionary matters which will have to be considered. Every day additional points are added, such as the submarine issue today, the issue of anti-aircraft artillery, etc. I would like to include more ideas and suggestions. Rommel read it once, so he is familiar with the general idea.

ROMMEL: Yes, indeed. It was presented to me.

KEITEL: He would like to use it as a basis for some other things. It's an intellectual exercise. Plus the orders for relief, bringing in forces, and similar such matters. But there are a few things that we have to do. Someone has to go over to the Commander-in-Chief West to discuss with him how he might be able to move forces to the West, and how he could take over that part of the Mediterranean coast that is now occupied by Italy.[435] The individual items come together gradually; you think of them only when you write them down. That's why we've written everything down now.

THE FÜHRER: Rommel, I assume you agree that it would be best to retain the two parachute divisions?

ROMMEL: Yes, absolutely!

THE FÜHRER: Then you can use the two divisions in coordination with your own operations.

KEITEL: They could be deployed in northern Italy.

ROMMEL: I'm very much concerned, my Führer, that the Italians will suddenly cave in and seal off the border, in particular the Brenner [Pass], because this lot has worked on it for many years, and Gambara[436] and also Navarini[437] have occasionally dropped a hint that they might possibly turn against us. I don't trust these guys. If they change sides, they could, as a sort of gift to the English, actually say, "Let's seal off the border and not allow any Germans in or out." That's why it might be good for these two divisions to stay outside for now.

THE FÜHRER: I can look at it later, on my own.

KEITEL: Yes! It's not yet in the right format, I should say; it still needs to be polished. But we would like to retain the ideas. They have to be written down, or something will get lost. If you'd like, the introduction could be changed or amended, but the bulk of the ideas—

THE FÜHRER: I will read it in my own time.

WARLIMONT: The part concerning the Southeast is down below.

KEITEL: That would be the basis for Rommel's work.[438]

WARLIMONT: If you still need the maps for that—

THE FÜHRER: No, I don't need any.

WARLIMONT: There are excellent maps. Maybe I could send them to you, my Führer.

THE FÜHRER: That might be a good idea.

End: 3:30 p.m.

* * * * *

MIDDAY SITUATION REPORT, MAY 20 OR 21, 1943[439]

(The beginning is missing.)

The East

BODENSCHATZ: This dam is said to be much stronger. We'll have to examine that.[440]

BUHLE: Ours are ...

BODENSCHATZ: These are made of reinforced concrete, and ours are stone.

THE FÜHRER: Zaporozh'e wasn't reinforced concrete, but compressed concrete. So we have to take one thing into consideration: that the torpedo nets ...

ZEITZLER: ... *(Presentation.)*

THE FÜHRER: ... The four-barreled gun?

BUHLE: Three or four.

CHRISTIAN: A four-barreled gun has three.

THE FÜHRER: ... includes something else, namely the 60-cm searchlights.

ZEITZLER: Yes, indeed! ... night fighting took place. That's good. In the South, several movements have been reported, my Führer—also further south. The picture didn't change. There is, of course, the possibility that these maneuvers could mean something more. There was … My Führer, I (sent) someone down here to the (Second) Army (which) … will (check) the precautionary measures against gas attacks, in this sector from here to here, from those companies all the way back to the rear. They had fabulous things here in a gas presentation several days ago. If you ask them to what extent … it is not quite clear. Now I intend to check a division from front to rear. That's one of those with heavy losses. There it would be best to … The … operations up here[441] suddenly made contact with the enemy—this is rather gratifying—all three of them. He's putting up stiff resistance here. In the center, too … and appears to have encircled them somewhat. I was concerned that they would slip through everywhere. I already issued the order concerning the Desna [River] position, to reconnoiter it closely so that we can get an exact map and start our actions. [—] Then I wanted to ask if these movements could be prepared at the General Staff level—only the chiefs—as a lot of work is involved, and that way they won't be completely surprised. I would ask the chief of Army Group Center and two corps commanders to come here. Or should I wait on that?

THE FÜHRER: Yes, wait a bit still!

ZEITZLER: Wait and see what else comes down there.

THE FÜHRER: Yes, I'll let you know as soon as I have a clearer picture of the situation down there.

ZEITZLER: Yes, Sir! A new unit appeared for the first time up here on the main road that otherwise goes to Smolensk. If it's confirmed, it would seem that a group is being formed here after all. It's amazing that he is … pulling troops away from this point … pressure point. But it may be pure coincidence. Nothing is happening further north. [—] Army Group North reports that systematic artillery fire started this morning south of Leningrad, and all connections, headquarters and supply lines are affected; the fire was more systematic than usual. It might be a coincidence, of course—maybe it is a response to our artillery firing on Leningrad. But it may also be … as we mentioned several days ago that something is happening up there.

THE FÜHRER: How many Tigers are there up here?

BUHLE: Six Tigers.

THE FÜHRER: Six Tigers, 12 assault guns and nine tanks …

ZEITZLER: Those are the small ones.

BUHLE: The accompanying tanks.

ZEITZLER: Then there is the decision regarding the construction of the Luga Position [Defense Line]. Where should the focus be—at the front in the Luga Position or on these things? I already told them that they should at least deploy up front in the Luga Position along this road.

THE FÜHRER: There they can use the inhabitants in that area.

ZEITZLER: So that we ... something more ...

THE FÜHRER: I don't see the need to take absolutely only ... people from the front line. In addition, I moved in five engineer construction battalions from the south. They should mainly—I believe the OT [Todt Organization] has about 14,000 men who can be employed. Now we must consider where to use them: in the rear area, ... in the Desna position or somewhere else entirely.

ZEITZLER: And what can be obtained there, so there aren't major transport movements.

THE FÜHRER: Yes, so we avoid major transport movements.

ZEITZLER: We'll use all we can get (for the) Desna position. All the others will be employed up here. Otherwise, there was nothing in particular, my Führer. Sepp Dietrich asked me to pass on his greetings. He sent me a letter: "I regret to report that we have now been put on hold."[442] He had waited for an occasion to launch an attack, but it didn't come, and they were all very disappointed; now they have moved back through ...

THE FÜHRER: ... His mood will improve as soon as he gets his Panthers.

WARLIMONT: (*makes a report to the Führer, which the stenographers cannot understand because of the noise made by removing and folding the situation maps.*)

ZEITZLER: ... also considered, because North, of course ... if I move this over there. But if the major transport movement is driven down at [speed] 60, I can't make a cross-connection. If something bad should start near Army Group North and the northern section of Army Group Center, I would not be able to bring anything else in up there. That's why I didn't want to move those reserves under any circumstances, but take them from these two points instead. That would be the 5th Mountain Division, and the 3rd [Division] is ... It will take quite some time, too, of course, ... and considering the large sectors, I don't really recommend it. I already thought that we could [—]

THE FÜHRER: But it's difficult, and there are many reasons for doing it this way. The other infantry divisions are available; they can be put on trains and taken there. This movement is such that they can simply be transported in large numbers from Khar'kov and Orël. ... Because relieving them always takes a long time.

WARLIMONT: The purpose of their employment takes priority, of course.

The Balkans

THE FÜHRER: What's the situation here?

WARLIMONT: We saw very little of the enemy, my Führer. The bulk of SS Division *Prinz Eugen*[443] has assembled here and is standing by to attack this large Communist group. The forward units of the central and northern groups have reached their final positions in the Piva sector. Three Communist brigades have been reported in this area, so it is possible that the staff is still here where it was before the start of the operation. There was contact with the enemy only by the (118th) Division, which forced its way through the position south of Foca and whose reconnaissance detachment advanced as far as the valley of this stream. The *Taurinense* [Division] [444] continues to pick fights as we hoped it would; it put out feelers toward the east and southeast, apparently—but the Commander-in-Chief Southeast wasn't sure—to ... and to smoke out the Communists who are supposed to be in this sector ... will follow the Bulgarians[445] behind the left wing of the 104th [Infantry] Division in order to take over the right wing of the 1st Mountain Division under the command of this German division. They will relieve the troops there and release this regimental group so that it can advance on Podgorica. There, at 6:30 p.m. this evening, the attack—initially by the *Brandenburg*[446] battalion—began, aimed at the relief of (Biroc). The Italians requested this urgently and were so shaken by the situation that they ... would have extended an almost cordial welcome to the Chief of Staff ...

THE FÜHRER: Maybe the telegram from the Duce contributed to this cordial reception.

WARLIMONT: They even offered to make trucks available to speed up the transportation. The Duce's instructions apparently hadn't been received yet. ...of the conversation was declined. It hasn't happened yet. In addition, they are weakening. After some difficulties, they ... made available the train from Mostar to ... Nicsic, which is extremely important for the supply lines. The Commander-in-Chief Southeast believes that the Mostar airstrip, which they had blocked until recently and, in spite of urgent relief requests, didn't make available to the Luftwaffe ... apparently cleaned out the ration supplies. The population of the region was being fed from these rations until now. The people can't survive without such additional supplies. Employing our services, the Commander-in-Chief Southeast urgently requested Rome to correct this situation and ensure that the people are again fed by the Italians.[447] The overall assessment made by the Commander-in-Chief Southeast is that he will ...engage the Communists ...except for those who slip through on forest trails, and that in a second action—according to Italian plans—an operation against the Četniks could soon be launched, because numerous Četniks got out. The Četniks won't go over to Albania. A Serb would be devoured there. (That is why) they are assembled here on this coastal sector and can be caught relatively easily—

THE FÜHRER: That's true. Everyone says that Albanians and Serbs hate each other—they're mortal enemies.

WARLIMONT: —while the Communists obviously have brought a train down here? control the railway down here. Because of our own movements in the Balkans, the Commander-in-Chief Southeast reported that one regimental group of the 117th Light Infantry Division will arrive at Argos on May 25, and another regimental group at Tripoli on May 27—both places more or less in the center of the Peloponnese. One part will follow there after replenishment is completed in its current assembly area around Thebes. The transportation chief reported that he will require 133 trains for the 1st Panzer Division, because only shortened trains can be used to cross Romania. The movements will start the day after tomorrow. Half of the forces in wheeled vehicles are scheduled to arrive in the Nish area between May 29 and June 6, and the other half in the Sofia area between May 31 and June 11. The forces in tracked vehicles will go to Athens, where they'll arrive between June 1 and 12. According to this schedule, the division won't arrive on the Peloponnese until the end of next month, with the first units arriving in the middle of next month.

THE FÜHRER: ... with tank spearheads leading ...

WARLIMONT: The order has been issued, my Führer: effective ... troops with tanks. [—] Then there is a situation report from Turkey,[448] my Führer; it doesn't indicate any major movements. There have been no shifts. The main focus continues to be eastern Thrace. But it is noteworthy, on the one hand, that the rumors about transports—which we allegedly brought in through Bulgaria and northern Greece—gave rise to Turkish reconnaissance activity, and, on the other, that there are also rumors that 517 armored vehicles have been supplied to Turkey from the beginning of this year through mid-April. That would put Turkey's total number of armored fighting vehicles at about 1,000—of which many are probably obsolete—with about 300 armored patrol cars.

THE FÜHRER: Maybe we could somehow make the Turks understand that ... it is a matter of ... It would be better for us to tell them now, so they don't find it out from the English once they have arrived there.

HEWEL: Yes, indeed!

THE FÜHRER: We could explain briefly that they are earmarked for the Peloponnese, for Greece.

KEITEL: We must ... as far as the time is concerned ...

ZEITZLER: The military attaché can go; then it wouldn't involve the diplomatic circles, if he just informs them.

WARLIMONT: ... movement of the light infantry division created quite a stir. Most of these tanks seem to be assembling in armored units opposite Istanbul. Other build-up is also reported from southern and eastern Anatolia—from eastern Anatolia as well.

Norway

The Commander-in-Chief Norway gives his weekly assessment of the situation, which deals primarily with the Luftwaffe. The daily reports indicate, my Führer, that the English … have stepped up their attacks in the southwestern area. In four days alone, from the 13th to the 16th, ships with a capacity of 24,000 tons were either damaged or sunk. Beaufighters[449] were seen for the first time, whereas previously only Hampdens[450] were used. In contrast, our Luftwaffe sorties have been quite limited, due to lack of fuel, (so that) reconnaissance of coastal approaches have been possible only in particular circumstances—

THE FÜHRER: Why?

CHRISTIAN: I looked into the matter. The general order, which has been misunderstood on several occasions, is to economize on fuel.[451] In places where sorties are imperative, of course, one can't save fuel. On the other hand, it must also be pointed out that the forces … were contained during the last few days by attacks on the Deutsche Bucht [German Bight]. We have to be able to get out there.

WARLIMONT: … reconnaissance only in particular circumstances … convoys near the Lofoten Islands will be covered only if the convoy is especially valuable. … of dive-bomber forces in the North is no longer possible. … tried to put down batteries on Fischer Peninsula … but by five batteries that are located in that area, so that there is a certain level of deployment.

CHRISTIAN: By fighter-bombers.

WARLIMONT: He also reports that the anti-aircraft defense of the industrial operations, following the successful attack on the (Gnaden-Heilbringer) mine,[452] must be considered insufficient. The Luftwaffe pointed out—Fifth Air Fleet, which … to defend emphatically…

THE FÜHRER: I would like to see a map where …

CHRISTIAN: Yes, indeed, my Führer.

WARLIMONT: The first gun of the Tondernaes battery was hit. Here, two new batteries ready for action … (*Map presentation*)

THE FÜHRER: If you look at it like this, of course, it looks wonderful. But I have a different map. I requested a 1:25,000 map; there you have to look through 12 pages before you come across one battery.

BODENSCHATZ: Except at Narvik …

THE FÜHRER: … it looks as if they were all over … That's just mad. (*Presentation.*) It's obviously different from when we first arrived there. If, when they came to Narvik, we had had just a fraction of what we (have there now), they would not have been able to enter. But in those days we didn't have anything there. [—] It looks great, of course. But it's all …

Situation in the air

What about the air situation?

CHRISTIAN: Several nuisance raids across Germany throughout the course of the day; incursions by Mosquitoes, which flew at midday north of Potsdam and Stendal via Hannover ... another Mosquito unit ... Neubrandenburg ... very high speed ..., 500 to 600 km. No attacks. (anti-aircraft fire) but without confirmed effect. Interceptors took off, but couldn't get close enough. Weather conditions: no clouds, good visibility. One Mosquito intruded over the Reich territory into southern Germany, via Colmar and Sigmaringen in the Munich area, and left from the area west of Augsburg ... Colmar. No attacks there either. The main attack was in the Munich area. Interceptors took off, but again couldn't get close enough. (Weather:) No clouds, visibility 10 to 20 km. To the south, another aircraft ... entered ... south of Stettin ... reduced its altitude to 1,500 and then ... again [—]

THE FÜHRER: I heard the following today: when these Mosquitoes fly at an altitude of 7,500 meters, they can't be seen; they are not visible to the naked eye. Today an aircraft expert was babbling about how, at an altitude of 7,500 meters, no plane is visible to the naked eye. And recently somebody told me—but those were fire police there, and their eyes aren't any sharper, because they aren't eagles ...

CHRISTIAN: The aircraft expert ... That is actually a difference ... the weather conditions, my Führer.

THE FÜHRER: In the winter you can see a vapor trail.

CHRISTIAN: In clear weather.

THE FÜHRER: There is a certain report—I've seen this several times—according to which when anti-aircraft gunners are so unsuccessful, they increase the altitude of the planes from one battery to the next—isn't that right? The speed becomes an enormous ... asked, above 7,000 to 8,000 meters a plane can't be seen by the naked eye. They flew at 8,000 meters, and the fire police were able to see them with the naked eye at an altitude of between 2,000 and 4,000 meters. A "miracle"![453] [—] Let's continue. It's not their fault. They also have ...

CHRISTIAN: Yesterday evening, a strong fighter group of 180 to 200 planes intruded slightly over the Dutch-Belgian (coast) ... western France ... Apart from that, nothing in particular from the West. Near Flensburg there are ... five batteries with 8,83/4 4-cm Beaufort and 3-cm and 2 4/5 2-cm.[454] Those batteries didn't fire. [—] These are the heavy batteries.

THE FÜHRER: They didn't fire?

BODENSCHATZ: ...

THE FÜHRER: That doesn't matter. But they didn't fire barrage fire.

BODENSCHATZ: They only fired for two minutes.

THE FÜHRER: No barrage fire.

BODENSCHATZ: ...

THE FÜHRER: (If they) had added barrage fire to that, ... we have 10,000 rounds ... shipyards were reduced to rubble, a submarine and several batteries were destroyed, and the enemy is getting ever more brazen. So if you take the view that, I admit—I'm not so stupid as to not (know) that you can't fire for half an hour at a plane flying at an altitude 6,000 or 7,000 meters, because it passes over so quickly. (But if we had replaced) directed fire with barrage fire,[455] ...

BODENSCHATZ: ... there must be barrage fire.

THE FÜHRER: Let me repeat: during the Great War we had no adequate measuring devices worth mentioning. Anti-aircraft directors were still in their infancy. But it was possible, with these ridiculous batteries, these 7.62 ... very few Russian guns—only a few 88 [mm] batteries—it was indeed possible to protect very important areas by adequate interdiction fire so that they weren't damaged by a single bomb. To be sure, the guns roared constantly. We had a few areas that had to be protected from bombs at any cost.

KEITEL: We never had any bombs land on the Bruges shipyards. We had an outer and an inner artillery defensive zone with barrage fire.

THE FÜHRER: Today I take (the position) ... that all the shipyards ... destroyed ... and then they say triumphantly, "My Führer, we only fired so many rounds."

CHRISTIAN: These batteries still don't understand what they have to do; they should be further out from the object.

THE FÜHRER: If there are only a few, they have to fire all the more!

CHRISTIAN: They can't reach them.

THE FÜHRER: They are too far away from the thing. They are outside anyway. ... there is no excuse. The same thing happened recently in Kiel. (2,800 rounds.) The second time, we saw the same result. Then they didn't return; they dropped all their bombs on the outskirts. The worst is that they gradually ... They don't risk anything. They won't achieve anything, firing at targets like that. With these fast planes, ours are always lagging ... behind anyway. The Navy ... always in front. ... It is generally said that the bursting points from the Navy anti-aircraft artillery are in front, while those of the Luftwaffe anti-aircraft artillery are further back.[456] Is that supposed to be symbolic? I don't know. I would rather have the bursting points in front. ... They should shoot earlier. ... The device checks the measurement and makes new settings ... The Navy bases the orders on observations ... and says: advance by two! This is ... on the device ... one after the other. At that time, I didn't want to spoil Göring's plans. Otherwise I would have had to make a devastating report. Earlier we were at the Schilling roadstead?[457] Then we went to Wustrow[458] and saw that the firing at the Schilling roadstead was about 75% better than the other. … I would also play the one off against the other.

(VOSS?): We were together at school. I studied at the Navy anti-aircraft school for four years.

THE FÜHRER: Then you … fame.

(VOSS?): They always claimed that our anti-aircraft director was behind, and that we would have to improve our technique by letting the men do the work, while the Luftwaffe always said, "No, it's an illusion; humans will make it worse."

THE FÜHRER: … but only through an anti-aircraft director, so that one doesn't know at all where the plane is …

CHRISTIAN: Maybe people with a … capability to understand … since ten years.

THE FÜHRER: The agreement will be implemented because I'll present it to the Reichsmarshal. One can't deny this. … gets a bomb on the roof, he says. They are not responsible, but people watch it … I get messages from everywhere saying that the Navy flak aims the bursting point ahead, and the Luftwaffe flak aims it behind. The other builds up even more steam and heads off even faster.

CHRISTIAN: … Yesterday the fighters have … That was probably because of the barrage fire.

THE FÜHRER: It is almost better if I … ahead than behind.

VOSS: Behind it is absolutely useless.

THE FÜHRER: Also psychologically it makes no difference to him … I imagine it's just the same as if someone were shooting from behind. That is uncomfortable …

CHRISTIAN: The Luftwaffe has … through every possible scientific … one couldn't see that with the naked eye because every shot in the curve—

THE FÜHRER: But it's interesting that other people can see in the third dimension.

CHRISTIAN: Only specialists can do it.

THE FÜHRER: But not all of them are specialists, there where the attacks are made. … constantly attacked. All of them are specialists. Take it from me.

CHRISTIAN: Any shot that falls short was aimed ahead; any one that over-shoots was aimed behind.

THE FÜHRER: No, the specialists—today they have only specialists— …

CHRISTIAN: No, they can't do that either.

THE FÜHRER: The enemy has already complained. … nothing happens except that they plunge down voluntarily.

CHRISTIAN: Thirty-five tactical aircraft and 9 torpedo bombers were deployed in the port of Oran last night and reported this morning.

BODENSCHATZ: Tactical aircraft, small and medium-sized armaments.

CHRISTIAN: Three Ju ...

THE FÜHRER: Four others ...

CHRISTIAN: Attacked, but without success.

THE FÜHRER: The Italians report that they have again torpedoed three 10,000-ton vessels.[459]

CHRISTIAN: This is today's preliminary report: ... airfield ... attacked in seven waves in Italy. Damage to the railway station. Numerous casualties. The two aircraft were destroyed. ... The island of Elba was attacked. No reports on damage. In addition, the airfield was attacked again today ... on Sardinia. Two enemy aircraft were shot down during aerial combat. Two Messerschmitt 322s were shot down by enemy fighters north of Alghero. ... Air Force 6 over Air Command East ... fought near (Rosslavl').

THE FÜHRER: It's called the Sixth Air Fleet now?

CHRISTIAN: As of today.[460]

THE FÜHRER: Good!

CHRISTIAN: ... Fighters struck convoys near Novgorod with low-level attacks—the First Air Fleet. Otherwise nothing near ... Tonight raids with fighter-bombers ... The weather situation is ... for enemy ...

VOSS: ... Should the Grand Admiral be on alert these days?

THE FÜHRER: That might be good.

VOSS: He was planning to go to Brest tomorrow. He will be back at noon on Sunday.

THE FÜHRER: Not before Sunday ...

Miscellaneous

KEITEL: This now is the work of the (Italian) ... about the issue of the North African campaign with the headline ..., written in quite a vivid style, that Field Marshal Rommel has come heavily to the fore, that in particular all those issues that have made our campaign so very difficult [—]

THE FÜHRER: We must be very cautious now. We should wait a few days until I've spoken with the Duce. ...

KEITEL: So it provides a vivid depiction for the German people: what have the troops achieved there? The Italians are not placed in the foreground but they are always mentioned, and mentioned decently, too. But in general it is an epic song about the (German Africa) corps and its general. (We must) acknowledge this, I suppose. ... once again around a ... (record) it that same evening?

THE FÜHRER: We should wait a few days. I would like to speak with the Duce first.

KEITEL: So I'll take it away long enough to ...

THE FÜHRER: Perhaps I can read through it by myself.

KEITEL: But I didn't want to bother you with it today, my Führer.

THE FÜHRER: Then we will take it to them.

KEITEL: The two drafts.[461]

THE FÜHRER: I want to take them with me ... I can hand over ... immediately.

KEITEL: ... everything prepared ...

WARLIMONT: West[462] doesn't know anything yet.

KEITEL: Of course West doesn't know anything yet.

WARLIMONT: Although he has to make his preparations, too, of course.

KEITEL: ... General Zeitzler and the Armed Forces Transport Chief ... during all these preparations ...

THE FÜHRER: ... (Norwegian) government ... This time I will finally rip the collar off these little states, so help me God! This is what I get! The insolence of these little states! The impertinence! ... Also according to current international interpretations, the government is deemed the legal government of a country which actually ... The hour will come ... When will we get any information?

(KEITEL?): (I think I) can report it to you at noon tomorrow.

HEWEL: Perhaps in the night.

KEITEL: ...

THE FÜHRER: I was asked by Prince (Phillip)[463] whether I should not ... the Duce ... in order to receive him there ... and then drive down.

(HEWEL?): ... says: At least for one night to ... Brenner ... half an hour. Then ... again as well. But I believe ... meeting at Brenner, continued at Klessheim.[464]

THE FÜHRER: ... called Klessheim.

HEWEL: But the headquarters. But the minister doesn't believe it will be necessary. The thought is good, of course. ... I will get suggestions.

THE FÜHRER: ... but not speaking. ... It's the old experience, ... He himself can ... in a ... can rest. If he arrives at noon like last time, [—]

HEWEL: 12:45 p.m.

THE FÜHRER: [—] then we should ... by 5 or 5:30 at the latest ...

(HEWEL?): ... I don't know. This evening he is still ... the contents of the telegram ... went down. But whether the Duce ... his ...

KEITEL: ...I will also stay with... my Führer, and Warlimont will come...

WARLIMONT: In the afternoon we will ...

* * * * *

MEETING OF THE FÜHRER WITH FIELD MARSHAL KEITEL AND GENERAL ZEITZLER, JUNE 8, 1943, IN THE BERGHOF[465]

Present:

The Führer
Field Marshal Keitel

General Zeitzler
Lieutenant General Schmundt
Colonel Scherff

Beginning: 9:45 p.m.

Eastern volunteers

KEITEL: From the overall standpoint, I see the issue of the treatment of the prisoners of war, the auxiliary volunteers—HIWISs[466] and the domestic battalions in the East as follows. General Zeitzler can correct me if this is incorrect. Vlasov's[467] whole propaganda, which he has invented himself, provides the basis for the current large-scale propaganda effort being executed under the code name "Silberstreifen."[468] Leaflets encouraging desertion to the enemy have been distributed there. We approved the leaflets back then with Reichsminister Rosenberg or the Minister for the East. They were discussed with him word by word, and he approved and authorized them. The major operation began there in early May, I believe.

ZEITZLER: One part was the decent treatment; that was the focus.[469]

KEITEL: If they come over now, they will be treated especially well. That is the basic Order No. 13, which has been turned into a leaflet.[470]

THE FÜHRER: I saw Leaflet 13.[471]

KEITEL: We have made sure that the deserters are received in special camps and are treated particularly decently.

THE FÜHRER: All this is quite all right.

KEITEL: And that they can report themselves for various options afterwards—firstly as normal workers, secondly as HIWIs, and thirdly perhaps also for the domestic units.

THE FÜHRER: That's not in it.

ZEITZLER: No, not in Leaflet 13.

KEITEL: It is later in the executive instructions. They should be transferred after a certain time. The General of Eastern Troops[472] has announced this, I found out. If they have proven themselves during a certain probationary period, they can request a reassignment and may possibly be approved for a transfer—either to the HIWIs or to the domestic units. This large-scale propaganda effort is based on these leaflets that are signed by the national or Russian national committee. In these leaflets, the decisive thing (and why I have to report it to you once again) is this: in addition to the usual list of things we always say—you will get good food, you will be treated decently, you will get work, you will go back to your country, and, for the future, the German Reich won't maintain the Bolshevik system, won't continue the expropriation of land, etc.—It also says: come over, if you come over you can join the Russian National Liberation Army [*Russiskaia osvoboditel'naia armiia*—ROA]. This in fact is written in the leaflet.

THE FÜHRER: I should have been shown the leaflet earlier.

KEITEL: We must correct it now. It is one of those points that is probably not so influential for these people, but which has at least played a role.

THE FÜHRER: We need not take it dramatically. I see one thing out of all this today, and that is the decisive point for me. We must not allow a wrong opinion to arise on our side. There is a difference between the propaganda that I make over there, and what we do ourselves in the end.

KEITEL: What we do behind our front lines.

THE FÜHRER: And, above all, what we believe. On our side we must not allow the slightest intensification in the belief that we could really, let us say, find a compromise solution in this way—similar to how it is in East Asia with so-called free or nationalist China. There are people among us who imagine something like that, but I should draw attention to the fact that this nationalist China hasn't yet detached a single soldier of a useful type.[473] We had a tragic lesson about this in the Great War—I referred to it recently—with Poland, where this thing got started indirectly by the Polish legionnaires who seemed totally harmless in the beginning.[474] But suddenly it got complicated. We must also be aware of one thing: I've always found that there are only very few people who keep their heads in times of major crisis and who don't give in to their imagination. That saying about the drowning man clinging to a straw is unfortunately too true. It applies not only to the drowning man but to all humans who are exposed to danger. Many people who are exposed to danger no longer see things as they really are. I could refer to documents that I received from Berndt[475] back then when the withdrawal was taking place. All of a sudden people took leave of reality and a vision arose, immediately after the landing of the Americans and English in North Africa. Now our salvation is there; now we must march there. Sheer madness—which I vigorously argued against at the time, but which suddenly obscured people's senses and, I'd like to say, confused calm, clear reason. I see a risk in that alone, if something like this gradually takes root among us. Now there are enough people. There are a great number with Rosenberg. But unfortunately we also have them in the armies. They are former Baltic aristocrats and other Baltic Germans. But they're also former Ukrainians who have settled in Germany—some of them, unfortunately, have even been naturalized—and who, of course, watch the German liberation action with great pleasure. But in the background they don't see our nationally defined goals; they see their own goals instead. It was that way in 1915-16, too. When the great crises began in 1916—Verdun failed in the West, the Battle of the Somme, the Brusilov offensive in the East, Romania attacked us, etc.—at this point everyone lost their senses. There's no doubt about it at all. Unfortunately, the soldiers were included. The only man who turned against it at the time was Bethmann-Hollweg, who always tried to swim against the current but was overridden by military arguments. Later, Ludendorff said, "They told me, too—I got it from military sources but it was incorrect; unfortunately, I was wrongly informed—that I would get 500,000 men."[476] Any thinking man would have said immediately, "You won't get 500,000 men to fight Russia; the Polish will build up an army in order to attack Germany and Austria if the occasion should arise, and to liberate Poland." Because every nation thinks only of itself. All these emigrants and advisers only want to have positions later on.

KEITEL: I may report in this context that when the Polish state stood against us, German officers, such as a commander of a cavalry regiment who had been in the German Army and had fought for four years, went to Poland in order to take over the command of a unit; old Polish nobility.

THE FÜHRER: The danger is the same today. Order No. 13 is totally out of the question. The other things can be done under the condition that not the slightest practical consequences will result—above all, that we avoid spreading a mentality like the one I have unfortunately already found among some gentlemen. Also Kluge has suggested it a few times, "Our job would be significantly easier if we were to build up a Russian army." All I can say on this point is that we will never build up a Russian army; that is a first-class fantasy. Before we do that, it would be much easier to bring the Russians to Germany as workers, because that would be much more decisive. I don't need a Russian army into which a have to install a lot of German corset stays. If I get Russian workers instead, they're of more use to me. Then Germans can be released, and I can re-train the Russians. The most successful production situation for us is the Russian worker who works in Germany—whom we naturally have to supply with rations of a different kind if we give him a top job. Only one thing is decisive—that a mentality doesn't arise suddenly among us. Someday we may not be in a good situation, claiming that now we just need to establish a Ukrainian state and everything will be all right, and then we'll get one million soldiers. We won't get anything—not even one man. That's a figment of the imagination, just as it was in the past. But we would commit mad acts. Above all, we would totally give up our war objective. I told Zeitzler this recently. I had a discussion with Rosenberg and Koch[477] and could establish only one thing; that there are, of course, enormous discrepancies between those two. Rosenberg has his political underworld shop from his own past as an emigrant.[478] Now we were quite sympathetic to these emigrants in 1919-22, because we thought there might be an upheaval in Russia. It turned out that all this was imaginary, too. The emigrants achieved nothing at all. They lived off of us in Germany and were fed by us. I had a dispute with Rosenberg on this issue as early as in 1921. I told him, "Rosenberg, keep one thing in mind—revolutions are made only by people who are inside the country, not by people who are outside." The Ukrainian Hetman [chief] came and introduced himself.[479] Then I said, "Rosenberg, what do you expect of this man?"—"Well, he organizes the revolution." I said, "Then he should be in Russia. Those people who want to create a revolution must be in that country. It's the same as if I were in Switzerland, saying, 'I am organizing a revolution in Germany from Switzerland.' That is downright childish. How do you imagine you can do this?" He said, "Lenin." I said, "Lenin didn't do it—we wrecked Russia and smashed it and brought Lenin into this broken-down Russia; then he was inside. But it really isn't possible to create a revolution from the outside. There the Tsar had been overthrown. First there was the Kerensky revolution. Russia was demolished on the battlefield, then the collapse happened within." I tried to make that clear to Rosenberg. But now he has this shop from that time. There is something more to this. Rosenberg is one of the sharpest thinkers on issues of world outlook. And this dealing with issues of world outlook has kept him from having very much contact with, I must say, ordinary daily affairs. So the issues of world outlook and the daily affairs can't easily be reduced to one common denominator. Now recently the two exponents were with me—the one of world outlook issues and great politics, and the other of ordinary daily affairs, Koch. Koch told Rosenberg straight to his face, "Party Comrade Rosenberg, what you're telling me is in fact very simple, but you must admit one thing. The policy that you want to pursue—that is, building up universities, forming national committees, etc.— I can only pursue after I have given these people a sphere of activity, because if I don't, all the work that you are doing there will just store up revolutionary energy that will be turned against us one day." Then Koch says, "It really is like that; someone comes to me—Backe[480] comes to me, and behind Backe stand the Armed Forces. The Armed Forces don't say, 'Dear Backe, let us negotiate; can you give us our rations or not?' No, the Armed Forces say, 'We demand it.' And at home the German people come and say, 'We demand it.' So Backe comes to me and says, 'You must deliver to me 5.7 million tons of grain.' And nobody cares where I take it from, whether I get it through love or not. Nobody cares what I give the others for it; I don't have anything to give away, I have no compensation, I can't offer anything, I simply have to take it away. Then they say, 'We need so-and-so many tens of thousands of horses and so-and-so many hundred thousand tons of meat and this and that.' Then they just purchase it anyway. [—] I have a similar case in the General Government [Poland], where the gentlemen had to agree with me in the end. Of course, it is quite clear. The gentlemen say, 'There is no economic order in the General Government. How can there be economic order in a country where there are 120 people per square kilometer—the French are not able to feed 80 people per square kilometer; they have a pigsty in their country—and where trash from the Reich is sent in and everything good is taken out?' Everybody says, 'I won't have that; I'll purchase what I need. The four-year plan purchases, the Luftwaffe purchases, the quartermasters' offices of the individual armies purchase, Speer purchases, and everyone outbids the other and thus demolishes the currency because everyone pays more. Why should a Polish farmer deliver anything for 12 Zlotys if he can get 4-5 Reichsmarks for it? We have given the workers their wages that are downright ridiculous. In the factories they get paid in Zloty, and then a worker is supposed to buy something with this couple of Zloty from a farmer who gets ten times the price in Marks, all from German agencies. Every agency says—and roars at you immediately, 'Don't you dare.' What would you do then? Then Frank says, 'After all, I have only 11,000 policemen in a country of about 147,000 square kilometers with a population of 16½ million or so. I need all the policemen to maintain order in Krakow, Warsaw, and these few places. How then could I do it?' These are assignments that can't be solved. [—] Now Koch says, 'Tell me Party Comrade Rosenberg, what should I do? Should I tell Backe, 'I am sorry, Party Comrade Backe, I have to build up a proper, clean Ukrainian state, so I can't give 5.7 million tons of grain; I will give you only 1 or 2 million and that's it, since my job is to build up the state.' So Rosenberg couldn't say anything either. Koch said, "My dear Rosenberg, you live in the Ministry of the East, in the nice world of territory organization. But I live in the hard world of satisfying thousands of requests that come to me. My only ambition is to satisfy these requests. I have been put into this position to do that. And I don't have any other option. How else could I do it?" He said, "I will lose 500,000 Jews here. I have to take them away[481] because the Jews are the element of unrest." But in his area the Jews have in fact been all the craftsmen. You want to establish universities and secondary schools now, so that we can build up the Ukrainian national state that will fight Russia someday. I'm not even in the position to cobble the boots of the worker who has to work here. I can't do it because no craftsmen are here any longer. All the Jews have gone. Which is more important: that I train the Ukrainian to cobble boots, or that I send him to the university so that you can build up the Ukrainian state? [—] Therein, of course, lies the enormous risk: that we too easily—enthused by the emigrants who naturally consider that their life task—lose contact with the ground under our feet, and that this slides on, gradually allowing people who don't have this political knowledge yet, and who don't know how things really are outside, to gain power suddenly. I have experienced one thing." Koch was also criticized for, among other things, allowing partisans to appear in his area. Koch said, "How dare you reproach me! Show me the army area where no partisans have appeared! What police units do I have? Give me enough police and I will remove the partisans. Take the troops away from one army area and you will see whether partisans are there or not. I don't have partisans in the fertile area, but in the northern area where there have always been bands anyway. The Army also has to take action against the partisans in the rear army area 50 km behind the front. I'm hundreds of kilometers behind the front, and I have no men. How should I do this? [—] All this is just building castles in the air—not to mention the fact that we can't even establish objectives for the future. I can't pursue any future objectives that might build up independent, autonomous states here. Because it starts out as a so-called affiliated state like Poland and ends up as an independent state. That is quite clear. End of story." So we have to take hold of things in such a way as to prevent mistaken opinions from emerging. As General Zeitzler already said, it might be important for me to explain my interpretations to the key officers, particularly the generals and field marshals.

KEITEL: Lammers is going to take down your opinions in a short memorandum. He already spoke to me about it, and I urged him to do it, as we have a difficult time making it clear to our generals. I can say that openly. I know it from Küchler and Kluge themselves. They see the setup and arming of the so-called domestic units as a release from the unrest in the rear army area.

THE FÜHRER: Now Zeitzler says one thing. There are, of course, no doubt certain units that could be immediately removed today, because they have to be replaced by something else.

ZEITZLER: Altogether we have 78 battalions, 1 regiment and 122 companies.[482] That is all. 47 of the 76 battalions are with the Field Marshal[483] in the "Eastland" [province of the Reich], the Ukraine and at the [BdE]. So there aren't very many ahead, and the ones that are ahead are all broken down. Then there is also a category with 60,000 men. They are some kind of guards. They are grouped together for the minor actions.

THE FÜHRER: That is necessary. We can't do without such things.

ZEITZLER: And the HIWIs are about 220,000 men. They are in with the troops, serving at a level of up to about Cannoneer Four, Five. They can't be removed.

KEITEL: I don't see any political or propaganda questions—or any other issues—with the HIWIs. The matter is more dangerous in the domestic units because they are combined in larger units there.

ZEITZLER: It's only a single regiment. All the others are only battalions. That's not really dangerous.

THE FÜHRER: The critical thing in my opinion is not the existence of these troops. The critical thing is that we must not deceive ourselves about the extent of what can be expected, or about what we can anticipate in return—that we don't adopt a mindset that one day allows the military men to come again like they did in 1916 and say, "Now politics must do something here: a Ukrainian state—" as in those days a Polish state was established. Later, Ludendorff had to go and say, "If only I had been informed about that earlier! My experts, my specialists, told me I'd get 500,000 to 700,000 men, and that was the reason." Ludendorff was held responsible for the foundation of the Polish state. He couldn't get rid of that or shake it off. But he talked his way out, and said, "I did it during the crisis because I was told I would get soldiers."

KEITEL: Then I would say that we should regard the author of these propaganda leaflets—the National Committee, signed by Vlasov—to be merely a propaganda instrument.

ZEITZLER: We have to draw a bold line. What goes to the enemy—there we can do anything; what remains inside—that is something else. There has to be a line between the two.

KEITEL: I explicitly asked Rosenberg this question again. I asked, "What do you intend to do with the National Committees?[484] Because we intend to exploit them for propaganda purposes, such as this deserter action. His answer was to join together these HIWIs—he calls them that—and members of the Russian, Ukrainian, Caucasian, Tatar, and other combat units—that's what he calls them—under the name "Russian Ukrainian Liberation Army," and also to exploit this measure for propaganda purposes, to which I agree. So it is in fact not only the propagandistic exploitation but also the joining together. And that is what the Führer doesn't want.

ZEITZLER: And we aren't doing that. At most we need to find something on the left of the line to give as a reward to the people who serve with us—to keep them with us—and that means something of positive value, whether it be money or a promise that they will get something afterwards. Joining these groups together is completely wrong, in my opinion, especially in divisions. Battalions are still workable because you can keep them in check. But it should never go beyond that—with the exception of the Cossack Division. That one is said to be quite good.[485]

THE FÜHRER: I would say that if we're successful in the Caucasus, we should be able to get some units, certainly not among the Georgians, but among the smaller Turkish peoples.

KEITEL: We exempt them because they are the most furious enemies of Bolshevism. They are beyond any discussion. Those are the Turkish legions. They are only domestic units. Let me point out again what we said last year, in early September: the domestic units that are especially experienced in fighting [partisan] bands—those are the companies—

THE FÜHRER: They were already there before.

KEITEL: —can continue to exist and even be expanded, as long as they are made up of absolutely reliable and willing elements that join together voluntarily. That's what we said then.

THE FÜHRER: Expanding is dangerous.

ZEITZLER: It was too much in the end.

THE FÜHRER: But now, of course, this expansion must be discouraged somehow. Because there is no limit to this expansion. One may understand it this way, and another may see it completely differently.

KEITEL: The General of Eastern Troops is also in favor of expanding.

ZEITZLER: No, I'll keep a tight rein on him. They should never expand beyond battalions.

KEITEL: In addition, it remains strictly forbidden to involve them in front-line combat or to use emigrants or former leaders of the intelligentsia. This was explicitly stated at the time. Such people must not get in. And we took them out, too. I myself took part in an action with Army Group Center. There, emigrants who had started out as interpreters had reached leading positions, but we threw them out.

SCHMUNDT: It is not quite true that Colonel General Lindemann[486] is extremely eager to form units. Instead, he says, "We have to distinguish between the propaganda directed toward the enemy—where it doesn't matter at all—and what happens in the rear army area." He says it's like this there, "We have now managed to get our soldiers free for the front line, due to the fact that I have 47,000 auxiliary volunteers in my army section alone, who, for example, build all the railways for me. They did this, this time, for food and shelter, so they had a living.

KEITEL: HIWIs or domestic units?

SCHMUNDT: HIWIs. But they are people who do it without supervision and without police—voluntarily for themselves—and the partisan war has died off. So far they've done it in exchange for bread and food, etc. Now Vlasov has come and is walking around like a preacher, preaching national liberation in the villages and to the HIWIs and the troops.

KEITEL: I've already forbidden that.

SCHMUNDT: Now, Colonel General Lindemann doesn't say, as the Field Marshal believes, something like, "We want to build up significantly." Instead, he says, "I draw your attention to the risk. People are already asking how Germany will reward us. Now he has gotten them all excited about freedom. No doubt he fought the partisan war even more. But the counter-question is asked, and Lindemann says that the moment has now come, that we either make a concession to Vlasov, even if we don't intend to keep it, and say, "You will get this and this for it—or we turn away from this thing significantly." Otherwise it could come back to haunt us, as people will become dissatisfied and will suddenly stop helping with the railways and start sabotaging them instead.

THE FÜHRER: I don't need General Vlasov in our rear area at all.

SCHMUNDT: But that is what he does.[487]

THE FÜHRER: It must be stopped. I only need him out ahead.

SCHMUNDT: The army leaders want to make this decision.

KEITEL: It has been made.

THE FÜHRER: Zeitzler, we have a clear position. We don't need that Vlasov behind the front lines. He can only have an effect on the other side.

ZEITZLER: Only on the other side, with his name and those pictures.

KEITEL: I'd like to ask the question which is urgently posed by Army Group North to the General Staff. They are asking to integrate Estonians, Latvians and Lithuanians as volunteers—as German soldiers—into the German units in order to make up for shortages.

THE FÜHRER: It can't generally be done that way.

ZEITZLER: There is the Latvian SS Brigade, too.

THE FÜHRER: Those are individual units. But for the majority one can't do it.

KEITEL: Integrated into the Army. They are not supposed to be grouped in special volunteer units on the basis of the compulsory labor law, but to be integrated with the German troops to fill existing shortages.

THE FÜHRER: Under no circumstances. In the end, it would mean that I made those units totally uncertain. It would be quite another thing if I went and made up a legion out of these people. It would have to be carefully selected, and drilled, too.

KEITEL: That is being done as well.

THE FÜHRER: But if you just put those people in with the normal troops, you never know what kind of poison they might bring in with them. One can't do this without careful consideration.

ZEITZLER: It is only in this one Niedermayer[488] Division where I had proposed to do it, in a ratio of 1:1. It is astonishing. Now the Russian soldiers are actually training our people on how to dig in and use the terrain. They have a way of digging in and lying down that it is just astonishing.

KEITEL: That is the Niedermayer Division that has Turkish people. It's number is 162.[489]

THE FÜHRER: Where is it actually?

ZEITZLER: It is in the [General] Government. It seemed insecure to me as well, although Niedermayer wanted to have it that way. Then I proposed 1:1 and now it is being restructured.

THE FÜHRER: One thing is very clear: We used those units seriously in only a few places, and they didn't cope with significant challenges there.

ZEITZLER: No, not significant ones. In one of the appraisals that I brought along, it also states that even though they have been there for a year and a half, they are not always reliable up to the end.

THE FÜHRER: One can't depend on that. So I must say again that where propaganda is concerned, we can do whatever we want over there. We can do anything. But on our side, we must be clear. It must not slip into a reappearance of what we had in 1916. That must not happen. Above all, one thing must not happen. We must not deliver those units to a third party who gets them and says, "Today you take part, tomorrow you don't." Then one day we will get something like a rallying cry for a strike. It will run along the whole front line, and then they are organized and can start blackmailing us.

KEITEL: To that I can only report that Vlasov has been removed from his position. He's not on the front any longer. He's been prohibited from engaging in his own propaganda activities and from doing any propaganda activities at all at the front.[490] There was just the one decision to be made, whether we let the call go out over there regarding the so-called Liberation Army.[491]

THE FÜHRER: Yes, anything can be done over there.

KEITEL: I didn't consider it dangerous because we are the army liberating them from Bolshevism.

THE FÜHRER: Nevertheless, I'm not convinced that the call of the Liberation Army is effective over there, because people don't want to fight; they don't want to be bothered.

ZEITZLER: I put the focus on the pictures, and how the situation is in the deserter camps. We'll get further that way than with political issues.

KEITEL: Now—the use of people from the deserter camps.

THE FÜHRER: I believe we should move them out and employ them in Germany. They are prisoners of war. If I could give 30, 40, or 50 thousand men to the coal commissioner![492] But we really must treat them decently.

ZEITZLER: I have established as a goal, out of ...[493] to make decent workers in Germany. At the front, not too much can be achieved with the deserters. I can use a few as HIWIs if there are shortages, but the majority of them should go to Germany as workers, to free the German people.

THE FÜHRER: I can only say that if we can't regulate our coal issue, the moment will come when I can't make any ammunition or any explosives anymore, when we can't continue to build submarines. It will affect hundreds of areas. It is ridiculous. But the moment will come. Even now it is tragic when the Italians come and ask why we don't deliver that. I must deliver it to them. But we can't because we don't have enough coal. This is, of course, carelessness.

KEITEL: So I will inform Minister Rosenberg that, according to your decision, we don't intend these things to have any practical effect behind our front lines, we will continue to use these means to carry out propaganda efforts aimed at the enemy, and we won't allow Mr. Vlasov to act in the Russian area any longer. If he wants to go across,——

THE FÜHRER: We don't have this with the others either. We would never permit, for example, the young son of the ... [494] to carry out propaganda efforts in Germany. After all, we don't give these things to the Channel Islands—we aim our propaganda efforts at our enemies. I am sure that the Russians, if they were in our position, would aim propaganda at us. We have to avoid raising false hopes on our side.

KEITEL: But it's really true. The generals, especially Kluge—I know it from him personally, and I have talked with him extensively about it—would see it as a relief.[495]

ZEITZLER: The clear message from above is what's missing. It must be stated point-blank from the top.

KEITEL: Now I'd like to express a request regarding an issue that's being processed right now. After establishing the regulations for the HIWIs, the question is now also arising in relation to the domestic units—regarding their composition, training, and such. It would be good if we were able to obtain this beforehand and show it to the Führer. It is still being processed in your organization department.

THE FÜHRER: Perhaps with the aid of today's shorthand report—since I have outlined my ideas today—Lammers can take a look at it and use that as the basis for this thing. We could do something more as well. We can see where the situation is heading. It might also be possible to gather some of our senior commanders together again so I can tell them personally.

SCHMUNDT: That would be wonderful.

KEITEL: That would be very good. I've seen a bit of self-deception. They hope for some relief and don't know what kind of flea they're putting into their bed.

SCHMUNDT: We could also tell them one day what you, my Führer, told the allies in Klessheim—a section of it.[496]

* * * * *

July 25-26, 1943

In the East, the spring peace brought by the muddy period ended on July 5, and two German armies prepared for the "Zitadelle" [Citadel] offensive against Kursk. Although they initially managed to drive some dents into the Soviet front line, the Germans had to discontinue their offensive after only one week in view of the strength of the enemy's reserves and the Russian attack against Orel that had started on July 11. Here in the North, the Red Army managed to achieve a 50-km-deep penetration and advanced to the city from the east. The Orel salient could no longer be held and would be evacuated as of July 31.

On July 17, the Russians also started attacking in the South between Izium and Taganrog—clearly with the intent to tie up German forces. They succeeded in forming bridgeheads on the Donets [River] southeast of Izium and on the Mius [River] north of Kuibyshev.

The developments in Italy also contributed to the termination of the "Zitadelle" offensive. There, the Anglo-Americans landed in southeastern Sicily on July 10. The Italian coastal units, as expected, surrendered practically without a fight or fled. The Americans collected the remaining Italian coastal divisions in the vast western part of the island. The English, however, have not succeeded in pushing ahead to Messina. A recently reinforced defense force—mainly consisting of German troops—forming a semi-circle around Etna, is holding the San Stefano-Nicosia-Agira-Catania line. However, dissatisfaction and war weariness are growing and spreading in Italy. On July 24, the Great Fascist Council gathered at 5 p.m. in the Palazzo Venezia, and the meeting lasted until early the next morning.
(*Maps 1, 4, and 7*)

* * * * *

MIDDAY SITUATION REPORT, JULY 25, 1943[497]

The East

ZEITZLER: The sign is actually a heavier attack, which started today near Trosna after stronger artillery preparation. Trosna is the western corner of the "Zitadelle"—the Center.[498] So far, the attacks have been driven back. There, the 4th Panzer Division was deployed. Apart from that, there's nothing particularly unusual on the other fronts. The North is also quiet today; he is apparently reorganizing there. Our counterattack has gained some ground. [—] My Führer! The counterattacks have been quite successful so far, and this corner is already cleared again. The reason it is going so well is that a German group that was between the Romanians—a motorcycle company—has held this height, even though they were cut off in the rear. That's why the counterattack went so well, because he could be supported by this. [—] It has also been going well here. [—] Here there was some artillery fire and a little thrust today. They wanted to move part of the 125th [Infantry] Division here as a precaution, but they probably won't need to deploy them.

THE FÜHRER: We will see. [—] Is that in order there?

ZEITZLER: So far it has been OK. This little thing here, where he was inside, is OK. Down here, my Führer, there were only scattered attacks on both fronts, again up to the 23rd … It looks as if reinforcements are coming nearer. An air force build-up has been reported—it's as if there's a stronger air force presence down there, while in return the force which was here went up to Rossosh. There is an advance party where the flag—this red flag—is entered on the map, where the blue radio signs are marked. They radioed that barracks should be made available for the air force officers. So it could be possible that this staff will go there. We can't say yet what conclusions should be drawn from that. It may be that he wants to go further around this corner. [—] Here are the captured materiel figures for the 16th Panzer Grenadier Division and here are the figures for the Sixth Army from the 17th to the 22nd. (*Presentations.*)

THE FÜHRER: 482 tanks!

ZEITZLER: Yes, he did in fact experience a huge loss here. The 16th Panzer Grenadier Division was primarily responsible for that. I would like to propose that we mention this in the Armed Forces Report.[499] I have already reported the numbers. Along this front, my Führer, large-scale regrouping actions have taken place in the rear area, as well as attacks by battalions and regiments, including a few individual tanks; they have been driven back. The movement down there is taking place as scheduled. It has been especially hard up at the corner again. There he attacked the 168th [Infantry Division] again. But now the 168th has taken back this hill in a counterattack. Then he boxed against the 106th [Infantry Division] here. [—] These two pressure points are still there, but under control.

THE FÜHRER: So they want to move back now?

ZEITZLER: Free until the 25th. [—] I brought along one more report, my Führer: The Condition of Forces in the Army Detachment Kempf.[500] (*Presentation.*) [—] That is clear, of course. They have been in there for a long time. It will be the same for those in the Center. Here is the report about the 16th [Panzer Grenadier Division] [—] These individual things are also quite interesting; those relating to the North and upward are on the same page. (*Presentation.*)

THE FÜHRER: Two T 34s [destroyed] by 3.7-cm antitank guns?

ZEITZLER: There must be something going on, because some of these tanks are not quite right anymore. This is cast steel, isn't it?[501]

THE FÜHRER: They must be getting worse—the steel is getting worse. If the front were shifted here, wouldn't this be a good obstacle in itself? The Donets [River] is it?

ZEITZLER: So far it has been. Now we wonder how things will continue when it starts to dry out. I'll find the position maps and see how it is in this respect.

THE FÜHRER: In a few weeks the dry period will be finished anyway, and then rain will start again.

ZEITZLER: I'll take a closer look at the position maps, and see what comes of it.

THE FÜHRER: Here around Khar'kov something has been built. Perhaps one could ... the papers ... 27 km they have built around here, primarily a tank trench.

ZEITZLER: Yes, after the battle back then.

THE FÜHRER: After the battle, with 6, 7, or 8,000 inhabitants.

KEITEL: That was the winter position of 1941-42.

THE FÜHRER: That was the winter position.

KEITEL: In front of this forest area!

THE FÜHRER: Perhaps it is still good today?

ZEITZLER: Let's see how it looks, and what's in it. In the rear area, we can build a blocking position; that won't hurt anything—there are enough civilians in Khar'kov.

THE FÜHRER: Hopefully not buried alive!

ZEITZLER: There was nothing in particular down here in [Army Group] Center's area. The 7th Panzer [Division] has now moved in to there. Here, my Führer, this large attack started today after prolonged artillery fire, in a sector of about 8 km, heavily concentrated. So far everything has been driven back. Along this front he has only pushed back during position recovery. Here, relatively little happened, except for the tank attack up here, which was north of the Lübbe[502] Group. Then he attacked near Bolkhov again, in regimental strength, supported by tanks.

THE FÜHRER: We must take care that nothing happens here!

ZEITZLER: He[503] wants to bring everything in here again. That's why I've given the order that he ... for this afternoon ... he has put them under the command of General Harpe.[504] This shows that he suddenly ...

THE FÜHRER: That is impossible! I categorically forbid that!

ZEITZLER: The SS [Panzer] Corps is the same—it is the whole thing that we need. He can go ahead here, in order to——

THE FÜHRER: … He may press ahead once here, in order to clear the way, but not here! The crisis here will be avoided by his going back here.

ZEITZLER: By his going back. I have the feeling that he will want to do that in order to force us to draw the 7th Panzer [Division][505] up.

THE FÜHRER: This is nonsense; that won't happen!

ZEITZLER: That's why I wanted to have it in writing.

THE FÜHRER: They have already destroyed the *Grossdeutschland* [Panzer Grenadier Division] this way once, near Rzhev.

ZEITZLER: He must have that as a last reserve, in case something happens.

THE FÜHRER: I remember the attack east of Rzhev, which was totally useless—totally ridiculous, with 2,700 casualties—total destruction of the entire division. Absolutely ridiculous!

ZEITZLER: It was distributed over 10 places at the time. Once I added up the figures of the enemy: 13 rifle divisions, 7 [rifle] brigades, 13 tank brigades, and up there 28 rifle divisions and 17 tank brigades. So he has critical points on the wings and especially up there. [—] Here there was a bit more traffic in the last few days. We can't conclude much from it yet, but it may be quite possible.

THE FÜHRER: There's the great risk that he could regroup.

ZEITZLER: That's why he must have *Grossdeutschland* for things like this. Here's his second line with the withdrawal. He has just now been telephoned; he probably wants to take an intermediate line today. Then, my Führer, I have sent staff to Orel with army patrols; they will survey all trains to see if anything is going out there. This could be possible very easily. Only vital things get in there.[506] [—] Regarding this line behind the salient, I have a report here from the General of the Infantry whom I sent there. (*Presentation.*) Now this Lieutenant General Dollmann[507] is coming in.

THE FÜHRER: I have read an evaluation of the fortress divisions,[508] Zeitzler, [they are in a] miserable state. I wonder if we shouldn't possibly—if we operate at all—go ahead, and in a pure fortress battle, if such a possibility arises—that means not when he comes at us with good assault divisions, but instead breaks through from the sides …

ZEITZLER: That's why I am generally in favor of it, too. Under no circumstances should … my feeling is that he has thrown way too many forces in here. He wants to throw everything in there. Today he wanted to make a written request again, asking to throw the 7th Panzer [Division] in.

THE FÜHRER: Absolutely impossible!

ZEITZLER: That's my opinion, too. We can't do that—throw something in here. He has a completely free hand if he wants to clear something. He'll be allowed to do it. On that basis he can draw something out. Now he came with the request today. He wants to place the 113th [Infantry Division]—which is arriving there now—in here, in order to free up 2 divisions in this area. This request has the advantage that if the 113th is deployed up there, he will cry every day that he wants it in down here. To put it in down here would be wrong. It is arriving from the West, it has a very good foundation, and it will be picked to pieces very soon. Basically, the only correct thing would be to move it into a position somewhere. Then we get two other divisions free. That is better than leaving it lying around.

JODL: But with the strength it has when it comes, it can replace two divisions of Army Group North, for example the 5th Mountain Division.

KEITEL: It's filled up one hundred percent.

THE FÜHRER: So, if it replaces the 5th? Useless!

ZEITZLER: My Führer! We must admit that he needs some reinforcement here, behind the Orel bend, because that's a difficult place to reach in time. But if a crisis occurs here—and I would tend to believe that it might start here—it would be good if we made it available for replacement, and kept one of the two divisions, the second, perhaps, in Smolensk.

THE FÜHRER: If he had built here instead of always talking and giving explanations![509] If he had built this here at least, we could take one or two divisions in here, pull the other gradually back, and keep a defensive position in this form here initially—which protects only this thing here, relying on the all-around defense here. That would be the simplest way. That is this position, and they can entrench immediately in the position.

ZEITZLER: Tonight I'll probably be able to submit a plan regarding his intentions on this matter. We haven't yet determined that, but we must finally have it. [—] Otherwise, there were only a few individual thrusts on this front.

KEITEL: If one sends the division there, its strength will drop within 4 or 5 days.

ZEITZLER: It's a pity for the nice division!

THE FÜHRER: If nowhere else, I would lead it straight in here and use it immediately for the construction of fortifications.

KEITEL: Then he will take parts of it later!

THE FÜHRER: Then we will just have to interfere. That shouldn't happen at all; the division ought to—

ZEITZLER: The situation, my Führer, is like this, if it is awfully urgent later, we might be forced to do it. Therefore, I think that the loss of 2 days, my Führer—if we relieve the division for 2 days—is not so bad. This loss, I think, can be recovered. The decision doesn't need to be made before evening, as they won't arrive until tomorrow. [—] South of the Il'men' Sea, nothing in particular. [—] In the area of Army Group North, relatively little happened today; here some smaller attacks. This breakthrough has been considerably narrowed. Here at this penetration, attacks started again today, and we counterattacked. Here the 28th Light Infantry is arriving in now.

THE FÜHRER: Nevertheless, I have the feeling that this has enlarged considerably.

ZEITZLER: Yes, it may perhaps be true that he is regrouping again and will strike once more. But he does have many casualties. Probably this is because they shot a lot of ammunition up here, and also because the sections here are quite reasonable. He can come there as often as he wants.

THE FÜHRER: He probably lost a lot of people here, too.

ZEITZLER: I agree. The losses must have been very high.

THE FÜHRER: You can see it in the pictures down below. The part that is the fortress division is quite disastrous. The other things, of course, he has built up. But once these pumped up units have been in combat for 14 days, no one can claim that only ours are becoming weaker, because his will keep shrinking as well. They are also human beings, of course, ...

ZEITZLER: If we could do it, we should go in with one or two divisions.

THE FÜHRER: The other map again! [—] This I thought in the South—whether it is correct, if we do anything at all—to use it here. This is the question mark. I don't know whether it might not be better instead to just divide something. Then we would use the SS [Panzer] Corps for a counterattack further north or further south in order to break through suddenly and come in from behind. The best, of course, would be that he attacks, a crisis comes, and we hold this firmly together until we have the feeling that he is at his limit, and then we strike his flanks.[510]

ZEITZLER: Yes, indeed. I'll discuss it with Manstein, my Führer.

THE FÜHRER: Here, one must screen. Kluge must not delude himself. He must move units out; that is perfectly clear. He has the shortest positions—it is ridiculous. He can't claim that the situation in his area is the worst. That's no procedure, if everyone tries to deceive everyone else.[511] That's not acceptable. Anyone can see that this here can't be held by one division in such an important area. If another division comes in, it is not much. We have to be clear about that. That is not much. Two are also not much. But only one division—that is almost 50 km—that's ridiculous.

ZEITZLER: The army group can't do it any other way. That's not a mistake by the army group—there's just no other way.

THE FÜHRER: There is no other way; he needs a number of divisions. They must come in anyhow—there's no way around it. Kluge may stand on his head but he will have to give in. That is ridiculous. One can't assume responsibility for that in the long run, that here are sections of only 18 km and behind them reserves—

ZEITZLER: Only 16 km on average!

THE FÜHRER: —while other divisions have 45 or 35 km or at most[512] 25 km, and no reserves behind. That is totally impossible.

ZEITZLER: So he can take that back?

THE FÜHRER: As far as *Grossdeutschland* [Panzer Grenadier Division] is concerned, we have to keep them back until the utmost ... Have the additional assault guns arrived at the 16th [Panzer Grenadier Division]?

ZEITZLER: At the 16th down there? [—] They have been there for a long time. They have already taken part.

THE FÜHRER: Those are the ones that have shot now?

ZEITZLER: Yes, indeed—they have shot now. [—] The ones for the 18th Panzer Grenadier Division are still on the train.

Sicily

JODL: In contradiction to yesterday's message, the enemy could advance only very slowly along the coastal road because of the mines and other barriers laid by the troops. The withdrawal of the enemy here in the middle was only temporary—obviously due to our artillery fire—whereas he really withdrew here further. But here it has been mined and wired, so we don't expect a continuation of the attacks, at least not on the ground. Part of the Aulig Group[513] is here in front and will go back to this covering position, then finally move into this main position, where both of the Italian divisions are located and have been organized for defense. Meanwhile, the 2nd Regiment of the 29th Panzer Grenadier Division has been moved up behind, with a battalion on the front line and two battalions staggered behind, as we may need to fear landings here. Later, as soon as we can overview the situation a little bit, we intend to the get the paratroopers over here—

THE FÜHRER: They haven't yet—

JODL: No, the 29th Panzer Grenadier Division has to assemble here, in order to ... the units then ...

THE FÜHRER: So here there are the *Hermann Göring* [Parachute Panzer Division]," the 15th [Panzer Grenadier Division], the 29th [Panzer Grenadier Division], the parachutists, and what from the Italians in addition?

JODL: From the Italians, something here in ...[514] and the two Italian divisions here. The enemy has further strengthened his forces here in Sicily.

THE FÜHRER: Make sure you get any information you can, Hewel!

HEWEL: They met until 3 o'clock this morning. The meeting was still going on then.[515] I will be informed shortly.

THE FÜHRER: That just underscores what I've said. What else could come out of such a gathering but useless chatter? Useless chatter in a moment when doing only one single deed would be better than all those meetings that last more than 6 weeks! [—] Go ahead!

JODL: The number of tanks ready for deployment has increased. The 15th Panzer Grenadier Division still has 28 tanks, and ten under short-term repair. *Hermann Göring* has 49 tanks, including 3 "Tigers," plus 17 assault guns, four under short-term repair.

THE FÜHRER: Twenty Panzer IVs are supposed to be added?

BUHLE: And 22 assault guns! If these numbers here are correct and don't include replacements, the losses seem to have been relatively low. The 15th Panzer Grenadier Division still has 38 tanks of the 46 they had originally, and the *Hermann Göring* still has 62 tanks and 4 "Tigers" out of its original 90 tanks and 17 "Tigers."[516]

THE FÜHRER: Three, I think?

BUHLE: One is undergoing repair; it's that one.

ZEITZLER: Through Quartermaster General Wege,[517] the following total losses—which are constantly being updated—have been reported: (*Presentation.*) This probably coincides with these reports here.

THE FÜHRER: Fifteen tanks, 6 Panzer IIIs, long, 7 Panzer IVs—also long—13 Panzer VIs. Those are the total losses.

BUHLE: That's absolutely correct.

THE FÜHRER: *Hermann Göring*: 7 Panzer IVs—also long—and 13 Panzer VIs.

BUHLE: In this matter it's absolutely correct.

THE FÜHRER: There it's totally correct: *Hermann Göring*: 7 tanks.

JODL: Not the 15th Panzer Grenadier Division!

THE FÜHRER: Seven Panzer IIIs, long, and 12 Panzer IIIs, short.

BUHLE: That's 19.

THE FÜHRER: That's 7 Panzer IIIs, short. There are 42 in total here. These 16—these are the long ones?

BUHLE: Those are command vehicles.

ZEITZLER: Those could be command vehicles.

BUHLE: Those could only be self-propelled antitank guns.

THE FÜHRER: Yes, self-propelled antitank guns. Then 12 Panzer IVs, long, 15 self-propelled mounts with 7.5-cm guns on the Panzer IIs, 14 assault guns.

BUHLE: The 14 assault guns would also be correct, according to this list.

THE FÜHRER: Well, if those 22 assault guns are still coming, along with the 20 Panzer IVs, then more tanks are available here than Rommel had in Africa most of the time.[518]

JODL: And above all, my Führer, they will probably only be used in a limited area.

THE FÜHRER: That is absolutely clear.

JODL: They can't move in the mountains at all. It will probably be in this area.

THE FÜHRER: A relatively small area. But might they possibly land something here? [—] So possibly for landings?

JODL: Along the coasts.

KEITEL: Assault guns: 126 and 117.

THE FÜHRER: That's more than Rommel almost ever had.

BUHLE: These are not those, my Führer—the 42 from the 29th [Panzer Grenadier Division].

THE FÜHRER: Oh, those aren't even included?!

KEITEL: Without them! I also haven't calculated them yet.

BUHLE: They haven't been taken over there yet; they're still here.

KEITEL: So he has a total of about 200 guns.

JODL: I have let it be said that as long as he has the advance element of the 26th Panzer [Division] here.

KEITEL: Once the supplies have arrived and these have been repaired.

THE FÜHRER: That's a good figure after all. [—] So I don't see any concern here, if that in the rear holds.

BUHLE: We don't need to send anything more in here; we can't deploy them.

THE FÜHRER: Here I'm not concerned at all, but over there I am concerned. I have a report from Calabria—you should take a look at it!

JODL: The enemy has brought in reinforcements here in Sicily. Here he has [—]

THE FÜHRER: Either he'll jump from up here—

JODL: —or possibly also over here like this. Five hundred and forty-eight aircraft here, including 500 single-engine planes on the airfields. A provisional American army corps recently appeared, as did the 22nd [Brigade]—apparently, since no one knows exactly where they are—the 22nd English Brigade, the 23rd Armored Infantry Brigade, and parts of the 1st and 4th Armored Infantry Brigades.

THE FÜHRER: Yesterday I talked to Prince Phillip about the weather. He said that in a few weeks it will start getting more and more unpleasant; it won't be nice all the time. There's always very rough weather, beginning in the fall.

JUNGE: Rough sea again.

THE FÜHRER: With small boats, he believes, one can do very little then—at least outside the ports, if one wishes to land.

JUNGE: We already had great difficulties unloading in the dilapidated ports when the winds sprang up in the winter—Benghazi, where the jetties were ruined.

JODL: These are all the forces that are in Sicily now. (*Presentation.*)

THE FÜHRER: Nine infantry divisions, one infantry brigade, two armored brigades, one armored detachment and airborne divisions. They are pretty broken down. But there was certainly an engineer landing brigade, a parachute battalion, an anti-aircraft group, a chemical detachment—what's that?—and a Canadian paratroop unit.

Rest of Italy

Here's what I received before the meeting. A trustworthy informant reports from Rome, "I had the chance to see the report by a reliable Italian officer who was on an inspection tour along the Calabrian coast ... (*Further reading aloud follows.*) "There are 50,000 men there, under the Duke of Bergamo"—it must be a duke!—"50,000 men." A Duke of Pistoia or Bergamo, but it must be a duke! If you know the dukes in person, they are such little things—one can really say they are just a little piece of meat wrapped in a duke's title.[519] "The defense facilities are described as being below even the most modest demands; what is available is known—also obviously known to the enemy...badly built machine gun emplacements...are criticized."[520] And now listen: "The mobile defense is criticized for placing the troops too close to the coast, because it's not the landing that's decisive but preventing the enemy from settling." You know, I should have...the Duke of Bergamo... "Regarding the armament situation, it was said to be insufficient for a real last-ditch defense; there was, in particular, a lack of automatic weapons, there was no protection against air attacks...up to 40% of the troops..."

[—] By the way, is the Antifibrin medicine[521] down there with us?

KEITEL: I'll have to check on it.

THE FÜHRER: Immediately! [—] "The anti-malaria medicine of the Montecatini[522] showed very bad results." I can imagine that—a profit-oriented company! ... "The inspector also found a lack of real fighting spirit among the troops. The soldiers had no idea about the threat facing their country; their concern was for their women and children, also because of a decrease of ... The officers' corps was corrupt—the older officers; the younger ones were skeptical. They reported themselves to... some frontline service time ... to acquire qualifications for political positions ... that the enemy won't carry out a landing operation in this location because of the terrain and the malaria risk." Those are "military aspects," too! But shouldn't we covertly circulate the rumors that the greatest losses there are caused by malaria? Shouldn't we do that? Who knows? Through our channels or something—through trustworthy gossips? They don't go only to Dircksen.[523] Maybe he has someone like that? It would probably spread surprisingly far.

JODL: We just have to mention it in the attaché department; that would suffice!

THE FÜHRER: One just says casually in conversation that injuries don't play any role; the disastrous losses are due to malaria.[524]

ZEITZLER: We could rename a field hospital "Malaria Hospital," with large signs! That would get out, too.

THE FÜHRER: Just to tell—the enemy likes to believe such things—the terrible thing was malaria, which had disastrous effects.

JUNGE: But it might also be an incentive, because the British know how to cope with malaria.

WARLIMONT: But the Americans don't.

JUNGE: They will say that all the Germans are in the hospital. They are not afraid of the Italians—they know they can deal with them.

THE FÜHRER: While the Germans are safe.

HEWEL: The British have had trouble with malaria throughout their colonial history.

THE FÜHRER: Then more then ever the "hope" of the Duke of Bergamo is [—]

HEWEL: I think they will verify it. It's not a secret at all.

THE FÜHRER: What do you mean, "secret"? We also have some things which are secrets and can't manage to do it—can't manage it reasonably.

JODL: By the way, he has a Bavarian princess, the Duke of Bergamo.[525]

THE FÜHRER: All the worse! All I can say is—that, too! If it weren't so sad it would be funny.

JODL: Then we get a report from the Commander-in-Chief West through Heckenrainer[526] regarding some admirals. Admiral Leonardi[527] was appointed commanding officer of the Augusta naval port in Sicily, where he ordered that the batteries be blown up before they even fired a single shot. … They intended to bring him before a military court on charges of treason. Leonardi had been chief of staff for Admiral … before, and even then he was removed as … by the Italian establishment. … faced heavy German and Italian criticism there because of his unwillingness to bear responsibility, his extreme fear and his lack of initiative. Despite his assertions to the contrary, he is not positively disposed toward Germany. He's a small person with an insincere personality, and he understands their main task at present to be a speedy removal of the Italian materiel from Toulon. [—] Then he reports on the effects of the requirements for the barricade: "The intended removal of the *Pusteria* Division"—the 5th [Infantry Division], which is behind the 4th [Infantry Division] Army in France, east of Lyon—"could be hindered by the Fourth Army. In return, the Army must hand over other troops from the Ligurian sector, mainly from the Alpine Mountain Divi-

sion. If the Sicilian situation deteriorates further, additional demands for ...
on the Fourth Army may be expected." This comes from Heckenrainer. The
desire is that it ... from us ..., but even outside the Fourth Army they still
have enough Alpine troops.

THE FÜHRER: Yesterday I heard something interesting again. In a conversation with Prince Phillip, it came up again. He asked me whether I thought
that a death sentence had been passed. I ask, "Why?" [—] "Well," he says, "I
saw the king, and there were two cases submitted where officers had been
sentenced to death by the military court." But he hopes and believes that
extenuating circumstances have been found, so that it won't need to be carried out. [—] Of course, one can't proceed that way. Disorganized troops
can't be brought to order again like that, of course. So if the king doesn't
stop "assisting," things won't get very far.[528]

(General Zeitzler excuses himself.)

JODL: Yesterday the Chief of Staff of the Commander-in-Chief South[529]
was in Sardinia. A telex with the details is expected. This [Italian] XIII Corps
Massow has been converted into an Army headquarters. Massow, the commander, is very old.[530] The commander of the 90th Panzer Grenadier Division[531] —which is a good division and is now positioned here—is also optimistic so far about the attitude of the Italians. He was explicitly told, as was
Westphal: it's always the same—before the shooting starts, these people are
charming, but then things change. But what we didn't know is that the 90th
Panzer Grenadier Division has actually joined up with the *Nembo* division,
the paratroopers,[532] and they are supposed to be quite impressive. They're
also here, so one could say that this area—even this Italian panzer division,
but only for fighting against paratroops, nothing else—is relatively well secured. Then he flew away over the eastern coast at very low altitude, in the
Storch, and has so far reported that as soon as an aircraft came, all the
Italians would run away. So he watched this here in particular, but didn't see
anyone running away, because obviously nobody was there. The eastern shore
seems to be manned very poorly because of the difficulties of landing, even
though there might be some landing points. I think the 90th Panzer Grenadier Division is there. We have to do all that ourselves; these people don't
seem to do anything at all. It seems that these roads can be blown up very
easily and thoroughly; the individual demolition squads are preparing the
blasts everywhere so that the enemy can at least be stopped here immediately. The most dangerous area is in the north, and there they have a certain
concern, because there is the possibility they could say, "There are only the
coastal divisions here!"[533] [—] There's a bit more there, but in this part
there's nothing but anti-aircraft and coastal divisions, and it will take forever
for the 90th to get up there. That's why they proposed—because General

Massow said he could provide German troops a regiment, 150 trucks from this area here—to take the assault brigade over there so that at least the German forces are together and all the sectors are secure, instead of having a few inadequate German forces everywhere.

THE FÜHRER: But if that is lost, this here is gone, too. There are two sides, of course: if the assault brigade were over there,[534] it would probably help to secure this area a bit.

KEITEL: Then he wouldn't attack Sardinia at all but Corsica.

JODL: The transfer is not difficult; it's only short distance.

THE FÜHRER: How large is the assault brigade? [—] I must tell you: I would have preferred to have all the German units there and to have taken over this whole island.[535] First of all, the French are here; they are more formidable than the Italians—they are real enemies—and then we would be a bit closer to Elba. From Elba we could come over.

JODL: That would be sufficient, of course, but then this here wouldn't be ready again. It's too much—the 4 fortress battalions and all the panzer divisions.

THE FÜHRER: If this here is lost! [—] The French land here, and the Italians—my God! But these parachute troops are here—they haven't been moved out, right?

JODL: No, they haven't been moved.

THE FÜHRER: And they are good?

JODL: They are reported to be good; they should make a good impression. So, as we already said, the gap is up there; a German regiment is missing there. Then it's already much better here than in Sicily. It's actually better than in Sicily, because they have the German battalions in the coastal defense lines.

THE FÜHRER: How are the battalions equipped here? With antitank guns?

BUHLE: At the moment, a heavy one and two medium-sized ones. Two are on the way, and by the end of the month … antitank guns per command are coming.

WARLIMONT: That is the old SS Battalion, the Reichsführer's[536] Battalion. That's the infantry battalion that has been assigned here, but it's still being transferred. [—] Here are the assault guns and anti-aircraft batteries—the allocations. (*Presentation.*)

THE FÜHRER: When will the additional assault guns come?

BUHLE: 20 assault guns are over there—two companies—and the third company will be ready in the next few days. The others are already over there.

WARLIMONT: Those are these first ones.

BUHLE: The second with staff.

WARLIMONT: An increase for Sardinia![537]

THE FÜHRER: So far, a total of 20 assault guns have been transferred?

WARLIMONT: Yes, indeed. This is the first battery.

THE FÜHRER: Those are two batteries?

BUHLE: A tank infantry detachment.

THE FÜHRER: What do they have?

BUHLE: 10.5.

WARLIMONT: Light howitzers, motorized.

BUHLE: One light one and one heavy one.

THE FÜHRER: Are those 8.8 cm?

BUHLE: 8.8. [—] Two batteries with heavy ones, one 3.7, one 2 cm, and three 7.5 tank infantry companies, of which two are over there and the third is still underway.

THE FÜHRER: It is a small, very brave group, of course. I'm convinced that these few thousand men—how many are there?

WARLIMONT: There were 2,500 at the time.

JODL: This danger exists. Of course, if he then lands here, our connection would only be across here—over here, like this. On the other hand, I believe he will now, if he has realized that [—]

THE FÜHRER: We should support these two things here and here again very heavily, also with flak, so that at least this connection is secured. This is 12 km here?

JODL: It should be 12 km there.

THE FÜHRER: If there were anti-aircraft batteries on both sides, we could provide relatively strong support for it.

KEITEL: Here in between it looks like there are Italian fortifications that have remained—very small islands.

THE FÜHRER: We should at least put some anti-aircraft guns on it. I mean here!

JODL: Then there's at least one more division there. [—] One of our fortification battalions is there, but there there's only one coastal division.

THE FÜHRER: That's nothing at all. We should see what we can do there. Can't we get a picture of them? [—] But here, reportedly, is a good commander?

WARLIMONT: Mallie.[538]

JUNGE: Here they ran away when a submarine fired at a barge—Porto Pacchio.[539]

THE FÜHRER: Is that confirmed?

JUNGE: It was reported by the Commander-in-Chief South.

JODL: That's one of those stories. When there's shooting, everyone scatters anyway, to take cover. If they were just fishing, they'll run away into the shelter. You have to be very careful in a situation like this. If there's shooting, and someone is not in his hole, everyone runs away at first.

Situation at sea: Mediterranean and Black Sea

JUNGE: There aren't any substantial new findings regarding the enemy in the Mediterranean, unless one wants to point to the discovery that the focal point is now supposedly—without any figures—on the southern coast instead of the eastern coast[540] where it has been so far. Even though this claim is not supported by proof, and it does certainly constitute an assumption, it does seem very likely. On the one hand, the movements on land indicate it, and on the other hand, our theory of the supposed focus on the eastern coast resulted not least from the fact that we had hardly received any reports on the southern coast after the first few days. The only observation here was a formation of seven, with a northern destination, and also seven ships here, with no course indication. Last night near Siracusa a submarine was able to strike a medium-sized warship, probably a cruiser. In principle, the cruiser should sink with a direct hit. If there were two hits, it is probably gone.[541] In Malta, the large warships are still in the harbor. Twenty-five cargo vessels have recently entered the roadstead; probably the convoys expected from the East in the last few days. Our own traffic there had a small loss: one Italian ship of 450 tons, which we have nothing to do with.[542] Aside from that, no other reports. There are 8 motor torpedo boats at Taranto, and two others are being taken there.[543] Significant operational difficulties at the moment. No reports from the Aegean Sea. [—] In the Black Sea there was an operation against the Machkov[544] beachhead in connection with the Army. It is aimed primarily at destroying the landing facilities. The boats shot all of their torpedoes and fired artillery against the landing sites; most of the landing stages—some are marked as bridges—were destroyed. Two light boats, 400 tons each, were destroyed at the landing stages. The others were unoccupied. A tugboat hit mines on its way to Temriuk and sank. There was an unsuccessful submarine attack against a returning escort, near Constanza.[545] Also reported from the West: there is stronger traffic going straight west—probably new additions—including particularly large troop transports.

Situation in the air: Mediterranean area

CHRISTIAN: We provided Luftwaffe support for the defensive ground battle, primarily with destroyers and fighter-bombers. There are no combat reports yet from the night. Enemy activity: continuation of the attacks, primarily against the transportation system. Bologna was attacked during the day by 43 four-engine aircraft. Hits on the railway station. One ammunition train ... numerous passenger cars and one railway-mounted gun were destroyed.

THE FÜHRER: A railway-mounted gun battery? What is that? An anti-aircraft battery?

CHRISTIAN: I just received it now.

JODL: The 12.8 cm!

THE FÜHRER: God almighty! That's really too bad! [—] Go ahead!

CHRISTIAN: Seven dead, 2 wounded. During the night 60 to 80 planes raided Livorno in several waves. Hits on the railway station and a gasoline refinery. Additional damage reports haven't come in yet. The planes flew out over western France to England. In the Straits of Messina, 5 fighter-bombers attacked Italian Navy units; one corvette was sunk, a torpedo boat slightly damaged.[546] Forty tactical aircraft, supported by 50 fighters, attacked Cantanzaro. I don't know what particular importance that place has. No one in the Navy or the Luftwaffe knows either. No damage reports yet. One anti-aircraft gun hit by a motor torpedo boat in the Straits of Messina.

JUNGE: Last night the submarines ... the protection ...

CHRISTIAN: There was an attack on Calamate using aircraft armaments; high-explosive bombs were dropped, but no damage. From these attacks, 21 aircraft have been reported shot down; the English themselves report seventeen.

THE FÜHRER: That's still a very heavy loss.

CHRISTIAN: With low-level attacks, light flak.

THE FÜHRER: Seventeen to twenty percent.

CHRISTIAN: They themselves report more than 100 aircraft, including Greek ones. The Greek air force was deployed. Seventeen losses. That's the report.

The Balkans

WARLIMONT: In the Aegean region and on Crete there is nothing new to report today. On the Peloponnese, there was the first air raid in a long time—carried out by a few planes against the Calamate airfield, without casualties. The 104th Jäger [Light Infantry] Division continued its march and has now reached the southern edge of the Gulf of Arta in this region, obviously fulfilling the order to add German support to the Italian occupation at the most critical points.

THE FÜHRER: I received a letter about that situation. We should pull the Italians out as soon as possible—that would ease the situation the most. We can do it immediately. Then it would be quiet at once.

KEITEL: I'm fully convinced that he's right.

JODL: They decided themselves to pull out the whole [Italian] III Corps.

KEITEL: They're pulling out the III Corps and the General Command VIII completely.

JODL: They are removing these three divisions. The *Brennero* [Infantry Division] is already on the march, and the second is next. We just said that we have to decide this, because we don't want to leave it empty until the 100th Jäger [Light Infantry Division] comes down. We want to have the General Command out.

KEITEL: To get rid of it, too.

JODL: Then we will have pushed the Italian divisions straight to the coast, where they can't do any harm. They are drawing the III Corps in there.

THE FÜHRER: And if they come in here, perhaps?

WARLIMONT: During the maneuvers of the 1st Mountain Division and the *Brandenburg* Regiment, it became obvious that we had pushed forward into the center of a system of organized [partisan] bands. Here they are avoiding us for the time being; here we have already made contact. The *Brandenburg* Regiment, coming east toward the Pindus Mountains, has fought its way through across the foothills of the actual Pindus Mountains. The bands seem to have retreated now into the Pindus Mountains. [—] We don't have any new information from the Serbo-Croatian area, because of problems with the line. [—] Then, the transport commander has reported that the first train of the 100th Jäger [Light Infantry] Division departed today for the Peloponnese.

THE FÜHRER: It would be good if this one mountain police regiment came into the Pindus Mountains later.

WARLIMONT: But that one was planned to go here, in this region.

THE FÜHRER: It's all the same.

KEITEL: It's quite a difficult scene here—Thermopylae and all those things, where we have so many objectives that are extremely unpleasant.

WARLIMONT: The SS Division *Prinz Eugen*, which is also going to be equipped for the mountains, should come into this area later. The commander of the German troops has moved his command post to Banja Luka. … of the 43rd [Infantry] and 100th Jäger [Light Infantry] Divisions toward the Dalmatian coast in the course of the overall movement. Otherwise, there is nothing else to be reported from the Balkans. [—] From the West only the incoming transport of the 265th. …

THE FÜHRER: When can this one regiment be expected—

WARLIMONT: Confirmation is still pending. But they have gone to Athens with their own transport trucks. So it depends on the possibility of leaving by ship.[547] It depends on the ship transport and escort, then. The order has been given.

THE FÜHRER: One more regiment here!

KEITEL: If possible, infantry units beforehand.

WARLIMONT: Yes, indeed—if we have the ship capacity in Salonika. If things go well, they will be on board there immediately.

KEITEL: The best thing would be for them to go straight down here by ship, in stages.

The West

WARLIMONT: From the West the only thing to be reported is that the incoming transport of the 265th [Infantry] Division, which will relieve the 94th [Infantry Division] in Brittany, has been completed.[548]

Situation at sea: Atlantic Ocean

JUNGE: In the West the submarines have achieved another success. A passenger freighter of 10,000 tons was sunk south of Rio.[549] Again, lively enemy air activity over the [Bay of] Biscay; figures have not yet been reported today. Outside the [Bay of] Biscay, near the Canary Islands, a submarine deflected an attack at first but then was damaged after all and had to return.[550] At the same time a submarine drove back an attack here, and here one of two returning submarines is reported; the other went out of sight. Inquiry is being made as to whether he is still alive. Another submarine near Novaia Zemlia was forced by air attack to return. A heavy enemy formation with a carrier was seen here again.[551] But one can presume that this wasn't only to block the submarines but also to protect the convoys that are traveling here. In the North Sea and the Channel there was very lively enemy activity by motor torpedo boats—all this here last night: 15 motor torpedo boats attacked a convoy of 2 steamers with protection, and 6 patrol boats or mine sweepers. The steamers are safe, but one patrol boat was sunk and one of the minesweepers was damaged. On the enemy's side, the sinking of one motor torpedo boat was observed for certain; others, at least three, were heavily damaged and on fire when they moved out of sight. A few hours later, the mine sweeper flotilla—still the same one—which was on its way south, was attacked by enemy motor torpedo boats three times at the locations indicated. They knew how to protect themselves, and didn't lose anything. At least 5 boats were on fire when they moved out of sight. We had one loss, however, somewhat further to the south, where a group of motor torpedo boats was moving from Boulogne to Ostende. The boats were attacked outside Ostende by motor torpedo boats; one boat was lost, but most of the crew members were rescued. [—] In Norway there was this air raid, which was already reported yesterday evening. The submarine that sank there in the harbor had no crew. The destroyer *Z 28*, which was in the shipyard there, caught fire in the rear part; the fire has been extinguished. Shipyard damages were to unprotected buildings only; most buildings are under concrete cover. The extent of the damage hasn't yet been reported in detail.[552] [—] Then there was an unsuccessful air attack against a convoy here, and the somewhat conspicuous approach of 3 motor torpedo boats yesterday afternoon on an eastward course—possibly preparing to provide cover for the returning planes. Traffic was normal, with 58 ships. [—] Nothing in particular in the Baltic.

The rest of the air situation

CHRISTIAN: Yesterday during the day there were 43 planes in this coastal area and 23 in the adjacent western region. Attacks mainly against railway stations and locomotives. Yesterday 9 locomotives were destroyed. No aircraft were brought down; the trains were partially protected by anti-aircraft guns. The attack against Norway took place roughly as follows: 100 aircraft flew toward the coast near Stavanger and split up. Fifty penetrated into the east and attacked here at the entrance to the Oslo Fjord; the others crossed over and raided Trondheim. The damage reported by our side: some halls in the arsenal, a tugboat hit, fire on a destroyer, ammunition in the Navy arsenal exploded.

THE FÜHRER: In both cases the fighters didn't approach. Or did they?

CHRISTIAN: There were a total of 4 aircraft shot down, all of them by anti-aircraft guns. The fighters took off. But the weather situation was such that the clouds started at 200 to 300 meters, lower in some places. The fighters were simply locked on the airfields yesterday. Usually, everything works well up there in Norway with the fighters, because the attack in the far north was very successful. There's the convoy that was attacked; it was engaged quickly by the fighters, and 17 out of a total of just over 30 aircraft were brought down, most of them before they attacked the convoy.

THE FÜHRER: Where was that?

JUNGE: Several days ago already, near Vardö.

CHRISTIAN: Near Vardö. [—] Last night the enemy finally used what we've been afraid of the whole time up to now.[553] He dropped hundreds of thousands of tin foil strips. Consequently, all radar equipment except Freya was jammed. That was also the reason for the relatively limited number of aircraft shot down by night fighters. They brought down 10, and flak brought down three. Hamburg itself was protected by 54 heavy batteries, 26 3/5 light, 22 spotlight batteries, 6 1/2 air barrage batteries, and 3 smoke batteries—altogether a very strong defense. It had been reported by the Air District that heavy guns had been removed. That is the case. Two railway flak detachments are to be moved to the Ruhr region—they're moving out today. That is planned but not yet carried out. In addition, the withdrawal of 8 to 10 heavy batteries for Italy.

THE FÜHRER: We can't do that. [—] Hamburg? I was told they would be pulled out here from the center, not from Hamburg. How many have they destroyed? And the ammunition consumption?

CHRISTIAN: That hasn't yet been reported, my Führer. The air raid itself lasted about an hour and a half,[554] so we can assume from that that the enemy was over the target for about an hour. With this huge anti-aircraft set-up, of course, one can assume that a lot of rounds were shot in an hour. The damages: several public buildings—

THE FÜHRER: You don't need to tell about it—I've already received the pictures. [—] But listen. This dropping of tin foil can protect the planes, right?

CHRISTIAN: It jams the Würzburg devices. Some of the night fighters are still guided by Würzburg devices. That's the guided night fight, which brings the aircraft to the enemy.[555] Now, the Würzburg devices display lots of targets, so one doesn't know where the planes should be directed. The Freya devices don't display that.[556] They don't pick it up.

THE FÜHRER: What kind of things do the British have there? Do their devices record this or not?

CHRISTIAN: I can't say, my Führer, but it is assumed so.

THE FÜHRER: They record it too?! [—] Confirm it!

CHRISTIAN: Yes, indeed. [—] And the Y devices that are being used more and more frequently in night fighting[557] also don't record this tin foil. So in principle we have the solution—that would put us ahead; however, it doesn't happen that quickly with these devices. In my opinion, the only reason the enemy didn't fly last night[558] was because an attack with 400 to 500 aircraft passing over the target within an hour was impossible due to bad visibility and weather conditions over England. It requires, as Colonel Peltz[559] once outlined to you, my Führer, …

THE FÜHRER: That's absolutely clear!

CHRISTIAN: We deployed 51 aircraft to mine the mouth of the Humber; 47 accomplished the mission. If these 47 aircraft had been over the English ports, I believe there wouldn't have been 500 aircraft over Hamburg. Whether all the aircraft are capable of doing it or only some of them, I don't know.

THE FÜHRER: When will this new mining process take place?[560]

JUNGE: In late August, with your approval, in order to take advantage of the favorable moon period.

CHRISTIAN: Here the night fighters don't pose such a great danger to the planes if we get into the enemy's take-off phase because during that time there's such a swarming in the air that their own night fighters have been prohibited from night combat here anyway, so that only their own aircraft—

THE FÜHRER: But I really believe that it would be better to attack towns over there. In this situation today you can't tell the German people that that has been mined; 50 planes laid mines. That's totally ineffective.

CHRISTIAN: Besides, it's not reported for reasons of secrecy, so that the enemy doesn't notice that mining is going on.

THE FÜHRER: I really don't know. If we come in with new mines—I don't expect what is always claimed, since he sweeps anyway.

CHRISTIAN: With anti-aircraft guns and fighters alone, it's obvious that we can't inflict enough losses on the enemy. Out of 400 to 500 planes, he has lost 13 so far. Even if we double the number that he's losing, it's still not a percentage that would suffice to make the attacks bloody enough for him to stop them.

THE FÜHRER: That was also the tenor of all the explanations during the discussion some days ago, when I drew attention to the fact that terror must be broken by terror! We have to make counterattacks—everything else is nonsense. All this mining is worthless, in my view; it doesn't affect the masses, and even over there it doesn't affect the people. It doesn't affect us, either. Or does it somehow have a psychological impact on the German people when there are casualties caused by mines here?! It doesn't touch the German people at all! And you can't say any longer, "Yes, but if a ship is destroyed because of it!" Here's another loss—when in Hamburg a hundred thousand people have to be evacuated in one night, when shipyards are destroyed—those losses are even higher. It's irresponsible now. In my view, we must use them to attack something on his side, especially if we notice that he's in the air with such huge numbers anyway.

CHRISTIAN: That's why we understood, my Führer, that we should no longer carry out terror counterattacks with 50 aircraft sorties against a small, insignificant place; that would not have any impact on him, once he knows about these successes. Instead, we should create an indirect effect with these 50 planes, so that he splits up his forces instead of coming with 500 planes. That's the only way, in my opinion.

THE FÜHRER: ..., because they certainly won't attack the airfields, ... I don't believe that they can do it. It's come to the point where we're supposed to be happy if we can find London today. I'm told nowadays, "We hope to find London anyway!" That's a crying shame, and I say so to the Reichsmarshal in the same way. I don't mince words. How will they find an airfield?! They might find 6 airplanes on that spot!

CHRISTIAN: There is so much night flight activity here that—

THE FÜHRER: Listen, if they can't even find London with certainty?!

CHRISTIAN: —that everything is illuminated here. Here there are 40 to 50 airfields, on which—

THE FÜHRER: Maybe one is illuminated, and 50 to 100 others can't be found at night. They hope they're there, but we don't have any confirmation. Terror must be broken by terror. It doesn't disturb me much that they attack airfields, but when they destroy our towns in the Ruhr area! And they are very sensitive—just a few bombs containing the new explosives have scared people, "The Germans have new weapons!"[561] I don't know why we beat around the bush in this matter. We can eliminate it only by affecting the people over there. Otherwise our people will go crazy in time. Things will go so far that people will lose their confidence in our Luftwaffe. They've already lost it to some degree. So you can't say, "We've laid mines over there." Because it's all the same whether 400 or 500 or only 200 or 300 come to Hamburg. But we keep beating around the bush. It would become effective only if we also systematically attacked the towns over there. But when I hear statements, "We didn't find it!" And next time, "We don't have enough aircraft!"—but then we do have enough to do something else. Next time it is said, "That wouldn't be really effective!" Plus, "We have to do the mining!" Then it's said on another occasion, "The flak was very intense!"—and then they say, "Anti-aircraft defense is insignificant." Most of the explanations that I keep hearing say, "We didn't find it." Not to be able to find London—a crying shame! And here I have to be told by a blockhead, "Well, my Führer, if he comes to Dortmund from England, he can precisely drop bombs on buildings that are 500 m wide and 250 m long, since he has the beam technique [*Strahlverfahren*] now."[562] Blockhead! But *we* can't even find London, which has a diameter of 50 km and is situated 150 km from the coast! I told this to the gentlemen here, too. Don't believe that I'm telling only you. You are not to blame. You're my adjutant.[563] I also say it to the other influential gentlemen.

CHRISTIAN: I just don't think we have the 400 to 500 planes that we could deploy to achieve the same effect on the enemy.

THE FÜHRER: That's not correct.

CHRISTIAN: They don't haul any more.

THE FÜHRER: But he has to cover longer distances. We have only a fifth of the distance he has to cover. To get to Hamburg he has to fly 600 km or more.

(JUNGE: 800 at least!)

Mostly over the water. Here, from these jump-off bases, we have only a short distance, so that makes up for the other things. Anyway, if we take the high-quality bombs, they will have great effect. The important thing is that they do notice it at all. I say, if there are 50 bombers over the center of Munich it would be totally enough; no one would sleep through that. In any case, it is better for 50 of our planes to fly over a town like that than to drop mines. That's really nonsense. They just send an aircraft to fly over it, and—brr!—it blows up behind them.[564]

CHRISTIAN: Our night fighters are standing like this, along this line, and the enemy's are standing crowded together like a—

THE FÜHRER: But you say yourself that they can't fly on such a day. If they can't get to the airfields, at least they can get to the towns!

CHRISTIAN: On days like that, when the enemy is flying out, he can't work with his night fighters.

THE FÜHRER: Good! Instead of doing such things we must attack here, prepare here, and select any target—it doesn't matter which one! [—] We can't do it like this. In time, the German people will become furious. When I hear statements, "We sent out 50 nuisance raiders, then such and such a number of mine-laying aircraft, and we raided an airfield somewhere"—it's all a stupid joke. It's avoiding the only effective means: terror must be broken by terror—there is no other way!

CHRISTIAN: We did the following, my Führer ... stopped if we ran out of bombs, so at least the enemy couldn't escape.

THE FÜHRER: All that can be done in addition. But the critical point is that the English will stop only once their own towns are destroyed—nothing else will do it. So he has no night operations once. But he'll stop when his towns are destroyed; that much is clear. I can only win the war by destroying more on the enemy's side than he does on ours—by inflicting on him the horror of war. It has always been that way and it's the same in the air. For just one year we've been making a virtue out of necessity, that we ... there is nothing positive about it. There's really no necessity, but conducting an air war with insufficient—but go ahead!

CHRISTIAN: In the East the operations have been continued at all focal points as they have been during the past few days. The Fourth Air Fleet was mainly deployed near Kuibyshev, a few [planes] near Izium, and with 45 planes up along the Belgorod front. Sorties at night in the area close to the front again, mainly against railway lines and airfields. The Sixth Air Fleet didn't fly at night—as the weather situation had worsened again—only during the day, but they had very strong operations with 1,367 combat sorties north and east of Orel. [—] Victories in aerial combat: ten by the Fourth Air Fleet, twelve by the Sixth Air Fleet.

THE FÜHRER: By the way, have you read the report by Stalin—that order yesterday, where he precisely cited the panzer grenadier divisions, panzer divisions, and infantry divisions?! [—] I believe it's literally correct.[565]

(WARLIMONT: At "Zitadelle"?)

At "Zitadelle." I have the following feeling: that this report actually represents the calling off of their own attack. He congratulates them on their success. I have the feeling that this signals the calling off of his own offensive, which means that he is turning this affair in such a way as to try to thwart our plan. But one has the impression that he is motivating his own actions with it at the same time. He has probably received reports in the meantime to the effect that the action isn't moving forward here, and that it has come to a standstill everywhere here, so he has given up this idea that things are continuing at a furious pace. One gets that feeling. Perhaps they will continue to push here, but they have probably lost a good deal as well.

CHRISTIAN: During the day—less so at night—the enemy supported his attacks yesterday as well, but with fewer forces altogether. Fighters brought down six, flak four; only fighters were deployed on our side. [—] Two fighter-bomber operations on the Fischer Peninsula. [—] Seventeen aircraft were brought down in the attack on the convoy.

THE FÜHRER: 1,829 sorties?

CHRISTIAN: Yesterday 7 aircraft in the West, one of those in the south; the enemy lost eighteen. (*Presentation: Armed Forces Report*)

THE FÜHRER: Have you already received a report about the enemy's aircraft losses, and what he reports about Hamburg?

CHRISTIAN: I will have that looked into.

THE FÜHRER: That 12.8 cm battery is there after all?!

CHRISTIAN: We don't yet have any information on casualties among the population.

THE FÜHRER: One district alone, out of ten, has suffered 800 dead so far! [—] I would write here: ...

CHRISTIAN: "Considerable and extensive destruction"?

THE FÜHRER: "Heavy destruction"![566] [—] But believe me, people really expect us to do something over there now, even if there are "only" 200 planes over them. No more monkey business! This experiment—today mines are dropped *here*, then we try to disturb *that* matter—doesn't work any longer! Our population expects retaliation strikes now. I hear wonderful things here: that the Heinkel 177 is coming now after all, that one can fly it at night, etc. Now we can carry out an attack against London with 100 Heinkels. I can give each of them six 1,000 kg bombs and whatever else as well. The Reichsmarshal also says—or his pilots and my Baur[567] say—that one time we should let them fly when the whole garbage is completely full. They fly over there in a Ju 52—fly over loaded and return—and say nothing happens at all; to be sure they would drop their garbage over London.

CHRISTIAN: I said that back in 1940 already.

DARGES: The British report that they dropped 2,000 tons of bombs and 12 bombers are missing.

THE FÜHRER: I want the exact locations where these 13 were shot down.

CHRISTIAN: Yes, Sir. It takes longer and longer now, because we don't spend fuel for it; they just dispatch individuals by bicycle.

THE FÜHRER: They must do it, or they can't make a report themselves. Someone has to be sent by bicycle.

Distribution of Army Forces (excluding the East)

JODL: Here is the proposal for distributing the overall forces by the fall, with the intention of adding an operational army in both northern Italy and the Balkans. (*Presentation.*) The 26 known coastal divisions, which we always have, will remain in the West, while all of the mobile divisions will be relieved by the fall, and only a reserve division will be stationed on the coast. What remains available in the second line, i.e., behind the coastal front line, are six infantry divisions, four of which are supposed to get more Russian guns, and the Commander-in-Chief West can then count on them permanently. It's done like this provisionally, so that he can group them now in such a way that will avoid continuous cross-shifting due to the ongoing withdrawal of divisions. Two additional divisions come into consideration, the 334th and the 340th, from these six [coastal reserve units]. They can be exchanged with Eastern divisions, with worn-out ones—perhaps two worn-out Eastern divisions for one triangular division[568] to go over to the East. In addition, there are six reserve divisions in the rear sector—for the time being, three reserve divisions further to the rear in the second line, six infantry divisions, and there are also six mobile divisions available. Therefore, the total number in the immediate coastal reserves amounts to nine infantry divisions and six mobile ones. That's sufficient. As for the mobile ones, the 21st Panzer Division, then the 715th [Security Division], which we were considering sending to Italy, are now planned for here. One 700 [series] division,[569] provisionally motorized, wouldn't stand heavy loads—nor would their vehicles, so it would be better to make them available as reserves for the Commander-in-Chief West as a semi-mobile division. Then the two SS divisions, the 9th and the 10th [Panzer]—these perhaps only until they are replaced by two worn-out panzer grenadier divisions from the East. Later they can join this Italian group. [—] Then the 14th Panzer Division and the *Feldherrnhalle*[570] [Panzer Grenadier] Division, which won't become fully serviceable until the end of the year anyway. In addition, two reserve divisions, motorized, have been brought in, so that of these six reserve divisions in the rear area, the two motorized and the Bosnian Division[571]—which is being built up now—would be available. That is absolutely sufficient to secure the Western region in the present general situation.

THE FÜHRER: Yes.

JODL: As central reserves here, there are initially the SS Division *Nordland*[572]—which is currently being built up and hasn't been moved yet—the SS Division *HJ* [Hitler Youth],[573] the 71st [Infantry] Division, and then the 2nd Parachute [Division], which is down here. Then in the South: the four known divisions in Sicily, then a group of four divisions in southern Italy, the two panzer divisions that are already there, and the newly brought in 76th [Infantry Division] and 305th [Infantry Division].[574] The 305th has already received the order. These island occupations are clear, and the formation of this group up here could take place as follows—three infantry divisions from the West: the 65th, 94th and 371st [Infantry Divisions]; then the 24th Panzer Division and the 3rd Panzer Grenadier Division, which is already there. That's five divisions. To be added from the East: the SS Panzer Corps with two or three divisions, and later the 9th and 10th SS [Panzer] Divisions here, as soon as they can be relieved. That would make nine to ten divisions in this area. So there will be a total of 19 to 20 divisions for the Commander-in-Chief South.

THE FÜHRER: That's more than the Italians have down there?!

JODL: Yes, Sir. We can expect that in such a situation these forces and these forces will somehow join together again.

THE FÜHRER: That's absolutely clear; they must join together.

JODL: The Balkans: First, Army Group E down there has 12 divisions altogether, which will arrive very soon. Already assembled there: the 297th [Infantry Division], the 11th Luftwaffe Field Division, the Peloponnese Fortress Division, and the 7th Bulgarian [Infantry Division], and from the Jäger [light infantry] divisions the 100th, the 104th, the 117th—which are there—the 1st Mountain Division and the SS Mountain Division *Prinz Eugen*, which has been brought in, then the Crete Fortress Brigade, the 22nd [Infantry] Division with the 92nd Regiment, and the Rhodes Assault Division.

THE FÜHRER: They're there?

JODL: They haven't been counted as a division, just drawn together.

THE FÜHRER: Where's the 1st Panzer [Division]?

KEITEL: It will come in here again.

JODL: Central reserves are coming here, along the railway line.

KEITEL: Only what's down there!

JODL: Rommel's operational army,[575] which is still to be formed, will be thrown in here or here, depending on the situation. The divisions under consideration for that would be the two mountain divisions from the East—the 3rd and 5th—then the Bosnian Division, once it's ready—it's now being built up in the West—and two Jäger [light infantry] divisions from the East, as I already said yesterday. The 1st Panzer Division is there, and the

Grossdeutschland Panzer Division is to be added later, once it's ready, along with the Bulgarian panzer division and a panzer grenadier division from the East. So this group ought to be formed with troops from the Eastern theater, for the most part, while the South is supplemented by the West—with the exception of these two and the SS [Panzer] Corps. Besides that, Army Group E then has a total of 10 to 12 divisions, when I count the available Bulgarian ones. These are the two Croatian ones, the two reserve divisions, the 173rd and 187th, then the Bulgarian forces, two Hungarian security divisions—which could free the German reserve divisions here—and the 104th and the 118th Jäger [light infantry] Divisions. [—] So they are all there, with the exception of the two Hungarian divisions, which may possibly be added.

THE FÜHRER: Then in this whole area here there would be about 33—let's say 30—divisions available?

JODL: Yes, indeed. Thirty divisions.

THE FÜHRER: An attacking enemy with 50 divisions?!

JODL: But the Bulgarian Army, except for the panzer division, hasn't yet been counted.

THE FÜHRER: Then the attacker needs 50 divisions.

KEITEL: If they are properly led right from the beginning, and if there's fighting there, yes.

THE FÜHRER: We have to make sure that some of them are choked off right from the very beginning. Now one thing is becoming clear—that it will happen wherever the German troops are.

JODL: The importance of the terrain is already obvious here.

THE FÜHRER: And that also has great significance for the whole because people realize what can be done with…forces deployed against Germans.[576]

WARLIMONT: And if the fortifications are added.

THE FÜHRER: They will tell themselves, "If we meet up with the Germans and are away from those others,[577] then this will stop." They know full well that a crisis will develop here because nothing can follow, whereas here the supply can be arranged.

JODL: As soon as we have mountainous terrain—and that is the case there—and troops that are able to move there, the superior effectiveness of the English and American tanks and air force will cease to be as significant. Then they won't be able to destroy the troops like they did in the African desert.

THE FÜHRER: With the air force!

JODL: Against pass roads the effect is of course great—against individual roads that must be used by vehicles. But apart from that it's rather limited.

WARLIMONT: Only against the rear connections.

JODL: The effect of artillery is also limited.

THE FÜHRER: So this is an organization that is feasible and probably sufficient for the beginning.

JODL: We may be able to achieve it by fall, if the East stabilizes to a certain extent. As stated earlier, bringing in the infantry divisions can now also take place continuously with these 5 divisions—these two and these three—which are supposed to come down here. And then subsequently the 24th Panzer [Division] should come down—that can be easily risked, with no doubt at all, because we are now gaining these reserve divisions to maintain forces in this area.

THE FÜHRER: Right now we also still have available what is guaranteed to be at our disposal in about 10 to 14 days: three complete Panther detachments. The one from the 26th [Panzer] Division will get their equipment back.

BUHLE: One in early August and the other one in mid-August; by the second half of August all three will be there. The *Leibstandarte* [SS Panzer Division] has just now been completed.

THE FÜHRER: These are 300 Panthers, which we have in three detachments. The personnel is complete.

BUHLE: All of them will come here.

THE FÜHRER: We'll have to see. I just mean that it's a reserve whose use has to be carefully considered now. If a crisis were to develop here[578] all of a sudden, we might have to act very quickly. A situation could occur in which I couldn't wait for anything to come from the East—we might have to take immediate measures. For example, we might have to move a detachment of the *Leibstandarte* or the *Reich* to one of the panzer divisions, which are quite weak here—or possibly even an SS division—so that we could lead them in here first. Then they would have tanks there, even though the infantry is not trained yet. That means that they have individual tanks—they are being trained tactically. The detachment itself has been trained.

BUHLE: The 9th SS [Panzer Division] should have about 30 assault guns now.

THE FÜHRER: They will have been trained tactically already. We could give that division the one Panther detachment.

JODL: The 24th [Panzer Division] is ready.

THE FÜHRER: It's ready anyway.

BUHLE: Concerning combat vehicles—

THE FÜHRER: How many tanks does the 24th have?

BUHLE: (46 assault guns.)

The 24th has only assault guns?

BUHLE: (46 assault guns.)

And the 26th [Panzer Division] down here?

BUHLE: The 26th Panzer Division has 60 Panzer IVs. The division has 60 Panzer IVs and 40 assault guns.

THE FÜHRER: Anyway, one assault gun unit is there, one Panther unit is there—the one from the 26th. We could give it to the 26th and, if necessary, it could be given to another one, so that we have solid support.

KEITEL: It will certainly be there by the beginning of August.

THE FÜHRER: We don't need just one—we need two!

KEITEL: The two SS divisions will also be ready then.

THE FÜHRER: The two SS divisions, too. I wouldn't transport them to the East any more.

BUHLE: We have to use the tanks to create another focal point when the East quiets down somewhat. All of the tanks are going there. It's only a question of tanks with all the divisions—that they get there eventually, and that they finally get tanks. The second detachment of the 1st Panzer Division only needs 60 tanks before it can depart.

THE FÜHRER: I don't regard it as so urgent at the moment that we bring the two SS divisions up to their complete number of Panzer IVs.

BUHLE: We can do it gradually.

THE FÜHRER: It's not necessary at all. If they're getting Panthers anyway, they'll have enough.

BUHLE: If they have the Panthers and assault guns, they can release the other detachment; they will be brought in again afterward.

THE FÜHRER: Then I would say the following to reduce transport—it would be best if they were to leave their Panzer IVs in the East.

BUHLE: That's what was intended. The personnel section stops here, they take along their Panthers, and their assault guns are handed over.

THE FÜHRER: No, so we understand each other correctly: the Panthers remain here anyway. The Panther detachments are here.

BUHLE: They take them along here?!

THE FÜHRER: …leave…in the East, and take only the personnel section.

BUHLE: They take them along, and they are detached here, replenished in Germany and follow later. They take the assault guns with them at once. A couple of days will be added for that. But everything is going forward more or less as intended to the East. Now 42 are going to the East; then the 1st Panzer Division will have its turn with the 52nd Panzer Detachment, then 33, 12, and 16.

THE FÜHRER: There are also the breakdowns!

BUHLE: But, of course, if we pull divisions out down below, the SS Panzer Corps—the entire 13th [Panzer Division], the 23rd [Panzer Division], and the 11th Panzer Division down there—can take over all the tanks from the SS [Panzer] Corps right away.

THE FÜHRER: Because of all these reports, I'm not quite sure whether it's even right to give one division—as it is now—this huge number of Panthers, even in the SS.

BUHLE The division can use 100. One must always check again, even with excellent divisions: 100 vehicles.[579]

THE FÜHRER: Granted. But consider one thing: the Panther has approximately the same—a nearly identical—effect as the Tiger; the gun has the same effect. This division had 12 or 14 Tigers. And what have they managed to do with them? … I have the feeling that they shoot quite a lot at infantry targets. That many enemy tanks don't appear there. If the Panthers take advantage of their superiority, and each of them shoots only 5 or 6 [times], then 500 to 600 enemy tanks would be destroyed by 100 Panthers. That many are not even in question. I have the feeling that this is superiority without any effect. They are fighting infantry. Assault guns would suffice against infantry.

Italian crisis

Have you received anything, Hewel?

HEWEL: Nothing concrete yet. Mackensen[580] just sent a telegram. He said, shall we say, that the Reichsmarshal's trip[581] could possibly be jeopardized because of the incidents. But we're still waiting for the details. So far he knows that the Duce was finally compelled by the Farinacci group to summon the Grand Council.[582] That was planned for yesterday, but was put off until 10 p.m. because no agreement had been reached yet on the program. He has heard from various sides that the meeting was extraordinarily stormy. Because the participants are bound to secrecy, he hasn't heard anything real yet—just rumors. One of the most persistent rumors he has heard says that they want to make the Duce appoint a head of government—a prime minister in the form of a politician: Orlando, who is 83 years old and already played a role in the Great War[583]—and then the Duce is supposed to become the president of the Fascist Grand Council. These are all just rumors; we'll have to wait and see. Then it is to have been said that this morning at 10 o'clock the Duce went to see the king, together with a number of generals, and that he was still there, meeting a continuing stream of important personages.[584] Buffarini, among others, is said to be with him currently.

THE FÜHRER: Who's that?

HEWEL: Buffarini is a Fascist.[585] [—] I'm still waiting for details from…that this crisis within the party spreads and becomes a crisis of the state. [—] It is also maintained that the Duce, especially as a result of the meeting in northern Italy,[586] is steadfastly determined to continue the fight. [—] That's all that's come through so far. Glaise[587] hopes to hear something concrete this afternoon from Buffarini, who's with the Duce now. Then this afternoon ... would—

THE FÜHRER: Good old Farinacci is lucky to have done this in Italy and not with me. If he had done that with me I would have had him hauled off by Himmler at once—immediately. [—] That's the result of such actions. What can be expected from it anyway? [—] Idle talk!

HEWEL: But, as I already said, Mackensen emphasized that these are just rumors. In any case, there is a considerable crisis there, and Mackensen thinks—because the Duce always told him that he would prefer not to have his birthday mentioned at all, and that nothing at all should be done—that we should be very careful in this crisis. But he will inquire there anyway, to find out what they think about it. Having the Reichsmarshal appear down there just now, at this particular moment, would, of course, be—but I'm getting additional details.

THE FÜHRER: That's one of those things. The Reichsmarshal and I have been through many crises together, and he is cold and calculating in crisis situations. In times of crisis one can have no better advisor than the Reichsmarshal. The Reichsmarshal is brutal and ice cold in times of crisis. I've always noticed that when it's do or die, he is a ruthless and iron-hard man. So you won't get a better one—you can't have a better one at all. He got through all the crises with me—the hardest crises, then he's ice cold. Whenever it got really terrible, he became cold as ice. [—] Well, we'll see.

Distribution of forces (continuation)

JODL: No Italians are included here!

THE FÜHRER: That's good, too.

JODL: But if we manage to do this, the southern European front won't be badly protected—(if) the East permits it.

THE FÜHRER: This must be given away. It's absolutely clear: *Here* we're dealing with critical decisions. If worst comes to worst, even more must be withdrawn from the East; that must be done. But, of course, I believe that if we do such a thing, a great deal will obviously have to be done by us. Out of all the liquidation materials from the Italian army, we will certainly get 10 or 12 or 15 divisions together quickly.[588] [—] What does this story in Hungary actually mean?

KEITEL: I'm having it investigated.

HEWEL: I've also ordered that it be investigated.

KEITEL: Perhaps it's the introduction of military jurisdiction and the installation of drumhead court-martials. I will have it investigated.

HEWEL: It may be the introduction of military jurisdiction for special offenses. I believe it's the old Austrian procedure.

THE FÜHRER: I want to have a diagram for this matter as well, Jodl—a map. A map is fully adequate for me. So if this could be drawn one more time!

KEITEL: As for the reserve divisions, we must write below: 6 reserve divisions plus two! [—] So review it once again!

Occupied territories (Belgium)

One more report has come in, my Führer, from the area of the Military Commander of Belgium and Northern France. During the last few days, the SD [security service—Gestapo] has thoroughly cleaned out the Belgian Communist Party—the printing press, the national headquarters. By penetrating the matter, they arrested the office, 53 top functionaries and 22 leading men. And the materiel, weapons, ammunition, all the propaganda materials, files—all kinds of things were confiscated. So it was a significant undertaking. It could be called a major strike.[589] The SD believes that in the Belgium-Northern France Command area—this works everywhere now—everything is in order, and that they have finally achieved something. Cooperation is good—very intensive and therefore also productive.

THE FÜHRER: You know, when we came to power, the police force wasn't up to the mark, of course, and it was for the following reason: pure ideological firmness is, of course, insufficient—although it is certainly very important. Criminal investigation skills are also needed. Criminal know-how and experience, and, unfortunately, part of the criminal know-how went with the former people. Now it was a difficult task to screen and check them to be sure—i.e., to find the decent people—and it wasn't entirely successful. They found out with this "Rote Kapelle" [Red Orchestra][590] that one rat had been in there since 1933 who had a permanent connection abroad. I have to say that our enemies succeeded in one thing: even with the dissolution of the control commissions[591] they had already installed a control mechanism in all the state apparatus, the party apparatus, and everywhere in the public apparatus, economy, and administration.

KEITEL: It was already there.

THE FÜHRER: That's why they could leave without trouble—the apparatus continued working, and was in contact with their embassies or consulate-general offices, attachés, etc. It worked splendidly. They didn't need any control commissions any longer—it worked splendidly. These people were also in the police force. In 1933 the police suffered from the fact that they consisted primarily of National Socialists with good will but very minimal knowledge of criminal investigation. They hadn't been trained in criminal investigation. Now, ten years have passed since that time. Now these people have gradually acquired skills and knowledge, and have gradually reached the level that the state police always had in the Romance countries—also in old Austria or in Russia, France, etc., which always used to have a good state police. That has emerged now. Now successes can be seen as well. There's hardly an issue on which the police are not totally informed. This is a very comprehensive apparatus, of course, which is necessary there and particularly great resources are needed.

HEWEL: Large resources and a lot of young people!

THE FÜHRER: Young people with the spirit of adventure, but also large resources. Paying bonuses of 100 or 200 marks will achieve nothing. To bribe a fellow like that, larger amounts must be spent.

KEITEL: ... young people were in there.

THE FÜHRER: We have to be very careful there. These people always have to be arrested and imprisoned as well, so that the others don't notice what kind of people they are. They are also put on trial and sentenced. In reality they are all agents. The others must never have a clue as to who blew the whistle on them. [—] Do you have anything else?

V. PUTTKAMER: No.

End: 2:12 p.m.

* * * * *

EVENING SITUATION REPORT, JULY 25, 1943[592]

Beginning: 9:30 p.m.

THE FÜHRER: So the *Leibstandarte* [Panzer Grenadier Division] will be the first panzer unit ready and shipped out.[593] [—] The situation report, please. Short—very short!

The East

ZEITZLER: Counterattacks down here. The situation there has intensified somewhat ... I have indicated once again: don't engage in minor actions. It's better to do something bigger later, so they don't ruin anything. Up there in the area of Army Group South there were individual attacks. They wanted to assemble here on the 29th or 30th to clear that out.[594] I pointed to that matter, and indicated that they'd be better off to do smaller things here; only minor things are being attacked. It was also somewhat quieter there than in the past few days.

THE FÜHRER: Has the decision already been made that he [Manstein] [595] is to pull back?

ZEITZLER: Yes, he wants to go back there into this green bend [north of Belgorod] tonight.

THE FÜHRER: That's the old position?

ZEITZLER: That's the old position, yes. Except that up there where the 168th [Infantry Division] is, the old position is not yet—this attack has, for the most part, been driven back; he couldn't really get close anywhere. Here, 50 tanks were knocked out. All reserves are being used at the moment. This attack here—there he broke through with 40 tanks. The results of our counterattack have not yet been reported. Nothing new on this front. This situation has become somewhat difficult, somewhat tense—coming in near the 3rd Panzer Grenadier Division.

THE FÜHRER: He [von Kluge] needs to make sure that he goes back here, too!

ZEITZLER: Yes, my Führer. I've brought along the documents.

THE FÜHRER: When will he move to that line? [—] He wants to move to *this* one today?

ZEITZLER: He's going to this line today. Then I should report the intentions, regarding *Grossdeutschland* [Panzer Grenadier Division] This intention is not in line with my opinion. First he wanted to push upward a bit. Nothing can be said against that. Now with the *Grossdeutschland* a little bit and then afterward up to here, in order to close this off. [—] It's totally wrong.

THE FÜHRER: Totally! There's no sense in it! He must take units out *here* and use the *Grossdeutschland* only for such purposes.

ZEITZLER: That's the only possibility. I'm also very disappointed about his further intentions. He reports that he intends to take 4 weeks for evacuation—by August 20. We can't afford that. Now I would like to ask whether I might fly there tomorrow.

THE FÜHRER: I must say—I'll have to see; perhaps I will go myself. No, I won't be able to get away.[596]

ZEITZLER: Should I fly there tomorrow morning?

THE FÜHRER: The best thing would be for him to come here.[597]

ZEITZLER: Yes, because he has other ideas. He has a totally different opinion, actually. That has been the case already for 2 or 3 days. So he must be brought into line in any case. [—] So he should come here?

THE FÜHRER: Yes, indeed.

ZEITZLER: He started attacking Army Group North again at 4:15 in the afternoon, when we had the radio message—he attacked again here in the same place. The attack was in part driven back and is in part still underway. Here there were severe attacks on both sides, where he attacked and we attacked.

THE FÜHRER: Are there any reports that the attacks—?

ZEITZLER: No, not yet. Some of them are still going on; some have been driven back completely. Then permission is requested to deploy the 113th [Infantry] Division[598] up there to relieve those two divisions. I believe that might be the right thing at the moment because it would free up two divisions. But I don't think we should immediately put both divisions at his disposal for down there—just one, and retain one of them in Smolensk. Otherwise, in the case of a crisis, one battalion after the other would come in.

THE FÜHRER: How did the 113th leave?

ZEITZLER: The 113th will arrive tomorrow afternoon.

THE FÜHRER: It's arriving already? So it has already left?

ZEITZLER: Yes, Sir. It will arrive in Smolensk tomorrow.

JODL: If he brings one out, he can take one down.

ZEITZLER: Yes, indeed—to keep the one in Smolensk and to take the other one, perhaps for the mountain division. That's the best thing at the moment, I think. Better than leaving them deployed there.

THE FÜHRER: Good!

ZEITZLER: This one is unusual. It's very bad—it has 15% Eastern troops.[599] [—] 15% Eastern troops; no other one has arrived that's so bad.

KEITEL: They must go into a quiet position at first—nothing else, under any circumstances.

ZEITZLER: They'll go into a quiet position first. Then he has again requested permission to take the 7th Panzer [Division] up. That will be rejected—it would be best if he came here tomorrow—because we need it down there.

THE FÜHRER: Yes.

ZEITZLER: Most of the evacuation trains[600] are underway. One hundred and ninety-three trains have gone, of which 33 were loaded and outward bound. All in all, it's progressing well. [—] I have here from the quartermaster general the ... losses from the Second Panzer Army. The results are certainly correct since they would only damage themselves if they reported too few. (*Presentation.*) That's the whole time from the 1st to the 25th [of July]. [—] Then here from the Ninth Army and the Second Army—from both, the whole time up to now: (*Presentation.*) [—] But it includes guns whose barrels burst from the shells and everything.

THE FÜHRER: Sixty-nine?

ZEITZLER: Nine of them are barrel bursts; that's still acceptable.

THE FÜHRER: So, 92 heavy antitank guns, 39/4 trench mortars, 42 light infantry guns plus 4 barrels, and 14 heavy and 69 light field howitzers.

ZEITZLER: And of those 9 are barrel bursts; that's still acceptable.

THE FÜHRER: ... eight 10 cm, two 21-cm heavy howitzers—and what does this mean here: field guns?

BUHLE: Those could be some kind of captured weapons.

ZEITZLER: Captured weapons are included. [—] This is acceptable for the long term.

THE FÜHRER: That's still not many.

ZEITZLER: Worn-out and damaged guns are also included. [—] Then reports from divisions that were withdrawn and brought all their equipment along. (*Presentation.*) They brought everything back—this was on the southern wing. [—] Then, my Führer, I would like to have access to the 300,000 field howitzer rounds in the West. I can replace them because I sent an officer to the front who can re-route the things that aren't quite finished yet—for example, 100,000 light field howitzer shells for … They are going to be filled this month and replaced later, so that way I would get 1 million additional rounds this month when they compress the right wing a bit. That's why I wanted to give the 300,000 rounds to the East and replace them out of the 1 million.

BUHLE: That is also possible since we are rearming divisions with Russian guns[601] at the same time—divisions that still have German guns.

ZEITZLER: These 1.2 million are helpful; we can squeeze that out. There will probably be a little less in September instead, but that doesn't hurt anything at the moment; we can give that up. [—] Nothing else regarding the situation, my Führer.

Italy

THE FÜHRER: Have you already been informed about the developments in Italy?

KEITEL: I just heard the last words.

THE FÜHRER: The Duce has resigned. It is not yet confirmed: Badoglio took over the government and the Duce resigned.

KEITEL: By his own initiative, my Führer?

THE FÜHRER: Probably at the king's wish, because of the royal court's pressure. I already said yesterday what the king's position is.

JODL: Badoglio took over the government.

THE FÜHRER: Badoglio took over the government—our harshest enemy.[602] We must figure out at once how we're going to find a way to bring these people here[603] back to the mainland.

JODL: The decisive question is: will they fight or not?

THE FÜHRER: They say they will fight but it is betrayal! We must be clear among ourselves—it is betrayal, pure and simple! I'm just waiting for the news about what the Duce says. What's-his-name wants to talk to the Duce now. Hopefully he will catch him. I want the Duce to come here immediately if he catches him. I want the Duce to come here to Germany at once.

JODL: If these things are in doubt, there's only one course of action.

THE FÜHRER: I've already thought—my idea would be that the 3rd Panzer Grenadier Division[604] would occupy Rome at once and clean out the whole government.

JODL: These troops here remain there until that is back. ... this whole action here in motion, up here. ... the fighting will cease, for this case ... so that in the region of Rome we combine these forces that we are bringing out with these that are still there, while the other flows together here. [—] This matter here will be difficult.

THE FÜHRER: Here, there is only one thing—that we try to get the people on German ships, leaving the materiel behind. Materiel here or there—it makes no difference. The people are more important.[605] [—] I'm still getting messages from Mackensen. Then we will give orders about the next steps. But this must be taken away immediately!

JODL: Yes, Sir.

CHRISTIAN: My Führer! May I remind you of the order that Colonel General Jeschonnek, who actually didn't want to leave Berlin before tomorrow afternoon, is coming back tomorrow morning?

THE FÜHRER: He must come earlier—as soon as possible![606]

(CHRISTIAN: Yes, my Führer.)

[—] The most critical thing is that we now safeguard the crossings in the Alps at once—that we are prepared to get in touch with the Fourth Italian Army[607] immediately, and that we get the French passes under our control immediately. That's the most important thing. To do that, we must send units down immediately, possibly including the 24th Panzer Division.

KEITEL: Out of all these things, the worst that could happen is that we don't have the passes.

THE FÜHRER: Has Rommel left already?

JODL: Yes, Rommel has gone.

THE FÜHRER: Where is he now? Still in Wiener Neustadt?

KEITEL: We can find out.

THE FÜHRER: Find out right away where Rommel is![608] We have to make sure now that we [—] So in principle, one panzer division—that's the 24th—is ready. The most important thing is that the 24th Panzer Division is brought down into this area at once so that the 34th Panzer Division[609] can be pulled through here immediately on any of the railway lines. That way we can concentrate this here immediately and make sure that the infantry division Feldherrnhalle [Panzer Grenadier Division]—which must be ready—occupies the passes at least. Because we have only a single division here, which is near Rome. [—] Is the entire 3rd Panzer Grenadier Division there near Rome?

JODL: It's there but not fully mobile—only partly mobile.

THE FÜHRER: What weapons and assault guns does it have?

BUHLE: The 3rd Panzer Grenadier Division has 42 assault guns.

JODL: But preparations for taking this sector over from the Fourth Italian Army are underway now.

THE FÜHRER: Thank God we still have the parachute division here.[610] That's why the people here must be saved at all costs. That's of no use here; they must come over, especially the paratroops and also the people from the *Göring* [Parachute Panzer Division] Their materiel is not important at all. They should blow it up or demolish it. But the people must come over. They are 70,000 men now. If it's possible to fly, they can be over here soon. They must hold a screen here[611] and then take everything back. Only small arms— everything else remains there. They don't need any more than that. We can deal with the Italians even with small arms. It makes no sense to hold this here. If we want to hold something, we could hold it from here on at most, but not from here. We can't take care of the matter from here, of course. Later we will certainly have to withdraw somewhere here—that's quite obvious ... The most important thing is that we get the units in here very soon, and that the *Leibstandarte* [SS Panzer Grenadier Division] comes out and is transported away!

ZEITZLER: Yes, Sir. I will give the order at once.

KEITEL: In the direction of the former ...

ZEITZLER: We have to prepare first. I have to get the railway materials here. I can go at a tempo of 36 convoys, 36 trains; it will take 2 or 3 days before I get the railway materials here. I will do that now right away.

(*General Zeitzler excuses himself.*)

JODL: We should really wait for an accurate report to see what's happening.

THE FÜHRER: Of course, but we have to start making deliberations now. There is no doubt about one thing—that they, of course, will declare in their betrayal that they will stick to their guns; that's absolutely clear. But that is a betrayal—they won't stick to their guns anyway.

KEITEL: Has anyone spoken with this Badoglio yet?

THE FÜHRER: Meanwhile we have received the following report: the Duce was in the Grand Council yesterday. There in the Grand Council were Grandi,[612] whom I always called a "pig," Bottai,[613] and above all Ciano. They spoke against Germany in this Grand Council in the following way, "There is no sense anymore in continuing the war; we should try to get Italy out of it somehow." Some of them opposed the idea. Farinacci, etc., seemed to have spoken against it but not as effectively as those who spoke in favor of this movement. The Duce sent word to Mackensen this evening that he will absolutely continue the fight and won't surrender. Then I suddenly received word that Badoglio wanted to speak to Mackensen. Mackensen said he had nothing to discuss with him, but then he insisted even more and eventually Badoglio sent a man—

HEWEL: Mackensen sent one of his men to Badoglio.

THE FÜHRER: He said that the king had just asked him to form a government after the Duce's resignation. [—] What does "resignation" mean? Probably this bum ... I said that the statements of this Phillip ..., one could gather it from that already.

KEITEL: The whole attitude of the royals! The Duce doesn't hold any means of power in his hands—nothing, no troops.

THE FÜHRER: Nothing! I told him that repeatedly—he has nothing! It is not true that he has nothing. They have also prevented him from obtaining any means of power. Now the minister has ordered Mackensen to go to the Foreign Office first. He will probably be notified of this there. I suppose it must be correct. Second, the minister asked whether I agree that he should go to the Duce at once. I told him that he should go to the Duce at once, and, if possible, prompt the Duce to come to Germany immediately. I would like to assume that he wants to speak with me. If the Duce comes it's good; if he doesn't, I don't know. If the Duce comes to Germany and speaks with me, it's good in principle. If he doesn't come here or can't leave or resigns because he doesn't feel well again—and that would not be astonishing with such a treacherous rabble—then who knows? But what's-his-name declared immediately that the war goes on; nothing will change in that respect. [—] These people have to do that, because it's betrayal. But we'll go on playing the same game on our side. Everything is prepared; we're ready to catch this whole mob instantly—to clean out all this riffraff. I'll send a man down there tomorrow who will give the order to the commander of the 3rd Panzer Grenadier Division to enter Rome immediately with a special group, and to arrest the entire government, the king, and this whole mob straight away, and especially to arrest the crown prince at once—to seize the riffraff, especially Badoglio and this whole rabble.[614] Then you'll see that they will weaken—down to their bones—and in 2 or 3 days there will be a coup again.

KEITEL: The only formation from the *Alaric* that's still on the march is the 715th.[615]

THE FÜHRER: Does it have all the assault guns at least? Forty-two?

BUHLE: He must have 42 assault guns; the assault guns were complete when they went.

JODL: Here's the organization. (*Presentation.*)

THE FÜHRER: How far are they from Rome?

JODL: About 100 km.

THE FÜHRER: 100? 60 km! More won't be necessary. If he starts with motorized troops he can enter and arrest the whole mob immediately.

KEITEL: Two hours!

JODL: 50 to 60 km.

THE FÜHRER: That's no distance at all.

WAIZENEGGER: Forty-two assault guns with the division.

THE FÜHRER: They are down there with the division?

(WAIZENEGGER: Yes, with the division.)

Jodl, draw it up now!

JODL: Six battalions.

KEITEL: Unconditionally ready for action. Conditionally ready for action: five complete ones.

THE FÜHRER: Jodl, draw up the order for the 3rd Panzer Grenadier Division to be sent down right away. An order—without talking to anyone—to enter Rome with assault guns ... and to arrest the government, the king and that whole group.

BUHLE: Perhaps all of the fast-moving units, the two reconnaissance detachments—

THE FÜHRER: Yes, so we have something there, too!

KEITEL: Are they there?

BUHLE: They're there—at least one from the 16th.

JODL: From the 16th.

THE FÜHRER: I want the crown prince in particular.

KEITEL: He's more important than the old man.

BODENSCHATZ: It must be organized in such a way that they are immediately loaded onto the plane and taken away.

THE FÜHRER: Onto the plane and immediately away—away instantly!

BODENSCHATZ: So we don't lose the *bambino* [baby] on the airfield!

THE FÜHRER: In eight days there will be another collapse here. You will see!

CHRISTIAN: Colonel General Jeschonnek had actually started when he got the call there. He hadn't intended to come before tomorrow noon, but he has already landed tonight. I haven't been able to speak with him yet. He just landed 10 minutes ago.

THE FÜHRER: How long will it take him to come over here?

BODENSCHATZ: It will take him an hour and a half by car.

THE FÜHRER: When he comes, he should come over here immediately. Tell him that! [—] And then I would really like to speak with the Reichsmarshal!

BODENSCHATZ: I will inform him at once.

THE FÜHRER: Of course, we will have to initiate it when we are ready enough with our forces that they can go over immediately and disarm that whole rabble. The watchword for the whole story must be that the traitorous generals at the top—Ciano is hated anyway—are striking a blow against Fascism.

(Telephone conversation between the Führer and Reichsmarshal Göring. The Reichsmarshal's questions and answers were not heard by the stenographers.)

THE FÜHRER: Hello, Göring. I don't know: do you have news yet? [—] So, it's not yet a direct confirmation, but it can hardly be doubted anymore that the Duce has resigned and Badoglio has taken his place. [—] Now, it's not a question of possibilities in Rome but of facts! [—] That's the reality, Göring. There's no doubt about it! [—] What? [—] I don't know; we want to make sure first. [—] That's nonsense, of course. It's carrying on as well, and how! They'll see how *we* will carry on! [—] So I just wanted to tell you this. Under these circumstances, I believe it would be good for you to come here as soon as possible.[616] [—] What? [—] I don't know! I will inform you about it then. But in any case, be prepared for the possibility that it's correct! (*End of telephone call.*) We've experienced a mess like this already: that was on the day when the government was overthrown.[617]

(KEITEL: At 10 in the morning in the Great Hall.)

But that turned different then, too. I just hope they haven't detained the Duce! But if they have detained him, it's all the more important that we go there.

JODL: That, of course, would be a different situation. Then we would have to go over at once. Because otherwise the essential thing would be that we can still get units over the passes. Otherwise the traitors could set up elements here, and we wouldn't be able to bring anything over anymore. The most important thing now is that the transports that are stacked up here come over. It was already ordered yesterday that everything should go over there—even if it's only to northern Italy and doesn't go any further from there—so that we still bring forces here to northern Italy. Because in this case—

BUHLE: These here will also be available again for that.

THE FÜHRER: Send those immediately! Just in case, of course, those should go at once!

KEITEL: That's the only reason we didn't pull them in there.

THE FÜHRER: We can do that at once—that's perfectly clear.

KEITEL: The next infantry division.

THE FÜHRER: Wonderful. They should expect something! If they are not deployed there, they would probably—because the betrayal changes everything, of course. I have the feeling that these people[618] here are already aware of the whole thing—this betrayal—and that's why they introduced martial law.

KEITEL: I clarified that. They have the following reason for it: so far, they've had martial law only for looting and robbery after air raids, should they occur. When asked for the date, they said they had already done it during the earlier raid on Budapest,[619] and had now expanded it for daylight raids: anyone who loots or robs during air raids, etc. It's a fine statement. This afternoon they sent me this back.

THE FÜHRER: We must be clear about this: This Badoglio pig was working against us all the time, here in North Africa and here—everywhere. Has Rommel left already?

(... ?): He's being held right now, my Führer.

THE FÜHRER: If he hasn't left yet, we should call him back immediately, of course.

KEITEL: It's possibly that he will still be in Wiener Neustadt tomorrow morning. He wanted to collect his belongings.

THE FÜHRER: Then have him brought here early tomorrow morning in a Condor, and then I'll give him instructions. Once the situation is ripe, everything will be put under the command of Field Marshal Rommel, of course—everyone will accept orders only from him.

JODL: So we have to send Weichs[620] the (order[621]) down there at once.

KEITEL: We can do that.

THE FÜHRER: Make sure Weichs is ready for anything that may happen!

BODENSCHATZ: Will the Commander-in-Chief South be informed?

(KEITEL: Yes.)

THE FÜHRER: Is the Reichsführer here?

DARGES: No, he's out at the moment; he had planned to come back tomorrow.

THE FÜHRER: Find out!

(DARGES: Yes, Sir.)

We have to draw up a list at once. It will, of course, include this Ciano, and Badoglio, and many others. First of all, the whole rabble—and Badoglio, of course, dead or alive!

(HEWEL: Yes, Sir.)

The first measures to be taken: first, we dispatch the units here to the border immediately, so that whatever can come over comes over. But these units here must immediately—Jodl, these units down here must be informed at once about their tasks, so they know that they absolutely must take control of these passes here immediately!

KEITEL: This battalion here in Innsbruck is informed about the secret instructions.

THE FÜHRER: Is it still there?

KEITEL: It's still there. The mountain school, relieved, ... the staff or a group of the *Feldherrnhalle* [Panzer Grenadier Division] has been instructed, the 715th [Security Division] has also been instructed, and the 3rd Panzer Grenadier Division. These three have been instructed; they received secret instructions at that time from the Commander-in-Chief West regarding the implementation of *Alaric*. Investigations and such like were forbidden, in order not to draw attention to these things. These three should do this. We had hoped to do it together with the ...

THE FÜHRER: They aren't there?

KEITEL: No, they're not.

V. PUTTKAMER: We should inform the Navy because of the transports. They are spread out everywhere in the ports, among the Italians.

THE FÜHRER: Certainly! But the crossing must still be made here, as far as possible.

GÜNSCHE: Field Marshal Rommel left for Salonika this morning and has arrived there.

THE FÜHRER: Then he can fly back tomorrow—he has his airplane there anyway.

CHRISTIAN: His old 111 crew.

THE FÜHRER: How long will it take him to come from Salonika?

CHRISTIAN: He can be here after 3 or 4 p.m., with one stopover.

THE FÜHRER: So 6 to 7 hours?

BUHLE: Six hours!

JODL: We flew from ... to Salonika in two and a half hours in the Heinkel.

SPEER: But he doesn't have my "lame duck"! That is something else!

THE FÜHRER: Your "lame duck"! As if! If good old Mackensen hadn't had it recently, he wouldn't have been able to land. As I heard it, our good man Hewel phoned Mackensen's wife directly and said, "Mackensen's plane is overdue." That's also very "diplomatic"! For that one must be promoted to the position of an ambassador first! [—] All the other things will go forward. So, Jodl, I repeat: first, an order to the 3rd Panzer Grenadier Division, and, if necessary, to these units here in order to support Rome; analogous orders to the Luftwaffe deployed around Rome—whatever is there: anti-aircraft, etc.—so they know right away. That's the one complex. Then immediately moving the other units in. This, of course, must be done in connection with that! The third is immediate preparation for the evacuation of all these areas by German units, which should be brought over here—while retaining the screen in front, of course. All units in the rear are to be removed immediately and brought over here. It doesn't matter at all: small arms and machine guns should be taken with them, but nothing else—everything else we can let go. We have 70,000 men down there, including the absolute best men there are. We must do it in such a way that the last ones go back in the motor vehicles and embark here. We have enough German ships anyway. There is a great deal of German ship capacity.[622]

JODL: Almost exclusively.

THE FÜHRER: The anti-aircraft artillery will remain here and provide uninterrupted protection. The anti-aircraft artillery that's over there will be the last to go. They will blow up everything and come over last.

CHRISTIAN: But no Italians will come over with the German troops?

THE FÜHRER: It must be done so quickly that they cross over during one night, if possible. If they transport only men, and don't take any equipment or anything with them, they will finish within two days—in one day.

JODL: The normal capacity under normal conditions is 17,000[623] men anyway. That's the standard capacity.

THE FÜHRER: Imagine all of this densely packed. It must be done like it was at Dunkirk back then. It would be ridiculous if they couldn't get the whole company across this narrow strait[624] under the protection of a Luftwaffe like this. What's critical is that they take the guns and machine guns with them. Trench mortars—all the light stuff.

JODL: They should be handed over to the two divisions that are there.

THE FÜHRER: They will immediately come here, to these two divisions. In any case, they will first get normal infantry reinforcements, and we must give them the weapons.

BUHLE: Also here, my Führer, the order ought to be given to the general staff today or tomorrow that from now on the focus in terms of motor vehicles should be shifted to here—meaning everything that is currently being built up and going to the East. Otherwise these units won't get there.

THE FÜHRER: We can still do that tomorrow. Then I have to take precautions about something else. We have to be careful with the Hungarian situation.

JODL: Then the Commander-in-Chief South must get a guard at once.

THE FÜHRER: Yes.

JODL: The 3rd Panzer Grenadier Division must provide a strong guard for the whole headquarters.

THE FÜHRER: Yes.

JODL: Otherwise they will round up the leadership!

THE FÜHRER: Yes, we can do that right away. I'll round up their [the Italian] leadership! They'll get the shock of their lives!

JODL: We should think it over carefully for half an hour first.

BODENSCHATZ: The Italian workforce?!

THE FÜHRER: They haven't arrived yet.

SPEER: We need personnel.

JODL: Don't let any more Italians cross the border—those who are still here in Germany![625]

SPEER: They work very diligently. We could put them to good use for the OT [Todt Organization], etc.

THE FÜHRER: When this thing blows up, I don't need to be concerned about the Belgian any longer either. Then I can lead this fellow away and lock all the relatives up together.[626]

SPEER: The Croatians could become very decent.

THE FÜHRER: Now, but—

SPEER: Better allies than all those Italians. If we could take this opportunity to recruit them, we would have 100,000 men. One day it will happen anyway!

THE FÜHRER: There is a possibility here after all. If they could have the chance to get Fiume on this occasion, it would be a chance to betray the Italians—a chance they would not pass up. They tried it earlier.[627] [—] Has anything else come in?

JODL: The day was relatively quiet. An assembly is reported south of Rivalcuto.[628] Minor attacks against the 15th Panzer Grenadier Division; the attacks were driven back here. And then since this morning an attack—still in progress—along the north coast. [—] Nothing else has been reported yet.

THE FÜHRER: Here, if it becomes necessary, they must retreat quickly and go back here on the roads. The vehicles must be emptied of everything else. All other things must be removed from the vehicles. All tractors, guns, etc., must be blown up! The critical thing is that the people get away.

JODL: A report from informers regarding a secret meeting at the headquarters in Cairo on June 20: the king of England[629] and General Wilson,[630] Commander-in-Chief of the Twelfth Army, which is intended for Greece.

THE FÜHRER: In connection with these people here, with the betrayal!

JODL: Then this message, which might also be connected to that. A controversial person from Switzerland—who, however, has often provided good, sound information—reports, "After stabilizing the situation of the Allies in Sicily ... attack from North Africa against the mainland, in the direction of Rome—with fresh troops—is intended. The occupation of Rome should be regarded as the most important action from a psychological standpoint. They intend to establish a provisional national government in Rome immediately. The Fascist Party would be dissolved, and Italy and Albania liberated from the Fascist dictatorship. Major new contingents of troops and weapons are said to have arrived in Africa from America and Canada."

THE FÜHRER: That's all certainly related to it.

JODL: That takes care of everything else that has been submitted.

THE FÜHRER: What else do you have?

JODL: This was for the Commander-in-Chief West.

KEITEL: The information about the issue you asked about today. The distribution of forces—the overview you asked for. [—] The Palermo port ... already as a motor torpedo boat base by the enemy ...

THE FÜHRER: "Reinforcement for Sardinia"—also outdated.

JODL: According to an aerial photo, the enemy is already using the Palermo port as a motor torpedo base. On the afternoon of the 24th, there were eight motor torpedo boats there.

THE FÜHRER: Shouldn't we prepare the 2nd Parachute Division[631] so they can be put on alert immediately?

JODL: Yes, they might possibly come into consideration as reinforcements in Rome.

THE FÜHRER: Yes, so we throw them in to Rome at once.

BODENSCHATZ: One of the Commander-in-Chief South's companies?!

THE FÜHRER: This is one of the most important things: to be strong here.

JODL: Otherwise, we won't yet be able to tell him anything.

THE FÜHRER: No, nothing else. He should prepare a strong guard. He must not go in person anywhere, either—not to any meetings. He must receive only in his headquarters. The best thing would be to say that he's sick. Or we could also say that he was summoned here to report.

JODL: He must stay there.

KEITEL: I would let him stay there. He is one who can lead and give orders immediately. He holds the apparatus in his hands. He absolutely should not leave his headquarters, and anyone who goes to see him there must have a military escort. He won't receive anyone else or leave his headquarters for any meetings, of course.[632]

THE FÜHRER: ...

HEWEL: No, I only spoke with the minister.

THE FÜHRER: Do you have anything else?

Situation in the air

CHRISTIAN: This afternoon there was another attack by 350 aircraft. First approach into the Flensburg region ... area between Kiel and Flensburg, then to Stralsund, then some started against ... again ... over the belt against Hamburg, mainly the port area; damages can't be assessed yet. Three hundred and twenty-four fighters were in the air. So far 10 have been brought down. The number of aircraft shot down is increasing steadily, as the

Reichsmarshal reports. Ammunition consumption last night: 50,000 rounds, including about 10,000 rounds of 10.5 and 20,000 rounds of 8.8.

THE FÜHRER: How many 8.8 [88-mm] barrels are there?

CHRISTIAN: In total, there are 54 heavy batteries here.

THE FÜHRER: Are these sextuple barrels or normal barrels?[633]

THE FÜHRER: Generally it's been sextuple barrels so far.

THE FÜHRER: So let's say 40 8.8s. That's 240 barrels, so 100 rounds per barrel, which is very little in an hour and a half. Very little has been shot!

CHRISTIAN: These are the locations where the aircraft were brought down. (*Presentation.*) Three are still missing.

THE FÜHRER: How could they report beforehand, then? They reported that 13 were shot down.

CHRISTIAN: They haven't found them yet—the wreckage itself. This is the report from the aircraft that shot it down.

THE FÜHRER: Do we always establish it so precisely afterward?

CHRISTIAN: It's established very precisely afterward. The locations where the aircraft were brought down are confirmed; usually they go there by bicycle to save fuel. It is determined very precisely.[634]

Italy

THE FÜHRER: So, Jodl, take care of the matter now!

JODL: These orders, yes.

THE FÜHRER: We have to go on with this game, of course, as if we believe they will continue!

JODL: We must do that.

THE FÜHRER: We have to do it like [—]

V. PUTTKAMER: The Grand Admiral will be here at the situation conference tomorrow.

End: 10:13 p. m.

* * * * *

SECOND EVENING SITUATION REPORT, JULY 25, 1943[635]

Beginning: 12:25 a.m. (July 26)

Italy

(*Presentation of an order*[636] *by General Jodl.*)

THE FÜHRER (*after inspection*): I don't know if this is possible, Jodl—this item here?

KEITEL: "Withdrawing anti-aircraft equipment"?

THE FÜHRER: Yes. I don't know whether this is feasible. We have to wait until—

JODL: It's just preparation, my Führer.

CHRISTIAN: That won't be possible in all cases because it mostly—

JODL: Just preparation!

THE FÜHRER: " ... telephoning strictly forbidden ... no order, all these instructions must be given only verbally by couriers or enciphered by telex or code. Telephone conversations—even in a disguised form—about these things is also prohibited, of course."

JODL: Yes, indeed. [—] So this is the border, and that's the border with Croatia. I had this idea in particular because I got hold of the message from the Tarvisio railway command today. For 10 to 14 days the Italians have been running ... ammunition transports by ... supplied with ammunition of all calibers.

THE FÜHRER: This is a bad story, of course—it's certainly connected to that.

JODL: " ... increased alert stand-by." These measures were presumably taken in case of the appearance of airborne troops or partisans.

THE FÜHRER: Then it's connected to that. The betrayal was systematically prepared by these people.

JODL: I think so, too. In addition there is a message from the Commander-in-Chief South: the communication from General Roatta indicates that the Duce, after hearing the report—this was certainly a while ago—renounced his plan to transfer the 3rd Panzer Grenadier Division into the vicinity of Rome as he had wished to do. [—] "Communication from General Roatta"! We have no idea whether all this is true.

THE FÜHRER: I don't believe Roatta is in cahoots with the others.[637] They hate each other, Roatta and Badoglio.

JODL: There are still a number of questions, my Führer. The Commander-in-Chief Southeast is asked to report immediately on how he can carry out Operation "Konstantin" with his forces in the current situation, and the Commander-in-Chief West Operation *Alaric*. Everything has changed now. But in any case, they have to make suggestions themselves concerning how they carry this out under the changed conditions, now that some divisions have been taken away. That should come by telex tonight. They knew about the news itself. Nothing further was said. What about the issue of the coal trains to Italy? So far we've left them running.

THE FÜHRER: We'll do everything we can to give the impression [—]

JODL: Now there is also the question: shouldn't at least trips to Italy, and private communications, be stopped?

THE FÜHRER: I wouldn't do that yet either.

KEITEL: No, not yet!

THE FÜHRER: All important persons have to give notice of departure anyway; they won't receive permission any longer.

JODL: Then I talked to Kesselring. Now that he has heard the appeal, he wants—he wasn't contacted, but there is in fact a new supreme commander and a new head of government—to take up contact with the king or Badoglio, which he must indeed do.

THE FÜHRER: Should he? Yes, he must!

JODL: He should do it tomorrow morning, at least to explore the situation.

THE FÜHRER: Good old Hube with his opinion, "Everything is tight here!"[638]

KEITEL: Hube didn't know anything. He only passed on what the—

THE FÜHRER: You see how dangerous it is for "nonpolitical generals" when they get into such a political atmosphere.

JODL: Then the order went out to alert the 2nd Parachute Division immediately, and to prepare for airborne transport, as far as capacity is available.

CHRISTIAN: We are still waiting for the report on what is available. But now another question, my Führer: Second Air Fleet, Field Marshal v. Richthofen, has been using 100 Ju 52 transport planes to supply the 1st Parachute Division in Sicily ... ten shot down again today. Consequently he wanted to withdraw them. The Commander-in-Chief South wanted to confiscate these planes at once, and he apparently also wanted to draw troops from northern Italy to central Italy, according to the developments of this situation. The Second Air Fleet then asked the Commander-in-Chief of the Luftwaffe. Then I said to the Commander-in-Chief of the Luftwaffe, "Any further telephone conversations on this matter are prohibited; from now on they go through the Commander-in-Chief South."

THE FÜHRER: The Commander-in-Chief South has to do all that, to pull everything together. I've just told the Reichsmarshal as well that no telephone calls are allowed.

CHRISTIAN: That came from below, my Führer. It didn't come from the Commander-in-Chief of the Luftwaffe; it came from the Second Air Fleet. [—] But now there is the question whether the 2nd Paratroop Division should have access to these planes?

THE FÜHRER: First the 2nd Paratroop Division. That's the most important—it's absolutely clear ...

KEITEL: The order reads, "If necessary without the heaviest materiel, which is to be destroyed if required. No transmission of orders by phone, not even in disguised form."

THE FÜHRER: No, I would write, "all the heavy materiel."

KEITEL: So, "If necessary without all the heavy materiel, which is to be destroyed if required!"[639] [—] Then here, "No transmission of orders by phone, not even in disguised form; instructions only by courier."

THE FÜHRER: By couriers whose letters must also be enciphered!

HEWEL: My Führer! There's a question of whether we shouldn't perhaps block the telephone connection from the postal service entirely. The postal service just called. That would let them get rid of the press calls. They're probably suggesting that now—that we should just block everything except the military lines.

THE FÜHRER: One could say that it's needed for military purposes, for government calls.

HEWEL: Above all the journalists, who now, of course—

THE FÜHRER: Only for government calls!

HEWEL: Only for ministries?!

THE FÜHRER: Only for ministerial and military government calls!

KEITEL: " ... whose written instructions must be enciphered." [—] So that there's nothing in anything they have with them.

CHRISTIAN: Encoded telex and radio?

THE FÜHRER: Encoded telex and enciphered radio. But this can't be deciphered?

KEITEL: No, it's done by the Navy as well.

THE FÜHRER: Encoded telex or enciphered radio!

KEITEL: " ... or encoded radio."

THE FÜHRER: Like that!

Sicily

JODL: Then the afternoon reconnaissance identified transport movement today along the northern Sicilian coast from Palermo to the east, consisting of about 50 vessels, including eight large, the rest smaller, probably landing boats. The course wasn't exactly established—probably eastward.[640] So it may have to do with a landing attempt at the rear of our right wing.

THE FÜHRER: Has all this been planned by the Luftwaffe?

JODL: The Luftwaffe is informed.

CHRISTIAN: Yes, indeed. It comes from the Commander-in-Chief South.

THE FÜHRER: Nevertheless, I think we must send another officer down there at once.

JODL: The aircraft is ready; we should just wait until tomorrow.

THE FÜHRER: An officer must come here, who can tell Hube how to do it: that they transport the rear people back at first, so that they come over, and that those in front have to keep holding and then rush back in one night. They must be pulled out in one night, with just the personnel. The last ones must shoot continually and make a spectacle.

Italy

JODL: This must be communicated verbally in any case—the fall of Rome.
THE FÜHRER: That must happen under all circumstances. That's absolutely clear. We can't get around it. It must be beaten back, and we must be sure to capture the entire government. The paratrooper division must plan it so that they jump around Rome. Then Rome must be occupied. No one can be allowed to leave Rome, then the 3rd Panzer Grenadier Division must go in.
JODL: And the troops that are on the way—those from the 26th [Panzer Division]
THE FÜHRER: That's not clear in the order in the words: "those being unloaded." It should be worded that they have to be unloaded there.
KEITEL: So let's add: "the troops to be unloaded," i.e., aside from the unloaded ones. I read it twice. I also thought, "Shouldn't we write instead, 'the troops of the 26th Panzer Division that have to be unloaded'"?
JODL: Some of them were unloaded because they couldn't get any further, and were supposed to—marching on land—
THE FÜHRER: That must be added: the unloaded troops and the troops that have to be unloaded. So: "Aside from the already unloaded troops, the rest of the 26th Panzer Division must be unloaded and placed under the command of the 3rd Panzer Grenadier Division."
HEWEL: Shouldn't we say that the Vatican exits must be occupied?
THE FÜHRER: That doesn't matter. I'll go into the Vatican immediately. Do you think the Vatican troubles me? It will be seized immediately.[641] First of all, the entire diplomatic corps is in there. I don't care. The rabble is there. We'll take out all the whole herd of swine. … What is already … Then we apologize afterward; that doesn't matter to us. We're waging a war there …
BODENSCHATZ: Most of them are sitting there…believing they are safe.
HEWEL: We will get documents there!
THE FÜHRER: There? [—] Yes, we will get documents; we will bring out something about the betrayal! How long will it take the Foreign Minister—what a pity he isn't here!—to draw up the instructions for Mackensen?
HEWEL: It's probably been sent out.
THE FÜHRER: So there!!
HEWEL: I'll find out right away.
THE FÜHRER: Will it be a journalist's work of 12 pages? That's what I'm most afraid of with you; it can be done in two or three lines. [—] Now I have

one more idea, Jodl. If he wants to attack tomorrow or the day after tomorrow[642]—I don't know whether the units are already together—I would have them attack in the East once more. Then the *Leibstandarte* [Panzer Grenadier Division] can strike together with them one more time, because if the materiel is just coming anyway—

KEITEL: The railway materiel!

JODL: They can do that, of course, because it's better if they leave a more consolidated position behind.

THE FÜHRER: That would be good, of course. Then the one division, the *Leibstandarte*, can be transferred out. That one should go first and can leave its things there. They can leave a lot of materiel over there; they don't need to take the tanks with them. They can leave them over there and bring them in again from here. So they remain over there for now. They will also get the Panthers here, so they're well equipped. It's ridiculous. Until this division gets there, they will have these tanks available as well.

HEWEL: I would like to ask about the Prince of Hesse, who is hanging around all the time. Do you want me to say that we don't need him?[643]

THE FÜHRER: Let him come, and I'll say a few words to him.

HEWEL: He goes around asking everyone, of course, and wants to know everything.

THE FÜHRER: That is actually a very good disguise—an iron wall. It's very good. In the past we often had people around us when we were planning something, but they had no clue, and the others were convinced that as long as those people were there, everything was in order. I'm afraid that Göring is overstepping his bounds.

BODENSCHATZ: I told him that very clearly beforehand.

THE FÜHRER: One has to be extremely polite. I would give him all those appeals—they are public anyway—that we've collected. He can read them, this Phillip—that would be totally harmless. But tell them that he's not to be given anything incorrect! I don't know where they are. Take care that they don't take anything incorrect! [—] And the outbound transport? When can it begin, the first one? All at once would be best!

JODL: We haven't received that yet. It's the 305th [Infantry Division] that's standing by.

THE FÜHRER: And the 44th [Infantry Division]?

JODL: It's ready; that depends on the shortages [in materiel]. The 44th won't be released until tomorrow; that depends on the shortage [in materiel]. But I assume that it will begin during the day tomorrow.

THE FÜHRER: Is the 44th motorized?

(JODL: No.)

But it's a triangular division?

KEITEL: A triangular and completely serviceable division. We wanted to bring it down there 4 weeks ago. Rommel wanted it because it was ready. You refused at the time, so we deployed the *Brandenburg* there because we didn't want it to become conspicuous.

THE FÜHRER: The *Brandenburg* is not there either.

KEITEL: It left again as well. It was in Innsbruck; things have gradually changed.

THE FÜHRER: Shouldn't we give these units—which might have to crack open these few bunkers[644]—some things? Either Tigers or something else, if there are difficulties somewhere? [—] Of course, a Tiger like that would shoot these few bunkers to pieces at once—the embrasures?

(KEITEL: No doubt!)

Perhaps we can find out from Buhle what there are in the way of Tigers in the schools, etc.

JODL: Whatever is available should be taken to Innsbruck.

THE FÜHRER: They only need a few to crack these few things open and... down to Krain, ... these few things will be cracked open soon. If a couple of Tigers come and shoot into them, they will go out at once. The concrete they have can be penetrated by the Tiger anyway. We might be able to take Panthers as well. Maybe we can see if it's possible to take something from the schools for this purpose—assault tanks as well, for example.

KEITEL: I will speak with Buhle.

THE FÜHRER: Tell Guderian to come here as well!

End: 12:45 a.m.

* * * * *

MIDDAY SITUATION REPORT, JULY 26, 1943[645]

Beginning: 11:46 a.m.

Italy

THE FÜHRER: Jodl, have any new reports come in?

JODL: No, so far only one meeting with Badoglio has been set down there, at 6 p.m. There was no time before that because he's overloaded ... some shout, "Pace, pace!" [Peace, peace!] while others are hunting Fascists.

THE FÜHRER: That's good.

JODL: But so far it's like the childishness before Ash Wednesday.

THE FÜHRER: But it will in fact become an Ash Wednesday. We've experienced this before ...

JODL: The supreme command has secured itself completely. A discussion took place some minutes ago regarding the fact that because of the danger he … has secured … an airfield totally in German hands …

THE FÜHRER: And another question. Do you have any news yet about when the paratrooper division will be ready to jump?

JODL: It's on alert but there's no news yet about when the additional troops will arrive.

THE FÜHRER: Jeschonnek must know.

JODL: They should come any time.

THE FÜHRER: Has this here been launched?[646] … Wouldn't it be possible to take the tanks over here at least?

JODL: … We especially have to take away the most valuable equipment, of course, during the time when no men can be brought back.

THE FÜHRER: Tanks above all! There are 160 tanks there … according to yesterday's description.

JODL: The new ones have not yet …

THE FÜHRER: No, they haven't been brought over yet.

JODL: What I received this afternoon is how all the trains are lying on the rails. (*Presentation.*) They're lying on all the tracks up to the Brenner [Pass]. From the Brenner to the southern wing it's not quite clear yet. But most of what was in last night's telex had already been launched by Kesselring.

THE FÜHRER: We just have to make sure that nothing nasty happens here with the Hungarians.[647] Which tank units can we send in there on short notice if necessary? … Panther detachments. Is it possible to improvise anything there? If something were to happen there … Now, I don't know where they are deployed. Where are they? In Döllersheim? That would be lower Austria.

JODL: Döllersheim, yes.

THE FÜHRER: Up here?

JODL: Between Vienna and Brno, to the northwest. The closest place for Hungary is Bruck.

HIMMLER:[648] Bruck on the Mur [River], not Bruck on the Leitha [River].

THE FÜHRER: Here, Untersteinfeld near … ?

HIMMLER: … I still don't have a thing … on the whole, if they haven't closed a lot before … everything that's sitting inside. There these fellows are sitting directly …

THE FÜHRER: With the Hungarians it's complicated because we have Hungarian security divisions in the East. They are out of the picture at the moment.

HIMMLER: I have two with me; they participated in the fighting decently this time.

JODL: They have a good commander.

HIMMLER: … we could really consider how we can manage it.

THE FÜHRER: It would in fact be possible—

HIMMLER: I think it's possible that …

THE FÜHRER: No, they won't do that.

HIMMLER: My Führer, …

THE FÜHRER: No, they won't do that. But it would be possible for them to declare—because they know— …

HIMMLER: But it could … economically …

THE FÜHRER: Very much!

HIMMLER: That they stop this with the divisions. I wouldn't put any cowardly stunt beyond them.

(GÖRING: Yes.)

THE FÜHRER: And what can we do with this one here now?[649] How can we get this one out—the people, in particular?

JODL: Yes, I would propose to take them … to Corsica, if possible, and pull them together there.

GÖRING: That's my opinion as well. Make Corsica as strong as possible.

JODL: The troops would have to give everything away, though, if they're to go to Corsica.

THE FÜHRER: Then we must discuss today how they would get over to Corsica.

JODL: Yes, indeed. Especially if I don't have enough capacity available to get them here. I can take them over here, of course. But there's still something there.

THE FÜHRER: Of course, we'll have to give this up here as well … bring over here. [—] How is this here, Jodl, with the paratroopers? [—] This here will be given up now!

GÖRING: Why will it be given up if we're holding this?

THE FÜHRER: … up there the ports, and you can't occupy everything with two divisions.

JODL: … the three divisions on the coastal front and the *Feldherrnhalle* [Panzer Grenadier Division]. But then the unit will come down which is intended for[650] —

THE FÜHRER: Which one is it?

JODL: The 715th [Security Division].

THE FÜHRER: It has arrived?

JODL: It's there.

THE FÜHRER: It's there, but not mobile.

JODL: It's partly motorized, with buses.

THE FÜHRER: We could put them in here.

JODL: Their task is to safeguard Mussolini anyway.

THE FÜHRER: And then perhaps to go on to Turin.

JODL: The next to come now are the 305th [Infantry Division] and the 44th [Infantry Division] by two routes, beginning tomorrow—the 44th into this area and the 305th into this area.

THE FÜHRER: And the 24th Panzer [Division]? When does it arrive?

JODL: It's not in yet.

THE FÜHRER: I believe the 24th Panzer is the most important one. That's the panzer division ...

JODL: It is, of course, the only panzer division that ...

THE FÜHRER: Granted.

JODL: It's just a question of whether we ... in the northern part. [—] He's closer to Italy now, of course. It's just that he has that huge flank. If the Italians ... to here, here from Trieste downward.

GÖRING: As I said outside beforehand, "If we don't get the weapons, the rebels will get them."

THE FÜHRER: Where is the 10th SS [Panzer Grenadier Division]? Is it here?

HIMMLER: It's here.[651] It came down there first.

JODL: It's not quite ready yet, but almost.

THE FÜHRER: I heard a very good evaluation of the *Göring* [Parachute Panzer Division]... actually a characteristic, because it's a general evaluation of our youth.

JODL: I read it.

THE FÜHRER: The young people fight fanatically, the ones from the Hitler Youth, ... young German boys, some of them 16 years old.[652] These Hitler Youth usually fight more fanatically than their older comrades. ... report over there that they didn't get them until all of them had fallen—down to the last man. So, if these divisions all fight like these two SS divisions fight—

HIMMLER: They are good divisions now, my Führer.

THE FÜHRER: ... that's how the *Hitlerjugend* [Hitler Youth] [Panzer Grenadier] Division will fight, and the youth in general. They have already been uniformly trained. They will get the shock of their lives there. These are young boys but they are now ... trained for a long time.

HIMMLER: These two divisions will have been trained from February 15 to August 15.

GÖRING: Fourteen ... were army officers.

HIMMLER: But now they are in very good condition. They were also inspected by Dollmann,[653] Blaskowitz[654] and Rundstedt,[655] and they said they were very satisfied.

THE FÜHRER: Each division has how many men on average? And what's the average age?

HIMMLER: They have 400 officers on average and about 3,000 to 4,000 older non-commissioned officers—"older" meaning also between the ages of 20 and 30. The two divisions have an average age of 18½ years for the whole division, i.e., from the commander to the recruits.

THE FÜHRER: So it can be said that the majority of them are 18?

HIMMLER: Yes, 18 years.

GÖRING: Recently it was said that people between 26 and 30 have proven to be the best fighters.

HIMMLER: On average—purely physically.

THE FÜHRER: If they're trained so long ... earlier the young people were mostly God knows what ... But they're all boys who enlisted already at the age of 17—many of them even earlier ... so that they come in ... But they certainly did fight with unparalleled bravery ... The others were poorly trained—two months' training ... some before April, some after April, some during April, and from the remaining months we have about 14 days ... those were all "wonderful" exercises—meaning exercises on the training grounds in Oberwiesenfeld ... They are certainly better.

HIMMLER: They are well trained, all in all.

THE FÜHRER: So these first five divisions are there now. But then you have the 24th Panzer [Division] ready as well?

JODL: Then the 24th Panzer is also ready.

THE FÜHRER: We must put them in here—that's quite certain. We have to make sure that we get a division down here from the East quickly, and that we pull this in behind.

JODL: Then, my Führer, Field Marshal v. Rundstedt is arriving at the Fourth Italian Army headquarters today.

GÖRING: For a visit.

JODL: Within the framework of these ongoing visits. The relationship has always been very good so far. I think it's quite a good—

GÖRING: Perfect!

THE FÜHRER: But he shouldn't stay there for long. He should leave again as soon as possible. The thing must be done quickly. We must look as quickly as possible—he must get an accurate picture of the situation today already.

GÖRING: What Italian formations are deployed in Rome?

HIMMLER: My Führer! We could try to get this division from the Duce. We gave them 12 assault guns, 12 Panzer IVs and 12 Panzer IIIs. That's 36—

THE FÜHRER: ... division, as much as they get.

JODL: There are people there anyway.

HIMMLER: Obersturmbannführer (Leinert)[656] from my staff is still there.

THE FÜHRER: He ought to make sure that we get the whole division—that it joins us.

GÖRING: At least the guns …

HIMMLER: Then the training commands are also down there.

JODL: When may I send this order down?

THE FÜHRER: … can give …

JODL: I've just transmitted an order to Kesselring.

GÖRING: Are we really giving these orders?

THE FÜHRER: They all come by encoded telex.

JODL: It's perfect.

THE FÜHRER: By encoded telex? What do you want? Otherwise we can't give anything—no orders at all anymore. Otherwise he won't know what we want.

GÖRING: I thought that in this case it could be done with special secret couriers.

THE FÜHRER: Couriers are even more dangerous, if they have anything on them. This must be enciphered again.

GÖRING: Memorized!

THE FÜHRER: But they can't memorize too many things. Besides, they memorize it anyway because … was also here; that's essentially how it was down there as well.

SCHERFF: Probably here … in the event of a coup.

HIMMLER: I can send something down to his people by radio.

GÖRING: It would certainly be most disastrous if they gave this here to the English. That would be disastrous, of course. That would be just fantastic. [—] They have the task of disarming them?

SCHERFF: Only very generally: to act if necessary. Then they usually lead them to the possibility—

THE FÜHRER: They are informed about the possibility of a coup, both of them, since in that case—

GÖRING: …

THE FÜHRER: No, they should get a signal. If we communicate it to them, it would cause difficulties. With them we can … radio …

HIMMLER: I can also radio to my division in Rome.

THE FÜHRER: Enciphered?

HIMMLER: Yes, indeed. Enciphered.

THE FÜHRER: And is that completely secure?

HIMMLER: Completely secure. We've agreed on a brand new key. Yesterday we made the last key. I can give them the order that they … with their …

GÖRING: … it must be secure.

JODL: That can only go to Kesselring, because otherwise he won't know what the further intentions are. The news that he then receives … a totally different situation again …

THE FÜHRER: Jodl, so for the march in here ... pull in to get in here first or to get across the Brenner?

JODL: I don't see any difficulties in getting across the Brenner [Pass]. The trains simply run through there.

THE FÜHRER: Yes, but if they suddenly occupy this?

JODL: Then there's the other point of view—

HIMMLER: And South Tyrol rebels![657]

THE FÜHRER: But there are no South Tyrolese. They've all been called up!

HIMMLER: There are still men there. The Italians are ... if we seize them ... They have to enter their bunkers anyway. I'm quite sure of that.

THE FÜHRER: ... Innsbruck garrison ... and makes his Tigers available for this purpose ... have you already spoken with Thomale about the affair? (JODL: Yes.)

Also about that?

SCHERFF: Thomale was here anyway.

JODL: We spoke with him already. At least over there in the east we have— the next closest regiment is there in Tarvisio.

HIMMLER: That's what I was going to say. This regiment came there ... this is now undamaged here ... this mountain regiment. We can bring it up easily.

THE FÜHRER: What kind of police regiment is this here?

HIMMLER: That's the police regiment that's in Marseilles. My Führer, we could ... this with Laibach and Trieste ...

JODL: The crossing points that we ... from Agram to ...

HIMMLER: It is important to me that we hold this in Laibach.

THE FÜHRER: But this we could bring over here.

HIMMLER: I can do that easily.

THE FÜHRER: Shouldn't we do that right away?

JODL: I suppose they will do this anyway because they have the order to safeguard ... —we will find that out today—to use increased security. We won't have anything else.

HIMMLER: Here I would get over much easier; we're located here already. So I would reach it more easily if I were to take Tarvisio from here. If I go in there, ... and then I have to say, of course: how far should we go up to this point we can ... go up.

THE FÜHRER: Well, if the tanks come the whole rabble will run away immediately like cowards. It's just good that I—

HIMMLER: Are our panzer units going down there as well?

GÖRING: They won't fight!

HIMMLER: Where are they going?

THE FÜHRER: Here, but we'll have to see. The *Leibstandarte* [Panzer Grenadier Division] will leave its tanks behind and get them back here.

GÖRING: I'm not concerned. That these cripples will oppose us at the Brenner [Pass]—that's totally impossible.

THE FÜHRER: If our Panthers come—

GÖRING: I think it's very good, the paratroopers jumping. Himmler's people can do it better than mine. Immediately!

THE FÜHRER: They can't jump. They have to land!

GÖRING: Some of them will land, yes.

KEITEL: ... Six o'clock in the morning goes up to ...

THE FÜHRER: He should come here!

KEITEL: He will come here at once. Yes, Sir.

THE FÜHRER: ...

GÖRING: Yes, that's my opinion as well.

THE FÜHRER: ... the Italians mad.

GÖRING: I mean that he did write the letter there!

LINGE: My Führer, Field Marshal Kluge and General Zeitzler have arrived. Would you like the gentlemen to come right away?

THE FÜHRER: Yes.

(*Meeting is interrupted by a discussion with Field Marshal v. Kluge.*[658])

The East

ZEITZLER: In the Seventeenth Army area, the counterattacks down here were somewhat successful. They started again today. Until 5 a.m. ... So far it has gone quite well. He has pushed only a little from the side. Then an attack began here ... Here, my Führer, the relief has already been reported: here the mechanized corps by the guards infantry corps and here the mechanized corps ... We ought to keep a particularly close eye on these movements, to see if they're being shifted by train or if they're just being pulled down ... and want to engage in a minor local action there. That could be possible. I spoke with Manstein ... He is already considering whether or not he should stay here with all the antitank guns. [—] The keyword—what's going on ... could last quite a while anyway. [—] The *Leibstandarte* [Panzer Grenadier Division] leaves tomorrow evening; they're already quite close. Here there was only local pressure, so we can assume that there might not be anything major going on at the moment, or he is still regrouping. He put the *Viking* [SS Panzer Grenadier Division] there and ... the downward movement from up above.

THE FÜHRER: But that's all that's going through?

(ZEITZLER: Yes, Sir.)

The 1st Panzer [Division] has 49?

ZEITZLER: But it will be here for weeks still.

THE FÜHRER: These here have 45 Panzer IVs and 10 Panzer VIs? That should actually be more. They can give those away at once. They only have 28 tanks anyway. They can give those to the *Reich*, [SS Panzer Grenadier Division *Das Reich*], and later, when the *Reich* is transported out, they will hand the package on again.

(ZEITZLER: Yes, Sir.)

How many assault guns does he still have?

ZEITZLER: Thirty.

THE FÜHRER: Thirty. And how many does he have?

ZEITZLER: Thirty-two.

THE FÜHRER: And how many (tanks) does he [SS *Viking* Panzer Grenadier Division] have?

ZEITZLER: One hundred and twenty.

THE FÜHRER: Then ... the *Viking* ... can give some away.

ZEITZLER: Yes, and this could be filled up somewhat.

THE FÜHRER: Perhaps we could give him more assault guns here. It makes no sense to take them along.

ZEITZLER: Certainly. It will be arranged so that this one will give them away, and, in return, will get those coming in that would otherwise be used as replacements. It will get a detachment when it gets there.

THE FÜHRER: It doesn't make sense to take the Tigers along, either. He can either give them to the *Reich* for the time being or—

BUHLE: A Tiger detachment for the *Leibstandarte* can be ready within 14 days, especially if the personnel—

THE FÜHRER: They will be ready in 14 days?

BUHLE: He can get ... 90 Panzer IVs by August 8.

THE FÜHRER: He doesn't need 90.

BUHLE: According to the thinking of the General Staff, though, some will be diverted from the 1st Panzer Division ...

THE FÜHRER: He doesn't need 90 if he's going to get his 90 Panzer Vs anyway.

ZEITZLER: If he gets his Panzer Vs, we can share ... with the ... so these stay here.

THE FÜHRER: It's enough if he gets 50.

ZEITZLER: He has the Tiger detachment and the Panther detachment.

BUHLE: The Panther detachment gets 71.

THOMALE: These are the companies ... until now four platoons ... four companies to be reduced from 22 to 17 ... so that he has a total of 21 vehicles.

THE FÜHRER: That's plenty.

THOMALE: Regarding the figure for the *Leibstandarte Adolf Hitler* formation ... Can I ... , my Führer, ... ?

THE FÜHRER: Yes.

ZEITZLER: Here east of Khar'kov there was more movement again. We have to watch and see whether it might possibly be these two things, which he may be regrouping. There are many indications that something could happen here [at Khar'kov], or up here [at Belgorod], at these two pressure points. Maybe this panzer can also ... or a part of it. Then something else new could happen—this matter here ... the 168th [Infantry] Division ... Here, another tank attack ... it began today.

THE FÜHRER: Those are these movements!

ZEITZLER: Yes, indeed. Those are probably these movements ... went ahead ... 6th Panzer [Division] now, after the sortie.

THE FÜHRER: Then here the 19th, the 11th and here the 6th [Panzer Divisions].

ZEITZLER: Then we left the 7th [Panzer Division] up here because ... pull in behind, of course.

THE FÜHRER: And the 3rd [Panzer Division] will be reserved ...

(Italy)

JODL: *(Presentation.)*

THE FÜHRER: July 25? What's today's date?

(JODL: The 26th.)

Is that in here?

JODL: Yes, Sir. I wrote it in here. [—] These are the instructions for the 715th [Security Division] regarding the safeguarding of Mussolini. [—] Then this is about the potential withdrawal of the forces from Sicily to[659] Sardinia.

THE FÜHRER: Has anyone spoken with the Grand Admiral [Dönitz] about the possibilities yet?

DÖNITZ: No.

JODL: He just knows that the embarkation area available for this purpose is at least as large as or even larger than the one used for the Strait of Messina.

DÖNITZ: ... up to 7,000 men daily in the Strait of Messina. Since the troops will be without equipment, we calculated 10,000 men.

THE FÜHRER: So they could be over there within two days?

DÖNITZ: In any case as many as in the Strait ... without equipment 1,500 tons, easily.

THE FÜHRER: But with guns, etc.

DÖNITZ: Yes, of course.

JODL: That was calculated based on crossing this way. If it has to be forced now, we should expect these figures to increase.

DÖNITZ: Yes, indeed. I believe that bringing the people in will require more time than ... the same applies to the strait between Sardinia and Corsica.

THE FÜHRER: ... if the matter is secured ... all their forces there.

DÖNITZ: Up here—from up here.

THE FÜHRER: ... or a part of it.

DÖNITZ: Yes, indeed. Because I think we should, if possible, take control of it up to La Spezia, because of the fleet ... would be a base in this area that is closer than that one. The only difficulty is that right now we have our supply base here, too. But we should get a base here in this area, maybe in Salerno. That's important.

GÖRING: Has the sequence of the crossing here been ordered?

THE FÜHRER: We have to leave that to the commanders here.

JODL: That's the responsibility of the XIV Corps. [—] Then this track is completely full at the moment. Eleven trains of the 26th Panzer Division are still underway here ... of the 1st Parachute Division four trains are still underway.

THE FÜHRER: What are these now?

JODL: Those are the units that are there in their entirety. [—] ... 4 trains in France. There is now the question of whether they shouldn't be stopped and deployed at the French coast.

DÖNITZ: ...that we ... ...not give them ... these four with the Italians ...

JODL: ... taking over by the Fourth Army.

GÖRING: For that, the paratroop things are with ...

JODL: Much more, even! Fifty trains of the 26th Panzer Division have not yet been loaded!

THE FÜHRER: Fifty?!

JODL: It's supposed to have more than 100 trains. These are all things that still ...

THE FÜHRER: Not loaded yet? [—] Then it's coming here anyway?

JODL: It will come here in any case. There are reports from the 1st Parachute Division that 45 trains have not yet been loaded.

THE FÜHRER: From the 1st Parachute Division?

JODL: From the 1st Parachute Division, yes.

THE FÜHRER: What are they? Probably not parachutists?

JODL: No, all the accessory equipment.[660] I don't know everything that is in there, of course.

JESCHONNEK: Rear staff, everything that—

THE FÜHRER: Then it has even more than ... rear things.

JESCHONNEK: Not only the 1st Parachute Division but also General Student[661] wanted to push down some additional things belonging to the corps troops; everything that was down there from the combat units of the 1st Parachute Division—

JODL: But they don't take ... These troops also have their winter equipment with them, of course.

JESCHONNEK: But they take these troops …

JODL: There are 6 trains that have not yet been loaded with Navy units.

THE FÜHRER: Regarding the sequence,[662] I would say: first the paratroops, second the Göring division, third the panzer division, fourth the remains of the Africa divisions, and last the 29th [Panzer Grenadier Division], because it also has the least there. But we have to leave this to the Army anyway. We can't do it schematically. But the whole front must … that goes back by leaps and bounds. The parachute division is, of course, the most important thing because it's the most valuable.

GÖRING: He urgently needs paratroopers. They are also the fastest to be redeployed again. The deployment of the 2nd Parachute Division should be discussed again. If we can't stop this … the corps actions … not clear yet.

JESCHONNEK: Absolutely. The 2nd is not coming down by rail. This division can be stopped at once.

THE FÜHRER: We shouldn't burden the rail system with such things.

JODL: It's urgent that these combat troops be transported on this railway line.

GÖRING: There's nothing down there anymore anyway, so we can stop them …

JODL: Then the decisive question is that the Italians stop these paratrooper units because … can't take in … at the Brenner.[663] Then the moment will come when I will no longer stop at this barrier. For now, of course, we must—

THE FÜHRER: That will happen the minute we occupy Rome.

JODL: Then the … together … must … acute.

THE FÜHRER: The occupation of Rome … has the 3rd Panzer Grenadier Division and all the units that they … must still draw in there. At the same time, that will also be the signal for ruthless action along the whole front. The critical thing is: the … absolutely must come down here.

GÖRING: May I ask again about the parachute division, my Führer? How do you see the dropping of the parachute division?

JODL: The dropping of the parachute division first aims at preventing anyone from escaping from Rome …

THE FÜHRER: It must be completely occupied—all arterial roads. That requires only very small teams. They will take up all-round defense positions, and then nothing else can happen anyway.

GÖRING: So not all of them simultaneously … The ones assembling on the airfield …

THE FÜHRER: Everything else that we bring into the city will be landed on an airfield. I don't know which one at the moment. We must make sure that we leave the airfield quickly, though, because we have to expect the

Allies to launch an attack very quickly. We have to leave the airfield instantly.

GÖRING: And blow up whatever we can blow up!

JESCHONNEK: That could only be done if a courier were sent down to southern France today or tomorrow, to General Student or the 2nd Parachute Division, to tell them where to go.

GÖRING: Where exactly it is that they have to jump?

JESCHONNEK: Because it won't be possible to have a clear view of the situation this afternoon or tomorrow morning.

THE FÜHRER: The situation will always be the same. Rome remains Rome. The arterial roads ... must be occupied. And that is something we absolutely can do.

GÖRING: Who would be best to block off the Vatican from the capital?

THE FÜHRER: That's the responsibility of the units coming in—first of all the 3rd Panzer Grenadier Division; they must do that. Then whatever is dropped afterward ... Now here are three so-called active Italian divisions. But I don't believe that they will do much if they're faced with force.

JODL: The 12th [Infantry Division] is in Rome. The others are further away.

THE FÜHRER: ... heard that Fascist Italy ... constitutes a world.

KEITEL: I thought they didn't have any military down there and that they wanted to take it out as far as possible?

HEWEL: They have apparently prepared everything very well—the newspapers ... the posters—everything is prepared. The president of the "Stefani" has shot himself, and such things.

THE FÜHRER: Who?

HEWEL: The president of the "Stefani" news agency has shot himself.[664] There are rumors to that effect right now, anyway.

HIMMLER: My Führer! People were also arrested—I regard this news as ...—Germans. At least as far as they don't belong to the embassy and aren't under suspicion somehow for having played a role in terms of intelligence or something. Also women.

THE FÜHRER: The Foreign Office must receive that immediately so that our ambassador there can declare at once, "All Germans must be released immediately or we will take the harshest measures." [—] The whole thing must be done very quickly, of course. That's the important thing. ... Speed is of the essence here. So, Rommel, it's a matter of first drawing the forces over here because we can't hold Sicily any longer; that's impossible. Whether you can hold the boot is also a question, but that really doesn't matter. The essential point is to maintain coherence so that we can fight at all.

JODL: I'd like to say with respect to the command: Field Marshal Rommel will have the command down there ... or we have to make a separation, so that Field Marshal Rommel ... this action. ... and that Field Marshal Kesselring will bring in these new forces from the south. As soon as they arrive there they will be put under the command of Field Marshal Rommel. It won't work otherwise; from Munich it is ...

THE FÜHRER: Granted, but nevertheless I think that the command ... must be given to Rommel.

JODL: Then ... to go to the south in order to ...

THE FÜHRER: Marshal Kesselring doesn't have the name. We have to go public with it the moment we jump ... Marshal Rommel![665] Second, all Fascist divisions and units that join ... We want to get the Fascists over at once; that must be our goal. ... destroyed units, also regular divisions ... and volunteers. Himmler had a very good idea there. We want Farinacci to declare that every man can go home—we want to involve him today already. Every Italian soldier can go home ... we will then get ... We won't get the others who go home. They are useless at the moment.[666]

HIMMLER: It might be better to take them to Germany afterward as workers.

THE FÜHRER: They are useless anyway, of course. [—] The second would be the attempt to take units away from here. This is the general task here, irrespective of the security here. The third is the occupation of Rome—by dropping paratroops and moving in the 3rd Panzer Grenadier Division.

GÖRING: But that must be ordered down there on site. It absolutely can't be ordered from Munich.

THE FÜHRER: It will be ordered, and the commanders will be responsible for carrying it out. And then, in parallel, the German units marching in. Unfortunately, we don't have enough paratroopers to do this here completely. I'm really sorry that we have this division over here. It would be good to have two divisions here right away. Then the German divisions would approach here. As far as border-crossing points are concerned, we should harmonize this then, of course. And it will take some time. The units ... Here's the *Feldherrnhalle* [Panzer Grenadier Division], even though it's not fully mobile—that doesn't matter. One task force is missing; the other will come afterward. But we must occupy this anyway... As soon as even one unit threatens to resist, ruthless shooting will start immediately. That's the only possibility. The action must be carried out ... Including the *Herman Göring*, there are six divisions—very good divisions instead.

GÖRING: Our opponents will, of course, call to the Allies for help and beg for their protection. So where will the enemy land then?

THE FÜHRER: But it will take some time before he is ready to land.

GÖRING: He can land paratroopers just as well as we can, of course.

THE FÜHRER: Of course he can do that, but that makes—

GÖRING: I just think it should be considered.

THE FÜHRER: At first, they are astounded—as always in such a case.

GÖRING: If Rome surrenders there will be no call for help to the Allies anymore.

THE FÜHRER: Actually, there will be. Some will run away because the Italians are ... Italy is divided and the Fascists are being pursued. [—] Who shot himself? The director of the "Stefani"?

HEWEL: Yes, the director of the "Stefani" shot himself.

THE FÜHRER: So, one can see that they were anything but unified. That will ... overthrow. That's one who ... himself Fascist ... that people wait for some signal, and then it will go on. We have to immediately ... , for example, the "Fascist Freedom Army."

HIMMLER: ... which has the panzer division, if we ... the commander again ...

THE FÜHRER: There we will have to see ... is the task of a ... We must establish a provisional Fascist government right away, which will sit there and give the orders that the ... All Fascist soldiers and officers immediately have a National Socialist [—] We must deliberately ... the National Socialist ... It is critical that these Fascist soldiers and officers join the National Socialist units immediately.[667] This elderly 73-year-old[668] [—]

HIMMLER: May I hand the order down to my Obersturmbannführer[669] ... urgent ... that have their training ... must come.

THE FÜHRER: He won't be able to do it.

HIMMLER: That's a different division. These are actually only militiamen.

THE FÜHRER: But there are so many others among them!

GÖRING: Then at least there are Germans sitting on the tanks and assault guns.

THE FÜHRER: Our people who are there. Otherwise nothing is done. There is time. They will get the order. If this has to happen, they'll get the order as well. They hear the appeals; hopefully they won't seal their ears. Then he won't need to keep anything secret anymore ... when the radio speaks openly. When "Stefani" radio publicly—

JODL: ... this training command has been initiated.

THE FÜHRER: Now, of course, many details have already been discussed here. There are divisions here ... the others must be eliminated. If the political propaganda in these Eastern divisions ... Many of these people don't want to be destined to die ...

KEITEL: They don't want to die. These are Eastern divisions. They'll disperse. Militia divisions, with very few—

THE FÜHRER: What do they have here? One moment! The 65th [Infantry Division], the 94th [Infantry Division], the 571st [Infantry Division], the 24th [Panzer Division], and the 3rd Panzer Grenadier Division ... I'm missing ... Where does it go?

JODL: This was the reverse compilation, to form an operational army together with the Italians. That has changed now. Now, the 305th [Infantry Division] and the 44th [Infantry Division] go in here to the north, while the 305th [Infantry Division] [670] remains down there.

THE FÜHRER: ... not there yet either?

JODL: No.

THE FÜHRER: It's coming here to the north anyway. Here there are more divisions coming. How many formations are coming here? The 76th [Infantry Division], the 305th [Infantry Division], then the 44th [Infantry Division]—

JODL: The 65th [Infantry Division].

THE FÜHRER: The 65th. All of them to the north.

JODL: The 24th Panzer Division, which is being planned on without the formations he's taking over here—he's taking over the 389th [Infantry Division], the 376th [Infantry Division] and ...

THE FÜHRER: So the 76th, the 305th, then the 44th, and then the 65th. Tell me, where does the 371st go?

JODL: ...

THE FÜHRER: And the 94th?

JODL: It comes in place of the ... the 44th, the 94th, then the 76th and the 65th—

THE FÜHRER: Just a moment! Once again!

JODL: The 44th, the 94th, the 76th, the 65th, the 305th, the 24th Panzer.

THE FÜHRER: And in addition the 3rd Panzer Grenadier, which is there anyway?

JODL: Yes, the 3rd Panzer Grenadier and the 2nd Parachute Division.

THE FÜHRER: And the 2nd Parachute Division. So that's eight divisions.

JODL: ... not the 26th Panzer [Division].

THE FÜHRER: Then to—Zeitzler, when does the advance guard of the *Leibstandarte* [SS Panzer Grenadier Division] arrive?

ZEITZLER: On August 2.

THE FÜHRER: Is the advance guard arriving?

ZEITZLER: The first train will depart tomorrow night. Then it will presumably arrive August 2.

THE FÜHRER: And it will need altogether?

ZEITZLER: At a tempo of 12 to 18 initially. Between the 2nd and the 8th it will be there in its entirety.

THE FÜHRER: So in addition the *Leibstandarte* will come, and right after that the *Reich* [SS Panzer Grenadier Division]

ZEITZLER: Yes, indeed. The *Reich*.[671]

THE FÜHRER: Then two additional panzer divisions will arrive.

JODL: They will be transported via Villach-Tarvisio anyway.

THE FÜHRER: That I don't know. But that's two again.

HIMMLER: When they come from the East, that's the most urgent.

THE FÜHRER: Then we have 10 divisions already.

ROMMEL: The supply from the East has, of course, the disadvantage that they...very many...are ... Then we are seriously delayed ... Isonzo [River].

THE FÜHRER: Then comes the next: the Indian[672]—the eleventh.

JODL: But by the time it arrives, all these routes to France will still be fully blocked. It might arrive at a moment when either ... do, or when it hasn't started yet at all—the other action.

THE FÜHRER: What do you think about this matter here, Rommel? That must happen very quickly ... The faster it happens the easier it will be ... all the other things ... in one moment ... that we go in; that's decisive. For this we have two divisions available, plus those units of the 26th Panzer Grenadier Division, plus those units that aren't yet very far along.

JODL: There is an urgent need for a general command. The SS General Command will come along anyway.

THE FÜHRER: ... comes after it. That will probably be—

ZEITZLER: Between the 1st and the 2nd, I think. Between the *Leibstandarte* and the *Reich*.

JODL: ... the General Command IV[673] is planned, as there is no corps staff at all down here ... to take over the Italians' sector, the Fourth Italian Army. Then we have released this one here from the front. But this one is not yet ready. That will take until mid-August—or at least it should take that long.

GÖRING: Where is the Parachute General Command?

JODL: We could take that for this thing. This is the only operations staff.

THE FÜHRER: Who is it?

JODL: Student.

THE FÜHRER: Excellent! That's the man for something like this—outstandingly qualified.

JODL: Now we need one for all these divisions that are coming in. It could perhaps be advanced to mid-August, so that this could come over here as well. It's not very much, though.

(*Presentation of a discussion between Mackensen and Badoglio by Ambassador Hewel.*)

THE FÜHRER: What untruthful nonsense! Listen! (*Reading aloud.*) "Fundamental cooperation"! [—] What impertinence!

HEWEL: Now he's making an effort!

THE FÜHRER: If I could catch this filthy pig!

GÖRING: The insolence with the letter!

THE FÜHRER: He's still a tricky old enemy of ours. He was the one who, on August 25, 1939, was at the forefront of those who saw to it that Italy didn't join the war—a fact that caused the English-French declaration of war and the signing of the Polish alliance.[674]

GÖRING: But a thing like this with his letter! A spectacle, really—a Punch and Judy show!

Sicily

THE FÜHRER: How are things here?

JODL: There was nothing in particular here ... The location of the 50 ships and larger units that were reported yesterday hasn't yet been further clarified ... The enemy has attacked more forcefully along the coastal route, on the right wing of the 29th Panzer Grenadier Division, on this line indicated in blue. The new commander has now taken over the 29th and reports that the division had only ... since it was rarely in combat ... crumbled further.

GÖRING: But if we ... here ... all this becomes a very strict German affair. This whole crossing here—

THE FÜHRER: Most importantly, the antiaircraft unit stays until the last man is gone.

DÖNITZ: We have to hold the entire width.

Situation at sea (Mediterranean)

THE FÜHRER: Where is this convoy that's heading east?

JUNGE: We have the following report about it: a convoy ... east of Palermo yesterday afternoon, with 8 larger ships and approximately 40 to 42 smaller ships, possibly landing craft ... [675] The precise location is unknown. A report that we received this morning might be connected to it—a report stating that 30 to 40 miles north of the Straits of Messina a convoy of 16 smaller vessels—presumably landing craft—was seen heading north this morning. It is likely the same convoy, but that hasn't been confirmed. No special significance can be drawn from it, except that the enemy is able to move fairly freely here.

THE FÜHRER: Is he being attacked here?

JUNGE: There are no combat forces here. There are only two submarines and the motor torpedo boats available here.

THE FÜHRER: No, by the Luftwaffe!

JUNGE: The report just came in.

CHRISTIAN: The intentions with regard to this matter are not yet known.

JUNGE: In addition, there will ... from the eastern Mediterranean Sea considerable enemy movement ... quite lively activity taking place on the northern coast and that ... already reported. There are also ... back from the 23rd, probably during the return transport from Palermo, 5 barges were attacked. Four of them were damaged so heavily that they had to destroy themselves. The rest tried to escape ... Sea rescue service by 10 Ju 52s. Out of three minesweepers that were used in this action, one was sunk. The minesweepers shot down two aircraft. Finally, a torpedo boat and an Italian corvette were damaged during an air raid against Messina yesterday. An attack carried out with a ... had no effect because of the already damaged state of the ship. They tried to recover the steamer ... a large ship of 8,700 tons, but the effort failed.[676] Then regarding our own situation, one significant thing is the report that along the entire southern coast all planned mine barriers were released in accordance with a coherent plan, i.e., there are German mine layers ... The reports about traffic here are sparse. No report at all about traffic from Sardinia; from Corsica only one vessel going back, and from here two submarines. [—] In the Greek area it should be reported as significant that ... the ... Navy commander of ... was shot down when he was flying over Corfu in a Ju 88 some days ago. [—] Convoy traffic in the Aegean Sea is running as planned. Here a larger troop convoy.

THE FÜHRER: Who shot him down?

JUNGE: An English ... In the Black Sea the enemy ... attacked, achieving the success that his ... was shot down ... continuous unsuccessful ... Traffic was disturbed again by the dropping of mines. ...

Italian fleet

DÖNITZ: My Führer! ... came back. It's just that there is a constant connection ... that 90% of his officers would come with us. I don't know.

THE FÜHRER: That couldn't be right.

DÖNITZ: That's too much. I can't do anything to prevent ... submarines ... were in La Spezia and Toulon and that 5 or 6 of them anchor near La Spezia. The right thing would be—if the propaganda didn't work—to seize the ships as soon as possible.

THE FÜHRER: They will be ... in Toulon ...

DÖNITZ: Yes, perhaps they can be seized before. I myself have submarine crews in La Spezia, too.[677] But they have nothing but shotguns or pistols, and they are not equipped with anything else. So if you want to seize the ships, the troops have to be equipped with the appropriate weapons. But I actually believe the Italians will let us seize them.

THE FÜHRER: Do you have any idea [—]?

GÖRING: We have people in there.

DÖNITZ: But they are not mobile—perhaps 300 men. We have 2 submarines in there. With 300 men you can't do much in the way of propaganda.

Obviously, they are not trained for this—they are sailors. I think, my Führer, we should try to prevent these people from putting to sea.

THE FÜHRER: I have said before that a special squadron or troop should be made available for this purpose.

DÖNITZ: Let's wait and see. You never know.

GÖRING: But you are there in front with submarines?

DÖNITZ: I will immediately be there with submarines if they put to sea. We have to wait and see how it develops. It's also possible that there will be a split within the fleet—that the young officers will arrest the old ones.[678]

GÖRING: But keep the group prepared for action!

JUNGE: You can let them know that there are submarines there.

FÜHRER: No, for God's sake, no!

DÖNITZ: That is still premature…

Situation in the air

CHRISTIAN: Near … it is noticeable that the enemy was very restrained in the air yesterday. One attack against … , specific damage not reported. Two aircraft were shot down then … also has, and that is striking, with 50 … , so that he simply has … this transportation … the island of Corsica and has a photo imaging system … shot down 10 aircraft. Then, the night before last, our Luftwaffe attacked with 99 aircraft … sank, one of them hit by a torpedo … , 13 other hits by torpedoes.[679]

THE FÜHRER: Altogether 56,000 tons. God Almighty! [—] Boy, do you have the thing, where this … happened? In the long run this would have become unbearable for the guy. It would have to become unbearable! Of course, if we did anything new here, it would have been the same.

CHRISTIAN: The information given by the police seems to be …

THE FÜHRER: I like it better that way.

CHRISTIAN: From…there is only the report…on the usage of destroyers.

THE FÜHRER: If I count a total of only 50,000 tons as temporary loss, and if I count a daily loss of 20,000 or only 10,000 tons here, that adds up to 300,000 tons per month and in 3 months it will be 1 million tons, which he loses in the Mediterranean region alone. And the damaged vessels—except for those that have been sunk—he has to bring back, to transport back. That's a loss of 90,000 to 100,000 tons. That is 300,000 per month, or 1 million per year.

HIMMLER: 20,000 a day!

THE FÜHRER: No, I calculate 10,000 tons a day. That's 300,000 tons per month, 900,000 in three months, so 1 million roughly. That is about half the ship capacity that he always has here.

DÖNITZ: If we finish them off, he will have nothing left for the operations.

CHRISTIAN: No further reconnaissance over La Spezia ...

GÖRING: It is very remarkable that he hardly flew at all yesterday, since he's always bombarding us with whole squadrons otherwise.

Action against Rome

JODL: In my view, the most important thing is to bring Student's staff to Kesselring immediately. Secondly, we need to send a courier to Kesselring, who can discuss the Rome action with Kesselring and Student verbally because he doesn't know about it, and who can then report back to us with what forces he might have and when he can bring them together so we can fix a rough date.

THE FÜHRER: We have to fix the date, or it won't actually happen—it will keep getting delayed, and that won't work. We have always determined this ourselves. We also determined it in the Serbian case and fixed it ourselves. We can't leave this to the organization down there.

JODL: But the organization down there can only tell me at the moment what is available there besides the 3rd Panzer Grenadier Division.

THE FÜHRER: The rest is up to us. We can ... the paratroop ...

JODL: ... only the people down there, Kesselring and Student, who ... the transport area [—]

GÖRING: We already know about the paratroops from up there.

THE FÜHRER: When can they jump?

GÖRING: There are 9 battalions.

JESCHONNEK: Nine infantry battalions have to be armed quickly. They have to fly in three waves. I would like to suggest that the second wave should possibly be undertaken in agreement with Field Marshal Kesselring, who has to determine where to land ... also involved will be the 1st Parachute Regiment ... Naples.

THE FÜHRER: The first wave can't land without ... impossible. The first thing we have to do is to close the exit roads instantly. Detached units must block them.

JESCHONNEK: ... the first wave, without the Italians recognizing ... when the intention is clear that Rome will be closed off.

JODL: We should do this under all circumstances. We could only afford a random drop if the whole division could fly at the same time and could drift down together.

THE FÜHRER: But who can guarantee that he won't get wind of it immediately? All the airfields are swarming with Italians, and if so many paratroopers come?

JODL: I think it will be possible, provided the paratroopers go to Sicily. That the Italians will act in a hostile way against the paratroopers as long as they are landing, [—]

THE FÜHRER: They won't do that.

JODL: I don't believe so. But the moment they jump, it will be completely different.

THE FÜHRER: Then a part of them will run away and the action will have failed—we must be aware of this.

GÖRING: There is a parachute division in Sicily.

JODL: It's all full of paratroopers ... will be unloaded.

GÖRING: Perhaps we can do it in such a way that all transport ... we ... directly with the Italians ... but that flights are only made to Rome and landings made there ... above all the transportation area ... need reinforcements here for the first wave ...

THE FÜHRER: Then I wouldn't say that the paratroops [—]

GÖRING: No, the 1st!

JESCHONNEK: The 1st Parachute Division.

GÖRING: Supply for them. We officially announce that here we don't ... anymore, that we need trains to bring them to Sicily. That would be the first wave. Then they fly back and we say officially, "We can only go to Rome because the places here are destroyed, and we can't fly over because of yesterday's loss." All this will be recorded. We have had the losses when flying over it ... In my view, we risk too many crews during the flight there, so we can only go to Rome ... Then, we officially announce to the *Comando Supremo*: we need trains for the paratroopers to cross to Reggio, since they are part of the division. And then the second wave comes.

JESCHONNEK: Not all the planes that arrive will be ready for paratroopers, if all of them want to jump.

THE FÜHRER: How many could jump?

JESCHONNEK: At the moment, with General Student—in the 2nd Parachute Division itself and in the region—which today ... southern Italy 90 Ju 52s plus 45 He 111s.

GÖRING: How many do they calculate on average now?

JESCHONNEK: On average, with weapons, 10 men ... together with these planes 2½ to 3 battalions.

GÖRING: That's landing space for—?

THE FÜHRER: That would be 1,200 men.

JESCHONNEK: If we add everything together, that would be 160 Ju 52s, 98 He 111s—so around a hundred 111s—6 Me 313s and 80 towing airplanes.

GÖRING: How many 111s did you say are ready to jump?

JESCHONNEK: I have 20 111s plus 70 equals 90 and now altogether 162 Ju 52s.

GÖRING: You just said 45!

JESCHONNEK: No, 20 plus 70 is 90 and 45 111s.

THE FÜHRER: ... different again; if they left, they can come down right away. They can be re-supplied later; they should stay for now.

BUHLE: The question of shifting the concentration and equipping the vehicles! The General Staff has considered it already... it's possible to move it there, including the 60.

ZEITZLER: I'll scrape everything together from the less important things ... come quickly.

THE FÜHRER: What kind of units are they?

BUHLE: Those are only units that are intended for assignment to the West, to northern Italy and to ... , which still have a larger reserve of vehicles—the 24th [Panzer Division], which is nearly complete, and the 60th [Panzer Grenadier Division *Feldherrnhalle*].

KEITEL: The 60th, i.e., the *Feldherrnhalle*, and the 24th.

ZEITZLER: It's on the way; it started this morning already.

GÖRING: Then we can use a strengthened regiment, 3½ battalions, in the first wave. We can finish it in three waves—the first wave tomorrow and the second following quickly in the early morning.

JESCHONNEK: The first wave starting tomorrow?!

GÖRING: In the early morning!

THE FÜHRER: Then I would start the first wave tomorrow evening.

GÖRING: This is the announced one; they won't get trains at once.

THE FÜHRER: But the other must be done in the morning. I can only do this together with the infantry advance. So the jump absolutely has to start at the crack of dawn, when the 3rd Panzer Grenadier Division drives in.

GÖRING: The first wave we want to land based on the need for it to come here. It lands here and then it meets over there. Then the second wave would come tomorrow for reinforcement.

THE FÜHRER: At the first light of dawn the second wave jumps.

JESCHONNEK: ... that the planes go back.

THE FÜHRER: That's two days, as I said before!

GÖRING: ... give the order immediately; this has to be emphasized.

JESCHONNEK: If it could still be postponed by one day, I would suggest that.

KEITEL: A telegram arrived from Rome, my Führer. The second-in-command of the *Comando Supremo* says: "Marshal Badoglio ... functions. Second: The Chief of the Luftwaffe High Command, General ... , reports directly to the king. Third: [—]" (*Further reading aloud.*)

THE FÜHRER: Things will most certainly change! They will see how things are going to change. That's the same fuss like with the Yugoslavs back then … "The Duce came on 24th. He would have remained in the minority, which resulted in his resignation … government by Marshal Badoglio. During the night of the 25th there was excited cheering—especially from young people—for the royal house and for Marshal Badoglio. Popular riots were mainly against …" *(Reading aloud.)* That's good. As I've always said …

JODL: … suffer a setback … to throw both operations together.

THE FÜHRER: I don't think so. They were scared back when the first German division showed up in western Epirus.

JODL: Maybe we should add support here and over there. [—] Anyway, the supply situation in Sicily is secured for the time being. *(Presentation of the Armed Forces report.)* May I ask for a decision? In my opinion, the following must happen: Today a courier should fly to Rome, who will verbally … give to Kesselring … regarding the Rome action, and Student must also go there to be informed at once.

THE FÜHRER: We don't need two; instead, Student comes here first and brings the courier along.

GÖRING: Student must come at once!

JESCHONNEK: That will take even more time, if I may say so. General Student is in southern France.

THE FÜHRER: In any case, this can't happen tomorrow morning early. How long will it take him to get here from the south of France?

JESCHONNEK: General Student can come here today. Then he can start early in the morning.

THE FÜHRER: I think it would be right to bring General Student here, to order him to come here. Then he can take over the matter.

KEITEL: Informing the government, too.

THE FÜHRER: We're not ready for that yet anyway. Finally, when could the first squadron from the [—]

JODL: That has nothing to do with the Rome action. Paratroopers will arrive, other troops will arrive, and this will go on step by step. But when they jump, Rome will be alarmed.

THE FÜHRER: They'll take it that way at first.

GÖRING: Kesselring will simply say that due to the threats here, the paratroopers—

THE FÜHRER: Because of the losses here!

GÖRING: No, because of the threat here they will be unloaded in Rome and from there a train will bring them to Reggio. But we have to wait, if possible, until the second wave can join in, so that they can come down together.

THE FÜHRER: Yes.

Southeast

WARLIMONT: There are no particular events to be reported from the Southeast or from the eastern Mediterranean. Our own movements also went as planned. This morning, Colonel General Löhr visited the commander-in-chief of the Eleventh Italian Army,[680] which Field Marshal Rommel had planned to do. The result is that this army didn't have an order from Rome yet. He declared that he approved of the regulation, but couldn't follow it until he received an order. Yesterday, it was agreed with Rome that the order should be … given. An inquiry should be made in Rome, and we should pressure them into giving the order.[681] Additionally, the Commander-in-Chief Southeast reported on the new distribution of forces, my Führer, which he thinks appropriate. (*Presentation.*) The situation on Rhodes and Crete is unchanged.

THE FÜHRER: And how is it here?

WARLIMONT: … strengthened the 92nd Regiment, because he believes it to be urgently necessary to fill this region between Montenegro and the northern Greek border, which otherwise would be empty of German troops …

THE FÜHRER: This regiment is here anyway. They don't need to fear that …

KEITEL: The transport always takes the longest time. The follow-up is always quicker …

WARLIMONT: For the same region he also provided the 100th Jäger [Light Infantry] Division, which originally should have gone to the Peloponnesian Peninsula, but which is going very slowly because all the trains are backed up. It should come here, too, to occupy the coast of Albania, if necessary.

THE FÜHRER: It can't do that.

WARLIMONT: It depends mainly on these two bases, my Führer, Valona and Durazzo, just as the whole "Konstantin"[682] Plan is set up without further support from troops from the East. These bases that are marked here once again should be occupied so that we will at least have the main ports—marked here—in German hands.

THE FÜHRER: But they are not secured.

WARLIMONT: With weak bases.

THE FÜHRER: When will Weichs arrive here?

KEITEL: He'll be here tomorrow. He leaves Nuremberg this evening and will arrive tomorrow morning.

ROMMEL: Weichs will probably come down here?

THE FÜHRER: Do you have doubts?

ROMMEL: No, … already said that the division would be here.

THE FÜHRER: I don't know how healthy Weichs is; he is a very quiet man.

KEITEL: I talked to him; he is ready for any assignment immediately.

THE FÜHRER: Then he must really be an extraordinary officer.

KEITEL: Weichs was a mountain man at first.

WALIMONT: Nonetheless, the Commander-in-Chief Southeast will ... the order ... to form ... The order of the divisions could come a little later.[683] The other proposals of the Commander-in-Chief Southeast are within the ... to bring the existing divisions closer to the coast, provided the 1st Panzer Division stays at the Isthmus of Corinth so that it can be used to the north.

THE FÜHRER: There is only one single division besides the 1st Panzer Division anyway. It should stay out there in front.

WARLIMONT: And the four siege battalions.

THE FÜHRER: Besides this division there's only one other one there.

WARLIMONT: The 117th [Infantry Division] he intends to shift closer to the western and southern coast. The 104th [Infantry Division] and the 1st Mountain Division have the same assignment. Then, another battalion from the *Brandenburg* Regiment, which is engaged in a mopping-up operation, will move in closer here. One division is already here in the region west of Belgrade, and the other is about to follow in the next couple of days.

THE FÜHRER: When will the police regiment arrive?

WARLIMONT: From Finland? It should depart from Danzig on August 1, but it will probably take two weeks to get down here.

HIMMLER: It would come down here.

WARLIMONT: The 18th Police Regiment should come to this area.

THE FÜHRER: And the *Prinz Eugen* [Division]?

WARLIMONT: It should come here, too, but as long as he doesn't have any other forces, it should stay here, since it could become necessary to occupy the bases on the coast. Then the same will apply to the 114th Jäger [Light Infantry] Division. There is also the 297th [Infantry] Division near Belgrade ... , which is not ready yet.

THE FÜHRER: It must ... quicker here...

WARLIMONT: If you, my Führer, agree, then the 100th Jäger Division should come to Crete, not down here, so we absolutely occupy at least these two main bases.

THE FÜHRER: Rommel, what's your opinion?

ROMMEL: ... then he breaks in from here, only where the Italians are. If he takes (Arkoudi) beforehand, he will certainly go ... ; if he doesn't take (Arkoudi), he will start from the air base to push in here. Here, he has—I saw this yesterday—... the indigenous units are more or less badly divided, but they have old regimental commanders turning up again from Greek regiments. So the two divisions ... are not in a very favorable situation. Yesterday, the southern division didn't make the connection ... backwards on the road ... was blocked and now receives supplies over the water, and is surrounded by water to the left and to the right. It can't reach the coast; it can only secure the road. As for the Bavarian division, the situation is very bad there, too. It also has water on both sides, and hasn't yet reached the coast. And it's no use with the Italians.

THE FÜHRER: They will drop out anyway.

GÖRING: As I said, my Führer, maybe we should give the order to try to immediately disarm the divisions that are there, because they are going to sell their weapons anyway.

HIMMLER: I already did that yesterday with the Italians.

WARLIMONT: The Commander-in-Chief Southeast issued the general order to take all weapons away from the Italian troops as soon as they start to waver in their current formation.

THE FÜHRER: They sell them!

GÖRING: They sell the last button of their trousers for English pounds![684]

WARLIMONT: He also asks if, with the addition of Bulgarian forces ... other divisions will be available in case of an attack. That had been discussed earlier with the king... will be maintained in the present situation.

THE FÜHRER: We have to wait and see.

WARLIMONT: Finally, he asks if the region of Fiume-Trieste will be placed under his command immediately if Italy breaks up.

THE FÜHRER: Löhr?—I can imagine that! Rommel should get that region; it is part of Italy.

WARLIMONT: Part of Italy, yes.

THE FÜHRER: He can't do it with his forces anyway.

WARLIMONT: Then we can proceed with this proposal with the exception of the 92nd Regiment.

THE FÜHRER: He can bring the other here for now. I think a big tank force is needed here, which can push through here as well as down there.

WARLIMONT: He has to prepare them for transport in Salonika anyway.

ROMMEL: Then it would be much better, ... then the motorized divisions ... squeezed in.

THE FÜHRER: An infantry division, and equip it with assault guns!

GÖRING: But the roads are very bad here; they will be very late.

THE FÜHRER: Here is a road that comes over from Larissa. It has been destroyed, but it must be repaired. Then the north-south road is good, and here, in the old Albanian part, and especially in the Austrian part, the roads are not so bad—at least you can drive better there than here.

GÖRING: That's for sure, but in front it is necessary to [—]

THE FÜHRER: Incidentally, we have waged war with panzer divisions here, too.

GÖRING: Right, but it became clear—

KEITEL: We went down to the Peloponnese!

GÖRING: —that for the infantry divisions, on the other hand ...

KEITEL: Sepp Dietrich at that time rushed through with his division immediately.

GÖRING: As soon as a firm decision is made. You can't evade him here ...

ROMMEL: We have to close off here completely, so they can't come in at all, and that they have a way out here.

WARLIMONT: A meeting of top Mihailovic people took place in the inner Balkans on July 23.[685] In a nutshell, it mean immediate activation of all sabotage ... , stopping the hostilities against Tito and cooperating with him by order of the King of Yugoslavia ... in addition to that, Roosevelt and Churchill have guaranteed to restore the state. Stalin had declared himself uninterested. Preparation to land 20,000 paratroopers—of course, that is a Balkan exaggeration—the implementation of a Serbian State Guard, a Serbian Border Guard and a Serbian Volunteer [HIWI] Corps.[686] Fighting with these forces will be forbidden in the future. There are also some other regulations against ...

THE FÜHRER: And the war here?

WARLIMONT: Nothing in particular, my Führer.

The West

Nothing new can be reported from the West, except the message that, yesterday in Paris, the military police seized a truck belonging to this well-known sabotage organization, which ... official orders from the London ... about the destruction of locomotives and railway installations in case of an Allied landing ... Otherwise, nothing new from the theaters of war, my Führer.

Situation at sea, additions

JUNGE: Nothing special from the Aegean region. Damage resulting from the air raids are mostly known. [—] It must be emphasized that in Novorossiisk the traffic with ... not known until now. In a ... 7 shot down by aircraft flak, without anything happening. ... submarine group ordered by the Grand Admiral toward the Mediterranean.[687] [—] One damaged blockade runner departing and ... torpedoing completed. A big tanker torpedoed near Durban in South Africa.[688]

THE FÜHRER: How big are the losses this month, until now?

DÖNITZ: Eighteen boats, tonnage up to now: 340,000 by the submarines.[689]

THE FÜHRER: So that is more than 300,000 tons. The Mediterranean theater costs him quite a lot.

DÖNITZ: That won't improve until the submarines, in terms of arms [—][690]

Situation in the air (cont.)

CHRISTIAN: Yesterday there was a daytime air attack by about 250 aircraft, Americans, in two run-ups—first a feint approach on the coast and then the main approach into this area, with the final attack against Kiel. Kiel was well screened by artificial smoke; nonetheless, there was heavy damage, including to the dockyard. There are no details as yet reported by the Luftwaffe.

JUNGE: The Howaldt Factory has serious damage; the Germania Dockyard and the Deutsche Dockyard seem to have only minor damages; 3 motor torpedo boats.

CHRISTIAN: There was an attack on Hamburg, primarily against the port area. Altogether, 25 aircraft were shot down by fighters, and another 6 by flak. There was a simultaneous attack by 80 aircraft in this area—in a purely diversionary attack against Amsterdam, against the Schipol Airport, and against smaller villages near Ghent. Only houses were damaged; no military damages. Fighters here shot down six aircraft. In this area there were a few incursions, but only as nuisance raids against locomotives; one locomotive was damaged in this raid, and a Mustang was shot down. A heavier raid with 300 to 400 aircraft reported so far, with at least 1,200 stick-type incendiary bombs… According to current findings, there were 180 killed, 300 injured … Hamborn, Gladbach, Mülheim; no damages reported yet. Night pursuit was initiated with 81 aircraft. The night fighter division had until now … minus 7 aircraft; four of them are used for the open night pursuit.

GÖRING: How many anti-aircraft guns are in Essen?

CHRISTIAN: Anti-aircraft artillery near Essen: 31 heavy batteries, 4¼ light, and 6½ searchlight batteries. In the rest of the area there were only a few nuisance flights, with no attacks reported. [–] Our Luftwaffe set off with 51 aircraft for Hull, 47 of them reaching the target. Exact results are not yet available. Three aircraft are missing, and hostile night fighters shot one down over our own territory. [—] Today, at about 11 a.m., stronger units flew against the Deutsche Bucht [German Bight]. At first, the target wasn't apparent. The units first flew toward Kiel-Hamburg, then turned to the south and, in the meantime, attacked Wilhelmshaven, Bremen, Hanover, and Hamburg. No details have been reported. Fighters were in the air, Herr Reichsmarshal.

GÖRING: ... The first units came here, and the fighters were deployed against them immediately, since the unit was quite strong. Then the formation went up there, and the fighters followed, but then turned off course here. At the same time, this big unit arrived here. As a consequence, the fighters were called back from here to be used against this unit. Then, when the other one noticed this, he made this turn, while the fighters ... hung on with the big unit. It shows how difficult it is to solve this matter with so few fighter troops available here. There is no doubt that this will improve within a short time, if the fighters are supported by the heavy [Model Me-] 410 fighter.[691] Then the success rate will increase. But everything possible was deployed, and it came closer at the end, etc. However, it also shows the extreme difficulty of maneuvering with so many units.

CHRISTIAN: One aircraft entered the circle of Berlin, near Brandenburg. Berlin had a public air-raid warning. At the same time, there was an incursion over Holland. Right now, there is an attack underway against the coast near Dunkirk. [—] In the East, the deployment is against the focal points near Krymskaia [in the Taman'], primarily the Fourth Air Fleet and the 16th Panzer Grenadier Division near Izium. Some of the close-combat forces were employed in the defensive fights near Belgorod. Parts of the Sixth Air Fleet also operated northeast and southeast of Orel yesterday, and ... the Sixth Air Fleet again reports 17 tanks destroyed and three others damaged. Four of the 17 tanks were shot by anti-aircraft artillery, and 13 were shot from the air; 19 were destroyed by the Fourth Air Fleet and 17 by the Sixth Air Fleet. The enemy operated only during the day in this area, especially south of Odessa. The First Air Fleet reports heavy support for enemy attacks, particularly south of Shlissel'burg, by hostile fighter-bomber operations. Our own fighters were used against them, and 7 aircraft were shot down; 20 others were shot down by anti-aircraft artillery. At night, the nuisance combat group was deployed, especially against hostile movements near the front, where 46 aircraft fought. In the North, the operations were against ship targets. Some aircraft didn't locate the ships and attacked alternative targets instead ... Yesterday in the East we had 13 losses compared with 60 enemy losses.

GÖRING: How many?

CHRISTIAN: Thirteen of ours, 61 of the enemy's.

GÖRING: That includes the 10 damaged aircraft. I've just seen the new Russian fighter-bombers[692] and also the Russian fighters, and I must say that I am relieved ... that it repels only machine-gun fire ... 2 cm and above and it gets through. I have clearly seen this, my Führer; you only need to see the profiling. This is the last type that was shot down. Its tank is in the rear. They will all burn; the tank is not protected. So this is very primitive, particularly their latest design—it's the weakest performance I've seen from Russia.

Panzer armaments

THOMALE: I must report on the Panther Detachment of the *Leibstandarte Adolf Hitler* [SS Panzer Grenadier Division]. The *Leibstandarte* has a detachment with 71 Panthers; there are 60 now, and we have another eleven left from Erlangen, so the division is ready to depart with 71 Panthers. It means that the company is ... with 17 vehicles instead of 22.[693] The motor vehicles are missing. Motor vehicles can be taken at once from the I/26 [1st Battalion of the 26th Regiment], which is there, and has given the Panthers to the 52nd [Panzer Detachment], that is in Russia. As a result, all motor vehicles must be taken at once, mostly they need the maintenance platoon. The rest will be brought in later, and will be there at the latest on Wednesday, so the *Leibstandarte Adolf Hitler* will be ready to depart from Grafenwöhr on Wednesday evening with the vehicles, the cars and the Panthers. Second: the [SS] *Reich* [Panzer Grenadier Division] is ready to depart on Saturday, the 31st, also with 71 Panthers. Now, it will receive ... agreed with the Army General Staff, including the maintenance platoon, so that this week on Wednesday evening the *Leibstandarte Adolf Hitler* will be ready with its vehicles, and the *Reich* detachment on Saturday evening with its vehicles, too.

THE FÜHRER: Are they trained, Thomale?

THOMALE: They are trained enough so that they can be deployed. The majority of the *Leibstandarte* is good. The *Reich* is good, too. They have young replacements who are not well trained with tanks, but it's OK, since we decreased from 96 to 71.[694] It can be corrected by doing that.

THE FÜHRER: That's quite good.

THOMALE: It means that two Panther divisions will be ready this week.

THE FÜHRER: Are all the innovations included in the Panthers?

THOMALE: Yes, Sir. They have all had modifications, of course. The optics are in order, as well as the rudder steering mechanism.

THE FÜHRER: The membrane?[695]

THOMALE: The membrane and all those things are fine, too. Additionally, we will get from Mr. Saur[696] of the Munitions Ministry the very experienced Lieutenant Colonel Stollberg,[697] who was the engineering officer there and who carried out this reconstruction excellently at that time. We will also get the support of the Munitions Ministry, so these figures were added in addition. The 71 for the *Leibstandarte* will be available already this evening, that's clear, ... and I now have ... until Saturday for the Panthers ... that will clearly be all right. I was concerned about the vehicles. But I have been promised for certain that I can immediately get the vehicles from the I/26 [1st Battalion of the 26th Panzer Regiment], which is ... in Grafenwöhr. That's one less thing to worry about. The other maintenance platoon for the *Reich*—at least Colonel Stieff[698] promised me this thing [—]

THE FÜHRER: When does the 26th Panzer get its Panthers?

BUHLE: The drivers are on their way with them toward the East.

THOMALE: I need to report that. We do have trained Panther detachments.

THE FÜHRER: The drivers are—?

THOMALE: They have to leave then. It has been ordered, that the I/26 ... the vehicles ...

THE FÜHRER: But then vice versa again, right?

THOMALE: Yes, Sir. Then vice versa. But now the 51st [Panzer Detachment], which has been filled up with tanks and now has 52, gives these two divisions ...

THE FÜHRER: But before you said 200, and now only 91!?

THOMALE: No, they are still at 96. They have been brought to 96; The 51st Detachment transferred its vehicles to the 52nd Detachment, so that it has at least 96, and the 51st was brought to 96 by the I/26th ... Now, there have been human losses in the meantime, due to the fighting, so we allowed them to take drivers from the I/26th so they will have drivers immediately. Drivers are, in fact, the most valuable thing. Only I sent Colonel Marx[699] there as a neutral observer to prevent them from taking too many. I told him to let them take only as many as they really need ...

THE FÜHRER: Then he simply takes the soldiers out?

THOMALE: That's clear.

BUHLE: In any case, many soldiers are taken out.

THE FÜHRER: So the I/26th loses its drivers. [—] But one detachment is ready, isn't it?

THOMALE: I have another detachment in Königsbrück, the I/201 [1st Battalion, 201st Panzer Regiment].It is in individual training in Königsbrück, with the 23rd Panzer Division. However, at the moment—just now found this out for sure; we've been having constant telephone conversations about it—I can't get it. It will take another 10 to 14 days. We won't get any other Panthers earlier, either; we have assigned all our Panthers through the end of the week. Then we have to start again to get an additional 71 Panthers. That's the maximum we could scrape together. [—] Also, we've trained the 1st Battalion of the 1st Panzer Regiment. But it's intended for the Balkans and should be equipped with Panzer IVs,[700] so the I/1 is out of question for the Panthers.

THE FÜHRER: The question is, where is it to go?

THOMALE: Yes, Sir. I would like to report, my Führer, that we still have trained tank crews there. First, there's the I/201, which is in Königsbrück, and the I/1, which can be brought in.

THE FÜHRER: When can the ones from the 1st Panzer [Division] finish their training?

THOMALE: The I/1 has completed individual training, but they need a little time still, probably about 10 days for company and unit training. Then it would just about be OK for the Panthers to start going ...

BUHLE: If the I/1 is equipped with Panzer IVs, that would be the first stronger fighting unit that could be brought in here—right into the Salonika region, not down there ...

THOMALE: From our side we also request that the I/1 ... can't use the Panthers in the Balkan region. On the other hand, ... because tanks can be used there. Thus, the Panzer IVs ... [—] Then, I must also report on the so-called Überrashungskkommandos [surprise commandos]. This evening at 7 o'clock ... ready to depart from Paderborn with 3 Tigers each ... enough armor-piercing shells, ammunition, trucks with fuel in Paderborn ... There are 2 Tiger groups with 3 Tigers each; additionally, 2 Hornet groups[701] in Coetquidan[702] with ... 4 each. They were trained in Coetquidan. That's the so-called V/25, with 45 Hornets altogether, so we could also take away 8 Hornets from them.

BUHLE: A complete division can be moved in here. One belongs to the 26th Panzer Division, but it hasn't started yet—a complete division still.

KEITEL: They should crack the bunkers ...

THE FÜHRER: Not the Hornets, but the 4 groups of Tigers have to be put in there...

BUHLE: They certainly will hack their way through.

THE FÜHRER: To Tarvisio and to the Brenner [Pass], so that nothing happens there!

BUHLE: The detachment can be brought here, to the *Feldherrnhalle* and to the 715th, here in this area.

THE FÜHRER: It would be good if they could also be available near Laibach.

THOMALE: That will be possible as well.

THE FÜHRER: Laibach or Fiume—into this region, anyway. That's the one; that's Tarvisio. [—] There are 3?

KEITEL: Three each, and the others have Hornets.

THOMALE: We structured the Hornets deliberately with four in each group.

KEITEL: Two groups of 4.

THOMALE: The detachment has 45.

THE FÜHRER: Forty-five Hornets—that's another tremendous waste, because there's no enemy here.

BUHLE: This is the antitank defense detachment of the 26th Panzer Division, which left. It has to go down anyway.

THE FÜHRER: Only there is no enemy here right now. [—] Continue!

THOMALE: Then, briefly, the equipment of the panzer divisions: the 14th Panzer Division currently has 30 assault guns, 28 Panzer IIIs with 8-cm long guns[703] and 4 Panzer IVs with the short gun, so altogether 62 vehicles and assault guns. That also includes the 5-cm long gun.

THE FÜHRER: That's the 14th?

BUHLE: One has Panzer IVs with the long gun, with 38 assault guns.

THOMALE: Thirty-eight assault guns. Yes, indeed.

THE FÜHRER: When can the 14th be ready?

THOMALE: It will be ready on August 31.

THE FÜHRER: Good!

THOMALE: The 24th Panzer Division has a complete assault gun detachment with 42 assault guns[704] and 5 Panzer IVs with the long gun—so 47 vehicles if you add them all together.

THE FÜHRER: The 24th Panzer Division?

THOMALE: The 24th Panzer Division. Yes, Sir.

THE FÜHRER: It's of no value.

THOMALE: It's supposed to go to the East now. In addition, it has 14 flame-thrower tanks to ... the enemy ...

THE FÜHRER: Then perhaps a Panzer detachment should be brought into the 24th Panzer, because otherwise the division is good.

BUHLE: It is very good.

THOMALE: The 201st [Panzer Detachment] could be brought into it. It will be the next one that's ready.

THE FÜHRER: We should do that.

THOMALE: Yes, Sir. To provide the division with a backbone. The *Feldherrnhalle* [Panzer Grenadier] Division has 30 assault guns, 18 Panzer IIIs with the short gun, 9 Panzer IIIs with the long gun ... and the old training equipment.[705] That equipment is not too valuable ... I'd like to report as well that the 24th Panzer Division has ... 300 vehicles...trucks ...

THE FÜHRER: We don't need them here. ...

THOMALE: These are the things that are still there. [—] Of course, these can't be separated from the detachments because it takes a lot of training time to be able to guide the remote-controlled tanks at distances of 900 to 1,000 meters.[706] It is possible to do it for the first 50 or 70 or 80 meters, but for greater distances the people have to work well together. Therefore, I urgently ask that they not be separated. There are also assault tanks[707] with cables laid inside and a remote-control unit built in, and certain lines are laid inside for it. But we would have to take new assault guns in order to modify them. [—] That's all, my Führer. [—] Colonel General Guderian will be here at 4 p.m., my Führer. ...

End: 2:23 p.m.

* * * * *

MEETING OF THE FÜHRER
WITH FIELD MARSHAL VON KLUGE, JULY 26, 1943[708]

Also present:

General Zeitzler, Colonel Scherff

Beginning: 12:10 p.m.

Italy/the East

THE FÜHRER: In general, has anything happened, Zeitzler?

ZEITZLER: Nothing in particular, my Führer.

THE FÜHRER: I don't know if you have been informed about the overall situation, Herr Field Marshal?

V. KLUGE: Via a radio broadcast today.

THE FÜHRER: The radio broadcast didn't reflect the truth, of course.[709] The situation, in brief, is as follows: the developments that I feared, which I recently mentioned in the meeting with the generals, has taken place in Italy. It's a revolt initiated by the royalty or Marshal Badoglio—so to say our old enemies. The Duce was arrested yesterday. He was invited to the Quirinal for discussions, and was then arrested there and dismissed immediately by this decree. Then this new government was established, which still officially declares, of course, that it is going to cooperate with us. But that's all a disguise to gain a few days to consolidate the new regime. It's obvious that no one is behind the new regime except the Jews and the rabble who draw attention to themselves in Rome. But in any case, they are there at the moment and it's urgent and necessary that we act. Actually, I've always feared this development. That was the whole reason why I was afraid to start in the East too early, since I always thought that everything would happen immediately in the South: the British would exploit it, the Russians would roar, the British would land, and with the Italians—I'd like to say—betrayal was in the air.[710] Under these circumstances I thought it best to wait at least until several units were ready. We do have units in the West. Because I am determined to strike like lightning, of course, just as I did in Yugoslavia. The resistance of Italy itself, I think, will be zero. The Fascists will come over to us. We also brought Farinacci over; he is with us. He is already in Munich, flying over here. I don't know where the Duce himself is. If I find out, I will go after him at once with the paratroopers.[711] This whole regime is, in my eyes, a typical *coup d'état* regime like the one in Belgrade, and one day it will collapse—provided that we take immediate action. I can only act if I bring over additional units from the East to the West. For this purpose, things have to be liquidated in case the offensive here fails. [—] Are these your maps?

ZEITZLER: The ones based on our reports.

THE FÜHRER: Would you like to tell me your situation now? [—] It's like this: I can't take the units the way they are now. I have to take politically sound units.[712] That would be, first of all, the 3rd SS Panzer Division,[713] which I can only take from Army Group South. But that means that you have to bring in other units, and you can only obtain them by eliminating this whole action, giving up this bend[714] here, and maybe also shortening the front in a few other places.

V. KLUGE: Well, my Führer, the current situation is as follows. Here[715] strong forces have been providing distinct pressure, which hasn't had its full effect yet since it is extremely difficult for that man to cross the Oka [River]. Yesterday, he unfortunately achieved quite a deep penetration in the 34th Army[716] lines here, which, however, we mostly counteracted through corresponding counterthrusts. But the forces we have here are relatively weak. The breakthrough in the 297th [Infantry] Division's lines was here; it was also somewhat compensated last night by our taking back this whole line.

THE FÜHRER: Are you on this line?

V. KLUGE: No, that line.

ZEITZLER: The other map shows the exact situation today—up there is what was taken back.

THE FÜHRER: It's better if you show it to me here.

V. KLUGE: The situation we have is momentarily such that yesterday there was a heavy attack—not as heavy as we expected, but weaker and over a narrower area. It only caused one penetration, which we were able to halt. They were primarily heavy tank attacks—150 tanks here, of which 50 were destroyed here alone. Now we are planning to move into this so-called Oka position and pull over here, and we will already shorten the Bolkhov bend here tonight. I'd like to take the order with me now that from Bolkhov we go down and across, and shorten this thing here a bit. The overall intention is to go back from here again, and then finally to move into this line here. [—] That's what we are planning first. Later, after the clearing action here has progressed, the general evacuation should take place. As the foundation for this movement—which is tied up quite tightly here, especially here in the north—*Grossdeutschland* [Panzer Grenadier Division] advanced with all its reconnaissance forces and threw the enemy back here, but then came across rather strong resistance at this point. I don't know yet how it will develop today. In any case, they should reach the edge of this area that is marked as "marshland." In fact, however, it is not marshland, but unfortunately, it is terrain that can certainly be crossed.

ZEITZLER: This morning the enemy attacked with greater strength.

V. KLUGE: Did he attack there?

ZEITZLER: Yes, also with a tank brigade.

V. KLUGE: We were informed of that yesterday. Here in this region he has two infantry [rifle] divisions—two good infantry divisions—and one tank brigade, and another tank brigade is being brought in.

THE FÜHRER: Tell me, where are the 100 Panthers?

V. KLUGE: They're not here yet; they are still in the formation stage. They have been unloaded.

ZEITZLER: The last trains all arrived on the 26th.

V. KLUGE: They are there with their crews, but are not quite complete yet.

THE FÜHRER: And where are they?

V. KLUGE: Berdiansk. [—] So we have strong pressure here, which is felt not only here, but also against this unfortunately very weak point, which, in my opinion, is the most dangerous. Everywhere here are units that were scraped together that tried to hold this line first and now they've been pushed back farther. It would be very unpleasant if things were to develop in such a way that this road, which goes up to the Reseta railway station, were to fall into enemy hands. For now, this is a castling line[717] from the south to the north that is being used by our side. Thus the request to deploy the 113th [Infantry] Division up here with the Fourth Army, on the Orel railway along the highway.

ZEITZLER: That was approved by the Führer!

V. KLUGE: And to pull out two divisions instead: first, one division that should be moved there immediately, and a second division, which we actually wanted to move into this region as well, to strengthen this wing. Because here we can't take another step backward—that would be a very bad development. Very strong forces are pushing forward here; they are much superior to our own forces—with tanks too, but relatively few tanks. The majority of tanks are pushing down here, admittedly down toward *Grossdeutschland*, and here, of course.

THE FÜHRER: His tank numbers must also gradually decrease.

V. KLUGE: Yes, of course. That's clear. We've also destroyed quite a few of them. But he's still attacking with strong tank units, so we have our hands full to finish them off. [—] That's the situation at the moment. Now we should retreat to this Oka position, slightly shortened, and from this foundation Orel should be evacuated along with everything necessary. Then, according to the plan [—]

ZEITZLER: The next point, Herr Field Marshal, would probably be down past *Grossdeutschland*?!

V. KLUGE: Let me say, my Führer, that I intended—as did Model[718]—to do the following in order to create a reasonable foundation here for the whole movement and to keep them from coming too close to us: first, to push forward here with *Grossdeutschland*, which is underway; and second, to attack and throw this thing back here, in order to reestablish the connection more or less along this line.

THE FÜHRER: I don't believe that will succeed anymore. *Grossdeutschland* is going through the forest?

V. KLUGE: It would never be considered there; it would have been forbidden. It was just that the push by the 253rd [Infantry] Division here [—].

THE FÜHRER: Let me review the general situation. The idea is to pull out a number of units within a reasonably short period of time. These units are, first of all, the 3rd Panzer Grenadier Division, which I have to take from Army Group South, and which has to cover the broadest front lines itself, of course. So it is a very difficult decision. [—] Do you have the overall situation available here—on the one to one million-scale map?

(ZEITZLER: Yes, indeed.)

It's a very difficult decision, but we have no other choice. Down there I can only use first-class units that support Fascism politically. Otherwise, I could also move some panzer divisions from the Army in there—but the whole thing won't come together without it, because I don't want to take away the Fascist metal,[719] and we are building up so many things in such a short time. That doesn't worry me, if we hold northern Italy. Not at all. In Rome, the *Messaggero* wrote a nasty article about the Duce, which cuts every Fascist to the quick.[720] That's clear; one should not imagine that the people are as fickle as those paid subjects. That's the rabble there—Jews and others like them; they raid Fascist Party homes.

(V. KLUGE: In Rome?)

That's how it always was with us, of course. That's what made the National Socialists fanatical in the end. So it will happen here as well. But I must have units down there that come under a political flag. It's not enough if I only have a good military unit down there; it must also be a unit that within a short time … annexes the … The Fascists have to run with us—because they are threatened by this fate we'll get them. In my opinion, we will build up divisions within a short time down there—not of regular soldiers, but of volunteers who come out of these divisions. There is nothing we can do about the current army, since everyone is running away.

V. KLUGE: My Führer! I must point out that right now we can't pull anything out. It's absolutely impossible at the moment!

THE FÜHRER: But nevertheless, it must be possible [—]

V. KLUGE: The only way we could pull something out would be if we move to the Hagen position!

ZEITZLER: Move up to here in the first stage, then we can take out *Grossdeutschland*, and keep *Grossdeutschland* here that long, and the 7th Panzer [Division] must go away soon.

V. KLUGE: We couldn't foresee this development in the general political situation; we couldn't suspect that it was going to happen like that. Now a new decision has to be made: first, the decision to evacuate Orel once we have our own vital things out.

THE FÜHRER: Quite clear!

V. KLUGE: But after that the evacuation can start, of course. However, I can't remove the whole population and all the supplies, etc. It can't be done in such a short time; a lot of organization is required. It is a very densely populated country, so it can't be done hastily. [—] Then another question arises about this position in the rear here, the so-called Hagen position, it is just beginning to be improved.

THE FÜHRER: Yes, unfortunately![721]

V. KLUGE: So this can't be done. We have numerous construction battalions and heaven knows what else. Every day there are torrential rains of a kind you can't imagine here at all. All the construction battalions have had to repair the streets everywhere when they should have been here in the back, working on this. They had to be thrown into the battle just to hold it.

THE FÜHRER: Perhaps the rain will stop soon?

V. KLUGE: I certainly hope it will. Today it's a bit better.

THE FÜHRER: But you have to admit one thing, Herr Field Marshal. As soon as this line has been reached, quite a number of divisions can be taken out here.

V. KLUGE: My Führer! I would note that four divisions—

THE FÜHRER: —are weakened.

V. KLUGE: I have four divisions here, which are extremely weak.

THE FÜHRER: I admit that, but how many divisions are smashed by the enemy?!

V. KLUGE: But in spite of all that! [—] Now the question of the so-called Karachev position, my Führer. If I move into a position there that is not completed, and I am attacked again with tanks and everything imaginable, they will break through with the tanks. And when they break through with the tanks, the moment will come here. I only mention this because it's a good opportunity—since we may run into a very difficult situation—and I would like to ask you to consider if it would not be more practical at least to go behind the Desna [River] at once. We must have the Karachev position anyway, at least as a skeleton—the way it is now and perhaps with another 14 days of construction—just to give the troops a place to stop while they're retreating further. I'm only calling your attention to it. So I wonder if it wouldn't be better to go behind the Desna [River] at once.

THE FÜHRER: Here they are safe, but here they are not safe [—]

V. KLUGE: Briansk—this part is good, but this section is not yet improved.

THE FÜHRER: That is no better than this part. If you imagine this Briansk position, and add this part, then this part with this one is equal to the whole—

V. KLUGE: But I have to have time for improvement, then; I can't do this—

THE FÜHRER: You have to improve this as well!

V. KLUGE: Yes, I have to develop that one as well, but here on the Desna [River] I don't need to build anything.

THE FÜHRER: Not here.

V. KLUGE: I have to build here—up to here—and there I don't need to build.

THE FÜHRER: But this is practically just as long as the one at [—]

V. KLUGE: But this is better, because here nothing can happen to me along the whole route.

THE FÜHRER: He won't attack here; he'll come down here.

V. KLUGE: That's extremely decisive, of course. But then, my Führer, I can't go back so early. First, I have to improve the Hagen position—I have to get it in order. I can't go back hastily.

THE FÜHRER: A hasty retreat is out of the question!

V. KLUGE: In any case, not much sooner than has been planned.

THE FÜHRER: What timeframe do you have in mind?

V. KLUGE: We have the following schedule: in about 5 days—

THE FÜHRER: In general, by when do you think you will be in here?

V. KLUGE: We didn't intend to go in before the beginning of September.

THE FÜHRER: That's impossible. Completely impossible, Herr Field Marshal!

V. KLUGE: Of course, now in this situation it's quite different. But the position won't be ready for another 4 weeks, of course.

ZEITZLER: First, this stage, and then that stage. Perhaps we can stay a little longer at this stage until it is built.

V. KLUGE: That's not possible for the following reasons—it might work for a certain period of time, of course, but there's another problem: the railway capacity, which at present is about 50 trains to Orel, will decrease to 18 trains per day as soon we lose Orel, and that will be a very unpleasant situation.

ZEITZLER: Then we won't need as many, either, if we are here.

V. KLUGE: I can't finish this. Up there, there are no unloading areas.

ZEITZLER: If I am here with the troops, this piece of railway is of no value!

V. KLUGE: No, not any more. I just wanted to say that as soon as I give up Orel, I must start retreating at the same time. But the decisive thing is that I must have my position in the rear.

ZEITZLER: If we could hold here for 6 or 7 days, we could gain 6 or 7 days here, and here we will free up some units.

V. KLUGE: But the calculation must always be done in reverse. How is the situation here in the rear? Because I have to have a position ready that can offer some degree of resistance; otherwise, he will run straight over it, and then I am in the same situation and can't pull anything out.

ZEITZLER: Herr Field Marshal, about 6 or 7 days would come out here.

V. KLUGE: Until then? What does that mean? The other one did this section in three days!

ZEITZLER: If we can hold for 6 to 7 days here, then the thing can go down here, so that after 10 days we could be here.

V. KLUGE: Already?

ZEITZLER: Yes.

V. KLUGE: That would be a terribly overhasty evacuation of the thing, which in my opinion is not—

ZEITZLER: Perhaps the army group can calculate it again.

THE FÜHRER: Nevertheless, Herr Field Marshal, we are not the masters of our own decisions here; in wartime decisions are often necessary, which—

V. KLUGE: My Führer! If the order is given that it must be done quickly—but then I have to point out that this idea conflicts with the "Hagen" position, which is not ready.

THE FÜHRER: This is not ready either. It is not ready here, and, of course, he won't rush into the completed position!

V. KLUGE: Perhaps I could do the following, my Führer: I could go back to this position, which is a bit further along—and here, too, more progress has been made, but here there is next to nothing. I have to take into account that I may have to evade more, but then this has to be built!

THE FÜHRER: That should be built as well, as a precaution; but I don't want to evade him here. It can be left until the winter, when the other will attack. Model improved this one very well. In principle, it should be possible to improve a position in this period of time—any position. When we advanced in those days, we would stop somewhere, dig out a position and hold it. This bastard digs a position in less than two days, and we can't get him out of it.

V. KLUGE: My Führer! Here it's mainly a question of tanks. That's the real problem—he plods along with his artillery and tanks until he finally breaks through.

ZEITZLER: If we go in here, Herr Field Marshal, in my view, half the divisions that are freed up could then be put in here. Let them dig for 6 days, and then we have the position.

V. KLUGE: That won't do it. In my opinion, the earliest we could move into the Hagen position would be in approximately—today is the 26th—four weeks; if we take the earliest calculation, in 3 to 4 weeks. That's the absolute earliest.

THE FÜHRER: We can't wait that long. Forces have to be freed up before then, or it's no use.

V. KLUGE: Then Sauckel can't pull out all of his workers.

THE FÜHRER: It must work! The other evacuates so quickly!

V. KLUGE: But my Führer, that's a huge number! He's going to jam all the bridges over the Desna.

THE FÜHRER: How many people are in here, anyway?

V. KLUGE: Several hundred thousand.

ZEITZLER: Two hundred and fifty thousand men, according to—

THE FÜHRER: Two hundred and fifty thousand men? That's nothing!

V. KLUGE: My Führer! But I need my forces now to fight; they can't do everything else.

THE FÜHRER: On the contrary, I would push the people back now and have them build first!

V. KLUGE: We tried that. Now all of them are harvesting; the rye is being cut now. They have no idea what lies ahead. They run away in swarms from the building sites at night—they run to the front to cut their rye. These are all difficulties. It's not organized at all.

THE FÜHRER: What happens to the cut rye? Is it burned?

V. KLUGE: We have to do it, of course. Are we going to burn it? Probably. But do we have the time for it? We have to destroy it—above all the valuable livestock we have here. Here we have the famous Kaminski,[722] who played a key role back then.

THE FÜHRER: Where is he stationed?

V. KLUGE: Here near Lokot, in this area around here. This is his empire—mainly here.

THE FÜHRER: Then, behind this line, I would in any case [—]

V. KLUGE: I have ordered that he not be touched initially, since we have to finish making all these treks over the very difficult Desna area. And here behind I have all these partisans who weren't killed after all,[723] instead, they stand up again and suddenly strengthen everything here with a huge parachute action. And these notorious railway demolitions in 400 places!

THE FÜHRER: Certainly, but all that doesn't alter the one fact that it must be done. I view the situation here [in the Donbas] as even worse. Look at the sectors he[724] has! There is one division—the 335th [Infantry]—that has 45 km.

V. KLUGE: But, my Führer, I don't know where the view originates that we didn't have that here. We have more than 50 km where the 56th [Infantry] Division stood, and the 34th [Infantry] had 48 km. They didn't calculate this correctly!

THE FÜHRER: It was correct at the moment we started—you had those sectors then.

V. KLUGE: When we started.

THE FÜHRER: All in all, Army Group Center has had quite different divisional sectors.

V. KLUGE: Due to the Buffalo Movement [withdrawal from the Rzhev salient],[725] we became a bit narrower, but we do have our 30 km and a bit more. I have the matter drawn out that far.

THE FÜHRER: But that is no comparison!

V. KLUGE: It's very thin up there with the 3rd Panzer Division, too.

THE FÜHRER: How is it here?

ZEITZLER: He didn't attack here. In fact, there is a new development. The motorized corps seem to have been pulled out and replaced by a guards infantry [rifle] corps. He may want to refresh the corps, and do something here. I'm a bit worried about this here, because he has the air force up there, too. It's not clear where he wants to go with it. Rail movements have increased slightly, so I'd like to believe that he's transporting troops out by train. Otherwise, one could believe that he is bringing them here. So we have to watch this movement. [—] This cost him a lot of blood here, so I think he gave up the matter with the motorized units; he is going out here. [—] I spoke with Manstein about this matter here and here. He phoned again today. Now that the *Leibstandarte* is gone, he wants to consider whether he is going to attack at all. I think it's reasonable for him to wait. There's no need to clear up this minor thing, since there's no enemy pressure.

THE FÜHRER: When can the *Leibstandarte* leave?[726]

ZEITZLER: The first train will leave tomorrow evening; 12 trains are scheduled per day, and then 20 after 4 to 5 days. The whole movement—there are 120 trains—will take 6 to 8 days.

THE FÜHRER: Only 120 trains?

(ZEITZLER: Yes, Sir.)

Well, Zeitzler?

ZEITZLER: It could be 130.

THE FÜHRER: I'm afraid it will be 150!

ZEITZLER: The number doesn't matter too much, if it's 10 or 15 more or less.

THE FÜHRER: What are they leaving here? Are they leaving the Panzer IV here, or will they take them along?

ZEITZLER: Last night they said they would leave them here and get new ones. I calculated on this basis—we just need to put a little pressure on the *Leibstandarte* to make them leave them here. If I know Sepp, he's going to take them along.[727] Someone should be sent down there to watch. It would be better if they were left here.

THE FÜHRER: Those two divisions are weak anyway. It's better to give them some others. And we should see if the Tigers can be given to one of them. He will get the two Tiger companies anyway.

ZEITZLER: I agree that on the way they don't [—]

THE FÜHRER: That's enough for the *Leibstandarte*. [—] How many Tigers is that—two companies?

ZEITZLER: He will get two companies, so 22 Tigers.

THE FÜHRER: And he will get the 100 Panthers anyway—his whole detachment—and then he has to get new ones for the Panzer IV on the way back.

ZEITZLER: I'll take the replacements that were designated to go there; he can still have them.

THE FÜHRER: Possibly assault guns, too. Then he can leave them here. That would strengthen the two divisions first. The next to go would be the *Reich*. Then the *Reich*, in turn, would leave part of its materiel to strengthen the other units, and would get its 100 Panthers in the meantime.

ZEITZLER: Then we save a lot of arming.

THE FÜHRER: Then we save a lot of arming, and the ones here will become even stronger. Then Manstein will get some materiel for his divisions; for example, the 16th Panzer Grenadier Division must also get something.

ZEITZLER: Then other armored divisions will arrive, and they can take them over.

THE FÜHRER: When the last leaves ... leave the weapons here.

ZEITZLER: Yes, Sir.

THE FÜHRER: I also want this matter here!

ZEITZLER: We're investigating it, my Führer. So far, the positions here have been very good, since we've always had our position here.

THE FÜHRER: A very good position, of course. In the end, a good position is better, even if it is a bit narrower. But one always has to build toward the rear, in case a crisis develops.

V. KLUGE: Yes, Sir. [—] So, my Führer, we face a new situation here then!

ZEITZLER: Perhaps the army group could draw up a plan outlining what can be done at the earliest, and the risks involved.

V. KLUGE: We're going to sit down together right now. I brought my Ia [728] along with me. We are going to consider it. But with everything there is a certain interaction in relation to the improvement of the Hagen position. I don't want to slip into a position that's nowhere near ready.

THE FÜHRER: The whole thing is like that for me. If this threat didn't exist, I would have said to immediately bring in the two divisions that you're getting now, instead of the 113th [Infantry Division]!

V. KLUGE: Yes, my Führer. Now, of course, they won't advance one step further. Now there aren't any more attacks here at all. There's no purpose to it; it's pointless. This was all under the precondition [—]

THE FÜHRER: To protect only the railway, so that we can use it!

V. KLUGE: Then the whole action could have taken place before the winter.

THE FÜHRER: But if it were possible, could you immediately bring in one of those two units to build the position?

V. KLUGE: So I should take them away from Model? Even though they push forward again every day, and with the miserable remains of the 111th, 212th, and 108th [Infantry Divisions], and with the 209th [Infantry Division] [—]

ZEITZLER: Those are the beaten ones.

THE FÜHRER: Good! If you bring the worn-out ones to the rear and replenish them, then they can build!

V. KLUGE: Good. I'll have to free something up. And, unfortunately, I also have to secure the routes with troops where all these treks are passing. They would all be killed behind the forest of Bryansk, since it's full of [partisan] bands—or at least they're reorganizing again.

THE FÜHRER: Yes, I also have difficult decisions, very difficult decisions.

V. KLUGE: I believe it.

THE FÜHRER: But there is no other way.

V. KLUGE: But before this thing here is carried out, I can't give up any troops; that's impossible. We'll have to see afterward how we can manage it.

THE FÜHRER: You should do this as quickly as possible. I can see it already, *Grossdeutschland* will be taken in a short time, and second, you will have to put something in here! A few panzer and a few infantry divisions will have to be [—]

V. KLUGE: No tanks; they are with me [—]

THE FÜHRER: They will be given away and will then be fixed up in the West.

V. KLUGE: But I need panzer divisions, too, of course.

THE FÜHRER: Well, you don't like this garbage too much, so it's easier for you to give it away!

V. KLUGE: What garbage?

THE FÜHRER: You said, "It's only garbage"!

V. KLUGE: I didn't say that!

THE FÜHRER: Yes, it slipped from your mouth, so we're taking it away from you.

V. KLUGE: No, I didn't mean it, my Führer. I have so little—not very much left. What I wanted to say was that it's nearly unbearable the way it is now.

THE FÜHRER: Yes, it's true they don't have tanks. That's why I said that they can be given away, and they will be fixed up in the West. Then I can bring them quickly from the West; they can be replenished there. In the end, the people have earned it. It's completely wrong to do it the other way round. In the West I can get them ready for action again, and I can pull in those from the West afterward. Above all, I have to be sure to finish the 9th and 10th SS [Panzer] Divisions as soon as possible. Today I got an evaluation on the *Göring* division, and how they are fighting. The English write, "The youngest—the sixteen-year-olds, just out of the Hitler Youth—fought fanatically, and would have let themselves all be killed. So they couldn't take any prisoners." [—] I'm convinced that these few divisions consisting of the young boys, who are already well trained, will fight superbly, because they have a wonderfully idealistic spirit. They will fight fantastically; I am solidly convinced of it.

ZEITZLER: Well, I still need to sit down outside with the Field Marshal.

V. KLUGE: I have to consider this again, my Führer. I know what's important now, so it will be done accordingly.

THE FÜHRER: As I said: the first thing that's necessary is that I get the SS [Panzer] Corps out. He needs something there, but I don't know what I'll give him. Perhaps the 7th Panzer [Division], which could be taken down, if he can free up something here so that he can cover here. But he has to have a replacement for it, or he won't be able to hold the thing. And he needs some infantry divisions! He can't hold this dangerous situation here. Of course, if worst comes to worst, there may not be any other option here but to shorten it. But this is a desperate situation—we have to understand that. It's not pleasant! These are very difficult decisions, which lead up to a critical point. But I'm also considering other things that we could do. Up here there's the issue of Leningrad, because of the Finns,[729] and down here I also thought: if we were to give this up [—]

ZEITZLER: If we decide to do this up there, we also have to do it down below.[730] ... to do it as painlessly as possible.

THE FÜHRER: There's not much point to it!

ZEITZLER: Well, there is a point to it; he isn't carrying out any major actions any more.

THE FÜHRER: At worst, we'd also have to take this away.

ZEITZLER: That's easier than to do this. Not much will come of this thing, and this here is much more valuable—if we wanted to give this away—than this here.

THE FÜHRER: How many do you think we will get out here [the Taman' region]? [—] Here we have to be strong, or he will start to land near Novorossiisk again. [—] First, everybody says, "We can give it away." But I can already hear Kleist,[731] or whoever is there, shouting afterward, "It can't be done that way; it can't be done with the forces in this position"— then afterward he will start here as well. Then we won't be able to bring ships in here anymore. Now we get our ships through; then that will be over. What I have in there is fine—it's good, but I can't bring in more.

ZEITZLER: First try the small bridgehead; we could still hold that for a while.

THE FÜHRER: I'm afraid we couldn't hold that. Of course, we can try. [—] We'll have to think it over.

V. KLUGE: We could pull back to the outermost northern wing, to our improved position, which I proposed at Velikie Luki. That would also improve our situation.

ZEITZLER: That is the intention in principle, but it won't free any forces for you, Herr Field Marshal.

V. KLUGE: No forces will be freed up. [—] Otherwise, we can't give up anything, except from this pot. We have to swallow Kirov and leave everything as it is now, although I would prefer to have worked a little bit here as well—but it's unfortunately not possible there.

THE FÜHRER: We can still move back here.

V. KLUGE: Here, one division can perhaps be taken out, but it's a stupid action anyway, since the situation there is already [—]

ZEITZLER: The positions are also exceptionally good!

V. KLUGE: The positions are good; they have been improved with incredible effort.

THE FÜHRER: You'd prefer Kirov?

V. KLUGE: I'd like to have it back as well; it's always an essential point for him.

ZEITZLER: It will cost more!

V. KLUGE: Under these circumstances it's now impossible, of course.

ZEITZLER: Up there you will get something free as soon as possible, if this moves back.

THE FÜHRER: Will I see you again?

V. KLUGE: No, I'd also like to go back at once. [—] Heil, my Führer.

(*Field Marshal v. Kluge excuses himself.*)

ZEITZLER: My Führer! I wanted to bring up the assessment of the situation again, so that I can have a timetable. Here, the first one can be saved right away—the other things are all connected with it, with the speed. This here is very tense; we have to let it go—everything has started. As for the SS [Panzer] Corps, we have to calculate that carefully, too. But I can report on this another time. There's no hurry.

THE FÜHRER: If only the SS [Panzer] Corps would get underway!

ZEITZLER: The *Leibstandarte* will start tomorrow at the earliest, at stage 12.

THE FÜHRER: The SS Corps is equal to 20 Italian divisions.

ZEITZLER: Then he must at least have the *Grossdeutschland* and the 7th Panzer [Division] down there. [—] If he stops here for 8 days, and takes nearly half of the free divisions over, it should work. If a division can dig itself into a sector for 6 days, it has something good. Mentally, however, he hasn't given up his slow movements. Maybe he's getting there—I think that would be good.

THE FÜHRER: If the penetration happens, then this part will be short, too. Have a look—this is half of what he has to do there.

ZEITZLER: Six to 7 days this way and 6 to 7 days that way, then we have another 8 to 9 days for evacuation here. The quartermaster general will come out with his big equipment in 7 days. If we urge a little a bit, we may get it a bit earlier. Then the next stage would come: 4 to 5 days this way, then he can stop for 6 days, then we'll get something out.

THE FÜHRER: Then he already has units in the rear area.

ZEITZLER: And above all, we won't be in a position where we have to throw in something out front.

End: 12:45 p.m.

* * * * *

October 3-4, 1943

The German Eastern Front has in the meantime been thrown back from 200 to 250 km in the central and southern sectors. After their success at Orel, the Russians attacked the German Belgorod-Khar'kov salient south of Kursk on August 3. German forces evacuated Khar'kov for the second time on August 22, this time permanently. In the meantime, as of August 16, the Soviets had crossed the Donets [River] on both sides of Izium, and, as of the 20th, had crossed the Mius [River] near Kuibyshev. The breakthrough succeeded in both locations; the Donets Basin (Donbas) territory was lost, and on September 25 the Russians arrived at Melitopol' and the Dnieper River between Zaporozh'e and Dnepropetrovsk. The northern wing of Army Group South has also been in dire straits since the end of August. Its Fourth Panzer Army was penetrated and pushed back to the Dnieper by the beginning of October; there, hoping for a break in the action so that it could replenish. The same fate was suffered by Army Group Center's Second Army, which—also penetrated—retreated back behind the Dnieper and Sosh [Rivers] by the end of September. It holds a bridgehead near Gomel, but at the mouth of the Pripiat' [River], along the boundary with Army Group South, there is a dangerous hole that it can't fill. Its retreat, as well as strong Russian attacks, forced the other armies of Army Group Center back to a position that was recently prepared along the Pronia [River] and east of Vitebsk, which protects the last railway before the Pripiat' Marshes—the line from Gomel to Mogilev to Orsha. These movements were concluded on October 1, after Smolensk and Roslavl' had been evacuated on September 24. Furthest south, the evacuation of the Kuban' bridgehead—which was attacked by the Russians on September 1 and involved the loss of Novorossiisk, Anape and Temriuk—is underway. Only Army Group North faces an unchanged situation.

On the Italian mainland, the Anglo-Americans landed on September 8 and 9 in Calabria, as well as east of Naples near Salerno, and announced the capitulation—which had been signed on the 3rd—of the Badoglio government. However, the hope they placed in these operations wasn't fulfilled. While the Italian Army disappeared from the picture without a trace, German troops were building a defensive position between Naples and Rome. The various river valleys running perpendicularly toward the coasts made this work easier. On the right wing, Naples was evacuated on October 1, and the German troops retreated behind the Volturno [River]. On the left wing, the paratroopers were thrown back to the Fortore [River], where they took evasive action and moved toward the Biferno [River].

In Yugoslavia, the departure of the Italians enabled Tito's troops to expand their area of operations, particularly in the coastal regions of the Adriatic.

(*Map 7*)

*****

EXCERPT FROM AN EVENING
SITUATION REPORT, PROBABLY OCTOBER 3, 1943[732]

1. During the presentation regarding the situation on the Eastern Front, Army Group North

(THE FÜHRER: The Spanish demanded that we withdraw the *Blue Division*) the Spanish one, immediately.[733]

ZEITZLER : Yes, indeed. I've heard it.

JODL: It's obvious that the weapons will stay there, since the people want to leave like vacationers. So only ... will go.

(ZEITZLER): ... should be discharged decently.

THE FÜHRER: Including provisions in Germany! All this has to be (prepared) carefully. These people are not responsible. These people must be treated well.

2. During the report on the situation in Italy

JODL: ... men assaulted a vehicle, an Armed Forces motor vehicle. ... They had been supplied with explosives and money. They were then arrested.

THE FÜHRER: What will happen to those two?

(JODL): ... arrested. They were normal uniformed paratroops, but they belong ... But that can also be found out about dead people. They won't say anything.[734] ...

3. During the report on the situation at sea

THE FÜHRER: Also, the British have admitted that a (passenger steamer) was sunk without rescuing a single person.

HEWEL: They announced the number of people. There (should have been) 500 on board.

THE FÜHRER: Plus the crew of 300—(altogether) about 1,000 people!

V. BELOW: Five hundred people in the cabin class, they say.

THE FÜHRER: Without rescuing a single person!

JODL: At that time it was ... (There must) have been others (besides) the first-class passengers. But the others are not counted.

THE FÜHRER: That's the "rabble."

VOSS: The Grand Admiral reports on the last convoy action[735] ... that he personally believes that out of all of these destroyers, not a single man would have been rescued except ..., but they died anyway. So one shouldn't (calculate) ... (men) as I did it today, but in his opinion the crews of the destroyers that were hit are in fact gone. ... He sees evidence for that in the present careful approach of the English ...

4. Regarding a presentation submitted by General Jodl concerning the combat command in Italy, especially the deployment of the German Luftwaffe

JODL: ... it[736] is no longer (able to attack the ships) without fighting the enemy air force.

THE FÜHRER: I think this is a ... Because at sea you fight with bombers (and against the enemy air force you take fighters. We pull back now) and say, "We'll attack the airfields." That's ridiculous—it's useless. (Such instructions) are impossible. Based on this story, there will be no air combat, nor will the (ships be attacked); then nothing will happen anymore. This is the flight into complete obscurity. This shouldn't be embellished with such timidity (then one should say), "We are not able to combat the ships and those things." What should be used to combat the air force? It can only be fought with fighter planes. Only those hit in the air have any purpose, not the others. If they tell me that they want to wipe out the airfields—they[737] will lose one or two (aircraft) that way. The result is basically zero. They spread them out. The results can't be (controlled) at all. It means nothing to destroy his planes. I must destroy his crews. Planes he produces in masses. That's ridiculous. [—] Submit this to me again tomorrow! Under no circumstances ...

JODL: Yes, Sir. This must be omitted. I can submit it again tomorrow.

(THE FÜHRER): They seek cover this way, so they can do nothing for a while. (Then) we can't control them. To combat ships—that's the decisive thing. That's quite clear.

JODL: That's what has been ordered up to now.

* * * * *

MIDDAY SITUATION REPORT,
OCTOBER 4, 1943, AT THE WOLFSSCHANZE[738]

The Balkans

JODL: ... In Greece, my Führer, there is nothing in particular except mopping-up actions in this area, ... where the commander was killed, ... again this battalion of this Probationary Brigade or Penal Brigade .... These are the regions where the 81st [Infantry Division], the 264th [Infantry Division] ... corps should come in. ... The situation in Tuzla is very unpleasant, too. This mountain Jäger [light infantry] brigade, which was intended to relieve Tuzla, ... attacked Tuzla with German forces, including parts of the 369th [Infantry Division], the (157th) and the *Brandenburg* Regiment and recaptured it again. In a company of the 369th Division, a plan was discovered to kill the German officers.[739] ... So in all these regions there are a lot of ... the whole division is useless, but such elements can exist anywhere. ... relatively quiet, at least no major ... impression that nothing would come out of the movement ... dissolves. He is in opposition ... and against the British as well.[740]

THE FÜHRER: Against the British?

JODL: ... would mainly be in opposition, since they ... requested that they unite with the Tito movement, while the Tito movement (has) the stronger impetus—which will get even stronger. I hope that due to these significant reinforcements, consisting of three full divisions—the 264th, the 181st (and the) Cossacks,[741] of which about half is there—we will be in a position to take on this group ... was done ... by the ... division ... in order to ... their mobility ... might be equipped with wheels in order (to be) able to move at all.

BUHLE: With French vehicles.

JODL: If they get more vehicles, it is not ...

THE FÜHRER: I am convinced we should take more out of Italy, and the interest ...

BUHLE: That will come out.

JODL: In addition, Kesselring requested another motor vehicle transport regiment from us.

BUHLE: He is, of course, ...

THE FÜHRER: Nevertheless, if one gets a whole country motorized, ...

JODL: Somewhere in this country there must be some cities, like Naples, that do have motor vehicles,[742] ...

BODENSCHATZ: They've all been taken away.

THE FÜHRER: Everyone took something for himself and won't give anything up. Everyone says: Who knows when I will get something again...

JODL: ... We don't get this via the normal report channel.

THE FÜHRER: It's quite ridiculous. We just have to calculate how many vehicles we have in this part of Italy ... everything will be taken away anyway ... There must have been at least 40,000 to 50,000 trucks.

The West

JODL: ... transport of the Bosnian Division.[743] The replacement is in progress here: the 242nd [Infantry Division] is moving in to relieve the 356th [Infantry Division].[744] Thirty-five trains from the 384th [Infantry Division] have arrived and are assembling here, and then the 245th and the 244th [Infantry Divisions] are beginning to form ... very lively again yesterday. The exposure created by pulling out the 371st [Infantry Division][745] can now be accepted in October ... strong. But major attacks can't be expected. Although the situation up here is completely ..., are still south of this line ... capable British divisions and approximately seven armored divisions.

THE FÜHRER: But wasted 20 divisions as well. (I have) the feeling that the British don't want to shoot their last powder, and they will say, "We will take care of ourselves; if something happens here [—]"

Situation at sea

(REPRESENTATIVE OF THE NAVY): ... Gibraltar nothing unusual. Again strong convoys. The coverage of Gibraltar is still unchanged. [—] At Philippeville ... report of a nice success has taken shape. The submarine *U 410* reported that they sank 8,000 tons on their way back to their home port. Additionally, five detonations were heard. Now the commanding officer reported when he returned that ... 6,000 ... 7,000 ... were sunk. That means the boat had a 39,000-ton success with one stroke.[746] The boat arrived in Toulon. [—] Up here: submarine chase. [—] The commanding admiral of Italy reports the commissioning of two Italian minelayers ... in La Spezia and one Italian minelayer in Venice. [—] The evacuation transports from Corsica should be ... 11 p.m. We haven't received the final report yet either.[747] ... A submarine chaser hunted the submarines that were reported here yesterday ... one submarine sunk.[748] [—] During the night of October 2 there was a motor torpedo boat advance against a convoy here, but ... In the Aegean region, one steamer here with Italians to Athens, one steamer to Crete ... carried out and the ... retreated back to ... That was reported yesterday evening already: ... cruisers and destroyers. [—] Attacks on the Crimea ... Kerch Strait as planned ... port facilities were blown up in Senaia and Taman'.[749] ... region, nothing unusual. [—] Twenty-three planes located over the North Sea. ... as planned. Lively activity in the air ... in the Baltic Sea. One patrol boat was sunk in an air raid. In the Channel area, a significant artillery battle took place between the opposing batteries, triggered initially by a single convoy. The steamer *Levata*, which was ... shot at by ... batteries ... Hostile batteries shot at a German convoy, which crossed here, a little later. That caused another duel between the two batteries. The artillery commander reports: Effective hits were observed in the area of the one battery over there. Last night, north of ... there was an engagement between German torpedo boats and English destroyers. There are no details yet.[750] Forty-two planes located over the [Bay of] Biscay. ... reports on the convoy ... that last night for the first time ... was warded off ... anti-aircraft artillery of these boats ... are going east toward this convoy, which is expected to come from the east. No further reports.

Situation in the air

CHRISTIAN: Yesterday during the day, a very strong ... activity with approximately ... attacks, primarily against airfields, against ... Despite the heavy attacks on the airfields—four-engine aircraft were also involved ... were caused. The airfields can be used. ... some damage to the airfield facilities, damage to hangars ... actually nothing serious. [—] ... deployed, in fairly strong numbers. 10 aircraft were brought down for certain, and probably eight others as well. The British report 15. In addition, there were these two, which were shot outside here—a Thunderbolt[751] and a Typhoon.[752] [—] During the night ... approached first in a relatively narrow front ... and a few high-explosive bombs. The return flight of some of the aircraft—so that we assumed at first that he was going ..., then assumed he would drop over Hanover and return. Then, he turned away with the rest toward the south ... our own fighters in this area between Hanover and Berlin, but had them positioned closer to Hanover. ... immediately went down to Kassel, where the majority of the forces have been in action. Two hundred and sixty-four fighters were in the ... In Kassel there are 28 heavy, 8 light, ... 8 searchlight batteries at the moment. Damage—it was determined that ... 600 mines and detonation bombs, 50,000 incendiary and 10,000 phosphorus bombs ...—were mainly in industrial ... No conflagrations. Numerous large fires and several hundred small fires. According to reports received thus far, 60 houses ... destroyed, ... damaged, ... Henschel factory: Factory I, seriously damaged. The Junkers factory wasn't hit. The Hohenlohe school was heavily damaged. Spinnfaser AG was seriously damaged, but it was already quite ineffective before. The Hansa weaving mill was damaged. In addition to those, a number of smaller factories as well. ... a church and hits on the Orangerieschloss [Orangerie Palace]. Heavy damage to the slaughterhouse. ... freight depot ... damage to various tracks. Casualties: 54 dead reported so far ... number of injured persons ... can't be determined yet[753] ... and had an air-raid warning for about 20 minutes. Reports so far of aircraft shot down: 15 for certain, plus another 21. England has just reported 24. The other 21 have not been confirmed yet. But 15 were definite. Now the English report 24. Defense was a bit handicapped again. There was a thick haze on the ground here, so the number of hits was lower than could have been expected from the number of fighters in action. In addition, during the day, one intrusion into this area ... and then after 20 minutes it flew out here ... In addition ... disappeared, for example; it was gone. We don't know if he was over Munich. All in all, 30 fighters flew on defensive patrol at the time of the first incoming flight. Then another defensive patrol was flown when the second group of aircraft was reported. Except for the two fighter patrols in two-ship formation that were already above, ... lines of planes in the air ... Only sound reported—no visual reports. Today during the day—the last report—there was an intrusion by about 100 aircraft into the area of the Deutsche Bucht [German Bight]. No bombs were dropped ... in the area of Frankfurt-am-Mein. Bomb dropping ... Heddernheim. Undercover agents informed us about the attack, so the Commander of the Center Sector had been warned beforehand. ... reception group near ... was accompanied for quite a long distance. An incursion by 100 aircraft with fighter protection to ... in the south of Germany ... the attack on Bolzano is still coming ... a connection was made through the attack from the south, so in fact a very [—]

THE FÜHRER: What was here? Did we bring aircraft in here or not?

CHRISTIAN: Yes, everything was brought in here, ... of the 3rd Fighter Division. In addition, the ... was deployed already during the approach, and during the departure as well. ... and pulled in the long-range destroyers from the south. ...

(JODL?): The Antimacchia airfield was taken after stiff enemy resistance. That's the essential thing. By October 3 at 10 p.m.—that was yesterday evening—800 prisoners had been taken, including 200 British. The landing craft are all returning.

CHRISTIAN: Disturbed ... the enemy's ... with 22 planes yesterday, including 14 Messerschmitts. All of the planes arrived at the target and dropped their bombs onto the airfields—on 10 ... altogether ... recognized the landing facilities.

THE FÜHRER: Yesterday I spoke with the Reichsmarshal. I prefer, despite everything that was explained to me, ... constantly attacking the towns.

CHRISTIAN: ... are so confused that way, ...

THE FÜHRER: They are confused, but they come.

CHRISTIAN: ... go there before, at the start. So far we have been there during the landing only.

THE FÜHRER: That makes no difference; but they come.

CHRISTIAN: ... when we constantly attack towns, ...

THE FÜHRER: Then we would have to ... a total of 10 to 12 ... over there ... every night ...

CHRISTIAN: This reverse encircling attempt was ... by five, and later by a second deployment—the number wasn't mentioned ... A tank landing craft was also damaged during this action[754] ... only limited deployment ... The total losses are low—I had them ... over here yesterday, but I can't remember them anymore—in 1,300 sorties, a total of 19 Ju 52s plus a few "Savoias"[755] and 4 or 5 Messerschmitt 323s[756] were lost; altogether very limited ... 14 Ju 52s are ... concentrated here. I don't know if we ..., because if he really ..., we should have had considerably more losses.

THE FÜHRER: Now a message has come, as ... announce officially, ... I must say, "Spiegelberg, I hear you running!" It was said yesterday out of the blue that the ships wouldn't be attacked anymore; instead ... again ...

CHRISTIAN: ... set up by the Armed Forces Operations Staff. We can't oppose it. It doesn't come from the Luftwaffe.

THE FÜHRER: No, first of all ... ships attacked ... What does that mean? In the air you can only use fighters to attack, and for attacking ships ... still fighting ships. Here, more fighters will be deployed. If fighter planes are free, we can take them here as well.

CHRISTIAN: ... the thing was set up here, and General Korten[757] and I were informed yesterday. I said, "Nothing to see" ... my inquiry—that I think it's wrong—has been answered, that is ..., this is the express wish of the Luftwaffe. The other way would not be possible. Because unless they ... the Luftwaffe ... It was a complete reversal ...

THE FÜHRER: Attacks are being made continuously with all units ...

CHRISTIAN: It's assumed that this version came about because one supposes that if ...

THE FÜHRER: That's just great. So they should go on attacking ships. Because they won't destroy the airfields here. They won't be able to do it. It's not feasible at all. [—] In addition, there's one more small thing: do they really think these little trees[758] that are planted here will (keep out) the gliders?

CHRISTIAN: That's another matter for the Führer Headquarters to address.

THE FÜHRER: I'm just asking if these little trees ..., if these would present the slightest obstacle at all?

CHRISTIAN: I saw them yesterday for the first time.

THE FÜHRER: They're put into the ground, and the first glider plane that comes along will pull them out ... I only want to ask one thing: if the place here is going to be mined, let me know beforehand so that my Blondi[759] won't be blown up.

CHRISTIAN: I mean, not to prevent the gliders, but because of the whole air situation.

THE FÜHRER: That can be done cheaper. This will come off soon. It will be disappointing. Overnight, the picture changes. I have nothing against it in the winter.

(... ?): ..., my Führer, that since our special equipment has become available, he has disturbed the shipping traffic, the ferry traffic, less than before ... this strange thing ... and this thing, too. In any case it's all a bit exaggerated. ...

THE FÜHRER: We will see what happens in (the Far East). Yesterday, the Japs—Oshima—told me that they will …; I can't say where … (With the) Japanese you never know. They are concluding major agreements as well, of course. … said something crazy: Matsuoka had to go because he wanted to … the fight against Russia.[760] The Navy said: we can't do that because we won't get any more oil; within a short time we will run out of oil.

(… ?): He's the one who … after our occupation …

JODL: The British didn't want to.

CHRISTIAN: The new figures for the contribution have arrived. The primary task of the Luftwaffe … continued attacks against aircraft … combating hostile landing operations …

THE FÜHRER: … when it reads: "The support of the Army must not be weakened by it," or "must not be adversely affected."

(… ?): … submitted these letters again, which were sent by a French minister from North Africa to his wife … as a fraud—but a very clever one—from the creator of falsified news…

THE FÜHRER: Those scoundrels! If they are a bit … in time they will get really …

JODL: It was absolutely implausible.

THE FÜHRER: It happened that way anyway.

JODL: It's happened similarly, anyway?.

THE FÜHRER: I say—if I only (wanted) to earn money, I could have earned something there … Some of these things …

(CHRISTIAN?): Strong deployment to support the Army near Kos.[761] Today, only dive-bomber units were deployed. Protection by armed reconnaissance units in this area, against returning Navy forces; preparation and assembly for new sorties. To the south … as well as … In addition, my Führer, the following is to be reported from this area: We have changed to standard time.[762] The Finns aren't joining in on that. … bad because of the oil region.[763] … transmission of all these times in the aircraft warning service … one comes …

THE FÜHRER: Why did he refuse it, anyway?

CHRISTIAN: It plays a role for them economically, of course. Then they have to go to bed by 3 o'clock, or [—]

THE FÜHRER: They don't have to.

HEWEL: It's shifting a bit.

CHRISTIAN: Now, we have Central European Time … on Eastern European Time … with daylight saving time … This might be economical for them, if they also …

THE FÜHRER: In the end, the one who has to bear the major load, must possess… also economic …

CHRISTIAN: All the others joined.

(... ?): ... the Russian shoots with artillery ... not much more can be done with smoke. In addition, State Councilor Pleiger[764] said ... again this 35,000 thing. He wanted to plan the smoke action for Nikopol'.

THE FÜHRER: This small bridgehead was disastrous from the very beginning. Of course, it's not unimportant ...

CHRISTIAN: We weren't asked at all, but I first said: ...

THE FÜHRER: ... we have to put in there ... to give to Nikopol'. Nikopol' itself is hard to attack from the air. Just a few minor things there—the power station, etc.—can be attacked ... The mine pits are ...[765]

CHRISTIAN: Shall we leave the smoke thing as it stands, my Führer?

THE FÜHRER: I would leave it at Zaporozh'e as long as we (have) the power station, yes![766] In any case, we still have time to build the other one up then. If we ... have to build up ..., then it's clear anyway ...

CHRISTIAN: ... improved weather conditions in general ... are due to this heavy precipitation. The danger is, ... dries out again. (*Presentation of press reports and the Armed Forces report follows.*)

WAIZENEGGER: I added 5 aircraft to the English reports.

End: 1:44 p.m.

* * * * *

October 26, 1943

In the East, the Red Army began its fall offensive on October 6, along a front stretching practically from Nevel' to the Taman' Peninsula. East of Nevel' the Russians succeeded in penetrating the lines between Army Group North and Army Group Center, tearing a broad gap in the front. Intense combat has been in progress since October 7 in the area around Kiev, which the Fourth Panzer Army has held thus far with only local losses. However, the Russians threw back the German Dnieper defenses southeast of Kremenchug on October 17, and on October 24 on both sides of Dnepropetrovsk. On the Sea of Azov, the breakthrough occurred on October 23 near Melitopol'; in less than one week, the land connection to the Crimea near Perekop will be cut. The Kuban bridgehead has been evacuated.

In Italy, the intermediate positions on the Volturno and the Biferno [Rivers], which are now being attacked by the English and the Americans, are still being held. To the rear, on the Garigliano and the Sangro [Rivers], another line is being prepared, which is to be held as long as possible.

(*Maps 5, 7, and 10*)

* * * * *

Evening Situation Report,
October 26, 1943, at the Wolfsschanze[767]

Beginning: 10:03 p.m.

The East

ZEITZLER: All in all, no fundamental change for the worse. Basically, it has remained as it was at midday.

THE FÜHRER: Is he[768] pulling the 13th Panzer Division down?

ZEITZLER: The 13th Panzer Division has been partially deployed already, and he put one regiment from the 335th [Infantry] Division in trucks and brought it in, so something has come down from there. He mainly set himself up in this one place here, which he has held bravely since yesterday. The occupation force in there is doing extremely well. They held it the whole day yesterday. Today there were heavy attacks, and they held the whole day again, so that he couldn't get any further. Here, only one reconnaissance patrol—more or less—continued in that direction, and the thrust went to … Parts of the 13th Panzer Division and the 17th [Panzer Division], plus the majority of the 97th Jäger [Light Infantry] Division are in there, as well as the 73rd [Infantry] Division and the 111th [Infantry] Division; one regiment of the 335th [Infantry] Division, which he took out above, has already arrived. The intention is to go back to this line, as was reported yesterday. The complete cavalry corps[769] is also in there. The 4th Mountain Division is still on its way over, as is the 50th Assault Division.[770] Then on this front, the retreat was completed back to this line, as the radio message reported two days ago. Here there is still fighting on the island. He hasn't had any success breaking through. In this place there was a penetration. At this location, he wasn't able to push any further. The situation there eased up due to the presence of the 14th Panzer Division. An enemy group is in down here, but should be cleared out. It's only a fairly small group. Nothing in particular on this front, either. There was a small engagement underway here. Here we don't know any of the particulars, but he doesn't seem to be pushing forward. He's not interested in it. A few reconnaissance tanks were sighted here. So he seems to be making the thrust here first. Up there, most of them were driven back again. [—] There was nothing (unusual) along this whole front. On the other hand, they believe that this action is going (to start) again tomorrow, and they want to assign the 7th Panzer Division to the Eighth Army, and to keep the 8th Panzer Division on hand near Kiev. I think we have to agree to it.

[—] Nothing in particular in the area of the Second Army. This matter has gradually been straightened out. Also here, only maneuvers were reported. Up there the breakthroughs are, for the most part, back under control. The 268th [Infantry] Division is approaching. Then there were a few minor things here. All in all, the line held completely, with the exception of this little dent here. Today he attacked again, but not to the extent that he did yesterday. Then new attacks started on the road to Orsha, but also not as extensively as on the previous days—just to the north. Here, certain reinforcements have arrived now. Here there have been a few shifts, so the thing will probably move to the north. The Luftwaffe field division brought back the first stage into this position.

THE FÜHRER: This is already the final position?

ZEITZLER: Yes, Sir. These points are the final line. The white part was the very first line. The position should be good. I spoke with ... [—] Army Group North has nothing in particular to report. Some movement was reported up near Staraia Russa. There were night frosts up there again, so we don't know if the muddy period is coming or if it's just a short transition period. Up there some movement has been reported—otherwise nothing. Here in this location there were a few maneuvers.

THE FÜHRER: What can we do now so that the 50th [Infantry] Division on the Crimea can be quickly replaced with something else? The biggest danger on the Crimea, as I see it, is not sea landings but airborne landings—he could drop an airborne brigade on the isthmus of Feodosiia.[771]

ZEITZLER: The agents report the following: An action is planned here, but it couldn't be verified. In my opinion, it's too much tonnage—they can't carry that much. I've given it to a Navy liaison agent.

THE FÜHRER: He's going to land here and here.

ZEITZLER: Yes, they say that simultaneously with this action, there will be an action in Feodosiia and another in Yalta.[772] I can hardly believe that he would be able do it with his shipping capability.

THE FÜHRER: No, I don't believe it. (He) will make an airborne landing. Perhaps he will try to support (it), once the airborne troops take possession of the batteries.

ZEITZLER: Some of the 336th [Infantry] Division has come in (here). But they are still there in the back. This (corner) is, of course, a bit unpleasant, because there is nothing there.

THE FÜHRER: That can't be allowed. He has to put in something from the 336th [Infantry] Division. He absolutely has to put in a unit.

ZEITZLER: Yes, that's actually more important than up there.

THE FÜHRER: And then the Navy again!

VOSS: I spoke with the Grand Admiral.

THE FÜHRER: This is the most important thing: that at least this flank is covered. Anything that can shoot must come over here. If there really is a landing, then it's do or die.

VOSS: Even the Navy landing craft must fight against destroyers then, if there's no other way.

JODL: Here, the Luftwaffe has proposed to withdraw the three light anti-aircraft batteries from Nikopol' back to Nikolaev, since it believes that no more air attacks will be made here.

ZEITZLER: The important thing is that we protect this railway bridge up here.

THE FÜHRER: Then they should leave one battery here. Two light batteries are enough there.

ZEITZLER: It seems that the Kherson Bridge is well protected. Another air raid was driven back again. The railway bridge near Nikolaev will probably be ready the day after tomorrow—since here we will gradually come under pressure with the supply if the weather is bad. Perhaps something should be prepared by the Luftwaffe, in case pressure arises there. We now have two movements[773] initiated by the quartermaster general. The first uses this railway, and the other one is here with large transport vehicles.

THE FÜHRER: How is this coming in here? When will the next division come after the 14th Panzer Division?

ZEITZLER: Thus far, things have gone as planned. Even the first trains of the *Leibstandarte* [SS Panzer Grenadier Division] left today as scheduled.

THE FÜHRER: The Panther detachment of the *Leibstandarte* has gone?

BUHLE: All of it has gone.

ZEITZLER: The 384th [Infantry] Division is coming … Then the 76th [Infantry] Division will arrive after November 2, and then the combat elements of the 25th Panzer Division (will follow), after November 5. Those (are) the dates at the (moment). Until now, we've been pushing them all up a bit.

THE FÜHRER: And the *Leibstandarte?*

ZEITZLER: The *Leibstandarte* arrives in Vienna on October 28.[774] The first trains have left. Then it has to get the order to pass through, so that it can (then) go on through immediately. Then the … combat elements will arrive, while the 1st Panzer Division will arrive all disorganized, since we're actually just driving it on the way it left from down there.

THE FÜHRER: I spoke with Goebbels. A message has come; an Englishman writes that interrogation of the British exchange prisoners produced the following picture: in Germany there is great pessimism. When the British left the hospitals they were told, "We hope you will be back again, before the Bolsheviks come. The Englishman now draws the following conclusion from this: it proves how effective our bomb raids are; therefore, it is of utmost importance that they be continued with the greatest energy. [—] We have to bring this, too—also into the hospitals. If such a bastard said such thing, ... to demoralize the German people ... to continue with new bomb raids.

Italy

JODL: There is a heavier attack underway against the ... Panzer Grenadier Division, against this town of Pietravecchio. The attack is still going on. Otherwise, there is no particular action, except here against the right wing of the 29th Panzer Grenadier Division, and here a few isolated attacks against the front in the middle of the parachute division, and against the right wing, with very strong fighter-bomber support. Fighter-bomber deployment was heavy today in general. Aside from that, no unusual action. [—] Here is a picture of how this position looks: (*Presentation.*) It was taken directly behind the front line. It's the Volturno valley. Tanks can hardly be used there. They have to cross the mountains there, and then there's this ground, and here is our position. It's quite a strong position already. Of course, all the [railroad] bridges and road bridges have been destroyed. This picture (*New presentation.*) was taken a bit further to the south, but also in this valley. He has to climb up the mountains there.

Finland

THE FÜHRER: ... received a (letter), and ... (given to) ... the prime minister. In this letter[775] he writes more or less that he ... consider how to proceed; it would (be) very serious. (One) has to understand one thing— that Finland has a different constitution—and he describes the whole thing. (The) envoy emphasized this. I said, "Democracy (here), democracy (there). Do you think that in America, which wants to be a democracy, it would be possible for someone to go to Switzerland to negotiate officially with the Germans, and then to make this public? Do you think (that) a democracy has no possibility of taking action against such treason? Then everything would end! Your theory, which you always preach—that it was a war of the Great Powers, which doesn't concern Finland and in which Finland is not interested, and that Finland could just go its own way to get out of this war of the Great Powers[776] —would give our people exactly the same right. Germany could end its war of the Great Powers as soon as some understanding could be reached, without taking the small powers into consideration." To this he replied, very subdued, that that would mean the destruction of Finland. But in the last few days they've been making fine declarations. They probably suspect by now that the others won't lift a finger for them anyway.[777]

The Balkans

(JODL): ... Then in the ... pushed through (as far as) Lipseni. So it is now our intention to create a connection along the big road tomorrow, and to push forward from both sides.

THE FÜHRER: We'll get the road, these pigs will go to the side, and when we're gone they'll go down again. Nevertheless, one can't say that we will do (nothing). To me, that would be like a lice-covered soldier saying, "If I take away the lice at one seam, they'll come back the next day anyway, so I'll just leave them. [—]" But one has to start the fight against the lice anyway. An energetic fight and the lice disappear. It's exactly the same here. All these territories were once occupied by one state. Then it was just like now, and he nevertheless managed to gradually pacify the territories. But now we must change to another system. We need to have a gendarmerie here that is not stationed in Agram and Laibach, but is everywhere out there in small groups, controlling things town by town. We have to take it by the root. The [partisan] bands can't keep forming—even in the towns the bandits have to be fished out individually. That is the prerequisite to pacifying this area. But if the British could cope with the nomads in the northwestern provinces of India, we can (manage this here, too).

JODL: I ... cause difficulties. Especially ... chased the heavy weapons off the streets ... captured (guns) and so on, so ... will ...

THE FÜHRER: It's quiet here now?

JODL: Yes, there it's quiet. Nothing more has been (reported) from there.

THE FÜHRER: So here we should already have a system to control the area town by town—who is there, who comes into the town, where he comes from—and to arrest such people immediately and send them away. In that way we could gradually free the area of drifting elements, because only the drifting elements are dangerous.

The East again

Zeitzler, two divisions are supposed to be set up in the Crimea now. When can we bring them in?

BUHLE: They are permanent staffs that had to leave the East.[778]

ZEITZLER: Today I gave the order to pull out the division staffs. We need to be very strict. They cling to their division staffs, of course, and come up with some sort of assignment. But that has no use anymore. They have to come out anyway.

(THE FÜHRER: If we) ... leave a division (at) the Kerch Strait, keep the (coastal) batteries sufficiently manned—and (also) the anti-aircraft batteries—and the Luftwaffe is ready for action here, and (the) Navy covers the whole territory between Feodosiia and Yalta, then, I believe, nothing more can happen.

THE FÜHRER: I just had an artillery officer down with me, who has taken a look at the Army coastal batteries. There they have a lot of (HIWIs) volunteers[779] as ammunition carriers, and these people are starting to deteriorate, too, which leads to fights among the HIWIs. Some of them want to participate and some of them don't anymore, so now they're beating each other up. This poses a certain danger in case of a landing. But we had to do it that way because at that time there were no men there.

Italy again

JODL: Here is a first general overview of the coastal batteries available on the parts of the Italian west coast occupied by us. The red ones are present but not ready for action yet, and the blue ones are ready for action. (*Presentation.*)

THE FÜHRER: This is quite a distance, of course. It's 200 km, but he can't land everywhere along these 200 km. ... (How is it) in Istria?

JODL: There's nothing there yet; (something) must go (there).

THE FÜHRER: Yes, something must go (there) as well. He won't land anymore. He's much too cowardly for that. This (landing) in Salerno he did in agreement with the Italians.

V-Weapons (Rockets)

JODL: A question concerning the deployment of the A 4[780]: Should it be announced? Should we speak about it or not? I ask because the various press reports are coming in now—also inquiries from Budapest—as a result of the speech by Ley,[781] which announced that within 6 weeks we will deploy a new weapon that is supposed to level entire cities in England. Should we speak about it in general?

THE FÜHRER: No!

JODL: I wouldn't give a time frame at all, because otherwise there will be disappointment again. It has been said on different occasions, in general terms, that we do have something, and that doesn't do any harm.

THE FÜHRER: Yes, indeed. They know that. The only ones who don't know are the German people as a whole. All the others know it. They ...

Sweden

JODL: This is the report from the military (attaché in) Stockholm, about the exchange in Göteborg.[782] (*Presentation.*)
THE FÜHRER: The Swedish crown princess (is) English. She's an enemy of ours, who is filled with (hatred). She's one of the main driving forces in Sweden. The fact that this worm speaks very fluent German makes her even more disgusting.[783]

Situation in the air

V. BELOW: Regarding the deployment of the Luftwaffe, it is to be reported that in the West, relatively little happened today because the weather conditions were bad. Nothing much is to be expected during the night, either. [—] In the East, the deployment of the Fourth Air Fleet has been quite good since 10 o'clock. The Sixth Air Fleet was unable to fly because of the fog and bad weather, and the same holds for the First Air Fleet. [—] In the Southeast, sorties were flown against Leros—about 55 fighters and dive bombers in total. [—] In the South, 34,000 GRT were damaged in attacks against the harbor at Naples the night before last. No other deployment was possible today.

Armaments
...
BUHLE: Except ... That makes about 140 altogether.
THE FÜHRER: And ammunition?
BUHLE: Five to six combat loads are sitting up there.
THE FÜHRER: We have to bring them there in huge quantities. They should shoot whatever goes out.
BUHLE: I hope that I can get another 23 out in 10 days. We will get 170 to 180 in total.[784]
THE FÜHRER: If we bring in 150 there and have 5,000 rounds everywhere, that would make 700,000 to 800,000 rounds.
BUHLE: But I hope another 30 might come together in the next 10 days.
KEITEL: We follow every single gun on its way.
BUHLE: The Luftwaffe field divisions in the West[785] are all unarmed; they don't have any guns like this anymore. But what we received from Italy was complete garbage.
KEITEL: Lots of stuff in bad condition!
THE FÜHRER: What's the overall picture of the Italian spoils we received?
(BUHLE: Concerning the) guns, it's terrible! ... one 12-cm gun. That is (a gun that) ... was in the approach.

THE FÜHRER: But we should do one thing: If the factory fittings are there, we should not impose our things on them, but just build the Italian ones; that is much easier. For example, a (12-cm) gun like that can be, if nothing else, deployed for coastal defense purposes. There we (are) happy to have them. We should also continue producing their 9-cm anti-aircraft gun. We can use it for coastal purposes then; we can use it for that without any interruption. That's much better than an alteration. If we convert the factory, nothing will be produced for at least two years. They always say the that conversion will be complete in one year. But if you take a closer look, one gun will come in January 1945, another gun in February 1945, another two in March, two guns in April as well—so practically nothing at all. Meanwhile, we could have continued production of at least 12 to 15 pieces a month. They should go on producing, if they're making the Ansaldo. We should immediately deploy the 9-cm anti-aircraft gun for coastal defense purposes, which will free up German anti-aircraft artillery. That way we can take advantage of it. In the other situation we don't use it, but do a conversion in hope of some future benefit. I would also say that we should continue building the 7.5 cm. We can always ... it for [—][786]

THE FÜHRER: They should not convert, (but) continue producing their things. (We) won't get anything for this war anymore. Before, if we had continued working instead of making that stupid conversion at Skoda, we could have gotten our howitzers there, and today we would have at least 1,000 good field howitzers.[787] So we got nothing at all. This conversion didn't help us much. It's the same here. People are focused on one kind of model. Before they can produce a second model, the machines have to be altered, etc. That makes no sense. With our immense need for coastal guns, this 9-cm anti-aircraft gun would also be excellent. Also the 7.5 cm can be deployed against landing craft and anything else. The 7.5 cm Ansaldo anti-aircraft gun shoots just as high as the 8.8 cm.

BUHLE: We shelled the small steel bunkers. But the way Speer reported it, with a reduced charge, it doesn't give a true picture—with the 15.2 cm reduced charge it would correspond to a range of 3,000 m. If I fire at it vertically with the 15.2—they can't (shoot) in any other way—it doesn't result in [—]

(THE FÜHRER): Was it mounted?

(BUHLE): No, it was just set down. (They) needed 6 shots to get the gravel and the earth off, to expose the bunker. So it was 7 shots altogether. (That) is not an accurate comparison. I have ordered another shelling in more realistic conditions, using the correct ammunition.[788]

THE FÜHRER: Yes, indeed. In more realistic conditions of war—and then we should do one more thing: put a layer of concrete blocks on top.

BUHLE: It took them 6 shots to get the concrete blocks away.

THE FÜHRER: Until they get 6 hits on such a small thing!

BUHLE: Several hundred rounds are needed for that.

KEITEL: It's a lucky hit; in the installations outside Verdun we waited months for a hit. A hit like that is coincidence. The dispersion over a normal distance is at least 100m.

THE FÜHRER: I would like to use the Italian armor-plate capacity for that. Then we could make it out of real armor material.

(BUHLE: If it) is 100mm of real armor material, then …

(THE FÜHRER: Then) we don't even need the … we have to put a cover around it.

End: 10:36 p.m.

* * * * *

November 19, 1943

On the easternmost tip of the Crimea, the Russians have now landed near Kerch, but even the very narrow peninsula with the town will be defended successfully until April. While the extended Nikopol' bridgehead is still being held on the southeastern side of the great bend in the Dnieper [River] bend, the enemy is already attacking Krivoi Rog again from the northeast, up to the point where the penetration had taken him in October. The major Russian attack on the Kiev area started November 3; the town was lost only three days later, and the Soviets drove the Fourth Panzer Army back—toward the southwest past Fastov and to the west past Radomysl' and Zhitomir, as well as on to Korosten'. On the southern flank of this penetration, in the Zhitomir–Fastov area, a German counterattack has been underway since November 11; this counterattack is halting the Russian progress and will allow the Germans to retake Zhitomir on the day of this meeting. Meanwhile, Army Group Center's Second Army, to the north, has been pushed back south of Gomel', whose evacuation Hitler had forbidden. Rechitsa, to the west of this town, was lost on November 17, and at Ovruch the enemy is already standing less than 100 km west of the Dnieper. The Soviets also achieved a breakthrough in the Ninth Army's lines at Propoisk, threatening Mogilev from the south and producing fierce combat. Along the Smolensk–Orsha highway, on the other hand, the Russians are trying for the third time—although in vain—to achieve a breakthrough. The penetration at Nevel wasn't cleared up, but the enemy is still refraining from taking operational advantage of his success.

In Italy, the German units have retreated to the Sangro and the Garigliano [Rivers], but are still holding the high position on both sides of Mignano, outside Rapido, which practically creates the connection. The Americans tried to take this position during their November 6-12 attack, but were unable to do so.

(Maps 5, 7 and 10)

* * * * *

MIDDAY SITUATION REPORT, NOVEMBER 19, 1943[789]

Beginning: presumably at 12:30 p.m.

The East

ZEITZLER: Today there is a lot of action in the area of Army Group Center. *(Presentation of the Armed Forces report follows.)*

THE FÜHRER: I've feared many times that they would station their submarines in our supply places.[790]

VOSS: We only have observations that there are carrier-based aircraft ...

WAIZENEGGER: So far the British have reported 32 aircraft shot down.

ZEITZLER: All in all it was rather a quiet day on the Crimea again yesterday. But there seems to be a tank brigade over there now, so, depending on the weather conditions, we could face a major attack.

THE FÜHRER: Assault guns?

ZEITZLER: The assault guns are coming now. Thus far 5 have arrived. The others are lying on that thing there, so the assault gun detachments will come in there. In general, the air transport went well yesterday. About 1,000 men came over. Today a total of 860 men on leave are supposed to come over. Here there was a small advance—otherwise nothing in particular. [—] I made tables showing all the losses and supplies once during the whole time. *(Presentation.)* These are the losses. [—] This is the overall situation during the whole time—ours and the Romanians. There you see the relation—many more Romanians are there nevertheless. That's what there was up to then, and this is two days later, because I receive the losses later. So with losses we are at least over that. In November I've scheduled another 8,000 men for about 10 days or so. Then it will continue at exactly the same rate. The pressure won't start before December, of course. Then we have to think about distributing this among all the replacements on the Eastern front. But for another ten days it's fine. [—] They can be very satisfied with the assault guns as well. This is what's coming over here. *(Presentation.)* There's nothing else unusual to report from Army Group A. The last of the 13th Panzer Division is now pulling up there. Here there's nothing special, my Führer, but the preparations for the attack are a little closer now.

Here there are movements, minor advances, 70 tanks. I counted all of this together here. In total, we have 118 tanks and assault guns in here, excluding the 13th Panzer Division. Manstein has pulled the 13th over here in order to have it available, because the 11th [Panzer Division] is leaving. He will also have it available if it becomes dangerous here. I think it's best to have it here for the time being. There were individual attacks on this front this morning, and one here, where they are still fighting. Here his assembly area was destroyed. Here the fighting continues. No other significant action. Here there is still quite a lot of garbage. The 11th and the 6th Panzer [Divisions] are going to close in here as quickly as possible. Parts of the *Viking* [SS Panzer Grenadier Division], which were supposed to block here, came in here. I have pointed out the Smela railway station to the army group.[791] That's the only German connection into here. Otherwise, the other connection will have to go via Transnistria afterward. That's probably why he's moving forward here with the 6th and the 11th, because he knows that. That could bring great pressure on us. I am only concerned that they might arrive too late, now that the weather conditions are so bad. If he comes in time, it would be good. [—] This is estimated at about two infantry divisions. Then down there [near Smela] [partisan] bands and some of the paratroopers have approached. Obviously this had been prepared with the parachutists for a long time.

THE FÜHRER: I have the same worry here: that it will start here all of a sudden.

ZEITZLER: Yes, Sir. That is just what the feelings are here at the moment.

THE FÜHRER: If it doesn't work here, he will attack here immediately. He'll do it quickly.

ZEITZLER: He is starting to throw up entrenchments here in this old bridgehead. It really does seem that he wants some sort of defense here.[792] It has been relatively calm along this front. Then here it's very orderly: The two combat groups of the 268th and 23rd [Infantry Divisions] have advanced to the highway and have driven back attacks. Then this ring was closed last night by the 7th and 8th Panzer [Divisions]. Parts of the 1st Panzer [Division] are in there. There is fighting in Schi ...[793]. Troops are also lining up against it from the south. Up there the attacks were driven back. He made a relatively strong attack, with tanks. Here again are the enemy losses from the 8th through the 17th: 9,300 dead, 658 captured, 332 tanks, 409 antitank guns. What's striking is the extensive equipment with antitank guns that's now being reported by all the regimental commanders. The panzer regiment commanders say that the enemy tanks haven't done them too much harm— it's the antitank guns.[794] Otherwise, the intentions are still the same as I reported yesterday: first clearing out this encircled area up to here, then preparing here with the left wing along the road.

THE FÜHRER: I'm afraid it will be very difficult here, because he's stopping a long time, building up one position after the other.

ZEITZLER: It's just because of the good road condition.

THE FÜHRER: Granted. But if we can't advance, the good road isn't much use. [—] But I'm still convinced that it will be easy and that we'll break out of this whole block.

ZEITZLER: Because of how it went yesterday and today, the army group is convinced that they will be able to come up here.

THE FÜHRER: The *Leibstandarte* has no attacking power here. That's almost 60 km.

ZEITZLER: The whole 1st Panzer, 7th Panzer and the *Leibstandarte* will go in there—so all three, not just the one. He wants to cover with the infantry and the 8th Panzer [Division], which is there. So he's creating a big focal point there, with the 19th Panzer [Division] from down here as well. The 25th [Panzer Division] has deteriorated greatly. Guderian has an officer down there, and I want to talk to him about the causes when he comes back. It has deteriorated drastically.

THE FÜHRER: And how long has it been in combat without a break now?!

ZEITZLER: The 1st Panzer [Division] has held itself together well—the best, actually.

THE FÜHRER: There are still 27 here, too.

ZEITZLER: Nearly 100 are out altogether.

BUHLE: Of these, 70 are out.

THE FÜHRER: I mean Panthers. That's an incredible loss.[795] Thirty of the others are out. So how did this happen? It's heavily armored and has double the losses of the Panzer IV.

ZEITZLER: And it even joined the battle later.

THE FÜHRER: So something must be wrong. It's impossible. This can't be. Both detachments were equally strong—they had about 90 [tanks]. There are 61 Panzer IVs, and only 27 of the others, which means that the one lost about 60 and the other 39. And its armor plating is better. He has 17 Tigers and 23 assault guns. It's like this: one-third of the tanks are gone, one-third of the assault guns are gone, one-third of the Panzer VIs—he had 17—are gone, and two-thirds of the Panzer Vs are gone. There must be some connection.

PFEIFFER: But they can all be repaired quickly.

THE FÜHRER: I don't care; at the moment they are all gone. I hear about quick repairs everywhere, but they never come back—they always stay away. I am curious as to when they will appear again. They always say: in a short time.

ZEITZLER: Short-term repairs do come back in and cover the losses a bit, of course. But with the Vs the number is too high.

THE FÜHRER: But the others have losses, too. There the losses reach 30%.

ZEITZLER: They were deployed a few days later.

HEUSINGER: The 25th [Panzer Division] came in on the 8th and the 1st Panzer Division on about the 12th [—]

ZEITZLER: They came in up there during the attack.

THE FÜHRER: But there must be some reason. This is ridiculous.

BUHLE: I was supposed to remind you again about the Panther detachment I/31 and the two Panzer Assault gun Detachments.

ZEITZLER: The Panther detachment of the 5th Panzer [Division] and the other detachment are coming. I haven't suggested anything yet because we still have 5 more days to decide. Then things might look different. The detachment that's departing first is the one for the 5th Panzer. It's leaving tomorrow. So initially I have them earmarked from us in the General Government [Poland], for the 5th [Panzer]. But if it becomes urgent—I will ask again in 5 days—we will put them in up there or down here. We'll do it that way with the others as well. At first they are assigned to an actual standing division. But when we have to decide in the General Government, I'll bring this up.

THE FÜHRER: Which standing divisions are here?

BUHLE: The 10th Panzer Grenadier [Division], and the other is in the 20th [Panzer Division].

ZEITZLER: So both of them would do well if they came down here. The only thing would be with the 5th Panzer. Then we would have to consider if we want to have a gigantic tank focal point here, and let them die out up there, or do we want to put something in there?

THE FÜHRER: With the 10th Panzer Grenadier, I still haven't made my mind up if it's right to put them in there. If they will somehow mature more quickly that way is a big question.

ZEITZLER: The critical point is up above. We can put them in there.

THE FÜHRER: I believe the critical point is more here instead.

ZEITZLER: But there are still 5 more days to go, my Führer. Down here he has pushed somewhat forward. Here [north of Kalinkovichi] the situation has grown increasingly tense. Here the 5th Panzer [Division] and 4th Panzer [Division] have lined up. But not much has come of it. Here there were very strong counterattacks. Everything is suffering from (the) weather as well. They can't get really close, so the whole thing has gotten stuck. Then here the enemy has advanced to the railroad, apparently with the 7th Guards Cavalry Corps, and has encircled this base of ours [Kalinkovichi]. As a result, Büsch[796] called half an hour ago and he's made up his mind to take out the 4th and 5th Panzer Divisions and to attack that man, because he is worried about the base. I believe, my Führer, that we have to do that. This base back here has the entire supply for the Second Army down there. It's a hard decision, but at the moment I can't see any other option. Later they will both be stuck, he won't be able to get them out, and everything will be cut off behind. Up here the thing is like this: some of the guards cavalry are advancing up to here, apparently with that as the target there. Parts of this tank corps here are crossing the Dnieper [River]. Now, Busch wanted to come over this afternoon, if the weather was favorable. But I don't believe it will be possible today. He won't be able to fly. He has great ideas about taking it back. In my opinion, we could at most come to the point where we say: forget about this attack at stage 1, and first push up with both divisions to cover the rear of Mogilev, then attack here with the 4th and 5th [Panzer Divisions] to cover this thing, and then we'll see what we can do after that.

THE FÜHRER: I also think that would be best.

ZEITZLER: It's the only thing to do, really. And the weather is horrible as well. Everything gets stuck in the mud. But we'll have to do it. So I may say that for the present?

THE FÜHRER: Yes.

ZEITZLER: And then we'll have to wait for today. He has gotten through with the cavalry. That's dumb. They'll come through the woods now.

THE FÜHRER: They don't have any assault guns for that.

ZEITZLER: Yesterday they had very heavy combat because they were continuously attacked from out of the woods and had to lead a very strong fight. Then a very fierce battle started here. That report arrived a quarter of an hour ago. He is also intensifying his attacks there a bit. [—] Then here, the battles are still going on. Some of them have been driven back. Very heavy aircraft deployment, while we can't fly.

THE FÜHRER: How can that be explained?

ZEITZLER: Because they can go out behind and we can't.

KORTEN: The weather is such that there is just a very narrow front. A high is coming in and we hope that by noon we will be able to get in and out. Tomorrow it will be better. It's because of this very narrow edge pushing in that he can fly and we can't.

ZEITZLER: In general, nothing unusual to report from the Ninth Army. [—] Those were the attacks against the border.

THE FÜHRER: This is a nasty thing.

ZEITZLER: Yes, it's very unpleasant. That happened just a quarter of an hour ago. It will be bad if that comes in still.

THE FÜHRER: Hopefully he has assault guns here.

ZEITZLER: He still has a few assault guns here.

THE FÜHRER: We don't know where they are positioned.

ZEITZLER: They're always marked with the combat group they belong to. [—] Nothing out of the ordinary with the Ninth Army on the northern wing. The Ninth Army believes that nothing will come here, and wants to loosen up somewhat here. I am a little bit concerned, because there is a great deal here.

THE FÜHRER: I am concerned, too.

ZEITZLER: Yes, this question mark has been around for quite some time now, so it will start soon. ... highway yesterday were driven back. Thirty-one tanks destroyed. The officers that were sent to the front say that the Russian losses were so incredible here—like we haven't seen for quite a while. They speak about large-scale slaughter. It could be.

THE FÜHRER: With the bad infantry, it had to come to that.

ZEITZLER: Here are some decent sectors. There are about 120 infantrymen for 1 km. We've hardly ever looked that good. The army group has done that very well.

THE FÜHRER: But it's just as good in the Army Group North area.

ZEITZLER: The North is good as well. [—] Here there is only a small concentration. Nothing has happened there yet. Today a strong attack started here and broke through here to some degree.

THE FÜHRER: We could have predicted that, after he pulled that away.

ZEITZLER: We will at least have to block off this narrow place here. There are fewer forces and lakes there. He won't be able to come through there so easily. Here a few tanks came over. These tanks have been destroyed. Here the action should start today.

THE FÜHRER: That won't get very far.

ZEITZLER: He'll have to do it. Otherwise he will be sitting on the road, and that would be terrible for him.

THE FÜHRER: I don't believe that will come too far.

ZEITZLER: If this pushes in here and destroys tanks?

THE FÜHRER: Would that have any effect, if this were pushed back here?

ZEITZLER: I believe so, yes. Because this up here will take another 10 or 12 days.

THE FÜHRER: Where is the assault gun detachment?

ZEITZLER: The assault gun detachment is in here. They arrived with 10. The others are on the train—the Tiger detachment, the one assault gun detachment and then the tank destroyer detachment.

THE FÜHRER: He must bring something more in here, so that nothing happens here. If he gets to Vitebsk, the whole affair will break down. Here there are two dangers: that he forces his way through, even if he doesn't come via the road to Vitebsk, but here.

ZEITZLER: Yes, Sir. That is a big danger, and there's a smaller one here.

THE FÜHRER: There they just have one road.

ZEITZLER: And here we will have to see, if nothing else can be done, how we can hold this narrow place at least. It's relatively short. If the attack comes in 10 days, we will have to do something up there, because it would be very hard for him to hold this here for 14 days. Here we heard some radio messages saying that he has very little ammunition, so we really can hope to get this thing in order. [—] My Führer, I wanted to hand this out in written form as well, to make it even clearer. (*Presentation.*) These are the things we had on the map yesterday. I wanted to give this out afterward for emphasis. [—] There's nothing much to report from up here in the Army Group North area. [—] There was a minor attack here, which was driven back. Then these radio messages that I mentioned before, stating that they had ammunition difficulties and that there were a few local shifts here. [—] Nothing in particular here, either, probably because of the bad weather.

THE FÜHRER: I must point out again that if we can fly here, that's the most important—these are the most important points—to destroy them as far away as possible. The further we go back, the better: Rzhev and so on. Every train that doesn't arrive here—every ammunition train that is destroyed—will be missed by those people at the front. Overland transport up here would be very difficult, considering the poor roads. Plus it always burns a lot of fuel.

KORTEN: Everything's ready. We can start right away, as soon as the weather permits.

ZEITZLER: On this front here, nothing unusual. Here a local shift was reported, here a few tanks and some artillery fire, and there one division has been brought to the front from the reserves.

THE FÜHRER: That doesn't mean anything.

ZEITZLER: No, these are insignificant things.

THE FÜHRER: I don't believe he'll do anything major.

ZEITZLER: He probably won't come until winter.

THE FÜHRER: And he doesn't have that many forces yet.

ZEITZLER: I can see no concerns, as Field Marshal Küchler said, up here. The worries are down here, for the Eighteenth Army as well. Stefflea[797] couldn't fly out today. He will come tomorrow.

THE FÜHRER: I won't be here tomorrow, unfortunately.

ZEITZLER: So he might have to wait another day. He's on the train; he wanted to ride to Lemberg [L'vov], then fly. But I don't believe he will be able to fly from there either, so it will be a day later anyway.

THE FÜHRER: I wouldn't let him fly anyway, if it's not very good. We can't afford a mishap there. Psychologically it's very bad if something happens.

We don't know—there are so many enemy swine down there who would say immediately that he has been killed.[798] We have to be unbelievably careful. Better by train.

ZEITZLER: Then, if possible, he could stay here until you arrive.

THE FÜHRER: With weather as bad as it is here, he shouldn't fly. I spoke with Giesler[799] yesterday evening. He told me how they circled around until they were able to come down. Then they were supposed to come back again, but on the way back there was nowhere to land, and then gradually they ran out of fuel. I've been on trips like that myself.

ZEITZLER: Also Busch, who wanted to come, has been warned against it. He wanted to try to come in the afternoon.

HEUSINGER: He called it off.

Panzer armaments

BUHLE: My Führer, I was supposed to speak to you about the Panther, concerning the turrets.

THE FÜHRER: Where are the Panzer experts?

ZEITZLER: I inquired about this myself, and they said the following: this can be operated by hand first, and then there is a small electrical thing that enables one to turn the tower. But the electricity has to be recharged by the engine again. The engine doesn't have to be running all the time, though; it only recharges this electrical thing from time to time. It's similar with the ventilation. It's supposed to be a hand-operated thing, which again is recharged by the engine.

THE FÜHRER: This is critical. But in the design that the gentlemen showed me—which they had discussed with the tank people—they just wanted to take the cupola off and put it on this concrete block, in the West. That was when General Jacob[800] was here. Weren't you there?

BUHLE: No.

THE FÜHRER: General Jacob was here and he brought this design, which had been discussed with the tank people. The idea was that initially we would only use a temporary foundation in the West—because I wanted to install 60 there, too ... but right next to it build concrete bunkers with revolving gun mounts ... Then I said, "You can't do that because you need the engine to turn the tower." Then he said, "No, the tower is turned by hand. It has a hand swivel. The only time it can't be turned by hand is if it's tilted."

BUHLE: It's a little slow, but it works.

THE FÜHRER: They say a thousand turns are necessary to turn the tower around. You can't destroy a tank like that.

BUHLE: A motor can be built into this little thing.

THE FÜHRER: I told those people, "A Volkswagen engine or something similar must be installed." Then they said, "No, it was only necessary for the ventilation." This has to be clarified. Get in contact right away. Otherwise none of these actions makes any sense.[801]

ZEITZLER: I told Guderian yesterday evening that he should speak with you about it.

BUHLE: Guderian brings out a weak personnel section for this, so that the driver and especially the gunner are there, so they can wait outside and be in heated boxes when danger is imminent

ZEITZLER: That's the danger of driving in.

THE FÜHRER: If they work, they can drive in. If they don't work, they can't go in. Usually they don't work.

ZEITZLER: And when they're out front, they have to run the engine from time to time, and that is unpleasant. Because the engine can't run on the front lines.

THE FÜHRER: Then they should be installed in such a way as to enable them to be heated at any time.

ZEITZLER: But the engine must run from time to time anyway.

THE FÜHRER: Why?

ZEITZLER: To recharge the batteries that runs the exhaust.

THE FÜHRER: Yes, when he's firing. But if he doesn't fire it doesn't need to run. But the engine must be heated, so that it will start immediately. Because the engine must always start. In the one situation he needs to drive in first, and in the other he is already inside. So we could build the roof over it in such a way that it can be completely heated. I have a feeling that these Panzer people are hanging around again, saying to themselves: it's a crime; look at this tank—they are going to dig it in, and it's running wonderfully. [—] It's ridiculous.

ZEITZLER: They are angry about it.

THE FÜHRER: But it doesn't run, so I can't use it.

ZEITZLER: One can tell that from the losses down there.

THE FÜHRER: If we had installed the Panthers—the more than 600 that we've lost in the East—solidly into the defensive front, we'd have had perfectly sound armor protection in the dangerous places. Then some things would never have happened. Like this we have nothing.

Situation in the air, the East

BÜCHS: In the East there was only limited action yesterday. Twenty-four of our nuisance raiders attacked troop targets north of Zaporozh'e. The enemy also made individual sorties in the area south of Gomel. Deployment won't be possible for us today until the improvement from the east reaches our units' quartering area. The ground condition in the areas of [Army Groups] North and Center is very muddy because of the continuing rainfall. The traffic in the South is not being held up too badly on the main roads; it is said to be worse on the smaller roads. In the Kiev–Zhitomir area there is a strip that is relatively good. There the smaller roads are also more or less passable. Because of the frost arriving from the south, an improvement in the road conditions is expected first in the area of Army Group South.

Italy

KEITEL: In general, no new incidents along this front. On the east wing, the only thing reported was that a few units have been observed in the Gulf of Gaëta. They are believed to be mine sweepers. Eight units there have moved further to the northwest. That obviously concludes the movement of the 50th British Division, which has been brought into this region. No other movements have been identified. The relief is finished in the 29th Panzer Grenadier Division sector. So they have taken over the sector completely. The 3rd Panzer Grenadier Division has come out. A few smaller operations after an artillery preparation—here in platoon strength, here in company strength—can only be regarded as reconnaissance measures. It's doubtful that a repetition of this attack in this strongly attacked sector of the front will take place in the next few days. For the present, there are no signs of it.

THE FÜHRER: The British put out reports that they have created the necessary conditions to push forward here. These are reports that have apparently been spread by journalists.

KEITEL: We can wait for that quite calmly. Then I already reported yesterday evening about the situation on the east wing with the 16th Panzer and the 65th [Infantry] Divisions. There were two attacks yesterday afternoon. A stronger one after an artillery preparation with smoke, past this town here against these crossings—this is the town of Arando—and the other attack against Archi. The occupying forces initially caused severe enemy losses and held the towns, but then after driving back the attacks they withdrew; now the battalion of the 1st Panzer Grenadier Division[802] has withdrawn back behind the Sangro sector. The enemy didn't manage to reach the Sangro anywhere or to cross it. Four tanks were reported destroyed yesterday. Altogether 6 tanks have been destroyed in the course of these attacks. Twenty tanks participated.

THE FÜHRER: But he is only advancing with a few things.

KEITEL: Obviously. But these are preparatory measures. It might be that they want to control the entrance to this valley. In any case, no other combat action has been reported today. On the other hand, all the coverage here has been taken back to the Sangro.

THE FÜHRER: A side note: to make sure that nothing happens here, we should take one of these heavy tank turrets—as soon as it's ready—down there and install it temporarily. We should temporarily install it on the firing range with the actual equipment that's inside now—with the engine they have now, with the pivot they have now—and cover it completely. I had another thought when I heard this. Hand me a sheet of paper. (*Sketch by the Führer follows.*)[803] There might still be some danger. Here's the turret with the gun. This is the upper level. Here is the way down to the lower level. If the gases aren't eliminated completely, there is danger of them sinking down where the people are.

KEITEL: The seats are on the sides.

THE FÜHRER: But there are two levels. If the gases come down here and get pulled through there, and they don't have ventilation from above down there, then I don't know if they can stand it. We need to find out now quickly. It's just a question of ventilation. Then we'll have to install a ventilation system.

BUHLE: One should be installed right away.

KEITEL: One has to say that if a real British offensive operation should develop out of these reconnaissance or advanced guard actions, it would be very unpleasant, of course. The 16th Panzer Division is being taken out right now—parts of it are already out—and the 65th [Infantry] Division's sector is becoming extraordinarily broad for only a six-battalion division. There is also this difficult obstacle at the front, and here as well there are some obstacles facing the front. But any major attack could become quite uncomfortable, of course. We'll have to wait.

THE FÜHRER: We can't wait. We have to tell Kesselring right away that the 16th [Panzer Division] is coming out.

KEITEL: The 16th is coming out.

THE FÜHRER: But in good time. Kesselring says to himself that for the moment, they still have the 16th here; if something happens I'll get it back immediately.

KEITEL: No, that's not possible.

THE FÜHRER: We absolutely must have them for the East.

KEITEL: This map only shows the movements in general—the departing movements. Now there are already 62 trains of the 2nd Panzer Division, which is quite a considerable addition of combat strength. From the 44th [Infantry] Division, 3 trains have left, and from the 16th Panzer Division the tracked vehicles have left.[804] Likewise the shifts here.

THE FÜHRER: I would like to know what that one has. But otherwise you'll never get it out of the Italian area. They should take whatever they can take along. At least that is out.

BUHLE: ... some vehicles out now—several thousand trucks.

THE FÜHRER: I'm a bit skeptical and would like to see the division that's getting weaker there.

ZEITZLER: There are also difficulties with winter clothing. Lots of winter clothes were lost at Zhitomir. I would to get some winter clothes out of the Italian supplies, but they're very difficult to get out of the Italian area.

KEITEL: And it's not much, anyway. It's just standard uniforms and underwear.

ZEITZLER: Underwear, primarily.

THE FÜHRER: It's very hard to get anything out of there. Back then, to keep individuals from stealing stuff for themselves, Rommel built up a barrier here and held everything back.

KEITEL: He can't do that very well. We sent off 36,000 railroad cars.

BUHLE: At the moment, the administrations are claiming that the first release took place because everything was blocked off where you yourself, my Führer, had decided this. The first troops were released for the East several days ago.

KEITEL: That happened four days ago.

THE FÜHRER: That's very good. I just don't want everything to be left in these rooms down below. There were 900,000 Italians ...

(... ?): ... already complaining that they don't have a jacket or a single boot anymore. How it can happen is a mystery to them.

THE FÜHRER: To me, too. But it's all the same whether their pants are taken off them by the British or by us.

KEITEL: We have ... moved 36,310 cars with evacuation goods and household goods across the border.

THE FÜHRER: They are not so much concerned about household goods; they are having the machines transported out.

KEITEL: The other things we had ready right from the start, military materiel. That's the essential part. There are 32 Armed Forces trains going over the border, 23 of them supply trains. They crossed the border yesterday.

The Balkans

Here, by withdrawing forces—there were still some parts of the 44th [Infantry Division] and the 14th Police Regiment, which have been pulled back now—the enemy has gradually started moving and is progressing toward this road again. Those are the forces that had been driven to the south before.

THE FÜHRER: If the British were to say that Germany has the assignment of putting the whole Balkan area back in order, we'd be busy for the next 30 years; march in, march out, turn around again, beat them up, and out again.

KEITEL: Here there was a mopping-up action in the area west and northwest of ... ; that is finished. But here parts of the 162nd Turkish Division, the Lefort group[805]—and also troops that were brought in from the north from the same combat group—have quite a hard battle against enemy forces on the heights between Tre ... and Stre ...[806]

THE FÜHRER: How many times has this area been cleared out by now?

KEITEL: In these areas there is always something coming together, to the east ... That's a very well-known point, where the enemy always ... [—] Here, the operation against the encirclement of these forces in the German area has been delayed and made more difficult by very heavy snowfall. The enemy has settled himself here on the Blegos[807] heights and is allowing himself to be attacked up there. The attack is underway by the Gevers group, which consists of a field replacement battalion of the 163rd [Infantry Division], two reserve mountain Jäger [light infantry] battalions, parts of the Italian militia battalion—which doesn't do anything—and the Karst Training Battalion of the Reichsführer.[808] They are attacking here. Here in the north, the 19th Police Regiment has been successfully blocked off, because at the moment no one can come into this mountain area without mountain equipment. This bridge is still blocked. It will be available again on December 31. It had been blown up. Departure of the 44th Division with 19 trains. The transportation movement of the 901st Regiment, to the main operation in the central Serbian area, and of the troops assigned to form the new Agram division, is in progress.[809]

THE FÜHRER: Are they running away down here?

KEITEL: The situation here looks like this. Here, from Rhodes, the commander of Rhodes explored this island, did some reconnaissance, and reported it to be clear of the enemy; then troops were sent over, and they also reported it clear of the enemy. However, it is reported—For ...[810] reported it this morning verbally—that an British Commando operation has obviously taken place in the area of Sidi. Sidi is manned by two officers and 50 Fascists, who had been, so to speak, dispatched there by us. We don't know yet what happened there. We haven't received a report yet. But it will be reported by the British as well. The islands are free now. They were all confirmed yesterday during the day. Also, on the island of Leros, 180 German prisoners were freed, while here 240 Italians in N ... For ... is clear of the enemy. Now the first observations have shown that the enemy is obviously fleeing to Turkey from Samos in small craft. It looks like they don't want to take up the fight on Samos anymore. And it hasn't been confirmed yet, of course. So, with the exception of some small islands that the Italians are still sitting on, the whole affair has been mopped up.[811]

THE FÜHRER: Those few will have to leave, as well.

KEITEL: We'll have to comb them out, of course, but that won't cause any difficulties. The main thing was this area, where naval forces kept intervening in the battles. [—] Again two heavy air attacks against the two airfields in Athens and in Larissa, which the Luftwaffe will report on. Departure of the 1st Mountain Division as before, to the operation that is being prepared up here in this area. Debar was taken yesterday and mopped up, and the forces that were deployed there will take on other mopping-up actions further north. And here is the town of Peschkopia. It was also occupied by hostile gangs, and has now been cleared out. An occupation force will stay there until the Bulgarian self-defense force arrives. Somewhat unexpectedly, a minor skirmish took place here in the assembly areas for the operation against Tito in this area. It was quite a successful skirmish, and was apparently initiated by the two *Brandenburg* regimental groups and Combat Group *Pfeiffer*,[812] with two battalions of the 197th [Infantry] Division and two *Brandenburg* battalions. Four battalions made surprise attacks in these two towns and cleared out Kachevo. This action resulted in 260 enemy dead, 150 captured ... reported, actually an operation to reach their assembly area later. Still weak enemy forces here; they tried to intervene in the fights yesterday, but will obviously come too late. Here a rather unpleasant situation. Bulgarians advanced against the town of Krem ..., and were driven back. The battalion can't be found at the moment; it seems not to have held out. Here the battle was fought through yesterday by both sides, Combat Group *Prinz Eugen* from the north, the other one penetrating into M ... There was an Ustasa [Ustaši] occupation force[813] that freed them. The enemy, unfortunately, could neither be caught nor destroyed, and some enemy troops escaped onto these two islands. There will probably be no other option but to clear these islands as well, after we've mopped these up. Yesterday movement was reported. We assumed that it might have been a retreat movement already, while no decision was reported up here. The enemy tried to relieve M ... An SS battalion was sent against it and was withdrawn from the attack against M ..., which is in our hands. The Ustasa [Ustaši] have been freed. Up here the usual local disturbances by [partisan] bands. Here the SS Battalion *Niederlande* ["Netherlands"][814] undertook a perhaps somewhat rash push against Krotovica, and didn't get through. The operation will be prepared again a little more thoroughly. It obviously started a little carelessly and thus wasn't successful. [—] Yesterday there was already a report saying that the battle on Leros had changed rapidly because of this—a report from the *Brandenburger*— ... that a first lieutenant stormed the bunkers with his platoon, captured the general, and demanded of him: either I will shoot you or you will capitulate immediately.

THE FÜHRER: Bravo!

KEITEL: Obviously he handled things well. That broke the resistance down completely. I wanted to suggest him for the Knight's Cross.

THE FÜHRER: He will get the Knight's Cross, especially because he declared right away: if you don't capitulate, I will shoot you. That's the right way to deal with these people.

KEITEL: Then there's another report, which sounds plausible. According to reliable sources, the Allies are supposed to be drawing up a unit of Yugoslav prisoners of war in Italy, consisting of about 18,000 men, who, according to Tito's order, will be brought to the country's Adriatic coast in about two weeks.

THE FÜHRER: It's not impossible.

KEITEL: No, it's not impossible, because they still have prisoners of war, though in limited numbers. It could be possible.[815]

THE FÜHRER: It's just that the prisoners of war don't want to fight anymore. That's a very old experience. Neither side will succeed. And that's why it's nonsense to believe that the Italians will fight. They won't fight on the other side either; they are of no value anymore.

KEITEL: A report from the Intelligence office [Abwehrstelle] in Hamburg— I can't judge if it is of any importance—says that according to sources in Portugal, Romanian and Hungarian consultations with the Allies are supposed to have ended in Lisbon on the afternoon of November 15.[816] Both countries are to request an armistice in the next few days on the basis of provoked unrest. I don't know if that's significant. It is definitely true that discussions like this have taken place in Lisbon again.

THE FÜHRER: Both of them certainly won't do it. One will do it, and the other will immediately march in because of the unrest. If unrest develops in Hungary and the Romanians tell us about it, then they would ask us to help them restore order in Hungary.

The North

KEITEL: From Finland, lively enemy reconnaissance patrols are reported on the southeastern front. That's coming from the Finns. On the northeastern front nothing unusual. Temperatures from plus 2 to minus 12. In Denmark a number of cases of sabotage have occurred, especially on one night— the night of the 17th. A signal box and transformer building at the Aarhus railway station and a railroad bridge near Langern were destroyed. Three km west of the Aarhus railway … damaged in several places by explosions. At the railway station … a railroad car filled with straw was set on fire. In the center of Copenhagen an Armed Forces staff official was shot on November 18. The upcoming sentencing of 15 saboteurs by the authorized authority is expected to be a deterrent; I don't know if it will be enough.

THE FÜHRER: I think the other procedure is better.[817]

KEITEL: The Reichsführer wanted to recommend this procedure to the commander and especially to the authorized agent of the Reich. It's probably the only thing that's effective against these acts of sabotage.

THE FÜHRER: We just can't wait until it's too late.

KEITEL: We have to do it as a precaution, before it happens.

THE FÜHRER: Best[818] will refuse it, I'm sure. I don't know about Hanneken.[819] Best will refuse because he is undiplomatic.

KEITEL: Hanneken is quite willing, if we tell him something.

THE FÜHRER: It's the only procedure.

Situation at sea

ASSMANN: A large convoy of 74 merchant ships was observed by air reconnaissance yesterday about 450 km west of Lisbon.[820] The submarines that were stationed a bit too far west in the reconnaissance patrol were then directed a little to the northeast. The convoy was then observed again several times in the afternoon and evening by the Luftwaffe. Yesterday afternoon one submarine approached the convoy, but was immediately subjected to heavy depth-charge pursuit from a group of submarine chasers, and reported strong air cover. Unfortunately, the boat wasn't able to report contact with the convoy until last night because of underwater pressure. Then another boat made contact with the convoy this morning. That boat will probably be able to stay with them, and the Luftwaffe will probably report again today as well. It reported the convoy again this morning, so the second reconnaissance patrol, lying further to the south, will hopefully make contact with the convoy tonight. The new 290th Reconnaissance Group—they didn't expect German aircraft to appear—managed to get as close as 300 meters to the convoy. They exchanged signals and then the planes flew on. In the Atlantic one wide shot was fired against an unaccompanied ship, probably missing because of the great distance.[821] Here an aircraft provided direction-finding signals for the convoy yesterday. Unfortunately the signals were heard by only one submarine. It is not yet clear if the distance was too great or if the boats didn't hear them for other reasons. [—] In the Finnish Bay, another Russian sweeper unit is clearing the area around Saiskaari.[822] It was fired on by land batteries—by the

"Bismarck" land battery. It has three 15-cm guns. One Russian vessel was sunk and another was damaged. There were Russian torpedo-bomber attacks against our steamer traffic at Baltischport [Baltic port] and west of Pernau, without success. [—] During sabotage actions in Denmark, a radio direction finding station at the entrance to the Aarhus harbor was also destroyed. During yesterday's flights into the Oslo Fjord, one aircraft was shot down in the Skagerrak by outpost forces, which were bombed as well. Very strong convoy activity along the Norwegian coast—84 ships in total. One of our troopships ran aground southwest of Tromsö. The salvage operation is underway.

THE FÜHRER: If we try to imagine it, we can only say that it's not that big in the Mediterranean with those forces either.

VOSS: One and a half million a month.

THE FÜHRER: Couldn't we get a list for some specific date, showing how much tonnage is located in the harbors of Oslo, Bergen, Trondheim, and Narvik, so we can get a picture?

ASSMANN: Yes, Sir. [—] In the North Sea no unusual events. Our own convoy activity, with strong cover, is going according to schedule. The very large convoys underway right now are quite gratifying; they are being led through the Ijssel-Meer and the Zeeland waters. Yesterday 5 convoys with 37,000 GRT were reported again. In the Channel, activity by the outposts and escorts is impaired by the continuing very strong swell. The weather situation in the Channel has now somewhat improved.

THE FÜHRER: Let's have some English voices now. One should not always criticize. ... (*Reading aloud.*)

ASSMANN: More enemy air reconnaissance in the [Bay of] Biscay, with 41 aircraft.

THE FÜHRER: It's too bad we can't get really clear pictures from East Asia.

ASSMANN: Yesterday in Gibraltar there was a convoy of about 53 freighters and 8 tankers. A convoy of 8 freighters sailed out of the Mediterranean. The only traffic at all in the Mediterranean yesterday was departing. Numerous cruisers, two submarines and destroyers arrived in Gibraltar, also coming from the Mediterranean. The weather conditions were so bad in the Tyrrhenean Sea and the Adriatic yesterday that reconnaissance was severely limited. Our mine operation in the Ligurian Sea went according to plan. In the Bay of Gaëta, as already reported, there were enemy mine sweepers. Supply traffic to Salerno. In the Aegean, our torpedo boats and submarine chasers set out with 240 prisoners and captured weapons to Syra, and from there to Piräus.[823] The clearing of the islands was carried out yesterday by three submarine chasers and three mine sweepers under the command of the Chief of the 21st Submarine-Chaser Flotilla. On Leros a naval battery has now been manned—I don't have the caliber yet—and the Leros radio station is ready for deployment. In the Turkish waters, no substantial enemy units were reported yesterday—only some small vessels sailing toward Samos, which might possibly be connected to an evacuation of Samos. [—] In the Black Sea, continuing enemy submarine activity by 5 submarines in the northwestern Black Sea and south of the Crimea. Our convoy of 10 Navy ferries left Odessa yesterday with 16 assault guns, 17 trucks and 80 tons of ammunition. That's 10 Navy ferries. The convoy was attacked from the air, but unsuccessfully. In the Kerch Straits, Navy ferries made contact with the enemy last night. One landing craft was sunk, and another with about 15 men—Russians—was destroyed by coastal batteries. Because of the very bad weather there were only 5 Navy ferries in the southern part of the Kerch Strait last night. One submarine—U 18—sank a freighter of 1,500 GRT off the Caucasus. [—] That is all, my Führer.

Situation in the air

BÜCHS: During the day yesterday, 100 aircraft flew into the Norwegian area, near Oslo, and attacked Kelle, the local front repair workshop ... and Daimler-Benz. Two hundred high-explosive bombs were dropped, resulting in severe damage—70 to 80% temporarily destroyed. The partial resumption of work is expected in about a week. Stocks of spare parts suffered few hits.

THE FÜHRER: I'll say something about that in a minute. I received another report. What's-his-name told me that he was ... in Schweinfurth ... 60,000 completed ball bearings ... I don't know if they were destroyed or not—because they were still in there.[824] It's left in the factory for a week or a month and is collected on such and such a date. He says we can't do this with such valuable things. He was, I believe, in Suhl and Zella-Mehlis, where there are at least 200 heavy anti-aircraft guns alone. They are standing there completely ready; they will be delivered later. We have to intervene. Buhle, the things that are completed must leave the factories immediately. We can store them anywhere away from there, wherever they are supposed to go to. We can't be responsible for these things being destroyed. And do the same with the Luftwaffe.

KORTEN: Yes, Sir. Immediately.

BÜCHS: Twenty bombs on the airfield ...; no damage. The ... jettisoned bombs ... and one freighter was attacked, without causing any damage. Nine aircraft were shot down by fighters. One of our own aircraft was destroyed, and two are missing. The only other incidents in the Norwegian area were coastal approaches by individual aircraft. One of them, a Mosquito, was shot by a Ju 88 at a height of 80 m. In this area during the night there were only nuisance raids.

THE FÜHRER: We can't not let those people fly here anymore. With that kind of flying they'll never get anywhere. I'll see that with the Reich Commissioner.[825]

BÜCHS: In the West ... mouth of the Seine ... before this fighter attack ... also railway stations. Two engines damaged. ... by 3 Liberators. One Liberator shot down. Also only a few approaches during the night in the French area. Bombs were dropped onto the airfield ..., no damages reported. No attacks in this area. [—] Regarding the intrusions into Reich territory,[826] it is reported that a total of 400 to 450 aircraft approached, in two large groups. One northern main group with about 200 aircraft came into the area around Berlin. Only 70 to 80 of the airplanes in this group flew against Berlin itself. Part of the group flew further to the north. Individual attacks were reported near Kremmen ... Greifenberg, about 30 aircraft in the Stettin area. Bombs were dropped on Pölitz, but nothing was damaged. From Berlin itself is reported that numerous high-explosive bombs and several thousand firebombs were dropped ... (*Reading aloud.*) I reported the individual districts yesterday evening already. About 20 houses destroyed. Then industrial damages—mostly fire damage to individual factories ... Public buildings were also hit. Personal losses so far are about 30 dead, the same number of slightly injured, about 900 homeless. [—] The second wave of attacks, with 200 aircraft, flew into the Frankfurt–Mannheim area, and individual aircraft continued on to the Stuttgart–Nuremberg area. This attack, with Mannheim as the main target, was a little stronger than the attack against Berlin; there were about 150 aircraft over the urban area.

KORTEN: Turning in like this, approaching from the south, while the other came like this. This here is wrong.

BÜCHS: It was reported that about 500 to 600 high-explosive bombs were dropped, primarily on the northern part of town, and fairly serious fires were caused in industrial plants. Isolated fire damage ... at Daimler-Benz, as well as the ... stock was hit. Some damage to public buildings. Personal losses were very limited. Reported thus far are one dead, six injured. In Ludwigshafen itself only very limited damage to houses, and no casualties. [—] There were attacks on the Rhineland-Westphalia industrial area in three waves—nuisance raids of about 20 Mosquitoes. Bombs were dropped on Essen, Aachen and Dusseldorf. There were no damages except from some minor damage to houses. Our defense was impaired to some degree by the weather. In total, 111 aircraft were deployed, and according to the latest reports 17 confirmed ... 18 confirmed and 10 probable are claimed altogether. This morning the British admitted to 32 losses. In addition, there were three emergency landings on Swedish sovereign territory. A few bombs were supposedly dropped on Swedish territory.

KORTEN: Here's what happened here. The weather was so bad that fighter deployment wasn't worth it. Because of this, those using the "Zahme Sau" ["Tame Sow"][827] snuck in and flew along as far as Greater Berlin, then veered off. Here the anti-aircraft fire was very effective. One hundred fighters had been assembled for the attack, but because of the bad weather, unfortunately, only a few of them came out.

BÜCHS: No activity on our part in the western Mediterranean or in Italy because of the bad weather. Limited enemy reconnaissance activity in the area around the front. [—] In the Balkans, two Spitfires attacked the Knin railroad station during the day; one locomotive was damaged. In the Greek area yesterday, there were renewed attacks against our ground organization; over Eleusis there were about 50 four-engines escorted by 15 fighters, and over Larissa 40 twin-engines with fighter protection. In contrast to the previous attacks, these attacks caused only minor damage. In Larissa two aircraft were damaged and in Eleusis one aircraft. That is partly because the fighter defense here apparently prevented the approaching units from dropping their bombs very precisely. Because the bombs were placed very badly—outside the field. Other than that, there were only a few other flights against the islands in the western Greek area. Nineteen reconnaissance aircraft in the area north of Crete. During the night some gang supply. Four aircraft attacked K ...; damages have not been reported yet. Six reconnaissance aircraft north of Crete. Ten aircraft attacked Iraklion; one was shot down by anti-aircraft artillery. [—] The overall weather situation in the East has been reported already: this increasing ... current, which is moving along the front here from the south ... will bring a gradual dispersal and ... from the east, and then the frost will arrive ... In the Mediterranean ... bad weather... also in the Po plain ... in the Reich territory and also in England considerable clearing. Before this layer of fog ... dispersing, moving in again during the night, so that gradually on both sides ... activity in the air ... will be made difficult. [—] There are intrusions over the Reich territory now; about 140 aircraft with strong fighter cover have been reported, approaching there from the south into the Rhineland-Westphalia industrial area. So far, reports have only been received regarding bombs dropped on Bocholt. All aircraft on opposite course again. According to an intercepted English radio message, all bombs are supposed to be jettisoned and the return flight should begin.

THE FÜHRER: It's the fog.

BÜCHS: Either on their side or ours.

THE FÜHRER: They're supposed to return home?

KORTEN: They're to return as quickly as possible. They probably do have great difficulty landing, if they land with bombs on board, my Führer. [—] The reinforcement of the fighter cover in the southern area has been carried out by the Reichsmarshal. One of the heavy fighter groups should come up here.[828] I don't yet have an answer …, if this thing is being prepared. These blue squiggles are the so-called tester beds, in which the night interceptors are guided. This blue has been developed, and the lightly marked part is the area that is being developed at the moment[829]—also this connection.

THE FÜHRER: What is this here?

KORTEN: That is the East Prussia connection, which is gradually progressing.

THE FÜHRER: So this is the night interception?

KORTEN: The night interception area—the Insterburg night interception area. It is supposed to be a demonstration for you, my Führer. The night interception area could be viewed quickly. [—] Then Romania is developed. That's not on here. All these are being developed.

THE FÜHRER: That will be good when all this is developed.

Miscellaneous

(VOSS?): We have received a report concerning the Allied merchant ship building program—new construction—saying that the British … converting this new construction program to fast ships—ships of up to 14 knots. A fast freighter is mentioned there, with a speed of 15 knots … (*Presentation.*) What is particularly remarkable about this ship is that it fortuitously combines the requirements of the shipping companies for a … especially for the East Asian freighter traffic, more or less with the requirements for fast troopships … It has especially heavy loading gear, and that … and is very spacious—especially suitable for tanks and trucks.

THE FÜHRER: It's 9,900 tons.

VOSS: Nine thousand nine hundred GRT and 12,000 tons loaded weight.

THE FÜHRER: So 10,000 tons the way we calculate it?

VOSS: Yes, Sir. Ten thousand tons.

THE FÜHRER: And the electric submarines go as fast as 18 knots?[830]

VOSS: Eighteen knots.

THE FÜHRER: So they're able to keep up?

VOSS: They can keep up and can also go ahead.

THE FÜHRER: But at 18 knots they can't go too long—only a few hours?

VOSS: Yes, that's true as well. But the great majority of convoys don't go at 14 knots either. We still count on 9 or 10 at the fastest.

KORTEN: This anti-aircraft thing in Bolzano will be all right, my Führer.
THE FÜHRER: Hofer[831] has asked that this be manned with 7.5s and
with some kind of 12.8 battery that can reach higher, in order to defend
this important place there. He says they can't reach up that far—they are
flying at an altitude of 8,000 or 9,000 m. Normal anti-aircraft artillery
doesn't reach that high ...
End: 1:35 p.m.

* * * * *

December 20-22, 1943

The winter battle in the East, with the main focal points of Gomel',
Zhitomir–Korosten, Krivoi Rog and Zaporozh'e–Nikopol', has continued
with unbroken intensity. In the south, near the mouth of the Dnieper [River],
the Russians have shattered the German bridgehead near Kherson; they
have also succeeded in expanding their own Dnieper bridgeheads at Cherkassy
and south of Iagotin. Between Army Groups South and Center, there is a
gap of 100 km that can't be closed—and the Pripiat' Marshes lying behind
are now completely frozen. Meanwhile, to the north, the evacuation of
Gomel' was approved, and completed on November 26; from the Sozh
[River] the Second Army has retreated behind the Dnieper [River]. On
December 13, in the penetration area around Nevel', the Russians lined up
for an attack toward the south and are now threatening Vitebsk. In the
area of Army Group North they are still quiet.

On the Adriatic coast, the British had forced German troops back across
the lower Sangro [River] at the end of November, but since December 8
they have been unable to progress beyond the next river, the Muro. In the
meantime, the Americans succeeded in breaking open the Mignano Gap on
the Tyrrhenian flank, but were only ably to push the defenders back to an
intermediate position before the Rapido–Cassino position.

All military arrangements at German headquarters are now carrying the
stamp of the "invasion." Hitler knows that it will certainly come in 1944 and
that he must defeat it. The former worries concerning a major operation in
the Mediterranean have evaporated in the meantime. Italy is now clearly to
be regarded as a secondary theater of war. The "invasion" will start from
England. Its target will be northern France or—as Hitler still believes—
Norway. The general guidelines Hitler issued on November 3, contained the
following:

The difficult and costly battle against Bolshevism has strained our military
resources to the limit during the last two and a half years. This was in accor-

dance with the size of the danger and the overall German situation. In the meantime, however, the situation has changed. The danger in the East remains, but an even greater danger is arising in the West: an Anglo-American landing. In the East the space for operations is still large enough that—if worse comes to worse—some ground could be given up without really endangering German territory. In the West, however, things are different. If the enemy breaks through our defenses on a broad front, the consequences can hardly be imagined. That is why I can't tolerate any further weakening of the West for the benefit of other theaters of war; indeed, I have decided to bring in new defensive forces in the West.

In spite of all planning, though, the suction of the bleeding Eastern front continues, and the Italian theater also feeds on the reserves of the West.
(*Maps 5, 7, 10, and 11*)

* * * * *

EVENING SITUATION REPORT, PROBABLY DECEMBER 20, 1943[832]

The East

(ZEITZLER): It was quiet during the day in the area of Army Group A. Something is coming together here. This corps seems to be going into this area, too, so there are pressure points here; Hube[833] is coming under pressure and therefore requests permission today to take this line in order to pull out one division.
THE FÜHRER: Where does he want to take it?
ZEITZLER: He wants to have them available in case he needs them in here.
THE FÜHRER: If only that position were a little better! (But if he goes out here) he will slip (a long way back, not just a) little bit. (That is the) concern I have. (Here he still has some sort of a) front. But if he takes forces out here during the (retreat movement), the other will pull ... that he ... in the bad position ... then there is nothing left to lose.
ZEITZLER: On this front (in general, nothing) out of the ordinary. The movements up there have gone (according to plan). The 11th Panzer Division has reached this point. (Starting from here) it will continue by rail. The ... is coming down from up above. [—] (No stronger enemy) cover identified ... (The) 5th Guards Mechanized Corps has been there the whole time.
THE FÜHRER: Where does he want to have them?
ZEITZLER: He wants to intervene up here [near Korosten'] with those three divisions, probably on the 20th, (when the) marching movements are

underway. Up here on the front it is generally the same as it was at midday. Only the middle corner pillar has broken away; he has taken it out from the side. That's why the 19th Panzer Division has been taken back to this line as well, so that there's a reserve behind. Right now there is still a hole here. Then he will go in here. [—] The 1st Panzer Division is … (on its) way as of today and will come into the area of …, following in the night and tomorrow … *Leibstandarte* is out. The 16th Panzer Division (is on) the march and will be (led) behind the 1st Panzer Division, (so it) won't get into the enemy area. The (regiment) that has been released is already marching in express transport to … (He wants) to pull (them) in even closer. I think he wants to (pull them in here); we can (let them go) up to here without worry.

THE FÜHRER: But I do have (the concern, and) and I can't get rid of it, that he might push into our lines here and (perhaps) here.

ZEITZLER: But on the other hand it is very difficult here [west of Kiev]. If we can do something with all the forces there, we'll probably be able to put it in order.

THE FÜHRER: Yes, when the two panzer divisions arrive.

ZEITZLER: But it might take a while before it gets up there. He primarily wants to have it in order to release the 25th Panzer [Division]. So then he might just let them go. Up there [—] and if we have this here and … get … we will (get) it under control. [—] … rifle divisions have been identified, (but only three tank corps) for the moment—one tank corps down here and two (up here). But the 1st Panzer Division has the command, probably with all its panzer corps. We have established by radio that it is commanding. … waited four weeks. But still (nothing) speaks positively (for it); there are no signs at the moment but (it is possible). Everything is all right with the Second Army. (This thing) went relatively well. I immediately ordered the army to withdraw the 18th Panzer Division as (reserves). We will need them (sometime). If they get this thing put right to some degree, (they can go off with the 16th Panzer Division.) The Panther (detachment is) ready now as well, so they can probably be taken toward Orsha (shortly). Then the (whole) Panther division will come together. If it has lost tanks, then the complete Panther detachment will be there right away. Then we will have very good combat forces in there. [—] On this front isolated attacks. Here [near Vitebsk] only one attack occurred. They still want to pull out the 131st [Infantry] Division. In principle, I think it's possible. It has a very small sector. … (They) want to have it available (as) a reserve. [—] (Here in the) afternoon the situation developed like this: … being shot, and it is … by evening, Reinhardt[834] said, he had no (reserves). So they pulled (in) the *Feldherrenhalle* [Panzer Grenadier Division][835] You had (already) given your basic agreement (to that), my Führer. It has been (pulled in) to here (already), but hasn't been released yet. But (we will) probably (have to) deploy it tomorrow for the counter-push (if) the thing here becomes precarious. I think (it's right) to do it up here, otherwise ... will come ...

THE FÜHRER: That's very clear.

ZEITZLER: That is (good) in any case. [—] Here on this front another penetration ... But that doesn't matter, because we are now taking it back. Here it's still relatively hard. This (position) was held all through the day today, while (here) [near Gorodok] the situation is somewhat unclear. But the 20th Panzer Division will come in here today and the combat groups of the 87th [Infantry Division] are attached as well and will join in, in order to take advantage of the artillery of the 20th Panzer Division. The 5th Jäger [Light Infantry] Division is already on the train with its first platoons and will be brought in here. Part of the 12th [Infantry] Division is on the train and part tomorrow at noon .... is. So we will have (a small assault group together here) by tomorrow. The 20th Panzer Division and parts of the (87th [Infantry] Division) will come in here, and here the *Feldherrenhalle*, (which we can) possibly use to attack.[836] So they are standing, ... will, available here.

THE FÜHRER: I believe ... winter battle. It began with that.

FEGELEIN: This highway ... From Vitebsk to Orsha is about ... It has been improved.

THE FÜHRER: Here we do have enough; I am absolutely convinced of it.

ZEITZLER: At ... we are stronger than ever before for such an action. (The important) thing (would be) to get the 16th Panzer Division in there as well, if (the thing) gets tougher. This detachment is (on its way) to Orsha. (Then) tomorrow with the 20th Panzer Division, the 87th Division, and parts of the 5th Jäger Division, they can put this in order, and with the *Feldherrenhalle* they can take care of this. There was only a minor local advance up there.

THE FÜHRER: Do you have anything showing how it looks up there now?

ZEITZLER: Yes, Sir. I have sent an officer over. That means he will depart tomorrow morning, and will then report ... what they have planned for (construction) rates. (For the next few weeks) there are 25 bunkers, 50 bunkers, and 100 bunkers scheduled. (*Presentation.*)

THE FÜHRER: So this is (in the first week from the) 18th to the 24th.

ZEITZLER: It's not much.

THE FÜHRER: In the second week (50 bunkers and) 5 km wire entanglement. The prerequisite (is) that it is (done) in time.

ZEITZLER: The materiel convoys have already (assembled) for it. For [Army Groups] Center and South I have two materiel convoys; they are (underway) at the moment.

THE FÜHRER: It is (urgent) that the bunkers be (built).

ZEITZLER: Yes, indeed. Whatever they can get (there).

THE FÜHRER: So this is what they have in the way of (manpower): 3,400 men for construction. That's not much.

ZEITZLER: That's why I sent some there. They don't have very many civilians down here either. Now they claim that most of the civilians had gone already, but it's not enough. We can't do this with 3,000 men. We need to get more civilians. That's why I called there earlier today. These numbers are nothing. The majority are soldiers. There has to be the principle: (the soldiers must) provide guidance. [—] Then Stefflea down here (had the idea) to stay in the Crimea for Christmas, (while) Antonescu (wants to be) in the Crimea for New Year's. Jaenecke[837] personally sent me a telegram (concerning the questions) Stefflea has raised. (It is quite) interesting, so we might possibly give him an answer to this. (*Presentation.*) I couldn't clarify this matter yet. … coming from the weapons office, he will go (down there) on the 26th, (because) officially no commission of ours has been down there yet. I can find out about that, so that Jaenecke can tell (him) something.

THE FÜHRER: He should tell us immediately who (is saying) this.

(ZEITZLER: Yes, Sir.)

So this one thing is unfamiliar to me. This second thing I have written anyway. This must be a misunderstanding. On the contrary, we were very relieved. I've even declared over and over that maybe this tank is of some value.[838]

BUHLE: I (spoke) to the infantryman yesterday, whom you sent to this tank course, (and) briefed (him). Tonight (they) will drive (down).

THE FÜHRER: I (told) them yesterday: (If I) suddenly (had) a 13-tonner for assault guns,[839] … could make … qualities.

BUHLE: I instructed the infantryman to (check this thing) from his point of view.

THE FÜHRER: Maybe you should take (the) Glump[840] along, because in principle we (won't) get an assault gun into a (normal) Panzer III. If we had designed it for an assault gun from the beginning, we might have come out differently.

KEITEL: We've initiated the matter with full …

THE FÜHRER: We have to make that known.

ZEITZLER: Then I had the commander of the Third Panzer Army give me a report concerning the 87th [Infantry] Division—how they did it and what happened.[841] These are the things: (*Presentation.*)

THE FÜHRER: Is this Strachwitz?

ZEITZLER: No, it's another man; this one was a tank man.[842]

THE FÜHRER: This can … concern …, only identification. … been.

ZEITZLER: No, I wanted to (know what) is (actually) going on (there), so we (asked) for details. (They had) given only general information. These are the numbers (that were in first), and the numbers that came out; (this is) the final figure.

THE FÜHRER: That's 4,500 men.

ZEITZLER: Out of 7,200.

THE FÜHRER: That's a loss of?

ZEITZLER: About 2,600 men. At that time (it was) reported that they had (lost) several batteries. That came as a radio report at the time.

THE FÜHRER: So how strong is it then? Because these were only the parts out front.

ZEITZLER: Actually, the whole (division) was in there, because the number was quite high—7,200 men.

THE FÜHRER: It says: 7,000 of them were encircled. Maybe you can find out how strong it is altogether, so we can get a picture.

(ZEITZLER: Yes, Sir.)

Nothing to report from the North?

ZEITZLER: ...

THE FÜHRER: It would be (bad if he) were to attack from the Oranienbaum pocket (and come out).[843] I have given an order of the day (to) the three Waffen SS divisions that are fighting there. (In addition), we absolutely have to pull (in) the Police Division from there and ... pull out ... one of the two other units ... again. We could send the *Niederlande* ["Netherlands" Division] ... to some other place.

Italy

JODL: It was (quiet) all along the right wing. Some livelier vehicle movements were observed in the Castel del Sangro (area). Up until noon there was only one attack against Orsogna, where the enemy broke through but was immediately pushed back by counterattack. Then there were two stronger attacks (in the afternoon), which hadn't yet finished by 7 p.m. this evening—one near Villa Grande and the other west of Ortona. The reserves there have been running counterattacks against both of them this afternoon. Other than that, nothing else happened there or in the other theaters.

The West, danger of invasion

THE FÜHRER: I have studied most of these files[844] now. There's no doubt that the attack in the West will come in the spring; it is beyond all doubt. I consider now once more that they want to do this along very broad fronts. But something even more interesting (follows from this:) ... certain moment not even ... that is to say, now they don't even have (forces) available (to) send off to the Mediterranean. They would have needed (five divisions), and there Churchill says: ... unfortunately we don't have 5 divisions available in the (Mediterranean). We don't have them there; (we are) strained (to the) limit there. But nevertheless, from this (agreement being suggested) to the Turks, one might assume that they will do it (with a second) front. We also have to expect (a landing in) Norway,[845] as well as probably a (diversionary) attack in the [Bay of] Biscay and maybe in the (Balkans), too. Then (we'd) have to (go over quickly—especially since our) submarines force can't ... fight with complete (confidence) anyway—in order to pull (our submarine) force together toward the north by early or mid-February. (Because) danger is imminent up there. It is entirely possible (that) they will make a landing there. (We can)not rely too much on being able to come up later, because we don't know what the ice conditions will be in the Baltic Sea. We have to operate with a mass of submarines up there. It would be a diversionary attack that they would make up there, but it would still be unpleasant enough for us if the swine were able to establish themselves up there and lure our Luftwaffe out. I don't believe he will make this trip with the ships now in order to lure our heavy (forces) out; instead, he will do it to check out our (force situation in the air). If he (isn't attacked) now ... he will know perfectly well that we don't have modern (aircraft) in Norway anymore. They have (airplanes up there but they can't) attack.

JODL: But he could be (wrong, because the weather) is bad up there most of the time.

VOSS: We have 4½ hours of twilight.

THE FÜHRER: (One) can attack (with no problem) in 4½ hours. That's the twilight. They attack ... during twilight. If they (attack in the Mediterranean), they always come at night. They can (always) fly. In any case, we have to expect (that he) will do something if this ... from mid-February, beginning of March ... Back then he landed in April, too. (He can) move it forward, too. It happens quickly there—(the) getting (lighter). Then it stays light for a very long time. He can (certainly) do this. We have to operate with a whole mass of submarines there, because we can't allow him to establish himself there either. If he establishes himself there it will be devastating for our entire northern army. Then we couldn't carry out any more transports. We know what it means in the south, when the pig sits on an island. That's one thing. [—] The second is the Biscay. We have to assign most of the submarines to the Biscay (and bring them in there. There we have to) operate (with) the majority of submarines and (with all those things) that are planned anyway ...

VOSS: That is (planned) very explicitly (and will) be done. If something happens in the West, (everything) there in the way of vessels will be (assigned) to this thing immediately; that has been prepared.

THE FÜHRER: We have to start that up above right away—(otherwise) it will be too late.

VOSS: There is a lot in Brest, (Lorient and St.) Nazaire.

THE FÜHRER: But they won't arrive (up there in time).

VOSS: Norway is a bit different.

KEITEL: Bergen, Trondheim.

THE FÜHRER: We have to go up there because we can't send any units up. It doesn't look too good with the Luftwaffe, either.

VOSS: This is only what we have marching through.

THE FÜHRER: Maybe he can consider this right away. From a certain point on, there has to be some sort of concentration there. The waters must teem with submarines up there. And we have to consider it in the West, too. I keep thinking about things that would (improve the defense—for example,) flame-throwers that start automatically, ... then tons of oil that can be thrown (into the sea and that will start burning there).[846]

ZEITZLER: Also the (new mines that) blow up mine detectors.[847] I thought of not deploying (them in) the East, but in the West. The (first) ones will probably be ready in January. If we deploy them (in the East first), only the Russians will get to know them. (They'd figure it out soon). Then we could give everything to the West. (If) the landings come and they (use) the mine detectors, they won't be prepared for the mines to (blow up).

THE FÜHRER: That will destroy (all) his confidence right away.

VOSS: The Commander-in-Chief[848] (already) gathered the commanders together recently and (made them) aware of this danger in the West, in particular.

THE FÜHRER: There is no doubt; they have committed themselves. After mid-February or the beginning of March there will be an attack in the West. I don't have the feeling that the British have their—shall we say—whole heart in this attack. There are too many naysayers who are already writing: if this is the case, we shouldn't do it; if that is the case, we shouldn't do it either. In England there is now a second current, which, (considering the) limited number of their divisions, wants to keep the divisions intact—just like we once (wanted) to keep our (limited number) of naval forces intact until the end of the war. That's obvious. Because (the armament) production capacity in England is decreasing rapidly. (We see it every) day. They blame the attitude (that the public) doesn't believe in the danger anymore. (Actually,) it is not (connected) with that, but with the (decrease) in steel production. If one (mines) one million tons of coal less every month, the steel can't increase; it's (all related).[849] And the idea that the Americans will send them more? (With them it is) just like with us. We were obligated to deliver the ... this and that. The fact of the matter is that even at the beginning we were hard-pressed to pull (the) deliveries together. Anyway, in war, everyone is his own best friend. No one would say, "First I will deliver the steel (to the others), and then I will take some myself." We (ourselves) couldn't (even) meet these very pressing demands. We always delivered a little less. We were supposed to deliver 1 to 1.2 million tons of coal, and only 900,000 tons remained.[850] If the Americans are supposed to deliver a certain thing that they suffer a shortage of themselves, they will certainly deliver less. And the British hold back from them, too. But they've actually brought in quite a lot. Just imagine what the British have in the way of units strolling around in the world—(it must be 50%) of their armed forces. If you look at India, (Africa, the Far East, and Australia, (they) must (have at least) 50% of their armed forces out there and (no more then 50% in Eng)land. And they want to (maintain that), of course, in order not to (lose any territory) at the last minute. But the attack will come; there is (no doubt) about it anymore.

JODL: On January 15 our ... will begin as well ...[851]

VOSS: The Grand Admiral has ordered his (commanders), like (on an island), not to give away a single meter under any circumstances, and has gathered (them) all together. I think it will work. That worked (on the Crimea) and it will work down there, too. (He has) made it clear to (them) what it's all about.

THE FÜHRER: If they attack in the West, (then) this attack will decide the war.

VOSS: Yes, Sir. That's what he told all the commanders.

THE FÜHRER: If this attack is driven back, the whole affair will be over. Then we can also take forces out very quickly.[852]

JODL: Very strong attack—(the strongest) so far, but with relatively limited (damage)—on the construction sites,[853] according to what I have (heard) so far.

THE FÜHRER: Smaller objectives are not (so easy) to hit.

JODL: They say the attack wasn't directed (toward) those objectives—they were alternative positions.

BÜCHS: The four-engines were initially approaching over the northern Netherlands in the direction of the Reich territory. (Then) they turned off to the west. It's not quite clear whether or not they (turned in) again. In any case, they ... attacked the construction sites afterward (with) ... aircraft.

THE FÜHRER: It's very clear that the (construction sites) disturb them. If (we) saw (such) objects being built up, and we knew that (they) would destroy Berlin, we'd become nervous, too, (and) would drive (our) Luftwaffe on as well. They are accurately informed about everything. They write that they are rockets. They have written that one to two tons of explosives can be shot over. They believe it now themselves. They write that the Germans started this thing first—they'd always worked in this field and had some experience. So it's not impossible that it could really work. But they'd take care of all these objects. Somehow, this certainly is (a threat to Eng)land. If the objects are built properly, (if we) make these small shelters—they (can't) attack that many (places)—nothing much will happen to the (soldiers) and the workers. And if (we) don't make (them) too big, it also can't … then it would be best to (build up) anti-aircraft artillery everywhere. To (hit) objectives that small from an altitude of 6,000 to 7,000 m would be pure chance.

JODL: Sometimes they attack from only 2,000 (m).

THE FÜHRER: Yes, but if we gradually bring in (anti-aircraft artillery) there, it will be different. We will also have to move a great deal of (anti-aircraft artillery) to the West—to Italy (and to the) West. I wonder if we shouldn't give an entire (monthly production) run of the (3.7 cm) to the West. We can shield ourselves with the 2 cm (somewhere) else.

BUHLE: The Army, for example, when it draws up its units, creates anti-aircraft artillery companies for infantry divisions with 2 cm and 3.7 cm, mixed. The East doesn't have the authorization to do so anymore at the moment. It doesn't matter if this infantry division does or doesn't have a company. But in the West or in Italy it would play a critical role. These divisions in the West really don't get the new formations because everything is going to the East.

THE FÜHRER: So we have to suspend (the deliveries to the East). That's the most important thing. (If we give) one or two months' (production) to the (West, that would be) 700 to 800 guns.

KEITEL: At the top is (the Navy), which gets so much because of the (submarines). I've given the order for this.

THE FÜHRER: And they get the (double-barrels) as well. (That) is starting very quickly now. The 3 cm (is good), too, (if) it lives up to what people promise. I (haven't) seen it. They say these double-barrels are fabulous.[854]

VOSS: I could imagine that if there were (an) accumulation of submarines, it could do (something); if just one is there it (wouldn't help that much). It is much better than what (we have now), of course.

V. PUTTKAMER: The double-barreled 3-cm gun is much easier to handle, while a double-barreled 3.7 cm in a submarine is rather heavy. There the 3 cm is better—not in its effect, but in its handling.

VOSS: It is better, of course—it pushes the enemy further away. That's very clear. But it's still not a cure for everything.

FEGELEIN: This caliber is decisive against (fighter)-bombers; there they tear them apart (in the air) …, while the 2 cm just doesn't go through. (The effect) of the 3.7 cm is huge. But it's (hard) for the infantry to handle because it's too heavy, (because it has a) weight of about 60 hundredweight.

VOSS: I am afraid that a break-through (in) this whole situation won't come until … with the …, my Führer.

THE FÜHRER: But there (we) would have to (make sure that) the submarines, at least, are there where (attack from) the air will be very difficult. That's (the way it is) in the Norwegian (area). We have to have them there en masse.[855] (For a landing operation,) 60 to 80 submarines should be there. Anything that can shoot must be moved there, so that at least we … on the part of the Army and the Luftwaffe doesn't direct too much (up there). We can't take any more up there. (That's) completely impossible; we will have to hold there with just our (own) forces. The dangerous thing is the airfields—if he gets (an) airfield somewhere. But in Norway—I have to point it out again—the total cover hasn't effectively decreased.

JODL: No. In addition, an infantry division has arrived from Romania.[856]

THE FÜHRER: (It has) decreased only numerically, I (believe).

JODL: Numerically it has (decreased) a bit.

BUHLE: The Panzer Division (Norway[857] has) … men.

JODL: In Norway there are 430,000 men.

BUHLE: There are some native (divisions) being established up there.

THE FÜHRER: Four hundred thirty thousand men correspond (roughly) to the strength of the French (Army in peacetime. That is) a huge number of men.

VOSS: What did we have up there in 1940? (It was) rather pitiful in the beginning. There we should always operate (with) … troops.

THE FÜHRER: It really was pitiful.

JODL: There it was much less. He did (not) have (much).

VOSS: I always say that if it succeeded then, it should definitely succeed now.

THE FÜHRER: Now, of course, he is landing with much better preparation and has equipped himself better.

VOSS: We are also much better prepared. That's what everyone up there says.

JODL: I'm afraid that in Norway …

THE FÜHRER: He just can't establish himself (on an) island. As soon as he (sits anywhere), he (endangers) all our transport.

JODL: Even Leros he had (to give up again. Here) we are able to attack with dive bombers.

THE FÜHRER: And the second is … that he can't make a landing down there. (It would be) unpleasant if he landed there and in the middle. That would (compel us) to bring forces down there. That would mean (that we) would fend him off up there first and then go there. But it's unpleasant.

VOSS: I don't believe he has the (penetrating power to) get through there. Because in the end he has (the example of) that big affair in Italy, where (he) got (completely) stuck.

THE FÜHRER: But we had good fortune in Italy, too. First, as defense. Second, we have a narrow shaft that is about 100 km wide, with natural obstacles as they are seldom seen. What's more, we have division sector-widths there that are almost like what we had in the Great War—but not with the very great combat distances. We had 9, 10, and 11 km in the Great War. That's about what we have there. This is good in Italy. Then he will have to (bring) everything (in) over long distances. But we have practically no (Luftwaffe) there. [—] (Now) we hope that if he attacks our (new aircraft) will come. Every month that we can (delay) this (will) be better for us. With every month the (likelihood) increases that we will be able to ... get ... at least one group of ... jet fighters.[858] The important thing is that he gets bombs on his head the moment he (lands). Then we force (him to) take (cover). And if there's always only one airplane (in the air, it has to) take cover, and that will cost him hour after hour. But (in) half (a) day we will (begin) pulling in our reserves. If he can be nailed to the beach for 6 or 8 hours, one (can) imagine what this would mean for us. (He is) nailed until our first reserves (arrive). In addition, that will give us a good picture. It would be (good) to have a glimpse right at the very beginning: where (is) the diversion and where is the real major attack? [—] I have one great concern—that in the end he will use those 4,000 kg apartment busters against the sluices at our submarine bases.

V. PUTTKAMER: Brest and Lorient don't have any sluices, only St. Nazaire, La Pallice[859] and Bordeaux.

THE FÜHRER: The pressure must be enormous. If 3,000 kg of high-quality explosives go into the water, it will send the whole thing up. Yes, we have to be worried here. But we have (one advantage): he will come with units (that are) not combat-experienced.

BUHLE: If we can (really get the) full-strength detachments for the West in January, (then) nothing can happen.

THE FÜHRER: That's what we hope.

BUHLE: But if we (take) everything (away) from the West! I barely get something together and it's (gone again).

THE FÜHRER: Who are you saying that to? (I won't let) anyone accuse me of taking away the units again and (again). You'll have to speak with Zeitzler about that.[860] ... But it is very hard for me as well. (Every day) I (see the) situation in the East. It is horrible. With 5 to (6 divisions) we might still be able to force the decision or obtain a major success. But I've always had these concerns in the West. I've never taken the position that nothing will happen. Rather, I am convinced that the moment will come when the English will be forced to end this war somehow, whether they want to or not. And the Americans have the presidential election. If Roosevelt doesn't gain a success and gets deeper and deeper into this, he might fail.[861] But if Roosevelt (fails, then) 6 months later he will be accused before the American Supreme Court. With what this man (has done), he can only get out of this as a winner—thereby eliminating the (national debt) to some extent. But as a (failed presidential) candidate he will be accused by his (successor), if only because of the instinct for self-preservation. (Because he) will take over the legacy that he ... That is why he will (let) his predecessor (be accused), because he has done this thing. All his ... financial manipulations already in the ... but also his later financial operations are such that this man won't be able to avoid the Supreme Court. The successor must do it. Because the one (who) comes (afterward) has to cope with the problem. This state, which is based on the liberal (capitalist) economic system—that's what they are fighting for—(has) a burden that might amount to some 100 billion dollars by then. Economically, that can't be digested. They can take on more and more debt, but how could they pay it off? With taxes? In that case they would need to tax away not two-thirds but nine-tenths. They just can't do that anymore. It will wash over them like a deluge. They will hold it up a bit by all kinds of manipulation. In reality, though, one can only maintain that through state authority, which means by brutal means. We can (do) it in Germany.[862] (They) can't. His successor has to (deal with) this. He will (have) nothing more urgent (to do) than to prove that this whole mess is Roosevelt's (work), no matter who his successor (is. That's the survival) instinct. They will (look for) a (culprit, and the) culprit is this man. That is quite clear. If one says: that's useless; (in four years he will be) there again. Yes, but in four (years' time—during those) four years the other one is hoping that (the situation) will change. In any case, the man will try (everything) to avoid losing the election. (His government) is also urging him on in that direction because it (must), and if the man wants to stay in his position, he needs to have some (success). That's why he wants to march in. [—] The British are extremely clever now. They want to give the supreme command to the Americans.[863] (They) do that very cleverly. Because one thing is quite certain: if the (Americans) have the Supreme Command, the British will let the Americans go first. They bear the responsibility if the whole thing goes wrong. If it went wrong for England, they would be responsible. And it's understandable that the British might not face the situation with such great confidence as Eisenhower. Eisenhower made a fortunate landing, but in both cases only with traitors. He won't find them among these people here, though. Here he'll get fired on, (and how)! It makes a big difference if one (lands in North Africa) and is greeted by Mr. Giraud[864] or (faces the Italians), who mostly wait in their hole and don't fire a (shot), or if one lands in the West (where) they actually shoot. As long as a battery (is able to fire), it (fires). That is certain.

BUHLE: And there are still (bunkers) behind. They first have to crack them one by one.

THE FÜHRER: Well, I am (absolutely) convinced that these ... are (not the right ones) to solve the problem. They can't do it. (If they) had troops with 2 years' Great War experience, one (could) say that they could do it. (But they're all) young units.

KEITEL: Totally inexperienced in war!

THE FÜHRER: That's why one can't say ours are young, too. Ours have more combat-experienced staffs, but they don't have that either.[865]

VOSS: Our men have been there for 2 years.

THE FÜHRER: I am convinced that as soon as it begins, it will be a relief. Last year we saw that in Dieppe.[866] It was actually a first-rate action. I saw Dieppe back then. How it was developed in those days! Since then, I've seen how it is now. What I saw is (a) small sector, (compared to those days) it's like 1:1,000. But when someone comes with such a large-scale attack, then it's important for him to have everything on hand (at a given) moment. (I) can (do) it (so that) I (give) a machine gun to an infantryman, and (also) a carbine, a couple of pistols, a ..., a flare pistol, also shells for (some special) purpose, smoke hand grenades—but he has to know what to take at the (right moment). When they (come) to land (and) have everything with them that those people have built, then it will work for the English and Americans only if everything really is there. If (something) goes wrong (during the landing) and those things are then missing, and (one waits for) a certain thing then, then it won't go any further.

BUHLE: And when everything has landed, he (must) advance 25 m to the bunkers. Only then he can fire with the flame-thrower.[867]

THE FÜHRER: Can't we make a special supply of flame-throwers for the West? Flame-throwers are the best for defense. It's a terrible weapon.

BUHLE: We have 1,200. There are thousands of the Russian ones, which are ignited electrically, in the West.

THE FÜHRER: But also direct flame-throwers. In the worst case we would have to have Speer carry out a forced action. He has workers available because of the (destroyed) factories. We could put them in somewhere and have them produce (flame)-throwers. Especially for defense, the (flame-thrower) is (the) most terrible weapon that exists. If someone comes along with (a shotgun), I can see the man. Besides, (he) has to come (close). But the defender is in a (hole. If) he attacks, he doesn't know that the defender has (a) flame-thrower. There's a foxhole in front of him—he has two small emplacements there and has, in addition to the machine gun, also the (flame)-

thrower. So then the other one advances, is 20 m (in front) of it, and suddenly it starts. That's a very (uncomfortable feeling).[868]

BUHLE: If we bring everything out in 2 months—(January and) February—there won't be any bunkers left without flame-throwers. We have 2,000. Then it will be 4,000.

THE FÜHRER: We have more bunkers than that in the West. We have about 7,500 already. So it will be nearly 10,000.

BUHLE: I mean assault troop flame-throwers—independent from the ones that are built in.

THE FÜHRER: It's the most terrible thing that exists. It takes away the courage of the attacking infantry, I would like to say, to engage in hand-to-hand combat. They lose all courage if they suddenly get the feeling that there are flame-throwers (on all) sides, wherever they (turn. Then) they lose all their courage beforehand. It's (the) most (terrible) thing that exists. Besides, there's also an uncomfortable (feeling); it is far more uncomfortable (when) it's burning there in front than (if you) get it in the neck. It's a (nasty situation). When we used the flame-thrower for the first (time in the Great) War, (we) unfortunately used (it) incorrectly. If we had saved the (flame-thrower) for a certain moment for a mass (deployment during) a major attack in the West, 15 to ... of them, it would have been devastating. (Because it is) certainly one of the weapons that causes (perhaps) the most terrible impression psychologically. But even (worse is) maybe the impression when one has it in the defensive position rather than when attacking. If the man attacks, you can see him—he jumps all the time—so you sweep him away. But with the defense, you don't know if he has a flame-thrower in his hole or not. If the hole is very narrow, the accuracy is better than that of the grenade thrower. It's difficult to throw a hand grenade into a hole from 30 m. It's certainly easier to reach someone with a flame-thrower from 30 m. Flame-throwers should also be in battery positions, for example. We must have flame-throwers everywhere. I've even thought that we might (also) use them also against low-level flights—but that's impossible. There are lots of ways. [—] Buhle, (remind) me tomorrow again! [—] We can establish (a connection) with Saur now.

BUHLE: I know we've put the (flame-thrower production) under huge pressure, (and that we) produce 1,200 a month. It (has) taken a (long) time. Now we've reached the point where we (get) 1,200.

THE FÜHRER: Due to the (destruction of) factories we always have a certain shock troop reserve as (a second) or third work shift. I don't know (if the factories) are being already run in two or three shifts. [—] With a major landing, we could, for example, also blow up barrels and set fire to them on the beach, so that they would have to wade through the fire to reach land. In certain places we could do that. Of course, we couldn't do that over a wide area. But we can think up all kinds of tricks in various places. One place, for instance, can be so heavily mined that no one can reach land at all. In another place oil barrels can start to burn. And in another place we can install the Russian flame-throwers, which will start spouting. In another place we will concentrate artillery from behind, (which) will produce a huge barrage. So (we) can think of all kinds of different things. (Then) afterward they can come together and (share) the experiences (that they) had during the landing.

BUHLE: I spoke to General (Jacob about) the fact that the Commander-in-Chief West ... keeps in reserve. He won't put them into (action) anymore.

THE FÜHRER: Then we have to (instruct) Rommel. (He) must take certain areas that have to be (mined completely). [—] I didn't know that a new (mine) like that had been produced.

KEITEL: It won't come (out) until January.

THE FÜHRER: We don't need (many, because) the other one searches for the mines and then they explode. Recently I've imagined a couple of times that we could maybe contaminate whole minefields with other mines, but also with antipersonnel mines, in such a way that certain minefields are not possible to enter, even for us. Because when someone steps on it, it blows up. We would have to take mines that are not laid in metal but in plastic.

BUHLE: The minefields along the beach are totally blocked, even for us. None of us can get in there except through the precisely marked lanes, which are only visible from our own side.

THE FÜHRER: (*Telephone call with Saur:*) Saur, (how many) flame-throwers do you produce per month now? [—] You ... exactly, how many you produce. [—] I need (three) times the number you're producing now—(in two) months' time. You must put (workers) in there as fast as possible. So in January/February three times the number you're producing now! (That's the) minimum requirement. [—] It's only 1,200? I thought (it was) 2,400. I wanted to have three times as much. (You) have already determined that the numbers come out. (So) higher, higher—quickly! We (urgently) need it. Thank you very much! Heil! Happy holidays! (*End of the telephone call.*) He says he made an increase up [to 1,200].

BUHLE: I reported that; we've already pushed hard.

THE FÜHRER: He says he thinks he can increase it. He can increase it because it's a production that doesn't require that many preliminary products. And, due to the bomb attacks, he has workers available, so he can put them in.

KEITEL: It's also a relatively simple thing.

HITLER AND HIS GENERALS

THE FÜHRER: We could (never be taken by surprise) if there (were) 20,000 to 30,000 flame-throwers in the West.

BUHLE: He has actually ... twice the number you ordered, my Führer, ... it. He has pushed it up to 1,200, (and he) says: I can't go any further.

End: 11:00 p.m.

* * * *

END OF THE EVENING SITUATION REPORT,
DECEMBER 21, 1943[869]

(THE FÜHRER): ... doesn't believe. Do you think the others don't know that as well?

HEWEL: I don't know if we have little injections like those.

THE FÜHRER: We don't need little injections. "Prisoners of war"! [—] We won't take it out on the prisoners of war, but on the war criminals in our hands. [—] He's doing it wrong again here.[870]

JODL: "Soviet," we said. It makes no sense. We can't even name the Soviet prisoners of war.

THE FÜHRER: So I will have it written again. Is there anything else? From the Navy?

VOSS: There's nothing to report from the Navy.

BÜCHS: Nothing from the air, either. Only in the West heavier attacks against construction (sites and air)fields in the area south of Boulogne. One construction (site was damaged).[871] (No particular) air activity on the rest of the fronts. Major intrusions are not (expected).

VOSS: Landing in the West is unlikely due to (bad weather).

End: 10:37 p.m.

* * * * *

MIDDAY SITUATION REPORT,
DECEMBER 22, 1943, AT THE WOLFSSCHANZE[872]

Beginning: 12:30 p.m.

The East

HEUSINGER: Regarding the general situation, my Führer, there have been no attacks on the front yet today. At Nikopol' the enemy has been quiet this morning. The counterattacks by Army Group South turned out favorably.[873] The Ninth Army's action on the right wing [north of Kalinkovichi] is progressing well. Other than that, there is nothing special to report from that front. In the (Army Group A) sector, the only combat action was up here.

(Here) there was increased enemy patrol activity and (our own assault) party activity. Two hundred seventy-five men on leave flew (over yesterday)[874] [—] Romanians. The Romanians are now being taken along all the time.

THE FÜHRER: From the 336th [Infantry] Division?

HEUSINGER: The last two battalions of the 336th Division will be relieved here now. They will be brought over to Odessa and then flown over here.[875] Those are the two battalions that were still here at the front and have now become free due to the withdrawal. There was no combat activity in the Sixth Army's area; the enemy has been quiet there. [—] In Army Group South's sector at the Nikopol' bridgehead, there were only two local attacks here this morning. During the night, the 24th Panzer Division was concentrated in order to make a concerted counterattack. It's not known yet if the counterattack will start this afternoon or tomorrow. Probably not until tomorrow. Up here a counterattack by the 3rd Mountain Division won ground and took a hill again. Yesterday the attacks were (primarily) by infantry, without any tank deployment worth mentioning, but with heavier artillery support. No combat action on this front. Here the enemy led two counterattacks that were driven back. The 13th [Infantry] Division is attacking now. The aim is to try to reach this line. We will see today, my Führer, if enemy resistance is so strong as to entail unnecessary losses, or if it will go on. It's progressing well at the moment. During this time—from the beginning of the enemy attack in here until the enemy was thrown back—the following numbers were achieved: 274 tanks and assault guns and 306 guns of all kinds. That is quite a good result from these actions.

THE FÜHRER: But all in all, it shows that the numbers on the other side are no huge thing at all. The sack was in here. The sack was then almost completely pinched off. He was stuck in here and was totally pinched off here. The result is 1,200 prisoners and 2,000 to 3,000 enemy dead. (But) those aren't huge masses anymore—otherwise, considering the situation we're in here, there would have to be completely different numbers [—]

(HEUSINGER): ... to push the projecting front forward a bit to achieve a shortened line. The enemy was quiet in this area. [—] South of Cherkassy, the enemy made two local advances today—here and here. They were driven back. Two battalions will be pushed in here today to comb through this wooded area again. Here, as reported yesterday, the 168th [Infantry] Division is out, and will remain here. We have put a blocking note on that. They also don't want to take down the one regiment here, my Führer, but must keep the division together here. They don't find it necessary here; instead, they think they can reach it this way. [—] The situation with the assault group near Kiev has developed in such a way that we had to regroup last night.[876] The attack by the *Leibstandarte* and the 1st Panzer Division began this morning at 11 o'clock, ultimately with the aim of reaching a line like this—so the shortest connection from here over there. In terms of the enemy picture here yesterday, altogether … appeared [—] still unclear. It was reported again this morning that the gaps the enemy put between his obstacles are closed again, so the army group has withdrawn its request concerning the 18th Artillery Division,[877] at least for the time being. It's still not clear. We still don't know where those corps will go.

THE FÜHRER: If it's successful with this line here, so that this holds out, at least two units will be free here. The 1st Panzer Division will be free and this one will be free. Then the danger won't be so great here. The danger will be greater here.

HEUSINGER: As soon as this is reached, they want to pull out these mobile units again and position themselves here. Other than that, there's nothing to report from [Army Group] South. [—] In the Army Group Center area, the engagement here [north of Kalinkovichi] progressed well. In a further attack this morning, these arrowheads everywhere have already been reached, and they have also started here. I spoke with the army group about the objective of (the) action. They said that they want to advance as close as possible (to this) sector and then over here [—] not yet ready for a decision. But they want to keep the 16th [Panzer Division] ready as a reserve.

THE FÜHRER: It would be good if we could put them here, so that we'd have one up there and another one here.

HEUSINGER: So that we'd have them at this runway.

THE FÜHRER: Yes. Then we can send them everywhere.

HEUSINGER: On the rest of the Ninth Army's front there was only enemy patrol activity, which was driven back. The Fourth Army's situation is unchanged. There was no action this morning. On the whole, the picture hasn't changed here, either. There are certain indications of dispersion. It seems as if the 2nd Guards Tank Corps, which has been in this area until now, has been pulled up here behind the 10th Guards Army, which has come up here [east of Orsha]. The army group has the one regiment from this area … taken out, in order to … its division [—]

THE FÜHRER: Any moment! Here he has the big [—]

HEUSINGER: The situation with the Third Panzer Army has developed in such a way that yesterday evening two more fairly deep penetrations occurred here [northeast of Vitebsk] in the 14th [Infantry] Division lines, and the division was pushed back to this line during the night. But it has held today. This morning there were only local advances here.[878] [—] The rest of the front is stable. There are pressure points in the 3rd Luftwaffe Field Division lines, in these three places, but they have not yet led to penetrations. Now enemy pressure is heavier there. There was patrol activity here this morning. It has been quiet so far along this entire front. Those two corps, the 2nd Guards Rifle Corps and the 5th Guards Tank Corps, which were originally here [north of Gorodok], have pulled more around here [west of Gorodok]. Regarding our own measures, the following is to be reported: When this regiment arrives, the (197th [Infantry] Division) will be compact (in this) area, in order to be ready in case the ... here [—] will first be pulled forward into this area, as ordered. Field Marshal Busch will probably come tomorrow—or, more likely, this evening—with the request for permission to make this turn in order to reach a front somewhere along here, which would be better in terms of terrain. But he only wants to do that after the 5th Jäger [Light Infantry] Division has arrived in its entirety. A wasteful deployment was refused him yesterday.

THE FÜHRER: Can we add some more assault guns here?

HEUSINGER: I will find that out, my Führer. But it should be possible.

THE FÜHRER: I would have preferred it if we'd tried to get further away from the railway, instead of doing this here.[879] Of course, that's more difficult to manage. But here it would have been more important than up there.

HEUSINGER: Here he fears—that was the [—]

HEUSINGER: The 5th Jäger Division is a strong division. It has six strong battalions.

THE FÜHRER: But he should also treat them with care! Sometimes it seems to me as if our men can't even look at a good unit before it's used up.

HEUSINGER: The main thing is that they're not deployed at all before all the units arrive—before they've arrived in their entirety. [—] This evening Army Group North should carry out the withdrawal movement to here, for which permission was granted yesterday. There were no attacks here today. Yesterday 18 tanks were knocked out. Furthermore, the army group—in my opinion this is very good—is now starting to put the 12th [Panzer Division] in motion.[880] It is supposed to come in here, so he still has something behind here. Altogether (on) this front there (are)—I had it added up [—]

HEUSINGER: That is not inconsequential, and it will probably also come in, if the 12th [Panzer] comes in behind as well, because then it has to be supported.

THE FÜHRER: Assuming that it will be developed well, he'll free up so many forces that we will certainly be able to support that. He just has to take care, though. I fear that the enemy will fight here with all possible means. If it doesn't work here, he'll come up again and try it up above.

HEUSINGER: The losses that the I Corps suffered—that's these five divisions from here to here [west of Novosokol'niki]—were quite severe during the last five days: 3,000 men. I told the army group again today that they must not bleed to death here, of course. That's why it would be better for them to propose smaller withdrawals in time. It would be allowed, if it's possible. (This) bend is useless afterward as well.

THE FÜHRER: It doesn't make sense. [—]

(HEUSINGER): ... this direction, and third, we have ordered the preparation of enough empty [railroad cars] at the railway, so that we can possibly even transport them here or wherever it should arise. [—] That's all there is to present regarding the situation.

BÜCHS: There is no air action to report on the East yesterday. Today there is also bad weather along the entire front, so no sorties are possible. (*Presentation of a paper on the Khar'kov show trial.*[881])

THE FÜHRER: So like this: an officer of the Army, one of the Waffen SS. Or an officer and a non-commissioned officer of the Army and an officer of the Waffen SS.

JODL: A lance corporal in the Army and a member ...

THE FÜHRER: Yes, that's how we have to do it.[882]

Italy

[—]

(JODL): ... the 44th [Infantry Division]. Right now there are some relief movements in progress.

THE FÜHRER: The English and also the Americans are complaining a great deal. The whole thing will gradually become very bloody, and they're asking themselves if it still makes any sense at all to continue the operation, or if it's completely ill advised.

JODL: I have the following impression: Their original goal was to take Rome with a breakthrough here before Christmas. Now they've realized that the terrain here is very difficult, that more positions are set up further to the rear, that new forces are being brought in—they already reported the 5th Mountain Division—and they have now moved their focus closer to the northern wing. There is no doubt that both armies now have the order to hold (as many) German forces as possible[883] [—]

JODL: Here is a report about it, but it's weak. The 5th Mountain Division is here for relief now; it will replace the 44th and one regiment of the 305th [Infantry Division]. This regiment has been pulled out already and will come up here now, because the plan is to gradually take the entire Group Schulenburg[884]—that is, the parts of the 1st Parachute Division that are still in here—up to the left wing as well, and to place the 1st Parachute Division there. In addition, a battalion that suffered many losses has been taken out. It will be replenished in Rome and can recover there.

THE FÜHRER: Rome is invaluable now. Shouldn't we establish a kind of prophylactic station in the Vatican?!

JODL: A drill ground?![885] [—] In any case, it is very good, of course, to be able to take really exhausted troops back where they can recover. It will then be [—] because it has never been in combat. The enemy has caught his breath again. There hasn't been any major combat action, as of early this morning. He seems to be assembling first. Here, a fairly worn-out regiment of the 90th Panzer Grenadier Division been taken out. The 65th [Infantry Division] is still being kept here; the artillery, in particular, has remained in position. Field Marshal Kesselring—or the Tenth Army—has decided to move these positions, which were on the front slope, away from the steady heavy artillery fire and place them a short distance away in safe territory. They will relocate them to the rear slope—without pressure—so that they aren't presented to the enemy artillery on a silver platter. [—] Advances that (were) attempted with strong combat patrols—an attempt to enter the southern edge of Ortona, and (an attack) in that direction with the strength of ... have been driven back. [—]

JODL: Actually, it is the same straight extension. They aren't any longer, either. That's the report. It obviously comes from the site manager there. (*Presentation.*)

THE FÜHRER: So there are basically only two that will be completed within reasonable time. That is nothing, of course.[886]

JODL: A fortification construction battalion has moved forward from the Apennines, and there are three more Italian construction battalions being kept here, too.

THE FÜHRER: It can only be built at night; that is clear. With 20, that's two per kilometer, at first. Until the first 200 are set up.

JODL: Usually it takes forever to get the OT [Todt Organization] started, because first they ... everything [—]

JODL: The transport situation is satisfactory, despite all the recent destruction. Actually, all routes are passable again—including Innsbruck, since yesterday—so no difficulties have arisen in the transport movements.

The Balkans

Increasing [partisan] band activity is reported from here: raids, sabotage—but only individuals, no larger groups. The 117th Jäger Division will clear that out now. This mopping-up action here will continue. Reported thus far: 107 dead, 39 prisoners, 265 suspects arrested, and many captured guns and parachutes again, which are evidence of the supply. There were 50 enemy dead and 60 captured in the mopping-up action by the 100th Jäger

Division in the coastal area west of Argirocastro. The (mission) at Tirana resulted in 20 dead; 172 Italians (have been) arrested. Also here some captured [—] that movements are going on over here. Here quite smooth progress—in the south, so far, without contact with the enemy. The enemy is avoiding us here. There is strong pressure only against the 369th [Infantry] Division's blocking troops. So here he is trying to get through in front of his own forces. Contact with the enemy only on the right wing of the 1st Mountain Division. There are two groups that had positioned themselves there—here and here—and they have been destroyed. There was also a battle up here; those troops have been driven back there as well. [—] The 901st and 902nd Regiments are clearing this out here. [—] These forces here have also been quiet during the last few days, although the enemy has been a little more active recently.

THE (FÜHRER): They are literally raging against the British … box on the ears! [—] I also have those [—]

JODL: … But that man has already been eliminated. Since a Russian ambassador or envoy found his way to him, his days will be numbered anyway.[887] No king will come here—absolutely not!

THE FÜHRER: That fits into our conception,[888] too—away with it! [—] The poor guy. Now he has lost his wife. She has also stepped back again, because she has seen that he is not that powerful. She has asked herself, "Why should I marry a king who is not a king?"

KEITEL: May I ask another question, my Führer? That Fritz—an Untersturmführer at the Taganrog Command—who hadn't been appointed until recently was transferred to the SD [Sonderkommando—Special Command].[889] Can we designate him a "(Waffen) SS officer"? That is (not) actually what he is; he is an (Untersturm)führer, but he has the official function [—]

KEITEL: That's how I wrote it. I just wanted to confirm it again.

JODL: Down here the enemy hasn't continued the attack against Plevlja, but has secured the area to the west. The Cetniks have secured this here. Minor advances were driven back. Part of the *Brandenburg* Regiment is securing Plevlja.

THE FÜHRER: In the end, Jodl, we are suddenly forced to step in on behalf of the Karadjordjevic dynasty and present Peter as a friend of ours.

JODL: Neditsch[890] has behaved very wildly.

THE FÜHRER: Does he not want him either? [—] Or does he want him?

JODL: (He) is leaving the question open, I believe.

(THE FÜH)RER: In what way did he behave wildly? [—] all those emigrant governments and counter governments lie their way through again and again. They always have to watch out and take note of what they've told everyone, so that they don't get it mixed up one day, the way it happened here with Schleicher.[891]

JODL: The most malicious remark in that report was at the end, where he said, "If the Turks don't play the card now—the trump card—it could be that their current fears about Russia may come true later." [—] So they have pulled out all the stops?

THE FÜHRER: But the Turks are so clever that ... like this or this. If we ... a failure [—]

The West

[—]

THE FÜHRER: What kind of experiences have they had?

JODL: We will get the experience reports. [—] We have now listed what can and should be brought together here from the Commander-in-Chief West himself and from other theaters in case of an attack here. But it won't be enough. As soon as the consensus is reached that the attack will start from here[892] and that it will go in a certain direction, we must begin to bring in troops beforehand, because what goes first—

THE FÜHRER: —is uncertain!

JODL: (It) is uncertain; at least it will take a long time. [—]

THE FÜHRER: We have to be very careful now with the rear positions that are not occupied, so we don't suddenly find paratroopers coming down and occupying the positions behind us. It can be done with transport gliders and parachutes. I wanted to occupy this National Redoubt[893] back then. That was the initial plan for the paratroopers. But it was ruined by that man who was captured there.[894] At first, the plan was to jump near Ghent in order to take it from behind and to seize this entire fortress, cutting the enemy off from his rear connections right away. That was our plan. The enemy could understand those ideas, too. If we have secondary positions here, which are not occupied, he will (come) in and suddenly sit in ... bunkers. Then we won't get him [—]

JODL: Other than that, no further reports from the West.

The North

Finland: Additional, somewhat livelier reconnaissance activity on both sides. In Denmark there was a sabotage mission against the Danish Industry Syndicate in Copenhagen, where infantry gun components and listening devices are produced; serious damage. [—] Also four minor sabotage cases, including one in which a member of the Armed Forces was slightly injured.

THE FÜHRER: Hanneken, Best, and Müller[895] must come here soon to discuss these countermeasures. I believe they disagree; each one of those three has a different view, which doesn't work. [—] sense; it's always: into trouble, out of trouble!

JODL: In general, the strike movement in Italy has ended.[896] All factories in Milan and Genoa have resumed work again, with the exception of a small factory 50 km northwest of Milan. In Milan itself eight Communists have been sentenced to death by an Italian war court.

Situation at sea

VOSS: No particular news regarding the submarine situation. The four outpost patrols were under water yesterday during the day and surfaced at night.[897] There haven't been any reports. Yesterday (after)noon the two boats started out ... boats should come here, hit the boat [—] in Skagerrak one destroyer—the *Lody*—*T 28* and one mine ship are deployed; yesterday afternoon they arrived at Kristiansand.[898] Yesterday there was extraordinarily heavy escort traffic along the Norwegian coast, without any enemy movements reported; 82 ships were escorted. South of Bear Island there is now a submarine outpost patrol, but we have no detailed reports.[899] No air deployment on our part. [—] Moderate enemy air action over the North Sea. The escorts north of Texel on the Dutch coast departed as planned with 7,850 GRT. There was no enemy action [—] point that—since an enormous accumulation of enemy ship capacity in the Mediterranean hasn't been identified—most of those ships are going through the Suez Canal toward East Asia. South of Toulon an enemy submarine was located on December 12[900]. The strike in Genoa is cooling down; the shipyards are back at work. Two motor torpedo boats from Viareggio were deployed last night in the Bastia region. There are no reports available yet. [—] The coastal traffic ran as planned yesterday. Air reconnaissance on the 21st produced no results.

Four mines were cleared around the island of Chalkis. [—] Air reconnaissance on the 20th produced no sightings in the direction of Cyprus and Alexandria. South of the island of Lemnos, a submarine attacked a motor sailboat; the submarine was then fired on by one of our land batteries and dived under. The sailboat was undamaged. Three Navy barges arrived yesterday at Ak Metschet[901] with five assault guns and additional materiel. [—] Another dock—a smaller 150-ton floating dock with 2 tugs— is on its way from Nikolaev to Odessa. The S-Boote [Schnellboote—motor torpedo boats] weren't deployed because of the weather conditions; they weren't used in the Kerch Strait either. [—]

Situation in the air

(BÜCHS): ... Seventy-two without sighting the enemy. Five aircraft shot down with the help of flak, with one loss on our side. Otherwise limited action. During the night, deployment of 5 aircraft against London; four reached the target and one broke away.[902] [—] Also very little action over the Mediterranean. Individual aircraft attacked railway installations near Tarquinia in the rear area, and an unknown number of aircraft made a deep attack against the Navy Airfield near Viterbo de Valle, without particular damage. Ten Spitfires[903] flew over the airfield at Viterbo; one Spitfire crashed for unknown reasons. In the area near the front, there were a few enemy fighter-bomber attacks. [—] Heavy clouds also over the entire Mediterranean area, with a low lower limit and extensive rain showers up to the front area. [—] In the Reich territory, the leading edge of this rain front is now at the Elbe. Behind it, the weather system breaks up considerably west of the Weser. Today intrusions will be possible with good visibility. But our own defense can get out as well. This rain front will reach the area of Berlin between the Oder and the Elbe in the evening. That's why the takeoff and landing from England—but also the takeoff of our own defense—won't be hindered. *End: 1:15 p.m.*

* * * * *

December 27-30, 1943

On December 24 the Russians initiated a new attack against the Fourth Panzer Army west of Kiev—in the same direction (toward Korosten', Zhitomir and Fastov) as their previous push, which had been blocked by the German counterattack in mid-November—to force the northern flank of Army Group North back even further. Brussilov and Radomysl' fell quickly, and by January 1 Zhitomir was also in Soviet hands again. A broad penetration to the southwest ripped a 45 km wide gap southeast of Berdichev and is already aiming for Vinnitsa.

Because of the critical situation between Korosten' and Fastov, and the ongoing threat posed by the 1st Baltic Front to Vitebsk, additional forces had to be withdrawn from Army Group North, which had already given away some divisions to relieve the central and southern sectors. But Hitler prefers to withdraw in the North rather than in the South.
(Map 10)

* * * * *

Meeting of the Führer
with General Zeitzler, December 27, 1943[904]

Present:

> The Führer　　　　　　　　　Major Borgmann
> General Zeitzler　　　　　　　Sturmbannführer Darges
> Major General Scherff

Beginning: 10 p.m.

The East

ZEITZLER: Nothing in particular to report from Army Group A. The first train won't depart until this evening. The railway was completed, but the troops weren't ready. Nothing unusual on this front or along this entire front. Here a local advance, which wasn't particularly significant. [—] This attack up here [east of Kirovograd] by the 11th, 6th and 3rd [Panzer Divisions] went as planned. The heavier resistance is here in the woods, so the army group[905] believes that the 3rd Panzer will probably have to go up against the woods to defend there; and this one should advance further toward this town. A smaller group is encircled here. He seems to have surprised them.

THE FÜHRER: When this is done here, the most dangerous spot will be here.

ZEITZLER: I think so, too. So he will try to reach that.

THE FÜHRER: So a deep [thrust] must be made here, above all. An officer of the 529th Infantry Division—

ZEITZLER: … Division.[906]

THE FÜHRER: —told me that their position was well developed; that is, they had a well-developed one behind the front position. They could go back there at any time if the situation became critical.

ZEITZLER: Down at that thing. [—] That was this attack here. It will be continued tomorrow up to here, while the 3rd [Panzer Division] is supposed to provide cover up above.

THE FÜHRER: And what kind of feeling do they have here?

ZEITZLER: Right now it doesn't seem like anything major is about to happen, although there are a large number of units here. The 17th [Panzer Division] is pulling out. But we don't know yet if he has already loosened something up.

THE FÜHRER: Will he take the 17th here?

ZEITZLER: The 17th will be taken up there by rail.[907] [—] Then the development of the situation up here [southwest of Kiev]. He's pushed a little more in that direction. On this front here, the 25th Panzer is mostly here and is being attacked from all sides. It was also attacked here. Here's a small blocking unit. At midday today there was still fighting here. Parts of the 20th Panzer Grenadier Division attacked from here. [—] On this front, the *Leibstandarte* [Panzer Grenadier Division] resisted here. The 19th Panzer [Division] fought through the woods here, where the enemy was, and is now here, together with the SS troops, holding the western edge of the woods. [—] Then he tried to cause the collapse of this corner post. For the most part, he failed. But he did push in a little further near the *Reich,* [SS Panzer Grenadier Division] so this corner has was taken again. [—] Then this afternoon, very heavy pressure began from above, but later it turned out that he wasn't that strong after all. In general he's been driven back, in some cases by these counterattacks. Now the 3rd Panzer [Division] will be positioned behind it up there. The intention is not clear yet; we don't know what they want to do with it.

THE FÜHRER: But it's just the 7th Panzer [Division] here. Nothing else is there.

ZEITZLER: Up here they still have only the reconnaissance detachment of the 7th Panzer.

THE FÜHRER: They've pulled the bulk of the forces over here now.

ZEITZLER: Yes, indeed. The ones that were in the inner wing. The numbers are generally the same. Twelve rifle divisions and 3 to 5 tank units have been confirmed; prisoners have been taken from the 4th Guards Tank Corps, the 9th Guards Tank Corps, and the 8th Guards Mechanized Corps, while there are two armored corps there that are not confirmed yet. It was reported that they were still there. [—] Up here there are three tank corps. Back here there are another four tank corps behind this one. Either he's taking them to—previously he'd taken them up to—

THE FÜHRER: He's trying to shake the whole thing up.

ZEITZLER: He's trying to become wider on both sides. [—] Then I'd like to report about [Army Group] Center again. From the Second Army, nothing in particular. We succeeded this morning in a local advance here, but it was thrown back again by a counterattack this afternoon. The bulk of the 16th Panzer [Division] is pulling out. The first train will depart this evening.[908] Here there was another local attack. Other than that, nothing unusual on this front. [—] There were some movements going up north here; we can't see yet where they're headed. Here a local advance and also here. Up here [south of Vitebsk] with the 60th—so where the *Feldherrnhalle* [Panzer

Grenadier Division] is—this thing actually held where the *Feldherrnhalle* pushed forward yesterday.[909] Today they were regrouping and advancing to here. There were sharp attacks from this side. A counterattack drove back this attack, and there was still fighting here at dusk. He'd reached the road, but then they threw him back. [—] Most of the attacks up here were driven back by midday—also this thing, where 7 tanks were knocked out, and also here around this bend … with some units of the 87th [Infantry Division]. They attacked here today at midday, south of the road, and were supposed go along this road. They were there—where the question mark is—until dusk. [—] Four trains of the 12th [Infantry Division] have pulled in now. And apparently the 29th [129th Infantry Division] has moved down here.[910] It could be that he'll expand some more there as well. We still have the 12th [Infantry Division] there, and it's coming relatively slowly. There are altogether 11 trains on this line. We still have a reserve until this is deployed. [—] Something is going on up north at the tip [of the salient west of Novosokol'niki]—maneuvers, training, or relief. We can't quite explain it yet.

THE FÜHRER: He'll go down here.

ZEITZLER: It was very unsettling during the two days when he didn't attack here. Either he's regrouping here … and this thing will launch, or he'll pull it down below. I don't think he'll attack this tip itself.

THE FÜHRER: No, he can advance on a very wide front here.

ZEITZLER: But it almost looks as if he isn't going to take this tip forward anymore.

THE FÜHRER: I don't think so either.

ZEITZLER: If I could just address three points.

THE FÜHRER: Zeitzler, I think he has to take out some mobile units here.

ZEITZLER: Yes, I actually think he should pull this tip [salient] back in now. It's not containing them anymore—it's containing us.

THE FÜHRER: He can leave outposts here. But he has to take units out so that only battle reconnaissance is left in there.

ZEITZLER: Then it's a withdrawal, so that only a rearguard remains with the enemy.

THE FÜHRER: Yes.

ZEITZLER: I will speak with Army Group North again this evening because I felt very uncomfortable during those two days when he didn't do anything. I feel like he must be rebuilding something. The North also thought it would be better to get back, in order to be able to rearrange in time. Otherwise we will be too late.

THE FÜHRER: Yes.

ZEITZLER: So we can allow them to take this back?[911]

THE FÜHRER: Yes.

ZEITZLER: But stronger rear troops near the enemy.

THE FÜHRER: Yes. He must be sure to get the units around here ... must bring them here at all cost.

ZEITZLER: I even thought that we might now pull the border down to about here. Because [Army Group] Center has a huge task here, and if he attacks here, he will probably come in that direction [from northwest of Vitebsk]. But we can still see how it develops over the next few days.

THE FÜHRER: It depends entirely on how long this thing here holds.

ZEITZLER: Because they didn't want to have the 32nd [Infantry Division] back there until January 10. That won't work.

THE FÜHRER: That's too late.

ZEITZLER: That's much too late. That's why I called. We can't give them any rest here. But if that is agreed to, and only rear troops will remain with the enemy, and they go into this line, they must release quite a lot. I will transmit this, then. [—] My Führer, I could stay with [Army Group] Center then. The request has been made to take the 292nd [Infantry Division] back into this improved position, which is also behind there.

THE FÜHRER: That's what what's-his-name said.

ZEITZLER: With a very detailed explanation.

THE FÜHRER: He says it's good.

ZEITZLER: The position is relatively improved. There are 60 shelters in here—32 under construction. Here there are 81 dugouts—6 under construction. This is the position here, and the explanation is that in the long run it won't be possible to hold that one anyway.

THE FÜHRER: Yes, I spoke with him.

ZEITZLER: I spoke with the regimental commander about this position as well. He also said it was good.

THE FÜHRER: Yes, they can do that.

ZEITZLER: Yes, I think so, too. So the permission can be given. [—] My Führer, an estimate of the situation has arrived from Manstein.[912] Perhaps I might present here my 1:1,000,000 map for the overall situation. First there are the answers to the two questions. One was this position, and the other was regarding the bridgehead [at Nikopol'], which you asked about yesterday, my Führer. (*Presentation.*) The Ilse Position [defense line] is the one marked here in front—this curve over here.

THE FÜHRER: I didn't say two small bridgeheads.

ZEITZLER: No, they shouldn't be—just the one thing. But they absolutely don't want to narrow it.

THE FÜHRER: The Kamenka position is this position.

ZEITZLER: I've marked these positions here. This is the Ilse position here, and this is the Kamenka position. (*Presentation of map.*)

THE FÜHRER: You should say, "in the Kamenka Line," because it's not a position.

ZEITZLER: Some shelters have been built.

THE FÜHRER: Because even the front one isn't a position, let alone this.

ZEITZLER: I had this given to me once—the Kamenka position. (*Presentation*.) At least it's something, though not much.

THE FÜHRER: How long is it?

ZEITZLER: Here it's 160 km long, and this whole thing is 360, my Führer. There are 21 units in here, and we save 200 km. That's what I presented about 10 days ago.

THE FÜHRER: Here is Nikopol'. (*Examination of the presented material.*) He hopes it, but he doesn't believe it. [—] He certainly can't seriously believe this: "completely exhaust the frontal attack"! It's not certain that he'll exhaust himself. [—] Yes, I want to talk about it again tomorrow.

ZEITZLER: Allow me to show this on the one to one million-scale map. I've marked the front here, and here the traffic routes. This double-track railway with an average capacity of 33 trains per day runs here.[913] He's quite close to there now. I believe it's only a matter of days. So the day after tomorrow this line will be gone. Now the other lines are left. I've already pushed this track here quite high. So far we've brought 4½ to 5 trains over this newly built bridge near Trichata.[914] I've now pushed it up to 10 to 12 trains. We came up so high because there was a certain amount of shifting in order to be able to help down here. But that railway will nevertheless be an immense loss, of course. We can compensate it here a bit with this single-track railway, which takes 7 or 8 trains, but it's threatened as well. Because it's about this distance. The position was here when he arrived on the 24th. That's about halfway to this railway line. Then this line down here is still left. It can handle relatively little, so we'll be under pressure in terms of railways if this corner post breaks out again. Then the border of Transnistria[915] is here already, so we'll also be under pressure in terms of roads. Down here, the main thoroughfare number 4 still goes along here.[916] If road 4 is eliminated, we will be under a great deal of pressure—then here we'll come into a … way back with the entire army wing, and that concerns me very much.

THE FÜHRER: This action here doesn't yet mean that he can cover this; to cover this thing here is a matter of how many forces he can get within the next few days.

ZEITZLER: Which will arrive within the next few days. That will get us a delay. He says that we can't get anything from the West; we don't have anything there. But the delay can only come through the 4th Mountain Division[917] and the small auxiliaries and the 17th Panzer [Division]. Nevertheless, they won't stop the thing entirely. That's why we need to look for new forces, and I see a way to obtain new forces from the tip [salient], for two reasons. First, that's the only route we can use to bring anything in here, and second, the tip can't be held over the long term. Because if he's in here, we have to do it, and at that moment we won't have anything to use to get this under control. We don't have the 4th Mountain Division, so the 17th Panzer won't be enough either.

THE FÜHRER: If he wanted to give up this here, why did he take the 4th Mountain Division away? Then we could have transported the 4th up here.

ZEITZLER: My Führer, I think we still need the 4th. We can't be too strong up there in that location.

THE FÜHRER: But with the forces he has now he can't hold this any longer. If we step back here, this here will be lost.

ZEITZLER: The Crimea will be lost anyway in the near future. Of course, this will lead to its loss earlier.

THE FÜHRER: It wouldn't have to be lost.

ZEITZLER: In my view, the Crimea can only be held if we can make a connection through here.

THE FÜHRER: The disposition of forces, and the recent moving around up here, may have been—

ZEITZLER: It's hard to say. Maybe we destroyed a few of his tank corps up here so that the attack hasn't come from up there. If we hadn't done that, we would have moved it here and carried out the Fastov action,[918] and then we might have run up against this difficult thing, and it certainly wouldn't have been any better.

THE FÜHRER: That doesn't matter now. The worst part was the bad weather.

ZEITZLER: At the beginning. And now the weather is such that the Luftwaffe absolutely can't get into action.

THE FÜHRER: Where is the artillery division now? Where does he have it?

ZEITZLER: It's now marching from Zhitomir downward toward Kazatin, where the 168th [Infantry Division] is arriving and where some units of the 25th Panzer [Division] are still located. It's supposed to protect this Kazatin connection.

THE FÜHRER: We should know how many forces he actually has here. Up there it looked very threatening for a while, and suddenly he's totally paralyzed.

ZEITZLER: My Führer, I think this is the winter offensive here.

THE FÜHRER: That's correct. But, nevertheless, how many totally new armies does he have here now? He has his old forces again.

ZEITZLER: He's replenished nine tank corps. He's had them there for weeks.

THE FÜHRER: That is correct. But those are still his old troops. He doesn't have anything new. Now, I don't understand one thing. The tanks alone aren't useful to him in this tank corps. They always claim that so many people are killed in the tanks—some of them are burned in there, and some are shot.

ZEITZLER: It's probably similar to the situation here. So far we haven't been terribly concerned about the tank crews. We will always have enough crew members.

THE FÜHRER: I'll think about it again tonight.

ZEITZLER: Yes, Sir. I would just be grateful if a decision were made, because every day counts.

THE FÜHRER: Well, this decision here is fine.[919]

ZEITZLER: May I send that out? At least it helps a bit.

THE FÜHRER: You can send it out. He will have one division free then. But to give up this thing—Zeitzler, we can talk big now and say that it is lost anyway. But when the time comes and it's actually lost, then Herr Manstein won't bear any responsibility at all. We will bear it.

ZEITZLER: That's clear.

THE FÜHRER: Then the difficult hours will come in which a major crisis will appear, with the consequence that this will immediately extend over to Turkey. ... are at stake there. On February 15 they want to blackmail Turkey into joining them.[920] If a crisis appears in the Crimea, they will do the propaganda then. Herr Manstein doesn't bear any responsibility; he says that politics should do that.

ZEITZLER: Yes, Sir. And it will be very difficult. First, because we can save very little—

THE FÜHRER: We can't save anything. The results are catastrophic. They will be catastrophic in Romania ... here's a major position. As long as we are standing here and here, and as long as we have the bridgeheads, an airfield installation here[921] is an endangered thing.

ZEITZLER: Yes, Sir. But if we can't do anything up here and allow it to continue, the same thing will result, and then we'll also have to deal with all the First [Panzer] Army developments.

THE FÜHRER: Be careful, because we've already experienced cases like this, where it was said that it couldn't be repaired. Then afterward it suddenly turned out that it had all stopped for good.

ZEITZLER: It's just that it's a very deadly place for us—so close.

THE FÜHRER: I agree completely. I haven't released the 4th Mountain Division for nothing. But it hasn't yet been proven that he has a totally new army now; they are refreshed forces. If we say that the winter battle has now started—it's the continuation of his battle. There's no difference.[922]

ZEITZLER: That's why I haven't called it the winter battle yet.

THE FÜHRER: He doesn't want to give us time to refresh ourselves, so he's continuing to fight. That's the whole thing. But you've seen here that he does get exhausted sometimes. He exhausted himself here and gradually became paralyzed.[923]

ZEITZLER: There's just the suspicion that he might have done that on purpose in order to continue up there.

THE FÜHRER: No, I don't think so.

ZEITZLER: He actually made it quite easy for us. He didn't advance any further here.

THE FÜHRER: Because he can't anymore. We must not assume that this is some ancient giant who becomes stronger every time he falls down to earth.

ZEITZLER: He's done that for so many months in a row.

THE FÜHRER: He has to run out of steam at some point. I read this report. In my view, the critical thing is that these troops really don't have good morale anymore. That's the decisive thing.

ZEITZLER: That's why I always hand in the reports. Because I have to expect such things.

THE FÜHRER: I've always been the one to point that out. I've also spoken here with the gentlemen from the Panzer forces. They say that the infantry doesn't fight at all. It's quite varied. There are divisions that fight well, and nothing happens there. If someone tells me that it's impossible to have any influence on the morale of the infantry—Zeitzler, I will tell you something. I am someone who has personally built up and led what is perhaps the biggest organization in the world, and who still leads it today. During this time I've learned that people send me news from local groups: Social Democracy is unbeatable here. Or: Communism can't be defeated at all here. It's absolutely impossible—we can't get it away from here. But that shows that it was always the commander. If this were a general judgment, then it would be acceptable. If someone tells me that attempting to influence the morale of the infantry has no value at all—I can only say that I once heard a major speak, and I said to myself, "This speech to the troops is useless." I listened umpteen times and it makes no sense. Of course, if an officer tells me that it's simply useless for this man, I can only say, "This proves that your influence has had no value. Because next door I put another team, and the people behave well under their commander. It was your influence, and you must go."

ZEITZLER: Yes, Sir. The troops resemble the commander.

THE FÜHRER: Always, fundamentally.

ZEITZLER: And I'm certain that when there are bad troops the commanders are either dead or are bad commanders.

THE FÜHRER: If they're dead, an even worse commander has come. That's very clear. [—] If that man gets exhausted here, too, and we can do this with these means, then we would tear out our hair afterward. Because it's not that the case is closed if we do this, but if we can turn the thing around here—those units here Manstein is fantasizing about. He knows perfectly well that they will attack here. He says that they might attack frontally, and then they will wear themselves out. He doesn't accept that; he's fantasizing to relieve his soul. Unfortunately, I can't do that. I see the hour coming when this action will develop into a crisis as well and will then affect this mission. Those are decisions. If we always say that it will be fought through successfully—the successful fight, in my eyes, consists today in being able to stop the thing somewhere.

ZEITZLER: That's quite clear. If we can stop it, it'll be a victory in our eyes. But we can't beat him.

THE FÜHRER: It's impossible to expect more right now. But we must not forget, either, that last winter we were in a tragic situation. Nevertheless, we advanced so far by May that we almost believed that we could attack ourselves, and in July we finally did attack.

ZEITZLER: It's just that the tension in the line is so very high. If we get this in order a bit and something new appears, we'll be under pressure again.

THE FÜHRER: When the troops have dug in and built themselves in, the psychological moment will also return. We just have to take away the commanders from the dreadful divisions as quickly as possible. We have to do that. I've studied the report and can only say that it clearly shows that there are divisions here that are terrible. But if a commander says that any influence on the people is useless, I can only say: your influence is useless. You don't have the power to affect that. He speaks the absolute truth. But it only means that he sees it from his perspective. *His* influence has failed entirely. I know that, too. During the four-year war [Great War] I got to know regimental commanders whose influence was ridiculous because no one took them seriously. We had other regimental commanders who—in the worst situations—got things in order again in the shortest time and stabilized the troops. It mostly depends on the man. In the units that are close to me, I know perfectly well if the unit has a good commander or not. Because you can see it in the unit itself, like in a mirror. Or I think of my local groups. Earlier I had Gaus at each election, where I knew exactly that when the evening of election day arrives, there will be a success. Why? I musn't say here, "Yes, it was Franken, or it was Cologne—because Cologne was black-red Cologne"—or East Prussia. What does East Prussia mean? It was totally reactionary, and turned away from us. Or Mecklenburg or Thüringia. Thüringia was bright red. But in this one case I had Koch, and in the other case I had Sauckel, and Ley.[924] It was those men. In other places I didn't have such intelligent men, unfortunately, and it was bad there. I knew for certain that the good Gaus had the good Gauleiters. It's still the same today. Recently I had a failure in Kassel. I can feel free to speak about it. The man, of course, will be dismissed. He'll be dismissed and removed. He wasn't up to his assignment.[925] We must not say, "Yes, it's easy for you in Berlin and Hamburg." On the contrary, in Hamburg it's even more difficult. But there's a tough man there who can't be broken by anything,[926] while the man in Kassel just collapsed. He wasn't up to this challenge. The commander basically reflects the condition of the troops, or the condition of the troops reflects the condition of the commander. Now, it can often be catastrophic as well. A good commander arrives there, falls, the next one comes, also falls, another comes, he also falls. Each of those falls affects the troops, of course. If the troops especially love a commander… When a good commander falls, it always has a worse effect than when a terrible one falls. That's the old experience. And it could be. But one thing's quite certain: If the troops are constantly in a bad state, it's always connected to the commander. [—] It's very easy to say things. We experienced it once, Zeitzler. We pulled back from an action to a short line. Unfortunately, we couldn't hold this short line. We could certainly have held it with better mobility and greater unselfishness on the part of the units. Then something could have been saved. We have a classic case. The whole Nevel' catastrophe up there is the fault of the egotism of the two army group commanders, who, as little egotists, just didn't want to advance.[927] Now we have to hold the bigger line. Now it's working and it has to work. [—] I see the consequences here. They are worldwide consequences.

ZEITZLER: Also for the troops and the position overall.

THE FÜHRER: It's catastrophic for the troops. We're obliged, if it's even possible, to defend this second Stalingrad[928]—if it can be done somehow. We can't just dismiss it coldly, because in this case it doesn't affect the army of Field Marshal v. Manstein. We can't do that; instead, we have to consider that the men here are lost. Number two. We could say: higher purposes. Maybe we could reach a higher purpose without it. But something else could happen. It could be that Turkey steps in. Romania depends on the national leader. If he loses his army here—.[929] You must read the letters he wrote me.

ZEITZLER: No, my only reason is this: the disaster might get even bigger. That's my only reason.

THE FÜHRER: Yes, we'll have to see. I've already considered whether or not we can risk it to throw the 16th [Panzer Division] down there.

ZEITZLER: Yesterday I fought a lot of internal battles with myself. Yesterday evening I also said that maybe we should think about bringing the 16th down here.[930]

THE FÜHRER: Zeitzler, we have to tell ourselves one thing. This decision is not as difficult as the decision about the Crimea. If we go there, the Crimea will be lost. We have to think a great deal about whether we shouldn't, under the certain conditions, take the 16th after all. We would then take the 4th [Mountain Division] up here and one division up here and the 16th. That's three units—until the other one gets mobile, at the worst.

ZEITZLER: At the moment we could do without it. But longer term it will get difficult up there. Longer term, we can only get this back into order afterward if we take back this corner up there. It was this bad in St. Petersburg, in my view.

THE FÜHRER: Not that bad. If I withdraw a bit there and save a few divisions, it's not as bad as this here. This here is worse and has the worst effects. Up there, if I were forced to withdraw a bit to save one division—

ZEITZLER: No, not so much that, but if we get the big solution.[931]

THE FÜHRER: Yes, that would be uncomfortable because of the Finns, but still not as bad as down there. I consider the loss of the Crimea the worst thing. It has the worst effects on Turkey. The Finns can't back out; in the end they will have to defend themselves. [—] With the 16th Panzer [Division]—I don't know. Can we take the map of Army Group Center once more? Could we keep the Panther detachment up here and add a few Panzer VIs again instead?

ZEITZLER: I have the following minor measures up my sleeve. First, one assault gun detachment will be in the General Government [Poland] tomorrow. We can give it to Manstein. Second, I put all the Tiger reserves for the Eastern front into the 503rd Tiger Detachment, which is here in the front near Kirovograd. I told Manstein that he should relocate the personnel from this detachment—which has one Tiger—up there, and bring in here the 45 Tigers that I'll get. Then we'll have a complete Tiger detachment up there. Second, the Panther detachment will arrive ... Finally, we could put that Panther detachment in there as well. The 23rd [Panzer Division] is here.

THE FÜHRER: We should put the 23rd in here, so that nothing can happen here.

ZEITZLER: With the Tiger detachment. Then we would have a detachment there.

THE FÜHRER: That would work better.

ZEITZLER: Because if I hadn't kept the Tigers together, but spread them out along the front, every unit would have received two or three, so they wouldn't be there either. So we'd have a good Tiger detachment there.

THE FÜHRER: In principle, he should be able to manage the action up here with the units he has here.

ZEITZLER: My Führer, I also believe that it'll work to some degree. I'm only concerned about the future.

THE FÜHRER: He'll get two divisions here.

ZEITZLER: Actually, I still have the feeling—even though it is just a feeling—that the heavier one will come to the northwest. But I can't prove it.

THE FÜHRER: First he'll try to break off Vitebsk to get the major highway and the railway junction.[932]

ZEITZLER: The main direction of the push will then be northwest, and then he'll start up there.

THE FÜHRER: Then it'll go up here. That's certain. But still, up here.

ZEITZLER: Now, we have very few mobile units here, of course. We can see it with the 32nd [Infantry Division]. They wanted to have it up there by January 10. That would be a mobile unit. If only it had arrived earlier!

THE FÜHRER: But if we have the 16th [Panzer Division] here, it won't come around either. We couldn't do anything more here, other than concentrating assault guns and trucking in infantry. Real armored divisions can't do anything in that terrain either.

ZEITZLER: Right now it's so dangerous down there that they would be very welcome down there, of course.

THE FÜHRER: So a "victorious penetration" down there. We must not get intoxicated by phrases.

ZEITZLER: No, it'll be good if we can get it to stop.

THE FÜHRER: There is no victorious penetration. The most we can achieve down there is to stop the thing. If we manage that, a lot will have been won. We can't expect anything more. How's the condition of the 16th right now?

ZEITZLER: In general it's still adequate.

THE FÜHRER: We should give them assault guns again.

ZEITZLER: It has 26 plus 18 or 19—so 46.

THE FÜHRER: If an assault gun detachment were to come, we might have to give it to them.

ZEITZLER: Yes, Sir. We can add the assault gun detachment and maybe the Tiger detachment as well.

THE FÜHRER: Just a minute! Shouldn't we rather do it this way? We give those assault guns to them—they can certainly provide crews for them—and then take the next assault guns for the detachment.

ZEITZLER: I didn't quite understand that.

THE FÜHRER: They have a complete detachment now. I mean that we don't deploy this detachment, but only the materiel—we give those 30 assault guns to the 16th [Panzer division] and hold back the crew and give the next thirty to those in the Homeland.

ZEITZLER: That would be a pity. They are already in the General Government [Poland]. They are trained, and have fired with them.

THE FÜHRER: That doesn't matter. They will still get the next ones.

ZEITZLER: Then it would be better to scratch together assault guns, because it's a complete, balanced detachment.

THE FÜHRER: But we can't get anything from Germany that fast. That's in the General Government. Then maybe we could do it this way, so that we give them Panzer IVs.

ZEITZLER: Because the next assault gun detachment with the skeleton, with the crew, is already in the Homeland. That's why those crews would actually become superfluous then.

THE FÜHRER: Then we'll have to see if can still add 30 Panzer IVs to them. The question is about the Panther detachment—if we should also take them away from up there.

ZEITZLER: I've now given thirty of those assault guns to Army Group A. [Army Group] South will get thirty in the next few days. So … there anyway. Then the 60th Panzer Grenadier Division will get sixteen. It's down there with the First Panzer Army around Krivoi Rog. Then another 30 assault guns will go to [Army Group] South as materiel reserves. We could maybe add them to the 16th Panzer [Division] when we get them down, because they will arrive here between January 1 and 2. We could give those to [Army Group] South then—not to stop and not to issue, but we could add them to the 16th Panzer. Then we'd have brought them up to the mark. Because the 16th Panzer won't arrive any earlier. Then the assault gun detachment arrives. Those are the 45 with the Tiger detachment, and these are the 76 of the 23rd Panzer Division.

THE FÜHRER: And with the Panther detachment here.

ZEITZLER: I don't have too much confidence in the Panther detachment by itself.

THE FÜHRER: Can they even man the Panther detachment themselves? Is there a division there that already has Panthers?

ZEITZLER: No.

THE FÜHRER: Not one?

ZEITZLER: No, they have little experience with them.

THE FÜHRER: Then we must either add the Panther detachment to a division up there or put it in here.

ZEITZLER: We could do the following: we leave the Panther detachment with the 16th Panzer and, in exchange, give the assault gun detachment from the General Government to [Army Group] Center.

THE FÜHRER: We could also do that.

ZEITZLER: That would give it more than the Panther detachment, which it can't handle. And up in that terrain assault gun detachments would certainly be good. If it gets a brand new, good assault gun detachment, it might be better than the Panther detachment. I can arrange that tonight still.

THE FÜHRER: Yes. The first part is already up there. But those are the Panthers.

ZEITZLER: The assault gun detachment is in the General Government.

THE FÜHRER: How will you pull the 16th down?

ZEITZLER: We can take it via Bobruisk–Minsk. There's a good rail line there, so we'll get it around there.

THE FÜHRER: How long will it take?

ZEITZLER: Not too long. Because most of our units that go south go around Königsberg anyway, to take advantage of this stretch. It will be good, of course, when the decision is made—as soon as possible.

THE FÜHRER: The 16th Panzer [Division] comes here, and will be taken back only to this small blocking position.

ZEITZLER: Yes, Sir. The 16th Panzer is coming down and the assault gun detachment is moving up.

THE FÜHRER: Yes. And then we'll see what we ... scratch together in the way of mobile things. Maybe we can still find something or other. Then we'll take this small regimental group, or whatever it is.

ZEITZLER: That's the *Langemarck* [Division][933] The first train will depart from there tonight.

THE FÜHRER: Where are we going to put that one in?

ZEITZLER: Initially, I've planned it for down there, in the direction of Berdichev, so it will join the *Leibstandarte* [SS Panzer Grenadier Division] or some other SS unit.

THE FÜHRER: If the 4th [Panzer Division] is gone from down there now, do you think that's enough? He will get an assault gun detachment.

ZEITZLER: I think we'll have to manage with that at first. On our orders, they've now established a mobile unit here with the assault gun detachment and two motorized battalions. So they have a unit like I suggested back then—a kind of improvised panzer division. I think it would be good if we would add a unit like *Langemarck*, which is new, to some SS unit, instead of sending it on alone.

THE FÜHRER: That would be better, of course. On the other hand, he'll get into a terrible mess.

DARGES: General, the *Reich* [SS Panzer Grenadier] Division is particularly short of supply troops, and could take this over immediately.

THE FÜHRER: Right, but the unit will get into a terrible mess.

DARGES: But they're good commanders.

THE FÜHRER: Has the unit fought yet?

DARGES: No, I think only a few of the core staff have.

ZEITZLER: We can't eliminate the possibility that he might get into a mess right off the train.

THE FÜHRER: That's why I ask if it might not be better to put a unit like that somewhere where it won't be hit so hard at first.

ZEITZLER: I'd like to think about it again. We don't need to decide until tomorrow or the day after.

THE FÜHRER: Yes, we still have a couple of days' time.

DARGES: I should remind you that some of the replacements are not trained with the 1st IG [infantry gun] and MG [machine gun].

THE FÜHRER: In the report it says that the people are trained with the infantry gun. What a fiasco.

ZEITZLER: I'd like to speak about it with Fromm[934] again. Reports have now arrived saying that they're not trained with the machine guns.

THE FÜHRER: That's absolutely impossible. They're not trained with the 1st infantry gun.

ZEITZLER: There are individual positive points, also with ammunition. I will check that. I have another copy of the report here.

THE FÜHRER: Now it's very easy to make such a big decision. Manstein will make it, because he'll reject the other thing right from the outset. If he were responsible for the Crimea himself, he wouldn't make the decision so easily. *End: 10:46 p.m.*

* * * * *

MEETING OF THE FÜHRER WITH GENERAL JODL AND, JOINING LATER, GENERAL ZEITZLER, DECEMBER 28, 1943[935]

Also present:

> *Field Marshal Keitel*   *Major Borgmann*
> *Lieutenant General Schmundt*   *Sturmbannführer Darges*

Beginning: 11:19 p.m.

The East

THE FÜHRER: Read this here,[936] Jodl. (*Presentation.*) No one reported that. I don't know where he came up with this. Two bridgeheads here? The question was rather if we would take one or the other. [—] To that I must say that it's not certain, of course, that we can't deflect the strike. It has been deflected once already. We recently deflected two divisions, which have now been thoroughly thrown back. What does "not to be deflected" mean? That assumes we credit him with some strength that we don't credit him with anywhere else. [—] The consequences he sees from that are as follows: he hopes that he can free up five divisions from there if he carries out the big action *here*. Because one thing is clear: some of the forces must move down here immediately. He assumes that he'll free up forces at the Dnieper [River] bend, and says, "We won't be able to bring them into the area around Berdichev so quickly this way." [—] He doesn't need to take them up there; it's not necessary. [—] "Within the next few weeks, the decision about the winter campaign in Army Group South's sector must be made, and therefore we must find it. We especially hope"—what does "hope" mean?—"... via Kirovograd or Krivoi Rog, to break through to the west at the lower Dnieper [River],[937] and that this will completely exhaust his troops." [—] How does he come up with the claim that he will get completely exhausted because of this combination of forces? He could also say here [Nikopol'] that he would get "completely exhausted." It's just juggling ... with words. Now, the first consequence is, of course—I've given the permission to go back here, so the 4th [Mountain] Division will go up here, and then the 16th [Panzer Division] should come down.

JODL: There he means the Kamenka position.

THE FÜHRER: This continues to the south.

JODL: He means this position [east of Kirovograd]; it continues further to the west of Kamenka.

THE FÜHRER: This position means the abandonment of the bridgehead here [Nikopol']. That's why I've thought again about this problem, and I wonder if we can keep a smaller bridgehead here—here's another smaller bridgehead—to force the enemy to leave forces here as well. Now I think, though, that this position doesn't go in here [east of Kirovograd], but here [Krivoi Rog], so we can't hold this [Nikopol'] anymore either. That would mean that Nikopol' and Krivoi Rog are lost.[938] He himself estimates that five to six divisions are necessary here [west of Kirovograd] to "operationally complete" the thing. He has now received three divisions.

JODL: It all depends on the assessment of the danger here. He judges that favorably because right now the enemy isn't pushing too much here, either. He obviously judges that [east of Kirovograd] favorably, and judges [Krivoi Rog and Nikopol'] very sharply.

THE FÜHRER: Here's Vinnitsa. That's clear.

JODL: Everything depends on that.

THE FÜHRER: But he can't do it with this. [—] Now read through the telegram. No, he's holding onto three divisions that he could have taken out. The 4th [Mountain] Division is better than any division he might take out there. The 16th [Panzer Division], which he's taking down from up there, is better, and he's pulling the 17th [Panzer Division] up himself. We just need to take his earlier prophecies, where he said back then that in order to take care of this thing here completely he needed five panzer divisions and three infantry divisions. He has received them.

BORGMANN: My Führer, General Zeitzler would like to speak with you. (*Telephone call with General Zeitzler.*)

ZEITZLER: My Führer, I have to call again. Manstein just called to ask what we can do with regard to his telegram.[939]

THE FÜHRER: I'm in a meeting with General Jodl here right now. The consequences he points at are, of course, all wishful thinking ... I first want to finish talking to General Jodl here. I may call you again later. Or would you like to come over here?

ZEITZLER: Yes, indeed, my Führer. I can come over.

THE FÜHRER: Maybe you should come over again.

(ZEITZLER: Yes, Sir.)

Thank you. (*End of the telephone call.*) Maybe Scherff can come over as well, if he's still up.

BORGMANN: He's ill, but I will ask again.

THE FÜHRER: Then leave him alone. We don't want to wake him up then.

JODL: He reports here: 47 rifle divisions and nine tank corps. So that would support the idea that the major strike will happen here. I admit that. And the fact that he's not going after the Crimea anymore right now is proof that he's waiting for a time when it will be easier for him than it is now.

THE FÜHRER: It'll be easier for him as soon as we're away from here. So he can do that as well. He needs a few divisions here. If he has no danger here anymore, then how many forces does he need here? ... When we're gone from here, he'll dominate us here. The conditions are very easy here, if he's not intending to cut all this off, as Manstein supposes here. That's very clear. The issue is that he can't force a decision in an operational sense anyway. He can't do it. He can't block it off somewhere. He can't do anything except deflect him somewhere. He can't do any more than that at the moment.

JODL: I don't think so either, because the forces that are coming out of here—

THE FÜHRER: He can't operate with those.

JODL:—are no longer in the condition they were last winter.

THE FÜHRER: That's ridiculous.

JODL: They've all been through extremely difficult times already.

THE FÜHRER: Here's a single division—the panzer division—that we're bringing out, and maybe the 3rd Mountain Division as well. Everything else is a fantasy.

JODL: Probably nothing much can be done with the others.

THE FÜHRER: The 4th Mountain Division has more value than three divisions from here because, first, it's a good division, and second, it's complete, while those are not.

JODL: It's quite certain that he still has to throw something up here. The 4th has already been ordered, though.

THE FÜHRER: The first trains of the 4th [Mountain Division] will roll up today.

JODL: And he'll also bring the 16th [Panzer Division] here.

THE FÜHRER: He wants to put the 17th [Panzer Division] in up above. It will also get tanks, I believe.

JODL: And the artillery division.

THE FÜHRER: The artillery division is also here. [—] "Rather, we hope"— that is nothing—"that the enemy will try to break through between Cherkassy and Kirovograd ... and will completely exhaust his forces." [—] What does "completely exhaust" mean? He doesn't have to break through there. He can break through here [Krivoi Rog-Nikopol' region] just as well as up there. That's no proof at all. Down here is this bridge, which goes over there. It might be important that we hold this lower bridgehead. As long as we have a crossing, the enemy isn't quite certain he can attack here. When the last bridgehead is gone, then [—] Another connection with General Zeitzler. [—] It's very clear that he's worried about Vinnitsa now. Here are his quarters.

JODL: That's the main railway line. That's already the last major line.

THE FÜHRER: Also via Zhmerinka.[940]

JODL: Zhmerinka is the main junction.

THE FÜHRER: "Operation"—I hate pompous expressions. This is no operation. It's just a pompous expression.

JODL: In short, he doesn't believe he can hold with the forces here [east of Kirovograd] . He needs more forces, and he doesn't know where to get them. So he wants to get them by shortening the line down there [Krivoi Rog-Nikopol'-Crimea].

THE FÜHRER: So that'll get him three divisions: one from here, one from here, one from [Army Group] Center. And another one, the 17th [Panzer], he's pulling away from here. That's four divisions. In his last telegram he demanded five divisions, and he couldn't have expected to get that division and the 16th [Panzer Division] at all. This one is worth more than the others.

JODL: It won't change much anyway. He's already received four divisions. The operational danger for the entire wing remains the same. It doesn't matter if we cut this off or not and pull in the bridgehead. He's always echeloned in front to the degree that he cuts the connection when he breaks through. We should go up from Odessa when he—but that can't be the reason. It's all about freeing up forces. We have to admit that he needs more there than he has now.

THE FÜHRER: An offensive clearance here is impossible. He can't do that anymore because he can't operate with these forces. It's ridiculous. It's just a phrase to cover himself again. [—] Then Zeitzler should bring the map that shows where the positions are marked. [—] He can't do anything with that anyway—maybe at most with the one or the other panzer division. Then he can pull one out here himself. He'll get the forces that he practically ordered himself—except with the difference that these forces are better than those he would have gotten out of here.

JODL: The question is if one of the Romanian divisions has been readied enough in the meantime—

THE FÜHRER: —to put it here? I've always wanted to reinforce this here. I can hold the Crimea as long as there's at least one bridgehead here. Those, I think, are not good?

JODL: Those two are not good. They're just the ones that he[941] is drawing up at home.

THE FÜHRER: He won't give away the ones from home. He's always looking at the Hungarians. It's idiotic, but [—] They are too close here, too. They also lose their nerve here. It would be good if he would move his headquarters away from here.

JODL: But he has to hold this railway junction, otherwise it'll get bad.

THE FÜHRER: That's the 4th [Mountain] Division. We can take it in first, and the 16th [Panzer Division] here, and he has to make a strike in here with the 16th, the *Leibstandarte*, and the 1st Panzer Division. But to claim that those are apparently 47 totally fresh divisions that can't be stopped anymore—here they can be stopped. Those are all bad units, but these are completely fresh ones.[942] It's all just reporting for his own purposes. He really has drawn everything in with unparalleled egotism. The pulling out of the 16th Panzer Grenadier Division, which should have gone here, caused the whole thing to collapse here. Otherwise the front would be here today. He can't do anything, especially not with those divisions. It's ridiculous to launch these divisions here offensively. He can't carry out an operation anyway. His hope that he'll be able to attack here as well with these forces—because the enemy will be worn out then—is all just talk. [—] "Likewise, bringing in additional forces from the West can't be avoided."

JODL: Something should be freed up here, too.

THE FÜHRER: If this can be done, something will be freed up.

JODL: The second concentration is just the same here. He's done only the first stage here, and hopes that that way forces will be pulled out.

THE FÜHRER: Here he's fortunate. He even hopes that he'll pull these forces in here, because he will "wear himself out with frontal attacks." He won't wear himself out with frontal attacks; rather, I'm worried that he'll break through here with the last remnants. [—] We also don't have a good picture of where the artillery division is.

BORGMANN: It was marked in the area around Kazatin.

JODL: There was a breakthrough from the rear just now. Back behind it there was a penetration like this today.

THE FÜHRER: We have to wait and see if the penetration is really that bad. He's just driving around with tanks there, where there isn't anything. Too bad this is only a 16-ton bridge, which also has to be retracted all the time, of course. [—] Here the 25th Panzer Division was an absolute failure from the very first day. It was the best equipped, with the best materiel.[943]

JODL: It also had very good people at the beginning.

THE FÜHRER: Dietrich told me that that division had vehicle materiel, of course! He says, "If only we had that! We have run-down vehicles, and there everything came brand new from the factory." [—] But here the guilty one is without doubt the divisional commander. He was incapable of making anything out of this division. [—] So we can't take away anything from here. On the contrary. They need it up there because the same crisis is there. [—] The 147th Reserve Division is a training unit from the Reserve Army? [—] And the 454th [Training Division]?

JODL: That's normal security—two training divisions put in there, the 143rd and ... three training regiments.

THE FÜHRER: Where are they, approximately?

JODL: As far as I know, they're being put in as continuous replacements for this division here.

THE FÜHRER: Would it be possible to take that one at a critical moment?

JODL: We could certainly take the staffs. [—] Then there are still two divisions being formed in the General Government.

THE FÜHRER: How do they look?

JODL: I can't tell. It's not my affair because Zeitzler is building them up.[944]

THE FÜHRER: If we were convinced that nothing would happen in the West for another 6 or 8 weeks, I'd say we should give those to the West and bring two divisions over from there.

JODL: Now only the young ones are there: the 9th SS and 10th SS [Panzer Grenadier Divisions].

THE FÜHRER: I can't give those away. Those are panzer units that he's forming in the rear.

JODL: There aren't any other divisions except for the 22nd wave,[945] which won't be ready until February. They don't have their weapons yet. They're up to 11,000 men now.

THE FÜHRER: And from the Balkans, if we take two there?

JODL: Certainly. They must give up two right away.

THE FÜHRER: They must give them to Rome.

JODL: They must send them to Italy so that the 90th [Infantry Division] and the *Hermann Göring* [Parachute Panzer Division] can come out.[946]

THE FÜHRER: And to stop that for the time being? To take two over here—the two training or reserve divisions?

JODL: We would have to do without one of them. We'd have to take away the 371st [Infantry Division]. That's a normal, reconstituted Stalingrad division, which has only engaged in these gang battles in its new composition. Otherwise it's complete.

BORGMANN: Some units of the 147th Reserve Division are deployed for railway protection and some are intended for new formations. We still need to find out what's happening with the others. I'll be notified immediately.

THE FÜHRER: We can't take them away from the railway protection either. So nothing will result from this action—that's why he won't get a unit anymore. That one won't come a day earlier. That just means the other one will get the additional forces free. [—] Now Manstein says he can't get them around that fast. But he doesn't need to go around there. He just needs to send them up here. He can take divisions out here. He only needs to relocate here and push in here. This is dangerous anyway, and makes me more uncomfortable than that whole thing there. The first thing is that I think he must relocate his headquarters away from here immediately—we can't get any reasonable decision under such pressure—unless the attack by the 1st Panzer Division breaks through.

JODL: This block formation presents the danger that this free space might fill up again, so that one day there could be pressure to the southwest.

THE FÜHRER: Where is the Luftwaffe, anyway? It doesn't appear much anymore.

JODL: The paratroopers?

THE FÜHRER: Yes, the paratroopers.

JODL: The 2nd Parachute Division is in there. The 9th is probably still quite good, next to the 4th Mountain Division

THE FÜHRER: The 9th? No, it's not good. [—] And this is the 3rd [Mountain Division] here?

JODL: The 97th Jäger [Light Infantry] Division.

THE FÜHRER: I believe that one is good. It's always been good. The 3rd Mountain Division and the 97th Jäger Division are good. The 9th, I believe, is bad. [—] So essentially he could have pulled only the 3rd Mountain Division from here, and it's not better than the 4th [Mountain Division], but significantly weaker. So he recently requested five to six divisions here. He has one division here, through the thing we agreed to in principle—that's one of these five or six—one division here and the other one there. That's three, while the upper ... In addition to that he's pulling out the 17th

[Panzer Division], so he's really getting four divisions out. He recently requested eight divisions. He's received three infantry divisions and five panzer divisions. So he can say that he had to give up the one. But in exchange he received another infantry division—the parachute division. So he really has received eight divisions. That fits in a barrel. He was very impressed, of course, by the unlucky fellow, Hoth,[947] outside Kiev. We learn about this bit by bit, how devastatingly this man has worked. It has been a source of defeatism of the worst kind. There are amazing things that gradually come out. The people are just now finding the courage to report this. [—] His quarters are very unfavorable here in this situation. He's now sitting right near the focal point. His quarters would be better somewhere else. It would be further away there, of course, but it would be better. Vinnitsa is certainly an unfavorable place for him. [—] But bringing in the infantry divisions from here doesn't go any faster, either. It doesn't matter. It always takes the same amount of time. What he's getting up here now he'll get up anyway. But he speaks of the "counter operation." He should not speak of a "counter operation," but call it by the right name: running away. [—] Then this thing won't work either, and he'll come back to here instead.

(JODL: Probably.)

Above all he should not speak of a "counter operation."

JODL: He's taking only that sector because with the time—

THE FÜHRER: Here he'll wear himself out in a frontal attack! What does "wear himself out in a frontal attack" mean? Then this won't play a role anymore. At least here I will definitely contain the forces. In the other case it's not certain if I can contain them. If he says he can't bring them around as fast as the other, then that's the question. All the forces he has in the rear will be brought around quickly if nothing is happening here anymore. [—] Those are just calculated tall tales. I can't call it anything else.

JODL: The worst was this action—this narrow piece, which had to be held here. Now we have this and this.

THE FÜHRER: And that there. That's also a characteristic example: We could have held it if he hadn't pulled the 16th Panzer Grenadier Division out back then—and directed it around, with this turning back and tearing off here. Then one division was missing here. That wasn't necessary. The 13th Panzer Division could have been pulled out earlier. Then we could have held the thing. It was also wrong that the line ... We ran into a theoretically improved line. Had we secured this here and had we ... something ... a sector, which is the last one, which must be held at all cost. Because if we go out there, it will be a catastrophe. Here we still have the possibility of going back into this one. [—] Here it's exactly the same. They go into a sector that absolutely must be held, and if they slide back further, this [Krivoi

Rog-Nikopol'] can't be held any longer either, and the whole thing collapses. [—] Back then he had five panzer divisions: the 1st, the 24th, the 25th, the *Leibstandarte* and—what's the fifth? So: the 1st, the 14th, the 25th, the 24th, and the SS. [—] The 14th was up here.

JODL: That's the 16th. [—] Here's the 14th.

THE FÜHRER: The 14th came afterward?

BORGMANN: I don't know that for certain, my Führer.

THE FÜHRER: Yes, it did.

JODL: The 14th came from the West.

THE FÜHRER: Yes, from the West. He just received the 1st Panzer Division from the Balkans, the 14th from the West, the 25th from the West, the 24th from Italy and the SS. So five panzer divisions[948] and three infantry divisions plus one parachute division. So now he has received more than he originally asked for. Back then he asked for eight divisions. Supposedly he could manage the thing with them. He has received nine divisions—all strong, like no others on the entire front. Now he's demanding five to six divisions. He can take one out here right now. He'll get one from here—that's the 4th Mountain Division—he will get the 16th Panzer Division from up there, and he will take the 17th [Panzer Division] from here; I can count these two for at least two divisions here. He acts as if hasn't gotten anything. His ratio of forces is still better than anywhere else on the front. The fact that some of his troops are very demoralized is related to the spirit that they absorb from above.[949] [—] It's catastrophic here. We can see that we were unable to hold this line simply because we didn't do the necessary shifting. Now we have to hold a line like this. These continual bulges are double, of course; they are also present for the enemy. But he speaks of "frontal attacks." He can't claim that at all. If he goes around here and over there, he must give up forces right away. Then this here can't be held anymore either. If this is taken back, then this can't be held any longer.

BORGMANN: The 14th [Panzer Division] came from the West and the 24th [Panzer Division] from Italy, at the end of July.[950]

THE FÜHRER: They brought at least 700 tanks along. The *Leibstandarte* brought 250, the 25th Panzer Division brought about 200 as well, the 24th—

BORGMANN: Also about 150. It was in northern Italy with us in that area.

THE FÜHRER: And the 1st Panzer Division?

JODL: It had less.

THE FÜHRER: Just over 100. And the 14th [Panzer Division]?

JODL: It didn't have any more than that either.

THE FÜHRER: It had more than 150. The others were all quite full.

BORGMANN: Altogether it's about 850.

THE FÜHRER: What he's received since then is a multiple of that—at least 400 to 500 tanks.

BORGMANN: About 100 a month. So 3 to 4 months.

THE FÜHRER: Many more came here. We also have to count assault guns. He's received a number of assault gun detachments. A Tiger detachment has also been brought in. In that time he's received well over 1,500 tanks.

BORGMANN: This arrived today at 11:10 p.m.

THE FÜHRER: That's probably one day later?

BORGMANN: Just a short while ago.

THE FÜHRER: Yes, he's in Vinnitsa and is worried here. He must get away quickly with his quarters.[951] It's useless. He can't be here, unfortunately. The right place would almost even be Chernovitsy. Or possibly L'vov [Lemberg] would be even better, unless the 1st Panzer Division's strike breaks through here. We actually should think that.

(*General Zeitzler arrives.*)

Zeitzler, first I would like to get two things clear. Field Marshal General v. Manstein has twice made demands. He made one demand several weeks ago, for five panzer divisions and three infantry divisions—thus eight divisions. That was his request at the time.

ZEITZLER: I will find out the exact number again.

THE FÜHRER: Five panzer divisions and three infantry divisions. He has received five panzer divisions—the five best ones we still had, some of them just completed—three infantry divisions and an additional parachute division. So he has received nine divisions. No other front sector has received as much as Field Marshal v. Manstein has received, although his ratio of forces is not worse than anywhere else. It's because of his frame of mind that not only is there no positive mood but there's a totally negative mood coming from his headquarters—especially very negative here, where Hoth was taken away.[952] It was particularly blatant here. So here he has received what he ordered before. Now, the day before yesterday we agreed to this withdrawal here, in order to free up five to six divisions, as he said. But he didn't expect more himself. He has this one here, and of these units—except the 3rd Mountain Division—none is of the same quality as the 4th Mountain Division. He has received the 4th Mountain Division. He'll get the 16th Panzer Division from up above [Army Group Center]. He has no panzer unit of this quality here. He's freeing up one division here himself, so he can take the best one out anyway. That's three, including two first-class units, which he would not get otherwise. He would never have gotten them from the withdrawal. Three first-class units—he can take one away here, plus he is also pulling out the 17th Panzer Division here and the 4th Panzer Division here—of which two are of a quality he couldn't have expected at all. But he's acting as if he has been allowed nothing at all. He has absolutely received what he requested. The opinion that he would bring that up here quickly or this down here is a fantasy. What is written in the telegram is all a fantasy. It is, I must say, dreamland. We can't operate here anymore. I will be satisfied if we can stop it. I don't expect any more than that—except from this. Those are just words. I don't expect a safe decision or a "victorious" decision. He says here, "I have to consider it impossible that the 4th Panzer Division, with the reinforcements now arriving, will be able to further prevent the cutting off of the railway connections, with Zhmerinka as the target. Therefore I consider necessary an immediate decision regarding the counter operations I suggested." [—] That is no "counter operation." They should just call it by the right name: retreat. I really hate these phrases. He should just say: "for the retreat," since nothing else is going to come of it. [—] "Particularly as its execution will be extraordinarily lengthy anyway. Likewise, bringing in additional forces from the West can't be avoided." He doesn't think about what's taking place in the West. If something happens in the West, it's not his business in the end. ... west in this direction in order to stop. Where they come from he leaves to us. Actually the 16th Panzer Division does come from the West. You have spoken with him again. What does he say now?

ZEITZLER: He considers it absolutely necessary that the withdrawal take place now. That will free up forces here.

THE FÜHRER: They won't be freed up. You see—it's always the same. He sang the same song here. The forces were released, of course, but they just slid around here, and now he has them here. It's always the same game: forces are freed up on both sides, not just ours. He has to admit that, too.[953] But here he says this: (*Reading aloud.*) Where are these consequences that he points out there? [—] Oh, I see!

ZEITZLER: The loss of Zhmerinka ... from the territory north of Cherkassy. ... are in transit to the Crimea.

THE FÜHRER: Do you have any news about this yet?

ZEITZLER: It could be right. We have a message from an agent saying that 33 trains are on their way there. It could be a mechanized corps. But it's only an agent's report so far.

THE FÜHRER: He writes here about five to six divisions being released. What is that? "This will free up about five to six divisions for the left wing of the army group." He'll get those five to six divisions anyway, for all intents and purposes. What comes next is just fantasy: "Certainly enemy forces will also be freed up in the Dnieper bend, but he won't be able to get them into the Berdichev area as fast as we can." [—] Who says that? He doesn't even need to bring them in here. If we're here, he will feel less threatened. Then he can reduce his units—his rear units—and bring them here quickly. He can take them out of that front. The units from the front are really not first-class; I have these things given to me every day. Today I saw that only one single unit is halfway there. The rest are not operational. What does he want to do with that? He has a division here, which would be the 3rd or 4th [Mountain Division]. That's the only unit that really has value. [—] Do you have the evaluation here, Zeitzler?

ZEITZLER: Yes, Sir. I have it.

THE FÜHRER: "But he won't be able to get them into the Berdichev area as fast as we can.[954] Rather, we hope that the enemy ..." [—] You know, when I hear such things: "We hope it!" Because it suits us, right? And the enemy will do what we hope for! Is this a military term at all? "Rather, we hope that the enemy will use the forces becoming available in the Dnieper bend and in the Nogai steppe to try to break through to the west via Cherkassy and Kirovograd, via Krivoi Rog or the lower Dnieper, and will completely exhaust his forces in a frontal attack." [—] What does that mean, "completely exhaust"? When he frees up these forces, he will break through again! Why not the same theory here, so that he also says here that he must completely exhaust them? There are at least as many forces here as we have here. [—] How many enemy divisions are in the area anyway? Do you have the data? Do you have it marked on the map?

ZEITZLER: No, it hasn't been compiled.

THE FÜHRER: Maybe someone can be called for the data, where the circles are.

ZEITZLER: However it was divided!

THE FÜHRER: So here the block, here the block, here near Cherkassy the block and the block here! [—] The enemy won't do what we hope for; instead, he'll do what harms us. He will carry out two operations: either he'll go over here with the freed-up forces and attack here from the bridgehead, and unhinge that right away, so he can immediately go over here—those forces can't prevent that—or, if he doesn't do that, he'll go around here and pull this further from here. Manstein expects that he will immediately bring them along from Cherkassy. From Kremenchug it's impossible, he says. He won't get them there. According to his theory, we will get up there faster from here than he will from Kremenchug. That can't be maintained. He's already up there with his forces, while we're dismantling here—faster than we can get up there. How is the railway transport situation? How do they have to get the forces up there, anyway?

ZEITZLER: They will go this way by rail, and here they can go along this bit. I marked it here—back here the major junction, and from Krivoi Rog the train runs more or less along here from Zaporozh'e. Then from this area, where the 17th Panzer Division is marked now, we have to—

THE FÜHRER: Those must go by motorized transit, but must those go on foot?

ZEITZLER: They have to bring the others around below here.

THE FÜHRER: The 4th Mountain Division is up here now anyway.

ZEITZLER: It's up here now.

THE FÜHRER: It will bear the weight of the whole action at first anyway.

ZEITZLER: It will be there for several days, but it will have left, of course, before those arrive by rail.

THE FÜHRER: Quite right. But a division will arrive there anyway. It's the second already. It must come up here as well. And the 17th [Panzer Division]?

ZEITZLER: It will be transported out from here. If he frees up infantry divisions here, he will release the motorized units now and be able to drive a bit—with *that* via land march.

THE FÜHRER: It's not entirely certain if they can drive now. The railway will be full to capacity with that one there during the next few days. I don't know if he's sending an infantry division up or something else.

ZEITZLER: Yes, Sir. It'll be free again until that one arrives.

THE FÜHRER: But it has to be transported down from here first?

ZEITZLER: This here is the railway that runs along here. It goes through.

THE FÜHRER: But he has to pull them up from down here. [—] We can't do anything else at the moment. [—] Those are the marks from today?

ZEITZLER: I marked that this evening. That's Kazatin.

THE FÜHRER: I consider one thing necessary: that he immediately leave Vinnitsa, so he doesn't lose his nerve. It makes no sense if he loses his nerve.

ZEITZLER: We've prepared that for the news service. Balti—that's in the middle. It'll work for the news service?

THE FÜHRER: L'vov [Lemberg]!

ZEITZLER: Yes, Sir. Lemberg is a bit far. I can try to see if we can find something. Maybe Tarnopol. He reported from Balti this evening that they are preparing that.

THE FÜHRER: He must leave Vinnitsa. It's useless. There must be a unit in Vinnitsa that burns the whole thing down and blows it up![955]

SCHMUNDT: Above all, no furniture must be left in there—otherwise it'll be sent to Moscow and exhibited.

THE FÜHRER: Burn everything down!

JODL: Balti won't work. It's not in Transnistria—it's already Romania.

THE FÜHRER: It's already Transnistria?

JODL: No, Balti is in Romania. It's in Bessarabia.

ZEITZLER: Balta is what was meant.[956]

THE FÜHRER: Where is Vinnitsa? [—] I think that's wrong.

ZEITZLER: Above all, the connections are very bad there. That's the major concern—if we can get the railway through Romania now. The Romanians have not given us the railway. I've tried everything possible.[957]

THE FÜHRER: I think it would be right for him to go to Tarnopol.

ZEITZLER: Yes, Sir. Then I'll prepare it.

THE FÜHRER: Do you have any news of the 1st Panzer Division's strike?

ZEITZLER: No, my Führer. No results yet, although I spoke with him earlier.

THE FÜHRER: I'm convinced that they will run through there.

ZEITZLER: It's hard to say. According to the 300 trucks that are following, we could run into a mechanized corps.

THE FÜHRER: How many men can fit on one truck? Twenty?

ZEITZLER: The Russians might take more, maybe also 20 men.

THE FÜHRER: That would be 6,000.

ZEITZLER: But it wouldn't have to be only men on the trucks. It could also be something else. The number of trucks corresponds approximately to what a mechanized corps would have.

THE FÜHRER: So then it would be 3,000 to 4,000 men.

ZEITZLER: My Führer, what worries me is that we won't have any effect on this enemy until the 30th. I am convinced that there will be a battle for Vinnitsa in 3 to 4 days' time.[958]

THE FÜHRER: That doesn't change anything.

ZEITZLER: It will change something, my Führer, because the thing can develop in such a way that this here becomes encircled. That's my concern.

THE FÜHRER: That wouldn't be able to prevent anything either. We can't do any more now than what's already underway anyway. [—] He can't prevent that either.

ZEITZLER: We could retreat into this Kamenka position.

THE FÜHRER: If he retreats, he'll be there. It doesn't matter if he's there or there.

ZEITZLER: Then 6 days will be gained, in case we have to retreat further.

THE FÜHRER: The decisive thing is that when he spoke of an operation, he was imagining going here.

ZEITZLER: If we continue thinking about this situation here, it can go in as far as here. Then we'll get into a very uncomfortable situation. Then we'll have only the Trichaty action [the encirclement east of Kirovograd].

THE FÜHRER: He won't change anything with that.

ZEITZLER: It'll be improved a bit, in case we have to break through later. Because if he leaves this connection, we'll have to break through.

THE FÜHRER: I consider it better, Zeitzler, to throw individual units in here as fast as possible and to block this off here. That's the decisive thing.

ZEITZLER: Yes, indeed, my Führer. Five days ago I was already in favor of leaving this thing alone and shifting the three panzer divisions up here right away. Then we would have had three units and would not have gotten into this predicament. This thing, in my opinion, is less important than taking something away from here.

THE FÜHRER: Then at least he can pull out a division quickly.

ZEITZLER: This thing should have been left to help itself. Then we could have marched up with three units and would finally have been able to push him in here. So far everything has been arriving bit by bit, unfortunately also with the *Leibstandarte* [SS Panzer Grenadier Division] and the 1st Panzer [Division], and I'm worried that the units down here will also—

THE FÜHRER: Anything he gets in the way of units must be brought in within the scope of the 1st Panzer or the *Leibstandarte*. He can't do it any other way. He has to bring them in within the area of the 1st Panzer or the *Leibstandarte* anyway. Are they coming into the line from Novograd-Volynsk to Zhitomir?

ZEITZLER: They're coming along the main line. When that's gone later, we'll have to go into this line.

THE FÜHRER: The critical thing is that they come within the area of the 1st Panzer and the *Leibstandarte*.

ZEITZLER: Then we can put them in here.

THE FÜHRER: Nothing else can be done, Zeitzler, other than to bring in forces to stop this. If the operation here [near Vinnitsa] doesn't work, this operation can be carried out. That won't change the overall result. Also, if they're here today or here, it's just a day. Then they would hastily have to run away again. This here won't change the result.

ZEITZLER: Units will be freed up. That's clear.

THE FÜHRER: The units that are released won't be brought up any earlier. It's absolutely useless.

ZEITZLER: Then we might take a greater risk here [east of Kirovograd] in order to close this [Vinnitsa] front again with the released units.

THE FÜHRER: How will they get them up there?

ZEITZLER: We'll bring the motorized units up here.

THE FÜHRER: Theoretically! If a motorized unit drives up from here [Kirovograd] to there [Vinnitsa], it won't make it!

ZEITZLER: We've also had major movements now.

THE FÜHRER: With tanks.

ZEITZLER: The tracked vehicles can go this way.

THE FÜHRER: Those have to take the train.

ZEITZLER: We can't get enough up here.

THE FÜHRER: Certainly. That's very clear, but they won't get them there anymore. They'll free up one division. He'll get one here and one will come out here. One is already on the way.

ZEITZLER: …

THE FÜHRER: If we had this thing here, and we had a division here, then we could bring it in here and follow after it here. But as soon as we do that, this will automatically slide in.

ZEITZLER: He's also bringing them in this way.

THE FÜHRER: Granted. But it's still contained here [Kirovograd]. You see—this block is here. If we go back, the block will immediately shift to here. He can run away immediately. What Manstein says is not true —that he'll be faster at pulling up these units. [—] But aside from that, what do they look like? Let's take the table for these units [in the Nikopol bridgehead and the Dnieper bend]. First the 335th [Infantry Division].

ZEITZLER: Solid, looks good, four medium-strong, three average battalions.

THE FÜHRER: The 97th Jäger Division?

ZEITZLER: The 97th Jäger Division: good, particularly solid.

THE FÜHRER: The 9th [Infantry] Division?

ZEITZLER: Solid, good. [—] The 17th [Infantry Division] is good, particularly solid. [—] The 211th [Infantry Division] is good, also solid. [—] The 67th [Infantry Division] was bad a few days ago. I asked about it a few days ago. But the ones down there were actually good. The 9th has always been good.

THE FÜHRER: What about the 24th Panzer Division?

ZEITZLER: No valuation is made for that. But it's strong, combat value 1.

THE FÜHRER: And what about the 258th [Infantry Division]?

ZEITZLER: Not solid.

THE FÜHRER: But the 3rd Mountain Division is good?

ZEITZLER: Particularly solid. Three medium-strong battalions, one average one, nine batteries. [—] The 302nd: [Infantry Division] is not solid, combat value 4; five average, two weak battalions. [—] The 294th: [Infantry Division] is not solid, one strong battalion, two medium-strong average ones, three strong[959] battalions.

THE FÜHRER: That one's not useful then. And the 123rd [Infantry Division]?

ZEITZLER: Not solid either, although it managed its thing well back then. [—] The 25th [Panzer Division] is not solid either; it got stuck back then as well. As did the 304th [Infantry Division].

THE FÜHRER: Those are the units that he'll get out here first. What about the 257th [Infantry Division]?

ZEITZLER: It's adequate.

THE FÜHRER: Now he has to put something in here. He can only take out one unit here. That would be the 257th. But here he has many units that are not solid. One unit will come out here. [—] Where is this line? It runs into here?

ZEITZLER: That's the Kamenka Line [at the base of the Dnieper bend].

THE FÜHRER: Where's the bridge? Is this it here?

ZEITZLER: The bridge is here.

THE FÜHRER: The Nikopol' one. And the lower bridge?

ZEITZLER: The lower bridge is here. Here's the one bridge, and there are ferries here.

THE FÜHRER: The ferries can't be used in the winter now. And the bridges?

ZEITZLER: The pontoon bridges are retracted?

THE FÜHRER: So they're not available either. So he has just one bridge anyway.

ZEITZLER: Now he has the 70-ton bridge, and then the weather could change.

THE FÜHRER: Change how? What do you mean?

ZEITZLER: So that they could be extended temporarily.

THE FÜHRER: It won't work anywhere. At most it'll freeze. It happens from the bottom up. Then the great danger is that he'll blast this when it's totally frozen again, and once the action is over it'll be fine again. Of course, there is one question. In those days it was always that if this here[960] is blasted, this will be mostly under water. Then it couldn't actually get so strong here anymore.

ZEITZLER: The water level is about 18 m, which will drop.

THE FÜHRER: Eighteen m is not so terribly much.

ZEITZLER: But those bridges would be affected.

THE FÜHRER: Another question, Zeitzler. How do these few divisions that you have in the rear look? [—] One moment. We just want to check these few units [west of Zaporozh'e]. The 46th [Infantry Division]?

ZEITZLER: Good, particularly solid.

THE FÜHRER: But weak. [—] And the 387th [Infantry Division]?

ZEITZLER: Not solid. [—] The 306th [Infantry Division] isn't either. It's also relatively weak.

THE FÜHRER: How does the 16th Panzer Grenadier Division look now?

ZEITZLER: Good, one strong, three medium-strong, one average, 17 batteries, 25 heavy antitank guns—the ones under Schwerin.[961]

THE FÜHRER: He wants to pull that one out.

ZEITZLER: No, not yet. That was the first assumption: if he gets them out.

THE FÜHRER: If he gets a unit free here?

(ZEITZLER: Yes, Sir.)

THE FÜHRER: *Grossdeutschland* is very weak?

ZEITZLER: *Grossdeutschland?* Yes, Sir. Solid but very weak. [—] The 9th Panzer [Division] has six solid, three medium-strong, four weak, 11 batteries. [—] The 15th [Infantry Division] is particularly solid: three average, two weak ones. [—] The 62nd: [Infantry Division] is solid, four average, one weak one.

THE FÜHRER: And if we reduce the size of the bridgehead here [at Nikopol']?

ZEITZLER: He couldn't do that either now. He said it was impossible to reduce the size. Personally, I would think that we could reduce it. Of course, that wouldn't free up very much anyway.

THE FÜHRER: He says two small bridgeheads.

ZEITZLER: I don't know how he understood that either. I told him clearly: a reduction across. First he wanted a lengthwise reduction. That's out of the question. We wouldn't save much then.

JODL: He means two small ones.

ZEITZLER: He probably means that, but we only want to hold one later anyway.

THE FÜHRER: I would certainly prefer to leave here as late as possible—if possible not at all. Because he won't get those forces anymore. It's a balancing of the forces. That one will come over immediately. He won't get any more forces from the Crimea—aside from the fact that it's none of Manstein's business anyway. Then he says: that's Army Group A—it doesn't concern me. You just have to look at the units here. [—] How many units are there? I would guess at least 30 to 35 units!

ZEITZLER: It was about that.

THE FÜHRER: We could put them here, and then he'll immediately blast the whole thing from the rear. If he wants to completely cover this here, he'll need these again here. He has to cover this line. So that doesn't save anything.

ZEITZLER: About ten units will be freed up—three to four down below and five up there.

THE FÜHRER: Five? One is already gone. It's already here. One is gone from here and must be replaced. You have to consider that as well. [—] Three to four down below? He won't get anything that way. This line must also be occupied. It's not occupied yet. You see that, when you look at the thing as a whole: we weren't in a position to hold this thing.[962] We are now in a position to hold exactly the same long bridgehead, and in addition we must hold that and give units away! There was a spirit in there in those days: Back! That was the typical retreat. Everyone lost his nerve, including Kleist. Everyone back! No one will claim that this here was harder than that or the entire front that we have here now. Now we have to hold the whole line from here on, and there we would have had to hold only this bit. Then we wouldn't have any difficulties with the Crimea, and we wouldn't need a unit here. We could have it here, and the two units that we have here now we could have here. We can't claim that we couldn't have held this. We could have held it. It was just the spirit in there: Everyone back! Sometimes it's a

real mania. [—] If it would have been a success at least! I've seen two re-
treats here, where I had to say to myself, "We can risk that." The one was the
Buffalo [Büffel] Movement.[963] There I said, "Not much will be lost." I agreed.
The second one I suggested myself: it was the Orel withdrawal—this sack.
If the offensive fails, we have to pack up. That was reasonable. But this here
was an idiotic retreat, I must say.

BORGMANN: There are 27 rifle divisions in this area, and four tank
corps in this area. [—] Here there are 17 rifle divisions, at this corner.
Then northeast of Krivoi Rog 16 rifle divisions and one tank corps. Then
there are 24 rifle divisions and five tank corps near Kirovograd.

THE FÜHRER: That's this here? [—] This also belongs to it?

BORGMANN: Then there are 13 rifle divisions and one tank corps in this
penetration area. Near Cherkassy there are four rifle divisions and one tank
brigade, and in this penetration area [near Vinnitsa] 42 rifle divisions, nine
tank corps and one cavalry corps on the front line and two tank corps behind, and—not confirmed yet—three tank corps.

THE FÜHRER: How many confirmed tank corps does he have in there
[the Vinnitsa penetration] now?

ZEITZLER: He has nine. The others may possibly be added as well—the
ones en route by train.

THE FÜHRER: I wonder if we shouldn't take something out of the bridgehead, even though the bridgehead contains the majority of the forces, of
course. [—] Oh, I wanted to ask you one other thing, Zeitzler. We have two
reserve divisions in the General Government?

ZEITZLER: Yes, Sir. With recruits. The one division is deployed up near
Korosten' for railway protection, where the big hatch is.

BORGMANN: That was the 147th [Infantry Division]. It has seven battalions, three of which are near Korosten'. Four battalions are recruits. It has
one engineer battalion and one artillery detachment. The 143rd [Infantry
Division] Division has ten battalions, of which seven are recruits. Three are
deployed in the Second Army area to fight bands.

THE FÜHRER: I thought there was something else further back.

JODL: Those are two new formations in the General Government. Is that
the 21st or 22nd wave?

ZEITZLER: That would be the 21st wave. If it's the 21st, the skeleton
should be more or less adequate.[964]

THE FÜHRER: I ask now for another reason: if possible, we could perhaps give one or both divisions to the West, in the hope that we'll have some
more time there, and take some other units over instead. But Jodl says there's
nothing in the West. He can't give any more panzer units.

JODL: There are no infantry divisions at all in the West that could be used in
the East. We could only take one that's supposed go to Italy now.

THE FÜHRER: Could this one be brought in? What kind would this one be?

JODL: That would be the 371st [Infantry Division].

THE FÜHRER: Where is it exactly?

JODL: It's now taking part in this action.

THE FÜHRER: In this action?

JODL: In the "Ernteeinbringung" ["Harvest"] action east of Agram.[965] It will be deployed there in the next few days.

ZEITZLER: In the Southeast? [—] The 371st [Infantry Division]?

JODL: It's still with the Commander-in-Chief Southwest, where it was earlier.[966]

THE FÜHRER: Combat value 2?

ZEITZLER: The 371st: two good ones, in principle. There are four; the first one is the best.

THE FÜHRER: When could it come here, if we sent one of those divisions in the General Government down there instead?

JODL: We don't need to do that. It wouldn't help. It will only cause unnecessary delays in the formation. And the result would be that then only one division and not two would go to the West. Then only the 71st [Infantry Division] will be sent to Kesselring, and the *Hermann Göring* will be handed over in exchange,[967] and the 90th Panzer Grenadier Division must remain here in the meantime.[968]

THE FÜHRER: When can that one there be on the train?

ZEITZLER: Where is it?

JODL: Southwest of Agram.

ZEITZLER: Then it'll take some time before we can get them out, because of the poor train connections and short trains.

THE FÜHRER: And how long once they are on the track?

ZEITZLER: It won't be long. We arrived there in 6-7 days.

THE FÜHRER: If I could just put something in here instead of the 24th Panzer Division! But if we take this away, we won't be able to hold this thing here.

ZEITZLER: Yes, indeed. We would put that at risk then. If we're lucky, it might be true. But so far we haven't been able to manage it. That one had to keep reestablishing the thing.

JODL: And what are these Romanian detachments doing there? The 5th and 14th?

ZEITZLER: We can't actually use them.

JODL: For security?!

THE FÜHRER: Here we need to put something in. How many good divisions are still here? Is there one good division still there?

ZEITZLER: There isn't anything prominent: the 101st [Infantry], the 307th [Infantry], and the Luftwaffe field division.[969] And they already have extremely long sectors. The 101st is adequate. It's good, but it has a wide sector. The 307th is not solid.

THE FÜHRER: How many battalions does the 101st have?

ZEITZLER: Eight strong battalions and a weak one.

THE FÜHRER: I thought of a different reason. We put this Balkan division here in the hope that we might be able to hold it that long. It's questionable whether or not we can do it. Then another unit would come out immediately after the 4th [Mountain Division].

ZEITZLER: I will calculate it taking the technical railway issues into account.

JODL: All the relief actions take quite a long time!

ZEITZLER: The Führer doesn't want relief. He wants to pull them out beforehand and create some pressure for a few days.

THE FÜHRER: Until the other one arrives.

ZEITZLER: The train thing down here will take a long time since we're going through Romania.

THE FÜHRER: It's useless. All the units they pull out of here must go out here.

ZEITZLER: We can see how long it takes with the 4th Mountain Division.

THE FÜHRER: Then we have to go around here. [—] They won't get around this. We can't give all the panzer units away here, or a crisis will occur. They can't do anything with those infantry divisions anymore. We must have a number of panzer units here. [—] Then following the 4th another good infantry division will come up again.

ZEITZLER: Yes, the 101st, we can say.

THE FÜHRER: Of course, it won't be able take along that much artillery. Something must stay here. Although they will get the artillery when the other one arrives, and I would rather put this division here initially.

ZEITZLER: Yes, indeed. So that it comes into the battle.

THE FÜHRER: That's what I'm also thinking with regard to *Langemarck* [SS Panzer Regiment]

ZEITZLER: I spoke at length with the Reichsführer about that today, and told him the options: either to the *Reich* or the *Leibstandarte*. The advantage of the *Reich* is that it can integrate them very well. The disadvantage is that they would come into combat immediately, and might even have to do something straight off the train. The second possibility, adding them to the *Viking*, is technically difficult because we would have to drive around before they could get close to it. The Reichsführer doesn't want the *Viking* in any case, because then the Walloons and the Flemish would be together.[970] Down here with this thing they would be put into a quiet position, but they wouldn't have the support of any unit. So the Reichsführer argues for the *Reich*. He said that the best thing would be to bring them to the *Reich*.

He said the German personnel was more combat-experienced. He wasn't too concerned about that.

THE FÜHRER: Today I asked for the organization of the new *Nederland* Legion.[971] How strong is it in total? 6,000 or 7,000 men?

DARGES: About 7,000 men.

THE FÜHRER: It has a combat strength that's downright enormous. Do you have that there? [—] You must take a look at it! We must consider an organization like this. Its combat strength is better than that of any other division here today, and it has 6,500 or 7,000 men. From an artillery point of view it's weak. It has only two detachments. But the third detachment wouldn't help much. Most of others have only nine batteries as well.

ZEITZLER: Nine batteries in most cases.

THE FÜHRER: So that would be a risk that we might have to accept. Would you like to speak with Kleist about whether or not he dares to do that?

ZEITZLER: Yes, Sir. You were already very concerned about the 4th Mountain Division.

THE FÜHRER: Instead of the 4th, these units came in.

ZEITZLER: These battalions?!

THE FÜHRER: He'll get an additional division in here, which is also equal in strength. We don't know what they'll do, of course, but in strength they are equal anyway. Though perhaps not in terms of artillery, because they won't be able to take all the artillery with them here. But let's not deceive ourselves here, Zeitzler—he can't operate with these units at all. Until he's there or here—if he can't stop that—there'll be a mess. But that doesn't matter at all. The critical thing is that we have to insist fanatically that this must be stopped. For the moment we can't do anything except provide cover here with these units. We can't fight offensively. The infantry divisions drop out of every offensive battle. They can't do it today. We see the limited successes of the 5th Jäger Division. Now, that's a good unit but the penetrating power equals zero.[972] If they would attack up above with the 12th [Infantry Division], the same thing would happen again. These infantry divisions don't have any penetrating power, and are also unable to attack during winter. They just can't do it. Last year we led attacks with only panzer units and panzer grenadier divisions. The infantry can't do it at all. They're also completely helpless. The infantry goes in there in the snow and gets shot. They can't take cover very well. We can't do anything but try to plug the hole. A few panzer units ... with them he has to drive around. It would be good if he could still get the 16th Panzer Grenadier Division out as well, but at the moment it's not possible to do more. If he engages in that thought: He withdraws with that army in order to operate freely—so he goes back in this direction—and now we have no idea how the army looks.

I read all the reports about these withdrawals. I could worry myself sick about the fact that I gave permission. It couldn't have been worse in front, either—on the contrary. But it's just like I said, that everyone was in a rush to go back, and the units arrived in the rear in terrible condition. The withdrawal was worse than any defensive fight. I am generally astonished. If we look at these units now, we can see how they've improved again!

ZEITZLER: My Führer! If they are more or less in position it will gradually increase. Then they'll get reserves and the convalescent men returning from convalescence leave.

THE FÜHRER: I'm astonished at how they've improved themselves in such a short time. So with this thing we could have held this, and then there wouldn't have been a crisis here. ... so that we aren't cut off. They feared that this would be pushed down here—so turn back immediately! That can become a mania, a real disease. In the end, it's not easy. That's 350 km—half the entire former Western front. We talk about the battle of the Marne, but we do this continually. In the case of a penetration, we give up a huge front of 350 km. Three hundred fifty km was the whole Army right wing in 1914.

JODL: But here, my Führer, we must not allow a crisis situation to develop. Otherwise they'll say one day: "Here an army is cut off again. That can't be—otherwise the whole thing will collapse. So the last mobile division has to come to here from the West in order to save one army, because otherwise the whole Eastern front will break!" Otherwise we'll lose the war because there's nothing in the West. A severe crisis situation, which might develop à la Stalingrad, must remain absolutely out of the question.

ZEITZLER: That's my opinion. I come to the same conclusion—to the same as Manstein—but for different reasons. I just have these reasons: they are now advancing 15 km per day, and will advance so far on the 29th and 30th that probably by the end of the year or around January 1st the battle for Vinnitsa will be fought. [—] Then the new units will arrive: the 16th Panzer [Division] still at timing 12 at best, then afterward the Jäger division from below with a timing of 3 to 6. Of course, that would not be very nice either, because by then the block will have widened. That's why I see huge danger from Korosten' down south.

THE FÜHRER: You are convinced, Zeitzler? You want to say that we take back the whole front here?!

ZEITZLER: First, I'm convinced that we need to initiate this thing. Then we'll free up some of the units.

THE FÜHRER: We won't bring them up by then either, Zeitzler, because then at that moment the others [Russians] will have new units free as well.

ZEITZLER: My Führer! The question is that we can either stop this situation to some degree so that it holds here [the Vinnitsa axis], and then this thing can be endured, let us say, initially. This Dnieper bend will always be a source of danger. We are extended so wide here that he will always be able to break through—here through this small corner. That'll always remain the big danger. So we want to try to come back here [the Kamenka Line]. The second thing is that if it doesn't succeed, then he'll come in here to Transnistria? [across the Dnestr River]. Then there will be nothing left for us. Then this thing will have to push through to the rear. That'll be difficult because we have only the one bridge at Trichaty.[973]

THE FÜHRER: If he pushes in with his divisions into this area, it can't be worse than if we voluntarily—

ZEITZLER: Voluntarily?

THE FÜHRER: We are voluntarily so far back. That has demoralized the people. These people have fought, Zeitzler! I have spoken with numerous men. They all say that they don't understand leaving a position that they've dug out so laboriously. Add up how many rifles we've produced in Germany during the last 6 months and how many rifles we possess right now; that's the best reckoning.

ZEITZLER: I've presented these lists every month, and this thing is included.

THE FÜHRER: That can't be right at all. We've produced more than 200,000 rifles every month. Now one could say, "Those are only new formations." [—] No! [—] How many rifles do we have? The stock sank from 6.1 million to 5.1 million. So it sank! So there was a loss of 1.5 million rifles. That happened here in the East. Where else were rifles lost? Just here! So it's impossible. The best proof is the number of lost rifles. Overall, there are fewer. It doesn't matter at all if one says, "We've made new formations." Because overall there are so many less, and they were lost here in the East during the "successful withdrawals," where the men got rid of their weapons. It really is like that. The men fought well, drove back the enemy, were well behaved and courageous, and improved many positions—and now they're told, "Back!" You can't say to a front of 400 or 500 kilometers, "There's a penetration up there, so you have to withdraw 500 km now!" [—] You can't explain that to them.

ZEITZLER: I just don't see any possibility, my Führer, if he really has advanced to here [north of Vinnitsa] already.

THE FÜHRER: Now, this situation is not such that we can say that. This Stalingrad was another case; that was over there. But here it's still ridiculous. Here there are connections everywhere.

ZEITZLER: The connections are very difficult here!

THE FÜHRER: They're difficult, but they can't be compared with Stalingrad. [—] This here is the worst thing. [—] So speak with Kleist to see if they'll risk that!

ZEITZLER: Yes, Sir. The one thing—and I'm considering the 371st [Infantry Division]—is that if we can exchange via Jodl, how will we bring them in here?

THE FÜHRER: If worse comes to worse we can take a course of action like this—we can perhaps go there and immediately throw some battalions forward, so that at least there's something there.

JODL: There we first have to know how long it'll take by rail, and how they are divided up.

THE FÜHRER: When can you find that out?

ZEITZLER: We can make the railway calculations. It'll still take a few days before the 101st [Jäger Division] can get underway because the 4th Jäger [Division] is on the line now.

THE FÜHRER: They can't do any more now. If they still get a division in the rear—

ZEITZLER: If worse comes to worse we can make that retreat there.

THE FÜHRER: We can take it back but it'll shake up this front, and we won't know if the other is going to push in behind immediately. We don't know that at all. We saw what consequences this withdrawal had.

ZEITZLER: Up here, he thinks he can hold a bit longer. We don't need to worry too much about that. The trouble is down below.

THE FÜHRER: Here he has a block and there he has blocks. The withdrawal here could cause him to attack again here immediately.

ZEITZLER: It could lead to that. But he could also attack that way if we don't withdraw.

THE FÜHRER: It's not like that. He has attacked the whole time. Today I received another report about the additional replacements that those brothers will get. Those are the most pathetic and dismal additional replacements that could possibly exist. Not very brilliant. [—] When can we get news on how this push here is going?! There could indeed be a few tanks—we can't judge at all.

ZEITZLER: It didn't look like it today. We won't receive that until sometime during the night because there was only radio contact just now.

THE FÜHRER: So be sure to figure that out immediately. Get in contact with the army group to find out how long they think they can hold out. That unit is a completely effective division with seven battalions. They have artillery.

ZEITZLER: Nine batteries.

THE FÜHRER: Assault guns and antitank guns? [—] Heavy or light?

(ZEITZLER: Heavy antitank guns!)

Nothing but heavy!

ZEITZLER: One engineer battalion, one field replacement battalion.

THE FÜHRER: They want to take that with them?

ZEITZLER: There are probably recruits in there. [—] There were actually eight battalions.

THE FÜHRER: And this one here has nine?

ZEITZLER: The 101st [Jäger Division] has eight strong ones and one weak one. But there are two Western battalions in there that have been added. Perhaps we should leave them there for now.

THE FÜHRER: We may be able to leave those here at the beginning.

ZEITZLER: We can also leave some artillery there.

End: 1:09 a.m.

* * * * *

MEETING OF THE FÜHRER
WITH GENERAL ZEITZLER, DECEMBER 29, 1943[974]

Beginning: 1:02 p.m.

The East

ZEITZLER: During the night I did the calculations for the whole railway thing. That's why I've come here before the situation report. There's nothing unusual with Army Group A. [—] Here along this front, on the whole, there's nothing unusual either. I spoke with Manstein again, and he spoke with the army again about this line—withdrawing here. The army is against that, for the following reasons. Here absolutely nothing has been built. They had to just lie in the fields. Second, they wouldn't save that much with the Dnieper front. That's why they oppose it internally. Besides, the pressure would then increase as well. I also believe that the savings won't be very great. Manstein himself believed that we could put in an infantry division in place of the 24th [Panzer Division]. I believe that if the army refuses that, we can't do it for now. [—] Here on this whole front everything went as planned. This attack here has started. Yesterday there was a wrong marking. The 11th [Panzer Division] was up to here. That was a mix-up. This town is correct as well: Bodenovka. The army had mixed that up. In reality it is as follows: the attack began here today, followed by a counterattack, which was thrown back. Nothing in particular on this whole front. Yesterday evening we entered Kazatin again, so there is fighting in Kazatin. We have taken back the railway station now. He then deployed up this morning where the purple arrows are. Relative calm during the night last night. The 1st Panzer [Division] never did arrive yesterday. It arrived an hour too late at the assembly point. It was already dark then. It deployed early this morning—where the blue arrowhead is, against here—and wants to push forward up to here.

In the meantime, he pushed forward below and came through with tanks here. Then there was a major attack against here, with these local penetrations that are marked here. Then he came in from the north against the 208th [Infantry Division]. There was the 7th Panzer [Division] again, which had struck forward and wants to throw him out again down below. Korosten' was retaken again yesterday evening. There is fighting on the eastern edge. This morning he entered Korosten'. Of the two in transit by train, one motorized corps came in. There we got a confirmation from the front, so this movement seems to bear out what happened here. [—] Perhaps I can quickly show [Army Group] Center first and the Z calculations.[975] With Center, there's nothing in particular going on down here. Büsch is coming again now because of this withdrawal of the 5th Panzer [Division]. I said that he should first give an accurate picture of what the position is like that they've improved. Now he wanted to take this back—and this corner, which already changed hands once.

THE FÜHRER: If it's improved well!

ZEITZLER: They should have improved it well. He first has to provide a positive picture, though. Then I'll bring it with me this evening. [—] On this front, nothing in particular. Here small local advances. Büsch has the impression that there seems to be quiet along this whole front here, and that he only wants to do something up above. I still have no evidence for that. Here the situation developed more or less favorably. He attacked early today, and at one place is inside again. [—] Here on this front relatively little. On the whole, this was deflected here. … Here he attacked again a bit at 11 o'clock with the 5th Jäger [Division]. … I spoke with him. He does want the railway to be kept free after all. A train went through again yesterday. But he is situated relatively close to the railway—1 km.[976] That's the reason he wants to attack after all. He considered it for a long time. I again expressed the concerns that you had, my Führer—that he will bleed to death with those few divisions if something happens there. His intentions are as follows. The 131st [Infantry Division] will be assembled here, so that there's something available here. He believes the enemy will attack again here and here, in order to take advantage of the two roads. In addition, he wants to bring the 299th [Infantry Division] over here, which he is taking over from the Ninth Army. Then he has two divisions here.[977] If he gets this in order to some degree, he wants to transfer one of them to the 6th Luftwaffe Field Division, because it's become a bit worn out now. Here on this front[978] he has the 5th Jäger and the 12th [Infantry] Division, and he wants to send the 12th Panzer [Division] up to Polotsk.

THE FÜHRER: He has no worries here?

ZEITZLER: None at the moment. Here there was a considerable relaxation. [—] There's nothing in particular happening with the [Army Group]

North. I had the two division shifts checked. From here two divisions went out there. We've confirmed that from prisoners now. They were actually very exhausted. It could also possibly be that he drew the exhausted divisions away from this situation and brought them to the other front. It wouldn't need to be because of a planned attack, but it could be.

THE FÜHRER: Calculate one thing: how much will actually be saved if we take that back?

ZEITZLER: I wanted to bring that with me this evening.

THE FÜHRER: On one condition: that this line will be rearranged. We can't do it the way it is now. They would have to try to get a connection over to here. So calculate how much would actually be saved.

ZEITZLER: Yes, Sir. In order to get that out. [—] My Führer, then I worked through the following, with all the possibilities. Let me show it to you here. (*Presentation.*) There are two movements underway: one movement on the main line to Berdichev, and the other movement, which is coming from below, from Odessa against Kazatin—so that two deployment groups would meet there then.[979] The one would come from west of Berdichev into this area, and the other group would come down here into the area of Vinnitsa. That's how they're arriving by railway. And that's correct, I believe. Now, up here the 16th Panzer [Division] would arrive first. The blue line is the 29th—today's date. The first train of the 16th Panzer will arrive during night of the 30th—tomorrow evening—and will start on January 4 with the combat element. So it will arrive well. Of course, he should hold it back now and not throw it in immediately. Down here the 4th Mountain Division will arrive first, also tomorrow evening, and will also start out already on the evening of the 4th. It'll arrive down below. Then we have two. At the same time, the tracked vehicles of the 17th Panzer [Division] will be added down below. The first trains are already arriving today, and it will also start on the 5th. Then we also have a double group down below: the 17th Panzer and the 4th Mountain Division. Up above we have the 16th Panzer. Now, my Führer, my suggestion is that if we now send the 1st [Panzer] Division via railway instead of the 101st [Jäger Division] up above, then I can drive them down with a timing of 12 and arrive 5 days earlier.

THE FÜHRER: Immediately! I also thought of that myself.

ZEITZLER: Yes, indeed. I believe that as well. I have a good group then: the 16th Panzer plus the 1st [Panzer] Division, which also starts on the 5th. Now the other question is whether we now put the 371st [Infantry Division] up above with the army group? Or should we still do this anyway, so that we can possibly still get the 101st here afterward? I'm actually leaning toward the latter.

THE FÜHRER: I wouldn't send anything else up above.

ZEITZLER: That's what I thought. Then we'll do it with the 371st, and also the 101st, so that we can supply it. I agree that it's not worth it up there.

THE FÜHRER: We need to figure this out. Now, I've considered all of this. Last night I mulled it over. Without a considerable addition of forces we can't settle this thing. In the North, at worst, it might become a burden on the Finns. That might possibly even be a relief for us. Because they have to fight anyway. Down here, if worse comes to worse, it could lead to the loss of the Crimea, then the loss of this ore area around Krivoi Rog and the loss of Nikopol'. So, if we don't take care of this thing here! But then this loss would also be more difficult for us from a supply and economic point of view than the loss up above, so I am determined to bring in the necessary forces. I can't bring any great quantities out of the West. The only way we can obtain the necessary forces is to pull them out from up there. I've thought about the following. At worst, we'd have to make do with the unit here in the Oranienbaum thing. That should be nearly sufficient to cover the affair at Narva. So in principle, this blocking unit here would have to hold the longest, so that he doesn't come in there. These units here would then almost be freed up. We could probably almost turn around with the ones that are here and basically occupy this line. I still believe today that we can free up 12 divisions from Army Group North.[980]

ZEITZLER: Yes, Sir. Then it's very convenient that Küchler is coming tomorrow. Then I can calculate that today and present it. This railway thing is going well. Then we have the two groups, the 16th Panzer and the 1st Panzer. So we have something with striking power there, and we have to concentrate that. Down here we'll get the 4th Mountain Division and the 17th Panzer out, and as a second element will then come the 101st and the 16th Panzer Grenadier by rail, and they'll start to go—the other two—from the 6th to the 8th or maybe the 12th. Then we have one more element. May I have it start this way?

THE FÜHRER: Yes.

ZEITZLER: Now there's the following question. Manstein complained that this front is getting a bit too much for the Fourth Panzer Army. He's right about that. Now I wanted to suggest that we take over the Sixth Army down below—the Sixth Army has only one general command, and the general command is directly subordinated to the army group. And then I would support the solution—I can speak with Manstein again—that we perhaps send the Sixth Army up in place of Hube, and put Hube in up above. I have more confidence in Hube than in Hollidt.[981] Mobile units are coming in up above, and Hollidt has no experience with mobile units.

THE FÜHRER: Here it's defense.

ZEITZLER: Yes, Hollidt can do more there, and Schörner[982] is with him there. There it's not so bad. If you agree, I can have that begin.

THE FÜHRER: Yes.

ZEITZLER: Then the tanks. Since December 7 the following have driven out: 294 tanks from the tip [salient] of First Panzer Army, 94 from the Fourth Panzer Army up above, and 154 from the Eighth Army, thus 542. Some of them are still en route by train and haven't arrived yet.

THE FÜHRER: But tell me one thing: how many tanks have we given to Army Group South, including the tanks for the five divisions that we've brought in here? I would guess that it's received well over 1,000 assault guns and tanks.

ZEITZLER: They've received all the supplies. I brought in 100 last month and 80 again this month.

THE FÜHRER: He[983] acts like he's the stepchild. In reality, he's the only one who has received anything.

ZEITZLER: He basically devours everything. Two to three weeks ago we started giving something to [Army Group] Center for the first time. Otherwise Center has been treated badly. [—] Then I will start that immediately, my Führer. They can head out with the 1st [Panzer] Division starting this evening. *End: 1:15 p.m.*

* * * * *

MEETING OF THE FÜHRER WITH FIELD MARSHAL VON KÜCHLER, DECEMBER 30, 1943, AT THE WOLFSSCHANZE[984]

Present:

The Führer	*Major General Scherff*
Field Marshal v. Küchler	*Major Borgmann*
General Zeitzler	*Hauptsturmführer Pfeiffer*
Major General Schmundt	

Beginning: 12:14 p.m.

The East, Army Group South

ZEITZLER: There was nothing unusual in the Crimea, on the whole. [—] Nothing on this front either. It seems as if there are preparations here again, and it also seems as if this tank corps is refreshing itself a bit. But we don't know for certain about that yet. We'll keep an eye on it. This movement is running according to plan. Up here the army group believes that this attack will be completed today. There are still fierce battles going on here. He seems to be pushing through here, but has been tackled by these two advance guard points now. They believe that they will reach here by this evening. Then they have some hilly terrain here, where they want to finish off. On the other front here nothing unusual. Here lively patrol activity. [—] Then the development of the situation here.[985] It's not completely clear what the situation is in here. Here there are definitely some individual units of ours. But there's no connected front in here. His main direction seems to have remained more southwest after all. He's still trying to break up this corner post a bit more now, and this corner post here, which he succeeded in doing on the 25th. On this front it went relatively well. They now want to create a completely contiguous front, which will enable the 1st Panzer Division to attack to the south, and the 7th Panzer Division to the south as well— because he has so many forces that he's even pressing this front back, and he's still outflanking the armies and forcing them back with these two things. Further to the north he's continuing to attack and is leading one or two motorized brigades up into the gap. Up here there seem to be only minor reconnaissance things—20 trucks that are going over there. The railway movements have gone well, also through Transnistria. I sent transport officers everywhere, and it's going faster than usual. Three trains of the 4th Mountain Division are arriving today, and from the 16th Panzer Division probably eleven trains. I have spoken again with the army group, so that they won't be thrown in piece by piece. Otherwise everything will be ruined. This afternoon I'll receive the reports regarding their intentions, and I'll present the intentions for this group this evening. The wheeled vehicles of the 17th Panzer Division will reach here today and will be there tomorrow. The tracked vehicles are underway as well. It's a bit slower because they can't be incorporated down here until later.

THE FÜHRER: The wheeled vehicles are driving over here?

ZEITZLER: They're driving on this road, via Uman'. Otherwise it would take too long and we wouldn't get them there. So far it's gone well.

Army Group Center

Here in the south there's nothing out of the ordinary. Here he's attacked again for the first time—a little bit stronger again. The battles are still in progress. [—] Here the report has just arrived by telephone. He's starting to attack the *Feldherrenhalle* [Panzer Grenadier Division] and the 6th Luftwaffe Field Division again. It's not marked on the map yet [south of Vitebsk]. Overall, there was a little bit less activity today—already early this morning. But those are probably the two attacks. Those also seem to be his two explicit focal points. We can see what units[986] have gradually been arriving here. It also seems to reach down below a bit. A bit more traffic has been reported from here, and here strong artillery fire was reported early today, as if he might try to expand[987] during the day today. [—] On this front [southwest of Vitebsk], from the 6th Luftwaffe Field Division down to here, the Jäger division[988] has pressed forward a bit in order to free this railway line.

THE FÜHRER: How is it here in the forest? If he's here in the forest he can reach the railway.

ZEITZLER: He's still in the forest with parts of a division. But they got a train through yesterday already: one train carrying men on leave drove through with armor protection. So he doesn't seem to be very close to it.

THE FÜHRER: The opening was removed here?

ZEITZLER: Yes, Sir. It has been eliminated.

Army Group North

In general, there's nothing unusual going on up above. The army group has now started the first movement.[989] I'd like to present the special map later. Field Marshal Küchler can show it later on the map. (*Presentation of a special map.*) This is the report from the army group regarding the withdrawal.

V. KÜCHLER: These movements have begun. I have not allowed a further withdrawal from this line into this line. This line was occupied last night, and tonight—the 30th—we will withdraw to this line, the so-called "Rollbahn" [highway] position.[990] This highway position is already prepared to some degree, so we can make a longer stop here. So I have initially given permission only to withdraw to this line, in order to see how this situation affects the enemy, and also to maintain the possibility of bringing this thing back, where there's still a great deal of immobile equipment, and also to have the possibility—if it takes longer—of remaining another day in this position. But in principle I suggest we carry out this withdrawal to the "Luchs" [position] quickly, for the following reason: not because the enemy might pressure us, but so that we can get the units over to here, and so that we can set ourselves up here in the new position. We don't want to come too late and have the enemy suddenly attack here—and then be forced counter push or counterattack again wherever we can in order to get to our actual main battle line.[991] In this position we can wait one or two days, because from here I can get the first division free; the 32nd [Infantry] Division comes out here. The 92nd [Infantry] Division is still here, and I can't take more than one on these bad roads and afterward on the railway. So there's no point in pulling out immediately or retreating faster. Not until this line will we free up two additional divisions—the 290th and 269th [Infantry Divisions]—and here the 122nd [Infantry] Division and the 58th [Infantry] Division as well.

THE FÜHRER: Where does this second position go now?

V. KÜCHLER: It goes like this—as it's marked here: (*Presentation of a special map.*) That's the precise trace. Here's where the "Panther"[992] [position] goes through. It goes from north to south, and in order to take advantage of the "Panther," a corner post like this should be made first. But here is the very good "Herbstnebel" ["Fall Fog"] position. I don't want to give up this town Novosokol'niki immediately, because from here he has dominating heights from which he can afterward look into this position. So I've ordered that we first move into this position, including these hills, in order to hold this Novosokol'niki a bit longer and in order to be able to take advantage of this railway. If he attacks very strongly later on, we'll go back to this "Herbstnebel" ["Fall Fog"] and occupy this "Herbstnebel" ["Fall Fog"] position. Here there's also already a blocking position under construction, so we can slant the thing here. I've said that it should initially be held and defended as a forward bastion.

THE FÜHRER: And from this thing you'll get 5 divisions in total?

V. KÜCHLER: Yes, Sir. 5 divisions. I would like to position one division—specifically the 58th [Infantry] Division—at Lake Il'men'.

ZEITZLER: Yes, I would be concerned there as well.[993]

V. KÜCHLER: I don't want to deploy them yet. But we still don't know yet what will happen—the enemy may not do anything here after all, and then I'd want to deploy a division here. (*Presentation of a new map.*) This is our final organization. Here's Group Gottberg[994] and here's the border. Here I would like to deploy the 290th [Infantry] Division. Here there's already the 132nd [Infantry] Division inside. It's already spread out a bit and will now come into a narrower area. Then the 122nd [Infantry] Division at this corner—the 81st [Infantry] Division, the 329th [Infantry] Division, the 23rd [Infantry] Division, the 263rd [Infantry] Division, and the 83rd [Infantry] Division—and then it continues as usual. Here's the 32nd [Infantry] Division. I want to have one division behind that as a reserve. That frees up Group Jäckeln,[995] and the Estonian Brigade will also be free. I ask that you leave Group Jäckeln with us in order to fight the [partisan] band. These are the police battalions—the Latvian and Estonian police battalions and the German police battalions. I actually wanted to suggest deploying the Estonian Brigade instead of the Latvian Brigade up on the Volkhov [River], so that they're fighting behind their own native country.[996] We wish to concentrate the Estonians and deploy the Latvian Brigade on this front now, and also to bring in the Latvians that are gradually being freed up, in order to provide reinforcement here. Perhaps that would free up the 8th Jäger Division. If that is manageable—all these movements will take approximately two to three weeks before everything is carried out—then we could take the Estonians up here, relieve the Latvians and deploy them here, and free up the 8th Jäger Division. Then, of course, we don't need to send the 58th [Infantry] Division in there. But that will take two to three weeks. I don't know if the enemy will allow us that much time. And once Lake Il'men' is frozen, he might attack there, so we have to keep one division here. Because when Lake Il'men' is frozen, it's no longer an obstacle—just the opposite. But it's right at the border between the two armies, and Lake Il'men' is free. Now he has motor sleds with trailers, and with those he can come across Lake Il'men' in a relatively short time—we calculated 2½ hours—from the eastern shore to the mouth of the Shelon [River], east of Sol'tsy. I'm worried that it might take too long before the 8th Jäger Division is freed up. That's why I want to ask your permission to place the 58th Division here first, just in case. Besides, it's by the railway here. If nothing happens here, we can still move them. [—] Now a second suggestion. Polotsk is here, and here are these roads that start from here and go diagonally backward into our space—into Army Group North's area. It's quite clear that Army Group Center has no great interest in doing anything about this matter, because it leads into Army Group North's sector. That's why I suggest that the army group border be drawn along this grid line[997] from here to here.

ZEITZLER: We had also thought of that.

V. KÜCHLER: Then we keep the 12th [Infantry] Division—because we have to deploy it here—and everything else stays. That also has the advantage that all the improvements on both sides of the army group are under unified command. That seems necessary to me because of the distribution of forces and because of the whole improvement of this position— that it's under single command.

ZEITZLER: With regard to supply, it's also possible to supply it from up above, down to Polotsk.

V. KÜCHLER: Yes, indeed! We have the railway and the road, and this rail line here will now be extended—I've already given the order—to here. That will be finished in about 2 to 3 weeks as well, so we can really strengthen this front.

THE FÜHRER: Has the extension already begun here?

V. KÜCHLER: Yes! That depends on the forces in Argen. The thing has started, as you ordered. But first of all, there are these forces—which are, after all, quite weak. They are not yet positioned like this; they're still like this—

ZEITZLER: The Reichsführer is building to here!

V. KÜCHLER: Yes, but I took one sector of the "Panther" [Position] down to here, because the Reichsführer was unable to provide enough forces to be able to build there as well—there are about 1,000 men. The staff of the 501st Construction Engineer Battalion and two Latvian construction battalions—in total 1,000 men—are now building in this sector down here. Then the building forces of the Reichsführer consist of four Ukrainian companies with 150 men each and two companies of 80 to 90 men each. So in total 770 men. So in this huge sector there are initially only 770 men from the Reichsführer and 1,000 men of ours working there. In addition, there are 250 civilian workers—which should be filled up to 4,000 men—currently employed by the IX Corps and Group Gottburg. That's to the south of us. But to unify the management—we would take the responsibility then—I'd request that the Reichsführer leave the forces with us, but also that the army group take responsibility for this expansion, as we've now also sent 1,000 men and a staff down there already. We have to defend it, after all; the Reichsführer can't do that. So we should get the responsibility then!

THE FÜHRER: This would be the new border?

ZEITZLER: I would like to speak with Army Group Center and check it from a supply perspective, and then it can be ordered. Especially if this railway here is gone later, this here should belong with that up above.

THE FÜHRER: What condition is the "Panther" [Position] in right now?

ZEITZLER: (*Presentation by Zeitzler.*) This is my engineering report with the obstacles, the improvements, etc., from December 23 of this year. Number of men deployed: 46,000—the numbers are pushed quite high—tank obstacles: 38 km, wire entanglement: 62 km, combat trenches: 56 km, combat positions: 1,880, shelters: 5,900, concrete bunkers with stones: 659, tank positions: 137.

(THE FÜHRER: Those are the new ones?)

Those are the iron emplacements. [—] Clearance of the field of fire: 10 km, roads constructed: 14 km, bridges: 1,250 m, field railway kilometers laid: 59. [—] Still under construction: 55 tank positions, 66 concrete bunkers and 3,000 other shelters. Then in front of the position, the creation of a cleared zone, where villages and everything else are eliminated, has already made good progress.

V. KÜCHLER: I have brought about an average improvement. (*Presentation.*) It's not the best sector, but it's far from the worst. We can accept it as average. This is an overview. That was the target on December 15. You can see that we've exceeded the December 15 objective in some sectors, and that we remained below it here in the Narva sector. Hardly anything has been done yet on [Lake] Peipus—first, because the forces were needed for other work there. We've now started them on this road, which leads from Narva to Krasnogvardeisk. That's why the thing is a little behind. But you can see that the goal was reached, by and large. (*Presentation of a map: Improvement of the 15th Infantry Division sector.*) Here is Pskov [Pleskau]. There, where the little boxes are filled in the shelters are ready, and the ones that are not filled in are under construction. These minefields have not been laid out yet, of course. It would be pointless to lay them out before the snow comes.

THE FÜHRER: Are the mines for that on hand?

V. KÜCHLER: The mines are on hand but are not laid out yet. You can see that it's a continuous obstacle along the whole front. This here is an occupied position, the "Pallisade" position. It's ready as well. The boxes that are not filled in are not yet ready.

THE FÜHRER: What does the red mean?

V. KÜCHLER: Red means artillery. Tank trenches are green and infantry is marked in blue.

THE FÜHRER: And yellow?

V. KÜCHLER: The yellow is the completed antitank defense trench.

THE FÜHRER: Down here it looks meager, of course. The total length of this "Panther" position, up to the new penetration,[998] is approximately what?

ZEITZLER: We had 655 km with the tip below, which is not being built.

THE FÜHRER: How much of that does the lake account for?

V. KÜCHLER: Lake Peipus is 180 km and the Gulf of Finland 75 km.

THE FÜHRER: Did you include the Gulf of Finland?

ZEITZLER: Only up to here.

V. KÜCHLER: Land 400 km, Lake Peipus 180 km, Gulf of Finland 75 km. We included the Gulf of Finland. That's a total of 655 km.

THE FÜHRER: And what would you need to be able to occupy the "Panther" Position under any circumstances? (*Presentation.*)

V. KÜCHLER: Now the average width[999] is 25 km. For the occupation of the "Panther" position, which has to be held at all costs, it's based on an average width of 15 km. With a land front of 400 km, this results in a need for 26 divisions, plus two reserve divisions on the right wing, plus one division at Pskov [Pleskau], two divisions on the Peipus front—we have to occupy them as well—and one division on the Gulf of Finland. So the minimum requirement, in total, is 32 divisions. And I especially ask that we get a panzer division somehow, or at least tanks in the strength of a panzer division, because we always need a striking force. That would be 32 divisions instead of 40 divisions now, so we would release 8 divisions.

THE FÜHRER: That's a land front of approximately 400 km?

ZEITZLER: Yes, Sir! Of which approximately 75 km are not yet constructed. That's the new thing down below.

THE FÜHRER (*after examining the documents*): Two thousand combat dugouts in 400 km—that's 20 in 4 km and 5 dugouts per kilometer.

V. KÜCHLER: There are 6,173 housing bunkers completed and 2,368 under construction.

THE FÜHRER: That would be about 10,000 altogether. In 400 km that's 25 per kilometer. [—] So concrete and tank positions together total approximately 1,000. That would be 2½ per kilometer. Have you thought about how you would carry out an evacuation here?

V. KÜCHLER: Yes, Sir! (*Presentation of a map.*)

THE FÜHRER: This up here is the lakefront?

V. KÜCHLER: Yes, Sir! [—] This here is the first zone, the so-called "Rollbahn" [Highway] position.

THE FÜHRER: How does that look, anyway?

V. KÜCHLER: It will be ready to defend on January 15. These here are the individual zones where there's always a certain stop—here a longer stop at the Luga Position—so we can send off the materiel that's moving back here. What worries us the most is the immobility of the divisions—the troops there. For example, the Luftwaffe field divisions, of which there are four here, are in general immobile or difficult to move. Then the Latvian Brigade, the SS Brigade—for the most part or at least a good share immobile or difficult to move. Then we have a great deal of heavy artillery, some of which is difficult to move. And the 7.5-cm guns are also difficult to move. Now, added to that, there is very unfavorable timing. There is still no snow. Or there is snow in some places, so that it's difficult to drive with wheeled vehicles, but in some places— right in this area—the snow has melted, so that it's hard to use the sleds.

THE FÜHRER: What kind of weather do you have now?

V. KÜCHLER: Mild weather like here. It's snowing. When we flew through to here there was snow. Then all of a sudden mild weather comes again. If you were to give the order today to carry out "Panther," we could begin the preparatory measures on January 6 and begin the evacuation itself on January 20.[1000] We need that much time to be able to bring back these things that are still immobile. I calculated it yesterday. The immediate measures could begin on January 6 because the mobility of the Luftwaffe field divisions, Latvians, Estonians, etc., and the artillery and the 7.5-cm guns is limited. (*Presentation.*) These are the dates when, according to the best calculations, we can say that this area is completely destroyed, at least for the most part, and we can bring away all the materiel. First day of troop movement is January 20. That would please us, because then we can expect that there will actually be snow and we can go by sled and tow our vehicles. [—] The duration is calculated at 28 days—so four weeks. With faster performance it could be done in 20 days. But in those 20 days we'd have to send some materiel there and blow it up, of course.

ZEITZLER: Why does it take so much time to start the immediate measures—until January 6?

V. KÜCHLER: Because for the immediate measures we have to bring in motor vehicles and horses, provide trains, load things on the trains, etc.

THE FÜHRER: The important thing is that these railways are destroyed, so he doesn't drive after us with full trains again. That's what has happened during all the evacuations so far.

ZEITZLER: Except for the "Büffel" ['Buffalo''] Evacuation [from the Rzhev salient]! With the "Büffel" it was good. That was the only one that went according to plan.

THE FÜHRER: We've carried out a few planned evacuations. The evacuation at Orel was systematic as well. It was ordered that they clear the Orel bend. But the trains weren't destroyed anywhere. They remained completely intact. For the dismantling and the complete destruction of these railways we have to provide vehicles, too!

V. KÜCHLER: Yesterday evening I spoke with Colonel General Lindemann[1001] again. He asks to be allowed to remain in his current position, of course, although the 1st [Infantry] Division was recalled. That, of course, was a huge blow to us.

THE FÜHRER: Granted. But now we have to endure completely different blows.

V. KÜCHLER: The 1st Division is an old line division of my old corps.[1002] So far I've carried out all three campaigns with the 1st, 11th, and 21st [Infantry] Divisions. In any case, I promised the Eighteenth Army that the 1st Division would remain up there for the use of the Eighteenth Army, and now the order suddenly comes that we have to give them away. That is, of course, extraordinarily hard. The division is experienced up there and knows every step of the way. It's been deployed everywhere already: at the Volkhov, in the Oranienbaum area—and it carried out attacks on Leningrad and was at the Luga front. Those are the divisions you can rely on best. The 1st Division is a very good division.

ZEITZLER: We could also use it very well down below.

V. KÜCHLER: As long as it's not smashed—if it's not thrown in straight off the train!

ZEITZLER: No, we'll assemble them into a larger group.

V. KÜCHLER: Then they can't do this as well, of course. That's why I suggested to you, my Führer, that we evacuate this thing as fast as possible, so that we don't have to reach our position first through a counterattack. Instead, we would come here and really have time to improve the thing first before the enemy arrives. He's not pressing forward, and I'm quite convinced that he doesn't want to press forward this far at all—except for here, perhaps, because he wants to have this railway here. He's gathered his assault group here and here, but I'm convinced that he's loosening up here. Because here in front there are old fortress divisions everywhere—precisely in these places that interest us most—which have no offensive strength. We're not sure right now about five to six divisions and panzer units. It's not clear if he has pulled them down toward [Army Group] Center or if he's concentrating his forces—as is possible—for a march against Nevel.

THE FÜHRER: I still need all the documents, Zeitzler! We need to get together again today to reach some decisions. Also the documents regarding the improvements!

ZEITZLER: Yes, Sir. I'll bring everything this evening.

THE FÜHRER: It seems to me that during an evacuation like this, the most important thing is that we are as strong as possible here during the evacuation, so that he can't push in here suddenly. That's the greatest danger.

V. KÜCHLER: That's why I wanted to have a division here or here.

THE FÜHRER: How is the improvement of your front position above Leningrad?

V. KÜCHLER: It's good. The position can be defended very well. There are obstacles and mines there. Everything has been newly laid out. The troops have enough dugouts. In fact, they have too many dugouts. That also has its disadvantages, because the enemy suddenly appears in the dugouts, which are often vacant now. He enters because our occupation is so thin that we can't prevent him from coming in somewhere—either secretly or with an artillery preparation—and all of a sudden he's sitting inside.

THE FÜHRER: You call it "thin." Take a look at the other divisions and compare their strengths and the condition of the improvements! You have the elite army—the show-off army for the whole Eastern army. That's downright provocative.

V. KÜCHLER: You already said that to me earlier. I've thought about it, and it bothered me, because during the earlier presentations you always saw how bad Army Group North was.

THE FÜHRER: That's completely misrepresented.

V. KÜCHLER: Yes, in relation to the others, but not in and of itself!

THE FÜHRER: In absolute terms yours is also very good, and in relative terms it's so good that it doesn't even bear discussion. It's only fortunate that the other army groups don't have an accurate look into these reports. Otherwise we couldn't save you at all anymore. Otherwise Zeitzler would pester me every day with blackmailing demands. Compared to you, the others are only poor wretches.

End: 12:50 p.m.

1944

* * * * *

ADOLF HITLER AND
THE NATIONAL SOCIALIST COMMANDING OFFICER (NSFO)

Preliminary remarks by Gerhard L. Weinberg

The preserved fragments of the stenographic records of Hitler's military conferences were published by Helmut Heiber in 1962.[1003] With few exceptions, these records were rescued in Berchtesgaden on the order of an American agency, after the German attempt to burn them. One exception is the transcript of the conference held on June 8, 1943,[1004] of which one copy went to the quartermaster department of the Armed Forces Operations Staff and was preserved in its files. Because the content of the conference transcript published here referred to the party chancellery, one copy was sent there; in this case, it was passed along "confidentially from hand to hand," and was then retained as a secret Reich matter. In this way the record was preserved, making its way to England with the Foreign Office files after the war, was microfilmed there, and finally handed over to the Federal Republic of Germany.[1005]

It's clear that the document is a copy of a piece belonging to the transcript collection. In the upper right-hand corner it carries the number "S 5/44" and in the upper left the mark "Dr.Hgn/Kr.," indicating, according to the system known from the other documents, that Dr. Kurt Haagen, a member, and Ludwig Krieger, the head of the Reichstag stenographic office, served as the stenographers for the meeting.

The main topics of the meeting are the organization, procedures, and personnel selection of the NS-Führungsoffiziere [NFSO—NS commanding officers] for the Armed Forces.[1006] After Hitler had ordered the establishment of an NS Operations Staff in the Armed Forces High Command on December 22, 1943,[1007] General of the Infantry Hermann Reinecke, named chief of the new staff, reported his plans for the new office on January 7, 1944. A meeting—the transcript of which follows—then took place, where Hitler presented his views of the problem of indoctrinating the Armed Forces with NS ideology. A few additional related problems were also discussed. The participation of the party chancellery in the NSFO work, already determined in the Führer order of December 22, 1943, explains the presence of Martin Bormann and the tone of the official party announcement of the Führer order, also dated January 7.[1008] That same day, Bormann also ordered the establishment of the relevant party chancellery working staff.[1009] The next day, Hitler signed an order regarding the ideological training of the soldiers.[1010]

During the weeks that followed, the questions that had been raised in the meeting of January 7 were addressed at headquarters. Following one suggestion given in this meeting by General Schmundt, Hitler began to gather the senior generals together for personal presentations on the importance of National Socialist education in the Army.[1011] The orders regarding the NS operations officers,[1012] issued February 6 and 9, must have taken their final form during those days.[1013] At the same time, the transcript of the January 7 conference was distributed in the party chancellery;[1014] the person responsible for NSFO matters in the party chancellery, Hauptbereichsleiter Willy Ruder,[1015] received the document for review[1016] on February 1. He incorporated some of Hitler's thoughts contained in it into a speech regarding the NSFO—given on Bormann's orders—to the Reichsleiters, Gauleiters, and unit commanders on February 23, 1944.[1017]

Thus, the conference of January 7, 1944 can easily be fit into the already known history of the NSFO, and it also sheds additional light on the sequence of events and the personal role of Hitler.[1018] Two themes in Hitler's explanations deserve special emphasis: first, his recurring reliance on real or supposed experiences from the time of the NSDAP struggle, and second, his concern about the possible influence of the propaganda of the German Officers' Union.[1019] Furthermore, the document is also significant because it reflects both Hitler's continuing mistrust toward the attitude of the Army and the inclination on the part of the leading generals to play up to the Commander-in-Chief of the Armed Forces.[1020]

Gerhard L. Weinberg

* * * * *

MEETING OF THE FÜHRER
WITH GENERAL REINECKE,[1021] JANUARY 7, 1944,
AT THE WOLFSSCHANZE[1022]

Also present:

Reichsleiter Bormann[1023]
Field Marshal General Keitel[1024]
Lieutenant General Schmundt[1025]

Major General Scherff[1026]
Lieutenant Colonel Borgmann[1027]

Beginning: 4:21 p.m.

REINECKE: My Führer, I report most obediently my appointment as Chief of the National Socialist Operations Staff of the Armed Forces High Command [OKW]. [—] May I present to you the underlying concept of this matter. [—] The order[1028] itself provides very clear guidelines. The assignments are very clearly outlined. Uniform guidance and orientation of all the people active in this area, together with the party chancellery. All instructions and guidelines in this area, which after the order possibly should and could come also from you, my Führer, should go to the commanders-in-chief. Not to the NS operations staffs of the Armed Forces branches, therefore, but to the commanders-in-chief, and from there go on to the commanders-in-chief of the armies, the air forces, and so on—always via the chain of command, just like all other orders. [—] That's why, in order to ensure these measures—I would almost like to say—there must be a revolution with regard to the appointment of all those officers who are to be active in this area now. They must be made equal in position and importance to the tactical command and the personnel command everywhere, and as such their commanders must grant them the same rights as, for example, the Ia [operations officer] of the division, the general staff officer or the personnel officer who deals with personal data, so that for all practical purposes they have a position in the staff—and also in the overall impact—that's necessary.

THE FÜHRER: That's absolutely necessary!

REINECKE: I believe that must be the foundation. There must therefore be a complete change in the meaning, so that externally it must be made clear in all guidelines and orders that the war can be won with 51 percent certainty through the ideological attitude and orientation of all officers. New methods, therefore also new weapons!

THE FÜHRER: There will be great resistance against it!

KEITEL: No, my Führer, we don't expect that.

SCHMUNDT: I don't believe it!

KEITEL: We've already come a long way with the education. I've also spoken about it with Reichsleiter Bormann. In some places there may be [*sic*] uncomprehending people, who will have to be convinced or brought to it by order. For the rest, there's absolute and unequivocal understanding.

REINECKE: I'm convinced that the assignment can only be carried out properly if all the men who are to be active in this area are personally selected and used in such a way that they can really master their assignments. We don't want intellectuals, scientists, and so on.

THE FÜHRER: They are totally useless and detrimental!

REINECKE: We're clear about the fact that these can only be men who are fanatical and believe within themselves that this task must account for at least 51 percent of the entire command. [—] I didn't want to suggest a vertical organization—for instance, beside the command structure there would now be NS operations officers everywhere who are guided vertically from above. Instead it would be like it is in the tactical area: orders from all command positions down to the very bottom, except that the official in charge is—just like in the tactical area—the NS operations officer.[1029] [—] Only the training and orientation of the uniform operations staffs of the three commanders-in-chief and their operations officers should be carried out vertically and horizontally. [—] I'd like to present how that is carried out organizationally! [—] In the OKW, or with me as Chief of the Operations Staff, there is now a representative of Reichsleiter Bormann, who has already established a very close connection between the two agencies. I don't want to establish a big bureaucracy here, just a very small operations staff without any officials, only with men who already have practical experience in this field. First, there are some old political fighters and a few young officers who have already proven themselves with the same fanaticism. The political fighters we want to bring into the small operations staff should also have proven themselves at the front as a prerequisite. I've already received a long list of names from the party chancellery, and I've looked through it myself. They all have front awards—some very distinguished. They all have at least the Iron Cross I or the bar for the Iron Cross I, so they all have significant front experience—which, unfortunately, was denied me personally in this war. [—] As a bureaucracy in this small operations staff, of course, there's nothing left except, for example, to take in the entire army welfare services, which does the "Strength through Joy" [Kraft durch Freude] employment, the employment of the propaganda ministry—so the morale-boosting care for the people, which also must be guided somehow—the organization of leisure time—and what I call the political bureaucracy, which deals with all questions of custom, marriage applications, and so on, which have a practical effect on the paper field, on the censorship field, etc. It should be a very small body. The same was planned for the commanders-in-chief of the Armed Forces branches, in order to bring all the assignments that we want to see from a strictly military perspective out of the correspondence and out of the bureaucratic procedure, which isn't that easy, my Führer. [—] Duplicate work should be avoided. Now it's quite chaotic, in that every one who means well and who can write well is starting or has started to write: each after his own fashion and in his own way. We wanted to avoid duplication at all cost. It affects all possible fields. Not only because down there no one knows anymore what is valid and what should be! We can also save a lot of work that has already been done—by the Waffen SS, for example—if we also use it here. I already spoke with the Reichsleiter SS about it a few days ago. He also promised to support me in all these areas, so that we can use much of what is already being done through Reichsleiter Rosenberg,[1030] through the party chancellery or in the Waffen SS. Then we wanted to orient the flowery speeches a bit, which are very prominent now, and hold them back a bit in favor of the political-ideological orientation. [—] Down below, in the divisions, armies, corps, air forces, naval high commands, etc.: the establishment of full-time NS operations officers. We wanted to press to fill these positions, so that if the positions aren't established and then it's said: there's no one I can put in there. But we have to use some pressure here; this position must be absolutely occupied. Orders have in some cases been used quite extensively there.

THE FÜHRER: The guarantee is in the fact that we really fill them with the appropriate men.

REINECKE: Yes, Sir. We wanted to carry out a purge. We wanted to clear out the intellectuals from all these positions. There are many philologists in there, as I've recognized. They should come out. On the other side, though, pressure should be used so that these positions are really filled. [—] On the other hand, we won't be able to go any further than to the divisions, due to a lack of officers! Down in the regiments, battalions and companies the tasks must be done on the side. But due to the fact that the pressure comes from the divisional staff, and the NS Operations Staff will have to be on the road a lot as well, the divisional commander will also be informed as to whether the regimental commander, the battalion commander, etc. really look after these things.

THE FÜHRER: What guarantee do we have that the divisional commanders will really promote this matter positively and not look at the whole issue right away from the viewpoint of doing anything to get the thing—

KEITEL: We have to check that, because they're in all the divisions. We have to check to make sure the man concerned is qualified. We'll do that together with the party chancellery. And we have to remove the unqualified ones. And third, by supervising all the activity—an inspection activity that, above all, requires those men who are employed with the commanders-in-chief, who travel around all the time, who look at the people, listen to them and judge them, and who must have a veto right in this area.

THE FÜHRER: I have experience in this field myself, from my time as an education officer in the Reichswehr.[1031] There I saw myself what, for instance, a regimental commander or even a battalion commander can do—that he can totally kill a thing like this.

KEITEL: It can only be achieved with continual supervision.

THE FÜHRER: We must not recoil from holding such commanders responsible for that. Because one thing is critical: this thing makes sense only if it isn't considered a kind of private issue, which one can either do or not do, and above all, it must be made clear right from the beginning that any criticism and grumbling about orders issued in the ideological field will be punished just the same as criticism of tactical or any other military matters, so that it will cost the officers involved position and insignia. Everybody must know that it's not a matter of free will, and that he must not say, "Actually it's nonsense—I don't believe this," and so on. That can't happen. He can't say that about other things either. He can't criticize any order he receives, especially to his subordinates. But it happens in this area. I receive dreadful news about that. The worst is—I can say it—in Hoth's Army,[1032] where Hoth constantly criticizes all the ideological measures in the presence of the generals. That's why the Fourth Panzer Army has had the worst attitude.

KEITEL: I'm aware of that as well.

REINECKE: I've discussed this matter with Schmundt. It's also necessary for the operations officer to work closely with the personnel officer and to communicate his observations to him. He also has to tell the commander, "I've observed on my visits to the troops there and there that no one is taking care of these things."

SCHMUNDT: The most important thing is that the responsibility of the commanders is maintained. The commander is the commissar.[1033] That's the trust that you, my Führer, have placed in him. Just as it is in the tactical, operational and educational command, he must have someone responsible for this—since the general staff officer and also the Ic [intelligence officer] are totally busy with operational assignments—someone who stands by his side in that respect, exactly like the IIa [personnel officer] in personnel matters. It's not the higher adjutant who makes the personnel policy; the commander is responsible. In the same way he's also responsible for the NS operations. Within headquarters, of course, cooperation is necessary between these three advisors to the commander. It's arranged like that within the headquarters. That's why it's also equally necessary that, just as the Chief of General Staff in the OKW is responsible to you for the entire tactical command, and just as I am responsible to you for the personnel policy in the Army, a person has to be identified in the Army who is responsible for the National Socialist operations. This person responsible for the National Socialist operations and I have, of course, to keep very close contact with General Zeitzler,[1034] since in the end the command of the field army is the most important thing, and we are jointly responsible to you personally for these things. The man chosen for this job receives his orders through the Armed Forces command, also in this case within the framework of the overall political leadership of the people, in the interrelationship between home-front-party, etc. So it becomes true what you, my Führer, declared already after 1933—that the two fundamentals this state and our people are based on are, on the one hand, the party, and on the other hand, the Armed Forces. The officers and commanders of the Armed Forces must also be just as much political ambassadors as the party officials—as you, my Führer, said it before the young officers.[1035] We must all speak the same language. We take over the young German man who has started in a certain direction: from the *HJ* [Hitler Youth] via labor service and party into the army. Here there must be no contradiction, no gap. My Führer, you may be one hundred percent convinced that there is a real yearning for this way to be clear. All the officers from the front have told me so. To some degree they've helped themselves, because they haven't been given these foundations from above yet. I have to keep emphasizing that in particular. That's why I'm convinced that this is a matter that will find only open doors.

REINECKE: I'd like to add here that especially the instructions for the NS operations officers must outline all these problems very clearly, so that the NS operations officer won't become a *Politruk* [political officer in the Red Army] or a complaint office—like a kind of republican complaint office again—on the one hand, but also not a priest on the other hand. He shouldn't go from the division to the troops and appear as a speaker like a preacher in the desert; instead, he should consider it his goal to teach the officers the art of really leading the people in a political-ideological way. That's where I see his main task—not to appear as a priest and speaker and give presentations everywhere.

THE FÜHRER: We just have to understand that only a very few of the officers will be suitable for this.

SCHMUNDT: In the distant past they received their wisdom in the Bible and from the drill regulations. As a consequence they will also need some sort of drill regulations here, and that's the booklet "What are we fighting for?"[1036] which they will receive initially, as ordered. In front there will be the obligatory order from you, my Führer, with your introduction.

KEITEL: We will certainly guide this correctly via the three headquarters and will also check it on site—how it's going—and then we have to intervene, since the personnel policy and the command are closely connected in this field.

THE FÜHRER: First one thing would be necessary: that we bring together here the selected officers from the armies, the corps and the divisions, and lead them through an eight- or fourteen-day course.

REINECKE: I had planned on that.

THE FÜHRER: I will speak to them myself then.

SCHMUNDT: I'd like to add a request to that, which is really extremely urgent. Everyone will be trained and drilled; only the commanders are never brought together. The fact is that the workers always know more than the commanders themselves, and that hurts the real front commanders. So that's why the request again that all generals, including the divisional commanders, be addressed once more by you, my Führer.[1037]

THE FÜHRER: It's hard to get them together.

SCHMUNDT: It must be possible—just like we get the adjutants together.

KEITEL: It's a bit more difficult. The IIa [personnel officer] can be replaced for eight days, but it's not that easily with the commander. But we have to aim for it.

BORMANN: If it were possible, it would be the greatest success.

THE FÜHRER: Let me explain here how we did the training in the party, to give you a picture of how difficult it actually was. When I established the party, the first training took place in the ongoing public meetings. These public meetings weren't really suitable for inner party training, though, as they were somewhat influenced tactically by the listeners we had. There were Communists, etc., so it was difficult to make the final aims clear without being kicked out immediately. That's why we had the so-called speech evenings. Only the party members, who were already absolutely convinced, came to them. To show you how I established a local group like Munich: when I started in Munich there was a mass rally initially twice, later three times a week. In addition, there was this so-called speech evening every Monday. At these speech evenings there were the confirmed party members, who were better, and of whom we could say that some of them are intended for greater tasks already. Then the individual sections held speech evenings like that as well. The people who participated in my speech evenings were mostly section commanders. They then held speech evenings themselves with their members, so the place was constantly worked over.

In addition, there were special training sessions for the SA, which also had its own courses in which presentations would be made. The SA commanders had their own course, which usually lasted ten days. I spoke to the SA commanders personally at least three to four times in these courses, and all the other leading men spoke there as well.

BORMANN: Absolutely all the men! Everyone was there.

THE FÜHRER: So we can say that there was such an enormous training effort that gradually absolutely identical conceptions were developed in all of them. In general it went so far that the measures that I had implemented in Munich, Goebbels had done in Berlin as well—as is the case in the purely military tactical field as well. There it's generally brought about by continuous training, so that if a second lieutenant falls in some phase of the battle, the other second lieutenant, who takes over the platoon, does almost exactly the same as the fallen one would have. Or that if a captain falls in a certain phase of the battle, his substitute who takes over the command of the company also does the same as the other one would have done. Or that if the regimental commander falls, the one who takes over the command does the same as the regimental commander would have done—because they've all had uniform training. We must reach that in this field, too.

BORMANN: In order to support General Reinecke and the other participants appropriately here, we've already selected some of our people. Each of the formations and various offices—the Rosenberg office,[1038] and so on—will send one man to me, who will be the official in charge of this special field, so that General Reinecke can really make use of all experiences of the party.

THE FÜHRER: I mention this because it's the complete opposite of what happened 1918. Back then it was real nonsense; there was no morale. The man who inspired it back then, Lieutenant Colonel Nicolai,[1039] had no idea and was completely up in the air. This must spread out in a uniform way throughout the entire Armed Forces, which reaches all the way down, so that we can say: if an ideological problem arises, it will be dealt with the same way in the 14th Division as in the 162nd, and the same way there as anywhere else. They will all be trained uniformly and will have the same views on all matters because they had the same basic training everywhere. That must be our ultimate goal.

REINECKE: For that reason we've included in the plan to start not only with the commanders, but also at the war academies, the military schools and the schools for non-commissioned officers, so that the people who teach this will all be oriented in one direction from the start. We have to bring them together straight across all three branches of the Armed Forces.

Then I had planned, for example, that also the departmental heads of the commanders-in-chief would be brought together once with the NS operations staff. That seems very important to me, because I believe that the work can't be done everywhere there in this way because of a lack of time. They always say, "We don't have time for that; we can't get it done by then." This must be achieved now through the same pressure we also bring to bear in the personnel field, so that everyone sees that whoever is not definitely active in this area will be demoted or will get an unfavorable comment in his file, just like he used to get them if he failed tactically or did some nonsense.

THE FÜHRER: But in the future it must not be seen as a recommendation for the one in question, if he gets an unfavorable comment. Until now it's been seen almost as a recommendation.

REINECKE: Recently we've also discussed all the material with Herr Junge.[1040] He told me some very interesting things. It doesn't seem to be the way it's supposed to be everywhere. At least I don't think we'll get through to the troops with very longwinded papers; instead, we'll have to bring along short, concise combat leaflets for the troops. But they really have to reach the troops.

THE FÜHRER: They especially have to take a stand on the issues that are critical at the moment. That was also the purpose of our speech evenings. During those evenings, the critical daily events were discussed from an ideological perspective, so that the people were trained on those issues. That's how the Communists' training used to be done as well, in their so-called discussion evenings.

REINECKE: We also wanted to intervene in the propaganda there, and request that this or that particular thing be done through the propaganda channel as well. That's why the field marshal[1041] has already ordered that some of the people who are active there are to work with me on the side. [—] In addition, I already spoke with Reichsleiter Bormann about how we will make sure that the commanding generals[1042] are informed quickly on timely matters. In the same way that the Gauleiters learn as quickly as possible how you, my Führer, think about this or that matter, it must also go to the commanding generals. Otherwise they get angry, feel left out, lose interest, and say, "We don't get this until two weeks later, or we learn about it only from talking with a Gauleiter." That's why I think we can get them here faster if we can guarantee them: whatever the Reichsleiter hands down through the party channel, you will also get in a clear form: this and this is my wish. The way it is with the troops—if the commander wants the people to go to church, then they go to church, whether they feel that way or not, and if he says: I don't want them to go to church, they don't go. That's how it is, for all practical purposes.

THE FÜHRER: According to my experience it isn't always like that, though. He says, "You don't need to go to church." But he has them line up, and whoever doesn't go to church has to peel potatoes or clean latrines, while those who go to church are free afterward.

BORMANN: I've already spoken with Goebbels about this field of active propaganda. He will support it extensively.

THE FÜHRER: It just has to work. That's quite clear!

REINECKE: It won't happen all at once, of course, but we must start now to have a wide effect.

THE FÜHRER: The critical thing is that we find the right people.

BORMANN: Yes, the right choice of personalities! We had the Gauleiters name all the people they thought appropriate, and asked the same of the Reichleiters, unit commanders, and so on.

THE FÜHRER: The best people are just good enough for that. In the Great War they did it in such a way that they turned the officer who wasn't good for anything else into a so-called education officer. We have to take the best people for that.

REINECKE: We'll take all the people who are political fighters to Weimar together. They'll come together now as company commanders, or whatever they were. First they have to become familiar with our ideas, and then we want to select the most qualified ones, who will join the operations staffs of the OKW and the three branches of the Armed Forces; we also want to see how we can use them as operations officers. The pressure must come from above. First there must be someone in the army group who mobilizes everything, then in the army, etc., so we get the pressure in from up above.

BORMANN: What General Schmundt said is correct. If we could win the commanders, we would arrive much faster. That's why we should consider getting the commanders together.

SCHMUNDT: It will have to be a couple of times more often, since we can't get everyone together at once; but it would certainly work, even if we only take the ones coming back from their leave. The commanders go on leave all the time, too.

THE FÜHRER: Certainly. They do go on leave all the time in a big rotation, but taking out the commanders of 60 divisions all at once will be hard.

SCHMUNDT: We'll do the calculations and make a recommendation.

KEITEL: We can't put too many demands on your time either, my Führer. It must be a fairly large circle, so it doesn't have to be repeated so often. But we'll find a way.

REINECKE: In any case, a great many senior officers complained that they weren't taken along to Bad Schachen and therefore couldn't see you, my Führer.[1043] They've written some very rude letters.

KEITEL: Nevertheless, we did have several hundred men here.

SCHMUNDT: But no front commanders!

KEITEL: No, only commanders in Germany, but they needed it badly.

REINECKE: That would be all for now concerning the plans. The guide-lines that we are developing and will then present to you, my Führer—the written materials that will go out—still need to be reviewed by Reichsleiter Bormann.

THE FÜHRER: The most dangerous thing happening at the front right now—several people have told me this now, most clearly Junge,[1044] because he's very thoroughly trained—is without doubt the appeals coming from General Seydlitz.[1045] It comes under a black-white-red flag, and the man doesn't know: is it true or not? It comes from officers, and the man so far has had the opinion that officers are men of honor. That man isn't aware that a number of such swine exist. There's no doubt that these are not people who are acting under pressure now. These people are not just being pushed forward—they're acting on their own. One just needs to read the writings. I know the dialectics and diction of the Jews very well. If I get an appeal today from someone, I can tell right away if it comes from the Reichsmarshal, from Goebbels, or from Ley. I can see that in the diction, just like, vice versa, my people know my diction very well. I didn't used to be able to write any articles, because my old party comrades told me im-mediately, "You wrote that yourself." When I asked, "How do you know that?", I was pointed to a few sentences. You can recognize immediately whether something has been done by a general staff officer or by a Jew. [—] Junge says that one thing that's been quite effective lately was a pre-sentation on how to make a photomontage. The common people don't know how they fake something like that. [—] We can't get around it any-more. I'm still considering: either we maintain the approach that the people are acting under pressure—of course, then we might be rebuked very un-pleasantly; if they go out and speak more and more sharply on the radio, no one will believe anymore that they're acting under pressure—or we could say that those are some characterless pigs who let themselves be bought. In the other case we can just be repudiated. What can we do if they go out and speak over the radio? They already talk on the radio all the time anyway. [—] I want to involve myself in this very heavily. I also want you [*to General Reinecke*] to report to me in short intervals. In my opinion, a gradual adoption of the National Socialist body of thought by the entire Armed Forces is the most important thing there is. How is a man sup-posed to be ready in the end to give his utmost if he doesn't know exactly why? It used to be said for Christianity. As long as it was a battle for Christianity, the Christians fought. Later, when the battles were about matters regarding the Monarchy, the Christian issue wasn't effective anymore. Despite all the doping, the Bavarians didn't become any braver either. That had nothing to do with Christianity anymore. Today, where it's about the basic elements of existence or nonexistence, about ruin or survival of the races, we must make it absolutely clear to that man. He must know what it's about. If someone goes out and tells his own people: if we lose the war, we'll experience a wonderful renaissance together with the Russians—that's a crime, an unparalleled disaster. They've removed their Tukhachevsky,[1046] and such an idiot like Kurt v. Seydlitz thinks that he'll remain then. Those creatures are dumb, or it's a lack of character that's completely without bounds—usually both together. We have to take a position against it.

REINECKE: I'd like to address two more points here. You brought up with the field marshal the issue of the German salute for the Armed Forces.

THE FÜHRER: Two things will be done on January 30. The regimental flags will be taken down and the German salute will be introduced for the Armed Forces.[1047]

KEITEL: I have two drafts here. They only represent the matter strictly from a command perspective. But you wanted to bring it in your proclamation.

REINECKE: I thought that propagandistically we could maybe direct the thoughts to the introduction of the German salute shortly beforehand, by telling the people who talk so much of tradition. If we're so attached to tradition, we could latch onto Fredrick the Great and reintroduce the old salute that was used back then. That's a tradition from a time when Prussia was at war.

SCHMUNDT: I don't think that's the most important thing. They all know that very well. The point is that there are still many officers who have always saluted that way, from their time as cadets up to field marshal, and they'll find it strange if they have to salute differently now. The important thing is that it not be issued as a military order: "Attention! As of tomorrow, use the German salute." Only you, my Führer, can express it in a proclamation, which at the end will prove: seen from this direction, no other conclusion is possible.

THE FÜHRER: That must be done in the context of a total standardization of the Armed Forces, party, and so on. We must face the other world as a total uniform body. [—] I will do that.

SCHMUNDT: The other point, which concerns the regimental flags, is absolutely clear.

THE FÜHRER: Yes, today there is only one ideological flag, no unit flag anymore. Every other state in the world fights united under its own "tricolor," its "star-spangled banner," and so on; only we have the unit flags.

KEITEL: Especially since no one has even fought under these unit flags.

THE FÜHRER: All the units that have newly arrived in the Reich didn't arrive under these flags, but under the swastika.

KEITEL: It would be an absolutely impossible situation for us if, for example, we could come to the armory hall on Heroes Memorial Day, and the unit flags would be there. It would give the same feeling as if someone were standing there in a blue Rock [coat] with the ball helmet.

REINECKE: That's why I wanted to suggest that we only display those flags that have been under fire, the flags of 1870 and 1914. Nothing else is of interest.

THE FÜHRER: The flags were made with lightening speed back then. First we didn't want any flags at all. But when the rumor circulated that I intended to introduce the swastika, Colonel General Fritsch[1048] did it all very quickly. The only branch of the Armed Forces that resisted was the Navy. The Luftwaffe was enthusiastic because it now had the hope of being able to go a bit further than others with decoration and embroidery.

KEITEL: The thing is so obvious that it's clear there won't be any trouble about it at all. The introduction of the German salute just means standardizing the salute that everyone has to make to you, my Führer, and actually does make. It won't do for the troops to salute their supreme commander with a different salute than they salute themselves.

SCHERFF: Everyone will welcome that.

THE FÜHRER: I don't care at all. Considering the great future tasks, we can only come out of this battle as an absolutely united ideological body.

SCHMUNDT: The important thing is just that we do it the right way. These are things that shake up all kinds of values, and they can't be done with a short order of five lines, like the order: As of tomorrow, no coats will be worn anymore.

REINECKE: It must not come through the garrison regulations.

BORMANN: It must be evaluated *positively*![1049]

REINECKE: Then on special holidays—for example, on Heroes Memorial Day—we may still display the old Army flags that were under fire?

(THE FÜHRER: Yes!)

KEITEL: But otherwise only the Reich war flag will appear. It will also be displayed if an honor-guard company appears. I've already put together the points that are under consideration here.

SCHMUNDT: Those are side issues. The main point I see is the following: that the flag really is carried and displayed at the front, when appeals take place at the front, when the dead are buried, when a unit is decorated—that the flags are decorated as well. If today a regiment asks: why hasn't our regimental commander been decorated? We've fought well. Yes, if the regimental commander is transferred after eight days, there will be another regimental commander there who isn't decorated either. The flag must be decorated when the regiment is to be honored as a whole. The regimental commander receives the award for his personal bravery and takes it with him when he goes somewhere else.

THE FÜHRER: If he got it for his regiment, he'd have to give it away again if he went somewhere else.

SCHMUNDT: It's wrong to claim that the units don't need a flag. It's only a question of down to the regiment or the battalion. Today with these weak forces we'll have to stop at the regiment. The regiment should have a flag, not to charge with, but which—as I imagine it—it could plant if it takes a fixed place.

THE FÜHRER: Our gentlemen in Stalingrad reported to me that the Russians would charge with unfurled flags. They were very shocked by this story.

KEITEL: They must not appear in the homeland. So far they've appeared at every opportunity. That must stop. Every honor-guard company or every honor-guard battalion has a flag along at home now. Lately there have been only a few, but, for example, last year at the Heroes Memorial festivities!

THE FÜHRER: The Navy wanted to avoid that back then. It was imposed upon them. They said, "We sail under a flag into a foreign country, and then we go ashore and have to show a unit flag, which no one knows."

KEITEL: Reinecke wanted to go to the Reichsmarshal already in the last few days, and speak with him also about those questions. Now it has been postponed because the Reichsmarshal didn't feel well. Reinecke spoke with the Grand Admiral,[1050] and the questions that are now to be solved have also been clarified.[1051]

REINECKE: Not with all the viewpoints that we have here, though; but the Navy has been quite active.

KEITEL: I would like to select another officer for the Army.

THE FÜHRER: Schörner[1052]—he's a fanatic!

KEITEL: Yes, he's a fanatic and pulls the people with him. I don't want to see how he handles the people who don't follow when he comes to the front and removes the people who don't fulfill their responsibilities. If we could have him for a couple of months! If he could be released from his command post for a time, so he could get this thing here underway, then we could release him later for another assignment after he had instructed and trained others. We need a fanatic, so that the thing will take the right shape first, and he would do that wonderfully. This is an assignment to which the greatest importance is attached.

(End: 5:09 p.m.)

* * * * *

January 28, 1944

The offensive that began on Christmas Eve 1943 against the Fourth Panzer Army has in the meantime brought the Russians west across the old Polish border to Sarny, and via Novograd–Volynsk to just outside Rovno, 300 km west of Kiev. On the other—also open—flank of the Fourth Panzer Army, the Russians reached Pogrebishche and the area near Vinnitsa on January 16, aiming for Uman' and temporarily even blocking the main supply line of Army Group South at Zhmerinka—as they had thrown back a counterattack on Pogrebishche and Zhashkov during the second half of January. Meanwhile, the 1st, 2nd, 3rd, and 4th Ukrainian Fronts pressed against the German lines that were still echeloned far ahead to the east, along the middle and lower reaches of the Dnieper River from Cherkassy to Nikopol'. Southeast of the Eighth Army, Kirovograd—situated upstream on the Dnieper from Cherkassy—was lost on January 9. Since then, the Russian attack has gained ground further to the northwest, and in the last three days, the Russians have also pushed out toward the southeast from their penetration area at Belaia Tserkov, where they were forced back a few days ago from the south. On this day, the panzer tips of both spearheads met at Zvenigorodka.

In Army Group Center's sector, during the first battle for Vitebsk from January 3 to 18, the enemy achieved little aside from a few successes south of the city. Between the Pripiat' and Berezina Rivers, the Second Army had suffered such deep penetrations since January 8 that, by mid-month, the army could barely pull itself out of the noose. Now the enemy is attacking—without decisive success—north of the Berezina as well.

Against the Eighteenth Army in the north, the Soviets attacked on January 14 from the Leningrad Front and on January 18 from the Volkhov River bridgehead. On January 19 the blockade ring was finally broken open. North of Lake Il'men', the Volkhov River front was penetrated and Novgorod was evacuated; from Leningrad and Oranienbaum the Russians have already advanced to just outside Narva. The Eighteenth Army is withdrawing behind the Luga River.

In Italy German units—attacked by the Americans on January 4—withdrew to the main position on the Rapido River. Since the night of January 17, the Anglo-Americans have been attacking the lower Garigliano River and, since the 20th, the Rapido as well. The threatening breakthrough into the Liri valley has forced the Germans to deploy their reserves. During the night of January 21, the American VI Army Corps conducted a surprise landing at Anzio and Nettuno. Only the hesitant way the bridgehead was developed, finally reaching a radius of 20 km, enabled the establishment of a German defense front by the Fourteenth Army. (*Maps 5, 7, 10, and 11*)

* * * * *

Midday Situation Report, January 28, 1944[1053]

Present:

The Führer	*Major General v. Buttlar*
Field Marshal Keitel	*Major General Scherff*
General Model	*Rear Admiral v. Puttkamer*
General Zeitzler	*Colonel v. Below*
Colonel General Jodl	*Captain Assmann*
General Korten	*Lieutenant Colonel Borgmann*
Lieutenant General Schmundt	*Major John v. Freyend*
Lieutenant General Heusinger	*Major Büchs*
Gruppenführer Fegelein	*Sturmbannführer Darges*
Ambassador Hewel	

(The completeness of the list can't be guaranteed.[1054])

Beginning: presumably 1:00 p.m.

The East (Army Groups A and South)

ZEITZLER: Here there were additional attacks, but seemingly not as strong as on the previous days ... good for us in general because of the ice thing. Stronger activity started here all of a sudden ... there's no indication if there will be anything significant or not. For the most part, we didn't see where the dispersal went ... (Here we learned the following from listening in on enemy radio communication): at these three focal points, each unit is to build 80 tank decoys.[1055] So apparently he's taking something away from all the focal points.

THE FÜHRER: Did this thing up there northwest of Berdichev, with the tank decoys across from the *Leibstandarte* [Panzer Grenadier Division], prove to be true?

ZEITZLER: Yes, indeed. There were decoys. He didn't attack strongly there either.

THE FÜHRER: In time one begins to worry that everywhere that fellow—

ZEITZLER: Yes, Sir. He does it on purpose. With radio things we have to be careful. [—] Here it's the same as what I said. Nothing in particular on this front. They still expect the attack *here*, because they say, "That's garbage there; that's why he moved it." Here on this front individual tanks have broken through. I don't consider this situation serious. Those are individual things, which came in to Shatalovka[1056] and are everywhere around here. Our thing is holding, for the most part. There are isolated small gaps in it. The 320th [Infantry] Division will be pulled forward. The results here were, for the most part, quite satisfactory during the last four days. On this front we're pleased that the attack spearheads met at 9:30 and that they got a very high result: 530 tanks disabled. If we add to those the 114 (that would be 644 tanks) that were destroyed altogether.[1057] Also the number of prisoners is certainly relatively high. [—] On the other hand, the situation became more serious here. Here it first seemed ... that he has a huge focal point here and presses in here a great deal. Now the army group had the idea that, during the night, when they ... the thing ... to come from above. That's a good idea. But now the situation became much more dangerous today, so they're still doubtful at the moment ... And now yesterday's request is repeated to withdraw this tip to inside this line ... and in order to be able to attack with these battalions. (Then) this attack up here (should) be carried out later after all.

THE FÜHRER: I don't believe that the attack here makes sense anymore.

ZEITZLER: ... still push in.

THE FÜHRER: That would be the theory—that they would stand here. Then they stand *there*, and then they push here into empty space. Here they won't get anything out.

ZEITZLER: My Führer, you would like that, but right now it still isn't possible that way. The fortunate thing is that they ... so fast ... They just did that under pressure in order to get something out. The bigger decision is, of course, if we ... here ... pull around to here. Perhaps it's relatively loose in his area, and we can reach here.

THE FÜHRER: Then it's all the more important down here that we don't go back under any circumstances. Because if they go back here, a flat line results and they push into the empty ...

ZEITZLER: It's very much at the point here. (The question is) whether the Kiev corps has come down here already—apparently not.

THE FÜHRER: ... At least four, probably five, of his (tank units) are eliminated.

ZEITZLER: We saw that in terms of the numbers as well. He threw in everything that was up here.

THE FÜHRER: That also indicates that his driving technique has become worse.

ZEITZLER: So I will pass this on then, my Führer. [—] On this front up here there is still nothing heavy.

THE FÜHRER: Can't you at least throw the *Viking* [SS Panzer Grenadier Division's] tanks out in front?

ZEITZLER: They're in here now. They also want to take something out of here as quickly as possible. But I don't believe it's possible today anyway. Then it will start to weaken here.

THE FÜHRER: They're in here?

ZEITZLER: Tanks came in here up to Zvenigorodka.

THE FÜHRER: An unpleasant thing!

ZEITZLER: So I don't consider this thing to be that significant, in and of itself. Except that here we can't easily see whether it's a strong thing or not. It could be a strong thing. He expected this attack. But, on the other hand, one can consider that ... where we can do something as well.

THE FÜHRER: Is this here an attack that was just made?

ZEITZLER: No, we came over there afterward, at 9:30. There was an attack there. The 7th Panzer Division has been deployed to counter that.

THE FÜHRER: If we could just release the 1st Panzer Division! It has 40 and 22 tanks ...

ZEITZLER: It has a relatively wide front.

THE FÜHRER: We might add them here! It's not quite enough.

ZEITZLER: In principle, Manstein[1058] wants—if this connection here is established ... That would be good. It would be better, of course, if we could add the 1st Panzer Division. But it'll be a while before it arrives.

THE FÜHRER: In the end they won't move.

HEUSINGER: We should find out whether Manstein's objective has changed.

ZEITZLER: And say right away that the Führer doesn't want to have the ...

THE FÜHRER: Even if he wants to make the thrust to the rear. Because if this goes back here, he's pushing into empty space. It all depends on when he expects to be ready here.[1059] You also see one thing: how good it is if a group defends itself somewhere for a long time. That ties up forces on our side, and it's the same on the other side.

ZEITZLER: ... Here he has again deployed machine-gun artillery battalions; so that doesn't interest him much ...

THE FÜHRER: ...

ZEITZLER: Up on that front the thing should start now after all, in order to press forward to the east and to press that forward ... that they go ahead and try it. There's a certain mobility in it; something is being held, and there's a certain activity ... still take it away afterward.

FEGELEIN: This sector here is still fortified from before, by the Polish. They're light fortifications.

THE FÜHRER: That's one thing then! With what could ...

ZEITZLER: The units that are being pulled out now are bad as well, of course. They wanted to replenish them first.

THE FÜHRER: If we could just give them the assault gun unit!

ZEITZLER: If we release them and bring them down from up above.

THE FÜHRER: He likes to have them in front of Rovno?.[1060]

ZEITZLER: He wanted to take them out from up above and put them into this area. Main reason: in terms of numbers it would ...

THE FÜHRER: ... something happened in Rovno.

ZEITZLER: At the moment, the danger seems to be much greater here than up above.

THE FÜHRER: Otherwise, my opinion is that it ... get out ... either the 7th [Panzer Division] or the 1st [Panzer Division]. It would be best if we would bring out the 1st, so that we ... the 7th, bring out the 1st and replace it with any infantry unit plus assault guns.

ZEITZLER: So that infantry comes in. I'd suggest leaving the 7th Panzer Division there still.

THE FÜHRER: We have to see how it looks up above. It's like this: Something else had better not happen either—that he can encircle the whole thing here. That's so thin that it'll be pressed together immediately. Then it goes together, he immediately gets a small ring, and then it's no use.

ZEITZLER: If he were to attack frontally here, they couldn't hold anymore anyway because it's become so thin. Here he personally has relatively few doubts about this line. Because our next action will push at least into here initially, to the area of (Karacha)[1061] ... If we can get the area from Karacha to Berdichev as the end goal, we can already be very pleased. For now it won't come any further north.

THE FÜHRER: If his units are smashed one by one, the thing will crumble anyway. Then he can't do anything in this whole area either.

ZEITZLER: So it doesn't matter if we have this tip. Then we can still push forward later on. Because we'll contain him ... He has released that; that doesn't interest him. He's bringing everything down here.

THE FÜHRER: I want to know when he believes he will be able to clear out this thing ... He's going to this line?

ZEITZLER: He's going into this green line here. He said yesterday that he had already (prepared) something.

(*Army Group Center*)

In the Ninth Army and Fourth Army areas there were, for the most part, no local attacks either. Up above, only some shifting was reported. Other than that, no real combat activity. He wants to take out the units of the 87th

[Infantry Division] here—we did order that—and wants to put in individual units, which he has in here. Then part of the 20th Panzer Division is being transported to Orsha, as he reported yesterday evening.

THE FÜHRER: I'm not quite comfortable with that idea. We have … of the opinion that we leave the 20th there.

ZEITZLER: Yes, Sir. He exerted himself very much yesterday for the thing with the 20th, as he said that they're worried about Orsha. So he wants to send them there. On the other hand, it's selfish if …

THE FÜHRER: The whole thing is, he wants to have the 20th out up there so that the 2nd doesn't slide away as well. If the 87th is gone …

ZEITZLER: The 87th is staying there.[1062]

(*Army Group South again*)

HEUSINGER: I spoke to Busse.[1063] The field marshal hasn't made his final decision yet.[1064] … But he believes that he unfortunately can't lead the attack in front of the current front because it'll take too long. … He's afraid that it will be too late, and that he'll unfortunately have to pull the forces in behind the front, because otherwise it would come too late. But he still wants to wait and see what happens today.

THE FÜHRER: But not that they release the 1st Panzer Division from up above!

ZEITZLER: Here's the old picture. We don't know if something bigger is really going to start there, or if it won't happen after all.

THE FÜHRER: It'll start up above.

(*Army Group North*)

ZEITZLER: Nothing in particular south of Lake Il'men', for the most part. North of Lake Il'men' the situation actually stabilized a bit early today. In the morning the attacks started again, where he came in here and here with units. The 58th [Infantry] Division will be turned away here and not to Narva. That's why the idea that they … the *Feldherrenhalle* [Panzer Grenadier Division]

THE FÜHRER: When will the 12th Panzer Division be thrown in?

ZEITZLER: … attack—first to the north, because in terms of the terrain it would be the only possible thing at the moment. [—] Here the thing actually turned out even better than it was yesterday evening. There does seem to be a connected position here. On the other hand, there is a hole here, and here the majority of the 212th [Infantry Division] was encircled. Parts … Then early this morning a slightly stronger crisis emerged here … toward the west in the direction of Narva …

THE FÜHRER: ... Then I can only say, "Get into trouble; get out of trouble." [change directions]. ... If we do the same thing, it makes no sense at all to do that. The good Küchler can't make it clear to me with all his artlessness[1065] ... to withdraw here, but it's in the course of a preconceived intention: we'll retreat here anyway, so don't stop! It's always this familiar theme ... What does he want to do up here? He's going back here already, too.

ZEITZLER: He wants to go to this line and here into this area with the right wing.

THE FÜHRER: So there are supposed to be huge installations—they've always claimed that—that were built. There's no doubt about one thing: that the whole thing here is pure wordplay—the pulling back here. (The thing in front here can't be held), but he wants to hold this thing at all cost. It's all wordplay. It was shown again: if we go out of an installation ... that's the experience of three years—a shorter line without solid fortifications and ripped-out troops ... can't be held. Experience has shown that again and again. Nothing worse could have happened up above either.

Situation in the air, the East

BÜCHS: In the East, sorties were only possible on the southern front yesterday. In the Crimea the majority—with 130 tactical aircraft and fighter-bombers—supported the battles on the Kerch Peninsula ... Deployment of 405 aircraft with the First Panzer Army. 157 of them in the penetration area to support ...east of Vinnitsa in front of our own attacking spearheads. Also 96 aircraft deployed in Army Group Center's sector. Very weak enemy deployment. Yesterday, hampered significantly by weather conditions, he (used) only 230 aircraft against Kerch, mostly as fighter protection for his artillery and his transports across the Kerch Straits. [—] In the north 8 aircraft attacked the Murmansk line and severely damaged one train with many hits; the railway line was interrupted by shelling. [—] During the night we flew only limited sorties, with 24, including marker aircraft,[1066] on the Kerch Peninsula, and with 6 aircraft ... fighting, without being able to observe any particular success. Also today on the entire front ... and then locally with fighter-bombers and fighters in this area. Otherwise with Army Group Center ...

THE FÜHRER: Zeitzler, when we look at something like this overall ... that we can't hold that.

Italy

JODL: The enemy attacked here[1067] on the outer left wing of the 3rd Panzer Grenadier Division, pushed the combat outposts back a bit to the main fighting line there … after yesterday's attack in the direction of Cisterna he didn't attack again[1068] … The goals of the attack are such that we can be ready with our forces on the 1st, according to present considerations.[1069]

THE FÜHRER: Then the Panther detachment is there as well?

JODL: Yes, the Panther detachment has already arrived with two trains. By then all the forces they need for the attack will be there. The focal point should probably be placed here: so the 3rd Panzer [Grenadier] Division with the 715th [Infantry Division] behind it.[1070]

THE FÜHRER: If they don't pull it all together!

JODL: With units of the 371st [Infantry Division] behind[1071] and with the 26th Panzer Division behind. So here a very sharp concentrated attack. I (still) expect to get the (report) today … Here the terrain would be bad for the armored unit; there it's supposed to be best.

THE FÜHRER: How many tanks can we employ?

JODL: I still don't have the numbers. The Panther detachment has 79.

THE FÜHRER: The ones from the Panther detachment have to be unloaded off the train. If they drive for a while …

JODL: More than 160 won't be ready for action, plus several assault guns and the 8 Tigers that are there … The 1026th Regiment, the transport is complete. The 1028th Regiment, transport is complete.[1072] …

(THE FÜHRER): … the numbers of Guderian, that there should be no more losses at all. It was very bad during the first few days; later on the numbers were slightly better. …

JODL: … From the Homeland there are two, and from the third regiment there are of 15 trains … from the artillery training regiment there are 3 trains. It has 16 trains. From the Panther detachment … of 15 … Then the heavy artillery detachment, Hause's mortar detachment, the 22 cm … in addition, there are in transit one railway construction engineer battalion from the West and one from the Southeast … [—] Yesterday on the southern front,[1073] east of Castelforte, the enemy … led another attack, the results of which have not yet arrived. Yesterday there were already these assault troop operations here … had a good result. In the course of this action, which has expanded a bit, they succeeded in throwing back the whole penetration area for 1 km. In total, the penetration area was approximately … [—] Quiet on the central front. On the left flank the only movement identified was in the area of Castel Fretone … also crossing during the night at Bari. Bari is illuminated … Also movements right by Nettuno.

THE FÜHRER: I don't know. I believe, if I judge it correctly, then ...

JODL: They don't write as enthusiastically as during the first landings. They consider the terrain horrible ...

THE FÜHRER: ... pour a small amount of water into this foaming sparkling wine. That will be a very cloudy soup.

JODL: They may not have been entirely correctly informed about ... what is brought in there relatively quickly.

THE FÜHRER: I think they have decided to do something, and when the execution comes, they implode ... On the basis of all the experience with ... They first make a huge, seemingly operational plan, and when it then comes to the implementation, they stand in front of a halt—how ... could jump ... that's too high for him—suddenly, and then comes the realization about the real toughness of German resistance, and then they don't dare do it anymore.

HEWEL: Also politics play a huge role. A general in these countries can't allow himself any major setbacks anymore. Then there are inquiries and further inquiries. They're attacked if they don't carry through with something that they've judged too risky.

THE FÜHRER: They've started it in order to carry out a very bold action for once.

HEWEL: They've worked on it for three months.

JODL: The start is quite good.

THE FÜHRER: If they ... a ... they could have achieved a bit. But here they want a big action. ... (*Presentation.*) There I wouldn't say "battalions," but "additional hostile forces." [—] Is that new again? ...

JODL: (In terms of) flak batteries, approximately 100 batteries will come together. The battery positions themselves are said to be well protected by light flak against air raids ... a great number of ... so that the danger that they will be eliminated at the beginning is not very great here.

THE FÜHRER: One hundred batteries?

JODL: ... the majority must be here.

THE FÜHRER: They can't be strong enough to push through here.

JODL: ... reason: because, of course, unbelievable little building material comes down, and besides, workforces were drawn away. (*Presentation regarding position improvements.*)[1074]

JODL: (*Review of the presentation by the Führer.*) There were none here earlier. They were there and have now been brought to the Fourteenth Army. But at the moment of the landing there were none here.

THE FÜHRER: ... they should not speak in such puffed-up phrases: "temporarily the improvement with field-like (construction methods)." When they report to me, they have to avoid all such phrases, and that is a phrase. One set of troops can do that in four hours. Either they don't have the work force, or if they do have the work force, then they can dig the steel shelters into the ground. Sixty-eight are still there. They only have to dig them in ... they declare that they're making field-like improvements, and then they leave the steel shelters outside ... one is only deceived. One unit can ... the field-like improvements ... But if they have people, they can at least (dig) the steel shelters into the ground, if they can't put them in concrete. Because a steel dugout with 10 cm thickness is still always better than if they create a field-like dugout. (*Further review of the presentation.*) The field-like improvement starts here now?

JODL: That's the cross block. The Slovakian Brigade[1075] is not mentioned because it's building on the plain ...

The Balkans

THE FÜHRER: Where exactly is this thing anyway?

JODL: That was supposed to have been here ... just (asking) about it.

THE FÜHRER: He must find that out exactly. That sounds so much like a fairy tale. It's almost too good to be true.

JODL: That seems not to have been communicated via radio, but by an agent ... Mopping up by the "Brandenburg" Regiment further to the south. 23 dead; 95 bandits and 19 Italians captured. ... right now they are entering their rest areas, in which they ... a certain time ... Then the 1st Mountain Division met heavy resistance while entering this area ... 53 machine guns, weapons, equipment and ammunition were reported as captured.

THE FÜHRER: Here there seem to be more equipment and weapons ...

JODL: ... This island should be attacked soon, so we'll probably get a paratroop battalion for that as well. Here some smaller enemy landings were reported at and north of Zara. The 114th Jäger [Light Infantry] Division[1076] is marching further in the direction of Fiume ... arrived near the border. Meanwhile the 392nd [Infantry] Division is fighting its way from this flank toward the front against relatively strong resistance. Yesterday 15 ... and ammunition captured on the left column ... The 2nd Croatian Brigade[1077] is now being transported out. It will be transferred to Döllersheim because we gradually want to bring these light infantry and mountain brigades to Döllersheim again for training, so that something can be made of them.[1078] [—] In the area of Tuzla, after the unsuccessful attempt to take Tuzla, the [partisan] bands have now seemingly ... succeeded ... the group that pushed forward from the north, and the one from the south, without having encountered the enemy. [—] Bulgaria: the 27th [Infantry] Division is now assembling forces for a mopping-up action here on the border.

THE FÜHRER: The Bulgarians have now ... an official declaration ... that everything ... unanimously in the Sobran'e[1079] ...

JODL: ... reported quite lively gang activity in the mountainous terrain. So it's said that this road can't be used any longer without escort, and that the people can only defend themselves with light flak against the firing from above—from the mountains. It's obvious that everything possible is assembling in this mountainous area.

THE FÜHRER: That could be dangerous during a landing.

JODL: It hasn't been very extensive so far, but if these divisions are a bit further, we'll also have to mop up a bit more radically. There's no other option then, except to possibly destroy the villages in these valleys. Because they live from them.

THE FÜHRER: My opinion is that the training of these units would take place best if they had enjoyed 14 days of training in the barracks yard, then they could (obtain) all the rest of their training while fighting against this riffraff. Most of all that would avoid the problem of providing training that doesn't have any practical value.[1080]

JODL: They only need one thing: to learn how to shoot.

THE FÜHRER: That is ... they will learn to shoot like the gods.

JODL: They won't learn that shooting at the enemy.

THE FÜHRER: If they've been trained for 14 days, ... that intelligent, and then we do the whole thing immediately in the field ... One thing would be eliminated here in a very short time: that they stand around half the time in vain, from one roll call to the next ... the soldiers will be trained. And what a lot of training there is to be done!

JODL: Yes, that's certainly the most difficult thing. There's nothing that's so difficult to push through with the troops ... would be nothing more to be asked of those people.

MODEL: At that time we carried out brief training within a month.

JODL: Back then we did it that way—last year. If they're there for 3 to 4 weeks, they say they still have ...

THE FÜHRER: Most of them have permanent staffs already anyway. Then we can immediately give them small security or combat assignments against poorly armed bands and let them fight. There they'll learn best ...

JODL: If that's true, then there's nothing else left. They can't live out of the high mountain region; they live out of the villages. So we have to start approaching the villages.

The West

THE FÜHRER: What kind of legion is the Eastern Legion [Ostlegion]?

JODL: Those are the replacement troops for all the Eastern battalions.[1081]

[—] Here General Jacob presented again, from building director Weise from

France,[1082] ... that construction during 1943 actually decreased; it initially increased until April, to 659,000 cubic meters, and then decreased until November, to 173,000 cubic meters. From there it increased again, and, according to the current (building materials received) and the construction program, they should reach approximately 500,000 cubic meters again this month.

THE FÜHRER: That's where the mistake was made, that the people from the OT [Todt Organization] were taken away.

JODL: ... why the firing positions[1083] are set so far back.

KEITEL: Dorsch[1084] said that himself.

THE FÜHRER: Pulling out the OT back then in favor of the Ruhr area, as the major Ruhr area attacks took place ... We lost the labor force that way. But, of course, we can also ask, on the other hand: Why did we do that? Why ... as soon as we go the opposite direction here and say: every man in the OT is ... and can't be brought in, at that same moment ... go away from home. We have to understand that as well. Then they have the feeling—it's made clear to them through propaganda—that in the Ruhr area ...

Situation in the air, Reich

(KORTEN): The British reported 34 aircraft shot down during the attack on Berlin. We had reported 23.

THE FÜHRER: My word!

KEITEL: We can report it again tomorrow.

THE FÜHRER: I would report it again next time. What was reported on our side anyway, as probable and certain?

KORTEN: Twenty-two as certain and one probably shot down, so an increase is possible.

KEITEL: Today it should remain as is. We can correct it tomorrow in the Armed Forces report.[1085]

Situation at sea

ASSMANN: No unusual events in the Baltic. In the Gulf of Finland, some light naval batteries were made available to the Army for the defense front—two 10.5-cm and five 7.6-cm-guns. The patrol station in the Skagerrak had to be eliminated, unfortunately, because the 17th Patrol Boat Flotilla has to be withdrawn for the[1086] ... is lying here in the shipyard right now.

THE FÜHRER: Don't we have anything here at all anymore?

ASSMANN: No, we have the destroyers here in Kristiansand and Oslo[1087] ... Nothing to report from the Channel either.

THE FÜHRER: Does Hammerfest have a harbor we can go into? Is Hammerfest a protected harbor?

ASSMANN: ...The air reconnaissance operated yesterday during the whole day ...They detected the convoy yesterday morning at 9:55.[1088] Unfortunately, because of a radio equipment malfunction, this news didn't reach the command post of the Commander of Submarines [F.d.U.] until the afternoon at 16:00. (The Luftwaffe) continued to reconnoiter during the night, and the convoy was identified again in the afternoon at 17:15—with a strength of 55 merchant ships and 9 destroyers—and during the night once again, at 0:23. The reports reached the Commander of Submarines Atlantic with a two-hour delay again. We can see that the air reconnaissance theoretically ... that it was only the reporting system that unfortunately caused the delay, through equipment failure. ...was very bad; it was southwesterly, the motion of the sea with a strength of 7 to 8, so that submarines actually couldn't get close to the convoy ... because in bad weather conditions with a ... must be expected, in order to still achieve success after all. [—] Then U532 reported sinking a 7,500 GRT steamer at the Lakkadives Island, south of Bombay[1089] ... Bay of Biscay. Then, of course, he comes out of St. George's Channel, can't be caught by us here, and in that time ...

(THE FÜHRER): ... not that we learn early that he has landed here,[1090] but we had to recognize it. That'll, in general, be the case in favorable weather conditions.

(ASSMANN): ... notice under all circumstances.

THE FÜHRER: Within what distance can we locate from here?

KORTEN: Approximately 150 to 200 km.

ASSMANN: Back then, during the operation against St. Nazaire, he came from far back in the west. He came by surprise.[1091]

JODL: Now he must come here with a huge action.

KORTEN: We fly daily up into about this area here. The submarines ...

JODL: That would be particularly important. He'll do it in weather conditions where the sea is calm and the visibility poor ... wants to carry out such actions, and then, of course, every hour earlier that we learn about this thing is extremely valuable.

THE FÜHRER: Can he go out here during bad sea conditions as well?

ASSMANN: He can post himself here.

THE FÜHRER: There he doesn't risk much at all; he goes out during rough seas and lands here.

JODL: There is a certain possibility that he'll be seen here by incoming and outgoing submarines.

ASSMANN: There are actually always 5 to 6 boats here ...

KORTEN: Every day we have about 20 to 25 heavy fighters and reconnaissance aircraft over there.

ASSMANN: ... of 12 U.S. transports. Protection for the convoy was provided by a U.S. aircraft carrier and four destroyers[1092] ... A submarine was reported in the Ligurian Sea; it fired 20 rounds yesterday evening on (Fredo) and San Rafaele ... The enemy was active again in the area of Elba, with destroyers and motor gunboats; there was no attack on our coastal traffic. The enemy wasn't reported in the area between Orbetello and the landing area. In the landing area, 27 transports were reported again yesterday and 50 to 70 landing craft ... There were 13 landing craft near the island of Ponza, on a northward course toward the landing area. Light forces appeared again in the Gulf of Gaeta and fired on the coast.

THE FÜHRER: Ponza is getting lively again as well.

ASSMANN: Yesterday evening the port commander's office reported a convoy from San Benedetto heading north. Flare signals were observed. It must have been the same forces that later fired here above Pesaro and Recanati and then changed course again. We carried out a mine assignment from Pola, in the area southeast of Ancona. Contact with the enemy didn't take place. Air activity in the Aegean again, some of which involved mines being dropped at Salamis and here. Our ... transported 350 prisoners of war from Leros to Piraeus[1093] ... the warships are, if we consider ... from up here, coming from England, went back on 5 battleships and 4 aircraft carriers. (It is not certain) whether the entry of this unit into the Mediterranean was really a British battleship unit. The only confirmed one is the *Warspite* in Gibraltar. All other reports about battleships ... and two French battleships, the *Lorraine* and the *Richelieu*, will be going to Algiers, and 2 British and 3 former Italian[1094] in the area of Malta and Tunis, and 3 battleships in Alexandria—2 Italians, which, according to agent reports, apparently wandered off in the Indian Ocean.

THE FÜHRER: They push the Italians into the Indian Ocean ... fight for the British Empire.

ASSMANN: There have been no further changes in the landing craft capacity in England, according to agent reports. According to the last agent report, it is still assumed that approximately 488 combat-vehicle landing ships are lying in the southern English defense (area).[1095] This number would actually be sufficient to transport 25 landing divisions ... for further waves, so that the total landing transport capacity is actually ... sufficient ... for a one-time[1096] ...

THE FÜHRER: They can go back again then.

ASSMANN: Yes, indeed. [—] In the Italian theater there are still to be received: 65 combat-vehicle landing ships, 130 combat-vehicle landing boats and around 1,000 landing craft ... [—] The traffic to the Mediterranean continues as planned, without notable changes.

Situation in the air (continued)

(BÜCHS: Intrusions) ... 18:00 received in the radio intercept picture, 18:45 first radar pickup at Norddeich, over the Frisian Islands with the majority of the aircraft flying in on a southeastern course, ... and then to an attack from the southwest and south against Berlin. Some units, a small number of aircraft, (went) north of the Frisian islands on an eastern course and turned away again at the coast. Departed on a wide front, very far to the south, south of the Ruhr area ... on the intrusion 37 positions already occupied, but which didn't shoot down any aircraft. ... speed of the enemy aircraft very fast at 120 and 150 km ... ... the 2nd and 3rd Fighter Divisions, first led in a northerly direction, could still be let in before reaching Berlin and had ... shot down an additional 7[1097] ... During the day, 68 tactical aircraft and fighter-bombers were deployed in 4 missions against the Anzio bridgehead; there were also 5 aircraft with 21-cm mortar shells.[1098] Very good effect on the landing areas. In addition, a 1,000 t landing boat was sunk,[1099] 3 merchant ships totaling 12,000 to 14,000 heavily damaged ... landing boats heavily damaged.[1100] Accompanying fighters engaged in aerial combat. Three aircraft were brought down, with 5 losses total on our side. During the night one mission with 31 tactical aircraft, primarily against Anzio and Nettuno—the town itself and as well against ships. One ship of 3,000 t damaged; 3 losses on our side. What's striking is that an enemy unit—it's still not clear yet, if was a bomber or night-fighter unit—flew up during the first half of the night, ... then circled there for a very long time and seemingly wanted to carry out attacks on our ground organization. But this attack didn't take place until the second half of the night. In the rear area an attack of 70 ... (in the Balkans) deployment of individual dive bombers to fight gangs ... Reconnaissance during the day in the Aegean ... [—] (Weather conditions) ... with lower limits around 1,000 m, only rising locally to 500 m in the Crimea and in the central sector of Army Group South; widespread rainfall in the area of Army Group Center and Army Group North. In the Italian area very good weather—nearly cloudless, very good visibility, unimpaired deployment conditions. In the Reich territory a rain front, which is now lying between the Rhine and Weser, is moving very quickly to the east, bringing a temporary worsening of the weather. Behind that it remains cloudy, mostly overcast, 10/10 cloud cover, (lower limit) 500 m— also across to England—upper limit around 3,000 m. Our defense can go out. The single-engines are somewhat hindered by the strong cloud cover.
THE FÜHRER: That's coming here as well?
BÜCHS: That can't be surveyed yet. The wind speed can't be determined until morning by the weather reconnaissance. We can't get a picture of when

it's expected to pull in here until the morning, after we have the determination of the speed by the weather reconnaissance. ...

THE FÜHRER: In East Prussia—hopefully the harvest won't be terrible, if the frost comes then ...

KEITEL: Maybe March frost, then we'll have ...

Miscellaneous

(THE FÜHRER): ... how important it is to have a bigger landing area. If the landing area is so small, one is completely dependent,[1101] and there ... can ... it is a prize question; it is as follows: where will he land? [—] Where are the clairvoyants?

MODEL: In Portugal.

THE FÜHRER: On the one hand, the people commit themselves so far with their cries that they can't go back anymore either, while on the other hand, of course, more and more voices are joining in about the ... Everything is put under the slogan: the election of Roosevelt[1102]; only under this slogan, and the nearer they come to (the election), the more worried they get. If we succeed (in carrying out) the action down there,[1103] there won't be another landing. There the Luftwaffe must also ... they have to supply what they can.

KORTEN: I just have the urgent request that no more units be ordered; the airfields are all bad ... (*Presentation.*)

THE FÜHRER: I ask myself: Can they accept that?

(KORTEN): ... in England it's been announced that the number of aircraft brought down has increased to 60 ... dominates the London urban area.

THE FÜHRER: Can they claim that now? I become quite unsure when I read the other British reports.

(KORTEN: We can) take out (the numbers) from before.

THE FÜHRER: We become quite uncertain. The impression during the conversation wasn't very convincing. One has the feeling that in the case of the He 177, virtually half failed immediately again. They don't even get over there. This garbage plane is, of course, the biggest piece of junk that was probably ever produced. It's the flying Panther, and the Panther is the crawling Heinkel.[1104]

KORTEN: But the Heinkel ...

THE FÜHRER: How can they maintain that only 30 were over the London urban area?[1105] We also claimed a lot. Someone said to me: 50 aircraft; there were no more than that over Cologne. Then they admitted to more and more, and afterward they reached 1,000. It must have been 300 to 400, though. You still have agents. Do we still have ...? That's not possible. We learn about the most secret happenings that take place in the others' war council, the most secret plans and thoughts ... but if 3 houses or 100 or 500 or 1,000 burn down in London, we don't learn about it.

JODL: There are Swedes and Swiss over there. ...

THE FÜHRER: I learn precisely what kind of war plans they have in the war council ... but if 10 houses burn down in London—

KORTEN: Our best agents are all working on it.

HEWEL: It takes some time. There we have to wait until someone comes to Stockholm. What censorship orders they've issued! They haven't let anyone out, not even an accredited envoy.

THE FÜHRER: I ask for the following reason: if that really was the explanation for this pathetic story—that the large majority didn't find London, but only 30 to 40 aircraft—then we can't do anything.

KORTEN: All the crews were questioned. The Reichsmarshal was out there with all the air commodores.

THE FÜHRER: Well, if that's true, we have to report something ...: there were more than 400 aircraft over ... they shouldn't deceive ...

End: 2:32 p.m.

* * * * *

TELEPHONE CONVERSATION
BETWEEN THE FÜHRER AND GENERAL ZEITZLER, JANUARY 28, 1944[1106]

Beginning: 5 p.m.

The East

ZEITZLER: My Führer, I wanted to report the following concerning the situation in Army Group South. The tanks that penetrated the Eighth Army and First Panzer Army lines met at Zvenigorodka.[1107] As a consequence, the First Panzer Army immediately ... around behind the 17th Panzer Division ... got underway, so in the direction of Zvenigorodka, in order to get that under control. That's why the push around to the front will be abandoned; the other units also seem to have been pulled in here as fast as possible in order to strike the penetrating enemy there. Thus the request of the Eighth Army, although: whether the tip up above[1108] in the Ros River position can be withdrawn, in order to be able to attack with a few battalions toward the south.

THE FÜHRER: Yes. How many tanks met there?

ZEITZLER: We can't say exactly. The ones that broke through from (Spoda)[1109] are certainly not too many. But now, of course, it will be at least 1 to 1½ days before the 17th Panzer will be able to attack. Then there will be more, of course. The crucial point is actually now that the attack around the front is being eliminated because of the short amount of time, leading to a withdrawal of the panzer divisions and an attack behind the front, they'll believe this large corner post is no longer necessary.

THE FÜHRER: That, of course, will mean the whole operation is lost again. That's a great pity. They can't bring across the 13th or 11th [Panzer Divisions] or whatever?

ZEITZLER: Not yet, my Führer, because they're worried that the gap there will then get bigger. Because by now they've brought it more or less under control. The worry is more from the west, where the gap is wider, of course.

THE FÜHRER: If they only put in the 6th and 7th [Panzer Divisions] here ...

ZEITZLER: First they could take out the 17th [Panzer], and if they add the 6th to it, ... come, then I don't believe that either.

THE FÜHRER: We have to ...

ZEITZLER: I discussed that with him as well. He wants to try ... But they've tried for quite a while and still haven't actually dared to take the whole 1st Panzer [Division] away from there yet.

THE FÜHRER: So that he employs the 58th and the 308th [Infantry Divisions] instead of the 1st Panzer.

ZEITZLER: That's what they plan to do.

THE FÜHRER: And that they possibly pull this assault gun detachment in here after all.

ZEITZLER: My Führer, we could do that.

THE FÜHRER: That would take a few days as well.

ZEITZLER: And that doesn't really come into consideration for the replacement either. The most important thing is actually that we bring in infantry.

THE FÜHRER: Infantry is fine, but it won't hold if there are no tanks behind it. That's been proven everywhere now. If there are assault guns behind them, it works well. But if there's nothing, they don't hold.

ZEITZLER: With the assault gun detachment we can still wait out the attack today, which seems to be meeting fairly heavy resistance, to see whether Bach ..., that we decide in the evening that it will just be drawn out immediately. Because there's no point in having this Bach Group get tied up there in heavy combat.

THE FÜHRER: I have only one thing to say: just now, when we've decided to stop this action anyway, it's even more unreasonable to take it out then.

ZEITZLER: ... 1st Panzer Division.

THE FÜHRER: No, not that, but that we then pull in the whole tip, if we're giving up the other anyway ... and move them over. Because what's there, of course, is not an encirclement. Those few tanks are just ridiculous.[1110]

...

ZEITZLER: It's just that around below, they say, the tip serves no purpose anymore.

THE FÜHRER: Everything that we don't have to withdraw has its purpose. If they can add the 17th Panzer and something else here, and destroy them, then why would they withdraw the tip then?

ZEITZLER: In order to free up some forces.

THE FÜHRER: Those aren't forces. Let's not deceive ourselves! Then they're just creating an attack front for the enemy, which he can immediately slide into again.

ZEITZLER: Then I'll refuse it for now and present it again this evening.

THE FÜHRER: Yes, if they're going over there with the 17th [Panzer Division] anyway, I don't consider this necessity as a given at all.

ZEITZLER: Yes, Sir. Then I'll present it again this evening.

THE FÜHRER: I would like you to come at 9 o'clock today.

ZEITZLER: Yes, indeed, my Führer. 21:00. Heil, my Führer!

End: 5:05 p.m.

* * * * *

EXCERPT FROM A SITUATION REPORT, PRESUMABLY FROM MARCH 1944[1111]

(THE FÜHRER): ... become ... If a person is constantly between ... of machines, he becomes ill. It's a ... to the nerves. By nature a man is intended for ..., but not for standing between buzzing machines. Life in cities like New York, ... St. Louis is unbearable. That's why the people are also ... If it's possible that a radio speaker ... reports about Martians landing ... in some places a panic breaks out, then ... how hysterically the whole population ... not ... that the Americans also only ... can be compared. There is ...

* * * * *

April 6, 1944

In the southern sector of the Eastern Front, the expected catastrophe has meanwhile developed. After the Russians had crushed the Nikopol' bridgehead in February, taken Krivoi Rog and pushed the German front back behind the Ingulets River, they deployed for a major attack at the beginning of March: Zhukov's 1st Ukrainian Front on the 4th on both sides of Shepetovka, and Koniev's 2nd Ukrainian Front on the 6th out of the Zvenigorodka region. Zhukov soon broke through the Lemberg [L'vov]–Odessa railway line between Tarnopol and Proskurov, then bent back the wide-open flank and pushed the covered German western flank to the Brody-Dubno-Kovel' line, and finally attacked again on March 21 toward the south. The First Panzer Army was encircled at Kamenets-Podol'sk, and the Dnestr River and the Pruth River were crossed as well. The Russians took Chernovtsy and Kolomia, and now stand on the east side of the Carpathian Mountains, having already— temporarily—reached the Iablunka Pass. In the meantime, Koniev also reached the Bug River on March 13, the Dnestr River on the 17th, and at the end of the month also pushed into Bessarabia. Army Group A (now "South Ukraine"), continually threatened with being cut off, has likewise been pushed back: withdrawing behind the Dnestr River, they still stand on the Tiligut River at the moment. In the Crimea, the Seventeenth Army awaits the Russian attack.

In Army Group Center's sector, the enemy achieved some successes along the Berezina River with a pincer attack against Bobruisk, but wasn't able to reach the objective. At Kovel'—400 km further to the west—the army group succeeded, along a thin front running exactly east-west, in reestablishing a connection with Army Group South (since April "North Ukraine"), which had been lost on November 12, 1943. The Pripiat' Marshes are now finally thawing. Outside Vitebsk the Russians achieved only local successes.

Army Group North had to begin its major withdrawal movement on February 18 and by the beginning of March had pulled back to the Narva– Lake Peipus–Velikaia Line, so practically to the Baltic States. In Italy the situation is unchanged. The German attempts to destroy the Anzio–Nettuno beachhead, on February 16 and again on the 29th, failed, as did the American attacks against the German Cassino position in the beginning of February, mid-February and mid-March.

(Maps 5, 7, 10, and 11)

* * * * *

MIDDAY SITUATION REPORT, APRIL 6, 1944[1112]

Beginning: 1 p.m.

The East (Army Group South Ukraine)
ZEITZLER: My Führer! ... yesterday local attacks in company and ... were at Kerch. Up here there were concentrations[1113] ... individual attacks, which, however, were ... by artillery fire [—] Then ... here a bridgehead ... will ... bridge here in order ...
THE FÜHRER: Three t.
ZEITZLER: A crossing ... one can hardly call it a bridge. Also here, a bridge(head) is now ... should also be a crossing. But that (still) isn't quite clear to me. [—] Heavy supply ... railway is gone here. ... Now we have to decide if ... take away ...
THE FÜHRER: There we'll have to see ...

(*Army Group North Ukraine*)

ZEITZLER: The First Panzer Army (was excellently) supplied,[1114] so that the supply ... is ... The army group is against that, of course, ... one or two days still ... the First Panzer Army some transport (capacity) [—]

THE FÜHRER: We must ... also the small roads—

ZEITZLER: That they possibly ... everything is occupied. For that reason the general (command) ... had this sector here up to up above ... there later, we can ... the one German ... pull in again. Then the general command has ... With the First Panzer Army it progressed as planned. [—]

ZEITZLER: He had ... stand near the unification. It is ... front itself under Zhukov[1115] advanced ... gave orders from here. He sees that ... and mixes them up a bit. From down here ... movements up to the north. The attack of the II SS Panzer Corps[1116] reached here. Right now there's a detachment here without fuel. [—] Then I had a ... with the First Panzer Army now ... (*Presentation.*) The last thing is positive. I had ... considered worse. This didn't ... Those were small combat groups.

THE FÜHRER: Three panzer divisions ... many.

ZEITZLER: The majority is actually still intact [—]

ZEITZLER: On this front ... The 100th Jäger [Light Infantry] Division had ... very good ... finished early today and is ... come. Also on this front,[1117] Friebe[1118] (actually) advanced quite well (despite the bands) in these forest areas, which are in here, so we can hope (that the) connection can be made, because they are also pushing forward now. (There) they've pushed a front line further forward into this corner now. There are actually only bands in here. [—]

THE FÜHRER: ... received, it would be nearly ... to be able to pull down.

ZEITZLER: I ... too, that they deploy down here, ... that they are assembled so far behind. ... but is because they ... not at the ... get into some kind of mess.

KEITEL: They're always bound to this ...

(*Army Group Center*)

ZEITZLER: In Army Group Center's sector today there is [—] The railway (fighting) ... Luftwaffe has ... backlog of 17 trains ... otherwise always 12 trains ...

KORTEN: There ... attack during the night. (*Presentation.*) The trains come out with difficulty ... during the night, immediately after the attack ... That's the additional second attack then ... result. There we can say that the whole … his engine-house and so on were pretty much blown. That was the first attempt by the corps. The bomb situation will continue to improve. Those are the destroyed railway trains, the burned out things. Regarding the attack on Korosten', the [—]

THE FÜHRER: Something … out, because as the last reserve we have only … 25th Panzer Grenadier Division. That is very little … is this huge stretch where there (is) nothing at all.

ZEITZLER: But here it also … relaxed.

THE FÜHRER: Yes, in the hope that it remains that way.

ZEITZLER: Something can come in there very quickly, of course. He can get there faster than we can. [—]

Yesterday there were 18 … here … yesterday 30. Today there aren't any … either … We can (be) pleased with yesterday's outcome here. Something is still (coming) down from above.

(Army Group North)

Up here the attack against the "Eastern sack" ["Ostsack]"[1119] has progressed satisfactorily so far. The 227th [Infantry] Division came in up to here, and the 122nd [Infantry] Division with the right column came to here. So the connection has almost been established. In here there are still strong enemy units. The left column is [—]

Situation in the air, East

BÜCHS: In the Crimea, 32 fighter-bombers deployed (on the) Perekop front. In the Sixth Army's sector, 123 tactical aircraft and fighter-bombers were deployed against tanks and enemy columns in the Rasdel'naia a penetration area, also with units in the area of Cornesti. Supply of the First Panzer Army[1120] from April 4 to 5, 18:00, very strong with 269 aircraft and 6 transport gliders. 261 t were … into [—]

ZEITZLER: … We had it over the … But from Odessa[1121] we get … large-scale transport capacity from the quartermaster general already … sent away … days ago. He can't get through on these roads now.

THE FÜHRER: For 400 t.

ZEITZLER: Transport capacity, so motorized vehicles. Those are the ones that have been sent, again 450 t. That's always the railway complaint now— I hope it will improve now as a result of the discussion—and the complaints about railway-related things, which are very impressive. I had [—]

BÜCHS: … Tarnopol, because the … in that way always a … Now they're trying … to execute better. Two hundred twenty-three tactical aircraft and fighter-bombers (were) deployed (on) the left flank of the army group in support of the attack by the II SS Panzer Corps; some units supported the battles in the Tarnopol area.[1122] Yesterday the Sixth Air Fleet supported the junction in the Kovel' area with 209 fighter-bombers.[1123] Otherwise only deployment in the rear area with 45 aircraft to combat the bands. The Fist Air Fleet 1 has 57 fighter-bombers in the area southeast [—] One mission during the night ... Alakurtti area. [—] Today deployment is severely affected by weather only in the area around Army Group Center. Flight is possible on the rest of the front.

Finland

WARLIMONT: In Finland there are still no major engagements so far, only reconnaissance and firing. There was also clash northeast of Kandalaska between German and Finnish hunter-fighters.[1124] [—] Above all he wants ... to regain the necessary freedom of movement.
KEITEL: We can't know if it's like that.
THE FÜHRER: It depends how long action is possible up here at all.
WARLIMONT: The weather right now is like this: within 24 hours the temperature varies from minus 10 to 12 degrees to plus 2 degrees, so major engagements are hardly possible.
THE FÜHRER: [—] government does everything to complicate the whole thing. The Swedes are also restraining themselves a bit now. The Swedes aren't putting them under pressure anymore either.[1125]
WARLIMONT: The German military attaché in Stockholm reports that the basis and size of Swedish mobilization efforts don't, according to his claims, seem to exceed the normal range.[1126] An interesting reference to the Aaland Islands.[1127] (*Presentation.*) [—]

Italy, etc.

Here[1128] additional ... our artillery has ... corps obviously very good ... hit camp and the ... long-range artillery bombarded ... the unloading places, especially at ... Here the enemy succeeded in attacking one of our own heavy flak batteries with Tomahawks[1129]—obviously an aircraft armament attack. The attack shows that they are quite unprotected. Three guns failed and three others were damaged. Five dead and 16 injured.
THE FÜHRER: They didn't have any light flak there. Probably they were taken by surprise.
BÜCHS: Two light guns are with the battery.
WARLIMONT: ... heavy movements ... of M. Cairo identified [—] Also the 334th [Infantry] Division ... the enemy front ... vehicles blown up and

also ... attacked. Some prisoners ... [—] The operation here ... which was described yesterday as very difficult because of the snowdrifts, was reported complete today, with 205 dead and 524 prisoners, including several—exact numbers are not reported—British and American prisoners of war. [—] Regarding the overall Mediterranean situation, it is notable that yesterday evening several troop transports went through the Straits of Gibraltar. Those were followed by others early this morning, making up a total of 27 observed transports. Seven of them are said to have entered Gibraltar. The majority are [—] The operational situation is ... that today can be ... expected. A number of (units) are ... prepared, which (should) then be sent through immediately. The route is partly just single-track in the main trouble spots.

THE FÜHRER: What's the situation in Hungary[1130] like?

WARLIMONT: Nothing new in Hungary. The 1st Mountain Division is going ahead as planned. Thirty-seven trains arrived with the majority in Sighet, while the rest are arriving in the area of Munkacs. All other movements are also on schedule.

[—]

The East again

THE FÜHRER: It's clear that (the link-up) is immensely important. But we can't count with great certainty on the First Panzer Army making the link-up. We can assume that the link-up will be made within two days. Then the First Panzer Army will detach enough units so that with the newly brought up divisions, the SS Panzer Corps and the strength of the First Panzer Army, a front will certainly be built up down here. Even if it goes badly the front will go about down here. This is Stanislaw here. But it will probably ... down here [—] build up a front ... unwilling to use ... here. One ... to make the link-up, but ... stuck. The mountain divisions must ...

KEITEL: That's Romanian territory.

THE FÜHRER: What does that mean, "Romanian territory"? Who defends it? Do the Romanians want to defend it?

ZEITZLER: The Romanians are extremely thin on that wing and have no ski battalions.

THE FÜHRER: That's the whole thing. I can't get involved in rivalries between those two,[1131] because the whole thing will solve itself if the Russians break in here [—]

The West

WARLIMONT: ... also ordered, you ... to pull out ... the Panzer Lehr Division [Panzer Training Division].[1132]

THE FÜHRER: No, under no circumstances!

WARLIMONT: He justifies it first with the ...

THE FÜHRER: I admit all that. We don't know that for sure, though. If I pull them out of here, we won't have any panzer units here at all.

WARLIMONT: We still have this reinforced infantry regiment and an entire assault gun brigade.

THE FÜHRER: One assault gun brigade for Hungary—that's 35 assault guns.

[—]

THE FÜHRER: It is ... to say honestly, the whole thing the British are performing[1133] looks like theater to me. The news about blockade measures, the defensive movements and so on—normally one doesn't do that when planning an operation like that.[1134]

KEITEL: Then you keep your mouth shut about those things.

THE FÜHRER: I can't get rid of the impression that the entire thing really is an impudent charade.

WARLIMONT: They did it absolutely methodically from the first day on ... to make ... for their own public ... and [—]

THE FÜHRER: ... West. A very considerable (change) took place, which in my opinion is having an effect. The great danger of Roosevelt staying lies in the Republicans' inability to agree on a candidate. Now, Wendel Willkie was defeated in the latest election in Wisconsin like never seen before. That shows that you can't offer just anything even to the American people—so that a scamp like him is rejected even there. Now comes Dewey. Willkie has personally already done everything he can.[1135]

KEITEL: He said he wouldn't be a candidate after this outcome.

[—]

THE FÜHRER: ... the meanest fellow ... a real gangster. What can you ... If someone else comes, ... an American politician ... This policy is so ... the Jews standing behind him ... a whole number of Jews already ... has brought them to Sing-Sing [Prison]. Recently he attacked Roosevelt. He was after someone whom Roosevelt had deprived him of. He said, "This fellow must be executed; there won't be peace until this fellow is executed." He was a Jew, too. Dewey himself is certainly a clean person. And that's something in this country of corruption. If someone comes who looks after American interests, then the story ends here. It is only a question of when such a thing could happen—if Roosevelt would still exert such heavy pressure here, or if he would pull back at the last moment. Even a very minor failure would be enough.

[—]

THE FÜHRER: ... make an advance by motor torpedo boat?

ASSMANN: Yesterday the weather was (very) cloudy, with heavy fog. They also tried to reconnoiter using the Luftwaffe, but it was useless.

KORTEN: We are gradually beginning to suspect that they have a new buoy, where they mark ships with radar equipment.[1136] Richthofen called me to say that he was hotly pursued.

ASSMANN: But it was observed here that they had moved out.

WARLIMONT: The same reports are coming from the northern coast of Brittany, but also unconfirmed. We ourselves were unable to fire yesterday, because yesterday our equipment ... [—] on good authority, but this ... : on the whole, a further opening towards the ... coast of England, a command formation.

THE FÜHRER: Now I ask myself: do they have to do it so ostentatiously? Would we do it so ostentatiously if we were planning something? We most certainly would not. That's not necessary for them at all. They can assemble their forces here, load them and bring them over here. We can't be certain what they're doing over there.

KEITEL: We would do it the opposite way and disguise everything.

THE FÜHRER: We would be over *here* for sure. Here we would [—] So I can't (get rid of the impression) that it may just be a very impudent bluff after all, because we weren't aware at all of those few landings they've made so far.[1137]

KEITEL: They were so secret that we didn't even suspect anything.

THE FÜHRER: The landing in North Africa.

KEITEL: We believed even on the very last day that they would go on through. They were at the level of Sicily with their advance point, and we said they would go through. But suddenly they turned right toward the coast.

THE FÜHRER: Today there was a report in the British newspapers where it says: at Nettuno not much can be done because [—]

ASSMANN: ... still around 2.5 million ... can figure out the purposes.

THE FÜHRER: Also ... that's 80,000 men. So they complain (now) that what they are doing is betraying their own native country. Reduction of the entire defense production by 20%, electricity by 10%, all the gasworks, and so on.[1138] [—] I agree that we should bring all these forces here,[1139] especially those we don't necessarily need somewhere else. Has the Navy moved across yet?

ASSMANN: That's in progress.

WARLIMONT: Also the movement of the 12th SS [Panzer] Division in this area is underway, even without the possibility for a temporary replacement. On the other hand, Student's Parachute Reserve and Training Division, which still has 12,000 men, now goes into the southern part of Holland [—] newly established here. ... *Reich* is in the ... Now the ... the request that he could ... the tanks, because here they ... can be moved, as well ... and the front on the southern coast.

FEGELEIN: When the (link-up with the First Panzer Army) is established, the *Reich* [SS Panzer Division's] combat group can be pulled out as well.[1140]

THE FÜHRER: It should be pulled out as well. It's supposed to come here.

FEGELEIN: It can be ready quickly.

THE FÜHRER: How strong is this combat group?

KEITEL: One thousand five hundred or 1,800 men.

FEGELEIN: No, it's even a bit stronger. It has 2,500 men. They haven't been pulled apart too badly. It's the original core.

THE FÜHRER: For over there it's nothing. But if we put them here we immediately have 15,000 men.[1141] Then it will ... very quickly again ... [—]

THE FÜHRER: ... the *Reich* Division ... a sense, how strong ...

FEGELEIN: ... 15,000 to 16,000 men strong ...

THE FÜHRER: Well, if they get a few thousand men from the HJ Division[1142] they will be ... fixed and ready to go.

FEGELEIN: The *Reich* Division has a total of 15,385 men.

BUHLE: The combat group and that one.

FEGELEIN: No, just that one itself.

THE FÜHRER: Then they're ready. Then they will be a division again—an old division.

KEITEL: With an outstanding pedigree.

FEGELEIN: The report is from April 3.

KEITEL: They even got Genesene and all that. But if they get that core!

THE FÜHRER: Probably they will also ... the last men on leave ... not into the East anymore [—]

FEGELEIN: ... 22,000 men.

KEITEL: The rear (services) still have the *Leibstandarte*, but it will be pretty thin.

THE FÜHRER: It couldn't take the artillery along anymore.[1143]

WARLIMONT: Could the individual units be transferred[1144]—the General Command, which is absolutely necessary for leading the panzer units in the West, the LVIII Reserve Corps, two engineer construction battalions and two bridge convoys?

THE FÜHRER: You can take the engineer construction battalions together with the bridge convoys.

WARLIMONT: The General Command means nothing to Hungary anymore, but it's very important to the West.

KEITEL: I think we can do that, my Führer.

THE FÜHRER: ... a big mess comes ...

WARLIMONT: ... command of Lang[1145] in ... pull in any time ...

KEITEL: ... give away the other units ...

The Balkans

WARLIMONT: From ... A mopping-up action ... Greece with the SS Police Division, which is spread over a huge area and couldn't be prepared yet, and now has the opportunity for training and action. The most important thing is the breakthrough of both the Communist crowds. They are disregarding their plan for the time being. According to intercepted radio messages, they'll meet more in the northwest, in this area, with the aim of resuming their march toward the southeast after regeneration, as they call it. That gives our forces the opportunity—with 12 Bulgarian battalions[1146]—to burst in on this withdrawal movement, while here in the south toward the Montenegrin border a barrier is being built up. We were advised by the Commander-in-Chief Southeast that the 4th Regiment *Brandenburg*, which you added from Hungary, in the rear of this (area) [—]

FEGELEIN: ... the others run away with all the stuff, when they[1147] go between. They kill them only with knives. A man who was there was wounded. He had his arm tied up and still killed 17 enemies with his left hand. Cases are also reported where they cut out the enemy's heart.

THE FÜHRER: That doesn't matter. [—] Another thing, Keitel. I read the press news yesterday. There was an ancient statue found in Corinth or Corfu—in Greece anyway—probably while our people were digging and building a fortress. We, as the generous and wonderful carriers of culture, said, "Look, we'll give it to the Greeks."[1148] The others were ready to take it. They shouldn't be such idiots. I ask that everything found by Germans be (brought) to Germany (immediately). What do these ... The ancient Greeks are ... from Schleswig-Holstein ... back. We must ... different from the ... The Americans would ... vermin and rabble ... come to Germany right away ... talked. They do (not) deserve (this) ... for the hard-working people.

KEITEL: Another case. I take this opportunity to ask if you really gave an order. In France a number of former Spanish gun barrels were found. Of these, according to Lorey,[1149] six at most possess a certain historical and cultural value. Those were made available to Franco by envoys in Madrid, as a present from you.

THE FÜHRER: I'm hearing it right now for the first time.

KEITEL: I said immediately that I don't believe it.

THE FÜHRER: They make presents on my behalf and I don't know anything about it. I don't even think about it.

KEITEL: The ... outcry, one can ...

THE FÜHRER: ... belongs to the Reich. The ... Kaiser, was at the same time ... Spanish gun barrels ...

BUHLE: They ... have. There are only six ... There were all together 24 barrels.

KEITEL: It was claimed by Ambassador Dieckhoff that you had given them to the Spanish head of state.[1150]

THE FÜHRER: That has nothing to do with Dieckhoff. I have no idea. I absolutely don't give anything historical away at all. I give away automobiles as presents. I was supposed to give Nefertiti as a present—they had involved Göring—so that we could establish further connections to Egypt. I said, "No, not Nefertiti." Then they proved that she came here through a nasty trick. A Jew had exported her through fraud.[1151] So I said, "Fine. I'll hand over the Jew." But they turned me down. Then Nefertiti would have been gone. You can't give away treasures just like that. What interest do we have in being stroked by those fellows ... not, I don't care. ... land rather than a few ... if they could do it, ... would. Make it public ... people find in the ground ... not to be communicated. That is not ... no catalogue, that comes from the ... pack it up immediately, wrap it, and send it to Germany. They can address it to me, because I won't use it for myself, but will put it in a public collection. If it's something very beautiful, it will go into the Glyptothek [Museum], or if it fits into the Pergamon collection in Berlin it will go there, or I will deliver it to Linz, where it will go to the art museum.[1152]

WARLIMONT: Another noteworthy thing is the mopping-up effort near Jajce. The majority of the so-called 1st Communist Division was driven back toward the west, where they seem to be mostly concerned with the protection of Tito's command center—which is again reported to be in this area. Tito's naval headquarters were supposed to be relocated from Lissa onto the Island of Pag, according to intercepted radio messages.[1153] So it is to be expected that he will want to establish a supply camp here, too, because access to the country was also more and more remote for him here. [—] Something else is notable here ... apparently after very ... attacked battle convoys ... thereby mismanage their ... partisan warfare.

Situation at sea

ASSMANN: In the Bay of Finland ... intervention of the naval battery (to fight) ... of land targets. The network ... Reval can be brought forward as planned.[1154] Nothing in particular on the rest of the Norwegian coast or in the Baltic Sea entrances. [—] Air reconnaissance over Jakonga[1155] showed 11 medium-sized freighters, and in the Straits of Gorlo 12 commercial ships and 9 security vessels at the entrance to the White Sea.

THE FÜHRER: This thing about the statue will be disposed of right now.
KEITEL: I wanted to check once more if it really was the case. The military attaché reported immediately that Dieckhoff had an order from the Führer.
FEGELEIN: The story about the statue was in the press.
THE FÜHRER: I mean the statue. It will be taken away in absolute silence. That was a mistake. Nothing will be in the press! It will be cancelled. I ... have brought. By this ... our people constantly ...
ASSMANN: ... ships. In the North Sea our own ... weather situation not possible yet. Regarding the location, it is already ... at the island of Ile ... A harbor-security boat ... sunk at Le Havre. Concerning the location, it must be said that with our location instruments we can only observe that enemy radar carriers are at sea. But we can't survey the area from a distance to determine distance with these instruments, because the instruments for that were ruined—on purpose—by the enemy days ago. [—] Further into the sea, near Cape Gris Nez, there were a few enemy units moving up and down, most likely acting as security for this minesweeping activity. A group of 20 mine aircraft contaminated the entrance of the Gironde. [—] U218 reported the laying of mines near San Juan in Puerto Rico. [—] We already discussed the entrance of the troop-transport escorts. Seven transports entered Gibraltar, 20 went into the Mediterranean. Enemy submarines ... reported from La Spezia. The harbor of Leghorn[1156] ..., so that now he ... can. Yesterday heavy (unloading activity)...that is 12 steamers in the morning ...
THE FÜHRER: There ... attack together.
ASSMANN: He must be very heavily supplied.
THE FÜHRER: Couldn't we fly attacks to certain areas with very small bombs—maybe with 1-kg bombs—so that we carpet-bomb a very large area and hope to blow up fuel and munitions depots?[1157]
KORTEN: I don't know where this report comes from. I didn't receive it.
ASSMANN: There are 12 steamers.
THE FÜHRER: That's an enormous thing. One must imagine that one steamer unloads about as much as 10 to 12 transport trains.
KORTEN: Richthofen called last night. He produced a major fire once and wanted to try it again. It's moonlight, so he can't do it now. But as soon as (the moon is on the wane) again ...
ASSMANN: ... put in the beachhead ... can. The detailed evaluation ... occupation with altogether ... occupation is, but different ... 2 large combat-vehicle landing craft ... ships, 4 landing boats and 12 ... in addition 3 artillery motor torpedo boats. At Cape Spartivento a departing escort of 8 freighters. Observed in the Gulf of Taranto: an escort of 20 steamers moving north toward Taranto. Coastal traffic again in the Bari–Brindisi area. Reported heavy enemy air observation in the area of Benedetto within the last few days. The occupation of Lissa was weaker yesterday, with only 5 smaller

naval units and 59 boats. [—] A certain increase in enemy submarine action in the Aegean. A submarine[1158] sank 3 motor sailboats near the island of Cerigo, and in the Bay of Suda one motor sailboat was sunk as well. [—] Limited ship traffic off the North African coast at the level of Derna. [—] In the Black Sea 2 Russian submarines were identified at Evpatoriia. Our own security forces were fired on in the Kerch Strait, from land. Then it was reported … in the course of the dispersal … underway, with very …

Situation in the air

BÜCHS: Yesterday … by fighter units, and … and single-engine aircraft … group in the area of Brandenburg … group down into the area of Augsburg … in both cases several airfields … attacked by aircraft armaments, only aircraft fire on aircraft and hangars.

THE FÜHRER: Our people seemed to have slept, because the airfields are equipped with light things.

KORTEN: No, the light weapons have all been taken down and brought to the West.[1159]

THE FÜHRER: Then he can destroy every airfield.

BÜCHS: Altogether 36 aircraft were destroyed on the ground—25 of them tactical aircraft and fighters—and a larger number were damaged.

THE FÜHRER: Then he'll repeat it today.

KORTEN: We will get light guns here from the new production. The … dams, important (bridges) …

BÜCHS: There were … shot down … Also in the West … airfields. Among them were … During the night entry of … (in the) southwestern area of France by … mined the coast and around 200 … against aircraft factories in Toulouse were carried out, namely against a Heinkel factory and a Junkers factory.[1160] Both factories suffered heavy damage, and there was additional damage to the airfields in Toulouse. At the same time yesterday there was an advance by a destroyer unit via Venice up to the area of the Bodensee. But it then turned around without attacking. [—] In Italy enemy action was limited yesterday because of bad weather. 3 aircraft making individual approaches were shot down by flak. [—] Attack against Bucharest. About 200 four-engine aircraft under fighter escort reached the Danube, and half an hour later another group of 50 four-engine aircraft attacked Nish. Our own defense flew again yesterday, with 192 fighters, 60 of them German, 93 Romanian and 39 Bulgarian. The Bulgarians are … because of the big … Through combined … in particular the … were hindered, so that … fell into … According to (reports) received so far … injured. Regarding damages … smaller refineries … refineries smaller fires … proved very well worth … were smoked in. According to (reports received so far) … oil burned. Our defense brought down 48 aircraft with fighters and flak, plus probably three more; 16 of them were shot down by flak, but haven't been confirmed yet. The losses are 12 aircraft in total—9 German and 3 Romanian.[1161]

THE FÜHRER: How could we lose 9 aircraft with the limited number that we shot down?

BÜCHS: Twenty-nine.

KORTEN: Sixty German and 93 Romanian fighters. Not all of the Romanians came near. We shot down 29, they shot 19.

BÜCHS: No further news from the Balkans.

KORTEN: General Fiebig[1162] definitely counts on 50 confirmed downed aircraft. On the other hand, the verification of the previous attack, where 44 were reported ... We had ... Romanians reported ... wasn't true ... General Staff, which 36 ... reduced.[1163] The English ... They will approximately ...

BÜCHS: In ... Army Group Center ... rest of the front, especially ... above zero during the day, while ... almost cloudless weather ... lie just above zero, in the ... In the Italian operation ... and also fields of ocean fog, which lie along the entire (eastern) coast and significantly hinder the mission. Defense is tight today in the Reich area, especially in the whole of north and northwest Germany. Also in the rest of Germany it is hindered by heavy rain, while drops over England are possible day and night. So far no intrusions have been reported.

KORTEN: A British report about an attack on Nuremberg. We reported 132, the English 96.[1164] Here is a reliable report, which ... of 143 four-engine bombers and also ... That is all ... something out. First ... will start. What ... fewer aircraft.

Production of gas masks

THE FÜHRER: ... show something.[1165] After ... military agencies ... produced. I have ... to construct, which ... was the product of ... (several) departments ... departments, as far as ..., are the biggest sleepyheads ... Months of work, and then it's all a mess. It collapses right away. This mask is the product of two weeks' labor. If our offices are not regressing, abolish the eight-hour day or rather the five-hour day! They even received a product briefing. I ordered that a standard mask be produced. Then it goes back and forth. Then a standard mask is produced that is suitable for carrying the new heavy filters that are much bigger. They have been strengthened once more. So we need a standard mask, which is absolutely uniform for military and civilian use, because it's a crime if I say today: I'm making a mask—and it's worthless. Rather ... can ... millions of people ... but for these ... must ... make a mask, which ... person knows, it ... take the responsibility for ... I have given the order … I have just now … When the gas war … put into a situation …

KEITEL: … 1939 we had … gas mask was totally different … mask.

THE FÜHRER: … a standard mask will be made. We can't make it just with Buna [rubber] anyway.[1166] We have to make it with textiles. That way we can get a standard mask that's very solid and firm.

End: 2:08 p.m.

* * * * *

May 18, 1944

There is spring peace in the East. Also the Southern front has come to a halt at the lower Dnestr River, before Kishinev and Iassy, at the foothills of the Carpathians and along the line eastward from Tarnopol through Brody and Kovel'. The Crimea has been lost.

In Italy the enemy began an attack between Cassino and the Thyrrenian Sea during the night of May 12. German troops were driven back over the Garigliano River, and Cassino was evacuated last night.

In the West they wait—so far in vain—for the invasion.

(*Maps 5, 10 and 11*)

* * * * *

EVENING SITUATION REPORT,
MAY 18, 1944, AT THE BERGHOF[1167]

Present:

The Führer	*Rear Admiral v. Puttkamer*
Colonel General Jodl	*Lieutenant Colonel Borgmann*
Major General Scherff	*Lieutenant Colonel Waizenegger*

Beginning: 11 p.m.

The East

BORGMANN: In the East no noteworthy engagements. As to the Sixth Army, the enemy continued to attack the left wing of the 4th Mountain Division up on the loop [—] In Army Group North's area, the 263rd [Infantry] Division experienced company-strength attacks for the first time. The attacks were driven back. Small penetrations were achieved, but our counterattacks and counterthrusts continue.

Italy

JODL: Today also there was heavy fighting. The enemy followed less on the southern wing, in contrast to here on the left wing of the 94th [Infantry] Division.[1168] According to reports received so far, those attacks were stopped at M. Carozzo and M. le Pezze. The next strong attack was on both sides of S. Oliva, there against the newly deployed 9th Panzer Grenadier Regiment. According to the latest reports, the enemy achieved small penetrations. Counterattacks are in progress. Also very heavy fighting east of Pontecorvo. There are no reports yet about the development of those battles. Here our artillery is concentrated strongly. (The Commander-in-Chief Southwest said to me: 200 guns.) Obviously that mortar is [—]

THE FÜHRER: Yes.

JODL: The Naples group is for the most part used up now.[1169]

THE FÜHRER: Yes.

JODL: Now the only thing left is the arrival of the North African group together with Nettuno.[1170] The Commander-in-Chief Southwest naturally considers himself forced to bring in stronger forces now. He offered the entire 26th Panzer Division, of which one regiment is already deployed, to the Tenth Army. He hands the whole Hauck[1171] Group—namely both Eastern divisions, the 334th and the 305th—over and also sends the entire 278th [Infantry] Division here, to cover the relief, and sends over the worn-out units of the 71st and 94th [Infantry] Divisions. So the reserves are naturally starting to be used up.[1172] After (consultation) with the Commander-in-Chief Southwest I (came) to the conclusion [—] (I) arrived at the following suggestion: (*Presentation.*)

THE FÜHRER: But outwardly we absolutely want to maintain the concept of the holding attack.

JODL: Yes, Sir.

THE FÜHRER: Only he must not use the Panzer Lehr Regiment [Panzer Training Regiment], unless—

JODL: He must not use anything from here at all, but he could—and he wants to—request reinforcements at Genoa and Leghorn.

THE FÜHRER: I agree with that.

JODL: Then possibly we could get the *Hermann Göring* [Parachute Panzer Division]

THE FÜHRER: Regarding the 20th Luftwaffe Field Division, (I'm not very excited.) It's the only mobile[1173] ... it will (take) a while [—]

—if we really want to do it—first of all, to take the Panzer Lehr Regiment, that's the best, and then the 16th Panzer Grenadier Division. If worst comes to worst we can combine it with the panzer grenadier division. Then we'll have a very strong group. I would do that first.[1174] Then we can decide in the next few days what should follow next. We can't do it all at once, anyway.

JODL: Yes, Sir. By then it may be clearer.

THE FÜHRER: We only have to make sure that the forces reach Hungary as quickly as possible.

JODL: Then we would put the one division into the area of the 16th Panzer Grenadier Division, and the other should be sent into the (area) west of Budapest [—]

The West

Today there were two reconnaissance missions—rather, we can't call them missions. They were attempts to locate obstacles off the coast and to photograph them. A patrol of the 18th Luftwaffe Field Division on the left wing eastward of Calais noticed some movement. An exchange of fire occurred. First we thought they were our own forces, clashing with each other. But flashbulbs, spades and American flashlights were found—one man was wounded—so we have to assume that Americans had tried to photograph the obstacles. Likewise, two British officers were captured at the mouth of the Somme [River]. They had gone in with a rubber dinghy and, according to interrogation completed so far, had been dropped by an British motor torpedo boat.[1175] Whose ... because of a clash with our own ... so that at daylight they ...in [—]

JODL: Of course it could happen once, although the beach is being patrolled continuously.

Italy again

THE FÜHRER: Here[1176] we really have to make sure that nothing happens again, not even against this line again. Because it uses up too many forces. The best line is the one that he has now. He can be pushed back here, of course—that doesn't matter—into a consolidated position.

JODL: So that is now the seventh battalion of the 305th [Infantry] Division. The 26th [Panzer] Division will arrive with the whole lot tonight. He also told me: the Polish have the greatest losses; the attacking English have about 50 percent, the Americans a bit less, and the French (have the) fewest (losses).

(THE FÜHRER): Because they are the best![1177] [—] ... been. If that had been able to hold in the Baltic region, all sorts of things would have come there. The best would have rushed down there, where they would have built up a resistance movement and advanced on Germany from there. That's absolutely clear. Those were the best people, too.[1178]

Hungary

Don't we have anything mobile here[1179] at all anymore?

JODL: Yes, we have the 18th SS [Panzer Grenadier Division] and the cavalry division.[1180]

THE FÜHRER: And the Hungarians are pretty burned out?

JODL: Yes. The last two divisions are coming out. And there's a new one in formation—the German *Volksdeutsch* Cavalry Division.[1181] (The) first parts (of) it have arrived.

Situation in the air

[—]

THE FÜHRER: Did nothing happen in Ploesti?

WAIZENEGGER: No, only insignificant damage. No reports have arrived yet regarding the success of our fighter defense.[1182] [—] Flying possibilities are limited today. However, there have been reports of units gathering in England. The defense has only limited possibilities to takeoff.

THE FÜHRER: We must reply seriously to this appeal by the Romanians. I don't know if you have received it. The Romanian government sent an appeal to the German government—that is, to me—regarding assistance with air-raid defense. And they took a very whining tone.[1183]

(JODL: No,) I didn't get it. ...

(THE FÜHRER):[1184] [—]

people of all nations, who didn't do the least to help keep the danger away. We even wanted to drive them out of Egypt. But unfortunately we weren't supported in that effort. We wanted to hold them back to who knows where in the East to prevent them from reaching the border. We Germans were the only ones who attacked anyway. And third, we have to tell them: we're doing everything we can. It's a direct appeal. Now the people will see it as it is. They could have had it easier if they had strained their forces like we strained our German forces. If they had accepted the sacrifices and those events, everything would have turned out differently. Now they see the consequences that develop (if someone) thinks that he (can get away) easily.

Italy again

[—]

(JODL?) : There are about 9 battalions besides the 29th [Panzer Grenadier Division].[1185]

THE FÜHRER: I'm curious! But it's clear: if he loses 50 percent of the attacking infantry it will be proof that he is doing a terrible job. Because the procedure he's following is quite an inexpensive one at present. He shoots at nonexistent shelters with a huge waste of ammunition. There's nothing there. Those few shelters in the rocks are absurd. They would never have gotten Monte Cassino if the breakthrough hadn't taken place in the south. There you see what you have. They write that they captured 500 men from the paratroop division. I don't believe that.

(JODL: That) is impossible.[1186]

THE FÜHRER: [—] ..., which are absolutely bulletproof, and for those calibers they are bulletproof, in any case—then they will be in for a shock.[1187] It will stop then. The fact that they still have those big losses shows that they are poorly led. And the fact that they have to bring up their divisions so quickly also shows that they had big losses. But we know from the East, too. If it doesn't go forward—if we can't get through, and if we have to fight constantly for 6 days, then the attack troops are gone. It all depends on getting through within the first few days. When Model told me at Zitadelle [Operation "Citadel"][1188] that he expected 3 days, I got cold feet. When he has to fight attacking for three days against an enemy that doesn't consist of newcomers—and (that was) the case (for him) in the end—6 or 7 days [—] they need to have new divisions. They can't expect that from them.

End: 11:18 p.m.

* * * * *

June 18, 1944

On the Eastern Front the Russians are still quiet, but there is growing evidence of the brewing thunderstorm facing Army Group Center. The storm will break out four days later, on the 3rd anniversary of the German invasion of the Soviet Union. Only on the Karelian Isthmus have the Russians already attacked; there they forced the Finns back behind Vyborg on June 10.

In Italy, the Anglo-Americans established a link-up with their beachhead on May 25 and forced the Fourteenth Army northward past Rome, which was evacuated on June 4. Only by taking huge risks—and because of the enemy's cautiousness—was the Tenth Army able to effect the link-up. Both armies are now retreating, and the front now runs along Lake Trasimenian, north of Grosseto and south of Perugia.

In Normandy, Eisenhower's troops landed 12 days ago. The defenders were unable to drive the troops back into the ocean at any of the landing areas, and the enemy now controls a strip up to 30 km wide on both sides of Bayeux. Today the enemy drove a 5-km-wide wedge from the southeastern corner of the Cotentin peninsula to the west coast.

(Maps 5 and 11)

* * * * *

Evening Situation Report,
June 18, 1944, at the Berghof[1189]

Present:

The Führer	*Rear Admiral v. Puttkamer*
Reich Minister Speer	*Colonel v. Below*
Reich Press Chief Dr. Dietrich	*Lieutenant Colonel Borgmann*
Colonel General Jodl	*Lieutenant Colonel Waizenegger*
General Buhle	*Major Büchs*
Lieutenant General Schmundt	*Sturmbannführer Darges*
Vice Admiral Voss	*Hauptsturmführer Günsche*
Major General Scherff	

Beginning: 11:03 p.m.

The West

THE FÜHRER: They have reported for certain that they are through now. Are they through now or not?

JODL: Yes, indeed. They are through.[1190] [—] The following is reported regarding the firing: from yesterday at 6 p.m. to 4:30 p.m. today (so 22 hours and 30 minutes), 206 shots were fired, with 37 of them bringing down aircraft—that's 18%.[1191] Reported with regard to the enemy: very heavy reconnaissance activity in the entire operational area, by both day and night; heavy combat action with isolated bomb drops. A supply station was also attacked, but seemingly without result. Tonight a different procedure is planned. First of all, in consideration of the troops, a pause in firing is scheduled for the entire regiment from 4:30 p.m. to 8 p.m. Then the reopening of fire today between 8 and 8:30 p.m., with a sudden concentration of fire, and then continuation only with concentrated fire—so no intermittent fire—from all positions approximately every 75 minutes until 1 a.m. Then a firing pause and then a concentrated discharge again and finally transition to intermittent fire, until dawn and, if the weather is good, even longer. So a totally different method, so they can't determine any rules over there. [—] From the beachhead itself it is reported that in the assault-troop-like continuation of the attack, the 21st Panzer Division,[1192] Group Luck, has taken a brickworks near Esqueville. Then there were smaller combined tank attacks, which broke through a bit west of here (Quinné)[1193] and reached the town of

Quinné. [—] Then behind the … 2nd Panzer Division a group was encircled. The attack hasn't been continued yet. [—] Nothing new is reported about these movements. Here's the order that the Commander-in-Chief West gave based on yesterday's directive from the command post. *(Presentation.)*

THE FÜHRER *(after checking the document):* This is even better. We even have another opportunity for an attack.

JODL: With the forces now available, he[1194] will hardly be able to do both: to take cover here—he'll expect counterattacks as well—and, at the same time, to lead the attack from here.[1195] He at least will have to bring in new forces.

THE FÜHRER: He'll need half of his available forces in here.

JODL: And in the Western part, where you don't know if the 15th is up there, which belongs to the American Army Group. [—] Very many aren't there. This one here is gone, with the exception of the 3rd British Airborne Division. This American one is questionable. Then the 38th British is still here. The 2nd Canadian Armored Division is also questionable. Another British one, which is also questionable—the 54th British. The 30th and 10th American [Divisions] are questionable. Then the 15th British Guard Division and one airborne division. But even this one is not completely verified. Well, that one is questionable—everything that was there. But nothing from this group is gone yet. Altogether 25 units. But that includes the brigades—two brigades counted to one division.[1196]

THE FÜHRER: That's why we must start to feed it, and put in artillery brigades, possibly such artillery brigades with … supply and get bodies that way.[1197] We see that with the Russians. He establishes his front with worthless units. We're too rigid. We have to build these units so that they consist only of combat forces and have very limited rear services, very limited bases.

JODL: On the 16th—writes the Commander-in-Chief West—Army Group B[1198] proposed to transfer a combat group from the islands to the mainland. The Commander-in-Chief West rejected that immediately.

(THE FÜHRER: No![1199])

Then I inquired again about further measures concerning the Eastern troops, and how those volunteer formations have fought.[1200] The Commander-in-Chief West reported expressly that, for the most part, they performed above the level expected, so they don't want to take any further steps—exchanges, etc.

THE FÜHRER: Then we should give those units German insignia,[1201] if they really fought here.

JODL: Yes, Sir!

SCHMUNDT: Yes, Sir. We gave them in the Balkans, too, and also in the East.

VOSS: The deployment of the pressure-box mines,[1202] which was asked about yesterday, has been taking place since the night of the 14th—in quantities of 50 to 60 mines, combined with other mines, laid out by the Luftwaffe. It is planned to increase this deployment through the use of motor torpedo boat and mine sweeper flotillas from Le Havre. The exact time can only be reported when the ... situation can be surveyed a bit.

THE FÜHRER: Especially that we put some blockades here in front of Le Havre with motor torpedo boats, so he can't do the same thing here again![1203]

VOSS: They first want to put a blockade at the mouth of the Orne [—]

Italy

(JODL: In this new line), where we don't yet know the exact course, we were largely successful in stopping the enemy and preventing penetrations. The only penetration happened here at (Stefani). The enemy enlarged the breach northeast of Grosseto as well as the one at the bridgehead further east. Then here the strong attacks pushed back the forces of the 90th Panzer Grenadier Division and the 20th Luftwaffe Field Division to the higher area north of [location illegible]. The group in S. Fiora, which is encircled, is still holding its position and has, according to monitored radio messages, driven back several attacks. Active preparation and assembly at the I Parachute Corps indicates the continuation of attacks against the 29th Panzer Grenadier Division. Here the enemy managed the only deeper penetration, at Radofini.[1204] In the afternoon, attacks were taking place up here, where the combat group of the 334th and 15th Panzer Grenadier Division ... the enemy won some ground worth mentioning. ... The attacks, which were led here on both sides of the major road to Perugia, were driven back. But here there are still combat outposts quite far south, and also down here north of Foligno. [—] On the western wing no particular action. Withdrawal to the blue marked line. He[1205] sent a telegram with regard to the situation in case the Elba should be lost,[1206] and the threat to this piece in the rear of this position.

THE FÜHRER: He has that threat everywhere—that doesn't matter. If he goes here, the threat is from the rear again, because he[1207] can go here from this island. He's not forced to go there. So that's no reason.

JODL: The only thing is the following. [—] On this map it's hard to see; it doesn't show the elevation differences properly. [—] (*Presentation of another map.*) Here he has the big Iron Mountains [Eisengebirge]: the Tuscan Ore Mountains [Erzgebirge]—I think they are called—begin here. He possibly wants to withdraw to those heights. He writes:

The developments on the island of Elba lead us to expect that despite the brave resistance of the occupation troops—which can't count on any support from land, sea or air—the island will be in the possession of the enemy within a few days. The loss of this island will create a new situation, at least for the western wing of the Southern front. From Elba the enemy (can) land and encircle the Fourteenth Army at any time, even without any notable reinforcement.

THE FÜHRER: He explains this now. A few days ago he didn't say it. Back then he wanted to (give up) the island.

JODL: He wanted to retreat further anyway. But now he has the order to hold.[1208] [—] (*A longer reading from the telegram follows.*) Until Elba is in the possession of the enemy, it's not urgent. A landing is easier for the enemy here in front rather than further back, where the terrain ... (*Presentation of a map with explanations by Colonel General Jodl.*)

THE FÜHRER: Is the "Albert" Line the green one?

(JODL: That's the green one.)

The "Albert" Line must be reconnoitered first of all. Nothing has happened. We can't say we want to take a position back when it hasn't even been reconnoitered yet.[1209] That's putting the cart before the horse.

JODL: Right at this moment it's not necessary. As it stands now, the block is quite good.

THE FÜHRER: It is different if he lands here, when he has a few little guys—from there alone. He has to bring forces over there first.

JODL: When he sits here,[1210] then we'll have to see if he adds forces here. As such, it's uncomfortable when he is here, the front is here, and he's so close to it.

THE FÜHRER: When he's here and the front is here,[1211] then he's just as close. The danger is *this* front here[1212] from a certain moment on. That's much more dangerous than that there.

JODL: The 715th and the 65th [Infantry] Divisions are now back here. Both will be enlarged by divisions from the 26th wave.[1213]

THE FÜHRER: Then we'll have fewer units again.

BUHLE: They were intended for that. The 26th wave is only infantry regiments—an artillery division and a tank destroyer company in one framework.

THE FÜHRER: How are the commanders of these units?

JODL: The 65th [Infantry] Division is good and has always been good. The 715th [Infantry] Division wasn't excessive. It is a 700-series division.[1214]

THE FÜHRER: That's a question of personality. We have groups that are theoretically old Landwehr people ... It only depends on the commander [—] In the Great War we never (had such inferiority in the air). I know that.

For example, during our offensive in the big battle in France we actually drove the British completely out of the battlefield. We didn't have such a pitiful situation during the Great War. In 1917 the situation was still such that in the battle of Arras the Richthofen wing totally cleared out the sky. British squadrons came through and were absolutely beaten back. I saw part of this myself—how the remains of 10 aircraft, down to the last one, were brought down. Then we had total freedom. Also in the Flanders battle, where the first really big air battles for those times took place. Already 70 to 100 airplanes were being used on both sides—that was a murderous strangle.... But one couldn't say that the enemy ruled the sky and flew where he wanted—that was never the case. Of course, they became quite bold too, and in 1918 it got worse.

JODL: Then the first squadron flights came. They came by the hundreds—400 to 500.

Situation in the air

BÜCHS: No particular reports from the air. During the attack on Hamburg, 11 aircraft were shot down by flak, according to reports received so far. The fighters didn't come close.[1215] Plans for tonight in the West: the IX and X Corps again—

THE FÜHRER *(interrupting)*: ... major damage in Hamburg?

BÜCHS: No. It's only the advance report stating that there was heavier damage at Blohm & Voss.

THE FÜHRER: But not to the submarine buildings?

VOSS: Apparently not.

SPEER: Nothing in particular happened at Blohm & Voss with the mass production, and at the shipyard[1216] there was somewhat more significant damage.

BÜCHS: Plan: the IX and X Corps again deploy mines and torpedoes, if weather conditions permit. Tonight it will be heavily clouded, 5-8/10, lower limits around 500 m.[1217] Tomorrow it will be similar. [—] In the East, deployment with units of the Meister[1218] Corps. The weather situation is still not favorable yet, as there is a heavy mist over the entire area, making it difficult to identify the targets. But they want to get some units out toward Sarny. Otherwise, there was no particular combat action in Italy or on the Eastern Front during the day.

THE FÜHRER: Still, we have to be prepared for this character in the East to bring big, thick waves on the day he attacks.

BÜCHS: Tonight, according to final reports, 4 airfields were indeed attacked by 50 to 100 of those long-range units—that was also written in Zhukov's operational instructions—in the area of Army Group Center. But damage was very limited.

THE FÜHRER: From our point of view I must say that when we can pass a place where there is a massive array of aircraft, then that's fine. But on the other side, it's not the destruction of the aircraft that is so decisive, but the destruction of the flying crew—and (we don't destroy the crew by attacking the airfields). The aircraft play a minor role for him. For us ... play ...

Defense production questions

BUHLE: From captured Russian materiel we still have more than 2,000 light field howitzers—12.2 cm with a firing range of 7,000 m. In addition, we have more than 1,200 15.2-cm heavy field howitzers with a firing range of 10,000 to 12,000 m. Ammunition is not available, and can't be produced either. We still have 1,000 infantry gun howitzers. Of those, 900 are still at home. That's the modern gun.

THE FÜHRER: Maybe we can possibly do something with the allies.

BUHLE: We gave several hundred of them to the Romanians, and the Finns will also get some of the 15.2-cm guns, because they have the ammunition for them. I wanted to suggest that we keep up to 300 ...

THE FÜHRER: ... I wish I had 600 barrels in here right now!

BUHLE: But I don't have a single round of ammunition.[1219]

THE FÜHRER: But I may be able to produce ammunition for them as well. Because if I produce ammunition for guns I don't have—if I lose 1,000 guns somewhere on the march back home—then I have to make ammunition for the other one, too. That's a change, of course.

SPEER: It is not only a change, but each new type of ammunition also requires a new type of casing.

BUHLE: If we wanted to use the 15.2-cm gun howitzers, we would have to make at least 100,000 rounds.

SPEER: Well, we always have to make the cartridge return a hundred percent initially, otherwise we will have 30 to 40% cartridge return.[1220]

THE FÜHRER: That's an extraordinary gun.

BUHLE: But it only shoots 7,400 meters.

THE FÜHRER: I want to have it exact. I want the whole thing written down.

Italy again

JODL: (*Presentation by Jodl.*) The provisional report about the condition of the divisions![1221] Are the numbers correct? Of the 90th [Panzer Grenadier] there is almost nothing left. There is also almost nothing left of the 20th, which was just deployed. The 362nd—that is correct—is pretty much gone.

THE FÜHRER: Where was 20th deployed?

JODL: It was in the battle for a day. … is still pretty good with four battalions. [—]

Defense production (continued)

[—]

THE FÜHRER: Then, in 1938-39, everything was leveled at the Czech situation. The most valuable guns … were all junked. There was a craze for unity. They just barely saved the Czech howitzers from being scrapped! At the demonstration, the Czech howitzer was presented as a monstrous freak. But it was even better than ours. Unfortunately, I made a big mistake back then. I should have continued building this gun from the start. … As well as the 21-cm gun! The Skoda gun was abandoned because the new German 21-cm gun was supposed to shoot even further—33 km, and the Skoda only fired 30 km. But this one was there and was tested—it was an excellent gun and had all-around fire, which is good in this case. I don't need to run around with the carriage trail, but I can continually turn around in any direction. Especially for coastal defense, for our needs, it's an excellent gun. The best proof is that everybody else desperately wants it. The Turks want it and also the Swedes. The Swedes have an excellent one themselves, but they fight over this gun. [—] Back then a huge order was placed, and someone—today we still don't know who—cancelled the order. That was after the war had already started. During the war the order was missing again, and many months had passed. Otherwise we would certainly be in possession of 160 21-cm guns today.[1222]

End: 11:40 p.m.

* * * * *

July 31, 1944

The extended front of Army Group Center broke down at the end of June under pressure from the Soviet offensive against the Ninth Army, the Fourth Army and the Third Panzer Army. The front has been torn apart to a width of 300 km. Now, at the end of July, the Red Army has reached Memel and is between Grodno and Kovno. In the meantime, on July 13, the Russians had also attacked Army Group North, whose retreat behind the Düna River had been prohibited by Hitler. On August 1 the Soviets reach the Gulf of Riga at Tukkum, cutting off the army group, which is still at Narva and Lake Peipus. At the same time, the enemy has almost reached the East Prussian border. [—] The Russian attack against Army Group North Ukraine's front began on July 14. After achieving breakthroughs at Brody and Kovel', the Red Army has now advanced over the Bug River up to the San River. In the direction of the Vistula River bend, Lublin has fallen on July 24, but the attack on Warsaw has failed for the time being.

In Normandy, by the middle of July, the Anglo-Americans were able to enlarge their beachhead to an approximately 30-km-wide strip up to the mouth of the Dives River in the east and including the Cotentin Peninsula in the west. On July 25 they began a large-scale attack. While the British were unable to progress very far in the direction of Falaise, the Americans succeeded in breaking through along the western coast. On the evening of July 30, Avranches fell into their hands. Brittany was reached, and the Anglo-Americans succeeded in breaking out of their beachhead into France.

On July 20, Count von Stauffenberg made his long-planned attempt on Hitler's life. He failed.

* * * * *

MEETING OF THE FÜHRER
WITH COLONEL GENERAL JODL, JULY 31, 1944,
IN THE WOLFSSCHANZe[1223]

Present:

The Führer	*Colonel v. Below*
Colonel General Jodl	*Lieutenant Colonel v. Amsberg*
General Warlimont Lieutenant	*Colonel Waizenegger*
Gruppenführer Fegelein	*Major Büchs*

Beginning: 11:53 p.m.

General overview

THE FÜHRER: Jodl, when I look at the big concerns today, there is first the problem of stabilizing the Eastern Front—we can't go beyond that at the moment—and I ask myself with regard to the situation if it really is that bad that our forces are concentrated relatively closely together. Because there are not only disadvantages, but also advantages. If the area that we are occupying now can be held, then this is an area that we can still live in, and we don't have those huge communication zones. Assuming, of course, that we really provide the combat group[1224] with what we created in those earlier communication zones. Then it will be a real force. If we don't do this, but the communication zone goes into Germany instead, if we develop an ever-deeper rear army service area, where no army area is necessary, and if we still link this with the idea of executive authority, where no executive authority is necessary, because all people administer authority only in the sense of the army anyway—then in 1939 I would have had to have given up executive authority in the West as far as Hannover, Minden it was all a single deployment area. When we do away with this homegrown but other-worldly ideology—which is not at all soldierly and is not even known in other armies—then the narrowing of the area isn't always a disadvantage, but can also be a gain. But only under one condition: that we really put that which we have developed or consumed in this gigantic area into the fight. If this prerequisite is met, it is my solemn conviction that we can stabilize the thing also in the East. [—] Italy. In Italy I would not remain in the Apennine position. I wouldn't do that because[1225] I couldn't contain a large enemy force, which will definitely be brought into action somewhere else. Because he won't pension off the forces if we go back now. But you could seal off Germany, of course, with a minimum of forces, when I go to the Alpine front. But I need the forces elsewhere anyway, and the other one's forces are freed up as well. In any case, it is still better if I lead a battle in a different country than if I bring it close to Germany and I have to draw the forces away when the mobility of the forces is quite limited—because his air force, as we know from experience, will move itself along. [—] In the West, in my view, there is actually one very decisive question. If we lose France as a war theater, we will lose our point of departure for the submarine war.[1226] We have to be clear about this. That's the point of departure for the submarine war. We'll still get some militarily important things out of this area, including the last tungsten—and the mines probably could be exploited more than they have been so far. We could do even more.[1227] But it's also clear that an operation in France—and I believe we must be fully aware of this at all times—is totally impossible in a so-called open field of battle under today's circumstances. We can't do that. We can move with some of our troops, but only in a limited manner. With the other ones we can't move, not because we don't possess air superiority, but because we can't move the troops themselves: the units are not suited for mobile battle—neither their weapons nor in their other equipment. They can't do it either. They haven't learned that. But the total strength of the forces in France can't be measured by the number of divisions—which we theoretically have here—but really only by the limited number of units that are actually able to move.[1228] That's only a very small fraction. If the territory weren't that important, a decision would be forced upon us—namely to clear the coast without hesitation and to lead the mobile forces immediately back into a line, which, I would like to say, we would defend unyieldingly. But one thing is already obvious now. I have here a certain number of forces. Those forces are hardly enough to defend this narrow front. If we can say that about 75% of all our mobile forces are here and a certain number of our immobile forces, and I transfer them to a line like this—then we can see the complete hopelessness of holding such a line with the forces that are available to us, no matter where I built it up. We have to realize that a change in France could only happen if we managed—even only for a certain time—to establish superiority in the air. That's why it's my opinion that we have to do everything—as hard as it may be right now—to prepare the Luftwaffe units, which we are setting up in the Reich now, to be used as last reserves in the worst possible circumstances. To use them—I can't tell now where the last dice will fall, but to use them where we can possibly create a change again.[1229] It's unfortunate that it will still take so many weeks and that we can't manage it faster. Because for me there is no doubt: if we could immediately draw in an additional 800 fighters, to reach 2,000 fighters at once, as we probably could do now, this entire crisis would be overcome immediately; there wouldn't be a crisis anymore. But even later we can only conduct the war here if we manage to rebuild the Luftwaffe to some extent. So I considered the question: what are the most dangerous moments that could occur during the entire war? First, of course, would be a breakthrough in the East with a real threat to the German homeland—whether in the Upper Silesian industrial area or in East Prussia—with the accompanying difficult psychological effects. But I believe that with the forces we are putting up now, which are slowly coming out, we are in a position to stabilize the East—I believe that—and that we will overcome this human crisis, this moral crisis. It can't be separated from the event that took place here.[1230] Because the action is not to be taken as an isolated action. But this act which happened here is, I would like to say, just a symptom of an inner circulatory problem, of an inner blood poisoning, that we are suffering from. What do you expect in the end from the front's highest leadership, if behind them (as we can see now) the most important positions are occupied by absolutely destructive people—not defeatists, but destructive people and traitors? Because it is like that. If the communications service and the quartermaster's office are occupied by people who are absolute traitors[1231]—and you don't really know how long they have been in contact with the enemy or the people over there—you can't expect that the necessary initiative to stop such a thing will come from there. Because the Russians certainly didn't improve so much in morale within one or two years. That is not the case. They didn't improve in a human sense either. But our morale doubtlessly became worse—became worse because we had this place over there, which constantly spread poison over the path of these General Staff organizations, the organizations of the quartermaster general, of the intelligence chiefs,[1232] and so on. So we only have to ask ourselves today—or rather, we don't have to ask ourselves anymore: how does the enemy learn about our thinking? Why are so many things neutralized? Why does he react to everything so quickly? [—] It's probably not the perception of the Russians at all, but permanent treason, constantly being carried out by some damned little clique.[1233] But even if it weren't possible to put it in concrete form, it would be absolutely enough that people sit here in influential positions, who, instead of constantly radiating power and spreading confidence and especially deepening their understanding of the essence of this battle brought to us by destiny—a battle of destiny that somehow can't be avoided or which can't be bargained away by some clever political or tactical skill, but that it really is a kind of Hun battle, in which you either stand or fall and die: one or the other. When those thoughts are not present in the higher positions, but when those idiots imagine that they are in a better position because the revolution was brought about by generals—instead of by soldiers as in 1918—then everything just comes to a stop. Then an army must gradually be taken apart from top to bottom. I have received so many individual letters from the front—about the Party—from good soldiers, who say, "We don't know at all what's going on; what's happening there can only be treason—it can't be explained in another way." So we also have to say, "Certainly there has been ongoing treason, and it's partly our fault as well. We always acted too late against the traitors, out of consideration for the so-called army, or we didn't act at all, although we already knew for a long time—for a year and a half—that they were traitors, again to avoid compromising the army."[1234] But the army is rather more compromised when we leave it to the little soldiers to handle the call that the Russians continue to give in the name of German generals—when we leave it to the little worm, to the little front officer, who must gradually come to the conclusion that either the whole thing is true or we are too cowardly to answer to it. [—] It must come to an end. It's not right. We have to repel and drive away those low creatures—the lowest creatures in history ever to wear the soldier's uniform—this riffraff, which managed to save itself from former times. That is our highest duty. When we have overcome this moral crisis, the Russians won't be better than they were previously, and we won't be worse than we were before. And with regard to our equipment and supplies, we're even better than before. Our tanks and our assault guns are better today, whereas the Russians' equipment has likely become worse.[1235] [—] In my opinion, we will also be able to fix the thing in the East. The great concern I see is obviously in the Balkans. I have the fundamental conviction: if today the Turks were persuaded—like the Finns—that we can hold out, then they wouldn't lift a finger.[1236] Everyone has only the one concern that they might sit on the ground between all the chairs. That's their concern. So if we managed through some act of extremely decisive resistance or even a successful big battle somewhere, if we managed to regain the trust of those people—the trust that we can hold this, and that this withdrawal is only in the end to shorten the front, because otherwise we couldn't do it on all fronts—then I am convinced that we could bring the Turks to a more-or-less waiting attitude, even though they severed the relationship themselves.[1237] The Turks are not pleased that the strongest European power opposed to Bolshevism and Russia is being eliminated in favor of a totally unstable counterweight: the Anglo-Saxons—who, furthermore, are questionable in their importance and firmness. They're not pleased. But also in Bulgaria they're slowly coming to the idea: yes, if Germany collapses, then what?[1238] We small ones can't do it. If the big one can't do it, we can't do it. There's also something else that depends on the stabilization of the Eastern Front, in my view. In the end the attitude of all the small Balkan states depends on it: the attitude of the Romanians depends on it, the attitude of the Bulgarians depends on it, the attitude of the Hungarians depends on it, and also the attitude of the Turks. Nevertheless, we must meet certain safeguards. The most critical safeguard is and will remain the initial securing of the Hungarian area—the only possible substitute for the sources of food that we lose otherwise, and also a source of many raw materials: bauxite, manganese and so on.[1239] But above all for transport purposes—the prerequisite for the Southeast. Securing the Hungarian area is of essential importance to us—so important that we can't overestimate it at all. We first must think about what in terms of new troop arrangements we can either bring in or build up there, to be able at any time, if necessary, to anticipate or prevent a Hungarian coup d'état against Herr Horthy.[1240] The second—just as important—is, of course, the attitude of Bulgaria. Because without Bulgaria it's practically impossible for us to secure the Balkan area so that we can get ore from Greece, etc. We need Bulgaria for that no matter what. Also in securing against bands, etc., we need Bulgaria. But it also depends partly on the fact that we really can stand in the East, and, of course, that we don't have a crisis in the rear or in the heart of Europe. So that's why any British landing attempt in the Balkans—in Istria or on the Dalmatian islands—would be very dangerous, because it will immediately affect the Hungarians. We shouldn't be surprised by the Hungarians. When we have such idiots or criminals with us, who say that even if the Russians come in we'll make peace, but if we have the Russians to ourselves not much can happen to us—so what right do we have to complain when some Hungarian idiot or magnate says, "We'll let ourselves be occupied by the British; they will have an interest in making sure that we aren't absorbed, so everything will be fine."

JODL: They might find out from those people.

THE FÜHRER: It's not impossible that they've been incited by those people in that way. So the danger is here, too, that the landing of the British could lead to catastrophic results. In my opinion, a landing on the islands, etc., can hardly be prevented in the long run, if it takes place with huge forces. There's only one question here. In the end I think it is the question of whether or not the Allies really act in agreement. If they act in total agreement, if the Russians say: we agree that you go onto the islands and we Russians in this case take, say, the Dardanelles—we would not be able to prevent it. Because I can't prevent the landing of four or six divisions on an island with 40,000 men, and even less on a small island. We just can't do that. We don't know if that's the case or not. I would like to doubt it. I don't want to believe that the Russians would leave the Balkans to the British. I would say that in this case a fierce Russian protest would follow. At most something could happen during a period of tension between the Russian Bolsheviks and Allies: that the British might try to get at least the Aegean islands for themselves. That would be theoretically possible. Together they wouldn't do it.[1241] [—] The Italian theater is now tying up a large number of forces that would otherwise appear operationally somewhere else. Even if a landing is made here, it would be partial units, though, that come. The great mass of all Allied forces is still concentrated there like before, whether we are in front of or within the Apennine position. One thing we have to be clear about: if we're thrown back in the Apennines, the operation is finished for us. Then it's over. We can't prevent him from coming over the Po plain. We probably can't even really prevent him from breaking up our retreat. So the Apennine position is decisive. If we're defeated there, in my opinion, we won't have the option of staying to fight somewhere in the Po plain. The only possibility left will be total retreat—sensible and accelerated retreat, if it even works—to the Alpine position. I don't see any other option. [—] Here the danger is that this whole position is just as much threatened by a landing from here[1242]—because you never know if he's going to turn here the next minute—with a landing from the West or with a breakthrough or with a new landing from Brittany. I've thought everything over now and I've come to the following conclusion, Jodl. If a crisis develops here, we can't leave all the responsibility to the Commander-in-Chief West. The headquarters must be here and we must, under all circumstances, lead from here. It's such a huge responsibility, and a solution can only be found if all forces work together. We may have to make the most difficult decisions. It could be that we'll have to accept a substantial reduction of the German living space again—possibly even to abandon the Balkans, even with the risk that our chromium will be used up within a short time. But it may be the only possibility to get the forces to operate here at all. We may at last have to deploy here, and then also draw back forces from here.[1243] And with that, I understand that it will be lost. We might have to retreat into the Alps directly in order to be able to operate here at all. Now I think the most important thing, Jodl, is that a number of orders are given here, which aren't connected to each other but which correspond to a certain plan of ours—but the plan must not be distributed to the army groups at all. You can't keep such thoughts from being immediately transmitted to the enemy these days, considering the lack of security within the inner army services. You can't avoid this. Because we don't know what's here in Paris. Stülpnagel[1244] was here. He took part in this mess. We don't know what relationships people have among themselves. We don't know which operational plans that we transmit here will immediately leak through and be in the hands of the British by tomorrow. Basically that's why I would say the following: first, we have to make it clear to the army group that, come what may, they have to lead the fight here with absolute fanaticism, because movement—or mobile combat—is totally impossible. We just have to imagine this in practice: if I turn back the whole front there, then it will go up to there. That's the same front. So I don't even cover a tenth or a sixth of the entire developing Western Front. You actually couldn't do that. Now you may say: let's take other forces. These other forces I couldn't really get here in time. In practice, that's impossible. We could bring some in here maybe, but it's not actually possible. I'm convinced a total collapse would happen. I'm not yet quite sure about which position is the best: if a Seine line—

JODL: No, that one is practically out of the question. Only this[1245] one could be considered. That's the best one. It is well reconnoitered, too.

THE FÜHRER: As I said before, that's the question anyway.

JODL: It's only for the start, because it's a clear line.

THE FÜHRER: Because it's a "break." The Seine line is very dangerous for us because he can destroy all the bridges over the Seine and can hinder all of our movements. That applies to every river that's in the way of a German retreat. In the long run, with the forces we have now in the West—

with 50 or 60 divisions—we wouldn't be able to hold either this line or that line, but at best this line.

JODL: Because it's improved.

THE FÜHRER: It's partially improved. We could prepare it further here. Then we have another line in the back, so it's questionable if he will interfere here at all, because he has to say to himself, "I can't get in too deep." He will likely lead his attack where it's the weakest—probably up here, where he assumes he can get into our industrial area[1246] the fastest. We have the connection here. Here it's the most decisive. Primarily he would also be in this area here, so we have a shorter line, and we have to secure this region to protect the industrial area. These are such wide-ranging thoughts that if I were to tell them to an army group today, then the men would be horrified. That's why I think it necessary that we set up a very small staff of ours here,[1247] which, if a crisis occurs, is prepared [to work] as an operations staff. The staff would be educated about the potential problems that could arise, and would, from the headquarters—we will probably have to relocate the headquarters here, too, or into the Black Forest[1248]; I have to discuss that with our Below again, where we would put it[1249]—but the Commander-in-Chief West can't carry the responsibility anymore. That is absolutely impossible. It's the fate of Germany. We couldn't sit up here—I assume that we will stabilize the Eastern Front— we can't sit up here while the fate of Germany is being decided. That is impossible. But in any case certain steps must be taken, and I would do this by giving out orders that are totally independent from each other, so that nothing points in any way to any intention or any particular direction. First, we must be clear about this among ourselves, Jodl. Which places do we want to hold under any circumstances, because they provide additional opportunities for the enemy? Because the only thing that can stop the enemy from obtaining an unlimited supply of materiel, troops and units is the number of airstrips available to him. So if he doesn't get a number of harbors, or ones that are efficient, then that's the only brake on his otherwise unlimited mobility.[1250] That's the only thing we can tell for sure, so we will simply have to decide to sacrifice certain troops in order to save other things. We have to do this ourselves. We have to identify these harbors in collaboration with the Navy. Their efficiency must be secured. And other harbors—which brings me to something else as well—must be handled in such a way [assuming] that the entire railway system is destroyed. And maybe it's more important to destroy all the engines, all the railway installations, all the pumps—everything—not just the rail lines. That might be even more important. Those are the only things that could buy us some time in the end. I can't operate myself, but by doing that I can make it immensely difficult for the enemy to operate deep into the area. I lead him into a war—I would like to say a scorched-earth war—that's different from the German one. But we must actually carry it out here then, and ruthlessly. [—] The one thing is the establishment of the harbors that must be held at all cost—without regard for the people there, so that it's impossible for the enemy to send in unlimited reinforcements. If he can send in unlimited reinforcements, then we absolutely have to give up the idea of withdrawing here with only our essential forces. We can't do that. Because you can see that a breakthrough like this can happen quickly! We can't do that at all. [—] This is the second point: now we have to demand from the Commander-in-Chief West that units which are not intended for fixed positions be made mobile—temporarily mobile—and that he report all of this. We must receive a report regarding each unit's degree of mobility and the quantity of weapons it can carry while mobilized. We also need to secure the destruction of the intermediate units in this whole front. When I have harbors, the intermediate units are not necessary. In fact, I have to give them up, because I would rather draw those people into the harbors and establish a solid defense there. Then we should be able to hold the harbor for, let's say, 6 or 8 or 10 weeks—and those 6 or 8 or 10 weeks will mean a lot in the months of August, September and October. Then we might be able to gain some time. That's the second step that he has to make independently from this. [—] Third: the line command, Jodl, must be established here by a senior officer, in my opinion. We can't leave it to the Commander-in-Chief West. We have to put in a staff that will set up this last possible line command, based on the entire battle experience that has been gained up to now.

JODL: It happened once already, my Führer, on your order.

THE FÜHRER: That happened once.

JODL: There's a fairly detailed report about that. Of course, we still aren't fully aware of all the effects of the carpet-bombing efforts, but the disadvantages of all the open and unprotected sectors are pointed out in the report. They don't have enough protection from the enemy's superiority in the air. That's the case in some areas. He already took that into consideration. He also discussed the various possibilities here. It's mostly wooded and covered terrain. It's excellent down there. The main problems begin here.

THE FÜHRER: That is the object?

JODL: That's the object.

THE FÜHRER: In those days it was meant as a pivot, as a kind of fortress.

JODL: That's why this line here is relocated forward. It's not only shorter, but it also occupies better terrain, because it's not so open as it is back there by the Somme [River] at Péronne.

THE FÜHRER: I would do just one thing, Jodl: I would set up your own development staff to improve this thing. Because it doesn't matter at all. Even if we managed it here, I would still come back to the idea—despite everything—that we should gradually reduce the further development of the coast and proceed with the development of this land front instead.

JODL: That's too much for the Commander-in-Chief West because he's an army group leader at the same time. He's not in Paris at all. He's leading the army group. They never see him any more—his army group has been abandoned anyway. Everything calls for another Commander-in-Chief. They want to have Rundstedt back, because Kluge is hardly accessible to them.[1251] There should be a dedicated staff here for these assignments anyway.

THE FÜHRER: And, Jodl, even in that case I come back to my previous opinion—even if we drive back all the attacks, even if fate changes, if we really could deploy more aircraft within 2 or 3 weeks, favored by the weather conditions that are gradually worsening and assisted by the Navy, and if the enemy develops problems replenishing his units, and if he has difficulties with the landings because he doesn't have any efficient harbors anymore—even if all that is the case, we need to have this line improved by the OT [Todt Organization]. It would be better to postpone other land missions and improve this line—in collaboration with the coastal defense from here northward, of course—because in the end it will be the most significant line for us.[1252]

JODL: The majority of the OT forces, aside from those building in advance of the Nineteenth and First Army, are now involved in the reconstruction of railways and roads.

THE FÜHRER: We'll have to see what we can pull out from there, especially what we can get in the way of cement. Because a position that isn't equipped with concrete bunkers—as we have seen—is worthless; it will be destroyed immediately. That works in terrain like they have in Italy. But it's not feasible elsewhere. This position seems important to me regardless, so we have to build this thing, no matter what happens. I would not call political units for the construction, because they really can't do this, but we have to establish a little shell organization here, which in fact consists of the OT. The political units can't do this. We could at most put political units in Lothringen, in Alsace, for those rear positions, and for the possible restoration of our German matter.[1253] But not much can be done except mining at the Western Wall. Except for wire, we don't need to do much. What's bad at the Western Wall is the antitank defense, because back then it was built for the 3.7-cm antitank gun. Now we have to see if the heavy gun will even fit at all. We need to investigate immediately to find out how much can be done.[1254]

[—] I would say the following, Jodl: we have to establish a very small operational staff now. This operational staff must deal with the different problems that could occur if a successful landing is made—either in the West, in Italian territory, or in Brittany or further north, which would be even more tragic. But this in itself shows that it can't be done by the Commander-in-Chief West by himself anymore. Finally, we must also consider the Italian matter, because a crisis could happen there as well. In my opinion, only our central staff can do that, because the Commander-in-Chief West by himself can't make the necessary resources available for such a purpose. In fact, one thing will happen right away: we will in fact establish such a thing—that will be decided—to arm certain positions that are not tank-secure from the beginning. That will happen very shortly, as we can't count on the returning units to arm them. It can only come from a central point—only from a point that is available to us. So again, I am convinced that it's wrong to give away 1,200 or 2,000 old Russian 7.6-cm or 12.2-cm weapons. Instead we should remodel them again—like we converted the Russian guns to split-trail carriages—and then we have to give them hollow shells, to add an extra level of antitank defense to our general antitank defense.[1255] But the operations staff has to think about all those problems carefully, so that we can in fact give clear direction to the Commander-in-Chief West right from the beginning—and on an ongoing basis. Also, we need to establish a headquarters immediately. It can't be too far away—preferably in the Vosges, and if that's not possible, within the Black Forest. In the Vosges would be best of all.

V. BELOW: The one at Diedenhofen is finished.[1256]

THE FÜHRER: Is it more-or-less secure against today's bombs?

V. BELOW: Against the 6,000s,[1257] I don't think so, my Führer.

THE FÜHRER: I don't think so either. [—] Is it camouflaged, so no one can see it?

V. BELOW: It's not at all visible from above because it's completely underground. It's located in some of the old forts on the Maginot Line, which are not visible from above.

THE FÜHRER: Can I see pictures of it right away?!

V. BELOW: We just have to take something that already exists. We couldn't build it anymore in that amount of time.

THE FÜHRER: I would like to have a foundation there again.

V. BELOW: Yes, Sir. Of course, I also consider this best. [—] Then, as mentioned, a OT construction staff to do the work. Then, I'd like to say, establish a demolition organization early, again with the help of the OT, because we have destroyed nothing so far. That's ridiculous. Then we need to work out general orders that'll be made available to the army group, of course, and to the Commander-in-Chief West and others who would be affected. Also the concern that it's based upon—and we have to tell this to the Commander-in-Chief West instantly: he has to make the units mobile. We'll tell him which units we need, and he must make sure that they reach a certain level of mobility within the shortest possible time. The units that we plan to pull out are to be made mobile. He doesn't need to know the purpose, because if he knows the purpose and it somehow goes through Paris, and if some Frenchwoman or Frenchman learns it the next day and the whole story immediately—

FEGELEIN: Rothacker[1258] was here 2 or 3 days before the attack—the Chief of Staff—and he helped plan the whole attack. He came from Paris.

THE FÜHRER: So it's impossible. We must play it safe. They don't need to know that—we'll simply tell them: this and this and this unit must be made mobile—improvised if need be. The army group, or rather the Commander-in-Chief West, hands in suggestions of his army groups, then we'll see to what degree they are mobile. Or better: he has to report to what degree they are mobile, how they're made mobile, and, especially, what they can carry in the way of weapons. That's the decisive factor. [—] And we determine the locations. We can't leave it to him; we'll determine them based on higher insight. We'll have to discuss that with the Grand Admiral and all the naval experts first thing tomorrow. This harbor will be defended at all cost, this harbor will be defended at all cost, this harbor will be defended. From here on out, the OT will provide everything for the defense of those harbors! [—] One thing became clear recently. It would have meant failure here at this little peninsula near Cherbourg if we had blocked this here, and there were some concrete-protected batteries that could always shoot into everything and into the harbor.[1259] It is not so much about the fact that we get harbors under all circumstances, but that we have a secure position from which we can shoot into a harbor constantly. Those few batteries must be put in concrete so that they can't be destroyed by the air force, and they must be supplied with ammunition so that we can shoot into the harbor no matter what. First we have to defend the harbor itself anyway, then finally destroy it—that is the most important thing. [—] But, as mentioned earlier, if we send out such an order in the usual form, it means that the enemy will be involved in everything we do. He is in it from the beginning and can neutralize the whole thing. We achieve no more this way than we achieve if we say that the Commander-in-Chief West doesn't need to know any more than necessary. First, he must know that he has to fight here in any case; second, that this battle is decisive; third, that the idea of operating freely in a free area is nonsense. He must know that he has to bring together all the forces that can possibly be brought together using human judgment. [—] That's one thing. Furthermore, he must know that certain units must absolutely be made mobile. That's also important. The third is that we ourselves, with the staff, must consider different contingencies right from the beginning—maybe without arranging everything in detail, but just for the sake of clarifying the exchange of units and determining the routes by which the units will be brought back. [—] It's totally clear that if he breaks through here,[1260] the railway system will still work for some time, but we must not risk that—we must not wait until it's too late. Then we'll have to make a decision. We'll turn one part back toward the Italian Alpine front, block that here, and pull the other part up from the Southern front right away. Then it's important that we transport those forces, which we'll bring up here, as far as possible by railway, and get them right into the planned reception areas, so that there are at least units there that are equipped with a lot of antitank guns, tank defense, assault guns, etc. That way we can immediately break up any advance we see, also from American units, and make it impossible. We can also let mobile units go further ahead—they'll always return—and they can catch something like that and win some time, so that the enemy doesn't run right into our line immediately. That must be done from the very beginning. It will be crucial to set up a staff of ours that can deal with this under clear orders. The moment the height of the crisis is reached, the main emphasis of the entire leadership shifts to the West again—as it once was, when, in the end, we led the way and the army groups received orders. It has to shift because it impinges immediately on the Italian theater. It just can't be done any other way. I have to turn one part down toward Italy at once to establish the front here. We can hold not only the Alpine front with those units, but with those units we can hold the whole Italian front, and maybe get one or two divisions free for the whole Ligurian front. That could be possible under some circumstances, so that we're at least totally secure here. The rest we would lead up here then. Positions that are key to our ability to continue the war, and which could fall into the enemy's hands right away,[1261] must be determined by a senior officer. Nonetheless, the Commander-in-Chief West himself will get the instructions to improve the positions. This and this position must be improved, this one is to be completed, this one is to be completed. He will also get instructions from us. He must in any case report which units he can shift into those areas. It's always presented as if they can't be moved at all. He has to make sure that the bravest officers get into those positions, not talkers like this character who went into Cherbourg and made a glorious appeal, who went ahead into the bunker at the very front and waited until the others approached, and then raised the white flag immediately. When the other one said then, "How can you reconcile this with your honor after you gave such an appeal?" he just shrugged his shoulders.[1262] [—] But we must find such officers. And so I've also come to the decision now that I don't care about this damned hierarchy at all. Here it's about men, nothing else! If I imagine what men we have—like this little major in Berlin who made such a hard decision.[1263] If I put a man like him into such a position, instead of some lieutenant general or commanding general, he's worth ten times as much. It really depends on one man, and the others are bastards. We raise them so they consider it to be obvious that others sacrifice themselves, but they don't even consider it themselves. They already have one eye squinting over here: what can happen to us? If we're imprisoned, we'll be treated according to our rank, especially those of us from noble families, so we'll be dealt with in keeping with our station and won't be put together with all the plebian masses. [—] Well, that's unbearable, and that's why we have to check all the commanders again. The Cherbourg case must be a warning. It can't be like that—it's a disgrace! It won't do to keep saying that we must not write about something like that in order to avoid damaging the army, and that it's better to praise such a person. [—] We do exactly the same thing that we have criticized in the Italians for years.[1264] Cowards are praised as heroes—characterless swine, who really behave worse than some Communist pig, because at least he's an idealist and is fighting for something. They're not mentioned, or they're even praised somewhere eventually, so that in the end this whole mess is camouflaged. I'm convinced that we can't do this! [—] I would put the staff together immediately; maybe you can bring some suggestions tomorrow, Jodl. Also concerning the fortress, so that we go over here if a crisis really occurs. I can't leave the Western campaign to Kluge. That's absolutely impossible because everything depends on it. The troops would not understand that either, if we sit in East Prussia while the decisive actions are taking place here. One can't know if we are here or here, or behind. Here are the most valuable parts, and behind it is the Ruhr area!

JODL: The one thing that concerns me is that in case something happens here [1265] within three, four or five days, we haven't yet ordered anything—

THE FÜHRER: You can't give any orders—or rather, you can order something, but nothing will be done.

JODL: Nothing has been prepared yet!

THE FÜHRER: You can give some orders, since we have to take on the responsibility anyway. That would be of no use. We would have to take it on anyway, if something happened within the next three, four or five days. We can order anything we want, but nothing can be done in the meantime. [—] So I can't leave the responsibility to Kluge even then. That's not possible. But orders regarding preparations that would be important in that case (in three, four or five days) can be given out right now. Mobilization of those and those units, determination of the harbors that are important to us, choice of commanders for those positions. And the people we bring here must know about a German officer's honor—not like those 16 people who handed over the Prussian fortresses one after the other in 1806,[1266] but like the one who held his fortress until the end!

JODL: That is the question, if General Warlimont should present verbally what was intended. He wanted to go there tomorrow[1267] because they wanted to have someone from us.

THE FÜHRER: I would only bring up those few things that don't have anything to do with the big story, but that have to be done anyway. We must not give these people the slightest hint, and we can't prevent that otherwise in this pigsty. It's as bad here as anywhere else. If I imagine that a man[1268] sits here for two years, who has done nothing in those two years but help to undermine the German front! Furthermore, the whole base in Paris is this man's fault. It's a fiasco! I didn't want him back then—you know that. A short time would have been enough. That man in the armistice commission and Mr. Abetz[1269] in Paris as our German representative—those two together would have given it all away within a few months. Everything that we had gained in our glorious six-week victory would have been gone within a few months! That was the best teamwork one could imagine: the one in the armistice commission and the other one in Paris. He is a totally incapable man, and besides he has taken his revenge. We should be able to find, say, 30 officers in the German Army that are heroes! It would be sad! But then I must not look at their insignias—I can put the insignias on them. I can do that. When I think of such people having received insignias—people who have become generals when they in fact deserved to be hung upside down—why shouldn't I name a good courageous front officer who has limited duties?! He doesn't need to operate tactically; I don't need a general who has proven to me that he led gloriously in the sandbox or on the troop training grounds somewhere! And by the way, I have seen myself what our generals have done on the troop training grounds, and how terribly they operate. They prove what they are capable of in organizational achievement, if they want to do something like this—a man like the Chief of the General Staff, Beck,[1270] who wanted to do this. That man has done nothing else in his life but busy himself with ridiculous little plans. How do I establish an army that, without ever provoking an enemy, is always in a position to take over the entire executive authority at home, without confronting the enemy at all? [—] This man doesn't travel to Paris without reason. He admired Gamelin.[1271]

When he came back, he shook his head ceremoniously.[1272] I said that I don't even consider Gamelin to be clever. If he had been a genius, he would not have watched while I armed! [—] It's interesting to read the assessment of Gamelin and Beck: those two big heroes of mankind met there! But if I imagine a scamp like Tito compared to a Gamelin or a Beck! But we have those people here, too, and if I want to defend a fortress here, you can't say, "My Führer, that doesn't work—the seniority of rank!" [—] I don't care about that at all! Here we need to bring in brave men who are willing to die if necessary, and we do have them! If we didn't have them in the German Armed Forces anymore—they are there among the German people—it would only be proof that the Armed Forces had made a totally negative selection. But that is not the case; they are there! Now, I've received letters from generals, etc., who are finally coming out and saying, "We saw this coming the whole time—it couldn't have turned out differently!" [—] So such people exist, and if the form is good enough, we still can do something. We'll go there in the name of God and promote the people! I'll do that with lightening speed because it absolutely doesn't matter. If a Napoleon could become a First Consul at the age of 27, I don't see why a 30-year-old man here can't be a general or a lieutenant general—that's ridiculous! We lead a revolutionary war! It is absolutely correct when they call Tito a marshal. A man who, with nothing, keeps an entire enemy war force constantly on the jump and continually recovers again, deserves the title of marshal more than anyone here deserves the title of Colonel General or field marshal who is not able to operate skillfully even with the best instrument that has ever existed. Such a man deserves this, and why shouldn't I treat good, brave officers in the same way here? We only have to give them the opportunity. [—] But looking at the big picture, we can't make any preparations from one day to the next that will be decisive in 5 days, or in 10 or 14 days. If it goes the normal military way, Jodl, absolutely nothing will happen. If it goes the normal way, only conferences will take place. I just spoke with a man who once again looked into the Apennine position. He says that it's a great fallacy if someone imagines that this is a position. This is no position at all![1273] [—] An expert who was down there—also an officer—says the same thing: this is no position at all; it's a big fallacy! [—] You know, in every position you have a display example that is presented. Now you wrote once yourself, Jodl, that a position is as strong as its weakest spot, because the enemy will discover its weakest spot and attack there, not at the strongest one.

JODL: See the Western Wall; see the Atlantic Wall!

THE FÜHRER: See the Atlantic Wall!! [—] Now the display examples are shown. They wanted to do it the same way with me. Had I had myself been in command at the Western Wall, I would have seen only the display examples: between Bingen and the Pfälzer Forest, the drilling area at Zweibrücken, Saarbrücken—a few spots. I didn't want that. I went everywhere—the entire wall, up and down—and looked at the weak spots. Then this fellow[1274] came and said, "There are only 5 emplacements per kilometer here because it's not an attack area anyway." [—] I asked, "How can it not be an attack area?" [—] He said, "Tank-proof!" [—] But tank-proof is absolutely out of the question." [—] So if I hadn't pushed back there, there would have been nothing in those spots. But then it was put in! Something must happen here, too. I can't leave it to the army group, who can't do it at all. They have other things on their minds and can't do anything. So if we leave it to the army group the same thing will happen as what we experienced in the East. I should have taken Kitzinger then—he offered himself. He would do that. He had the people and would round them all up.[1275] But then the Army was indignant at such an idea. That wouldn't work—it could only be done by the army group; the army groups should rule in their rear territory. This is what we were told, with the result that nothing—absolutely nothing—happened. Not a single spade thrust. And the positions that supposedly existed between Melitopol' and Zaporozh'e were faked.[1276] I was simply lied to—nothing had ever been there. In the fall of 1941 a few minor efforts were made there. That was all. It was a pure swindle, and it would be the same here. I've seen on a large scale what happens in reality. The people have had lots of time to develop the Black Forest at least. They know themselves—I don't need to repeat this—what is in the Black Forest: nothing. Absolutely nothing! [—] So we really will have to set up a small staff here, and we need to get Jacob and the OT here. Jacob and Dorsch[1277] together must put in a staff which will be in charge of making the developments, without regard for anything else. If we can't make the extension solid here, it will be at most a very short delaying line. A proper defense can only be established where we have either the Western Wall or at least ground conditions to permit this—and that would be the Vosges [Mountains]. There we can organize resistance.

JODL: But it hasn't been reconnoitered yet. That must be done first.

THE FÜHRER: It must be done immediately, and as far out as possible, so that we have the option of going back to a main line—and especially so that we can blow up the streets. Here in this country we can do something, of course. There must not be a single bridge that isn't prepared for demolition—not one bridge! It doesn't matter if the enemy blows it up or we do.

JODL: Quite a few are already destroyed here.

THE FÜHRER: Many have been destroyed already, but also the last that remain! The tracks must be destroyed. Those are all general orders; it must all be prepared. Of course, it can't be done by a central staff; the local authorities should destroy all the track in such a situation. Everything must be prepared so that we can destroy at least the most critical sections of each track. We won't be able to destroy all the lines. That will be a problem because we need, for example, to provide rail cutters. Here's a question. Some time ago I ordered rail cutters to be made for usual railway tracks and also for steel posts. These were rejected—some agency has forbidden further construction! We ask ourselves how an idiot like that could dare to do such a thing? I give Speer the order to build these things, and a different department comes along and just says, "Not for steel tracks!"[1278] [—] That means I can't demolish anything in the West because almost all the tracks are steel. But that's no problem. We can give the order right now to carry it out. [—] But in the basic combat instructions,[1279] the first part has to be agreed to absolutely, and we have to make it clear to him. That it must be held at any cost! If he loses this he can't operate. That's the decisive factor—we must take away from him every thought of being able to operate. The forces are ridiculous for that, of course.

JODL: He doesn't mean that. He's absolutely determined to hold it.

THE FÜHRER: Maybe tomorrow we can already—think about it!—put together a staff of some equally intelligent and inventive heads. Because if we really want to transport this back, it's not so much systematic work— nothing happens systematically, because the enemy is able to destroy everything systematically—but it must be intelligent work. If we don't do it intelligently, the whole thing will be lost. Then we can't do anything about it. Then, as mentioned before, the second point: I have to push the Luftwaffe so that these 12 or 15 groups will be finished, which initially, I would like to say, must be led in an informal and flexible manner. We can't make a long-term plan because it might have to be thrown out in the next few days. All we need is for a revolt to break out in Hungary or something like that. So what we need to secure we must secure now! So I would think about what we can still pump into Hungary.

JODL: Replacement formations, except for those two brigades.

THE FÜHRER: Yes, put them in there, so that at least something is in the country.

FEGELEIN: There are still two cavalry divisions in there, and they're also getting stronger.[1280]

THE FÜHRER: What do they look like? What do they consist of?

FEGELEIN: They have three regiments.

THE FÜHRER: And the people?

FEGELEIN: Ethnic Germans [Volksdeutschen] and Reich Germans [Reichsdeutschen].

THE FÜHRER: There are Reich Germans?

FEGELEIN: Yes, Sir. One division has about 60% Reich Germans right now. The other division, the volunteers, also has 30% Reich Germans—all the commanders and so on. But there are three strong cavalry regiments, one artillery regiment with three detachments (two heavy and one light), one engineer battalion with two companies, one intelligence detachment with one radio company, one reconnaissance detachment with a Volkswagen reconnaissance detachment.

THE FÜHRER: They are already mostly mobile?!

FEGELEIN: Yes, Sir, with three squadrons. [—] Then they also have one assault gun detachment.

JODL: Readiness for action?

FEGELEIN: Two were made out of the one—that's why it will take until October 1 for them to be ready. But if we have a revolt within the country they can be used right away. The one has to pull up the other one, though, or it won't work.

THE FÜHRER: And to what extent are they still mobile at this time? Can we at least everywhere—

FEGELEIN: It always works in Hungary because they can make themselves mobile in the customary manner.

THE FÜHRER: I really wanted to go over here to the West, but I can't do it now, as much as I would like to. For at least the next eight days, I won't be able to fly because of my ears.[1281] It is also questionable for the second one, but when one is completely better, then I don't care anymore—then I would risk it. But if I get into an airplane now with the roaring and all those changes in pressure, it could be catastrophic. And what would happen if I suddenly got a middle-ear infection? I would have to be treated. The risk of an infection is there as long as the wound is open. It didn't go off without affecting my head, either.

FEGELEIN: Everybody suffered from a light concussion.

THE FÜHRER: Of course, I can stand and I can also talk for a certain length of time, but then I have to sit down suddenly. Today I wouldn't dare speak to 10,000 people. A speech like the one I held at the Obersalzberg recently[1282] I wouldn't dare to hold today, because I might suddenly get a dizzy spell and collapse. A moment like that can even occur while walking, and I have to pull myself together in order not to make a false step. But, of course, if all else fails, I'll do anything; then I don't care at all. Then I'll go in a single-engine aircraft and be the target shooter up front, so I get there quickly. I don't care at all. Of course, it would be better if I were well again. [—] Only we have to lead very flexibly within the next few days. So I consider it necessary that the Reich Foreign Minister comes over here more frequently, since you[1283] don't go to the Reich Foreign Minister. I really would like to talk through everything with him myself, but it's too long for me, and I can only tell him what you would tell him anyway. You are also exhausted, no doubt, but I get so many matters all the time that deal with other things, including absolutely critical ones. Normally I would have stayed in bed for 10 or 14 days, but altogether I have worked at least 8 hours every day, not counting reading the dispatches. Eight hours went by anyway, reading memoranda and other things. So in my current state of health I do about the same amount of work as our gentlemen in their stressful offices in Paris, etc. But if it is not necessary I don't want to push it and possibly cause a collapse; that's not necessary. [—] Otherwise, the amazing thing is that this blow seems to have caused my nerve problem to almost disappear. I still have some shaking in my left leg, if the meeting takes too long, but this leg used to shake in bed. It has suddenly disappeared almost entirely because of the blow, though I don't want to say that this is the best cure.[1284]

End: 12:58 a.m.

* * * * *

August 31-September 1, 1944

On August 6 the Red Army forced its way to the Vistula River at Sandomierz. In the meantime, however, the Russians have also reached the river further downstream and have established two more bridgeheads on the western shore. Between the Vistula and the Narev Rivers, they pushed the Second Army back over the Narev during the second half of August. Near Tukkum, to the north, between August 16 and 20, the Third Panzer Army succeeded in re-establishing contact with Army Group North, which had lost Dorpat [Tartu] in the meantime, but which had prevented an enemy breakthrough here as well as north of the Dvina River.

While the northern edge of the Carpathians—after the loss of the Galician oilfields on August 8—could be held, the Russians, after destroying the German-Romanian front in a three-day fight, broke across the Dnestr River and pushed through on both sides of the Pruth River in Romania on August 22. The Antonescu regime collapsed the following day; the German units that couldn't fight their way over the Carpathian Mountains were captured by the advancing Russian forces. On August 31 the Red Army enters Bucharest; only in the oilfields of Ploesti does fighting continue.

In the West, the Americans advanced south to the Loire River after breaking out of their beachhead, then, to the west, attacked the rear of the

German Army that was facing the English. West of Falaise-Argentan the
Seventh Army and the Fifth Panzer Army (Panzer Group Eberbach) were
practically encircled and for the most part destroyed in early to mid-August. Without further serious resistance, the Allies approached the middle
of the Loire and the Seine, established the Orléans-Chartres line on August 16, and entered Paris on August 25. On August 29, the Marne River
was crossed and Châlons and Reims were taken. On August 31, Verdun on
the Meuse River had already been cleared of German troops; on this day,
Amiens is reached, in the direction of Belgium, and the Somme is crossed.
In the meantime, on the Riviera, the American Seventh Army landed between Toulon and Fréjus on August 15, encircled Toulon on the 20th and
Marseille on the 22nd (both harbors fell on August 28), conquered the Du-
rance region, and is now advancing northward along the Rhône valley. The
Americans are currently busy breaking through a weak German barrier at
Valence.

In Italy, the German armies have drawn back to the Green Position
[—] in the Apennines during the last two months. The last withdrawals
from the area north of the Arno River are now taking place. The previous
night on the Adriatic, however, the Allies threw the eastern wing of the
Tenth Army back over the Foglio—which was already part of the Green
Position—toward Rimini.
(*Maps 5, 1, and 12*)

* * * * *

MEETING OF THE FÜHRER WITH
LIEUTENANT GENERAL WESTPHAL[1285] AND LIEUTENANT GENERAL
KREBS,[1286] AUGUST 31, 1944, AT THE WOLFSSCHANZE[1287]

Also present: Field Marshal Keitel

Beginning: 3:35 p.m.

THE FÜHRER: You know that Field Marshal Kluge has committed suicide.[1288] There are very strong suspicions that if he hadn't committed suicide, he would have been arrested immediately anyway. Yesterday the trial at
the People's Law Court was interrupted.[1289] Unfamiliar with this (procedure, the chairman) turned to Field Marshal (Kluge) [—] (It is to be assumed that the thing failed due to an enemy fighter-bomber) attack. He sent
away his General Staff officer. The action didn't succeed then, though. British-American patrols advanced forward, but apparently no connection could
be established. He also sent his son into the pocket. The British have re-

ported that they are in contact with a German general, and the officer, who was probably the contact, has been arrested.[1290] It is claimed that he was exchanged out of British captivity because of malingering. But he was arrested for other reasons. That was the man who was supposed to mediate in this thing, who was, in those people's opinion, supposed to bring about a change of fate. The idea was that we would surrender to the British and then join together with them against Russia—a totally idiotic concept. Especially with the criminal abandonment of German territory in the East! They thought we would have to (abandon) up to the Vistula [River] anyway, maybe up to the Oder ... up to the Elbe [—] August 15 was the worst day of my life. Thanks to a coincidence, this plan wasn't fulfilled. All the army group's measures can only be explained under those circumstances; otherwise, they would be absolutely inexplicable. The staff of the Seventh Army—I must also tell you—is not in good shape.[1291] It would be good if you, General Krebs, could take all the men you think are worth your trust, and give the orders necessary to clean up this staff entirely. Unfortunately, Field Marshal Rommel[1292] is a very great and enthusiastic leader in successful times, but he is an absolute pessimist when the slightest difficulties arise. Before, I faced the difficult question of whether I should send Kesselring's staff there or if I should hand the task over to Rommel.[1293] Before, I always blamed (Kesselring) for (seeing things) too optimistically [—] North Africa totally lost his nerves, so that after the abandonment of El Alamein he got worked up about an idea that couldn't be accomplished. He had to stay out front—that was the only possibility to save everything.[1294] Because the enemy's superiority wasn't balanced out when he went into the wide-open area—it made it even more effective. At this narrow spot, 60 km wide, an attack could possibly be withstood. Once pushed out of there, and without the coverage of Schott on the left side,[1295] then, based on desert warfare experience, there was the possibility of constant overtaking, and then he wasn't able to maneuver, but the enemy could maneuver. When I was informed about the decision that night—unfortunately I learned about it only the next morning—I ordered right away that it shouldn't happen. As a result of the unfortunate tangle of circumstances, the matter remained here and was handed over to me too late, and my order to cancel (the thing) immediately[1296] [—] he did the worst that could be done in such a case for a soldier: He looked for non-military solutions.[1297] In Italy back then, he also predicted that the collapse would come very soon. It hasn't happened yet. In fact, it was totally disproved by those events, and I have been justified in my decision to keep Field Marshal Kesselring there. I see in him an unbelievable political idealist, but also a military optimist, and I think that one can't lead militarily at all without optimism. I consider Rommel in certain circumstances to be an extraordinary bold and also clever leader. But I don't consider him tenacious, and that that is also the opinion of all the others.

KEITEL: Yes, that has become more and more obvious.

THE FÜHRER: As long as things (go) well, (he) is shouting for joy. When the first [—] imagined the further development at all. I said right away: It's not yet time for a political decision. I think I have proven enough in my life that I am able to gain political successes. I don't have to explain to anybody that I wouldn't let an opportunity like this pass by. But it is, of course, childish and naive to hope for a convenient political moment to do anything during this time of heavy military defeat. Such moments can arise if we have successes. I have proven that I (have done) everything possible to deal with the British. In 1940, after the French campaign, I offered my hand to the British and renounced (everything). I didn't want anything from them. On September 1, 1939, (I) made a suggestion to the British—rather, I repeated a suggestion, which had been transmitted by Ribbentrop already in (1936)—the offer of (a) union, whereby Germany would (guarantee the British) Empire[1298] [—] recommended. Churchill, in particular, and that entire circle of hatred around Vansittart,[1299] opposed all those suggestions; they wanted the war and can't go back now. They are staggering toward their ruin. But there will come moments in which the tension between the Allies will become so great that the break will happen then nevertheless. Coalitions in world history have always been ruined at some point. We must only wait for the moment, no matter how hard it is. It is my duty, especially since 1941, (not to) lose my nerve under any circumstances, but if there is a (collapse) somewhere, to (find) a way out and a means to repair the mess somehow. I could (well say): you can't imagine a bigger crisis than the one we have experienced already in the East this (year). When Field Marshal Model came, Army Group Center was in fact only a hole.[1300] There was more hole than front, and then finally there was more front than hole [—] has, to say that those divisions were completely immobile, that they didn't have any German materiel, that they were equipped with God knows what kind of guns, that we sent all the prepared divisions into the East, that there were only training divisions in the West, that we had the panzer divisions in the West only to fill them up, and once they were ready we sent them to the East.[1301] If I had had the (9th) and 10th SS Panzer Divisions in the West, the (thing) probably would not have happened at all. But this wasn't done, due to a—I must say—(criminal) urge[1302] to (cause) an overthrow here. The people imagined they could go either with the British against the Russians or—in the second, (Schulenburg,) direction[1303]—with the Russians against the British or—in the third and stupidest direction—to play one off against the other. Pretty naïve![1304] (The judgment) of all the people who have (seen) the guilty in court now goes as far as a shocking [—] continue the fight, until the opportunity for a reasonable peace arises—one that is acceptable to Germany and that can secure the life of later generations. Then I will do it. Because everyone can imagine that this war is not comfortable for me. I've been cut off from the outside world for five years now; I haven't visited a theater, listened to a concert, (seen) a film.[1305] I live only for the single task of (leading) this battle, because I know that if there is no strong will (behind) it, the war can't be won. I reproach the General Staff, because instead of always exuding (this) iron will, it weakened front officers who (came here), or spread (pessimism) from the General Staff to the rest of the forces, when (General Staff) officers came to the front. It is tragic when the young officers, who face sentencing now, declare in front of the court: [—] department of the General Staff, in which the chief was absolutely fine, namely with Gercke,[1306] where not a single man has been found so far who is involved in this thing,[1307] while in the other departments, the quartermaster general, the organization departments, foreign armies, etc., the leaders supported this base action. What happened here was directed against me. If it had been successful, it would have (been) a catastrophe for Germany. The fact that it didn't succeed gives us the possibility to finally get rid of this abscess (inside) our organization. We can't foresee, though, how badly it may have damaged our foreign policy—with (the Romanians), the Bulgarians, the Turks, the Finns, the other neutrals, and so on. How it has hurt the German people—(now), of course, the speech restrictions have been loosened, and things have come to light that are hair-raising. Until now the German people were silent, but now everyone is speaking out. [—] have experienced. The fact that we've had to experience terrible things here with Army Group Center, which are just now slowly becoming clear[1308] —the disgrace that German officers can be found, who deliver speeches over there, and that German officers and generals capitulate—all that can't be compared with what happened in the West. That's the most outrageous of all.[1309] I believe that you, Westphal, are joining a (staff that) is basically sound. First of all, Field Marshal Rundstedt (is) absolutely clean and a man of integrity. (Further), Blumentritt[1310] is very sound and personally (decent; I) just think he lacks a bit of experience to command (such a staff) and that he was heavily affected by this whole (thing). But absolutely (nothing) has been submitted against him. KEITEL: The only one in this staff was the quarter(master, who) had been sent there a few weeks before, Colonel Finckh.[1311] He was one of (Wagner's[1312]) men [—]

THE FÜHRER: [—] thought very highly of. I promoted him twice my-self, gave him the highest awards, gave him a great gift to help him get settled, and gave him a large bonus in addition to his salary as field mar-shal.[1313] So for me, this is the most bitter and disappointing thing of all. The way he came here, it (might) have been tragic. Maybe he slipped into it by accident—I don't know—and maybe (then he) couldn't (see) any way out anymore. He saw a number of (officers) being arrested, and he feared their statements. His nephew is blamed the most, who stated this in front of the court,[1314] and, as a result, President Freisler[1315] —which was correct—interrupted the trial immediately to (get proof) of this and to hear the field marshal. But he (was no) longer alive. Freisler also said, of course: there is a limit; all (trust) in the German Armed Forces com-mand will collapse. [—] It is like a Western. When you look at the people—Stieff[1316] and all those people—the level is really shocking. I got rid of a man like Colonel General Höppner[1317] back then not only because he disobeyed a command but (because) he was really a small character. Kluge himself[1318] (was also) convinced that he had to go. Now I've been (justi-fied). The trial showed everyone (in the courtroom) how little they were. The observers said, "How could those (people ever) become officers at all?!" Yes, how could they? I had to take what was available, and I've tried to make the most of it. [—] (The staff) that you, Krebs, are taking over, is no doubt (messed up)—we have to be clear about that. I can only (tell) you: take care that you (clean up) this lot as fast as (possible), that you ... Field Marshal Model the [—] We will fight—if necessary even at the Rhine. That doesn't matter at all. We'll keep fighting this battle at all costs, until, like Frederick the Great said, one of our damned enemies gets tired of fighting, and until we (get) a peace that will secure life for the German nation for the next 50 or (100 years) and that (doesn't) damage our honor a second time the way it (happened) in 1918. Because this time we would not (be silent) anymore. (Back then) we were silent about it.[1319] (Destiny) could have gone in a different direction. If my life had ended, personally, for me—(I can say)—it would only have been a relief from worries, sleepless (nights and a) serious nervous disease. It's only (a fraction) of a second, then you are freed from all of this (and have) everlasting peace and quiet. But I nevertheless thank providence that I (survived), because I believe [—] I don't want to spread it any further. I don't want to disgrace the German Armed Forces by talking about this thing any longer. If it became public knowledge that Field Marshal Kluge wanted to lead the entire Western army to capitulation and go over to the enemy himself, it might not lead to a collapse of (morale) in the German nation, but at least to (contempt) for the Army.

That's why I want to (be silent) about it (now). We have informed only the generals that he has committed suicide.[1320] He did commit suicide. The (things that) were said before were wrong. That was ... It was said that he had already earlier ... and had suffered from a stroke. In (reality), he was waiting for the British patrol, which ... They missed each other. He lost his ... in the fighter-bomber attack. Now he was (in the area), couldn't get any further, and (drove back) again. [—]

* * * * *

MIDDAY SITUATION CONFERENCE, SEPTEMBER 1, 1944, AT THE WOLFSSCHANZE[1321]

Present:

The Führer	*Vice Admiral Voss*
Field Marshal Keitel	*Gruppenführer Fegelein*
Grand Admiral Dönitz	*Envoy v. Sonnleithner*
Colonel General Guderian	*Major General Thomale*
Colonel General Jodl	*Rear Admiral Wagner*
General Buhle	*Lieutenant Colonel Waizenegger*
General Warlimont	*Lieutenant Commander Hansen-Nootbaar*
Lieutenant General Burgdorf	*Major John v. Freyend*
Lieutenant General Kreipe	*Major Büchs*
Lieutenant General Wenck	*Major v. Freytag-Loringhoven*
Lieutenant General Westphal	*Hauptsturmführer Günsche*

Beginning: ...

The East

GUDERIAN: From Army Group "South Ukraine"[1322] it is reported, my Führer, that the enemy has entered Bucharest, taken Ploesti, and is pushing into the mountains here. Also from Group Winkler[1323]—the units have already come around and put pressure from there on the retreat roads. Some Group Mieth is in this area south of Bacau. According to Russian radio, General Mieth was unfortunately killed.[1324]

THE FÜHRER: Oh!

GUDERIAN: Not confirmed yet, but reported by the (Russians).

THE FÜHRER: Such an officer here [—]

GUDERIAN: Here a Romanian defense front has been (established near) Brasov.[1325] Russian (attacks) have been stopped here; the (counterattack) has thrown some of his forces back in here ... Further attacks are (planned. A defensive block) has been established with flak [antiaircraft units]. Came ... to an unfortunate ..., where an entire ... ; according to the report by ... published by the Army ... the Army ... immediately in contact ... has developed.

THE FÜHRER: That's what I said yesterday: interference can also have terrible effects on the other side.

GUDERIAN: But the people really don't have anything else. The enemy is everywhere here. Of course, it's hard to decide what's important. In any case, we have to check immediately to see if the flak reserves are too (large). [—] (On) the rest of the mountain fronts there were no particular actions. (Also) nothing in the area around the Hungarian border. So far the formations are going as planned.

THE FÜHRER: The cavalry school is still in German territory?

GUDERIAN: Yes, the cavalry school is still ... according to a report, which I couldn't (confirm), though.

THE FÜHRER: When the Communists move in here[1326] ... —believe me— not the ... Regent Council comes from ... have reports that they ... among each other. Now ...

GUDERIAN: ... over the Danube. That was ... on the Carpathian front ... the enemy preparations to attack the Hungarian Army and also toward the Dukla Pass. [—] The disarmament in Slovakia has progressed without any major interruptions.[1327] The right of the two divisions has voluntarily handed over its guns. Some of the troops from the left division went into the villages and woods and obviously want to remain there. But the mission is in progress there, too. The first units of the 357th [Infantry Division] have arrived. Furthermore, the army group has stopped portions of the 359th [Infantry Division], which hadn't moved (toward) ... But I will work on Harpe[1328] to make sure that this thing continues, because otherwise (we) won't finish with the relief of the panzer forces in time. They have to get out there for refitting.

THE FÜHRER: If the 357th (accomplishes) this mission, we'll have to see if we can't ... a few ... at the passes, so that we ...

(GUDERIAN: The) ... stands here. It will ... ready in ... The refitting should take place ... (at the) Neuhammer (troop training ground). (I have arranged for it to be done here ...) September—complete with full ... division in this area ... of the 101st Jäger Division, which ...

THE FÜHRER: Where is the 75th [Infantry Division] now?

GUDERIAN: The relief will start today.

THE FÜHRER: We'll have to see if we need them to extend this mission.

GUDERIAN: In my opinion, they must be used in any case to lengthen the right wing and reinforce (it), no matter how [—]

THE FÜHRER: In any case, to make sure that nothing happens to us there, so that (we) are not cut off at the end, and we can take it back at the right moment.

GUDERIAN: In my opinion, this action can be a pure holding attack; however, it could get out of control, of course, due to (the) unreliability of the Hungarian troops. The same with this one here. (Preparation) for an attack is also in progress here. The attack will be very soon. (It can't) take much longer. The artillery battle has (already begun) ... the attack is still making good (progress).

(THE FÜHRER: Have they) brought in ammunition?

(GUDERIAN: Whatever we) had in the way of ammunition, ..., partly with the army group ... taken into the area of Warsaw.

THE FÜHRER: They should not pick them up backwards.

GUDERIAN: No, there are special officers of mine on their way to stop that nonsense. The ammunition reserves of all the army groups and armies everywhere are being checked. I had the armies instructed once again by General Berlin.[1329] He has the order to call on the artillery commanders every day to check what they've done and where their ammunition is, and to see if the ordered artillery combat assignments were started and completed on time.

THE FÜHRER: It really is better if we drive back an attack using artillery, rather than being forced back and leaving the ammunition to the enemy.

GUDERIAN: We can see how that works at the bridgehead ...That is a ... thing. With the strong ... The mission will be continued. ... are (available). ... (advances) by the enemy. Yesterday ... be fought. The ... attack is ... on both sides ... the army group counts on this, ..., so that the enemy apparently ... moves over there now. Here is mostly just infantry. Smaller advances. The rest of the troops are destroyed, the entire bridgehead totally cleared. Here everything is gone. [—] That was near the Ski-Jäger-Division,[1330] where this strong artillery attack took place during the night. So that worked very (well) then.

THE FÜHRER: And do we know anything yet about what they will do next?

GUDERIAN: Not the new plans, my Führer. They wanted to finish this mission first, and possibly get a bit farther here, then a new plan will be developed based on their strength and the enemy situation. They are considering advancing here in the direction of Sandomierz or on the other wing.[1331] [—] Here there is mostly infantry; here tanks are everywhere. From here ... has ... taken away tanks. So under certain circumstances it could be (the best) solution if they would not ... this thing first ... bridgehead up there in Pulavy ... concentrated ammunition. ... at the Vistula front ...

(THE FÜHRER): ... lined up. There are ...

(GUDERIAN): ... the Vistula. ... at Corps Detachment E a ... hold against it right away. [—] There's nothing in the bridgehead yet. It's still quiet there. Then here there were attacks against the SS "T," [*Totenkopf* SS Panzer Division] [1332] at the intersection between the SS "T" and the *Viking*. So far nothing in particular. [—] In Warsaw progress has been made. [1333]

WENCK: That's the old map—and here's the new one.

GUDERIAN: The comparison of both battle territories shows that quite good progress was made.

THE FÜHRER: This here is the most important.

GUDERIAN: The bank is in our hands now.

WENCK: Probably this part, too.

FEGELEIN: That's the central part of Warsaw, (according) to the aerial view. (*Presentation.*)

WENCK: That was the ghetto.

(THE FÜHRER: That has) been eliminated now?

(FEGELEIN): ... as such already everything [1334] ...

(GUDERIAN: I had an) officer there; he came back yesterday (and reported a) high level of absenteeism among the officers and (sergeants).

(FEGELEIN: Especially) the non-commissioned officer problem is very (urgent. We still have) men but no commanders—very few non-commissioned officers, in particular. The relation of troop absence to non-commissioned officers is about 2 to 1. So we urgently need sergeants.

GUDERIAN: The house-to-house combat costs us a lot of sergeants. If the officers and sergeants don't lead out, the men don't follow.

FEGELEIN: A change will come when *Viking* really [—]

GUDERIAN: My Führer, I had already suggested putting the *Viking* in down here.

FEGELEIN: The blocking lines are blocked off toward the south—Makotow—they won't come through anymore—with an air force unit or anything else.

THE FÜHRER: We get the impression that (nothing is leaking) through into the city from outside.

(... ?): ... they take after the round ...

(... ?): ... the current picture. That will be ... to totally eliminate ...

(GUDERIAN): Last night they (tried to establish contact). But they (failed).

FEGELEIN: We're having difficulties taking all the housing blocks down, my Führer.

GUDERIAN: It costs us a lot of ammunition.

FEGELEIN: There's hardly anything left standing there.

THE FÜHRER: Here, where things are really burned out, we should really use the Luftwaffe—they can drop mines and destroy the whole thing then.

MILITARY CONFERENCES 1942-1945

FEGELEIN: For the ghetto, my Führer, it took us half a year in those days, I think.[1335]

THE FÜHRER: Look at the towns in our country here, where mines are dropped. When the houses are burned out they aren't strong anymore. They're only walls standing there, which can be taken down immediately by the mines. How many mines do we have? 8 or 10 thousand?

(KREIPE): I don't know the exact number in stock. ... probably.

(GUDERIAN: He also made) small advances here. ... with the 3rd Cavalry Brigade, which ... has. ... penetration, which is blocked off ... up to Courland ... conveyances, so that with ... count on, with renewed ...

THE FÜHRER: What about the Hungarian cavalry division here?

GUDERIAN: We wanted to pull out a division that had proven itself up here in the area of the Fourth Army—the 542nd [Infantry Division]— and relieve it with a new formation that's arriving now, and then relieve the *Viking* and the Hungarian cavalry division with the reliable 542nd. Both will work. The cavalry division has only a relatively small sector there. We will manage both of them. In this way, we can bring a battle-experienced young division in here. The *Viking* will get a quick refitting behind the front in the territory south of Warsaw, and can then relieve the Hungarians, so the Hungarian cavalry division will be free. The transportation of both the reserve divisions and reserve corps is in process. The Hungarians have no particular value to us anymore. [—] (Then), up here, there were no unusual battle actions. (The enemy has) ... gotten closer again ... with some parts. It is ... successful. Here also a ... shortening of the front by ... Colonel General Reinhardt ... that the entire march ... and not toward the north, ... the opinion that he ... As consequence, the ... Army Group North with General Kleffel[1336] ... reported on it yesterday. [—] Here we succeeded in pulling out the majority of the 7th Panzer Division, which we'll initially have prepared as a reserve. Here in the panzer divisions of the XXXIX and XXXX [Panzer] Corps, some of the tanks have been taken back behind the front for repairs and renovations. Those divisions' fronts are quite extended, though, and therefore very weak from an infantry perspective. Artillery ammunition was all that could be put in up there. The artillery battle has been initiated as much as possible. [—] Here we have a considerable deployment in depth with Group Kleffel. Everything has been done—considering our circumstances at least, and the conditions in the East—that could be done, according to our best judgment, to prepare the defense for the upcoming attack.[1337]

THE FÜHRER: Guderian, we need (a success) here. It's very important today. That is (decisive).

(GUDERIAN): ... especially today, my Führer.

(THE FÜHRER: I don't) care at all. We have to (become active again), ...
that (we take hold of the law of action) again. And I still see the possibility
of success in it, that we (actually) ... take position.

(GUDERIAN): That's why (I've) initially forbidden that ... be used in an
attack against the Russian assembly area east of Stockmannshof. That would
be of no use.

THE FÜHRER: That would be of no use. We should let them get going
and see what happens there. If they suffocate and keep lying there themselves, then it's like this, according to Schörner's[1338] judgment: the infantry—the commander of the infantry regiment of the 20th Panzer Grenadier Division,[1339] who was just in there, also told me this yesterday—the
infantry is bad, so awful that the men somehow turn around, and if they
don't have tanks, they run away immediately. So that's bad. It may not be like
that in general, though. Of course, this is different. They also have motorized units.

GUDERIAN: They also have good ones.

THE FÜHRER: Those are the better units.

GUDERIAN: But up here, in Schörner's opinion ... was actually also ...
that the division ... will be squeezed in... first lets itself get picked off.

(THE FÜHRER): ... isn't enough either. These ... if we want to get rid of
them ... They must be well ... decisive, that we ... this thing ...

GUDERIAN: That's the precondition.

THE FÜHRER: Maybe we can make a surprise movement and get in the
rear of this whole thing,[1340] and obtain what's necessary for the panzer
divisions again: open territory, so they can be employed in their own element. If this were to turn out well it would provide relief there anyway. He
would be forced then to bring in units from up there. He doesn't have
anything else here.

GUDERIAN: We still have something: the 6th Panzer Division, which is
located behind the front of the Second Army.

THE FÜHRER: I would take this one here, too, if there's something here.

GUDERIAN: If that happens, and the thing remains (solid) down there, we
can also get the 6th up here.

THE FÜHRER: Then we can bring it up here as well.

(GUDERIAN): ... I would leave it.

(THE FÜHRER): ... of course, here a total ...

(GUDERIAN): ... had a defensive success, ... maybe even very ...

(THE FÜHRER): ... must ... the *Grossdeutschland* ...

GUDERIAN: The *Grossdeutschland*, at least. Possibly the 6th from below
up here.

THE FÜHRER: The 6th and maybe also the 5th Panzer Division, because
the 5th is still relatively good with regard to the number of tanks.

GUDERIAN: The 7th, too.

THE FÜHRER: And the 7th and the 14th.

GUDERIAN: The 14th must go in there.

THE FÜHRER: We must really break in here near Bauske with a great push into the depth, so we don't fight laboriously where he has built up his anti-tank weapons.

GUDERIAN: They tried right there, too, recently.

THE FÜHRER: Exactly. That's clear!

GUDERIAN: Especially here as well, at this always ... superiority no surprise.

(THE FÜHRER): One thing became clear. I ... this thing here is successful ...

(GUDERIAN): Immediately!

(THE FÜHRER): Immediately! Then it will stop anyway. ... He pulls out troops here ... make, then the ... would ... is done and we can smooth this out here if we don't do the second thrust here. But we won't attack again directly into here—that wouldn't make any sense if we can't lead it in such a way that we really overtake them the depths—we'll just cut him off. We can then retreat to the Sehne [River] and pull everything together for the final success. We must think about where the last attack will take place. We can't say that today.

GUDERIAN: First we must do the thing near Mitau [Elgava]. If that can be completed in a positive way, we'll also have the panzer forces free for operations. [—] Nothing unusual has happened here. Nothing up here, either.

THE FÜHRER: Here we have the possibility of three strikes, which, if successful, could possibly take away 50 or 60 enemy divisions.

GUDERIAN: It may also be that the situation ... takes away something for ...

(THE FÜHRER): Absolutely (right)!

(GUDERIAN: I consider that to be) correct.

(THE FÜHRER): ... on the one side so ... can't take any further steps. ... free from us, with which we ... Then I would also suggest that we not go down there right away, but that we get rid of the thing east of the Vistula.

GUDERIAN: Yes, Sir.

THE FÜHRER: The big penetration—we'll gather together what can be gathered together to eliminate it, and only when this is done will we really have free units to go down there.

GUDERIAN: Temporarily, still!

THE FÜHRER: In my opinion, we can continue to operate in the South later. We can still operate there in November. Further up it stops anyway.

GUDERIAN: At Dorpat [Tartu] we succeeded in pushing the enemy back ... to the river. Another push is planned to reclaim Dorpat [Tartu] itself. The preparation ... the Sturmbannführer again ... tanks—they are not ... enemy weaknesses ... They want Dorpat [Tartu] ... goes, push into here, ... we want those tanks...

(THE FÜHRER): ... you one thing, though: before a ... that we were faced with the question: ...

GUDERIAN: Yes, Sir.

THE FÜHRER: It really is like that: Here, if we [—]

GUDERIAN: If this were successful here, no matter how it ends, my Führer, if we get Dorpat [Tartu] or not—when we get to the river, the tanks should come out. That way we will have the next panzer reserves here, whether we put them here or there—better in this area—so we can also send them, if necessary, to this front in combination with the 14th [Infantry Division].

WENCK: The plan was to break through here in combination with Lauchert[1341] and the newly arriving division, and to come out here with the 61st [Infantry Division] and maybe the 14th.

GUDERIAN: That was the big plan.

THE FÜHRER: Again, that's such a minor (action, with which we) ... accomplish this thing here ...

(GUDERIAN): ... finish this thing quickly. ... right away here. ...

THE FÜHRER: We might (possibly) be able to do it like that ... that we ... here at all ... we are in the back. That's how (we) achieved (our) big successes (earlier). Then we shifted the focus onto smaller operations, due to a lack of forces, but also due to a lack of imagination and self-confidence—and a lack of knowledge about the use of tank weapons, which we just rammed straight into the largest antitank and artillery fronts.

GUDERIAN: And fragmented at that.

THE FÜHRER: To let them drive in there!

GUDERIAN: The worst mistake is the fragmentation.

THE FÜHRER: While we always have to hit the soft spots. Because the tank isn't there to attack when the other one has the bull by the horns, but to attack the weak places. That has arisen entirely from tactical considerations, I would say.[1342] (*Presentation of the Armed Forces report.*)

Situation in the air

(BÜCHS): ... supported yesterday at the ... The enemy has here in ... from Italy. He is before ... group of about 80 four-engine and 100 single- and twin-engine fighters. Attacked individual targets probably in the area north of Bucharest. Since the flights out didn't take place until late afternoon, it must be assumed that the units stopped off here, took off again, and didn't fly back to Italy until afternoon.

KREIPE: Some of them.

BÜCHS: Ten dive-bombers were used in surveillance of our ship movements on the Danube, and three of them led an attack against a Romanian ship near Calafat. The ship was left heavily damaged and listing. Our units are not through the Iron Gate yet; according to this morning's report, they were with the ... of the Iron Gate.[1343]

(KREIPE): ... our reports.

(BÜCHS): ... on the airfield were ... including 64 aircraft altogether ...

(THE FÜHRER: That's only) possible if they were building up during peacetime.

(BÜCHS): ... is so. In two places ... in the Romanian area ... here at this end to ...

THE FÜHRER: But it's quite certain that it's a peacetime buildup. Even if we invade in two places, that doesn't matter. Either we can use the fields or not. If they're too small, why don't we move further back right away? That doesn't make any sense!

KREIPE: They were all aircraft with short range. Then they couldn't be deployed anymore at all.

THE FÜHRER: If there are so many, they can't start from two places. Are they ready for action now, those 64?

KREIPE: No!

BÜCHS: Fifteen aircraft were used in Slovakia ... airfields.

(THE FÜHRER): I have seen pictures—just ...the 87th Squadron—likely ... fantastically. ...

(KREIPE): ... have a couple of weeks ago ... is, gave during an attack ... airfield in Germany ... only came out afterward that ... kept in fragmentation boxes ... The fighter-bombers have ... led deep attacks without a break and have taken on every single fragmentation box.

THE FÜHRER: Do you have anti-aircraft guns on this air field?

BÜCHS: Yes, Sir. Light anti-aircraft guns. There were 70 planes, of which about 30 continuously carried out deep attacks against the anti-aircraft positions. The others singled out individual boxes to shoot up.

THE FÜHRER: How many anti-aircraft guns were there, anyway?

BÜCHS: I can't tell.

THE FÜHRER: Probably three 2-cm.

BÜCHS: The Slovakian fighter squadron at Pressburg [Bratislava] hasn't been seen anymore. Altogether about 20 aircraft have flown from the Slovaks to the Russians ... are probably on the ... and the army group ... only limited use ... bad, so that only ... sorties are flown ... only with the army ... and due to the bad (weather conditions) ... greatly hindered.

Situation at sea

VOSS: The Lake Peipus fleet was further damaged by repeated air attacks. 10 boats and 2 Navy artillery lighters are still ready for action.[1344] [—] In the Gulf of Finland and in Narva Bay there was lively clearance activity by the enemy.

THE FÜHRER: What does the enemy have now on Lake Peipus?

VOSS: He has some gunboats and faster vessels—smaller vessels.

DÖNITZ: But actually, my Führer, they have been fairly heavily damaged by air strikes.

THE FÜHRER: I ask because it has never been possible to destroy (even a single enemy thing) with the Luftwaffe at Lake Ladoga],[1345] and he can ...

(VOSS: The transport traffic) to Army Group North went ahead as planned. ... fire damage, had to (be towed) in.

(DÖNITZ): ... reported belatedly that the ... was destroyed. In the ... heavy damage, partly ... Navy arsenal, German ... almost 100 % out of commission.[1346]

VOSS: The enemy has also heavily mined southern Norway and the entrances to the Baltic. Yesterday 65 vessels and 12 aircraft were deployed for mine sweeping. 22 mines were cleared. [—] The traffic along the Norwegian coast in that area had to be temporarily blocked due to the intrusion of 150 enemy mine-laying aircraft. The rest of the Norwegian traffic continued as scheduled. The traffic in the north of Norway was also reopened. [—] Nothing in particular to report from the North Sea. [—] Our batteries near Cape Gris-Nez, the *Todt* and *Lindemann* batteries—a 38-cm and a 20-cm battery—fired on Dover. During the withdrawal of our minesweepers and patrol (boats) ... to Boulogne ... again there were lively ... and a battle with ... There was no significant damage.[1347] Dieppe and Fecamp were ... Le Havre have started.[1348] At ... with the battery ... battery has ... on the 30th and ... must ... and with the exception of ... is ... from the sea at 25 km (distance) ... last 19.47 gun[1349] is out of commission. I personally believe that he still has anti-aircraft guns for his defense, and that's why he still has some combat strength. But it seems to be ending.

DÖNITZ: There's nothing left there.

THE FÜHRER: He has defended like a hero.[1350]

DÖNITZ: Yes, it was worth it, my Führer. Because St. Malo hasn't been used yet.

VOSS: In Brest the destruction of the naval station has started, and will be carried out thoroughly. The Ile (Amorique) has been evacuated. There was a light Navy artillery detachment there. It will be added to the defense of St. Nazaire. Otherwise, no reports from this area.

(DÖNITZ): My Führer, may I (point out the following) again: The weak spot is still ... push into this area,[1351] especially ... weather conditions.

(THE FÜHRER): ... you ... not possible?

(DÖNITZ): ... not, my Führer. ... not.

(THE FÜHRER: Why) don't you (think) so?

(DÖNITZ): ... on-shore weather, mostly ... only very few days in the month. I don't think he will do it after September. He won't do it. Instead, he will try to get in here, and then in here, under cover of the prevailing west winds in the fall.

THE FÜHRER: When does that kind of weather start?

DÖNITZ: We should expect it within the next few days. From September 15 on for sure.

THE FÜHRER: So?

DÖNITZ: Well, my Führer, it's like this: we have tried by all possible means to steadily strengthen the implementation of those blockades with mine production. We will put about 2,500 mines and 700 underwater defensive weapons[1352] in here in September, so that the thing will be ... strongly ... But we are unable with the help of ... of the enemy, to prevent a clearing, ... delays, but no prevention ... necessary that we also ... in this ... 15,000 beach mines ... are ... laid out. We must ... here only in the summer ... we can't (work) here ... laid out along the coasts ... in September we ... 1,500 ground mines ... or to block special landing sites here. We have already started here. The red one is already a ground mine barrier. Into this area we will put three 12.7-cm batteries from the destroyers, which are delayed, and five 7.5-cm guns or batteries from Navy artillery lighters with trained submarine crews who are waiting for submarines that either aren't going to be ready or haven't gotten ready yet. In the end, my Führer, that is all the Navy can do—it's all they have available. Lastly, I'd like to report that as a preventive measure we can put 60 Biber ["Beavers"], 60 Molche ["Salamanders"] and 60 Marder ["Martens"]—those are midget craft[1353]—into this area in September.

THE FÜHRER: We'll get two 21-cm. We must now ... give it. There are two new 21-cm (guns) ... 30 cm. Perhaps they will be ...

(DÖNITZ): ... make—and actually ... so that our ... to risk things. ... to go into those areas ... he ... a huge ...

THE FÜHRER: Exactly! That is the most dangerous spot. Besides, if he settles in here, a counterattack will hardly be possible because it's cut off by that tributary. It's practically an island.[1354] If he settles in here, then he'll just sit here.

DÖNITZ: He blocks off Norway, has influence on Sweden, and blockades the entrances to the Baltic Sea.

THE FÜHRER: That's absolutely clear.

DÖNITZ: I'll try, my Führer, to pump everything I have in here.
THE FÜHRER: Yes!

The West

Well, Jodl, the attack by these two divisions here is ...
(JODL: It's) not quite clear if he ... at all ... At least the divisions are on (their way).
(THE FÜHRER): ... now then?
(JODL): ... Bar-le-Duc in the battle.
(THE FÜHRER): ... frontal combat. That is ... here?
(JODL): ... not over Amiens ... southern edge of Albert ... into the lead. Strong ... Commander-in-Chief West ordered. In particular, the right wing is behind the Somme [River]; the left wing apparently not yet. But the report on that hasn't arrived.
THE FÜHRER: Is that behind the Somme already?
JODL: The right wing is behind the Somme.
THE FÜHRER: We should make sure we can still move it.
JODL: He's trying that right now. He's approaching from above, and wanted to get parts of the 10th Panzer Division as well. He has even pulled out a battalion from a local division—the 712th [Security] Division—to bring in more forces there. So here there are currently attempts to clean this out. The right wing behind the Somme. More precise news hasn't yet been received from the left wing, but it is in retreat. ... south of the Somme: Laon. There is ... area of Vervins. With it the ... would be—up to Vervins. Then ... front, by the three American (divisions) ... in the direction of Charleville, ... the third over Bar-le-(Duc) ... divisions. ... by the 2nd Armored Division, ... these bridgeheads ... west of Pont-à-Mous(son) ... Western Wall, namely with ... Metz in the Western Wall in general, because the labor forces can't be led any further forward.
THE FÜHRER: And here?
JODL: Here in the Vosges—but everything else will be at the Western Wall, while only the two infantry divisions will be deployed in front.
THE FÜHRER: What is coming here then?
JODL: The one from Military District [*Wehrkreis*] V[1355] comes here. The Gau [local leader] is pushing the labor forces forward right now.
THE FÜHRER: So if we can't hold this here for quite some time, this[1356] won't come back. Now where are these forces here?
(JODL): ... reported in general; the ... Reserve Division is the last, ... and the middle marching group ... That is obviously the ... both divisions, which ... fight with terrorists ... the 338th broke through ... the Isère,

even if ... built up the anti-aircraft defense ... [—] is there. An orderly officer arrived there where the army group is. In this area, various security lines are being developed.

THE FÜHRER: If Blaskowitz[1357] can manage this, then I will solemnly apologize to him for everything.

JODL: Another corps has come here, the (Luck)[1358] Corps. It's very good.

THE FÜHRER: Probably the best chance is to build up a group in this area here.[1359]

KEITEL: If we can get it all together.

THE FÜHRER: As long as we bring together a group west of the Vosges, there's the possibility of an operational follow-up; if not now, then by ... not now; that ... forces, and the ... to defend the front ... it is very ... will be in the perpetual ... just have to ... ourselves from ... no winter war ... free it completely.

...

(JODL): ... we can only ... in the winter. Fog, night and snow are best.

THE FÜHRER: That's the best chance.

KEITEL: That's our best ally in the fight, without a doubt.

JODL: The first two trains of the one infantry division have arrived in Diedenhofen. So this division goes into the Diedenhofen—Metz position. The next division goes in toward the south, and behind the 36th [Infantry Division]—this infantry division must be used to lengthen this again right away and to build up as far out in front as possible.

THE FÜHRER: If the first forces here [—]

JODL: Here with the (panzer) divisions.

THE FÜHRER: ... forces in here ...at all, really ... massed troops, and these ... (most valuable) labor forces, ...which were in there...if there are 11,000 ... do? He would...leave... There ... would ... bring into the position. If we can't do anything else, we'll send them to the Western Wall.[1360] I have spoken with Guderian, and we'll now bring all 8.8-cm antitank guns into the West, because that is the best.[1361] But he is right: No matter how improvised it is, they have to come with crews—otherwise it would not make sense.

BUHLE: Organized detachments are being built up, which will be ready in the next few days.

GUDERIAN: My Führer, I prepared some fortification antitank detachments weeks ago.[1362] They must go there.

THE FÜHRER: First, all 8.8s; second, all Tiger IIs with the long (gun) ...; third, all tank destroyers. ...

(... ?) .... bring ... Metz, for example .... deployed .... 65 trains of gas ammunition ...

(... ?): ... now important.

(... ?): ... 175 German ... ready

(... ?): ... Metz, in a ...

(... ?): ... troop units ... I would like to advise against it.

THE FÜHRER: The infantry school[1363] will handle the antitank guns.

GUDERIAN: They don't take up much. There can't be more than about 12 guns—fortification antitank guns. We can handle that with no problem.

THE FÜHRER: It won't be enough.

THOMALE: My Führer, we still have the two antitank gun detachments, the 501st and 502nd.[1364] They have left already. Each can take 36. Then the 503rd and 504th, which will also be ready in two days. They will also get a 7.5-cm detachment. And the fourth will become an 8.8-cm detachment, so that we will have three 7.5-cm detachments and one 8.8-cm detachment. [—] [1365]

THE FÜHRER: Schroth! A fabulous man.[1366] In his case it is like this—I know him very well—he has a severe heart disease. It can change into periods of total lethargy. We once had to send him on leave for a long time because of that. I don't know if you remember.

KEITEL: Last year he was quite all right again. He was the first to report about those unpleasant appearances over there. He is terrific.

THE FÜHRER: An excellent man.

KEITEL: An absolutely steady character. He immediately took control.

JODL: The men that he has in reserve, he has ... pumped into the military districts [—]

JODL: The panzer brigade is also going down there. That is the first thing reported right now from the Replacement Army—the first that is there. Those are two police battalions. That is the ensign school with three battalions, one combat group: one battalion, two combat groups with two battalions altogether.

THE FÜHRER: We also have to give them antitank guns, of course. That's the one near Metz?

JODL: That's Metz. [—] There's Diedenhofen. Right now the 353rd [Infantry] Division is arriving there. Two trains are there. The others are following. Up there, two combat groups with two reinforced battalions are on their way. That one is in front. Furthermore, everything that the Military Districts XIII and V[1367] can get will go in here. [—]

(THE FÜHRER): ... We just have to make sure ourselves that we really get an area in which we can concentrate our forces.

JODL: That's why I told everyone—Gauleiters, military district commands— that it's fundamental that we now build up everything within the Western Wall and within the Maginot Line from Diedenhofen to Metz. We will then push forward from there if the situation allows it, so that everything won't be destroyed in front again, with that crowd fleeing back again and the actual western wall in back lying useless—blocked there.

THE FÜHRER: Guderian, how could you best [—] add (a few) Tiger IIs.[1368]

THOMALE: We've already done that.

GUDERIAN: In principle it would be best to give the Tiger, which has a weak detachment, to the others—send the entire detachment to the front and give it the new equipment, because they have to be trained quickly and there are still some weaknesses that the troops need to understand. We experienced it with the 501st Detachment—it came out and stood there only with three Tigers on the second or third day. That's catastrophic. The commander is always blamed, even though he can't do anything about it.

THE FÜHRER: Under these circumstances, wouldn't it be useful to set up a racially pure detachment? [—]

GUDERIAN: I'm for racial purity.

THE FÜHRER: I read an American description, which established with envy that that is a weapon the Allies unfortunately don't have.

GUDERIAN: My Führer, we can't let ourselves get pushed in, not even by such an urgent situation. It costs us the equipment, which can't be replaced.

THE FÜHRER: You know my opinion. We have to hold tight here. We can't let ourselves be seduced into acting hastily.

GUDERIAN: I just want to warn you of one thing, my Führer: that we'll load the stuff on the railway and take it in there. [—] get infected (by this panic); rather, only troops can go in front and not materiel.

THE FÜHRER: Three regiments being activated will come in here? Or what is here?

JODL: That's the first thing Military District V has reported. Three regimental groups and six battalions are being built up from the Replacement Army here in front, in order to push it forward—in addition to the two police battalions that are on their way already.

THE FÜHRER: Of course, they all have to get antitank guns and close-combat weapons, because otherwise they will be overrun by tanks in this stretch up here. [—] Guderian, these [—] (There is no worse defense—this has to be) repeated again and again—than the Rhine.

GUDERIAN: The Rhine is no defense at all. It's nothing compared to the Vosges.

THE FÜHRER: The Rhine fortifications are totally outdated, of course.

GUDERIAN: Hardly existing anymore—everything collapsed.[1369]

THE FÜHRER: We built it right at that moment, when the recognition came that something like that could be destroyed by direct fire with high V_0

[initial velocity]. But we finished it in the hope that the enemy doesn't know that yet. But the Rhine defense—

GUDERIAN: (It's) more than (thin). I know that.

(THE FÜHRER): ... 17 to 20 positions per kilometer [—]

(THOMALE): ... called ... up, we can set up mobile panzer brigades there. Such a panzer brigade looks as follows: one to two detachments, and I would suggest that we fill up one panzer detachment with Panzer IVs from the relevant military district, which is actually intended for the supply of the West, then they go into regular units. Second, we have also three Panther detachments being built up in the Homeland, where only the Panthers are missing. I would suggest that we add those Panthers then to the 1st Battalion, 29th Panzer Regiment, the *Hermann Göring* [Parachute Panzer Grenadier Division] and to the 1st Battalion, 30th [Panzer Grenadier Regiment]; they would then be the second detachments for these brigades— one Panther detachment with 45 Panthers. In addition, two to three infantry battalions and [—]

GUDERIAN: So now the Reichsmarshal just needs to give his permission for this.

THE FÜHRER: I give permission immediately.[1370] We already have a kind of Reich defense General Staff. We have an establishment for which we were envied by all the countries of the world: the Commander-in-Chief of the Armed Forces. No one else has anything like it. It just hasn't become public because the General Staff didn't like it.

KEITEL: Fought it tooth and nail!

THE FÜHRER: Fought it tooth and nail! After we have been fought against for years because of this establishment[1371] [—]

THOMALE: It must be refreshed.

GUDERIAN: The Third Air Fleet has so many trucks!

KREIPE: We lost so many of those in the Army deployment. All the trucks are destroyed. Most of the trucks that we are said to have don't exist anymore. We're unable to equip the 9th Anti-Aircraft Division— which is in formation and refitting, and which is now to be brought over here—with the necessary trucks; it can only be taken there as mobile.[1372] I have tried myself, the Air Intelligence Troops, because we (lack) all-terrain vehicles [—]

THE FÜHRER: But I'm convinced that the Luftwaffe is still better equipped with trucks—measured against their duties—than the Army. There's no doubt about it. Now, that's not the issue—we don't want to quarrel over trifles ["the Emperor's beard"—des Kaisers Bart]—but the issue is that the front must be stabilized here, so that we can at least start marching in units. Because as it is now, we can't march in units or do any refitting, because the refit units must be put back in again. It doesn't matter where I do the refitting. Because if I [—] had been up to 1939, that is: the panzer unit works together with the infantry as a kind of battering ram, while I had the opinion back then—already when we entered Czechoslovakia—that the panzer unit is there, operationally evaluated, to establish a situation that actually leads to the collapse of a great number of enemy forces. However, we can only do that if we are able to bring in enough units and if we can do it in an orderly way. If I get three panzer grenadier divisions here, and there are three platoons there, and I throw those three platoons into the fight, then that's ridiculous. That way we waste practically [—]

THOMALE: Within 48 hours.

THE FÜHRER: Immediately! Immediately!

THOMALE: Then I wanted to request that all units that are still in the West—service troops and all of the panzer units—be gathered behind the Western Wall, so that we—the Inspector General—can get them in order.

THE FÜHRER: I agree with that.

THOMALE: Otherwise, we won't get them in order.

GUDERIAN: Especially the tank destroyer formations that don't (have) any equipment left [—]

(THE FÜHRER): … to hold the Somme. The coastal artillery, which will be freed here, should, in my opinion, be brought up here in order to concentrate it.

GUDERIAN: We also have very little at these very important points on the North Sea coast.

THE FÜHRER: That's now only [—]

GUDERIAN: It's not that we're trying to take them in. We only want to arm them and pull them up front.

THE FÜHRER: Of course, the enemy will try [—]

DÖNITZ: Down here it was a success. We have packed everything in the heads down there.

THE FÜHRER: That won't work any more. Everything has no doubt been blown up there. The batteries that are installed here will certainly not be brought back, unless they were taken down before. I don't know. But we could give them, for example, Russian gun howitzers again. We also have captured and possibly 17-cm guns. Günsche, I have the big album of the Western Wall; find out—maybe Schaub[1373] knows—if the [—]

THE FÜHRER: Of course, I would prefer to have completely uniform ammunition.

GUDERIAN: Here we have to take modern German guns with quite a bit of ammunition.

THE FÜHRER: That would be best. Unfortunately, the German field how-itzer is worse than the Russian one, until it gets the new shells.

GUDERIAN: I don't know what the production of the Russian 12.2 cm is.

BUHLE: We get ... pieces [—]

(GUDERIAN): ... sense. In my opinion, the first priority should be to send German guns.

THE FÜHRER: We can't get them in there,[1374] because we need the German guns first for the building up of our German divisions.

GUDERIAN: The entire 8.8 production can easily go in here.

THE FÜHRER: That is something else. The 8.8 has to be put in here abso-lutely.

KEITEL: That's very good. Excellent!

[—]

GUDERIAN: This number is too small. It won't work for these assign-ments.

THOMALE: My Führer, then there will also be a Panther detachment ready with 17 destroyer Panthers 8.8[1375] and 28 assault guns, as you ordered.

THE FÜHRER: When will they be ready?

(THOMALE: Ready on September 5.)

Get them here immediately!

GUDERIAN: They were also intended for the West.

BUHLE: They were intended for the West; will [—]

THE FÜHRER: Everything else here is nonsense. We won't be able to make a real attack, a major attack, earlier.

GUDERIAN: We can form two more detachments by then.

THE FÜHRER: By then we will have the 25 divisions![1376]

GUDERIAN: The Tigers, which we don't have at the moment, will also be ready by then.

BUHLE: The Tiger II is not (ready for deployment) at the moment; (there are still several difficulties.) [—]

150 and 100; all that has to come from the East [—]

GUDERIAN: This has to be reconstructed, which will take months, and this is an immediate measure!

FEGELEIN: This one here will be there in August. (*Presentation.*) He can come up to 150 here and up to 100 here, but that will take several months.

BUHLE: My Führer, the guns that will actually be (available) during the next few weeks, considering our current ammunition situation, are already (des-ignated for) the 12th Artillery (Corps.)[1377] [—]

THE FÜHRER: Is this the light infantry gun?

BUHLE: The Russian 7.62 infantry gun howitzer, firing distance 7,000, but unfortunately with a flat trajectory.

THE FÜHRER: What do you mean, "flat trajectory"? It is also a high trajectory gun—it has a very small charge. That's what our infantry gun is, since it shoots much further.

BUHLE: It is not a high trajectory gun! [—]

GUDERIAN: All the guns and ammunition that we have in the German Reich have been taken by the General of the Artillery and organized into fortress artillery detachments—everything!

BUHLE: One hundred fifty new guns have just become available; we must give them to these reserve detachments, which are pulling in here.

THE FÜHRER: If I look, for example, at the occupation of Metz, they seem to be high-quality troops, but if they don't have any artillery, then (I will have to) put something in there [—]

(JODL): ... available. Two-thirds or three-quarters of the available Norwegian batteries will come to the West—if the ammunition is actually usable.

THE FÜHRER: The issue is that in these next few days—today, tomorrow, and the day after tomorrow—the battle for Metz might start, and it is critical that we immediately put antitank guns and artillery in there!

GUDERIAN: That will be done, too.

THOMALE: Seventy-five antitank guns are available immediately [—]

(THE FÜHRER): ... don't give them any antitank guns, they can't hold it; then these six battalions will be gone within a few days.

GUDERIAN: My Führer, it is also moving; everything that we could organize and arm in the way of antitank guns, machine gun battalions, antiaircraft artillery, and Army flak battalions is already being drawn up. I don't know exactly which of these troops have already been given to the West, but I've made everything mobile that we can make mobile. The OKW must know that. [—]

(JODL): ... stand, as Thomale has just said, and a great number of antitank close-combat weapons that must be given to these troops in here. The Commander of the Replacement Army"[1378] has to distribute these, since he is also leading the troops here. It must be made available only to him, since he won't be free to decide what to do with it until he receives it.

GUDERIAN: Everything is possible, within 24 hours.

THE FÜHRER: That must be done!

THOMALE: That is clear. The only thing is that the troops ... to their [—]

THE FÜHRER: Of course, this here is more the preparation. [—] The connection to the group should take place here!

GUDERIAN: The Vosges are easy to defend—that is a definite ridge. We can do that. I know it quite well.

THE FÜHRER: So Commander-in-Chief Blaskowitz is here in Dijon, and he still seems to feel quite safe here. He built up some coverage here?

JODL: There are some [—]

THE FÜHRER: How many divisions are here altogether right now? Five?

JODL: Four plus the panzer division.

THE FÜHRER: So five divisions. So we have to consider that maybe one division has to be held back. Then three divisions and the panzer division will come here; three divisions from here and two divisions from here—that makes five altogether—so five divisions plus one panzer division. In any case, the divisions are such that they [—] brings them here under all circumstances and not to any other area; we have to lead them into this area. That's the most important place strategically, so we have to build up the assault group there.[1379]

GUDERIAN: Before Besançon!

THE FÜHRER: It has to be built up here, because here there's the best connection over there. If we build it up here, then nothing can happen at all. And in the worse case, there's still the Black Forest behind us. So not (much) can happen here. [—]

THOMALE: What we have beyond the Western Wall will go even quicker in the replenishment—it goes very quickly; then troops with good combat strength will result.

THE FÜHRER: Now comes the question that everyone asks again. They drive back—all young people—and the others have to go in the front! [—] That is very difficult. The things we see from above are always great, but unfortunately we have to give our orders to subordinates, and whether these orders are always sensible and [—]

(GUDERIAN): ... pulls, maybe it would work with the Inspector General. I have a number of officers who are there for nothing beyond orderly duty.

THE FÜHRER: Good! [—] The whole thing is a real shame. If we weren't closely pursued here, I would say that we should gather the group together even further south, under the condition that we still keep the connection and that we immediately push forward in the direction of Troyes. In any case, we have to ... with this pathetic messing around [—] and what distance we have to cover with our railway network—a few kilometers.

KEITEL: It's unbelievable, how he does the supply.

THE FÜHRER: They're starting to grumble already as well. I don't know if you read it, but they've already complained today. There isn't enough of anything, it can't go on like it is right now with the supply, the troops in the front would starve to death ... materiel, and so on [—]

(KREIPE): ... not been delivered yet. We received radio messages from General Ramcke,[1380] and he urgently asks for aerial delivery containers, for materiel and such things. Unfortunately, we haven't received the containers from the Army yet.

THE FÜHRER: Does the Army make the aerial delivery containers?

KREIPE: They are delivered by the Army.

THE FÜHRER: Aerial delivery containers?

[—]

THE FÜHRER: They must have raced!

JODL: The enemy has pushed forward from Amiens to here, at Villers-Bocage. There are covering forces there. This group near Albert is being attacked—the one from Corbie out to the southern edge of Albert; Albert itself has held. Here ...by parts of the infantry divisions in replenishment ... and the 352nd [Infantry Division] and with a combat group of the 10th SS Panzer Division. ...The 9th is moving in to St [—] not sure if it took over the units—the II SS Corps, the combat group of the 1st, the 9th Panzer Division, the 12th, bringing in the 116th, and also the 47th Infantry Division further back in the bend. Then east of Montcornet the enemy has advanced with 60 tanks in here.

THE FÜHRER: That's an impertinence!

JODL: Then from Rethel, where fighting is still going on [—] to the north and then to block the Meuse here in this sector from south of Verdun to Commercy.

THE FÜHRER: That is the "right start" for a panzer unit!

JODL: We need them in any case in this extension ..., there it belongs on the outside.

[—]

THE FÜHRER: Of course, it would be good if that were to stay in the front, so we could have an occupation force here if necessary. We can't occupy 250 km with six battalions.

JODL: Some of it is here anyway.

THE FÜHRER: This reconnaissance detachment?

JODL: These here are the individual things that I [—]

JODL: Here it is reported that, as rearguard, the 338th [Infantry] Division—which is fighting extremely well, but which is actually not complete, since the one regiment had already been transported out before—made the entire withdrawal possible, so that the last troops have come across the Isère [River]. So one has to assume that the 338th Division is in the process of going back over the Isère[1381] here [—] condition from—or one of the panzer brigades suggested by Thomale. It would be best to put them into the 11th Panzer Division.

THE FÜHRER: That one won't come up here that quickly.

THOMALE: From the 11th Panzer Division, ... detachments, as far as they are ... as Panzer IV crews [—]

JODL: One from each military district who pulls it through. We don't need to talk about that.

THOMALE: It will happen in any case.

GUDERIAN: So, another position appears![1382]

[—]

JODL: The enemy no doubt started immediately when he recognized the withdrawal. It was reported that everything went according to plan during the night. The 71st [Infantry Division] is very … worn out, has only a narrow sector.

THE FÜHRER: I have the feeling that it (has been dealt with) here in the same way as it was down there at that time. [—]

Italy, the Balkans

[—]

JODL: It was that way with the 1st Parachute Division, which was here.

THE FÜHRER: It was already in there?

JODL: On the left wing there were very strong (attacks). That is clear from the fact that 51 tanks were knocked out despite the mountainous terrain.[1383]

[—]

JODL: The surprising thing for me here is that this traffic was quite smooth today, despite the fact that there aren't any bridges across the Po [River][1384] there any more. Also the supply went without difficulties. Yesterday I (had a report.)

(WESTPHAL: Yes, I brought it with me.)

Quite a lot has (been organized in the course of time) [—]

THE FÜHRER: We can't leave that out; we have to proceed in (quite) a barbaric way so that everyone knows what will happen to him (if he) betrays us!

(JODL): …, if it is proven, it would be best to (hang) him.

THE FÜHRER: Hanged!

[—]

(JODL): … bring back … the fortress battalion from the island of Kos, … the 47th Regiment of the 22nd [Infantry] Division. The air (transport forces) and the fuel are sufficient for (that).[1385]

THE FÜHRER: Fuel that is on the islands themselves [—] places, … (the) forces, which are marching in here, and which would put him, the field marshal, (in the situation) in the next … there in Sofia some emphasis …

(GUDERIAN: My) Führer, I'd like to request that German soldiers not be allowed to let themselves (be disarmed.) [—]

(THE FÜHRER): … The connections (are less clear); people[1386] have decided to (betray) us. It's no use. The stronger we appear, (the better); then we

get the (tanks[1387]) at least. (We fight with) weapons and with honor. The ...
Suggestions have also been made, ... not to take possession. We [—]
GUDERIAN: The Bulgarians have blown up the railway. The (railway connections between) Salonika and Nish were ... by[1388] ... !
THE FÜHRER: That's all just a theory; if we [—]

* * * * *

September 17, 1944

After Finland withdrew from the war on September 2, the Twentieth Mountain Army began its retreat to northern Norway on September 9.

The Russians broke through along the Narva River on September 15, and are now pushing forward along the Gulf of Finland to Reval. In Latvia they attacked through the German Düna bridgehead south of Riga. In Lithuania—on the Narev, the Vistula and the Visloka Rivers, as well as at the northern edge of the Carpathian Mountains—the Soviet offensive came to a halt after achieving its aims.

The German-Hungarian front in Transylvania, which had been established out of remains and reserves along the former Hungarian-Romanian border, was forced to clear the Szekely/Scucules salient after September 7 and pull back to the upper Maros; however, a counterattack near Klausenburg [Cluj] delayed the Russian advance on Arad and Temesvar, and with it the penetration into the Hungarian lowlands.

The evacuation of Greece has begun.

In the West, Montgomery invaded Belgium after the hopeless German attempt to defend along the Somme River failed from the very start. Brussels was captured on September 3, and Antwerp on September 4. The British, however, were brought to a stop at the Albert Canal. The isolated German Fifteenth Army was able to fight its way through from the Somme along the canal and through Flanders to the mouth of the Schelde River, which it occupied; there the Germans established an initially adequate defensive front north of Antwerp. The Americans, who were struggling with supply problems, had meanwhile reached the border of the Reich at the Eifel on September 11, but here—shortly thereafter outside of Aachen and Trier—they were stopped by the Western Wall. In Lorraine they also reached the Moselle River near Toul and on September 15 they took Nancy, but were driven back by the German defenses before Metz and Diedenhofen. The American and French troops advancing in the Rhône Valley had meanwhile reached Besançon on September 8 and Dijon on September 11; they also couldn't get beyond Belfort. Between the two Allied landing groups, the remains of the First Army fought its way through from the south of France, in continuous battles with the Maquis [underground].

The British-Polish attack on the Italian Adriatic coast remains stuck for the time being outside of Rimini, but the enemy has also been attacking a relatively exposed front north of Florence since September 10. It succeeded in breaking through in the direction of Bologna on this day, September 17.
(*Maps 6, 7, 11, and 12*)

* * * * *

EVENING SITUATION REPORT,
SEPTEMBER 17, 1944, AT THE WOLFSSCHANZE[1389]

Present:

The Führer	*Envoy v. Sonnleithner*
Field Marshal Keitel	*Lieutenant Colonel v. Amsberg*
Colonel General Jodl	*Lieutenant Colonel Waizenegger*
General Buhle	*Major Büchs*
Lieutenant General Burgdorf	*Hauptsturmführer Günsche*
Vice Admiral Voss	

Beginning: …

Finland
(WAIZENEGGER[1390]): … In Finland the withdrawal movement of the 7th Mountain Division behind this sector here has been carried out according to plan and without any pressure from the enemy.[1391] A reinforced company is still holding here as rearguard. To the north, the 6th SS Mountain Division[1392] has driven back various thrusts in company strength on both sides of the red (road) here. The strong enemy pressure … continues. The enemy is … attacked the front of the 163rd. [Infantry Division] [—]

Hungary
[—]
The enemy pressure against the eastern front of the LVII Panzer Corps was stronger. The enemy achieved a deeper penetration in two places along the 46th [Infantry] Division lines,[1393] on the right wing. Counterattacks have been launched. There was a stronger penetration on the left wing, where the enemy tore open the front across a breadth of about 3 kilome-

ters, and penetrated to a depth of about 2 kilometers. Some enemy troops are supposed to have ... themselves in this (wooded area). Countermeasures have been initiated here. (More detailed reports have) not arrived yet.

The East

[—]

depth. Two tanks were destroyed in these battles. The fighting is still in full swing there. Several hostile thrusts were driven back by the 68th and 75th [Infantry] Divisions. A nice defensive success by the 1st Panzer Division: the connection has been established. That cut off the cavalry corps and an additional infantry battalion here. Tomorrow (the 1st Panzer Division) is to push north in order to make the connection even tighter and to prevent (these encircled enemy troops) from breaking out [—] couldn't continue his attacks today either. Other than that, there wasn't any particular combat activity on Army Group Center's front, except our own attack on the left wing of the 3rd Panzer Division,[1394] which advanced quite well. We won ground throughout—about 5 kilometers to the east.

THE FÜHRER: But that's quite bad!

WAIZENEGGER: But (the army group reports) that it went well, my (Führer) ... with the spearheads about ... carry out the attack. [—]

(THE FÜHRER): ... 30 to 40 km. [—] It's extremely difficult for the people to simply break off something that is unsuccessful—it's difficult to accept that. That's been our experience.

KEITEL: Yes, to stop then.

THE FÜHRER: That's been the experience—then it tenses up.

WAIZENEGGER: ... The enemy's very strong deployment of fighter-bombers ... essentially all attacks ... (on the) left wing a local (penetration) ...[—] In the area of the VI SS Corps, this front is supposed to be straightened today—up to the green line for the time being. That will free up a battalion of the 83rd [Infantry] Division, which should then be moved into the penetration site with the 21st Luftwaffe Field Division. There is a battalion of the 218th [Infantry Division] further south, which will ... the XXVIII Corps in the area south of Lake Wirz. (Several hostile attacks) against the 21st [Infantry] Division lines failed. However, the enemy was able to (achieve) two deeper penetrations toward the south. (The) 31st Infantry Division has (lined up) here for a counterattack. [—] start was, as it is marked here. The planned withdrawal will take place tonight to this green line. This penetration here is currently being blocked by a battalion from the 11th [Infantry] Division. An additional regiment from the 11th Division is coming from the north, along with parts of the SS panzer reconnaissance detachment and a police battalion. There is nothing unusual at Narva.

The Southeast

In the Southeast, in the area of ... (strong) hostile air reconnaissance reported ... Our own air reconnaissance reported today ... Thera[1395] a hostile aircraft (carrier) ... a destroyer, an additional [—] Here in the area of Bozovice there is local fighting with the Romanians.[1396] The course of the battles around Temeschburg: An attacking group from the south has reached the road running toward Lugos, just east of the town. West of this there is an additional combat group on the southern edge of town, which has destroyed four hostile companies there. Combat Group Behrends,[1397] attacking from the northwest, (pushed into) the town but was driven back by a counterattack. A Hungarian reserve division ... is now supposed to ...take part (in the attack) against the town (from the northwest). [—]

WAIZENEGGER: The Bulgarians still have 88 Panzer IVs available, plus two assault gun brigades with about 50 assault guns altogether.

KEITEL: Nevertheless, we should try it with the combat group of the 4th SS.[1398]

THE FÜHRER: We shouldn't just try it, of course—it has to (be) taken ... where the assault guns have come back, (we must) move them out by train [—]

The West

[—]

(WAIZENEGGER): ... is supposed to be here in this area, according to the most recent report. However, it hasn't been confirmed yet. A series of communiqués with individual airfields has clarified the picture slightly.[1399] The following is reported from the airfield at Soest: no enemy at 6 p.m. [—] These are telephone reports. The airfield at Deelen—I think that's what it's called—has actually not been attacked itself, but from there (enemy) landings were observed west of (Arnhem). 30 transport gliders were (observed). [—] This area was also (free of enemy forces) between 5 and 6 p.m. On the other hand, it is certain ... where our own forces are in action. [—]

JODL: That's not a whole lot. Essentially there are the fortification crews, reinforced by the entire SS combat group—what is it called? Demelhuber[1400]— and alarm units, since the bulk of the division has been pulled out of here. There's the fortification crew, the Navy, the coastal batteries—

KEITEL: —and the Supreme SS and Police Commander.

THE FÜHRER: We (still) haven't found anything out that will tell us whether or not this goes all the way (over to the coast)?

JODL: That is ... I'll read that in a minute. [—]

THE FÜHRER: 1,500 with 10 each—that would be 15,000. [—] How big are they?[1401]

JODL: Approximately the strength of a division. [—] From the supply area, the advance guard point of the 107th Panzer Brigade will drive through Wesel between midnight and 1 a.m. However, the unloading area is supposed to be Venlo-Roermond, probably for technical reasons related to the railway.

THE FÜHRER: That's not such a bad idea.

[—]

(WAIZENEGGER): ... the division: to take the Wilhelmina Canal bridges at Son and Best. One *Hermann Göring* battalion is encircled in Son. At the same time as the airborne landing, the enemy moved northward out of the Neerpelt bridgehead, and he is supposed to be located with his spearheads 2.5 kilometers south of Valkenswaard, according to a report that hasn't yet been confirmed. The First Parachute Army is pulling all available forces together in order to destroy the airborne enemy. The combat group from the 59th [Infantry] Division is coming here quickly from the Fifteenth Army Headquarters. WB. Netherlands, near Arnhem (reports that the enemy has landed with a) focal point 10 kilometers west of Arnhem ... between Ede and Veenendaal and [—] the 406th Division.[1402] In addition, a battalion with four light field howitzers is deployed there. Another 24 guns are in Goch. A battalion of the 10th SS Panzer Division is being brought in via Emmerich. In addition, alarm units are being formed in that whole area. The landing at Goch and in the area of Xanten–Cleve hasn't been confirmed. Summary: the impression we have so far is that the enemy will try, together with the assault group from the bridgehead ... out of the areas of Eindhoven–Nijmegen and ... airborne troops ... the crossing ... over the Meuse, Waal and Rhine [Rivers] ... and to reach the Ijssel-Meer. [—]

(BÜCHS?): ... the air. Total deployment strength hasn't been reported yet. Two wings of the 1st Fighter Division have been transferred over here from the Berlin area. They arrived in the area of Bonn and Paderborn this afternoon and will be ready for additional deployment tomorrow morning. The 262s weren't able to fly yet today, since the Rhine airfield was still not ready because of the attacks during the night. It is being repaired as quickly as possible, and they hope to be (able to go out) again very soon.

THE FÜHRER: How many (262s were ready for deployment?)

BÜCHS: Yesterday there were ... aircraft. [—]

THE FÜHRER: Of course, if we let them go without bazookas[1403] and such things!

BUHLE: That's completely new—I'm just now hearing it. It was probably done quickly by Student,[1404] since it happened without anyone saying anything to anyone.

THE FÜHRER: Exactly. But we have to see that they get something in ...

BUHLE: Immediately. That is ... (That) is the most urgent thing (there is.)
[—]

(THE FÜHRER): ... is ... overcome ... than the whole Siegfried Line—because it is a gigantic water obstacle—to break through from the rear.

BÜCHS: Night fighting has been concentrated in this area, in order to be ready when four-engine units approach.

THE FÜHRER: But they don't come here.

BÜCHS: According to the (reports) we've received, Air Command Holland has reported in total ... transport aircraft and about ... (transport gliders. That would be) capacity for two divisions ... (with) weapons.
[—]

BUHLE: That is the better-armored patrol car, the 18-ton one.[1405]

THE FÜHRER: The greatest danger is the penetration here! This here must hold under all circumstances, of course, to prevent a land connection.

KEITEL: Here are the preparatory measures from the Commander of the Replacement Army, which I ordered today at noon, ... for Military Districts X and XI[1406]; all the forces that he could (draw together) there, we have concentrated here ... One division, a second is coming [—] the build up of our panzer troops is under great strain. We didn't want to take the staff of the "Schwiebus" Panzer School either.

THE FÜHRER: Panzer IIIs make no sense.

KEITEL: Just like the Army school for non-commissioned officers. Those are the things we're doing the build-up from. There are five companies, (so) that does no good. (That would be) two divisions, which we could get initially, one with ... men, the other about 10,000 (men strong.) [—]

BUHLE: It will be ready at the end of October.

KEITEL: [—] somehow endanger them by pulling out one of the combat groups, or we destroy the whole thing. [—] First of all, here are the two divisions that were designated for it. [—] So I would not be for it. Likewise the 363rd Volksgrenadier Division in Military District XI, which Jodl has talked about. That would mean an (anticipation of) the final formation,[1407] but will (certainly) facilitate the whole thing[—]

(THE FÜHRER): ... namely that we hold this line here on the Rhine, and that we send them up here or here. The most important thing is that we hold the Rhine here. When it has been fought free here, then we'll soon have the big canals—that is the most important thing, aside from the fact that our line goes here. We can connect here, and we have this thing here anyway—the fortress is there. If we have it nearby at least, it'll be better, in case something (happens) here.

KEITEL: Load and transport! Then we can still give orders about the areas (into which) they will be brought. [—]

THE FÜHRER: V1, but from airplanes?[1408]

JODL: From airplanes. [—] Here the line has been pushed back slightly by this attack. Here the connection has been established in the area north of Aachen, via Heerlen. [—] Here an attack on the southern outskirts of Aachen has been driven back.[1409] Here the forces are in the same positions as before. The 12th [Infantry] Division, which is gathering here near Mausbach,[1410] is regrouping in order to start fighting tomorrow together with the rest of the division that has arrived in the meantime. [—]

THE FÜHRER: This seems to be closed here?

JODL: Yes, this line here is closed up to Nomeny.[1411] Nomeny is being held here, and is being strongly attacked from the east. Then there's the connection between the 553rd [Infantry] Division and the 106th Panzer Brigade, which is blocking this off again, and behind the front there is an additional enemy attack from this direction [—]

THE FÜHRER: He's trying to get in this way.

JODL: Then here against the 553rd Division (front) [—]

JODL: Yes. [—] Assembly areas here, then. [—] It was reported this morning that the enemy is through south of Epinal, with 25 tanks. This hasn't been confirmed. He is assembling the troops west of Jussey. Fighting near Fougerolles,[1412] where the enemy threw back the combat outposts. Attacks on Lantenot, in approximately battalion strength, have been driven back here. We have received no reports from further south.

THE FÜHRER: The further south he attacks, the greater the [—] he marches forward, he will have all the town inhabitants inside his front.

JODL: He[1413] asked expressly—before the order—that it be explained. He drew attention in particular to the unfortunate state of the Nineteenth Army's forces after the loss of the 16th [Infantry] Division.[1414]

THE FÜHRER: He has to make sure that he gets the forces from these 100,000 men—200,000[1415] came back. The other[1416] takes (everything), but we don't do that. We've done it much too (carelessly), and they have to get out. [—]

THE FÜHRER: To take the Cossacks out?

JODL: The Reichsführer[1417] is taking them over now. [—] The 183rd Volksgrenadier Division will arrive today between 1 and 2 in Bonn. The unloading area is supposed to be near Düren.

THE FÜHRER: That's the second; when is the third coming?

JODL: The third will be here on the 20th. [—] The 108th Panzer Brigade with 5 trains ... near Gerolstein, ... trains on their way. Then the border is ... been transferred, [—]

JODL: Completely reinforced! That's the only place where the Western Wall has faced a serious threat up to now.

THE FÜHRER: Of course, he is lying entirely on the left wing—what we did back then the other way around on the right.[1418] And that is right. That's why this thing here has to stay absolutely in our hands, because we can (only) cause a change in the overall situation if we come from here as well. Have you (received) the relief map of the West yet, which we used to (have) back in Berlin?

[—]

JODL: He has to pull the 11th Panzer Division out. I don't think he can do it without it.

THE FÜHRER: He can't do it with just the fortress formations, since there isn't a position there. They are not capable of such a thing. He can only put them into a position—along the Western Wall.

GÜNSCHE: The relief map was burned during an air attack in Berlin.

THE FÜHRER: Is it not possible to (get another) one? Find out immediately!

BUHLE: [—]

(THE FÜHRER): ... it now. [—] But we'll leave it anyway, if it consists of East Prussians.

KEITEL: They're the volunteer East Prussians. We have to leave them here.[1419]

JODL: Yes, but the other would be possible.

THE FÜHRER: How does the 349th [Infantry Division] look, anyway?

BUHLE: Right now, my Führer? With regard to personnel the 349th is probably not quite full, and with regard to weapons it has about 50%.

JODL: It must ... Lötzen ... here and Arys? [—] That would be [—]

BUHLE: It's supposed to be ready on October 1, but I doubt it will be. It'll be delayed slightly because of the motor vehicles, but only by a few days.

THE FÜHRER: I wonder whether we shouldn't possibly earmark these. I know Guderian will complain. But here it is much more dangerous than in the East.

BUHLE: The Führer Infantry Brigade[1420] should be ready at the same time.

THE FÜHRER: We (must) keep the Führer Infantry Brigade here now, under all circumstances.

[—]

THE FÜHRER: We have to keep in mind—we don't want to be careless anymore—the possibility that they might make a similar mess[1421] here.

KEITEL: We now have one battalion from it.

JODL: If the 349th leaves, then there will be nothing left in this area, of course. As long as it is still here [—]

THE FÜHRER: Here there is also an SS battalion of the Reichsführer, and here there's a police battalion and this, which we have here. Otherwise we don't have anything else here?

KEITEL: Here? No.

[—]

THE FÜHRER: This thing is so dangerous that we have to be clear: if a disaster happens here—here I am, here is my entire Supreme Command, here is the Reichsmarshal, the Army High Command is here, the Reichsführer SS is here, and here is the Reich Foreign Minister![1422] So that's the most valuable catch—that's clear. I would risk two parachute divisions without hesitation if I could get the entire Russian command in one stroke.

KEITEL: The entire German command!

[—]

(... ?): ... brought the staff. I demanded it; it was discussed with Kreipe beforehand.

THE FÜHRER: Where is the 25th Panzer Grenadier [Division] being readied?

BUHLE: In Grafenwöhr.

THE FÜHRER: It should come over here[1423] immediately as well then, if it's going to. We should consider that, in any case. We don't have to decide that yet, but we might possibly (have to) do it.

BURGDORF: It has been (reported that the) equipment is extremely difficult to (come by, and that) it won't (be ready) until the end of [—]

(THE FÜHRER): ... We really have to be careful now. If something terrible happens, it will be of no use to say afterward, "I suspected that—I knew it!" The reports arriving now should not be taken casually. These reports are quite alarming. They reported this back then, too. Looking back, of course, the whole thing seems like a fairy tale now. But they say that the man at headquarters has been found now, so we don't need to worry about it—it will be done by the Germans themselves; they will (eliminate) the Führer. That such pigs ... find, we are just now seeing. But to report now ... that (they) now have a new ... (We would rather be) on the safe side.

[—]

KEITEL: We can't interfere right now, but we can order it anyway.

V. AMSBERG: Actually it has already pulled out. It's standing on German soil again now. Combat Group Werthern[1424] only has about 700 men now.

THE FÜHRER: In the old Reich territory, though!

V. AMSBERG: Yes, in the old Reich territory. It is in the area of Insterburg again ... General Wenck said to me recently, that if ... (something) happened, he could give it away.

[—]

BUHLE: Six divisions—of that size—have also been added through the formation of the Valkyrie formations[1425] and the formations created from the returning men. The worst thing is that the artillery is lacking.

THE FÜHRER: When will these fortress artillery brigades finally arrive?

BUHLE: They are on their way—the first four. Additional ones[1426] will come in the next few days.

THE FÜHRER: They only have ...

BUHLE: No, that's not ... (A) part, in any case well over (half), ... available French [—]

(THE FÜHRER): ... He says to himself, "Maybe I'll get guns!" He does it like the well-known man who goes to someone and says, "Do you have a match for me?" Then the other one gives him a match, and then he says, "Could you spare a cigarette?" Then he has one. He does it the other way around! It would be interesting—and I'd like to know—how many spare parts for our tanks are actually here now. It would be interesting to find that out for once.

Italy

Here he was driven back again?

JODL: Continuation of the attacks. (The attacks on the) pass road itself were driven back ... has been lost. [—]

The West again

BÜCHS: My Führer! We have just spoken with the airfields at Deelen, Soesterberg and also Leeuwarden. There it's quiet. The report from Leeuwarden hasn't been confirmed. There's no action in the air either. According to radio intercept, no assembly of transport units or heavy units has been identified. But we have to expect that they'll come back tomorrow.

THE FÜHRER: They will definitely come tomorrow, since they are so loud—calling up the Dutch, etc. So we have to assume that they will (come) tomorrow.

BÜCHS: Then of the ... there are ... which also ... Luftwaffe side ...

The Balkans

[—]

THE FÜHRER: They aren't doing anything much either!

JODL: Probably on both sides! It has been established that there are British among the nationalist partisans and among the Communists as well.[1427]

THE FÜHRER: When they are with the nationalist partisans they help it along, and when they are with the Communists, they hinder it.

BÜCHS: The appearance of the carriers has been confirmed by the corresponding model. It ... identified yesterday and today ... and Martlett. Those are both (aircraft types that) indicate that he is evidently deploying (aircraft carriers in that) area of the sea there.

Political reports

[—]

(THE FÜHRER): ... negotiations with Germany. The last few weeks should have shown that Stalin is by no means willing to enter into commitments for the post-war period ... (*Reading aloud follows.*) That's all nonsense! [—] What kind of events are these in Brazil? Does anyone there have a clue?[1428]

V. SONNLEITHNER: Nothing has arrived from there.

THE FÜHRER: I have the (feeling that) ... has started against the Americans.

[—]

(THE FÜHRER): ... executed. (*The reading aloud of additional press reports.*) The Pope has made a new statement against Communism—in the sense of a revision of his previous position regarding Communism. (*Reading aloud.*) The Holy Father will have a hard time soon! [—] Now there'll be worries about the Balkans. (*The reading aloud of additional press reports.*) This is the proclamation by Eisenhower.[1429] Have you (read it)? (*Reading aloud.*) The question is whether we should make a brief statement (about it) ... and that we...the guerillas [—]

JODL: Should we even try to legalize this?

THE FÜHRER: I wouldn't do that. Just the proclamation—period! The best thing is to make clear to everyone that this battle is a struggle for life or death. If someone gives himself up as a prisoner, then he can't expect us to show consideration for American or British prisoners because of him.

V. SONNLEITHNER: An official attempt will probably fail. They only fear reprisals.

THE FÜHRER: Here come ... already ... the successor of the Finnish ...

[—]

THE FÜHRER: This doesn't leave here!

BÜCHS: According to British reports, they have been transported into the north of Russia.

THE FÜHRER: Otherwise, there is nothing else here that needs to be fought with that. They know full well that it's quite heavily developed here!

V. SONNLEITHNER: The Turkish ambassador in Chungking reported that the Americans had said that it would come to armed conflict between America and Soviet Russia. As he said, this was from both official and unofficial American circles. (*Presentation.*) This is a report on ... Serbia.

[—]

V. SONNLEITHNER: He is actually only reporting what the Djuiric[1430] told him. I don't think he has first-hand knowledge.

THE FÜHRER: No, not that. But he reports whatever fits into his concept. With those people there is always a little bit of truth. But it would be good,

Jodl, if you would read through it. Take a look at it. I regard it as nothing more than idle talk.

V. SONNLEITHNER: Kasche[1431] is not satisfied with the Četniks. (*Presentation.*)

THE FÜHRER: Now he is coming all of a sudden. Oh, my God! These poisoned flowers—that is all I can say. [NDT: "meadow saffron," poisonous autumn flower.]

[—]

V. SONNLEITHNER: Here he writes about the interruption in the communications equipment. (*Presentation.*) Then he says that the Poglavnik's[1432] speech was of some use after all. He still hopes that it will improve there someday. (*Presentation.*) The Albanians are falling more and more heavily into Communism. There's nothing else in here. (*Presentation.*) Here is a report on the railway workers' strike in Denmark.[1433] (*Presentation.*) Blücher[1434] says that Hackzell was so healthy that he thinks he must have gotten quite a shock in Moscow, if the stroke hit him immediately.[1435] (*Presentation.*)

THE FÜHRER: ... gets ... a clean lawyer ... then it's over!

V. SONNLEITHNER: ... means that it ... not ... back to Lisbon at the moment [—]

THE FÜHRER: Yes it is! That is very good if he doesn't ...

V. SONNLEITHNER: Yes, Sir. That is also the opinion of the Foreign Minister.

The West again

BÜCHS: My Führer, I would also like to present the report from the Reichsmarshal concerning the formations that are designated for the ground operations in the Dutch area. The strength is still missing for the individually numbered [formations]. (*Presentation.*) The other is actually only about 100 men. The main thing is the field replacement battalion. These 1,600 men are the main component of the field replacement battalion, plus an officer instruction staff and the tank destroyer detachment.

THE FÜHRER: They shoot our German ammunition as well?

BÜCHS: Yes, these are the drilled ones—these 20 Russians. [—] Then here are the anti-aircraft combat troops again.

Yugoslavia

JODL: I thought we had a unified policy. But here there is a Neubacher[1436] policy and a ... policy: "Long live the Četniks!" ... : "Down with the Četniks!" We (only damage) ourselves that way.

THE FÜHRER: That has (nothing to do) with a unified policy—those are the men like ...

JODL: It also varies from location to location.

THE FÜHRER: But one thing is certain: that Neubacher ...

V. SONNLEITHNER: Unfortunately, it is always the case that people who are located somewhere become victims of this local psychosis.

THE FÜHRER: In the same way, Kasche is a dreamer!

JODL: He doesn't need to call up anti-Četnik passion. It's already there, as evidenced by everyone joining Tito because he is passionately fighting against the Četniks—but also against us! It's there anyway, with the exception of the Ustasha. They don't do it since they would be killed, but the others do it.[1437]

THE FÜHRER: That's right. That is indeed the situation. Except that Kasche doesn't know that everyone is defecting to the other side again. He is convinced that the flow is in the opposite direction. Kasche said that they've joined in great masses. Where are they?

V. SONNLEITHNER: He has corrected the numbers already.

THE FÜHRER: (From) over there to us!

V. SONNLEITHNER: He recently (admitted) himself (that the) opposite movement is taking place. He (also) gave (an) explanation (for it). We still have it ...

THE FÜHRER: One really has to admit that I can be wrong by 10 degrees (about something), or 20 degrees or 50 degrees. If one is wrong by 90 degrees, then it is rather difficult to maintain. But if one is 180 degrees wrong—completely on the opposite side—then it's a masterly performance.

V. SONNLEITHNER: Concerning Kasche, my Führer, the Foreign Minister has always suggested that you replace him, since the Foreign Minister thinks that Kasche is quite a respectable man but in a certain respect obsessed.

THE FÜHRER: He is a respectable man. It's just that respectable men go to the dogs as soon as they get into the Foreign Office.

V. SONNLEITHNER: Because they can't cope with the difficult tasks.

THE FÜHRER: Kasche used to be a daredevil of the first order.

V. SONNLEITHNER: My Führer, the reason is that the people, when they come out, measure the conditions there by theoretical standards. That is wrong, of course. That's what Kasche does.

THE FÜHRER: Our military men next door have judged the situation correctly. He has to (pass it on) objectively.

V. SONNLEITHNER: Glaise-(Horstenau)[1438] was the military ... who knows that already.

KEITEL: No, Rendulic![1439]

V. SONNLEITHNER: Rendulic knows it as well.

THE FÜHRER: At least he has to listen to those two things.

JODL: Kasche has stressed that it is completely wrong to put somebody who knows the situation there. A former Austrian should never be put there.

V. SONNLEITHNER: He says they are prejudiced. That is one point of view. But on the other hand, one can't understand the mentality of those tricksters if one doesn't know them.[1440]

THE FÜHRER: That's what I've always said! Just recently Neubacher reported that if we don't arm the Četniks or the Mihailovic people immediately with 50,000 guns, they will immediately go over to the other side and oppose us. I said before, "They won't do that—they will go with us or they'll be killed, if we … disarm them." Now he says, "They fight like crazy." [—] That man really changes his statements all the time. It is quite astonishing. But that can't be connected to the fact that the people knew this before. It must be connected to your office, since Neubacher is also an old …; he knows that, too. He used to be completely sensible. Six or eight years ago Neubacher was still completely normal.

V. SONNLEITHNER: But still he was always in accordance with his military colleagues and coworkers.

THE FÜHRER: They talked him into it!

V. SONNLEITHNER: I don't know. They influenced each other.

THE FÜHRER: No, they just realized it very quickly! Weichs became suspicious immediately.

V. SONNLEITHNER: But Neubacher also became suspicious at that same moment—it happened at the same time. It was surprising, but it was at the same time.

GÜNSCHE: Obergruppenführer Phleps[1441] knows the situation down there quite well. He was also quite successful with his units.

The West again

BÜCHS: My Führer, the phrase "of which" was wrong in the previous report. There are three marching groups with 1,600 men, a field replacement battalion with 1,500 men, and also an officer-training course.

THE FÜHRER: That makes quite a difference.

BÜCHS: There are 1,600 men.

THE FÜHRER: There are even more. Three marching groups with 1,600 men each, the field replacement battalion with 1,500 men [—]

BÜCHS: My Führer! Three marching groups with 1,600 men altogether!

THE FÜHRER: Oh, together?

BÜCHS: That's what it says. It also says in the report: "of which 1,500 are in the field replacement battalion." That "of which" is wrong; there are 1,600 men in three marching groups, then 1,500 men in the field replacement battalion. That makes 3,100. Then 450 men in the officer training course. That makes 3,500. Plus 250 men in the tank destroyer company. So about 3,750 men.

THE FÜHRER: That makes a great difference! [—] When can we expect the entire assault gun brigade to arrive? It only has a few trains. How many trains does it have?

BUHLE: It has 31 assault guns, so four or five trains.

THE FÜHRER: So it can arrive all at once?

BUHLE: It depends how it left up there.

JODL: The first train arrives at 6 p.m. in Koblenz.

THE FÜHRER: I hope they pull the other trains through quickly!

JODL: There was an interruption because of the strike.[1442] However, it was reported that the first trains have started again—so they should be close together.

THE FÜHRER: And the panzer brigade? It only has 36 tanks and one tank destroyer company as well!

BUHLE: The tank destroyer company will probably not be with them. It has 36 Panthers. But it has the three-barreled gun on this armored personnel carrier.

THE FÜHRER: So? That is quite good! How many do they have up there?

BUHLE: One on each vehicle.

THE FÜHRER: How many carriers do they have?

BUHLE: I can't say from memory. It could be about 70.

V. AMSBERG: Eighty, I think, is the authorization.

THE FÜHRER: Do they have the short 7.5 [cm gun]?

BUHLE: Some of them have the 7.5. I think 36 vehicles have three-barreled guns, the others have 2 cm and 7.5.[1443]

End: 2:07 a.m.

* * * * *

November 6, 1944

The 20th Mountain Army is withdrawing further into northern Norway along the few roads in Lapland.

Army Group North was forced to abandon Estonia to the Russians in September. The second Russian attack on Riga in the first half of October led to the evacuation of the last districts of the city, while on October 10, German troops were pushed back to the border of East Prussia and the Soviets reached the Baltic Sea at Polangen. Army Group North, which the

Russians didn't succeed in encircling near Riga, is defending—and will until the end of war—the Courland bridgehead, currently with 26 divisions. The Russians broke through into East Prussia on October 16, and weren't stopped until they reached the west side of Ebenrode and the Angerapp. Since then, counterattacks have closed this gap and the enemy has been driven back to the western side of the Romint heath. On the Vistula River the situation is unchanged.

Hungary remains the main focus of the battles on the Eastern Front. On October 5, the Russians advanced from the Romanian-Hungarian frontier area between Arad and Oradea [Grosswardein] and pushed toward the lower Tisza [Theiss], reaching the river quickly; the German troops barely managed to hold a large bridgehead between Sombor and Baja before the Danube. On the southern flank of this attack, Koniev conquered Belgrade on October 18, after a three-day siege, and crossed the Morava River in several places. The other Russian attack, also aimed in a northwesterly direction from the region of Gyula-Szalonta, was less successful: the breakthrough over the middle Tisza failed, and, on the way to Budapest, the Germans were able to hold a strong bridgehead in front of Szolnok. A new push to the north on October 17 reached Tokaj on the upper Tisza via Debrecen, but a German blocking force managed to stop the retreat of the German and the Hungarian troops from Siebenburgen [Transylvania] and the Carpathian Mountains on the Tisza—west of the Uzhgorod [Ungvár]–Wisloka line. Meanwhile, however, the Hungarian positions between the Danube and the Tisza were penetrated on October 30 near Kecskemét, and the first Russian tanks have reached the southeast edge of Budapest. While the situation in this area will be cleared up by bringing in new reserves and will be eased on November 6, the Soviet attacks between Szegéd and Szolnok are getting stronger and will crush the German Tisza bridgehead.

Army Group E, encircled in southern Serbia and Macedonia, fends off the Bulgarians east of the Vardar River, in the Amselfeld, and east of the Ibar River. The army group must now hinder the Russian breakthrough to the west and must march along the Samtschak road and from Kraijevo through partisan territory to Bosnia. On the last day of October, Salonika was evacuated; now the march ends just outside Skopje, which will be evacuated a few days later.

In Italy, the Anglo-American attack on Bologna was blocked 10 to 15 km south of the city. On the Adriatic coast, German units are fighting their way back from river valley to river valley, and are standing now outside Forlì and Ravenna on the Rabbi and lower Ronco Rivers.

In the Netherlands, the enemy airborne landings have created a curved front line, reaching far to the north at the lower Rhine in North Brabant.

West of this area, the Canadians started on October 1 to free the mouth of the river Schelde, facing tough resistance. At the same time, the German bridgehead east of the river Meuse was crushed. The German troops are now withdrawing over the Meuse to the Waal. On the Belgian border, the last defenders of Aachen surrendered on October 21 after a bitter fight, but, nevertheless, the American successes are only local. On the Moselle and in front of the Vosges the situation is basically unchanged. The bridgehead outside Metz and the Belfort fortress are still in German hands, and between these two points the Americans are slowly fighting their way forward between St. Dié and Baccarat over the Meurthe River.
(Maps 6, 7, 11, and 12)

* * * * *

MIDDAY SITUATION REPORT, NOVEMBER 6, 1944[1444]

Present:

The Führer	*Vice Admiral Voss*
Reich Press Chief Dr. Dietrich	*Major General Christian*
Field Marshal Keitel	*Envoy v. Sonnleithner*
Colonel General Jodl	*Lieutenant Colonel Waizenegger*
General Buhle	*Sturmbannführer Schulze*
Ambassador Hewel	*Major Büchs*
Lieutenant General Linnarz	*Cavalry Captain Scheidt*
Lieutenant General Wenck	*Hauptsturmführer Günsche*
Gruppenführer Fegelein	

Beginning: 3:12 p.m.

The East

WENCK: My Führer, the Army Group South situation is still tense, especially in the region of Szolnok.[1445] In the Budapest area it has become more stable, primarily because of yesterday's first advance of the panzer group. So far, the group has thrust into a long column and caused quite a disaster,[1446] but during the night the group stayed behind because they want to act together with the 13th, which will come out of here tonight, and the 1st Panzer Division against these two tank corps. They do this because the army group believes they'll have to regroup in the region of Szolnok tomorrow, where the enemy is putting a lot of pressure, and bring up these forces from this area—the Sixth Panzer Army—especially because they are worried about the Danube line, since two corps from the area of the Commander-in-Chief Southeast are coming nearer and are getting closer here around Baja. This corps has also been confirmed, and another corps from the south which will be brought in here. The question, my Führer, is if we can afford it, but they'll probably be needed, in order to bring in another division down here.

THE FÜHRER: This one probably will have to go to the West.

WENCK: One is going to the West now; it is being transported right now from Slovakia. Now there is only one Hungarian assault brigade and one training regiment left here. That's not much.

THE FÜHRER: Yes, that won't help.

WENCK: We could certainly bring in more Hungarians, but they are not reliable enough.

JODL: There is a possibility—I just thought of it: if we could bring in one division from Istria, if we could bring in the 44th [Infantry Division], which is in the region of Istria for replenishment right now, then they'd be outside Vienna.

THE FÜHRER: Outside Vienna. We could do that.

KEITEL: The *Hoch- und Deutschmeister* [Division][1447]

WENCK: Because these forces will be engaged around here.

THE FÜHRER: I think we can take that risk.[1448]

JODL: In the region of Istria we do have the 71st [Infantry Division]. That means the loss of another division, of course, which later on was supposed to move to the Southern front. But now, in the winter, I think it is [—]

THE FÜHRER: We could do that. How does the 44th look at the moment?

JODL: They are not at their best, but one couldn't say that they are unable to fight. They will be about [—]

THE FÜHRER: What strength?

JODL: Numerically—I have that here—it won't be that much.[1449]

THE FÜHRER: This would be another possibility, to bring them in here—anywhere, it doesn't matter—to bring one division in here and—

WENCK: —the Hungarian one further down, and here we should take another German division.

THE FÜHRER: We take it between them.

WENCK: There are still Germans here—some of them police regiments. Then the 10th Hungarian Division [—]

THE FÜHRER: There are Germans here anyway.

WENCK: Yes, here are Germans and police.

THE FÜHRER: We'll have to see what we can scratch together. What kind is the 31st?

FEGELEIN: That's a Russian one again, my Führer.[1450] One is Siegling,[1451] the other one is Kaminski.

THE FÜHRER: This one doesn't appear to have any value.

FEGELEIN: It has about 8,000 to 10,000 men. But at that time you had authorized them to come into this area.

THE FÜHRER: Back then there was nothing there. But if it's no good, if the Russians now [—]

FEGELEIN: I can find out right away.

THE FÜHRER: If the Russians attack!

FEGELEIN: They were put in there because they had the whole baggage train with them. They were the ones who joined in the shooting on the train in Hungary. There were two different groups: one was Siegling and one was Kaminski. That one is with the whole baggage train. Some Cossack units have been pulled in here, because they haven't done well elsewhere.[1452]

THE FÜHRER: Do you believe they will do better here?

FEGELEIN: Yes, Sir. They have not caused any trouble lately. The Russians will kill them all, if they get them. I don't believe they will desert and go over to the enemy.

THE FÜHRER: Really? They won't go over to the enemy?

FEGELEIN: They are their greatest adversaries. But I can double-check again.

THE FÜHRER: Find out what kind of unit this is, and how it is equipped, ...

FEGELEIN: Yes, Sir, my Führer!

THE FÜHRER: I don't ask for the reasons. They were officially cited lately; they are embarrassed, anyway.

WENCK: Then, my Führer, there were several attempts to cross the Tisza, in many places; these attempts were repulsed where German troops were stationed. Only here with the Hungarians—in this place and in this place— did the enemy manage to cross. Here parts of the German 3rd Division are being brought over. It's the same thing with the Hungarians; there is a bridge-head there as well. Here they were all turned away, and here two battalions of the 3rd Mountain Division were brought over to remove this bridge-head. Two more battalions were brought in here, to take action against these. You can't always depend on the Hungarians.[1453] Otherwise, there is nothing particular on this front, only a few isolated attempts to get closer to the Tisza. Here there are mostly Romanians. I believe there is no need to worry. Besides, the reconnaissance detachment of the 8th Jäger Division will be brought in here, and the same will happen with the Hungarians—the reconnaissance detachment of the 4th Mountain Division will be placed behind the Hungarians. In addition, the army group plans at the end to pull out the 15th [Infantry] Division, after the 4th Mountain Division is in here, to build up another reserve here, in order to either bring them in here later or pull them in over here. The 18th SS Panzer Grenadier Division comes[1454] [—]

THE FÜHRER: Of course, the affair didn't go the way we expected. Bashing our heads into the wall[1455] has become an obsession with us; it doesn't lead anywhere.

WENCK: The forces have to be concentrated again, anyway. With these forces we can't build a line. It is impossible.

THE FÜHRER: But they start building up a line, instead of concentrating them in here. I had doubts right from the start, as they moved away from the Tisza. As soon as something like this comes up, it can only be a sign of something fishy for us. It's getting rotten already. Running around here in front makes no sense. It's useless to build up a front here. When it is built, they will move over here. What then?

WENCK: My Führer, unfortunately all the divisions are very exhausted [—]

THE FÜHRER: It's worse when they go at the head than if we pass by here.

WENCK: The break in the fighting continues for Army Group A and also for Army Group Center. There is nothing new to report. There are the same preparations. Today there was quite a significant night air-reconnaissance mission: 1,400 vehicles here, 2,500 vehicles here, which are all moving into the supposed areas in night marches. We will probably get the 68th [Infantry] Division up here in time—before the attack, I believe—to get these divisions out of here. Otherwise, the transport of the 19th Panzer Division is going according to plan as well, with 26 trains, and will be completely assembled, together with the combat element, in three days.

THE FÜHRER: This one here is stupid, of course.

WENCK: Yes, indeed! I don't believe he will attack here, my Führer; he will probably attack here in this area on both sides of Debica[1456] and around here.

THE FÜHRER: He will attack here!

WENCK: We have created local reserves here.

THE FÜHRER: He might want to unite forces. His major attack will no doubt be here, to break out of this situation.

WENCK: Yes, but we'll get together four or five divisions around here as well. If the infantry division comes out in time, we'll have the 3rd [Panzer], the 17th Panzer, 16th Panzer, 20th Panzer Grenadier Division and the 19th Panzer—and perhaps the 25th Panzer, which doesn't need to go to the Magnushev bridgehead.[1457] Then it probably will be contained. But two reserve regiments have also been pulled out. [—] Here the replacements arrived, with some livelier traffic; all the well-known features. 26 trains out of 60.

THE FÜHRER: As strong as 60 trains?

WENCK: Sixty trains with replacement elements, 45 trains with combat elements. The 25th is complete here. Here there are the two battalions of the security regiment, which is brought in here and which will go behind the 337th [Infantry Division] as reserve. Here there are movements as well, but not much above usual strength: 330 trains. There is another regiment of the 3rd Panzer Division in here—it should move out. The 6th Panzer Division is quite competent. The 104th Panzer Brigade, which came out of here, will go to the 25th, and will be pulled out. Thirty-four trains left from here.

THE FÜHRER: Can't you strengthen the SS "T" [*Totenkopf* SS Panzer Division][1458] a little bit here? That way you might—there are so many battalions there—bring in a few battalions, to maybe give the whole sector to the SS "T," so we can get the *Viking* [SS Panzer Division] out of here anyway?

(FEGELEIN: Yes, Sir!)

If we brought in some more battalions, we could then possibly draw on them later.

WENCK: That would be very good.

FEGELEIN: The Reichsführer will come over here afterward anyway.

THE FÜHRER: To get the *Viking* out of here. It will certainly be the case that one would be glad—at worst, we take something out here to change something here, or we might let them stay together so the division won't fall apart. How does the 73rd [Infantry Division] look at the moment?

WENCK: The 73rd is in much better condition with 5 battalions. It has done fairly well again, and, according to reports, it should be fit for action again as a division.

THE FÜHRER: I don't want to tear apart the corps; that is very clear. Here we could ... back behind and the 3rd Panzer Division [—]

WENCK: Anyway, my Führer, we wanted to schedule the 3rd for East Prussia.

THE FÜHRER: To save a division here—you can get in contact right away—we might put in a few battalions.

FEGELEIN: Yes, Sir!

WENCK: The 102nd Panzer Brigade will be brought down here, to provide a little reserve against this local reinforcement. [—] The battle for Goldap: In the three days of fighting for Goldap, the Soviets lost 1,739 dead, 246 prisoners, 59 tanks and assault guns, 134 guns of all kinds, 54 mortars.

THE FÜHRER: That is why I crossed out "1,739 dead" in the Armed Forces report, my dear sirs, because the number of dead and captured—2,000 altogether—bears no relationship to 59 tanks and 134 guns of all kinds. Because 2,000 men are one regiment, practically, and for one regiment 134 guns is a lot. That's a gun for every 15 or 20 men.[1459]

WENCK: Probably quite a lot have run off.

THE FÜHRER: They have probably gotten out as well. But the other deduction is also possible, as everyone says, that the divisions are so weak that this character is making a huge bluff with his so-called "divisions." That's what's being said on all sides. He's counting on his artillery. He is concentrating it. Apart from this, his divisions are so weak—just a few thousand men.

WENCK: It was also quite strange that he had to call forces down from here in order to bring in reinforcements at Goldap. He didn't bring them from the same area.

THE FÜHRER: We have to look at a thing like this in an exacting manner. How is it possible? We have to take the results again. We formed quite a number of pockets. The results in terms of deaths and prisoners were always minimal. We've had pockets with 7 divisions inside, where we took 2,000 prisoners and killed another 2,000. But where are the rest? And then it is said that he attacks with huge crowds of infantry. But if we ever made such an encirclement, there was never anything in it. But it has always been like this. It was like this already in 1941. Except for a few major attacks, the results have been very meager in general.[1460]

WENCK: My Führer, the 21st [Infantry] Division will come in here, starting tonight, and will relieve the 5th Panzer Division and the 547th Volksgrenadier Division. That way the 5th Panzer Division will be in reserve again, and the 547th will be refurbished a bit—and the 561st as well—to relieve additional panzer forces afterward. We'd like to try, maybe with a division, when one of the two has been filled back up, to pull *Grossdeutschland* [Panzer Grenadier Division] out up here, if it is strong enough. But we'll have to support Memel adequately with assault guns, so nothing happens.

THE FÜHRER: We'll have to drive whatever we can there.

WENCK: *Grossdeutschland* has 6 battalions up there right now, so we could use this division here. [—] The dispersal here in this sector continues. There are 32 fewer battery positions.

THE FÜHRER: The dispersal was here?

WENCK: Yesterday the reconnaissance report was here, at this corner. We don't quite believe it, but the army group [—]

THE FÜHRER: Maybe he's stopping because the whole matter seems too costly to him, this whole system here. He must have had doubts. He always has a certain fear of sending his units into a good area, because there Bolshevism becomes absurd. So it's possible that he might move them here to the south[1461] and that he says he's reached his goal here—to break the whole thing out.

WENCK: But there he has had very heavy losses.

THE FÜHRER: That's why!

WENCK: In the North, my Führer, the heavy defensive battle continues.[1462] But everything held yesterday as well, except for some local penetrations, which were generally cleared up or sealed off. Yesterday 41 tanks were knocked out again. Here there are quite a few gaps. But the 205th [Infantry Division] will come, which will probably be deployed today; likewise units of the security division. A local focal point is obviously still forming here.

THE FÜHRER: There is no doubt that his strength is decreasing. Just imagine—he storms in here with 90 divisions, which he can only assemble in one or two groups in the strength of one regiment [—]

WENCK: Today is the eleventh day. So far, 522 tanks have been destroyed.

THE FÜHRER: He has an enormous number of tanks.

WENCK: Compared with that, our materiel losses thus far have been: three 3.5-cm [guns], seven 1.FH [Model 1 field howitzers], nine 12.2[-cm] Russian [guns] and one 15-cm [gun].

THE FÜHRER: Small losses; that's right. Small losses, if we stand! All our losses have taken place because of the "glorious" retreats—those retreats we make to achieve "operational freedom."

WENCK: Here no changes are reported in the enemy situation. In the region of Sworbe only reconnaissance activity.[1463] (*Lieutenant General Wenck excuses himself.*)

THE FÜHRER: Take care! How will you get there?

WENCK: I will go partly by train and partly by car.

THE FÜHRER: Just leave the train in time, so you ...[1464]

Situation at sea

VOSS: There is nothing new to be reported regarding the Navy situation, my Führer. The enemy continued to be quiet yesterday in the Baltic Sea as well; enemy submarines are positioned here.[1465] All the transports and all other movements are going according to plan. Nothing unusual in Norway. In the North Sea and off the coast of the Netherlands, the weather is bad, so action at sea has been impossible. On the other hand, Navy artillery barges and Navy artillery lighters have fired at the enemy positions in the Schelde [Estuary] again. [—] A submarine returning from the Atlantic reports the sinking of an 8,000-ton steamer. Only the first part of the radio transmission was received; the other part was garbled. It's possible that we will hear more when the submarine returns.[1466] No other reports.

HEWEL: The Navy would like to extend its operations in the Baltic Sea, and has asked us to inform the Swedes of this, mainly because of the mines.[1467] (*Presentation.*) The new picture will be like that. [—] I wanted to present this.

Situation in the air

BÜCHS: In the Hungarian combat area in the East there are 118 fighter-bombers southeast of Budapest deployed against the traffic from Szeged to

Kecskemet. There's also fighter-bomber deployment at the Drau. [—] In the Reich territory, there have been—according to our reports—17 planes shot down by anti-aircraft guns. The enemy admits an astonishingly high number: 61 losses altogether—31 heavy bombers and 30 fighters.[1468] Yesterday 11 Lightnings attempted to attack the Eder dam again with heavy bombers.[1469] All the bombs fell on open fields or into the water. No damage to the dams. Our deployment in the area near the front: 92 airplanes without enemy contact. One loss on our side. [—] The main focus of the railway fighting [—]

THE FÜHRER: Do you ever read these reports, too, or are they presented to the Reichsmarshal?

BÜCHS: Yes.

THE FÜHRER: Like the one by Gauleiter Hoffmann[1470] on the attack on Bochum?

CHRISTIAN: They are not presented to the Reichsmarshal.

THE FÜHRER: Why not?

CHRISTIAN: I don't know. They go to the party chancellery.[1471]

THE FÜHRER: From us here! After you have read them.

BÜCHS: Gruppenführer Bormann[1472] brought them over this morning.

CHRISTIAN: The last one from Essen I got from Büchs.

BÜCHS: I got a copy today and might be able to pass it on.

THE FÜHRER: I have been assured that he is carpet-bombing during the night, and they're hitting fantastically. [—] And how many? There are 85 aircraft here. Seventy-one are for the hydrogenation plants.

BÜCHS: They had started. The weather was cloudless here in the area of Brüx.

CHRISTIAN: We thought the attack was going to be against Brüx.

THE FÜHRER: Of the 3,100 we are supposed to have,[1473] these 85 are [—]!

BÜCHS: Without the replacements, my Führer, it would be 3,100.

CHRISTIAN: The Reichsmarshal has ordered that all these new groups now standing by should be deployed in a single day—a day when the weather doesn't pose a problem—all together, in one strike.

THE FÜHRER: I'm just afraid that when this day comes, the groups won't come together and that they won't find the enemy and won't be able to make contact with him. I would prefer, in such a situation, that we had focused on one thing, even if we only had 300 planes, and destroyed it.

CHRISTIAN: Yes, Sir!

THE FÜHRER: Instead, we scatter again in all directions. If he comes with 300 planes, we should tackle them. We should throw everything at them. That doesn't matter. If we should ever get 1,000 [—]

BÜCHS: Fighters from the Fourth Air Fleet were deployed against the approach to Vienna yesterday. Sixty-two, including some Hungarian fighters, engaged in aerial combat, and we shot down four four-engine planes—plus five were shot down by anti-aircraft guns, so nine altogether. The British admit to losing 12.

THE FÜHRER: I have thought it over, recently—I don't know if it has been reported to the Reichsmarshal or not—I've thought the whole thing over recently, and I have come to the following conclusion. Eighty aircraft have been shot down recently.

BÜCHS: Eighty-two.[1474]

THE FÜHRER: Of these 80, the fighters shot down 50 and 30 were shot down by anti-aircraft guns. These 30 we have to leave aside for the moment. Four hundred and ninety aircraft have engaged in aerial combat.

BÜCHS: Three hundred and five!

THE FÜHRER: All right, 305 have engaged in aerial combat. You recently said 490.

BÜCHS: No, 305. None of the Frankfurt fighter wing has had aerial combat, and of the 4th Fighter Wing—

THE FÜHRER: All right, 305! It doesn't matter. Including—he said—an assault squadron, which was deployed with 42 aircraft. This assault squadron alone has shot down 30.

BÜCHS: Both assault groups. There were two assault groups.[1475]

THE FÜHRER: With altogether—?

BÜCHS: With altogether 62 airplanes. Sixty-one of them have engaged in aerial combat.

THE FÜHRER: All right, 61!

BÜCHS: They have shot down 30 four-engine planes.

THE FÜHRER: So there are 20 left. If you subtract the 60 planes from 305, there are 240 left. So 240 planes together have shot down only 20 in aerial combat and have themselves lost: the assault squadron 30—

BÜCHS: The assault squadron: 30.

THE FÜHRER: —and the others have lost 90. So with 90 losses they have shot down 20 altogether in 240 sorties.

CHRISTIAN: Something else. The assault group has another group with it to give them cover.

THE FÜHRER: I don't care. I say, the covering group has to shoot as well—it's not just bombers that have been shot down, but also fighters.

BÜCHS: Of course.

THE FÜHRER: So the result is totally unsatisfactory.

CHRISTIAN: The deciding factor in this issue is that the 30 shot down by the assault groups [—]

THE FÜHRER: Is there anyone among you who goes through all these matters and analyses everything closely? The Reichsmarshal doesn't know this anyway.[1476] When he was here recently, he didn't even know that our losses are bigger, because they are confusing the whole picture with those damned "failed-to-land reports."[1477]

CHRISTIAN: That's presented daily.

THE FÜHRER: I want this calculation. This is striking evidence that either the fighter pilots or the aircraft are useless. The fighter pilots—we can't claim that, because they are shot down. So the planes are useless. But I get the opposite judgment from the Luftwaffe. The planes are good. It's ridiculous. If I do the calculations on this matter, I get a devastating result.

BÜCHS: Of the 65 airplanes that originally went missing during this mission, 38 have been found and 27 are still missing. The 38 airplanes were totally destroyed; of the pilots, 32 were dead and 6 were wounded or returned safe and sound.

THE FÜHRER: How many are still missing? 28?

BÜCHS: Twenty-seven are still missing.

THE FÜHRER: It is very clear. Those that they found ... with every such loss.

BÜCHS: In Italy there was a very heavy deployment of twin-engine fighters against the railway yesterday, especially against the routes in the region of Trent. The Italians deployed 23 fighters; 4 twin-engines were shot down without any loss on our side.

THE FÜHRER: This is a miscalculation, too. I was recently presented a calculation. One needs some time to catch on to this. I was presented with a calculation a month ago, but it should have said how many sorties have been flown. For one month alone it looks great. But the number of sorties is—

BÜCHS: I do present the number of sorties. But I don't have them for the complete month.

THE FÜHRER: That's why! It's so minimal.

CHRISTIAN: But they are percentages, my Führer.

BÜCHS: My Führer, from the first of the month I'll pursue these sorties, especially for missing-person reports.

THE FÜHRER: There must be somebody to go through all of these issues and draw some conclusions and consequences. One can't simply say, "That's the way it is!"

CHRISTIAN: My Führer, there's an ongoing planning session at ... Reich Air Force, Colonel General Stumpff,[1478] is responsible for it. Galland, as the inspector, can talk to the troops.[1479] The Reichsmarshal always has with him [—]

THE FÜHRER: I must say—such a calculation has never been presented to me.

CHRISTIAN: My Führer, I have lots of tables like this.

THE FÜHRER: But I never get any analysis. I have to do it myself.

CHRISTIAN: That was the first impression: the assault group has shot down 30 four-engine bombers.

THE FÜHRER: Thirty. And the anti-aircraft guns 30 as well. So there are 20 left. These come from 260 aerial battles. That's a very bad result. I deploy 260 fighters and shoot down 20. So if I deploy 2,000, I shoot down 200. So I can't count at all on the fact that somehow with these planes—and there are still tons of them being produced. They're only eating up labor and materiel![1480]

CHRISTIAN: The boys haven't flown for 10 days, and that, my Führer, is the real reason.

THE FÜHRER: We always had "reasons" before, too!

CHRISTIAN: It has an effect. On the other hand, the wing that started in the West with bad weather has landed without losses—because it flies every day, even in bad weather. That has an effect, surely.

THE FÜHRER: I won't say anything against the airmen, just against the results; nothing changes there. Because with 2,600 planes I have the possibility of shooting down 200. In other words, the hope of decimating the enemy with a mass deployment is not realistic. So it is insanity to go on producing the aircraft, just to give the Luftwaffe the chance to operate with numbers!

BÜCHS: Reconnaissance reports from the Balkans indicate that there is a significant stream of supplies coming from Italy to the bands, both day and night. Reconnaissance reported this movement of motorized units yesterday already. Then these corps northwest of Belgrade were also confirmed by reconnaissance again yesterday. Supplies are coming from the region of Budapest. Nothing in particular from the Kecskemet area.

Reinforcements for the Eastern front

THE FÜHRER: So how does the 44th [Infantry] Division look?

JODL: I don't have the last strength report, because there it says: "being relieved at the moment." At least they seem to be equipped with enough artillery and antitank guns. They seem to have lost a few heavy infantry weapons. But with a small amount of refitting from the Vienna area, the division should be usable anyway.

FEGELEIN: The 31st [Infantry] Division, my Führer, consists mainly of Hungarians, of volunteers. There is almost nothing left of the Russian personnel.[1481] There's only the German permanent staff of the Kammerer division,[1482] which was down there. But that'll take about two more months. It still doesn't have any fighting strength, since it's all untrained men. We could bring 2,000 men from the *Viking* into the *Totenkopf*, and get the *Viking* out that way. But we must check to see if they can really use 2,000 men from the *Viking*, because of their junior officers. We have to give something from the *Viking* to the *Totenkopf*, even if it means they'll be ready later. That doesn't matter.[1483]

THE FÜHRER: ...

FEGELEIN: I've told him that already.

Situation in the air (continued)

BÜCHS: Sorties during the night against columns in the region of Kecskemet and deployment of 10 fighters against the railway station at Arad. Reconnaissance reports strong movements in front of Army Group A, generally toward the northwest. Tonight reconnaissance of the San-Vistula triangle and into the Baranov bridgehead.

THE FÜHRER: We have to be careful here. This is all distraction, what he's doing here. He's trying to break this thing out of here. He must have the feeling that he will have to leave lots of blood on German ground up here.

BÜCHS: In the West there were incursions as far as Stuttgart by two Mosquito units, each with about 36 aircraft. We deployed 36 He 111s for the V 1 shelling of London,[1484] and 17 aircraft to supply the fortresses.[1485] [—] From Italy only modest fighter-bomber sorties near the front region south of Bologna. [—] The weather situation: On the back of this bad-weather front, which is passing through central Germany from East Prussia, there are dispersing clouds from the West with good visibility for fighters; lower limit 500 to 1,000 m. At the moment, incursions in the region of Hamburg and the Ruhr area; almost complete cloud cover, upper limit reaching very high. Perhaps the approach was supposed to have gone further to the east, but the units turned to the northwest and dropped bombs on Hamburg and Neustrelitz. [—] In Italy, deployment wasn't hindered. In the Po Valley the fog is quite heavy already and probably won't lift today. Above the fog there is good visibility in the direction of the Alpine railway routes. [—] In the East, deployment in Hungary is impossible. Along the rest of the front, especially in the area of Army Group North, deployment is seriously hindered.

The Southeast

JODL: No new reports from the islands. No new reports from Greece, either. In the overall picture of the forces, there's a report from our combat reconnaissance, that here—relieving the Bulgarians—Russian forces, including tanks and also ... parts of troops, are coming to the Turkish-Bulgarian border here.

KEITEL: Those that are relieving the Bulgarians.

JODL: Those that are relieving the Bulgarians there.

THE FÜHRER: So, is this report confirmed?[1486]

JODL: One can't swear to it yet, my Führer. But if they build up and come from several sources, then they will probably be right. There are people being sent across the front—so probably through Bulgaria, Macedonia and Greece.

KEITEL: We'll wait for confirmation.

JODL: It'll show after a while.

THE FÜHRER: Do we have anything from Turkey?

HEWEL: We haven't received a report yet.

JODL: Turkey would have to confirm it in the end, when they get to the border. ... Then, in the Kraijevo area, this movement of forces toward the west has been confirmed, but not as far as we thought, to the road between Kraijevo and Uzice, but only within the front. In the area west and south of Belgrade, the Russians continue to disperse. On the other hand, two Russian corps that used to be in the region of Belgrade are now between the Tisza and the Danube, for certain.

THE FÜHRER: We really have to go there and pull this one division away even faster.

JODL: Yes!

THE FÜHRER: But if it is already here in the area—tell me, Sonnleithner: if we bring the 44th Division, the Vienna Division, down here to the Danube, do you think that is good?

V. SONNLEITHNER: I do believe they'd feel like they were protecting Vienna.[1487]

THE FÜHRER: Good!

V. SONNLEITHNER: Because it is obvious that the Viennese are afraid of the Russians. They're beginning already.

THE FÜHRER: Good! [—] I don't want them to say: let's go to the Prater! [an amusement park in Vienna]

JODL: The left wing of the Fourth Bulgarian Army was thrown back by a counterattack. Afterward the rear guard of the regiment of the 22nd cleared off. The rear guards are assumed to be along the Daruma line and to the west of it.

THE FÜHRER: Here the opponent has been thrown back?

JODL: These attacks around Kocane were repelled. [—] Here the enemy was thrown back again near Kumanova. Here heavy losses in some parts. This will all be covered. Further to the north, near Prinjavac, the Russians were quiet.

THE FÜHRER: The only difficulty is fighting our way across the road.[1488]

JODL: Here's the difficulty. The mopping-up group, starting from Prijepolje, pushed out quite a ways over the Bistrica. Quite a bit of this road is destroyed.

THE FÜHRER: I have only one big worry: when winter comes.

JODL: On this part there were damages. They were just confirmed by the air reconnaissance. Otherwise, I don't see any other difficulties there at the moment. In the Kravaljo area the local actions have become a bit livelier as well. But there were no more major attacks. The 223rd [Infantry] Division is tied down by prisoners. So it didn't withdraw there, not in that direction. West of it is the 93rd Russian [Rifle] Division and then one Yugoslav brigade. In comparison to their usual combat actions, the Russians are rather cautious here.

THE FÜHRER: That's clearly hard to supply—these units here.

JODL: Also in this region there is nothing remarkable except for the Tito bands and some Russian reinforcement. There must be a unit in here, a Russian one, one or two. At least he mounted a strong attack against the 118th Jäger Division on the north wing. They tried to take that back by counterattack. After this failed, the seizure of this position, which was supposed to be held, is now demanded.

THE FÜHRER: That's nonsense.

JODL: They are quite ... Then all of a sudden very strong air reconnaissance started.

THE FÜHRER: And what happens if they are pushed back here as well into the final position? And if they are pushed back from there, nothing will bring them back. I believe the Commander-in-Chief Southeast[1489] will be as unconscious of its importance here, as he was here.

JODL: He'll stop here, just because he has to stop here and he has extended the positions at least a bit. Because he has to stop here. Because we don't have anything else around here. There is nothing up there.

THE FÜHRER: He should go further ahead here. This is probably ... extended.

JODL: At the moment we can't bring anything up too fast. There is only one section that's passable. That is this one here. Everything else is marching cross-country. And nothing can be freed up from this region either,[1490] because the Sarajevo area will probably be seriously threatened by bands [partisans] soon. Yesterday 150 supply planes flew in here all of a sudden, so one can see that these forces are being replenished.

THE FÜHRER: How is it back here? Are there gangs back here, or is anything coming up from behind?

JODL: No, that runs right through. That's where all the rear services of Army Group E and everything come; usually that goes up in the back and covers the street. So we'll be able to move through this one road.

THE FÜHRER: Go on!

JODL: In Croatia the front has stabilized south of Mostar with the regiment from the 118th Jäger Division. Several attacks by bands from the south were all repelled. There were no English with them, only gangs; at one time parts of the (51st) Airborne Division had been mentioned.

THE FÜHRER: I think it is quite funny. They obviously didn't reach very clear agreements in Moscow, regarding this being British territory, because they do it so timidly.[1491] The Greek government came here now and dispersed all these gangs. I don't know if you read this, but they're disbanding all the Communist gangs. It was reported today.[1492] They are certainly doing it because of British pressure. But the British don't even appear around here. So, if they had reached such a clear agreement—just imagine: if the Russians appear in this area, the British would appear quite officially. But they don't do it officially.

JODL: This one division up there is certainly there as support, the 31st, and 34th is there ...

CHRISTIAN: There are two things that might still give us something to think about. In the Sarajevo area there are planes flying in continually with supplies. Second, two close-combat corps have been deployed here on the Italian front: one American corps—that one was comparably weak—and on the right wing a very strong British one. The British corps has been pulled out—the American one has taken over the whole front—but we still don't know where it has moved to and there are no good indications yet. But it may have some kind of relationship up here.

THE FÜHRER: That they would move over here? They could hardly go over here.

JODL: I believe that could come, too.[1493]

THE FÜHRER: First of all, they won't come here into Hungarian territory, because there are Bolsheviks there anyway. They can't go westward, in here.

CHRISTIAN: They could possibly move over here.

THE FÜHRER: It's possible that they are freeing up a close-combat corps just in case, because the tension seems to be steadily increasing, in spite of all the polite phrases they exchange. It's possible that they might free up a close-combat corps for Greece or for in here. It is certain that the Russians will attack here. I would guess that the whole story will be finished in two or three weeks. And whoever holds the Dardanelles won't stay on one side—that is very clear: he has to occupy the other side as well; he has to get it, too. One only has a thoroughfare if both sides are controlled. So he[1494] also takes the second action here, and with that, the whole building starts to collapse.

CHRISTIAN: If those forces really are pulled out of here, my Führer, it certainly does affect the whole Italian front, if they take the strong air force away from here.

THE FÜHRER: I'm surprised by one thing. This explanation they have given, now by Alexander,[1495] that this whole front[1496] has become so weak, that the withdrawing of French and American divisions [—]

CHRISTIAN: Rear services!

THE FÜHRER: They say the whole thing wasn't any stronger than here; they were no stronger than we were. So if they continue boxing here, they will need the close-combat corps even more.

CHRISTIAN: Yes, Sir!

THE FÜHRER: I don't believe that they would just jump over with the close-combat corps; they can't do that. They need to have a base first. And they don't have any at the moment. They certainly won't go in here. That's Russian territory. So they can only stand by, either for the French territory, and it could be possible that they withdraw them over there, or—what I believe—they stand by, ready for anything, to come in here.

JODL: But here they are withdrawing four-engine bombers.

CHRISTIAN: So far very insignificantly, Colonel General

JODL: In the region ...

CHRISTIAN: A few in southern France.

THE FÜHRER: Either they go to France, or they come up here. I would think—

CHRISTIAN: It is apparently not yet possible to get supplies for the four-engine in France.

THE FÜHRER: But I would think, rather, that they are standing by, because for England this is a very important question.

JODL: So the British could have done something around here, with the situation we're in. He only needed to land somewhere here[1497] and he'd cut us off completely.

THE FÜHRER: With the help of the gangs around here! He would just have to push in here.

JODL: That would be totally cut off.

THE FÜHRER: He does have relatively good roads in Albania. They're not bad. The Italians have built them up somewhat.

JODL: Even if he didn't want Albania, he could have landed in northern Greece.

THE FÜHRER: But here!

JODL: But in Albania he could have done it at any time.

Finland

THE FÜHRER: Where's the press?

DIETRICH: My Führer!

THE FÜHRER: The "VB" has commented on this Finnish Ministry of the Interior statement in the most idiotic way. Look at this.

DIETRICH: I only read the first one yesterday, my Führer, in the Sunday evening paper.

THE FÜHRER: That one is good.

DIETRICH: That was because of your order. The "VB" [editor] did it himself, before he read this.

THE FÜHRER: That doesn't matter. It is childish. They can repeat that. But even better [—]

DIETRICH: Yes, Sir. Then we will do that.[1498]

Southeast again

JODL: The Second Panzer Army has, for the most part, taken this mountain pass position; also now in the center, with the XV Corps, where the last units have fought through from Drnis[1499] to Knin. On these passes the front is blocked off to the west. Nothing out of the ordinary has happened in Croatia or the area around Agram.

Finland

In Finland it was reported this morning that these Russians and Finns have actually been united starting from Ivalo. Not the Russians but the Finns are pursuing along the road to Varanger Fjord.[1500]

THE FÜHRER: News is now coming from Finland—and not from us anymore, but from other sources—that the resistance in Finland is really starting to organize. The disbanding of the White Guards: they'd have refused that; they couldn't allow themselves to be disarmed. The statements of the Minister of the Interior are to be understood in this context. They certainly did have their reasons. This worsening mood didn't appear out of nowhere. I am convinced that clever propaganda should be able to subvert this.[1501]

JODL: If we come here now, and if we stand here, and they might likely be forced to attack here—the Finns—then I think it might be possible—if we might possibly undertake a counterattack in winter—that we could, in conjunction with the propaganda, cause this to be disbanded.

THE FÜHRER: We should really set up a Finnish Free Corps within our own forces,[1502] and they should make an appeal. We shouldn't make it; they should.

JODL: No pressure at all on the XIX Mountain Corps. The 6th Mountain Division has withdrawn to here.

THE FÜHRER: That's very surprising.

JODL: He doesn't push here; at the moment it is only the Finns. Here there's no particular pressure. The 6th Mountain Division with its spearhead is moving over to (Narvik) with its motorized units. The majority of the 6th Mountain Division is marching up here to the Lyngen Fjord.[1503]

THE FÜHRER: They don't have the vehicles for transportation.

JODL: The Navy doesn't have vehicles yet.

THE FÜHRER: By columns. Are there vehicles there?

JODL: With vehicles, that might work. They do it more intensely here, my Führer. But I believe we'll be in time, because the demands on the Navy are quite high at the moment. The 560th has to transport them. Up here they have transport vessels as well, because they're taking out the wounded and everything else, and obviously have to deploy heavily while clearing the coastal batteries. But this is being hurried along as much as possible.

THE FÜHRER: And this is the 2nd [Infantry Division]?

JODL: The 2nd has now reached Porsanger Fjord. The 163rd [Infantry Division] is at the border and the 169th [Infantry Division] north of Ivalo.[1504] (Presentation.) This is another overview of the battery clearings. The red batteries have been destroyed, the violet ones have been cleared or are being cleared right now, and of the violet ones, which are dismantled up here, these green ones have been build up again already. One can see that these batteries here are still ready for action. They're being dismantled.

THE FÜHRER: A green one has been built up here?

JODL: Yes, indeed. One has been built up there! But that can only be a mobile one. Because it won't stay. That was there where they brought a battalion in as well.

THE FÜHRER: Where is the Tirpitz?[1505]

VOSS: Here!

THE FÜHRER: Couldn't we bring something more over here?

JODL: A new one just arrived there.

THE FÜHRER: On this island. This one is most at risk; there's no doubt about it.

VOSS: Tomorrow morning I will get another map of the Navy batteries, my Führer. Maybe we can put this aside until tomorrow.

THE FÜHRER: So he evades the heaviest Navy batteries. I am convinced he will give the 40-cm batteries a wide berth.

Sweden

JODL: I have confirmed this press report from Stockholm about the pursuit onto Swedish territory of a Norwegian man with wife and child; the following was reported. It was quite far to the south—here is Oslo—it was in this location. It is more or less correct.[1506] (Presentation.)

THE FÜHRER: We have to give a very clear order now.

JODL: It's doubtful that it's necessary to punish someone.

THE FÜHRER: Don't punish anyone!

JODL: That wouldn't make any sense. And the other question up there, about this straw—that comes next—that seems exaggerated. (*Presentation.*)

THE FÜHRER: Violation of neutrality of the Finns; Sweden: building up a Norwegian corps.[1507]

JODL: Up there we are in a region where nobody knows where the border is. So this will be a regular request; that's why we will get an official from the Foreign Office.[1508]

THE FÜHRER: Do you know what I feel? I personally have the feeling that the Swedes will take this as an opportunity to bring up reinforcements themselves. They won't be bringing up the reinforcements because of us, though, but because of the Russians. But they are afraid to declare this officially.[1509] That's why they come here and say we took a small heap of straw. That's the whole reason. That's why they're moving a division up here. We should say this calmly, "They should not be so cowardly about why they're coming up here." We should say it quite openly. Wouldn't that be the best way? Talk to your minister, and see if it wouldn't be best to write calmly in the press that they're planning to bring some divisions up here, and they motivate this by a man having taken some hay from a Swedish barn. They should not be so cowardly and should just admit that they're afraid of the Russians.[1510]

West

JODL: Concerning the situation in France: this corps is still dispersing around—Hertogenbosch and is pulling forces—the 15th—probably in the direction of Nijmegen and Arnhem, and the 7th Division in the direction of the bridgehead at Venlo, where the attacks have increased significantly.

THE FÜHRER: The bridges at Moerdijk have been blown up?

JODL: The bridges at Moerdijk have been blown up, although the bridgehead is still holding; it's been pushed in at one place here, and also here, but the bridges are gone. Here the counterattack made quite good progress. Some of the Americans—including parts of the 28th American [Infantry] Division, which is new—have been cut off here and encircled.[1511]

THE FÜHRER: This is Steinhoff, or what's his name?

JODL: Schmidt, the one with the ... transport movements,[1512] in spite of the unbelievably strong attacks, have been quite good, so the 272nd [Infantry] Division with 30 trains is there. The 9th Mortar Brigade is approaching and will reach the region of (Düren) on the 7th. The 12th Volksgrenadier

Division has arrived with 6 trains, and the 212th [Infantry Division] is here—it departed from East Prussia, from Lötzen—with 8 trains arriving on the 7th. Twenty-two trains are there from the 25th Volksgrenadier Division. The 277th [Infantry Division] will arrive here between November 7 and 18. Of the 25th Panzer Grenadier Division, 14 trains have arrived. From the 401st Volksartillerie [Peoples Artillery] Corps, 3 trains have arrived. From the 708th [Infantry] Division, the first trains will arrive on the 7th, having departed with 7 trains from Slovakia. [—] The plans of the Commander-in-Chief West have arrived now. [—] Then another [formation], the 401st Artillery Corps, which has arrived with 3 trains, will come in here. Here in Middelburg—on an island in a town with 30,000 men—is a group of some hundred Germans, mainly supply troops.[1513]

THE FÜHRER: With 30,000 men?

JODL: Thirty thousand inhabitants.

THE FÜHRER: You said: with 30,000 men.

JODL: With 30,000 inhabitants. There are about a hundred soldiers facing fire from all sides. It must be quite chaotic in the city. The forces down here are still partly holding here and here, and a group here. The battery was even taken again, but it has been lost again. No entry into the Schelde [Estuary] yet. But in the mouth of the Schelde there is minesweeper activity.[1514] [—] In the area of the Fifteenth Army, this westernmost corner post, near Willemstad at the mouth of the Rhine, was pushed in during the course of the concentric attack against the 346th [Infantry] Division along this road and along the eastern road. The attack against the bridgehead in front of the Moerdijk bridges, against the 711th [Infantry] Division, has pushed back the west wing. The bridgehead is still holding. The heavy equipment has been pulled back.

THE FÜHRER: That's good.

JODL: And not by using the bridges—but they [the bridges] weren't being used even before, because they had continuous artillery fire. So it didn't make any sense to keep them. Otherwise an explosive charge or cable might have been shot through. [—] Then the bridgehead of—Hertogenbosch has been pushed back by an attack, mainly from the southwest, but also from the south. [—] Here the situation is more difficult at the moment, because the crossing—the bridge was destroyed beforehand—didn't go as smoothly as here, because of the strong waves. Maybe the ferries here are not as good. So here it seems that not all the equipment is safe yet. Consequently, a counterattack was led by the 712th Division to gain time. [—] Then the opponent attacked our small bridgehead again. But we held him off, and he was thrown back again by a counterattack. [—] There's very heavy artillery fire here. It's starting to get livelier. There's nothing more down to Aachen, except a very strong sudden concentration of fire against the 3rd Panzer Grenadier Division, with 10,000 rounds impacting in their sector.

THE FÜHRER: Against the 5th or the 3rd?

JODL: Against the 3rd Panzer Grenadier Division. That means that here our movements toward the front have been crushed. But 10,000 shots were fired against this sector of the 3rd Panzer Grenadier Division. The penetration area around Germeter looks like this: the 116th Panzer Division took Vossenack, then came up over these hills here into the area south of Vossenack, then turned to the south and connected with the regiment of the 89th [Infantry Division]. That cut off the American forces here in Kommerscheidt.[1515] Then down here some of our bases are still holding.

THE FÜHRER: Anyway, here's a whole [—]

JODL: Here it's blocked off.

THE FÜHRER: Here's a group of bunkers.

JODL: Here's the connection. [—] This is to the south on the next map.

THE FÜHRER: Where's the atlas? (*Presentation of the maps of the Western Wall.*)

JODL: On November 4 and 5, there were 63 V1 launches with 5 failures and 14 V2 launches on Antwerp. [—] No changes along the whole front. It is still just the American V Corps, with thin occupation; there are about four divisions in the whole corps sector.[1516]

THE FÜHRER: Which sector is it?

JODL: From here up to south of Monschau. It's not entirely clear if this is the 4th [Infantry] Division. Here's the 2nd [Infantry] Division and the 8th [Infantry] Division.

THE FÜHRER: So it's 60 or 70 km as the crow flies. Each division has 20 km.

JODL: Nothing has changed with regard to the occupation. On the other hand, there have been new attacks from the region south of Luxembourg against our combat outposts south of the Moselle [River]. They were attacked suddenly and quite fiercely. In one place there was very difficult close combat around these small villages. Three tanks were destroyed. In the end, he threw the combat outposts back over the Moselle, and the southernmost bridgehead was given up. This could be preparation for an attack north of Diedenhofen, or maybe it's only cover for this area. Maybe he just felt uncomfortable using this as the starting point for an easier reconnaissance in depth. [—] In the region of Metz nothing new has come up. The divisions here are quite numerous. No immediate preparations for attack can be identified yet.[1517]

THE FÜHRER: Twenty km per division!

JODL: The left wing of the First Army hasn't been attacked anymore. The Nineteenth Army is fighting [—]

THE FÜHRER: One can only imagine, if we consider our own proportions: the attack against Verdun at that time took place with 7 divisions on a front of ... km. Here there are ... divisions on 11 km.

JODL: There were never more than 3 battalions in the first wave.

THE FÜHRER: Very close to each other—it was practically a division every 2 or 2½ km.

JODL: The Nineteenth Army has faced some quite lively battles. One was around Raon l'Etape, where our counterattack threw the enemy back to the edge of the forest west of Raon l'Etape. The other group was at St. Dié. This forest block held there as well, and a breakthrough further to the south was thrown back during a counterattack. Two or three battalions attacked here, so almost a regiment's strength. The attacks around here were weaker but recurring.

THE FÜHRER: What happened here?

JODL: Here a small breakthrough was eliminated. [—] The attacks in battalion strength from the southeast against Gerardmer were weaker, but repeated six times. But they were driven back. Down here the French are keeping rather quiet. The only group still fighting here is the 2nd French Armored Division. [NDT: 2nd DB]

THE FÜHRER: They're very harsh, though. Also the statement by de Gaulle. He shouldn't be so impertinent—not so impudent![1518]

JODL: I think I reported this yesterday already—this thrust at La Rochelle.

THE FÜHRER: He shouldn't forget that they've been defeated! Even more amazing is the impudence of Herr Franco.[1519]

HEWEL: Lovely! We don't need to do anything.

KEITEL: He really deserved it.

HEWEL: He deserved it.

THE FÜHRER: One always counts on the decency of others.

KEITEL: I'm surprised he wasn't struck dumb—to even say something like this!

THE FÜHRER: What would he do now if we said that the thing only failed back then because we weren't willing to relinquish our colonial clause, and we made the agreement with Pétain out of loyalty and only under the condition that the French [—][1520]

HEWEL: Do we have any interest in making him even more impossible?

THE FÜHRER: I only ask, "What would he do?" We are so decent [—]

JODL: That'll cost him his neck.

THE FÜHRER: That'll cost him his neck—that's for sure!

Italy

JODL: The weather was better, but nevertheless there was trial fire by numerous new batteries, using phosphorous [bombs] and smoke. There were no infantry attacks except in the sector of the 305th [Infantry] Division. The 305th is positioned over a broad area, and by moving reserves over from the right half of the sector it was possible to intercept the enemy again. Different groups are being relieved. Here the 34th American [Infantry Division] is being relieved and substituted by another one. We don't know yet which one it will be. Also the 1st Canadian [Infantry Division] is being relieved and substituted by another one. The only thing that worries the Commander-in-Chief Southwest at the moment is this extremely strong activity in the last few days against the railroads. He doesn't have any railways at the moment. The section from Trent to Verona is destroyed in eleven places. The alternate westward route is damaged. The only possibility at the moment is to come in through Villach and Udine to Treviso, a bit further, because all the routes are interrupted right now. Maybe it will get a little better when it gets foggy, but then he'll go against this part.

THE FÜHRER: We have to put up a smokescreen around this.

JODL: He certainly has heard about "many fighters," so he comes asking if we can't suddenly—they were so impudent that they would train all their students in bomb-dropping—if a single appearance of a hundred fighters wouldn't lead to a noteworthy success.

THE FÜHRER: That would lead to no success at all. That would lead to a success for the other side, because then the fighters would be destroyed.

JODL: We can't move anything to Italy. At most, if the northern section was to be attacked, we could appear once with fighters from the Munich area. Yesterday some fighters came; they shot two down right away.

CHRISTIAN: Italians!

JODL: They were Italians.

CHRISTIAN: Italians with German commanders, German squadron captains.

THE FÜHRER: What does that mean? The Italians are in the airplanes?

CHRISTIAN: Yes, Sir.

THE FÜHRER: So! ...

Miscellaneous

JODL: Yesterday 130 prisoners were taken in Slovakia, 15 tons of explosives were captured, 1 billion rounds of infantry ammunition, and large stores of supplies.[1521] [—] This group has been cleared out. Some went through here, about 500 men, and are now positioned for battle on the western edge of the High Tatra [Mountains]. Some of them have already been destroyed up here.

THE FÜHRER: They'll have problems getting through here. The High Tatra is an immense obstacle.

JODL: That's why they went in here. They couldn't hold in the valleys anymore. One regiment of the 18th is gone. The 154th Field Training Division has been moved here into the Rosenberg area.

THE FÜHRER: And here?

JODL: The 167th [Infantry Division] is arriving here in place of the 708th [Infantry Division].[1522]

THE FÜHRER: I thought it was in place of the 371st [Infantry Division]?

JODL: Nothing is going in there, my Führer—that one is coming down—apart from the Replacement Army, which is supposed to go in here. But no divisions. For the infantry, though, a division will come in here. Here, the Replacement Army has been ordered to fill in some more. But, I believe, we still can get this area under control. It has now been covered so closely [—]

THE FÜHRER: When can the 44th [Infantry Division] be moved out? We have to do this very quickly.

JODL: I have already spoken to him.

FEGELEIN: It is possible, my Führer, to bring up 1,250 men for the *Viking*? They are ready to march immediately. There are also 1,680 men standing by up here for *Nordland*, for the III Germanic Corps.[1523] But that'll probably be used up there for Schörner. We can't really take that away.

THE FÜHRER: How do they look? I don't know how much they've deteriorated.

KEITEL: We have to keep them for him.

FEGELEIN: They are both available now, and they do have 9 weeks of training, these 1,200 men, while the other 1,600 are ready. That's *Danmark* and *Norge*, which were once scheduled for here, in case something were to happen. But I believe we should give them to Colonel General Schörner.

THE FÜHRER: Find out how the corps looks up there with Schörner. I don't believe they were even in the battle.

FEGELEIN: They were in it more or less.

KEITEL: They were out for part of the time.

THE FÜHRER: Find out how strong they are, and the losses.

FEGELEIN: Yes, Sir!

BUHLE: Here's the compilation of the railway batteries. (*Presentation.*) The ones in the East that might be considered for the West are checked in red.

THE FÜHRER: So there are four.

BUHLE: Yes, four 24-cm. There the ammunition is running out. That will be filled up.

THE FÜHRER: End of November. [—] Anyway, I would go over with the 104 rounds once again. Are there two or three?

BUHLE: There are two. They are in the East. One is ready for action at home. They are the Bruno N.[1524] This one is just moving over here, and two more are coming in a few days.

THE FÜHRER: What kind of high-explosive shells are these?

BUHLE: They're from the Belgian guns.

THE FÜHRER: Stop! That's our gun anyway. It can absolutely be shot. This is a German gun. These are 38 cm. We can shoot with this.[1525]

BUHLE: There are four here in the Southwest. Twelve K 5s are already in the Southwest, and four K 5s are still supposed to come up to the Southwest.[1526] Another 150 rounds are supposed to arrive, my Führer.

THE FÜHRER: Where are they? [—] They are of no value in the East.

BUHLE: This must have just come over, my Führer.

THE FÜHRER: Make sure this goes to the West. There are 700 rounds there. Where are they?

BUHLE: Also in the East.

THE FÜHRER: We can't take them away from Army Group North.

BUHLE: I don't believe they're with Army Group North.

THE FÜHRER: Some of them will be with Army Group North. Find out! [—] 32 cm? Southwest?[1527]

BUHLE: There are nine in Italy. Here's one. It's just moving over here.

THE FÜHRER: Absolutely not! From East to West! Also these railway howitzers.

BUHLE: That is the equipment that's still in Warsaw—60 cm.[1528]

THE FÜHRER: They'll be moved out; that's clear.

BUHLE: Then there are still 4 38-cm guns with 90 rounds in Warsaw. The four were intended for the West. There I still have 43 rounds.

THE FÜHRER: We have to take them away from Warsaw. [—] They aren't in Warsaw anymore—I'm sure they're already in Budapest!

BUHLE: They were there. They've been taken away from there. They are up with Army Group Center.

THE FÜHRER: They're with Army Group Center? They must be taken out.

BUHLE: Also to the West?

THE FÜHRER: Yes, all four of them.

BUHLE: To the West!

FEGELEIN: About 10 days ago, the two divisions had 12,000 men and 4,000 men—so 16,000 men altogether. I have to find out by radio—I won't know until tomorrow—what losses they have and how they look now. (*Presentation of press reports.*)

THE FÜHRER: The conservative *Daily Mail* writes: (*Reading aloud concerning General Franco.*[1529]) Now the first Communist Finnish papers are appearing. A weekly magazine is planned. The press might be able to use this.[1530] [—] The Spaniard can do anything, although it's bothersome. Maybe we can keep this, and lay it aside and use it again sometime. [—] TASS is agitating very intensely. Now the matter with Iran.[1531] [—] The Japanese have sunk four more aircraft carriers with their "kamikazes" again and have damaged another one.[1532] If only we could at least damage an aircraft carrier! Where's the Luftwaffe?

CHRISTIAN: Here!

THE FÜHRER: Take this for the Luftwaffe to study. [—] In New York there are 18—in other towns there are additional mass gatherings for this Communist affair, for the Soviet-USA. (Hues) has expressed himself quite brutally against Communism in the last few days[1533] ... (*Reading aloud.*) Then there is a note about the governmental crises in Finland. Two Communists entered the cabinet.[1534] And there were various bloody clashes in different Finnish garrison towns. (*Reading aloud.*) In addition, the Americans have been snubbed with their whole air force affair. We should do something clever with the press. The Russians didn't come at all.[1535] The others refuse. And we should do it in such a way that it makes the whole affair look like it was directed by the British—that the British succeeded in winning the other countries over to their plans...[1536] Here it says that I am a prisoner in my own house at Obersalzberg, in my own "residence."[1537] (*Presentation.*)

HEWEL: A report about the Americans appeared in the *Schweizer Kurier* yesterday. So I converted the American itemization based on the statements of that man who was disabled in the war, and the numbers are too big. If we just took it like this, it would be implausible.

JODL: It's too high.

HEWEL: I would suggest that we do the following with these numbers [—]

JODL: He must include among the injured those who work in industry, etc. Otherwise it's impossible.

THE FÜHRER: They don't have the strict standards that we have.

HEWEL: So we'll just leave it.

JODL: May I report something about the operations in the West[1538] to a smaller group?

End: 4:32 p.m.

* * * * *

December 12, 1944

In the East the situation is unchanged.

In Hungary, the Soviet push over the middle Tisza [River] has thrown the German-Hungarian troops back to the Gödöllö-Egor [Erlau]-Miskolc line. Beginning on December 5, the enemy pushed northeastward against the Ipol [Eipel] River and the Danube [River] bend, where Vac [Waitzen] fell on December 9. In the meantime, the Soviets lined up in southern Hungary at the end of November and reached the Nagykanisza-Lake Balaton [Plattensee] south of Szekesfehervar [Stuhlweissenburg]-Lake Velence [Velenzesee]-Budapest line.

On the Croatian border, the front against Hungary has been stabilized in Syrmien and at the Drau, covering the further movement of Army Group E from southern Serbia to Bosnia.

In Italy, in the Adriatic sector, the English took Ravenna on December 5, and three days later Faenza on the Lamone, thus leaving the eastern part of the Apennines behind permanently.

In the West—after heavy fighting that began on November 16—the Anglo-Americans advanced east of Aachen to the Roer, first near Jülich and then upstream to Düren. They don't dare cross the river, however, as long as the dams in the upper course are in German hands. In the Lorraine region, between November 8 and the beginning of December, Patton pushed the German front back to the Saar. On November 14 the French attacked the Burgundian Gate, while the Americans attacked in the direction of the Zabern valley via Saarburg. The encircled city of Belfort, along with Mülhouse, fell on November 22. Strasbourg fell on the 24th, and on December 12, the day of this meeting, Hagenau would fall into enemy hands. In between, in central Alsace, the 19th Army is still standing west of the Rhine in a large bridgehead around Colmar. In the Aachen and Lorraine region, German units have assembled and—according to Hitler's wish—and will penetrate into Belgium four days later and push forward to Antwerp.

(Map 8)

* * * * *

THE FÜHRER'S SPEECH TO DIVISION COMMANDERS, DECEMBER 12, 1944, AT ADLERHORST[1539]

Beginning: 6 p.m.

THE FÜHRER: Gentlemen! A fight like the struggle in which we find ourselves right now, which is being fought with such unlimited bitterness, obviously has different aims than the quarrels of the 17th or 18th Centuries, which might have concerned minor inheritances or royal dynastic conflicts. People and nations don't start a long war of life and death without deeper reasons. One can't deny that the German nation, in terms of size and value, has (earned the claim) in central Europe to become the leader of the European continent. Politically, however, especially since the Thirty Years' War, Germany hasn't been able to realize this claim, as it was the goal of the peace of Münster and Osnabrück to prevent the German nation from unifying and regaining the German Reich's dominant position in Europe. Political disunity kept the power of the German people from coming together, and is responsible for allowing the establishment of the British world empire, for the American continent being English instead of German, and for the predominance of France on the continent itself. Likewise, only political impotence can be blamed for...[1540]

Both states have taken every opportunity to resist a German political recovery—meaning a union of individual states and tribes or even the formation of a German empire in the sense of a unified state. The attempts to bring about this unification are very old. Whenever Germany breaks up, many German rulers and leaders—princes as well as generals—as well as politicians, writers, artists, economists, and so on, feel the necessity of reestablishing a unified (Reich of all Germans. All these attempts to erect a unified German Empire have been fought) relentlessly by these opponents. The peace of Münster in 1648 almost achieved the status of a European Magna Charta. It was said that the so-called balance of power thus created, and the impossibility of one nation achieving predominance in Europe—and this could only be Germany—corresponded to a more or less divine order and served a general human legal order as well, and that the attempt to change this situation was a crime against human rights, against the freedom of the people, and later against democracy, the parliamentary democracy, and so on. Nothing but words! The foundation (for this argument was the attempt to prevent a German union under any circumstances. They recognized), as this war proves once again, based on the cultural history and the general history of man's development, that the unification of 85 million people of this quality would certainly have solved the problem of hegemony right away. They realized this and defended themselves against it by all possible means.

Bismarck suffered from it. When, let us say, especially after the age of Bismarckian union, the power of this unifying thought spread and—in part economically, in part also politically—inevitably brought the unified Reich into being, (they started a policy of uniting against Germany, and the war against Germany) was seen and proclaimed as a sort of holy war. The father of this idea was Churchill, but one has to admit that international world Jewry stood behind it, for obvious reasons.

Now, today, this battle is being fought as a continuation, not only, as it sometimes is said in the press, of the World War of 1914 to 1918, but really as a continuation of the wars of 1870-71, 1866, 1864. Because the so-called unification wars were different from the liberation wars, as they had the aim of unifying the German nation once again, it was a natural requirement that this aim be reached only in stages, and not completed right from the start. But the goal was clear. In the end, the goal could only be—even if this wasn't obvious (to everybody)—the complete unification of all Germans. I have made it part of my lifework to reach this goal. This goal has to be reached, not because of any (theory) or political will, which can also be changed or postponed, but because of the recognition that otherwise the requirements of a people of millions can't be adequately pursued. Life without *Lebensraum* [living space] is unthinkable. *Lebensraum* can only be secured by a corresponding political power. The deployment of political force is again required by the organization of the factors from which the political power can or should arise. Germany can only realize its right to existence in this world if all Germans are unified and (defend this right to exist. This became very clear to the others when they saw in National Socialism) also the ideological possibility of unifying all the German tribes. That's why National Socialist Germany has been fought so fiercely—right from the start, when we first took over of power, and even before—again supported by international Jewry.

So today we are facing a fight that was inevitable—it had to come, sooner or later. The only question is whether it is the appropriate time. I showed yesterday[1541] that the first objection can be eliminated easily—the objection that we've acted in too preventive a manner.[1542] All of man's successful wars, gentlemen, have been preventive wars. Whoever recognizes that a battle can't be avoided and doesn't ... the (best moment), in his view ... The political situation (is always changing, and there is—if one wants to reach a political goal that is recognized as necessary—no stability) guaranteeing the achievement of such a goal. Such stability doesn't exist politically because likes or dislikes in the life of the people are constantly changing concepts. I read a memorandum this year, which I wrote in 1939 right after the Polish campaign. I could publish it even today. In the meantime, reality has proven its truth not once but ten times over. It showed that the theoretically positive situation of 1938-39 didn't have to remain stable, but, on the contrary, it was dependent on many factors that could change at any moment.[1543] (It is like this) ... as long as one is not convinced that they have a certain lifespan, but that the death of a single person can bring about a complete change in the political situation, and that the changing of a regime can turn the political goals completely upside down. In other words, one can't say that in six or ten or twelve or twenty years there an especially fortunate situation will exist to carry out, let us say, a political union or the attempt to achieve a union, which is recognized as necessary.

But the military factor also supports this. There is no moment in which a weapon can be seen (as final). Once we were lucky enough, because of a gigantic effort following the previous lack of armaments—I spent 92 billion up to 1939[1544]—to create complete predominance in most armament areas. But it was obvious that this predominance couldn't last. Because at the same moment in which we—to name just one example—introduced the new heavy field howitzer, other countries were already poised to move from the construction of a gun with a range of 15 km to a range of 17 km. The Russians already had a gun with a range of 18 km. At the same moment in which we introduced a certain type of tank, the Russian KV 1 and 2 tanks—but especially the T 34 type were already designed and under construction.[1545] In other words, this war has already shown us after one or two years that some of our models, which were the state of the art when we started the war, were already outdated in the course of the first two years.

In war it is possible to catch up again because there is complete disregard for the usual economic conditions. In peacetime, one can never completely overtake other nations year after year in the technical aspects of one area of armament or the other. Not to mention the tactical perceptions, the training, etc., not even the leadership. Because no armed force can swear that it now has the best training or the best leadership. That won't be proven until the war. One can't claim it beforehand. And regarding the fortunes of war, one can be completely silent in this context. ...

It was impossible to achieve such technical superiority in five or ten years. There couldn't have been a luckier moment than we found in 1939. It was very clear—right from the moment in 1936 when the 2 billion pound [sterling] credit was granted in England and they converted to practically universal conscription[1546]—that the Tories in England, together with the Jewish underworld, were determined to return to their old policy of gagging Germany, and that because of this, sooner or later it would come to a fight.

But there was another moment to be considered, and that was decisive for me personally. I have had to make hard—infinitely hard—decisions in my life. (Such decisions can only be made by a person who is willing, by sacrificing all personal life, etc.,) to offer himself to one thing alone and to devote himself to it completely. I was convinced that in Germany, in the coming ten, twenty, thirty, maybe fifty years, no man would come with more authority, more possibilities to influence the nation, and more decisiveness than myself. I also believe that after I am gone, time will prove that I assessed things correctly.

That is why I thought it personally correct to clarify—even in my younger years—after evaluating the situation, the conditions that were necessary, not to create the war, but to bring about the security that would be necessary if Germany were attacked. That security was based on: 1. Immediately introducing universal conscription and total armament of the nation; 2. Restoring German sovereignty by occupying the Rhineland and regaining sovereignty in the west, through measures that included the construction of fortifications; 3. Immediately annexing Austria, settling the Czechoslovak issue, and finally settling the question of Poland, to bring the German Reich territory into a defensible condition. These were the prerequisites for maintaining peace in the future. Because even peace can only be maintained if one is armed. And there is not only military armament, but also, I would say, a territorial armament, which, with our infinitely small *Lebensraum* is very difficult to achieve.[1547] You can see that today's bombers can (fly from England to the heart of Germany) in less than two hours ... Additional problems arose: (the impossibility for the German people to) exist (in such a restricted *Lebensraum*) in the long term, and the impossibility of feeding the German people without a sufficient agricultural base.

And, finally, there were psychological factors—namely in the mobilization of the power of the German people. You can't put enthusiasm and the willingness to sacrifice oneself into bottles and just save them. This happens once in the course of a revolution and will slowly fade away again. The gray weekday and the comforts of life will captivate men and turn them into *petit bourgeois* again. What we were able to achieve by National Socialist education, by the immense wave that (took hold of) our people, (we couldn't let pass.) ...

But even if (the circumstances were fortunate), some conditions had to be carefully fulfilled in any case: the restoration of German sovereignty, the armament of the nation, the reintroduction of universal conscription—but also the occupation of the Rhineland, the freeing of the states annexed by the treaty of Versailles and the treaty of Trianon, etc., and the creation of a unified territory went in that direction. If this led to war, we had to accept this war. Because it is better to accept it right away, at a time when we were armed like never before. (Otherwise we might have had to) accept it at a time when this arming had been lost again. The Great War proved in the end that one can't avoid a war by not striking. Because starting in 1898-99, when the right moments for initiating a conflict arose, we let years pass, always expecting to keep the peace through flexibility and compliance, or to achieve even better armaments by waiting, until finally—in spite of all attempts to maintain peace—the war was imposed on the German Empire. Anyone today who examines the wishes of Moltke in the years 1876, 1877 and 1878—when he wanted to strike against France once again, to nip the newly strong France in the bud[1548]—and the political arguments that were brought up against it, (will recognize clearly how wrong it wasn't to fulfill Moltke's wishes at that time. Instead,) based on political factors resulting from the internal German parliamentary situation and from other difficulties within the country, they held back—and then finally got mixed up in it anyway, at the most inopportune time.

It is very clear, gentlemen, that such a conflict is now progressing like a grand historical struggle, with its ups and downs. Anyone who believes that the great epochs of world history are nothing but a series of successes has never understood history, or has perhaps not even read it properly; it is very clear that success and failure come and go. In the end, the one who gains the laurels of victory is not just the most capable one, but, most importantly—and I want to emphasize this—(the boldest). The building of states—no matter whether it is the Roman Empire, the British Empire or Prussia—has always been achieved by toughness, stubbornness and durability. Not so much by a single blaze of genius or by a burst of energy that flares up once and then vanishes, but much more by stubborn tenacity, which is the greatest help in overcoming all crises. Rome couldn't have been imagined without the Second Punic War. England would not be imaginable if crises hadn't been overcome within England itself. Prussia would be unimaginable without the Seven Years' War. And the greatness of the leading personalities, as well as of the people themselves, wasn't born in times of fortune but is always confirmed in times of ill fortune. People who can endure good luck are quite common. People who don't become weak when faced with bad luck are rare. (There are) few people (of this kind). History has always awarded success to these few.

So it is understandable that this type of struggle—which is really about bringing up a new world power, which is very necessary if Europe is not to fade away—can't progress like, let us say, a short battle over a minor conflict such as an inheritance or something. In this case the war might last years, with high points and low points, and in the end the winner will be the one who survives all this with the most stubborn tenacity. The objection that there might be moments when technical superiority could decide the final outcome is totally invalid. Because even in technical matters there is no superiority that remains with one side right from the start. Rather, there is (superiority first on one side, then again on the other. Our current situation) is connected with a temporary decline in our armaments in certain technical areas—not in quantity, but in value, due to new inventions that have also been useful to our opponents. I only have to point out that one single invention, which wasn't made by the English, but which they unfortunately developed better than we did—I am talking about the invention of electric locating [NDT: radar]—in a matter of a few months practically wiped out our prospering submarine war.[1549] And now we have unfortunately lost valuable bases at a time when we were just about to make this invention obsolete through the construction of new submarines, which are now ready and being launched. I hope they will be deployed again in the course of the winter, and then they might change the course of fate substantially.[1550]

(The war is certainly) an endurance test for all participants. The longer the war lasts, the (harder) this endurance test becomes. This endurance test will be withstood as long as there is still hope for success. Without hope of victory, endurance tests are usually not undertaken with the same strong will with which, for example, a fortress might fight as long as there is hope for relief. So it is important to rob the enemy of his certainty of victory from time to time, and to show him through offensive strikes that his plans are doomed to fail anyway, right from the start. This is never achieved as effectively by successful defensive as by successful offensive strikes. Long term, then, one can't believe in the principle that defense is the stronger part of the fight. It might ... be useful to others. One can't forget that the total sum of men deployed on our side is just as great as on our opponents' side of. And we must not forget that some of the enemy forces are tied up in East Asia against Japan—against one state that, excluding China, contains well over 100 million people and represents a valuable force in technical armament.

Nevertheless, one has to recognize that too much time spent strictly defending will undermine one's endurance, and that these periods must be relieved by successful strikes. So I attempted to lead this war in an offensive way, whenever possible, right from the beginning—to lead it in an operational way, and not get pushed into any kind of world war situation. When this happened anyway, it was only in connection with the defection of our allies,[1551] which naturally had operational effects. ...

But wars are finally decided by the recognition on one side or the other that the war can't be won anymore. Thus, the most important task is to bring the enemy to this realization. The fastest way to do this is to destroy his strength by occupying territory. If we ourselves are forced into defense, our job is to teach the enemy by ruthless strikes that he hasn't yet won, and that the war will continue without interruption. It is just as important to strengthen these psychological moments by not letting a moment pass without showing the enemy that no matter what he might do, he can never count on a capitulation—never, ever. This is crucial. The smallest sign of such a (mood for capitulation will raise the enemy's hope of victory again) and will fill a generally hopeless mass with new hope, causing them to willingly take on all burdens and sacrifices again. That's why publishing defeatist memoranda is so dangerous, as it happened in 1917, and the danger of files, as we saw that year—which, although known to the enemy for years, still helped maintain the hope that a miracle might happen that would suddenly change the situation.[1552] The enemy must know that he won't be successful under any circumstances. If this is made clear to him by the attitude of people, by the Armed Forces, and even more by the severe setbacks he experiences, his nerve will break in the end. The same thing will happen as Frederick the Great experienced in the seventh year of war, and which he could (count as his biggest success in life). One can't say afterward, "Yes, then (the situation was different." It wasn't different), gentlemen; rather, at that time almost all the generals, including his own brother ..., almost despairing of possible success. His government presidents, his ministers in Berlin, appeared in delegations and asked him to stop the war right away—this war couldn't be won anymore. The steadfastness of one man enabled the fight to continue, and in the end the miracle of a turning point did occur.

Also, the objection that this would never have happened without the accession to the throne of a new tsar in Russia is of no importance at all. Because if the capitulation had happened in the fifth year of war, then the succession to the throne in the seventh year, i.e., two years later, would have been completely insignificant. One has to bide one's time.

And the following must also be considered, gentlemen. (Never in the history of the world) has a coalition existed like that of our opponents, which has been assembled from such heterogeneous elements with such extremely different and conflicting goals. What we have as opponents are the greatest extremes that can be imagined in this world: ultra-capitalist states on one side and ultra-Marxist states on the other; on one side a dying world empire, Britain, and on the other side a colony seeking an inheritance, the USA. These are states whose aims are now diverging even more every day. And the one who recognizes this development, let us say, like a spider sitting in its web, can see how these oppositions develop by the hour. If a few heavy strikes were to succeed here, this artificially maintained united front could collapse at any moment with a huge clap of thunder.[1553] (Each of the partners joined the coalition in the hope of) realizing (its political aims this way), ... to be able to dupe the others or to win something: the USA trying to be heir to England; Russia attempting to win the Balkans, the straits, Persian oil, Iran, and the Persian Gulf; England attempting to hold its position and to strengthen its Mediterranean position. In other words, someday—and it could be any moment, because on the other side history is also shaped by mortal human beings—this coalition will break up, but always with the prerequisite that this battle should under no circumstances lead to a moment of weakness by Germany.

Of course, we also had great weaknesses, right from the start of the war—weaknesses that lay primarily (in our allies. For us it was a very significant weakness that we didn't) have very strong states, (but) very weak states as allies. But at least they ... fulfilled their duty for a while. We can't complain and lament about it; rather, we have to thankfully acknowledge that at least for a time these states fulfilled their purpose. We were able to conduct the war for years at the periphery of the Reich. Now we have been partly pushed back to the borders of the Reich, and partly we are still far from the old Reich borders. In any case, we are still fighting this war from a position that gives us every opportunity to get through and to survive, especially if we are able to eliminate the danger here in the West.

Now, gentlemen, I have accepted sacrifices on other fronts—which weren't necessary—to create the necessary conditions that will allow us to move forward offensively. If I speak about an offensive here, the one who is in the thick of battle, suffering especially from the total air supremacy of the enemy, might be a bit concerned and might say right from the start, "How can one even think about something like that?" The situation in 1939 or 1940 was also not to convince nearly everyone that the battle in the West could be decided by taking the offensive. Just the opposite, gentlemen! I have not written memoranda in order to run through open doors, but to open up closed doors. It would not have been necessary back then, in countless and repetitive meetings, to present my ideas about the required offensive means of conducting warfare[1554] ...

(Conducting a defensive war was) the official position that I argued against in those years. They accepted the idea of an offensive war against Poland, but an offensive war against France and England was considered insane—a crime, a Utopia, a hopeless pursuit. The fact demonstrated the opposite. Today, we can hardly imagine where we would be if we hadn't conquered France back then. ...

One could object that the difference between 1940 and today (was in a certain view) immense. At that time we faced an unproven enemy army, and now we face an army that is known to us already and is engaged in war. That is true, gentlemen. But where strength is concerned, not much has changed[1555]—with the exception of the Luftwaffe, which is a very critical factor, and I will come back to that point. Concerning strength: at that time, in the West, we lined up for the offensive with a total of about 100 divisions—110 divisions, 86 of which were deployed offensively. Not all of them were first-class divisions; some were improvised and hastily assembled in only a few months, and only some could really be called first-class. ...

(Also for the upcoming offensive we don't have only first-class units available.) But on the enemy side (they are not all first-class) units either. We have many worn-out troops, and the enemy has many worn-out troops as well, and has suffered severe losses. We now have the first official report from the Americans, and they really have lost about 240,000 men in just three weeks.[1556] These numbers are just gigantic—far higher than what we thought they might lose. So he is also worn out. Technically, we are about equal on both sides. With regard to tank weapons, the enemy might have more tanks, but with our newest types, ours are better.

(*End of the fragment.*)

* * * * *

December 28-29, 1944

In the East it is still calm; the Russians are attacking only in Courland, where they have been n the offensive since December 21, but without real success.

In Hungary, the enemy lined up on both sides of Lake Velencze on December 20, as the last German reserves had moved away to the penetration area north of the Danube River as a result of the threatening situation on the Ipol [Eipel] River. In the region between the two lakes, the Soviets were only able to conquer Szekesferhervar [Stuhlweissenburg] during the night of December 22, but they also forced a breakthrough between Lake Velencze and Budapest. The capital was encircled from the rear on the 24th, and to the northwest, the enemy advanced to the Bakony forest. North of the Danube, the German units were thrown back over the Gran River and eastward to the Slovakian border.

In the Southeast, the last rearguards of Army Group E are now moving back toward the Drina River. This will complete the evacuation of Greece, Macedonia, Albania, Serbia and—except for a strip in the north—also Montenegro.

In Italy the situation has changed very little. The enemy attacks that started on December 20 north and west of Faenza have—like the German push around Galliano—achieved only local successes in the last two days.

In the West, three German armies lined up for an offensive on December 16 at the Belgian border and in northern Luxembourg. In the northern section, where the main focus of the attack should have taken place, the Sixth SS Panzer Army was only able to reach Malmédy with its southern wing, while the Seventh Army was able to advance only with its northern wing along the Sauer. In the center, the Fifth Panzer Army managed a breakthrough. In the Ardennes they pushed over the Ourthe and Rochefort Rivers to about 7 km outside of Dinant on the Meuse River. Here the offensive was able to advance no further, and German units finally had to move into the defensive on the 27th. On the German southern flank, the Americans were able to free the encircled Bastogne on December 26. Because the Allies' reserves were able to ward off the German offensive, battles along other sectors of the front are ending. On the border of the Palatinate, the next German offensive is being prepared.

(*Map 11*)

*****

MEETING OF THE FÜHRER
WITH COLONEL GENERAL BLASKOWITZ, DECEMBER 28, 1944,
AT ADLERHORST[1557]

Present:

The Führer	*Lieutenant General v. Obstfelder*[1558]
Colonel General Blaskowitz	*Lieutenant General Westphal*
Field Marshal Keitel	*Major General Scherff*
Field Marshal v. Rundstedt	*Colonel v. Below*
Colonel General Jodl	*Colonel Meyer-Detring*
...	*Major Johannmeyer*
Later: Reichsführer SS Himmler	

Beginning: 6:02 p.m.

The West

BLASKOWITZ: According to the directive, the advance has now been ordered as follows. The right [flank] assault group on the outermost right wing: the 36th Volksgrenadier Division, next to it, the 17th SS [Panzer Division]; Command: the SS Corps. Orders: break through, disregarding the fortifications, in a straight southerly direction. The 36th Division should then begin, when they arrive here, ... veer off. This part ... by the left wing ... Volksgrenadier Division. Then ... must ... first the further ... Then I want to ... army engineer battalion ... is weak. That should ... be strengthened, so it ..., the right pushed in ... the 17th SS later freed up ... through, then (followed) ... both panzer grenadier (divisions) ready for action, (first the) 25th, then the 21st, but the 25th ... is very weak. The 21st is in good condition at the moment. The 21st Panzer Division is on the left wing at the moment. I wanted to let it stay there until late afternoon on the 31st—because the left wing is very weak, as there are very weak forces there—so a safety coefficient will be there until the very last moment; then in a night march they will pass by here, so they arrive on time here. The two divisions will then be able to go through behind there, in the direction of Pfalzburg and Zabern, and take Pfalzburg as well as Zabern.[1559] [—] The 2nd Assault Group is composed of four divisions: the 559, 257, 361 and 256. The advance: the inner division turns around the south edge of Bitsch and then turns in the direction of ... should then ... the remaining free ... roll up from the back ... 257 and 361 will initially stay ...

THE FÜHRER: ... Are they the ones here in front? ...

BLASKOWITZ: As they said recently, the ... there are a lot (of small roads), ... more or less to the side ..., in assault units up to battalion strength ... only what they have with them. They're (not allowed to take more) with them. They're in a ... line, so behind our position, which can't be crossed without the permission of the Army. They have to leave everything behind.

V. RUNDSTEDT: The 361st [Infantry] Division is the one that fought its way back through this whole thing. They know every inch of ground around there.

BLASKOWITZ: That's the division that is now clearing the same path that they made there.

V. RUNDSTEDT: While roads come out everywhere around here.

BLASKOWITZ: The left division, the 256th [Infantry], will first make the flanking movement to the southeast, then go along this through road while the spearhead turns in here; ... if the forces are insufficient ... further: when we have reached...with the lead elements of the 257th and 361st, we will have the report (that the) divisions are (through), and a clarification (has been made) as to whether a threat to the flanks has developed, (then) it'll be time for the heads of the 257th and 361st to turn, ... initially the 361st.

THE FÜHRER: Here there is just one question to be asked. In principle ..., how it is possible, so that ... for their part are still in the woods the ... otherwise we can't get here at all ..., unless we refrain right from the start from going in here, and only go here. But that is a decision I would not make until after we've really seen it. Because it could also happen that—if the further, deeper advance fails—if we then stay too deep in here, he might be able to put a block across it immediately with very few forces. That's why it's still desirable to push it back as far as possible. But if faced with a superior attack, we move back.

V. RUNDSTEDT: I believe that if the enemy recognizes the attack, he will never push out here. Instead, he'll come out here to reach the open area, especially if he still has some tanks, to press into these points. That he might ... in this difficult terrain ... But I am of the same ... : if the forces ... to the exit routes from the mountains ... for barriers, for min(ing operations) ... directs himself ... So it must be ... with a certain ...

THE FÜHRER: (I have) the feeling that he ... with ... our forces ... advance offensively, can ... on his side ... him ... carry out mining operations ... finally (make) them stop ... but run into him here. But it could be ... possible that we might have difficulties here. We have to ... take into account that we might not be able to support a long covering front, and that we might possibly have to push through to Ingweiler earlier, so that this would be the outermost border we reach. Also, we should not leave too many units here to provide cover. Otherwise we won't get in here anymore. Then it would be good to be near the exit route. Then we have to turn a few units out here right from the start, to push into here. One or two panzer units should be pulled through here. We'd have to see, then, that we carry out a much tighter pincer movement. That would not be the ... for the ... but good, if we ... until we see what ... can, that we back ... in case of a ... to hold.

(BLASKOWITZ): ... Division is also with ...

(V. RUNDSTEDT): ... they should then ... with ... will be launched, and, if ... go. If the ... the direction of the march in ... should. I wanted them ... bring, thinking of the best case, so they can build a pivot here.

THE FÜHRER: We could also use them for that at first, if difficulties arise anywhere. We assume he lies somewhere in front here, and the normal divisions can't just move cross-country, so we could use them to create an opening. So I would keep them totally mobile. But certainly we could set a final goal.

V. RUNDSTEDT: That belongs in the area of the 361st. That's the plan.

BLASKOWITZ: This is the plan. This here is the favorable area. ... in all (directions) ...

THE FÜHRER: ... another case: first ... tough. Here is a ... the 100th Division.

BLASKOWITZ: ... along quite a broad (front). ... That is the 100th Division that (has) spread itself out.

THE FÜHRER: Does anybody know how he has organized (his defense)?

(BLASKOWITZ): He has pulled (back), ... pulled very far back. He has ... set cover out front. Otherwise (he has) recently pulled back quite far.

V. RUNDSTEDT: Defense of bases! If the resistance here in front is very tough and heavy, and I come along here maybe with the 559th, I just take the 21st Panzer Division behind it and shut the door from behind. Don't attack it from the front; that makes no sense. There are enough roads everywhere.

BLASKOWITZ: The territory is not too rough.

V. RUNDSTEDT: It only looks wild because woods are marked here. It's not that hard.

KEITEL: The valleys are narrow, though, and we have to be prepared for barriers.

(BLASKOWITZ): One battery has already gone ahead. ... if the thing is set free ...

(KEITEL): There are plenty of (roads) in here. Here ...

(V. RUNDSTEDT): The center, the 361st, is the most difficult (one) ...

THE FÜHRER: The decisive factor is that they (don't) ... and block the way with stuff that ... they don't even need.

(BLASKOWITZ): No, it's very strict.

(V. RUNDSTEDT): After what we unfortunately had to experience up there, there is now a flood of unneeded vehicles standing around.[1560] (They) came along—empty cars to carry captured materiel.

THE FÜHRER: Then in the north[1561] something else has proven necessary. We can't push the covering forces far enough away from the main fighting line. What we can do in the beginning in an open space with comparably modest forces, we can't achieve later. Because when the enemy arrives, it's too late. So if we could just set up small barriers everywhere [—]

V. RUNDSTEDT: This sector offers itself. Besides, he is so weak around here. He can't risk, with the few tiny divisions he still (has) there on the left ... doing ... He will ... everywhere ...

(THE FÜHRER): (I believe) also, that the threat to the (flanks) ... will ...

(BLASKOWITZ): The only thing he has in the ... is the ... Armored Division. If it will still be there, ... is questionable.

(V. RUNDSTEDT): I ... that it will stay, ... It is unlikely that ... away.

(THE FÜHRER): ... deploy them. If ... panzer units are entirely adequate, ... He can ... the whole thing here ... leave the mobile forces in this area. We don't need to pull the 559th in here if this is cleared out; in that case, it can be pulled out and used here for cover.

BLASKOWITZ: We had thought, once they cleared this out, that we would first bring them together and pull them over here to see how it looks, and where I might need them.

THE FÜHRER: In the most extreme case, we could pull them out to cover the flanks, so that we would come out here with the 36th and the 559th— two infantry divisions—and one panzer unit. The two other units we could ... with the forces that ... can bring down here. ... then in here ...

(BLASKOWITZ: Two) panzer divisions and four in(fantry divisions) ...

THE FÜHRER: ... we could also make ... available to settle this affair.

BLASKOWITZ: ... being led after: ... coming after.

THE FÜHRER: ... We want to rush them.

BLASKOWITZ: No, I mean that it comes from ... (I believe that) this moment will be the decisive one for us. (If this) starts, he will now gain the impression that all the pressure will be against the southwest at first—

THE FÜHRER: He won't believe that.

BLASKOWITZ: —and that later we will hook around.

THE FÜHRER: He'll never believe that we are going to the southwest. If everything works out and stays secret, he won't expect us to attack here. Or do you have some indication that he's concerned about something here? He ...

(BLASKOWITZ): No.

(JODL): We hope that the attack (plan) won't be (taken along) to the front line, like in every other (operation).

(V. RUNDSTEDT): It's not planned, according to the distribution list.

THE FÜHRER: (If it doesn't) come up by accident, (he) won't (expect it). He thinks (it's impossible that we) would line up against him there. He won't guess (that we are lining up again.[1562] The deciding factor is) that we have to (arrive) down here so early that he can't move away to the south under any circumstances. The one thing that must not happen is that we are forced to follow him onto the Rhine plain. If he starts pulling down right away and goes to the south, we'll have to turn in as fast as possible, so he can't get away. Otherwise, there's a great danger that this guy will go down here.[1563] We don't know to what degree this bridgehead will really be successful, and how deep it will become. I told Himmler[1564] that he should make himself a few very small commands—with only a few assault guns, armored person- nel carriers and Volkswagens, which he should be able to scratch together— and drive them ahead ruthlessly to blow up bridges. Here's a line, which, if everything turns out well, we won't cross. That would be this line here. If we push through here, we'll be north of ... north of the railway. So we could ... the cros(sings, which) are ... all easily blocked over the ..., so he won't be able to (escape to the south) ... and if there are only a (few) ... (that) cause confusion (for him), so he ... It is still possible (that he) could pull through the forest via Hagenau to (try) to get into Strasbourg. We (have) to be pre- pared for the worst. That would be (the) moment (then), when he could force (us), if we ... get the street, around Ingweiler ..., that we turn in with ... as fast as possible.

V. RUNDSTEDT: If the thing comes out right and the (tanks) turn off and the infantry turns off, then I'll still have the mountain division. I'll chase them forward to the south and block the pass that goes through here from Strasbourg.

BLASKOWOTZ: The Schirmeck valley!

V. RUNDSTEDT: Right down here, from Zabern to the south.

THE FÜHRER: That is not a great distance.

V. RUNDSTEDT: No, and the territory is not very rough for a mountain troop. That's on condition that this works out well. Then he'll say to himself, "What shall I do? So out with that stuff, especially with the French!" But ... just keep it in mind.

(THE FÜHRER): ... the 361st [Infantry Division] comes cross-country?

(V. RUNDSTEDT): Yes, Sir.

(THE FÜHRER): ... the condition of the roads ... There one can't ...

V. RUNDSTEDT: I have to point out again and again. (That division has, in the) battles from here ... fought back (up to this line), and (they know) every step and stone (in this area). That's (why it is important that we) relieve them of the things (that they don't) absolutely need [—]

KEITEL: They'll probably find roads around here.

V. RUNDSTEDT: There are roads everywhere. It's not a high mountain area.

THE FÜHRER: The northern Vosges are flat.

BLASKOWITZ: Attack beginning at 11 p.m., sneaking in without a sound, so at first he won't know if they are raiding party operations. We are very clear about this: without artillery support in the moonlight. The moon is up from 7 p.m. until 7 a.m.; the moon is full for two days. There are only a few assault guns along. With artillery support we (couldn't work) in this (situation). ... batteries everywhere out front ... no artillery behind ...

(THE FÜHRER: How did he react) to raiding party (operations) ... in the area of the First Army?

(BLASKOWITZ: It was) different ... That time there were ... there were predominant ...

(V. RUNDSTEDT): Everywhere where we are still standing in front of the Saar, the (action) has turned out fine. ... our raiding parties had these difficulties. (At) ... or whatever it's called, it worked out well. Where the salient still extends forward around Forbach, everything worked well.

BLASKOWITZ: Yes, there they always get through.

V. RUNDTSTEDT: Now, all of this is still in front of the Maginot Line. The difficulty arises only when our attack hits up against the Maginot Line.

THE FÜHRER: Now this heaviest 653rd Tank Destroyer Detachment should come here.[1565] It would be desirable, of course, if they could come here for the attack, because they, working together with any ... (unit)—if any engineer battalion could (join—) would be invincible. That is ... with the 12.8 cm and armor (of 250 mm) ..., maybe has a (speed of) 12 to 15 km, not (more). But it is very durable ... if the other ... with his ..., he will position himself in front of the bunkers ... after which he ... places himself 30 to 40 m in front of the bunkers and shoots them to pieces. (It) will shoot every bunker from a distance of 2,000 to 3,000 m, (guaran)teed. The heaviest bunkers lie deep, the ... (The French have) no works that are (stronger than) 1.60 m from the back. In general he has 1.20 m. But it usually shoots through 2.40 m with a concrete shell from 2,000 m. It has armor plating of 250 mm. Against this he has no weapon. We've already seen how his weapons fared facing the Königstiger. This is the assault gun designed to completely eliminate the heaviest obstacles. If difficulties arise anywhere along the Maginot Line—he doesn't have any artillery inside the Maginot Line, because we took the artillery out back then.[1566] I hope that the few batteries that were in there—that we destroyed those few barrels at least, and that the breech locks were taken out. He doesn't have anything in the towers—as far as the towers that are still there. So he can't defend the Maginot Line in front at all. It is in fact an (installation) that's mostly underground. (There are a few) machine gun emplacements and a few armored (cupolas). But these (works) are damaged. (Back then) we ... (removed) the electrical installations, the ventilation systems ... electrical machines, and especially ..., because we needed them elsewhere, ... One can ... the towers, ... not lift ... I also don't (believe) that he has learned to manage the (works) in this short time. I don't think it's (possible). So (he places) himself (in) several in-between installations, which one can reach from the rear. (These things) deployed here will, in my opinion, have the greatest effect. [—] Where is the detachment (now)?

WESTPHAL: I already reported that it is doubtful that they will arrive in time. The commander has already reached the First Army. He doesn't help too much. He claimed that one train had left.

THE FÜHRER: It would have been better if he had stayed with his detachment and led it here.

WESTPHAL: He's been sent back to bring them here. They are at several railway stations.

THE FÜHRER: It doesn't matter. That's such a valuable weapon, that three or four pieces are of more value than ... (takes others. But I have to) point out that (they can't) cross (weak bridges). The vehicles have (a weight) ... about 90 tons.[1567] So (they are immense) hunks of metal.

(V. RUNDSTEDT): Everything has been done to (bring) the (detachment) in ... on time.

THE FÜHRER: Especially if it concerns clearing out individual installations afterward, where the enemy (still resists)—at the 559th—that would be (the best weapon) imaginable.

BLASKOWITZ: The 559th in this line!

THE FÜHRER: I don't know if it might not be easier to pull through in this terrain. We'll have to see. Bitsch is here. I believe that what comes through east of Bitsch will be easier, because here the Maginot Line is still in our possession, while here the Maginot Line is not in our possession anymore. I just don't know how it works in these sectors here. I can't judge. It can't climb very steep slopes. It's not a weapon that can take on very steep slopes like other tanks. At most, it can climb slopes of 20%. It's best to take only 15%.

(... ?): ... the mobility ... the very best on the barrel...that we have, and ... (THE FÜHRER: Even if he) builds himself an antitank-gun blocking position, (it can) eliminate it. (It's) also wonderful against antitank-gun blocking positions. The moment they fire, they're (given away, and when they're) given away, they can't do anything against (this weapon). If the 12.8 (fires at the antitank-gun position) with high-explosive shells, every round from 2,000 to (3,000 meters is a hit). So every antitank-gun position is (worthless. How are the people) outfitted in terms of footwear?

WESTPHAL: The footwear is not first-class, of course. But we have now brought in quite a lot and are also working on resoling them.

V. RUNDSTEDT: The question of clothing is a very dark chapter anyway. One has to ask if it might not be possible to take something away from the good Luftwaffe, which is sitting around on the airfields. The head doctor visited me recently, and he said that when an airman is being deloused, he brings along three changes of clothes. We could take boots away from them as well.

(THE FÜHRER: There are) several different possibilities. (One possibility is) that I first find out, (from all the storehouses of the three) branches of the Armed Forces in Germany, what exactly it is that they have.

(KEITEL: That's been) prepared: (confiscation—initial) inspection, taking in and (confiscation).

(THE FÜHRER: The) second possibility is that because (so many things) are kept secret (anyway), the (different branches of the Armed Forces) won't get anything new (until they) report their supplies very thoroughly, and also very thoroughly ...

KEITEL: We know the storehouses.

THE FÜHRER: How many storehouses are there? I heard the number today.

KEITEL: There are thousands of storehouses.

THE FÜHRER: It's very clear that it has deteriorated significantly because of the of the air defense measures. Before we regulated it very closely, but now it is out of control because of the air defense measures.

HIMMLER: Dispersing and hiding!

KEITEL: It was a hard battle, to break up the clothing depots.

THE FÜHRER: The infantryman is still the poor (devil. He has to) carry everything along. He only has (what he carries with him.)

(HIMMLER: Because I) couldn't equip the Volkssturm [peoples' militia] on the Upper Rhine ... or my ... either, (I have) ... confiscated ... the supplies of the customs (border guard) in Württem(berg and in Baden), which I have taken over.[1568] (There were) thousands of boots and (uniforms).

V. RUNDSTEDT: In the little village where (I am located, there is a) storehouse with hundreds of police uniforms.

HIMMLER: Wonderful! Send it on over!

KEITEL: You gave Reich Minister Speer the authority to dispose of all resources in the Armed Forces' stores.[1569] Now I've seen an order—it was delivered to me—for the confiscation of all Armed Forces' supplies of fabrics and leather. It was delivered to me, because at that time it was said: in agreement with the Chief of the OKW. Minister Speer signed the order on December 16 or 17 and it is now being carried out.

THE FÜHRER: I'm afraid, if Speer has signed it—did I sign it?

(KEITEL: The basis of the) order! It was an (authorization) at that time.

(THE FÜHRER: The) authorization will be denied (for this matter) immediately. (It was only a very) general authorization: (Reich Minister Speer) was authorized to take the measures necessary to continue to wage war.

(KEITEL): We can do it again right away.

(THE FÜHRER:) I just spoke with Frank.[1570] (He said: The) Navy has (large stores), of course. (There) every man has three or four shirts. [—]

WESTPHAL: With us everyone has only one set of underwear.

THE FÜHRER: [—] If I take away one set from everyone there, I'd gain at least one to one and a half million sets of underwear for the Army. That would certainly satisfy the most urgent needs. [—] That's one measure. But then another measure has to be taken—he also said that things have to be done more economically. It's strange, but there's a continual loop. In Germany we take up a fabric collection, while things are constantly coming home from the front. It's a constant (loop. Today you can) go into tens of thousands or (hundreds of thousands) of households and you will find (Armed Forces things everywhere).

(HIMMLER): ... millions of blankets since ...

THE FÜHRER: With what? The bombed-out men (say to themselves, "I have to) care (for) my wife"—and send the (blankets home. Or) they take three blankets on leave (and come) back (with only two). Everyone turns a blind eye (because he says to himself: we've) done the same thing ... On the other side, I have to make a fabric collection in order to get hold of the stuff.

HIMMLER: The measure requiring them to pay ten times the price—270 marks—is of no value either. Everyone is happy to pay that. He says, "270 marks—that's cheap; I'd have to pay more on the black market."

THE FÜHRER: For a blanket they pay more than 270 marks at home. So he doesn't lose anything. He then buys two blankets and sells one on the black market. So he still has one for himself, and with what he gets for the one on the black market he easily pays what the second one cost him.

KEITEL: At least we've managed, (from the stocks) ... of the (Navy and the Luftwaffe) ... especially the Luft(waffe)—to give more to the Army) in many areas.

(THE FÜHRER: If someone) hasn't (reported in more) than a year, (it's proof) that he has huge (supplies in his depot). We just have to go after that.

(KEITEL): The Navy and Luftwaffe have much lower (consumption. What) wear and tear on clothing (they) have, and what (wear) and tear the man in the trench has!

THE FÜHRER: We can say that the man in the infantry gets one to two sets a year, and the man in the Navy and the man in the Luftwaffe also get one to two sets a year. But the men in the Navy and Luftwaffe collect them. It's clear that the men in the Luftwaffe paratroop divisions have the same consumption as the infantry, but the others—the ground staff, for example—don't. We have to bring some things out, just like we brought men out—even though it's getting harder, since everyone clings to them, for a thousand reasons. I assume that all the commanders-in-chief say only what they think is true. (The commanders-in-chief report what) has been reported to them as true. (But many things that are) reported to them as true are (not true. If I'm given a) report saying that we can ... (not) give it out ... (No) one wants to be the one who wrote (it. It is said: That) is a careless, stupid (remark, that I) need (half a year) to train a female Luft(waffe assistant, who) does nothing but (operate a searchlight).

(KEITEL: It was said that they) also had to be (trained to radio). ... also in the Army...

THE FÜHRER: Only a small amount is reported by radio. They don't need to radio—only to (illuminate). But these gentlemen expected that I wouldn't look at it or read it.

BLASKOWITZ: So can it be carried out this way?

THE FÜHRER: Yes! Hopefully you'll get through.

BLASKOWITZ: We'll get through.

THE FÜHRER: I have the feeling that not much more can happen during that operation, if it doesn't get stuck right at the start or experience unusually bad luck. Because the other one doesn't have anything. He has a few (divisions) here. (What can he do with them?) Here he also has ... has (pulled) away anyway. (It's possible that he) will suddenly bring something back. (But it's ... un)likely that he would (do it). ... we will also ... him ... That could (lead) to a (major success—that we might possibly (destroy) five divisions. (That) would eliminate (one) piece, and then we (could be sure to get another) piece out (with a second strike).

(V. RUNDSTEDT: At least) no danger could (result) from it ... could never (become a danger for us).

HIMMLER: That's what happened near Hagenau, where I'm forming a bridgehead.

THE FÜHRER: I said this before: go ahead with the forces you have, and place them in front everywhere, even if many are lost. That doesn't matter—they'll hold for several days, especially if they have a few assault guns.

[—] Another important thing is that if we build an all-round defense any-where, we have to spread the assault guns out and dig them in immediately, as far as possible, even if that means they aren't as mobile. We have to set them up in an all-around defense position. But when they're dug in, they're almost unreachable. If the 38-ton[1571] is in the ground, dug in well, it can't be (hit) at all.[1572] [—]

(HIMMLER): ... of the Rhine-Marne (channel [canal?].) ...

(THE FÜHRER: ...Zabern,) to ... push ... to here ... (If), as mentioned earlier, (we) meet difficulties here—and (we) move away too much there, so that sealing it off here is impossible—there would still be the possibil-ity to pull in here. But we also have to block it to the south. We can't stay on the road. That would still be a possibility as a last concession. But it's not ideal. It would be ideal, of course, if we could get Zabern—and even more ideal if we could pull through the 6th SS Mountain Division to block off the Schirmeck valley so he can't move out here anymore either.

HIMMLER: The American divisions are located in here. This here is a rela-tively empty space. There (is not much in here).

(THE FÜHRER: Here) there are still two ...

(HIMMLER): ... American divisions ... pull out first ... still in the area of ... so that he ... in the current ... these units ...

(THE FÜHRER: They will) certainly be picked apart ... available ...

HIMMLER: That's not of much value (either). (It) has company strengths of 40 to (50) men. For American proportions that's quite weak.

THE FÜHRER: The Americans are writing now that they could save 6 divisions if they'd cut back their rear services. That improves the troops' morale unbelievably, if one takes out the rear services and puts them in the front! We know this ourselves. Anyone who hasn't really tested the proce-dure will be greatly surprised here.

HIMMLER: The engineer battalion was deployed with the 36th, and it was said that it (hadn't been deployed) since Nettuno. (Now) they are (sup-posedly) deploy(ing) it again ... because the infantry (had such great losses.)

(THE FÜHRER: It must) be going poorly for them. Otherwise (there would not be such extensive) new conscription.[1573] (One only has to cal-culate). They have an air force (of 3 million men; they have a) navy of 3 million (men. That already makes 6 million) men that the Americans ... have, today (even more, probably.) ... (Then) in East (Asia) they have ... have 40 or ... (divisions).

HIMMLER: The Americans certainly don't have a higher conscription rate (than 10%) of their population. (That) makes 13 million out of 130 million people. They certainly don't have more than that yet.[1574]

THE FÜHRER: But that is a great deal for democratic states. They can't do it with the industry, either. Everything starts to get squeezed.

KEITEL: They're supposed to have an army of 7 million men, plus 6 million men in the air force and navy—that makes all in all only 13 million men.

THE FÜHRER: Now they do have big rear services. They have a completely motorized army. It is … (their situation is anything) but perfect. (In America) criticism of the whole (way of conducting the war is starting, so that one …, instead of concentrating on *one* thing,) divides it along the whole front …

(*End of the meeting.*)

* * * * *

THE FÜHRER'S SPEECH TO DIVISION COMMANDERS, DECEMBER 28, 1944, AT ADLERHORST[1575]

Beginning: 6:48 p.m.

THE FÜHRER: Gentlemen! I have asked you here before an action, the success of which will determine the course of further strikes in the West. First, I would like to quickly show you the significance of this individual action. I would like to put it into the context of the overall situation we are in, and of the problems that exist and which have to be solved—problems which, no matter whether we solve them well or poorly, will certainly find a solution: in the one case in our favor, and in the other leading to our destruction.

The German situation can be characterized in a few sentences. In this war—as in the Great War— it is not a question of whether Germany will be granted any kind of merciful existence by our opponents if they are victorious. Instead, it is a question of whether Germany will continue to exist at all or if it will be destroyed. Unlike the wars of former times, such as perhaps in the 17th or 18th Centuries, no question of state organization will be decided, nor any question of the membership of any people or tribe or former federal state in the German Empire; rather, it will be a decision about the continuing existence of the essence of our German people. A victory of our enemies must undoubtedly lead to Bolshevism in Europe. Everyone must and will understand what this Bolshevization would mean for Germany. This is not a question of a change in the state, as in the past. State changes have taken place innumerable times in the life of the people; these changes come and go. But this concerns the existence of the essence itself. Essences are either preserved or eliminated. Preservation is our aim. The elimination could destroy a race like this, possibly forever.

Battles such as those taking place at the moment have the character of ideological conflicts and often last a very long time. So these battles can't be compared with the battles of the times of Frederick the Great. Then it was about a new German Great Power working itself up within the framework of the German Empire, which was gradually crumbling or had already fallen apart. This Great Power, I would like to say, had to fight for its status as a European Great Power. But today it's not about Germany having to prove itself as a European Great Power—the validity of that is plainly evident. Instead, it's about the German Reich taking part in an ideological war for existence or nonexistence. Victory in this war will finally stabilize this Great Power, which already exists in terms of numerical strength and worth; the loss of this war, however, will shatter and destroy the German people. Some of us will be evacuated. Just a few weeks ago you heard the explanations and remarks of Churchill in the British parliament, where he said, "All of East Prussia and parts of Pomerania and Upper Silesia—maybe the whole of Silesia—will be given to Poland, and in return Russia should get back something else; the 7 or 10 or 11 million Germans will have to be resettled."[1576] In any case, he hopes to eliminate 6 to 7 million more through aerial attacks during the course of the war, so that resettlement won't cause too many difficulties. That's the rational explanation of a leading statesman today in a public assembly. In the past this would have been considered a propaganda slogan—a propaganda lie. Here something is said (officially) that doesn't correspond in the least to what would actually take place, because England is not at all in a position to resist Bolshevism in the case of a German breakdown. That's a weak theory. Right now, when Mr. Churchill has to withdraw from Athens after a pitiful disgrace and is not able to stand up to Bolshevism in any way[1577]—in this moment the man tries to create the impression that he is able to stop the advance of Bolshevism at any border in Europe. That is a ridiculous fantasy. America can't do it; England can't do it. This war is waged over one state's fate. Germany will either save itself or—if it loses this war—perish.

I want to add right away, gentlemen, that when I say this, don't conclude that I've had even the slightest thought of losing this war. I never in my life learned the meaning of the term "capitulation," and I'm one of those men who has worked himself up from nothing. So for me, the situation we find ourselves in today is not new. The situation was different, and much worse, in the past. I only say this to make you see why I pursue my goal with such fanaticism and why nothing can weaken my resolve. I could be tormented with worries and even damage my health by worrying, but this would not change my decision to fight until the balance shifts to our side in the end.

The objection that one has to think in rational military terms in these circumstances can be countered best by a very quick glance into world history. Rational military consideration in the time after the Battle of Cannae would have convinced absolutely every man that Rome was lost. Abandoned by all friends and betrayed by all allies, having lost the very last combat-ready army and with the enemy at the gates, nevertheless the steadfastness of the senate—not of the Roman people, but the steadfastness of the senate, of the leaders—saved Rome at that time. We have a similar example in our German history—not on a worldwide scale, but nevertheless extremely decisive for German history, because the later establishment of the German Empire was also brought about by this hero or was made possible because of his historic actions. This was the Seven Years' War, when already in the third year, in countless military and political organizations, the dominant feeling was that this war could never be won. Based on human judgment, it should have been lost, because there were 3.7 million Prussians against 52 million Europeans.[1578] But that war was won nevertheless. So in conflicts of a worldwide nature like this, the cast of mind is a decisive factor, making it possible to find new ways out and mobilizing new possibilities. It's especially important to realize that the enemy consists of men of flesh and blood, too, who have nerves and who don't have to fight for their existence the way we have to. That means the enemy doesn't know—like we do—that it's about existence or nonexistence. If the British lose this war, it would not be as significant for them as what they've already lost in the war. America won't lose its state or its people. But Germany is battling for its very existence. You will all notice that the German people have understood this. You need only look at German youth today and compare them with the youth of the Great War. You need only look at German cities today and compare the attitudes with those of the German people in 1918. Today the whole German nation stands unshakable and will remain unshakable. In 1918 the German people capitulated unnecessarily. They have now come to recognize the danger of the situation and to understand the problems we face. I want to say this quickly as an introduction, and then address the strictly military part.

How is the military situation? Anyone who follows the familiar great conflicts of world history will find similar situations very frequently—perhaps even worse situations than we face today. Because one must not forget that even today we defend a Reich territory and an annexed territory that is far larger than Germany ever was, and that we also have armed forces that, in themselves, are no doubt even today the strongest on earth. If one really wishes to see the whole situation clearly, he only has to imagine one thing: just take one of our opponents as a world power—Russia, England or America—and there wouldn't be any doubt that we could handle each one of them alone in an instant. That proves the strength of the

German people, but also the strength of German military might—which, in the end, arises from the strength of the people, and can't be imagined in a vacuum.

Militarily, it's critical that in the West we transition from this unproductive defensive posture to offensive warfare. Offensive operations alone can turn the war in the West in a successful direction. In a defensive war we will soon get into a disastrous situation—to the extent that the enemy manages to use his materiel more and more effectively. He won't sacrifice men—at least not in the future like he does now—as one usually imagines. The idea that offensive warfare is always bloodier than defensive warfare is wrong. We have seen this on our side. The bloodiest and costliest battles for us were always our defensive battles. The offensive battles were—if one takes into account the enemy losses and ours, including the men captured—actually relatively favorable for us. It's similar in this offensive. If I imagine the total number of divisions that the opponent has thrown in here,[1579] and estimate his losses in captured men only—captured men are worth no more than dead men; they are eliminated—and if I add his casualties and losses of materiel and compare this with our losses,[1580] then there is no doubt that the brief offensives that we've already made have led to an immediate easing up of the situation along the whole front. Even though it unfortunately didn't lead to the decisive success we might have expected, a huge easing up has occurred already. The enemy has had to give up all his offensive plans.[1581] He's been forced to reorganize completely. He has had to re-deploy units that were worn out. His operational intentions have been totally thrown out. The criticism at home is enormous. The psychological moment is against him. Now he has to declare that there is no possibility of concluding the war before August, maybe even before the end of next year. So there has been a change in the whole situation—which one certainly would not have thought possible two weeks ago. This is the result of a single battle, in which we haven't even deployed a large number of divisions against the enemy; a large number of the armored divisions are still marching back or have been involved in the battle for only a few days. In my opinion, a defensive war would be unsustainable for us in the long term, because the casualties during the enemy's offensives are steadily decreasing, and the deployment of materiel is increasing. He'll stop these stubborn head-on pushes. The criticism at home is one decisive factor here. But on the other hand, there is also the gradually improving flow of ammunition and war materiel. To the extent that he's able to repair the harbors and solve his transport problems, he can—assuming the supplies[1582] are adequate—bring in more materiel. He'll get used to the kind of tactic we already learned outside Aachen: bombarding a position, shooting out single bunkers with tanks, and then occupying a completely dead area with comparably few infantry forces.[1583] In the long term, the loss of men won't be as great on his side as it will be on ours. During this time he'll slowly but surely demolish our railroad connections and increasingly reduce our transport options. We don't so much force him onto the battlefield with his bomber units; rather, we expose our German homeland to him—which affects the front through a reduction in the supply of ammunition, fuel, weapons, equipment, vehicles, etc., which therefore has negative affects on the troops. In other words: continuing our current or former tactics, which were forced on us by circumstances—we simply couldn't line up any earlier—would probably cause severe casualties for us while decreasing the enemy's losses significantly.

Thus, we will abandon these tactics as soon as possible—as soon as we believe we have sufficient forces to take offensive action. In principle, it is possible. The first action in our Western offensive has already made the Americans bring in at least 50% of the troops from other fronts, which has significantly weakened the other assault groups to the north and south of the penetration area. It has also brought in the first British divisions, along with a large share of the armored forces. I believe that eight or nine out of fifteen armored divisions have already appeared. So now he has to concentrate his forces there. This sector where we are going to line up now has also already thinned out considerably.[1584] He has pulled out division after division, so we really need to hurry if we're going to be able to destroy a large number of divisions. There may only be three or four. If we're lucky, there might be five—probably not six anymore.

I want to emphasize that the aim of all these offensives, which will occur in quick succession—I am already preparing a third strike[1585]—is first to eliminate the American troops south of the penetration area.[1586] We will destroy them one by one and wipe them out division by division. We will then see to what degree we can move directly into the penetration area from this operation. The troops in the penetration area have the assignment of containing the enemy forces. The penetration area is in a critical location for the enemy. A crossing over the Meuse would be immensely dangerous for the Americans and the British. An advance against Antwerp would be catastrophic. The advance didn't succeed. But one thing did succeed: Now all the essential available forces have been brought together to block off the danger. This is the first positive achievement. now it's about using lots of individual strikes to first destroy the forces lying south of the penetration line.

The task that the new offensive requires doesn't go beyond what is possible—beyond what can be achieved by our forces. On our side 8 divisions are lining up. Except for one division coming from Finland,[1587] the other seven are worn out; some of them have been rehabilitated. But the enemy—who face us with five divisions if everything goes well, or maybe only three or four—is not fresh either. His troops are worn out, too, except for one division on the Rhine—we will have to see first, how it proves itself—and the 12th Armored Division, which is still not certain to be deployed at all, and which in any case is a young unit that hasn't yet been in combat. But all the other units on the enemy's side are worn out, too. We certainly couldn't wish the circumstances to be any better.

If this operation is successful, it'll lead to the destruction of part of the group of divisions that faces us south of the penetration area. The next operation will follow immediately. It will be connected with another strike. In this way, I hope first to smash the American units lying to the south. Then we'll continue our attack and will try to bring all this into relation with the actual core operation.

So this second attack has one clear aim: the destruction of enemy forces. This is not about questions of prestige. It's not about gaining territory. It's only about destroying enemy forces wherever we find them. It's also not about freeing all of Alsace in this manner. That would be wonderful. The effect on the German people would be immeasurable, the effect on the world decisive—psychologically significant—and the effect on the French people depressing. But that's not important. It's much more important, as I said before, to destroy the human forces.

But in this operation it will also be necessary to give speed a high priority. That means that whatever we can take instantly, without departing from our original aim and direction, we must take, in my view. Sometimes one can try for weeks afterwards and still not succeed in taking what could have been taken before in three or four missed or wasted hours. One reconnaissance detachment and a small motorized unit or an assault gun brigade or panzer detachment might possibly cover 20 to 40 decisive kilometers—a distance one couldn't achieve in six weeks of fighting afterwards.

Unfortunately, we have experienced that in this operation. There were a lot of good omens for this first operation, and also some bad omens. One good omen: generally we managed, for the first time, to keep this operation a secret[1588]—for the first time, I might say, since the fall of 1939, since we've been at war.[1589] But even here some nasty things happened. Once again an officer tried to reach the front line with an order and got caught. It can't be determined today if the order was found and evaluated, or if it wasn't believed. In any case, the order did fall into the hands of the enemy. But, thank God, it didn't have any effect. At least no one reported that the enemy felt alarmed. That was a good omen.

The very best omen was the development of weather that had been forecast by a young meteorologist who was actually right—a weather development that gave us the opportunity, two or three days beforehand, to really disguise this last assembly, which almost couldn't be disguised, so that the enemy didn't see anything. The same meteorologist who forecast this weather with absolute certainty was right again. Then the total failure of air reconnaissance—partly as a result of the weather, but also partly as a result of a certain arrogance. The people didn't think it necessary to look around. They didn't believe in the possibility that we could line up again. Maybe the conviction that I'm already dead also contributed, or the idea that I'm suffering from cancer and can't live and can't drink anymore, so that danger is also eliminated. They were only dealing with their own offensive.

And there was a third thing. The conviction that we would not have the necessary forces. I can tell you something right here, gentlemen: our forces are certainly not inexhaustible. It has been an extremely hazardous business mobilizing the forces for this offensive and for the strikes to come—a hazardous business that has, of course, been connected to immense risks. So if you read today that it isn't going well on the south of the Eastern Front in Hungary,[1590] you need to know that we can't be equally strong everywhere, of course. We have lost so many allies. Unfortunately, we are forced to withdraw to a much smaller circumference area as a result of the betrayal by our dear allies. But despite all this, it has been more or less possible to hold the Eastern Front. We will bring it to a stop in the south as well. We will block it off. It has nevertheless been possible to draw up many new divisions, to give them weapons, to refresh old divisions, to re-arm them, to refresh panzer divisions, to save fuel—and especially to get the Luftwaffe in order again. It is now able to fly numerous sorties a day—if the weather permits—and is now coming out with new models[1591] that are finally able to attack the enemy from behind even by day, and against which he currently doesn't have anything to deploy. In other words, it has been possible for us to bring up enough artillery—mortars and so on—and panzer and infantry divisions to at least restore the balance of forces in the West. This is a miracle in itself. It required continuous investigation, months of work, and drilling down into the smallest details. I'm still not anywhere near satisfied. Every day something else comes that still isn't ready, that didn't turn out right. I just have received the bad news that the requested 21-cm mortar, which I've been chasing like the devil for months, probably won't arrive.[1592] But I hope they'll arrive anyway. There's an ongoing battle for weapons and men, for materiel and fuel, and the devil knows what else. It can't last forever, of course. So this offensive really must be successful.

If we can halfway manage to clear it out in the West again[1593] —this must be our one and only aim—then, above all, we'll get the iron situation in order again. Because we don't need only the Saar area; we especially need the Minette. That's one of the prerequisites. The more critical our situation becomes in the rest of Europe, the more important this ore region becomes. We can't continue this war—or go on existing as a nation—without certain raw-material resources. So this is critical as well. I hope it succeeds in the course of these operations.

But the enemy didn't think it possible. He was absolutely convinced that we were at the end of our rope. That was an additional third point that initially allowed our offensive to be successful.

Difficulties that arose then were, first, the unbelievably bad roads, and second, the repairs to the bridges that took more time than scheduled.[1594] Here we discovered for the first time what ten lost hours can mean—for a panzer division, ten lost hours can mean the possible loss of an operation. Someone who doesn't get through in ten hours might not be able to make up for it afterward in eight days. That's why speed is everything here. That's one point.

The second point is that as a result of getting stuck on bad roads, and as a result of several destroyed bridges that couldn't be repaired quickly, we didn't line up here with the fluidity that would otherwise have been desired; instead, we had an immense weight of materiel and especially vehicles.[1595] I don't know why those vehicles in particular were taken along. It was even claimed that vehicles were taken along to (take things away), so that everyone could take away whatever he could get a hold of. I don't know about any of that. But one thing is certain. We do have too many vehicles. We have to learn from the Russians in this respect.

One thing has been proven from the start. In this attack the infantry divisions advanced just as fast as—sometimes even faster than—the panzer divisions, even though these infantry divisions were on foot.[1596] It reminds me of 1940, when, for example, a division like the 1st Mountain Division—which I really worried about, wondering if it could catch up—suddenly started running like a weasel.[1597] All of a sudden they arrived at the Aisne almost as fast as our panzer units. Quite a few infantry divisions proved themselves here—some young divisions, whose progress really was hindered by the panzer units blocking the roads. They would have advanced more quickly if the roads hadn't been blocked by panzer units. So one thing is certain. Theoretically, of course, with panzer units where everything is motorized—I always hear that they are 75 to 80% or 85% motorized, which is usually too much already because then everything is driving, and there are 8 or 10 men on a truck, while in the past there were

30 men in a truck—one can certainly cover 100 km in a day with panzer units, or even 150 if the terrain is clear. But I don't remember a single offensive where we even just for two or three days covered only 50 or 60 km. In the end, the speed is usually not much higher than that of the infantry units. They only made shorts jumps. They could take something quite quickly—also the advance detachments of the infantry units—but then they'd have to again. As soon as the panzer division is unable to drive, too much motorization is a burden. Because if they can't get off the roads and have to drive at air raid intervals, it means that in the end some weapons will certainly not be in position. Either the artillery or the infantry won't arrive. It has usually only been small advance guards that have actually fought the battles. That emerged in the engagement of Army Group Model—also, for example, with the *Leibstandarte*. In the end, only the advance guards were in combat. From the 22nd SS Panzer Division, it was the advance guards that were in the battle. But an immense road leading to the rear is completely barricaded and blocked. One can't move forward or backward. In the end the supply of fuel can't even be brought in. This is almost like driving in place—it really is driving in place. To prevent frost damages, etc., they drive at night.[1598] And the people are warming themselves as well. It demands a huge amount of fuel. There are bad roads everywhere, and one has to drive in first gear. ... doesn't matter.

We really can learn only from the Russians. If I receive a report today about a Russian road that leads into a front sector where there are 36 rifle divisions and tank units, a certain number of tank regiments and several other units, it means that last night 1,000 vehicles drove on a road—and tonight 800, then 1,200 and 300 vehicles. That's an alarm that runs through the whole Eastern Front. It means an attack is imminent. With us, one panzer division has 2,500, 3,000, 4,000, 4,500 vehicles and reports then that it's only 60, 75 or 80% mobile. By chance I caught two mountain divisions, one of which has 1,800 and the other 1,400 trucks. These are mountain divisions! Certainly they will be picked apart now, if they haven't done it to themselves already. This development wouldn't be so bad if we could afford all this, and if we really could operate in wide open [terrain]. But when we're pressed in and crammed onto a few roads, this motorization can even be a misfortune. That's one of the reasons the right wing got stuck at first: bad roads, obstacles—bridges that couldn't be repaired fast enough—and finally, third, the difficulty of handling the mass of vehicles. And with that again the difficulty of fuel supply, which can't be brought in by the Luftwaffe as it was in previous offensives, and then, of course, the threat of a potential clearing in the weather. We must be clear about this. The Luftwaffe has done well. They have certainly engaged themselves very much and have done everything they could, considering the number of sorties possible with the aircraft they have available now. But nevertheless, in good weather we can't cover the air space in such a way as to prevent all (fighter-bombers) from coming. Then a crammed-full road like that is really a mass grave for all kinds of vehicles. We were nevertheless extremely lucky, because when the good weather came, we were already, for the most part, able to disperse.

These were, as I said before, the moments of bad luck that accompanied the moments of good luck. Nevertheless, for a brief moment the situation offered the hope that it might be possible to hold out. I also didn't believe at first that he would expose himself so much. But now that this exposure has occurred, it's time for us to do what we can in other spots along the front. And we have to do it quickly. So I come to something extremely critical: the objections that could be raised against a continuation of the operation. The first objection is the old objection. The forces are not yet sufficient. Here one can only say, "We have to take advantage of unique situations, even at the risk that we're not that strong yet ourselves. Because we've deployed very strong units now. If the attendant circumstances had been more fortunate, weaker units would certainly have achieved even greater success than the strong units in less fortunate circumstances. So strength can only be measured relatively. The enemy is not at full strength either. The enemy also has weaknesses."

The other moment that—as everybody knows—always comes up is that a longer break is necessary for refurbishing, etc. Gentlemen, speed is of the essence here as well. I believe that if we give the enemy time to think, we've already lost half our chance. Nineteen-eighteen must be a warning for us in this regard. In 1918 the breaks between the individual attacks were far too long.[1599] The reasons have been given. But there's no doubt that if the (second) offensive at the Chemin des Dames had taken place sooner (after the first),[1600] the results would have been quite different. Certainly the connection with the wing of the first big assault group could have been established via Compiègne, and the situation might have taken a decisive turn. Perhaps we could actually have reached the sea. So the breaks aren't always desirable, of course.

I must also emphasize something else, gentlemen. I've been in this business for eleven years now, and in eleven years I've never heard anyone report to me, "Now we're completely ready." Rather, in these eleven years there have always been reports that say, "The Navy urgently requests that we wait for such and such a time, because this and that must still be done; it will be ready on this date." The next time, when the Navy was ready, something came from the Army. It would be unfortunate to do it right now, because the Army is just about to introduce this and that and wants to wait for it. When the Army was ready, the Luftwaffe came and said, "It's absolutely impossible to do this before the new model is introduced; there's no way of attacking or exposing ourselves to such a danger." When finally the Luftwaffe was ready, the Navy came again and declared, "The former submarine didn't prove effective; a new model has to be introduced, and this new model won't come before the year such and such. We were never ready. And that's true for every offensive. The most tragic was perhaps the fall of 1939. I wanted to attack immediately in the West.[1601] They said, "We aren't ready." Afterward I was asked, "Why didn't we attack? We just had to order it." I said then as well, "It was a mistake." We should have just declared, "We will attack in the West on November 15 at the latest; that's it—no objections." Then we would have lined up. I'm convinced that we would have shattered France by winter and would then have been totally free in the West.

One is never really ready. That's quite clear. And it's also unthinkable in our situation. The big issue is always that if one theoretically gets ready, the things that are ready are not available anymore, but are needed somewhere else. We also aren't in a position today to put divisions on ice. All this is observed Argus-eyed. Whenever it's quiet in the East for 14 days— or at least no major battle—the commander of the army group in the West comes and says, "In the East there are still panzer units available; why don't we get them?" But as soon as it's quiet in the West, the same commander in the East declares immediately, "There's total quiet in the West; we could bring over at least four to six panzer divisions to the East." As soon as I get one division free, someone else is eyeing it. So I'm pleased if the divisions are there at all. Now I do it like some clever army commanders or commanders-in-chief, who don't pull out any divisions at all. Instead, they leave the divisions in, make very tiny sectors and say: I don't have any divisions available; they're all at the front. So I have to find a division on my own. Otherwise you won't get one at all.

So I must say, "We don't have unlimited time available either, because events march on." And if I don't act quickly in one area, a situation might occur in another area in the meantime forcing me to pull something out again. Time is of use only for those who take advantage of it.

Then there are other concerns about ammunition. I'm convinced that we'll come out better in terms of ammunition in this offensive, because experience shows that offensive engagements require less ammunition than defensive ones. And I have to emphasize something here, too. The general opinion is that we can't match our enemies for long in terms of ammunition. Usually, according to the troops' reports, even in the West we've had

ammunition consumption of about … of the Allies. In the East we've had
ammunition consumption that's almost 100% higher than that of the Russians. So if you hear sometimes that the Russians come up with immense
masses of ammunition, it's very clear today that German ammunition consumption in the East is exactly 100% higher than the Russian consumption.[1602] And I'm not even including the ammunition we leave behind on
our retreats. That can't be calculated. [—] So we will be able to supply this
offensive with ammunition. It's more a problem of transport.

In principle, the question of fuel is also assured for this operation. We
will get all of these things; there's no doubt. The general transport situation is more difficult. But the transport situation will improve to the extent that every commander of a unit conscientiously considers, "What I
have to take and what I don't necessarily need." Everything we take along
that isn't really necessary is not only a burden on the troops, but also a
burden on the supply and a burden on the whole fuel situation—and thus
a burden for these upcoming operations. That's why I think it's important
to consider very rigorously again and again: What do I not necessarily
need? It is by no means a desecration of the character or the honor of an
armored division—it doesn't matter if it's from the Army or the Waffen
SS—if a battalion marches on foot for once here. Because if they can't
catch up after a halt, they'll have to march anyway. They must go forward
regardless. So if the operation led into the Sahara, for example, or to Central Asia, I would say: I understand that one has to keep the vehicles. In
this operation, when at the most (50 to 60) km will be covered, one can go
on foot. After all, the infantry has to do it as well. They've never known
anything else. That's why they see it as their God-given fate or their honorable duty, while the armored unit sees it as a kind of insult if some of their
troops have to march on foot for once.

I believe this is one of the most decisive factors in the success of this
operation. In general, the plan for the operation is clear. I totally agree
with the measures that have been taken. I especially hope that we'll be able
to bring the right wing forward quickly to open the entries to Zabern, and
then immediately push into the Rhine plain and liquidate the American
divisions. The destruction of these American divisions must be the goal. I
hope that the fuel situation will then allow us to assemble a new grouping
and carry out another strike, which I absolutely expect—with even larger
forces—to destroy even more American divisions. Because the number of
our forces has increased somewhat again. I hope that I will be able to
support this next attack with … additional divisions, including again one
very good division from Finland. So unless this thing is haunted by bad luck
right from the start, it must work out, as I see it.

I don't need to explain to you a second time how critical this is. Also the success of the first operation is very much conditioned by this. Because as soon as we carry out these operations A and B and they succeed, this threat to our left flank will stop automatically. Then we'll have our third battle there and will totally smash the Americans.[1603] I'm absolutely convinced that we'll be able to turn to the left then.

It absolutely must be our top priority to clear out this matter in the West through an offensive. It must be our fanatical goal. If one or the other secretly holds this against me: Yes, but will it succeed? Gentlemen, those objections were raised to me in 1939, too! In documents and statements I was also told, "We can't do that; it's impossible." Even in the winter of 1940 I was still told, "We can't do this. Why don't we stay at the Western Wall? We've built the Western Wall; we should let the other one storm it and we can maybe attack him in from behind—but let him come first, then maybe we can advance afterward. We have all these wonderful positions and we're taking a risk!" What would have become of us if we hadn't attacked back then? It's just the same today. The balance of forces is no worse today than it was in 1939 or 1940.[1604] On the contrary—if we succeed in destroying these two American groups in two strikes, the ratio of forces will be clearly and absolutely turned to our favor. But I'm counting on the German soldier to know what he's fighting for.

The only thing that's not working in our favor this time is the air situation. But that's what is now forcing us to take advantage of the bad weather—the winter—at all cost. The air situation is forcing us to do it. I can't wait for good weather. I would also prefer it if we could hold out tolerably and put it off until spring. By then I will have drawn up 10, 15 or 20 more divisions, and in the spring we attack. But, first, the enemy will also bring over 15 to 20 more divisions. Second, I don't know if I will rule the air any more in the spring than I do now. But if I don't control it better in the spring, the weather situation will be decisively in the enemy's favor, whereas now there are still weeks when they at least can't carpet-bomb troop assemblies. That's already significant.

But to show how important it is to decide this affair, I will give you only one thing to consider. Now the enemy knows all about the flying bombs. Today he has reconstructed them completely, of course. We know that. He's already producing them. There's no doubt that he could almost completely demolish the Ruhr area with a massive firing, just like we're continually disrupting the industrial areas in England.[1605] There's no protection against it. We also wouldn't be in a position to fend this off with fighters. I don't even want to mention the heavy rockets. There's absolutely no defense against them. So everything points in one direction: that we should clear up this situation before he is able to deploy large weapons as well.

The German people themselves have been able to breathe again during these last few days. We must not allow this respite to turn into lethargy again—lethargy is wrong, it can turn into sadness. There has been a sigh of relief. Only the idea of advancing offensively has had a cheering effect on the German people. And if this offensive is continued, when the first big successes emerge—and they will occur, because our situation is no different from that of the Russians from 1941 to 1942, when they, too, were standing under the most unfavorable conditions, and when they maneuvered us backward with individual offensive pushes against this long front where we had transitioned into a defensive mode—when the German people first see this development, you can be sure that the German people will make every sacrifice that is humanly possible. We will be successful with every single appeal to the German people. The nation won't shrink back from anything—if I do another fabric drive or collect something else, or if we need men, the youth will volunteer enthusiastically. But in any case the German people will react absolutely positively, as I must say that the nation is as decent as can be expected. There are no better people than our German people.[1606] Individual bad incidents are certainly the exception that prove the rule.

So, in conclusion, I would like to appeal to you to stand behind this operation with all your fire, with all your energy, with all your strength. This is a decisive operation. Its success will absolutely and automatically bring about the success of the second one. The success of the second, follow-up operation will automatically cause the breakdown of the whole threat to the left side of our attack. Then we will actually have taken half of the Western Front from the enemy. Then we will see. He won't be able to withstand long against the German divisions—about 45 will line up then. Then we will master our fate after all.

The date has been scheduled for New Year's Eve, and I am very grateful to all participating staff who, first, have taken on this huge amount of preparatory work, and second, have accepted the risk of taking responsibility for it. I see it as a particularly good omen that this was possible. In German history, New Year's Eve has always meant good military fortune for us.[1607] For the enemy, New Year's Eve is an unpleasant disturbance because he doesn't celebrate Christmas, but New Year's. And we couldn't start the New Year any better than with a blow like this. And if the news arrives in Germany on New Year's Day that the German offensive has started again in another place and that this is leading to success, the German people will conclude that the old year ended badly but the new year has started well.[1608]

That's a good omen for the future. Best wishes to all of you, gentlemen, for yourselves.

One thing I might add, gentlemen: the secrecy of this operation is the prerequisite for its success. Anyone who doesn't have to know about this doesn't need to know. Anyone who must know something about the matter should only find out what he needs to know. Anyone who must know something about the matter should not find out about it any sooner than he has to.[1609] This is critical. And no one who knows anything about this matter—and who could possibly get caught—should come into the position and be sent to the front. This is decisive.

V. RUNDSTEDT: My Führer! In the name of all the commanders assembled here, I can assure you that on the part of the leaders and the troops, everything—really everything—will be done to help this offensive succeed. We all know where mistakes were made during our first offensive. We will learn from that.

End: 7:38 p.m.

* * * * *

MEETING OF THE FÜHRER WITH MAJOR GENERAL THOMALE, DECEMBER 29, 1944, AT ADLERHORST[1610]

Also present: General Buhle

Beginning: 1:15 a.m.[1611]

The West

THOMALE: I just spoke with all the divisional commanders again about your wishes and concerns.[1612] The divisional commander of the 21st Panzer Division, Feuchtinger,[1613] and the commander of the 25th Panzer Grenadier Division, General Burmeister,[1614] were there. The commander of the 17th SS [Panzer Grenadier Division][1615] was absent, unfortunately. But I know his concerns and will follow up on this matter myself.

THE FÜHRER: I think he has the fewest concerns.

BUHLE: He's in the best situation, by far. He has been supplied with a complete Training Regiment—a compact regiment. He is by far in the best situation.

THE FÜHRER: If it works out right with his crews—that I don't know. They do have some issued materiel. I have ordered that all SS unit crews be pulled back, so we have a certain reserve at home. I don't know if it's been carried out yet or not. He certainly doesn't have any crews.

THOMALE: Just half an hour ago I was told—it's a rumor, I want to emphasize—that he is short 30 crews. So without finding out more about this rumor, I ordered that 30 army crews in this area of the West be assembled and prepared for departure, so that they can be sent there in wood-gas vehicles—that way a shortage of 30 crews won't cause trouble for us under any circumstances. So I've assembled them there preventively. Whether they're necessary or not, at least they're there.

THE FÜHRER: At least he only has a few materiel concerns.

BUHLE: I do have a compilation here from December 10, from SS Command headquarters[1616]: In the 17th SS Panzer Grenadier Division there are 20 crews without Panzers but with assault guns, and 20 crews without tanks with Tank Destroyer IVs.[1617]

THE FÜHRER: For crews he's had to deploy mostly infantry because he has no men. That's the tragic thing about it—that these men might be deployed as fighters too quickly. In principle, one shouldn't do that. Because I can't replace them in that short amount of time. I can't take out an old tank driver.

BUHLE: It's the same with the drivers. We're always training thousands of drivers. They must be there somewhere.

THE FÜHRER: Many of the drivers go into the companies, of course, when they don't have anything else. They say that the division must hold. They don't have any vehicles anymore, so they take some of their men.[1618]

THOMALE: The supply lines are just being combed out.

THE FÜHRER: Those are the healthiest ones, of course. They're taking the best boys. They're the best drivers, too.[1619]

THOMALE: I'd like to summarize the results of this meeting. The divisional commanders have the greatest concerns about the staff composition, of course. The staff composition has been thrown into great disorder. So the training condition is not in order either, and—what's the worst for the tank people—the radio can't function then. That puts the mobility on the battlefield in question. That's unfortunately what happened to the *Leibstandarte* on the first day. They hadn't been allowed to radio for weeks before.[1620] They were out of practice. In the first days, for example, the radio didn't even work in a good division like that. One can't hold it against them. I've been speaking about it with General Buhle. This regulation— that radioing is forbidden—may have been issued by some intelligence man gone wild. People in foreign countries know that the *Leibstandarte*, *Das Reich*, and so on are here. So then they can radio, too. They can do some harmless practice exercises and radio something. This teamwork can't be carried out for the first time on the battlefield.

BUHLE: Obviously, the people back in the operational rear area can't radio. Also here, this armored army was recorded as present by the British weeks before.

THE FÜHRER: They knew it was there.

BUHLE: So we should and must allow these people to radio as well. Otherwise they can't train.

THE FÜHRER: We only have to find a way to maintain this radioing, even if the unit has moved away. I don't know how it can be done, but it's critical.

THOMALE: It can be done.

THE FÜHRER: So they continue radioing, and the normal radio communication goes on with the help of substitute machines that we bring in, or we move the radio operators out at the very last minute! Because they recognize the different radio operators—they recognize by their personality if they're new or if they're different people.

THOMALE: As a further summary, it can be said that of these three divisions, the 21st Panzer Division is in the best condition, in my view, and that the mobility of all three divisions can be considered absolutely sufficient.

THE FÜHRER: I think so too.

THOMALE: So now I come to the individual divisions. The 25th Panzer Grenadier Division looks like this: (*Presentation.*) The units that are not outlined are the units that have been in combat already. The blue-outlined units are the units that have been in Grafenwöhr for rehabilitation and training so far, and will now be brought in. The panzer grenadier then looks like this now at the beginning of the attack: two panzer grenadier regiments with two battalions each. These red colored battalions won't come until January 31—therefore, later. Regimental staffs are there already. The second is missing only the heavy infantry gun company. That will follow on the 31st as well. Then the Panzer detachment will come here, with 36 Panthers and 11 Panzer IVs long L 70, and a tank destroyer detachment with 31 Panzer IVs long L 70—so this division has more than 78 tanks available in total.

THE FÜHRER: That's what they'll actually have when they deploy?

THOMALE: When they deploy. I just requested the train departure times again this evening—how it stands at the moment. For the 25th Panzer Grenadier Division, I just reported: 36 Panthers is the target and 42 Panzer IVs long. It actually has—this is what Burmeister admitted: 6 and 19. In the allocation there are 30 Panthers and 22 Panzer IVs. Of those 30 Panthers, 10 departed on the 25th at 9 p.m., and the other 10 on the 25th at 10:45 p.m., at one-hour intervals. They were handed over on the 27th in Landau to the Saarbrücken transport command, and on the 26th—one day before—from Soest to Wuppertal. They will certainly be there tomorrow morning. But this evening it was impossible to find out where they are because of the telephone connection. They should be there. If the first 10 were in Saarbrücken yesterday and the second ten were in the area of

Wuppertal the day before yesterday. We should assume that these first 20 will arrive tomorrow during the course of the day. The last nine of these 29 or 30 left Soest on the 26th. They were there on the 26th as well, so we can assume that they were also in Landau on the 27th. The train couldn't be reached in such a short time this evening. There are 29; there should be 30. The one, the command vehicle, broke down in Grafenwöhr. It will be sent on afterward. Then the 22 Panzer IVs long—17 and 5, so that makes 22—are allocated. They left Breslau, were in Kohlfurt on the 28th, and are now in the Halle district. I'm a bit concerned about whether or not they will be there in two days. But I want to assume they will. And these are also in the Halle district.

THE FÜHRER: If they're in Halle, I don't know if they'll come.

BUHLE: I'm not worried about the 21st Panzer Division and the 25th Panzer Grenadier Division because they're in the second line. I am worried about the 17th [Division]—that they will get their tanks.

THOMALE: But I believe that if they're in Halle today, they will arrive in two days.

BUHLE: They'll all be there by the 1st.

THOMALE: That's the situation with regard to the tank allocations. The personnel reinforcements: they have all departed. I had all the specialists with me here today. As I just reported to you, they will be full with two regiments of two battalions each. With regard to the weapons, everything that's missing is on its way except for the carbines; we're still short on those. There are no carbines at the moment. The 13 missing medium mortars and—

THE FÜHRER: What good are the people if they don't have any carbines?

THOMALE: Most of them do have machine guns and pistols. All of them are more or less specialists. There are relatively few who are still equipped with carbines in a panzer division. It's the baggage trains that have the carbines. [—] One light field howitzer is missing. It's there, too. [—] To summarize, we can say, with regard to tanks, the division will presumably be full. With regard to weapons it will be three-quarters full, considering that the carbines, for example, are missing. With regard to vehicles it's also three-quarters full, but that means it's sufficiently mobile. With regard to personnel it's been brought up to 90%. A few individual specialists in the artillery, the engineers, the infantry, and so on, might be missing. I've already spoken with the divisional commanders about whether they agree with this summary. They completely agree with it. These blue, newly allocated units of the 2nd refurbishment [installment] are not integrated with the combat units yet, of course. This battalion doesn't know this battalion. The commander of this regiment doesn't know this battalion. So the bonding and the teamwork are still missing.

THE FÜHRER: It's the same in the 17th Division. They don't know their training regiment yet either. But if we have to bring up people during the battle, it's just the same. If I suddenly subordinate an unknown battalion, it's just the same.

THOMALE: The 21st Panzer Division looks like this: again two panzer grenadier regiments of two battalions each, of which one is an armored personnel carrier battalion,[1621] just like in the 25th Panzer Grenadier Division. The 25th Panzer Grenadier Division looks better than the 21st Panzer Division with regard to armored personnel carriers. It's a little behind there. But the 21st Panzer Division is much better in terms of tanks. It has two Panther companies with 19 each, two Panzer IV companies with 17 each, and a tank destroyer division with 21 tank destroyers. If we calculate the target: two times 19 equals 38 Panthers, two times 17 equals 34 Panzer IVs, plus 21 tank destroyers. Adding those numbers together makes 93. So it's going up against the enemy with 93 tanks. It has an actual supply of 32 Panzer IVs, 16 Panthers, and 4 Panzer IVs long. Feuchtinger has admitted this. So in the allocation there are 2 Panzer IVs, 22 Panthers, 17 Panzer IVs long. Their status: the 2 Panzer IVs departed on December 25 at 4 o'clock; we don't need to worry about them. The seven Panzer Vs were in Eppingen already on the 26th, in Karlsruhe. They have already arrived. He has reported that already. The ten Panzer Vs were in Crailsheim today, the 28th. So they're there as well. The five Panzer Vs were also in Crailsheim today. So the 22 missing tanks are there. The 17 missing Panzer IVs left on December 27, but tonight it wasn't possible to find out where they are at the moment. So these 2 and 22 are certain, so the Panthers and the Panzer IVs are guaranteed. And they left on the 27th. They will all be there by the 31st. I'm not worried. All the weapons are on their way, too. One-third of the missing machine guns have arrived already. The 6 light field howitzers that are missing will arrive by December 31. All of the heavy infantry weapons will arrive as well. The personnel allocations have also all already left. They will be there in time, too. So the division will be one hundred percent complete except for a few specialists. To summarize: the 21st Panzer Division is the best-equipped in terms of staff and materiel. The training situation again: units are not yet integrated, even down to the crews. [—] Then comes the 17th SS, where I have not personally spoken with the tank man in question. I can only report that the 17th SS Panzer Grenadier Division has 45 Panzer IV assault guns and 31 [*Vomags*],[1622] which makes 76. Here the target is 76. They have 19. 57 are in the allocation. These 57 all left Alten-Grabow[1623] today. That was because the crews weren't made available before yesterday. I'm not worried. Leaving Alten-Grabow today, they will make it without any trouble.

THE FÜHRER: With them it certainly is important.

BUHLE: Everything is going with special transports. If it doesn't get there in time—we should double-check it tomorrow, Thomale—then we'll have to give this division assault guns from other divisions and the arriving—

THOMALE: Wouldn't it be easier to put the 21st Panzer Division into the first wave?

BUHLE: That's not possible anymore.

THOMALE: The 21st is the best. I've always emphasized that the 21st is best of all.

THE FÜHRER: I don't think it will work out.

BUHLE: They've already been instructed. We can't do that anymore. Part of the 17th is in front already and will stay in its sector.

THOMALE: I will be here all day tomorrow. I wanted to go there straight from here for the day of the attack. Back then I was with Sepp Dietrich, Manteuffel[1624] and the divisions right away as well. It's always good to be there on the first day.

THE FÜHRER: I hope the new method works out well, and that they can cheat their way in without artillery preparation. We can't do any artillery preparation because we'd only be shooting into the empty space. He doesn't have anything in the front. That's why it's all the more important that the heaviest tank destroyer detachment, the 653rd, comes in.[1625]

THOMALE: I spoke with Westphal[1626] today about the tank destroyers with the 12.8. Westphal told me that they've "set heaven and hell in motion" to make sure they arrive.

THE FÜHRER: That's by far the most valuable, of course. In the future, too, these things have to be either deployed or pulled out. We can't let them hang around like this. Have they been deployed at all?

THOMALE: Westphal said that the one company hasn't been deployed.

THE FÜHRER: And the second one?

THOMALE: The second one was still on its way.

THE FÜHRER: So neither of them has been deployed?

THOMALE: No, neither of them has been deployed.

THE FÜHRER: One can only say that they are insane. That's the strongest weapon. If the others run against our fortifications with 10 or 12 heavy tanks, there is so much noise that everything is literally exploding. But if we have 24 of the absolute heaviest in the world, they're not even deployed at all.

BUHLE: The second company wasn't there yet.

THE FÜHRER: Hopefully they will be deployed now. Otherwise I'll go crazy. Buhle, you may tell Westphal: it is not acceptable to not deploy such special weapons. It's a outrageous. These gentlemen have no idea of the value of such a weapon. That's because our whole leadership doesn't think technically enough. They can't imagine it because it's only two companies. We won't make 10,000 of this weapon anyway—not even 1,000.

THOMALE: The 17th SS still is designated as two regiments with three battalions each. The third one, the training regiment, has never been deployed.

THE FÜHRER: In reality there are only two regiments. The training regiment makes one, and the other two will be merged. Has he done it yet?

BUHLE: Yes, Sir. He has done it. He still has one battalion from the second regiment, and from the other regiment he has taken over the other battalion completely. It wasn't difficult to bring them together.

THOMALE: So it's two regiments with three battalions each again.

THE FÜHRER: I don't know if the second regiment, the training regiment, has three battalions.

BUHLE: Yes, it comes with three battalions—three panzer grenadier battalions. This regiment has one heavy infantry gun company, one anti-aircraft company, and one engineer company.

THE FÜHRER: How strong is the regiment?

THOMALE: It should be 3,000 men strong. The battalion will have about 750 men.

THE FÜHRER: Today he says it's only 2,000 men.

BUHLE: He'll have 2,500.

THE FÜHRER: If we say a number that's too low, they don't say anything. They only cry if we name a number that's too high.

THOMALE: Now there's the reconnaissance detachment. There I can report that for the entire 17th SS Panzer Grenadier Division, 1,000 men have arrived. Thirty assault guns are, as mentioned, missing. I've had them supplied as a precaution. Two hundred and twenty reconnaissance tanks have arrived as well.[1627] The third panzer grenadier regiment is on its way in. It will arrive on time. All the missing weapons are on their way. The 14 light field howitzers that are missing—with the artillery this seems to be where the biggest shortage is—are supposed to be there by December 31. It's the same with the 29 medium mortars. I will call the senior quartermaster about that again right away, to have him expedite this matter.

BUHLE: I already spoke with him last night.

THE FÜHRER: But the most important are these two heavy tank destroyer companies, the 653rd.

THOMALE: Westphal reports every day about their great problems with the bridges, because they have to reload there.

THE FÜHRER: It really is outrageous that they haven't even deployed them there at least. That's because those people don't know anything about special weapons like this.

THOMALE: Then to report on what you ordered before: the 257th Volksgrenadier Division and the 559th Volksgrenadier Division have received the assault gun companies—they received them from the 79th and the 712th [Infantry Divisions].

THE FÜHRER: Will receive!

THOMALE: No, they'll arrive tomorrow. The 559th will get the one from the 712th and the 257th from the 79th. The 79th is already in the Stuttgart area today with its assault gun company, so it will be with the 257th tomorrow. The 559th, which is supposed to get the 712th's company, has already been in Utrecht and is now on its way down. So it will be there by the day after tomorrow.

THE FÜHRER: I just thought of something, because people are always complaining that they get the replacements too late. We marched off for the second offensive in 1918 on the evening of the 25th. On the 26th we spent the night in a forest and on the morning of the 27th we lined up. We marched off at 5 o'clock. One day before, in the afternoon, we received the replacements for the big offensive on the Chemin des Dames.

BUHLE: Replacements totaling 60,000 men have gone to the West. I purposely stopped the third installment on the 15th, when it was supposed to leave, because more had obviously come out—because the operation began later—than were needed. Then everything is shared among all other divisions. That's why I stopped the last 12,000. They're rolling out right now. Otherwise they would spread them over all the divisions in the Netherlands, etc.—that's why the Dutch divisions have grown so strong—and the replacements Model is already crying for[1628] would then be missing.

THOMALE: The ordered assembly: as I reported already, the following have been supplied and brought forward first: 40 Panzer IVs, 6 Tigers, 6 Hunter-Tigers [Jägd-Tiger], 34 tank destroyer IVs and 44 tank destroyer 38s. These were present in the form they're in here. Of those, these have already been distributed to these divisions, and today there are again 32 Panzer IVs, 25 Panthers, 13 assault guns, 6 Tigers, 6 Hunter-Panthers, 23 tank destroyer IVs, and 16 tank destroyer 38s ready. These are over and above what's needed to replenish the 21st, the 25th, etc.; so the things I was able to send in here afterward are not included.

THE FÜHRER: I spoke with Saur today. He says he hopes to produce about 1,500 tanks and assault guns this month.[1629] Here the issue is, above all, getting the replacements to Model as well—and doing so quickly enough that we can line up again then.

THOMALE: Here's what we have again today. If I add these together, it makes 121. So at least there's something there today. So here I have the distribution for December 1 through 28. In total, 532 went to the East and

774 to the West, plus the 121 here, which makes 895—so around 900. The other theaters are Italy and Hungary. All in all, the total I received in December was 1,526. The projection is for 2,235. I'm not convinced that we'll get them. For example, he says 380 Panthers. I know that only 280 will arrive.

THE FÜHRER: That's impossible. He has projected a total of 1,500 tanks and assault guns. This projection, of course, is based on a plan that was made a long time ago.

THOMALE: That's what was still being said at the beginning of November. But it keeps changing all the time.[1630]

THE FÜHRER: It's the destruction.

THOMALE: So now I have 1,500 already on the 28th. This is the spillover from November. I calculate very strictly: from the 1st until now I've received 1,526. Now it turns out again that in this month of December, I will have at least 1,700 vehicles. At the very end of the month—these three days—is when most of it always arrives.

THE FÜHRER: I asked him what he'll be able to bring out by January 10. He hopes to bring out several hundred tanks and 300 to 400 assault guns—so between 600 and 700 altogether.

THOMALE: Then I have the 121 at first, and if he sends me another 600 I'll have 721.

THE FÜHRER: And we have to count on that, in order to be able to follow right away with the next operation.[1631] Speed is of the essence now. One thing has become apparent again—there's no doubt about it. We had very bad luck in the first operation. Bad luck in a great variety of respects. That's why more tanks were lost than necessary. But nevertheless, we destroyed at least 600 to 700 enemy tanks. We can say that 6 to 7 divisions were completely smashed.

THOMALE: You ordered me to supply 100 armored personnel carriers by December 20. Of these 100, I supplied 143 by the 20th. They have been distributed as follows: (*Reading aloud from the presentation follows.*) By the 31st I was to provide another 100. So I still need to bring in another 57. That's no problem for me. Because of the refitting ordered for the 21st, etc., 43 beyond the originally ordered 100 armored personnel carriers had to be allocated. (*Reading aloud follows.*) If more come in, of course, I will supply more. What hurts me this month is that the 500 promised medium armored personnel carriers won't come—only 400. If I only receive 400,[1632] I'll get there with my 57 armored personnel carriers. [—] That's the personnel replacements. I have received 3,850 infantry replacements and 7,800 replacements for the Luftwaffe. From myself, from the panzer grenadiers, I've taken another 4,900, so that altogether there are 16,550 replacements in the march [trained replacement] battalions. In addition, the Commander-in-Chief West has received 2,800 specialists, so altogether we have brought in an additional 19,350 men in December for the panzer troops in the area of the Commander-in-Chief West.

THE FÜHRER: That's a lot.

BUHLE: There's a bit of misappropriation everywhere. In the formations' tables you were shown this morning, there were only 14,000.

THOMALE: For the panzer divisions being deployed in the East, I need a supply of 5,550 tanks and for the Commander-in-Chief West[1633] 600. The East has received almost four times as many as have gone to the West. [—] That's a personnel plan for January. I don't want to present that now. [—] That's everything that I wished to report to you tonight.

THE FÜHRER: Saur told me again that he's trying to build as many of these heavy antitank guns as possible right into the armored patrol cars.

THOMALE: As you ordered, I've started with all the armored personnel carriers in the East. They're standing around out there, so they're already starting to build.[1634] All the new production is going to the West now anyway, and will be delivered with the 7.5 L 48.

THE FÜHRER: There's no doubt that that's the most decisive thing we can possibly do today.

THOMALE: For me, the 352nd and 353rd Flame-Thrower Panzer Companies, which are already on their way to the operation, have been a disappointment. I must report that they have a flame-throwing range of only 35 m.[1635]

THE FÜHRER: That's insufficient.

BUHLE: Saur told me yesterday that it was 60 to 80 m.

THOMALE: That was reported to me by the weapons office. I can only pass on the report from the weapons office.

THE FÜHRER: Get in touch with Saur right away! We need to have a flame-throwing tank with a range of at least 120 m.

BUHLE: We do have a flame-throwing tank with a range of 120 to 140 m, but in order to do that the tank needs to be equipped differently, of course. A barrel like that can be installed in eight days. An extension has to be mounted.

THE FÜHRER: I would suggest that we take tanks only where only the hull is still tolerably usable, add armor plating—strong, if possible—get rid of the turrets completely, and instead strengthen the armor plating.

THOMALE: Yes, Sir. The 38-tons don't have turrets anyway. These here are two 38-t companies. This here is another Panzer III company. That one does have a rotating turret. It couldn't be taken off in this short amount of time.

THE FÜHRER: We need to create another detachment that is really very heavily armored. Because they need to be able to approach close enough to actually hit.

THOMALE: But I would nevertheless suggest that we let them go in the third wave—we can't let them go in the first wave—so that the cleaning out can follow immediately. They really have to paint the trenches with their flames.[1636] [—] I just wanted to report this soon enough to avoid disappointment.

THE FÜHRER: Only tanks with the heaviest armor plating are suitable as flame-throwing tanks, of course.

THOMALE: Yes, Sir.

THE FÜHRER: It would be better if we could take a Tiger—maybe in the form of a Hunter-Tiger —turn it into a flame-throwing tank, and bring in a stream of 200 m.

THOMALE: We can take all the Tiger I's coming out of the repair service, where only the turrets are damaged. We can do that without any problems. We still have enough Tiger I's. I have to gradually convert Tiger I detachments to Tiger II detachments anyway.[1637] I don't need them at all. I already have a remote-controlled detachment of Tiger I's.[1638] So it can be done easily. But it's not possible to do it within the short time that you ordered. I must give the ordnance office and Saur the credit for being unable to manage it in such a short time.

THE FÜHRER: Above all a very long flame jet.

BUHLE: I made some investigations. We have one that throws 120 to 140 meters.[1639]

THE FÜHRER: That's the minimum.

BUHLE: Saur told me, as I reported yesterday, that the first attempts to shoot flames were apparently quite successful. He said it reaches to about 1,000 meters.[1640] [—] Let me also present a notice about a question that has been posed repeatedly by the troops and the antitank-gun people in the West—and also by Thomale's man[1641]—concerning the installation of the 7.5 into the 3.7 gun ports. (*Presentation.*) In my view, the most important thing is that these gun ports were built under other circumstances and for other conditions.

THE FÜHRER: Granted, but—

BUHLE: Here he writes at first only what people outside say to him. He contrasts it later, on the next page.

THE FÜHRER: That's rubbish. It's real nonsense. I could just as well refuse every rifle because of the risk of fragmentation effects.

BUHLE: In my opinion, the most important fact is that they installed all these ports in an area that was considered suitable for tanks at the time, and that the rest of the area is completely vacant—

THE FÜHRER: We have to add something to it. There we can take all those 8.8-cm guns in depth.

BUHLE: —and that these antitank guns are all more or less concentrated on the front line.

THE FÜHRER: If it's the other way around the troops will start to shout if they have nothing in front.

BUHLE: Now, this man offers a suggestion that I agree with. He says we must not attack now; now everything must be thrown in [—]

THE FÜHRER: We'll get more of them.

BUHLE: —and afterward we can find a balance. He only wants to have this very clear command relaxed—which I gave in response to your order that these gun ports must all be equipped with the 7.5—so that he can equalize later on.

THE FÜHRER: You have to understand. The forward line will be covered to a depth of 1,000 to 2,000 meters. In a situation like this, with concentrated artillery action, based on experience I would say that an antitank gun wouldn't be possible. If I put them further behind, the penetration won't be adequate. They can reach no more than 1,000 meters today—and even there I couldn't reach the Sherman.[1642] Then they'll complain again out front that the tanks will drive up to within 30 to 40 meters of the emplacements and blow them to bits. So that contradicts the other facts. It's obvious that I have to find a reasonable balance everywhere. The realistic balance would be for me to erect more 8.8-cm antitank guns in depth on the battlefield, as they have an effective range of 2,400 meters and can reach even to the foremost point. That's for the deployment in depth. Then we have a lot of 8.8-cm guns that weren't installed in the tank destroyers, as we were unable to produce them in greater number.[1643] We should get 80 of them. They should be arranged in depth and, along with the others, they should fill up the emplacements initially. It's quite clear that not every one will have the opportunity to shoot. But the probability of one or the other having the opportunity to shoot is greater than the probability that they would be preserved if they were positioned in the forward area. Above all, the crew wouldn't stay long. Those men won't fool me. Here they want me to believe that the crew, when they're standing at 1,000 meters, where they can't operate—with a range of 1,000, I won't hit anything today—won't run away. The crew runs away and the antitank gun stands there completely alone. That, too, is understandable because they're being beaten up. There we can only answer: everything remains.[1644] Whatever else comes they will erect in depth, above all the 8.8. They should really bring the long-range flak in depth. That's open to them anyway. They don't need to build emplacements for that. Since the 8.8 is delivered with a provisional cross artillery mount, you can place them everywhere in no time; I think it would take only one night or a couple of hours. They should camouflage them completely so they're not visible. That's what will best prevent a breakthrough in depth. [—] The old view about terrain that is safe or unsafe for tanks is wrong—I've fought against this mistake for years—because they've never tried it. It was the General Staff that ruled: here tanks can operate, but not here. I've seen terrain where I had to laugh. One General Staff officer, who had surely never driven a tank, ruled: tanks can't operate here. I said: "How can you claim that?" What was built at that time was already completely insufficient back then. It wasn't created for the huge number of antitank guns that the infantry divisions are sup-posed to have. Instead, it was already a consideration at that time, that some of the antitank guns—we didn't reckon primarily with air strikes then, but with heavy barrage, which is now emerging as very troublesome again.[1645] Because if you listen to the people who are at the front near Aachen, they say: everyone is pounded at once. You have to ask someone who comes from there. Someone who comes from there, of course, is going to say that everyone is pounded at once. But it's the fortification specialists who stand in a quiet area and say, "Here you can't cover every-thing, so that has to go away." I have to bring something else additional in. [—] One more thing. In the past, these specialists built the so-called anti-tank-gun dugout, the antitank-gun Remise[1646]—not the antitank gun em-placement. I said to the people at that time, "Do you seriously imagine that in an emergency situation the crew could pull an antitank gun out into torn-up terrain?" The men looked at me as if I were insane. [—] And now those emplacements have been destroyed. All the emplacements that are built high above the ground are being destroyed now. But no one can destroy the ones that are hidden underground. No one can stand in front of them; no one can hit them. The emplacements that are really dug in were only built for air defense because the Luftwaffe—in Kitzinger[1647]— had taken on a man who had already built such things during the Great War. [—] In 1939 I fought for the flame-throwers, but the idea was re-jected by the general in charge of the engineers—this genius was called Förster[1648]—with the claim that they hadn't proven useful during the Great War. I said, "How can you maintain that, Herr General?" He said, "It is a known fact." I said, "How can you say such a thing? The flame-thrower was one of the most effective weapons used during the Great War." I participated in that mess myself, but the general hadn't. He said, "You could see at Douaumont that it was dangerous for our own people but not for the enemy." Now, of course, Douaumont blew up because a couple of people tried to make coffee with a hand grenade. One went off, which set fire to the munitions, and that set off 1,600 liters of flame-thrower oil. Douaumont burned down because of that, of course.[1649] That could hap-

pen anywhere. With the same right you could say: ammunition is something completely obsolete; did you hear that a munitions train blew up
again? [—] That was the general who distinguished himself at Rzhev again.
I shunted him aside back then. He would have built a German fortification like the Maginot Line, with an unbelievable expense of materiel and
without any fortifications above. Now people come to such fundamentals
and say: the … must out. That was indeed one of the differences between
the western wall and the Maginot Line, where there was nothing outside.
Above there were two machine guns and down below there were 167 men
attending to the two machine guns. They were attending to elevators. Down
below were electric elevators, electric lines, etc. It was complete madness.[1650]
But the whole thing was built by those people back then, or it was at least
influenced by them. This is also crazy. The condition of the position on
the river Saar is a crime. Instead of going up, they built it down. At first
they had it behind Saarbrücken. Then I demanded that it be erected in
front of Sarbrücken. But I didn't specify the line myself. The result was
that they remained down in the valley. And in front of that is a cliff 60, 80
or 100 meters high, which goes down vertically and is perfectly suited to
setting up the whole ammunition storage and supply behind the cliff. Then
you leave and let others take over the observation.[1651] In this case I can
only say: that's how the German General Staff has been under the leadership of Herr Beck[1652] and later Herr Halder.[1653] Those were the guns they
made in the end.

THOMALE: You said today that the panzer divisions should be humble
and ride bicycles again. I only wanted to say that we in the Inspector General's
staff had the idea and put them on bicycles ourselves. I support that very
strongly.

THE FÜHRER: I'm not so much in support of bicycles per se, but we
really must analyze carefully what needs to be driven. I know how they
waste people in the military, also horses—today I had a long conversation
with Frank,[1654] who said to me, "We can't afford this long term with
horses—or motorized vehicles." It's that way with people as well. I experienced it earlier, when I was a messenger. For example, if a commander at
the front received a postcard, a man had to run forward that day—at least
in our regiment in 1915 and 1916, before we received a decent regimental
commander—and had to bring him the postcard, which was announced
by telephone from the rear position. That could cost the life of a man, and
it could even endanger the staff itself, because by day one can see from
above where the people are going. Genuine madness. But this ridiculous
waste of people had to be gradually brought to a halt from above. They
did the same with horses. At that time, for example, they would drive from

Messina to Fourne for a pound of butter, and would bring forward a pound of butter from Fourne to Messina. That's nonsense, of course. It was the same in industry: a 4.5-ton truck drives somewhere to fetch a small machine that weighs 12 kg. We've gradually put a stop to that now. [—] Something else has to be considered. I believe that the current panzer divisions—from the point of view of future effectiveness—are improperly designed, because in the end it will be shown after all that one can't undertake such deep operations in the limited European space. Because in the future, after a few days, one can't count on such an empty space as in 1940.[1655]

THOMALE: We hold the same view. On the one hand, based on the reason you just said. Also, the company, battalion, regiment, and division commanders are unable to lead such mammoth units today. I've also argued about that problem with Sepp Dietrich: why this unbelievable number of trucks? That must be ordered regularly now. There I have the support of General Buhle.

THE FÜHRER: What would really strengthen the panzer divisions would be an increase in the armored personnel carriers.[1656]

THOMALE: Yes, Sir.

THE FÜHRER: Because there I can also come down from the road relatively quickly, and on average terrain I can disappear sideways across relatively long distances, where I would otherwise be bound to the roads anyway. If I don't dominate the air completely, I am forced to drive at air raid intervals. If it stops up front, everything else has to stand still as well. Then I have distances of 40, 60 or 80 km for the whole column. Those foot marches are much harder than if I had organized them a little more primitively from the start.

THOMALE: I started immediately with the reorganization of the panzer corps. I went so far as to have only one panzer grenadier regiment for three battalions. The SS and everyone are going crazy. They say there must be two regiments for three battalions again. I said, "We'll get to that." Now I've already taken the whole supply away from them. We have to organize these divisions to be as small and as strong—in terms of tanks—as possible.[1657] [—] I need to add one more thing: if you install too many heavy weapons in the armored personnel carriers—three-barreled guns, 7.5s, etc., then I can't put people on them.[1658] Then I need too many armored personnel carriers again in order to take the people away.

THE FÜHRER: The ideal would be if we had enough tanks so that we didn't need to take the armored personnel carriers. And we would give to the reconnaissance detachments—which sometimes have to be very fast cross-country—a few armored patrol cars and enough antitank guns so that they aren't immediately destroyed.

THOMALE: But the reconnaissance detachment has eight. Because of your suggestion, I would like to ... the tank destroyer detachment now, which until now had twelve motorized platoons. [—] The tank destroyer detachment in the panzer division was equipped as follows—for example, the 21st Panzer Division: two assault gun companies and one motorized platoon. Those I want to change to self-propelled guns with 38's.[1659] Then, first, I will have my tractor-pulled weapons below me. The whole thing becomes much shorter. And I will make twelve armored personnel carriers with the 7.5 L 48s. Those I want to cut out of the armored personnel carriers and save somewhere, maybe with the engineers, so that I end up with the same number of armored personnel carriers. That way I get twelve more 7.5 L 48s in total. The reconnaissance detachment gets eight, and here they have twenty.

THE FÜHRER: The reorganization will never end. The manufacturing conditions at home change, the training status changes, the leadership capabilities change as well. That's nothing new. A short time ago, I read in a volume of letters from Fredrick the Great—in one letter he writes the following: "I entered the war"—this was the fifth year of the Seven Years' War—"with the most wonderful army that ever existed in Europe. Today I have a mess. I have no more leaders, my generals are incompetent, the officers are not leaders anymore, my troops are miserable." It's a devastating judgment. But, nevertheless, the man persevered in the war. If you read the judgment about the Russian troops, it's terrible. But the people do persevere anyway. Those really are the eternal and most fundamentally genuine soldierly qualities. Because soldierly qualities show themselves not in some game in a sandbox somewhere, but in the moral quality of perseverance—in toughness and persistence. That's the decisive factor in every success. Brilliance is just a phantom if it isn't supported by persistence and fanatical toughness. That's the most important thing in all of human life. People who only have ideas and thoughts, but who don't have firmness of character or toughness and persistence, won't be able to achieve anything. They are soldiers of fortune. When things go well, they're on top of the clouds; when things go wrong, they back down immediately and abandon everything again. You can't write world history like that. You can only write world history if—behind intelligent reason, a lively conscience and eternal alertness—there is a fanatical persistence, a strength of will, that makes a man an inner warrior. The soldier feels it as well in the end, in critical moments—that his leadership represents these qualities. Some don't like that; they are the worse ones. But the good ones can identify with that and feel secure, because they say to themselves: why have we made so many sacrifices? Because the war won't last as long again as it has lasted until now. That's very true. No man can stand that. Not us; not the others. It's only a question of who can stand it longer. The one for whom everything is at stake will stand it longer. For us, everything is at stake. If the other says one day: now we've had enough—nothing will happen to him. If America says, "Out! Finished! We're not giving up any more boys for Europe"—nothing will happen. New York will remain New York, Chicago will remain Chicago, Detroit will remain Detroit, San Francisco will remain San Francisco. Nothing will change. If we say today, "We've had enough; we're stopping"—then Germany ceases to exist.

End: 2:10 a.m.

1945

* * * * *

January 9-10, 1945

On the Eastern Front, it is obvious that fighting will soon resume. In Slovakia and northern Hungary, the German troops have been thrown back across the Hron [Gran] River, and the front has come to a halt south of the river, along the Bakony Forest–Lake Balaton–Nagy Kanizsa line. The Soviets are currently attacking north of Szekesferhervar [Stulweissenburg].

In Italy, an unusually hard winter has forced the Anglo-American forces to halt their operations.

In the Ardennes, the Fifth Panzer Army has withdrawn to Houffalize under pressure from heavy attacks against both of its flanks since January 3. The minor German offensive in lower Alsace has brought only limited improvement to the front between Bitsch and the Rhine River. Otherwise, the situation in the West is unchanged.

(Maps 5, 7, 11, and 12)

* * * * *

CONCLUDING PORTION OF A MIDDAY SITUATION REPORT, PRESUMABLY, JANUARY 9, 1945[1660]

THE FÜHRER: ... We have such a huge number of radio operators that our communications should function splendidly. And as you saw with Kesselring, if someone does it right, it does work.

KEITEL: Berlin had been everywhere along the front.[1661] He visited me before that situation arose. He had just spoken to me about it.

GÖRING: It's best the way. It is with Sepp Dietrich, to whom we immediately gave the entire unit.[1662]

THE FÜHRER: But he complains that his radio operators are bad, too[1663] ... The Luftwaffe has even ordered butter via radio transmission. Surely they must be able to transmit.

GÖRING: Radio operators have also been released from flight crews.

THE FÜHRER: We observe this thing here from above, of course. How it actually works out in reality—that is the same as if I take the Reich Court in Leipzig and the policeman outside, who has to transform the orders of the Reich Court into practice. Those are two different worlds. Here it is a non-commissioned officer or watch officer or sergeant who has to decide in the end where the man is placed. Then they are asked, "What were you, actually? Radio operator? What did you do the whole time? Did you ever hear a shot?" ...

(GÖRING): ... the people arrive somewhere else, then they have to turn in their weapons again and are sent away without weapons. I gave that to you;[1664] they changed weapons three or four times. It's quite natural that this doesn't increase their courage and eagerness to fight.

JODL: Anything can happen. I also read today that the people who were supposed to be sent to us by the Luftwaffe were shuttled from one barracks to another for eight weeks. They didn't even have one day of training, and then they were given to the Army. For eight weeks they did nothing but move from one barracks to the next.[1665] You wouldn't believe what can happen.

THE FÜHRER: Here you experience everything until the last ... and in the eleven years of experiences that I've had in my current capacity.

GUDERIAN: Wöhler[1666] has just brought a new report from the field: that during these battles [northwest of Budapest] the 1st Guards Mechanized Corps showed up with 150 new tanks, which hadn't appeared since the invasion of Romania; a corps about whose presence we haven't been informed. ... The earliest time for the attack [German counterattack] is the 14th or 15th.

THE FÜHRER: That doesn't matter then. Under that precondition, I would say that we would want to move the Tiger detachment here.

GUDERIAN: Up here [north of the Danube River east of Komarom] is initially the push from north to south ..., because the enemy is weakest here, and then a sharp turn toward the east. He has just strengthened himself with the 4th Guards Mechanized Corps up here, with the 5th Guards Mechanized Corps here and here. If we immediately push around here, we would take the bull by the horns, according to Wöhler. The weakest place will be here ...

THE FÜHRER: ... can scratch together at all. For this purpose, we have to hold the view that this is the main action, so we need to continue to push here. The deception must be good here.

GUDERIAN: Yes, Sir. He is of the opinion that we must nevertheless reinforce strongly here [near Esztergom-Gran] later on, in case Gille[1667] comes out. The 3rd Panzer Division and the 3rd Cavalry Brigade must come in here. Otherwise it won't hold.

THE FÜHRER: The 3rd Cavalry Brigade as well?

GUDERIAN: He doesn't believe he can hold it this way ... should leave them here because they can get out of the woods better ...

JODL: I still have to present a message from an informer in Antwerp, reporting that a V2 crashed into the "Rex" cinema during a crowded show on December 17, 1944. There were 1,100 victims, including 700 soldiers.

THE FÜHRER: That would finally be the first successful launch. But it is so fairytale-like that my skepticism keeps me from believing it. Who is the informer? Is he paid by the launch crew?

JODL: The informer has the strange name "Whisky."

THE FÜHRER: That's a bad chief witness.[1668] [—] If the Russian won't join in, he's refusing for political reasons.

GUDERIAN: Because of the English.

THE FÜHRER: ... You have to consider that there are a huge number of Polish voters in America. The Polish have a strong influence on the Catholic clergy, and the Catholic clergy are gradually starting to rebel against Roosevelt's Christianity. The Greeks are Orthodox; they have less influence in America. They give them up. A suggestion was made by the Americans now—it has just been aired, and I assume it is a trial balloon. It would be unbelievable if it were really done like this; the British would be absolutely furious. Europe should be divided into several spheres of influence ... and only because they intend to engage in blackmail. On the other hand ... have hesitated. They have presumably not signed the new delivery contract because of the Lend-Lease law. That is the Americans' blackmail.[1669] For the Russians, the question is what they would prefer: getting the deliveries, giving up some things and attacking Germany again in order to take some of the burden off the others, or doing without the deliveries, keeping their people and assessing the situation in Europe. Stalin has a huge fear of Germany. ...

GUDERIAN: ... not concerning pilots either.

THE FÜHRER: When the two squadrons come it will be better.[1670]

GUDERIAN: Then it will be better.

THE FÜHRER: But it doesn't make a big difference.

GUDERIAN: The big question is ammunition. If we get ammunition now we can do a lot.

THE FÜHRER: Now our departure from the East is gradually starting to take its toll. We should already have had a monthly allotment of 2 to 3 million rounds for the Eastern Front alone, from our factories here.[1671] Back then they said: What point is there—some iron mines! And the front was even shorter then than it is now.

GUDERIAN: It is getting longer with every step backward in Hungary ...

THE FÜHRER: ... brilliant thoughts, that they said, "We stand on Crete, and so on—and we lose Königsberg." That was the phrase. The fact that I didn't stand on Crete for pleasure, but that I stood on Crete in order to ... all the Balkan countries, Turkey ... was brushed aside. They also didn't realize that I wasn't in Petsamo for pleasure. One can't say that it's fine without nickel. It is not fine without nickel. We were able to stock a supply for a certain time. We have lived, after all, for four to five years. It's because of the aircraft that we can live without that. It's not as good as it was before.[1672]

GUDERIAN: That's why the Hungarian area is so important.

THE FÜHRER: For me, the greatest concern is that we build the jet factories now (for the Me 262), but we don't know yet how great an effect the deterioration of the material will have ... outlets. For the engine it can be said that an engine block consisting of 65% nickel is better than one of 10% nickel. ... With the new electro-processing we are making progress. But these major revolutions—war is the father of all things; they have invented the most during the war—require years to get from the awareness to the experiment, from the experiment to the first prototype, from the first prototype to reality.[1673]

THOMALE: To mass production!

THE FÜHRER: And then to mass production anyway. Many years go by. You can't do that. It's a catastrophe. Now the absolute worst that can happen to us is the destruction of the German transport system.[1674] We have enough coal. They mine so much from the pits that it can't be carried away ... We have more than 80,000 railroad cars too many. But we can't run them ... This means that we will drop from 2.9 million steel to one half that, or less. At first, this will primarily affect ammunition, since ammunition has the shortest production cycle. Those are all the people who continually attacked me earlier because of my "mad" policies of holding large areas. They would have preferred that we remain in the cramped space. Memoranda of Herr Beck![1675] The people wanted to make war in a vacuum. In my opinion, there must be courses in the future that teach what is necessary to conduct a war.

GUDERIAN: The War Academy!

THE FÜHRER: In the past, they judged it from the point of view of food. They knew that you can only feed armies if you have space. That is the whole Wallenstein tactic. I have read criticisms of Wallenstein, also by military men who have made God knows what kind of accusations ... vanished like a swarm of locusts. They could only stay for a certain amount of time in one area. His operations were determined by the necessity of feeding 50,000 men. Such a playground strategist, of course, ingeniously rejects that 250 years later and says: That was a mistake; he should have marched to there. Wallenstein wasn't as stupid as a minor strategist might imagine.[1676] He also had no railways. At that time living space [*lebensraum*] was important for food supply. Living space is important for the delivery of supplies. You can't make war in a vacuum, and if Germany hadn't extended its living space ... Holland. These worthless countries exist only because some European powers couldn't reach an agreement on devouring them. If this decisive great power Germany weren't present, these countries would vanish from the map. You see that with the Hungarians and ... It makes me furious when they come again and again and say, "Don't harm them; it damages their honor!" They don't even have honor. These worthless countries are the most sensitive that exist on earth. Others trample on them. [—] I gave another order yesterday that 50% of the Me 262s must be modified for the 500-kg bomb again.[1677] Because I have to be able to drop it. If we don't attack the traffic network of the others, we are simply handicapped. It must also be possible to make a few attacks on Antwerp during the day. We can't rely on the V1 or V2 launches.

GÖRING: Antwerp is only a question of range.

THE FÜHRER: I have ... he says the question is if they can accommodate the 500-kg bomb with four guns. Then I said: Good—take out two guns and see if the operational radius increases.

GÖRING: It's always the same again, what we bring out in the front.

THE FÜHRER: Then we'll have to see if we can make it work with small changes. I consider the range to be most important. Without a doubt, the bottom line for us is that we cause the enemy the same replenishment difficulties. Because he is more sensitive to supply problems, since he lives off of materiel alone. He doesn't have railway repair facilities like we do. He has fewer locomotives than we do. While we have 1,800 more locomotives ... only 60% of his earlier locomotives altogether. Of that 40% the majority have been destroyed. If I destroy something there and demolish the trains, I hand him a devastating blow. Without materiel, he is even less able to conduct war than we are.

GUDERIAN: That is very important in the Romanian and Bulgarian area.

THE FÜHRER: There we can do it.

JODL: A memorandum that Ganzenmüller[1678] gave me proves that it doesn't work to supply armies long-term without railways.

THE FÜHRER: Long-term it is impossible to supply an army without trains. The English have published a very ingenious document that contains a truism. It says that our weakness in North Africa was the absence of a railway network. That is very simple. But it wouldn't have helped us because we didn't have superiority in the air. Railways plus air dominance were necessary. Railways alone are of no use. But if I can break into his protected airspace with some modern machine—that can only be done at high speed—and hit him at the railway stations! He is much more sensitive than we are. He is not at all prepared. We have lived through this misery for years. There is another letter from Ganzenmüller, describing how the Reich railway improvises. It is really a wonder how people can improvise today, with a minimum of labor. That is already astonishing. Imagine: according to earlier views, a country would be paralyzed after a week of such attacks. Our air raids on foreign railways were child's play, and even then we paralyzed them in a short time. The others can't do that either. They don't have the power behind them. There is no one there who registers the people. They are not organized. They have complete disintegration of the civil authorities. You can do that only in a country that is organized very tightly. The Russian—that pig—has managed it. If someone starts to whine among us, I can only say: take the Russian in his situation in Leningrad.

GUDERIAN: He leads brilliantly. The boys in Hungary lead well—very fast.

THE FÜHRER: The way they have survived this crisis!

GÖRING: They let a million die of starvation.

GUDERIAN: They lead very energetically, very quickly, and very decisively. It is a lot.

THE FÜHRER: That's why I am strongly in favor of quickly reorganizing, Guderian.

GUDERIAN: If it doesn't work, we'll regroup tomorrow. Wöhler has been instructed accordingly.

End: 8:18 p.m.

* * * * *

EVENING SITUATION REPORT,
JANUARY 9, 1945, IN ADLERHORST[1679]

Present:

The Führer	*Rear Admiral v. Puttkamer*
Ambassador Hewel	*Lieutenant Colonel Waizenegger*

Beginning: 12:55 a.m.

The West

WAIZENEGGER: Enemy advances north of Nijmegen failed. Some prisoners of war, among them several Canadian officers, were brought in here. Otherwise, no particular combat action on the Army Group "H" front. In the Elsenborn area, in front of the 277th [Infantry] Division's front, several assembly areas—up to battalion strength—were destroyed by our artillery fire. Also here, in the Aisomont area, our artillery faced hostile movements and fire from enemy infantry. Along the Sixth Panzer Army's front, the enemy attacked strongly again, but not until noon. Numerous hostile attacks failed in the area east of Otré. Attacks were renewed again this afternoon. Here in the area east of Odeigne, there is a penetration of approximately 1 km in depth. Counterattacks by parts of the 9th SS Panzer Division have begun. Southwest of Odeigne, the situation here in this forest area is still unclear. From the area of Dochamps, the enemy advanced to the south, pushing approximately 500 meters into our main battlefield. A combat group from the 2nd SS Panzer Division is launching a counterattack. Cielle was lost here. The 2nd SS Panzer Division is also counterattacking here. West of that is another penetration, also approximately 1 km deep, which parts of the 116th Panzer Division are attacking. These assembly areas here were smashed by artillery fire. A hostile thrust failed here on the northwestern front of the 116th Panzer Division. On the western front of the XXXXVII Corps, no major combat activities. But the enemy also pressed very strongly against the southern front of the Fifth Panzer Army again. He achieved a local penetration northeast of Tillet ... employed for the expected attack after very strong movements were reported in the last few days. He achieved breakthroughs on both sides of Longchamps, each approximately 1 km in depth. Counterattacks were launched. Here our advances to the west towards Bastogne failed. An attempt to clear out this penetration here didn't succeed either. There were stronger hostile motorized movements from the south, which then turned to the east in the area south of Bastogne, so we also have to plan on reinforced attacks against this front soon. Lively fighting near Nothum. The enemy attacked here to the northwest and north, supported by approximately 20 to 30 tanks. The push to the north failed. To the northwest, he achieved a slight local penetration here, which was blocked. Otherwise, no major action on this front. In the LXXXII Corps area, the enemy attacked several times against Fraulautern and Roden, but without success. The 17th SS Panzer Grenadier Division is still fighting here in Rimlingen. They hold the southern part of the town. The enemy has started a counterattack from the southeast, and fighting for the town is still in progress. South of that, here in the area north of Guising,[1680] a hostile push supported by five tanks was driven back by our artillery fire. 250 prisoners were taken during the battles here in this area. North of Lambach,[1681] the enemy attacked the 559th Division front with two to three companies, supported by two tanks; they were stopped in front of our main battlefield. Northeast of Lemberg our attack to the west … hostile artillery activity. Fighting by the XXXIX Panzer Corps: here the 29th Panzer Grenadier Division broke through the Maginot Line at noon and advanced to the area of the railway station 500 m west of Hatten. The 21st Panzer Division took Hatten and pushed the enemy back toward the west. In the afternoon, both divisions met a stronger antitank barrage here, east of Rittershorn. The divisions are regrouping now and will continue the attack tonight at 2 a.m.—the 25th in the direction of Suburg,[1682] and the 21st north of there toward Sultz. 300 prisoners were taken during these battles … South of Niederrödern, the woods here are strongly occupied by infantry. Very heavy mining was reported from this location. This town, Forstfeld, was reported enemy-free by our reconnaissance. Stronger occupations southwest of there. No enemy in Neuhausel either. As expected, the enemy began stronger attacks against the bridgehead north of Strasbourg today. After moving a regiment into position, supported by approximately 40 to 50 tanks, he attacked from the northwest and pushed our covering party back to the street between Herlisheim and Drusenheim. During the fighting, the enemy advanced to Herlisheim but was then thrown back to the northeast by our push. A counterattack by two battalions was started in order to bring the old main battle line [HKL][1683] here southeast of Rohrweiler back into our possession again. Thirteen enemy tanks were destroyed, and three of our own.

THE FÜHRER: In general, it's still three to one with the panzer forces. It's like that in the East as well. Regarding the tank numbers Guderian gave today, one questions unfortunately didn't come to mind at the time: the problem of ammunition. I could have said that immediately. The barrel number is a farce. ... It was the same with Army Group North. If I add up the totals, we have approximately 3,000 tanks and assault guns in the East today. If I plan on the normal destruction ratio of approximately three to one, the enemy needs 9,000 tanks to destroy our last one. He doesn't have 9,000 tanks—not yet, anyway.

WAIZENEGGER: Also our own firing rate in the East is far higher than that of the enemy. We fire much more. [—] On the northern front of Nineteenth Army ... that is practically cut off. A combat group from the 106th Panzer Brigade is attacking to the south from the area of Gerstheim. Further details about this attack are not yet available. Other parts of the combat group have reached this bridge here near Haussern. In this area near Herbsheim, and also near Rossfeld, groups of enemy forces have been encircled. They are receiving heavy fire from antitank guns and mortar. The enemy is now trying to attack from the northwest to free these groups again. But all his attacks failed in the area southeast of Sand and near Huttenheim. Two tanks were destroyed during that action. Southwest of there, in the area west of Rossfeld, our own main battle line was strengthened. So the fortifications of this newly won main battle line should be noted. In the backcountry, there are still these two enemy groups that are heading toward their destruction.

THE FÜHRER: Of course, if it goes well we could probably indeed break through to Molsheim. That's not impossible, with the 269th [Infantry Division] in addition.

WAIZENEGGER: I also think he has positioned himself with his forces mainly in the area north of Strasbourg, so he won't have very much here. [—] Further south there was nothing.

Italy; Southeast

In Italy no major action; nothing in the Southeast either.

The East

In the East there was no major action with the Second Panzer Army or the Third Hungarian Army. But there was heavy fighting here [north of Szekesferhervar], with Breith's[1684] assault group. Today the breakthrough of 80 enemy tanks here to the southwest. ...

THE FÜHRER: ... with the Luftwaffe the whole problem is that we have desperately bad aircraft.

WAIZENEGGER: There are 80 tanks. Yesterday evening I ordered the final assembly of approximately 70 tanks in the area of Zamoly. They were employed during this attack.

THE FÜHRER: That is the one corps that is theoretically supposed to have 150. But half of it is gone. Here I see the chance of attack as quite high. Fighting the antitank-gun blocking position here is pointless. I see a much better chance of breaking through here.

WAIZENEGGER: Yes, indeed. [—] During the attack up above, this newly forested area, which has been cut up badly, proved very unfavorable. The assault troops are arriving here a bit weakened, and in order to tear through here we need a supply of new forces.

THE FÜHRER: Yes, especially infantry.

WAIZENEGGER: We can't attack the antitank-gun blocking positions with tanks.

THE FÜHRER: What they have achieved is very good. But even those very bold things were accomplished by the infantry.

WAIZENEGGER: Yes, indeed. [—] Here [south of Esztergom—Gran] this combat group has pushed into the forest terrain, advancing on average about 3 km, against quite tough enemy resistance. The assault group of the IV SS Panzer Corps didn't advance any further. Stronger hostile counterattacks from the south and east were driven back.

THE FÜHRER: They will also fail; that is quite sure. It's coming to a halt here now. But now we have to get in motion. We certainly can't do that here anymore, and the faster we regroup, the ... I consider the whole thing impossible.

WAIZENEGGER: The timing isn't easy either, I believe. It was ordered this afternoon. It will take quite a lot of time before the assault group has assembled and the supply and organization are complete. [—] In the area north of the Danube River, the situation hasn't substantially intensified or changed. The enemy attacked again with tanks against Komarom [Komorn], and 7 tanks were knocked out. The enemy tank losses in the whole area here are still enormous. Yesterday 51 tanks were destroyed north of the Danube.

THE FÜHRER: Something else is noteworthy: the gradually increasing use of antitank grenade launchers [*panzerfaust*]. If I had millions of them in the troops, then eventually a few hundred tanks would not approach a certain point, if there were 10,000 antitank grenade launchers, even if there were still a lot of misses.

WAIZENEGGER: A couple of days ago, we mentioned a panzer division in the Armed Forces report—I'm not quite sure which division it was—that destroyed 80 tanks within a certain period of time, 60 of them with short-range weapons. The antitank grenade launcher has proven valuable, and the people now have confidence in the weapon; they know how to use it and have very great success with it.[1685] [—] Here the enemy attacked via the Esztergom [Hron]-Novy Zamky [Neuhausel] railway line toward the north, but was thrown back. Otherwise, the situation between Komarom [Komorn] and Novy Zamky [Neuhäusel] hasn't changed. Today at noon 30 trains of the 20th Panzer Division arrived [at Nitra]. It has 55 trains in its combat elements, plus another 15 in its advanced training element. The division is arriving at Speed 8.[1686] [—] Here, west of the Hron [Gran] River, the enemy broke through our defenses northward and turned toward the east. He took Bina on the Hron [Gran] himself. Otherwise, there was no particular combat action on the Hron [Gran] front. The northern part of Pukanec, which was lost yesterday, was taken back again during the counterattack. Other than that, there was no major action in the Army Group South area. [—] Here in the area of Army Group "A," the enemy achieved a local penetration along the boundary between the Hungarian 16th Infantry Division and the 1st Ski Jäger Division.[1687] A battalion of the ski Jäger division is counterattacking right now. ...

THE FÜHRER: There they are launching a few attacks.

WAIZENEGGER: During the last days, we received reports of very strong logistical operations in the Baranow bridgehead. They have the impression there that he will start soon.[1688]

THE FÜHRER: So here he is supposed to have—if we take the general figures, and if it's true that he has 150 guns here on a 1-km front[1689]— that's 1,500 guns on over 10 kms [of front]. That can't be true at all. That would be 15,000 guns over 100 kms [of front] and about 20,000 guns over [a front of 150 km]. And the Russian forces don't consist only of artillery, either. Besides, what does he shoot out of those guns? Ten or 12 rounds per gun?

WAIZENEGGER: He has certainly strengthened his artillery enormously, but not to that extent, of course.

THE FÜHRER: He can focus on a few main points here. This operational idea of pulling back here [to the west], forming two groups, and then attacking with them is quite a dangerous idea.

WAIZENEGGER: Otherwise there is nothing, my Führer.

THE FÜHRER: The weather for tomorrow?

WAIZENEGGER: Very good weather for us in the West, my Führer. Low clouds. ...

End: 1:12 a.m.

* * * * *

MIDDAY SITUATION REPORT, JANUARY 10, 1945, AT ADLERHORST[1690]

Present:

The Führer	*Colonel v. Brauchitsch*
Reichsmarshal Göring	*Captain Junge*
Field Marshal Keitel	*Oberbereichsleiter [?] Lorenz*
Colonel General Jodl	*Lieutenant Colonel Borgmann*
General Buhle	*Lieutenant Colonel Hermani*
Ambassador Hewel	*Lieutenant Colonel Waizenegger*
Lieutenant General Winter	*Lieutenant Colonel Weiss*
Lieutenant General Zimmermann[1691]	*Major Büchs*
Vice Admiral Voss	*Major John v. Freyend*
Major General Scherff	*Sturmbannführer Göhler*
Rear Admiral v. Puttkamer	*Sturmbannführer Günsche*

Beginning: 5:06 p.m.

THE FÜHRER: Did you see this, Göring? Something leaked through there again! (*Presentation.*)

GÖRING: My Führer, by chance I experienced this myself. A few days ago I was making a phone call, and suddenly a long conversation came on the line—I don't know who was calling—about V2 and V1, about supplies that had to go there, and two missing "Meilerwagen." That struck me—that strange expression "Meilerwagen."[1692] It was the first time I had heard it. They had to go to there, that would take until tomorrow, etc., etc. It lasted about a quarter of an hour. I listened in on everything over my phone ...

The West

ZIMMERMANN: ... Up here, for the moment, nothing changed since yesterday.

THE FÜHRER: And here?

ZIMMERMANN: Nothing there either—nothing established at all. Here he is still very weak, so we have no clue if anything has been added to it, but nothing seems to have been taken out, either. [—] Army Group "H" saw virtually no action. Just a single small reconnaissance push here at Gravenwegen, which was driven back. Besides our own reconnaissance patrol activity, no major combat action, just intermittent fire. [—] At Army

Group "B," the fierce and repeated attacks of the last few days ... against the north flank a bit ... The pressure point is again the area of Bastogne and eastward around Lottre ... Here are individual tanks. It is also assumed that right now the whole division ... Here, for the most part, all attacks yesterday and today were driven back ... In the area of Tillet, which was given up voluntarily yesterday, he pushes with ... that these units are thrown into battle in groups, delaying their assembly. Strong pressure on the Führer Grenadier Brigade here, but it's not considered threatening by Army Group "B" because an extraordinarily strong antitank-gun front has been built up here. Otherwise, there were only smaller raiding party attempts here in the Seventh Army area. Other than that, nothing unusual. [—] The bringing forward of reserves is currently as follows, my Führer: you sent an order today regarding the I and II SS Panzer Corps with the four divisions. The order was passed down by the field marshal[1693] immediately with the following wording: "The Führer has ordered that the I and II Panzer Corps with the 1st, 2nd, 9th, and 12th SS Panzer Divisions, beginning immediately, ... are to assemble for rapid refitting behind Army Group "B," and placed at the disposal of the Commander-in-Chief West in such a way that they no longer become involved in combat ..." Field Marshal Model reported on the order that the postponement ..., that the established organization of the divisions ... during combat the relevant unit has to ... his ... every atomization [dispersion of forces] is a tactical [blunder] ... [which will lead to the] relief of army leaders, commanding generals ...[1694]

THE FÜHRER: We will do that! [—] Where is Burgdorf?

ZIMMERMANN: ... division commanders down here.

THE FÜHRER: Division commanders can't be called to account because they don't want that at all. They fight tooth and nail to avoid being split up. It's only the army commanders and the army group commanders who are the culprits in this case. [—] But get it [the order] ready immediately.

ZIMMERMANN: A new word has been coined: atomizers [—] So right now the Army's 9th Panzer Division is outside [the bulge], along with the *Leibstandarte* and the 12th from the SS.

THE FÜHRER: Is the *Leibstandarte* outside now?

ZIMMERMANN: Yes, Sir. The *Leibstandarte* is outside. Only Group Peiper is missing, as it lost its way a bit at Malmedy at the time and is now being pulled back by Field Marshal Model.[1695]

THE FÜHRER: We have to make sure that we reactivate the units again as quickly as possible, because the long time ... Field Marshal Model doesn't believe it either. He's not that stupid ...

ZIMMERMANN: In the area of Army Group "G," in general, on the whole ... bridgehead of Saarlautern ... the enemy has a single bunker ...

THE FÜHRER: We have to consider one thing here: whether we really shouldn't send in one or two dozen Hunter-Tiger. Of course, we must have sufficient artillery at the same time. But they could pound a bunker like that to bits. But that's not possible right now?

ZIMMERMANN: ... because they are difficult to move. [—] These attacks out of the Wimmenau area to the north against the 6th Mountain Division were all thrown back; in one place they attacked with tanks, and they were also thrown back. But those are units ... committed as decoys. The attack of the 21st Panzer Division was successful today, although it is still only of local nature; fighting through the different bunkers that kept resisting again and again—while some of the crews first hid in the small towns and then reappeared again later—did cost a lot of time. But according to some still unclear radio reports, the 21st Panzer Division should be north of Rittershofen now. Rittershofen was supposedly captured in a difficult engagement this morning, and this road was reached. But that is not confirmed yet—it's only a radio report. [—] This morning five bunkers were taken. A small error was made with one of them. It was at bunker 361, the uppermost bunker here. We would have noticed it afterward; that was the one 300 m to the southeast. So it was a false report. [—] According to the report, they were here; the town itself was strongly occupied by the enemy. This wood here, part of the Hagenau Forest, ... also tanks inside. ... one was shot out; after that the others turned away again. [—][1696] After that the field marshal ordered, "The stronger enemy resistance in the Hattingen area has probably resulted in a weaker hostile occupation near Roschwoog— that's up there—so the plan remains for the 10th SS Panzer Grenadier Division to start in the general direction of Bischweiler, via Selz. The designated combat group of the 10th SS Panzer Grenadier Division—that should be an infantry regiment, a panzer detachment, an artillery detachment, and we still hope to get an assault gun detachment there in time as well—is to be brought forward to Selz as quickly as possible and must attack no later than the morning of January 12, 1945." [—] Beforehand it will probably ... and won't be possible ... the slipperiness of the roads. [—] "Secondly, the 7th Parachute Division must immediately close ranks at the front in the area southeast of Weissenburg, and, depending on the development of the situation, move immediately behind the XXXIX Panzer Corps, so that the 10th SS Panzer Grenadier Division can be brought in there."

THE FÜHRER: Of course, here we have the old experience. If they get through quickly with the tanks, then it will work. But to get through the forest here with the tanks is, I think, a difficult undertaking. [—]

JODL: Now, a number of Army troops are being unloaded up there. There are 15 trains in total; ten are unloaded. Have they been assigned yet? [—] There is a mortar detachment, a field howitzer detachment, a light field howitzer detachment and two ...

ZIMMERMANN: All the artillery has been pulled over here on the field marshal's orders.

JODL: That's what's still missing here, a few mortars [—]

ZIMMERMANN: The bridges near Selz are only ... the others are going over here a bit further north, but otherwise all the artillery should come here.

THE FÜHRER: Buhle, where exactly are all the Hunter-Tiger now? There's one company with the 14th here. Where is the second right now?

BUHLE: The second was still here and should go to Boppard for loading. My Führer, I just got here this morning.

ZIMMERMANN: Two Tigers from the one company departed on a transport train. They left during the night. The others that are still coming down from the mountains north of Boppard are in need of serious maintenance. The maintenance platoon has been moved everywhere. Now they need cranes and such things. They are mostly in short-term repair, but it must be done first.

THE FÜHRER: They are not employed at all? ... But they are in need of maintenance, of course, because of all the pointless driving.

ZIMMERMANN: ... comes a bit earlier. But it should take until March 15.

THE FÜHRER: And where exactly is the other company now? ... I ask for the following reason: we should at least be able do some small things here with the other company, because in principle they are not at all vulnerable to further air strikes.

[—]

ZIMMERMANN: The field marshal has explicitly forbidden anyone from going into the woods.

GÖRING: That is one of the biggest forests down there.

THE FÜHRER: Of course. We only ask ourselves, where are they going here? I don't know. That area is an enormous flank. If enough infantry follows, it's possible, but otherwise [—]

GÖRING: If he has forces! But he doesn't have many forces either.

THE FÜHRER: This counterattack here with the 256th [Infantry Division] can't break through; they're too weak. That's why I keep coming back to the idea that we should add a mountain division to it.

KEITEL: The 256th is too weak.

THE FÜHRER: It's also not well suited for this battle. They should probably not be employed in this battle, I fear. I have the feeling that there are too few; then you'll get a small hump [penetration].

JODL: ... here pulling out again in the mountains with weak forces; then there is the chance that we can push through there. But he has no further reserves. He can only shift from one front to the other now, and our pressure is still increasing. This whole heavy artillery regiment, the 7th Parachute Division, two assault gun brigades and the 10th SS Panzer [Grenadier Division]—that is surely a useful addition of forces, which is still ... now [—]

JODL: The escort battalion of the Reichsführer is located there.

THE FÜHRER: He called it back, of course, but when will it come?

ZIMMERMANN: Not until later.

THE FÜHRER: When does that one come, anyway?

ZIMMERMANN: The 47th departed yesterday evening on the first train out of the Siegburg area. So the first trains can be here—with the advance guard—in three days, if no major air actions interfere again.

THE FÜHRER: Now comes ... the units set out [—] There's something I don't like: the 6th Mountain Division has suddenly become a sort of fortress division now, and stays here.[1697] Now, it is without doubt still the best assault division of all the units here. Even if they are picked apart for a regimental group, the other two regimental groups are still there. But, in any case, together they are still stronger than any of the other divisions here—even today still. Besides, it's also physically a first-class division. Those are trained people who have all lived through God knows what. The forest is not frightening to them—it's favorable terrain for them. If we had had them here, we could have let them scour the woods. A division like that does more there than three others. Such a division wouldn't be bothered by that, because they're accustomed to constantly ...

JODL: Eventually, we may be able to relieve them with the 36th. If something comes in there, and still more artillery comes in there [—]

THE FÜHRER: I am of the opinion that we must deploy offensively in one direction or another. Either/or! Either we deploy them here to increase pressure here, or we take them out entirely and transport them over here in case we want to comb through the forest afterward. But the question is still whether we can't finally attack him from the rear for once.

JODL: The two together must go in that direction.

KEITEL: And they will manage it—that small sector.

ZIMMERMANN: The second combat group will be thrown in first. They're not yet at the front, but we can bring them there quickly.

JODL: There is probably only one regiment in front, since two-thirds of the divisions are outside anyway.

ZIMMERMANN: That can be managed.

THE FÜHRER: Until now, only the 1st Regiment has been in combat; the 2nd and third 3rd have not been involved at all yet. That can be done with this division's strength. They weren't involved in combat in Finland, either; they were drawn out and are completely intact. It would actually be crazy to hold a unit, which must feel almost at home here, in such an area. I don't promise anything here. The most we could accomplish would be to obtain a finger [projection]. But maybe we could block off the road here. But he would fight from all sides again against this finger. He has enough routes here. Then he would just exit via Zabern here. [—] How does it look south of Strasbourg, Jodl? Do you have a picture there? (*Presentation.*) Is that the current picture?

JODL: The whole main fighting line—the way it was before—is back in our possession again. The enemy had enormous losses here: out of 40 or 50 tanks, 19 were destroyed and two were captured—so nearly half. Down here, where parts of the 1st French and 5th French Armored Divisions have been established, the clearing of this bend is underway. Three groups are encircled: one in Herbsheim itself, one in Rossfeld, and a slightly larger group near Obenheim to the north, which tried to break through to the west today but was thrown back. Relief pushes from Benfeld were driven back, so we can assume that these forces will be liquidated today. It didn't quite succeed yesterday. With regard to artillery, they are quite strong here; they have eleven batteries, including some heavy ones. [—] The 198th, which is weak in the area of infantry, is quite strong in artillery. The others available [—]

KEITEL: ... reserves!

JODL: Right now the enemy has patched everything with temporary staff, like we've done a hundred times in the East, moving men from one front to the next. He has tried to eliminate that in order to avoid this threat, which ... here ... so that could stop, then.

THE FÜHRER: ... that we actually go in like that; there we can use the road anyway, and then pull that behind. I would also deploy the 7th Parachute Division here immediately, which, of course, could start the attack here [—] It is, of course, a question of whether—in the long term—it is correct to attack in that direction, or if—in the long term—if we push through here, we'd actually also have to bring in the additional forces here as well, if we get a connection here at all.

JODL: That's clear. Because if it loosens up at some point, we will immediately pull the mobile parts in behind.

THE FÜHRER: But Himmler believes it will be the loosest here. In any case, he also succeeded in using a transition to get even this action under control.

JODL: But there was nothing here—only a few minor posts.

THE FÜHRER: Is this in our hands now?

JODL: Forstfeld, yes.

THE FÜHRER: [—]

ZIMMERMANN: On the 12th—the day after tomorrow—early in the morning, with at least a reinforced regimental group. Whatever can come in will be allocated there.

JODL: Forty-seven trains are on their way; 14 were there last night.

[—]

JODL: There's not much in there; on the edges, of course, there are some fighter commandos.[1698]

THE FÜHRER: It's probably full inside; they've mined everything there.

JODL: ... made a mess, but nothing else. He needs all that for the battle now.

ZIMMERMANN: There are four to five tanks that appear, and he pushes them forward on the roads where he's received a report.

THE FÜHRER: Can't we at least still bring the one platoon here to the attack?

JODL: ... both Hunter-Tigers, yes.

THE FÜHRER: It doesn't matter how many there are. There may be two or three bunkers, but they can hold something like that. But if we have Hunter-Tigers there in front, it's possible that we might be able to break through [—]

It will be a similar story here ... There's nothing in the rest of the sector anyway?

JODL: It's quiet on the rest of the front. [—] That was after the situation report at four. He has to cover the withdrawal of the forces there, of course, and spread out over the whole front.

[—]

THE FÜHRER: One thing I have to say. Himmler has done very well with the few minor actions he has undertaken. He has investigated everything very well.

JODL: The transfer of the XIV Corps was well prepared. That was in coordination with the Ia [operations officer] of the 553rd, who is very good.[1699] According to reports from my General Staff officer who was there, the transfer across the Rhine was a textbook transfer. It was like a peacetime river crossing—admittedly without resistance. But still, a Rhine crossing is a matter that requires some engineering and technical ability.

Italy

THE FÜHRER: Italy?

JODL: There were no battles in Italy. Although the weather improved and the aerial activity increased again yesterday, ... According to the available reports, it appears as follows here: this whole area ...

THE FÜHRER: But he can come in here later, through these canals? [—] Or how is it? Can we even determine what we have available there now, and what kind of forces we can count on?

JODL: Two heavy antitank guns, two Nashörner [Rhinoceros],[1700] and a regiment of the 114th Jäger Division is coming in here now. In total there are 17 light field howitzers employed in two detachments—one to sweep the front, another detachment to sweep the ... That will now be reinforced by the 114th Jäger Division, which is coming over, and by five ..., which will also be brought over here. Then the Navy is there ... with two torpedo boats standing by, various motor torpedo boats ..., to step in if any landings are attempted.

The Southeast

There was a small operation near [the island of] Rhodes. A sailing vessel appeared here—escorted by three destroyers—which wanted to land on Alimnia, but it was sunk by antitank guns there. Then 20 to 30 persons, probably from the destroyer, landed on Calchi, which is not occupied by us.[1701] [—] Tonight Prijepolje will probably be cleared out by the rear guard. At the end there are now two regiments of the 22nd [Infantry Division] and 966th Fortress Brigade. The third regiment of the 22nd Division is marching in the direction of Visegrad. The previous rear guard, Combat Group Steyrer,[1702] is approaching Sarajevo and will then be disbanded. The fortress battalions will join other divisions. [—] No particular action here. After this situation here... fairly ... we left a regiment of the 7th SS Mountain Division as an occupation force.

[—]

THE FÜHRER: Have you heard that the Fifth Bulgarian Army was disbanded? It was announced over the radio—because of the total unreliability of the officer corps and the men.

[—]

JODL: ... reinforce parts of a regiment of the 11th Air Force Field Division ... Cossacks located ..., without leading to larger-scale combat action. [—] The report about the lining up of these two regiments hasn't yet arrived, and there was no fighting here in the whole area of Bihac. There have been reports in the inner circles regarding a few cases of unreliability in the Ustasi units; two companies disobeyed, left the position, and ... marched off.

West again

Here I have another overview of the artillery, my Führer. (*Presentation.*) First, these are the lengths of the fronts, if you include the coast of the Netherlands: 1,175 against 1,800 km.[1703] With regard to fortress artillery we are relatively good, with 1,145 guns against 1,062 in the East. But most of these are positioned at the front and on the coast. This here is a second security line, where the fortress batteries are standing. In the Army artillery, without mortars, we have 51 1/3 motorized detachments against 94 in the East. We're somewhat better in the immobile or partially mobile category: 41 against 15. [—] This is the observation artillery. It is much stronger in the East: 39 observation detachments against 13. The assault artillery in the East is also considerably stronger, with 31 detachments against 11.

THE FÜHRER: Yes. Now, this is not decisive. The critical question is: What is being fired by the Russians, per German round? ... That, of course, gives a different picture.

[—]

JODL: ... will be done by the end of the month, ... the entire division won't be there before the 24th.

THE FÜHRER: It's unfortunate that they're coming so late. Those are two divisions that we could send to the East.

Sweden

JODL: ... Sweden's entry into the war on the other side.[1704]

THE FÜHRER: ...

JODL: I don't think it's likely either. The preparations, of course, would include blocking the Small Belt completely, and possibly pushing up north near Narvik to a more favorable position. But that has its advantages and disadvantages. Should we make special preparations?

THE FÜHRER: No.

JODL: I believe it will happen the way the statement indicates at present.

HEWEL: Here's the report on the Swedish/Scandinavian issue. (*Presentation.*)

JODL: They would become allies of Russia, then. The same direction ... we can think about it, but I don't believe anything more is necessary either.

GÖRING: It is the intellectual left-wing circles ... but they have concerns about them. ...[1705]

[—]

Situation in the air

BÜCHS: My Führer! There are no particular reports from the Reich area or the West or East, because of bad weather. The delivery of supplies to Budapest was only possible with very limited forces, because of the bad weather.[1706] Yesterday 39 aircraft were employed during the day; 22 of them reached the target, including four Ju 52s that landed. [—] Regarding the weather situation: the center of a low-pressure area is currently over Germany. There is only limited cloud cover but extensive banks of fog and high fog, which, in the course of the day, only burned off in a few places, especially in the West. It cleared up today in the upper Rhine area, in the south of Germany, and in the Po [River] plain, because the temperature on the ground ... In northern Italy it's minus 16 degrees.

THE FÜHRER: In northern Italy minus 16 degrees, in Königsberg minus 3 degrees, and in Hammerfest probably minus 1 degree.

The East

[—]
HERMANI[1707] : No action in the area of the Second Panzer. The 118th Jäger Division has taken over the sector of the 3rd Combat Brigade, which was relieved with the rest. One detachment has been ordered to stay down below. The tank battle continues north of Szekesferhervar [Stuhlweissenburg]. This morning there were attacks again from the south against Sarkeresztes and the salient west of Patka. So far this morning, four tanks had been destroyed. I haven't been able to find out about our own tank losses yet. Here 70 tanks were seen by ground observation.[1708] We are making a counterattack against a hill that was lost here. The attack against the Waldgebirge [Forest Mountains] is gaining ground again, against stiff opposition. New here is an attack against the whole front at Bicske, Zsambek and Dag; it was driven back. The operation yesterday evening, to break through to Budapest [from the southwest] ... has met with strong antitank resistance ... Prisoners confirmed the presence of the 93rd Guards Rifle Division, which was previously up here at Lacenes, and which has now obviously been pulled down to here.

THE FÜHRER: So there will be a rest pause up there [south of Esztergom]?!
[—]
THE FÜHRER: But that makes no sense!
HERMANI: ... but hasn't started yet.
THE FÜHRER: Absolutely useless! Three days have now been wasted here, while we go on hoping, when we've run into a barrier—while the enemy is

steadily adding reinforcements and we're not getting any stronger—that some miracle will enable us to advance.

HERMANI: He managed to ... not only the road, but also both of these ... [—]

The situation at the Budapest bridgehead is very serious. Here's where the attacks against the Eastern front took place. (*Presentation.*) Because there's no place to land, the supply is very strained, and an airfield absolutely must be built up somewhere in this area. I have a city map of 1:25,000, which we can use today to review the blocks of houses that have been lost, my Führer. (*Presentation.*) This is a fortification on the outskirts of town; it's not shown on the map because the map unfortunately doesn't reach that far. That was the position on January 8, and this morning we got a radio message with the position of the current main battle line. I drew it in quickly here. The occupying forces are pushed together in this area.

THE FÜHRER: There's no airfield there anymore.

HERMANI: No. The one was over here in this area, and the second was built up on Czepel Island ...

THE FÜHRER: That doesn't help; there's no airfield in this area anymore.

HERMANI: No, there's no airfield anymore. [—] I'd like to present the figures that the Russian Army reported regarding the battle in the Budapest area: "several residential areas" were taken on December 30, 1944, "several residential areas" on December 31, 1944, and from January 1 to 8—taken together—1,761 [city] blocks. ... the outer suburb.[1709] It is generally correct, while in detail ... I just received a radio message about the daily report from yesterday, which says: ... heaviest defensive battles at the eastern bridgehead because of the shortening of the main battle line ... led to deep penetrations ... heavy street fighting and sustained ... heavy casualties on both sides; on the western bridgehead sudden concentrations of fire. [—] The supply situation forces us to be extremely economical. Air supply ... up to now 3 tons in the castle ... from the ship, which is on the Danube ... food secured ... How it came to that, I don't know either. [—]

THE FÜHRER: How long is this here, anyway?

HERMANI: The scale is 1:25,000.[1710]

KEITEL: One centimeter equals 3 kilometers.

HERMANI: Yes, that's 3 kilometers.

THE FÜHRER: Is this ice?

HERMANI: There's ice on the Danube, yes.

THE FÜHRER: That's too bad! This is 1½ kilometers. Can you land a seaplane on 1½ kilometers?

GÖRING: Yes, it depends, my Führer.

THE FÜHRER: With the Ju!?

GÖRING: We've landed on the Danube with a Ju before.

CHRISTIAN: In principle it needs only … with heavy bombs …

GÖRING: But the area is very short, …

JODL: Now, Guderian has developed this idea[1711] —

HERMANI: General Wenck will come this evening. The Colonel General has just spoken with the Führer—he called him.

JODL:—the idea to go to the west bank and then get more space up here to create an airfield.

THE FÜHRER: Impossible! All these airfields are just ideas that can't be employed because every location is under artillery fire.

JODL: I don't know if the idea was developed internally.

THE FÜHRER: It doesn't matter who had the idea, but every airfield … , which is not set back 4 to 5 kilometers, … When they fire on it with mortars, they can't land; it is impossible. They see every plane that arrives at night, …

CHRISTIAN: The report from yesterday, which claimed that four aircraft landed—I don't know where—must be confirmed.

THE FÜHRER: Perhaps they landed on the troop training ground.

HERMANI: That was here on the …

CHRISTIAN: Here it was still possible yesterday. [—]

THE FÜHRER: Could you find out what's happening with the ice floes here? If the ice is breaking up, nothing will work—that is clear—but it could be that the ice is not flowing. [—] We don't have light planes or anything like that? [—]

GÖRING: But we do that with the piggy-back plane,[1712] too.

THE FÜHRER: Yes, and do we have gliders?

GÖRING: We have gliders.

THE FÜHRER: Gliders—they could land. There are enough of them.

GÖRING: We brought them in quickly. They were in Graz.

THE FÜHRER: Gliders can always land.

GÖRING: They could certainly land here.

THE FÜHRER: There are countless places for gliders. They're the only ones. Send the gliders here at once—all that we have!

GÖRING: There are areas here and here for gliders. They just have to avoid the tall houses.

THE FÜHRER: Gliders can go anywhere. If worst comes to worst, we could land them on streets like this one—Andrassy [street]. [—] How wide are the gliders?

GÖRING: That varies.

THE FÜHRER: They have to open up a street like Andrassy, by tearing out the streetlights and everything. [—]

GÖRING: But a glider is always more or less lost.

CHRISTIAN: He has 200 gliders.

THE FÜHRER: (How much will they carry? [—] One ton?)

CHRISTIAN: One ton, yes. [—]

CHRISTIAN: ... but actually only in limited numbers.

GÖRING: We still have them, but I always say: if something is broken, adjustment a half year later it comes ..., when we need it.

THE FÜHRER: For gliders I don't need a lot of stuff.

GÖRING: No, that's not a major concern. The Hitler Youth do it. The Hitler Youth have gliders at their schools.

THE FÜHRER: And then we don't risk the expensive tow planes.

GÖRING: No, they release.

THE FÜHRER: They will float down in the night.

WEISS: There is a parade ground below the castle—800 meters long, as smooth as glass ..., open area ... landing and starting again.

THE FÜHRER: Gliders can definitely get in?!

WEISS: We'll have to examine it again, to be sure.

THE FÜHRER: We have to try everything, anyway! [—]

HERMANI: Right now there are attacks here.

GÖRING: You know that area, Weiss?

WEISS: Yes, Herr Reichsmarshal. In the spring I saw it with General Schmundt—I drove there. At least one regiment was being drilled on it. It's as smooth as glass. There are no barracks or ...

JODL: I'm familiar with it, too. It's the best anyway, because the castle is right next to it, with all the cellars.

GÖRING: I can confirm it with a radio message.

WEISS: It is very easy to find; it's below the castle.

GÖRING: The castle protects it from the wind, which is very good. [—] Could you arrange for that whole area to be cleared of every obstacle—trenches, etc., so that it's leveled off?

THE FÜHRER: Flak is definitely [—]

CHRISTIAN: I'd like to report the following. We have gliders in four locations: in the southeastern area around Linz and Wels—they have already been ordered here, but the others are in Wittstock, and they must be driven to southern Germany ...

THE FÜHRER: At first we can use those that are in the East already; the others will be brought by train, by priority transport.[1713] [—]
They don't have much there, so it would be good if they were actually to get the Tiger detachment brought in for the attack, because there's no sense in having Tigers, etc., here! [—]

HERMANI: At least you can drive them around.

THE FÜHRER: And further north?

HERMANI: North of the Danube [River], the 20th Panzer Division began its attack early this morning and pushed through to Ogyalla. Another group from the 20th Panzer Division is attacking Perpeto. Parts of the 208th [Infantry Division] that pushed ahead from Komoram [Komorn] forced an enemy tank group to turn away. We took Naszdav and Imely yesterday. They are attacking further to the southeast now. An attack—which has been held off thus far—against the front of the 211th [Volksgrenadier Division], which has built up a blocking front again, ... At this time there are enemy attacks against Kürt from the southeast and east.

THE FÜHRER: It's a mystery where this guy brings these tanks from again. [—] But here there's a very strong relief attack.

HERMANI: In the Eighth Army area, only battles near (Putna); Putna has been lost again. Attacks to the east of it were driven back ... an attack against the Hungarian 16th [Infantry Division] was driven back. Here there was a small penetration, down there. Apart from that, no battle action here ... our anti-aircraft fire in this area was very good, according to a radio report. ... should be taken out after the reconnaissance mission [—]

GÖRING: And that we bring as many troops in there as possible, or there's no point to it!

HERMANI: We also found out by aerial reconnaissance that there are two ice bridges here, eight ice crossings here and twelve here. ... [—] Reinforcements are being brought to the Magnuszew bridgehead, where there is also mine-clearing activity, according to radio intelligence. [—] Army Group Center reports no combat action. Here, according to prisoners' reports, tank bridges are also being built over the second trench, and artillery is being pulled forward over the ice. Orders have been given to lay mines in the Romint Heath area, according to a radio report. Here north of the Romint Heath, again according to aerial reconnaissance, is a concentration of artillery—about 170 guns per kilometer. That is a confirmation of what was reported as 150 guns a few days ago. Otherwise, no battles or other incidents.

GÖRING: Could you send a few more tanks? I would suggest *Grossdeutschland* [Panzer Corps] first. That division has only 36 Panzer IVs instead of 81, only 45 Panzer Vs instead of 79, and instead of 42 assault guns—that's not bad—only 32, and only 18 ... instead of 45.

THE FÜHRER: I believe they are being added continually, as far as I know. In any case, Thomale recently said again that they are being added all the time. [—]

THE FÜHRER: Just imagine—there is division after division there! That can't continue long term.

KEITEL: ... what kind of organization of forces the East still has [—]
I read it, too.

THE FÜHRER: It can't be any other way.

KEITEL: Artillery has held up quite well, but some of the numbers, including heavy weapons, have been reduced considerably.

THE FÜHRER: It can't be done any other way. Then his combat strength is also [—] he does it for two or three days, then the action will end.

KEITEL: Average combat strength: 5,000 men.

HERMANI: From the 31st [Infantry] Division, two ships have left.[1714]

JODL: In contrast to the attacks in Russia itself, the force of the attacks here has weakened significantly. He never attacks anywhere with [—]

THE FÜHRER: But the normal division—only with 10,000 men ... would be 120,000 men. If you take the total, it would be 360,000 men. Of those, he doesn't have 130,000 men here—more than 1 million men ... he doesn't have at all. Those look like Chinese divisions. [—] Is Wenck coming this evening? [—] I am always horrified when I hear something about having to retreat somewhere in order to be able to "operate." I've seen it for two years, and it always leads to disastrous results. (*Presentation: Incendiary shrapnel ammunition, February 1944.*[1715])

Armament issues

"Smoke trail"? I don't know how to assess it. I don't know how they designate "smoke trails" as victories in aerial combat. Are they all counted?[1716]

BUHLE: No, they're not counted—only these confirmed numbers. Wherever it says, "smoke trail," it wasn't counted. This is the Luftwaffe report from that time.

THE FÜHRER: I just saw this column—I hadn't seen it before.

KEITEL: That's the number that produces the total here.

BUHLE: And there are 25 smoke trails in addition to those.

THE FÜHRER: One aircraft shot down with every 205 rounds—that would be huge, of course. It would already be a lot if we could get an aerial victory after 1,000 rounds, because that would mean for every million rounds only 1,000 aerial victories [—]

BUHLE: Ten times what it is now.

GÖRING: One thousand would also be a good result.

BUHLE: The current average is such that altogether we ... without those that are shot down in training, ... only one aircraft shot down per 10,000 rounds, ... to bring down an aircraft.[1717]

THE FÜHRER: We should deploy them where real mass attacks are made. The way they are used now, it's hard to get a clear picture. We have to protect some obscure place with just those for once—outfit 30 or 40 batteries with just those. [—] We never know who does what, which always leads to deceptive reports. The fighters come and claim they've done it, then another battery comes and claims it did it. [—] Here's a letter to the editor of an English newspaper—it shows again what crazy things are happening over there. Here's another thing—but first: this is the B 29, isn't it?[1718] [—] It flies in formations of 20 to 40 aircraft and holds the division together ... then a few of our little fighters come between them, and they're shot down before they even have a chance to shoot. Because they bring a few little guns against this giant, and tumble down without ever hitting the colossus. That's why it's not ... That is a complete developmental failure, like the Heinkel 177[1719] and all the dive bombers—the inadequate arming of the fighter. All developmental failures by people who lack the imagination to see what is necessary.

GÖRING: The dive bomber wasn't a development that [—][1720]

THE FÜHRER: But to continue it with the big one! It is not because of a developmental failure that I have fighters, either. But I am opposed to fighters with inadequate weapons, since they have no effect against these formations at this range. One sees that it's totally useless, unless they can ... the fight from below... but then these little fighters come and tumble down—most of them head off at once, and disappear.[—] showed that it is utter nonsense ... I see the development coming: he exchanges this heavy four-engine bomber for a heavier one, and comes with absolute security ... up to 20 and 24 guns ... It is nonsense—technical nonsense, nothing more. It is irresponsible not to introduce long-range weapons that are effective from a greater distance. He can't have any effect with the 5-cm gun, or with the 3.7 either; he is dependent on all the small guns. But, of course, he would ... probably not ... the fighter at all ... if he gave away all the small guns ... The only possibility is that we ... the bomber wings ... they shoot out with four. That is much better than ... But he flies around here as if there were nothing there at all ... a complete developmental failure, without doubt; we can't do anything with it. I spoke again with Saur today ... and Galland told me personally, ... the probability of approaching ... The fact is that they can't do it anymore, although we build more and more aircraft, and the number of our sorties is ... When I imagine that we now [—] That is technical nonsense and childishness— just as dumb as ... if we knew that the ... would come in a group. We couldn't assume that we would fight it this way long term. In the end, we could only do it in the East, and we can do it today only because the Russians don't have masses of small defensive weapons. If they had those defensive guns, like the British and the Americans, we couldn't do it there either. But with them, the low-level flights and the ... of aircraft stop when we have enough defensive guns. When we plaster them with 2 cm, with 12 mm, etc., it stops at once—that is quite clear. It is a complete developmental failure, that month by month [—] They haven't taken them for fighter combat anyway, because they're too slow. They are too slow at low altitude and too slow up high. Down there it's the same. I always get the combat results from down there when fighter-bombers are involved: 1:4, 1:5. One can't say every time: Yes, because they can't fly there! [—] That is all the more unfortunate. Then I have to ... come to something else. The only possibility is to come in with a weapon that is effective even at greater distances and to which the opponent can't respond. Because with his 12 mm and those other things, he couldn't shoot 1 or 1½ km, and I realize that the possibility of hits will be low. But every hit by a heavy projectile like the 5 cm will destroy the plane. Then even the big ones will crash, while we can't do anything with these small guns.[1721] I say, yes: the best proof is our armored assault aircraft, of which 30 or 31 were recently destroyed in an attack by 43 ... Then I really have to ask: how long can we allow ourselves to do this? Also a ratio [—] ... if I want to build in advance in such cases ... the B 24[1722] or 29 is now being added ... we can't afford that ... I've always been told that we don't have a fast enough rate of fire ... have to come closer to reach it at all ... aircraft have better armor, ... so the losses will probably decrease. That's the situation, right? I see a huge danger. We can't take it easy and say, "That won't happen—he won't deliver that!" He'll deliver it! The Japanese are seeing it today already—he flies these enormous distances, and in a short time he will fly them here in our area as well. They have been used, so I can't say: I don't believe it. I have to believe! ... He has no losses, or only very limited losses ... That's a parade exercise on a sunny day! And with them he can do it even better and more easily; no one is in any danger, and then one day he won't need fighters anymore either. Then it's possible that he could eliminate his fighters entirely. If I imagine that German aircraft, on the one hand, defend against fighters, and, on the other hand, also need to attack, then they come into a hailstorm and the effect is—I've spoken with many people and they saw the same—like Bormann said of Mecklenburg,[1723] a fox hunt, and our planes just can't do that forever. One can imagine how it affects the population; the impression on the population is disastrous. [—] So that is a technical dead end. At the beginning of the war, our fighters were equal to the others or superior. [—][1724] Now the fighters are of less interest to me. We can handle the fighters with our new defensive weapons, if they make low-level attacks. But the bombers are our destruction. If we can't take action against them, and continue stubbornly along a path that has been proven false, because the fighter still has its mad fascination—I find that unbearable, and I see a great danger there. That's why I mention it today, too. One has to understand the developmental failure. It is such that in a case like this, the Air Force takes the point of view ... : "It's not as hot when you eat it as when it's cooked," they won't come! [—] That's not the case; these planes will come. No one can say either, "He won't attack Japan!" But now he attacks it, with 70 to 100 aircraft. But in a short time these 70 to 100 aircraft will be 200, then 500, then 1,000 and 2,000. He shifts everything. He can manufacture it industrially in mass production. And what else does he need? He can destroy everything with it. The bravery of individual airmen is of no use then, because the aircraft are not equal. ... One can't say that he does (not) have 18-ton bombs.[1725] In the past, we didn't believe a lot ... That the 6,000-kg bombs and more ... it was said: There is no such thing, ... they have no penetration depth. And today they fly almost to [—] For the last year, test flights have been underway with the biggest aircraft in the world—enormous planes, carrying 18 tons or 124 fully outfitted soldiers, wingspan of more than 70 meters, 2,600 horsepower engines. ... If the first 200 to 300 come here, they could carpet-bomb with 2,000-kg bombs ... so we can't say, "Get to work—that will be taken care of again!" It won't work—it is completely impossible. And we build our little fighters with 2-cm [guns] and test to see if we should change to 3-cm, etc., short guns. Then he would have to come within 50 meters, and even then he won't destroy it. The 5 cm caliber is the smallest that can be used here today, in my opinion. I spoke with what's-his-name today. He thinks we can install the 5 cm even in the 262 ... that doesn't matter. But it would be a major victory if it could be installed at once, ... then the fighter wouldn't have to go within 50 meters ... doesn't matter at all ... If they don't shoot down 4 aircraft from every formation on every incursion, that's enough. He can't sustain that long term, either. Now, when we lose 10, 20 or 36 planes in every attack—and the enemy less than a quarter of that, sometimes nothing—I have to say: that's no mission. What should the people do, if they don't have good planes? Here we have, I'd like to say, ... on the wrong object ... do against these formations? [—] He has enough fuel ...

GÖRING: The range is not important to him. It's just important that we protect the tactical aircraft from the enemy fighter cover—that's the danger. ...

[—]

THE FÜHRER: But at first it's so fast that the enemy fighter [—]. Our victory, of course, now consists of the fact that I absolutely can't reach the same penetration depth with a jet aircraft as I can with the normal engine fighter.

GÖRING: At this moment, not yet. No.

THE FÜHRER: I am happy if we can eliminate them in 6 months or a year—that is a victory. And he can't escort them with jets. He doesn't have them—at least not at this time. He can't escort them. So that gives me another possibility.

GÖRING: With the gun, the 262 can still maintain a speed of 700. That can be done, although 650 [—]

THE FÜHRER: He claims it would be the same weight.

GÖRING: That doesn't matter. It's the armaments that are decisive.

THE FÜHRER: If they fly in and shoot with a 5 cm [gun] from a distance of 1,000 m, a whole swarm of 40 [Me-] 262s can shoot from a distance of 1,000 m—so only 2 or 4 will fly out, and if we have no losses and the enemy has 10 or 12, then the action is as it should be. ... They may even shoot into the formation from a distance of 2,000 m—then it will certainly break apart. [—]

GÖRING: So far that's quite clear. We don't have the latest reports on how the [Me-] 262 works in its current state against the four-engine aircraft; that's being tested.

THE FÜHRER: ...

GÖRING: It can approach differently from below—it can go below them.

THE FÜHRER: The closer they have to come, the greater ..., if they approach to 50 m.

GÖRING: It has to get into the dead space.

THE FÜHRER: If the current fighter has a speed of 600 km, then the fantasy numbers that the Air Force has always given are clearly impossible. But even at a speed of 600 km, 8 or 12 guns can defend against it, so it will achieve no result—as is the case today. That's no fantasy of mine—I don't invent such things. You can see that that is not the case. It means gaining 120 km and doubling the aircraft armaments ... So I double the defensive strength and increase the offensive strength by ... about 20%. Otherwise we won't reach the goal—it's the wrong route. The more we insist on it, the worse it will become, and then nothing will be of any use ... and shoots in all directions. [—]

I once had a meeting with armor specialists in Berlin.

KEITEL: I was there, too.

THE FÜHRER: They told me the following: we prefer a 2 cm or at the most a 3.7 cm [gun] with ... and a high rate of fire, rather than a big heavy gun. That means that if someone is well armored he won't be destroyed, but if you shoot at him at length, perhaps he will turn away. That's what the specialists said.

(KEITEL: Yes, indeed.)

I was completely alone in my theory that the most important thing is to destroy the other with one strike. Better to make one shot that kills him. It's the same with the Naval weapons. Witzell[1726] told me once: I prefer a 28 cm [gun] with more ammunition rather than a 38 or even a 40 or 42 cm. [—] I even wanted to have a 53 cm [gun], but take less ammunition along ... I have always said: But if you think [—] Then I couldn't care less about the enemy fighters. Then he must destroy the bombers. That's the key factor.

GÖRING: No doubt.

THE FÜHRER: Everything else is unimportant.

GÖRING: He would have to be able to destroy the fighter first and then destroy the bomber. But that won't work.

THE FÜHRER: No, that won't work. The key factor is that I destroy the bomber. For that, the heavy caliber is absolutely necessary. They say to me: yes, if we only had a faster rate of fire. [—] I would prefer that, too, although we now have 140 rounds per minute.

GÖRING: So that he delivers at least two or three rates of fire.

THE FÜHRER: I would also prefer that they have 600 instead of 140 rounds. But that won't work. [—]

GÖRING: They harass the covering fighters, too. For the jets they are out of the question. [—]

THE FÜHRER: We can't just say: "I don't believe it" or "That doesn't interest me" or "I don't believe he will bring them in large quantities!" Then I wouldn't have needed to introduce the long 8.8 cm [gun]. For the existing tanks, the 7.5 [gun] and the short 8.8 are fully adequate. But I said back then already: we have to give the impression of continually advancing. And they wanted to make trouble for me over the Tiger ... because we didn't know if that character wouldn't suddenly appear with a tank that had 250 mm of armor. [—] That is the perpetual experience of 1,000 years in the technical area. ... That's why I wanted to give this thing to Reich Minister Speer. But unfortunately it was drawn up incorrectly ... This book only discusses wars and what emerged from them. It should really be a general technical overview of all the known wars from antiquity to the present. Then one could see how often wars were decided by weapons that were minimally superior from a technical standpoint—with very little superiority. It is said that if Hannibal, instead of the seven or 13 elephants he had left as he crossed the Alps, or instead of the eleven—you should actually know this—had had 50 or 250, it would have been more than enough to conquer Italy. [—]

GÖRING: But we did finally bring out the jets; we brought them out. And they must come in masses, so we keep the advantage. The others can be quite a bit better with their engines and aircraft because they ... very much [—]

THE FÜHRER: The V1 can't decide the war, unfortunately.[1727] [—]

GÖRING: … with all possible things. This gun is good. But just as an initially unpromising project can finally succeed, … the bomber will come, too, if it also [—]

THE FÜHRER: But that's still just a fantasy!

GÖRING: No!

THE FÜHRER: Göring, the gun is there; the other is still a fantasy!

GÖRING: I think we will have some success with that as well.

THE FÜHRER: OK, good!

GÖRING: That is also… a major project. [—]

THE FÜHRER: They say it comes in at 9,000 m, and the Americans claim it can fly at altitudes of up to 12,000 m.[1728]

GÖRING: We should count on ten—with nine to ten.

THE FÜHRER: Even then, a good share of our anti-aircraft guns will be useless. Like I said [—]

GÖRING: Thus the "Treibspiegel"![1729]

THE FÜHRER: Like I said, I suffer from such things—if I see something like that coming in on the horizon, and everything argues for continuing along the proven path, because it's a path that has stood the test … had a light anti-aircraft gun, I would support further production of the dive bomber. If I don't build anything, on the other hand, … I would say that we should make fighter-bombers …

CHRISTIAN: It says in his own press that he will go in that direction, because he attacks this way. Different people there say: we can't build so many B 29s, because then too few Fortress … [—] Otherwise, that couldn't have been written in the press at all.

THE FÜHRER: … already increased to 70, which he uses to attack. And the number of victories in aerial combat? [—] All right, but before they attacked a ship. That was a ratio: If a pilot attacks a transporter or a battle-ship[1730] … Nevertheless, we can see how the defensive strength is, and how long he can continue in spite of it. [—]

But he doesn't need it. The aircraft themselves have almost infinite defensive strength; that's clear. I recently read a report. Now he has 12 to 18 guns, and the new one should have 24 12.7 mm. That's a cloud of projectiles penetrating a fighter.

GÖRING: Of these 24, he can use at least half of them at one time.

THE FÜHRER: He has many of them in revolving turrets now, so he can shoot in all directions. He flies echeloned so everything can be brought to bear—in every direction. In any case, it's a huge danger! [—] So, Göring, drive them on! I implore you!

GÖRING: Yes, Sir! I will examine it with Speer, too.

THE FÜHRER: ... after he had been here three days before. [—]
There is, of course, the danger that they will attack all the gun production facilities again. But we have to be clear about it: it could only have been betrayed by someone in a military position or in the industry. It couldn't have been given away by the workers, because they didn't notice anything. Or by telephone?

JODL: A telephone conversation is always the most likely.

GÖRING: Nothing was to be telephoned from here; it was arranged with Speer and Saur, ... and the Führer had given the order. They called a meeting then.[1731]

THE FÜHRER: Someone at headquarters must have given it out; it couldn't have come from a production plant.

GÖRING: They called a meeting. That is correct. Now I want to find out what meeting they called, to see if we can't find something out—because nothing was discussed with those people. That narrows the circle, because nothing further was done from here. Nothing was discussed that evening, as the Führer signed the order and gave it to Speer. He put it in his pocket and drove away with it.

KEITEL: He went by train with me.

GÖRING: That's the territory of Saur and Speer ...

End: around 7:15 p.m.

* * * * *

January 27, 1945

    The expected Russian winter offensive began with staggered attacks between January 12 and 15 along the Vistula River and in East Prussia. As early as the first day, the Fourth Panzer Army was torn up in numerous locations along the Vistula, and its lines were penetrated in the direction of Kielce. On the following day, the lines of the Ninth Army, also south of Warsaw, were penetrated as well. That same day, the Russians attacked in East Prussia between Ebenrode and Schlossberg, and, two days later, attacked from the Narew River north of Warsaw, where they penetrated the lines of the Second Army in the direction of Thorn and Soldau. Also on January 15, in the south, the enemy forced the Seventeenth Army back over the Wistoka River. After the German front had collapsed almost everywhere like a house of cards, the Red Army rolled through Poland. Czestochowa fell on January 17, the enemy took Krakow and Lodz on the 18th and 19th, and on the 20th the battle for the Upper Silesian industrial region began. That same day, the armored spearheads of Koniev's 1st

Ukrainian Front also crossed the Lower Silesian border east of Breslau. Three days later, Russian forces reached the Oder River between Oppeln and Ohlau. They crossed the river at Steinau and now stand just outside Breslau. To the north, Zhukov's 1st Belorussian Front pushed past Poznan and reached the Oder River-Warta River bend, threatening Eastern Pomerania to the north. The attempted defense of the Notec River [Netze] Line failed. Russian forces have already reached Schneidmühl and have taken Bromberg. Meanwhile, in eastern East Prussia, the enemy pushed the Third Panzer Army back behind Deime, Pregel and Alle, while, in the western part of the province, he advanced through the collapsed front of the Second Army to Allenstein and via Deutsch Eylau up to Marienburg and Elbing on the Nogat River. Without orders, the Fourth Army attacked the spearhead of the Russian penetration from the Masurian Lakes westward, to reestablish the connection with the Second Army, which is now west of the lower Vistula River.

In Hungary—where the fighting occurred primarily southwest of Budapest—and in Yugoslavia, the situation is mostly unchanged.

Italy continues to be quiet.

In the West, the German troops were forced to withdraw from the Ardennes back to their position at the beginning of the offensive. In Lower Alsace, a few cities changed possession on both sides; in Upper Alsace the French have been attacking the German Colmar bridgehead since January 20. The situation hadn't changed otherwise.
(*Map 13*)

* * * * *

MIDDAY SITUATION REPORT, JANUARY 27, 1945, IN BERLIN[1732]

Present:

The Führer	*General Buhle*
Reichsmarshal Göring	*Ambassador Hewel*
Field Marshal Keitel	*Lieutenant General Winter*
Colonel General Jodl	*General Koller*
Colonel General Guderian	*Vice Admiral Voss*
General Burgdorf	*Gruppenführer Fegelein*
Major General Scherff	*Lieutenant Colonel Waizenegger*
Rear Admiral v. Puttkamer	*Major Büchs*
Colonel v. Below	*Major v. Freytag-Loringhoven*
Colonel v. Brauchitsch	*Major John v. Freyend*

Captain Assmann   Sturmbannführer Göhler
Hauptbereichsleiter Zander   Sturmbannführer Günsche
Director Schuster

Beginning: 4:20 p.m.

Weather conditions

SCHUSTER: The weather conditions, my Führer, are characterized by the arrival of low-pressure areas over the Atlantic, then here over France. They cross Germany here, with areas of snowfall, and settle in the eastern area—this is caused by a mass of cold air that is lying over Russia and being pushed into the area around the province of East Prussia by strong winds from the south and east. The edge of this low-pressure area then moves away over Italy, which means considerably more difficult take-off conditions for the enemy. A significant change in the weather is not likely in the immediate future. As before, low-pressure areas will come in from the west, with some isolated areas of precipitation, then spread out from west to east, settling longer here in this area because further movement to the east is blocked. For England, this will result in severely worsening take-off conditions, due to the east winds up here that are blowing across England. For the last three days, there has been a low cloud cover with continuing snowfall over all of eastern and central England, with bad visibility and ice forming in the clouds. But the conditions over England are not such that flight is completely impossible; western England has better conditions due to off-shore winds. There the clouds have broken up and the visibility ... good ... better weather. So the complete cessation of flights over England is not caused by the weather alone.
THE FÜHRER: What else?
GÖRING: They have no airfields here; they're all here.
SCHUSTER: Herr Reichsmarshal, we have established that in December England had similar conditions, and in that period of four weeks the British did fly in those conditions. In one month they had to divert about 2,800 aircraft to other airfields—up here to the north and to western England.
GÖRING: They have lost a lot in the last few weeks with these diversions.
SCHUSTER: But it is true that the vast majority—around 90%—of the British airfields lie in an area of bad weather. England itself reports heavy snowfall and low temperatures. [—] Then a new area of precipitation has moved in over France and the Western combat area. The whole area from the Eifel south lies under snow today, with low clouds and bad visibility.

Over the Reich territory the weather conditions were quite varied. Areas of snowfall alternate with areas of fog, especially in the northern part of the Reich. The conditions in the area south of Stettin [Szczecin], down to Breslau [Wroclaw] and including the Posen [Poznan] area, have improved somewhat. The cloud cover is unbroken, but it's 800 to 1,200 m high, and visibility below the clouds is 5 to 10 km, so flying is possible today. It's the first day in a long time that has had somewhat favorable conditions. The area including Pomerania and the Vistula down to Krakov [Cracow] has had poor visibility all day, in this snowfall zone. Here the units are unable to fly. In East Prussia the cloud cover is unbroken, 300 to 500 m high, and the temperature is minus 15 degrees. Yesterday there was also a strong east wind of about 40 km per hour. These strong winds from the east are destroying the ice conditions very quickly in all these areas. Down toward Hungary, the weather is such that there are good flight conditions over the whole Hungarian region today—cloud cover at 1,000 m. Budapest is in the snowfall zone. Clouds at night, 400 m high. Heavy ice formation was observed. [—] Regarding the condition of the ice: the Oder [River], with the exception of a few places, is covered in a sheet of ice throughout the whole area. The ice is strong enough to walk on, and vehicles can be driven on it. The ice is about 50 cm thick. If it reaches 60 cm, we can drive tanks over the area. On the Danube [River], there is ice in the area of Budapest. From the Baltic Sea harbors it is reported that Pillau—even with these strong east winds and low temperatures—stays clear the whole winter, but Königsberg has heavy ice in these low temperatures. The Königsberg channel must be kept open with icebreakers. Then the Stettiner Haff froze very heavily. But Swinemünde has remained relatively free of ice. The other Baltic Sea harbors, which connect to the west of Swinemünde, up to Mecklenburg Bay, already have very thick ice, especially in the area of Rügen and to the southeast. Regarding the Neisse [River], it is reported that the river is frozen south of Ottmachau. Only in the city of Neisse itself has the ice on the Neisse broken up. Now, it's like this: if we want to break up the ice on the Oder by changing the water level, then we'll need to have a significant supply of water at our disposal.[1733]

THE FÜHRER: Smaller ones aren't enough?

SCHUSTER: Because the waves level out during the long trip down to the Oder. One must have an enormously strong jet of water—then the ice will break up. The ice floes will float over the sheet of ice, but then freeze together again very quickly. The temperature should also be near zero, because then the structure of the ice changes and it breaks more easily.

Hungary (Army Group South)

GUDERIAN: My Führer, the situation has intensified in the area of Army Group South.

THE FÜHRER: Stop right there! That makes no sense anymore.[1734] You must make sure that they fight back and build up a defensive front here—and they have to throw that back.

GUDERIAN: The enemy attacked here. So far, he has been driven back everywhere here. But it is clear that the 18th Tank Corps was reinforced with the 7th [Guards Mechanized Corps], and it is possible that Pliev [Cavalry-mechanized Group][1735] will also either be taken in here or come down there.

THE FÜHRER: In any case, with the forces that are here now, we can't do it. That is clear.

GUDERIAN: That is clear now. [—] The enemy achieved a penetration to here and shot out to the center. We are continuing to push them back further. So far, 10 tanks have been knocked out. The bridgehead has been pushed in. Very heavy attacks here. Numerous heavy attacks here from all four sides. Altogether 15 tanks have been destroyed up here. Then here a counterthrust against the attack by the 23rd Panzer Division. The 356th [Infantry] Division is arriving; the first transports are there.

THE FÜHRER: We can't rely on that one at first.

GUDERIAN: Then the 23rd Panzer Division is pulling out, to build up a reserve here. The advance of our 6th Panzer Division has moved inside the red circle. Here an enemy attack was driven back.

THE FÜHRER: The thing here must be adjusted. We have to shift to defense here, take that back, and shift the mortar corps and the Volksartillery Corps to a defense here. The units must go here in order to throw it back.

GUDERIAN: In Budapest the situation is intensifying because the enemy has shifted his focal point to the center of the western sector and has reached the so-called Blutwiese [Blood Meadow], which, until now, was the main drop point for supplies brought in by air. The counterthrust has begun. Whether it's possible to do it with the available forces—to clean this thing up—is uncertain, because the casualties have increased significantly. He is trying to build a bridge here over the Danube to Margaret Island. The situation is visibly intensifying. [—] Along the rest of the front, there were some thrusts up here. Here they were driven back; here a small, insignificant penetration. Here an advance was driven back. There was regrouping and replacement of the Russia troops in this angle up here through Romania. The Pliev corps [Cavalry-mechanized Group] withdrew in this direction.

THE FÜHRER: To here.

GUDERIAN: Either he will relieve the 6th Guards Tank Army here [north of the Danube River] [—]

THE FÜHRER: No, he'll be added.

GUDERIAN: —or he'll be added to them, or he'll go over here.

THE FÜHRER: No, he'll be added, in order to break through over here [north of the Danube]. He knows that the 20th [Panzer Division] is gone.[1736] How is it going with the Sixth Panzer Army now?

GUDERIAN: It rolled off in the direction of Vienna. I don't know the exact status of the transport movement at the moment.

KEITEL: Six trains pulled out.

WINTER: The advance guard of the 12th SS Panzer Division has reached the loading area. The conditions have improved and relaxed somewhat. The fuel supply is now adequate, the street conditions have improved a little since it hasn't snowed any more, and even the action in the air decreased yesterday evening. But even so, everything that was hoped for and ordered hasn't been achieved. But we can assume that the pace will pick up now.

THE FÜHRER: I said right away that it makes no sense to hypnotize oneself with something and say, "I need it here, so it must happen like this."[1737] In the end, I have to rely on things as they are. Marching out a considerable force from the West is unthinkable in less than 6 to 8 weeks, because it's impossible. Whoever says otherwise is dreaming—he's living in a state of wishful thinking, but not in reality. It's the same as the recall of troops from Greece back then.[1738] It takes time—it's no use. I'll be glad if they get so far along that the I and II [SS Panzer] Corps arrive here [west of Budapest]—say, in 14 days. If that can be achieved, it will be something huge. But I expect that only the combat elements will arrive, at best. But even there one can't say, "I will assign the combat elements"— because it will come how it will come. I can't wait for a long time, either. I have to make sure I keep moving forward. Otherwise, whatever stops moving will be destroyed as well.

WINTER: They were explicitly ordered not to show consideration for that, but to leave.

THE FÜHRER: It is very clear that there is no other possibility: it must go, or it will congest everything. Then all of it will be destroyed, and in the end nothing else can move out at all. Based on all human experience, the parts that can be used here at least[1739] will come first; they were the farthest behind, so they will arrive first.

GÖRING: How does he[1740] come out with such strength from the interior?

THE FÜHRER: He has moved everything together.

GUDERIAN: He has scraped everything together.

THE FÜHRER: I believe he will start the next attack here [north of the Danube northeast of Komarom]. Here I am not entirely sure if the 44th [Infantry] Division can hold it.

GUDERIAN: That's why the 46th [Infantry] Division is pulling out—so that the front will move back and become shorter.

THE FÜHRER: But then we have to lead them forward here, not further back. We can't hold it any longer. If something breaks through in front, it can't be repaired in the back. This must be brought in quite close. The attacks will certainly be made in the direction of Komarom. That is very clear. That way he will block even the railway.

GUDERIAN: This here is occupied by the 357th [Infantry Division], which is moving in. The 271st is not so far yet. It could possibly be available for that. Now we have to consider whether we should bring the 356th over here. In any case, the 46th Division would then have to go here.

THE FÜHRER: How does the 46th [Infantry] Division look?

GUDERIAN: It's a good division.

THE FÜHRER: We have to do it, so we can stop this whole thing here without having to use the corps or the army here, which I want to deploy in the south. But one can see how dangerous it is. That must be cleared out. I am not completely sure if we can do it from here—because we'll get frontal attacks again—or if we'll have to come from below after all. Because if we get involved in time-consuming frontal attacks, it won't work. But it won't work with the strength of this army. So they have to shift as quickly as possible to defense, before it's too late. They have to build up a front between Lake Velencze and the Danube, and they may have to break through with a panzer corps to the south.

GUDERIAN: According to General Wöhler and General Balck,[1741] something is being brought in here slowly. The turning toward the west happened too slowly. Certain complications in the transmission of orders and in the reporting system have caused delays.

THE FÜHRER: I also believe that it's too narrow again. The other one has pressed in. It's like this: If you push into an enemy who has concentrated his troops, than the panzer division concept is meaningless. Then a panzer division is not much more than a poor infantry division with assault gun and tank support. It is tanks accompanying artillery—nothing more. Here we have to learn this even now from the English and Americans. We have to pay more attention to this. Even the tanks are then additional accompanying artillery. They aren't suitable for breaking through anymore, because there are minefields, etc.

GUDERIAN: We have established everywhere a very close connection between the panzer grenadiers, the engineers, and the tanks themselves.[1742]

THE FÜHRER: I believe the firing practice for the tanks still focuses on very short distances. The tanks will be damaged like that.

GUDERIAN: No, my Führer, as Inspector General I extended it personally to the farthest range possible with our optics.

THE FÜHRER: The optics have to be improved as well, because it is clear that when I pull the tanks so far forward, they destroy them with artillery strikes. Then the tanks will be destroyed. Our tanks, especially the older ones, with 30- to 40-mm armor[1743] on the sides, are not at all safe from heavy explosives. So that has to be decided today now.

GUDERIAN: It will be decided.

THE FÜHRER: Pushing through[1744] makes no sense anymore—it won't succeed. How he stops it doesn't matter. The right thing to do would be for him to withdraw here, go into defense, and try, by pulling in a unit— possibly the strongest parts of the two SS divisions and the 1st Panzer Division—to take charge of the action from below and to lead one [division] up, so that the area is not lost.

GUDERIAN: The 23rd Panzer Division, which was in the reserves until now, is also here.

THE FÜHRER: So it makes no sense anymore.

GUDERIAN: He has no tank reserves now, anyway.

THE FÜHRER: I would not pull the 23rd out of here.

GUDERIAN: It's already underway. He wants to stretch out the cavalry.

THE FÜHRER: That is very unfortunate. As soon as it's taken back, Guderian, he will push in again here. He will make the major attack in the direction of Szekesferhervar [Stuhlweissenburg], because that way he will cut off the whole bunch.[1745] So this here has to be secured. That's the most important thing there is. The second is this here [northeast of Komarom].

GUDERIAN: Yes, it will be said again.

THE FÜHRER: He will push in with full strength here. That is just the beginning.

GUDERIAN: If we take it back, certainly. The question is if we should hold this here.

THE FÜHRER: Then they will be destroyed here. With these forces nothing can be done anymore. A defensive line has to be taken here and also here. In this area, he has to make an attack against the weaker enemy first, which he can do. Otherwise he will get a defensive front that is so long he can't hold it with his forces. Then he'll have to go back. It calls for lightning—quick decisions. We can't tinker around for such a long time like up there—it has to be done with lightning speed. So I order that he turn to defense at once and that he strengthen this by every possible means. Here he has the Volksartillery Corps. Here he has to have other units, or he can't do anything. This division unfortunately can't be counted; it's an illusion.

GUDERIAN: It will take a long time.

THE FÜHRER: The rear services will probably arrive first. One train is there?

GUDERIAN: One train has arrived; six will arrive. There are some combat troops included, but not many—some artillery and a battalion.

THE FÜHRER: With cavalry I can't stop a tank attack—which will come with deadly accuracy. And if he breaks through here, the whole thing is lost. Then I have to make sure that I can get it out. Nothing more can be expected. The whole attack has come in a moment when he has the forces free here. That's too late. He should have pulled through at the beginning, three weeks ago—then it might have been possible for a thrust to break through and establish a connection.[1746] Whether or not we could have held it is another question; that I don't know. Because on the other hand I don't disregard the fact that then the enemy would not have been here, but here. So that's an issue as well; if he pushes forward here, then [—] But that must reported at once.

GUDERIAN: It will be done at once, my Führer.

Silesia (Army Group Center)

Army Group Center's[1747] movements are progressing smoothly. The other final position, which should be captured, is this line here. The enemy pushed in only very weakly there. The withdrawal of the 208th [Infantry] Division is in general going quite smoothly. Transport is stalled by interruptions in the railway line. Some will be loaded in Briesen.

THE FÜHRER: Is this [south of Breslau] its final position?

GUDERIAN: Yes, indeed. It should reach it by January 30.

THE FÜHRER: That would be good, of course, because behind it we would still have the big Rochade Line.[1748]

GUDERIAN: It should connect with the Eighth Army down there. Up here [between Oppeln and Ratibor] is the 100th Jäger Division, which has mostly finished withdrawing. Behind it is the Ski Jäger Division, of which the first two battalions were employed up here. It is not completely out yet. Here [southwest of Katowice] is the part of the Ski Jäger Division that had to be employed because the enemy was pushing here so strongly. Very heavy battles have developed in the area of the Seventeenth Army. The attacks along a continuous line from the Tichau area to Auschwitz have been deflected; however, Auschwitz [Oswiecim] itself was lost. Further north, the 371st [Infantry] Division separated into three combat groups, with only a loose connection between them. Five tanks were destroyed. [—] The situation in the industrial area itself is difficult. With a penetration from both north and south, the enemy surrounded Myslowitz [Mislowice] from both sides and pushed forward to Kattowitz [Katowice]. Fighting is going on in Kattowitz now. Enemy tanks pushed into Kattowitz from the south.[1749] Combat groups composed of various quickly gathered units, including parts of the 20th Panzer Division, have started a counterattack to push them back out again. Also further north, in various places, there were very heavy attacks and penetrations were achieved. Nevertheless, Colonel General Schörner has decided to pull a number of battalions out, and to move them toward Hindenburg and further south, in order to check the enemy penetration at Gleiwitz [Gliwice]. In these battles, 30 tanks from the 20th Panzer Division were disabled yesterday, and 10 today—so 40 altogether. However, the 20th Panzer Division itself is operating on a broad front, in a heavy and unequal defensive battle. Further to the south, the enemy has enveloped them once more. Three battalions of the 1st Ski Jäger Division are approaching, and should be used to intercept this thing. The 8th Panzer Division, now for the most part—31 of 39 transports—present, will now assemble at Ratibor [Raciborz] and will be used in a counterattack in the direction of Rauden [Radlin].

THE FÜHRER: Where is the main coal area?

GÖRING: Rybnik and Mährisch-Ostrau [Morava-Ostova].

BUHLE: Here is a very important area.

GÖRING: High-grade steel and everything.

GUDERIAN: As of this evening, the regiments of the Gneisenau units[1750] will begin marching out of the protectorate; they will all be sent to join the army group at Mährisch-Ostrau. The Russian 3rd Guards Tank Army is here, with all its corps employed next to each other—altogether five tank corps, which are now pushing sharply toward the south to envelop the Kattowitz [Katowice] industrial area from the west. Here is a heavy and, at the moment, unequal battle. Further north, up to the edge of the army group area, fighting has begun for the Oder [River] crossings. At Krappitz [Krapkowice], we succeeded in throwing the enemy back yesterday. He broke forward over the Oder again early this morning, and counterattacks to push him back again are in progress. Most of the 100th Jäger Division is employed here, as is Group Stegmann[1751], which is a panzer group from the 103rd Panzer Brigade. The bridgehead, which was connected here, has been split in this one place and divided. We're not yet sure if that will last. North of Oppeln [Opole] is an extension of the bridgehead, which should be reduced in size through a combined counterattack by combat groups under General Hoffmann.[1752] Here we succeeded in reaching the river again—also here in the center. This wide south of Schurgast is causing difficulties and concern. The enemy also crossed the river between Brieg [Brzeg] and Ohlau [Olawa]; counterattacks have started, but haven't broken through. Then here at Zedlitz [—where yesterday the attack pushed forward far over the street and the railway—the enemy was pushed back to the street by a combat group under the Commanding Officer at Ohlau. We'll try to clear the thing up completely today, by using the 1st Battalion of the 39th Panther Detachment from the northwest. Thus far, four enemy tanks have been destroyed. There is no change in the situation at the Oder bend southeast of Breslau [Wrocław]. The 269th [Infantry] Division, under very heavy attack, has—despite a few limited penetrations—held its position so far. The situation south of Steinau [Stinawa] and at Köben is difficult, where the enemy succeeded in making deep penetrations in the direction of Herzogswalde and Raudten[1753] this morning. Here, under the command of the LVII Panzer Corps, General Kirchner,[1754] some units of the combat group of the 408th [Volksgrenadier Division] are used. Down here the staff of the 16th Panzer Division, which was just pulled out of the pocket, began a counterattack with a number of armored personnel carriers from the Glogau [Głogów] area. We haven't yet received a report confirming that it has actually started.[1755] So far it has only been ordered.

THE FÜHRER: What is this here?

GUDERIAN: That's the objective of Saucken's[1756] Corps and Jauer.[1757] They have reached the area of Köppelstädt here, and should now be pulled forward into the area of Schmückert, then turn to the south to defeat the enemy forces here—especially the 4th Guards Tank Army and the two tank corps [actually the 10th Guards Tank Corps and 6th Guards Mechanized Corps] that have already pushed ahead to the river, at the endangered bridgeheads—and thus free the area north of Breslau.[1758] Saucken's group was attacked from the south today at Horlen. Sixteen tanks were knocked out in this area. The north flank of Group Saucken group is being protected by the 19th Panzer Division, which is in a reasonably strong condition in the area of Gostyn and Storchnest. They also have quite a few assault guns and their artillery, so we hope that this protection will be enough to cover the attack to the south. [—] The Ninth Army will be transferred to the Reichsführer—to Army Group Vistula—today.[1759] In Glogau the command was taken over by the XXIV Panzer Corps under General Nehring,[1760] who is pulling the forces still under his command—primarily the 19th Panzer Division[1761]—down here. He's organizing them for new resistance on the Oder—east of the Oder, as far as possible. For the time being, the enemy is pushing forward up here with a tank corps. It was primarily reconnaissance units that trickled across the Glogau–Grätz line—a bit stronger into the Wollstein area, and only weaker from there on. We succeeded in holding the Tirschtiegel Position, with the exception of some reconnaissance parties that slipped through in a few places.

FEGELEIN: The Reichsführer has just ordered that the Tirschtiegel Position be occupied only by the Volkssturm [Home guards], while everything else goes forward.

THE FÜHRER: That's the goal.

FEGELEIN: That's correct.

THE FÜHRER: The goal is for Volkssturm men to come in here, and everything else that he can pull together will go forward and push down here.

GUDERIAN: In principle, all the units have already been ordered. They should be brought into the Lissa [Leszno]–Kosten [Koscian]–Posen [Poznan] line right from the beginning. It's interrupted here. Without my knowledge or the knowledge of the Reichsführer, these units were stopped in the Tirschtiegel Position by Military District III.[1762] I asked twice a day if the units would move forward. So that didn't happen with the necessary emphasis.

THE FÜHRER: But now it will be done with the necessary emphasis.

FEGELEIN: He has two assault gun companies there now. The goal is for him to get into the Posen [Poznan] area.

GUDERIAN: That's Group Saucken. The Reichsmarshal's[1763] division and the Brandenburg[1764] Division are here. They are to lead this attack and destroy this whole group in the Steinau Oder bend.

THE FÜHRER: That's good.

JODL: There's just one thing I don't understand. Didn't you say that the 19th [Panzer Division] would be pulled out there?

GUDERIAN: No, the 19th is in Gostyn.[1765]

JODL: Then these are other forces, because they must shield the rear.

GUDERIAN: No, up to now only rear services, maintenance facilities, etc., have been pulled out. These are across the Oder. Everything else will be kept on the Oder. [—] I request authorization to deploy the members of the War Academy, which will be closed in the next few days anyway,[1766] in order to establish—together with two companies of the Berlin[1767] Guard Regiment—a dense regrouping line, heavily occupied by officers, in this area straight west of the Oder, to prevent anything else from flowing out there.

THE FÜHRER: Yes. [—] And this is where the cavalry is to come?

FEGELEIN: The cavalry replacement and training regiment. It's about 1,500 men and will be brought in behind Colonel General Schörner.

GUDERIAN: The men will be divided.

GÖRING: Only this, which is coming back here, is weak in terms of officers. If these good, choice officers could come in there—

THE FÜHRER: I'll allow that. Here there are tens of thousands of men going back; they must be pulled together. They must have officers as well—the best ones. Otherwise we won't be able to catch them.

GUDERIAN: You want to catch this thing here, get it in order, and bring it forward.

GÖRING: But not closed, I don't think.

THE FÜHRER: No, as an interception line, to take them and get them in order. That can only be done with the best.

GÖRING: That's my opinion, too.

THE FÜHRER: And the cavalry should come here.

FEGELEIN: They will come the day after tomorrow.

THE FÜHRER: What's the unit's name?

FEGELEIN: It's the cavalry replacement and training regiment. There are about 1,500 men.

THE FÜHRER: It will be under Schörner, to block the roads to the rear.

GUDERIAN: The War Academy should cover the roads from Breslau to Glogau.

THE FÜHRER: And from Breslau to the east it can be done with the cavalry regiment. There are 1,500 men?

FEGELEIN: It could be even more. I don't know for certain. The commander is en route. They are available to the 8th and 22nd SS Divisions,[1768] but that's not an option.

THE FÜHRER: That's not an option. The important thing is that they take care of this assignment.

GUDERIAN: The formations that are going back with marching orders are in order and don't have any excess people with them, but during these treks and in the railway trains coming back there are many shirkers acting as coachmen and assistants for the soldiers during the treks, and some have put on civilian clothes. The whole control should focus less on the military formations—which are marching in order under the leadership of officers, motor sergeants and inspectors—and more on these treks.

THE FÜHRER: They'll be caught in the line anyway. They won't get past it; everything that drives through individually must be brought out to the rear. Schörner says he's brought out 13,000 men so far.

Pomerania, Prussia (Army Group Vistula)

GUDERIAN: In Army Group Vistula's area, the new boundary line comes into effect today with the takeover of the command by the XXIV Panzer Corps and the Ninth Army. The line runs north of Glogau, south of Lissa and north of Krotoschin [Krotoszyn], in the general direction of Kalisch [Kalisz]. Then the XXXX Panzer Corps is deployed here; it has the sector from Lissa to Posen excluding Posen, then the Posen post headquarters, then in the north the V SS Mountain Corps—which has a bad telephone connection at the moment because of the many interruptions caused by enemy reconnaissance patrols working mischief in their rear. Here in front is a consolidated line in the Tirschtiegel front, and in front of that a closed block. It's not totally clear if Grätz is in our hands. Then the Posen Fortress, which had to withstand several attacks from the south and northwest. Here a fort has apparently been taken, but it's not clear yet if it's here or here. In any case, something unpleasant has already happened there as well.[1769] [—] By decoding enemy radio messages, we succeeded in confirming through enemy radio communications the concentration of the 1st Guards Tank Army. It should follow this line. Its flanks stretch out like this—the way it's marked—in this general direction.

THE FÜHRER: During the next few days, I want a clear picture of the findings we have so far about the concentration—also about the enemy situation, the projected objective direction and the concentration locations, because our own measures depend on it.

GUDERIAN: Yes, Sir. In this area at least, which includes Posen, the 1st Guards Tank Army is reported to be concentrating.

THE FÜHRER: With how many corps?

GUDERIAN: With tank corps. That's four corps.

THE FÜHRER: They normally have 1,600 tanks. How many would they still have?

GUDERIAN: Half at the most. [—] In between is the Posen Fortress, which has held. According to the news in the radio messages, the enemy infantry is for the most part dependent on the railway line running from Nakel [Naklo] southward via Gnesen [Gniezno] in the direction of Jarotschin [Jarocin].

THE FÜHRER: The more they push in here, the more difficult the supply will become.

GÖRING: The railways are all intact; they drive through by train without any complications.

THE FÜHRER: I hope all our trains and all our engines weren't stuck.

GUDERIAN: It was likely quite a jam. Not everything came out. [—] Then to the north is the 2nd Guards Tank Army with its corps. Now, the situation got a bit more complicated here as well. The enemy sent strong reconnaissance elements from the Scharnikau [River] over the Netze [Notec] River], and is pushing against Schönlanke [Trzcianka], Schloppe [Czlopa] and Filehne. He attacked Schneidemühl [Pila] today.[1770] This Usch [Ujscie] bridgehead was still ours this morning. But the enemy passed it sideways and crossed the Netze.

THE FÜHRER: The Netze is no obstacle.

GUDERIAN: It's frozen now, too.

THE FÜHRER: It's totally frozen.

GUDERIAN: He attacked this Schneidemühl position, made contact from the east and northeast and was driven back here. The army group headquarters is going to Crössinsee.[1771] The situation in the area around Nakel is unclear. Nakel itself was lost. The Latvian division has withdrawn further to the north.[1772] The army command has gone as far as Preussisch Friedland, and the enemy pushed through in between. The situation at Krone [Walcz] is questionable. Bromberg [Bydgoszcz] is in enemy hands. The occupying forces are in this railway triangle and the enemy is advancing from here with the 2nd Guards Cavalry Corps to the Vistula valley road and along the railway line in the direction of Schwetz [Swiecie]. From there the XXXXVI Panzer Corps began a counterattack with the 4th Panzer Division, the 337th [Infantry] Division[1773] and the 542nd [*Volksgrenadier*] Division. The Kulm [Chelmo] bridgehead, which is smaller now, is being held only by the 251st [Infantry] Division on the eastern edge.

THE FÜHRER: It might possibly have to be given up.

GUDERIAN: It will have to be given up. The Reichsführer intends, as he discussed with you earlier, to give up this bridgehead as well.[1774]

THE FÜHRER: The big one; he wants to have a small one.

GUDERIAN: He wants to hold Graudenz [Grudziadz][1775] and the small Marienwerder [Kwidzin] bridgehead, and to take the rest of the forces over here as well.

THE FÜHRER: No, he would rather hold Graudenz. Marienwerde is so far away.

GUDERIAN: Graudenz is better, too. It's a fortress. There's the position here.[1776] Here the enemy attacked and achieved a penetration at Gransee. He also attacked at Graudenz, but was driven back. Then the enemy pushed against the Mewe River bridgehead. South of Mewe he came over the river with weaker units; to the north he was driven back. At Marienburg [Malbork] there is fighting for the castle and the railway, which are in our hands. Here there's still a naval battalion approaching.

THE FÜHRER: They've fought very well so far.

GUDERIAN: Yes, indeed. This position along the Nogat [River] is being held by the Navy. The 7th Panzer Division is being brought forward in the direction of Neuteich [Nowy Staw], to strike the enemy—who has crossed over the Nogat—in coordination with the Naval regiment that was in the bridgehead before, and to clear out the thing on the left bank of the Nogat. South of Elbing [Elblag], the bridgehead is still in our hands. The enemy pushed into the city from the north with a few tanks—15 in total. The fighting continues there. The Reichsführer wanted to pull the 32nd [Infantry] Division into the Nakel area.

FEGELEIN: He just reported that a regiment has arrived now.[1777]

THE FÜHRER: Where?

FEGELEIN: I don't know.

GUDERIAN: The 227th [Infantry] Division, which also came down from Courland, is here. Most of the units—the majority—are there, while the 32nd Division is coming over now.

THE FÜHRER: This is our problem child now.[1778]

GUDERIAN: The attack by Army Group North began this morning and had good results. Here, the first units of these tank destroyers[1779] and Arko [Artillery Command] 302[1780] reached halfway to Frauenburg [Frombork]–Elbing. They were there this morning already. The panzer groups that went ahead here reached here; the 28th Jäger Division reached Karwitten and Liebemühl [Milomlyn] and engaged with the enemy to the north here. Group Einem[1781] should be pulled in afterward in this direction, to make it decisive. The 170th [Infantry] Division and the 131st [Infantry] Division also made good progress in the attack, as the blue arrows indicate here. Further to the south, in the area of the 18th Panzer [Grenadier] Division[1782] and the rest of the 299th [Infantry] Division, our attack—which is for holding purposes primarily—didn't break through; instead, they are still continuing to defend in this position. The intention is to push forward here again, in order to hold the enemy forces. Down here an enemy thrust was driven back. *Grossdeutschland* has been pulled out, but without fuel at the moment, and one other division.

THE FÜHRER: *Grossdeutschland* goes where?[1783]

GUDERIAN: *Grossdeutschland* will go up there, as will the 562nd [*Volksgrenadier* Division]. The plan is to pull the 562nd Division in here by overland march, in order to be able to employ it up there or here if necessary. The withdrawal movement was completed without enemy pressure. The enemy didn't follow. Combat outposts and rearguards are still far behind near the enemy. Here there was pressure on Friedland [Pravdinsk], without result. Then the enemy attacked fairly heavily south of Königsberg. Opposing this were the 547th [*Volksgrenadier*] Division, remnants of the 61st [Infantry] Division, and some units of the 2nd Division *Hermann Göring* that were mobile. The main enemy pressure is on the northeastern front and north of Königsberg, where the remnants of the 551st [*Volksgrenadier*] Division and the 286th [Infantry] Division have apparently lost almost all of their fighting strength—which led to a crisis situation this morning. We're not quite sure if the front is still how it's marked here, or if it has already been taken back to this line.

THE FÜHRER: If they're on this line, they won't come back here again.

GUDERIAN: Then nothing else will come back on the Nehrung. I spoke with Colonel General Reinhardt and discussed these circumstances.[1784] The commanding general of the Königsberg Fortress, Lasch, has been authorized with that command up to the Samland coast.[1785] I request retroactive permission.

THE FÜHRER: Yes, indeed. Of course.

GUDERIAN: He's the most notable personality we have up there. Koch[1786] telephoned himself, and General Lasch as well, to say that there is a fairly significant crisis here [at and south of Memel]. General Lasch went himself to collect and bring in the disorganized crowds up here. We hope the people will come in time to catch this. There are now three battalions of the 95th [Infantry] Division, three battalions of the 58th [Infantry] Division, three battalions of fortress troops, a mortar brigade, and the 278th Assault Gun Brigade.[1787]

THE FÜHRER: I just don't understand one thing. The fortress troops should be kept here until the end, and the infantry brought here first.

GUDERIAN: Yes, the other way round.

THE FÜHRER: You can see the most primitive actions if you don't say exactly what to do beforehand.

GUDERIAN: It was said that one division should come out immediately. That happened. Here there's a battalion en route by truck. Hopefully they will arrive in time to catch this.

THE FÜHRER: Where are the assault guns?

GUDERIAN: The assault guns are already here, for the most part. That has rolled off already. The 278th [Assault Gun Brigade] and the Tiger detachment are still in here.

THE FÜHRER: I hope they weren't pulled down here.

GUDERIAN: They were ordered here.

THE FÜHRER: Find out. That's 60 things.

GUDERIAN: That's the weakest part in front there.

Courland

There was another defensive success for Army Group Courland. Because of heavy enemy pressure, it had finally become necessary to take the front back to the previously approved line. Here the enemy attacks failed, and assemblies were broken up. Here there was a penetration; the 14th Panzer Division and units of the 218th [Infantry] Division are engaged in a successful counterattack. Here all enemy attacks were driven back with fairly heavy enemy losses—10 tanks were knocked out. Limited local penetrations will be cleared out by the units of the 12th Panzer Division that are being brought in. The enemy is now also reorganizing from here out toward the west, which points more and more clearly to a concentration against the southern front in the direction of Libau [Liepaia].

THE FÜHRER: That's quite clear, because the harbor is there and they hope to get it. That's why we have to protect Libau very heavily.

GUDERIAN: Fairly heavy night flight sorties on the part of the enemy.

Miscellaneous regarding the Eastern front

GÖRING: There are 10,000 captured air force officers at Sagan [Zagan]; under the custody of the Commander of the Replacement Army.[1788] Guard and transport forces are not available. The idea has been suggested that we might turn the prisoners over to the Soviet Russian allies. They would get 10,000 pilots.

THE FÜHRER: Why didn't they transport them away earlier? That's incredibly sloppy.

GÖRING: It's the Commander of the Replacement Army.[1789] We have nothing to do with it. I can only report it.

THE FÜHRER: They must leave, even if they march on foot. The Volkssturm will be mobilized for that. Anyone who runs away will be shot. That must be done by all means.

GÖRING: That's from Sagan. There are 10,000 men.

GUDERIAN: The entire 4th Panzer Division has rolled out, as has the 227th [Infantry] Division. The rest of the 32nd [Infantry] Division is underway now. Then the headquarters of the III SS Panzer Corps will arrive tonight, and tomorrow night the *Nederland* Division, which is already out. Some units of the *Nordland* have also been pulled out of the front already.

THE FÜHRER: Will they get replacements now? Is that on the way in already?

GUDERIAN: Fegelein arranged that. He has been ordered to replenish them at once.

THE FÜHRER: It's quite clear that right now Army Group Vistula has nothing except the Nehring corps, the one group and what they have on the Vistula. That has to be organized. They will come from here now—in part from Germany. That must be done anyway!

GÖRING: How many cattle wagons are needed for 10,000 men?

THE FÜHRER: If we transport according to German rules, we need at least 20 transport trains for 10,000 men. If we transport according to Russian rules, we need three to five.

GÖRING: Take off their trousers and shoes, so they can't walk in the snow.[1790]

GUDERIAN: Then Vlasov wanted to make some statements.[1791]

THE FÜHRER: Vlasov is nothing.

GÖRING: They shouldn't run around in German uniforms there. You see young people everywhere. That just provokes the people. If someone wants to catch them, then they're Vlasov people.

THE FÜHRER: I was against dressing them in our uniforms. But who was for it? It was our beloved Army, which had its own ideas.

GÖRING: They're going around like that right now.

THE FÜHRER: I can't dress them. We have no uniforms. Back then I wanted the foreigners—but Herr von Seeckt sold German steel helmets to the Chinese. There's no sense of honor there. Every poor devil wears a German uniform. I've always been against it. I was against putting Cossacks in German uniforms. They should wear Cossack uniforms and badges as proof that they're fighting for us. That's also much more romantic. It never occurs to the British to dress an Indian in an British uniform. That shamelessness is ours alone, because there's no character inside. Otherwise we wouldn't put German steel helmets on others. The British let the Indians go as natives.

GÖRING: The Vlasov people are certainly so hostile over there that they'll be punished if they're caught.

THE FÜHRER: Don't say that. They will desert to the other side.

GÖRING: That's the only thing they can do: desert to the other side. They can't do anything else.

GUDERIAN: Should the division that's being drawn up in Münsingen be finished more quickly?

THE FÜHRER: Yes, indeed. We should finish that.

FEGELEIN: The Reichsführer wanted to have the supreme command over these two divisions.

THE FÜHRER: Vlasov won't desert to the other side.

GÖRING: They can't do anything except desert to the other side. Then they won't eat anything else up.

FEGELEIN: The men won't desert to the other side either. I've seen them.

THE FÜHRER: They look fine. In France we experienced it: they deserted to the other side.[1792]

FEGELEIN: The Russians will kill them all, because they kill even the Russian workers who worked for us. We have the proof already. They'll kill them all.

THE FÜHRER: We do the same with the ones who worked in West. The Allies are having difficulty finding another mayor.[1793]

GÖRING: I would still use the Vlasov people.

FEGELEIN: And the officers from Sagan?

GÖRING: Obergruppenführer Jüttner[1794] is to transport the 10,000 prisoners from Sagan.

THE FÜHRER: They must be moved out with every possible means. The Volkssturm must be mobilized with the most energetic people. Escape attempts will be punished by shooting.

FEGELEIN: We have a man for it, who guards the KZs [concentration camps]. It's Gruppenführer Glücks.[1795] He must do it.

GUDERIAN: Schörner is complaining about Group Rudel[1796] being recalled. He wants written instructions about it and is beside himself. That is irresponsible; we have to give the Reichsführer something.

THE FÜHRER: Because he has absolutely nothing. Rudel can work better in the open than in the industrial area.[1797]

GUDERIAN: I can tell Schörner that that's your order. I spoke with Koller about it again. He's of the same opinion. [—] Then in Rastenburg there are 1,800 men from the SS tank destroyer replacement and training detachment. They should be moved out at once. I believe we should leave them in Königsberg, so the man will have something.

THE FÜHRER: But there's no SS unit here. I would make that available to Himmler as well; he needs them. There's nothing at all there. We have to give them to Himmler so he can gradually start building up a skeleton.

GUDERIAN: Right now they're under the Hauser[1798] combat group, which was in Lötzen.

THE FÜHRER: If they would defend Lötzen I wouldn't say anything. But after it's gone anyway!

GUDERIAN: The question is if we should leave them in Königsberg, so it doesn't turn into a complete bloodbath.

THE FÜHRER: I'm afraid they won't go to Königsberg, but to the West.[1799]

GUDERIAN: That can be ordered

THE FÜHRER: You can order it, but will they follow? No one would follow the order.

GUDERIAN: Yes, they would.

BURGDORF: Rendulic[1800] has arrived up above.

GUDERIAN: The command has been taken over by Rendulic and Natzmer.[1801]

GÖRING: The weapons issue is the important one. We're combing people out. The people are there but they receive no weapons.

GUDERIAN: Here are the strength returns. I don't know if you requested it from Wenck. (*Presentation.*) The 203rd [Infantry Division] has 3,400 men and the 541st [Volksgrenadier Division] still has 3,100. From Group "Hannibal"—that's a police group—there are 900 men. Combat Group Hauser and the 21st [Infantry Division] couldn't obtained. *Grossdeutschland* is still reasonable: two medium-strong, one average, three weak battalions, four light batteries, 39 heavy artillery guns. That's the corps artillery and the Army artillery. Tank strength has decreased considerably. Still about 25 altogether. Then, my Führer, I wanted to request authorization to pull the recruitment age group 1928 out of all the eastern military districts, so that they're brought only to a reasonably safe military district for training.[1802]

KEITEL: Otherwise the Russians will catch them. Every month there are around 50-60,000 men—we absolutely must have them.

GUDERIAN: Military Districts I, XX and XXI; VI and XXI are out, and VIII is out as well. We should also take away II and III.[1803]

KEITEL: For the next three or four months. I had everything discussed with Jüttner again today.

GÖRING: Weapons, weapons!

THE FÜHRER: That's perfectly clear. We're constantly losing industrial areas and don't have so many weapons.

GÖRING: But we make people mobile, which reduces the readiness everywhere.

THE FÜHRER: What does "readiness" mean? We can't work at full capacity industrially anyway.

GÖRING: No, I mean military readiness. Everything is being pulled together extremely carelessly in order to free people up, and we don't have the weapons. I'd like to draw attention to just one thing. I was obliged to give away all the small arms from the anti-aircraft [units]. And I did it. Now the anti-aircraft stands there with its heavy guns and has no small arms. So many heavy batteries have been overpowered in battle because they had no small arms and couldn't shoot with the heavy guns.

THE FÜHRER: A major program is starting. I hope that it can be carried out with the available forces, but I can't say. 900,000 assault pistols[1804] should be produced per month.

BUHLE: That will take a while still.

THE FÜHRER: And what's happening with the peoples' gun [volksgewehr]?[1805]

BUHLE: The people's gun is starting now. This month we'll get the first 8,000, next month we'll get 25,000, and the month after that 50,000. That's the projection.

GÖRING: The weapons that Field Marshal Keitel took away from us.

THE FÜHRER: Where is our gun production? Mainly in Upper Silesia?

BUHLE: No, the gun production is more in central Germany, in Suhl and Oberndorf. But there's a lot in Württemberg, and there they have terrible trouble with power and coal.

THE FÜHRER: The gun and machine gun production won't be affected, as far as I know.

BUHLE: It will be shortened now. It will be completely stopped under the coal and power emergency program, so that everything else will stop suddenly and something will come in there. So this month will be very bad.

Hungary again

GUDERIAN: Then regarding the behavior in Army Group South I can say that the army group believes that it doesn't have enough with one division in this area. It suggests leaving the entire Gille Corps with two divisions in, pulling out the 1st Panzer [Division] and the 23rd Panzer [Division], and bringing everything together under Breith.[1806]

THE FÜHRER: But this must be covered here, too, because the next big thrust will come here. As soon as we go away here, the next big thrust will come here. That's even more dangerous.

V. FREYTAG-LORINGHOVEN: Six trains of the 346th [356th Infantry Division] have arrived.

THE FÜHRER: That's still not a fighting force. We can't count these trains. The ones that come from Italy are rear services first.

GUDERIAN: But there are some combat troops with them. I'll find out what it is.

THE FÜHRER: Here, when he takes out the 23rd, he has only the cavalry. When it changes to defense, he'll come over here with his tanks. That's a serious danger.

GUDERIAN: He has to leave the panzer group here until the danger is completely eliminated.

THE FÜHRER: He absolutely must leave the panzer group here.

JODL: The combat element is out ahead; it has left. Now all 31 trains down there have left.

WINTER: It's coming at about Speed 7.

THE FÜHRER: But this is the important thing. If he breaks through here, everything is lost. We have to be clear about that. As far as I'm concerned, the Gille Corps can change to defense.

GUDERIAN: The 1st Panzer Division out, added to the 3rd [Panzer Division] and what can be released from the 23rd [Panzer Division], plus the Breith army command?

THE FÜHRER: He doesn't think he can do it with just the 1st [Panzer Division].

GUDERIAN: I don't know. I'll have to review that myself.

THE FÜHRER: How does the 1st look anyway?

GUDERIAN: It's not that strong anymore. It was filled up with men again. The 23rd is certainly the stronger one. It's better.

THE FÜHRER: When I speak of dangers, I'd like to say that danger point 1 is here. Danger point 2 is here. Danger point 3 is here. If he pushes through here, it's all over. If he pushes up here, that will collapse, too.

GUDERIAN: That's the 1st, the 3rd, the 23rd.

THE FÜHRER: The 23rd is the best.

GUDERIAN: Yes, it's tolerable; also the 6th and then the two SS divisions. That's the condition on the 24th. It suffered a bit in the battles, of course. But in terms of replacements it's still the best. [—] I will review this.

THE FÜHRER: Say it again. This is the most dangerous point. The next point is here. If he breaks through here, everything is lost. That's also a dangerous point.

GUDERIAN: Artillery and mortars are here.

THE FÜHRER: If we're pushed into a corridor, this will go back slowly. But here we have the wide plain. If he comes here everything will collapse. That's the most dangerous.

The West

JODL: No significant changes have been identified on the part of the enemy, except that the 6th British Airborne Division pushed into the Venlo area, causing a limited compression of these very wide divisional sectors. No additional divisions were sent in for the attack against the Roer bridgehead, except for some armored brigades, so the British Armored Guard Division, the 50th British Division, and also the 11th British Armored Division are still in the rear here. The American group around Lüttich is probably still there.

THE FÜHRER: What's happening with the British air attacks in the south, considering the weather conditions?

KEITEL: No major attacks.

JODL: It was bad—snowstorms and fog.

GÖRING: There was nothing on either side. So I don't think it was just the weather.

KEITEL: There were no major attacks.

JODL: Only 5 trains of the 1st SS Panzer Division have left so far.[1807] That division is now moving into this area. The fuel is there. So if there are more delays now, it's because of the execution of the march or the heavily snowed roads. [—] It didn't intensify there, either.

THE FÜHRER: One day without flying is more helpful than five days with flying, of course, if they pull through quickly on the day when there's no flying.

GÖRING: Today there's no flying, Büchs?

BÜCHS: No.

V. BELOW: Not much so far.

JODL: The 12th SS Panzer Division is now coming into loading area B with its advanced guard. The 9th SS Panzer Division is moving now as well. We don't know which route the 2nd will take.

THE FÜHRER: If we have one or two days of weather like this, do you think he will attack then?[1808] When can we expect at least the combat portions of this panzer army to arrive in Vienna? Not before two or three weeks?

JODL: The one corps will be there in 14 days.

THE FÜHRER: And the second corps?

JODL: That will vary.

WINTER: This will take 12 days. The second corps can be there in an additional four or five days, if the movement progresses as it has so far.

THE FÜHRER: They'll come just in time, because the next crisis is coming down there.

JODL: The railway should be able to move smoothly. If they're open now, we should plan on 16 days for all four divisions to arrive, and the timing should be fairly smooth then with 40 trains.

THE FÜHRER: That's the first real fighting force.

KEITEL: It will go quickly through Germany.

GÖRING: In 14 days they can be assembled up there.

JODL: Twenty-three trains are there from the 2nd Mountain Division. The 25th hasn't moved yet.

THE FÜHRER: How has the 2nd performed? I heard that it supposedly had a minor failure.

JODL: Yes, I heard a report on that. I'll get a report from the divisional commander.

THE FÜHRER: But it has proven itself well up there. Even the best divisions can get a shock somewhere sometime.

JODL: These are totally new conditions here. It's always like that. Whenever a division comes to a completely new theater, there's always a little crisis at first.

THE FÜHRER: Even the best division can get a shock.

JODL: Besides, every new division is looked at askance.

THE FÜHRER: Especially when it arrives in good condition, with good soldiers and good boots and is well maintained and the guns are not rusty. Then they immediately say, "Where do those people come from, where something like that still exists?"

JODL: The 3rd Panzer Grenadier Division started moving as well. It's coming up to Erkelenz.

THE FÜHRER: One time I experienced the kind of messes that are made there. A brand new division came from home. A regiment came to the town where we were. They moved through, but stopped there for a rest and to put the guns together. Our people made a big scene there. Before they could turn around, the beautiful new guns were gone and the old, completely rusty and dirty ones were there. They had to continue forward. It was a fiasco, but nothing could be done. Then you hear immediately: Where do those people come from, where something like that still exists?

JODL: The Führer Grenadier Brigade and the Führer Escort Brigade have not moved yet, but they have assembled now. For the Führer Grenadier Brigade I have the strength: 4,229 men in daily strength; two Panzer IVs, three in for repair; eight Panzer Vs, ten in for repair; five assault guns, eleven in for repair, 27 coming in. That would be 60 tanks altogether.

THE FÜHRER: And the Führer Escort Brigade is a bit stronger.[1809]

JODL: I don't have that one yet.

THE FÜHRER: I think it has 7,000 men.

GÖRING: Can't we put tanks in little groups—six or ten—and have them drive around the forefield disabling the tank point.

THE FÜHRER: That happens anyway. They approach in small groups of ten to fourteen assault guns, with armored personnel carriers.

GÖRING: They look for the tanks.

KEITEL: Tank-destroyer reconnaissance patrols.

THE FÜHRER: And armored patrol cars with antitank guns, which drive very fast. They will be used there now, to hunt there.

GÖRING: Fighter commandos [*Jägdkommandos*] can be very promising.

JODL: During the thrust against the 6th Parachute Division on the 26th, the enemy lost 25 dead, which were counted, and two flame-thrower tanks were destroyed. Heavy firing from the batteries southeast of Nijmegen.

THE FÜHRER: When can we expect the 7th Parachute Division to be brought up from down there back to its own unit?

JODL: That will take a long time—at least 14 to 20 days.

THE FÜHRER: That's fine, but we must bring them up because a very serious crisis point will emerge here. And the 5th Parachute Division?

JODL: There are no stronger forces there yet, but the 5th and 3rd are here.

GÖRING: We have to merge them. The fighting strength of four combined parachute divisions is equal to five divisions.

JODL: Then here concentrations were broken up with artillery fire. The attack here is being continued with the existing forces. He had pushed into Ottilienberg[1810] and was thrown back with a counterattack there.

THE FÜHRER: They complain and protest terribly about the whole situation here on the Western Front.[1811]

JODL: Here the front was pushed back. There are now two flat bridgeheads in front of the Roer [River]. On the rest of the front it was quiet; movement there. The attacks here weren't as concentrated as in the last few days, but weaker and more isolated. South of Nevenbach the enemy broke through. There the counterattack is in progress. Further to the south he was thrown back again. Northwest of St. Vith he was also pushed back.

THE FÜHRER: Here is the Schnee-Eifel.

JODL: No, the Schnee-Eifel is further back. There's where the Western Wall runs. That's the wooded hill line that should then be held. So this line will be a bit further back from here then. They're still a little in front. This was the piece the enemy had. Here is the Western Wall. The attacks further to the south were also isolated and weaker. Three heavy attacks in the direction of Burgreuland were driven back. [—] This salient will be taken back into this straight line. In this place here the Roer has already been reached. From there on the salient projects out again. Only a minor thing was carried out there today. Various enemy follow-up thrusts were repeatedly stopped by counterattacks. The enemy had considerable losses here.

THE FÜHRER: They write that the Americans have lost 85,000 men this month. That's 50 percent of what they lost in the entire Great War.[1812]

JODL: Further south it was quiet. On that corner, with Remich,[1813] the enemy broke through again yesterday to Schlossberg and beyond. There he was thrown back in counterattacks to the north of Tetting. Further attacks were driven back. The panzer group turned back after the lead tank was knocked out. Lively movement in the area southeast of Saarburg. At Saargemünd some sort of relief or supply movements seem to be in progress. Heavy assembly of railway material in the area around Metz, and heavy vehicle assembly in the area of Zabern and Saarburg. It was quiet yesterday on the newly won Moder front,[1814] where the Moder-Rotbach sector was reached everywhere. The bridge in the rear at Merzweiler—over this sector—is ready, although enemy artillery fired on it. It's a 40-ton bridge, which makes the supply easier here. The engagements were still heavier down here, where the enemy continued his attacks from south of Erstein and then down east of Colmar.[1815] But yesterday all attacks here were successfully driven back. One tank was knocked out. Likewise, these attacks at Markolsheim were driven back while eight tanks were disabled.

THE FÜHRER: This thing here absolutely must be fixed.[1816] It is actually such that we have to try to get this salient here after all. This must be the withdrawal?

JODL: That's the withdrawal he has ordered now; on the 27th this line and on the 28th this position.

THE FÜHRER: But the most important thing is that we get this salient in our hands. For that purpose we have to seriously consider whether we shouldn't pull out the 6th SS Mountain Division from here, relieve it with some other unit, transport it around and join it with the 2nd Mountain Division, in order to carry out the operation with both of these mountain divisions. Only mountain divisions can do it, because this is the decisive thing: that Breisach remains completely secure in our hands. If this remains in a big bridgehead, the danger is low, in principle. Perhaps you could speak with the Commander-in-Chief West about that. We have to try to get the 6th SS Mountain Division out somehow, and bring it in with the 2nd Mountain Division so that both mountain divisions can carry out the attack together here. That can be done in stages. Here the enemy can't do much with tanks. This attack must be led into here. That has always been Himmler's idea, too, because in this terrain he can't do much with tanks. And that could be a success. That's 30, 50 km. A mountain division can do that. Otherwise we can't do it. If they clear this thing out here, it would fit well with the connection here. Schlettstadt can be left out; it's not that important. It can also be smaller. That doesn't matter—just that we have greater security here, because Colmar is so near.

JODL: And all the artillery is there.

THE FÜHRER: Above all, the bridges must be outside the range of artillery fire. Aircraft send a signal when they are arriving, the artillery fire doesn't. [—] Up here the action has now come to a halt.

JODL: This has come to a halt.

THE FÜHRER: Speak with the Commander-in-Chief West, to see if he can't bring out the 6th SS Mountain Division. Also defensively this line could later be held more easily than the other one.

JODL: Much more easily.

THE FÜHRER: If there were two mountain divisions here on this front, everything could be held.

JODL: This order went out yesterday. (*Presentation.*)

THE FÜHRER: Above all, a careful defensive line must still be built up here.

JODL: That's the old one; the new one is a bit further forward.

THE FÜHRER: It must be improved.

JODL: Then the question about the command structure in the West should be discussed today.

THE FÜHRER: Yes, I wanted to discuss that with you, Göring. So the people who spoke with him today think that Student[1817] has become very tired.

GÖRING: He doesn't need to stay. They don't know him. They don't know his outrageously slow speech. They don't understand that. That's the judgment of everyone who speaks with him. But aside from Model, he's still one of the greatest steadying influences when it gets hard. I'm convinced of that. He's so outrageously slow. They think he's crazy because they don't know him. But I'll take him with pleasure.

THE FÜHRER: In those days during the operations in Italy he had it, too.

GÖRING: He spoke so slowly. They all thought he was stupid. I'll take him gladly because I know—these gentlemen are witnesses—that he will be needed again in a critical situation. I'll take him gladly because I need him, because he gives his paratrooper army spirit again. He says, "Yes, the Führer also told me"—I know him; the others don't know him. I don't blame them because they can't judge him any other way. Someone recently asked me if I had a fool up there. I said, "No, he's not a fool; he spoke that slowly before." Now he's been hit on the head, so they think that's the reason. But it was that way earlier. But with every operation he says, "It's best if we jump into the enemy area."

THE FÜHRER: He has done the most incredible things.

GÖRING: I'll take him with pleasure, so he won't be seen wrongly. I know that at the critical hour he'll be needed. He's steady. He's not a big genius otherwise, but he's a straight, upright tenacious man, who knows that his troops have to hold. But I'll take him away gladly, so you can see later how it holds then, when he's gone.

THE FÜHRER: I would be very sorry; I don't know how much. Is Blaskowitz a steadying influence like that?

GÖRING: No, he is much more voluble. Student's little toe is worth more than all of Blaskowitz.

THE FÜHRER: That's just the question.

GÖRING: But I'll take him gladly because I know. A critical moment will come, and then you'll complain and take him back. I look forward to that day.

THE FÜHRER: I don't look forward to that day.

GÖRING: No, but then you'll give him back. Why should I expose such an excellent man to this gossip? You know him; he has always spoken so slowly.

THE FÜHRER: When I presented the action in the West back then, he developed a slowness like that, too. But in the end he did do it. It was the same with the operation to free the Duce.[1818]

GÖRING: Also in other actions in Italy he did his job.

THE FÜHRER: He absolutely did clear up the thing in Italy.

GÖRING: If he had stayed there, that bridgehead would not have come either. But I need him urgently. He should tighten up the parachute army again and bring in those divisions. Then you have someone you can always put somewhere else when it's do or die. He will never yield or waver. He may speak more slowly then. It's possible. But he'll retreat even more slowly.

THE FÜHRER: He reminds me of my Fehrs, my new servant, the Holsteiner. When I say something to him he thinks about it for a long time. He needs minutes. He is stolid. He does his job well—he's just extremely slow.

GÖRING: Then Student is someone who has clever ideas. That can't be argued. He puzzles something out by himself.

THE FÜHRER: But it was suggested that we take Blaskowitz up and give that to Hausser, or vice versa.

JODL: That we put Hausser in up above.

GÖRING: Hausser is already familiar with this here[1819] now.

JODL: There are more SS units here.

THE FÜHRER: That, I would like to say, is pure improvisation. If I want to do this thing, I would like to have Hausser here, too.

FEGELEIN: Especially because there's always pressure from the Reichsführer, even if he can't order anything else—he still pushes constantly.[1820]

THE FÜHRER: So that he does this thing. The Reichsführer also lives this thing completely. He says: My Führer, if we have this here, then he has one important access line less, we have one beautiful position more, and then I can guarantee that nothing will happen in Breisach. The whole bridgehead depends on that in the end—the ferry traffic back and forth. A bridge is better.

JODL: In any case, difficulties are already arising from the separation. Now Hausser immediately ripped out everything he could pull out and brought it down there, so we don't know at the moment how we can get these mobile units out. So for that reason alone it's necessary that we bring these[1821] together, because having so many higher staffs there causes nothing but difficulties. Besides, he has no quartermaster staff. I would suggest that we leave Hausser here and give him the First Army as well. I think that would be the right thing.

THE FÜHRER: Hausser is a crafty devil. He gives the impression of a shrew.

JODL: An incredibly sarcastic, funny man. At least he was.

THE FÜHRER: He has a fox face.

GUDERIAN: He tells very good jokes.

KEITEL: Very quick at repartee.

THE FÜHRER: With his sly little eyes. But I'm just not sure if he suffered from the last heavy injury.

FEGELEIN: No, he didn't suffer; he was tested. The Reichsführer said he doesn't quite like the look of the thing. He said that if he lines up down there with a successor, and he does something unsuitable, he's not quite all there intellectually, then that's the most unpleasant for him. The Reichsführer is so clever that he wouldn't have proposed it if he didn't know for certain: That works—because he would make a fool of himself, and the Reichsführer is quite sensitive about such things.

THE FÜHRER: We all are.

FEGELEIN: But the Reichsführer is always criticized, of course.

THE FÜHRER: If something goes wrong.

GÖRING: I can only ask that the relief of Student be done in such a way that it doesn't look as if he were a failure, because he hasn't failed at anything—nothing—I can confirm that. Rather, whatever his assignment was, he did it faultlessly, even if there wasn't much action. He did the flooding there, etc.[1822] I would like to do it like this: I need the Parachute Army urgently and will file the application.

FEGELEIN: Besides, Hausser has the following profound maxim. He says, "As a soldier I'm nearly 65 years old; the greatest achievement I can ever accomplish is to die on the front lines due to bravery in the face of the enemy."

THE FÜHRER: I don't want that at all.

FEGELEIN: But he pushes.

THE FÜHRER: That is no profound maxim.

GUDERIAN: I know him very well. It doesn't necessarily have to be that way. He's a person who loves life.

FEGELEIN: Above all he does his utmost until the end, without considering the risks. He goes through artillery fire, and when his adjutants lie down, he says: Why are you so sensitive?

THE FÜHRER: I would lie down, too. I had only one general who didn't lie down. But he didn't hear it.

JODL: I would suggest it anyway. This is a little weak. Christiansen[1823] is not exactly a born army leader either.

GÖRING: I admit that.

JODL: Up there it's already a little thin in terms of leadership.

THE FÜHRER: Good.

JODL: I believe that would be the most expedient. Then the Reichsführer will get his staff in the East as well.[1824]

GUDERIAN: That's particularly important because the Reichsführer's current staff is a terrible improvisation—he can't do anything with it. The intelligence system doesn't work, and that's bad. That's not acceptable. Something must be sent there quickly.

KEITEL: Especially designed for him.

THE FÜHRER: That will be done. Hausser will stay here; Blaskowitz there.[1825]

The East again

FEGELEIN: My Führer, I have another immediate decision. I've just checked. In the *Leibstandarte* barracks outside, there are 6,000 men who are intended for the I [SS] Panzer Corps. Right now it will still take some time, so I request that we put at least 4,000 to 5,000 of these men with the best officers behind Schörner. For the next 14 days it doesn't matter if they're in the barracks or on the road.

THE FÜHRER: We can't do that because they have to be trained. When the *Leibstandarte* comes out, they must follow again immediately.

FEGELEIN: They are trained.

THE FÜHRER: Then I can't bring them in again. This corps doesn't have much time. Take the cavalry—that's 1,500 men. You can add a few Volkssturm people as well.

FEGELEIN: Should I bring the commander in?

THE FÜHRER: If you want. I don't need to speak with him.

FEGELEIN: So these can't be taken away?

THE FÜHRER: No.

Ammunition allotment

V. BELOW: Then the ammunition assignments.

THE FÜHRER: Yes, the thing with the ammunition assignment. He[1826] says he can't conduct the defensive battle with five or eight rounds for the heavy field howitzers.

JODL: That's the calculation of the quartermaster general, and he added that it will become worse.

THE FÜHRER: But he can't conduct the defensive battle with that in crisis situations like that.

JODL: I assume that it's calculated so as to—

THE FÜHRER: If someone has a large front with quiet positions, it will work. But if someone has the misfortune —

JODL: That's apportioned to every gun on the Western Front.

THE FÜHRER: That's precisely why. But if someone has the misfortune to be in a sector that's constantly being hit, and he gets his five rounds there, then it's not enough. Then he needs 500 to 600 rounds per day for defense. In the Great War we fired up to 500 to 600 rounds with small batteries in major defensive battles.

GUDERIAN: These calculations are for the entire front.

THE FÜHRER: That's precisely why. If someone has a big sector, it's better.

JODL: It has also been ordered for the entire Western Front.

THE FÜHRER: Now he's doubly unlucky. All the others have divisions, while on the Rhine he has a hodgepodge with no artillery at all. That's why the assignment is so bad for him, because he has artillery only where there's firing—where the big trouble is. He doesn't have any other artillery. Otherwise, he has Russian guns, etc., where there's no firing anyway. Let's say he has 100 field howitzers there where there's always major fighting. If he can fire 500 rounds per day with 100 field howitzers, then nothing can be achieved in a big battle. One should consider that when one gets a bigger sector—it must balance out.

JODL: No, it's for the whole Western Front.

THE FÜHRER: In the Great War we actually had a horrifying ammunition supply in normal times, in 1915-16.

GUDERIAN: One to two rounds per tube per day.

THE FÜHRER: The regiment begged all day to be allowed to shoot retalia-tory fire. Then in the evening six shots were regularly granted: four Brennzünder [incendiary fuses] and two impact fuses. That was the entire artillery support for an infantry regiment. They usually came when the en-emy had finished, and then he started again. Then we were absolutely furi-ous and said: We shouldn't have started with those six rounds! But I must say that if we were attacked during a major engagement, ammunition was unlimited. We shot whatever the barrels could shoot.

GUDERIAN: That's not the case now.

THE FÜHRER: Normally there was just a huge restriction. But where an attack was imminent or had started, we really fought. I know that on May 9 the battery of our Major Parseval shot nearly 5,000 rounds.[1827] They fired as fast as possible the whole day—so more than 1,000 rounds per barrel.

Italy, the Allies

JODL: In Italy it was quiet—snow and fog. Now the last units of the 29th Panzer Grenadier Division have been relieved and the last units of the 4th Parachute Division have moved in. The 1st and 4th Parachute Divisions are now together under the I Parachute Corps.

THE FÜHRER: I don't know. Do you believe the English are still watching the whole Russian development with internal enthusiasm?

JODL: No, of course not. The plans were quite different. The full extent of it probably won't be recognized until later.

GÖRING: It's certainly not in their interests to have us keep holding in front while the Russians conquer all of Germany.[1828] If it goes on like this, we'll get a telegram in a few days. It's not on their account that we don't let them take one step inside, and that—according to the enemy's current inter-pretation—we hold like crazy in the West and the Russians push further and further into Germany and take practically all of Germany.

THE FÜHRER: To that extent, the National Committee, that traitorous organization,[1829] could still have a certain significance. If the Russians really proclaim a national government, then fear will grow in England.[1830]

JODL: They've always viewed them with mistrust.

THE FÜHRER: I've ordered that something be passed to them now: the report that they're drawing up 200,000 of our men under the leadership of German officers, totally infiltrated by Communists, and that they want to let them march off then.[1831] I've requested that this report be passed to the British. I gave it to the foreign minister. That's something that will have an effect on them—as if we were to stab them right there with a shoemaker's awl.

GÖRING: They entered the war so that we wouldn't reach the East, but not so that the East would reach the Atlantic.

THE FÜHRER: That's quite clear. Something like that is abnormal. British newspapers are already writing very bitterly. What is the purpose of the war?

GÖRING: On the other hand, I read a report in the "Brown Paper"[1832] that they can support the Russians with their Air Force—because they could come with their heavy bombers into the areas where the Russians are moving in, even if it's a fairly long flight. But the report comes from absurd sources.

THE FÜHRER: They can't support him tactically, because we don't know ourselves where the Russians are and where we are—so they certainly couldn't know that.

JODL: Thirty-one trains of the 356th [Infantry] Division departed [for Hungary] at Speed 8.[1833]

THE FÜHRER: I still have unpleasant work to do today. I have to "hypnotize" Quisling today—or I'll have him come tomorrow at 3 o'clock. Below, try to find out if that's possible. I would like to speak with the foreign minister briefly after this, if I can see Quisling tomorrow at 3 o'clock, if it's possible—if he can wait until we're no longer in a war situation. That's a terrible story. He's totally crazy—the people have made him go nuts.[1834]

Croatia

JODL: This mopping-up action at Travnik is finished. The 104th [Jäger Division] will be pulled up here now. We can't go through here diagonally. Then he requested—I have no objections—that the Visegrad bridgehead be pulled in. It no longer has any importance because we don't want to attack in that direction anymore. He requested that they be allowed to go behind the Drina [River] because they can save more forces there, which will allow them to widen.

THE FÜHRER: Yes.

JODL: The 22nd [Infantry Division] is fighting up here, and has now reached the Drina. There the bridge has been blown up. Now they're going along the west bank to the north.[1835] Here, in this area, there's a significant relaxation because of the evasive movements of the [partisan] bands in connection with the Četnik battles here. The connection with Plevlja has been restored, so the situation here is better. The 297th [Infantry] Division is marching up, and is just now beginning to reach Brod. The supply situation has improved because yesterday—on the 25th—the 8-ton bridge was completed, therefore, traffic can go here again now. The hospital train was attacked here on this road by low-flying planes. Ten dead and seven new wounded. [—] It was quiet on the Syrmian front. Assault party action on our side. By around February 1 we will be able to assemble about two divisions here. Three to four divisions by around February 6.

THE FÜHRER: So it won't be any earlier.

GUDERIAN: If there's no crisis, my Führer, it's better to wait.

THE FÜHRER: Absolutely. I won't reveal myself beforehand; instead, we will build up very secretly here and then the thing will be done concentrically from both sides.[1836]

JODL: It's not certain yet if the 233rd Infantry Division is finally away, but we can assume it. Various attacks against the Group Fischer[1837] again; they were driven back. In the Virovitica area it was quiet. Then a new operation is planned to the south[1838] by the Cossacks, who have performed well otherwise.

THE FÜHRER: The Cossacks are good. But why do we have to put them in German uniforms? Why don't we have those beautiful Cossack uniforms?

JODL: Most of them have Cossack uniforms.

GUDERIAN: Red fur hats.

THE FÜHRER: Do they still have those?

JODL: They have red trousers with silver stripes.

THE FÜHRER: We have to leave that. It's wonderful: Cossacks are marching with us.

BURGDORF: The commander of the Cossack Division, General von Pannwitz,[1839] always visits his troops in Cossack uniform. I saw a photo of him. He looks very wild—he put the scimitar in front.

JODL: They were also drawn up as a national unit. They have their replacements now, too, because their families were there. I don't know where they are now. They were there in East Prussia.

GUDERIAN: They left there a long time ago. They went somewhere.

GÖRING: They were in Belgrade.

JODL: They have their children there.

GÖRING: They always do their military expeditions like a peoples' migration—they take everything with them.

JODL: There was no other action here, except for these attacks that were driven back. [—] In this area it was quiet, too, because there's a huge amount of snow—as there is at the Brenner [Pass] in Italy as well.

The North

In the north 57 trains of the 163rd [Infantry] Division have now arrived in Oslo. Thirty-nine trains of the 2nd Mountain Division left Aarhus. [—] Now I would like to present the report by General von Uthmann[1840] from Stockholm. (*Presentation*.[1841]) This is a case where even the envoy could pound on the table a little bit.

THE FÜHRER: Can the envoy pound on the table? Thomsen[1842] always has such wonderfully clever comments—world-political views inspired by Stockholm's atmosphere.

Miscellaneous

GÖRING: My Führer, I'd like to read the following from the 27th [of January] about the panzer division that's fighting down with the Saucken corps, "After successful defensive battles in the Litzmannstadt [Lodz] area, the division is fighting ... according to orders, back toward the west." (*Reading aloud*.) Five Panthers have knocked out 25 tanks.

THE FÜHRER: An American or British correspondent had an angry outburst and said he couldn't be forbidden to write the truth. The truth would be, for example, that the Germans are simply far superior with their tanks.[1843]

HEWEL: He gives a lot of examples.

THE FÜHRER: He gives examples of where they have to lie.

HEWEL: For example, they lost just as many tanks as they knocked out, but he had to write that they had lost only a few.

THE FÜHRER: He says that the German tanks are superior; there's nothing wrong with that.

GUDERIAN: Our main problem is the fuel issue at the moment.

THE FÜHRER: That's why I'm concerned, Guderian—if something happens down there [the Lake Balaton region], it's over.[1844] That's the most dangerous point. We can improvise everywhere else, but not there. I can't improvise with the fuel. Unfortunately, I can't hang a generator on a panzer. At home I could do that. I've seen that the training tanks have it.

GUDERIAN: Yes, they've had it for a long time—several months.

THE FÜHRER: Buhle, I also wanted to say that a report came that they have a big tank, the Boxer ... gun L 48 ...[1845]

BUHLE: The notice I gave you, yes.

THE FÜHRER: They fight it from 200 or 300 m. Maybe we should produce a new shell now, either with a bigger explosive charge—I don't know if we can still use the hollow-charge principle—or we could even shoot a kind of stick-shaped charge shell, a shaped bomb, which, of course, could only be front-loaded, but with which we could drive up close. We could shoot one anyway.

BUHLE: I think we should provide an L 70 first.[1846]

GUDERIAN: That would probably work with the 38 t, too.

THE FÜHRER: But it's not certain if we can actually penetrate the new tank with that.

GÖRING: Will the heavy bazooka penetrate it?

THE FÜHRER: That hasn't been tried.

BUHLE: We can assume it would. A 15-cm hollow charge would also penetrate.

THE FÜHRER: If we shoot a shaped-charge shell or bomb, that would certainly knock it out. With that we can only shoot one shot, of course.

BUHLE: We have to drive loaded, if something like that comes.

THE FÜHRER: If he notices something like that.

GUDERIAN: And then he has to hit it with the first shot.

THE FÜHRER: They come up within 150 to 200 m.

GÖRING: Will the 8.8 still penetrate?

THE FÜHRER: That hasn't been proven. We couldn't confirm that. The long gun of the King Tiger [Königstiger] might be able to penetrate.

BUHLE: He also seems to have a flat roof on the side.

THE FÜHRER: It's something new, anyway.

BUHLE: I spoke with Saur about it yesterday.

GÖRING: Has a Hunter-Tiger [Jägdtiger] been disabled?

KEITEL: So far not a single Hunter-Tiger has been knocked out. It broke down from the rear. Not from the front yet. The Hunter-Panther is something different. The Hunter-Tiger is the heaviest blaster [Knacker] there is anyway.[1847]

THE FÜHRER: So far it has blown away every bunker with one shot.

BUHLE: We'll bring out those 25 as well on the 5th.

THE FÜHRER: It moves very slowly—12 to 15 km.[1848]

V. BELOW: Reich Minister Lammers says that Quisling could come tomorrow. One day doesn't make much difference.

THE FÜHRER: He'll be happy if he can stay here. But I want to see the Foreign Minister after this meeting; he should be ready.

V. BELOW: Yes, Sir.

THE FÜHRER: Do you have anything else?

HEWEL: Just one thing. In connection with this story, the Swedish papers are also putting out huge sensational reports that the inventor and designer of the V-weapon has supposedly arrived there. They've put out interviews with a Prof. Hartmann. I've already spoken with the Luftwaffe and General Buhle; he doesn't know him at all.[1849]

THE FÜHRER: They haven't made contact with a V-man, but with an S-man—a swindler.

HEWEL: But they do this regularly—they suddenly disclose things like this with huge sensational reports.

GÖRING: They're attuned to huge sensations.

THE FÜHRER: They must know everything, if they believe they have the inventor.

HEWEL: Now they even have the man who worked on the V4. He's supposedly ready to give detailed information.

Situation at sea

ASSMANN: In the Arctic, movements by Russian and English forces. U 292 has supplied the meteorological detachment on the Bäreninseln [Bear Islands].[1850] Three of our destroyers from the 4th Destroyer Flotilla will now be moved from Narvik back home, because in the spring we will urgently need them in the Baltic area.[1851] During an air attack on a convoy heading south, we unfortunately lost a 2,900-ton ore steamer due to bomb damage. It was hit three times and was still afloat, but then sank afterward while being towed. In the area south of Haugesund numerous mines were cleared. We laid a coastal mine blockade at Stavanger. According to a radio communication, British motor torpedo boats are active again along the western coast of Norway; they haven't been sighted yet. The traffic between Oslo and Aarhus suffered again from the weather yesterday. The weather is unusually bad. The convoys can go, but they're delayed 7 to 10 hours. A troop transporter arrived in Aarhus with 776 men from the 163rd Infantry Division, 328 horses and 191 vehicles. In Oslo, 5,500 men from the 163rd Division are now ready for embarkation.[1852] [—] From the eastern Baltic, we can report that these transports[1853] have continued as scheduled. Three ships have arrived, and four will arrive today. Then these four ships will probably leave again today, loaded. Then, there are no more vessels in Libau [Liepaia] at the moment, because the traffic from Gotenhafen and Danzig was halted yesterday due to stormy weather conditions. Yesterday's transport results: 3,294 men from Courland, plus 1,122 horses, 713 vehicles, 115 tons ammunition and a few prisoners of war. [—] The Memel traffic went according to schedule as well. 211 men, 40 vehicles and 2,000 tons were transported to Pillau. The ferry *Deutschland* is en route to Swinemünde with 1,500 wounded. [—] The evacuation of East Prussia continued with 34 vessels. Twenty-five thousand refugees were carried across the western Baltic. That makes a total of 45,360 refugees that have been transported from East Prussia to the Reich so far.[1854] A small refugee steamer with 150 vehicles ran aground here on the Hela Peninsula. Rescue attempts are in progress. [—] Yesterday there was a regrettable explosion in Pillau while the mines were being loaded. Two hundred and seven mines exploded. They were aerial mines with time-delay fuses. The accident probably happened when a mine fell and activated the fuse. It caused heavy damage and 19 men were lost. [—] The employment of the cruiser *Prinz Eugen*[1855] is planned for the area north of Elbing, but it couldn't take place today because of the bad weather. There was a snowstorm with very poor visibility. But the necessary preparations have been completed. The cruiser can be employed at any time, as soon as the weather improves.

THE FÜHRER: Can we deploy the old ships here—the *Schleswig-Holstein*, the *Schlesien*?[1856]

ASSMANN: They aren't in running order any more. They're only good for training; they're docked in Gotenhafen.

V. PUTTKAMER: One of them also sank.

ASSMANN: Yes, the *Schleswig-Holstein* is not in running order at all anymore.

THE FÜHRER: If it's sunk, then it can't shoot.

V. PUTTKAMER: The 15 cm aren't on board anymore either, only the worn out 28s.

THE FÜHRER: Why can't you re-bore them?

V. PUTTKAMER: I don't know.

THE FÜHRER: Then you're don't run the danger that they will suddenly be used somewhere.

V. PUTTKAMER: There is probably other work to be done that has priority right now.

THE FÜHRER: Re-boring those eight barrels could have been done any time since the days of the Westerplatte.

ASSMANN: A minesweeper in the Pommerschen Bucht [Pomeranian Bay] struck a mine. The boat was towed in. [—] It's snowing in the North Sea, wind force up to 7. Off the peninsula, some of our offshore mine barriers exploded because of thawing ice. Using our motor torpedo boats and small submarines wasn't possible because of the bad weather conditions. [—] No particular reports from the Mediterranean.

Situation in the air

BÜCHS: In Hungary yesterday only limited sorties north of the Danube in the area southwest of Ipolysag. Supply[1857] was attempted with a total of 19 aircraft. Only 7 came in, though, and dropped 6 tons of ammunition, 1.6 tons of provisions. [—] The focal points of employment in the Silesian region were between Oppeln and Steinau. One hundred and three aircraft, with some at Bentschen, Gleiwitz, and—stronger for the first time, with 114 planes—in the Marienburg area as well. Three hundred and ninety-one fighters, mostly in low-level strikes. Five tanks knocked out and around 178 vehicles—many horse-drawn ones—destroyed. In addition, two bridges between Oppeln and Breslau were also hit. [—] In the West, only fighter-bomber employment, with a focus on the Ruhr area and a weak twin-engine unit. [—] Yesterday evening in London, there was a radio report that commented on the question of why they haven't flown; it said that they've had bad weather over England for four days, but that they would use this time to bring their aircraft to the highest level of preparedness. They have apparently brought in another 70,000 men and women for this [purpose]. Their technical preparedness obviously decreased sharply because of the heavy employment during our offensives—unless it's just an excuse in response to the question. Because it came publicly over the radio. [—] During the night the only intrusions were by 20 Mosquitoes, which dropped bombs on Recklinghausen. Bad weather in Italy. No intrusions of bomber units from the west or south today either.

Political reports, personnel questions

THE FÜHRER: The meeting seems to be taking place in Teheran again.[1858]
HEWEL: If it takes place at all now. I'm quite sure it will be postponed.
BURGDORF: Then here's an excerpt of measures by Frederick the Great and Frederick William I. I can send it up to you so you can read it.
THE FÜHRER: If people always think that I'm so brutal—all high-ranking people should read this. [—] It's always been this way. These things should be given to our officer corps to read. They have taken in only the Schlieffen spirit, not the spirit of Moltke, Frederick the Great, Frederick William I, Blücher, etc. That was also a good spirit. The 73-year-old Courbiere shows that as well.[1859]
GÖRING: There you can see that age makes no difference.
THE FÜHRER: No, on the contrary: when they become old, they become stubborn old mules. I've experienced that as well.
BURGDORF: Schörner has encroached heavily on matters that are yours, my Führer—discharges, etc. But I don't think we should disavow that afterward. Otherwise we can't move ahead. He writes here, too, that he would like to hang a commander if he can't get things in order. (*Presentation.*) Then the thing about the officers, which I presented, has been taken up again by the Reichsmarshal.[1860] The Reichsmarshal is of the opinion that we have to leave the people in their rank and employ them according to their ability.

GÖRING: I have, for example, a commanding general [serving] as a company commander in a parachute regiment. Until now, demotion was part of the punishment if someone committed an offense. Now, if someone is honorably discharged, and he's brought back in, only to be given a lesser responsibility because he can't lead anything else, then we can't call him up as sergeant. That's a demotion. I don't know who would want to become an officer at all then. Because then even with honorable performance, there's no protection anymore.

THE FÜHRER: But it's very difficult if you let a general lead a company today under a battalion commander who is maybe a first lieutenant.

GÖRING: In this case it's going very well, but he can't be demoted.

BURGDORF: I'd like to point out a development that's very extensive in the Army. We now have several thousand officers, who have never served with a weapon—or [at least] not since the end of the Great War. Since then—because the front was far away and these areas had to be covered—they've been used in office positions and administrative positions or as railway station commandants and in train security. Now these people have accumulated. Now Reich Minister Goebbels has made the legitimate demand[1861] that these people should not be dismissed simply because we can't use them as officers, while everyone up to age group 86 has been called up. Because if we discharge them from the active Armed Forces, younger people would very likely be discharged as Class A, while older ones would be called up as privates. Herr Reichsmarshal doesn't attack the issue of leaving them in active military service. It's clear that they must go in. Now the question is: How can we use these people?

GÖRING: In the Great War the people did their duties as officers and were discharged.

BURGDORF: But they haven't been trained with weapons at all. We have an officers' training regiment in Wildflecken.[1862] There the people are divided into three groups: those who will be dismissed because they are not really capable anymore and can be better employed in industry—that will be checked very carefully—then those who can be used advantageously with the troops in some position, and then those who have systematically shirked throughout the entire war. We've identified people who were in 15 different positions in a single year, which shows that wherever they went they were repeatedly sent away again.

GÖRING: If you have a shirker, send him to court and remove his responsibilities. I just think it's impossible for a profession—there's no such thing in the whole world—to take someone against whom nothing can be proven, who served with honor, and reduce his rank just because he was employed in a subordinate position.

THE FÜHRER: We do it; the British don't.

GÖRING: He always remains an officer.

BURGDORF: A retired officer can only start again. Hewel spoke about a colonel who entered the service again and was shot down as an aerial gunner.[1863]

GÖRING: You have to ask why he was discharged.

BURGDORF: He thought it was done quite respectably.

THE FÜHRER: In England rank is associated with position.

GÖRING: I've checked it carefully. If someone is a captain and would become a major in ten years, and tomorrow is brought into a position that's ranked as a major, then he will usually be promoted to a major. And if he's placed in a captain's position after that, he goes back to captain. But when after ten years of development it comes time for him to be a major, then he becomes a major, regardless of what position he's in. That applies only when he's promoted out of that rank.[1864]

THE FÜHRER: I want a detailed presentation of how it is in England. Who can do that?

FEGELEIN: General Christian knows it well. I spoke with him; he was in America.[1865]

BURGDORF: Then we would have to decide whether or not to create officers' units, where it would be said in the officers' units that a lieutenant colonel might possibly lead a group and a captain the platoon—thus where ranks are pointless. But I warn against it, because I've seen these people. It can lower respect for the officer corps, so that a whole officers' battalion runs away. Because the people I saw would run away.

GÖRING: That's correct. But do you really want to let a man become an officer, who knows: I can be demoted at any time without doing anything?

BURGDORF: As soon as the Führer began promoting people without consideration for what they were, only for what they could do, then, at that point, we logically also have to inform the people who can't perform, "Unfortunately, you can't do it."

KEITEL: But these are totally different people. They wouldn't even have come if we had said that to them; they would have chosen another profession.

BURGDORF: There's no officer in this war who hasn't been promoted three ranks during this war.[1866]

GÖRING: Of course he's been promoted; if an officer has retired because of age or temporarily because of illness—illness is not the issue—

THE FÜHRER: I think, in short, the issue is the following, Göring. The whole bureaucratic apparatus, which, is in some ways overstaffed, will be mucked up, so that, in comparison the civilian bureaucracy, it is like a rabbit against a dinosaur. And it's connected to the fact that, in the military, everyone is automatically called up at the beginning of the war—anyone who ever served and was earmarked for anything. Now they're called up based on their previous rank. Now they're promoted further. These people have become old, and can be leaders only up to a point. Because they're Great War officers, they have the rank of general now and are not in a position to lead a battalion. Now that would lead me, in any other country, to call up only some of them, or only certain ones fit for active service, who have God knows what positions in civilian life, and to dismiss others who are in superfluous positions and send them home. Because I can't use them. I can't give the general a division or a regiment, because he can't do it. I can't give the colonel a battalion, because he can't do it at all. He is constantly promoted and can't lead a company. That's the problem. It has nothing to do with his claim for a pensions. But when I call up the Volkssturm, and bring God knows what kind of people into the Armed Forces, while lowering the age, I go out and send people home who are completely fit for active service, simply because they're in a position that obviously doesn't need to be filled, and which they don't fill because it's completely superfluous because it's in a bureaucracy that we want to streamline. I send home these people who are fit for active service and are soldiers, and call up others who are only conditionally fit for active service and are not soldiers.

GÖRING: It's true. That shouldn't happen. He should be placed in a position where he can work, but within his rank.

THE FÜHRER: Yes, I can't use him in his rank.

GÖRING: Not in his assignment. In the Great War, he did his job and became an active officer.

THE FÜHRER: Granted. But that man is now a colonel because of me, and to trust him with a regiment would mean the assassination of 3,000 men.

GÖRING: He shouldn't get a regiment.

THE FÜHRER: He may not even be in a position to lead a group; then it's difficult.

GÖRING: Then he stands sentry. I've offered that to some of my generals. I've told them that I can't give them anything else.

THE FÜHRER: Did the generals accept that?

GÖRING: Some did, some didn't.

THE FÜHRER: And these?

GÖRING: These I want to call up with a more clear-cut system. So far I've left it up to them, and haven't ordered them.

THE FÜHRER: What does he do then?

GÖRING: If nothing else, he stands sentry.

THE FÜHRER: As a general?

GÖRING: As a general.

THE FÜHRER: Do you believe that that's useful?

GÖRING: This general fought bravely in the Great War as a battalion commander, was discharged as a colonel, and was called up again because we needed him.

THE FÜHRER: In the Great War, no battalion commander was discharged as a colonel.

GÖRING: As a lieutenant colonel.

THE FÜHRER: My regimental commander was a major, was given a brevet rank later, and I made him a colonel.[1867] In the Great War, people weren't promoted. The promotions were the worst ever.[1868]

GÖRING: Some of them were promoted. But he was given the brevet rank of lieutenant colonel, was called up as lieutenant colonel because we needed him for some bureaucratic thing, and then he was promoted further. That demotion was the most disgraceful ever in the officer corps—there's no doubt about that—and our men don't understand it.

THE FÜHRER: I'm also of the opinion that we have to do it in a fundamentally different way. We have to do it so that the rank is equal to the appointment, as a matter of principle.

GÖRING: That's right. I totally agree with you. For three years I've asked for this.

THE FÜHRER: In England it's like that, in principle. If someone leads a division, he's a division general; if he leads a regiment, he's a colonel; and if he leads a battalion, he's a major. After he's led a regiment for a while, he goes back again.

GÖRING: Only someone totally without self-respect would have endured a demotion. If he wasn't, he committed suicide.

THE FÜHRER: That's not a demotion.

GÖRING: If he was a colonel, and was called up as a sergeant, that's a demotion. When he comes into the duty position, he can—

THE FÜHRER: His pay shouldn't be touched either.

GÖRING: I would just throw the pay at his feet and say, "You're taking away my honor; you know that this is the worst disgrace the officer corps has experienced so far."

THE FÜHRER: It's not really like that. That's your opinion. It was also a disgrace if I promoted a man very quickly. The officer corps considered it a disgrace when I promoted Major Remer to colonel right away.[1869]

GÖRING: Not for him, though.

BURGDORF: If I, as a general, were to serve as a major, I would rather do it in a major's uniform, because otherwise I would constantly be disparaged publicly, and everyone would know it.

GÖRING: You say that because you won't be in that position. Then you would do it. It would be a shining example.

BURGDORF: I trust that I can still be employed according to my rank.

GÖRING: Then we have to rebuild everything. In this case, it's considered a demotion without a trial.

THE FÜHRER: It's not a demotion. This man is not being demoted; rather, he's being placed in a rank whose responsibilities he can actually fulfill, and beyond which he had progressed without being capable of performing at the level of the new rank. Then it's also a demotion if I draft the general manager of some factory into the Army and he becomes a normal soldier.

GÖRING: No, he's not an active officer. He hasn't chosen the officers' profession.

THE FÜHRER: But he has chosen a profession and he has to be able to perform those duties. If he can't, it's not a demotion.

GÖRING: If he can't perform as general manager, he will be dismissed.

THE FÜHRER: Then he can't be general manager anymore, but probably only manager.

GÖRING: Or somewhere else probably a consultant.

FEGELEIN: In political leadership, it's always been that way.

THE FÜHRER: Basically, I believe that the British principle is healthier, which says that whoever leads a division is a division general, and whoever doesn't do it, isn't. And if a division general leads a regiment one day, he's a regimental commander again.

KEITEL: In the Reichswehr we used to be of the opinion that generals must never lead regiments and battalions, and thus we did away with rank insignia as useless in the old army. We simply said that we wear no uniforms, just stars—so that a general could also lead a battalion then. We couldn't do it any other way.

GÖRING: In my case, a general led a group.

THE FÜHRER: What insignia did they have?

KEITEL: In the Reichswehr only stars.[1870]

FEGELEIN: Hausser was discharged as a lieutenant general and was our Standartenführer.

THE FÜHRER: Now, an example. I just want to say something quickly. How many generals were discharged from the Army, came to the Waffen SS and took subordinate positions?

GÖRING: They weren't forced to do it.

THE FÜHRER: What does "forced" mean? We have an emergency now. The question is this: I have to think like a company commander. A company commander is a [second] lieutenant and is capable of leading a company, but he has a colonel who is completely unable to lead a company because he hasn't done it for 25 years. But now he's in as a platoon commander—maybe not even that——and there he is in his uniform. What kind of a confusing mess will we have then? Does the company commander salute his colonel?

GÖRING: That's something fundamental that upsets and revolutionizes everything that existed before, from the ground up—an idea that wasn't even thinkable until now. I just want to point that out.

THE FÜHRER: It's already that way in the rest of the world.

GÖRING: Not in the whole world. It's never been that way in England. That's why I made the suggestion that we should differentiate between the rank and the position.

KEITEL: It hasn't caused any problems in the Volkssturm so far.

GÖRING: No, not there. You said in the Reichswehr. So you want to say that it was introduced in the Reichswehr—that someone who was a general and led a battalion was only a major?

KEITEL: Yes, indeed. He didn't wear a general's uniform, but the man was called battalion commander instead of major, lieutenant colonel or general.

GÖRING: How long did that last?

KEITEL: It was done in the Reichswehr. It disappeared later because it was said, "How can we do that?" It's insanity. I was the one who said, "We have no rank—no lieutenant, captain, major, or lieutenant colonel; instead, we have platoon commander, company commander, battalion commander, and regiment commander."

GÖRING: When was a general, for example, a platoon commander?

KEITEL: I should know. I was Chief of Organization in the Army General Staff.

GÖRING: What years are you speaking about?

KEITEL: Nineteen twenty-five to 1930. The mobilization instructions, which applied to the entire Armed Forces, were introduced officially and accepted. There was no rank anymore, just rank corresponding with position.

GÖRING: That's what I've been proposing for two years. But it never happened that a general who was a general suddenly became a non-commissioned officer.

JODL: I would do it like this. Lieutenant Colonel X will be called up as platoon commander.

THE FÜHRER: He won't be demoted. That's a definition that was suddenly thrown in here. But in principle his rank remains.

GÖRING: If someone was a general and is called up as a noncommissioned officer, then according to the previous interpretation he's been demoted.

THE FÜHRER: I can't call him up as a general.

GÖRING: If he's being called up as a platoon commander or group commander, that's something else.

KEITEL: We were in an emergency situation then, and couldn't do anything else with the enormous officers corps in the Great War.

JODL: These extreme cases probably won't even come up.

BURGDORF: If someone becomes a group commander, wouldn't need to have any leadership charisma anymore.

GÖRING: How would you like to change the rank? You said yourself as a sergeant or non-commissioned officer.

BURGDORF: That's what the many captains and majors that I have are.

GÖRING: You spoke about generals. But a colonel would be unhappy, too.

BURGDORF: I can still use a colonel as an officer as well. But most of these people were never soldiers.

GÖRING: Correct. I agree completely with your definition if we take the service designation.

THE FÜHRER: But he can't go around in a general's uniform then either. Because what kind of company will you get if every company commander is in the uniform of a [second] lieutenant, and the platoon commander is in the uniform of a general, to give an extreme example? I don't know which is the bigger demotion. On the one hand, I can't give the general a unit that corresponds to his rank if he can't do it. How can I give that general a young volunteer division if it's going to be destroyed? He may have been a bad company commander in the Great War, and it was common knowledge. In normal peacetime he wouldn't be in a position to lead a company. Then he would have had to take courses, just like today. We promote many people and know that under normal circumstances, in peacetime, they couldn't do it.

JODL: Can't we say that Colonel X will be called up as a Volkssturm company commander, even if he ends up somewhere else?

BURGDORF: He'll be subject to a different judgment there.

THE FÜHRER: I've had people in the SA and SS who climbed laboriously. In the Army it's impossible. Imagine a company in practice, which is led by a hard-working [second] lieutenant who became [second] lieutenant, who can and must lead them, but who has under him a few lieutenant colonels or generals in their uniforms. During this time, the rank absolutely must be suspended, in my view. There's no other way.

GÖRING: So that he keeps his rank off-duty, and during his term of service it's suspended.

THE FÜHRER: One thing must be avoided. The people who are fit for active service don't fight only because they can't perform the duties of a certain position, while those who are only conditionally fit for active service have to lead the battle. Today I have to take psychological moments into account not only for the officers, but for the German people as well. In the end it's no disgrace.

GÖRING: But that must be made clear.

JODL: We can't have people feeling like they're being demoted without fault.

BURGDORF: We'll give them six weeks' training to demonstrate whether they are the men or not. I've seen these people, and they would say immediately, "Herr Reichsmarshal, that chap must take that uniform off." If I had to make thousands of legally based demotions, I wouldn't even have the people to work it all out.

GÖRING: Then I would say at once, "Out of the Armed Forces and into the Volkssturm."

BURGDORF: There are old people in the Volkssturm. There's a 46-year-old man who's fit for active service, who has successfully shirked—he was in the West before.

GÖRING: That one you can demote.

THE FÜHRER: He can't lead anything. He's never been in such a position. I can't entrust him with the smallest unit.

GÖRING: Then you have to take some people out of the units as well.

BURGDORF: In the combat troops you'll see it rather quickly.

FEGELEIN: The Reichsführer did it, too. With the Nineteenth Army he only said, "I am of the opinion"—and it was done.

THE FÜHRER: In the end, the soldier's profession is a fighting profession. That must be the goal.

GÖRING: We just have to make it fundamentally clear, because it's a completely different interpretation.

THE FÜHRER: It's not a demotion, but the rank is suspended during the time of employment. If the man is able, he'll get his old rank back in a short time. He has it much easier than someone else. But we have to find some way out. One thing must be avoided: that a military screening action takes place and people go out of the military bureaucracy and into civilian inactivity. I can't use them in labor service because, in some places, we have a surplus of manpower. But aside from that, the people would say rightly that he is fit for active service and the other isn't, and this other one is conscripted.

BURGDORF: In the officers' training regiment, the departure of a mortar platoon to the Reichsführer in the Black Forest worked miracles. But down there it had a bad effect, when a first lieutenant and three [second] lieutenants carried mortars around.

THE FÜHRER: In my eyes, that's more degrading than the other procedure. The other procedure involves giving a man a position that corresponds to his abilities and in which I can trust him totally. The other way, I let him run around in his uniform and do work that normal infantrymen and noncommissioned officers do.

GÖRING: Then we must do what we can do—stop promoting, etc.

BURGDORF: Promote only the commander.

GÖRING: Then there would be no one left in the staff.

BURGDORF: We do have privileged positions.

KEITEL: We have assignments that must be done by people near the front. We can't do anything with cretins.

BURGDORF: It's much worse to pull out the people who are fit for active service.

KEITEL: Would you like to read my order regarding pulling out the people who are fit for active service? It's gradually becoming unbearable.

GÖRING: I also can't leave someone in the staff who says, "In the staff I can't be promoted; I have to prove myself as a commander. I won't stay there; you can't demand that. Today I can lead a company. You've taken me out for a year, and now I can't even lead a group—and that's not my fault." That's what he says.

BURGDORF: We promote those. We take over paymasters as company commanders and battalion commanders as soon as they're able to do that.

THE FÜHRER: I think it's worse today to put together so-called officers' battalions, because if they fail, it gives a very bad impression. It circulates among the other troops. Then they're considered disciplinary battalions. I think it would be better to incorporate them, because that would be a total defamation.

GUDERIAN: In the mortar battalion we mentioned, there's a lieutenant colonel who was my supply commander in Poland, France and Russia. He was excellent, and received the Iron Cross I from me. This man was denounced by one of his compatriots from the upper Danube for alleged remarks that he never made—which were before the annexation—and because of that, he was removed from his position and was put in this mortar battalion in Wildflecken. So as a decent, faultless lieutenant colonel—who in his case was an exceptionally hard-working and particularly faultless man— he's carrying mortars around. He has written me the most terrible letters, which are downright heartrending. He says, "I've been slandered without any fault on my part, without any reasonable inquiry or investigation, just because of some mudslinger who denounced me, and I don't know how to help myself." I don't believe he's rehabilitated yet.

THE FÜHRER: The issue is the cases where we have to dismantle five-sixths of our administration today. The defamations aren't the issue at all. The administration must be reduced, and we can't make these five-sixths not be soldiers anymore, just because they can't get a military command that corresponds to their rank.

GUDERIAN: Then we have to use them some other way. If a colonel can only be used as a battalion or company commander, then that's what he will become, and for the duration of this assignment he will remove his shoulder boards.

THE FÜHRER: That's the issue.

GÖRING: But he doesn't become a non-commissioned officer.

GUDERIAN: No, he remains a colonel or a general with all the pay and allowances.

GÖRING: Leave the pay aside.

FEGELEIN: In the escort command there are many Hauptsturmführer who serve as non-commissioned officers in the *Leibstandarte*. That has never posed any problems.

GÖRING: The Waffen SS is an active force. The others are inactive. If they serve there, they do reserve service. Someone can be a colonel and also a private. That's something different. Now no one will stay in his command because he'll say: I run that risk.

THE FÜHRER: Under no circumstances will I, first, dismiss these people and send them home. At the same time, when I'm conscripting men almost up to age 56, who are only very conditionally fit for active service, I'm also dismissing 45-year-olds, even though they've been soldiers the entire time. That doesn't work. Second, it doesn't work for me to take people who aren't capable of leading a unit and give them a unit anyway.

GÖRING: And third, I can't say afterward to people who were capable of leading a unit, but who I took out into staff service: Because you've been working in the staff, you won't get a unit.

THE FÜHRER: If they're capable of leading a unit, they'll get one.

GÖRING: No, they were capable.

THE FÜHRER: Then, in a short time, they'll be there again. They have to learn it. That's no disgrace. I had to learn to be Reich Chancellor, too. I was party leader before—my own master—and, as Reich Chancellor, I was subordinate to the Reich President. I was government councilor for a time in Braunschweig.

GÖRING: But not practicing.

THE FÜHRER: Don't say that. I was very useful to that State.[1871]

BURGDORF: We let them all take courses, and train them further. Besides, we always have the request to the higher command authorities to give the relevant people back to us after two months, so that that person comes back. That way he doesn't become a stranger.

THE FÜHRER: I can put the born commander in any staff today—if I bring him back, I can't say he skips all that. That's impossible. Because they have to learn a great deal. Everyone who's commanding out there says that. But in just a few months he will obviously prove his capacity as a leader again. Then he'll have a position that corresponds to his rank again, if he's a born commander anyway. That's quite clear; it's no trick. Take a born commander today, and in no time at all he'll be whatever corresponds to his rank.

Sagan [Zagan] again

FEGELEIN: The 10,000 officers and non-commissioned officers—the English and Americans in Sagan—are marching off in two hours, on a trek. In addition, there are 1,500 men who were somewhere nearby in the General Government [Poland], who are marching to Sagan itself. Because they couldn't be transported, they were given the offer of remaining with the Russians. They rejected that and offered to fight with us …
HEWEL: They want guns.
JODL: If we can get Englishmen and Americans to fight against the Russians, that would create a sensation.
HEWEL: But it hasn't been confirmed yet.[1872]
THE FÜHRER: Maybe one person said something like that, and then it was immediately generalized. I'm extremely suspicious of that.
FEGELEIN: If it's possible and we can do it, fine.
THE FÜHRER: But not because one person said so.
FEGELEIN: The 1,500 were marching by foot; they wouldn't go by truck because they were afraid they'd be driven to the Russians. They were marching because they saw that the Russians had driven into a German civilian trek. That had such an effect on them that they marched off.
HEWEL: We could easily let a few English officers across.
JODL: They could be aviation specialists.
End: 6:50 p.m.

* * * * *

February 24, 1945

The Russians are attacking the German bridgehead in Courland for the fifth time now, again without great success.

In East Prussia the Third Panzer Army has been compressed into a 10- to 20-kilometer wide strip on the west coast of the Samland Peninsula. The connection with the encircled town of Königsberg, which was lost on January 31, was reestablished on February 19. The Fourth Army tried in vain to hold the Heilsberge triangle, and has now been pushed by the Russians into a semi-circle around Heiligenbeil on the Frische Haff. There is no longer a land connection to the west. Elbing fell on February 12 and the Vistula River valley was lost as far north as the Mewe River. To the west, an improvised southern front extends from Tucheler Heide via Konitz-Jastrow-Arnswalde to the Oder River at Greifenhagen. Attempts to support the front in the Oder-Warta River salient were unsuccessful and the Ninth Army was pushed back across the Oder at Küstrin and Frankfurt, while building bridgeheads on both sides. In Silesia the Russians destroyed the Oder River defense line between Brieg and Glogau at the beginning of February. The German front now runs behind the Lausitzer Neisse River and along the eastern border of the Sudeten Mountains, and along the Lauban-Goldberg-Zobten line. The industrial areas in Upper Silesia are in Russian hands and German forces have been pushed back behind the upper Oder River.

In Slovakia, Soviet breakthrough attempts failed in the Tatra Mountain region. To the south, Russian forces were thrown back behind the Gran River once again after hard fighting. The situation in Hungary and also in Yugoslavia hasn't changed significantly.

In Italy the break in the fighting was interrupted by a limited local American attack outside Bologna.

In Alsace the enemy had destroyed the German Colmar bridgehead by February 9, taking the whole Rhine line south of Strasbourg. The day before, Montgomery's units lined up between the Meuse and the lower Rhine Rivers, but advanced via Cleve and the Reichswald [forest] with difficulty, as the other part of the planned pincer movement, the American attack across the Roer River, had to be postponed until yesterday, February 23, because of flooding caused by German bombing attacks. In the Eifel, in the Moselle River region, and along the Saar River, the Americans are carrying out holding attacks.
(*Map 13*)

* * * * *

EVENING SITUATION REPORT, FEBRUARY 24, 1945, IN BERLIN[1873]

Present:

The Führer	*Lieutenant Colonel Borgmann*
General Burgdorf	*Lieutenant Colonel v. Humboldt*
Ambassador Hewel	*Oberbereichsleiter Lorenz*
Rear Admiral v. Puttkamer	*Major Johannmeyer*

Beginning: 12:53 a.m. (February 25)

The East

V. HUMBOLDT: Nothing in the Second Panzer Army area. At the Plattensee [Lake Balaton] nothing. The bridgehead on the Gran [Hron] has been cleared out.[1874]

THE FÜHRER: Really?

V. HUMBOLDT: Yes, it has been cleared out completely—it's in order. The two SS divisions are already pulling out.

THE FÜHRER: Wonderful!

V. HUMBOLDT: The 1st and 12th SS [Panzer] Divisions are pulling out. The army group intends to pull out another division, but it hasn't yet been decided whether it will be the [44th] *Hoch- und Deutschmeister*, the 46th *Volksgrenadier* Division, or the 211th *Volksgrenadier* Division.

THE FÜHRER: I would always leave the *Hoch- und Deutschmeister* here, because we'll get a bit more from that division under the motto that they're protecting Vienna than if they're stationed elsewhere.

BURGDORF: The 46th is a good division, too.

THE FÜHRER: So that's completely cleared out?

V. HUMBOLDT: Yes, it's completely cleared out.

THE FÜHRER: That went well.

V. HUMBOLDT: Up here just movements—no engagements. Army Group Center is planning a regrouping on the south wing, which has probably already been presented. The plan is to deploy the 320th [Infantry] Division on the right wing, coming from up here, to deploy the 545th [Volksgrenadier] Division here, and instead to pull out the 4th Mountain Division, which has a higher combat value, and deploy it up here. It hasn't been finally clarified yet, where specifically it should be employed. In addition, the 359th [Infantry] Division will be added to the Seventeenth Army. The 4th Mountain Division will probably be brought into this area here. At the bridgehead north of Ratibor, the enemy led only a minor advance against the southern part. Continuous regrouping by the enemy has been reported. In addition, units of the 8th Air Army are being shifted, which in principle belong to the 2nd Belorussian Front that's commanding down here.

THE FÜHRER: Burgdorf, where's the report by Hanke[1875] from Breslau[1876]?

V. HUMBOLDT: In the front area south of Breslau, the enemy attacked again, but was unable to achieve any success. The attacks are weaker and not so cohesive anymore. It's assumed that the enemy hasn't attacked with greater strength because of the heavy losses he's had. I have a 1:100,000 map of Breslau here. (*Presentation of the map.*)

THE FÜHRER: I received a report. They say that the battalion that was flown in was again apparently the very worst ever.

V. HUMBOLDT: Here he has the Cürassier Barracks under his control and is attacking again here in the southern part. Our attacks couldn't get through. He's also putting constant pressure on the (Gladow)[1877] airfield here. Yesterday nothing came in because of the weather. For today, 48 Jus with ammunition and 27 Jus with the rest of the battalion that's still missing—they went down in other places—are scheduled. In the northern sector, the enemy is very weak. Our combat patrols were able to advance quite far and come back with captured materiel. [—] It hasn't yet been reported in detail how things are going at the airfield.

THE FÜHRER: If he's very weak here and we could enlarge it here, we should do it, in order to maybe build another airfield here as a precaution.

V. HUMBOLDT: Yes, Sir. [—] These here are all weaker enemy advances. [—] In the Goldberg area, the enemy attacked with greater strength. The situation held for the most part, because the 10th Panzer Grenadier Division attacked from the west against a penetration that the enemy was able to achieve here, and was mostly able to close the gap. Here this thing is sealed off. But the situation is still quite tense. In addition, the three mobile corps in this area here, attacking Lauban, have been confirmed. In Lauban itself the fighting continues. In the south the situation held because periodic counterattacks against enemy penetrations were, for the most part, able to hold our front here. In the northern sector a positive development is noted. [—] The intensity of the battles is indicated by the number of tanks that were knocked out: here ten, here 23 tanks and 12 heavy antitank guns. Of these 23, ten were captured in working order. Here in this area a group of forces is still encircled and is being destroyed right now. [—] On the Lausitzer Neisse [River] only weak enemy advances. Here an attack in battalion strength against a forward base; the attack was driven back. The southernmost bridgehead is now this one here at Treibel.[1878] Both of these bridgeheads here have been cleared out. There are some weak units still inside. Forty prisoners were taken here. Then northwest of Treibel there's another bridgehead that's supposedly being cleared out right now—plus another bridgehead here. In Forst itself an insignificant penetration against which a counterattack is in progress. Here 20 heavy antitank guns were knocked out. Everywhere, wherever he can hold ground at all, he immediately brings in very strong antitank guns. Stronger attacks against the Guben bridgehead along the whole front. Hill 107 in the northern part has been lost. A counterattack is underway. Bismarck Hill is still in our hands, as well as the hill over here, the Uhlig Hill. Here the plan is to clear out this bridgehead at Forst from the south, with panzer units and units from the XXIV Corps, and also to pull out the 16th Panzer Division here. Other than that, no particular engagements in Army Group Center's sector. [—] No combat in Army Group Vistula's sector along the Oder [River] front—only local reconnaissance on both sides. The tank army hasn't been confirmed by radiophotography [—] Here, another division of the 47th Army, which is in this area, has now appeared, and it isn't completely clear yet whether it's at Prignitz or Bahn. In any case, it has been confirmed by prisoners. In addition, a rifle corps of the 47th Army is in control here. Attacks against Pyritz from the southwest and southeast. A total of ten tanks appeared in this area; seven of them were knocked out. All attacks were driven back. Here there was a small penetration that was blocked off. Lively reconnaissance action; infantry being brought into this area. [—] A considerable intensification on the right wing of the Second Army where the enemy was able to break through; he lined up with five divisions in total—confirmed—from the former front in Finland, probably—this hasn't been confirmed yet—controlled by the 19th Army. The 19th Army operated on the Finnish front as well. The five divisions that have appeared so far come from the 7th and 14th Armies, which were in Finland. The enemy was able to penetrate the 32nd [Infantry] Division's front this morning, which was only weakly occupied, and his spearheads crossed the Konitz-Landeck road this afternoon. There were only weak armored forces, probably made up of assault gun regiments or separate tank brigades—never more than five or six in the spearheads. For the moment, no countermeasures were possible in this area other than to pull in the units of the French Volunteer Brigade *Charlemagne*,[1879] which were assembling in this area anyway.

THE FÜHRER: They won't help.

V. HUMBOLDT: They are armed very poorly at the moment and won't be able to restore the situation in this area. It's not quite clear yet what the army group is planning in detail. [—] The 8th [Guards] Mechanized Corps has been confirmed in this area by radiophotography, and there's a possibility that the enemy, with the success he has achieved here, will also put a mobile unit in here. He attacked with 30 tanks here, penetrated at a weak spot south of the lake, and has supposedly reached the road. But in the afternoon it wasn't reported that he had reached it. The attacks against the left wing of the 32nd [Infantry] Division—which had assembled on the other side of the focal point at Konitz—that were stronger on the left wing were driven back. The panzer group of the 7th Panzer Division was originally supposed to help clear out these penetrations up here, but it was brought back and employed in this combat area here. In addition, the plans call for the 226th Assault Gun Detachment, with 31 assault guns, to be brought down here by rail transport—expected arrival tomorrow morning. New here since this morning or yesterday evening: The enemy attacked out of the penetration area to both the west and the east, but was driven back. He also brought some units into the penetration area from the south, through the marsh. The 4th Panzer Division, with its panzer group, attacked to the south and took (Best) again, and also built up security here, so this thing can be considered sealed off. The attacks on both sides of the penetration area were driven back. Here's another penetration in the 81st [Infantry] Division's lines. Here weaker advances up to regimental strength. But everything has been driven back. A concerted attack—with an artillery preparation—hasn't been detected.[1880] Because he certainly has three or four artillery divisions in this area, although it's strange that the 1st Guards Tank Corps, whose employment was always expected in this area, has now appeared here in radiophotography and no longer over there. So over there there's actually only a mobile corps, the 3rd Guards Tank Corps. Graudenz is still reporting heavy combat in the southern sector, with attacks from the east and artillery fire. The plan is to fly 12 Jus in tonight. [—] In East Prussia ongoing battles, particularly on the southern wing—

(THE FÜHRER: That's terrible.)

—and here from the west. Here's the deepest penetration: 1 km deep. Starting against that is the reconnaissance detachment of the 2nd Parachute Division, plus a regiment of the 50th [Infantry] Division, which was here on a front behind the 562nd [*Volksgrenadier*] Division and which is now being engaged with this regiment here. Strong artillery—46 minutes of heavy fire. The other attacks were, for the most part, driven back. Here, in this area, the gap has been blocked off to some degree now. There is still an insignificant gap here, but the enemy didn't advance through it to the north. Here there is a regiment-strength penetration, leading north from Hohenfürst.[1881] There he has been thrown out again. The penetration itself is not completely cleared, though. On this front everything was driven back except for this minor penetration here. The attack up here progressed quite well. The 5th Panzer Division is pushing forward and is just outside Ragitten. Combat in Ragitten. Seerappen is still occupied by the enemy. It was bypassed on the right wing. The left wing of the 561st [*Volksgrenadier*] Division was able to move forward only a little. These enemy units in the woods are still holding out. Relatively hard combat. The 5th Panzer Division moved around them here and some units have already turned in against them. The 93rd [Infantry] Division also advanced well, and won about 1 km ground. He has set up antitank-gun and artillery blocks in depth here. Relief thrusts in company and battalion strength up here, in order to divert the opponent up here.

THE FÜHRER: In addition to getting that tolerably under control, we have to immediately regroup and lead the next advance up here right away. I'm convinced that he'll be weak here. He's packing everything together here.

V. HUMBOLDT: Yes, he can only bring it in from here. He has nothing else in this area.

THE FÜHRER: How is it in Courland?

V. HUMBOLDT: In Courland the heavy attacks are still underway. According to the picture so far, the army group has reported that the 3rd Guards

Mechanized Corps and the 10th Guards Army have not been employed yet, and also that the command post of the 51st Army has been moved forward. Generally the attacks against the left wing of the X Corps have been driven back. But here the enemy was still able to gain 1-2 km ground. There are counterattacks underway. Some units of the 12th Panzer Division are moving in. In addition, the 205th [Infantry] Division, which is also a good division, has been relieved and will also be moved over into this combat area. [—] Here absolutely no radio activity; regrouping underway. Sixty percent of the combat elements of the 215th [Infantry] Division have gone.

THE FÜHRER: Here's the story from Gauleiter Hanke. It's all in agreement with his commanding officer. (*The Führer then reads from a telegram from Gauleiter Hanke of Breslau.*) He says that the MG 15 is not reliable in ground operations.[1882] That's what I've said the whole time. They fire extremely rapidly but they're worthless because they get dirty so fast. The MG 34 is better. At least that fires. [—] The commanding officer also thinks it necessary to have a second battalion with good combat strength. My position is that we have to do that; we have to supply something there. That's quite clear. [—] Hanke is a devil of a fellow. He's a Silesian.

BURGDORF: Should I tell Below that he—

THE FÜHRER: Yes, a second battalion must go in there—one that has proven itself in combat.

The West

V. PUTTKAMER: On the right wing of the II Parachute Corps the enemy is trying in vain to enlarge the penetration area southwest of Üdem. Counterattacks by the Panzer Lehr Division gained 2 km of ground to the west in heavy combat, but then stopped. South of Goch, the enemy, in the strength of two regiments, succeeded in gaining some ground in an attack to the south. The penetration in the Oberheusburg[1883] area has been sealed off. [—] Army Group "B": in the XII SS Corps area west of the Roer, the forward security forces were pushed back to these two places that are still in our hands—south of Kamp and Hilfahrt. On the right wing of the LXXXI Corps the enemy pushed forward from Gürzenich and Kofferen in the direction of Lövenich. Hottorf was lost. Some units of the 59th Infantry Division and the 183rd Volksgrenadier Division have been employed here to block this off. The combat group of the 11th Panzer Division has reached ... On the left wing of the 59th Infantry Division the enemy is advancing out of Jülich to the north and east. A counterthrust from the Mersch area has begun. Southeast of Jülich the enemy pushed into Hambach and Niederzier. An attack against Oberzier is in progress at the moment. A regiment of the 9th Panzer Division is being moved into the Steinstrass area.

THE FÜHRER: Their second day of fighting is even messier than ours was on our second day of fighting back then.

BURGDORF: Krebs[1884] said to me today that he had inquired again about the new wave that's supposed to come down at the Roer dam.[1885] The situation would be like this: so far 25 cubic meters[1886] have come down. These bombings would cause 25 cubic meters more to come, so that would be 50 cubic meters coming down—i.e., only two-thirds of the previous 75 cubic meters. So a bigger wave is not expected. He spoke about it with General Westphal and discussed it at length.

V. PUTTKAMER: In the LVIII Army Corps sector, the enemy pushed into Arnoldsweiler with 15 tanks and was thrown back again in a counterattack on the western edge of the town. There's combat noise in the northern and southern parts of Düren. The situation there is still unclear. South of Düren, Niederau was taken back in a counterattack. A subsequent enemy counterattack was driven back. In the XIII Corps sector, the enemy pushed into Waxweiler and Nieder-Pierscheid with 8 tanks. In the LIII Corps area the enemy pushed into Neuhaus with 50 tanks and is carrying out attacks to the north and south from there. A counterattack with assault guns from the Neuerburg area has begun. On the left wing of the LXXX Corps the towns of Oberbillig, Wasserbillig and Könen were lost. In the LXXXII Corps sector, changeable battles with bunker groups east of the Saar. No details have been reported there. An enemy attack at Fraulautern was driven back. East of Forbach, a few individual bunkers were repossessed in a counterattack from the Spicherer Hills to the south. Enemy attacks against the right wing of the XIII SS Corps since 7 a.m. Wietrigshofen[1887] was lost there. The counterattack has been launched. Klein-Bittersdorf was taken again.

Italy, the Southeast

The Commander-in-Chief Southwest has reported only enemy attacks in battalion strength on the left wing of the 232nd Infantry Division, in the same place as before. Details about the course of the battle are not yet known. [—] No reports from the Commander-in-Chief Southeast.

Situation in the air

Regarding the situation in the air,[1888] the following can be reported. Reich territory: major intrusion by some 1,000 American tactical aircraft from the west, attacking transport network targets in Harburg, Wilhelmshaven, Bremen, and Quakenbrück with a total of 750 [aircraft], and attacking Hannover with approximately 200. Also attacks by partial units on Bielefeld, Gütersloh and Wesel. In addition, 400 British tactical aircraft flew in to attack industrial and transport targets in Dortmund, Unna and other cities in the Ruhr area. In the western combat area, around 400 twin-engine tactical aircraft and very strong fighter-bomber activity with a focus on Münsterland and the Ruhr area. From the south, an intrusion by approximately 350 American tactical aircraft for attacks against Graz and some against Klagenfurth. [—] Our engagement: 213 fighters to combat low-flying aircraft in the area east of Linnich. So far four aircraft have been reported shot down. Nine of our aircraft are missing. [—] Italy: Approximately 400 enemy fighter-bombers in the front area and 120 twin-engine tactical aircraft attacking the Brenner route in the Ala-Brixen sector. Also attacks by some 350 tactical aircraft on transport installations in Verona, Ferrara, Padua, and Udine. [—] East: due to bad weather, only very limited fighter-bomber activity in support of our own attack in the Guben area and in the area around Lauban and Neukirch. A total of 450 aircraft were employed.

Submarines

JOHANNMEYER: Here's an article from the *Times* on the employment of our snorkel submarines, which is very interesting. (*Presentation.*)
THE FÜHRER: This device wouldn't have harmed us at all. Our boats were only destroyed from the air.
V. PUTTKAMER: Especially in shallow water and near the coast it's quite ineffective.[1889]
End: 1:18 a.m.

* * * * *

Early [1] March 1945

In the East, the southern front in eastern Pomerania was torn open by Zhukov, initially on February 26 west of Rummelburg, and, later, in other locations. On March 3 the Russians enter Köslin, and the following day reached the outskirts of Kolberg on the Baltic Sea.

In the northern Rhineland, Montgomery's Canadians moved forward to the Rees-Xanten-Geldern line during the first days of March. Here, on March 3, they linked up with the Americans, who had advanced to the north and east from the Jülich area and the Meuse River, and who had taken Neuss

and Krefeld the day before. To the south, the enemy has pushed forward from the Roer to the Erft; now there is fighting for this last obstacle before Cologne and the Rhine River. On the Moselle River, the German units have been thrown back over the Kyll; Trier is lost on March 3.
(*Map 13*)

* * * * *

FRAGMENT OF A MIDDAY SITUATION REPORT, PRESUMABLY MARCH 1, 1945[1890]

The West

JODL: ... here the 3rd and 36th American Divisions, which we hadn't located before.
THE FÜHRER: I spoke with Burgdorf, so that we can get a man here[1891] who has a talent for improvisation. If it's a colonel, that's fine, too. I'll make him a lieutenant general immediately. I don't care about that at all. It must be a talent that's capable of making something out of nothing. I have no use for people who only move around divisions that are already complete and write: this division will be ready on June 1, this division on July 1 and this division on August 15.
JODL: He takes them from the Replacement Army. He only gave away cadre. The employment of these cadre as they are has been prepared, of course. It's clear that the last man will be employed.
THE FÜHRER: No, that it's improvised at the front, regardless of the formations!
JODL: Here it will be strengthened with Volkssturm, as much as we can. (The cadre in the rear will be filled up by) year group 28 [the age group born in 1928].
THE FÜHRER: That's something completely independent from that.
KEITEL: That should continue independently.
THE FÜHRER: That they'll be used ... that goes without saying.
JODL: Here we have the divisions that are being formed. They received the remnants of other units. They've been thrown together and reinforced. They are being reinforced by Volkssturm battalions and are defending the Rhine [River]. Here,[1892] observations differ somewhat from each other. While the Navy considers the traffic here normal and has identified only three smaller landing craft, the Army observation reports indicate that there are ... freighters, which are coming in here.
THE FÜHRER: What in the way of Luftwaffe replacements have been coming into this area here? What has already arrived here in the area, in terms of Luftwaffe training and replacement units?

CHRISTIAN: I spoke with Colonel General Student about that today at midday. He said he had given an order again yesterday …

THE FÜHRER: It has been destroyed, Jodl. Others report that such and such a number have surrendered. You can see it yourself from the numbers reported missing.

JODL: Many people have surrendered, of course.

THE FÜHRER: That's the result of our Geneva Convention policy.

CHRISTIAN: According to our reports, there are large numbers missing from the parachute divisions, so that replacement will be necessary. We'll probably have to take them from the reinforcements right away, especially for the 6th Parachute Division.

JODL: In the area of this penetration, which already occurred yesterday, various things have been built up here in the rear as a precaution. The combat group of the 84th [Infantry] Division has come here, and a battalion of the 190th [Infantry] Division, and then some units of the 32nd Parachute Regiment have gone to Kempen to make contact here with the First Parachute Army, so the enemy can't get through between them. I would consider it a major mishap if the parachute army were to be caught in the rear here. Because without it we can't hold a bridgehead in front of the Rhine. It's still the strongest in combat.

THE FÜHRER: It's still the best.

JODL: Then further south … the British bridgehead. Further south of that the combat group achieved a success, even if it's not that significant. In any case, it pushed forward in front of the Erft again, threw the enemy back, and held off further attacks against this bridgehead in front of the Erft. From here down toward the south, this high plateau has been held for the most part, with the exception of small, weak bridgeheads that were already there yesterday. In one location here the enemy broke through to Konnertsheim.[1893] The battles further to the south have diminished here. Here this piece of 1 to 1.5 km was lost yesterday. Other than that, the front held. A question mark must still be placed here regarding the situation west of Plate. [—] The bridges over the Rhine: in Cologne the last bridge is … (The enemy report) about the bridge left intact by the Germans is not correct, according to reports by the army group.[1894] The Erft Bridge has been destroyed. In front of the Erft there is a smaller canal bridge. The destruction of this bridge wasn't successful, although three engineers fell during the attempt to blast it, due to a malfunction of the Italian safety fuse. But the Erft bridge has been destroyed. [—] In the search for additional things we could do to secure the Rhine on the east bank as well, the question of the *Hamburg* Division was raised again.[1895] In fact, a division from the Hamburg Military District, from Military District X, could be formed within five days—

THE FÜHRER: Form it!

JODL:—from two infantry regiments with two battalions each and regimental units, a Füsilier battalion, and a tank destroyer detachment ... (But I see here) that the formation of a division for the East was recently ordered in Military District X.

THE FÜHRER: That doesn't matter. It can be formed in any case.

JODL: Because it could be that the enemy, with the paratroopers he still has, might (make an airborne landing) if he reaches the Rhine somewhere.

THE FÜHRER: That's why I want to get all the paratroopers here, even if they're still armed so poorly.

JODL: There is no report on the pulling out of the 246th [Infantry] Division and its whereabouts. The movement of the boundary, i.e., the takeover of the Seventh Army, hasn't happened yet today—the arrangement regarding the communication lines still had to be made—but it should occur tonight or tomorrow at the latest.[1896] Here our counterattack has begun against a penetration north of Prüm, which was achieved in limited depth and with weaker forces. Then the enemy, as I reported before, has grabbed forces up here, in order to ...

(*End of the fragment.*)

* * * * *

FRAGMENT OF A MIDDAY SITUATION REPORT, PRESUMABLY MARCH 2, 1945[1897]

The West

THE FÜHRER: ... But what he has at the front aren't divisions.[1898] They're junk. But he has to make something out of that junk anyway. He has lots of unit symbols here. There's where I see the great danger. We have unit symbols here, and these unit symbols drive themselves into a situation like it was at the Nineteenth Army from the beginning, where it isn't supported.

JODL: That's why I had the map given to me. It's not that bad with this defensive front, which has the Western Wall here first and then the Rhine.

THE FÜHRER: Unfortunately, the Western Wall is the weakest here because the bunkers in front are worthless.

KEITEL: The commanding general has been here from the beginning. Military District Command V is in command down here. Here's the LXIV Corps. In my opinion, that has to be occupied again. Then we'll get commanding generals there who can improvise in their area. They can do that with the commanding general of Military District V.

THE FÜHRER: If they can do it!

KEITEL: I'm convinced. The Reichsführer got them himself. He took Bach, who was up here, with him. They were both improvisers who were brought into action back then. The one was Bach and the other Reinefarth.[1899]

THE FÜHRER: If I had Bach-Zelewski here, I'd be completely reassured. He would scrape together prisoners, convicts and everything. Where is Bach-Zelewski now, anyway?

KEITEL: The Reichsführer took him along.

THE FÜHRER: If I had Skorzeny[1900] here, I'd also be content.

GUDERIAN: He[1901] had the X SS Corps for a while. I think it was changed. He wasn't quite well for a while.

KEITEL: Those were both people the Reichsführer took for himself back then.

GUDERIAN: The Reichsführer is Commander of the Replacement Army at the same time. That's a big advantage.

GÖRING: Bach-Zelewski has the Oder Corps.

KEITEL: Back then he employed General Pfeffer here. He had the front against Switzerland.[1902] There was an SS corps here and there was an SS corps here. He[1903] did all this. He was the one here in Strasbourg.

BURGDORF: He has the X SS Corps now.[1904]

GUDERIAN: It's located east of the Oder in the Dramburg area.

THE FÜHRER: There are old tanks that are no longer capable of operating. Someone else would throw them away … (He installs them) at some intersection.

FEGELEIN: Obergruppenführer v. d. Bach is on the Oder front.

KEITEL: If you want this reassurance, I believe you should take the two men that the Reichsführer himself brought in. That's proof that they're right.

FEGELEIN: That was Reinefarth and Bach.

THE FÜHRER: I want Feuchtinger to get an order to build something up again. We can't afford the luxury of holding such people. The same goes for Hanneken.[1905] I don't care about that at all. We can deal with this thing later. Now it's about every man. I don't care if he got himself some more furniture or not. If I give Feuchtinger some junk—he still managed to make a division out of garbage first. If someone said later, "He can't command"—that was, of course, the aversion right from the start because, against all predictions, he had made something out of garbage. Here we have to make something out of garbage, too.

FEGELEIN: The original organization was that Reinefarth had the south wing …

THE FÜHRER: … failed, because he gives orders that can't be followed because he has no troops to do it. The troops aren't there. It's a waste of command energy. He can give out commands to his two corps every day, and the two corps give the orders to the divisions, and the divisions pass the orders on, but there's nothing there.

JODL: Then it would be best to give the army a rich army commander, because nothing comes from nothing. Even if we put an SS commander there, he'll get something from the existing SS people. He doesn't make them from nothing either. They're there. And the Army man has nothing.

THE FÜHRER: That's not the way it is either. We have Army men who have just as much as the others. Some of the Army men make something out of nothing and others make nothing from a lot. I met an Army man who said that, for the defense of Zaporozh'e, he would have to have at least ... (men. But there were only) 80,000 men (in Zaporozh'e). But he didn't see that. It was the same in Dnepropetrovsk.[1906]

JODL: That doesn't happen anymore.

THE FÜHRER: It's still happening today. We haven't changed them. They're still living and we still have to use them. Those are two completely different talents. In my opinion Manstein is an absolutely first-rate operational talent. There's nothing to criticize there. I'm the last one to contest that. And if I had an army today of, say, 20 divisions that were complete and standing there as if we were at peace, I would say that I couldn't think of a better operator than Manstein. That's what he can do; that's what he will do. He throws things around like lightning. That's on condition that he has first-class units, fuel and enough ammunition. But if something of his breaks down, he can't make it work again. If I come into possession of an army again today, it's not to say that I wouldn't use Manstein somewhere. Because he is certainly one of the most capable officers we have. But those are two different talents. You've seen it as well. The great generals of the Great War didn't manage to draw up even one army themselves. Leaders appeared out of nowhere. They built up the liberation army then and saved Germany for a time. Afterward they were kicked out and sent away, except in the Navy. The Navy was decent and employed this whole illegal bunch of OC[1907] people.[1908] But the Army kicked them out in disgrace. They were very different. Some of them were only organizers—I know them all—but never fought. For example, Petersdorf[1909] and Pfeffer[1910] were never at the front.[1911] Pfeffer is a born organizer. I would have him organize something, and when it's finished let him go.

GUDERIAN: (Primken)[1912] just raised money in the Rhineland and with that money recruited the jobless people who were there. Then he brought the Freikorps to the forefront.

THE FÜHRER: Without a doubt, Pfeffer got a Freikorps together and used it to blackmail the German government. I would have cured Pfeffer of that. Later I would have had him hanged. But the Freikorps was there in any case.

GUDERIAN: People like Petersdorf were very doubtful in combat.[1913]

DR FÜHRER: Petersdorf's Freikorps did fight; Pfeffer didn't. Pfeffer looked after his Freikorps ...

GUDERIAN: That was an active Jäger battalion.

THE FÜHRER: But in any case, those people got it done. I still think Kirchheim is quite well suited for jobs like this, even today.[1914] After all, these people didn't become great commanders with me because their abilities were limited. I'm not saying that Feuchtinger would be able to lead an army. But he did draw up a division, and he did it out of garbage. Why shouldn't I use a talent like that? I have nothing to do with Feuchtinger. I'm not a stockholder in some company. I've seen Feuchtinger three or four times in my life—once or twice at the Nürnberg Party Day. Once he agitated the people against me, who almost tore me apart. I've seen him two or three times during the war.

KEITEL: He demanded 275,000 marks from the state for a three-room apartment. That's an achievement as well.

THE FÜHRER: I would let him work that off through organizational work. We can still get him afterward.

BURGDORF: I can't do anything about Feuchtinger. Feuchtinger and Hanneken are under the jurisdiction of the Reich war court.

KEITEL: Then the Führer would have to order that they be released from custody.

THE FÜHRER: Both of them have to do service now for what they did. That's what it depends on. If they don't serve, they'll be put in the chain gang. [—] Hanneken used to be the man who would shout the loudest about the steel distribution, so the Reichsmarshal made a very clever move and said, "You distribute the steel!" That's how Hanneken rose up so quickly. These people can only be used for assignments like that.

(*Rear Admiral v. Puttkamer calls in*)

JODL: The Commander-in-Chief West is waiting for a decision on whether he can bring the wings together.

THE FÜHRER: That can only be because he wants to run away and cross the Rhine. I would only go as far as the western wall at first ...

JODL: His part of the Meuse, which he's holding, is the last finger left.

THE FÜHRER: That doesn't matter. The western wall goes here. It goes behind our line.

JODL: Now he's through here and has packed up here. The report arrived just before I came to the meeting.

THE FÜHRER: That's not so certain, either. That could be two or three tanks.

JODL: But he still has a connection over here.

THE FÜHRER: That's nothing.

JODL: That's a blocking position. That's the real Western Wall.

THE FÜHRER: In any case, he should hold at the Western Wall as long as humanly possible. We have to cure him of one idea above all: that he can go back here. Because at that very moment the other will free up the entire 6th English Army[1915] and all the American troops, which he would immediately deploy here. Those people don't look any further. It just means moving the catastrophe from one place to another. As soon as I move away from here, he'll free up the whole army. He[1916] can't assure me that he'll stay here; instead, he'll go over here. There's no doubt that the building up of reserves at this most endangered point here hasn't been done with as much energy as possible. That's not so much Model's responsibility—he can only take his own area—as the responsibility of the Commander-in-Chief West.[1917] The Commander-in-Chief West had to try right from the start to get a division like the 6th, for example, out. He should have sent the 11th up here and not down there to the lower place. The Panzer Lehr Division should have been put in here. They didn't work on building up reserves there. There wasn't much regard for the future. You have to admit that, Jodl, if you're fair!

JODL: He saw the dangers down there as too acute. He wasn't right at Saarbrücken and he wasn't right at the Weissenburg valley. At the Moselle he was right.

THE FÜHRER: I want to ask you something: Even if he had been right at Weissenburg, what would have happened to us there?

JODL: Of course. But he gave very strict orders before, too.

THE FÜHRER: Then we would just have been pushed back to the Western Wall again.

JODL: No, the main reason was that he would have been up above with his reserves long before if the Sixth Panzer Army hadn't had to be moved with the little remaining fuel.[1918] There were dozens of tanks back then that couldn't be refueled ...

THE FÜHRER: Can't we keep chasing a few officers in there? We need a few officers here—even if they only have one leg or one arm—who are very capable fellows, who can be sent there so we can get a clear picture. [—] Burgdorf, we must have officers here who can be sent forward there—even if they're so badly wounded that they only have one arm left. They're completely suitable for this purpose—so that they can convince themselves about what's happening here. Because I don't trust reports at all. Reports are made to throw sand in one's eyes. Everything is explained, and later it turns out that nothing happened at all. Suddenly he's sitting on the emperor's throne or somewhere up there, and then they say, "My Führer, the story was different; it was reported, but something wasn't quite right."

BURGDORF: Yes, indeed. Then I would still like to make the suggestion concerning the supreme command on the upper Rhine.

JODL: Obstfelder is there now.[1919]

BURGDORF: The Commander-in-Chief West got him there by command. Förtsch was down there.[1920] They took him away, supposedly because he was needed on the Saar.

THE FÜHRER: The man who has this here can only improvise. The formations in the rear are formed by the Commander of the Replacement Army anyway. They only appear when something is happening. But the formations themselves are formed by the Commander of the Replacement Army.

JODL: By the Commander of the Replacement Army!

THE FÜHRER: They're none of his business, of course.

JODL: No. His only business is the employment of these forces in the event of a major attack.

THE FÜHRER: Then they have to be employed, of course. But he's responsible for using every possible improvisational means and scraping together everything there is in Germany to build up a front—even women, as far as I'm concerned. That's a matter of complete indifference to me. There are so many women coming now who want to shoot, that my opinion is we have to take them immediately as well. They are braver. If we put them in the second line, at least the men won't run away. Here no one can go over the Rhine anyway. That's what's so wonderful about it. Here one can only run away to the rear. We have to have this part here completely and safely under control … activity … operate over there.

JODL: Yes, indeed. That's happening. Everyday it happens.

THE FÜHRER: The brother over there must become so uneasy that he gets no rest at all.

JODL: I don't know what a man like that should do here. Even for improvisation he needs something; it must be given to him. He has no authority in the local state. Otherwise he comes into conflict with the Gauleiters.

THE FÜHRER: I want to tell you something: I have great officers, without a doubt, but I'm convinced—to name one example—Captain v. Petersdorf, who's a rogue, by the way,[1921] and Captain Pfeffer, who was also a rogue, organized a Freikorps and never had any authority. Manstein could never do that. Manstein can operate with divisions as long as they look good. If I had an army here consisting of 10 to 20 first-class divisions, I would give it to Manstein. If the divisions are damaged, I have to take them away from him as fast as I can. He can't do it anymore then. But the commanders of the Freikorps managed it in a hostile environment ... That has to be a person who doesn't follow a pattern. He speaks up, he moves, he gets things from all kinds of places.

JODL: He'll get something from the Gauleiters. But otherwise it's quite simple: I just need to put someone in there who cares about nothing else. Then he'll steal everything from the Replacement Army—whatever he can get in the way of recruits, etc.

THE FÜHRER: What does "stealing" mean here? He takes men who wouldn't have been taken at all otherwise. We saw it recently when the first crisis arose. It was possible to build up something like a defensive front here in a very short time. If someone goes out and says, "I require a division, the division needs so-and-so much artillery, first-class detachments consisting of three batteries, etc."—then it won't work. He has to take everything. There's so much running around out there that's not being spit on at all. If I were to offer to a normal division commander what Himmler got for himself back then, he would spit it out and say, "Are you crazy? Stay away from me with that garbage!" But in such a situation one has to take it. It doesn't matter what he's shooting with. Because he doesn't make the divisions that are there; the Commander of the Replacement Army makes them. All he can do is employ them.

(End of the fragment.)

* * * * *

**FRAGMENT OF A MIDDAY SITUATION REPORT,
PRESUMABLY MARCH 2, 1945**[1922]

The East

THE FÜHRER: ... how the enemy was and how the enemy is today.

GUDERIAN: Those were completely different circumstances for us and for the enemy. They can't be compared anymore. He's expecting continued attempts to break through.[1923]

THE FÜHRER: Here there are 531 tanks and assault guns. We have nothing like that on the whole front. How strong is the whole front in Italy?

GUDERIAN: It has around 400.

JODL: About 356.

THE FÜHRER: After this battle he still has around 500 tanks and assault guns—as many as we have in all of Italy.

GUDERIAN: *(Presentation by Colonel General Guderian.)* Then here is a report by the Army doctor regarding the losses since January 14—for the period between January 15 and February 14—on the Eastern Front. The numbers ...

THE FÜHRER: Jodl, take a look at this! (*Reading the numbers from the document follows.*) This is the product of our humane convention, our Geneva Convention, which we will uphold under all circumstances because it "offers us enormous advantages." Enough with this story![1924] This is what's decisive. If I make it clear to everyone that I have no consideration for prisoners, that I treat enemy prisoners ruthlessly, without consideration for reprisals, some will consider whether they shouldn't desert right away. Because it's no fraud—it corresponds with that—if they report that they've taken 8,000 prisoners in one day alone. Otherwise the numbers of people missing would be incorrect. They report that they've taken 22,000 prisoners in … days.[1925]

GUDERIAN: There are some dead included with the missing.

THE FÜHRER: A very small percentage. Here (in the West), by far the greatest majority of those missing are guaranteed to be prisoners … partly a fanatical resistance, which … completely inexplicable and stupid, with the British and Canadians. That's where the paratroopers are. On the other side they write: in some places no resistance at all—immediate and easy surrender to the Americans. It's a disgrace.

CHRISTIAN: The intelligence services state that the Russians intend to advance up to and including Vienna. (*Presentation.*) Otherwise only near the front. It's important that he reconnoiters the Baltic Sea. (*Another presentation.*) No changes in air force concentrations in the Hungarian area, or here either. Here a sharp thrust forward. The majority is still in the area east of Breslau and in the area around Posen.

GÖRING: In deployment, the strength is here right now.[1926]

CHRISTIAN: And a strong regrouping from up here … corresponds with the concentration of the two main Russian groups with four tank corps.

GUDERIAN: These tank corps are already down here. One is still up here.

THE FÜHRER: I'm curious as to how he'll react to our advance. He has to react somehow.

Italy

JODL: Three hundred and eight tanks and 215 assault guns!

THE FÜHRER: In Italy there are (400) tanks and assault guns.

JODL: The majority of them are Italian weapons, which are not as good.

THE FÜHRER: There's nothing happening again?[1927]

KEITEL: No, nothing at all.

GÖRING: May I ask what kind of general orders there are concerning the handing in of weapons by the lightly wounded? We see an awful lot of lightly wounded men coming back, who are very lightly wounded—and some a little more seriously as well—who all have no weapons. They had weapons before.

KREBS[1928]: The lightly wounded are still supposed to carry their small arms. (*End of the fragment.*)

* * * * *

FINAL PART OF THE MIDDAY SITUATION REPORT, MARCH 2, 1945[1929]

Hungary

THE FÜHRER: If we had a parachute battalion here, we could put that down here! But it just isn't there. In an instant we could close the whole main entrance.[1930]

GUDERIAN: There's not so much difference in terms of the distance. Angelis's[1931] front line goes here near Nagybajom.

THE FÜHRER: There's where the strongest resistance is.

GUDERIAN: We can get through there. As soon as we have the area around Kaposvar, it will go very quickly.

THE FÜHRER: Until we get through there, he'll build up these little anti-tank-gun blocks to the rear. At least he'll expect something like that here, I think. It's very unlikely that he would have antitank-gun blocks here.

GUDERIAN: The Cossacks!

LÖHR: The plan is to put the Cossacks in here. This here is a bit far for cavalry. They also have very weak artillery with them.

THE FÜHRER: These two bridges here are the most important.[1932] Can't we think some more about whether it's possible to do anything there?

LÖHR: I have nothing. I have no motorized forces. They would have to be brought in, and that's not possible before the 6th.

THE FÜHRER: Can't we bring in a single train with something at least?

JODL: ...

THE FÜHRER: That's lovely. Here you have Kaposvar. Here you have a center. Here you will certainly have the biggest problems; here, in terms of people, you'll have the greatest resistance. Here he has no resistance at all. Anyone who reaches this road can drive through here. I guarantee you that there's nobody there, whereas here there's the main supply line.

LÖHR: Maybe we could drive down like this. That's a good road there.

GUDERIAN: That's what's already intended in this plan. If we're out here—the soundest road goes from here, I believe—we may be able to get through here.

LÖHR: Yes, it would work.

GUDERIAN: And then down here.

LÖHR: This across here is a highway.

GUDERIAN: That's all right again.

LÖHR: Maybe at Barcs [on the Drava River]!

GUDERIAN: I don't think we can get through here. Angelis has planned that already—as soon as we're out of here and reach the junction with the road down from Kaposvar.

THE FÜHRER: It's incredibly important that we get this action here under control.

GUDERIAN: I will tell the army group they absolutely must try—if the thing is blocked here, without getting stuck at the beginning—to throw a mobile unit forward, which will reach around here and march toward Baja.

THE FÜHRER: The 16th SS [Panzer] Division must have …

LÖHR: There's a bicycle detachment here. The 11th has a fusilier battalion. There are four assault guns here; two are here. We don't have any more.

GUDERIAN: The 92nd [Grenadier] Brigade—that's two battalions with some reconnaissance and tanks—could possibly be brought around here. I'll review that again.

JODL: The 92nd is still a reserve behind the Second Panzer Army.

THE FÜHRER: Hurry them through! We have to chase a unit through here. But it must have commanders who are familiar with the area, so that no time is lost. It would have to go through Fünfkirchen, of course.

GUDERIAN: That's very heavily occupied. The Bulgarian Supreme Command [1st Bulgarian Army] is there. We have to try to get through north of it.

THE FÜHRER: This Kaff backwater here is important. This here won't work. I'm convinced that we'll reach the target faster through here than through here. We'll probably capture the whole supreme command as well if we take this here, because they'll run away in that direction.

JODL: Here there's a reconnaissance detachment starting out.

LÖHR: That's Speed 2. It's coming from here.

THE FÜHRER: Couldn't we start it so that the reconnaissance detachment has the assignment, above all, to take hold of this thing here? … Granted. But if we come down after all, they'll only need to hold for two or three days. After two or three days the whole thing will be decided, and then we will have pushed through. As long as the bridges aren't damaged! We can't build the bridges. We have no materiel for that. We're not in a position to build a huge bridge like that these days. Those are still the old peacetime bridges?

LÖHR: Yes, Sir.

THE FÜHRER: There's a railway bridge and a road bridge?

LÖHR: Road and railway on one bridge, with stone pillars.

THE FÜHRER: That's the most important thing of all. If I had paratroopers, I'd put them down there.

The Dodecanese

JODL: From the Southeast I must report a landing on Piskopi, northwest of Rhodes.[1933]

THE FÜHRER: Not on the island of Rhodes itself?

JODL: No, on the island of Piskopi. That's northwest of it. The landing was protected by two destroyers and six gunboats; a stronger detachment that landed in the northern part was driven back in the southern part. The report says that a hill taken by the enemy in the north has been recaptured by the occupation troops. There seems to be fairly strong artillery support from the enemy destroyers. The radio connection was interrupted during the night. The occupation forces are not very strong.

THE FÜHRER: The quarrel between the Greeks and the Turks is already beginning, because the Turks expressed the opinion that they would intervene in this war in order to get Rhodes.[1934] The whole Greek press is protesting: it would be a mean trick to give that to the Turks, because all the Dodecanese are completely Greek. There's a big scene! This year all that is hailing down at once!

Situation at sea

ASSMANN: Nothing in particular to report regarding the Skagerrak transports. The transport movements in the Baltic and the Skagerrak are heavily restricted by the weather at the moment. For example, in Sassnitz the transporter carrying the refugees and wounded couldn't be unloaded. Right now there are still some 10,000 wounded people and refugees on board in the Bay of Sassnitz, who can't disembark because of the weather. [—] Here there are also nine transporters en route to Libau. They had to turn around again, not because the steamers couldn't travel in that weather, but because the smaller security ships accompanying them couldn't make it in the rough sea.

THE FÜHRER: I once crossed over from here to Pillau. I threw up.[1935] That's a really nasty sea. It's not a sea at all. It's the meanest there is.

ASSMANN: The Baltic really is more unpleasant than the Atlantic, with its small, short swells.

THE FÜHRER: I thought it was a small pond. And then it acted up!

ASSMANN: ... Army engineers and the Army 787th Artillery Regiment, to Gotenhafen, Danzig still units of the 32nd, 389th and 215th Infantry Divisions, to Libau the last units of the 93rd Infantry Division. Yesterday 800 tons of supplies were shipped from Pillau to Rosenberg[1936] during the course of the day. The Grand Admiral reported that it was actually everything there was to be transported out of Pillau yesterday.

THE FÜHRER: Guderian, it's like this. Anything that gets to Pillau can be brought over. We can't bring over any more than what gets to Pillau. The bottleneck isn't there; the bottleneck is Pillau. And here again the bottleneck isn't Pillau; it's the quantity of supplies.

ASSMANN: The quantity of supplies is what really matters.

CHRISTIAN: The Luftwaffe emergency service has brought back a total of 43,415 refugees and 7,000 wounded people out of the Eastern regions, using air traffic control boats and also air traffic control ships.[1937] (*Presentation.*)

THE FÜHRER: You are transporting more by sea than in the air. You fight better on land than in the air ...

ASSMANN: Refugee transport now completed: 491,000. [—] Also to be reported from the Baltic: light enemy air activity in the areas of Windau and Courland. The destroyers and torpedo boats from the Königsberg sea canal couldn't be employed yesterday because of the weather conditions. It was due in part to heavy seas, and in part to the ice in this area. An enemy submarine has been located north of Stolpmünde. Then I must report that the day before yesterday the Kaiser Wilhelm Canal had to be closed because of mines that had been dropped. [—] Strong southwest winds in the North Sea. Also northwest winds at the canal exit, so that motor torpedo boats couldn't be employed. With regard to employment during the night before last, I must add that two flotillas of motor torpedo boats were employed against a convoy heading south near Great Yarmouth. Our motor torpedo boats couldn't reach the convoy because of the defense, and also because they didn't get the actual convoy itself. It must have passed through already. In the south there was mining in the area of the Thames-Schelde traffic. The mines were laid according to plan. Torpedo attack on a convoy heading to Ostende with landing craft—those are supply convoys using landing craft—but without success. [—] Regarding the submarine war: a submarine reports the sinking of 25,000 GRT in the North Channel and in the Irish Sea.[1938] The boat is now on its way back. The report so far is only 25,000 tons. We calculate that to be four ships. The boat will give a detailed report after it arrives. Another boat reports sinking a freighter and a destroyer off Gibraltar.

THE FÜHRER: If only we still had the Atlantic harbors!

ASSMANN: Then we would be in a position to have a stronger presence in the Atlantic, whereas now we're restricted to the English area.

THE FÜHRER: Although the submarine bunkers don't have the necessary strength anymore either. 7 meters would still work for a while.

ASSMANN: Also from the Mediterranean: air photographic reconnaissance photographs of Leghorn. The occupation ... Also aerial photographs of Bari, Brindisi and Taranto. In Taranto, in addition to two old Italian battleships, there are 20 destroyers, but then also three combat-vehicle landing craft, three troop transporters and special-purpose ships. Landing boats have not been identified here. But in Bari there are 50 auxiliary landing boats. In Brindisi there is a special-purpose ship and 35 auxiliary landing boats.

THE FÜHRER: But it's possible that they'll be used for transport over there.

ASSMANN: We can't yet conclude from this that he's collecting transport space here. He has also used a lot of auxiliary landing boats for supply service. He still has about 120 combat-vehicle landing ships and 230 combat-vehicle landing boats in the Mediterranean right now, so he would be able to move five or six divisions simultaneously for a landing operation in the Mediterranean. But the reports we've received in the Adriatic area are such that we can't yet conclude that a serious landing operation is planned.

Situation in the air

BÜCHS: In Hungary, sorties again in search of locomotives in the area southeast of Budapest. Two locomotives were destroyed. This employment, escorted by fighters, took place at the same time some units flew back into the Hungarian area after their approach on Vienna and dropped isolated bombs on Plattensee [Lake Balaton] as well. Six of the fighters entered into aerial combat. They shot down three aircraft—two four-engine planes and one fighter. However, four of the six fighters were shot down. Two pilots were killed. The fighter-bombers engaged here in the area east of Budapest reported—but the report has yet to be confirmed—that American units have landed at Zombor airfield. They saw 20 four-engine aircraft on the airfield, and 15 more that were in the process of landing. In addition, two more were shot down by flak during this intrusion. [—] In the Breslau area ... in the Zobten area and for free intercept in the area of Breslau itself, where the enemy was engaged very heavily yesterday. Thirty-five motor vehicles were destroyed and three aircraft were shot down. Successful engagement again yesterday with bridge attacks by 65 fighter-bombers with fighter protection. The bridges were photographed afterward. It showed that a 30-meter section of the Görlitz bridge was destroyed, and that there were two direct hits on the Lebus bridge. In Pomerania 97 aircraft were engaged, primarily against convoys in the Rummelsburg area. About 50 motor vehicles and 8 guns were destroyed, and 18 tanks damaged. In East Prussia we engaged in limited free intercept activity. One aircraft was shot down. [—] Regarding enemy activity, we can report that until midday when the cold front ... was stronger in the area close to the front, in support of the battle: about 300 fighter-bombers in the Cologne-Düsseldorf area, plus about

300 aircraft in overlapping waves in the Ruhr area. Our own sorties were early at first, with five Messerschmitt 262s dropping bombs on Düren and Linnich. That was done without losses. Then 129 fighters from the 17th Fighter Division were employed in two fighter missions in the morning, to provide support in the area of Munich-Gladbach. The first mission had 62 aircraft, of which 51 engaged in aerial combat in individual groups with a total of 100 enemy aircraft, mostly the Thunderbolt model. Most of the aerial battles took place at an altitude of about 1,000 meters, only for one unit from 1,000 to ...

THE FÜHRER: At the altitude where the others are absolutely superior, or at least equal!

BÜCHS: Eight aircraft were shot down. Six Thunderbolts and two Austers[1939]—those are artillery observation aircraft, which were flying with a very strong fighter protection of 30 Thunderbolts—were shot down. Our own losses, in this first action for the moment: 11 aircraft missing. Then we flew a second fighter mission with 67 fighters, all of which engaged in aerial combat with numerous enemy fighter groups of 20 to 40 aircraft, again at an average altitude of 1,000 meters. These fought less successfully than the first and were only able to shoot down two aircraft. Our own losses, according to current reports: ten missing and another four total losses. So, for these two employments, that's ten certain and two probable aircraft shot down against—still provisionally—21 missing and 4 total losses. In the Rhine–Main area 31 aircraft were employed to fight low-flying airplanes. They engaged in aerial combat at an altitude of ... m with a unit of ten Thunderbolts, of which they shot down five, with two of ours missing. In the Mannheim-Ludwigshafen area 31 planes were employed, which also engaged in aerial combat with 25 Thunderbolts at an altitude of about 2,500 m. They also shot down three aircraft. Two of our aircraft are missing and there were two total losses, but without losing the pilots. So in total, with a employment of 199 fighters—188 of which engaged in aerial combat—18 enemy aircraft were shot down, with 25 planes missing and six total losses on our side.

THE FÜHRER: The missing ones are gone.

BÜCHS: We can calculate that on average, one-third of the crews return.

THE FÜHRER: I want a report every day about which missing ...

BÜCHS: The enemy is attacking the V2 launching positions mostly with Spitfires and Tempests,[1940] with bombs in diving attacks. Flak [antiaircraft] platoons have been used, which have successfully shot down aircraft. In the last few days, five fighter-bombers have been shot down by light flak at the V2 positions themselves.

THE FÜHRER: What kind of platoons are those?

BUHLE: They are four-barreled platoons, which Kammler[1941] has at the V2 sites. They belong to the batteries.

BÜCHS: The heavy units flew into the southwestern German area yesterday to carry out major terror attacks on a number of cities.[1942] Ulm was especially affected. Then there was a very heavy attack on Mannheim. In all the attacks, in addition to damage to houses, there was also very strong damage to railway installations. There were eight Messerschmitt 262s from a group currently in transfer, which happened to be carrying out practice sorties; two had enemy contact. They shot down two aircraft themselves—a bomber and a fighter. But they were both shot down as well, apparently by fighters. The exact reason they went down is unknown.

CHRISTIAN: The two were flying single or in a two-ship formation. The other six had no contact with the enemy. The two saw the unit and threw themselves on it—which is forbidden. They just went into the enemy unit without orders, and reported it via radio message. They were shot down themselves.

THE FÜHRER: But that's exactly the result I predicted. It can't be done like that. That will only change if we have different armaments.

BÜCHS: In the southwestern German area a total of seven aircraft were shot down by flak. The enemy admits to 34—12 bombers and 22 fighters.[1943] The intrusion to attack Moos-Bierbaum[1944] yesterday was in a different form; it was one attack spread out over four hours. The enemy flew in 14 waves, in numerous small groups, apparently with the intention of confusing the defense that way. A total of 2,500 high-explosive bombs were dropped, most of which fell on open fields. ... According to the reports received so far, total cessation of production, again for an indefinite time. [—] In the East only limited employment during the night.

THE FÜHRER: Especially if they're coming in very small groups, we should be able to destroy them. Then we can't say, "These are enormous masses; this is superior power"—instead, we should be able to destroy them.

GÖRING: That's right.

BÜCHS: From the West yesterday a Mosquito intrusion toward Berlin. Then very strong night fighter-bomber employment of our own, with 265 aircraft. We had very good success, especially in the area west of Cologne, against villages near the front, movements, and with some units also in the Goch area. Five Ju 87s are missing and there was one total loss, but the crew was saved. Only individual nuisance raids into the Erfurt and Kaiserslautern areas.

GÖRING: The performance of the Ju 87 should be emphasized.

BÜCHS: Using the moonlight. [—] Regarding the weather conditions: Over the Reich there are heavy showers today with very high wind speeds—on the coast up to 100 km on the ground, and in the interior up to 80 km. Also, especially on the north side of the mountains, there were very strong snow and sleet showers, which very much hindered our employment in the Münsterland again this afternoon around two o'clock. These rain fronts will continue to move further east and will diminish during the night, as will the cloud cover. High pressure is moving in from the northwest, so tomorrow we can expect limited clouds in the whole area and only a few isolated showers. Wind speeds will decrease as well. [—] One hundred ninety-six fighters started against the attack in the central German area today, despite the weather conditions. The attacks took place at exactly the time when the main showers were moving over the Berlin area. The groups had isolated contact with the enemy, because they couldn't assemble. Other groups landed again because they couldn't get through in these weather conditions. There was also quite heavy icing, which varied considerably in the degree of coverage. It must be expected that aircraft will also have been lost due to weather conditions.

CHRISTIAN: It was impossible to supply[1945] tonight due to the weather conditions. There was a 100 km wind.

Armament questions

(*Presentation by General Buhle.*)

THE FÜHRER: What does that mean in practice?

BUHLE: Using a different head,[1946] we've managed to achieve the same penetration effect with half the explosives. At the same time, I can reach a range of 150 m—50 m further—because the head is lighter. I save 0.9 kg per round. That's exactly the explosive content of one field howitzer round. That's an enormous gain.

THE FÜHRER: Who did that?

BUHLE: It was various people.

THE FÜHRER: The people who do something like that really must be honored. We can't look at that from a small, bureaucratic point of view. We have to give every such man 200,000 to 300,000 marks. It must be an incentive. We can't be petty.

BUHLE: Some of them are soldiers.

THE FÜHRER: That doesn't matter—all the more, then. Why should I pay less to a soldier?

KEITEL: It's a sizeable savings and a greater firing range.

THE FÜHRER: If we get the explosives for one million field howitzer shells, we can't pay the man enough. The Panzerfaust [antitank grenade launcher] goes 100 m further, has greater penetration, and takes half the explosives. That gets me a million field howitzer shells.

BUHLE: One hundred fifty m range. Yesterday someone fired from 200 m and hit. It will become the weapon. It is actually such that a man has a tube today and can load it again and again. Before he had to throw it away. That was one of the limitations. We have to reach 1.2 million again. We can't drop below that again. (*Further explanations of the presentation by General Buhle.*)

THE FÜHRER: How about the 7.5 cm? What do you have there?

BUHLE: The 7.5 works, as I recently reported. The shell case is reusable— at the lowest load 6,400 m, then up to 10,200 m with an intermediate load— so I have two additional loads and always only have to put one into the field and can do the next load with tubular powder.[1947] But for that I have to use the good powder. That reaches 11,400 m. That's our calculation for the maximum distance for now. I can reach 13,000 m. The dispersion is very high. It's the same load with a powder usage that's more than double. I jump immediately from 1,200 gr to 3 kg; it's huge.

THE FÜHRER: That's not possible now. We can do that later. [—] And how often can one shoot the cartridge?

BUHLE: I shot it more than five times. Nothing ever happened. But in practice, it really can't be shot more than five times, so let's say five times. Regarding the powder, there is daily testing to see how it can be done most inexpensively. The powder issue is really the bottleneck.

THE FÜHRER: It's particularly important that we be able to use inferior powder.

BUHLE: It makes hardly any difference. [—] You should speak to me again about the production of the 10-cm gun, Saur told me: "We had ordered ten percent initially."

THE FÜHRER: I'm still convinced that we have to start doing the mixed things again. I have divisions in Courland that have done it that way on principle. Every detachment has two 15-cm batteries and one 10-cm battery.[1948]

BUHLE: A good share of the Army artillery still has it. It's just bad in the infantry divisions. The 10-cm gun can't be drawn by horses at the moment. ... They have to be driven separately.

THE FÜHRER: In the Great War, the 10-cm guns were already transported in two loads. The 15-cm was transported in two loads. I have to transport the 15-cm howitzer in two loads, even if it's possible to do it with horses. That doesn't change anything. Why is that still being discussed? I have to transport the 15-cm howitzer in two loads, too.

BUHLE: Yes, indeed. The heavy field howitzer is driven in two loads.

THE FÜHRER: What results have the 8.8-cm anti-aircraft ammunition had this month? I would like to know our stock sometime. ... I want to tell Saur that he should go out and, instead of letting the Hunter-Tiger just stand there, he should install the 8.8.[1949]

BUHLE: That's what has been ordered.

End: 7:45 p.m.

* * * * *

FRAGMENT OF A MIDDAY SITUATION REPORT,
PRESUMABLY MARCH 10, 1945[1950]

BÜCHS: An 80 m section of the canal was torn up then; the water has leaked out of that part of the canal.

THE FÜHRER: Is that this part here?

CHRISTIAN: It's not at Ladbergen; it's between Ladbergen and Gravenhorst.

BÜCHS: Until now it was always at Ladbergen. Yesterday at ... the junction of the Dortmund Ems Canal and the Lippe was attacked; an 80 m section was torn up. [—] Our employment, initially only in the upper Rhine area, [was] against low-flying aircraft. Seventeen aircraft saw the enemy, with Typhoons. The losses were caused by technical reasons ... 29 aircraft employed in very bad weather yesterday to reconnoiter the bridges—three were Arado 234s,[1951] which ... attacked with 500-kg bombs from 500 m without closer observation of the effect. One of those aircraft is missing. In addition ... employment of 24 fighters with bombs, which reported these hits. Individual planes engaged in aerial combat with the fighter protection over the bridge; one Mustang[1952] was shot down. Then two aircraft were employed, Fw 190s, with SC 500 Trialen, but the results couldn't be observed because of the fighter defense, which engaged in aerial combat at the same time. There were ten fighters over the bridge at the time of the attack. A total of three aircraft are missing.

[—]

BÜCHS: The ceiling above our telephone exchange[1953] is exactly 80 cm.

THE FÜHRER: If a military agency built that—

JODL: ... a 15-cm concrete thing, with a floor in between!

BÜCHS: Both floors in between have 15-cm concrete ceilings, then here the main ceiling, which is above the telephone exchange, is 80 cm—all with pressure doors. This part here is underground; this here above ground.

THE FÜHRER: Where repairing the cracks is much more difficult then, if something goes in from the side.

BÜCHS: ...

THE FÜHRER: Exactly. That's even worse. It happened to me twice: at my place two bombs went directly in. If (the ceiling) hadn't been so strong, it would have pressed them right together. Your little bunker here would very likely be completely gone. And those were just light little bombs of no more than 250 kg. I don't think they were 500s. If a 2000-kg bomb had come in here, it would have given us some bad cracks. Even the 250s were enough to cause cracks so bad that water ran in. How strong is the ceiling out there?

V. BELOW: Fifty cm concrete.

CHRISTIAN: Our bunker has 42 m of earth over it. It was built in 1936.[1954]

THE FÜHRER: You have ... in clever foresight ... bunkered in!

CHRISTIAN: Into the mountain.

THE FÜHRER: But the question is how the concrete is put in on the inside.

CHRISTIAN: It has about 2 m concrete.

THE FÜHRER: You believe that! [—] Reinforced concrete?

CHRISTIAN: I believe it's reinforced concrete.

THE FÜHRER: Children, don't make fools of yourselves!

V. BELOW: I don't think it has more than 2 m.

CHRISTIAN: And then inside the mountain!

THE FÜHRER: Forty-two m? I don't believe that, because there isn't even a 42 m high mountain here.

V. BELOW: It's the tunnel down inside.

THE FÜHRER: Bring me the plans; then you'll see how that shrinks! [—] And I also want to see the plans for those "magnificent buildings" out there! [—]

BÜCHS: ... the area of high pressure stretching further east, the sudden drop in temperature more in the eastern Ruhr area. In the western combat area a certain improvement has taken place.

THE FÜHRER: "Improvement"? A worsening!

BÜCHS:—a worsening has taken place. Today it was still very bad in the central sector of the Rhine; low clouds were rolling in at around 150 m. It was a little better only on the upper Rhine and in the lower-lying areas.

THE FÜHRER: If we could get out of here, all our [Me-] 262s and whatever we have would ...

GÖRING: (The number of sorties) would be much higher if we ... had more engines.

THE FÜHRER: How many 262s were in action?

BÜCHS: In the bomber formations only?

THE FÜHRER: In action altogether?!

BÜCHS: I'll have to get those numbers first.

THE FÜHRER: And for the Arados as well!

GÖRING: They would be even higher if we ...[1955] the aircraft that are at the front. As I just said, the teething troubles are behind us; they've already been through follow-on equipment 1, 2, and 3 and have everything built in now. ... The others have to get the follow-on equipment first.

THE FÜHRER: ... civilian population ... behind the labor forces. Even if the workforce is really bad, I need 800,000 additional workers just to (bring) the railway (into working order). We can't afford that. It's sheer lunacy. The people come and say: we want to start doing this. [—] If I don't (get that in order) everything else will be wasted as well. In the end, the workforce is one of the most critical factors today; whether it's girls or women, it doesn't matter at all: everyone has to be employed. At first, we had doubts here because of the gigantic treks. But fine. We have 1.3 million horses [—][1956]

CHRISTIAN: During the ... a total of 187 (Me 262s) delivered. The most always come out in the first few days. At the end of the month, there's always a hold-up in the industry, and then the planes always come in fairly high numbers. ... We put them into the follow-on equipment, and then they'll be delivered.

THE FÜHRER: By the way, the rumors from Krems regarding the nickel. Now I'm hearing from all sides: yes, we calculated that without this and without that. Now I'm curious!

GÖRING: I know what was said about the nickel back then. I was there. I thought it was complete nonsense. It was said back then that we had almost unlimited supplies of nickel.

THE FÜHRER: Now they say they're calculating ... But that's always the case if we expose something. Then the military authorities came (and told the scientists what had to be done) because there are big military advantages, and then the leading economic men are so stupid and say the same, instead of right from the start ... We could just as well have stayed at Petsamo[1957] as down there, I guarantee you—it's all the same.

GÖRING: It would be a great help to us, my Führer, if you could push hard for us to get engines as well as aircraft.

THE FÜHRER: I push and push, but all the pushing is of no use if a factory is built and then destroyed!

GÖRING: But we have them down inside the mountain now. It's already going![1958]

THE FÜHRER: I've pushed so much that I've said: I'm not even going into this mine, because 25 percent of all engines— that makes a difference! (*End of the fragment.*)

* * * * *

March 23, 1945

The Soviet attacks in Courland have still gained only limited ground. In East Prussia the remnants of the Fourth Army at Heiligenbeil and the Balga Peninsula have been pressed together even further. The situation in Samland is unchanged. In West Prussia the remnants of the Second Army are fighting on a stretch of coast that is now only 10 to 15 km wide, between the mouth of the Nogat and Rixhöft Rivers; on this day the German forces are cut in two by a Russian penetration to Zopot. On the lower Oder, the Soviets have now thrown the German troops back over the river and the bay, and have completely occupied Eastern Pomerania. A last bridgehead east of Stettin had to be given up on March 20. In Upper Silesia the enemy attacked the German Oder front between Oppeln and Ratibor on March 15, and—

as before in Lower Silesia—advanced to the eastern edge of the Sudeten Mountains. At Plattensee [Lake Balaton], the German offensive that began on March 9 has been unable to advance, and now the Russians are penetrating into Hungary and Slovakia with the objectives of reaching Vienna and Brünn [Brno]. In Yugoslavia the situation is unchanged. The break in the fighting in Italy is only occasionally disturbed by minor operations.

On the Rhine, the Americans reached Cologne on March 5 and, two days later, were able to build a bridgehead on the right bank of the Rhine River at Remagen. In the meantime, the Eifel had been crossed and Andernach occupied on March 9. Since the following day, the entire Rhine line from Emmerich to Koblenz has been in Allied hands. Then on March 15 Patton's concentric attack against the Moselle–Saar–Rhine triangle began as well. The First Army on the Saar River and the Seventh Army on the Moselle River were smashed. The German forces that weren't cut off by American tank spearheads attempted to reach the Rhine in a state of chaotic disintegration. On March 20 the Americans were already in Worms, in Bingen the following day, and in Mainz on the 22nd. Now, on the 23rd, there is fighting in Ludwigshafen. Only between Speyer and Karlsruhe are the German bridgeheads on the left bank of the Rhine able to hold until March 25. Patton crossed the Rhine the night before at Oppenheim.
(*Map 13*)

*****

EVENING SITUATION REPORT,
MARCH 23, 1945, IN THE FÜHRER'S APARTMENT IN BERLIN[1959]

Present:

The Führer	*Lieutenant Colonel Borgmann*
General Burgdorf	*Major Brudermüller*
Ambassador Hewel	*Major Johannmeyer*
Colonel v. Below	*Sturmbannführer Günsche*
Stabsleiter Sündermann	*Sturmbannführer Göhler*
Lieutenant Colonel de Maizière	*Hauptsturmführer Kersten*
Later:	*Hauptbereichsleiter Zander*

Beginning: 2:26 a.m. (March 24)

The West

BRUDERMÜLLER: Here in the area south of Arnhem there was artillery fire as in the previous days. 1,375 motor vehicles were identified here through air reconnaissance, including 233 tanks. Also strong concentrations of motor vehicles identified in this area. On both sides of Rees, the enemy—in company strength, according to reports received so far—crossed the Rhine with amphibious tanks. The 8th Parachute Division assesses the situation to be such that they can clear this thing out with their reserve regiment.

THE FÜHRER: No.

BRUDERMÜLLER: The army group immediately released the 15th Panzer Grenadier Division for that purpose anyway; it's coming down to clear it out and throw the enemy into the water.[1960] The 116th Panzer Division is moving up into the area of the 15th Panzer Grenadier Division. [—] Strong fighter-bomber employment during the entire day, far into the rear area. Also here very strong artillery fire since 5 p.m., and conspicuously strong fighter-bomber and tactical aircraft activity in this area, so the Commander-in-Chief West expects an attack here in the Wesel area. [—] I can report on the bridgehead[1961] using the small map. Here in the northern part strong motorized movements. Otherwise, here on the eastern front of these two corps there was only artillery fire and fighter-bomber activity into the rear area. Among other things, the command post of Army Group "B" was attacked again. The enemy continued his attacks to the east here, and succeeded in achieving a few deeper penetrations. A blocking position was erected here. Down here the enemy was caught up along this line. According to an unconfirmed report, there are 30 tanks in Niederbieber. No new reports about the occupation of Neuwied. A counterthrust by a regimental group of the 18th Volksgrenadier Division stalled in front of an antitank gun defensive line here. [—] Here west of Mainz smoke screening and vehicle traffic reported. Army Group "B" reports that they don't believe they can pull out the 6th SS Mountain Division right now. A battalion is being kept on alert, though, so that it can be driven over here at any time on short notice. [—] Fighter reconnaissance reported a bridge here.[1962]

THE FÜHRER: Is the entire Luftwaffe in position here to eliminate this at least?

V. BELOW: Today Me 262s and Arado 234s were sent out, as well as Otto fighters.[1963] The fighters barely got through, though, because they became involved in aerial combat beforehand.

BRUDERMÜLLER: The Luftwaffe is now asking whether the main focus should be up here at Wesel or over here.

THE FÜHRER: It must be established down here immediately.

BRUDERMÜLLER: Colonel General Jodl suggests that the main focus remain here, first, because we are much weaker on the ground here than we are up there, and also because we couldn't fly here or up above tomorrow if the units are transferred.

V. BELOW: We've already flown here today.

BRUDERMÜLLER: According to the latest telephone reports from the Commander-in-Chief West, a counterattack started from north to south in the late hours of the evening. An attack from west to east is planned for tonight. We don't know if that has started yet or not. Field Marshal General Kesselring[1964] has driven in this area here himself. [—] The Commander-in-Chief West has ordered that the bridges from the lower reaches of the Main [River] up to Höchst be blown up, and that the bridges in Frankfurt be ignited. The other bridges on the Main up to Miltenberg are to be prepared for demolition. A senior engineer officer has been assigned the responsibility for the technical preparation of this operation.

THE FÜHRER: The best thing would be to try to get a few Hunter-Tigers as well.

BRUDERMÜLLER: The serviceable Hunter-Tigers from the 653rd Detachment are so caught up in combat in the area left of the Rhine that they can't be pulled out now. The tanks that were brought over for maintenance—there are 16—are to be sent to the Oppenheim bridgehead immediately after the maintenance is completed. There's no report yet on when that will be, though.

THE FÜHRER: Then we have to supply them with the necessary spare parts by air immediately. It must be ordered immediately, so they get them right away. Has Saur been contacted yet?

BRUDERMÜLLER: I'll speak with General Thomale again right away. [—] In the Ludwigshafen area the enemy pushed through into the center of the city. Heavy house-to-house combat and very severe losses are reported. It's emphasized that the district leader has provided outstanding support for the fighting here. In the Ludwigshafen area there are still 70,000 civilians who are hindering the combat. [—] The Commander-in-Chief West has now ordered—because a cohesive command is no longer possible, and also because there's no relevant time savings in his opinion, if the fighting continues here—that Lieutenant Colonel Löffler,[1965] the former commanding officer of Coblenz, move over with the remnants of the occupation force, because he's badly needed as a combat commander in the western sector.

(THE FÜHRER: Yes.)

[—] During these battles seven tanks were knocked out. The ferries and bridges at Speyer were blown up. Here the enemy is attacking Speyer from the north. Also attacks here. He has taken Bergzabern, in order to advance toward the east then and push forward to Herxheim.

THE FÜHRER: According to American reports, there's hardly any resistance here. They report sixteen thousand, seven thousand, nine thousand prisoners per day.[1966]

BRUDERMÜLLER: The bulk of 16th Volksgrenadier Division's artillery is there; no reports on the infantry yet, though. The bulk of the 36th Volksgrenadier Division's artillery is there, plus a regimental group; one regimental group is still missing. [—] I must correct myself here. From the 16th, twelve guns are there. [—] The position of these divisions, which are marked in here, is unknown at the moment.

The Southeast, Italy

In the Southeast and in Italy nothing significant. [—] I'd also like to present an evaluation that came in tonight from Field Marshal Kesselring. (*Presentation.*)

(*Hauptbereichsleiter Zander enters.*)

THE FÜHRER: Show me all the reports that have come out of the Breslau Fortress so far.

(ZANDER: Yes, Sir.)

The East

DE MAIZIÈRE: In the Second Panzer Army's sector, the fighting in this salient here is over. 150 prisoners taken so far, and here[1967] built up. [—] With the Sixth Army, the situation continues to intensify.[1968] This town of Balatonfüzfö,[1969] which was fought over today, is securely in our hands. But the Russians advanced with tanks to just outside this town. Veszprem is in enemy hands. To the east of Veszprem, and west in the direction of the railway, security has been built up, as well as here in front, by units of the 3rd and 4th Cavalry Divisions, the 9th SS [Panzer] Division, and here the 3rd Panzer Division.

THE FÜHRER: The connection to the lake[1970] must not be lost under any circumstances. If it's lost, it's all over.

DE MAIZIÈRE: Yes, that has been ordered already. [—] Here are the still preliminary numbers of the units that came out from the 1st Panzer Division and the [44th] *Hoch- und Deutschmeister* Division. The commander of the *Hoch- und Deutschmeister* Division and his 1a [operations officer] have supposedly fallen. That's General Rost.[1971] There's a gap between Markö and here, but we don't have any further details yet. Bases of the *Leibstandarte* Division are being held here and here.

THE FÜHRER: Is Fegelein here?

GÖHLER: No, the Gruppenführer is in bed. He's not feeling very well.

THE FÜHRER: I demand one thing now: that the last man, wherever he may be hidden, be sent immediately to the *Leibstandarte*, to the entire Sixth Panzer Army. [—] But immediately!

(GÖHLER: Yes, Sir.)

Sepp Dietrich has to be informed of that immediately. Right now! If I catch only one man, then God have mercy on him!

GÖHLER: Yes, Sir. He has already received a telegram from the Reichsführer yesterday; the Reichsführer gave him specific orders that the troop strength should not be allowed to decrease under any circumstances.

THE FÜHRER: What does "decrease" mean? It means nothing. The last man that the Sixth [SS] Panzer [Army] has must be sent in.

(GÖHLER: Yes, Sir.)

DE MAIZIÈRE: North of that is another gap. It's not yet clear how far the Russians have penetrated into the woods. It's holding here, along the Klara position. This town has been lost. Here a counterattack by units of the 6th Panzer Division and the 2nd SS [Panzer] Division. Strong attacks against the whole front south and southeast of Komarom, in each case in battalion or regiment strength in various places; all were driven back. However, that made it necessary to pull back these units of the 2nd SS Panzer Division, which had been taken forward in the attack. Here's the small bridgehead, and in here there are still five battalions that have the order to fight their way through tonight.

THE FÜHRER: Over here or here?

DE MAIZIÈRE: Over here, like this!

THE FÜHRER: Do we want to hold the bridgehead?

DE MAIZIÈRE: No. It's up to the army group. I have orders to present this order here, which the Chief of General Staff issued this evening. (*Presentation.*)

THE FÜHRER: We can't count on that at all yet.

DE MAIZIÈRE: Yes, indeed. That will take quite some time. [—] Up here on the Gran [Hron] [River], at this little bridgehead, this town was taken back. The army group has now been ordered to carry out the final evacuation of the rest of the bridgehead. No other engagements up here on the Gran.

THE FÜHRER: I don't understand that. What happened there on the Gran? What was taken back there?

DE MAIZIÈRE: This town was recaptured by us, and now there's only a small bridgehead here, and the army group has the order to evacuate it for good.

THE FÜHRER: It's quite clear: it's better for them to go over here, so that there won't be trouble here, too.

DE MAIZIÈRE: Yes, Sir. [—] Artillery ranging along the Gran front, clearing mines, bringing in forces. About 1,500 vehicles identified by air reconnaissance. The situation in the area south of Neusohl is becoming increasingly tense. West of the Gran, the enemy advanced into the area southwest of Neusohl, eastward not quite so far. A regiment of the 15th [Infantry] Division has launched a counterattack. Here's another penetration, which led across the road toward the west—there where there are Hungarian units. Here the army group has ordered the withdrawal of the left wing up to here, while leaving hunter commands [*Jägdkommandos*] in front here, which are to maintain the connection with the right wing of the First Panzer Army.

THE FÜHRER: If the left wing is withdrawn to here, how should it be reestablished?

DE MAIZIÈRE: The hunter commands are staying on the previous line here, and they are to maintain the connection with the right wing of the First Panzer Army, over the mountains. Here, there's still about 2.5 m snow on the mountains. [—] In the Army Group Center sector, the focal point of combat was in the area of Leobschütz and Neisse. Down here in the mountains, forces were brought in, including 50 guns, to the border between the 304th and the 16th Hungarian Division. Only limited attacks against the Ratibor–Schwarzwasser bridgehead; they're judged to be holding attacks, especially since the 5th Guards Mechanized Corps, which is here, was identified in this area today.

THE FÜHRER: I want to see that more precisely on the map.

DE MAIZIÈRE: Here an attack with three tank corps and the two armies, the 60th and 59th Armies. For the most part, no intensification of the situation since this afternoon. The enemy only pushed further forward here; he was stopped here first, with only thin security forces. Here a combat group of the 17th Panzer Division is still encircled, and has the order to fight its way through today in this direction. This salient north of Leobschütz hasn't been attacked. But instead the enemy attacked out of this area with 30 tanks. The army group is now planning to build up a new front tonight, withdrawing this salient back into this line, and using these people who are supposed to fight their way back. The Führer Escort Division arrived with the first transport at 7:30 p.m.—sooner than expected. In total, 16 transports are underway. Here two battalions of the 1st Ski Jäger Division are being brought in. A similar picture in the Neisse area: attacks brought under control with loss of ground—it was here this morning. The cohesiveness of the front was maintained, except for one gap here, where tank combat is taking place. About 60 enemy tanks against 21 German tanks tonight. The front north of the Neisse [River], like at Leobschütz, wasn't attacked. But west of Neisse they advanced with 40 tanks, which penetrated as far as the northwestern part of Neisse. Here also building up a front, while withdrawing this forward salient, which wasn't attacked, back. In terms of enemy forces, the 4th Guards Tank Army is here with two mobile units—one from here and one from here.

Strong employment of fighter-bombers. Tanks knocked out: here 25, here 24, here 18. Here we can also report that in this small corner, where there were units of a mechanized corps of the 4th Guards Tank Army, the enemy was pushed out and this thing was straightened. In Breslau only weaker attacks against the southern front.

THE FÜHRER: I want to find something out again: A few days ago, a report arrived from Breslau that the enemy was using the heaviest weapons against which the city—or, rather, the fortress—had no equivalent countermeasures. Now it's presented as if bringing in six heavy infantry guns would hinder the transport of ammunition. I won't have that. The heavy infantry guns will be flown in and the ammunition will come as well. That's only six aircraft in total; everything else is transporting ammunition anyway. That has been arranged by the Luftwaffe again, of course.

DE MAIZIÈRE: Three of the heavy infantry guns were flown in last night. One made a crash landing, so two are there ready for action. The next three should come in tonight. [—] Weaker attacks against the southern front; they have been driven back.

THE FÜHRER: Pass that on immediately. They absolutely must be flown in. Hanke is a panzer man; he has no idea what a heavy infantry gun even looks like. They were just complaining that they don't have any weapons to combat the heaviest things. So I ordered that heavy infantry guns be sent in immediately. Go to your chief of transport; he's responsible for that.

V. BELOW: Yes, Sir.

DE MAIZIÈRE: Concentrations in the southern part of Glogau. Otherwise no particular engagements. Daytime reconnaissance identified 25 tanks here today, along a wide front. It could almost be a deception, if tanks are appearing here so openly during the day.

THE FÜHRER: I have one great worry here. Here's the one panzer group.

DE MAIZIÈRE: Here's the panzer group of the 21st Panzer Division, which has about 50 tanks, according to the latest data.

BURGDORF: He wants to pull out the entire 21st during the next few days.

DE MAIZIÈRE: With the fortress battalions that are being brought in, either the bulk of the 21st Panzer Division or—it hasn't quite been decided yet—some units of the *Brandenburg* Division should come out. [—] Notable up here is a employment of 200 fighter-bombers in the rear section of the front, especially against small villages. In the Küstrin[1972] area there were attacks against the Klessin base from north and south. The occupation forces pushed together in the town. Here the Russians attacked again all day, without success. The main focus of the attacks was on both sides of the road leading out of Küstrin to the west. Here is a minor local penetration, against which an attack is taking place. The number of tanks disabled was reported as 116 yesterday—20 of those by the Luftwaffe—and 42 today, according to reports received thus far. Tonight the 20th Panzer Grenadier Division and the 25th Panzer Grenadier Division were to attack side by side in an east-southeast direction, toward the Oder. The report on the execution hasn't yet been received.

THE FÜHRER: These numbers of tanks disabled seem so fantastic to me because they contradict the number of attacking enemy tanks that were reported at first. At first it was said that there were 60 tanks attacking.

DE MAIZIÈRE: Yes, indeed. According to the number of units employed—they're listed here—it would still be possible. Here there are: the 259th Tank Regiment, two tank brigades of the 11th Tank Corps, another separate tank brigade and an assault gun regiment. That's about 240 tanks.

THE FÜHRER: If they're all complete!

DE MAIZIÈRE: Yes, indeed—if they're all complete. According to a radio report, a unit of the 2nd Guards Tank Army was deployed in here [Kustrin area] yesterday. It couldn't be proven, though, whether it's a brigade or less or more. Without a doubt, the numbers reported do seem very high.

THE FÜHRER: The first report said there were 60 tanks in total attacking here. That's not unimportant. If they've disabled that, that's good; I just don't believe it.

DE MAIZIÈRE: Other than that, no combat in Army Group Vistula's area. [—] In the Second Army's area there are penetrations that have been sealed off. This attack was still in progress. No new reports from the Zoppot area since the afternoon situation. Here local penetrations have been sealed off. There was a new strong attack against the front southwest of Danzig, with strong penetrations. The situation here is not completely clear yet. Attacks against the southern front were driven back. All mobile units facing the Second Army confirmed again: six mobile units.

THE FÜHRER: We can only do something here with an enormous concentration of all Naval forces, and really only at this one point here, abandoning all other actions. There's no other option but to give up this thing here and to go to the Vistula here. That will cost us the road from the Nehrung, of course. We'll have to see about that tomorrow.

DE MAIZIÈRE: Fourth Army: All day long attacks in battalion and regiment strength against the front, leading to no success during the day. The report just came in about a strong Russian attack against the XXXXI Panzer Corps, in which this town and the heights here were lost. That's all the more regrettable because from here one can overlook all the lowlands. The employment of aircraft limited today due to the weather. [—] The Chief of the General Staff gave the following order to Colonel General Weiss[1973] tonight. (*Presentation.*) No unusual occurrences in Courland here. Here all attacks were driven back except for one local penetration, which is still in progress here. Here a local penetration and bringing in of forces from the east and northeast. Here a new pressure point could develop. The Chief of the General Staff has already indicated that the army group should assemble this panzer brigade of the 12th Panzer Division in this area, so that there are reserves here in time. Here the attacks were driven back. Here there are still local difficulties. There's still a small group behind there, and there's another one there.

The West again

THE FÜHRER: When will the two parachute regiments come up from Italy?
BRUDERMÜLLER: I can't report on that at the moment. I'll find out.
DR FÜHRER: He asks for units that have great combat effectiveness here. At least 15 strong units were lost by leaving the Western Wall, because one could supposedly fight better in the open. There you see the result of all this talk. It wasn't Kesselring's fault.
BURGDORF: No, he's done all he could now.
THE FÜHRER: The worst thing is this second bridgehead here at Oppenheim. Is there still one of our panzer brigades or anything at all operating? [—] Didn't the others[1974] get through at all?
V. BELOW: There were 117 fighters employed to attack with bombs and on-board weapons. Some of the units didn't reach the bridgehead because of previous aerial combat. Nine aircraft are missing. Some did reach it.
THE FÜHRER: Some, so not only the Me 262s?
V. BELOW: No, also some of the other fighters.
THE FÜHRER: Have they been able to attack the bridge?
V. BELOW: There's no report on that yet.
THE FÜHRER: What shocks me with the Luftwaffe are the so-called numbers of aircraft missing, where it just says: Missing—over German Reich territory! One can't imagine them to be completely blown up so that nothing can be found. In a few days that should be clarified. What's-his-name mentioned a certain suspicion today—totally independent from me, but it's also my conviction—because they don't report on these things anymore; they maintain complete silence.[1975]

Situation in the air

V. BELOW: The American four-engine units attacked traffic installations in the Rhine, Münster and Osnabrück areas today, with another group in the Bochum, Essen, Iserlohn, Hagen and Dinslaken areas. The British four-engines also attacked traffic installations in the area of Bocholt and flew attacks with some units against Bremen and the Quakenbrück air base. According to reports received thus far, a total of 17 Me 262s were employed. In total, according to reports so far, four aircraft were shot down without any losses on our side.[1976]

THE FÜHRER: By the 262s?

V. BELOW: By the 262s!

THE FÜHRER: The others don't get close?

V. BELOW: No, the others don't get close. [—] From the south there was an attack of 600 American four-engine aircraft on the Schwarzheide hydrogenate plants[1977] and industrial targets in the same area of the Lausitz. In addition, 200 aircraft attacked traffic installations near St. Valentin and in the Vienna area. [—] In the East fighter-bomber employment against the bridges. There were three hits on the bridge at Lebus and one hit on the bridge at Göritz-Mitte [central Göritz]. Tonight there's another employment of a few Ju 88s—six of them. That's basically all.

The West again

THE FÜHRER: The greatest danger I see is really in this second bridgehead—the Oppenheim bridgehead.

BURGDORF: Also because he got the bridge-building equipment there so fast.

THE FÜHRER: A pontoon bridge!

HEWEL: The Rhine isn't that wide there either.

THE FÜHRER: It's a good 250 m! It just takes one person who's asleep at a river barrier, and there could be a terrible disaster. The upper bridgehead is probably the reason some units were rescued down there. If it hadn't been built, and the enemy had advanced with all his forces straight south along the Rhine, nobody would have gotten out. The instant we allow ourselves to be pushed out of the fortifications, it's all over. Here the leadership acted in an absolutely pathetic way. They've fed the troops the idea—from above—that one can fight better in the open than in here.

Miscellaneous

BURGDORF: Reich Minister Dr. Goebbels requests permission to convert the east-west axis in Berlin into a runway. For that it would be necessary to take away the streetlights on both sides and to cut away a further 20 m of the Tiergarten [zoo] on each side. He thinks it would be good, in that we could widen the east-west axis sometime later.

THE FÜHRER: He can do that. But I don't think it's necessary. Fifty m width should really be enough.

ZANDER: I just have the last three radio messages from Hanke here. (*Presentation.*)

THE FÜHRER: I want to have all of the latest radio messages.

ZANDER: They're in the alternative quarters of the party chancellery. I'll have to request them.

THE FÜHRER: Ask for them immediately! A telegram came in, in which he wrote that the enemy is now using the heaviest weapons, against which they have no countermeasures. After that the heavy infantry guns were requested. Now the heavy infantry guns are being played around with, as always in these cases. The army group was to provide them. But I ordered that it be done from here, from the headquarters, and I had it confirmed whether the heavy infantry guns were there at all. Buhle acted surprised then. In reality they should be provided by the Commander of the Replacement Army. The army group has no heavy infantry guns. It took ages then. Then it was said that they wouldn't fit into the aircraft. Then, they would fit if taken apart. Then again, they couldn't land. In truth it's the aversion to landing. Now they explain, "If we bring in the heavy infantry guns, we can't bring in any ammunition." In reality that's six aircraft—six transport gliders. The rest are available for ammunition. But Hanke is a panzer man; he has no clue about that. If they really need weapons to shoot the enemy out of individual blocks accurately, there are, of course, even better things; but those can't be brought in. There's no weapon that's more effective that can be brought in than the heavy infantry gun. If we bring in 18 rounds of ammunition, though, that's a fiasco. We can't do anything with 18 rounds of ammunition, even though a heavy infantry gun can tear a house down to the cellar with one shot, of course.

BURGDORF: Can I allow Reich Minister Goebbels to do this?

THE FÜHRER: Yes, but I don't see why it would have to be made wider. We don't land there with "Goliaths." It's 52 m wide.

V. BELOW: If the Ju 52 has to land there in the dark later, it would be difficult with the streetlights.

THE FÜHRER: The streetlights—fine. But to cut down 20 to 30 m of the Tiergarten to the left and right—

V. BELOW: That's hardly necessary.

THE FÜHRER: We don't need any more than 50 m width. And it's useless anyway, because it can't be reinforced to the left and right. It's completely pointless.

JOHANNMEYER: It's only the sidewalk and then the embankment.

V. BELOW: I don't think it's necessary to cut down 20 m either, but the streetlights should be removed.

THE FÜHRER: He can take away the streetlights.[1978]

BURGDORF: I will send that out.

THE FÜHRER: But it just occurred to me: we could also let Me 162s and Me 262s take off on the east-west axis.

V. BELOW: Yes, indeed, with this length!

HEWEL: But not with the victory column on it.

BURGDORF: That would have to be taken down.

THE FÜHRER: It's almost 3 km up to the victory column. That's long enough.[1979]

BURGDORF: Lankeit has led the 12th [Infantry] Division so far. He will be free now, so I wanted to suggest that we take him down to the [44th] *Hoch- und Deutschmeister* Division. He did very well with the 12th Division. He's from upper Bavaria.[1980]

THE FÜHRER: With the 12th Division in the West?

BURGDORF: Yes. He was in the East before and is familiar with the thing. [—] Then again the question: what is the intention with regard to Guderian's leave at this time?[1981]

THE FÜHRER: I want to finally get the doctor's definitive decision on Wenck, and I mean binding. He'll answer for it with his head. In this amount [of] time he will be well or not well—period, end. They make excuses all the time, saying: he can leave the hospital on such and such a day. Now they apparently don't even know whether he'll have to be operated on or not.

BURGDORF: The doctor told us he thought it would be necessary until April 15, even if Wenck doesn't want to keep resting anymore.

V. BELOW: Is it acceptable if—when you, my Führer, are not staying there— the smoke screening is reduced on the Obersalzberg? There's smoke with every intruding aircraft now, and that takes a lot of chemical/acid used to produce smoke...

THE FÜHRER: Yes, but then everything is gone. We have to understand that. That's one of the last alternative locations that we have. Nothing will happen to the bunker, and it's not about my house, either; but the whole installation will be gone.[1982] If Zossen is badly hit one of these days, where will we go then? A heavy attack on Zossen, then it's gone. A large part of it is probably gone right now.[1983]

BURGDORF: They are completely serviceable. All the houses remained intact, and there are enough barracks. If the barracks are all destroyed, though, the last possibility is gone.

THE FÜHRER: I saw that one picture. It was a 1-meter concrete wall. That's Army concrete that they used there. That shouldn't even be pushed in by a bomb like that, since it was above[1984] the ground.

BURGDORF: Because I've been there as a guest, I don't want to bring the facilities of the German Air Force to your attention; but if I had known that such an installation was in the immediate proximity of Berlin, I would have said: It's crazy. Because both operational staffs would fit in there besides you, my Führer. There at Wannsee—Air-raid Defense School—they have a high bunker with 3.5 m reinforced concrete on top of it and with four floors—one underground and three above ground. I saw that by chance.

THE FÜHRER: That has been completely concealed from me until now.

V. BELOW: It's the German Air Force bunker. Before, the Air-raid Defense School was out there, and then the bunker was built by the German Air Force about two years ago.[1985]

THE FÜHRER: It's like this. Nothing is absolutely safe, of course. That's clear. But against bombs of up to 1,000 kg these bunkers here[1986] are generally safe. So some can always be accommodated here. I can still throw some other things out here. We can do that, in principle. Some can be accommodated there. Zossen isn't safe out there, and that's not because it couldn't be safe in principle, but because it was built by the Army and not by a building contractor. If the OT [Todt Organization] and a real building contractor had built it, 1 m concrete walls would hold at least so that those underground wouldn't be penetrated easily. But I saw a bomb come in sideways and go through 1 m underground right away. Then I've also seen the armoring. On the outside an armoring of two layers at most and on the inside also an armoring of two layers at most. That's a joke, of course. That just means we've built concrete buildings. The earlier buildings of Speer are not that excellent either—we have to be aware of that. Even these buildings here are only very massive because these huge buildings are standing over them and because the buildings offer a protection that's enormous in itself. But it's not completely safe. The Army[1987] buildings are completely fraudulent. We have to say that very soberly. The people who did that fooled themselves. If really heavy carpet bombing comes down on it, the houses in Zossen will all be swept away—all the buildings that are there. First, what's above ground, anyway, but also the two underground bunkers. They're weak, too. Now the question is: can this whole thing work if all the buildings above ground are gone?

BURGDORF: Yes, indeed. They can work down below.

THE FÜHRER: Is that enough for the staff?

BURGDORF: Yes, for the smaller operations staff that's already in there now.

DE MAIZIÈRE: Many are already working underground there, where the facilities up above haven't been repaired. For example, General Krebs, the Chief of the Operations Section,[1988] works mostly underground. For the staff that's there now, it works, even if the buildings above ground are destroyed.

THE FÜHRER: We have to count on that, of course. Because they obviously get the news now about what's been destroyed. Now I fear that here, just like at the Reich Chancellery, foreign workers will ingeniously have been used to clear the place. Then they get the news via their organization 14 days earlier, about what has been damaged.

V. BELOW: I'll find out about that.

THE FÜHRER: Because the attack will be repeated—that goes without saying—and when the attack is repeated, one day we have to expect them to blast the installations away. I presume that with the underground bunkers the second floor—the first-floor ceiling is only 1 m thick, which is nothing, and I don't even know, since it doesn't show in the drawing, whether the ceilings have girders at all—

JOHANNMEYER: They do have girders. You can even see some of them. I lived down there for four weeks myself one time.

BURGDORF: You see them running along the ceiling, just like here[1989], even above, when you come in.

THE FÜHRER: Main girder?

(JOHANNMEYER: Yes, indeed.)

Normally, one can expect that 1 m won't be penetrated by a 1,000-kg bomb, but it blows up, it comes in about 50-60 cm, and breaks through the whole thing immediately—so the upper floor would be gone with a bomb like that.

BRUDERMÜLLER: The first two battalions of the 6,000 paratroopers have marched out of the engagement area today and are to be loaded near Bolzano [Bozen]. But right now, the Brenner route is still being interrupted by air attacks. So we're calculating three days into the Bolzano area. Empty convoys will be used as far as possible; there are very few, though, because there's very little shooting right now. But the majority will have to march on foot into the Bolzano area.

THE FÜHRER: Then they won't reach Bolzano in three days. From there to Bolzano is a three-week route—20 days, or 14, or at least 10 days.

BURGDORF: From Trent to Bolzano is already a one-day march.

BRUDERMÜLLER: A time calculation is very difficult at the moment, and there are very few empty convoys driving back because they have relatively [little] to drive forward at the moment, because they don't shoot much and therefore have relatively limited supply.

BURGDORF: Couldn't they go at least part of the way by train? They can always get off and get on again. There's nothing to unload—it's just the people with their small arms.

THE FÜHRER: The important thing is to have the other 7,000 men ready for these 6,000, so they can be immediately integrated when they come in. The 6,000 men should be instructed en route already, so they know what it's all about and they can form divisions from them immediately. At least they'll be suitable for defensive purposes then. We'll have to see then, where to bring them. We don't have to determine that now. [—] These are two units that could arrive. The other two units—I don't know yet; they must be homeland units, so we'll have to improvise a little with that.

BRUDERMÜLLER: Now he'll get the "Donau" [Danube] Shadow Division [Schattendivision] as well.[1990]

THE FÜHRER: It won't work with only that.

BRUDERMÜLLER: He can, of course, fill up other worn-out divisions with it.

BURGDORF: In my opinion, Military Districts XI, IX, and VII haven't drawn anything up so far,[1991] at least not the way all the other military districts have been plundered. We should be able to do something there, somehow.

THE FÜHRER: Would you take that up with Jüttner right away? That absolutely must be done.

BURGDORF: Yes, Sir. I will say again that Military Districts XI, IX, and VII must make some kind of contribution now.

THE FÜHRER: We don't know what all is strolling around out there. Now I hear for the first time, to my surprise, that a Ukrainian SS Division has suddenly appeared. I didn't know anything about this Ukrainian SS Division.

GÖHLER: That has existed for a very long time.

THE FÜHRER: But it's never been mentioned in our discussions. Or do you remember?

GÖHLER: No, I don't remember.

THE FÜHRER: Maybe it was reported to me a long, long time ago. I don't know. How strong is the Ukrainian Division?

GÖHLER: I'll find out.

THE FÜHRER: Either the unit is reliable or it's not reliable. I can't draw up units in Germany today because I don't have any weapons. It would be nonsense for me to go and give weapons to a Ukrainian division now that's not completely reliable. Then I'd rather take the weapons away from them and draw up a German division. Because I assume that they are very well armed— probably better than most of the German divisions we're forming today.

BURGDORF: It's the same with the Latvian 20th. It shattered immediately down there as well.

DE MAIZIÈRE: The Latvian [division] is fighting up in Courland right now, and very well. The one down there was the Estonian [division].[1992]

BURGDORF: Yes, the Estonian one was gone immediately. We have to imagine it psychologically as well. It's asking a bit much of these people.

THE FÜHRER: What are they still supposed to be fighting for, anyway? They're gone from their homeland.

BURGDORF: If there are a lot of fainthearted people even with us, we really can't demand it of those people.

THE FÜHRER: We need to find out exactly what's still there now in terms of foreign formations. For example, the Vlasov division is either good for something or not. There are only those two possibilities. If it's good for something, it has to be addressed like a fully effective division. If it's good for nothing, it's idiocy to arm a division of 10,000 or 11,000 men, while at the same time I'm unable to draw up other German divisions because I have no weapons. Then I'd rather go draw up a German division and give all the armaments to them.

BORGMANN: The Indian Legion![1993]

THE FÜHRER: The Indian Legion is a joke. There are Indians who couldn't kill a louse, who'd rather be eaten themselves. They wouldn't kill an Englishman either. To have them face the English of all people is really a stupid idea, I think. Why should the Indians fight more courageously for us than they fought in India itself, under Bose's[1994] leadership? They put Indian units into action in Burma, under Bose's leadership, to free India from the English. They ran away like sheep. Why should they be braver with us? I think that if the Indians were used to turn prayer wheels or something like that, they'd be the most untiring soldiers in the world. But to use them in real bloody combat is ridiculous. How strong are the Indians? [—] Besides, it's nonsense. If we had an abundance of weapons, we could afford such jokes for propagandistic reasons. But if we don't have an abundance of weapons, these propagandistic jokes just can't be justified. [—] What's with this so-called Galician division anyway? Is that the same as the Ukrainian division?

BORGMANN: I can't tell.

THE FÜHRER: There's still a Galician division wandering around out there. Is that the same as the Ukrainian? [—] If it consists of Austrian Ruthenians, we can't do anything other than take their weapons away immediately. The Austrian Ruthenians were pacifists. They were lambs, not wolves. They were terrible, even in the Austrian Army. It's all just self-deception. Is this Ukrainian division the same as the so-called Galician division?

GÖHLER: No, the Galician [division] is the 30th and the Ukrainian is the 14th. I think the 30th is being refitted in Slovakia.[1995]

THE FÜHRER: Where has it been fighting?

GÖHLER: The Galician, the 30th, was originally employed in the Tarnow area and hasn't been used again since then.

DE MAIZIÈRE: The division was employed under the command of First Panzer Army during the fighting for Lemberg [L'vov]. I believe it was encircled back then with the XIII Corps, and only a few units returned. It hasn't been employed since then, as far as I know

THE FÜHRER: And it's constantly being refitted?! Does it have weapons as well?

GÖHLER: I'll have to find out.

THE FÜHRER: We can't afford this kind of joke when I can't equip other divisions because I don't have the weapons. It's ridiculous.

GÖHLER: The Ukrainian division has an authorized strength of 11,000 and an actual strength of 14,000.

THE FÜHRER: Why is the actual strength greater than the authorized strength?

GÖHLER: They probably have that many more Ukrainian recruits than the target, so they've integrated them in.

THE FÜHRER: And the arms?

GÖHLER: They handed over a large share of their weapons to the 18th SS[1996] back then.

THE FÜHRER: If they're ready for action now, they seem to have weapons again. I don't want to claim that we can't do anything with these foreigners. We can certainly do something with them. But we would need time for that. If we had them for 6 or 10 years, and the areas themselves were in our own hands, like in the old monarchy, then they would be good soldiers, of course. But if we get them, and the areas are somewhere over there—why should they still fight at all? They're receptive to every form of propaganda. I assume that there's still a very strong German presence in there as well.

(Presentation by Sturmbannführer Göhler.)

GÖHLER: They have the following actual stock of weapons: 2,100 pistols, 610 submachine guns, 9,000 rifles, 70 guns with telescopic sights, 65 machine carbines 43,[1997] 434 light machine guns, 96 heavy machine guns, 58 trucks, four armored personnel carriers (see footnote)[1998] —

THE FÜHRER: We could equip most of two divisions with that.

GÖHLER: —22 flame-throwers, one medium antitank gun, eleven 7.5 cm antitank guns, 17 light infantry guns, three heavy infantry guns Model 33, nine 3.7 cm anti-aircraft artillery pieces, 37 light field howitzers, and six heavy field howitzers.

THE FÜHRER: I have to know now what they're worth. Tomorrow I'd like to speak with the Reichsführer right away. He's in Berlin anyway. We have to go through that very conscientiously now, to determine what can be expected from a unit like that. If we can't expect anything, then it makes no sense. We can't afford the luxury of having units like that.

GÖHLER: The Indian Legion has a strength of about 2,300 men.

THE FÜHRER: We would do them the biggest favor if we told them, "You don't have to fire anymore."

GÖHLER: They have 1,468 carbines, 550 pistols, 420 submachine guns, 200 light machine guns—

THE FÜHRER: Imagine that. They have more weapons than they have men! Some people there have two weapons in their hands!

GÖHLER: —24 heavy machine guns, 20 MKWs,[1999] four light field howitzers, six light infantry guns, six antitank guns—it doesn't say which kind—

700 horses, 81 vehicles, 61 cars, five motorcycles, and twelve eastern model caterpillar tractors,[2000] of which eleven are ready for action.

THE FÜHRER: What is the Indian Legion supposed to do?

GÖHLER: I can't say. It's been getting refurbished for a quite long time.

THE FÜHRER: But it hasn't fought yet.

GÖHLER: No.

THE FÜHRER: I consider a unit to be in refurbishment if it has fought heavily and is now being refurbished again. Your units are always refurbishing replenishing themselves and never fighting.

The West again

BRUDERMÜLLER: Army Group "H" reported at three o'clock that the enemy has also deployed for an attack 1.5 km south of Wesel and at Mehrum. No reports on strength or further developments yet. That was to be expected. There had been remarkably strong fire since 5 p.m., both here on the main battle line and far into the rear area.

THE FÜHRER: Since 1 o'clock?

BRUDERMÜLLER: No, at 3 the message reached the Commander-in-Chief West. Now it's 3:30.

THE FÜHRER: But it must have been expected here, in principle.

BRUDERMÜLLER: We expected it here. The Commander-in-Chief West announced already this evening that he expected the attack on Wesel as well after there had been very strong artillery fire since 5 p.m. and also conspicuously strong fighter-bomber and artillery observation aircraft activity.

THE FÜHRER: Are there paratroopers here?

BRUDERMÜLLER: The 180th [Infantry] Division is here. But it's relatively strong.

THE FÜHRER: It should have 8,000 men.

BRUDERMÜLLER: It has already been filled up. It has nearly full battalions. (Presentation.) In terms of artillery, including the secondary batteries, it has 22 batteries altogether right now—so 22 are in this sector—including eight heavy batteries.

THE FÜHRER: These[2001] are the subordinate ones?

BRUDERMÜLLER: The ones with the squares that aren't filled in are the subordinate ones, and the filled-in squares are their own.

BORGMANN: General Thomale and General Buhle report that there is no unit ready that can be moved to Oppenheim right now. In the Sennelager[2002] there are only five Hunter-Tigers that will be ready today or tomorrow and could be employed in the next few days. There will be two more in a few days, so the unit could be increased to seven. All the others are already in action, and there's nothing else that's almost ready at the moment.

THE FÜHRER: They're at the Sennelager?

BORMANN: Yes, Sir.

THE FÜHRER: They were originally intended for the upper bridgehead.

BORGMANN: Yes, indeed. For Remagen—for the 512th Detachment.

THE FÜHRER: When will they leave?

BORGMANN: They'll be ready today or tomorrow. They can probably roll out tomorrow evening.

THE FÜHRER: Then we'll see about that tomorrow. If we only knew which of the 16 or 17 that were brought back could be repaired, and when! That would be the most important thing.

BORGMANN: I'll ask again, so that General Thomale can give us a clear picture of those 16 by midday or afternoon tomorrow.

BRUDERMÜLLER: I've already informed General Thomale that everything must be done to repair them as quickly as possible, even if the spare parts need to be brought in by air transport, and that if necessary, it's possible that an engineering officer from here, who knows about things, could be sent there. He also reported that he has relieved the detachment commander, the adjutant and the intelligence officer of their duties, because his officers who were down there had told him that they were lacking in energy. He is sending the best man he has by car tomorrow morning.

THE FÜHRER: I didn't get the impression from the detachment commander that he was a real lion.[2003]

JOHANNMEYER: He was in "Adlerhorst" back then.

BURGDORF: If I want to speak with the Inspector General[2004] about filling a detachment on the basis of our information, I immediately have a quarrel .... It's not possible at all. They keep all the special detachments for themselves.

THE FÜHRER: He didn't give a particularly lively impression back then. Or did you have that impression?

JOHANNMEYER: No, he didn't make a particularly good impression. He talked a lot, but in my opinion there wasn't much behind it. General Thomale was very convinced by him at the time.

THE FÜHRER: I don't know.

JOHANNMEYER: He's a man who was very severely wounded. He was wounded eight times, I think. He couldn't be that capable physically, either.

THE FÜHRER: Granted. But that doesn't always prove anything.

BURGDORF: Especially in the panzer troops we have a great number of young, fresh people because they've all come from active units. There we have very good new blood—much better than in the infantry. *Miscellaneous A telegram has also arrived from Gauleiter Forster.[2005]* (*Presentation.*) It concerns pulling out 450 specialists for the security service. There are 12,000 men up there in total.

THE FÜHRER: They claim they don't have enough. But if it's psychologically wrong, we have to refuse.

BURGDORF: Should I respond that they must stay?

THE FÜHRER: Contact Kaltenbrunner[2006] immediately! Kaltenbrunner said he could hardly do without them. But he says that if it's psychologically bad for keeping the thing there, they have to stay.

V. BELOW: I'd like to ask again about the aircraft. Should the 335 be built now, with the units that are planned?[2007]

(THE FÜHRER: Yes.)

When we end production, Speer has suggested stopping the [Me-] 109 totally, right then, so that all the people who are busy with the preparations now won't be used for that anymore, so that everything will stop immediately.

(THE FÜHRER: Yes, indeed.)

And the [Me-] 190 should be turned out in the next four months.

THE FÜHRER: Yes. The 190 is better than the 109?

V. BELOW: Yes, indeed. It's better. It has a better engine and it's more useful as a fighter-bomber than the 109. It would be phased out and be replaced as a fighter-bomber by the 152. It shouldn't be used as a fighter at all.[2008]

THE FÜHRER: Yes. I just think we need fast aircraft with an absolutely superior speed and great security, so they can land even when one engine fails, in order to fight the Mosquito attacks that are becoming more and more frequent. They don't disturb us much, because we're sitting in this deep basement, but they're very unpleasant for the people. A twin-engine aircraft is better for that than a single-engine aircraft—there's no doubt. That's the case with this plane,[2009] and I would prefer it to the tank fighter.

V. BELOW: The tank shouldn't be used in the Reich area or as a fighter at all, but only as a fighter-bomber.

THE FÜHRER: But then we'd still need a plane, as long as the 262 isn't completely safe. I'd think those things would be better for that.

V. BELOW: Then I wanted to suggest that we have a meeting with you some time, with all the people who are involved with the Me 262 now. I would suggest getting together the Reichsmarshal, General Koller, then Kammhuber,[2010] then General Peltz, who is leading the engagement, then Speer, Saur, Degenkolb,[2011] Messerschmitt[2012] and Dorsch—perhaps at the beginning of next week. There are still some questions that only you can clear up.

THE FÜHRER: What what's-his-name said today, I've said the whole time: there's such a disparity between the production and the actual engagement numbers. No other country in the world has that, and it wasn't like that with us before either.

End: 3:34 a.m.

* * * * *

HITLER'S SITUATION REPORTS, APRIL 23, 25, AND 27*

Monday, April 23, 1945

Marshal Zhukov's 1st Belorussian Front and Marshal Koniev's 1st Ukrainian Front—with 2.5 million soldiers, 41,600 guns, 6,250 tanks, 7,560 aircraft—are tightening the screws on the Reich capital. On this day, Red Army units occupy Potsdam and Döberitz west of the city. Fighting is already taking place in the northern and eastern city districts of Frohnau, Friedrichshain, Tegel, Pankow, and Köpenick. Underground [subway] lines C, D and E cease operating, and in Kantstrasse the inhabitants hang the first white flags out of their windows. In the Führer bunker under the Reich Chancellery, not far from Potsdamer Platz, Adolf Hitler appoints Artillery General Helmuth Weidling as commanding officer of the Berlin defense area. Using random units—44,630 soldiers, 42,531 Volkssturm men, 3,532 Hitler Youth, Labor Service men, and members of the Todt Organization— General Weidling is supposed to withstand the pressure of the 2.5 million Soviet soldiers; only one of every two German defenders has a rifle. Wenck's "army" (three weak divisions)—ordered by Hitler to carry out a relief operation on behalf of the capital—still remains 60 kilometers southwest of Berlin. To the south of the Reich, American and French troops reach the Danube River on this day, in the area of Donaueschingen; to the northwest and north, British and Canadian forces attack Delmenhorst and Hamburg; and in the east, Soviet troops are fighting in the Lausitz and in East Prussia. From Berchtesgaden, Reichsmarshal Göring telegraphs to Führer Headquarters that if no other order is issued, he will take over governmental responsibilities. At 9 a.m. Hitler orders—in vain—that Göring be arrested.

* * * * *

Present (April 23):

Adolf Hitler
Field Marshal Wilhelm Keitel, Chief of the Armed Forces High Command (OKW)
General Hans Krebs, Provisional Chief of the Army General Staff
General Wilhelm Burgdorf, Chief Adjutant of the Armed Forces

---

* [NDT: In these final transcripts, Hitler is identified by name, rather than as "The Führer."]

SS Gruppenführer Hermann Fegelein, Deputy to the Reichsführer SS at the Führer Headquarters

Colonel Ernst Kaether, from April 22 to 23 commanding officer of the Berlin Defense Area

HITLER: When can we expect the auxiliaries to arrive?

KREBS: That issue is still unresolved. Except for the two promised battalions, additional forces are not immediately available. Whatever we could get has been brought in here.

KEITEL: The two battalions won't be here before tomorrow morning, even if everything runs smoothly.

HITLER: It's very late. By then he [the Russian] could already be standing in the city center. There can be no discussion of a real defense if no troops are there. [—] I heard shocking news again: in one area the troops withdrew. The Volkssturm and Hitler Youth repaired the thing again. The troops had received withdrawal orders from someone.

KREBS: There was action there. The thing was brought under control again at the cost of numerous and bloody losses. Except for the *Nordland* Division, there are no units of foreign origin on any part of the front.

HITLER: An entire corps has disappeared completely. Only the SS Division *Nordland* is there. Everything else has disappeared, including the corps commander. The only unit that didn't follow that is *Nordland*. That's so disgraceful! If I think about it all, why then still live at all!

KEITEL: The Wenck unit must throw something in the way of motorized vehicles into Berlin immediately.

BURGDORF: Wenck has four German Labor Service Divisions and no weapons!

HITLER: Then naval units must come as well.

KREBS: The enemy's general offensive is becoming dangerous, because, for the moment, he's still making no attempt to go into Berlin, but instead to seal it off.

HITLER: All available reserves must be provided to Wenck, even if they're poorly armed, in order to fill in the gap. No additional reinforcements are to be given to Steiner.[2013] Keitel, find out what battalions are still coming in.

KEITEL: Yes, my Führer, everything will be done.

* * * * *

2ND SITUATION REPORT, APRIL 23, 1945

HITLER: Forces must be brought into Berlin by all possible means in order to cover the Grunewald. Berlin is now the main point of attraction for the enemy. The enemy knows I am here. The enemy will do everything in order to concentrate here. That could provide the best opportunity for us to lead him into a trap here. But that presupposes that we finally recognize the significance of this hour on our side, and work very obediently according to the plan ordered from above. Everyone must work honestly! This up here [indicating Army Group Steiner, which was to line up from the north for a relief attack on Berlin] is not honest! Steiner has too many doubts in view of the defensive front standing before of him.

KREBS: I believe we still have four days' time.

HITLER: In four days the thing will have been decided

* * * * *

3RD SITUATION REPORT, APRIL 23, 1945

HITLER: The following should be brought in during the course of the afternoon, if at all possible: two battalions of the *Grossdeutschland* Division. It may be possible to add some other battalion to that. In the government quarter, there are the following reserves: the Führer Escort Company, except for two platoons that are already employed; a Volksstorm battalion from the Propaganda Ministry with three companies; and a Volksstorm company of the Reich Chancellery. Together a strength of around 3,500 men. The Reichsführer SS wanted to send his battalion over here as a last reserve as well.

KREBS: Volunteer soldiers and SS men have strengthened the forces manning the innermost defensive ring in the government quarter.

HITLER: We have to watch out that Seydlitz's soldiers and officers don't come in here as well.[2014] Up here on the Havel [northwest of Berlin] a difficult situation arose. If this threatens to collapse, it will be a mess and a serious mistake on the part of the command. Everything that comes in should be employed against that now. We also have to pull everything out from here. The 7th Panzer Division must be employed here in order to eliminate this mess. [—] The current enemy pressure indicates that the enemy's initial intention is to encircle Berlin and thus cut off the supply lines to Berlin. The Luftwaffe must take absolutely everything they still have and concentrate it up here, and quickly! We're dealing with minutes. Also here between Treuenbrietzen and Schwielowsee, everything must be thrown forward in order to cut this off here. The thing up on the Havel must also be brought under control as quickly as possible.

FEGELEIN: The important thing is to clear the street system.

HITLER: In Potsdam we must hold at all cost. Group Steiner has to move down the Havel [River].

KAETHER: New reports just arrived. There are ten to twelve very heavy enemy tanks on Landsberger Strasse east of the main fighting line, supposedly Stalin models. Behind that, innumerable additional tanks. Therefore, [they are] considerably stronger than originally reported. Not only the stated 40, but considerably more. As far as the eye can see. Luftwaffe support was ordered, and engagement has been announced. Artillery commands were ordered to act against that with concentrated fire.

HITLER: We have to go down low with bombers and really destroy them. Our assault guns are a bit too weak when faced with these things.

* * * * *

WEDNESDAY, APRIL 25, 1945

The Soviet ring around Berlin closes. At around 1 p.m., the attacking spearheads of the 4th Guards Tank Army, advancing from the south, and the units of the Soviet 47th Army advancing from the north, link up at Ketzin, twelve kilometers northwest of Potsdam. In the Reich capital, the Soviets push forward from the south to the Neubabelsberg-Zehlendorf-Neukölln line. In Spandau, Hitler Youth under the leadership of National Political Education Institute chief, SS Gruppenführer Heissmeyer, are encircled. Weidling, the city commander, explains to Hitler with the help of a standard city map that the German front is being systematically pushed back to the city center. Acting against a Führer order, General Busse's Ninth Army doesn't fight its way through to Berlin from the southeast of the German capital, but instead attempts to break through to the west into American captivity. On the front east of Berlin, the Soviets reach Görlitz, Bautzen and Kamenz, and, in the southeast, Brünn. The British reach a line between Bremen on the Weser and Horneburg on the Elbe. The Americans advance through the Bavarian forest to the south; in central Germany they meet the Soviets' western advancing spearheads at Torgau: the remainder of the Reich is cut in half.

* * * * *

HITLER: The British and the Americans are being quiet on the Elbe [River]. They've probably agreed on some kind of demarcation line. In Berlin it looks worse than it really is. The Berlin area must be cleared, emptied of people, in so far as possible. The 12th [Wenck] and 9th [Busse] Armies, which are forming fixed fronts in the west and east, must be pulled into Berlin. The divisions in Berlin must be filled up, however possible, using the local population. Recruiting columns must be set up in order to bring everyone in. In Berlin, General Weidling has the central command; Colonel Kaether is his deputy. One division staff or another will still come in. The cadre units will be put in order and replenished again, so we'll have divisions. Everything else that comes in will be integrated into these divisions so that a real order will develop. [—] Southwestern Germany is fragile. Even my influence from Berchtesgaden couldn't have prevented that. The defeatist mood was there [even] earlier. The three men responsible are no longer alive. They have poisoned the whole Western Front from the beginning—a society corrupted by its luxury. [—] I can achieve success here alone. If I do achieve a success, even if it's only a moral one, at least it's an opportunity to save face and gain time. One thing I do know. It's totally useless to go south, because I have no influence and no armies there. I would be there with just my staff. I could only hold a southern German Ostmärk mountain block, even though Italy could also be maintained as a war theater. But there as well, total defeatism dominates the leadership, which is devoured from the top down.

GOEBBELS: In Berlin we can achieve a moral success on a global scale. This success can only be achieved here, where the eyes of the entire world are directed. The fact that the Russians are marching into Brandenburg won't be regretted as much as if Berlin were to be taken into their possession. But if they are driven back in front of Berlin, then that would be the basis for a great example for the world.

HITLER: If it's really true. I received news that the talks between Eden and Molotov apparently didn't reach a compromise. The Russians demand the whole area. That would mean the whole war would be lost for the British. England started this war because I demanded a corridor to East Prussia and Danzig, with approval under Allied control. And now they're supposed to allow a power that now dominates practically the whole of Europe already and extends into East Asia to advance even further? [—] I believe that the moment has come when the instinct for self-preservation will cause the others to stand up anyway against this immoderate and proletarian-Bolshevist colossus and Moloch [Devil]. If I were to run away from here today like a coward, the result would be that the others would try to erect in southern Germany a kind of neutral line, and that would be all. Then National Socialism would be eliminated and the German Reich as well. If I strike here successfully and hold the capital, then the hope might grow among the British and the Americans that they might possibly be able to oppose this danger with a Nazi Germany after all. And I am the only man for this.

GOEBBELS: If such a conception is possible at all, which is debatable, then it would only be possible through you and only in this place. If you leave this city, you lose everything else as well. You can't give up Berlin with the idea that you can defend yourself here or somewhere else.

HITLER: I have said that to the gentlemen as well. I said, "The situation is not such that I have a completely stable front down here in southern Germany and have a buffer zone and don't want to leave Berlin out of sheer obstinacy." I see where the development is going. All my attempts to influence the tactics are simply useless. Insane and catastrophic mistakes were made during the defense of the Rhineland as well as in other places. All the plans I worked out failed simply because the ground was pulled out from under them through the arbitrary acts of junior commanders.

KREBS: Field Marshal Keitel has issued the following orders. The combat group of the 7th Panzer Division goes to Nauen and then to Berlin. One of our assault gun groups will go to Berlin immediately. The command structure according to Jodl's proposal. Subordination of Army Group Vistula under the Armed Forces Operations Staff in Rheinsberg, as of this evening. Wenck will take over the command as soon he has influence over Group Holste. The thrust to the south from Löwenberg will start this evening.

GOEBBELS: The war situation is such today that only a visible symbol can achieve something.

HITLER: As an inglorious refugee from Berlin, I would have no authority in either northern or southern Germany, and in Berchtesgaden even less.

GOEBBELS: In 1933 the party was so weakened that without your personal action only further failure would have come. Only by means of your personal effort was everything else swept along. If you had left Berlin on Sunday, Berlin would not be in our hands today.

HITLER: With what was I then supposed to hold the south against the west? You see, it's like that everywhere: a name guarantees a certain order. Wherever there's a name, a personality, there's order. As long as there was a personality in Italy, there was a certain order here. Under Vietinghoff, the demoralizing influences again became stronger.[2015] [—] It was those smartasses that Clausewitz warned of—people who always see the easier way as more intelligent. Actually, the easier way is stupider. And then the false cleverness on top of that. For me there's no doubt: The battle has reached a climax here. [—] If it's really true that differences will arise among the Allies in San Francisco—and they will arise—then a change can only come about if I strike at the Bolshevik colossus at one point. Then the others might come to the conclusion after all that there is only one who is in a position to stop the Bolshevik colossus, and that is I and the party and today's German state. [—] If fate decides differently, then I would vanish from the stage of world history as an inglorious refugee. But I would consider it a thousand times more cowardly to commit suicide at the Obersalzberg than to stand here and fall. [—] One shouldn't say, "You, as the Führer…" [—] I am the Führer as long I can really lead. I can't lead by setting myself on a mountain somewhere; I must have authority over armies that obey. Let me achieve a victory here, and even though it may still be difficult and hard, then I will have the right again to eliminate the lazy elements that are constantly creating obstructions; then I will work with the generals who have proven their worth. Only a heroic attitude can enable us to stand this difficult time. [—] Also earlier in history, the Asian assault wasn't broken by the fact that everyone surrendered; somewhere he must be stopped. We experienced ourselves once, how difficult it is to negotiate with Molotov. We were at the height of our power then. Here stands the Asian khan, who wants to conquer Europe. England realizes quite clearly that Bolshevism will continue to devour beyond the points already reached today. This is now the decisive battle. [—] If I win this battle, then I expect nothing from it for my personal name. But then I will be rehabilitated. Then I can eliminate a number of generals and lower officers, including in the SS, who have failed at decisive points. But for all those I accuse of withdrawing, I have to provide an example, so that I don't withdraw myself. [—] It's also possible that I will fall here. But then I will have perished in a decent way. But that would be still better than if I would sit as an inglorious refugee to Berchtesgaden, giving orders from there that are of no use. This so-called southern fortress is not self-sufficient. That's an illusion. The armies down there are fragile. There's just nothing that can be done in the south. [—] I can see the possibility of repairing the thing only if I achieve a success in some place. Bear in mind the repercussions on the British. If we defend Berlin successfully today—and certain signs of an anti-Russian mood are emerging—then they will see that the people who possess the appropriate farsightedness will again take a bit of courage in the face of this colossus. These people might then say to themselves: if we were to go with Nazi Germany, then maybe we could hold our ground against this colossus after all.

GOEBBELS: It would also be encouraging for the other side. If Stalin sees this development in the Western States that's based on a German victory in Berlin, then he would say to himself, "I won't get the Europe that I had in mind. I'm only bringing the Germans and the British together. So I will strike a balance with the Germans and make some sort of agreement." Frederick the Great was once in a similar situation. He also got all of his authority back after the Battle of Leuthen. If the Führer proves that it can be done—that one can stay, and that one can win a battle by staying—then these executions will have an educational meaning and not a crushing effect.

HITLER: It's simply unbearable for me personally to have other people shot for things that I do myself. I wasn't born just to defend my Berghof alone.

GOEBBELS: If the thing in the south and west had been different, and if it had just been about a Battle for Berlin—like, for example, for Breslau—then I would have strongly protested against your coming to Berlin and making a prestige issue out of it. But the developments have now made this Battle for Berlin into a prestige case after all. The Führer has decided to oppose the Russian enemy in this place, and has appealed to the German people of Berlin to follow him one last time. This situation must be fought through now, in one way or another.

HITLER: There was no problem for me here at all. It's the only possibility at all to restore my personal reputation. Somewhere, the power of the Greater Asian Khan must be broken. Back then it was the Battle of Vienna [1683]. Now it's the Battle for Berlin. When Vienna was freed, the entire Turkish power wasn't broken instantly. It took years still. But it was a signal. If the Viennese had surrendered like cowards at that time, then Turkish power would have continued to advance.

GOEBBELS: It seems important to me that as long as we're not getting any relief from the outside, we have to keep our defense area around Berlin as large as possible.

HITLER: The narrower we are, the worse it is. [—] The Allies will have created a demarcation line on the basis of diplomatic agreements. But the Russians certainly aren't thinking about observing it. I know how it was in the winter of 1940. I didn't go to war against Moscow out of carelessness, but because, on the basis of certain information, I knew that an alliance between England and Russia was being prepared. The question was whether we should begin to strike ourselves or whether we should wait and be crushed to death sometime. [—] Now, I became acquainted with Molotov at that time. The Russians hadn't achieved any overwhelming international successes at that time. They were defeated in Finland. Then they occupied a few areas. In the Polish campaign they waited too long—until we were well past the agreed demarcation line. Then came our campaign in the West, in which we achieved a huge victory. The Russians hadn't expected that at all. It was the biggest victory in the history of the world. Then came the various demonstrations by our Luftwaffe against England. And in this whole situation, Molotov demanded things from us in Berlin that were outrageous. [—] He demanded from us that we withdraw from bases on Danish territory at the exit to the North Sea. He had already announced a claim to that back then. He demanded Constantinople, Romania, Bulgaria, Finland—and we were the winners at that time! How will this Molotov act now toward the British and the Americans with such victories and after these catastrophic failures of the Allies. [—] Now this Asian conflict is added to that. In America, sober thinkers will say: what do we want here anyway? Capital investment, perhaps? But we won't gain markets here. There are resources for us in China. On the other hand, they don't want Russia to enter the war against Japan. They say: we'll handle Japan alone.

GOEBBELS: If the Soviets advance up to the Elbe, including the Protectorate [of Bohemia], then the Americans will disappear from here. Only 20 to 25 British divisions will remain. Pacifist and salon Bolshevik propaganda will begin among the British troops. Stalin will militarize his area, including the German area. He will fight with propaganda against the Western forces because they destroyed the cities. He's a better propagandist than the British. [—] The Soviets can play on all pianos. A conflict will arise here in a very short time. I can't imagine that there are intelligent Englishmen who don't see that.

HITLER: Now it's going to happen. What Lloyd George[2016] once told me: the provisional peace treaty. Back then Lloyd George declared in a memorandum, "The Peace of Versailles can't be maintained and is insane. England is destroying the European balance." It was a classic prophetic memorandum by Lloyd George. [—] If we were to leave the world stage so disgracefully, then we would have lived in vain. It's completely unimportant if we continue to live for a while still or not. Better to end the battle honorably than to go on living in shame and dishonor for a few more months or years.

GOEBBELS: If the thing goes well, it's fine anyway. If it doesn't go well and the Führer were to find an honorable death in Berlin and Europe were to become Bolshevik, in five years at the latest the Führer would be a legendary personality and National Socialism a myth. He would be hallowed by his last great action, and everything human that they criticize in him today would be swept away in one stroke.

HITLER: That's the decision: to save everything here and only here, and to put the last man into action—that's our duty.

* * * * *

2ND SITUATION REPORT, APRIL 25, 1945

HITLER: There's a formal denial from TASS, which implies that the demarcation line is definitely fixed. [—] I've thought about the situation in East Asia. If the Americans have any interest in winning something from this war now, then the war must prove useful for them in some way. It can only be useful if they

1. Destroy as much as possible in Europe. European industry will then need the next ten years to build itself back up again, and won't provide any competition during that time.

2. America must maintain East Asia as a permanent market. And the Americans are now supposed to fight so that the Dutch and British colonies will become free—only so that the others can make deals and the Soviets can sit in China and Manchuria. [—] It's all madness! The Americans can calculate, too. The change that has taken place now is a far-reaching change of regime.[2017] [—] If the thing comes to a halt here, what will the result be? The result will be, under the precondition that we really persist and that we really strike the Russian and give him a blow somewhere and don't

collapse—the result will be that the Americans will say, "We want to concentrate on East Asia and secure ourselves a gigantic, lasting market in this enormous area of half a billion people, including Korea, the Philippines, and Manchuria."

GOEBBELS: It's a political development that is striking, but which needs an external impulse to become virulent—like the Great War, for example. They themselves admit that the enemy coalition is ready to break. They talk of the Third World War, etc. The notion of a Third World War is a set formulation of the Anglo-American press. The death of Roosevelt was one of the impulses, but that still wasn't sufficient. If a second impulse comes along here—if Germany proves somewhere that it's capable of action—then that could be the second impulse needed to break up this hostile coalition.

HITLER: It could happen that the isolationists say: American boys can only fight for American interests. Why should the Americans die for non-American purposes? In all those countries there's no democracy at all—for example, Romania, Bulgaria, Finland. The Americans could withdraw here and throw themselves against East Asia alone, thereby binding the Russian here at the same time—because they would free us—so that the Russian can't engage himself so much in East Asia.

* * * * *

FRIDAY, APRIL 27, 1945

Soviet soldiers cut the Reich capital off from its last connections with the outside world; they occupy the airports of Tempelhof and Gatow. Now Berlin can no longer be supplied by air either. On both sides of the Hohenzollerndamm, after strong artillery preparation, the offensive against the city center begins at five o'clock in the morning. Soviet units encircle Potsdam and occupy Spandau; they fight in the Schöneberg and Kreuzberg districts. In Mariendorf the occupation power sets up the first mayor's office. Soviet war reporter Guss observes on this day: "The Germans run from one street to another: they search for underground storehouses and pull out women's handbags, hats, gloves…The 'master race' covers huge distances on foot in order to loot." The center of the battles in the northwest of the Reich is at Bremen. In southern Germany, the Americans push against the Danube line at Deggendorf and march into the northern part of Ulm. The Soviets take Pillau (East Prussia), break through to the west at Prenzlau, and push forward to the Lychen-Templin line. On this day it is revealed that Reichsführer SS Heinrich Himmler had offered the Western Allies surrender negotiations through the Swedish Count Folke Bernadotte. Berlin defender Weidling states, "The moment had come to settle the bill for the sins of the past years."

*****

Present (April 27):

Adolf Hitler
Joseph Goebbels, Reich Propaganda Minister and Reich Defense Commissioner
Arthur Axmann, Reich Youth Leader
General Hans Krebs, Provisional Chief of the Army General Staff
General Helmuth Weidling, Commanding Officer of the Berlin Defense Area
SS Brigadeführer and Major General of the Waffen SS Wilhelm Mohnke, combat commander of the Berlin government quarter "Zitadelle"
Colonel Nikolaus von Below, Hitler's adjutant (Luftwaffe)
Vice Admiral Hans-Erich Voss, Representative of the Commander-in-Chief of the Navy in the Führer Headquarters

KREBS: Brünn is lost. [—] Schörner is now starting to advance in a northerly direction.[2018] Strong attack against the Ninth Army from the south by the Russian 28th Army, which had been pulled out of East Prussia.

HITLER: The best relief for that would be the thrust by Schörner now.

KREBS: Wenck has reached the southern corner of the Schwielowsee. The Potsdam Defense Area wants to create a bridgehead at Caputh. Very strong attacks against the southern group of the Ninth Army [General Busse]. The enemy broke through and turned in to the east. We reached Müggendorf in an attack to the west, but we're being attacked in the deep flank by the enemy. Serious supply difficulties, no fuel. Fuel will be brought in today by the Sixth Air Fleet. Stronger enemy attack from the northeast and east.

HITLER: I don't understand the direction of the attack. He [General Busse] is pushing into completely empty space.

KREBS: The freedom to move has diminished considerably.

HITLER: He's pushing into the void. If he had pushed forward to the northwest and had reached the same as now, then he would be considerably further west now.

GOEBBELS: The Gau just reported that Group Wenck has linked up with the Potsdam bridgehead.

HITLER: If an energetic thrust really does take place here, this whole thing here will come into motion, because the enemy has only rear units here.

KREBS: No further enemy progress toward the west. Keitel reports that Group Holste has won ground with weaker assault groups at Nauen and Kremmen, and that these groups will be reinforced by units from the 199th [Infantry] Division.[2019]

HITLER: It is getting very urgent that they start.

KREBS: If that were to happen, the prospect of establishing a connection would certainly be possible.

HITLER: I repeat once again how much better the Ninth Army would have been able to operate. The connection between Wenck and the Ninth Army would already have been established by now.

KREBS: It's very unpleasant in the Third Panzer Army's sector. Relatively thin front lines have been penetrated in depth at Prenzlau. It has been ordered that a new line be formed and defended. No reports about Stettin. The enemy has set foot on the island across from Kammin. No change along the Elbe.

HITLER: It almost supports the idea that they have a demarcation line. They're not appearing in the air either.

KREBS: Wenck has three divisions: *Körner, Hutten,* and *Scharnhorst.* He's pulling additional forces in behind him. Report from Wenck: "The significance of the task is understood. Proceeding with all forces against ordered objectives." [—] By tomorrow morning considerable reinforcement should have arrived in the northwest. The last units of the 7th Panzer Division, the *Schlageter* division, and some units of the 199th Division, of which the first units supposedly already arrived in Kyritz yesterday, without a regiment. General Holste will command that then. [—] In Wannsee the 20th Panzer Grenadier Division is holding. No new reports from Gatow, but it probably held. The bridges are being held. The connection has been interrupted.

HITLER: If Wenck really comes up, he'll immediately connect with the Wannsee group.

KREBS: If that happens tomorrow, the group could face the enemy with 40 tanks and assault guns.

HITLER: The thrust to the Schwielowsee should take effect soon.

KREBS: In Berlin the enemy has advanced far to the north. He supposedly pushed forward across Bülowstrasse up to the corner of Lützowstrasse. On the bridge at the Halleschen Tor there are supposedly two enemy tanks on fire. Three companies that made the counterattack are encircled at Moritzplatz. Jannowitz Bridge is unchanged. The enemy came closer to Alexanderplatz. In general, it held in the northeast. Unpleasant penetration at the Humboldthain railway station. Flak towers encircled here. Back-and-forth battles at the western harbor. The enemy supposedly drove around with assault boats. Supposedly enemy tanks north of the Witzleben railway station. A panzer thrust is in progress against it. In the Grunewald, the Reich Labor Service is holding out with assault guns and is connected with the right and left. The bridges of Pichelsdorf and Stössensee are holding. The enemy advanced at the Ruhleben Race Track but was stopped to the south.

HITLER: A city of millions can't be occupied by 400 tanks. That will crumble.

KREBS: In general, it has been confirmed that the intention of the enemy in the past six days must have been the following:
1. Encirclement in general;
2. Isolation in small parts, which succeeded in the west;
3. Now he will push against Potsdamer Platz, Alexanderplatz, and the Charlottenburg railway station, in order to try to divide the city center into individual parts.

HITLER: We must hold a number of assault guns ready here in the middle, as a central reserve. [—] The only thing crippling us is the fact that we don't know exactly what's happening and that we don't have precise data and are dependent on chance news. We have to push again and again.

BELOW: Air supply should start now with the help of He 111s and Ju 87s. At […] the Jus should come with the rest of the SS battalion and the units of Navy soldiers.

VOSS: The Luftwaffe must free at least one airfield where we can fly the people in. But without an airfield it's bad. One hundred men are coming in on the east-west axis today for your personal protection. Those are fellows who will help us here. If Wenck frees the Gatow airfield, then there's no problem at all.

HITLER: The decisive thing is the attack from north to south, and now also from the northwest. We have to tackle it from all sides so we can achieve a success somewhere again.

KREBS: It looks like the Russian didn't send such strong forces against the Elbe as was first assumed. Perhaps he turned in because he hoped to be able to take Berlin with weaker forces.

HITLER: If the thing goes well here—if action is taken from all sides, and if everything available is committed to the operation we're planning—then it's critical that not everyone believes it necessary to still secure a rear cover for himself, as does Steiner, unfortunately. If we can hold two, three or four days here, then it's possible that Wenck's Army will arrive and possibly also Busse's army. Otherwise, it would have been better if Busse had lined up further to the north.

KREBS: A withdrawal of forces from Berlin still can't be identified. It should have started to become noticeable against Wenck as of today—in the Grunewald area, which is very awkward for us. Wenck is moving with tremendous speed, which is also due to the fact that the enemy is relatively weak.

HITLER: And to that fact that Wenck himself is a man.

KREBS: If Holste gets it in motion in the same way, then I would consider it possible that this relief could come from the northwest and southwest and allow us to establish connections right in those locations where the enemy broke through to the west. We'll have to wait and see to what degree a relief attack materializes on the eastern front.

HITLER: If only we could get a completely accurate picture! I am very worried that Busse's Army is blocking itself off. Colonel General Hube of the First Panzer Army, for example, always kept his situation wide back then, if he was encircled. [—] Wenck can't do it either with only three divisions. That's sufficient to clear out Potsdam and to establish a connection somewhere with the forces that have come out of Berlin. But it's not sufficient to crush the Russian tank forces. But Busse has the panzer forces necessary for that. The panzers that Wenck is bringing are too few. Wenck isn't really motorized. He has three assault gun detachments with 38 T. He has two assault gun training regiments employed as infantry units. Of his three divisions, he'll need at least half to cover the south block. It depends how fast we take away the forces from the east and seal off the opponent at the place where he has to come out.

GOEBBELS: God grant that Wenck comes! I imagine a horrible situation: Wenck is near Potsdam and here the Soviets are pushing on Potsdamer Platz!

HITLER: And I'm not in Potsdam, but at Potsdamer Platz! The only thing that makes me nervous in all this tension is the fact that we want to do something and can't do anything after all. I can't sleep anymore; if I ever really fall asleep, then comes the bombing. [—] The decisive thing is that someone who attacks first and then gets slower and slower doesn't advance! The one who advances is the one who attacks with concentrated power and starts attacking immediately like an idiot. It's a question of disposition.

VOSS: Wenck is coming, my Führer! The only question is if he can manage it alone.

HITLER: You have to imagine. That will spread through Berlin like wildfire when it is said, "A German army broke in from the west and made connection with the fortress." The Russian won't be able do anything but throw in new things again and again in an attempt to hold his widely scattered positions. There will be a first-rate focal point here. The Russian has used up much of his strength crossing the Oder, especially the northern army group. Second, he's using up a large number forces in the house-to-house combat. If up to 50 T 34 or Stalin [tanks] are knocked out every day, then in ten days that's 500 to 600 tanks destroyed. [—] Today I will lie down a bit more at ease, and I only want to be awakened if a Russian tank is standing in front of my room, so I have time to make my preparations. [—] With all this back and forth, there's no other possible way we can cause the opponent real damage other than by the method we're using. We had to hold Berlin because here the Russian can be forced to bleed to death. What else is supposed to stop the Russian if he can even march straight through here? [—] Richelieu once said, "Give me five lines written by a man! What have I lost! Dearest memories!" But what does that all mean? Eventually you have to leave it all behind anyway.

* * * * *
2ND SITUATION REPORT, APRIL 27, 1945

MOHNKE: Four enemy tanks and two Czech tanks advanced to the Wilhelmplatz. They were knocked out by tank destroyer troops. The tanks had Swastika pennants. We captured the crew of one tank.

HITLER: The identification order must be scrupulously maintained.

MOHNKE: The main battle line still runs across the Moritzplatz. The battalion at the Moritzplatz has been fought free again. Behind the block we want to form small intervention forces everywhere, so that if any penetration should occur, they can eliminate it again in a counterattack. I've brought 10.5-cm light field howitzers into position at the Gendarmenmarkt, aimed in the direction of the Belle-Alliance-Platz, and to the Pariser Platz, aimed in the direction of the Unter-Den-Linden-Palace, also in Leipziger Strasse, aimed in the direction of the Spittelmarkt. Every gun has twelve rounds. As soon as these are fired, the crews will fight like infantry. The enemy firing has decreased somewhat for the moment. An 8.8-cm self-propelled gun came back from Adolf-Hitler-Platz. It stayed there until 14:00 and didn't see a single enemy tank.

GOEBBELS: The Soviets really are motorized robot people. A deadly danger! [—] If the western harbor is lost, we still have individual supply stores in the subway tunnels. The western harbor was the last major reserve. During the last few days, we brought materiel out of the western harbor under artillery fire. But there are 24 tons of grain stored there.

HITLER: By assaulting a city of 4.5 million, the Russian has brought a colossal load upon himself. How many wounded do we have every day?

GOEBBELS: We have 9,000 wounded in the hospitals; so maybe 1,500 wounded every day. [—] If relief actually comes to Berlin, then the supply won't create huge difficulties for us. Because the Russian won't be in a position to transport away such huge amounts in a few days. The supply in Berlin is sufficient for ten weeks. The Russian can't devour in four days what three million are supposed to eat up in ten weeks.

HITLER: If I were ever to be in a position to build government buildings again, then I might equip them with appropriate precautionary measures.

GOEBBELS: I believe every one of us resolved some things for his life.

MOHNKE: What we wanted in 1933 we have not completely achieved, my Führer!

HITLER: You know, I said recently, "It might have been better if I had waited another year to a year and a half."

GOEBBELS: In 1932 you only wanted to come to power as Reich president.

HITLER: I said at that time. The time hasn't come yet, because I had the conviction that if such a total revolution comes, everything else will be completely ruined. If someone is still there, there's always someone else in the background—for example, Hugenberg or Schleicher.[2020] If I had waited still longer, the death of Reich President Hindenburg would have come. He would have died half a year earlier because I would have upset him so much in the opposition. If anyone was called to be German Reich president, it was I…. Then I could have stepped in without being hindered by anything. If you don't settle such accounts immediately, you become sympathetic and don't settle them at all.

GOEBBELS: That happened because you had to make a number of personnel compromises. If, for example, you had received power as Reich president, then you would never have made Admiral Levetzow police president of Berlin. The fact that such a huge number of elements came from abroad at that time can be traced back to the fact that we had such idiots as police presidents.

HITLER: I had to work my way through from one compromise to the next. That lasted until Hindenburg's death. I had intended beforehand to ruthlessly call to account people like Colonel General Hammerstein, Schleicher and others, and the whole bunch around that scum. But after a year and a half, this resolve gradually became weaker. The big building-up work came. Otherwise thousands would have been eliminated at that time. In the meantime, they were assimilated.

GOEBBELS: I know how back in March [1933] so many of these "March casualties" got into the party. There was real fury about that at the time. When we didn't want to accept those elements then, we were asked if we didn't want reconciliation. It would have been better to close the party and say: no one else can join anymore.

HITLER: We could have done that if I had come to power by an explicit act of popular will or by a coup d'état. We regret afterward that we're so good.

GOEBBELS: All the Austrian Gauleiters also said at that time that the revolution had a cosmetic defect. It would have been better if Vienna had resisted [in 1938 during the Anschluss of Austria to the Reich] and we could have destroyed everything.

MOHNKE: Those are two examples: 1933 and 1938. And if it goes well now, my Führer, we shall not let this hour pass by again.

HITLER: That's also why I'm staying here, so that I have a bit more moral right to take action against weakness. Otherwise I wouldn't have the moral right. I can't keep threatening others if I myself run away from the Reich capital in the critical hour. We have to introduce certain codes of honor into the entire Armed Forces. A basic principle that the Navy has always followed must be brought into the party and must apply to every individual: in this city I've had the right to give orders; now I must also obey the orders of fate. Even if I could save myself, I won't do it. A captain also goes down with his ship.

VOSS: Here in the Reich chancellery it's just the same as on the bridge of a ship. One thing is true for everyone. We don't want to go away either. We belong together. It's just important that we are a decent community. The people who are together with us must be decent fellows.

HITLER: It is possible to educate people to have an attitude like that. It's not true that the Japanese are supposed to be better soldiers then we are. They're just better educated. If we hear today that the Americans captured a total of seven Japanese officers who were all seriously wounded, and that all seven committed hara-kiri immediately after their capture, then you can see what kind of heroism can be created through systematic education.

KREBS: I told Jodl that we have only 24 to 26 hours; by then the link up between the armies of Wenck and Busse must be completed. Assuming, of course, that we succeed in receiving the announced transmissions this evening. [—] The situation with the Third Panzer Army is considered serious. Keitel wanted to turn in from the south to the north. I said that was impossible. We first have to free Berlin. I said that the enemy attacks must be parried, of course. Grand Admiral Dönitz is with Keitel today. Everything seems to be coming together so that the Navy forces can be flown in to Berlin. In the northwestern area a stronger panzer group is to be formed, whose task it is to work toward Wenck's Army.

HITLER: I have two concerns. We no longer have any oil areas. As long as we had them, anything could be done. The two oil areas in Austria provided us with a total of 120,000 tons. That could be increased to 180,000 tons. That is catastrophic because it makes large-scale operations impossible. Once I finish this thing here, we'll have to make sure that we get the oil areas back again. The others are fighting using oil areas that are far away across the oceans. We have them right in front of our gates.

* * * * *

3RD SITUATION REPORT, APRIL 27, 1945

KREBS: In contrast to yesterday evening, a consolidation of the situation and an absolutely cohesive front can be identified. Overall picture: primary pressure right now from the east and north. Relatively stable in the southwest. To that extent, a different picture from yesterday. That could be associated with the fact that the enemy has achieved his aim—to close off —here. But it could also be related to the withdrawal of forces to the southwest. [—] Regarding the situation in detail: Situation of the Reich Sports Field unclear. Smaller German groups are still holding without connection to each other. South of Pichelsdorf Bridge, a larger bridgehead is being held. Individual vehicles came through from there to here. Cohesive front along Bismarckstrasse, including the radio tower and the Grunewald quarter, where the Reich Labor Service, under the command of General Labor Leader Decker, is particularly distinguishing itself. Only a very thin communication line to Bülowstrasse via the Wilmersdorf railway station and the ring railway to the Schöneberg station. The enemy penetration up to the corner of Lützowstrasse no longer exists. There's a penetration in the direction of Spittelmarkt that hasn't been cleared. The eastern front has held despite the heaviest pressure now. The battle for Friedrichshain has been influenced especially positively by the commander of the anti-aircraft artillery, who is supporting the land battle extraordinarily well from the flak tower. This front has already held like this for several days. Pressure against the Wedding railway station driven back. The details of the situation in the western harbor are unclear; part of it is still in our hands.

AXMANN: The bridgehead south of Pichelsdorf Bridge was strengthened by a company. Attack on Heerstrasse driven back.

KREBS: The Russian will probably come with his main pressure from the east, north and south now. We have to expect an attempt at a surprise break-through from various sides tonight, especially if the enemy assesses the threat from the southwest as stronger.

AXMANN: The Russians are in the Charlottenburg Palace as well now.

MOHNKE: Individual Russian snipers appeared at Potsdamer Platz.

HITLER: The shafts of the subway and city trains are a danger.

KREBS: We assume that the connection has been made at Schwielowsee. The connection with Potsdam has been interrupted. In Wannsee a combat group is holding the bridgehead. The Gatow airfield is still in our hands. Fighting with tanks for barracks north of the airfield.

HITLER: The catastrophic mistake of the Ninth Army was to begin the attack to the west and not to the northwest. The army allowed itself to be forced away from its real objective.

KREBS: Our attacks in the northwest are continuing now. Regarding the attack by Group Steiner: The 7th Panzer Division has stepped in and the attack is underway. Plus there will be a regiment of the 199th Division, regiments of the *Schlageter* Division and an additional division—so a considerable numerical reinforcement. The enemy to the west hasn't concentrated to attack from the Elbe bridgehead so far. Strong pressure against Wittenberg has been identified from the east. As of tomorrow, we can expect pressure from Schörner toward the north, in the direction of Senftenberg.

HITLER: The Ninth Army did the worst thing possible. If there's no radio activity for a fairly long time, that's always the sign of a bad development. Is it possible that something could come into Berlin tonight?

VOSS: A company commander just reported from the escort company of the Grand Admiral. He fought his way through from Bernau to the Tirpitzufer [bank of the Tirpitz] in Berlin with approximately 120 men. He's in the Bendler block now and will then come here.

BELOW: The supply should have started at 21:30.

HITLER: I haven't been able to understand why the Ninth Army pulled itself into such a narrow area and why they lined up to the west and not to the northwest. It's impossible to lead if every plan that's made is changed by every army commander according to his pleasure.

KREBS: Busse probably can't move. He reported supply difficulties. He's starting to attack again now. As a result, forces that otherwise could have turned against Wenck's rear will now be diverted by Busse.

HITLER: If something like that isn't done quickly, it's over. The other one always reacts faster to that. The Ninth Army was one of the best armies we still had: eleven divisions! If he had placed the main force to the north-west, he could have made the thrust. I just want to state how impossible it is to lead if every army commander or corps general does what he believes to be right without concerning himself with the overall plan. Such disobe-dience never existed in the party. Not following one of my orders meant, for a party leader, immediate destruction and being thrust into nothingness. It's the same with the Russians. If someone there acts against an order, then it's no different. Now, it's come to what I said about taking up an all-round defense position in the narrowest space. [—] On the entire front, only one man has proven to be a real field strategist. The one who has to endure the worst attacks has the most orderly front: Schörner. Schörner had terrible equipment; he put it in order again. With every assignment he was given, Schörner achieved excellent results. Schörner together with Wenck—that was the best team I could imagine. And Schörner, within a few weeks, made a front out of a mess—and he didn't just built it up, but filled it with a new spirit and held the front. When he left it disappeared again. It's all just a leadership problem. You can't lead with a disobedient and high-handed or-ganization. In a company it doesn't work without obedience either. But in general this happens continuously. In contrast to that stands the fantastic achievements of individuals. [—] If you lived through these surprises again and again for twelve years, you'd find it difficult. Many can't understand my bitterness. I can't imagine that a party leader to whom I had given an order would dare to refuse to carry it out. The overall result is damaged by that, and the individual suffers again under the overall result. The bigger the individual's sphere of responsibility, the more obedience must be practiced.

GOEBBELS: Stalin introduced a mechanical obedience. With us, obedi-ence should be more of a moral principle.

HITLER: Blomberg[2021] already said to me that obedience only goes as far as the general. It was a mechanism that made it possible to avoid an action through false reports, etc., if difficulties arose. [—] We must establish a connection with the Ninth Army after all. We still have radio communication for half an hour a day. Tito and his partisans radio across the whole Balkan area with short-wave transmitters.

WEIDLING: In the southwest: the 18th Panzer Grenadier Division gave up only limited ground in mobile combat. The connection with the Hitler Youth and Reich Labor Service was established at the Westkreuz railway station. Fortunately, the Russian was stopped here to a certain degree. We've found out that some of the Russian units in the northwest were pulled out, probably due to the relief attacks from the outside. Charlottenburg Palace was lost. Western harbor still in our hands. In the northeast the main battle line held for the most part, with support from the encircled flak tower. In the east, strong attacks in which the opponent advanced to the Spittelmarkt. At the Spittelmarkt the enemy was thrown back again, but later pressed forward again. [—] Two hours ago the alert report arrived that hostile tanks were advancing across Belle-Alliance-Platz into Wilhelmstrasse. The situation was cleared again. The Grossgörschenstrasse railway station is in our hands. In the last four days, 230 enemy tanks have been knocked out; today, according to partial reports, another 40 to 50. So up to this evening, a total of 280 to 300 enemy tanks, which certainly doesn't include all enemy tanks destroyed. Today was a day of "Tatar" [frightening] reports. During this war I've kept nerves that are thick as ropes. But the kinds of reports that came in from the various sides today were terrible.

HITLER: Communists always work with false slogans. [—] I must have absolute certainty that I won't be taken out of here by some clever trick by a Russian tank. This security consists in the fact that here in the city center is a unit that's in the hands of a man who knows me personally, and who's then also a bit stronger in the end. It's not a regular unit either, but an improvisation. [—] The whole defense is a bit peculiar. A city is being held which previously gave away its entire defensive strength. One part was pushed in, not through the fault of the sector commander, but by means of enemy pressure. If I leave a central reserve in the hands of a single man, then in a few days there will simply be nothing left. [—] I had this unit placed under my command because I see in it a kind of central reserve that's there to hold the "Zitadelle." So now I keep giving away the Zitadelle crew, just like earlier the 20 battalions of the Volkssturm. It has turned out well that I receive reports from numerous places, because that gives me an accurate assessment. Either we'll stand this test or we won't stand it.

KREBS: Basis for the solution: The Mohnke Defense Area remains under the command and responsibility of Mohnke, with the exclusive assignment of protecting this main battle line against every attack. If this main battle line were to be pulled into the area of the fortress, as is the case on the southern front, then Mohnke would take over this sector and withdrawn units would be placed under his command. Mohnke's duties remain unchanged. Mohnke must report all observations from his area of command to Commanding Officer Weidling. But we would probably have to step back from the current radical division of the defense districts, since Defense Commander Weidling must, under all circumstances, be guaranteed freedom of movement in the southwest area, in consideration of the relief attempts.

HITLER: Grand Admiral Dönitz has detached Navy soldiers for the personal protection of the Führer. They are the bravest men he has. He wants to make a certain number of them available to me. This offer comes from Dönitz himself. He'll bring them in at any cost. When I have them, it will be a certain relief for you, because it's the highest elite of a commander-in-chief of one of the branches of the Armed Forces. Of the 600,000 men in the Navy, Dönitz will give the bravest 150 men for my personal protection. The moment could come when extreme steadfastness is everything. With the calibers he's shooting now, the Russian can't destroy us. But the Russian has already announced that he's bringing in 40.6-cm guns and 37-cm mortars. It's just a problem of the speed with which he brings it in. It will take some time, but he'll do it. Then it will come to the heroic battle for a last small island. For this, only very few people can be used. Otherwise it would be a Taubenschlag [Waterloo situation]. [—] I can imagine that the few men who are then standing by me as last protection will all move in here as well, and if the relief doesn't come, we must understand: It's not a bad end to a life if one falls during the battle for the capital of one's Reich. If it were different, within a few years we would be unable to find a single musketeer who would die within the Reich for his Reich. I can't demand of anyone that he fight outside if I myself don't even want to fight in the center of the Reich. [—] The decisive thing will be that you, Weidling, try to balance out the difficulties among the various kinds of units without losing sight of the operational aims in the west and southwest. [—] We have to obtain the maximum possible from every force we have. The important thing is that we always hold back a sufficient panzer reserve for the city center. The whole defensive zone of the inner Zitadelle [Citadel] of Berlin has become larger, so the value of the troops inside is therefore less.

WEIDLING: We have to change the defensive zone according to the situation on the main battle line.

MOHNKE: No, I have to maintain the inner area.

HITLER: Two complete infantry regiments from the *Grossdeutschland* Division should arrive. The Navy wanted to send in 2,000 men every night for three or four days. The Luftwaffe also wanted to send some very good units. Some of them should be held back for the central reserve. A guard battalion should come from the Reichsführer SS. If I want to hold Berlin to the end, I must also have the best means here. I can't carry out the last resistance with the worst things; I need the best. For example, it's wrong that 300 Frenchmen still have to help to defend the Reich capital as well.

MOHNKE: I would like to have whatever else is flown in.

WEIDLING: We have huge difficulties because of the water shortage. That's an enormous burden on the troops. It's very important that we hold the Tiergarten.

HITLER: Who would have believed that the connection with the west would be ripped out because a well-meaning act took 7,000 to 8,000 of the best soldiers away from me? A completely thoughtless document that they gave out. We had to order: Whatever has been ordered into Berlin must come in! Everything that wants out must be caught. Fifty aircraft with one and a half tons each are announced for tonight.

BELOW: The first drops have already been reported. Landings are still expected.

HITLER: The things that have been dropped must be transported instantly to the focal points.

WEIDLING: Provisions must be improvised.

* * * * *

Forty-eight hours after this situation conference, the resistance in the Reich capital ceases. On April 29, Berlin defender General Weidling reports to the Führer that Berlin could be held for one more day at most. The ammunition is running out. "In a tired voice, the Führer asked Brigadeführer Mohnke," as Weidling later reported, if that was also true for his "Zitadelle" command sector. Mohnke said it was. On this day Red Army soldiers advance further into the government quarter. Coming from the south, they fight their way across Tempelhof, Lützowstrasse, and Hohenzollernplatz to the zoo railway station. The last shots fall on the Reich sports field, Alexanderplatz and the Spittelmarkt. Weidling's evaluation of the situation provides the cue for Hitler's last decision: On April 30, 1945, at 3:30 p.m., he commits suicide together with Eva Braun, who had been married to him only hours before.

LIST OF PARTICIPANTS

A) COMMANDER-IN-CHIEF OF THE ARMED FORCES

1. *The Führer and Commander-in-Chief of the Armed Forces*
   Adolf Hitler
2. *Chief Adjutant of the Wehrmacht to the Führer and the Commander-in-Chief of the Armed Forces (additionally Chief of the Army Staff Office)*
   a) **Rudolf Schmundt** until October 1, 1944 Major General (April 1, 1943 Lieutenant General; July 27, 1944 General of the Infantry); born August 13, 1896; 1914 officer candidate; 1915 Lieutenant, Infantry regiment 35; Reichswehr; 1931 Captain; 1935 Major; 1936 on the Staff of the 18th division; February 1938 Chief Adjutant of the Army to the Führer and (October) Lieutenant Colonel; 1939 Colonel; 1941 Major General; October 1942 Chief of the Personnel Office of the Army at the same time; April 1943 Lieutenant General; July 20, 1944 seriously wounded during the attempt at the Führer's headquarters and died of his injuries October 1.
   b) **Wilhelm Burgdorf** from October 12, 1944 on: Lieutenant General (November 1, 1944 General ("Infantry"); born February 15, 1895; 1914 officer candidate; 1915 Lieutenant grenadier regiment 12; 1930 Captain; 1935 Major and teacher of tactics at the War College in Dresden; 1937 Adjutant at the General Command IX. Army Corps; 1938 Lieutenant Colonel; May 1940 Commander of Infantry Regiment 529 and (September) Colonel; May 1942 Chief of the 2nd department of the Personnel Office of the Army; October 1942 Major General and deputy Chief of the Personnel Office of the Army; October 1943 Lieutenant General; October 12, 1944 Chief of the Personnel Office of the Army and at the same time Chief Adjutant of the Armed Forces; missing since May 2, 1945.
3. *Adjutants of the Wehrmacht (Army) to the Führer and the Commander-in-Chief of the Wehrmacht*
   a) **Gerhard Engel** from March 15/September 26, 1943: Major (March 1, 1943 Lieutenant Colonel); born April 13, 1906; 1925 Reichswehr; 1930 Lieutenant Infantry Regiment 5; 1937 Captain; March 1938 Adjutant of the Wehrmacht (Army) to the Führer; 1941 Major; October 1943 Leader (February 1944 Commander) Infantry regiment 27; May 1944 Colonel; July 1944 Leader of the 12th Infantry Division; November 1944 Major General and Commander of the 12th [VGD]; April 1945 Lieutenant General and Commander of the Infantry Division *Ulrich v. Hutten.*
   b) **Heinrich Borgmann** September 26/October 22, 1943-end of March 1945: Major (January 1, 1944 Lieutenant Colonel); born August 15, 1912; 1932 Reichswehr; 1935 Lieutenant; 1940 Captain and Commander III./Infantry regiment 46; end of 1942 at the 3rd Air Force Field Division and Major;

January 1943 Ib 327th Infantry Division; June 1943 Ia 94th Infantry Division; September 26, 1943 sent to the of the Wehrmacht Adjutancy and from October 22, 1943 on Adjutant; end of March 1945 leader of a officer candidate division in the 12th Army; killed April 1945.

c) **Colonel Erik von Amsberg**, Lieutenant July 21, 1944-October 24, 1944; born October 21, 1908; 1929 Reichswehr; 1932 Lieutenant Reich's Regiment 14, there Regiment Adjutant (1936) and Squadron Chief (1938); September 1939 at the General Command XI. Army Corps; May 1940 Adjutant Chief OKW; June 1941 Commander Reconnaissance Department 46; April 1942 Major; April 1943 Official in charge of the cavalry at the Staff of the General of the Infantry/Army High Command (OKH); April 1944 Lieutenant Colonel; July 21, 1944 sent to the of the Wehrmacht Adjutancy to the Führer; end of October 1944 1st Adjutant of the Headquarters of the Army 19.

d) **Willy Johannmeyer** Major from April 1945 on; (see 6).

4. *Adjutant of the Wehrmacht (Navy) to the Führer and the Commander-in-Chief of the Wehrmacht* **Karl-Jesko v. Puttkamer**, Captain at Sea (September 1, 1943 Rear Admiral); born March 24, 1900; 1917 Cadet at Sea; 1921 Lieutenant at Sea; 1930 Lieutenant Captain; 1935 Navy Adjutant to the Führer; 1936 Lieutenant Commander; September 1938 Commander (*Hans Lody*) in the 4th Destroyer Fleet; October 1939 again Adjutant of the Wehrmacht to the Führer and (November) Frigate Captain; April 1941 Captain at Sea.

5. *Adjutant of the Wehrmacht (Air Force) to the Führer and the Commander-in-Chief of the Wehrmacht* **Nicolaus von Below** Major (March 1, 1943 Lieutenant Colonel, March 1, 1944 Colonel); born September 20, 1907; 1928 flight training at the [DVS]; 1929 Reichswehr (Infantry Regiment 12); 1932 Lieutenant; 1933 change to Air Force; 1935 Flight Group Döberitz; 1936 Squadron Captain in the [J.G.] 134 *Horst Wessel;* 1937 Captain and Adjutant of the Wehrmacht to the Führer; 1941 Major.

6. *Officer in the [Adjutancy] of the Wehrmacht* **Willy Johannmeyer** Major; born July 27, 1915; 1936 officer candidate; 1938 Lieutenant Infantry regiment 64; 1942 Captain; 1943 Commander II. Grenadier regiment 503; end of 1943 Oak Leaves and Major; 1944 Personnel Office of the Army; November 1944 sent to the Adjutancy of the Wehrmacht to the Führer as "Staff Major"; April 1945 successor to Borgmann as Army Adjutant.

7. *Personal Adjutants of the Führer*

a) **Fritz Darges** SS-Major (January 30, 1944 Lieutenant Colonel); born February 8, 1913; commercial training; 1933 SS; 1934 Junker school Tölz; 1935 2nd Lieutenant 2nd Standard SS; 1936-39 Adjutant to Borgmann; 1937 1st Lieutenant; 1940 as Battalion Adjutant and Company Leader Western Campaign respectively, Captain; October 1940 Personal Adjutant to the Führer; March 1942 until March 1943 sent to the tank department/SS-division *Viking;* January 1943 Major; August 1944 Department Commander and later until the end of war Leader of the Tank Regiment in the 5th SS-Tank Division *Viking*.

b) **Richard Schulze** SS-Captain (February 24, 1943 Major, November 9, 1944 Lieutenant Colonel); born October 2, 1914; 1931 HJ; 1934 SS (LSSAH); 1935

SS-Junker school Tölz; 1936 2nd Lieutenant; 1938 1st Lieutenant; autumn 1938 Adjutant Chief SSHA and Napola; April 1939 Adjutant to Ribbentrop; January 1941 LSSAH; August 1941 Orderly Officer to Hitler; October 29, 1942 Personal Adjutant to the Führer; November 15, 1943 sent to the SS-Junker School Tölz as Tactics Teacher and Class Commander; July 25, 1944 again Personal Adjutant to the Führer; January 1945 SS-Junker school Tölz.

c) **Hans Pfeiffer** SS-Captain; born December 5, 1915; 1930 HJ; 1933 SS, tank training; 1937 2nd Lieutenant; 1939 as 1st Lieutenant Orderly Officer at Hitler's Escort Command; January 1942 Captain; August 1942 as Officer at the headquarters sent to the 1st SS-Tank Division; October 1942 Personal Adjutant to the Führer; June 10, 1944 died as Company Leader in the 12th SS-Tank Division at the invasion front; posthumously promoted to Major with effect from April 20, 1944.

d) **Otto Günsche** SS-2nd Lieutenant (April 20, 1943 1st Lieutenant; April 20, 1944 Captain; December 21, 1944 Major); born September 24, 1917; 1931 HJ, 1934 LSSAH; from 1936 on Colonel at Hitler's Escort Command; June 1942 SS-2nd Lieutenant after Junker school and duty at the front; January to August 1943 Personal Adjutant to the Führer, August 1943 Company Chief 1st/SS-Tank Division *LAH*; February 1944 until April 30, 1945 personal Adjutant to the Führer.

8. *Orderly Officer of the Führer.*
   Heinz Kersten SS-Captain; born November 28, 1920; 1933 HJ, bargeman; 1938 as volunteer to the LSSAH, Poland Campaign at LSSAH; 1941 2nd Lieutenant SS-Division *Viking*; 1942 Platoon and Company Leader 1st SS-Division *LAH*; October 1944 Führer Escort Company; November 1944 Captain; December 2, 1944 sent to the Führer's headquarters as Orderly Officer.

9. *Hitler's Servants*
   Heinz Linge *SS-1st Lieutenant* (April 20, 1944 Captain; February 24, 1945 Major); born March 22, 1913; bricklayer, College of technology; 1932 NSDAP, 1933 SS; from 1935 on personal Servant to Hitler; 1939 2nd Lieutenant in the Escort Command; 1942 1st Lieutenant.

B) ARMED FORCES HIGH COMMAND (OKW)

10. *Chief of the OKW*
    Wilhelm Keitel General Field Marshal; born September 22, 1882; 1901 officer candidate; 1902 Lieutenant Field Artillery regiment 46; 1908 Regiment Adjutant; 1914 Captain, during the World War Battery chief as well as in different General Staff positions, [Freikorps] in Poland, Reich Forces; 1920 Tactics Teacher at the Cavalry School; 1922 Chief 7th/Artillery regiment 6; 1924 Major; 1925 in the Organisation Department of the Army; 1931 Colonel; 1933 Infantry Commander III (Potsdam);, 1934 Major General and Infantry Commander VI (Bremen); October 1935 Chief of the Wehrmacht Office as successor of v. Reichenau; 1936 Lieutenant General; 1937 General

of the Artillery; February 1938 Chief of the OKW; November 1938 Colonel
general; July 1940 Field Marshal.—Sentenced to death at the main trail of
Nürnberg September 30, 1946 and hanged October 16.

11. *Adjutant (Army) to the Chief of the OKW*

Ernst John von Freyend Captain (April 1, 1943 Major); born March 25, 1909;
1936 Lieutenant in the Artillery regiment 28; 1937 activated; 1941 Captain,
February 1942 OKW; March 15, 1942 Army Adjutant to the Chief of the OKW.

12. *Chief of the Wehrmacht Operations Headquarters in the OKW*

Alfred Jodl General of the Artillery (January 30, 1944 Colonel general); born
May 10, 1890; 1910 military training; 1912 Lieutenant 4th Bavarian Field Artillery Regiment; 1921 Captain; 1931 Major; 1932 RWM (T1); 1933 Lieutenant Colonel; 1935 Colonel and Chief of the Department of Country Defense; November 1938 Artillery Commander 44 (Vienna); April 1939 Major
General; from August 26, 1939 on OKW/Chief of the Wehrmacht Command Office (January 1, 1942 renamed into Wehrmacht Commanding Headquarters); 1940 general of the Artillery.—Sentenced to death at the main trial
of Nürnberg September 30, 1946 and hanged October 16.

13. *(1.) General Staff Officer to the Chief of the Wehrmacht Operations Headquarters (WFSt)*

a) **Eckhard Christian** Lieutenant Colonel until August 25/October 31, 1943
(April 1, 1943 Colonel); born December 12, 1907; 1926 Reichsmarine; 1930
Lieutenant at Sea; 1934 as 1st Lieutenant to the Air Force, Reconnaissance
Flight School (Sea) Warnemünde; 1935 Captain; 1938 General Headquarters
of the Air Force (1st Department); 1939 Adjutant Chief of the General head-
quarters of the Air Force; March 1940 Ia X. Flight Corps; June 1940 Major
and Group Commander 26; January 1941 WFSt; 1942 Lieutenant Colonel;
August 25, 1943 (after the death of Jeschonnek) at Hitler's order Ia Air Force
Command Headquarters; September 1944 Major general and Chief of the
Air Force Command Headquarters; April 22, 1945 Leader of the Connection
Command of the Chief of the General Headquarters of the Air Force to the
OKW/Headquarters North.

b) **Heinz Waizenegger** Major November 1, 1943—February 28, 1945; (April
1, 1944 Lieutenant Colonel); born October 22, 1913; 1932 National Police;
1934 Police Lieutenant; 1935 taken over into the Army Adjutant III./Infan-
try Regiment 56; 1938 as 1st Lieutenant (1937) Chief of the 9th/Infantry
Regiment 56; 1940 Captain and [O1] at the General Command V. Army Corps;
March 1942 sent to the Tank Headquarters of the Army 3; August 17, 1943
General headquarters Officer at the WFSt; May 1943 Major; March 1945 O1
at the Headquarters of the Army (AOK) 2.

c) **Hermann Brudermüller** from March 1, 1945 on: Major (April 20, 1945
Lieutenant Colonel); born July 22, 1914; 1933 officer candidate; 1935 Lieutenant [A.R] 15, 1939 as 1st Lieutenant (1938) regiment Adjutant A.R. 51,
1940 O1 129th Infantry Division; 1941 Captain; 1942 sent to the 110th Infantry Division and respectively to the General Command XXIII. Army Corps;
November 1942 Ib 122nd Infantry Division; June 1943 Major; August 1943
OKW/WFSt (Operations Department).

14 *(2.) General Headquarters Officer to Chief of the WFSt (Adjutant Chief WFSt)*
  a) **Heinz Waizenegger** Captain (May 1, 1943 Major) until October 31, 1943: (see 13b)
  b) **Herbert Büchs** from November 1, 1943 on: Major; born November 20, 1913; 1937 Lieutenant; 1940 Staff K.G. 77; December 1941 Air War Army; October 1942 Captain at Headquarters of the Air Force Command Don; March 1943 Ia [op] VIII. Flight Corps; August 1943 Major at the Air Force Command Headquarters; November 1943 WFSt.—1957 German Armed Forces.
15. *Vice-Chief of the WFSt*
  a) **Walter Warlimont** until September 5, 1944: Lieutenant General (April 1, 1944 General of Artillery); born October 3, 1894; 1913 [officer candidate]; 1914 Lieutenant of the Foot Artillery Regiment 10; during the World War Adjutant and Battery Commander, Reichswehr; 1925 Captain in the [RWM]; 1929 Command to US Army; 1933 Major in the RWM (1934 Department Commander WaWi); 1935 Lieutenant Colonel; 1936 Commander II./Artillery regiment 34; 1937 Commander Artillery regiment 26; 1938 Colonel and (October) Chief of Department Country Defence in the OKW, at the same time (from November on) until the beginning of war Chief of the Armed Forces Command Office; 1940 Major General; January 1942 Vice-Chief of the WFSt; April 1942 Lieutenant General.—October 1948 life sentence at Nürnberg; released from Landsberg 1954.
  b) **August Winter** from November 5, 1944 on: Lieutenant General (April 20, 1945 General of the Mountain Troops); born January 18, 1897; 1916 [officer candidate]; 1917 Lieutenant of the Bavarian 2nd Telegraphy Battalion, Reichswehr; 1933 Captain; 1934 War Academy; 1936 Major; 1937 Army High Command/1st department; 1939 Lieutenant Colonel; October 1940 Ia Army Group A (April 1941: South, July 1942: B); 1941 Colonel; April 1943 Chief of the General Headquarters 2nd Panzer Army; August 1943 Major General and Chief of the General Headquarters Army Group E; March 1944 chief of the General Headquarters Army Group F; August 1944 Lieutenant General; October 30, 1944 sent to the OKW/WFSt; November 15, 1944 Chief of the WFSt.
16. *1st Officer of the General Headquarters of the Army in the WFSt*
  a) **Horst Baron Treusch von Buttlar–Brandenfels** until August 1944: Colonel (January 1, 1944 Major General); born September 2, 1900; 1918 Lieutenant Hussar Regiment 10, Reichswehr; 1933 [Rittmeister]; 1937 Major (January) at the [December] General headquarters of the Army; 1939 Lieutenant Colonel and (December) Ia 81st Infantry Division; 1940 Ia Group XXI. Norway and respectively (December) AOK Norway; January 12, 1942 1st Officer of the General Headquarters of the Army in the WFSt; February 1942 Colonel; November 15, 1944 Führer Reserve; January 1945 sent to the Commander-in-Chief West as Division Commander; April 1945 Commander of the 11th Tank Division.
  b) **Wilhelm Meyer-Detring** from August 20, 1944 on: Lieutenant Colonel (September 1, 1944 Colonel); born May 9, 1906; 1925 Reichswehr; 1928 Lieutenant Infantry Regiment 7; 1936 Captain; 1938 Id IX. Army Corps; 1939 Quarter-

master IX. Army Corps; February 1940 Ia 229th Infantry Division; July 1940 as Major Ib Armed Forces Representative to the Reichsprotektor of Bohemia and Moravia; October 1940 Ia 137th Infantry Division; 1942 Lieutenant Colonel (April) and Ic Army Group D (July).—1956 German Armed Forces.

17. *1st Admiral Officer in the WFSt*

a) **Wolf Junge** until August 24, 1943 as well as November 4, 1944-January 10, 1945: Frigate Captain (April 1 1943 Captain at Sea); born January 5, 1903; 1922 Reichsmarine; 1926 Lieutenant at Sea; 1934 Lieutenant Captain; 1936 Guard Officer tank ship *Admiral Graf Spee*; 1937 Navy Academy and Corvette Captain; 1938 Referent in the OKM; April 1939 Referent and respectively Group Commander in the WFSt; 1941 Frigate Captain; August 5, 1943 First Officer (May 1, 1944 Commander) battleship *Tirpitz*; November 4, 1944 again WFSt; January 11, 1945 First Officer of the Command Headquarters Navy High Command Eastern Sea.

b) **Heinz Assmann** from August 25, 1943 on: Captain at Sea; born August 15, 1904, 1922 Reichsmarine; 1926 Lieutenant at Sea; 1934 Lieutenant Captain; 1937 Referent in the OKM, from October on Navy Academy; 1938 Corvette Captain and Officer of the Admiral's headquarters at the Navy Group Command East; November 1939 Referent in the OKM (1/SKL); between that January/March 1941 Frigate Captain (April) and First Officer battleship *Tirpitz* (September); June 1943 Captain at Sea, August 25, 1943 WFSt.—Died October 15, 1954.

[The 1st Officer of the General Headquarters Air Force in the WFSt (Colonel Berg or respectively Lieutenant Colonel Boehm-Tettelbach) usually did not participate, as well as the 1st Officer of the General Headquarters of the Army, in the situation conferences, since both Army and Air Force were represented by the Officers of the General Headquarters at the Chief of the WFSt.]

18. *Chief of the Army Headquarters at the Chief of the OKW* and (from January 15, 1945 on) *Chief of the Armed Forces Armaments*
Walter Buhle Lieutenant General (April 1, 1944 General of the Infantry); born October 26, 1894; 1914 Lieutenant Infantry regiment 124; Reichswehr, 1926 Captain in the Reichswehr (T1); 1930 Company Chief Infantry Regiment 13, 1932 Reichswehr (T2); 1933 Major; 1936 Lieutenant Colonel and Commander II./Infantry Regiment 87; 1937 Ia General Commander V. Army Corps; December 1938 Chief 2nd Department of the General Headquarters of the Army; 1939 Colonel; 1940 Major General; January 1942 Chief of the Army headquarters at the OKW; April 1942 Lieutenant General.—Died December 27, 1959.

19. *Representative to the Führer for Military History*
Walter Scherff Colonel (September 1, 1943 Major General); born November 1, 1898; 1915 entered the army; 1917 Lieutenant Infantry Regiment 122; 1920 Infantry Regiment 13; 1929 Headquarters 5th division; 1931 Command Berlin; 1932 Reichswehr (T2); 1933 Captain; 1935 General Headquarters of the Army (2nd department); 1936 Major; 1937 Headquarters 21st division; 1938 General Headquarters of the Army (7th department); 1939 Lieutenant Colonel OKH/AHA; February 1940 headquarters [BdE]; November 1940 WFSt;

February 1941 Chief of the War History Department OKW, September 1941 Colonel; May 17, 1942 Representative to the Führer for Military History.— Suicide in American captivity May 24, 1945.

a) *Adjutant*

Wilhelm Scheidt 1st Lieutenant (April 1, 1944 [Rittmeister]); born August 28, 1912; 1938 Lieutenant at the Regiment Reconnaissance department 6; 1941 Lieutenant Colonel of the Regiment OKW/War History Department.

C) ARMY HIGH COMMAND (OKH)

20. *Commander-in-Chief of the Army*
    Adolf Hitler

21. *Chief of the General Headquarters of the Army*

   a) **Kurt Zeitzler** until June 9/August 14, 1944: General of the Infantry (February 1, 1944 Colonel General); born June 9, 1895; 1914 Lieutenant Infantry Regiment 72; 1919 moved over to the voluntary troop; 1920 appointed as Battalion Adjutant into the Reichswehr; 1928 Captain; 1929 Headquarters 3rd Division; 1932 Chief Captain of Infantry Regiment 09; 1934 Reichswehr [Minister Office, later WA (L)] and Major; 1937 Lieutenant Colonel; 1939 Commander of the Grenadier Regiment 60 and Colonel; August 1939 Chief of the General Headquarters XXII. Army Corps (renamed December 1940 into Tank Group 1; October 1941 1st Tank Army); February 1942 Major General; April 1942 Chief of the General Headquarters High Command West (Army Group D); September 24, 1942 General of the Infantry (skipping the rank of a Lieutenant General) and Chief of the General Headquarters of the Army; August 15, 1944 Führer Reserve, released January 31, 1945.

   b) **Adolf Heusinger** June 10, 1944—July 21, 1944: Lieutenant General (see 23a)

   c) **Heinz Guderian** from July 21, 1944 on: Colonel General; born June 17, 1888; 1903 Cadet Institute Lichterfelde; 1908 Lieutenant Fighter Battalion 10, in the World War Commander of the radio Station, News Officer among others General Headquarters Position; 1915 Captain; December 1918 Boarder Police East; 1919 Iron Division, Chief 3rd/Fighter Battalion 10; 1922 Reichswehr; 1924 General Headquarters 2nd Division; 1927 Major in the Reichswehr (TA); 1930 Commander of the Motorist Department 3; 1931 Lieutenant Colonel in the Reichswehr (In 6); 1933 Colonel; 1934 Chief of the Headquarters Inspection of the Motorist Troops; 1935 Commander of the 2nd Tank Division; 1936 Major General; February 1938 Lieutenant General and Commander of the General Command of the Tank Troops (April 1938 XVI. Army Corps); November 1938 General of the Tank Troops and Chief of the Rapid Deployment Troops; August 1939 Commander General XIX. Army Corps; June 1940 Commander of the Tank Group Guderian (later: 2); October 1941 Commander-in-Chief of the 2nd tank Army; July 1940 Colonel General; December 1941 Führer Reserve; February 20, 1943 General Inspector of the Tank

Troops; July 21, 1944 at the same time Chief of the General Headquarters of the Army; March 28/April 1, 1945 suspended.—Died May 15, 1954.

d) **Hans Krebs** from April 1, 1945 on: General of the Infantry (see 24b)

22. *Adjutant of the Chief of the General Headquarters of the Army*

[a) **Günther Smend** until June 9, 1944: Major]

b) **Bernd Baron Freytag v. Loringhoven** from July 25, 1944 on: Major; born February 6, 1914; 1934 enters the army; 1937 Lieutenant; 1939 1st Lieutenant in the Command of the 1st Tank Division; 1940 in the General Command XIX. Army Corps; 1942 Captain and Chief 2nd/Tank regiment 2; March 1943 sent to the Command of the 111th Infantry Division; October 1943 War Academy; April 1944 Operational Department of the General Headquarters of the Army; November 1943 Major.—1956 German Armed Forces.

23. *Chief of the Operational Department in the General Headquarters of the Army*

a) **Adolf Heusinger** until July 20, 1944: Major General (January 1, 1943 Lieutenant General); born August 4, 1897; 1915 [officer candidate] 1916 Lieutenant Infantry Regiment 96; Reichswehr, 1922 Adjutant III./Infantry Regiment 15; 1927 Headquarters of the 5th Division; 1931 Reichswehr (T1); 1932 Captain; 1934 Captain Chief Infantry Regiment 18; 1935 Ia 11th Division; 1936 Major; April 1937 General Headquarters of the Army (1st Department), 1938 Lieutenant Colonel; 1940 Colonel and (October) Chief of the Operational Department; 1941 Major General, June 10—July 21, 1944 Representative of the Chief of the General Headquarters of the Army; July 22 until October 1944 in Gestapo arrest.—1952 Military Expert; 1955 German Armed Forces.

b) **Walter Wenck** July 21, 1944-August 30, 1944: Lieutenant General; born September 18, 1900; 1919 officer candidate Free Corps; 1923 Lieutenant Infantry regiment 9; 1929 Adjutant II./Infantry regiment 9; 1933 War Academy, 1934 Captain; July 1936 Headquarters Command of the Tank Troops; September 1936 Reconnaissance Department 3; April 1938 General Headquarters XVI Army Corps, November Chief 1st/Tank regiment 2; 1939 Major and Ia 1st Tank Division; 1940 Lieutenant Colonel; February 1942 Teacher at the General Headquarters Instruction Courses; June 1942 Colonel and (September) Chief of the General Headquarters LVII. Tank Corps; November 1942 Chief of the General Headquarters of the Romanian 3rd Army; December Chief of the General Headquarters Army Department *Hollidt* (before 6th Army); February 1943 Major General; March 1943 Chief of the General Headquarters 1st Tank Army; April 1944 Lieutenant General and Chief of the General Headquarters Army Group South Ukraine; July 21, 1944 Chief of the Operational Department in the General Headquarters of the Army; February 17, 1945 accident with motor vehicle; April 7, 1945 General of the Tank Troop and Führer reserve; April 16, 1945 Commander 12th Army.

[September 1, 1944 shift of different functions to newly established office "Chief of the Command Group" (see 24).]

c) **Bogislaw v. Bonin** September 1, 1944-January 18, 1945: Colonel

d) **Götz Bennecke** from January 18, 1945 on: Colonel

24. *Chief of the Command Group in the general Headquarters of the Army*
   a) **Walter Wenck** September 1, 1944-February 17/April, 6, 1945: Lieutenant General (see 23b)
   b) **Hans Krebs** I.V. from February 17, 1945 on: General Infantry; born March 4, 1898; 1914 War volunteer; 1915 Lieutenant Infantry Regiment 78; during the World War Captain Commander and Adjutant, Reichswehr; 1925 1st Lieutenant, 1928 Chief 13th/Infantry regiment 17; 1931 Captain in the Reichswehr; 1933 Assistant of the Military Attaché in Moscow; 1935 General Headquarters 24th Division; 1936 Major; 1937 General Headquarters of the Army (11th Department); 1939 Lieutenant Colonel and (December) Chief of the General Headquarters VII. Army Corps; 1940 Colonel; March 1941 Representative of the Military Attaché in Moscow; January 1942 Chief of the General Headquarters of the 9th Army and (February) Major General; March 1943 Chief of the general headquarters Army Group Middle and (April) Lieutenant General; August 1944 General of the Infantry; September 1944 Chief of the General Headquarters Army Group B; February 17, 1945 Chief of the Command Group OKH (substitute for Wenck); April 1, 1945 Chief of the General Headquarters of the Army.—Missing since the beginning of May 1945 in Berlin.

25. *Officers in the Operational Department in the General Headquarters of the Army*
   a) **August Herman** Lieutenant Colonel; born May 31, 1911; 1928 Reichswehr, 1934 Lieutenant; 1938 as 1st Lieutenant (1937) Adjutant of the Infantry Regiment 42; 1940 Captain; 1941 General Headquarters of the Army/Chief transportation System; September 1942 Commander Transportation Area Poltava; November 1942 Ib 304th Infantry Division; January 1943 Major; June 1943 Quartermaster LII. Army Corps; August 1943 Ia XXXXII. Army Corps; April 1944 Lieutenant Colonel and Ia 26th Infantry Division; September 10, 1944 general headquarters of the Army/Operational Department; April 1945 Chief of the General Headquarters Corps Reimann.—1956 German Armed Forces.
   b) **Hubertus Baron von Humboldt Dachroeden** Major (December 1, 1944 Lieutenant Colonel); born July 24, 1912; 1932 Reichswehr; 1934 Lieutenant; 1938 as 1st Lieutenant (1937) Adjutant Artillery Command 6; 1940 Chief 5th/Artillery regiment 42 and Captain; January 1942 Headquarters Higher Artillery Command 302; August 1942 Ib 168th Infantry Division; 1943 Id Army Group B; May 1943 Major; March 1944 Ia 87th Infantry Division; September 10, 1944 General Headquarters of the Army/Operational Department; April 1945 Führer Reserve.
   c) **Ulrich de Maizière** Lieutenant Colonel; born February 24, 1912; 1930 Reichswehr; 1933 Lieutenant Infantry Regiment 5; 1937 as 1st Lieutenant (1935) Adjutant Infantry Regiment 50; 1939 Captain; September 1940 Ib 18th Infantry Division; January 1941 General Headquarters of the Army/Organisational Department; April 1942 Major; May 1943 Ia 10th Infantry Division (10th Tank Grenadier Division); June 1943 Lieutenant Colonel; November 1944 as Army-Ia sent to the High Command West; February 15, 1945 General Headquarters of the Army/Ia Operational Department; May 1945 WFSt.—1955 German Armed Forces.

26. *Deputy Chief of the Personnel Office of the Army* (Chief HPA see 2)
   a) **Wilhelm Burgdorf** until October 11, 1944: Major General (October 1, 1943 Lieutenant General) (see 2b)
   b) **Viktor Linnarz** October 12, 1944-January 15, 1945: Lieutenant General; born August 19, 1894; Cadet Corps; 1914 Lieutenant [Tel] Battalion 2; 1920 Motorist department 5; 1929 retired as Captain; 1930 employed again Motorist Department 6; 1935 Major and Commander II./Tank Regiment 6; 1936 Headquarters Command of the Tank Troops; 1938 Lieutenant Colonel in the OKH/PA (P1); August 1940 Colonel and (October) Chief 3rd department/Office Group P1/HPA; June 1941 Commander 5th Tank Brigade; October 1942 Chief Office Group P1/HPA; January 1943 Major General, April 1944 Lieutenant General; October 12, 1944 Deputy Chief HPA; January 15, 1945 Führer Reserve; March 1945 Commander 26th Tank Division.
   c) from January 15, 1945 on: Lieutenant General Ernst Maisel
   Adjutant of the Chief of the HPA
   Rudolf Weiss Major (April 1, 1944 Lieutenant Colonel); born September 27, 1910; 1931 Reichswehr; 1934 Lieutenant; November 1938 OKH/Adjutant PA, 1940 Captain; 1941 Adjutant 1st Tank Division; April 1942 at the Chief of the Army Armament (Office Group K), Adjutant General for Motorization in the AHA, June 1942 Major; from October 2, 1942 on Adjutant Chief HPA.—Died September 19, 1958.

27. *General Inspector of the Tank Troops*
   Heinz Guderian Colonel General (see 21c)

28. *Chief of the Headquarters of the General Inspector of the Tank Troops*
   Wolfgang Thomale Colonel (February 1, 1944 Major General; March 1, 1945 Lieutenant General); born February 25, 1900; 1918 enlisted in the army; 1919 Lieutenant Motorized Department 3; 1926 1st Lieutenant and Adjutant Motorized Department 6; 1929 Infantry School; 1933 Captain in the Motorist School Command Zossen; 1935 Tank Regiment 5; 1937 major in the Headquarters 3rd Tank Brigade; June 1938 OKH (In 6); 1939 Lieutenant Colonel; May 1941 Commander III./Tank Regiment 25; July 1941 Commander Tank regiment 27; March 1942 Colonel; June 1942 at the Headquarters Chief of Army Armament; February 25, 1943 Chief Of the Headquarters General Inspector of the Tank Troops.

D) LUFTWAFFE HIGH COMMAND (OKL)

29. *Commander-in-Chief of the Luftwaffe*
   a) **Hermann Göring** until April 23, 1945: Reichsmarshal; born January 12, 1893; Main Cadet School Lichterfelde; 1912 Lieutenant Infantry regiment 112; 1914 Battalion Adjutant in the Infantry regiment 112; October 1914 Flight Troop; Observer Field Flight department 25 (AOK 5); 1916 Fighter Squadron 26; 1917 Commander Fighter Squadron 27; June 1918 Commander Fighter Squadron 1 *Baron v. Richthofen*; 1919 retired as Captain; August 1933 General of the

Infantry; 1934/March 1935 General of the Luftwaffe and Commander-in-Chief of the Luftwaffe; April 1936 Colonel General; February 1938 General Field Marshal; July 1940 Reichsmarshal; April 23, 1945 removed from all his positions and arrested.—Sentenced to death by hanging September 30, 1946 at the Main Trial of Nürnberg; committed suicide October 15, 1946.

b) **Robert Knight v. Greim** from April 26, 1945 on: General Field Marshal

aa) *Chief Adjutant of the Commander-in-Chief of the Luftwaffe*

Bernd von Brauchitsch Major (March 1, 1943 Lieutenant Colonel, March 1, 1944 Colonel); born September 11, 1911; 1931 [DVS]; 1931 entrance into office Rider Regiment 3; 1934 Lieutenant and shift to the Luftwaffe, testing position Rechlin; 1936 1st Lieutenant in the [K.G.] 162 *Immelmann*; 1939 Captain and Commander IV./[Stuka] [L.G.] 1; July 1940 Adjutant of the Reichsmarshal; 1942 Major; January 1943 Chief Adjutant of the Commander-in-Chief of the Air Force.

30. *Chief of the General Headquarters of the Air Force*

a) **Hans Jeschonnek** until August 19, 1943: Colonel General; born April 9, 1899; Cadet Corps; 1914 entrance into office and (December) Lieutenant; 1917 Flight Troop (Fighter Squadron 40), Reichswehr (Rider-Regiment 11 and respectively 6); 1932 Captain; 1933 shift to Air Force, Adjutant of Milch, Group-Commander in the [K.G.] *Hindenburg*; 1937 Lieutenant Colonel and Chief 1st Department/General Headquarters of the Luftwaffe; February 1938 Chief Luftwaffe Command Headquarters; November 1938 Colonel; February 1939 Chief of the General Headquarters of the Luftwaffe; August 1939 Major General; July 1940 General of the Luftwaffe; March 1942 Colonel General; suicide during the night of August 18/19, 1943.

b) **Günther Korten** August 24, 1943-July 22, 1944: General of the [Flg.]; born July 26, 1898; 1914 [officer candidate] Field Artillery Regiment 34; 1915 Lieutenant, Reichswehr (Tank Battalion 10 respectively 6), 1932 Captain; 1934 shift to Air Force and Major in the RLM (General Headquarters Officer at the Secretary); 1936 Commander reconnaissance Group 122; 1937 Lieutenant Colonel and Department Chief RLM (LP IV); 1938 Chief of the General headquarters of the Command General of the Luftwaffe in Austria; 1939 Colonel; 1940 Major General and Chief of the General Headquarters Air Fleet 3; 1941 Chief of the General Headquarters Air Fleet 4; August 1942 Lieutenant General and Commander Command Don; January 1943 General of the Luftwaffe; February 1943 Command General I. Flight Corps; June 1943 i.V. Commander-in-Chief Air Fleet 1; August 24, 1943 Chief of the General Headquarters of the Luftwaffe; wounded at the attempt on his life July 20, 1944 and died of his injuries July 22, 1944; posthumous Colonel General July 23, 1944.

c) **Werner Kreipe** August 1, 1944-September 19, 1944: Lieutenant General (September 1, 1944 General of the Luftwaffe); born January 12, 1904; 1922 Reichswehr; 1925 Lieutenant; 1934 Captain and shift to Luftwaffe; 1936 RLM; 1937 Major; 1938 Commander Reconnaissance Group 122; 1939 [K.G.] 2, March 1940 Commander III./[K.G.] 2; June 1040 Department Chief in the RLM (training system); November 1940 Lieutenant Colonel; 1941 Chief of the General Headquarters I. Flight Corps; 1942 Colonel; August 1942 Chief of the General Headquarters Luftwaffe Command Don; October 1942 Chief of the Headquarters at the Chief of the Training System in the RLM; March 1943 Major General; July 1943 General for Flight Training; July 1944 Lieutenant General; August 1, 1944 Chief of the General Headquarters of the Luftwaffe; 1945 Commander Air War Academy.

d) **Karl Koller** from November 29, 1944 on: Lieutenant General (January 30, 1945 General of the Luftwaffe); born February 22, 1898; 1914 War Volunteer, 1917 Aircraft Commander; 1919 released as Vice First Sergeant; 1920 Police Flight Squadron; 1922 Country Police; 1933 Captain of the Police; 1935 shift to Luftwaffe (Headquarters Air Fleet 3); 1936 Major in the General Headquarters Air Fleet 3; 1938 Lieutenant Colonel; March 1943 Major General; August 26, 1943 Chief of the Luftwaffe Command Headquarters; May 1944 Lieutenant General, November 29; 1944 Chief of the General Headquarters of the Luftwaffe—Died December 22, 1951.

31. *Chief of the Luftwaffe Command Headquarters*
   a) **Hans Jeschonnek** until May 31, 1943: General Colonel (see 30a)
   b) **Rudolf Meister** June 1, 1943-August 23, 1943: Lieutenant General
   c) **Karl Koller** August 24, 1943-September 4, 1944: Major General (May 1, 1944 Lieutenant General) (see 30d)
   d) **Eckhard Christian** from September 4, 1944 on: Major General (see 13a)

32. *Permanent Liaison Officer of the Reichsmarshal to the Führer*
   Karl Bodenschatz General of the Luftwaffe; born December 10, 1890; 1910 officer candidate Infantry regiment 8; 1912 Lieutenant; 1916 1st Lieutenant and shift to Flight Troop; 1917 Adjutant 1 *Baron v. Richthofen*; 1919 sent back to Infantry regiment 8; 1921 Captain; 1932 Major; May 1933 Chief of the Air Protection Office in the RWM; September 1933 shift to Air Force as 1st Adjutant of the R.d.L.; 1934 Lieutenant Colonel; 1935/36 at the same time Adjutant to the Führer and the Reich's Chancellor; 1936 Colonel and Chief of the Headquarters Office/RLM; December 1937 Chief of the Minister's Office; 1938 Major General, September 1939 at the same time permanent Liaison Officer of Göring to the Führer; January 1941 General of the Luftwaffe; severely wounded during the attempt of April 20, 1944 and unfit for service until the end of the War.

33. *Head of the Weather Station at the Chief of the General Headquarters of the Luftwaffe*
   Oskar Schuster [General Manager] (1944: [Director]); born October 31, 1909, 1929-34 studies at College of Technology in Munich and Dresden; 1934 [Referendar]; 1935 entrance into Reich's Weather Office; 1939 [Manager] and Head of the Weather Station at the Chief of the General Headquarters of the Air Force.

E) NAVY HIGH COMMAND (OKM)

34. *Commander-in-Chief of the Navy*
   a) **Erich Raeder** until January 30, 1943: Great Admiral Dr.
   b) **Karl Dönitz** from January 30, 1943 on: Great Admiral; born September 16, 1891; 1910 Sea Cadet; 1913 Lieutenant at Sea; 1912 Cruiser *Breslau*; 1916 to the Submarine-Navy; October 1918 imprisonment; 1919 Reichsmarine; 1928 Corvette Captain and Torpedo Boat-[Halbflottillenchef]; 1930 Officer of the Headquarters Navy Station Northern Sea; 1934 Commander Cruiser "Emden"; 1935 Frigate Captain and Commander 1st Submarine-[Fleet]; 1936 Captain at Sea and Head of the Submarines; 1939 Counter Admiral and Commander of the Submarines; 1940 Vice Admiral; 1942 Admiral; January 30, 1943 Great Admiral and (at the same time) Commander-in-Chief of the Navy; April 1945 Commander of the Armed Forces North; May 1, 1945 Head-of-State and Commander of the Armed Forces.—sentenced to 10 years of imprisonment October 1, 1946 in Nürnberg; released from Spandau 1956.

35. *Encourage of the Commander-in-Chief of the Navy*
   a) *Adjutant of the Commander-in-Chief of the Navy*
   Jan-Heinrich Hansen–Nootbaar Lieutenant Captain (October 1, 1943 Corvette Captain); born April 19, 1911; 1931 Sea Officer Candidate; 1935 Lieutenant at Sea; 1937 1st Lieutenant at Sea; April 1938 First Officer *Grille*, 1939 Lieutenant Captain; March 1940 Commander Torpedo Boat *Falke*; 1941 at the 9th War Ship Production Academy Department; March 1942 Commander *T22*; May 1943 under the Commander-in-Chief of the Navy (for training as Adjutant); September 1, 1943 Adjutant of the Commander-in-Chief of the Navy; April 27, 1944 Chief 4th Torpedo-Boat-[Fleet]; August 26, 1944 again Adjutant of the Commander-in-Chief of the Navy; October 11, 1944 Chief 5th Torpedo-Boat-[Fleet].

   b) *Admiral at the Commander-in-Chief of the Navy*
   Gerhard Wagner Rear Admiral; born November 23, 1898, 1916 Sea Officer Candidate, 1918 Lieutenant at Sea, 1929 Lieutenant Captain, 1933 OKM (Ref. I op), 1935 Corvette Captain and Armed Forces Academy, 1937 Commander of a destroyer, 1939 Frigate Captain and Ia Operational Department/Sea War Command (SKL), 1940 Captain at Sea, June 1941 Chief of the Operational Department/SKL, 1943 Counter Admiral, June 1944 Admiral with the Commander-in-Chief of the Navy.—1956 German Armed Forces.

36. *Permanent Representative of the Commander-in-Chief of the Navy at the Führer Headquarters*
   a) **Theodor Krancke** until February 28, 1943: Vice Admiral; born March 30, 1893; 1912 Sea Cadet; 1915 Lieutenant at Sea; 1922 Lieutenant Captain; 1930 Corvette Captain; 1935 Frigate captain; 1937 Captain at Sea and (October) Commander of the Navy Academy; October 1939 Commander Tank Ship *Admiral Scheer*, February 1940 OKM/Special Headquarters "Weserübung" respectively (April) Chief of the Headquarters Command Admiral Norway; June 1940 Commander of the Heavy Cruiser (formerly Tank Ship) *Admiral*

Scheer, April 1941 Counter Admiral; June 1941 Chief of the Quarters Master Office SKL; April 1943 Admiral and Commander-in-Chief of the Navy Group Command (from October 1944 on Navy High Command) West (Commanding Admiral in France); April 1945 Commander-in-Chief of the Navy High Command Norway.

b) **Hans-Erich Voss** from March 1, 1943 on: Rear Admiral (August 1, 1944 Vice Admiral); born October, 30, 1897; 1915 Sea cadet; 1917 Lieutenant at Sea; 1928 Lieutenant Captain; 1934 Corvette Captain; 1937 Frigate Captain, 1938 Commander 3rd Navy Sergeant training Department; August 1939 Admiral Headquarters officer Navy Group Command East; November 1939 Captain at Sea and Chief of the Fleet and Training Department respectively Command department in the Quarters Master Office SKL; January 1942 Chief of the Command Office Group in the Quarters Master Office SKL; October 1942 Commander of the Heavy Cruiser *Prinz Eugen*; March 1, 1943 Counter Admiral and Permanent Representative of the Commander-in-Chief of the Navy in the Führer Headquarters.

F) REICH'S SS COMMAND

37. **Heinrich Himmler** Reichsführer SS (from July 21, 1944 on at the same time Chief of the Army Armament and Commander respectively Commander-in-Chief of the Substitute Army); born October 7, 1900; 1917/18 officer candidate in the 11th Bavarian Infantry Regiment, farmer; January 1929 Reichsführer SS; July 21, 1944 Chief of the Army Armament and Commander of the Substitute Army (August 1944 Chief of the Army Armament and Commander-in-Chief of the Substitute Army; January 7, 1945, at the same time December 1944/January 1945 Commander-in-Chief Upper Rhine; End of January/March 1945 Commander-in-Chief of the Army Group Weichsel.— Suicide in British captivity May 23, 1945.

38. *Liaison Leader for the Military SS to the Führer*
   a) **Karl Wolff** until the beginning of 1943: SS-1st Group Commander
   b) **Hermann Fegelein** from October 1943/January 1, 1944 on: SS-Brigade Commander (June 21, 1944 Group Commander); born October 30, 1906; 1925 Temporary Volunteer Rider regiment 17; 1927-29 Officer Candidate Bavarian Country Police, Rider School; 1932 NSDAP, 1933 SS-2nd Lieutenant; 1936 Major and Commander SS-Main Rider School; 1937 Standard Commander; 1940 taken over into the Military SS as Lieutenant Colonel of the Rider School and Commander of the SS-T-Rider Standard respectively SS-Cavalry Regiment 1; August 1941 Commander SS-Cavalry Brigade; May 1942 Inspector of the [Reit-und Fahrwesen] in the [SSFHA]; December 1942 Senior Colonel and Commander of Fight Group Fegelein; April 1943 Commander SS-Cavalry Division (later 8th SS-Cavalry Division *Florian Geyer*) and (May) Brigade Commander; wounded September 30, 1943; after getting well into the Führer Headquarters; January 1, 1944 Chief of the Office VI/SSFHA

under the [Kdrg.] to the [RFSS] as Liaison Leader of the Military SS at the Führer.—Demoted because of desertion April 27, 1945 and executed at Hitler's order during the night of April 28/29, 1945.

aa) *Adjutant of the Liaison Leader of the SS*

Johannes Göhler SS-Captain (December 21, 1944 Major); born September 15, 1918, 1933 Hitler Youth, commercial teaching; 1936 SS, 1937 SS-TV; 1941 2nd Lieutenant Rider regiment 1 (SS-Cavalry Brigade; later 8th SS-Cavalry Division *Florian Geyer*); 1942 1st Lieutenant and Chief 4th/SS Rider Regiment 1; November 9, 1943 Captain, August 1944 Adjutant to Fegelein.

G) REPRESENTATIVES OF THE HIGHEST REICH'S AND PARTY AUTHORITIES

39. *Permanent Representative of the Reich's Foreign Ministry (RAM) at the Führer*
    Walther Hewel Envoy I. Class (March 31, 1943 Ambassador); born March 25, 1904; 1923 College of Technology in Munich, participant in the November Putsch 1923 as Flag Carrier of the *Stosstrupp Hitler*, sentenced to 1¼ years of imprisonment (Landsberg); export trader (1927-36 in Java at the Anglo-Dutch Plantations of Java Ltd.); 1933 re-joins the NSDAP; 1936 Gau Main Office Leader at the AO in Berlin; February 1937 Ribbentrop Office (1st referent for German-British relations) and SS-Major; June 1938 entrance into the Foreign Ministry as Legation Councilor I. Class and leader of the personal headquarters RAM, SS-Standard Commander; 1939 Presenting Legation Councillor; September 1940 Envoy I. Class as Ministry Conductor and permanent representative of the RAM at the Führer; 1940 SS-Senior Colonel; 1924 SS-Brigade Commander; March 31, 1943 Ambassador—Died probably May 2/3, 1945 in Berlin.

    a) *Representative*
    Dr. Franz von Sonnleithner Envoy I. Class; born June 1, 1905 (Salzburg), 1924-28 Studies of Law and Political Science in Vienna, Rome, Paris; 1927 Diploma Trader; 1928 Dr. in Jurisprudence; 1929 Police Director Vienna; 1931 Police Commissioner; 1932 Police Director Salzburg; 1932 NSDAP; 1934 Federal Chancellor Office (Code Department); October 1934 removed from office and sentenced to six years of strict imprisonment because of high treason in favour of the NSDAP; March 1938 Reich Government Vienna; October 1938 entrance into the Foreign Office as Legation Secretary; 1939 Legation Councillor in the Minister's Office; 1941 Presenting Legation Councilor; March 31, 1943 Envoy I. Class as Ministry Conductor and put in charge of the Leader of the Personal Headquarters of the RAM.

40. *Reich Minister for Armament and Ammunition* (from September 2, 1943 on: *Reich Minister for Armament and War Production*)
    Albert Speer (Professor); born March 19, 1905; College of Technology (TH) in Karlsruhe, Munich and Berlin, Diploma Engineer; 1927 Assistant TH Berlin; 1932 self-employed Architect; 1932 NSDAP; 1933 Reich Propaganda Command (Office Leader for artistic design of mass rallies); 1943 Leader of the

Office "Beauty of Work" of the NS-Union [K.d.F.], as successor of Troost Hitler's Architect (Reich's Party Day Buildings and so on); 1937 Professor and General Construction Inspector for the Reich Capital, High Command Leader; 1938 Prussian Privy Council; 1941 MdR; February 1942 as successor of Todt Reich's Minister for Armament and Ammunition, Chief of the Todt Labor Force, General Inspector for the German road system and general Inspector for water and energy; March 1942 General Authorized Person for Armament tasks in the four-year-plan; May 1942 took over the Armament Office/ OKW.—Sentenced to 20 years of imprisonment at the Main Trial of Nürnberg September 30, 1946; released from Spandau in 1966; published *Inside the Third Reich* in 1969; published *Spandau: The Secret Diaries* in 1976; died 1981.

a) *Contact at the Führer* from May, 1944 on: Colonel Nicolaus v. Below (see 5)

41. *Reich Chief Press Officer*

Dr. Otto Dietrich Reich Leader; born August 31, 1897, 1915 War Volunteer (Lieutenant), studied in Political Science and Philosophy in Freiburg, Frankfurt and Munich; 1921 Dr. Political Science, economy, trade editor *Essener Allg. Zeitung*; 1928 leader of the trade editing "Münchener-Augsburger Abendzeitung," NSDAP; 1931 deputy Chief Editor *Essener National Zeitung*, 1931 Reich Chief Press Officer of the NSDAP; 1933 Vice President of the Reich Government and Permanent Secretary in the Reich Ministry for National Information and Propaganda; 1941 SS-Lieutenant General.—Sentenced to seven years' in prison April 1949 in Nürnberg; released 1950 from Landsberg; died February 22, 1952.

a) *Deputy Reich Chief Press Officer*

Helmut Sündermann Main Office Leader; born February 19, 1911; 1930 University of Munich (history, political economy and journalism), 1930 NSDAP; August 1931 Headquarters Leader of the Reich's Press Office NSDAP and SS-member; November 1933 Chief in Office NS-Party Correspondence; 1934 Leader of the Press political Office of the Reich Chief Press Officer; 1937 Headquarters Leader of the Reich Chief Press Officer of the NSDAP; 1938 Main Office Leader; 1941 SS-Lieutenant Colonel; 1942 Deputy Chief Press Officer of the Reich's Government and [MdR].

b) *[DNB]-Representative*

Heinz Lorenz [Oberbereichsleiter]; born August 7, 1913; 1931 NSDAP, 1931 Press Stenographer; later Script Leader in Wolff's Telegraph Office (from December 1933 on at DNB); Hitler Youth-[Hauptbannführer]; Adjutant to the Reich Chief Press Officer, as News Contact of the DNB for presentation of foreign news material at the Reich Chief Press Officer at the Führer Headquarters.

42. *Adjutant of the Leader of the Party Office of the NSDAP*

Wilhelm Zander [Hauptbereichsleiter] SS Colonel; born April 22, 1911; Trading School, employee in the wood trade and Correspondent; 1931 NSDAP and SS (1932 full time); 1933 Lieutenant in the Personal Department [RFSS]), 1935 Adjutant SS Northwest; 1936 Adjutant SS Central; 1937 sent as Major to the Headquarters of the Deputy of the Führer/Reichsleiter Bormann; 1943 Lieutenant Colonel; September 1944 Colonel.

INTRODUCTION TO THE NOTES

by Helmut Heiber

The bibliographical references within the notes on the text are not intended as a bibliography of the particular subject addressed, but refer only to the works that were used. If both the original edition and the German translation of a book are included in the bibliography, and the name of the author is listed without additional comment in the reference, the page numbers refer to the German edition. For the commentary, the only documentation available, for the most part, was part of the collection in the library of the *Institut für Zeitgeschichte* [Institute of Contemporary History], but not, for example, file materials. An exception is the map section, which was compiled by General of Artillery (retired) Walter Warlimont, on the basis of maps similar to those used during the situation reports.

The present edition was already completed by the end of 1957, but in some parts the notes were still corrected during the final revision using literature published in 1958. At the end of 1958, the complete text was ready for typesetting. The printing was delayed for more than two years, however, by circumstances beyond the control of the publisher and editor. A further revision of the text, which had already been completely set, may have been desirable from a scholarly point of view, but could not be justified given the additional work and disproportionate costs involved. If this editorial shortcoming is to be accepted in connection with the publication of a work that was edited some time ago, the following must be kept in mind: the book presented here is a collection of source material, whose value and significance is much less tied to a specific time frame than, for example, a monograph would be. Thus, the source will continue to be used even when the comments in the notes will have become outdated not only by years but by decades. Very soon it will be irrelevant whether it represents 1958 or 1960. The commentary is only a tool to understanding the text.

Only in one case did the editor decide to deviate from this rule. During the final revision in 1958, the first installments of the personal data on the Army generals were published and were used in the commentary (compiled by Wolf Keilig within the framework of the loose-leaf collection *Das deutsche Heer 1938-1945*). In order not to stop halfway, personal data from the following installments was added as well, which was not too difficult technically. The same applies to the personal data section of Walter Lohmann and Hans H. Hildebrand: *Die deutsche Kriegsmarine 1939-1945*.

The listing of sources does not imply that the entire commentary is based on these sources. In fact, the sources listed may apply only in some relatively trivial details, while the primary material was derived from oral or written information and communication with the editor, which were used extensively. The editor also wishes to take this opportunity to thank again all those who made themselves available for questions and inquiries and provided information. Deserving of particular mention are:

General of Infantry (retd.) Walter Buhle (deceased), Stuttgart; and

General of Artillery (retd.) Walter Warlimont, Rottach-Egern,

who reviewed the texts and provided valuable comments as regular participants in a large number of the discussions. The same effort was made by:

Dr. Jürgen Rohwer, Working Group for Military Research in Frankfurt (now [1962] director of the Library of Contemporary History, Stuttgart),

to whom the editor is indebted for numerous facts and details of the history of the war at sea. In addition, the editor is obliged to all who have helped with their specialized knowledge or their recollections—often through numerous discussions or extensive correspondence—providing explanations, comments and opinions:

Rudolf Absolon, Central Certification Bureau of the Federal Archive, Kornelimünster at Aachen;

General of Anti-Aircraft Artillery (retd.) Walther v. Axthelm, Traunstein;

Lieutenant General (retd.) Hugo Beisswänger, Ulm;

Gottlob Berger, Gerstetten;

Walter Blume, Heisede at Hildesheim;

General of the Infantry (retd.) Günther Blumentritt, Marburg;

Lieutenant General (retd.) Hermann Böhme, Munich;

Ministry of Defense, Bonn;

Ministerial Director, Dr. Cartellieri, Bad Godesberg;

Colonel (retd.) Torsten Christ, Munich;

General of Parachute Troops (retd.) Paul Conrath, Hamburg-Stellingen;

Lieutenant General (retd.) Paul Deichmann, Study Group, History of the Air War, Bad Ems (later Luftwaffe Study Group) at the Bundeswehr Command Academy, Luftwaffe Section, Hamburg-Blankenese;

Minister (retd.) Fernand Demany, Brussels;

German Department for the Notification of Family Members of Fallen Soldiers of the former German Wehrmacht, Berlin-Wittenau;

German Chamber of Commerce, Vienna;

Major General (retd.) Hans Dörr, Grosskarolinenfeld b. Rosenheim;

Brigadier General Kurt v. Einem, Neumünster;

Lieutenant General (retd.) Gerhard Engel, Oberbolheim b. Cologne;

Colonel (retd.) Dr. of Engineering Willi Esser, Grafrath über Frechen;

General of the Engineers (retd.) Otto Förster, Walsrode;

Research Group for the Post-war History of Berlin, Berlin-Dahlem;

Colonel General (retd.) Hans Friessner, Bad Reichenhall;

Major General (retd.) Walter Grabmann, Steinebach/Wörthsee;

Colonel General (retd.) Paul Hausser, Ludwigsburg;

Lieutenant General (retd.) Otto Heidkämper, Bückeburg;

Colonel (retd.) Heinz-Danko Herre, Munich-Solln;

Hans H. Hildebrand, Hamburg-Bergedorf;

General of the Engineers (retd.) Alfred Jacob, Munich;
General of Panzer Troops (retd.) Georg Jauer, Greven/Westphalia;
University Assistant Professor Dr. Ludwig Jedlicka, Vienna;
Lieutenant Colonel (retd.) Ernst John v. Freyend, Essen-Heisingen;
Dr. F. W. Kärcher, Munich;
Major General (retd.), Dr. of Engineering] Werner Kennes, Farchant/Upper Bavaria;
Major General (retd.) Helmut Kleikamp, Kiel;
Field Marshal General (retd.) Georg v. Küchler, Garmisch-Partenkirchen;
Major Robert Lammineur, Antwerp;
Professor Emile Lousse, Blanden b. Löwen;
Lieutenant General (retd.) Carl Hans Lungershausen, Hamburg-Wellingsbüttel;
Rudolf Lusar, Munich;
Lieutenant General (retd.) Bruno Maass, Munich;
Field Marshal General (retd.) Erich v. Manstein, Münster;
Colonel of the General Staff Dr. Hans Meier-Welcker, Military History Research Department, Freiburg i. Breisgau;
Field Marshal General (retd.) Erhard Milch, Düsseldorf;
Lieutenant General Max-Josef Pemsel, Ulm;
Colonel (retd.) Horst v. Petersdorf, Berchtesgaden;
General of the Signal Troops (retd.) Albert Praun, Neumarkt-St.Veith;
General of the Infantry (retd.) Enno v. Rintelen, Deidesheim;
Lieutenant General (retd.) Carl Rodenburg, Lübeck;
Joachim Ruoff, Munich;
General of the Panzer Troops (retd.) Dietrich v. Saucken, Munich-Solln;
Karl-Otto Saur, Munich;
Lieutenant General (retd.) Dr. of Engineering Erich Schneider, Bensheim-Auerbach;
Reich Minister (retd.) Lutz Graf Schwerin v. Krosigk, Arenberg;
Major Dr. Ferdinand v. Senger u. Etterlin, Cologne-Rodenkirchen;
General of Panzer Troops (retd.) Fridolin v. Senger u. Etterlin, Happach, Kreis Lörrach;
Diplomat (retd.) Dr. Franz v. Sonnleithner, Ingelheim/Rhineland;
Administration of the cities of Berchtesgarden and Cologne;
Colonel General (retd.) Hans-Jürgen Stumpff, Bonn;
Lieutenant General (retd.) Wolfgang Thomale, Peine;
Diplomat (retd.) Dr. Hans Thomsen, Hamburg;
Colonel (retd.) Werner v. Tippelskirch, Stuttgart;
Major General (retd.) Alfred Toppe, Duisburg;
Lieutenant General (retd.) Bruno v. Uthmann, Hamburg;
Wasag-Chemie AG, Factory, Neumarkt/Opf.;
General of the Panzer Troops (retd.) Walther Wenck, Bochum;
General of the Cavalry (retd.) Siegfried Westphal, Dortmund;
General of the Mountain Troops (retd.) August Winter, Munich-Pasing;

General of the Infantry (retd.) Otto Wöhler, Grossburgwedel b. Hanover; and Colonel General (retd.) Kurt Zeitzler, Hamburg.

Without their help, the clarification of many open questions would not have been possible.

The editor cannot close this list without his sincere thanks to Fräulein Sybille Becker for her untiring help with proofreading and indexing.

H.H. [Helmut Heiber]

For maps 3, 4 and 6, sketches from the book by Kurt v. Tippelskirch, *Geschichte des Zweiten Weltkriegs* [*A History of the Second World War*], were used with the kind permission of Athenäum-Verlag, Bonn.

NOTES

NOTES TO THE PREFACE

[1] Helmuth Greiner: *Die Oberste Wehrmachtführung: 1939–1943*, Wiesbaden 1951, p. 407.

[2] Greiner, p. 409.

[3] Alan Bullock: *Hitler: Eine Studie über Tyrannei*, Düsseldorf, p. 689. [NDT: *Hitler: A Study in Tyranny*, London, 1962]

[4] Greiner, p. 12.

[5] A foreign guest could sometimes find himself not as a participant in a military conference but a spectator in a specially choreographed presentation having only an approximate connection to reality. In these cases, the term "show conference" was used.

[6] An affidavit by ORR Krieger, dated March 31, 1946 (Document Keitel No. 15), states: "On the one hand Hitler tried to *protect himself through the stenographic records against false or incomplete reports*. He repeatedly said at meetings: 'That is why I allow this to be recorded.' Obviously, he didn't trust certain officers as a result of false or inaccurate reports, especially regarding production plans and production results as well as the readiness and capability of weapons and aircraft, etc. He was already skeptical before the establishment of the Stenographic Service, and this mistrust increased even more after 1944. With respect to false or unclear reports and data, he frequently expressed regret that he 'didn't have everything recorded earlier.' He frequently admonished meeting participants with express references to the stenographic record, urging accuracy, particularly with numerical data. In telephone conversations he also occasionally inserted the comment, 'Be careful. I'm having everything stenographed here.' On the other hand, Hitler also wanted to use the stenographic record to provide historians with documentary material regarding plans and decisions—and also to clarify *responsibility*. He repeatedly stated that he 'took responsibility for his orders, for history and for posterity, and that is why he has everything recorded verbatim.' Sometimes he would explain in this context, 'If it goes well, gentlemen, you will earn the glory, and you're welcome to it. But I take full responsibility for everything, even if it turns out badly, for posterity and for history.'"

[7] The "Reichstag Stenographers"—the original designation—were, at the time they were ordered to move to the Führer Headquarters, already given rank in the Regierungsratsgruppe [Government Council Group] of the government salary system. Only later were they awarded the designation Regierungsrat [Government Councilor] that had already been introduced by some regional assemblies. The director of the Stenographic Office, Krieger, and the head of Stenographic Service at the Führer Headquarters, Dr. Peschel, received the designation Oberregierungsrat [Senior Government Councilor].

[8] A vivid description of such a meeting, in February 1945, is found in Gerhard Boldt: *Die Letzten Tage der Reichskanzlei*, 4th ed., Hamburg and Stuttgart 1948, p. 11.

[9] The stenographers using the Gabelsberger system (Krieger, Dr. Reynitz, Thöt) deviated from the usual practice of the Plenar rotation service, instituting a new procedure intended to prevent the unconscious loss of attention that easily occurs when a stenographer is recording a text which he knows he won't have to edit himself: they decided only afterwards which meeting portion to assign to each person.

[10] A few meetings in the fall of 1944 were exceptions, when Hitler was bedridden and the lack of space in his bunker room meant that only one stenographer was called in.

[11] In May 1945 the stenographers incorrectly told the Americans that the second copy was intended for the Army archives and had been delivered there. That statement, although it found its way into the literature, was false.

[12] The stenographers do admit to one incident where Hitler requested to review a transcript. The discussion concerned the security of a North Sea convoy—strong or weak—and at least one of the two passages in question contradicted Hitler's later statement. But even in this case he changed nothing and did not order another review of the stenographic notes when (as was characteristic for him) he believed there were discrepancies in the transcript.

[13] Privately, and to a certain extent also between the lines, Scherff did express criticism, but this did not damage the assessment of his official work.

[14] The List of Participants provided by the stenographers at the beginning of each transcript (since the end of 1943 for the situation conferences and earlier for the special conferences) gives the false impression of a constant number of participants from beginning to end.

[15] The May 1945 stenographers' estimate of 200,000 pages—a figure later repeated by Allen—is too high; however, it is possible that the 103,000 figure does not include the special conferences.

[16] Dr. Haagen's and Herrgesell's shorthand notes were destroyed with the rest of the materials at Berchtesgaden. Fourteen days later, however, Herrgesell gave an eyewitness report from memory, discussing the dramatic meeting of April 22, 1945. This report was cited in essays in two American periodicals ("Adolf Hitler's Last Hours" in *Time*, May 21, 1945, and "How Dead Is Hitler?" in *Cosmopolitan*, August 1946).

[17] Especially ORR Krieger, who had accompanied Dr. Peschel to Scherff's quarters, argued forcefully against destroying the documents. He maintained that every effort should be made to preserve them, and claimed that General Scherff was in any case not authorized to order their destruction.

[18] When Sergeant Allen later wrote: "The men in charge of burning did not want to finish the task, because they felt the papers would prove how much Hitler was responsible for the fall of Germany," this was pure speculation. It is not true that the work was performed reluctantly and carelessly. The fact that various pieces more or less survived is explained below.

[19] See also the description by Wilhelm Scheidt in *Echo der Woche*, September 9, 1949.

[20] At least according to a second-hand report by Dr. Peschel. Dr. Haagen, who was staying in the same basement where this nocturnal burning operation took place, remembers only large quantities of annotated situation maps. Helling also doubts the Berlin burning, since he had taken the third copy to Berchtesgaden together with the first part and shorthand notes. So the question remains open: Where are these third copies? In any case, only originals and shorthand notes were found at the site of the burning. The version given above is therefore more probable, even though a sudden reappearance of the working copies cannot be excluded.

[21] At the first meeting, one of the two Reichsleitung party functionaries appeared as well. He later disappeared into a camp, however, since he was neither very talkative nor indispensable to the transcription work.

[22] In addition to Allen, Special Agent Eric Albrecht and Captain Palmer worked with the stenographers.

[23] It is impossible to give an exact figure, since in some cases it cannot be determined if the fragments are from the same conference or not.

[24] The originals are in Washington D.C., today.

1942

[25] Almost immediately after the beginning of the Eastern campaign, Mussolini offered his allies assistance in Russia, and by July 1941 the Italian XXXV Corps, known as *Corpo di Spedizione Italiano Russia* (CSIR)—consisting of the *Pasubio*, *Vicenza* and *Torino* infantry divisions and the 3rd Mobile Division of Principe Amedeo Duca d'Aosta (usually abbreviated as *Celere*)—had already been transferred to the Ukraine. In October of the same year Mussolini offered an additional twenty divisions in order to compensate for the deployment of German forces in the Mediterranean area. However, the Italian High Command thought it possible to send only six divisions. Indeed, because of lack of materiel (especially trucks), only some of the originally intended forces were sent to southern Russia in May 1942: in addition to two militia divisions (see note 97), the Italian II Corps with the *Ravenna*, *Cosseria*, and *Sforzesca* divisions and the *Alpini Corps* including the *Tridentina*, *Julia*, and *Cuneense* divisions (see note 96). From June 1942 on, these forces—along with the Eighth Army under General Gariboldi (after Hitler had curtly rejected Italian inquiries about the possible assumption of the Army High Command by the crown prince)—operated in the area of Army Group South. Like all its other Axis allies, the Italian troops had to endure the onslaught of the Soviet attacks during the winter of 1942-43. The Russian push against the Italians on the Don (which had obviously been expected by Hitler) was to be delayed for two weeks. On December 16 the hostile attack across the Don destroyed the Italian Eighth Army. The still intact Alpine Corps, which had formed the northern flank, was surrounded one month

later near Rossosh' and destroyed during the second half of January—because Führer Headquarters had forbidden a timely retreat. At the beginning of February 1943 the staff officers of the Eighth Army were pulled out and the rest of the formations returned to their homeland, which was now itself under threat of attack.—*Source: Rintelen, p. 147; Tippelskirch, pp. 316 and 324; Messe, passim.*

[26] This refers to a Soviet fleet formation, identified by air reconnaissance and the radio signal observation service, which consisted of a cruiser and 6 to 8 destroyers. The fleet advanced into the western Black Sea and, divided into two groups, briefly bombarded the coast near Fidonisi and Galisera. Contrary to Jodl's assumption, which is clear here, the Russian Black Sea fleet—consisting of a battleship, 5 cruisers, 30 destroyers, over 50 submarines and innumerable small units (Conrady: 2 heavy and 4 light cruisers, 3 flotilla leaders, 10 to 12 destroyers, 6 torpedo boats and 30 submarines)—was, despite its immense superiority, never used in operation, apart from one instance shortly after the beginning of the hostilities. The fleet withdrew to the eastern harbors after the loss of the main military base at Sevastopol', and only supported the tactical moves of the Red Army in small deployments using motor torpedo boats with (often makeshift) landing vehicles. The Soviet submarines were not particularly successful either (sinking 9 ships, totaling 25,000 GRT in 130 verified attacks).—*Source: Ruge: Seekrieg, p. 160.; Conrady: Die Kriegsmarine…, passim.*

[27] This question relates to the three German submarines of the type II-B (*U24, U9* and *U19*), which had arrived in the Black Sea shortly before. Altogether six 250-ton submarines were transferred overland (along the Elbe to Dresden, on the expressway to Ingolstadt, along the Danube to Linz, where they were assembled) to the Black Sea. These submarines fought particularly against Soviet convoy traffic on the eastern coast. With the help of motor torpedo boats and occasionally also aircraft, they were able to destroy two-thirds of the Soviet transport fleet of 300,000 GRT during the course of the war. Not a single German ship was lost during this time; the Germans finally sank their own ships in 1944 during the evacuation of the Black Sea. As a result of the long-distance transfer overland, the raising of sunken vessels, and new construction from the Nikolaev shipyard, the German Navy in the Black Sea had, altogether, a fleet of 10 motor torpedo boats, 23 mine sweepers, 5 blockade breakers, 6 submarines, 3 mine layers, 8 submarine hunters, 13 troop transport ships each of 800 tons, and about 200 flat-bottomed light craft and artillery carriers. In partial contrast with the numbers provided by Ruge, Conrady lists the boats which were transferred to the Black Sea via the Elbe, expressway and Danube as follows: 30 motor torpedo boats, 23 mine sweepers, 6 submarines, 50 marine flat-bottomed boats, and 26 submarine chasers, as well as various launches, coastal defense ships and motorboats. There were also additional small units as well as several Italian motor torpedo boats and small submarines.—*Source: Ruge: Seekrieg, p. 222; Conrady: Quer durch Europa, p. 63.*

[28] Incorrect division number.

[29] The Soviets began a large-scale attack along the Don northwest of Stalingrad on Monday, November 19, and on November 20 they began to attack to the

south of Stalingrad as well. In the afternoon of November 22, Soviet tank forces linked up southeast of Kalach, surrounding the Sixth Army in a pincer attack. Apart from innumerable small independent units, the IV, VIII, XI Corps and LI Army Corps and XIV Panzer Corps (44th, 71st, 76th, 79th, 94th, 99th, 100th, 113th, 295th, 297th, 305th, 371st, 376th, 384th, and 389th Infantry Divisions, the 3rd, 29th, and 60th Motorized Divisions, and the 14th, 16th, and 24th Panzer Divisions), and the 9th Artillery Division were surrounded. In addition, parts of the Romanian 1st Cavalry Division and the Romanian 20th Infantry Division, as well as the Croatian 100th Infantry Regiment, were also surrounded.—*Source: Schröter, pp. 51 and 80.*

30 Different meanings are possible for this abbreviated term "group," since panzer or army groups as well as combat or marching units could be referred to. Here, however, it generally means combat units, i.e., formations that are tactical and restricted in time (reinforced or combined staffs, battalions, regiments and also divisions), assembled according to the conditions and needs of the particular tactical situation and under temporary suspension of the regular chain of command.

31 It is probably Colonel Schweitzer who is referred to here—the former commander of the military sub-district of Essen.—*Source: Das deutsche Heer, p. 865; Rangliste 1944-45, p. 209.*

32 Walter Hörnlein, born January 2, 1893; cadet institution in Lichterfelde; 1913 Second Lieutenant 140th Infantry Regiment; 1914-1919 in French captivity, became First Lieutenant in the Reichswehr; 1927 Captain; 1935 Major, Commander, 69th Infantry Regiment; 1937 Lieutenant Colonel; November 1939 Commander, 80th Infantry Regiment; 1940 Colonel; 1941 Commander, Infantry Regiment *Grossdeutschland*; 1942 Major General and Commander, *Grossdeutschland* Panzer Grenadier Division; January 1943 Lieutenant General; at the end of 1944 Infantry General and Commanding General, LXXXII Army Corps; and 1945 Deputy, II Army Corps as well as XXVII Army Corps.—*Source: DNB of March 16, 1943; Order of Battle, p. 568; Das deutsche Heer, p. 324; Rangliste 1944-45, p. 23; Seemen (page numbers are dispensed with in citations of this book; the awards can be seen from the alphabetical list of the recipients of the Knight's Cross); Keilig 211/140.*

33 Kurt von d. Chevallerie (not to be mistaken with Lieutenant General Hellmuth von d. Chevallerie; the Chief of Staff of the Crete fortress later on, Colonel General in the General Staff von d. Chevallerie; or Lieutenant Colonel Botho von d. Chevallerie, who was killed in action on November 16, 1943), born December 23, 1891; 1911 Second Lieutenant, 5th Infantry Guard Regiment; during World War I Reichswehr Company Commander and Adjutant; 1935 Colonel; 1938 Chief of the Zentralabteilung (Central Department—GZ) of the Army General Staff; 1939 Major General and Commander, 83rd Infantry Division; 1940-41 Commander, 99th Mobile Division; 1941 Lieutenant General; February 1942 Infantry General and Commanding General, LIX Army Corps; and May-October 1944 Deputy to Blaskowitz (Commander of the First Army). Kurt von d. Chevallerie has been missing since 1945 (Kolberg).—*Source: VB of*

December 24, 1943; Order of Battle, p. 536; Das deutsche Heer, p. 10; Rangliste 1944-45, pp. 16 and 316; Seemen; Keilig 211/53.

[34] Erich Brandenberger; born July 15, 1892; 1911 6th Regiment Sentinel Bavarian Field Artillery; 1913 Second Lieutenant; and during the World War Adjutant, Artillery Battalion Commander, Reichswehr. Among other assignments; teacher at the War Academy; 1935 Squad leader in the Army Training Department of the RKM; 1936 Colonel and Commander, 76th Army Regiment; 1938 Commander, 74th Artillery Regiment; 1939 Chief of Staff, XXIII Army Corps; 1940 Major General; 1941 Commander, 8th Panzer Division; August 1942 Lieutenant General; January 1943 Deputy Commander, LIX Army Corps; May 1943 Commander, XXIX Army Corps (from August 1943 General of the Armored Troops); August 1944 Commander, Seventh Army; and end of March 1945 Deputy Commander, Nineteenth Army.—*Source: Army High Command Staff Files (Nbg. Dok. NOKW-141); Siegler, p. 114; Order of Battle, p. 553; Das deutsche Heer, p. 525; Rangliste 1944-45, pp. 17 and 420; Seemen; Keilig 211/43.*

[35] Otto Tiemann; born February 12, 1890; 1909 Second Lieutenant, 8th Engineer Battalion; 1934 Colonel; 1937 Major General and (since 1936) Senior Engineer Officer 3 (Dresden); 1939-43 Commander, 93rd Infantry Division; February 1944 Commanding General, XXIII Army Corps; May 1944 General of the Engineers; and December 1944 Commanding General, XVII Army Corps. Tiemann died on May 8, 1952.—*Source: Order of Battle, p.634; Seemen; Das deutsche Heer, p. 219; Rangliste 1944-45, pp. 18 and 319; Deutsche Soldatenzeitung of May 8, 1952; Keilig 211/341.*

[36] According to Hitler's order of September 18, 1939, a Police Division under SS-Brigadeführer Pfeffer-Wildenbruch was established in October 1939 with members from the Ordnungspolizei and special army troops such as artillery, engineers and so on (in 1942 they were released again). They were first used as armed SS and later (Reichsführer SS decree of February 10, 1942) they were fully integrated in the forces of the SS as 4th SS Police Panzer Grenadier Division. This division was put into action during the campaign against France and in Russia until May 1943, in the siege of Leningrad and at Volkhov (February-March 1942). From the summer of 1943 on, they were located in the southeast. A second division with members from the police was established in 1945: the 35th SS Police Infantry Division.—*Source: Hausser, pp. 15 and 68; Order of Battle, p. 338; Vortrag Chef Orpo über den Kräfte- und Kriegseinsatz der Ordnungspolizei auf einer Dienstbesprechung der BdO and IdO on February 1-4, 1942 (Nbg. Dok. NO-084).*

[37] As Army Chief of the General Staff, Zeitzler repeats in detail here what General Jodl, Chief of the Armed Forces Operations Staff, has to a great extent already reported. This custom was later altered, and only the Chief of the General Staff reported on the Eastern Front (see Introduction). It is also possible that in this case Zeitzler was absent for other reasons and Jodl only operated as a deputy reporter.

[38] Term for the German front wedge to Lake Ladoga (Shlissel'burg), which since 1941 separated Leningrad from the rest of Russia, making the besieged town dependent on supplies coming over the lake.

[39] Erich Jaschke; born May 11, 1890; 1910 Lieutenant, 132nd Infantry Regiment; 1938 Colonel and Chief of Staff of the Infantry in the Army High Command; 1941 Commander; 90th Infantry Regiment; October 1941 Major General; January 1942 Commander, 20th Motorized Division; 1943 General of the Infantry (May) and Commanding General, LV Army Corps (March); and October 1943 General of the Infantry in the Army General Staff.—*Source: Order of Battle, p. 571; Seemen; Das deutsche Heer, p. 24; Rangliste 1944-45, p. 17; Keilig 211/152.*

[40] Paul Klatt; born December 6, 1896; 1915 Second Lieutenant, 51st Infantry Regiment; Infantryman, then Engineer during the World War; 1936 Major; 1938 Commander, 83rd Mountain Engineer Battalion; 1939 Lieutenant Colonel; 1941 Colonel and Commander, 138th Mountain Light Infantry Regiment; May 1943 Major General; July 1944 Commander, 3rd Mountain Division; and December 1944 Lieutenant General Klatt was in Russian captivity from 1945-1955.—*Source: DNB of December 30, 1944; Order of Battle, p. 577; Seemen; Das deutsche Heer, p. 653; Rangliste 1944-45, p. 36; Keilig 211/164.*

[41] A genuine fuel problem within the Wehrmacht was not yet felt that year or the next. The problem noted here, as in other similar cases—especially in Africa—is more a problem of transportation and supply. Trains carrying the fuel were not able to reach the front on time, or the distance between the unloading point and the fighting troops had become too great because train connections were absent or destroyed. Motor transport columns, which in any case were only available in insufficient number, consumed large amounts of their fuel load themselves while moving from the train station to the front. Shortly after the beginning of the German summer offensive in late June 1942, several panzer divisions repeatedly came to a halt because of this problem. Some even had to be left behind, and were withdrawn from southern Russia and assigned to other fronts. They were missing at the decisive turning point.

[42] From this one can clearly see that "down there" means southern Russia; the general fuel situation was not yet a problem. The Germans at the beginning of the war had already attempted to reduce the effects of possible enemy action against their fuel supply by intensifying synthetic fuel production. Gaining control over Romanian petroleum did the rest. So in early 1944, the total monthly requirements of about 600,000 tons could still be met, with a few insignificant exceptions. A serious situation arose when the Allied air force began destroying the Romanian and Hungarian oil fields, the German hydrogenation plants, and the transportation routes in April and May of 1944. [—] The following chart provides information about the production and consumption:

in 1,000 t	1940	1941	1942	1943	1944
German fuel supply	3,963	4,839	5,620	6,563	4,684
German total amount received	6,389	8,120	7,619	8,956	(5,554)
Consumption	5,856	7,305	6,483	6,971	—
(By the Wehrmacht)	3,005	4,567	4,410	4,762	—

—*Source: Schramm, P.E., p. 394; Die deutsche Industrie, p. 171.*

[43] Erich von Lewinski, known as von Manstein (after his stepfather, the husband of an aunt); born November 24, 1887; 1900-06 Cadet Corps; 1907 Second Lieutenant; 1915 Captain, during the First World War served mostly in adjutancy and general staff duties, Reichswehr; 1927 Lieutenant Colonel; 1929 RWM; 1931 Lieutenant Colonel; 1932 Commander, 2nd Battalion, 4th Infantry Regiment; 1933 Colonel; July 1935 Chief of Operations in the Army General Staff (OKH); October 1936 Senior Quartermaster I and Major General; 1939 Lieutenant General and Commander, 18th Infantry Division; August 1939 Chief of the General Staff, Army Group South; October 1939 Chief of the General Staff, Army Group A (plan for the Western campaign); February 1940 Commanding General, XXXVIII Army Corps; March 1940 Commander, LVI Army Corps; June 1940 General of the Infantry; September 1941 Commander-in-Chief, Eleventh Army; January 1942 General; July 1942 Field Marshal; November 1942 Commander-in-Chief, Army Group Don (renamed Army Group South on February 14, 1943); and March 31, 1944 awarded Iron Cross with Swords. Manstein was sentenced to 18 years in prison by a British military court in Hamburg in February 1950 (sentence was reduced to 12 years) and released in February 1952 on parole, and finally discharged in May 1953.—*Source: Army High Command Staff Files (Nbg. Dok. NOKW-141); Munzinger Archive.*

[44] Paul Tzschöckell, born September 11, 1895; war volunteer; 1915 Reserve Second Lieutenant; 1919 in police service; 1935 appointment as Captain in the Army; 1938 Lieutenant Colonel in Smoke-shell mortar training and experimentation department; 1939 Commander, 3rd Smoke Battalion; 1941 Colonel and Commander, 53rd Rocket Artillery; October 1942 until March 1943 Commander, 2nd Smoke Division; later at the Celle Gas Defense School (November 1944 Commander as Major General); and April-May 1945 Commander of a combat group.—*Source: Das deutsche Heer, p. 826; Rangliste 1944-45, p. 49; Order of Battle, p. 635; Keilig 211/344.*

[45] Erich Abraham, born March 27, 1895; 1914 war volunteer; 1915 Reserve Second Lieutenant; after the First World War served in police service; 1935 appointed Lieutenant Colonel in 18th Infantry Regiment; 1938 Colonel and Battalion Commander, 105th Infantry Regiment; 1941 Colonel; 1940-42 Commander' 230th Infantry Regiment; 1943 Major General and Commander, 76th Infantry Division; January 1944 Lieutenant General; December 1944 Commanding General, LXIII Army Corps; and March 1945 General of the Infantry.—*Source: DNB of July 2, 1944; Order of Battle, p. 521; Seemen; Das deutsche Heer, p. 364; Rangliste 1944-45, pp. 28 and 331.*

[46] Heinz Fiebig, born March 22, 1897; 1914 Ensign; 1915 Second Lieutenant, 156th Infantry Regiment, Reichswehr; teacher at the Dresden Military School; 1939 Lieutenant Colonel and Commander, 1st Battalion, 192nd Infantry Regiment; 1941 Commander, 448th Infantry Regiment; 1942 Colonel; September 1943 Commander, 246th Infantry Division; October 1943 Army Weapons School, Fourth Army; and December 1944 Major General. In addition to him there was also a Lieutenant Colonel Fiebig, who was commander of the military district in

Perleberg and Bernau.—*Source: Keilig 211/84; Order of Battle, p. 546; Das deutsche Heer, pp. 796 and 913; Rangliste 1944-45, pp. 51 and 215.*

47 Karl Hollidt, born April 28, 1891; 1910 Second Lieutenant; company commander and adjutant during the World War; taken on as a Captain in the Reichswehr; 1935 Colonel and Chief of General Staff, Military District I; 1938 Major General and Commander, 9th Infantry Division; 1939 Commander, 52nd Infantry Division; later Chief of General Staff, Fifth Army and Commander-in-Chief, East; 1940 Lieutenant General and Chief of General Staff, Ninth Army; October 1940 Commander, 50th Infantry Division; February 1942 General of the Infantry and Commanding General, XVII Army Corps; from December 27, 1942 Commander, Army Detachment Hollidt (establishment of the Chir front after the encirclement of Stalingrad), which, on March 5, 1943, was renamed the reconstituted Sixth Army; September 1943 General; and April 20, 1944 Führer Reserve. Hollidt was appointed representative and military adviser to the Gauleiter of the Ruhrgebiet at the end of February 1945, where the Americans captured him. During the Armed Forces High Command trial in 1948, he was sentenced to 5 years in with his sentence reduced due to time spent in captivity.—*Source: Armed Forces High Command staff files (Nbg.Dok.NOKW-141); Munzinger Archive.*

48 The above-mentioned push by the Soviets under Marshal Rokossovsky and General Eremenko northwest and south of Stalingrad on November 19 and 20, 1942, separated the fronts of the Romanian Third and Fourth Armies. During the penetration in the northwest in particular, two of the four Romanian divisions located there fought literally down to the last man; however, they lacked heavy weapons and armor-piercing long-range artillery when faced with the superior force of the three tank corps and the three cavalry corps of the Soviet Don Front.—*Source: Schröter, passim; Tippelskirch, p. 312.*

49 Undoubtedly refers to a magnetic charge.

50 During the first campaigns, the Panzer III and IV tanks proved successful, until at the end of July 1941 the first Russian T 34 tank (26 tons, 7.62-cm gun) appeared quite unexpectedly east of Orel. While the Panzer IV was only able to destroy the T 34 from a distance of 500 meters or less—and then only from the side or from behind—the T 34 could shoot frontally through the Panzer IV from a distance of 1,500 to 2,000 meters. Reproducing the T 34, which was the first attempted countermeasure, failed due to technical difficulties. Instead, new construction of the Panzer V and the "Panther" tank was begun. The "Panther" was comparable to the T 34, with a 7.5-cm gun (final weight 45.5 tons), and it accelerated the construction of an already developed 55-ton Panzer with an 8.8-cm gun (the Panzer VI "Tiger," later expanded to 72 tons with the "Königstiger"[King Tiger] VI-B). Production was delayed by constant interference in construction, frequent improvements, and new assignments—such as, for example, a 100-ton tank (the "Maus," with a 12.8-cm gun; two prototypes built with a final weight of 180t), and even for a monster 1,000-ton tank (copied from Russian attempts and which actually got to the wooden model stage)—as well as the forced increase of assault gun production. This is why the very im-

portant element of surprise was abandoned in the fall of 1942 near Leningrad—in an early deployment of the Tiger tank in a relatively unimportant attack in a limited area, on terrain generally unfavorable for tanks. The problem with the Tiger tank, which was otherwise generally outstanding, was its complicated production. The monthly production of 13 tanks, which was achieved in November 1941 (and which would soon be interrupted again for a longer time), could later only barely be doubled. Counting Panthers and Tigers together, the Wehrmacht had 72 units available in early 1943; by the end of that year it had more than 1,823, and a monthly production (of both types) of 375 pieces. While the production of Tiger tanks never exceeded 25 units per month, it was later possible to build up to 400 Panther tanks per month (including tank destroyers) for a time. The highest tank production altogether was reached in December 1944—with 1,817 vehicles, including tank destroyers and assault guns. But the fact that many tanks were only deployed after long delays, since special equipment was still missing must be kept in mind. This caused considerable differences between production and deployment numbers, particularly as a result of increasingly frequent air raids and the ensuing losses. [—] Technical details:

Armor thickness (mm)		Weight			Consumption		
	Front	Side	Guns	(t)	km/h	(l)
V "Panther" (Sd.Kfz.171)	60-80	50	7.5 cm long, 1-2MG	45.5	46	732
VI-A "Tiger" (Sd.Kfz.181)	100	80	8.8 cm, 2MG	55	38	569
VI-B "Königstiger" (Sd.Kfz.182)	100-150	80	8.8 cm long, 1MG	68	38	864

—*Source: Senger-Etterlin, pp. 21 and 190; Guderian: Erinnerungen, pp. 21 and 253; Schneider, p. 223; Der Frontsoldat, 1953, p. 26 and 1955, p. 50; Görlitz I, p. 340; Lusar, p. 28; Wilmot, p. 155; Guderian: Panzer; Marsch, pp. 15 and 234; Wiener, p. 57.*

[51] See List of Participants. The mention of Thomale by Buhle refers to an inspection of new departments for the Tiger. As Fromm's liaison officer to the Speer ministry, Thomale was already at that time entrusted with special missions concerning guns.

[52] This refers to the correction of an incorrect report by Göring.

[53] The German tank force was developed from 1925 on and from 1929-33 was tested in the Soviet Union. (1929: 9-ton "Kleintraktor" [Small tractor] with 3.7-cm and 18-ton "Grosstraktor" [Large tractor] with 7.5-cm short gun; 1932: the so-called "Neubaufahrzeuge" (Nbfz.), which, however, were not sent to the USSR; illustration in *Der deutsche Soldat* 1957, p. 140). 1935: Panzer I (6 tons, 2 machine guns) participated for the first time in a larger-scale practice exercise; Panzer II (9.5 tons, 2-cm gun) was still being tested at that time and was introduced in 1937. In 1937 it was put into production and in spring 1938 Panzers III (23t, originally 3.7-cm, then 5-cm and finally also 7.5-cm short gun) and IV (23.6 tons, 7.5-cm short gun, later long) were introduced. [—] Technical details:

| Armor thickness (mm) | | | Weight | | Consumption | | |
	Front	Side	Guns		(t)	km/h	(l)
I (Sd.Kfz.101)	15	15	2 MG		5.5	20	145
II (Sd. Kfz. 121 and 122)	15	15	2-cm, 1 MG		9.5	40	200
III old (Sd. Kfz.141)	30	30	3.7- or 5-cm, 2-3 MG		23	32	227
III new (Sd.Kfz. 141/1 and 141/2)	50	30	5-cm long or 7.5-cm short, 2 MG		24	40	318
IV (Sd.Kfz. 161-161/2)	50	30	7.5-cm short or long, 2 MG		23.6	40	477

—*Source: Guderian: Panzer-Marsch, p. 234; Lusar, p. 28; Senger-Etterlin, pp. 15 and 190; Wiener, p. 55 (according to Wiener, Panzers III and IV were not introduced until fall 1939).*

[54] Until the Western Campaign in 1940, the two heaviest German tanks at that time were equipped with the following, according to the regulations of the General Staff: the Panzer III had a gun that was able to destroy tanks—meaning a long-barrel gun with a caliber of 3.7 cm for action against Panzers, fortifications and so forth; Panzer IV, on the other hand, was equipped with a 7.5-cm gun with a short barrel ("Stummel"), which was intended for use against infantry targets. However, in 1940 it was discovered that the French had tanks against which a 3.7-cm caliber was wholly inadequate. Therefore, it was decided that Panzer IV tanks had to be equipped with a long gun of 7.5-cm caliber so that it could also be used against armored targets. This revision definitely took some time, as the installation of the new weapon required a completely new construction for the turret.

[55] Rudolf Witzig; born August 14, 1916; 1935 Ensign in Engineer Battalion Höxter; 1937 Second Lieutenant; December 1938 transferred to the Luftwaffe; 1939 Lieutenant Colonel; May 1940 conquest of Fort Eben-Emael together with a parachute division, Captain; and November 1944 decorated with Oak Leaves as Major and Commander, 1st Battalion, 21st Parachute Panzer Regiment.—*Source: Seemen; VB of May 13-14, 1940.*

[56] The railroad under discussion is the electrically run train connection between the northern Swedish iron ore area of Kiruna and the Norwegian harbor. The power source for the train was threatened by sabotage and air raids.

[57] The motor torpedo boat operation in the Channel refers to an attack by the 6th Motor Torpedo Boat Flotilla. The deployment of motor torpedo boats in the Channel was easier to manage than in the Black Sea, as it was possible in the Channel to detect hostile convoys from the coast with transmitters and to launch the motor torpedo boats directly without having to cover great distances. Deployment was much more difficult in the Black Sea because of the great distances—only air-reconnaissance reports could be used, and these were often imprecise (because of inaccurate air navigation) and usually several hours old. By the time the motor torpedo boats reached the reported location, the targets had already significantly changed their position, making it more or less a matter of luck if the motor torpedo boats found the enemy.

[58] At that time (at the beginning of December 1942), only one German submarine was located in the Tuapse operational area.

[59] The motor torpedo boats of the 1st S-Flotilla in the Black Sea were equipped with, among other things, a 4-cm Bofors anti-aircraft gun, which in some cases came from captured enemy supplies.

[60] After the Anglo-Americans landed in French North Africa on November 8, 1942, German and Italian troops marched (on November 11) into the part of France that had not yet been occupied. As of November 27, the French Army, which had been newly trained after the armistice, was disarmed.

[61] This refers to the Vichy police. Hitler's statement, unusually frank considering the relatively high number of meeting participants, reveals one of his essential traits in the treatment of people: the attempt to turn subordinates into accomplices and dependent "tools" by forcing them to take reprehensible measures.

[62] This news comes from an announcement by the Military Commander in France, reporting on the results of the completed measures of the Deputy General for Manpower for his command area. By the summer of 1942, approximately 150,000 French voluntary workers had come to Germany. On July 10, 1942, 76,493 Frenchmen were actually employed in the Reich (not including the Eastern areas). That summer, Deputy General Fritz Sauckel ordered an additional 350,000 French workers, including 150,000 skilled workers. The government in Vichy provided these workers by the scheduled date at the end of the year, with only a slight delay (as Jodl reports here, 200,000 by the end of November). The Germans, in return, implemented the so-called "relève" to allow French prisoners of war to be transferred to a civil employer-employee relationship, or to be released completely, according to a predetermined quota. In January 1943, Sauckel's second program required 250,000 additional French workers, including 150,000 skilled metalworkers—by March 15, in return for relief for French prisoners of war and continuation of the "relève." This demand was met (though somewhat behind schedule) through business support and the calling-up of the 1920-22 age group. In total, 266,331 workers arrived in the Reich from France (excluding the two northern departments) between January 1 and June 30, 1943.—*Source: Abetz, p. 241; Verschiedene Statistiken des GBA, Berichte des Militärbefehlshabers Frankreich u.a. in den [Various GBA statistics, reports from the Military Commander in France, including] Nbg. Dok. NG-109, NG-940, N-G-1648, NG-1700, NG-3996, NG-4936 und NG-5029.*

[63] According to the agreements, the highest military command in North Africa lay with Mussolini and his Armed Forces commander-in-chief, the *Comando Supremo*, in Rome. Hitler had gained considerable influence over North African operations in early 1941 after Rommel's arrival —despite the fact that Rommel was officially under the command of the Libyan governor general, Marshal Ettore Bastico, and the *Comando Supremo*—and, after the occupation of Tunisia in November 1942, he acquired more formal military control as well by appointing a German commander-in-chief (General von Arnim after December 1942). Harmonizing intentions and orders with Rome—which was the responsibility of Field Marshal Kesselring, Commander-in-Chief South—

become more and more of a formality, but nevertheless required a certain amount of tact. Tunis was a sensitive issue for the Italians, who didn't want to lose control of this important part of their territorial "aspirations." In any case, the German army group command led at the front in Tunis, with one Italian army and one German army under its command. The sharp tensions that one might expect from such a difficult situation, however, did not come to pass.—*Source: Kesselring, passim; Rintelen, pp. 155, 172, 181 and others; Westphal, pp. 189; Siegler, pp.21 and 96.*

[64] Hitler still thought at that time that he would be able to disengage a larger number of armored divisions from the East and transfer them to Tunis, which proved impossible. The majority of the German units fighting in Tunis later belonged to Rommel's army—which, despite all hopes at the time of this meeting, was driven back.

[65] Partisan fighting was an intentional and well-prepared element of the Soviet national defense plan, although German commanders were unaware of it before the outbreak of war. Shortly after the hostilities began in June 1941, Stalin himself called for men to join this guerilla war. He found willing followers in most parts of the country, especially since the German occupying regime proved eager to plunder the country and enslave the population. After the heavy reversals suffered by the Wehrmacht in the winter of 1941-42, the partisans— or, as they were called by the Germans, the "bands" [*banden*]—gained particular strength in the rear area of Army Group Center. Because they were able to control large, connected areas and organize mass attacks against the few railways in the region, they became a dangerous threat to those fighting at the front. German countermeasures, which were initially limited to passive protection, began to develop into real attack and encirclement operations, in which SS, police and army units participated. The fight was conducted with extreme cruelty on both sides.

[66] This regulation was issued on November 27, 1942, which means that it was already in effect at the time of this meeting. This is confirmed by the statement by Jodl at Nuremberg. The text of this regulation has apparently not survived. Hitler passed on the "preamble" mentioned here in an order dated December 16, 1942, and signed by Keitel, stating: "The Führer has received reports indicating that several members of the Wehrmacht who were involved in the guerilla fighting were afterward called to account for their behavior during the fight. In response, the Führer has ordered: "The enemy is using fanatical, Communist-trained fighters who don't hesitate to commit any act of violence. More than ever this is a question of survival. This fight has nothing to do with military chivalry or with the agreements of the Geneva Convention. If we don't engage in this fight against the bands with the most brutal means possible—in the East as well as in the Balkans—the available forces will soon be unable to control this plague. Therefore, the troops are authorized and required to use all means possible in this fight, without any restrictions—including against women and children—as long as it leads to success. Considerations of any kind are a crime against the German nation and against

the soldiers at the front. Our soldiers have to bear the consequences of the attacks and cannot accept considerate treatment of the gangs and their members. These principles must also be applied in the combat instructions for the guerilla war in the East."—*Source: IMT (dt.) XXXIX, p. 128 (Dok. 066-UK).*

[67] The self-defense clause is understood to be Section 53, which says: "It is not a criminal action if the action was taken in self-defense. Self-defense means defensive measures that are necessary to stop an unlawful attack that is being attempted against oneself or another. Overstepping the bounds of self-defense is not a criminal act if the offender has done so out of dismay, fear or shock." Although the German law of self-defense in Section 53 is relatively broad, and—in contrast to Swiss law—does not require a fundamental proportionality of the two opposing legal rights, Hitler's observations concerning the practical consequences (for police officers, for example) are not entirely incorrect. Nevertheless, it would be difficult to express the legal version—in which complex and diverse real-life situations have to be reduced to a concise statement—differently. Thus, the text of Paragraph 53 was not changed during the Third Reich.

[68] In November 1913, in Zabern (Saverne) in Alsace—where friction between army and civilians already existed—Second Lieutenant Baron von Forstner addressed the issue in a lecture discussing how one should react if there were indeed attacks by civilians. He said: "Anyone who stabs one of those "Wackes" [insulting name for a person who comes from Alsace] to death during such an attack will get ten marks from me." Because Forstner's punishment for this remark was minimal (only a few days' confinement to the barracks), the anger of the population continued to rise. Tension reached its climax during a riot in front of the Schlossplatz on November 27, 1913, in which the commander of the regiment, Colonel von Reuter, ordered a platoon of soldiers to move out with loaded weapons; they immediately arrested 27 people. The colonel, who was accused of unlawful detention, was exonerated by the court-martial in Strasbourg on a flimsy pretext. The "Zabern affair" led to intense debates in the Reichstag and a vote of censure against the government.—*Source: Eyck: Wilhelm II, p. 666.*

[69] Hitler is probably referring to the bloody riots in Paris on February 6, 1934, which resulted in sixteen dead and several hundred wounded—mostly in front of the Chamber of Deputies. The riots (which were started by front-line veterans but soon included all political persuasions, including the Communists, and the man in the street) were instigated by the right against the cabinet of Edouard Daladier. They were triggered by the circumstances surrounding the Stavisky scandal, which threatened to become another Dreyfus Affair. Indeed, Daladier was forced to resign, although he could have obtained a majority at the heated [parliament] meeting on February 6. The attacks that later broke out from several tendencies—because of the police action against the demonstrators—were mainly aimed at the minister of the interior in Daladier's resigned government, attorney Eugène Frot. Paris police prefect, Jean Chiappe had already been removed from office on February 4, two days before the riots. Chiappe, according

to Daladier, hadn't taken drastic enough measures against demonstrations by political groups before the riots, which were aimed not just against Stavisky but also against the Third Republic in general. Thus, this was not a consequence of but more likely a reason for these bloody clashes. There was also a law suit filed against Frot. Whether there were suits filed against police officials as well—as Hitler claims here—could no longer be ascertained.—*Source: Baumont, p. 355; Frankfurter Zeitung of Feb. 5-12, 1934.*

[70] There had already been several previous debates regarding the draft of these "guerilla war" regulations, but Jodl repeatedly resisted any relaxation of the orders expressed in it. His cynical statement after the longwinded comments by Hitler is typical of the annoyed Jodl. It was ironic, and, according to the participants, caused smiles all around. On June 7, 1946, Jodl was interrogated by Colonel Pokrowsky at the Nuremberg Trial, and said the following regarding this statement: "The draft of this memorandum had been lying for weeks with the Führer. He constantly complained that by issuing regulations, the troops would be limited in their ruthless fighting against the gangs. And since I had already issued these regulations without his permission—and he still wasn't giving his permission—I became slightly irritated. When he again started in on longwinded discussions about his fighting experiences, about experiences in Chemnitz while fighting against the Communists, I said in order to finally break through: 'My Führer, what people do while fighting is not written about in these regulations. I don't care if they cut them in four pieces or if they hang them upside down.' Had I known that the Russians are so poor at understanding sarcasm, I would have added: 'and roast them on a spit.' That is what I said, and then I added: 'But these regulations deal with retaliation after the fighting, and that has to be forbidden.' At that, all of the officers laughed, including the Führer, and he gave me permission to issue the regulations."—*Source: IMT (dt.) Vol. XV, p. 594.*

[71] Jodl seems somewhat uninformed about Himmler's intentions and measures, as the Reichsführer SS had at that point already decided how to prevent the male population from leaving a cleansed area and moving into another partisan-infested area. He had already given the order to senior police and SS commanders on November 3, 1942, requiring that "during all actions against the gangs, in areas which are cleared out and occupied by us, all non-essential people who are able to work will be immediately captured. They will then be marched to Germany to work." During the year 1943, this system was improved to the point where children from partisan-infested areas were herded into camps on the outskirts of their home territory and made available to work in the Kok-Sagys area extension.—*Source: Nbg. Dok. NO-491, NO-1665, NO-2623 and NO-745.*

[72] Erich von dem Bach-Zelewski; born March 1, 1899, active officer until 1942, then became a taxi driver and farmer, since 1919 member of the people's movement, 1930 NSDAP, 1931 SS as Standartenführer [Regiment Commander], 1934 SS Gruppenführer [Group Commander] and Führer [Commander] of SS Oberabschnitt Nordost [Command Northeast], from February 1936 Führer of SS Oberabschnitt Südost [Command Southeast] (Silesia) after being de-

feated in power struggles with Gauleiter Koch, in June 1938 Senior SS and police commander in Defense Area VIII, June 1941 Senior SS and police commander for Russia-Center (formally until June 1944), November 1941 Obergruppenführer, September 1942 RFSS deputy for guerilla warfare and after June 21, 1943 head of the anti-guerilla units. After a lengthy illness, he was given responsibility for the suppression of the Warsaw uprising in August 1944 as Commanding General of the Corps Group von dem Bach-Zelewski; in October 1944 head of the operation "Panzerfaust" against the Horthy regime in Hungary, during the last months of war, Commanding General of several corps (January 1945 X SS Corps, February 1945 Oder Corps). Von dem Bach-Zelewski appeared as a chief witness in the Nuremberg Trial; he was sentenced by the Munich court to 10 years in a labor camp. —*Source: Nbg.Dok.NO-1621, NO-1661, NO-2026, NO-2042, NO-2451; SS DAL; various legal files.*

[73] After the disarmament of the French army all its equipment and weapons were confiscated. It can no longer be determined exactly which actual equipment is being discussed here, but presumably it concerns motor vehicles, which were always scarce in the Wehrmacht. This interpretation is supported by Hitler's sudden statement about replacement parts; he always said "replacement constituent parts."

[74] Buhle uses this opportunity to repeat a request that has already been made by the Army armaments department: that a second engine should be delivered with the tank when it leaves the factory, as is done in aircraft production. However, this requirement was never met, as the Ministry of Defense Production was of a different opinion, not least because of insufficient production capacity.

[75] The incident discussed here happened shortly before "up there," i.e., in the Leningrad bottleneck. During the deployment of the first Tiger unit a tank was seriously damaged by the use of incorrect brake fluid. According to statements by all the people questioned, however, it was merely carelessness and not a case of sabotage.

[76] Transcript number unknown—Fragment No. 8—A partially burned shorthand record, the transcription of which was only possible with gaps.

[77] Aksai sector.

[78] The year before, during the siege of Sevastopol', the Russians had attempted two landings in the Crimea, which were thought to be relief efforts: on December 29, 1941, at Kerch and Feodosiia, where the Kerch Peninsula was lost until May 1942, and on January 5, 1942, at Evpatoriia, where the attacking Russian forces were thrown back into the sea after a three-day fight. Later, especially during this Stalingrad winter, no Russian landings occurred.—*Source: Tippelskirch, p. 276.*

[79] Probably in the western Caucasus.

[80] First Panzer Army.

[81] Meaning the First Panzer Army again.

[82] Already at the end of 1941, Professor von Mende from the Reich Ministry for the Occupied Eastern Territories had created commissions with Turkestani and

Caucasian emigrants and had given orders to search for Turkestanis and Caucasians in the prisoner-of-war camps—of whom the great majority, however, had already been "specially treated as Asians" by the SD Einsatzcommandos. Under the code name "Bergmann units," Captain Prof. Oberländer formed units with the people who had been collected; these units were supposed to support the German forces in their home territories during the following campaign. In the spring of 1942, the Armed Forces High Command finally give permission to set up regular legions of Turkestanis, North Caucasians, Armenians, Azerbaijanis, Georgians and Volga Tatars, after military command posts had already started doing so on their own. Like all the other "Eastern troops," these units were under German commanders; however, they were also interspersed from the position of company commander down with non-commissioned officers of the concerned nationalities. These minorities from the Eastern areas always had the support of the Ministry for the East, as the ministry wished to weaken the dangerous numerical superiority of the Russian military areas. Initially, however, all attempts to use people from the Eastern nations met with stiff opposition from Hitler. But due to the developments of the war, eventually more and more of these units were set up within the Wehrmacht as well as the Waffen SS. Altogether, approximately 100,000 Caucasians were armed by 1945, of which 48,700 were in the legions and field battalions, 21,500 in building and supply units, 25,000 in German units and 7,000 in the Waffen SS and Luftwaffe.—*Source: Thorwald: Wen sie…, passim; as well as the material collected by Thorwald, which was stored in the IfZ (particularly the Caucasian Committee report of March 26, 1945); NOKW-1604 and further numerous Nbg. [Nuremberg] documents.*

[83] Cannot be identified. Colonel von Pannwitz could possibly be meant here.

[84] The Armed Forces report was prepared by the Press and Propaganda Department of the Armed Forces Operations Staff, and was regularly checked by Hitler before being released for publication.

[85] The 5th SS Panzer Division *Viking* (until the summer of 1942 a panzer grenadier division) was the first SS unit with European volunteers. In November 1940 the division was established—under Steiner, who would later be SS Obergruppenführer—out of the *Germania* regiment of the SS Support Division and troops from other sources. Up to half of its members were Dutch, Danish, Norwegian and Flemish. From June 1941 on, the division was deployed in the southern part of the Eastern front.—*Source: Order of Battle, p. 389; Hausser, pp. 41 and 46.*

[86] A transcription error occurred here. There was no Army Group South at that time, as Manstein's Army Group Don was not renamed "South" until February 14, 1943. This part had been corrected in the text; originally it said, "to the south." The stenographers probably corrected it erroneously.

[87] Allusion to the supposedly belated intervention (claimed by Hitler and also pursued in legal action) of a German panzer division during a Russian attack on the Romanian Third Army on November 19-20, 1942.

[88] Hitler's fear of losing a great deal of materiel during a retreat was not without merit. Aside from the fact that materiel always gets lost in retreats that are not

planned far in advance, this danger was considerably increased due to motorization. Tanks and motorized vehicles that could not be driven had to be abandoned in great numbers, as they often could not be transported back. These vehicles were especially hard to replace, however, as this type of production was affected by the German war economy bottleneck. Bad weather—for example, periods of mud—considerably increased the losses. On top of that, propaganda exaggeration of German armaments had relaxed the troops' attitude toward materiel losses, which had initially been quite careful. Aside from such considerations, Hitler was also in principle opposed to backward movements—especially since he succeeded, through a draconian order, in stopping the German front from continuing its retreat from Moscow during the Russian winter of 1941-42, and probably prevented a collapse of even greater proportions. He applied this experience equally and increasingly to all situations, all seasons, and all theaters of war. In reality, however, the constantly changing assumptions and the refusal to allow any retreat—and the resulting repeated encirclement of entire armies—led to heavy losses of both men and materiel during the course of the war, not to mention the effect on morale.

[89] The 16th Motorized Division supported the deep northern flank of the 1st Panzer Division in the Kalmyk steppe at Elista in the northern Caucasus.— *Source: Manstein, p. 358.*

[90] The thrust of Army Group Hoth (Fourth Panzer Army and the remains of the Romanian Fourth Army) in the direction of Stalingrad. On November 24, Hitler forbade the Sixth Army from breaking out of Stalingrad, which it was already prepared to do. The following day, Field Marshal von Manstein was taken away from Leningrad and moved to the south, together with his Army Headquarters. There, the Fourth Panzer Army, the Sixth Army (which was encircled at Stalingrad), and the remains of the Romanian Third and Fourth Armies were assembled together in the newly created "Army Group Don" and placed under his command. While the General Staff was arguing with Hitler for permission for the Sixth Army to break out, Manstein put together an attack group in the area of both sides of Kotel'nikovo, 150 km south of Stalingrad, under the command of General Hoth. This group consisted—in addition to the mostly useless remains of the Romanian VII and VI Army Corps—initially only of the LVII Panzer Corps with the 6th Panzer Division brought in from France, and also the 23rd Panzer Division, which had slowly been moving there from the Caucasus since December 1. Later, the 17th Panzer Division was also added. Originally, Hoth's forces east of the Don and Hollidt's forces west of the river were supposed to lead the relief attack. The beginning of the attack was delayed, however, because of the weather—rain and a few degrees above freezing—because of the slow arrival of the 23rd [Panzer], and because of the uncertainty about the 17th Panzer Division. Because of the situation in Stalingrad, Hoth decided to line up on December 12. At the same time, according to Manstein's plan, General Hollidt was supposed to attack in a generally eastward direction from the small Chir bridgehead at Verkhne-Chirskii, turning the Russians away and holding up some of their forces. The Sixth Army was to line up for an attack at

its southern front in order to establish a connection with the Army Group Hoth, once this group had approached within 30 kilometers—to the outer defense ring—since the stores of fuel available in the Pocket wouldn't allow the tanks to operate extensively. By establishing the "corridor," the Sixth Army was supposed to receive reinforcements and supplies, allowing the ring around Stalingrad to be completely destroyed under double pressure from inside and outside. Stalingrad and the Volga position would still remain under German control. For all practical purposes, however—as Manstein and the Army General Staff acknowledged—breaking out in the direction of the relief army would have involved a direct pursuit of the Russians, and with that the abandonment of Stalingrad. Hitler would basically have to accept that, just as he had done in other cases.—*Source: Tippelskirch, p. 314; Manstein, pp. 353 and 359; Schröter, p. 98.*

[91] This reference is again to the Army Group Hoth attack.

[92] At that time, Manstein often transmitted such situation assessments in short intervals via the teletypewriter, in order to emphatically state his opinion to Führer Headquarters. One such assessment, regarding the situation three days before, on December 9, 1942, was published by Manstein in his *Verlorenen Siegen*, p. 651. He also described the circumstances of the reinforcement for the relief attack on Stalingrad in detail in the following text. The importance of this problem justifies the inclusion of Manstein's statement also, as a comparison:

> The second question was the reinforcement of the relief forces. Reinforcement of the Fourth Panzer Army was essential after it became obvious that of the seven divisions originally promised for a relief attack by Army Detachment Hollidt, at most the XXXXVIII Panzer Corps with two divisions would be available for this purpose. It didn't require a long discussion to determine that with only two divisions (the 6th and 23rd Panzer Divisions) it would not reach Stalingrad.
>
> There were two possibilities for reinforcement. The Army Group High Command requested again and again that Army Group A send the III Panzer Corps with its two panzer divisions, which would be out of place in the mountains anyway. This request was always refused …
>
> The second possibility for a timely reinforcement of the Fourth Panzer Army for its thrust toward Stalingrad consisted of the Army High Command bringing in new forces. The 17th Panzer Division, and behind it the newly established 306th Infantry Division, were approaching Army Group Don. The former could have just managed to line up against Stalingrad, because of the delay suffered by the LVII Panzer Corps at Kotelnikovo. But the Army High Command gave the order to unload the division as a reserve behind the army group's left wing, as it feared—not without good reason—that a crisis would develop in the case of a full-scale enemy attack, which seemed imminent. However, one could not have both things at the same time: success for the 4th Panzer Division and security from a crisis on the left wing of the army group—which the 17th Panzer Division, if it joined in, would not be able to

control anyway. We preferred the success of the Fourth Panzer Army, while Hitler opted for the false security that he hoped to achieve by holding back the 17th Panzer Division. As a result, the division—when Hitler finally released it, after the arrival of the 306th Division, which was following it, joined the Fourth Panzer Army too late for the first part of the relief attack. Perhaps the decisive opportunity was lost there because of this! ...

It was a race to see whether the relief troops—the Fourth Panzer Army—would succeed in holding out their hand to the Sixth Army east of the Don before the enemy forced the break-up of the relief operation. If they were successful in overrunning our weak front at the Chir or the left wing of the army group (Army Detachment Hollidt) or the right wing of Army Group B, it would open up the opportunity to cut off all the rear connections of Army Group Don and Army Group A at Rostov.

Launching and sustaining an attack operation east of the Don in the direction of Stalingrad—with the danger described above posing more and more of a threat—must have meant taking a risk that we had rarely dared to take before. I don't think Hitler recognized the real significance of the risk at that time. Otherwise, he probably would have taken more drastic steps, at least for a reinforcement of the Fourth Panzer Army, in order to bring rapid relief for the Sixth Army. Instead, everything he did, as General Zeitzler himself says, 'was always to throw a monkey-wrench in our plans.' For example, when he held the 17th Panzer Division back for decisive action in the wrong place, or released the 16th Motorized Division far too late, as was already mentioned earlier. Hitler constantly claimed that the General Staff—meaning the generals—could only 'calculate' and not risk. There is probably no better proof against this claim than the risk which the High Command of Army Group Don took when it ordered the thrust of the Fourth Panzer Army on Stalingrad, and when it held out until the very last possible moment in a situation which could have meant the destruction of the entire German southern wing ...

While east of the Don the LVII Panzer Corps, which was intended for the relief attempt, was completing its assembly around Kotelnikovo, the enemy had been attacking our front at the lower Chir, west of the Don, with heavy forces since December 10. It became obvious that the XXXXVIII Panzer Corps would not be freed from this front to move out of the Chir-Don Bridgehead and work together with the LVII Panzer Corps.

Thus, the lining up of the LVII Panzer Corps became even more urgent. After the corps had completed its discharge and assembly around Kotelnikovo—in heavy fights against strong hostile forces, which tried to break up the final linking—and had destroyed the enemy to a great extent, the corps started off for the attack in the direction of Stalingrad on December 12. Its flanks covered the Romanian VII Army Corps to the east along the Volga and the Romanian VI Army Corps to the west up to the Don. It seemed as if the attack came as a surprise to the enemy—at least he probably didn't expect it so early. At first the corps made quite good progress, but the enemy quickly brought up forces from the Stalingrad area. He didn't restrict himself to defense at all, but constantly tried to counterattack and retake the territory that had been won by our two armored divisions, or he tried to encircle parts of them with his tanks, which outnumbered ours by far. The LVII Panzer Corps succeeded again and again in destroying strong groups of enemy forces. In the course of this unpredictable battle, a key decision was not made until December 17—when the 17th Panzer Division east of the Don was finally able to join in the operation. Under constant urging from the Army Group High Command, the Army High Command had finally released the division from its unloading area behind the left wing of the army group. However, the division had quite a long march to the Don bridge at Potemkinskaya and across, before it could attack east of the Don."—*Source: Manstein, p. 357.*

93 Army Group Hoth.

94 The reference is to the front at the Don, which had been taken by the Italians.

95 It was these two weak "last reserves." The leader of the Schulte brigade, mentioned frequently in the following text, could not be identified. The Führer Escort Battalion was a fully motorized Army battalion. It consisted of selected officers, non-commissioned officers and troops, and it was reinforced by tanks, assault guns, anti-tank guns and light anti-aircraft. Generally they were assigned to protect the Führer Headquarters, but in particularly critical situations, such as in this case, they were also often temporarily sent to the front.

96 Regarding the Italian divisions on the Eastern front. The Italian divisions were named in part after provinces (for example: *Piemonte, Calabria, Sicilia, Puglie*), in part named after towns (for example: *Roma, Napoli, Como, Cremona, Pavia, Siena, Verona*), and sometimes they also had other names like *Re, Regina, Cacciatori delle Alpi, Lupi di Toscana*, etc. So the names were not synonymous with their places of origin.

97 During the reorganization of the Italian infantry divisions from three to two infantry regiments in 1938-39, plans called for each division to be assigned two militia battalions in case of mobilization. The reference here is to the so-called Black Shirt battalions, 132 in all at the end, which had been formed by members of the "Fascist Militia," a party organization. This extension of the army divisions was actually carried out at the beginning of the war, but it did not prove effective in the least. The four militia divisions *3 Gennaio, 23 Marzo, 28 Ottobre,* and *Giovani Fascisti* were set up from the spare Black Shirt battalions and all of them were stationed in Africa. The two divisions mentioned first were destroyed during an English attack in December 1940. Both divisions—"March 3" is a mistake, it must be "March 23"—were later reestablished and were transferred together with the Italian 8th Army to the Ukraine. A fifth militia division was the Armored Militia Division "M," which was set up in the spring of 1943 in Italy and which was trained by SS staff and received German materiel. Hitler and Himmler wanted it to be a special Lifeguard unit for Fascism and particularly for Mussolini, but it was not used. —*Source: Martin, p. 70; Rintelen, p. 55.*

[98] The reference here is to Rychkovskii, at the mouth of the Chir on the Don, and the Don bridge located there. However, the bridge was not lost that day; it was not lost until December 14, when it was blown up.—*Source: Manstein, p. 361.*

[99] The consumption rate indicates the number of liters of fuel that this type of tank consumes in 100 kilometers.

[100] From the end of 1939 on, the Army General Staff compiled division evaluation lists. The divisions handed in so-called "condition reports" every month, which were written on prescribed forms and evaluated by the organization department in the Army General Staff. The prior combat performance of the relevant unit was recorded in a second document. The combination of these two factors led to the overall evaluation, which ranged from "fighting value 1" to " fighting value 4," with 1 being completely combat-ready. This arrangement, which was initially intended only for the replenishment periods of individual units, was later extended to all divisions as an ongoing evaluation. (See the following statements by Hitler.)

[101] Georg von Küchler; born May 30, 1881; 1901 Second Lieutenant; 1914 Captain in the General Staff; during the First World War mostly in General Staff positions, Reichswehr; 1929 Lieutenant Colonel and instructor at the artillery school; 1932 Artillery Commander in Königsberg; 1934 Major General; 1935 Inspector of military schools; April 1937 General of the Artillery and Commanding General, I Army Corps; Commander-in-Chief. Third Army during the Polish campaign; Commander-in-Chief, Eighteenth Army in the Western campaign as well as at the border between German and Soviet interests and later outside Leningrad and at the Volkhov; July 1940 General; January 16, 1942 Commander-in-Chief, Army Group North, as successor of von Leeb; June 30, 1942 Field Marshal; and January 29, 1944 transferred to the reserve command. At the Nuremberg trial of the Armed Forces High Command, von Küchler was sentenced to 20 years in prison (reduced to 12 years in 1951) and released in 1953.—*Source: Berliner Boersen-Zeitung of March 12, 1940; VB of May 30, 1942; Munzinger Archive; Keilig 211/185.*

[102] The Italian divisions.

[103] Stalingrad is meant here. It should not be concluded from Hitler's following statements that he didn't want to give up Stalingrad only because he wanted to prevent the loss of materiel. As usual, he wanted everything at the same time: to keep the materiel and also the men, of course; to keep the town and with it the symbol of overcoming Bolshevism; to stay on the Volga as one of the (finally) achieved aims of his war plans; and, finally, to push from the protection of this position forward into and over the Caucasus as soon as possible. Despite the strong words he used for it, the prevention of materiel loss was only a partial motive.

[104] At the beginning of the 1942 summer offensive.

[105] Hitler means the Soviet penetration over the Donets near Izium in January 1942. The Russians started to attack Khar'kov on May 12 from the Krasnograd salient, which was up to 100 kilometers deep, as well as from north of town, near Belgorod and Volchansk. Through significant local penetrations, they were able

to come quite near their target from the north and south, until German counter-attacks not only pushed the Soviets back over the Donets but also turned the former salient into an enormous pocket in which, according to the Armed Forces High Command report, 240,000 prisoners were taken and 2,026 guns and 1,249 tanks were captured.—*Source: Tippelskirch, p. 278.*

[106] To go from Rastenburg to Berchtesgaden, where Hitler wished—as he had already said before—"to free his head for new decisions" and where he had intended to meet with Mussolini and Antonescu between the 17th and 21st of December. This trip was permanently cancelled on December 15.

[107] To Stalingrad.

[108] The 7th Panzer Division had been ordered out from the West after the encirclement of Stalingrad.

[109] Soon after the beginning of the summer offensive in the southern sector in late June 1942, Hitler made two panzer divisions—which were stuck due to lack of fuel—available to Army Group Center. Contrary to the strong opinion of Commander-in-Chief von Kluge, who wanted to support the heavily threatened Rzhev front with those forces, the divisions—at Hitler's wish—were used at Sukhinichi in a pincer attack from north and south to clear out a deep breach of the German front, left behind from the winter fights. This operation then stalled at the beginning, due to a lack of forces.

[110] Oak Leaves awarded before and after the date of this meeting:

	June 13–Dec. 12, 1942	Dec. 13, 1942–June 12, 1943
to Generals of the Army	6	21
to other members of the Army	12	40
to generals of the Luftwaffe	–	2
to other Luftwaffe members	27	20

—*Source: Seemen, p. 24.*

[111] For the West.

[112] From the spring of 1943 on, Hitler—in view of the increasing threat of "invasion," i.e., a large-scale Anglo-American landing operation—always wanted to maintain eight mobile units as operative reserves in the occupied Western areas. But after the Allied landings in North Africa in November 1942, two of the units were scheduled for Tunis, and additional ones were supposed to follow there. Thus, eight mobile units could not be counted on for the West anymore.

[113] The loss of Soviet production capacity due to the German advance is estimated at around 40 to 45 percent, and not until early 1943 were the industrial centers in the Urals, Siberia and Turkestan able to fill the gap completely. But by the summer of 1942—not least because of American help—the Russians had overcome the worst of the serious materiel crisis that they had experienced in the winter of 1941-42. The following list provides insight into the scope and allocation of American assistance for Russia in three of the most important armament categories. Altogether, American assistance totaled more than 15 million long tons.

	Aircraft	Panzers	Trucks
Allied assistance (according to Allied records)	14,800	13,300	427,000
Allied assistance (according to Soviet records)	6,900	10,200	300,000
Soviet production, 1940-45	106,600	128,500	950,000

Nevertheless, of course, considerable supply shortages still existed in the Soviet Union at that time. Soviet-produced oil, for example, was of low quality due to inadequate refining and did not work well as aircraft fuel, while the American deliveries of large quantities of aircraft fuel could only remedy the situation slowly.—*Source: Deane, p. 84; Kalinow, pp. 40, 53 and 58; Goudima, p. 251.*

[114] A captured Soviet T 34 tank, which had been shown at the Führer Headquarters, suggested quite low-grade production. For instance, the seams of the armor plates were welded so badly and incompletely that they must have fallen apart at every hit. It was supposedly a production sample of a series that had been built for some emergency situation.

[115] At the time of the German attack against the Soviet Union, the 2,500 German tanks at the front faced 10,000 Soviet tanks. Furthermore, the Russians possessed a reserve of 10,000 tanks, while the German panzer force had only 500. The Wehrmacht, though, prevented the reestablishment of an operative Soviet tank force, and succeeded in almost entirely destroying the existing Russian tank force. According to German reports, Soviet losses reached 18,000 tanks by October 6, 1941, and even the Soviet records admit to losing up to 7,000. Not until the encirclement of Stalingrad—as is also shown here—did larger Soviet tank units appear. Their tactical leadership, however, was relatively weak—then as well as later—so that even in 1944-45 the successes of the Russian tank force did not reach the level of German victories in 1941, although the Russians were finally able to increase their yearly production of tanks and assault guns to 30,000 units.—*Source: Galai, passim; Görlitz I, p. 261.*

[116] The so-called "Radschlepper Ost" ["Wheeled Tractor East"], made by Porsche, was a later development of the Austro-Daimler wheeled tractor from World War I. This tractor, with its extremely large wheels of around 1.5 meters in diameter, had pulled the Austrian heavy howitzers at that time and is said to have impressed Hitler at Maubeuge, where those canons were used. The "Radschlepper Ost" had four iron-plated wheels and reached a speed of 8 km per hour. It was used to pull equipment, and also for troop transport. Due to the resistance of the Army Weapons Office, only 100 units of this model—which the professionals regarded as nonsense—were built, and they soon disappeared again.

[117] The "Raupenschlepper Ost" (RSO) [Caterpillar Tractor East] was built by the Steyrer factory and owed its existence to the initiative of the Steyrer manager, Hacker. It was a full-tracked vehicle, a simpler tractor for pulling heavy anti-tank guns and also field howitzers, on which the crew could be transported as well. The faults of the RSO were its low speed and poor steering capability. De-

spite—according to the judgment of professionals—insufficient tests, the RSO went into production in 1942-43 and was produced in quantity by Steyrer and Magirus, since, in Hitler's opinion, the latent shortage of tractors could not be overcome any other way. As feared by many military experts, the frontline troops were not satisfied with the tractor, and reported this—as in the present case— many times. The RSO was lost by the thousands on the front in the following years, in part due to its shortcomings.

[118] Heusinger had, in the meantime, checked the latest status by long-distance call.

[119] Joseph (Sepp) Dietrich; born May 25, 1892; agricultural worker, hotel employee; after 1911 became a professional soldier, ended the war as deputy sergeant, Landespolizei, Munich; 1920 Freikorps Oberland; 1923 NSDAP and SS member; 1931 Commander, *Leibstandarte Adolf Hitler*; 1934 led in the shooting of Röhm and other SA commanders; July 1934 SS Obergruppenführer; during the war Commander, 1st SS Panzer Division *LAH*; July 1943 Commanding General, I SS Panzer Corps; August 1944 Commander-in-Chief, Fifth Panzer Army; SS Obergruppenführer and decorated with the Iron Cross with diamonds; and from October 1944, until the capitulation, Commander-in-Chief, Sixth SS Panzer Army. At the Malmedy trial, Dietrich was sentenced to life imprisonment; he was released on parole in October 1955 and sentenced by the Munich court in May 1957 to 18 months' imprisonment for the execution of the SA commanders in the summer of 1934.—*Source: Munzinger Archive; Krätschmer, p. 10; Seemen; Siegler, p. 116.*

[120] If and to what extent the Waffen SS was favored over the Wehrmacht in the allocation of replacements is still the subject of ongoing debate between the groups' respective members. Of the 120,000 Reich Germans who were called up and made available to the Waffen SS—which had a total of 860,000 men, including 320,000 Reich Germans—some had been transferred from the Army or the Luftwaffe, and some had been members of the conscripted (and, in the case of members of the general SS, also older) age groups. These were divided according to a fixed quota, which had been established by Hitler on Keitel's suggestion and after input from the Commanders-in-Chief of the Armed Forces branches and the RFSS. The Waffen SS percentage was still so small at the beginning of the war that it did not appear independently at all, while the Army, Navy and Luftwaffe divided the replacements in the ratio of 66:9:25. But the Waffen SS manpower agencies, established in 1940 by the deputy General Commands, were now in charge of obtaining their quota of RAD-selected "human material." This was done through their recruitment efforts, which were not always carried out according to the rules, as well as through special agreements with the Reich Youth Leadership (e.g., concerning the patrol teams). Their penetration of all national and party establishments allowed, for the most part, favorable access. During the final years, recruitment became coercive, and finally regular drafts took place when the number of volunteers did not cover the quotas anymore. That applied in particular to the establishment of the 9th and 10th SS Panzer Divsions, whose personnel, on Hitler's order, had been inspected and called up outside the quota in the winter of 1942-43. As a consequence, the

standard of leadership over the highly valuable personnel of the SS divisions sank—which was considered inexcusable by the Army officers, considering the gaps in their own noncommissioned officer corps. Within the Waffen SS, the *Leibstandarte* received special preference in the personnel distribution (in the Army, correspondingly, the *Grossdeutschland* Division).—*Source: Berger, passim; Guderian: Erinnerungen, p. 406; Görlitz I, p. 212; Nbg. Dok. NO-535, NO-1109, NO-1477, NO-1642, NO-1825 and NO-2280.*

[121] The reference is to the small radio-controlled Raupenschlepper [caterpillar tractors], which were filled with dynamite and blasted via long-distance ignition.

[122] Otto Wöhler; born July 12, 1894; 1914 Second Lieutenant, 167th Infantry Regiment; 1918 Lieutenant Colonel, Reichswehr; 1934 Ia [operations officer] 8th Infantry Division; 1935 Lieutenant Colonel; 1937 Ia, VII Army Corps; 1938 Colonel and Ia, Army Group Command 5 (later Fourteenth Army); December 1939 Chief of Staff, XVII Army Corps; October 1940 Chief of Staff, Eleventh Army; March 1942 Chief of Staff, Army Group Center; October 1942 Lieutenant General; April 1943 Commanding General, First Army Corps; June 1943 General of the Infantry; August 1943 Commander-in-Chief, Eighth Army; December 1944 to April 1945 Commander-in-Chief, Army Group South. Wöhler was sentenced at Nuremberg to eight years' imprisonment.—*Source: Trials X, pp. 13 and 53; Siegler, p. 143; Order of Battle, p. 644; Seemen; Das deutsche Heer, p. 73; Rangliste 1944-45, p. 17; Keilig 211/369.*

[123] Theodor Scherer; born September 17, 1889; 1910 Second Lieutenant; 1920 Bavarian Landespolizei; 1935 transferred into the Army as a Lieutenant Colonel; 1937 Colonel; 1938 Commander, 56th Infantry Regiment (in 1939 the 56th Light Infantry Regiment); 1940 Major General; October 1941 Commander, 281st Infantry Division; May 1942 Commander of a combat group [Kampfgruppe] in the area of Kholm; November 1942 Lieutenant General and Commander, 83rd Infantry Division. Scherer was honored that year with the Knight's Cross and Oak Leaves within a span of only 2 months.—*Source: Order of Battle, p. 618; Seemen; Das deutsche Heer, p. 309; Rangliste 1944-45, p. 22; Keilig 211/292.*

[12] With Army Group Hoth.

[125] Meaning the Aksai sector.

[126] Here and in the following reference it must be "62nd" instead of "262nd." The 262nd Infantry Division was located in the central section.

[127] The development of the military situation around Stalingrad since the beginning of the encirclement operation.

[128] Field Marshal von Manstein.

[129] With this statement, the decision was finally reached regarding Manstein's request for an armored division for the relief attack in the direction of Stalingrad—the primary topic of this meeting so far. The attack, however, which got another push on December 17 with the arrival of the division, had to be stopped on December 23, despite a relatively positive outlook. The successes of the Soviet offensive on the western shore of the Don threatened to cut off Army Group Hoth at the Chir front, and the threat to the northern flank of the army group—due to the Soviet breakthrough near the Italian Eighth Army on the Don—

forced Manstein to take "steps of wide-ranging significance," including the re-location of the 6th Panzer Division to that location. At that time, the LVII Panzer Corps had already reached the Myshkova [River] a few days earlier and had established a bridgehead on the northern shore—still 48 km from the south-ern front of the Sixth Army. In view of the risks associated with this mission—and considering his limited fuel resources, his mostly immobile artillery and his exhausted and already partially starving troops—Paulus decided against the "ur-gent" attack in the direction of the LVII Panzer Corps, which Manstein had ordered on December 19. In the end, under the influence of his Chief of General Staff, General Arthur Schmidt, he obeyed Hitler's contrary order.—*Source: Manstein, p. 362; Schröter, pp. 102 and 105.*

130 This time it wasn't only the Romanian corps in Army Detachment Hollidt—the Italians also had their turn. Four days later, the Soviet thrust struck the Italian Eighth Army at the Don, which was penetrated two days later; the Italians re-treated in a steady stream toward the West.—*Source: Tippelskirch, p. 316.*

131 Rommel was returning from the position at El Agheila, the so-called "Mersa-el Brega position," which the retreating German-Italian armored army had tem-porarily occupied. Montgomery had planned to go around Rommel's troops at the straits of El Agheila and capture them. To provide a distraction from the movements of the flanking convoy (New Zealander 2nd Division), he had sched-uled a frontal attack against Rommel for December 14, which was to tie him up in combat. In preparation, Montgomery had ordered heavy artillery fire and air bombardments for two days before—which, however, due to some over-eager-ness, had already started on the 11th. Rommel knew about the general English preparations for attack, of course, and he had already started on the 6th to withdraw his Italian troops toward the west into the Buerat position outside of Tripoli. Because he misinterpreted the bombardments of the 11th and 12th and the individual raids as the beginning of Montgomery's general attack, he or-dered on the night of December 11 to 12 that his motorized German troops also evacuate the Brega position, whereby—without realizing it initially—he es-caped the planned encirclement.—*Source: Montgomery, p. 51; Rommel Papers, p. 370; Tippelskirch, p. 338.*

132 Buerat position.

133 Göring had spoken with Mussolini and the Italian Armed Forces leadership on November 30 in Rome, when he accompanied Rommel back to Italy after his report at the Führer Headquarters on November 28. This discussion also ad-dressed the defense of Tripoli. Contrary to Rommel's opinion, requesting the evacuation of Libya and the retreat to Tunis, the decision was made to defend Tripoli behind the Syrte in the Buerat position after the expected loss of the Mersa-el Brega line (El Agheila). It didn't help. On January 15, the British threw the Axis forces out of the Buerat position as well.—*Source: Rommel Papers, pp. 365 and 384; Ciano, p. 494.*

134 Meaning Rommel's attack against the British position south of the El Alamein front, with the goal of breaking through to the Suez Canal. The attack started during the night of August 30, 1942. By the morning of September 1, however,

Rommel was already forced to halt all significant attack movements—in part because of the failure of the fuel supply. That evening, some tanks had only a single consumption unit left. The next day, 2,600 of the 5,000 tons of fuel promised for September 3 had already been sunk and 1,500 were still in Italy. So for the sake of precision, it wasn't Rommel's first offensive, but his last.—*Source: Rommel Papers, p. 276; Ciano, p. 466.*

[135] The "4,000-ton steamer" mentioned here would probably be the *Sant' Andrea*—the most serious Panzer loss at that point. Furthermore, the fuel situation was not the only reason Rommel was forced to halt his offensive after 48 hours and draw his troops back to the starting position—the fierce resistance and skillful operation of the English also played a role, as did, in particular, their strong superiority in the air.—*Source: Gilbert, p. 11.*

[136] Albert Kesselring; born November 30, 1885; 1906 Second Lieutenant (Artillery); in the First World War served as Captain primarily in staff positions, Reichswehr; 1922 Ia of the Chief of Staff for the Chief of Army Command, Sparkommisar [Budget Commissioner] of the Reich Army; 1928 Chief of Staff at the Wehrmacht office; 1931 Detachment Commander, 4th Artillery Regiment; October 1933 left the Army as Colonel; Head of Administrative Office in the RLM (Dept. D); 1935 joined the Luftwaffe as Major General; June 1936 Head of the Air Command Office; 1937 Commander in Air District III; October 1938 Chief, First Air Fleet; July 1940 skipped General rank to become Field Marshal; January 1940 to June 1943 Chief, Second Air Fleet; December 1941 to March 10, 1945 Commander-in-Chief, South (November 21, 1943 re-designated Commander-in-Chief Southwest); July 1943 to March 1945 Commander-in-Chief, Army Group C; July 1944 awarded the Iron Cross with Diamonds; March 11-25, 1945 Commander-in-Chief, West; and March 25, 1945 until the German surrender, Commander-in-Chief, South (from April 22 on for the entire Southern territory). Kesselring was sentenced to death by a British military court in Venice in May 1947 (later reduced to life, then to 20 years' imprisonment), released on parole in July 1952 and finally freed in October 1952.—*Source: Kesselring, passim; Munzinger Archive; Seemen; Siegler, p. 126.*

[137] Bernhard Ramcke; born January 24, 1889; 1905 shipmate in the First World War promoted from sergeant to officer due to bravery; Reichswehr; in the Polish campaign Regiment Commander; during the Crete mission in May 1941 took over the Parachute Assault Regiment as Colonel; 1941 as Major General transferred to the Afrika Korps (Commander Parachute Brigade Ramcke); subsequently during the Italian campaign, Commander, 2nd Parachute Division; in spring 1944 to Brittany and later Commanding Officer of the encircled (since August 4, 1944) fort at Brest. Ramcke defended Brest until September 20 and received the Iron Cross with diamonds on the day of his surrender. He was turned over to France in 1946, and there—after a temporary disappearance from his place of residence—he was sentenced in 1951 to five years' imprisonment and released shortly thereafter.—*Source: Munzinger Archive; Hove, p. 155; Seemen.*

[138] Hitler refers here to Kesselring, who, as the one responsible for the supply over the Mediterranean and the Luftwaffe support for Rommel, was likely to have a

different opinion. The identical judgment by Ramcke might be explained by the fact that he could only see the section of the battlefield where he had to attack with his troops. Hitler's explanations, though, were proven wrong by the further developments in the North African campaign. In the end, the ever-greater enemy superiority in the air—over Africa as well as the Mediterranean—was decisive to the negative conclusion of the campaign.

139 Erwin Rommel; born November 15, 1891; 1912 Second Lieutenant, 124th Infantry Regiment; Reichswehr; 1937 Colonel and commander, training group, Potsdam Military School; October 1938 Commanding Officer, Führer Headquarters; November 1938 Commander, Wiener Neustadt Military School; 1939 Major General; during the Polish campaign, Commanding Officer, Führer Headquarters; during the Western campaign, Commander 7th Panzer Division; 1941 Lieutenant General and (February) Commanding General, German Afrika Korps (September 1941 Armored Group Africa); July 1941 General of the Armored Troops; February 1942 Commander-in-Chief, Panzer Army Africa (January 1943 Army Group Africa); January 1942 General; June 1942 Field Marshal; March 9, 1943 recalled from Tunis; and in mid-1943 Commander-in-Chief, Army Group B (August-November 1943 in northern Italy, but after December 1943 in northern France). Rommel was injured in a car crash near Lisieux on July 17, 1944, during an air attack. Because of his involvement in the July 20, 1944 events, he was forced to commit suicide—by Generals Burgdorf and Maisel, on Hitler's orders—on October 14, 1944.—*Source: Rommel Papers, passim; Das deutsche Heer, p. 803; Siegler, p. 135; Munzinger Archive; Dt. Soldatenzeitung Sept. 1952; Keilig 211/276.*

140 Göring was in favor of Kesselring at that time and against Rommel. Rommel's nerves really had been strained.

141 It seems that an advance notice of this Soviet explanation had been presented to Hitler at this point in time—around noon on December 12, 1942. The full text of this special report was not made public by Radio Moscow until the night of December 12, and could hardly have been known to Hitler here, even considering time differences. Furthermore, the text disproved Hitler's claim that it was almost all Romanians, and it also spoke of 94,000 dead, not prisoners. The relevant section of this special report says: "The materiel captured by Russian troops in the battles around Stalingrad during the offensive of November 19 to December 11 consists of: 105 aircraft, 1,10 armored fighting vehicles, 2,134 guns of various calibers, 1,714 mortars, 28 flak batteries, 4,175 machine guns, 317 anti-tank guns, 4,196,000 artillery shells and 20 million cartridges. 62 radio transmission stations, 522 km of telephone wire, and various other war materials also fell into Russian hands. During the same period, 72,400 prisoners were taken at the Stalingrad front, while 632 enemy aircraft—including 353 transport planes—548 armored cars, 934 guns of all calibers, 194 heavy machine guns and 138 large trucks were destroyed. In the time period mentioned, more than 94,000 officers and soldiers were killed, 80 percent of them Germans and the rest Romanians."—*Source: NZZ of Dec. 14, 1942 (morning edition).*

142 In Africa.

[143] Rommel.

[144] The next line back—the Buerat line.

[145] The asphalt coastal road in Libya, built in the 1930s by the Italians and opened in 1937—the "Litoranea Libica." After its major supporter, Governor General Air Marshal Italo Balbo, was shot down during an inspection flight on June 28, 1940, by friendly naval anti-aircraft fire during an English air attack over Tobruk, the road was given his name (officially "Litoranea Italo Balbo," usually called "Via Balbia").

[146] The supply traffic along the Tunisian coast was mostly Navy barges, as well as a few small coastal boats, sailboats and motorboats, which traveled southward close to the coast.

[147] These were merchant ships that had fallen into German and Italian hands during the occupation of southern France. When German troops occupied Marseille on November 12, 1942, they found nearly 700,000 GRT [gross registration tons] of French merchant ship capacity. After "negotiations" with the Vichy government, the Reich was given 645,000 GRT as a "French contribution to the defense of the Reich," while 50,000 GRT in small boats remained for French coastal navigation. This acquisition—according to the opinion of the German Commander-in-Chief South—brought temporary improvement of supplies for the troops in Africa during a time when tension was at its peak. According to a French report, the following were taken over:

87 freighters	with 316,400 GRT
16 tank carriers	with 96,300 GRT
19 passenger ships	with 151,200 GRT
31 smaller ships of various kinds	with 81,400 GRT
Total:	645,300 GRT

At this time, Italy still had 1 million GRT merchant ship capacity, of which 400,000 GRT were available to transport supplies to Tunisia. 325,000 GRT of that was lost by the time Tunis surrendered.—*Source: Kammerer, p. 465; Kesselring, p. 153; de Belot, pp. 197 and 203.*

[148] Unlike the other previously free zones of France, Toulon was not occupied by German and Italian troops on November 11-12, so, according to the conditions of the armistice agreements, the Axis powers respected the French fleet for the time being. But on November 27, a German-Italian attack, Operation "Anton," was carried out against the harbor to prevent French ships from putting to sea and joining the free French forces in North Africa. The action failed to capture the French fleet, however, which mostly scuttled itself as the Wehrmacht entered Toulon. It is not known to what extent merchant ship capacity was secured; in any case, it would have been an insignificant amount in comparison with the tonnage captured at Marseille.—*Source: Mordal, p. 248; VB of Novon 28, 1942.*

[149] The escort traffic from Sicily to Tunisia and initially also to Tripoli was led around the western tip of Sicily (Trapani) and was usually escorted by Italian destroyers and torpedo boats. During this time, mine barriers were set up in the

Sicilian straits, parallel to the German-Italian traffic routes, to protect against enemy surface forces.

150 Meaning French fishing steamers and yachts, some of which were remodeled into submarine fighters for the 22nd Submarine Fighter Flotilla in December 1942 and January 1943, and which were mostly used in the Tyrrhenian Sea.

151 The *Wecke Police Detachment* was established under Major Wecke on February 23, 1933, as fully motorized support troops within the Prussian Schutzpolizei [Security Police] and as Göring's personal troops. Shortly thereafter, it was enlarged to the *Wecke Police Group*, put directly under the command of the Prussian Interior Ministry, and renamed the *Landespolizeigruppe* [State Police Group] *General Göring* on December 22, 1933. Its duties, which initially consisted primarily of anti-Communist raids and guarding concentration camps, acquired more and more of a military character. As *Regiment General Göring*, the group was transferred to the Luftwaffe on September 23, 1935, and received the blue flyer uniforms with white collar patches soon thereafter. Colonel von Axthelm, later Inspector of Anti-Aircraft Artillery, as commander from 1936 to 1940, created a military formation—which only lacked submarines, as was said jokingly at the time—out of Göring's mixed private army. In early 1942 the regiment, whose original duty was securing tactical support for paratroop units after they jumped, was expanded to the *Hermann Göring Brigade*, and in late fall of the same year to the 1st Parachute Panzer *Hermann Göring*. A General Command by this name was finally also established in October 1944.— *Source: Jürgens, passim; Koch: Die organisatorische…, passim; Bertram, passim.*

152 The following exchange probably deals with observations regarding Allied supply traffic along the North African coast.

153 The German submarine U 602 off the North African coast on December 9, 1942 torpedoed the British destroyer *Porcupine.*

154 At this point, Germany had already fallen irreversibly behind in electric or radio location technology— generally known as "radar" after the war (radio detecting and ranging). This deficiency now led to more and more significant defeats at sea, and especially in the air war. At the beginning of the war, German researchers were able to counter the English developments with at least something of comparable value: e.g., the already mass-produced "Freya" general locating device—without altitude specifications—which had a long range of 120 km and was used in the air-raid warning service; or even the first models of the altitude-specific and more refined locating instruments of the "Würzburg A" type, which were being tested at that time. These instruments—later improved and known as the "Würzburg-Riesen"—were used to guide anti-aircraft fire, to lead night fighters, and to identify more specific air positions. The primary reason Germany fell behind so quickly was a fatal scientific mistake: the misjudgment of the revolutionary use of high-frequency waves (less than 10 cm). But the enemy was also able to take the lead in another respect. The German Navy, which carried out its own development work, had entered the war in 1939 practically without radar equipment, and, due to the large size of the instruments, was able to equip only the largest units with radio location technology. At the end of

1941, however, a smaller instrument, the "Liechtenstein" Bordsuchgerät [onboard search device] was produced based on the Würzburg principle (that is: target as signal) for the Luftwaffe night fighters. This device was necessary due to the enemy's ability to disappear into the darkness at night, but could only be used against targets in the air. Thus, the German submarine force was taken completely by surprise during the English air attacks of July 1942, which were carried out with great daring in bad weather and at night, with the help of [onboard radar devices] ASV devices on 1.5-cm wavelength with 6 km range). After March 1, 1943, makeshift defense facilities for detecting enemy radar ("Biscaya-Kreuz," "Metox" receiver) were able to remedy the problem until the Allies were forced by the German submarine stranglehold to prematurely deploy the decisive Rotterdam instruments; however, Hitler's remark shows that German replica construction had not yet been successful up to the time of that situation conference.—*Source: Bley, passim; Hoffmann: Geheimnis radar, passim; Busch, p. 179; Churchill IV/1, p. 326; Lusar, p. 113.*

155 Because of the RAF night attacks on Berlin, which began in the late summer of 1940 (August 25), the Luftwaffe High Command placed General Weise, an experienced anti-aircraft specialist, in charge of the command and reorganization of III Luftwaffe Command. As a result, the flak and searchlight batteries were deployed in a more concentrated fashion. On March 21, 1941, Weise became head of the Luftwaffe Commander Center and received, in addition to his II Anti-Aircraft Corps and II/IV Luftwaffe Command Unit (Berlin/Dresden), VI Luftwaffe Command Unit (Münster), and XI (Hamburg) and the night fighter division, as well as VII Luftwaffe Command Unit (Munich) and XII/XIII (Wiesbaden/Nuremberg) for matters of air defense. From Hitler's remarks here and in other situations, it is clear that the increasingly prominent role of flak in air defense was due in part to his influence.

156 These statements are correct. Before the war, plans called for an expanded defense of Berlin, with flak batteries overlapping in triple layers at 5,000-meter range. The 150 heavy batteries necessary to achieve this were not brought together, however. On the contrary, more and more flak had to be withdrawn from Berlin for use in the Western campaign. General Weise then brought the Berlin defense up to 80 batteries again, and orders were given to increase the number further, to at least 100. For this effort, more and more of the so-called "large batteries" were built in the Berlin area—as well as everywhere else—which, instead of the normal equipment of 4 guns, were supplied with 6, 8, 12 or at the end even 18 guns in order to produce a truly massive fire. At 900 guns in 1944, Berlin's air defense exceeded by far the peacetime goal—though not in terms of the batteries, but in the number of guns. The considerable strength of its defense, however, could not save the Reich capital from the extensive devastation that began with the Battle of Berlin—from November 18, 1943, to March 24, 1944.

157 Hitler refers to the serious losses due to the sinking of transport ships carrying materiel from southern Italy to Africa. The Tiger tank was superior to the English and American tanks and was especially well suited for use in Africa because of the long range and penetration capability of its gun.

[158] Here Hitler expresses for the first time a consideration that he often repeats later: the possibility of Allied landings in the eastern Mediterranean. In fact, however, the Allies never seriously considered giving up the planned operation in the central Mediterranean in favor of actions in the eastern part—although there may haven been discussions before Casablanca regarding the usefulness of an attack in the Mediterranean at all, or regarding the exact direction of the push (Sicily-southern Italy or even Sardinia-Corsica). Later, whenever Balkan operations were discussed, they were always connected to the Allied plan to force Turkey into the war and roll up the German southeast position. Churchill, in particular, always wanted to see operations in the eastern Mediterranean and especially in the Balkans—in addition to and in support of Operation "Overlord" (the invasion of northern France). But his plans were spoiled by defensiveness—less on the part of the Russians than from the Americans, who even allowed local operations against the Dodecanese (which had been started by the English after Italy changed sides on September 8, 1943) to fail, after the German decision to evacuate the area south of Rome, became obvious in October 1943. In contrast to the unsuspecting Americans and especially to Roosevelt, Churchill actually thought politically in terms of the peace to be won for the democracies. At the Teheran conference (November 28 to December 1, 1943), it was finally decided to forego any action in the southeast in favor of a faster invasion of northern France.—*Source: Montgomery, p. 113; Churchill, passim, esp. IV/2, pp. 46, 271, 309, 320, 324 and V/1, pp. 33, 329; Beyer, passim; Wilmot, p. 132.*

[159] This "mopping-up" wasn't a lasting success, however, as the second meeting of the pro-Tito AVNOJ ([Anti-Fascist National Freedom Council] of Yugoslavia) took place in Jace almost a year later, establishing a provisional Yugoslavian government after finally taking a position against King Peter and his government-in-exile. The date of the Jace meeting, November 29, 1943, was later written on the ribbon of the Yugoslavian national coat of arms.

[160] Meaning the border of the German-Italian control zone in Croatia.

[161] Colonel of the General Staff Draza Mihailović, who, contrary to official opinion, called the defense of the Yugoslavian border impossible and had argued for conducting warfare from a limited national territory, saw his opinion vindicated by the rapid capitulation of the Yugoslavian Army on April 16, 1941. He used the already existing village militias (Četniks) to organize the resistance against the occupiers. Ever since Turkish times the political underground movement was as traditional to this area as the heroic robbery by the underdogs who had fled into the mountains. Mihailović was able to establish a connection with Allied headquarters and the London government-in-exile, which promoted him to Army General and in which he served *in absentia* as War Minister from January 1942 to May 1944. After the Communist Party of Yugoslavia had shifted to actively fighting occupation on July 4, 1941, they soon had quarrels with the Četniks, whose warfare had become weak because of sharp reprisals against the civilian population—especially against the many wealthy and well-known Mihailović followers in Belgrade—and whose policies, dictated by the ultimate goal of restoring the monarchy, the Communists soon feared more than the

declining Axis powers. After initial contact attempts, open battles broke out on the upper Ibar as early as the beginning of November 1941. From that point on, aside from collaboration with the Nedic government, the Četniks made more frequent local tactical compromises with the Italians and finally also with the Germans. Thus, due to an English initiative (the United States and, surprisingly, the USSR were more reluctant) Allied support shifted increasingly toward the more active Tito partisans, until Churchill's speech at the House of Commons brought the formal break with Mihailović on May 24, 1944. Mihailović was thereby forced into further collaboration (for example, the joint combat offer rejected by Hitler on August 17, 1944). This mysterious maneuver gave Tito the welcome opportunity to eliminate his rival, who, after a long hunt through the Serbian mountains, was captured on March 13, 1946, put on trial in a Communist court, sentenced to death, and executed on July 17, 1946.—*Source: Matl: Jugoslawien im...,* *passim; Fotitch, passim; Lazitch, passim; Dedijer, passim; Yourichitch, passim; Sava, passim; Zilliacus, p. 125; Churchill V/2, p. 166; Rendulic: Partisanenkrieg, p. 99; Kiszling, p. 181.*

[162] According to a statement by the stenographer, this number is doubtful. It must also be remembered that Hitler shortly thereafter speaks of a "major attack" by 16 aircraft.

[163] On December 14, 1942, the Anglo-Americans released the following communiqué regarding this air attack: "USAAF heavy bombers attacked targets at Rouen on Saturday afternoon. The weather was bad and results couldn't be verified. Squadrons of Allied fighters supported and covered this operation. Strong opposition was encountered from enemy fighters, 14 of which were destroyed by the bombers and 4 by fighters. 2 bombers and 4 fighters are missing." Since that Saturday was the December 12 on which this situation conference took place, there is obviously a mistake or a misunderstanding reflected in the text: Christian did not mean "yesterday" but "today." This is confirmed by the Armed Forces High Command report, which did not report any daytime enemy incursions on December 12, but reported on December 13 regarding the preceding day: "Enemy bombers and fighter units, under the protection of cloud cover, carried out daytime attacks against several towns in western France. The population suffered losses. The enemy lost 7 aircraft, including 2 four-engine bombers."—*Source: Gilbert, p. 14; VB of Dec. 14, 1942.*

[164] The Armed Forces report for this day, December 12, 1942, reported: "During the night, a fighter unit attacked the important Sunderland harbor and shipyard. Widespread fires occurred, and 2 German aircraft are missing."

[165] Read as: over.

[166] The number 1,000 stands for the weight of the bomb (1,000 kg) and the letters SC are the code letters for the type of bomb—in this case mine bombs with a large amount of explosive and relatively weak walls. The other major type of demolition bomb was the SD bomb, with relatively les explosive power and thick walls for greater penetration.

[167] According to the recollection of a participant in this meeting, this was a false report released by the Luftwaffe, which Hitler had discovered through reports

from the commanders responsible for that same attack. Based on the figures given, the reference must be to the first 1,000-bomber attack of the RAF, which was carried out during the night of May 30-31, 1942, against Cologne. 3,300 houses were totally destroyed and 7,200 damaged in this attack. No earlier attack had caused anywhere near this degree of devastation, and Cologne was not mentioned in the Armed Forces report again. In contrast to Hitler's statement here, however, the Armed Forces High Command report of May 31—at least in the version the daily papers published June 1—spoke of "heavy damage ... especially in residential areas."—*Source: Rumpf, p. 78; VB of June 1, 1942.*

[168] Hitler's explanations, which reflect the shift from optimistic propaganda to "strength through fear" that took place during the Stalingrad months, were apparently in response to the latest SD report, as Goebbels remarked in his diary under the same date: "The latest reports of the SD and the Reich propaganda offices were presented to me. In both of these, as well as in the reports of the Gauleiters, there is very sharp criticism of our news policy regarding the situation at the front. I feel absolutely not guilty of this obvious fizzle. I have always urged greater frankness in news. ... We need to make the gravity of the situation clear to the German people, also at the front. The German people can endure things; they will only become uncomfortable if they have the feeling that they are being spared excessively. I will be concerned again that at least our supplementary report to the OKW High Command report will handle these things better."—*Source: Goebbels Diaries, photocopy in the IfZ, Bl. 1553 and Lochner ed. Doubleday, 1948, p. 239.*

[169] Renamed Luftwaffe Command Southeast at the end of the year in southern Greece and Crete.

[170] The designation "Luftwaffe Don" is incorrect. The General Command First Air Corps, under Lieutenant General Korten, had the name "Luftwaffe Command Don" during those fall and winter months (according to Siegler: October through March; according to Korten's personnel data: August 24, 1942, to February 25, 1943), and was therefore directly under the command of the Luftwaffe High Command. This was supposed to lead to a stricter command and better support of the Army in the decisive battles in the southern sector.

[171] The Air District Commands 1 to 7 (6: Sea) had been established in April 1934. On the basis of Führer order of February 4, 1938, the Luftwaffe was reorganized. Luftwaffe Group Commands 1 to 3 were established, to which the Luftwaffe Commands East Prussia and Sea (later disbanded) were added as well, as was the Luftwaffe Command Austria (later Ostmark) after the *Anschluss*. The first Luftwaffe areas were established in February 1939 by renaming the Luftwaffe Groups. The German Luftwaffe contained the following eight air fleets (Luftwaffes):

First Air Fleet (Luftwaffe 1)—(formerly Luftwaffe Group 1) February 1, 1939 until the surrender (Berlin, later Polish campaign and Eastern campaign)

Second Air Fleet (Luftwaffe 2)—(formerly Luftwaffe Group 2) February 1, 1939 to October 27, 1944 (in Luftwaffe Command South) (Braunschweig, later Western campaign and African/Italian campaign)

Third Air Fleet (Luftwaffe 3)—(formerly Luftwaffe Group 3) February 1, 1939 to September 27, 1944 (in Luftwaffe Command West) (Munich, later Western campaign and in the West)

Fourth Air Fleet (Luftwaffe 4)—(formerly Luftwaffe Command Ostmark) March 18, 1939 to April 7, 1945 (in Luftwaffe Command 4) (Vienna, later Southeastern campaign and in the East/Balkans)

Fifth Air Fleet (Luftwaffe 5)—(new) April 12, 1940 to October 10, 1944 (disbanded) (Norwegian campaign, Norway/Finland)

Sixth Air Fleet (Luftwaffe 6)—(formerly Luftwaffe Command East) May 11, 1943 to capitulation (Eastern campaign)

Reich Air Fleet (Luftwaffe Reich)—(Luftwaffe Commander Middle) February 5, 1944 to capitulation (Reich territory)

Tenth Air Fleet (Luftwaffe 10)—(new) July 1, 1944 to end of March 1945 (in replacement Luftwaffe) (training and replacement)

—*Source: Siegler, p. 51.*

[172] There are several versions of the figures denoting the exact extent of the Stalingrad supply catastrophe. Where there are differences, the numbers provided by the last head of the Military Science Department of the Luftwaffe, Herhudt von Rohden, are used here. There seems no possible doubt that Hitler's decision to leave the encircled Sixth Army in Stalingrad was not, in the end, based on firm supply promises from Göring, who was again misled by the successful supply of 300 tons a day to the pockets of Kholm and Demiansk, despite serious reservations by the Luftwaffe General Staff. The extent of the promises by Göring, which can no longer be verified, varied between 300 and 500 tons per day, while the reported requirements of the Sixth Army were 750 tons—or, at the minimum, 500 tons. As a result of unfavorable weather conditions, an inadequate number of transport planes, heavy losses to Soviet antiaircraft (246 aircraft in December alone; 488 altogether, or even 808 according to other statements), increasing flight distances due to the retreating German front, and the steadily shrinking space for landing or dropping supplies near Stalingrad, supply drops reached only the following daily averages:

Nov. 25–29	(Beginning of supply attempts by air)	53.8 t
Nov. 30–Dec. 11	(Supply by VIII Air Corps)	97.3 t
Dec. 12–21	(Relief attempt)	137.7 t
Dec. 22–Jan. 11	(Until Russian assault)	105.45 t
Jan. 12–16	(Loss of Pitomnik)	60 t
Jan. 17–21	(Loss of Gumrak; from then on many night drops, with corresponding losses)	79 t
Jan. 22–23	(Loss of Stalinsgradskii)	45 t
Jan. 24–Feb. 2	(Only night drops)	77.9 t
	Overall average:	94.16 t
	Total supply:	6591 t
	Highest daily quantity, on Dec. 19:	280 t

—*Source: Herhudt, passim; Schröter, pp. 90, 142 and 149; Feuchter, p. 199.*

1943

[173] Transcript number unknown—Fragment No. 47—A shorthand record taken by the stenographer Berger, who died on July 20, 1944, was preserved. Large portions of the individual pages—more than half—were destroyed by fire. The shorthand fragment was transcribed again by the second stenographer who had participated in the original meeting, but whose control record was not preserved. As it was an unusual handwriting, not all the words could be deciphered perfectly.

[174] Meaning before the start of the actual situation conference, because initially only Hitler, General Zeitzler and Lieutenant Colonel Engel were present.

[175] The question was whether or not the Donets area—whose wealth of coal, in Hitler's opinion, would be of decisive importance for either the German or Soviet war effort—could be held. On January 18, Zeitzler had suggested to Hitler for the first time the possibility of evacuating the area, as there was the danger of a huge gap developing in the front between Voronezh and Voroschilovgrad after the collapse of the Hungarian Second Army, and Army Group Don was thus threatened with encirclement. In a long-distance call with Zeitzler the following day, Manstein identified timely relief from the direction of Khar'kov as a prerequisite for holding onto the Donets area. If forces for this purpose could not be freed up in time from the Armed Forces High Command theaters, from Army Groups North and Center or through new call ups at home, or if the railway systems did not permit such a rapid assembly of forces, the district could not be held, and the attempt to remain anyway—isolated on the lower Don and on the Donets—would be an operational mistake. In a teletype message to the Army High Command the day before this conference, Manstein had expressed his opinion once more: the timely defeat of the enemy northeast of Khar'kov, before the beginning of the muddy period, or—if, as unfortunately might be assumed, the forces were insufficient for that—the abandonment of at least the eastern part of the Donets region.—*Source: Manstein, p. 430.*

[176] The SS Panzer Corps' divisions assembled in Khar'kov to push into the rear of the enemy forces advancing on the German Donets front. So far, however, only the General Command, the 2nd SS Panzer Division *Das Reich,* and parts of the First SS Panzer Division *Leibstandarte Adolf Hitler* had arrived. The rapid advance of the Soviets and the threat it posed to the assembly area, however, frustrated the planned concentrated counterattack by the corps.—*Source: Manstein, p. 435; Hausser, p. 82.*

[177] The 13th Panzer Division belonged in principle to the First Panzer Army, whose withdrawal to Rostov, in order to strengthen the threatened Army Group Don, was finally agreed to by Hitler on January 24. But the 50th Infantry Division—which was also under the command of the First Panzer Army—could no longer make the connection as a result of this hesitation, and had to join the unit of the Seventeenth Army that was withdrawing to the Kuban. After much vacillation, Hitler then decided that the 13th Panzer Division should

go with Army Group A back to the isolated Kuban bridgehead, which Hitler considered particularly important due to the Crimea's influence on the attitude of Turkey.—*Source: Manstein, p. 429.*

[178] The following discussion applies to the suggestion to pull the front back in the southern sector, thus abandoning the Donets area. Hitler had strongly emphasized the need to significantly increase German armament production, because he realized—to a certain extent—that from the beginning of 1943, American armament production would accelerate dramatically. Because the production increase seemed possible in the long term only with the help of the Donets area, extensive production programs had been planned for the region; these programs would disappear if the area were evacuated. But one has to bear in mind that the discussion refers to plans only, because in reality—and this was also indicated in a memorandum by Speer written at this time, possibly as a result of this meeting—successful economic use of the Donets area had not been achieved thus far, because the destruction was too extensive and repairs were therefore very difficult. Only in the coal mining sector were some successes achieved; however, after the ore mining and steel production did not materialize, a grotesque situation arose that—because of the great distances— the locomotives transporting the coal away were using almost as much coal as they were pulling.

[179] Meaning per battalion sector.

[180] In the context of this discussion about the clearance of the Don River's mouth and the eastern Donets basin to the Mius River—requested by Manstein in order to reinforce the west wing of Army Group Don, which was continually threatened by encirclement—Hitler refers here to the previous disagreements concerning the withdrawal of Army Group A from the Caucasus after the collapse of the southern sector of the Eastern Front. The First Panzer Army and the Seventeenth Army constituted Army Group A; the former retreated past Rostov and reinforced the defense of the Fourth Panzer Army and Army Detachment Hollidt, while the latter withdrew to the Kuban bridgehead. Although Hitler claims here to have saved Army Group v. Kleist, that is not quite in accordance with the facts, as it required several requests—and took literally until the last minute—to obtain permission from him to withdraw from the Caucasus. Thus, the last incomplete sentence is particularly unclear.— *Source: Manstein, p. 379; Tippelskirch, p. 320.*

[181] The *Reich* Division (Second SS Panzer Division) was an SS support division, formed in 1939 from the SS support troops after the end of the Polish campaign. After the Western campaign, the division received the sobriquet *Reich*, and later *Das Reich*. The division fought under Küchler in France, was among the first German units to invade Belgrade a year later, and was deployed until March 1942 in Russia with Army Group Center. After being refitted in France, the unit was transferred again to the East and in March 1943 took part in the battles in the Ukraine (Khar'kov), after June 1944 on the invasion front, and in Hungary in 1945.—*Source: Hausser, passim; Order of Battle, p. 337.*

[182] The following discussion refers to the Russian report that Field Marshal Paulus and other generals, including v. Seydlitz and Schmidt, were captured in the southern pocket of Stalingrad.

[183] General Giraud—who had already been in German captivity during World War I, and escaped from a field hospital—on May 19, 1940 drove into the headquarters of the Ninth Army, which he had taken over, without knowing that it was already occupied by German troops. He was captured by German officers and imprisoned. Later, through his successful escape from the Königstein fortress, he added considerably to the strain of the Berlin-Vichy relations.—*Source: Aron, p. 513 and others; Abetz, p. 235; Munzinger Archive.*

[184] On January 26, the Soviets had attacked the pocket at Stalingrad—which was stretched the furthest in the north-south direction—in the middle, and finally divided it in two. After January 27 at 2 a.m., there was no further connection between the main pocket and the troops of the XI Army Corps under General of Infantry Strecker, which were pushed together around the tractor factory in the north of Stalingrad. On February 2 at 11 a.m., the Russians lined up for the final attack on the tractor factory, after the main pocket had surrendered two days before. Three hours later a German reconnaissance aircaft reported: "No further combat action in Stalingrad."—*Source: Schröter, pp. 196 and 231.*

[185] Arthur Schmidt; born October 25, 1895; studied architecture at Karlsruhe Technical College; 1914 war volunteer, 26th Infantry Regiment; activated and taken into the Reichswehr; 1937 Lieutenant Colonel and Ia [Operations officer], VI Army Corps; 1939 Ia, Fifth Army (after November Eighteenth Army); 1940 Colonel and Chief of the General Staff, V Army Corps; June 1942 Major General and Chief of the General Staff, Sixth Army; and January 17, 1943 Lieutenant General. Contrary to Hitler's fears, Schmidt did not cooperate with the Soviets and also did not join the National Committee later. He returned to Germany in 1955 from Soviet imprisonment.—*Source: DNB of Jan. 14, 1943; Order of Battle, p. 620; Das deutsche Heer, p. 118; Rangliste 1944-45, p. 24; Manstein, p. 365; Keilig 211/297.*

[186] Hitler's Luftwaffe Adjutant v. Below had received this letter from a relative who had been a general staff officer in a unit in Stalingrad.

[187] Friedrich Paulus; born September 23, 1890; 1911 Second Lieutenant; during World War I mostly in adjutancy and general staff; 1918 Captain, Reichswehr; 1931 Major in RWM; 1933 Lieutenant Colonel; 1934 Commander, Motor Transport Detachment, Wünsdorf; 1935 Colonel and Chief of General Staff, Armored Troops Command; 1939 Major General and Chief of Staff, Fourth Army Group (later Sixth Army); 1940 Lieutenant General and 1st Senior Quartermaster in the Army General Staff; January 1942, General of Panzer Troops and Commander-in-Chief, Sixth Army; November 30, 1942 Colonel General; and January 30, 1943 Field Marshal. On the following day capitulated in Stalingrad. Paulus declared after the execution of the July assassins that he had joined the National Committee to Liberate Germany. He was released in November 1953 from Soviet captivity and took up residence in Dresden, where

he died on February 1, 1957.—*Source: Army High Command staff files (Nbg. Dok. NOKW-141); Munzinger Archive.*

[188] Walter v. Seydlitz-Kurzbach; born August 22, 1888; 1910 Second Lieutenant; 1930 Major and Adjutant to the Chief of the Army Weapons Office; 1936 Colonel and Commander, 22nd Artillery Regiment; Major General; 1940 Commander, 12th Infantry Division; 1941 Lieutenant General; spring 1942 Commander, Special Corps Demiansk; May 1942 Commanding General, LI Army Corps; and June 1942, General of Artillery. In Soviet captivity, Seydlitz became president of the German Officers' Association and vice president of the National Committee to Liberate Germany, but he refused after the dissolution of the committee to take a position in the German Soviet zone. In October 1955 he was released from captivity.—*Source: Munzinger Archive; Seemen; Order of Battle, p. 626; Das deutsche Heer, p. 479; Keilig 211/317.*

[189] Hans Hube; born October 29, 1890; 1910 Second Lieutenant, 26th Infantry Regiment; lost an arm during World War I; Reichswehr; 1936 Colonel and Commander of an infantry school; October 1939 Commander, 3rd Infantry Regiment; 1940 Major General and Commander, 16th Panzer Division; 1942 General of Panzer Troops and Commanding General, XIV Panzer Corps; summer 1943 in Sicily as commander of Group Hube; and after November 1943 Commander-in-Chief, First Panzer Army in the East. On April 21, 1944, after being promoted to Colonel General and being awarded the Diamonds, Hube was killed in a fatal accident—which he himself caused—on a return flight from the Führer Headquarters (Berchtesgaden). As Commanding General of the XIV Panzer Corps, Hube had left the Stalingrad pocket on December 28, 1942, in order to receive the Swords award and had reported to Hitler on this occasion about the situation in Stalingrad. He did return into the pocket, but was flown out again on January 18, 1943, in order to manage the overall supply of Stalingrad. (See also below note 638.)—*Source: Schröter, pp. 150 and 203; Manstein, pp. 382 and 553; Seemen; Munzinger Archive; Das deutsche Heer, p. 804; Keilig 211/145.*

[190] Hitler's information agrees with the suicide statistics published in the statistical yearbooks of the German Reich (1932–1939/40). There, with surprising consistency, the following numbers are given (after 1935 including the Saar area and Austria):

1930	17,880	1935	20,928
1931	18,625	1936	21,984
1932	18,934	1937	22,171
1933	18,723	1938	22,398
1934	18,801		

[191] On January 8, Lieutenant General Rokossovsky had sent Colonel General Paulus, via his representatives, a request for capitulation—which expired on January 9 at 10 a.m.—promising the Sixth Army life and safety, return to their homeland or to any country after the end of war, normal provisions, and the preservation of their personal belongings, uniforms, badges of rank and decorations. Paulus

did not reject this request immediately, but sent it to the Führer Headquarters and asked for freedom to act as he saw fit. Not until the following day was the Soviet ultimatum refused, on Hitler's orders.—*Source: Schröter, p. 153.*

192 As far as it could be deciphered from the individual legible words, Hitler explained further that it must be clear to everyone and impressed upon everyone that a surrounded fortification must fight to the very end. (Note by the stenographer.)

193 These words, according to the recollection of the stenographer, probably refer to Udet, who committed suicide after he failed in his role as the general in charge of aviation production.

194 Karl Becker; born December 14, 1879; 1900 Second Lieutenant; 1908 Instructor at the Berlin-Charlottenburg Military Technical Academy; 1911 Assistant in the Artillery Experimentation Commission; 1914 Captain and Battery Chief (42-cm mortar); 1916 Head of the Ballistics Office of the Artillery Experimentation Commission in the Reichswehr: Army Weapons Office; studied at the Berlin Technical College (1922 Diploma and Doctor of Engineering); 1921 Major in Weapons and Equipment Inspection; 1930 Colonel and Head of the Balistics and Ammunition Detachment in the Army Weapons Office; instructor and 1932 honorary professor at the University of Berlin; 1933 full professor of Defense Technology, physics and balistics, and permanent Dean of the Defense Technology Faculty of the Berlin; October 1932 Head of Examination System in the RWM; 1933 Major General; 1934 Lieutenat General; 1936 General of Artillery; 1937 President of the Reich Research Council; and February 4, 1938 Chief of Army Weapons Office in the RKM. Becker was the first active general to be a member of the Prussian Academy of Sciences.—*Source: Berl. Börsen-Ztg. [Berliner Börsen-Zietung] of May 27, 1937; DAZ of Dec. 14, 1939 and April 9, 1940; VB of July 16, 1938 and April 12, 1940.*

195 Becker was a brilliant artillery officer who nevertheless may have been a bit too conservative in carrying out the duties of an office that demanded a great deal of organizational ability, and he may not have been quite equal to the techniques of the defense industry, which it was his task to lead. He also failed in his effort to convince Hitler to establish an operations staff to supervise the three weapons offices, which would be above the various branches of the Armed Forces. Hitler withdrew an order to this effect the same day, at the urging of industry interests that wished to maintain the fragmentation. Instead, Becker suffered the affront that, with the establishment of the Reich Ministry for Armament and Ammunition on March 17, 1940, the new Reich Minister Todt was granted the right to give orders to the Army Weapons Office as well. Added to that was a criminal affair in which the general's son was involved. Becker apparently no longer saw a way out and reached for his pistol on April 8, 1940.—*Source: (regarding the Army Weapons Office): Schneider, p.241; Mueller-Hillebrand I, pp. 101 and 121; Dornberger, pp.78 and 87; Leeb, passim.*

196 Nothing is known about Paulus being wounded. But the foreign correspondents in Berlin also heard about it that same day, February 1. The transmitter of the Sixth Army, in the GRU [Soviet intelligence service] building in Stalingrad

should have included in his last report that Paulus was seriously wounded.—*Source: NZZ of Feb. 2, 1943 (morning edition).*

[197] Hitler had made General Paulus, who had become Colonel General on December 1, 1942, a field marshal on January 30, 1943. But at the same time he reminded him by telegram to take a pistol in his hand, because—as Hitler wanted it to be understood—a German field marshal had never surrendered before. Hitler did not keep his promise in any case: not only was the promotion of Colonel General v. Kleist, Busch and Baron v. Weichs to field marshal announced that same day, on February 1, 1943, but later Hitler also promoted to field marshal Colonel General Model and Colonel General Schörner, of the Army, on April 1, 1944, and March 1, 1945, respectively, and, from the Luftwaffe, Colonel General Baron von Richthofen on February 16, 1943, and Colonel General Ritter v. Greim on April 25, 1945.

[198] Hitler was badly informed: the promotion of Colonel General Paulus to field marshal was already published, among other places, in the *DNB Morning Report* of the previous day, January 31. Puttkamer was probably just an adjutant on duty at the time.

[199] Hitler means Lubyanka, the GRU [Soviet intelligence service] prison.

[200] Major in the General Staff Coelestin v. Zitzewitz (born January 11, 1907) of the Army High Command, who, as liaison officer, was already with the Sixth Army in June/July 1942, and remained, along with his own radio transmitter, in the Stalingrad pocket from November 25, 1942, to January 20, 1943, with the assignment of reporting as quickly and as extensively as possible. After his return he was ordered to report to Hitler for a presentation regarding the question of flying out specialists. Thus, Zitzewitz belonged to the first "pocket flyers" of the Army High Command, who then were called into action more and more frequently later, also to encourage encircled troop leaders.—*Source: Schröter, p. 190; Manstein, p. 389.*

[201] The reference is to a Captain Adam, a son of the former head of the Troop Office [Truppenamt], General of Infantry Wilhelm Adam, who, as an orderly officer, led his division back brilliantly after the loss of the men at the front.

[202] In the old Army at the time of the Kaiser, the next generation of general staff came from voluntary applications. Seeckt, on the contrary, in 1921, after the founding of the Reichswehr, extended the selection principle across the widest base: every officer now had to undergo, during his years as First Lieutenant—i.e., after about ten years of service as an officer—a so-called "Regional Army Examination" (later: "academy examination"), which lasted for a week and took place at the headquarters of the military district [*Wehrkreis*]. This examination determined the officers' suitability for general staff education, which then consisted of a three-year (temporarily only two-year) visit to the Berlin War Academy, that included approximately 100 to 150 officers per year group. Approximately one-third of the participants were considered suitable for general staff service, which translated to about 5 per cent of a whole officers' age group. Some of these men went into the departments of the Army General Staff, or served as Ic's [intelligence officers] or transport com-

manders for the general commands, but most were Ib's in the divisions. Those who did not pass the academy examinations still had the opportunity for a career in a ministry or in the higher adjutancy, or as a tactics instructor at a war school. After 1937, a small number of older officers without the military district examination were sent to the academy at the suggestion of their commanders. And finally, during the war, general staff candidates were recruited straight from the troops—also without the examination—after success at the front or through selection by their superiors.—*Source: Teske, p. 35; Erfurth: Generalstab, p. 124.*

203 The correct name could not be determined.

204 Hitler's happiness came too soon. But he was not the only one who did not realize that the commander of the Romanian 6th Infantry Division did not die in the Don bend, but, on the contrary, had been captured by the Soviets. Lieutenant General Mihai Lascar was the first foreigner to whom Hitler gave the Oak Leaves, on November 26, 1942. (Then followed: Lieutenant General Muños Grandes, Grand Admiral Yamamoto, Major General Teodorini, Colonel General Dimitrescu, Major General Dumitrache, Grand Admiral Koga, Colonel General Lakatos, Marshal Baron v. Mannerheim and SS Sturmbannführer Léon Degrelle.) The Oak Leaves recipient Lascar reappeared at the end of 1943 at Special Camp 20, in Planernaia, near Moscow, as a member of the Communist Romanian Legion and rose to be Romanian Minister of Defense in Groza's second cabinet, from November 1946 to December 1947.—*Source: Manstein, p. 276; Schröter, p. 49; Puttkamer, p. 58; Seemen, p. 49 (incomplete) and p. 281; Keesings Archive 1946-47, p. 937.*

205 Not until a year and a half later, after the execution of the July conspirators and after he had joined the National Committee to Liberate Germany, did Paulus speak via the Moscow radio station—on August 13, 1944.—*Source: NZZ of Aug. 14, 1944 (evening edition).*

206 According to the recollection of a participant at the meeting, this and the earlier reference to the "proud, beautiful woman" concerned one of Göring's secretaries. She committed suicide after an unjust accusation by the Reichsmarshal, and received as a reward for her heroic attitude a state funeral.

207 Erwin Jaenecke; born April 22, 1890; 1912 Second Lieutenant, 12th Engineer Battalion; taken into the Reichswehr as a cavalry captain; 1936 Colonel; November 1938 Chief of Staff at the Inspectorate of Fortifications; 1939 Major General and Senior Quartermaster, Eighth Army and Commander-in-Chief, East; July 1940 Senior Quartermaster, West; 1941 Lieutenant General; February 1942 Commander, 389th Infantry Division; November 1942 General of Engineers and Commanding General, IV Army Corps (on January 27, 1943, flown out of Stalingrad); April 1943 Commanding General, LXXXVI Army Corps; June 1943 Commander (October Commander-in-Chief), Seventeenth Army; February 1, 1944 Colonel General; May 1, 1944 Führer Reserves; and January 31, 1945 honorable discharge. While in Soviet captivity, Jaenecke was sentenced to 25 years' imprisonment; he was released in October 1955.—*Source: Army High Command staff files (Nbg. Dok. NOKW-141); Munzinger Archive; Keilig 211/ 150.*

[208] Ugo (as of 1928, Count) Cavallero; born September 20, 1880; Alpine troops officer; General Staff training; November 1917 Chief of the Operations Department, of the Italian Supreme Army Command; 1920-25 in industry; 1925-28 Under Secretary of State in the Ministry of Defense; 1927 Lieutenant General; 1938 Commander-in-Chief in East Africa; December 12, 1940 to January 30, 1943 Chief of *Comando Supremo* (in addition, from the end of 1940 to May 1941, Commander-in-Chief Army, Group Albania); and July 1942 Marshal of Italy. After November 1942, Cavallero had obviously played one side off against the other, and it had ended badly for him. He was arrested on July 26, 1943, after the overthrow of Mussolini, by the Badoglio government, but was freed by the Germans—whose compliant tool he was considered to be, at least in Italian military circles—immediately after September 8. Two days later, however, he committed suicide, as he was to be brought to Germany and thus before Mussolini, who he probably assumed possessed compromising material about him.—*Source: Munzinger Archive; Kesselring, p. 244; Rintelen, p. 116; Siegler, p. 93; Anfuso, p.142.*

[209] This remark of Jodl could hardly relate to the preceding discussion. It more likely refers to the conference of Adana, where, after Casablanca, Churchill quite surprisingly met with the Turkish president Inönü and Prime Minister Saracoglu on January 30-31. The meeting was considered at that time to be an English success that would lead toward Turkey's participation in the war, so Jodl's words might be meant ironically. It is certainly not impossible that Kesselring could already have been informed about the fact that Papen would be received by Foreign Minister Menem Encioglu on February 2 and be briefed on the Adana talks. With this gesture, the meeting between Churchill and the Turks lost much of its initially sensational and spectacular character.—*Source: NZZ of Feb. 2 (midday edition), Feb. 3 (evening edition) and Feb. 4 (morning edition), 1943.*

[210] Meaning German, not Italian.

[211] Jodl was reporting here on Allied air raids against the German-Italian supply routes on the Mediterranean.

[212] The 105 ships from France were vessels that had been raised along the southern coast of France and were being brought to Italy for repairs.

[213] The British Combat Group H, with one to two battleships, one carrier, and also cruisers and destroyers, generally protected the Allied convoys that ran from Gibraltar eastward into the Mediterranean Sea.

[214] Meaning a group of long-range tactical aircraft.

[215] On January 29 and 30, an air-sea battle developed in the waters of the Solomon Islands, near the Rennell Islands, when Japanese fighters attacked an American fleet convoy. As the Japanese imperial headquarters had announced on the day of this meeting, February 1, two battleships and three cruisers were supposedly sunk, and one battleship and one cruiser seriously damaged. Seven Japanese fighters, diving directly onto their target, were lost, and three others did not return. Hitler, who clearly reproached his Luftwaffe with the Japanese

success, did so unjustly, as in reality the Americans lost only the heavy cruiser *Chicago* during this Rennell Islands battle, while the destroyer *La Valette* was seriously damaged.—*Source: VB of Feb. 2, 1943; Morison: Guadalcanal, p. 351.*

216 Karl Strecker; born September 20, 1884; Lichterfelde Cadet Institute; 1905 Second Lieutenant, 152nd Infantry Regiment; Captain during World War I; at the end of the war left the service as Major, then Captain in the Ruhr Area Security Police; 1927 Head of the Pankow Berlin Police Inspectorate; 1934 Major General of Police; 1935 reactivated; 1937 Commander, 4th Infantry Regiment; 1938 Infantry Commander 34; 1939 Commander, 79th Infantry Division; 1940 Lieutenant General; 1942 General of Infantry and Commanding General, XI Army Corps. Strecker was encircled with his corps in the Stalingrad pocket and was captured by the Soviets on February 2, 1943, in the Tractor Factory. He joined the National Committee to Liberate Germany at the end of 1944 and was released in October 1955.—*Source: Munzinger Archive; Order of Battle, p. 631; Seemen; Das deutsche Heer, p. 166; Rangliste 1944-45, p. 16; Keilig 211/ 331.*

217 Accordingly, the Armed Forces report of February 1 said: "The northern group under the leadership of General of Infantry Strecker..." In contrast, the report of the following day said: "During the night [the enemy] managed ... to break open the defense ring of the XI Army Corps, which had remained connected until then."—*Source: VB of Feb. 2 and Feb. 3, 1943.*

218 The reference here is to British submarines.

219 Hitler assumed correctly. Seydlitz had been with Paulus in the southern pocket.

220 Otto Förster; born March 16, 1885; 1904 Second Lieutenant, Guard Engineer Battalion; in World War I company commander and General Staff officer; Reichswehr; 1929 Lieutenant Colonel and Commander, 4th Engineer Battalion; 1932 Colonel; 1933-1938 Inspectorate of Engineers and Fortifications (5th Inspectorate); 1934 Major General; 1937 Lieutenant General; April 1938 General of Engineers; and end of 1938 Commanding General, VI Army Corps (Münster). Förster had led this corps in various campaigns until he was suddenly relieved of his command by the Army Commander-in-Chief, Colonel General Strauss, on December 30, 1941, in Staritsa (in the Rzhev area), on Hitler's order. Without bidding farewell to his troops, he was to turn over his responsibilities immediately to his successor, Luftwaffe General v. Richthofen. The Armed Forces Honor Court initiated investigations into the allegation against Förster—that he had arbitrarily given withdrawal orders. However, with the help of his corps war diary, he was able to prove that this accusation was unfounded, and that he had only recommended such a withdrawal in a situation analysis—which was passed on without his knowledge to Hitler—because the position in his sector had become untenable. The case was dismissed, but Förster received no new assignment; he was honorably discharged in February 1944. The whole affair was related to Hitler's "cleansing action" during the winter of 1941-42, to which also Rundstedt, Guderian, Ritter v. Leeb, Hoepner and others at that time fell victim. On this occasion, of course, Hitler

could not overlook Förster, who had been out of favor with him since 1938 (Hitler will again mention General Förster and his alleged failure later on).

221 Walther Heitz; born December 8, 1878; 1899 Second Lieutenant; 1914 Captain; Reichswehr; 1930 Colonel; 1931 Commander of Königsberg; 1933 Major General; 1934 Lieutenant General; 1936 President of the Reich War Court; 1937 General of Artillery; September 1939 Military Commander of Danzig-West Prussia; and after October 1939 Commanding General, VIII Army Corps. Heitz, surrounded with his corps in the Stalingrad pocket, was separated from the main pocket into a smaller "central" pocket by a Russian advance on January 28, 1943. This pocket was the first to be forced to surrender, on January 31. Heitz—promoted that same day to Colonel General—was taken into Soviet captivity and died there in February 1944.—*Source: DNB of Jan. 31, 1943; Munzinger Archive; Schröter, pp. 210 and 221; Keilig 211/127.*

222 Meaning in the Soviet report.

223 Alexander v. Hartmann; born December 11, 1890; 1911 Second Lieutenant; Reichswehr; 1934 Lieutenant Colonel; 1937 Colonel and Commander, 37th Infantry Regiment; 1941 Major General and Commander, 71st Infantry Division; and September 1, 1942 Lieutenant General (subsequently January 1, 1943 General of Infantry). Hartmann died on January 25 in Stalingrad.—*Source: Keilig 211/121; Schröter, p. 207.*

224 Luftwaffe Command East under Luftwaffe General (after February 17, 1943 Colonel General Ritter v. Greim was established in April 1942 from the V Luftwaffe General Command and was then renamed Luftwaffe Command 6 on May 5, 1943. Luftwaffe Command East, like Luftwaffe Command Don directly subordinate to the Luftwaffe Commander-in-Chief, operated in the area of Army Group Center.—*Source: Siegler, p. 53.*

225 Almost exactly a year before, on February 8, 1942, the Soviets had surrounded Demiansk during their winter offensive in the central sector, encircling the six divisions of the II and X Army Corps. Two and a half months later, these divisions succeeded, on April 20, in pushing forward a corridor from the area southeast of Staraia Russa and reestablishing a connection between the pocket and the front; however, this connection was rather unreliable and Demiansk continued for the most part to depend on supply by air. Russian attempts to smash the pocket failed in August, and also when repeated again during the winter. Now, Hitler would finally be forced by the enormous tension in the southern sector to evacuate Demiansk later in the month, after having thus far ignored all suggestions to that effect.—*Source: Tippelskirch, pp. 247, 290 and 328.*

226 Hitler's question about the fighter-bombers touched on a weak point in the German air war. Because the only aircraft that were further developed at first were types that had already existed at the beginning of the war—new methods were not pursued in a timely fashion, or were discontinued because of various obstacles—German aircraft designs became more and more disadvantaged in comparison to new Allied construction. After diving attacks—the method the German Luftwaffe had used so successfully in the early part of

the war to make bomb attacks on tactical targets—ceased to play such an important role as they had during offensive mobile warfare, and after such attacks were rendered somewhat obsolete by increasingly sophisticated defense and position-finding methods—and the strong English defense also made the horizontal attacks of the He 111 unprofitable—three of the fighter wings situated in the West were temporarily converted to fighter-bomber wings, as the German fighters (such as even the old pre-war He 51 and Ar 68 models) could also be equipped as multi-purpose aircraft for the transport of bombs. Among the aircraft used in this way—and also considered as a successor to the Ju 87—was the FW 190 fighter (250 kg, later a maximum 500 kg bomb load). But the losses suffered in this type of attack were also disproportionate to the successes obtained—and this was only partially a pilot issue. Not until the end of 1942 was the tactic of deploying fighter-bombers in attacks against England repeated again—with the FW 190—on the personal order of Hitler; however, this also had to be given up after a short time because of high losses. The Allied long-range fighters, on the other hand, especially the "Mustang" and the "Thunderbolt," obtained amazing results with their fighter-bomber tactics during the final battle for the Reich. (See also note 1720.)

[227] When the Army personnel situation became extremely tense during the fall of 1942, the Luftwaffe was, on Hitler's orders, supposed to provide support in the form of approximately 200,000 men. Based on departmental reasons, Göring defended himself successfully against having to give up men to the Army; however, he declared himself ready to establish his own Luftwaffe divisions with the requested personnel. These divisions would be assigned to help relieve the Army in the ground campaign (announcement by Göring on September 12, 1942). Within a short period, 21 so-called Luftwaffe field divisions (the 22nd did not come into action) were actually established. They first fought under their own direction in the Luftwaffe, with only tactical subordination to the general commands of the Army, but by year's end they were incorporated also organizationally into the Army—to the extent that they still existed. The fatal disadvantage of these units, causing high casualties, was that relatively high-quality staffs were placed in the hands of a completely combat-inexperienced command cadre. The negative technical term "to use up" [*verheizen*] came to pass here in the fullest sense of the word. Only the 21st Luftwaffe Field Division was established from the volunteers of the old Luftwaffe Field Regiments 1 to 5—who already had ground battle experience—and the Meindl Parachute Brigade.—*Source: Denzel, passim.*

[228] Regarding the Donets area.

[229] The shortage of personnel and later also of fuel was indeed a significant contributing factor in the catastrophic defeat of the German Luftwaffe, although the primary factor was no doubt German aircraft design. The German designs remained practically unchanged (until the last models, which came too late) and were thus increasingly disadvantaged in relation to the constant improvements and new development on the enemy side. While the German aircraft construction figures are impressive,

	1939	1940	1941	1942	1943	1944	1945	Total
Bombers	737	2,852	3,373	4,337	4,649	2,287	–	18,235
Fighters	605	2,746	3,744	5,515	10,898	25,285	4,936	53,729
Jet aircraft	–	–	–	–	–	1,041	947	1,988
Fighter-bombers	134	603	507	1,249	3,266	5,496	1,104	12,359
Reconnaissance planes	164	971	1,079	1,067	1,117	1,686	216	6,299
Total production	2,518	10,247	12,401	15,409	24,807	40,593	7,540	113,515

it is necessary to bear in mind that, for the most part, these models were practically obsolete by the time they came off the assembly line and were unable to challenge enemy air supremacy. In the bomber category, for example, there was nothing comparable to the American four-engine planes and in the fighter category there was nothing equal to the American all-weather and long-range fighters. (In addition, repairs must also be considered, and in the figures for the last years, "production" did not necessarily mean "ready for action" or "received by the troops.") But while the production curve continued to increase until 1944, the shortage of personnel was felt earlier, particularly after 1943. The primary cause was the incorrect estimate of the war's duration by Göring and Jeschonnek in the first years of the war. This led to a massive consumption of fuel at the front, at the expense of training, which received only 15 to 20% of its requirements. The Germans paid for this imbalance in the later years of the war, particularly when the heavy losses during large-scale Luftwaffe supply operations—on Crete, at Demiansk, in Africa to El Alamein, and especially in Stalingrad—created gaps that could no longer be filled. Later, after the enemy side implemented permanent fighter cover, the shortcomings of the Luftwaffe were felt above the Reich as well.—*Source: Baumbach, p. 313; Kesselring: Die deutsche Luftwaffe, p. 145; Rieckhoff, p. 265.*

[230] Meaning the low number trained.

[231] The He 177—called the "Flying Tinderbox" by the troops—was the unfortunate result of the need to develop a distance bomber. Göring had neglected this aircraft type following the decision not to build up a German strategic Luftwaffe after the death of General Wever in 1936, and the breakup of the coordinated Luftwaffe leadership the following year. The original, senseless demand of the General Staff (Jeschonnek) for a four-engine aircraft with diving capability forced the designers to use double aggregates, i.e., arranging each pair of engines on one crankshaft and with one propeller (tandem arrangement). This double-V engine did not stand the test, though part of the problem was also the fact that it had been rushed to deployment prematurely. From the first day of deployment in September 1942—after the diving requirement had been abandoned—there were problems with piston seizure, inadequate cooling, and oil leaks that caused vibration and frequent engine fires. Of the aircraft participating in the air supply of Stalingrad, for example,

four planes were lost through engine fires in one squadron alone, and the rest were soon out of action as well. Later, the He 177 was brought to the front for use—as originally intended—as a heavy bomber, after the elimination of the many problem areas and this time as a new development with four single engines, lifting surface [wings] that had been lengthened by 1 m and a fuselage lengthened by 2 m; however, production was cancelled in July 1944 in favor of the fighter program. (Data: Tiefdecker aircraft, 5-man crew, 540 km/h, 1-ton bomb load, 6,000 km range; production numbers: 1942: 166, 1943: 415, 1944: 565.)—*Source: Baumbach, pp. 151 and 314; Schneider, p. 235; Bartz, p. 83; Lusar, p. 45.*

[232] Dr of Engineering Ernst Heinkel; born January 24, 1888; technical college; diploma and doctoral examination; 1912 engineer for the Berlin-Johannistal Aviation Company; 1913 chief designer, Albatros Factories; 1914 technical director, Hansa Aircraft Factories; and 1922 founded the Ernst Heinkel Aircraft Factories. Heinkel built mopeds, motor scooters, etc., since 1950, as well as aircraft engines and licensed models since 1957, died on January 30, 1958.— *Source: Munzinger Archive.*

[233] There were various plans during the second half of the war for a distance bomber that could attack the industrial areas of the Urals as well as the USA (the best-known example was the Me 324). Unless the discussion concerned the possibility of further developing the FW 200 "Condor" or the FW 191, the reference here was probably to further discussion of a project study that had been presented in May 1942 by Focke-Wulf but never executed. The proposal was for a six-engine distance bomber, FW 400, originally with a range of 10,000 km and a 5-ton payload.—*Source: Baumbach, p. 158; Lusar, p. 68.*

[234] The name cannot be identified, but the reference was to a Soviet industrial area in the Urals.

[235] Meaning no Russian flak.

[236] The following table gives an approximate—but not necessarily completely reliable—overview of the enemy air raids against the Reich during World War I:

	1914	1915	1916	1917	1918
Bombs dropped	33	940	1,817	5,234	7,717
Dead	11	116	160	79	380
Wounded	42	329	352	323	797
Property damage in millions of marks	1	0.83	1.38	6.3	15.5
Number of attacks	–	ca. 50	–	376	657

Most of the attacks in 1914, 1915 and again in 1918 were made during the day, while in 1916 and 1917 the raids were primarily (1916: 78%) flown at night. Targets were the armaments industry, some military installations, and—during the final phase—also the civilian population. Most of the damage was caused not by the raids themselves but by the confusion and frequent disturbances that followed. The trouble that nightly air-raid warnings caused for the armaments factories on the western border of the Reich forced Commerce Councilor Röchling, chairman of the board of the Düsseldorf Steelworks Association, to send a letter to the Supreme Army Command on November 20, 1916. The letter included the following: "At today's board meeting, the significant disturbances caused by air raids against the steel factories on the western border were discussed. The continuing reduction in the nightly production as a result of these disturbances has caused not only a 30% drop in the steel production, on average, but has also led to fears that night operations may soon be discontinued altogether. ..." So Hitler was not entirely wrong in this case.—*Source: Der Luftschutz, pp. 64 and 135.*

[237] Hitler addressed this topic again in detail nearly two years later.

[238] The "Mosquito" was a light twin-engine two-seater introduced by the RAF in September 1941. It was used for close reconnaissance and as a single-seat fighter (Mosquito model 11)—with eight rockets of 27.2 kg each to attack ship targets—and also as the "Pathfinder" during large-scale attacks on German cities after August 1942. Above all, it was used as a medium bomber with the ability to carry initially 900 and later 1,800 kg. The Mosquito appeared for the first time at the front in this capacity on May 31, 1942. As a result of its high speed of nearly 700 km/h—which could not be matched by any German fighter except the Me 262 jet fighter—the Mosquito could, until the end of the war, eliminate all armaments in favor of a larger bomb load. In addition, the only attacks on these aircraft that promised any success—diving from a very high altitude—were impossible due to the high altitude of the Mosquitoes' flight. The Mosquitoes were also very difficult to locate electronically because of their timber construction (Canadian spruce). The result of the continuous annoyance by these planes—deployed more and more frequently in small formations—was the introduction of the public air-raid warning in Germany. Due to the grumbling of the vexed population ("The fat one can't even finish off a few lousy Mosquitoes!"), Göring established two special units with highly tuned engines and the soothing designation "Fighter Wing 25" and "Fighter Wing 50," though they were actually only reinforced squadrons. The two units did not shoot down even a single Mosquito and were disbanded in the fall of 1943.—*Source: Rumpf, p. 82; Feuchter, p. 214; Galland, p. 227; Hébrard, p. 197.*

[239] See also p. 59. Only small pieces of the remaining pages of this shorthand record were preserved, with no coherent sentences. The only thing that could be gathered from the remaining fragments was that Hitler continued to discuss Luftwaffe issues, particularly relating to the He 177.

[240] Transcript number unknown—Fragment No. 38—The transcript was burned in the upper left-hand corner. Hitler had been staying since February 18 in his "Wehrwolf" quarters in western Ukraine, on the road from Vinnitsa to Zhitomir. He had also directed the war effort from there the previous year, from July 13 (Greiner: July 16) to November 1. A few days after this meeting and the following one, he moved back again to Rastenburg, where he arrived on March 13.

[241] From the summer of 1940 (1940: 22 admitted English raids) until the battle of Berlin on November 18, 1943, the capital of the Reich was the target of periodic Allied air raids of increasing strength. These attacks caused serious losses, but did not significantly alter the appearance of the city. During the first quarter of 1943, for example, the Armed Forces High Command report noted the following attacks on Berlin: January 16 and 17 in the evening, January 30 during the day, March 1 in the evening (Armed Forces High Command report of March 2, 1943: "British aircraft came over Berlin last night and dropped demolition and incendiary bombs onto the Reich capital and towns nearby. There was damage from incendiary and demolition bombs in residential districts and to public buildings. The population suffered losses."), as well as during the nights of March 27 and 29. During the same time period, the German Luftwaffe attacked London on the evenings of January 17 and 18, and on January 20 at midday, as well as the night of March 3 mentioned here (Armed Forces High Command report of March 4, 1943: "During night of March 3 the German Luftwaffe bombed the area of greater London with heavy demolition bombs and thousands of incendiary bombs.")— *Source: Armed Forces High Command reports; Rumpf, pp. 61 and 67; Galland, p. 193.*

[242] The Mareth Line—the border fortifications between Tunisia and Libya—were dismantled after the French armistice with the Axis powers at the end of June 1940, but the concrete bunkers, though light, still provided good support for Rommel's withdrawing army.

[243] The 8.8 cm [88 mm] anti-aircraft artillery gun 41—an advanced version of the 8.8 cm anti-aircraft artillery guns 18, 36 and 37—was then being deployed and tested in Tunis for the first time. The essential characteristic of this weapon, which was unrivaled even several years after the end of the war, was the significantly increased initial velocity (V_0: 1,000 instead of 820 m/sec), which thus increased the range (vertical 14,930 instead of 9,750 m, horizontal 19,700 instead of 14,800 m). As a result of the enormously increased stress on the barrel, however, the barrels' number of rounds (lifespan) sank initially from 8,000 to 250. By using low-heat powder, the number of rounds was again increased to 4,000. Additional advantages of the new gun were the low trunnion height and strengthened carriage, as well as the electronic discharge and mechanical ammunition rammer, which increased the rate of fire from 15 to 20 rounds per minute.—*Source: Koch: Flak, pp. 114 and 209.*

[244] For the fluctuations in the tank forces in Africa, see below.

[245] After the complete abandonment of Italian North Africa, the German-Italian panzer army under Rommel was placed directly under the command of the *Comando Supremo* for a time. In this arrangement, Field Marshal Kesselring represented the German interests.

[246] Rommel proposed to restrict the final defense of Tunis to a position approximately 150 km long, in the northern part of the country ("Enfidaville position").

[247] Regarding the takeover of French tonnage, see above. It turned out to be particularly difficult to arm these vessels with a sufficient number of anti-aircraft guns.

[248] In the Mediterranean, the tanker capacity in particular was extraordinarily limited, so the sinking of tankers always had very serious consequences. From November 1942 to February 1943, British submarines, surface forces and aircraft repeatedly caught Italian tankers and sank them. By January 22, 1943 (the end of sea traffic to Libya after the evacuation of Tripoli), the Italian merchant fleet had lost a total 1,345,000 tons, with an additional 1,195,000 tons damaged—equivalent to all the available ship capacity at the beginning of the war, plus 275,000 tons of newly constructed, confiscated, conquered and German tonnage.—*Source: Trizzino, p. 53.*

[249] The 999th Probationary Troop was formed by order of the Armed Forces High Command on October 2, 1942, originally as "the 999th Africa Brigade." Included in this formation were, after special selection, those who had been designated as unfit for military service during war and peace, according to section 13 WG, and were now considered conditionally fit for military service. Unfit for military service, according to section 13 WG, were those who had lost their civil rights because of subversive activity or imprisonment, those who were subject to section 42a of the criminal law code (protective custody, institutionalization, emasculation, etc.), or those who had lost their fitness for military service according to military judgment.) With delivery of the induction order, the so-called Military service exclusion certificate was removed and a service record was issued. The first inductions took place on October 15, 1942. The replacement unit was initially situated on the Heuberg training grounds, later at Baumholder training grounds. After the evacuation of Africa, the remains of the field unit were renamed the 999th Fortress Brigade; it was deployed primarily in Greece. The brigade was later expanded to the 999th Fortress Division, then, toward the end of the war—probably as a deceptive measure—renamed again, this time as the 41st Infantry Division. After the capitulation, a large portion of this unit fell into Yugoslavian captivity. If they displayed particular courage and exemplary behavior, the members of the Probationary Troops could have their unconditional "fitness for military service" restored by the Army Commander-in-Chief upon transfer to a regular formation. If they failed, on the other hand, they could be discharged as permanently unfit for military service and be turned over to the police for internment in a concentration camp. Unsuitable persons, such as those with more than five years' imprisonment, were separated again at the end of 1943 and were handed over to the OT [Todt Organization] as unfit for military service.—*Source: Die Sondereinheiten, p. 29.*

[250] Helmuth Felmy; born May 28, 1885; 1896 to 1904 Cadet Corps; 1905 Second Lieutenant; 1910 War Academy; 1915 to 1918 Captain and commander of various field air detachments; Reichswehr; 1924 RWM; 1927 Major; 1933 Colonel and commander of an infantry regiment; October 1933 left and entered the RLM; April 1935 Senior Air Commander of the 5th Air District (Munich); 1936 Major General and Commander, 7th Air District (Braunschweig); 1937 Lieutenant General; February 1938 Air General and Commander, 2nd Luftwaffe Group; February 1939 to January 1940 Chief of the Second Air Fleet; 1941 Head of

the German Military Mission in Iraq; June 1941 to August 1942 Commander, Southern Greece and Special Staff "F"; 1942-43 Commander of the Brandenburg Units; June 1943 to October 1944 Commanding General, LXVIII Army Corps, and then Commanding General, XXXIV Army Corps. During the Nuremberg trial of the southeastern generals (Case 7), Felmy was sentenced in February 1948 to 15 years in prison; he was released in December 1951.—*Source: Jahrbuch der deutschen Akademie..., p. 64; Siegler, p. 117; Order of Battle, p. 547; Munzinger Archive; Trials XI, p. 779.*

251 In the southern sector of the Eastern Front, following the uprising in Iraq (in the spring of 1941), General Felmy was ordered by the Armed Forces High Command to the creation and training of German-Arab units for desert combat. One of the three formations gradually built up this way—each in about regimental strength—was deployed in September 1942 in the Kalmuck steppe in the southern sector of the Eastern Front.

252 Tunis.

253 In 1941 the Australian government had already—against the wishes of Churchill as well as English Supreme Commander, General Auchinleck—forced the relief of the Australian troops stationed in Tobruk. Additional military disagreements of this kind between Australia and England followed. The status of the dominion troops and the reservations of their home governments varied, as did the positions of the dominions at the outbreak of war—ranging from nonparticipation (Ireland) to participation based on the dominion's own decision (Canada, South African Union) to automatic participation (Australia, New Zealand). The position of auxiliary troops varied as well. The Canadians, based in the British Isles, were actively involved in the war, and in February 1940 the first brigades of Australians and New Zealanders arrived in Suez and were welcomed by Foreign Minister Eden. South African troops, on the other hand, were permitted to operate outside the country, but only in "southern Africa." Despite the best intentions for a broadminded interpretation of this geographical concept, deployment in Kenya (on the border of Italian East Africa) was questionable, so the South Africans limited themselves initially to providing volunteer units, then formally reorganized their territorial army into a volunteer organization. The frequently inadequate equipment of the dominion troops also added to the difficulties and demanded heavy sacrifices from the motherland. The dominions declared themselves prepared to adopt the English organizational structure, training methods and equipment types, but retained full responsibility for achieving this assimilation.—*Source: Mansergh, pp. 366 and 376; Playfair, pp. 57, 84 and 105; Toynbee: The Initial Triumph, p. 313.*

254 The 7th SS Volunteer Mountain Division *Prinz Eugen.*

255 Appendix 20 of the Armed Forces Operations Staff war diary entry for March 1, 1943, stated: "By the order of the Führer, a fully motorized assault brigade, consisting of Army and Luftwaffe units, will be established. It is to be ready for operation by March 10. The German general at the headquarters of the Italian Armed Forces is to prepare temporary accommodation in the region of Leghorn and take steps to swiftly transfer the forces to Sardinia. (By the order of the Chief of

the Armed Forces Operations Staff, he had already obtained the agreement of the *Comando Supremo*; the latter had requested that the brigade be placed under the command of the Italian Corps in Sardinia.)"—*Source: Nbg. Dok. 1786-PS*

[256] After taking on the role of Commander-in-Chief of the Navy in February, Admiral Dönitz, with a view to better protecting the blockade runners, ordered Z 23, Z 24, Z 32 and Z 37, the four largest German destroyers with the most armaments, to be grouped together as the 8th Destroyer Flotilla under Captain S. Erdmenger. The destroyers were to be transferred to the mouth of the Gironde in March (until then, German destroyers had only been stationed in the Bay of Biscay between June 1940 and September 1941). However, the successes that this measure was intended to bring did not materialize. Effective use of the destroyers' guns against light enemy forces proved impossible in the heavy swell of the Atlantic Ocean and the Bay of Biscay. In March 1943, the destroyers' task was to escort the following ships returning from East Asia: *Doggerbank* (8998 GRT, torpedoed and sunk by mistake by U 43 on the previous day—March 3), *Irene* (4793 GRT, cornered and scuttled on May 17), *Pietro Oresolo* (6344 GRT, which arrived in Bordeaux on April 2, leaking) and *Karin* (7322 GRT, cornered and scuttled on March 10). They also escorted the following ships out to sea: *Osorno* (6951 GRT, arrived in Yokohama on May 4), *Portland* (7132 GRT, cornered and scuttled on April 10), *Himalaya* (6240 GRT, returned to port) and *Alsterufer* (2729 GRT, arrived in Japan on June 19). After the beginning of the Eastern campaign, blockade runners were the only way to transport vital commodities such as rubber, sweet oils, fats, metals and ores from East Asia. Rubber—the only reason for launching this risky enterprise—was so important to the war economy that the Germans were prepared to take considerable risks. From East Asia, the number of ships leaving for Europe was:

	of which:	arrived	were sunk	turned back
Nov. 28, 1940–July 20, 1941	5	3	1	1
Aug. 21, 1941–Feb. 26, 1942	12	9	3	-
Aug. 8, 1942–Feb. 7, 1943	15	4	7	4
Oct. 2–29, 1943	5	1	4	-

From Europe, the number of ships leaving for East Asia (to collect raw materials) was:

	of which:	arrived	were sunk	turned back
Sept. 1941–May 1942	7	6	-	1
Aug. 1942–April 1943	19	11	4	4

Several Japanese, Italian and German submarines were assigned to the transportation of raw materials, but without significant success. The overall balance is as follows: of the total load of 217,415 tons (of which rubber made up 93,879 tons), 113,805 tons (44,595 tons of rubber) arrived—that is 52.3% (47.4% of the rubber). 16 cargo ships (including one Italian), three tankers, one destroyer, two torpedo boats, and 13 submarines (including two Japanese and two Italian) were lost.—*Source: Michaux, passim.*

257   Rear Admiral (1941: Admiral) Dr. Otto Groos; born July 17, 1882; 1931-1934 Chief of Naval Headquarters and 1939-40 Chief of the Armed Forces Academy, served as head of the special staff for economic warfare from June 1940 until the end of the war (with the exception of several months in mid-1944).— *Source: Siegler, p. 121; Lohmann/Hildebrand 291/102.*

258   The reference is to the Italian Fourth Army, commanded by General Vercellino and stationed in southern France as part of the occupation force.

259   The militia divisions could not be organized as new Fascist divisions before the collapse of the regime; the only exception was the "M" panzer division of the militia.

260   The Armed Forces High Command report of March 4, 1943, read: "Last night, the British Air Force attacked territory in western and northwestern Germany. Explosive and incendiary bombs damaged numerous buildings in the area of Greater Hamburg and the surrounding rural communities. There were losses among the population."

261   This place, the name of which the stenographer recorded several different ways, was probably Wedel near Hamburg, but according to the text of the communiqué of the High Command, it could also have been Wesel on the Rhine.

262   This is the time when the first practice flights of the U.S. Air Force were being flown over the territory of the Reich. In the first years of the war, the RAF had carried out a few daylight raids. Under the Lend-Lease Agreement, the British had received 20 "Flying Fortresses" in the spring of 1941, with which they had flown 39 missions by September. Because of the high altitude (10,000 to 13,000 m instead of the optimum of 8,000 m to 9,000 m) and uncoordinated action, the British complained about ineffectiveness and great losses. Apart from the Lancaster Special RAF Unit, which began making precision daylight attacks—including low-level attacks—from the summer of 1942 on, the English resumed attacking under the cover of night. The Americans came to Europe in 1942—a first advance detachment arrived in February, the first 1,800 men of the Eighth Allied Air Force embarked on April 27, the majority of the personnel were transferred in June, and the transfer of aircraft began the following month. Hesitation by the leadership, along with the support required for operations in North Africa, gave the Reich a breather. The Eighth Allied Air Force did not fly its first daylight raid against the city of Wilhelmshaven until January 27; on April 17, 1943, Bremen was the target of the first large-scale American attack. This was the beginning of the so-called around-the-clock bombing: the RAF operating during the night, the Eighth Allied Air Force during the day. *Source: Galland, p.190; Rumpf, p. 83; Churchill IV/2, p. 304.*

263   Southwest of Khar'kov, near Krasnograd, where the Fourth Panzer Army succeeded in destroying parts of the Soviet 3rd Tank Army (12th and 15th Tank Corps, one cavalry corps and three infantry divisions) before March 5.—*Source: Manstein, p. 464; Tippelskirch, p. 326.*

264   *Rückseitenwetter* refers to the wake of a bad weather depression going from west to east, from area A to area B, so that Air Force A, taking off from A, can

ride behind the depression and attack B without fearing Air Force B, which is temporarily prevented from taking off. This *Rückseitenwetter* worked against the defense from Anglo-American air raids because the weather situation in Germany is primarily influenced by westerly winds.

265 It was common practice in the Armed Forces to refer to a "Lücke" (gap) as a "Luke" (hatch), such as in the saying, "to stand on a hatch." Zeitzler uses this expression several times.

266 One of the three inferior—as the description indicates—covering divisions, which the Hungarians had left in occupied Russia following the collapse of the Hungarian Second Army at the Don River. It is understandable that the fighting morale of these units was anything but excellent in view of the widespread war-weariness in Hungary. Several weeks later, Hitler gave Goebbels another explanation for this state of affairs. On May 8, 1943, Goebbels noted in his diary: "The Führer drew the lesson from the past winter of having war waged in the East hereafter exclusively and solely with German troops. The Romanians made the best showing; second best were the Italians; and poorest the Hungarians. The Führer regarded this as owing mainly to the fact that there has been no social adjustment in Hungary, not even an indication of it. As a result the troops just do not realize the necessity of the fight. Whenever officers here and there gave a good account of themselves they were left in the lurch by their men."—*Source: Goebbels Diaries (ed. L. Lochner, p. 356, New York 1948).*

267 Günter v. Kluge; born October 30, 1882; 1901 Second Lieutenant in the 46th Field Artillery Regiment; during World War I General Staff officer in the 236th Infantry Division; Reichswehr; 1930 Colonel and Commander, 2nd Artillery Regiment; 1934 Major General and Inspector of Signal Troops; 1935 Lieutenant General and Commanding General, VI Army Corps (Munster); 1936 General of Artillery; 1938 Commander-in-Chief, Army Group 6 (Hannover); in Poland, France and Russia as Commander-in-Chief, Fourth Army; fall 1939 Colonel General; July 1940 Field Marshal; December 1941 to October 1943 Commander-in-Chief, Army Group Center; from July 2, 1944, to August 16, 1944, Commander-in-Chief, West (Army Group D); and—from July 19—Commander-in-Chief, Army Group B. Hitler relieved Kluge of his post and replaced him by Model on August 16, 1944.—*Source: Munzinger Archive; Das deutsche Heer, p. 74; Siegler, p. 127; Deutsche Soldatenzeitung of Nov. 13, 1952; Keilig 211/168.*

268 It is unclear whether he is referring to the 2nd or 6th [Panzer Division]. Regarding the Luftwaffe field divisions, see note 227 and note 1173.

269 Transcript number unknown—Fragment No. 39—The left upper edge of the transcript is slightly charred.

270 On the north wing of the Second Army.

271 This was probably a rumor, as a Soviet tank with two turrets and this type of armor is unknown.

272 Again a reference to the gap in the northern wing of the Second Army that was mentioned at the beginning of the meeting.

273 The northern flank of the Orel salient.

[274] During the siege of Leningrad, Shlissel'burg [Schlüsselburg] on Lake Ladoga was the northernmost point of the bottleneck separating the area east of the city from the rest of the Soviet territory. On January 18, 1943, the Soviets finally succeeded in recapturing Shlissel'burg; from then on, the main supply lines for Leningrad passed through that point.

[275] Just two days after the Germans attacked the Soviet Union, a representative of the Spanish Foreign Office stated in a press conference that the Spanish government was extremely pleased with the outbreak of the war and that it was the sincere wish of thousands of Spaniards to join the battle. A manifesto issued by Arrese, Party Minister and Secretary General of the Falange [Party], on June 27, 1941, called for the establishment of a corps of volunteers to fight against the Soviet Union: "That is why we allow our young people to join the best of all battles, the European crusade!" In late July and early August, the Spanish battalions arrived at Grafenwöhr, where they received their field equipment and were fitted out with German uniforms. They were deployed as the "Blue Division" [División Azúl] (250th Infantry Division) in the area of Leningrad. Having visited the division in Novgorod on Lake Ilmen in October 1941, Erwin Lahousen, an assistant to Admiral Canaris, said: "In spite of the German uniforms, the Spaniards stand out in their appearance and attitude. Whereas the officers are career soldiers without exception, the men are volunteers. They are very brave in battle, but allow their horses, equipment and, in particular, vehicles to go to pieces. They don't take prisoners. The commanding officer of a division can never tell precisely where his regiments are at the moment. But the mood is good, in spite of heavy losses among the officers. There are strong political tensions within the officer corps and between the officers and troops." The Spaniards did not live up to the German standards, and, in this harsh climate, they were unable to meet the expectations placed on them, so they were pulled out of the front by late 1942 and deployed to fight partisans. In addition to the División Azúl, four Spanish fighter squadrons (Esquadrón Azúl), which relieved one another consecutively, were deployed in the East.—*Source: Keesings Archive 1941, p. 5090 and 1945, p. 364; SIGNAL, August 2 issue 1941 and January 1 issue 1942; Pattee, pp. 453, 456 and 469; Order of battle, p. 214; Nbg. Dok. NOKW-3146; Haupt, passim.*

[276] A rapid reaction corps was created by the Piedmontese General La Marmora in 1836. It was made up of 24 battalions and received specially selected recruits and special physical training. They were conspicuous for their broad-brimmed felt hats with characteristic plumes and peculiar quickstep marching style. Originally conceived as infantry, they were later fitted out with bicycles and finally with motorbikes. Mussolini, who had been a Bersagliere in World War I, held them in high esteem.—*Source: Bossi Fedrigotti, passim.*

[277] He refers to a local attack on the western front in Tunisia.

[278] Rommel's Panzer Army Headquarters Africa [Pz.AOK Afrika] was converted to an Army Group Command in late February 1943. Under this command, Colonel General v. Arnim commanded Fifth Panzer Army, which had been reorganized in late 1942.

[279] The teething problems of the new Panzers V (Panther) and VI (Tiger) were far from being overcome at that time.

[280] The English Eighth Army assembling in front of the Mareth line.

[281] He mentions a convoy that reached Tunis thanks to the protection provided by several Italian destroyers.

[282] Seiskaari was a Soviet-occupied island base in the inner Gulf of Finland; the island could be reached by truck when the water was sufficiently frozen.

[283] This was the Convoy RA 53, from which three vessels were sunk by U 255 and U 586 between March 5 and 10. Two submarines had been operating in the Arctic Ocean since July 1941 and four since September 1941. Hitler had ordered these submarine deployments because he feared an attack on Norway, on the one hand, but also because he wanted to hamper the expected delivery of supplies to the Soviet Union. (The first English convoys, PQ 1 to 7, left for Murmansk and Arkhangelsk as early as summer and fall of 1941.) Starting in January 1942, a battleship, two armored vessels, three cruisers and three destroyers were moved to the Arctic Ocean and the number of the submarines operating in that area was increased to 16 or 20. Furthermore, in cooperation with long-distance bombers, these submarines extended their zone of operation to the White Sea, the region of Novaia Zemlia, and the Kara Sea in 1942. As a result, the convoys bound for Russia were interrupted for several months beginning in the summer of 1942, and the Allies once more stopped sending convoys along the northern route in March 1943, after the end of the polar night—this time because all available naval forces were involved in submarine warfare in the Atlantic. It was not until November 1943, after the beginning of the fall darkness and many urgent Soviet requests, that convoys left for Murmansk again. The danger stemming from the German presence along the northern route was considerably reduced by the elimination of the *Tirpitz* and the eventual destruction of the *Scharnhorst* around Christmas 1943. All in all, a quarter of the Allied assistance for the USSR was transported along this seaway, with 21% of the cargo being lost.—*Source: Ruge: Seekrieg, pp. 173, 196 and 208; Churchill V/1, p. 296.*

[284] "Checking the route" means checking the German sea lanes for enemy mines.

[285] German convoys operating between Kirkenes and Petsamo were usually attacked by Soviet coastal batteries positioned on the Fisherman's Peninsula before they entered the harbor of Petsamo.

[286] Weather conditions permitting, Navy ferries [lighters] operated every night between Kerch and Anapa in order to supply the bridgehead on the Kuban. Anapa was situated on the southern side of the bridgehead, i.e., on the Black Sea; Temriuk was on the northern side, on the Sea of Azov.

[287] Already during the "Phony War" [drôle de guerre], the French, operating from Alsace, had laid mines in the Rhine. In the night of April 13 to 14, 1940, the RAF started dropping magnetic mines on German inland waterways (initially the Kaiser Wilhelm Canal and the mouth of the Elbe River). Starting in mid-1943, an ever-greater number of missions were flown, causing several waterways to be closed from time to time. In 1944, navigation in the Dortmund Ems Canal

and on the Danube was temporarily paralyzed (on the Danube, some 125 ships were lost, amounting to around 5% of all Danube vessels; these losses were caused by 1,382 mines which were dropped between April 8 and 9 and October 4 and 5, 1944).—*Source: Ruge: Seekrieg, p.244; Royal Air Force I, pp. 88 and III, p. 225.*

[288] The reference is to attacks by the 2nd and 6th Motor Torpedo Boat Flotilla conducted along the English coast.

[289] Eight large submarines operating in the seas around southeast Africa sank 300,000 GRT during one venture in the fall of 1942, while losing only one vessel. In spite of this not entirely satisfactory result (in view of the long approach and supply difficulties), other large submarines (up to 1,600 tons) and also Italian submarines began to operate between South Africa and Madagascar in February 1943. Because the Japanese had made available the port of Penang on the west coast of Malaysia to permit the regular re-fuelling of tankers, fuel was no longer provided by the submersed tankers known as "milk cows" (large submarines that could pass on up to 600 tons of fuel). Jodl's report refers to one of these ventures: On March 3 and 4, *U 160* attacked convoy DN 21 in the area of Durban and sank four ships, heavily damaging two others; it has not been confirmed whether the seventh ship was torpedoed or not. From December 1943, two to five submarines operated with varying degrees of success in the Indian Ocean. Some of them moved back to Europe after 1945, while others were taken over by the Japanese.—*Source: Seekrieg, p. 226 and p. 237.*

[290] The *California Star* was sunk by *U 515* on March 4, 1943.

[291] Reference is made to the sinking of the British steamer *City of Pretoria* by *U 172* on March 4, 1943.

[292] A convoy to the North African ports on the Mediterranean was assembled in Gibraltar at that time.

[293] The English cleared the mine barrier that had been placed by *U 118* in February, which had caused several losses.

[294] The reference is to the Greek submarine *Papanicolis.*

[295] The mass-produced "Tigers" and especially "Panthers" were initially used to replenish armored detachments in the West; they were released for use in the East only after faulty parts had been replaced.

[296] According to Hitler's views and plans, the invasion would be stopped on the coast by combined fire from all weapons.

[297] Dive bombers were often used quite successfully in the East to combat tanks.

[298] A hollow-charge projectile is comprised of a powder charge contained in a cast cylinder with a conical hollow, the base of which points to the top of the projectile. The softer the material (such as copper sheeting) of this conical insert—whose tip melts as the powder charge burns down and opens the way for the accumulated powder gases—the higher the penetrating power. The following hollow-charge projectiles were developed for the German Armed Forces:

Pioneer hollow charge HL 15 and 50 (each weight is given in kg)

HL antitank projectiles (penetrating power for armored steel was roughly equivalent to caliber)

Large rifle cartridges

Limpet and ground mines

HL bombs (SD 5 H) designed for use against tanks and against battleships and bunkers (SC 500 H)

HL missiles

"Panzerschreck," ("Ofenrohr" [stovepipe], "Bazooka") and "Panzerfaust" [antitank grenade launcher]

Lieutenant General a.D. Dipl-Ing. Erich Schneider describes the technology of the hollow charge as follows: "The hollow charge throws the detonation gases against the target in a shooting flame, at a velocity of thousands of meters per second; the strength of this mass of gases pierces the armored plates. This was a perplexing physical phenomenon whose precise action could only be determined and explained after the advent of electric spark photography. Before the war, a patent had been issued which was taken up by the Army ordnance depot when the engineers were faced with the task of attacking modern fortifications. Eben Emael went down in history by demonstrating how this could be done. The principle, which was earlier applied in limpet mines used against armored vehicles and by frogmen against battleships, was later transferred to artillery projectiles and missiles."—*Source: Lusar, p. 151; Schneider, p. 236.*

[299] The antitank defense always played a special role in Hitler's technical considerations. Following the invention of the hollow-charge shell in late 1941, he often said that this shell, which could be fired from any gun, would possibly mean the demise of the tank force. The events of the war—based at least on the developmental stage at that point—refuted this assumption. But whenever new enemy tanks appeared that could not be penetrated by the antitank shells then available, Hitler returned to the subject of the hollow charge. Both developments—the hollow charge and the increased capacity of the armor-piercing gun—progressed in parallel until the end of the war.

[300] Ironically intended comparison between the encirclement of a small group of partisans with Moltke's classic battle of encirclement.

[301] Reference to the battle in the Bismarck Sea, which took place March 2 to 5, 1943. U.S. B-25 bombers attacked and destroyed a supply convoy sailing from Rabaul to Lae. The convoy was made up of eight ships, and was escorted by eight destroyers under the command of Rear Admiral Kimura. Only four destroyers escaped back to Rabaul. On orders from General MacArthur, the U.S. motor torpedo boat group fired at the survivors floating in the water to prevent them from reaching the coast and reinforcing Japanese garrisons. Immediately after the Japanese attack on Pearl Harbor, the 51 U.S. submarines stationed in the Pacific Ocean launched an all-out submarine war against Japanese ships. Because of the long distance to the target and defective torpedoes (faulty

ignition and controls that were too deep), initial success was rather limited. But the Americans soon improved their performance, because until late 1943 the Japanese continued to send out single unescorted ships to increase the utilization of their tonnage. The average monthly tonnage sunk was 50,000 GRT in 1942, 120,000 GRT in 1943, and 200,000 GRT in 1944. U.S. submarines sank a total of 4.9 million GRT, the U.S. Air Force 2.7 million GRT, and surface ships 0.1 million GRT. 0.8 million GRT were destroyed by mines and 0.4 million GRT sank as a result of naval accidents. 52 of 288 submarines were lost. The tonnage of the Japanese commercial fleet—6.1 million GRT at the beginning of the war—was reduced to 5 million GRT at the end of 1943, 2.8 million GRT at the end of 1944, and 1.8 million GRT (of which 1.2 million GRT were operational) at the end of the war. The construction of new ships, which was increased only in 1943 (a total of 260,000 GRT in 1942; close to 800,000 GRT in the first half of 1944), could make up barely half of the huge Japanese losses even in the best of times. The Japanese submarine force, on the other hand, was only occasionally involved in economic warfare and was used almost exclusively in combating enemy battleships, especially the terrifying aircraft carriers. All German attempts to persuade the Japanese to participate more actively in economic warfare failed—including the transfer of two German submarines to the Japanese in hopes that they would be copied.—*Source: Ruge: Seekrieg, pp. 196, 225, 237 and 290; Rohwer: Die japanische Ubootswaffe, passim.*

[302] In the spring of 1942, the Japanese, on their way to occupying Australia, had also occupied the Island of Guadalcanar (or, more accurately, Guadalcanal), which is part of the Solomon Islands. On August 7 of that same year, the Americans landed 13,000 men there, but failed to drive the Japanese from the western part of the island. In the following period a number of naval battles were fought for supplies, the climax being two battles involving Japanese convoys on November 13 and 15, 1942. The deployment of an increasing number of U.S. battleships put a strain on Japanese supply lines, eventually forcing the garrison of 30,000 troops to be evacuated. The Japanese evacuated the final 11,700 men during the nights of February 1 and 2, 4 and 5, and 7 and 8, 1943. The retreat could indeed be considered successful, because it was superbly disguised. According to American opinion it was "the most clever evacuation in the history of naval warfare." Not until the morning of February 8, after the last Japanese had left the island (which had been hotly contested for six months), did the enemy realize that the island had been evacuated. The Americans had mistaken the evacuation transports for reinforcements.—*Source: Ruge: Seekrieg, pp. 240 and 244; Ruge: Entscheidung, p. 129; Tippelskirch, p. 265; Morison: Guadalcanal, passim.*

[303] Dr. Hans-Heinrich Dieckhoff; born December 12, 1884; joined the diplomatic service after his graduation in 1912; 1914-16 cavalry officer; 1916-18 Embassy secretary in Constantinople; after being posted in Santiago and Prague, he served from 1922-26 as councilor at the Washington Embassy, then later at the London Embassy; 1930-36 he was head of Dept. III (England-America) of the Foreign Office; subsequently head of the Political Department; and in

the winter of 1936-1937 he temporarily attended to the business of the Undersecretary of State. From March 1937, Dieckhoff served as ambassador to Washington. Because of the violent reaction of many foreign countries to the "Kristallnacht" ["Night of the Broken Glass"], he, like many other delegation heads, was recalled and did not return to his post. Beginning in April 1943 he represented the Reich in Madrid as the successor to Moltke, and in early September 1944 he was recalled for consultations and was then relieved of his duties. Dieckhoff died in March 1952.—*Source: Berliner Börsen-Zeitung of March 25,1937; Frankfurter Zeitung of April 19, 1943.*

[304] Meaning those who express such opinions. This assessment of American public opinion regarding the primary importance of the Pacific theater of operations was as correct as the above-mentioned Japanese presumption that the Americans would still give priority to the battle against Germany, as had been decided by Washington ("Arcadia") as early as the beginning of 1942 ("Germany first").

[305] Sonderführer Baron von Neurath.

[306] The underestimation of American soldiers revealed in this comment was to have fateful consequences in the battles accompanying the invasion during the summer of the following year. The American part of the landing stage in Normandy was neglected, and the Americans eventually succeeded in breaking through in France.

[307] The naiveté with which Hitler judges the American farmers (based on photographs!) could hardly be surpassed. The man who had led Germany into another world war based his judgment of opponents on these criteria!

[308] A statement most likely made during a visit to the Obersalzberg in October 1937. Whether the duke (whose sympathy for Hitler's Germany was well known) actually made this or a similar remark is open to debate.

[309] This comment by Hewel does not make sense at all, of course. Although Australians of German descent were the most important component of the non-British population of the country, they amounted to less than 2% of the population before World War II (approximately 90,000 out of a population of 5 million in 1925). Although the cultivation of fruits, vegetables and grain was indeed advanced by the German settlers, the superlatives used by Hewel come from the nationalistic arrogance that was widespread in those circles.—*Source: Lodewyckx, passim; Nowack, p. 91.*

[310] Perhaps Hitler is referring to the acerbic statement issued by TASS on March 2, 1943, in reply to the February 25 announcement by the Polish government in exile, stating that the 1939 eastern border of Poland was inviolable and irreversible. The Russian statement, accusing the Poles in London of usurpatory policy, imperialist tendencies and a friendly attitude to the Fascists, read: "Leading Soviet circles hold the view that the Polish government, by denying Ukrainians and Poles the right to unification, gives expression to its imperialist tendencies. Their claim is based on the stipulations of the Atlantic Charter, but in the Soviet view the Atlantic statutes do not contain anything that would support these claims…" Apart from this, no differences between the Western Allies and the Russians are

known to have developed during the previous weeks, not even regarding Asian or Pacific issues.—*Source: NZZ of March 2, 1943 (evening edition).*

[311] General Hirosho Oshima, successor to Togo (who was transferred to Moscow), was promoted to head of the Japanese mission to Berlin on October 8, 1938, after having served as military attaché for four years. He disappeared in late 1939. Probably at German request, he was appointed ambassador on December 23, 1940, to succeed Kurusu, but, because of his extremely pro-German attitude he was sidelined by his government—in particular during the Japanese-U.S. negotiations in 1941, but also afterward, when he was not always informed of things that one would expect someone in his position to know. The then Undersecretary of State in the Foreign Office, Weizsäcker, noted on September 4, 1941: "Oshima was grateful for it [i.e., information on the Japanese-American talks], because his Foreign Minister has left him almost completely in the dark until now. According to him, even private information which he used to get from his Tokyo friends, bypassing the Japanese Foreign Office, has not been available since the beginning of the Russian campaign." Similar information was noted by a representative of the Foreign Office at the Army High Command, VLR v. Etzdorf, on September 22, 1941: "Ambassador Oshima complained that he was not informed by his home country and had to get information and advice in Berlin." After the collapse of the Reich, Oshima was captured by the Allies but survived the post-war trials.— *Source: Nbg.Dok. NG-4017 and NG-5156; NZZ of May 14, 1945 (morning edition).*

[312] The two Japanese super-battleships *Yamamoto* and *Musashi* were, at 63,659 tons, the heaviest units in World War II (in comparison: the *Iowa* was 45,000 tons, *Vanguard* 42,500 tons, *Bismarck* 41,700 tons, *Jean Bart* 39,000 tons). The two ships were put on keel in 1937-38, launched in 1940 and commissioned in December 1941 and August 1942. They were armed with nine 45.7-cm guns in three triple turrets (*Iowa*: nine 40.6-cm, *Vanguard*: eight 38.1-cm, *Bismarck*: eight 38-cm, *Jean Bart*: eight 38-cm guns), plus six 15.2-cm and twenty-four 12.7-cm anti-aircraft guns and 150 2.5-cm guns. In spite of their novel armor, the two battleships were hit and sunk relatively early: *Musashi* on October 24, 1944, and *Yamamoto* on April 7, 1945.—*Source: Hadeler, passim.*

[313] From the beginning of the war the Japanese had ten aircraft carriers compared to a total of seven U.S. carriers, of which only four were operating in the Pacific Ocean. The Japanese completed additional aircraft carriers during the war, but these had little impact, as Japan was unable to provide the required number of planes and, in particular, skilled crews after the losses it sustained in the Battle of Midway. At Midway, the Japanese had lost their four best aircraft carriers on June 4, 1942, so that with the commissioning of the new U.S. carriers built under the "Two Ocean Navy" building program, the American superiority increased constantly from mid-1943.

[314] In the large air-naval battle near the Midway Atoll (west of the Hawaiian Islands), which was decisive for the progress of the Pacific war, the Japanese lost four carriers and one heavy cruiser due to enemy bombing. The Americans, in contrast, lost only one carrier and one destroyer. This compelled Grand

Admiral Yamamoto to not attack Hawaii. Hewel's remark about "down there" probably refers to one of the battles in the waters of the Solomon Islands, as details on the complete elimination in the Bismarck Sea of the Japanese convoy headed for Lae (March 2 to 5, 1943) certainly were not available in the Führer Headquarters.—*Source: Ruge: Entscheidung, pp. 95 and elsewhere; Ruge: Seekrieg, pp. 241 and elsewhere.*

[315] Saburo Kurusu; born in March 1886 to an American mother; and a career diplomat from 1910. Kurusu was Japanese Ambassador to Berlin from December 1939 to December 1940 and signed the Tripartite Pact on September 27, 1940. In November 1941, he was sent to Washington to assist Ambassador Admiral Nomura in the negotiations of the peaceful settlement of the Japanese-American differences. When Kurusu, following the destruction of secret papers, handed the declaration of war to Secretary of State Hull on December 7, Pearl Harbor had already been attacked an hour earlier. Although Kurusu later claimed that he had no knowledge of the attack, Hull believed he did. This remark by Hitler, on the other hand, backs the view that Kurusu, like Nomura (who was considered to be the main advocate of an American-Japanese understanding), was left in the dark about the true intentions of his government until the very end.—*Source: Munzinger Archive; The Memoirs of Cordell Hull II, p. 1062; Langer/Gleason, passim (in particular p. 932).*

[316] The Japanese disguised their raid against Pearl Harbor, at least in part, based on German advice. For instance, briefly before the action, the Japanese ship *Taturo Maru* left for San Francisco, and the War Ministry invited officers and their ladies to an event on the evening of December 7. On the other hand, foreign radio stations had reported Japanese fleet movements as early as December 6, and British, U.S., and Dutch naval forces were alerted—showing that the attempted disguise had little effect. [NDT: Despite many disputes, most historians have concluded that President Roosevelt was not aware of the specifics of a Japanese attack, although the Pacific forces had been on the alert many times in the months leading up to December 7. It is also agreed that FDR expected and hoped for an incident that would put America at war with Germany, not Japan. See Gordon W. Prange, *At Dawn We Slept*, McGraw Hill, New York 1981.]—*Source: Feis, passim; Langer/Gleason, passim; Tansill, passim; Wagner, passim (see further references noted); Rohwer: Zum 15. Jahrestag..., passim, Nbg. Dok. NG-4396.*

[317] Hitler's hopes were unfounded, as the Japanese never brought out anything spectacular in the development and production of tanks.

[318] Following the shelving of operation "Sea Lion" ["Seelöwe"] and after defeat in the Battle of Britain had shown that the war against Great Britain would not end soon, Germany began in the winter of 1940-41 to try to persuade Japan to declare war against England. Beginning in February 1941, the Reich government urged Tokyo to take action against Singapore. However, after careful preparations and Matsuoka's visit to Berlin at the end of March, the Wilhelmstrasse changed its course during the summer and requested in late June and early July that Tokyo launch an attack against the Soviet Union. Although Foreign Minis-

ter Matsuoka backed this plan, a different decision was reached due to the influence exerted by part of the Japanese armed forces. At the imperial conference on July 2, Japan decided not to take part in the war against the Soviet Union for the time being, but to engage instead in southward expansion, even at the risk of becoming embroiled in armed conflicts with Great Britain and the U.S.A. This decision remained unchanged despite the subsequent diplomatic moves by the Wilhelmstrasse, which stuck to its guns and favored Japanese action against Vladivostok, or Singapore if need be, but certainly not what actually came about: an attack against the United States. The German leadership overestimated the Japanese potential, and never lost hope in subsequent years that the Japanese would eventually fight against Russia and thus relieve the German Eastern front. However, peace between the two countries in the Far East continued until the Soviet Union declared war against Japan shortly before the Japanese capitulation on August 8, 1945, so as to have a say in Japanese affairs.—*Source: Nbg. Dok. NG-1433, NG-1951, NG-3437/38, NG-3459, NG-3825/ 26, NG-4371, NG-4423/26, NG-4448/51, NG-4640, NG-4657, NG-5156, etc.; Feis, passim (in particular p. 213); Langer/Gleason, passim (in particular p. 625).*

[319] This is not entirely true. The first armed Japanese-Russian conflict in these border skirmishes took place as early as July and August 1938 on Lake Khasan at the Manchurian-Soviet border, where the Japanese were defeated and had to concede to the evacuation of the disputed no-man's land border strip. They also came off second-best the following year, in the battle for a 20 km-wide border strip east of Khalkhin Gol, on the border between Manchukuo and Inner Mongolia. This was almost a regular campaign, which began in May 1939 and ended with the expulsion of the Japanese from the contested area after a major Soviet attack on August 20, 1939. The War Ministry in Tokyo admitted 18,000 dead, while Moscow even spoke of the elimination of the Japanese 6th Army.— *Source: Jones, pp. 180 and 183.*

[320] The old armored cruiser *Izumo*, which was deployed as the flagship of the China fleet.

[321] See note 1841.

[322] The Armed Forces report of that same day read: "A U.S. bomber formation yesterday intruded on Dutch and western German territory. Bombs caused civilian losses. A large number of Dutch children were killed."

[323] The code name of the Führer Headquarters near Münstereifel, which was used during the first part of the Western campaign in 1940.

[324] The supposed 6 destroyers were in reality the 8th Destroyer Flotilla comprised of the boats Z 23 (commander's boat), Z 24, Z 32 and Z 37. It was transferred from the northern area to the Bay of Biscay in order to support the torpedo-boat flotilla in pursuing blockade runners. They were the largest and strongest destroyers of the Navy, equipped with five 15-cm guns and eight torpedo launchers. Z 25 was originally scheduled to take part, but was forced to stay behind due to engine problems. The boats left the mouth of the Elbe River, passed the Dover-Calais straits during the first night (during which they were fired upon by the long-range batteries in Dover, and drove back a motor torpedo boat attack),

and arrived in the Le Havre harbor in the morning. During the second night, the boats were transferred from Le Havre to Cherbourg, and during the third night they passed Brest and arrived in the Bay of Biscay, where they entered the mouth of the Gironde River on the following evening. They moored in the harbor of Bordeaux and were immediately camouflaged. *Source: Michaux, p. 494.*

[325] The name is unclear. Perhaps Hitler was referring to the then Air General Otto Dessloch, who commanded Luftwaffe Group Kuban at that time and commanded the Fourth Air Fleet beginning in June 1943. Dessloch did not take over the Third Air Fleet, which had been leading in the West, until August 23, 1944. Until then Field Marshal Hugo Sperrle remained the Commander-in-Chief.

[326] The reference is to the British steamer *Château Roux*, which was damaged during this raid.

[327] A Panamanian tanker of 7,000 GRT was sunk during the raid on Philippeville (East Algeria).

[328] Robert Ritter v. Greim; born June 22, 1892; Cadet Corps; 1913 Second Lieutenant in the Field Artillery; 1915 joined the Luftwaffe; 1917 First Lieutenant and Commander, 34th Fighter Squadron, later of the fighter formation Greim; "Pour le mérite"; 1919 law studies; junior lawyer; 1924-27 served with the Chinese Air Force in Canton; returned to military service in January 1934 and was appointed commander of the first fighter squadron of the new Luftwaffe; February 1939 Commander, 5th Air Division; 1940 Lieutenant General and until March 1942 Commanding General, V Air Corps (in the West, then after June 1941 in the East), which was reorganized as Luftwaffe Command East on April 1, 1942, and renamed Sixth Air Fleet on May 5, 1943. He was promoted to Colonel General in February 1943. On April 25, 1945, Hitler appointed Greim to be Field Marshal and Commander-in-Chief of the Luftwaffe—and for this purpose he had to fly into the encircled city center of Berlin. After being captured by the Americans, he committed suicide on May 24, 1945.—*Source: Munzinger Archive; Siegler, p. 120, Seemen; Geschichte der Ritter... I, p. 402.*

[329] Major Gustav Pressler, who was awarded Oak Leaves, was born October 13, 1912; joined the police in 1932; was transferred to the Luftwaffe as a Second Lieutenant in 1935; and became a member of the *Immelmann* dive-bomber squadron in 1937 (serving as group commander in the end).—*Source: DNB of January 28, 1943; Seemen.*

[330] Erhard Milch; born March 3, 1892; 1911 Second Lieutenant; 1915 joined the Luftwaffe; in World War I as a captain and Commander, 6th Fighter Group; discharged in 1920; and served with border troops and the police flight squadron in East Prussia. When the squadron was disbanded, he joined Lloyd-Ostflug, a civilian aviation company, then Danzig Airmail; he worked as head of flying operations at Junkers from 1923, and in 1925-26, after the merger of the aviation companies, he sat on the board of Deutsche Lufthansa. He was appointed Göring's deputy in the Reichs Commissariat for Aviation on February 4, 1933. From February 22, 1933, Undersecretary for Aviation; October 1933 Colonel; 1935 Lieutenant General; 1936 Air General; October 1938 Colonel General and

Luftwaffe Inspector General; July 1940 Field Marshal; November 1941 (following Udet's suicide) General in charge of aircraft production and also Commander, Fifth Air Fleet in Norway from April 12 to May 10, 1940; and head of the Stalingrad relief mission from January 15 to February 3, 1942. On June 20, 1944, the positions of Undersecretary for Aviation and General in charge of aircraft production were eliminated; on January 7, 1945, Göring relieved Milch—who, as a matter of form, had served as Speer's deputy in the Ministry of Armaments and War Production—of his post as Luftwaffe Inspector General and deputy of R.d.L. and Commander-in-Chief of the Luftwaffe. In April 1947 Milch was sentenced in Nuremberg (Case 2) to life imprisonment (the sentence was reduced to 15 years in 1952); he was released on parole in 1954.—*Source: Munzinger Archive; VB of March 20, 1942; Frankfurter Zeitung of Nov. 3, 1938; Siegler, p. 132.*

[331] Transcript number unknown—Fragment No. 32—The (destroyed) date of this meeting can be more or less reconstructed as follows: Hitler had returned to Rastenburg from Vinnitsa (Wehrwolf) on March 13, and he made a speech in Berlin on March 21 to mark Veterans Day, which had been postponed by a week "because of the military situation" (Völkischer Beobachter wrote on March 22, 1943, that only now the situation in the East was such that "the Führer dared to spend a few hours in Berlin"). He then traveled to Berchtesgaden, where he received the first of a series of satellite leaders on March 31. Since the date of March 20 is mentioned, this meeting could not have taken place any later than March 18, or Zeitzler would have spoken of "tomorrow" or "today." In addition, the "Buffalo Movement" [Operation Buffalo] was apparently still in progress, so the discussion may have taken place on March 16, the day on which that operation was completed. Preparations for "down there," on the other hand, indicate that it took place at Wolfsschanze—as the stenographer noted—that is to say not earlier than March 11. The reference to a strike in Turin gives another clue. The Fiat factory there was the center of the strike action, where 40,000 to 50,000 employees failed to report for work on March 12. Therefore it may be assumed that this fragment dates to a period between March 12 and 15. [—] Of the two original sets of shorthand notes, one was completely destroyed while the other was so heavily charred that only about half of the text—spread over the page—is legible. According to a note on the fragment, the first transcription of the text yielded 45 typed pages; the second yielded only 28.

[332] Panzer Grenadier Division (Panzer Division after the winter of 1943-44) *Grossdeutschland* was an elite army force with members from all the German ethnic groups. It was not included in the regular division numbering system and, among other duties, it had to assign guards to the Führer Headquarters. The division was established in May 1942 from the *Grossdeutschland* Regiment, which was set up in the summer 1939 from the *Wachregiment Berlin*—probably including parts of the Doberitz Infantry Training Regiment and 92nd Infantry Regiment. The regiments and battalions that were given priority in terms of replacements and armaments were all called divisions. *Grossdeutschland* was deployed on the Eastern front until 1945. *Source: Order of Battle, p. 303; Görlitz II, p. 195.*

[333] Planned evacuation by Army Group Center of the salient projecting along the front between Iukhnov and Rzhev.

[334] Smoke mortars consisted of a mobile launcher that could fire multiple powder rockets (15-cm and 21-cm caliber) at targets several thousand meters away at very short intervals. Originally designed in the inter-war period for the delivery of gas or smoke ammunition, they were relied on more and more heavily by artillery units as the war progressed. The name is probably derived from their original use; some, however, believe that it is a reference to the inventor, Dr. of Engineering Rudolf Nebel. During the war, the smoke mortar troops were grouped in special brigades and regiments.—*Source: Lusar, p. 88; Order of Battle, p. 474.*

[335] Alpini and Bersaglieri divisions were always considered to be the best Italian units.

[336] Vittorio Ambrosio; born July 28, 1898; Second Lieutenant of Cavalry; took part in the Italian-Turkish War as a Captain; 1915 to 1918 Chief of Staff, 3rd Cavalry Division; 1918 Colonel; 1923 commanding officer of a cavalry regiment, later at the Cavalry Academy; 1927 Brigadier General and Chief of General Staff of an Army Corps; 1932 Division General and Commander of the 2nd Mobile Division; 1935 Commanding General of an Army Corps on Sicily; December 1938 Army General and Commander-in-Chief, Second Army (he was in Croatia from April 1941 to January 1942 with this army, where he openly favored the Četniks); from January 1942 to January 1943 Army Chief of General Staff; and on January 30, 1943 succeeded Cavallero as Chief of the *Comando Supremo*. Ambrosio was one of the conspirators against the Fascist regime and was appointed Inspector General of the Army by the Badoglio government, but soon applied for his discharge.—*Source: Munziger Archive; Alfieri, pp. 214, 220 and 222; Siegler, p. 93.*

[337] Regarding Hitler's comments on his allies' troops, the reader should bear in mind that the Italians and the Hungarians did not adopt as their own objective the German invasion to conquer Russia's space (and the winter battles that such a campaign required). The Romanians, after recapturing of Bessarabia, did not have a clear war aim anymore either. In addition, the characteristics of the three allies didn't prepare them for the stress and strain of heavy fighting. The brave and persevering Romanian soldiers had the best record, and the original Italian Expeditionary Corps (CSIR) had proven its worth. But even these formations lacked suitable non-commissioned officers, and inadequate combat training caused relatively large losses that had a negative impact on the morale of the troops. Weapons—in particular antitank weapons—and equipment were obsolete and inadequate, and the relationship between officers and men was cold (think of the different rations). The command—with the exception of the outstanding commander of the Romanian Third Army, Colonel General Dimitrescu, or General Lascar—were not up to the challenges of the Russian campaign either. In addition, there were political differences within the officer corps and national tensions between individual allies (Hungarians and Romanians, for example, could not be deployed together!). In view of this situation, independent

deployment of allied troops, as required by the High Command, caused considerable problems to the German commanders at the front. Because Hitler had ordered the assault across the Don towards the Volga River, it was not possible for the Germans to take any precautions. With many misgivings (which proved justified in the end), the allies were entrusted the area of the Don that was relatively easy to defend. After that disaster, Italians and Hungarians disappeared from the Eastern theater of war—the Italians forever, the Hungarians until July 1944; only the Romanians stayed, with 8 divisions at the bridgehead on Kuban and in the Crimea.—*Source: Manstein, p. 210; Schröter, p. 49; Hillgruber: pp. 162, 171, and elsewhere; Friessner, p. 233.*

338 This refers to the outfitting of 700,000 Italians in addition to the Germans' own large needs. Mussolini always generously offered troops, but they lacked the required equipment and weapons.

339 After the Polish campaign, the former Sixth Army, which was established at the beginning of the war from the command of Fourth Army Group (Leipzig), was renamed Tenth Army. It was commanded by Field Marshal v. Reichenau until December 30, 1941, then by Panzer General Paulus. After the capitulation of the Sixth Army at Stalingrad, the Sixth Army was reestablished from the command of Army Detachment Hollidt and remained at the Eastern Front until the capitulation.—*Source: Siegler, p. 27.*

340 Fritz Sauckel; born October 27, 1894; trained as a sailor; 1914-19 prisoner of war in France, then blue-collar worker, enrolled for two years at a polytechnic; 1919 Deutschvölkischer Schutz- und Trutzbund; 1921 joined NSDAP [Nazi Party]; 1927 Gauleiter [Party leader] of Thuringia; 1930 member of the Thuringia State Assembly; August 26, 1932 appointed Chairman of the State Ministry and Interior Minister of Thuringia; 1933 Member of the Reichstag; May 5, 1933 appointed Reichsstatthalter of Thüringia; on September 1, 1939 Reichs Defense Commissioner in Military District IX (Kassel); March 21, 1942 appointed General Representative for Work Assignment for the commissioner of the Four-Year Plan (GBA). Sauckel was accused at the Nuremberg main trial (primarily in connection with the slave labor issue), sentenced to death by hanging, and executed on October 10, 1946.—*Source: Der Grossdeutsche Reichstag.*

341 In 1943, in addition to the 550,000 men whose birth year made eligible for military service, the Armed Forces were able to add 1.5 million persons from earlier age groups who were released from other industries. Due to the increase in foreign labor and women entering the workplace, the work force in the Greater German Reich was (despite conscription) increased by some 1,765,000 individuals that year—from 26,935,000 on January 1, 1943, to 28,700,000 late in December 1943. (The GBA report, "Die deutsche Industrie..." indicates even higher numbers—16 million men, 14 million women and 7 million foreign workers and prisoners of war for mid-1943.) The screening of the potential labor force through compulsory registration and the requirement to close businesses based on the regulations of January 27 and 29, 1943, added 833,000 full-time and 793,000 part-time workers to the labor force; the reorganization (AZS action) carried out in the second half of 1943 added another 396,000

workers to the armaments industry.—*Source: Weidermann, passim; Die deutsche Industrie…, p. 46; GBA Report of Dec. 12, 1943: "Der Arbeitseinsatz im Grossdeutschen Reich vom 1. Januar bis 31. Dezember 1943" (Nbg. Dok. NG-3996).*

[342] It is no longer possible to identify exactly what output was to be tripled. Generally speaking, the German ammunition output tripled from 1940 to 1944, while the weapons output experienced a nine-fold increase. For individual weapons whose output was especially accelerated, the multipliers were as follows: submarines 4 to 6, aircraft 4 to 5, tanks approximately 17. It should be kept in mind, though, that the differences between output figures and absorption figures grew tremendously during this period, so the number of operational weapons did not grow at nearly the same rate.

[343] Racial policy measures were introduced by Italy at the time of the Abyssinian campaign, but application of the provisions was initially limited to the colonial territories (in order to prevent the development of a mixed population). Apart from a few sectarian and fanatical organs and spokesmen (*La Vita Italiana*; Farinacci), these issues were not taken up by official publications until spring 1938, after the stabilization of the Axis. Mussolini made his first comment about the matter at the end of July. According to the decision of the Fascist Grand Council of October 7, 1938, the position of Jews was settled by a statute and relevant legislation was adopted, but numerous privileges were permitted for mixed marriages, old Fascists, veterans, etc. The removal of Jews from the Italian armed forces began in 1938, but most of them reappeared in their previous (or other) positions later. The resistance of the Italian people (who were not particularly enthusiastic about racial measures) was backed up by the Catholic Church, which protected Jews who had converted to its faith. As early as September 18, 1938, Mussolini spoke of "unexpected friends who suddenly appeared." Priests continued to give their blessing to "mixed marriages" that were prohibited by the "law for the defense of the Italian race." These marriages could not be sanctioned through the civil ceremony that was optional in Italy at that time. In addition, primary and secondary schools run by the Catholic Church had become a refuge for Jewish children of the Catholic faith when they and their Jewish teachers were expelled from public schools late in 1938.—*Source: Blahut, passim; Roehrbein, pp. 74 and 78; Pini, p. 301; Wagenführ p. 9.* [NDT: see also Renzo De Felice, *The Jews in Fascist Italy: A History*, Enigma 2001, pp. 278-284]

[344] Matthias Erzberger; born September 20, 1875; elementary school teacher and editor; from 1903 Member of the Reichstag (left wing of the Center), initially annexationist, then in favor of a negotiated peace during World War I; in 1918 undersecretary without portfolio, signatory of the armistice on November 11, 1918; from June 1919 to 1920 Finance Minister; on August 26, 1921, shot dead by two former officers, Schulz and Tillessen.

[345] Roberto Farinacci; born October 16, 1892; a railroad worker who became an attorney, was a right-wing radical Fascist who distinguished himself by his vitriolic attacks against the Jewry and political Catholicism and therefore was held in high regard by leading German national socialists. After the slaying of

Matteotti, he was appointed Secretary General of the Fascist Party in 1924, but resigned in 1926 to protest the rapprochement between Mussolini and the Vatican. He then lived a secluded life as the publisher of *Regime Fascista* in his hometown of Cremona, which he developed into a power base. A strong proponent of the Axis alliance, he also promoted anti-Semitism. He was executed by partisans in 1945. In 1938 he was given the position of a state minister; he was also a member of the Fascist Parliament.—*Source: Munzinger Archive; various mentions by Wiskemann, Ciano, Rintelen and Anfuso.*

[346] Eduard Wagner; born April 1, 1894; 1914 Second Lieutenant in the 12th Bavarian Field Artillery Regiment; Freikorps [Free Corps] Epp; Reichswehr; from 1933 in the Quartermaster Division of the Army General Staff; 1935 Lieutenant Colonel; 1936 Chief of the 6th Detachment of the Army General Staff; August 1940 Major General and Army Quartermaster General; 1942 Lieutenant General; and August 1943 General of Artillery.—*Source: Munzinger Archive; Keilig 211/353.*

[347] This statement could be completed as follows: ... "without attacking the Russians, and limiting myself to defense."

[348] He probably refers to Guderian, who was appointed Inspector General of Panzer Troops and given extraordinary powers by Hitler on February 20, 1943 (see note 385).

[349] Wolfram Baron v. Richthofen; born October 10, 1895; regular army officer during World War I; hussar, later airman in the Richthofen Fighter Wing; left the service in 1920, enrolled at the Technical College in Hannover; recommissioned and in 1929 Captain and academic degree of Dr. of engineering; left service again in 1933 and joined RLM; was officially accepted into the Luftwaffe as a Major in 1935; January 1937 Chief of General Staff of the Condor Legion; November 1938 Major General and Commander of the Legion; during the campaign against France and Russia, Commanding General, VIII Air Corps; June 1942 Commander, Fourth Air Fleet; after his mission in Stalingrad, promoted to Field Marshal on February 17, 1943; and from June 1943 to fall 1944 Commander of the Second Air Fleet in Italy. Richthofen underwent brain surgery in August 1944 and died on July 12, 1945, of complications resulting from the surgery.—*Source: Munzinger Archive; Siegler, p. 134; Seemen; Order of Battle, p. 611.*

[350] The term "commander-in-charge of division clear-out" was probably coined by Zeitzler; at any rate, this or a similar designation is not known.

[351] Applications for compensation could be filed for private property lost during withdrawal. This regulation applied mainly to officers' uniforms, which were private property, because—except for the clothing allowance—they had to pay for their uniforms out of their own pockets. The processing of applications for property lost during the major withdrawals in the winter of 1942-43 indicated the volume of superfluous things that was carried along.

[352] According to the 1935 military criminal law, section 81, paragraph 2, self-mutilation was punished with one to five years' imprisonment; according to the special wartime penal regulation of November 1, 1939, section 5, para-

graphs 1 to 3, this offence was regarded as "demoralization of the armed forces" and carried the death penalty.

353 After "Veterans Day," Hitler went to Berchtesgaden and used the following month to receive his satellite leaders and bolster their morale, which had been sapped by changing fortunes in North Africa and Russia. He received the following personalities "down there":

> on March 31, the Bulgarian Tsar Boris
> on April 7-10, Mussolini
> on April 12-13, the Romanian "Conducator" [Leader] Marshal Antonescu
> on April 16-17, the Hungarian Admiral v. Horthy
> on April 19, the Norwegian "Prime Minister" Quisling
> on April 23, the Slovak State President Tiso
> on April 27, the Croatian "Poglavnik" [Chief] Pavelic
> on April 29, the French Prime Minister Laval

In spite of the expression "at his headquarters" that was used in the communiqués, the receptions usually took place at Klessheim Castle or the Berghof, as shown by the published photographs.—*Source: Keesings Archive 1943, pp. 5893, 5898, 5902, 5902, 5907, 5910, 5913, 5917 and 5919 and also VB of the relevant period.*

354 As far as has been determined so far, the German field army included eight so-called field training divisions (the 147th, 153rd,* 155th, 381st, 382nd, 388th,* 390th,* and 391st*). They were stationed in the occupied territories and served as both training units and occupation forces. Another purpose was to deceive enemy intelligence and, as their food had to be made available by the country in which they were stationed, ease the strain on supplies from the Reich. These were skeleton reserve armies, which continued to report to the Reserve Army in the West, whereas in the East they were incorporated into the field army and received orders from the army groups. The latter could train their replacements as they saw fit, based on their experience. In addition, the regular divisions in the East had special field training battalions for refresher and other courses, familiarizing the reserve troops with conditions in the East, etc.— *Source: Order of Battle, pp. 18 and 358; Keilig 15/63 (the four field training divisions listed as belonging to the field army in the "organization of the field army, as of mid-September 1943" are marked with an asterisk).*

355 Again, the reference is to Berchtesgaden.

356 In March 1943, the "General Staff Courses" (organized after 1940 as a replacement for the War Academy, which had been closed at the beginning of the war) were increased in size to 150 participants and designated again as a "War Academy." During this discussion, they were probably speaking about this institution, unless they were referring to a special course for General Staff officers that might have taken place at Sonthofen.—*Source: Erfurth: Generalstab, p. 223.*

357 These were just words. Hitler, in particular, should have had no doubt about the year 1943; at best it could bring some relief, but never a positive change in the military situation. Any statement to the contrary simply reflects the dan-

gerous political wishful thinking to which he succumbed more and more frequently (without actually taking any steps to make his dreams come true).

358 Transcript number unknown—Fragment No. 50—One of the two sets of shorthand notes was completely destroyed, while the other was charred to such an extent that only one quarter of each page was legible. These gaps, amounting to three-quarters of the page, are indicated by dotted lines. The first transcription yielded 35 typewritten pages. Date, place and time are probably not correct, because on that Sunday Hitler attended a celebration and made a speech at the Berlin memorial to mark Veterans Day, which had been postponed by a week. Although the hour of that event cannot be ascertained because of the security measures taken, the shadows in an available photograph suggest that it was the afternoon (according to the report by the NZZ the celebration took place "at noon"). The date given is confirmed by the following text, and the hour cannot be determined, but the location was probably wrong; the discussion most likely did not take place at the Berghof, but in the Reich Chancellery. In another preliminary remark to the second transcription made in May 1945, the stenographers stated that at that time they did not remember whether the 1943 Veterans Day had been moved, but gave March 14 as the date and thus the date of Hitler's presence in Berlin. They probably relied on a pocket calendar or some other printed calendar. It may therefore be assumed—and it seems reasonable to do so—that the locations were added only during the (first) transcription of the original text, so that the locations given in the preserved minutes and the second transcription or the fragments of the minutes were later reconstructions (1945).

359 Karl Schneider; born August 10, 1881; 1902 Ensign; 1920 discharged as Lieutenant Commander; May 1940 reinstated as Commandant of Dünkirchen Port until the capitulation, June 1941 Commander z.V., April 1944 Captain z.V.

360 Probably supplies for Tunis.

361 There is no doubt that this number is wrong. A Tenth Army did not exist at the time, the 10th Panzer Division fought outside Tunis, and the 10th Panzer Grenadier Division fought in the central sector, while the 10th SS Panzer Division was stationed in France.

362 Hans-Karl v. Scheele; born May 23, 1892; 1912 Second Lieutenant, 3rd Guard Infantry Regiment; Reichswehr; 1935 Lieutenant Colonel; 1937 commanding officer, Training Group A; Hannover War Academy; 1938 Colonel; 1939 Commander, 191st Infantry Regiment; 1941 Major General and Commander, 208th Infantry Division; March 1943 Lieutenant General and (after February) Commander of the Scheele Corps, then LIII and LII Army Corps; December 1943 General of Infantry and head of the Armed Forces Patrol Service; and November 1944 President of the Reich Military Court.—*Source: Order of Battle, p. 617; Seemen; Das deutsche Heer, p. 798, Rangliste 1944-45, p. 17; Keilig 211/290.*

363 A comment by Manstein: "When Khar'kov and Belgorod were captured, the army group's second counterattack ground to a halt. The operations could not be continued because of the worsening mud. The army group had planned to complete it by cooperating with Army Group Center to shorten the front by

clearing out the Kursk salient, which projected far into the German front in the west. This plan did not materialize, since Army Group Center was not in a position to help."—*Source: Manstein, p. 467.*

364 The first SS General Command, commanded by SS Obergruppenführer Hausser, was established in Germany in May 1942, and later on in France. Until further SS general commands were set up during the second half of 1943, it was known as SS Panzer Corps (without number), later on it was known as II SS Panzer Corps. At the end of the war, there were altogether seven genuine SS general commands:

I SS Panzer Corps (*Leibstandarte Adolf Hitler*)
II SS Panzer Corps
III (German) SS Panzer Corps
IV SS Panzer Corps
V SS Mountain Corps
VI SS Volunteer Corps (Latvian)
IX Waffen SS Mountain Corps (Croatian)

plus five SS general commands which were formed at the end of 1944 from the Reserve Army, the customs border guards, Volkssturm [militia], Eastern battalions, etc., some of which were commanded by police generals and one even by an Army general (XI, XII, XIII, XIV and XVIII SS Corps). The Waffen SS was not in a position to set up the staffs of the latter corps, so personnel had to be recruited from the Reserve Army. They were established because Himmler wanted to have as many "SS units" as possible.—*Source: Order of Battle, p. 333; Hausser, pp. 17, 76, 104, 189 and 270.*

365 Transcript number unknown—Fragment No. 4—The preserved shorthand record was somewhat charred; only parts of it could be used for the second transcription.

366 At this time, Hitler was again worried about the Balkans. Following the German-Italian collapse in Tunis, the Allies had open access to the southern flank of "Fortress Europe" via the Mediterranean. Theoretically speaking, their next target could be either the Balkans or Italy. Even after the Allied landing on Sicily (July 10, 1943), and later in the Bay of Salerno (September 8, 1943), Hitler remained concerned about the Balkans.

367 Bauxite deposits: Transylvania, Dalmatia, Phokis (northwestern Greece), island of Naxos; chrome deposits: northern Albania, northern Greece, eastern Bosnia, Banat.

368 Copper is mined primarily in the largest European copper deposit at Bor (Serbia), southwest of the Iron Gate. Other deposits: northern Serbia, Macedonia, Banat, northwestern Bulgaria.

369 The 11th Luftwaffe Field Division.

370 "Gisela" was the code name for a planned German operation that was to advance from southern France toward Spain. Suggested by the Navy, it was a late revival of the old Felix Plans, aimed at Gibraltar and Portugal. It soon became clear that the implementation of this plan depended on Spanish sup-

port, which was now even more out of the question than before. The main purpose of the venture was a thrust into the flank of the Anglo-American concentration in North Africa. The operation, which was first discussed in December 1942, was finally called off by Hitler on May 14, 1943 (i.e., five days before this meeting), because of increasing danger from the Spanish guerilla war and in consideration of the Tunis disaster.—*Source: Hinsley, p. 226.*

371 The 9th SS Panzer Division *Hohenstaufen* and 10th Panzer Division *Frundsberg* consisted of draftees and were new regular units that had been built up in France during the winter of 1942-43.

372 A reference to the sub-units of German divisions which, because of transportation problems, had stayed behind on the Italian mainland or on Sicily while the rest of the divisions were destroyed in North Africa.

373 According to the order of battle of (October) 1943, the 21st Panzer Division was equipped only with light tanks, while the 15th and 10th were panzer grenadier divisions.—*Source: Keilig 15/52 and 15/58.*

374 This is a reference to a situation report in which the *Comando Supremo,* in contrast to its earlier view that the next Allied push would be directed exclusively against the Italian islands, included in his considerations an enemy landing operation on the Balkan peninsula. [NDT: Some of these opinions about a possible Balkan landing by the Allies may have been planted as disinformation by French intelligence through its double agents inside the SIM (Servizio Informazioni Militare). See Paul Paillole, *Fighting the Nazis,* Enigma, New York 2003.]

375 "Command tanks" were special Panzer III models (Sd.Kfz [Sonder Kraftfahrzeug—Special Motor Vehicles] 266, 267 and 268) manufactured by Wegmann in Kassel. The guns were replaced by wooden dummy guns, and the tanks carried wireless communication equipment consisting of two transmitters and two receivers. These command tanks were used in the Panzer III and Panzer IV units. The Panther and Tiger units had command tanks of the same type (Sd.Kfz 172 and 183), but because more space was available in these models they kept their guns and simply carried less ammunition.

376 The number of tanks produced during this month could not be ascertained. The following output can be assumed for the first half of 1943: 500 Panzer IIIs, 1,400 Panzer IVs, 300 to 400 Panthers and 60 Tigers. The overall German annual output of armored vehicles (i.e., including tank destroyers and assault guns) showed the following trend:

	1940	1941	1942	1943	1944
light	800	2,300	3,600	7,900	10,000
medium	1,400	2,900	5,600	9,400	12,100
heavy	—	—	100	2,500	5,200

A Swiss source specifies only the medium and heavy armored fighting vehicles (it can be proven, however, that the number of Tigers listed was several times the actual output):

	1940	1941	1942	1943	1944
Panzer III	895	1,845	2,555	349[?]	—
Panzer IV	280	480	964	3,073	3,366
Panther	—	—	—	1,850	3,964
Tiger	—	—	78	674	623
Königstiger	—	—	—	—	379

– Source: Die deutsche Industrie, pp. 71 and 182; Wiener, H. 3, p. 72.

[377] Flame-thrower tanks were 12.6-ton special-purpose tanks (thickness of armor: 15 cm, speed: 50 km/hour), equipped with two powerful flame-throwers (range: 60 m) in addition to a machine gun. Some of them used trailers to carry the flame-oil tanks.—Source: Guderian: Panzer-Marsch! p. 235; Lusar, p. 35.

[378] The 9th and 10th SS Panzer Divisions.

[379] Meaning that if the attack near Kursk had been launched in mid-April as originally planned, instead of waiting—at Hitler's insistence—for further shipments of tanks, especially the new Panther model.

[380] This should read: panzer command vehicle.

[381] Design plans for the Tiger tank had originally been submitted by Henschel and Porsche. Both prototypes were then demonstrated at Berka in May 1942. While Hitler preferred the Porsche design—not the least because of his close relationship with Volkswagen—tank experts decided in favor of Henschel's Tiger. Irritated, Porsche built about 50 units of his model (later known as tank destroyer Ferdinand)—more or less on his own initiative.

[382] At Kursk.

[383] Sepp Dietrich established the first units of the Leibstandarte Adolf Hilter as armed units as early as 1933; in 1936 the Leibstandarte reported to the new "Support Troop Inspection" at the SS headquarters. When the war broke out, the Leibstandarte was initially deployed as a reinforced motorized regiment and expanded into the 1st SS Panzer Division Leibstandarte-SS Adolf Hitler in 1940 and early 1941 (until the summer of 1942 it was classified as a panzer grenadier division). The I SS Panzer Corps general command Leibstandarte Adolf Hitler was formed in 1942-43 with personnel who had been released from the division. The LAH, which had priority with regard to supply of men and material, participated as part of the Tenth Army (Reichenau) in the Polish campaign, and was deployed on the right wing with the Eighteenth Army (Küchler) in the Western campaign. It was deployed in southern Yugoslavia during the Southeast campaign, and in the East it fought in the southern sector from the beginning of the campaign until summer 1943—with an interruption in mid-1942. It was deployed briefly in northern Italy, then in the fall of 1943 again in southern Russia, then in mid-1944 during the invasion in France and eventually in 1945 in the final battles in Hungary.—Source: Hausser, passim; Order of Battle, pp. 333 and 336.

[384] Two days earlier, on May 17, 19 British Lancaster bombers of the 617th Squadron—formed specifically for that purpose—had bombed the dams of the Eder, Möhne, and Sorpe reservoirs. They used cylindrical special-purpose

bombs containing a device that set the bomb spinning upon release. When released at a predetermined speed, altitude and distance, the bomb would damage the dam at the most effective depth. The dam of the Sorpe reservoir was missed, but the damaged Eder and Möhne dams (which held, respectively, 130 and 202 cubic meters of water) released huge floods into the valleys, causing tremendous losses—in human lives and material assets. This disaster also had a major impact on the water and power supply of the Ruhr area. The Armed Forces High Command report of May 17 stated: "Weak British air squadrons penetrated the territory of the Reich last night and dropped a limited number of high-explosive bombs in several places. Two dams were damaged; the resulting flood wave caused heavy losses among the civilian population. Eight of the attacking planes were shot down…"—*Source: Brickhill, p. 78 and elsewhere; Galland, p. 213. (Galland speaks incorrectly of a daytime attack.)*

[385] After having been in disgrace for more than a year, Guderian was appointed Inspector General of Panzer Troops on February 20, 1943. Having the rank of a Commander-in-Chief of the Army, he was the superior officer over all panzer troops, panzer grenadier, motorized infantry, panzer reconnaissance troops, tank destroyer troops and heavy assault gun units. He had requested that Hitler put all assault gun units under his control, but the General Staff succeeded in pushing through this limitation, which in the end resulted in quite a lot of friction. In his area, Guderian was responsible for organization, training, technical development, vehicle distribution, and the activation and rehabilitation of units.—*Source: Guderian: Erinnerungen, p. 260.*

[386] Code name for the attack on Kursk.

[387] Like the Army General Staff, Hitler held the view that the rehabilitation of battle-weary divisions was the most appropriate way of creating or maintaining combat-ready units. The development of the overall situation repeatedly forced the High Command to set up new operational reserves, as the existing ones were completely worn out. However, such reserves were only available to the High Command if they were stationed in Germany, the then General Government [Poland], or France. So the required number of battle-weary divisions ("skeletons") had to be transferred to those areas for rehabilitation. But despite weeks of preliminary planning, these initiatives often failed, as the command posts at the Eastern front—usually justified by the circumstances—would not release the divisions earmarked for rehabilitation. Then the High Command had no other alternative but to set up the required reserves through new activation.

[388] With Zeitzler, who did not wish to release the rump divisions that were still in combat in the East, despite the fact that they were only "skeletons."

[389] A conflict flared up between the Italian governor of Montenegro, General Pirzio Biroli, and the German commanders, during a joint German-Italian operation against partisans in the Balkans. A great stir was caused when a Montenegrin citizen, who was a relative of the Italian queen and who had cooperated for a long time with Italian authorities, was arrested. This incident, which could not be resolved locally, caused Hitler to write a letter to Mussolini in which he accused the Italian generals of playing into the hands of the en-

emy, thus sabotaging joint efforts. Von Rintelen, the German general at the *Comando Supremo* and military attaché in Rome, delivered this letter to Mussolini the following day.—*Source: Rintelen, p. 202.*

390   Having been reconstituted in France after its destruction in Stalingrad, and prepared for transfer to Italy, the 16th Panzer Division remained on the mainland. The 90th Panzer Grenadier Division, commanded by General Lungershausen, was formed for Sardinia—primarily from march battalions.— *Source: Order of Battle, p. 296.*

391   Paul Conrath; born November 21, 1886; war volunteer; 1917 Second Lieutenant; 1920 joined the Prussian State Police force; promoted in 1924 to Captain and in 1934 to Major; 1935 transferred to the Luftwaffe; 1938 Lieutenant Colonel; 1940 Colonel and Commander, *General Göring* Anti-Aircraft Regiment; July 1942 Major General and Commander, Panzer Parachute Division *Hermann Göring*; September 1943 Lieutenant General; May 1944 Commanding General, Parachute Training and Replacement/Reserve Troops; and January 1945 General of Parachute Forces.

392   Bulgaria was the only friendly country whose army Germany substantially assisted in organizing and supplying with modern weapons. The first discussions about this matter were held by the chief of the operations branch of the Bulgarian General Staff at the Armed Forces High Command headquarters as early as the summer of 1941. The first weapons were delivered to the Bulgarians in the winter of 1941-42. By August 1944, 10 infantry divisions, 1 cavalry division and 1 armored division were equipped.

393   Erich Fellgiebel; born October 4, 1905; Lieutenant, 2nd Signal Battalion; 1914 instructor at the Spandau Telegraphers' Academy; during World War I, primarily General Staff positions; Reichswehr; 1930 Commander, 2nd Intelligence Department; 1934 Colonel and Inspector of the Signal Corps (in the Seventh Army, later also entrusted with the responsibilities of the Inspector of the Armed Forces communication lines in the Armed Forces High Command; 1938 Major General; and 1940 General of the Signal Corps. Fellgiebel belonged to the group of conspiring officers and was to sever the communication lines of the Führer Headquarters following the assassination attempt of July 20, 1944. He was arrested on the evening of the same day, sentenced to death by the Volksgerichtshof on August 10, 1944, and executed on September 4.—*Source: Munzinger Archive; Pechel, p. 329; Wheeler-Bennett, p. 760 and elsewhere; Das deutsche Heer, p. 27; Rangliste 1944-45, p. 15; Keilig 211/82.*

394   Transcript No. S 97/43—Fragment No. 5—Completely preserved.

395   Alexander Löhr; born May 20, 1885 in Turnu-Severin; infantry officer in the k.u.k. Army Detachment; after 1913 in the General Staff; played a leading role in the organization of the Austrian Air Force after World War I, in the end Major General and Commander of the Air Force and Chairman of the Luftwaffe Department of the Defense Ministry. He was accepted into the German Armed Forces at the rank of a Lieutenant General; April 1938 Commanding General of the Luftwaffe in Austria (changed in August 1938 to Luftwaffe Command Austria, and in March 1939 to Fourth Air Fleet), Commander, Fourth Air Fleet

in the campaign against Poland and the Southeastern and Eastern campaigns until June 1942; May 1941 Colonel General; July 1942 Armed Forces Commander Southeast (Twelfth Army) which became Commander-in-Chief Southeast (Army Group E) in 1943 (from August 26, 1943, to March 24, 1945, he was only Commander-in-Chief of Army Group E, as the Commander-in-Chief of Army Group F, Baron v. Weichs, served as Commander-in-Chief Southeast). Löhr was extradited to Yugoslavia in May 1945 and sentenced to death in early 1947 because of the bombing of Belgrade in 1941. He is said to have been executed on February 16, 1947.—*Source: Munzinger Archive; Seemen; Siegler, p. 130.*

[396] Probably the then Commander of Crete (1942 to June 1944), Lieutenant General Bruno Bräuer, previously Commander of the 1st Parachute Regiment (Iraklion Task Force during the Crete operation). Bräuer, who had been appointed General of the Parachute Forces, was executed by a Greek firing squad on May 20, 1945.—*Source: Order of Battle, p. 532; Hove, p. 133.*

[397] Appointed "Representative of the Führer for the Recording of War History," Colonel Walter Scherff was asked by Hitler to attend as often as possible and probably attended the previous meetings as well. His task was primarily to write essays for newspapers; these essays were also collected and published in the following brochures:

Zwölf Kriegsaufsätze, Berlin 1943

Feldherr aus Schicksal: Der Feldherr im Urteil seiner Zeit, Berlin 1943

Vertrauen und Glaube: Ein Bekenntnis zum Feldherrn dieses Krieges, Salzburg 1944.

It is striking that these publications center around one subject only: the "military genius," "the Führer's qualities as a military leader" and include almost intolerable flattery and praise, but still raise a number of questions which—though they were naturally answered in conformity with the political line—were more or less taboo at the time. "Die grosse Bewährung" (April 1942) states: "There were skeptics who alluded to the many sycophants even at a time when—in the midst of the victorious Balkan campaign—on April 20, 1941 the Führer's qualities as a military leader were duly praised by the German press. Even the great success of the Eastern campaign in 1941 did not bring about a change. Even these people who, based on their education, had preconceived ideas of military leadership qualities and the conduct of war, found it difficult to believe in the phenomenon embodied in the person of Adolf Hitler." In "Der Feldherr im Urteil seiner Zeit" (April 1943), he wrote: "The German [sic!] people are fortunate to have such a leader. Unconditional confidence and trust in him will bolster the fighting power of the entire nation. He who doubts him might ask himself where he could find a man to take his place and fulfill his numerous responsibilities as well as he does."

[398] This is probably a reference to the Ia [operations officer] of the 22nd Infantry Division stationed on Crete who is referred to as Löhrs' companion: Heinz Langemann; born August 27, 1905; 1935 Captain, 1938 Ib; 1940 Ia [operations officer] 22nd Infantry Division; 1942 Lieutenant Colonel; July 1943 Chief of General Staff, XXIII Army Corps; August 1943 Colonel; August 1944 in Army General Staff; and February 1945 Chief of General Staff of the Fourth Army.

[399] Constantin Alexander v. Neurath, the only son of the former German foreign minister, had earlier, as SS Sonderführer, been sent as the representative of the Foreign Office to Rommel's army in Africa. Recently he had been dispatched to Sicily, presumably to deliver a message from Ribbentrop or Himmler.—*Source: Speidel, p. 85*

[400] General Mario Roatta; born February 2, 1887; 1934-1936, founder of the Servizio Informazioni Militare (SIM), the main Italian military intelligence unit operating from 1934-1943; 1936-38 Spanish campaign; July to October 1939 military attaché in Berlin; November 1939 under Graziani (who was not trained for a position in the General Staff) he was Deputy Chief of General Staff of the Army; March 1941 he was appointed Graziani's successor as Chief of General Staff of the Army; 1942 Commander-in-Chief of the Second Army in Croatia; later and up to this period, Commander-in-Chief of the Sixth Army on Sicily. He returned to the post of Chief of General Staff of the Army at the end of May 1943. Later, Roatta joined Badoglio, but was replaced by General Bernardi in December 1943 because of a pending Yugoslav indictment for war crimes. He was given a long prison sentence in 1945, but managed to escape to Spain. The Supreme Court of Appeal annulled the sentence in 1948. The following year, the military tribunal in Rome also cleared Roatta of the charge of having surrendered the Italian capital without a fight in September 1943.—*Source: Munzinger Archive; Kesselring, pp. 234 and 242; Rintelen, pp. 78, 201 and 240; Badoglio, pp. 104 and 147; Westphal, pp. 216 and 288.*

[401] Friedrich Ruge; born December 24, 1894; active officer; POW after Scapa Flow; Navy (among other things involved in mine development and mine sweeping); 1937 Commander of Mine Sweepers; 1941 Commander of Security, West, February 1943 Vice Admiral, March 1943 Special Staff for Escort Matters (Tunis) with the German Naval Command Italy, May to August 1943 Commander German Naval Command Italy and German Admiral at the Italian Admiralty, November 1943 Admiral with Army Group B (Rommel) and later with Commander-in-Chief West, and November 1944 Chief of the Design Office Naval High Command/Naval Armaments. Ruge was accepted into the Federal Navy in 1956.—*Source: Munzinger Archive; Wehrkunde 1956, p. 206; Lohmann/Hildebrand 291/311.*

[402] Umberto of Savoy, Prince of Piedmont, was Commander-in-Chief of the Italian Army Group *Crown Prince*, which he commanded in southern and central Italy from April 1942 until the Italian capitulation on Sicily.—*Source: Siegler, p. 94.*

[403] May 16.

[404] Hitler had made a similar comment about Roatta as early as February 1942: "This Roatta is a spy. He sabotaged the plan to enter the Rhône valley in June 1940." Hitler was so suspicious of this Italian general that he endeavored to have him appointed Ambassador to Berlin two months after Mussolini was toppled, in order to remove him from the top of the Italian army. Kesselring and Rintelen, on the other hand, evaluate Roatta positively—they described him as open and honest and doubted the "general accusation of Roatta as an enemy and traitor." They said that he was very sarcastic and that they did not like his

manner, but he was more forthcoming than his comrades who only exchanged pleasantries and said comfortable, polite things (see also pp. 134 and 213).— *Source: Picker, p. 204; Kesselring, pp. 234 and 242; Rintelen, pp. 78, 201 and 240.*

405 Enno von Rintelen; born November 6, 1891; 1912 Second Lieutenant, 2nd Grenadier Regiment; during World War I in the adjutancy and General Staff; accepted as a Captain by the Reichswehr; 1934 Battalion Commander, 48th Infantry Regiment; 1935 Colonel; after October 1, 1936 military attaché in Rome; 1939 Major General; September 1940 keeping his rank, he served as a German general in the headquarters of the Italian Armed Forces; 1941 Lieutenant General; and 1942 General of Infantry. On August 31, 1943—a few days before the Italian capitulation—Rintelen was recalled and replaced by General Toussaint; he was not given another assignment.—*Source: Rintelen, passim.*

406 Allusion to Kesselring's trust in the reliability of the Italians and his unflinching belief in their professed loyalty. According to Kesselring's own account, the headquarters considered him to be an Italophile and suitable only for friendly dealings with the Italian royalty. Rommel was used for the times when a tougher course had to be steered. Others also criticized Kesselring for his unshakable trust in the Italians and his great optimism in assessing the situation. Hitler reputedly said of him: "Kesselring is too decent for these people, who are born traitors."—*Source: Kesselring, p. 233; Rintelen, pp. 194, 201 and 240; Westphal, pp. 224 and 257; Hagen: Unternehmen Bernhard, p. 124; Skorzeny, p. 111.*

407 During the ten days preceding Neurath's report, Mussolini had adopted the following reforms:

1. Increasing work discipline.
2. Instruction to prefects to make confiscated hoarded goods available to needy families or works canteens.
3. Closing down of renowned fashion boutiques for violation of price controls, with the requirement to continue paying wages.
4. Expulsion of an industrialist from the party for unjustified price increases and obtaining orders by unfair means.
5. Stricter tax controls of the real estate and share markets.
6. Handing over confiscated black-market goods to hospitals and charities.

—*Source: NZZ of May 10 (noon edition), 14 (evening edition) 18 (morning and evening editions) and 19 (evening edition), 1943.*

408 When the number of air raids against Italian towns increased during the last months of 1942, people wondered whether Rome, the Holy City, would be spared. Using the good services of the Vatican, the Italians contacted the British ambassador to the Holy See, Sir Francis Osborne, and were given an evasive answer; with references to the importance of the city as a railroad junction, to air fields and to the *Comando Supremo* and other Italian and German command centers. As a result, the military headquarters were transferred to areas outside the city. The Italians had the impression that the British were mainly interested in the removal of the German operational headquarters. Although there was no real German headquarters in Rome (the staff of Commander-in-Chief South, for

example, was already stationed at Frascati), but only liaison staff which kept contact with the Italian authorities and worked together with them. Because not all Italian military authorities and German soldiers could be removed from Rome, the order was issued that the staff of the German authorities in Rome had to wear civilian clothes and their official cars were to have civilian number plates. On May 19, one day before this meeting, Undersecretary of State in the British Ministry of Aviation, Balfour, when asked whether there was a tacit understanding to abstain from bombing Rome, stated in the House of Commons, "Rome is not an open city and there is no agreement to this effect. We will not hesitate to bomb Rome if this action is dictated by the progress of war and seems to be useful." Exactly two months later, the severe air raid on July 19, 1943, preceded the overthrow of the Fascist regime.—*Source: Rintelen, p. 184; Ciano, p. 496; NZZ of May 20, 1943 (morning edition).*

[409] Tables prepared by the authorized representative for the deployment of labor indicate the following number of Italian civilians employed in Germany in 1942 and 1943:

July 10, 1942:	211,618 (of which 17,906 were women)
August 20, 1942:	207,398 (of which 18,386 were women)
October 10, 1942:	205,005 (of which 28,792 were in agriculture; 170,575 in industry; 1,742 as household help; 3,896 in commerce, authorities, technical service, etc.)
June 30, 1943:	160,000 (negotiations were held about their return)
August 15, 1943:	131,491 (to which 500,000 military internees were soon added)

—*Source: Nbg. Dok. NG-447, NG-940, NG-1153 and NG-3996.*

[410] Hitler had made such an assertion on several occasions, as confirmed by Göring and Ribbentrop, whereas the English and the Italians rightfully denied such a connection. It is correct that the mutual assistance pact between England and Poland was indeed signed on the afternoon of August 25, 1939, when Mussolini, who had been undecided until the last minute, was persuaded by his foreign policy consultants to have a thinly veiled refusal delivered to Berlin. This made it clear that the Italians declined entry into the war, at least for the moment. However, the two events have their own independent history: the English-Polish negotiations on one hand (the English guarantee of Poland's sovereignty on March 31, 1939) and the Roman indecisiveness concerning participation in the war on the other. It is true, however, that London was very well informed about the behind-the-scenes fighting in Rome and the uncertain Italian attitude, so that when Mussolini finally made the decision in the morning or at noon of that day, the English were probably very quickly informed of its content. But there is no evidence that the signing of the pact, which had been pressed by the Polish party and delayed by England, was speeded up by news from Rome, especially by the events that had taken place in Palazzo Venezia one or two hours earlier. To what extent the British attitude was reinforced by Italy dissociating itself from its Axis ally is hard to say, as it is difficult to identify intangible factors in

the piles of relevant documents. But one thing is clear: between "Munich" and August 1939, there had been the "Kristallnacht" and the entry of Hitler's forces into Prague.—*Source: Hofer, pp. 81 and 107; Ciano, pp. 130 and 136; Documents 3/ VII, pp, 168, 220, 224 and 249; IMT (in German) IX, p. 660; Ribbentrop, p. 187.*

411 The reference is to the Italian battleship *Vittorio Veneto.*

412 Reference to the orders to be prepared by the Armed Forces Operations Staff in the event of a turnaround in Italy. Because of the anticipated blockade of the straits of Sicily and Messina, ships sailing on behalf of the Germans had to get out to the eastern Mediterranean in good time.

413 Those units of the 1st Panzer Parachute Division *Hermann Göring* that had not stayed in Tunis were scattered across Sicily, southern Italy and southern France.

414 Kesselring, who disagreed with Rommel and Keitel, was correct. When it happened in August, in spite of strong enemy pressure, all four German divisions crossed the straits, taking the bulk of their material along. This success was due to the skillful and lasting destruction of the withdrawal routes in the area of Messina, which were filled with numerous man-made obstacles.

415 Giuseppe Bastianini; born 1899; journalist; early member of the Fascist party; 1921 Deputy Secretary General of the Fascist Party; 1923 member of the Fascist Grant Council; 1927 joined the Foreign Service (Envoy in Tangiers, Lisbon and Athens, Ambassador to Warsaw); 1938 Undersecretary of State for Foreign Affairs; October 1939 to June 1940 Ambassador in London as Grandi's successor; May 1941 appointed Governor of Dalmatia; and after February 1943 after Ciano's dismissal he served again under Mussolini as Undersecretary of State for Foreign Affairs. As early as Mussolini's visit to Klessheim in April 1943, Bastianini had unsuccessfully tried to make it clear to Ribbentrop that Italy could not continue the war. Perhaps Hitler's aversion dates back to that period. Bastianini survived the war; a Yugoslav request to extradite him in December 1947 was not granted.—*Source: Munzinger Archive; Wiskemann, p. 296.*

416 On the day of this meeting, May 20, 1943, Undersecretary of State Bastianini gave a speech at the Senate Foreign Relations Committee on the occasion of the budget deliberations for 1943-44. He said (excerpts commented on by Hitler): "Once again, it is necessary to emphasize the importance of the fundamental principles to which Italy and Germany wish to remain faithful in order to lay the foundations of the new world order. The small states will not be oppressed in any way by the great powers. Their distinctive national qualities will not be eliminated or restricted… Our policies have always defended this principle of nationality, for the others as well as for ourselves, and it was never our goal to oppress or enslave other European peoples. Italy has always been the first to speak out against territorial injustices and unequal administration of law… Our country did not join the war with the intention of or the stupid ambition to impose this or that political institution on the peoples of different races; rather, we were imbued with the ideal of genuine justice and fairness that is directly related to the Word of God in which we believe…Italy is not in the habit of renouncing her honor—the only possession of poor peoples. From Novara to the Piave it has had a king and an army to defend it. In view of the terrorist methods employed by our enemies,

who expect an unconditional surrender—which can only be imposed on rebellious tribes—we invoke everything our people did in order to become a nation. Italian-French relations are grounded in the principles formulated by Italy and Germany as the basis of the new European and world order. We do not intend to destroy or humiliate France. However, in order to be able to take part in the reconstruction of Europe, France must understand the need to make sacrifices and not only to take part in the production and the military effort of the Axis countries, but also to settle all matters that are still pending in her relationship with her conquerors."—*Source: NZZ of May 20, 1943 (evening issue)*.

[417] Regarding his conduct and the measures to be taken in his area of command in the Balkans in the event that Italy collapsed.

[418] As indicated in a memorandum written by Speer in the fall of the following year, chromium, which was required for the production of high-grade steel, was a bottleneck for the Germans, while the supplies of copper, nickel and bauxite were sufficient for the time being.—*Source: Wilmot, p. 466.*

[419] Rintelen was to deliver a letter from Hitler that he had received as a telegram regarding the matter of Pirzio Biroli. In his reply, Mussolini covered the Italian generals, stating that they only carried out his orders and that he was responsible for their actions.—*Source: Rintelen, p. 202.*

[420] When Austria's annexation by Germany was accepted without opposition by Italy, the Great Power most directly concerned, Hitler sent a telegram to Rome on March 13, 1938, "Mussolini, I will never forget this!"

[421] In May 1938.

[422] Count Galeazzo Ciano; born March 18, 1903, as the scion of a politically important family from Leghorn; early member of the Fascist party; entered the diplomatic corps in 1925; married Edda Mussolini in May 1930; 1934 Undersecretary of State for Press and Propaganda; 1935 served as Air Captain in Ethiopia; and June 1936 to February 1943 Foreign Minister, then ambassador to the Vatican and member of the Fascist Grand Council. There, on July 25, 1943, he voted against his father-in-law. Nevertheless, he and his entire family were placed under house arrest by the Badoglio administration. With German assistance, he escaped to Germany at the end of August, and there he initially made amends with Mussolini, who had been liberated in the meantime. Later, though, after his return to his home country—probably at the urging of family and friends—Mussolini had him and the other disloyal members of the Fascist Great Council tried by a special court in Verona. There, Ciano was sentenced to death on January 11, 1944, and executed that same day. Attempts by his wife Edda to buy his life—in exchange for the delivery of his dreaded diary—failed.—*Source: Munzinger Archive; Anfuso, passim (especially p. 258).* [NDT: see also Galeazzo Ciano, *Diary 1937-1943*, Enigma 2002, the complete edition, edited by Renzo De Felice; Ray Moseley, *Mussolini's Shadow: The Double Life of Count Galeazzo Ciano*, Yale 1999]

[423] Philip, Prince of Hesse, from the family of the Electors of Hesse whose property was confiscated in 1866; nephew of Kaiser Wilhelm II; born November 6, 1896; 1915 joined the Army as a private; 1918 discharged as a lieutenant; after 1922 worked in Rome as an interior designer; 1925 married Princess Mafalda of

Italy, daughter of King Victor Emmanuel III; 1930 joined the NSDAP [Nazi Party]; June 1933 to September 1943 served as Senior President of Hesse-Nassau; and 1938 SA Obergruppenführer. Hitler sent Philip to Rome as a courier on several occasions, especially to announce unexpected foreign policy moves. After the defection of Italy, he was arrested at the Führer Headquarters by Rattenhuber and Müller on September 8, 1943, and spent the rest of the war in the concentration camps of Flossenbürg and Dachau.—*Source: Munziger Archive.*

424 Mafalda; royal princess of Savoy; born on November 11, 1902; daughter of Victor Emmanuel III of Italy; and after September 23, 1925, wife of Prince Philip of Hesse. After the abolition of the Italian royalty, Hitler had the princess, who was in Rome at that time, arrested. She was lured to the German Embassy under the pretext of a telephone call from the prince, driven to the airport on the alleged request of her husband, and put on a waiting airplane and flown to Germany. She died in the Buchenwald concentration camp on August 28, 1944, from injuries sustained during a recent Anglo-American air raid on the camp.

425 Since the end of September 1942, Mussolini, who had previously had a stomach ulcer, had again been plagued by severe stomach trouble. For a considerable amount of time, he could take only liquid food, and suffered a significant physical decline.—*Source: Rintelen, p. 218; Ciano, Diary, numerous notations of Mussolini's ailments in 1942-1943, pp. 548, 549, 552, 553, 554, 555, 559, 563, 567.*

426 Unless the stenographer misheard, this was a "echte Fehlleistung" (a real slip), as Mussolini certainly addressed Hitler as "Führer" and not "My Führer."

427 Hitler's ideal was a leader who would stand out both because of his firm political and ideological attitude and his excellent military skills—more or less the type of leader the Waffen SS sought to develop.

428 According to Italian reports, Mussolini must have mentioned his domestic concerns to Hitler for the first time when he visited Berchtesgaden in January 1941. The Duce, who had been reduced to a mere "wing man," could not get over—according to Anfuso—confiding in a friendly, condescending foreigner. The reawakening of a certain anti-German resentment in Mussolini dates back to that time. Ciano noted in his diary on January 20, 1941, "Mussolini said that he brought Hitler up to date on Italian matters, including the undecided attitude of the King, which, however, has no influence and finally also about the Badoglio case, which Hitler compared to the Fritsche case." It must not have been easy for a dictator, speaking "among colleagues," to admit that he was a "paper tiger." The comment of October 28, 1940, to which Hitler last referred, may only have been intended as motivation for the attack on Greece.—*Source: Anfuso, p. 143; Ciano, p. 415.*

429 Colonel Pavle Djuršic was one of Mihailović's subordinates and the commanding officer of the Četnik units in Montenegro. Djuršic, who—as is shown by this comment—had already cooperated with the Italians, was among the first Četnik leaders to conclude an agreement with the Nedic Administration in the fall of 1943, following the re-orientation of the German Balkan policies under Neubacher. In those September days, all the national Serbian forces, including

the Serbian State Guard and the Nedic Administration's Serbian Volunteer Corps, actually united under Draza Mihailović.—*Source: Matl: Jugoslawien, p. 111; Fotitch, p. 164; Kiszling, p. 183.*

[430] Another one of Hitler's allusions to the German-Italian disputes which should have been settled at "the highest level": a battalion of Četniks, led by a Montenegrin brother-in-law or nephew of the Italian king, had been taken prisoner by German forces some time before.

[431] Prince (1860–1910), later (until 1918) King Nikolaus or Nikola (mistakenly called Nikita most of the time) of Montenegro, born 1841, died 1921. Gained independence from Turkey in 1876-78 and added territory to his country. Later, he followed the Russian political line more and more closely, which may explain the resentment that Hitler—who, after all, was an Austrian—expressed here. The king immediately sided with Serbia in August 1914, but after the occupation of his country he concluded a special peace treaty with Austria—which he later revoked on Allied urging. In November 1918 he unsuccessfully opposed the unification of Montenegro with Serbia (Yugoslavia), which had been decided by the Yugoslav parliament. Nikolaus became famous for his private war against Skutari after the end of the First Balkan War, when he took the town in contravention of the decision made by the Great Powers (and probably by bribing the commanding officer) and, with his intransigent attitude, again raised the specter of a world war. Nikolaus yielded surprisingly, and, as a result of his bull market maneuvering, earned millions from a stock market speculation. He also became known as a clever father, since the husbands of the seven daughters of this "sheep thief" included King Peter I of Serbia, Grand Prince Nikolai Nikolievitch, and, finally—this is the reason for Hitler mentioning it—Victor Emmanuel III.

[432] Emperor Franz Joseph had made generous gifts to King Nikolaus of Montenegro on various occasions. In view of the emperor's sense of propriety, it can hardly be assumed that he was prepared to cover the Montenegrin's supposed fraudulent activities at the Universal Postal Union from his own private coffers. Hitler liked to tell anecdotes and make up stories for the officers at his headquarters— who had very little knowledge of Austrian affairs—in order to give the impression that he had a profound understanding of the Balkan political background. Hitler never seriously dealt with the problems of the multinational Habsburg Empire, although he occasionally purported to be an expert on issues relating to the Danube region.

[433] General Ferenc Szombathelyi was the Honved [Hungarian] Chief of Staff from September 1941 to March 1944.

[434] At this time, Rommel was beginning the establishment of his "Munich Labor and Rehabilitation Staff," later known as Army Group B, which was initially intended to lead Operation *Alaric*, as Hitler planned to have Kesselring replaced by Rommel at a suitable time. In July the decision was made to present this change to Mussolini at Feltre as part of the general reorganization of the command structure in Italy. Göring and Ambassador v. Mackensen, in particular, succeeded in changing Hitler's view at the very last minute before his departure. They argued that Rommel, who was regarded as the person responsible for the

loss of Libya, would not be welcome in Italy. So the topic "change of command" was not discussed at Feltre; the status quo was maintained for the time being, and Rommel was earmarked for the Balkans a few days later.

[435] While "residual France" was being conquered after the landing of Anglo-American forces in North Africa in November 1942, the Italians took over the securing of the French Mediterranean coast and the hinterland up to a point west of Toulon.

[436] General Gastone Gambara commanded the corps of Italian volunteers in Spain and served as ambassador in Madrid until Italy joined the war in June 1940. After October 1941 he was Chief of General Staff with Marshal Bastico in Libya, where he had several disputes with Rommel—some of which were personal in nature, but others concerned fundamental strategic differences. An investigation instituted by his personal nemesis, the chief of the *Comando Supremo*, Ugo Cavallero, because of incidents during the war in Spain, resulted in Gambara's dismissal in March 1942. After having held a command post in Bolzano for a short while, he was put up for consideration for a new command. Although Gambara had emerged untainted from the proceedings, he was not given another front line command. After the Italian defection, Gambara and Marshal Graziani put themselves at the disposal of Mussolini, although, strangely enough, another reason for Gambara's dismissal in Libya had been an offhand remark made at the officers' mess, "I hope I live long enough to lead an Italian army to Berlin." Gambara was married to a woman from South Tyrol. Before the Italian capitulation, the German side suspected him of cooperating with the Allies.—*Source: Ciano, p. 449; Anfuso, p. 310; Rommel Papers, pp. 152, 171, 175, 178 and 186.*

[437] General Enea Navarini commanded the Italian XXI Corps in Africa and, in contrast to Gambara, was highly valued by Rommel.—*Source: Rommel Papers, pp. 253, 357 and elsewhere; Westphal, p. 199.*

[438] According to instructions given by the Armed Forces High Command, Rommel was to prepare his own more detailed orders for a possible assumption of the High Command in Italy. Keitel's remark does not apply to Warlimont's preceding comment, but follows on his own earlier remarks.

[439] Transcript number unknown—Fragment No. 48—One of the two shorthand records was completely destroyed, while the other was so severely damaged that only part of each page could be deciphered. The first transcript had consisted of some 35 typewritten pages. The date of the meeting was determined on the basis of the events reported. It certainly must have taken place between May 17 and 24, as the dates on pp. 243 and 244 indicate.

[440] These comments were probably prompted by the British air raids on the Eder, Möhne and Sorpe dams a few days before.

[441] Against partisans operating in the rear area.

[442] The 1st SS Panzer Division *Leibstandarte Adolf Hitler*, which at that time was still commanded by Sepp Dietrich, was set aside for use either in the planned attack in the Kursk area or in Italy.

[443] The 7th SS Volunteer Mountain Division *Prinz Eugen* was established in the Serbian Banat in late 1941. The division's first commander was the former Ro-

manian division general Artur Phleps, who had joined the Waffen SS as a volunteer; the troops were composed of 15,000 ethnic Germans from the Southeast regions. The term "volunteer division" was soon significant only for psychological and propaganda reasons, as the character of the volunteer unit was officially revoked as early as 1942, and all ethnic Germans living in the Serbian Banat were drafted on threat of punishment. The inconsistent prior training the troops had received in the various armies caused considerable difficulty, and also the weapons consisted primarily of captured weapons of diverse origins. In October 1942 the division was used on Ibar for the first time and fought bravely until the end of the war, but not without the customary atrocities against Yugoslav partisans that were the trademark of other troops fighting in the Balkans. In July 1943, together with three Army divisions and the Muslims of the 13th Waffen SS Mountain Division *Handschar*, the division was merged into the V SS Mountain Corps commanded by SS Obergruppenführer Phleps.—*Source: Hausser, p.106 and elsewhere; Krätschmer, p. 203; Nbg. Dok. NO-1649.*

[444] Name of an Italian division.

[445] Bulgaria was also an occupation force in Yugoslavia. The southernmost part of the territory—northern Macedonia and a strip of southeastern Serbia—was placed under Bulgarian civil administration by the Germans in 1941. The Bulgarian occupation zone remained generally free of partisans until the end of the war; however, at German request, units of the Bulgarian occupation corps, whose strength was equivalent to several divisions, took part in the fighting in other areas.

[446] Originally established by and reporting directly to the Defense/Foreign Detachment of the Armed Forces High Command, this detachment, initially the 800th Training Regiment for Special Duty, was made up of hand-picked, specially trained staff and was responsible for the administration and pooling of military agents, and later also for special missions, commando operations and acts of sabotage behind enemy lines. This unit was also known as the *Brandenburg* Regiment because the core established in the spring of 1939—originally just a company which had been enlarged to battalion strength (800th Construction Training Battalion) by 1941—had General Ordnance Services barracks in Brandenburg on the Havel. The unit was made up of volunteers, including numerous ethnic Germans living outside the Reich; parts of it were put at the disposal of army groups when required. When military developments caused the preconditions for commando operations to deteriorate after early 1943, the bulk of *Brandenburg* was employed against partisans in the Southeastern theater, while only individual battalions stayed on in Russia, Italy and southern France in 1943-44. These units, in contrast to their original purpose, were also increasingly deployed as regular infantry units. During the last years of the war, the regiment was expanded to a panzer grenadier division; it included— in addition to a legion battalion, a coastal fighter detachment, and an intelligence detachment, and the 1st through 4th *Brandenburg* Regiments. A 5th regiment—the *Kurfürst* training regiment, which had been given the original tasks of the *Brandenburger*—became independent.—*Source: Koch: Division Brandenburg, passim; Kriegsheim, passim; Görlitz II, p. 75; Order of Battle, p. 312.*

[447] The local command of the Italian occupation forces in this economically important area, which formed part of the Italian occupation zone, refused at that time not only to take part in joint actions against the strong groups of partisans operating in the area, but even threatened to prevent the entry of German troops into the Italian zone by force of arms. The reason for this very unusual behavior between allies was the quiet deal-making between the Italians and the Četniks. Italy, which as early as 1941 had been anything but confident of victory, intended to try to retain as much influence as possible in the Balkans, and erect a barrier against the frightening German aspirations. Because the Italians also held the view that they would not be able to defeat both enemies—Četniks and Communists—at the same time, the idea of establishing contacts with the Četniks presented itself. These contacts resulted initially in local truces and later on in actual alliances. In addition, the practice developed among the Italians of exchanging their prisoners for food and ammunition. This resulted in serious German-Italian friction, as the Italian-occupied parts of Yugoslavia (Montenegro, New Albania, western Croatia) were seen as "soft spots" and were naturally preferred by partisans as concentration zones. In September 1943, 16 to 18 battle-weary Italian divisions capitulated in that area. These divisions were so demoralized that for the most part they did not want to wait for the Allies' arrival, which was expected by their commanders, but just discarded their weapons.—*Source: Yourichitch, p. 49; Ciano; Fotitch, p. 208.*

[448] During the war, Turkey maneuvered between the British demand to join the war (based on the English-Turkish Assistance Agreement of 1939), the fear of a German invasion, and the fears of a Soviet victory. At the Adana conference on January 30-31, 1943, between Churchill and President Inönü and several high-ranking military officers, Turkey once again managed to resist British pressure, but did accept military assistance. The Turkish national assembly gave in to the pressure of the Allies only in the final stages of the war, and broke off diplomatic relations with the German Reich on August 2, 1944. Hitler, on the other hand, whose original concept had been based on maximum quiet in the Balkans— quiet which had been disturbed in an unwelcome and embarrassing way by Mussolini's unsuccessful raid against Greece—never really considered operations against Turkey. The situation would have become awkward for Turkey only if the German pincer movement against the Near East had not been forced open at El Alamein and Stalingrad.—*Source: Papen, p. 515; Churchill IV / 2, p. 324.*

[449] The Bristol *Beaufighter* was an English twin-engine two-seater fighter, with four guns and six machine guns, 500 km/h. *Beaufighters*, first deployed in early 1941, were mainly used as night interceptors and light bombers.—*Source: Hébrard, p. 329; Feuchter, pp. 172 and 183.*

[450] The Handley Page *Hampden*, a medium-range two-engine bomber, was one of the RAF's standard bombers (six machine guns, top speed 425 km/h) in the early years of the war, before the advent of four-engine bombers. By late 1941, Hampdens were no longer deployed in sorties against the Reich, but

were mainly used for convoy and coastal protection and as transport planes. The reference here is to the first attacks with *Beaufighter* planes against German convoys off the southwestern Norwegian coast between May 13 and 16, 1943. Before then, the older and slower *Hampden* was mainly deployed in that area.—*Source: Hébrard, p. 192; Feuchter, pp. 98, 183 and 216.*

[451] The protection of convoys—and the leapfrogging deployment this required—and maritime reconnaissance required quite a great deal of fuel. Fuel had been rationed as early as 1942 for Luftwaffe training. Explicit orders had also been given to reduce private flights and travel, etc., so as to save fuel. On the front, however, economy measures were probably not ordered before 1944.

[452] A reference to the Knaben molybdenum mines near the Flekke Fjord between Stavanger and Kristiansand, which, after the loss of North Africa—were the only molybdenum deposits controlled by the Germans (molybdenum is required to harden steel, especially in the production of armor plating). The Knaben works were attacked by two Mosquito units on March 3. While the actual mines remained intact, the ore washing plant and the crushing installation were destroyed, and five civilians, including the German manager, were killed. The pre-war output of this mine reached 700,000 tons, and that figure had increased in the meantime. Two-thirds of the output was made available to the German armaments industry, while one-third had to be supplied to Sweden, as the Swedish Johnson group held the majority of the shares in the mine.—*Source: NZZ of March 5, 1943 (evening edition).*

[453] From a technical point of view, the German anti-aircraft artillery was certainly up-to-date and perhaps even superior to the weapons developed by the enemy. The German artillery was successful against daylight precision attacks flown in clear weather, but was initially almost powerless against nighttime terror attacks—following the elimination of radar equipment through the Düppel process—and even later was effective only to a limited extent. However, the guns developed at the beginning of the war were no match for the technical developments in enemy aircraft design, particularly where altitude and speed were concerned. A more effective massed deployment of the newly developed guns with their high v_0 (e.g., 1,000 in the 8.8-cm anti-aircraft gun 41, compared with 820 in the 8.8-cm anti aircraft guns 18, 36 and 37) failed, like so many other things, because of the limited production capacity of the German armament industry. The bottleneck affected primarily the ammunition sector, as the strong armor of enemy planes required larger calibers (increased use of the 10.5-cm anti-aircraft gun 39 and 12.8-cm anti-aircraft gun 40), despite the German gunpowder shortage. Remote control and rocket supplements were also hampered by the shortage of raw materials; the German anti-aircraft rockets *Schmetterling* ["Butterfly"], *Wasserfall* ["Waterfall"] *Rheintochter* ["Daughter of the Rhine"], *Enzian* ["Gentian"], and *Feuerlilie* ["Fire Lily"] did not advance beyond the trial stage. From the tactical point of view, it should be pointed out that one battery, even if it has maximum mobility, could only protect one particular object—meaning that in a target area as

large as Germany, the protection of any given site always took place at the expense of other potential targets. Enemy bombers frequently attacked unprotected locations for this very reason, so as to establish new focal areas. This gave rise to the impression that the mobile anti-aircraft forces were "chasing" the attacks. During the last year of the war, the key armament industry sites were transformed into "anti-aircraft artillery fortifications," at the expense of less important potential targets. These sites were built up to include as many as 900 guns (Leuna, Heydebrack). In the meantime, the light and medium anti-aircraft artillery—a total of 6,000 guns at the beginning of the war—had grown to more than 40,000 guns at the end of the war, while the heavy anti-aircraft artillery was up from 2,600 to 15,000 guns. Hitler's comments must not hide the fact that he was always convinced of the value of anti-aircraft artillery, and always—unless his decisions were moderated by the senior military commanders—gave it priority until the very end, even at the expense of other weapons.—*Source: Koch: Flak, passim; Lusar, p. 38; Feuchter, p. 304; Baumbach, p. 216; Hébrard, p. 433.*

454 The 4-cm Bofors was a captured anti-aircraft gun. With regard to the 3-cm gun, this was probably either misheard or written down incorrectly; he probably referred to the 3.7-cm German gun. The designations 3/4 and 4/5 meant that these made up 3 or 4 platoons of the total battery.

455 Experts deemed anti-aircraft barrage fire—one of Hitler's favorite ideas— feasible only in cases where no measurement data were available. So barrage-fire zones were established for certain barrage-fire batteries, i.e., captured heavy batteries, which were not equipped with anti-aircraft directors. In addition, when streams of bombers approached—the technique was useless against individual small formations—other batteries could also be forced to shoot barrage fire without sighting by using the Düppel technique or active interference with radar devices; however, this type of fire was regarded more as a measure aimed at pacifying the civilian population and the operational headquarters than as effective defense. In contrast to Hitler's insistence—in principle not unjustified—on keeping the enemy away from certain objects, the ambitious anti-aircraft gunners, who wanted to score as many hits as possible, pointed out—out of consideration for the morale of the troops—that bringing down a plane was the best form of defense, and that attempts to create a psychological effect through mere firing was futile, particularly against the later, primarily instrument-flown attacks. Motivated by Hitler's frequent insistence on barrage fire, the Luftwaffe officers that summer calculated a "barrage fire cube," which indicated the number of rounds required to protect a space against enemy bomber formations. For a formation that was 2 km wide, 3 km deep and had an altitude variation of 1 km, 6 million shells would have to be fired simultaneously—i.e., 6 million guns would have been required. With object protection provided by 200 guns, the chances were 1:30,000 that the enemy formation would be hit. Even when effective anti-aircraft centers were eventually established, it was argued that directed fire from 30 or more batteries produced barrage fire as a secondary effect.

[456] The Luftwaffe's anti-aircraft artillery indeed put great store in shooting rather too long than too short, if it was not possible to reach the target exactly, because in that case the trajectories cross the target area, creating at least the opportunity for a direct hit. In addition, the above-mentioned difference could also have been due to the different types of fire control predictors, and, last but not least, to personnel. While the Navy anti-aircraft artillery, up to the very end, had active personnel with complete Navy training, the Luftwaffe anti-aircraft artillery had eventually become the largest branch in the Armed Forces, comprising 1,190,000 "men." But because the majority of the active personnel had to be released for ground duty or for the Luftwaffe field divisions, prisoners of war, women and children made up a large percentage of this figure. Thus, in reality, about half of the personnel were practically unusable.

[457] In Kiel.

[458] Target range and arms school of the Luftwaffe anti-aircraft artillery in Mecklenburg (already renamed "Rerik" at that time).

[459] In the first months of 1943, quite a few night air raids against harbors on the North African coast were flown from southern France and Italy, also resulting in the destruction of a number of Allied troopships.

[460] The renaming of Air Command East into Air Force 6 was done by order of the Luftwaffe Commander-in-Chief on May 11, 1943. Apparently (see above note 439), this modification was made effective about 10 days later.

[461] Draft orders of the Armed Forces Operations Staff in the event of Italy's defection or collapse (*Alaric* for the Italian area, *Konstantin* for the Balkans.

[462] Reference to the Commander-in-Chief West. The Fourth Italian Army was deployed in his area on the French Mediterranean coast.

[463] Phillip, Prince of Hesse.

[464] If a meeting between Hitler and Mussolini was considered here—as it appears—it did not take place at that time. Altogether the two dictators met seventeen times:

June 14-15, 1934	Venice
September 25-29, 1937	Munich, Essen, Berlin
May 3-9, 1938	Rome, Naples, Florence
September 29, 1938	Munich (Munich Conference)
March 18, 1940	Brenner
June 18, 1940	Munich
October 4, 1940	Brenner
October 28, 1940	Florence (originally planned for November 6; advanced because of the Italian adventure in Greece)
January 19-20, 1941	Berchtesgaden
June 2, 1941	Brenner
August 25-29, 1941	Rastenburg, Lemberg, Uman (visit to the Army Group Rundstedt and the CSIR)
April 29-30, 1942	Klessheim

(A meeting scheduled for mid-December 1942 was cancelled because Hitler didn't want to leave Rastenburg, and Mussolini, who was annoyed, pretended to be sick and sent Ciano instead.)

April 7-10, 1943	Klessheim
July 19, 1943	Feltre
September 14, 1943	Rastenburg (after Mussolini's liberation)
April 22-23, 1944	Klessheim
July 20, 1944	Rastenburg (after the assassination attempt)

—*Source: Wiskemann, passim; Anfuso, passim; Ciano, passim; VB.* [See also, Santi Corvaja, *Hitler and Mussolini: The Secret Meetings*, Enigma 2000.]

[465] This transcript is not from the Berchtesgaden collection. It seems to be a surplus copy for the quartermaster's department of the Armed Forces Operations Staff (see also Hitler's remark during his meeting with Field Marshal Keitel and General Zeitzler, June 8, 1943: "Perhaps with the aid of today's shorthand report..."). It bears the circulation stamp of this department and the initials of the Deputy Head of the Armed Forces Operations Staff, General Warlimont, Colonel Baron Treusch v. Buttlar-Brandefels for the Army Operations Department, Colonel v. Tippelskirch for the Quartermaster's Department, and also the officials of this department. The document, which was incorporated into the Nuremberg series and was given number 1384-PS, is incomplete. On the last available page (27), the last line was transferred—obviously from the following page—by handwriting, most likely by Warlimont. The adjournment time is missing. This transcript was published in German by George Fischer in the *Journal of Modern History* (Chicago) vol. XXIII, no. 1 (p. 62), and in English as Appendix II to his book *Soviet Opposition to Stalin*, Cambridge (Mass.) 1952, p. 176.

[466] Aside from the closed "domestic" formations that were established later, the German field troops in the East had tried from the very beginning to replace some of their losses on-site by using Soviet prisoners of war as interpreters, grooms, cannoneers, baggage drivers, kitchen aids, craftsmen, etc., in their units. In the middle of 1943, the number of these "Hiwis" (Hilfswillige—auxiliary volunteers) was, according to Herre, about 320,000 men, with 70 to 80% of them being used as noncombatants. In the rear services, the "Hiwi" portion of the overall personnel was often 50% or more; in the combat units, one could find up to 20% auxiliary volunteers. During the course of the war, the "Hiwis" reached at least an approximate equalization under law with the German soldiers. In the present discussion, Zeitzler gives the number of auxiliary volunteers as only 220,000; however, he may have had every reason to keep that figure as low as possible when discussing it with Hitler. The statement given by Schmundt that the Eighteenth Army alone had 47,000 auxiliary volunteers, also contributes to the greater credibility of the figure mentioned above by Herre. A list compiled by the staff of the generals of the Eastern troops that same month (June 1943) also included the estimated number of those "Hiwis" who were concealed by the units; it estimated 600,000 auxiliary volunteers. The largest

number estimated is that of 1 million auxiliary volunteers, a few months before the end of war.—*Source: Thorwald: Wen sie ..., pp. 129 and 245; Heinz Danko Herre: Deutsche Erfahrungen in der Verwendung von Kriegsgefangenen gegen die Sowjetunion (Thorwald materials in the IfZ); Ernst Köstring: Erfahrungen mit den Freiwilligen aus dem russischen Raum im Kampf gegen den Bolschewismus 1941-45 (Thorwald materials in the IfZ); Dallin, pp. 536 and others; Fischer, p. 45.*

[467] Andrei Andreewich Vlasov; born September 1, 1900; in Lomakino near Nizhnyi Novgorod; 1919 Red Army; 1930 Communist Party member; 1938-39 military adviser to Chiang Kai-shek; 1939 Commander, 99th Rifle Division; 1941 Commanding General, 4th Tank Corps and defender of Kiev; then, Commander, 20th Army under Zhukov as defender of Moscow; Lieutenant General after the battle of Rzhev; and March 1942 Deputy Commander, Volkhov Front and Commander, 2nd Shock Army. There, Vlasov was captured in June or July when he tried to lead his army in an escape from encirclement south of Leningrad. His group was encircled and gradually destroyed. This experience made him an anti-Bolshevist, and he put himself at the disposal of the Germans, with the aim of overthrowing the Soviet system from the head of a Russian National Army. On September 10, 1942, he signed the first leaflet that was dropped over the Russian lines. That same month, accommodations were provided for him in Berlin, and German military agencies began to promote Vlasov's plans. The entire action, which in late fall led to the formation of a "Experimental Central Unit"—which was dissolved by Field Marshal v. Kluge in December—had to be organized with extreme caution. Considerable difficulties could be expected from the disclosure of the unit's activities—both from Rosenberg's Ministry for the East, which pursued a policy of "decomposition" of the Eastern area by promoting the minorities, and from Hitler and his headquarters, where Vlasov was viewed as a mere pawn to be shifted on the propaganda chessboard.—*Source: Fischer, p. 26; Thorwald: Wen sie..., p. 135.*

[468] Operation "Silberstreifen" ("Silver Stripe") was a large-scale desertion-promotion action planned by the Foreign/Defense Intelligence Office. It was intended to support the spring offensive near Kursk, and was to start simultaneously with the military action. The organizers had prepared 18 million leaflets, which they intended to drop along the entire Eastern Front. "Leaflet No. 13" had been written specifically for this purpose; it contained general phrases and a printed pass. They also intended—and the originators of the plan expected the most from this—to drop older leaflets from the so-called Smolensk Committee, in which the opinions of the Vlasov people on the reconstruction of Russia were stated. "Leaflet No. 13" was countersigned by General Gehlen and also approved by Zeitzler, while the rest of the plan, including a personal assignment for General Vlasov, was forbidden by the German leadership. Because the offensive against Kursk also had to be postponed, "Silberstreifen" was launched separately during the night May 6, 1943. It was a failure. Only a few hundred deserters turned themselves in along the entire Eastern front.—*Source: Heinz Danko Herre: Die Aktion Silberstreif (Thorwald materials in the IfZ); Thorwald: Wen sie..., p. 220; Dallin, p. 570).*

[469] This sentence is deleted by hand in document 1384-PS.

[470] This part of the text was subsequently corrected in document 1384-PS. The original version read: "...That is Leaflet 13." Regarding Leaflet No. 13.

[471] Number "13" is deleted by hand in document 1384-PS.

[472] The position "General of the Eastern Troops" (later "General of the Volunteer Units") in the Army High Command was established in mid-December 1942 as inspector of the Hiwis [auxiliary volunteers] and volunteer units from the East. The General of the Eastern Troops was initially General Heinz Hellmich (1941 Commander of the 21st Infantry Division, replaced before Moscow and from then on commander of a reserve division in Poland), who had been in Russian captivity and had learned adequate Russian. Hellmich was replaced by General of Cavalry Köstring at the end of 1943. As field agencies, there were "Commanders of the Eastern Troops seconded for special duty" in the army groups, the armies and the Armed Forces Commands.—*Source: Thorwald: Wen sie..., pp. 126, 248 and 322; Fischer, p. 45; Dallin, p. 543.*

[473] On March 30, 1940, the Japanese had proclaimed a so called "National Government of the Peoples Republic of China" headed by Wang Ching-wei, a former friend of Sun Yat-sen and deputy of Chiang Kai-shek who had been expelled from the Kuomintang Party because of his pro-Japanese and pro-surrender position. Although this satellite government appointed a Minister of War and a Chief of General Staff on August 23, 1942, and formally declared war on England and the United States on January 9, 1943, Hitler's comment might not have been too far off the mark. After Wang's death on November 10, 1944, the "National Government" faded away until the Japanese surrender, unnoticed and insignificant.—*Source: Jones/Borton/Pearn, p. 13; Schulthess 1939-40; Keesing's Archive 1940-1944.*

[474] Since the beginning of World War I, a "Polish Legion" consisting of three brigades—led, for all practical purposes, by Pilsudski (de jure Commander of the 1st Brigade)—had fought Russia within the framework of the Austro-Hungarian Army. After the proclamation of a Polish satellite state by the Central Powers on November 5, 1916, the Central Powers tried to use the Polish forces for the further benefit of the German-Austrian war effort by forming a Polish Army. The collapse of Tsarist Russia in the following year and the Bolshevist renunciation of Poland, however, thwarted these plans, as the Polish could be offered better chances in the other camp now. On February 15, 1918, after the Treaty of Brest-Litovsk, the last Polish unit, the 2nd Brigade, crossed over to the other side in the Bukovina region. The Polish change of sides was not in the least caused by machinations of the legionnaires. It took place rather inevitably because the Poles had chosen the lesser of two evils, and now that the greater one had disappeared, they naturally started trying to do away with the lesser one as well. Nevertheless, the situation of the Eastern volunteers was, of course, somewhat similar.—*Source: Komarnicki, p. 91.*

[475] Alfred Ingemar Berndt; born April 22, 1905; 1922 NSDAP; 1929 Editor at W.T.B; 1933, Editor-in-Chief of DNB; 1936 Ministerial Councilor in the Ministry of Propaganda and head of Dept. IVa (German Press) and Reich Deputy

Press Chief; 1938 Assistant Director and head of Dept. VIII (Literature); 1939-41 head of Dept. III (Broadcasting), Ministerial Director; 1941-44 head of Dept. II (Propaganda); 1941-43 Rommel's Ordnance Officer in Africa; 1943 Air War Damage Inspector; late 1944 Commander of a panzer unit of the Waffen SS; and died in Hungary on March 28, 1945.—*Source: Börsenblatt f. dt. Buchhandel of Dec. 29, 1938.*

[476] As the Russians were able to call up only a few age groups prior to their withdrawal, the number of men between 17 and 43 years of age who were available in Congress Poland and Polish Lithuania in 1916 was estimated at 1.4 million, in addition to 100,000 Poles in the German and Austrian prisoner-of-war camps. Indeed, Ludendorff, Falkenhayn, and other military leaders were particularly impressed with the idea of mobilizing these resources. Ludendorff wrote after the war that he, like Bethmann Hollweg, would have preferred to have made a special peace with Russia rather than allowing the Polish question to become serious, but he had not believed that this was a possibility.—*Source: Komarnicki, pp. 81 and 93; Bethmann Hollweg II, p. 94; Ludendorff, p. 313.*

[477] Erich Koch; born June 19, 1896; Business College; apprentice in business; Railway Assistant (1926 dismissed because of his membership in the NSDAP); 1922 NSDAP; 1928 Gauleiter of East Prussia and leader of a parliamentary group in the province's parliament; 1930 member of the Reichstag; 1933 Prussian State Counselor, June 9, 1933; Chief President of East Prussia; October 1941 also Reich Commissioner of the Ukraine; and late 1944 entrusted with the leadership of the Reich Commissariat for Ostland ["Eastern Territories"].

[478] On May 19 Hitler had received Rosenberg and the Reich Commissioner of the Ukraine, Gauleiter Koch, to discuss with them the dispute about the German policy in the East that had been smoldering between the two for some time. The cause of the disagreement was that Rosenberg was pursuing a political objective in the East (diminution of the Russian colossus through deliberate nationality-based policies and the relative promotion of the "minorities," especially Ukrainians), whereas Koch pursued a policy of pure colonialism and exploitation for the benefit of the German war economy—as Göring and Bormann also would have done. In the course of that discussion (during which Hitler generally took Koch's side), the Minister of the East was also forbidden to use "members of alien races" in his agency—meaning the emigrants with whom Rosenberg had maintained close contact since settling in Munich in 1919. Despite police prohibitions, he used many of these emigrants in his ministry—hundreds if not thousands of them in the Eastern regions.—*Source: Dallin, pp. 111 and 160.*

[479] The Ukrainian Hetman Paul Skoropadsky was head of a Ukrainian government under German occupation in 1918, and since then had been living as a prominent emigrant in Germany. This monarchist reactionary was a close acquaintance of Rosenberg from his time in Munich and received a not insignificant "honorary pay," as well as further financial support for propaganda purposes. He supported—in contrast to other leaders of the Ukrainian nationalists—Germany's policy in the Ukraine uninterruptedly until the end of the war.—*Source: Dallin, pp. 111, 114 and 622; Nbg. Doc. NG-3055 and NO-339.*

[480] Dr. Herbert Backe; born May 1, 1896 in Batum; interned during World War I; 1918 exchanged; 1923 NSDAP and. Diploma in Agriculture; 1924 Assistant at the Technical College of Hanover; 1927 administrator of a farm, later tenant farmer; 1932 member of the Prussian parliament; 1933 Undersecretary of State in the Reich Ministry of Agriculture and Food Supply, after the elimination of Darré in May 1942 manager; and from 1944 on in the rank of a Minister of the Reich. Backe committed suicide in Nuremberg on April 6, 1947.— *Source: Munzinger Archive.*

[481] One should bear in mind that behind the euphemisms "lose" and "take away" is concealed nothing less than a significant part of the infamous "Final Solution" to the Jewish question.

[482] A reliable compilation of all the Eastern battalions in the German Army is nearly impossible without the relevant Armed Forces files. However, an American list of the German Army units, dated 1945, gives a fairly complete overview of the total strength:

76 (Turk.)	403	556	622 (Cos.)	654 (Rus.)
94 "	404	557 Cos.	623 "	658 "
126 (Cos.)	406 (Rus.)	558 "	624 (Volga Tat.)	659 "
134 (Rus.)	407	560	625 "	660 "
198 (Georg.)	409 (Georg.)	561	626 "	661 "
213 (Cos.)	412 (Rus.)	570 (Cos.)	627 (Rus.)	662 "
229 (Rus.)	423	572 "	628 "	663 "
236	427 (Rus.)	574 "	629 "	664 (Tatar)
263 (Rus.)	429	580 "	630	665 (Rus.)
268 (Rus.)	439 (Rus.)	587	631 (Cos.)	666 "
274 (Rgt.)	441	600 (Rus.)	633 (Rus.)	667 "
282	443 (Cos.)	601 "	634 "	668 "
284	446 (Rus.)	602 "	635 "	669 "
295 (Turk.)	447 "	603"	636 (Georg.)	674 "
297 "	448	604 "	640 (Rus.)	680
305 "	450 (Turk.)	605"	642 "	681 (Rus.)
308 (Rus.)	452 "	612	643 "	687 "
339 "	454 (Rus.)	615 (Rus.)	646 "	690 "
350	456"	616 "	647 "	698
360 (Kos.; Rgt.)	469	617 "	648	727
370 (Turk.)	545 (Cav. Rgt.)	618 "	649 (Rus.)	729
371 "	550	619 "	651 "	776 (Turk.)
384 "	553	620 "	652	780 "
389 "	555		653 (Rus.)	781"
782 (Turk.)	796 (Georg.)	809 (Armen.)	822 (Georg.)	835 (N. Cauc.)
783 "	797 "	810 "	823 "	836 "
784 "	798 "	811 (Turk.)	824 "	837 "
785 "	799"	812 (Armen.)	825 (Tatar)	838 "
786 "	800 (N. Cauc.)	813 "	826 "	842 "

787	801 "	814 "	827 "	843 "
788 (Turk.)	802 "	815 "	828 "	844 "
789 "	803 "	816 "	829 "	868 (Azerb.)
790 "	804 (Azerb.)	817 (Azerb.)	830 (N. Cauc.)	871
791 "	805 "	818 "	831 (Tatar)	932
793 "	806 "	819 "	832 "	1059
794 "	807 "	820 "	833 "	
795 (Georg.)	808 (Armen.)	821 "	834 "	

According to an incomplete compilation of the structure of the domestic units, made by the Ministry of the East on January 24, 1945, nearly 600,000 members of the "Eastern peoples" served in armed German units. In detail they are as follows:

1.	Lithuanians (Army, Luftwaffe, police, RAD, OT)	36,800
2.	Latvians (SS, Army, police)	104,000
3.	Estonians (SS, police, border police, etc.)	10,000
4.	Turkish Tatars (Army, legion)	20,550
5.	Crimean Tatars (SS)	10,000
6.	Armenians (Army, SS)	7,000
7.	Azerbaijanis (legion, Army, SS)	36,500
8.	Georgians (legion, Army, SS, RSD)	19,000
9.	Kalmucks (SS, Army)	5,000
10.	Northern Caucasians (legion, Army, SS)	15,000
11.	Russians (ROA, Eastern battalions)	310,000
		573,850

This list does not contain, in addition to several splinter groups, the Cossacks (SS: XV Cossack Cavalry Corps, Domanov Regiments; Army: one brigade, three regiments, eleven battalions; police: one security regiment, five Schuma battalions), the huge number of HIWIS [auxiliary volunteers], or, probably, the Russian, Ukrainian and Belarus SS divisions. Thus, estimates of around 400,000 Eastern troops (excluding Hiwis) for early 1943—and the highest number of nearly 1 million a few months prior to the end of the war—might not be terribly exaggerated. (See also below notes 1200 and 1201.)—*Source: Order of Battle, p. 383; List of the units of volunteers from the East within the German Armed Forces (Thorwald Material in the IfZ); Nbg. Doc. NO-5800; Fischer, p. 45; Dallin, p.536.*

[483] It is unclear which field marshal is meant here. Either Kluge or Küchler could have been referred to in the context of "ahead."

[484] The head of Dept. I5 (Caucasus) in the Ministry of the East, Prof. v. Mende, had, as an ethnologist, many connections to emigrants, and had been in charge of several national committees (Turkestani, North Caucasian, Georgian, Armenian, Azerbaijani, Volga Tatar) since 1941-42. Some of these committees had been established previously and others were founded under the auspices of the Ministry of the East. These committees had little more to do than to search the German prisoner-of-war camps for fellow countrymen willing to

help. The above-mentioned "Russian Committee of Smolensk," on the other hand, founded in December 1942 by Vlasov, stood for a broader objective and placed greater demands on its members.—*Source: Thorwald: Wen sie..., pp. 31, 71, 110 and 170; Dallin, p. 557; Fischer, p. 20.*

485 The Cossack Cavalry Division was then being formed at the new East Prussian training area Mielau (Mlava), using existing Cossack units of the Army Groups South and Center (see below note 1417).—*Source: Thorwald: Wen sie..., p. 249.*

486 Georg Lindemann; born March 8, 1884; 1904 Second Lieutenant, 6th Dragoon Regiment; 1914 Cavalry Captain; during World War I mostly in General Staff positions; Reichswehr; 1926 Major; 1931 Lieutenant Colonel and Commander, 13th Cavalry Regiment; 1933 Colonel; 1935 Commander of the Hanover Military College; 1936 Major General and Commander, 36th Division; 1938 Lieutenant General, breakthrough at the Maginot Line during the Western campaign; fall 1940 General of Cavalry and Commanding General, L Army Corps; from January 16, 1942 Commander-in-Chief, Eighteenth Army at Leningrad and along the Volkhov; July 1942 Colonel General; March 31 to July 3, 1944 Commander, or (from May 6 on) Commander-in-Chief, Army Group North; and after January 27, 1945, Armed Forces Commander-in-Chief in Denmark, later (until June 4, 1945) Army Headquarters Lindemann Dissolution Command.—*Source: Army High Command Staff Files (Nbg. Do. NOKW-141); Munzinger Archive; Siegler, p. 129; Keilig 211/199.*

487 Vlasov had traveled to Army Group Center from February 25 to March 10, 1943, and then a month later spent a few days (until April 10) with Army Group North. In both cases, he was received by the commander-in-chief. He had also spoken to various Eastern battalions and the inhabitants of several towns; he had made remarks about his planned Russian national policy, and these remarks were passed on to Hitler. These events formed the background of this meeting, which brought the entire Vlasov policy to a halt—until the following year, when, after disastrous developments in the military situation, Himmler took up Vlasov's cause and backed Russian national aspirations.—*Source: Thorwald: Wen sie..., pp. 192, 205 and 210.*

488 Prof. Dr. Oskar Ritter v. Niedermayer; born November 8, 1885; 1907 Second Lieutenant, Bavarian 10th Infantry Artillery Regiment; Reichswehr; 1921 left the service; 1924-32 head of military work in the USSR; 1932 rejoined as Major; 1933 left again (January) and rejoined again (November); Lieutenant Colonel (Engineers) in the Armed Forces High Command; 1936 Professor in the Military-Technical Faculty of the Berlin Technical College; 1938 Colonel (Engineers); May 1942 activated and Commander, 162nd Infantry Division; September 1942 Major General; May 1944 Commander of the Eastern Troops 703. Niedermayer went missing at the end of the war.—*Source: Keilig 211/236.*

489 In the spring of 1943, the Azerbaijanis and Turkestanis were pulled out of the Eastern legions deployed in the Ukraine and the General Government and were mixed with the German personnel in a 1:1 ratio. Because the staff of the 162nd Infantry Division—which had been crushed during the battles of Army

Group South—was chosen to be the core of the new division, the new formation was named the 162nd (Turkish) Infantry Division. Initially, the commander was Major General v. Niedermayer, who had participated in several World War [I] operations in the Middle East and had converted to Islam. After its formation in the Neuhammer training area and after a temporary deployment against partisans in Slovenia, the division was transferred to Italy in early 1944. There it fought briefly on the front lines under General v. Heygendorff in June and October, but was pulled out due to unreliability and lack of success. From November on, the 162nd Turkish Division was used against Italian partisans. In 1945 the division was captured by the Americans, who delivered the Azerbaijanis and the Turkestanis to the Soviets under the usual unpleasant circumstances via Tarent-Odessa.—*Source: Order of Battle, p. 188; Thorwald: Wen sie…, pp. 312 and 572; Ralph v. Heygendorff: Das Schicksal der 162. (Turk) Inf. Div. (Thorwald Material in IfZ); Major i. G. Adler: Die 162. (Turk) Inf. Div. (Thorwald Material in IfZ); Ernst Köstring: Die 162. (Turk) Inf. Div. (Thorwald Material in IfZ).*

[490] On April 18, Keitel had ordered that the "Russian prisoner of war General Vlasov"—in view of his "unqualified, impertinent statements during a trip to Army Group North"—be immediately transported to a prisoner-of-war camp and be delivered to the Gestapo if he appeared again in person. Though Vlasov's friends in the Armed Forces High Command were able to prevent the literal execution of this order, Vlasov was prevented from engaging in any political activity for the time being.—*Source: Thorwald: Wen sie…, p. 219; Dallin, p. 572.*

[491] Russkaïa Osvoboditel'naia Armiia (ROA—Russian Liberation Army), the propagandistic joining together of the widely dispersed Eastern troops. The ROA was a phantom, but the term was adopted by advocates of Vlasov's cause in order to promote the organization of a real Russian Army out of these units.— *Source: Fischer, p. 42.*

[492] More precisely, it should read: "… the Reich Commissioner for Coal …" The office of the Reich Coal Commissioner—established in the summer of 1939 to raise the efficiency of mining, and led by the DAF functionary Paul Walter— had in fact been dissolved again in early 1941, instigated by the coal industry. At the time, on March 3 and 4, Paul Pleiger (see note 764)—the General Director of the Reichswerke Hermann Göring, in his capacity as the new head of the "Reich Coal Agency"—was appointed "Reich Commissioner for Coal" and also chairman of the newly established "Reich Coal Association," which encompassed coal mining and trade activities. Now, in June 1943, the Reich Coal Association attempted to obtain from the rear area army services 200,000 Soviet prisoners of war who were able to work in the mining industry. At the end of the month, 50,000 Soviet prisoners of war were allocated to them, and on July 8 Keitel informed Pleiger that permission had been given to transfer 200,000 Soviet prisoners of war into the mining industry.—*Source: VB of March 20, 1941; Nbg.Dok. NI-2840, NI-3342, NI-3498, NI-4151, and NI-4202; IMT XI, VDB Pleiger XII and Closing Vert. Pleiger III.*

[493] Rendered by Fischer: "… this should …" But the text obviously reads "out of," clearly to be followed by "them" or "deserters."

[494] The name is missing because the stenographer apparently didn't understand it and kept the place open for inquiry or completion later. John Amery could have been meant here. He was the talented but somewhat unusually predisposed son of Leopold Stennett Amery, Secretary of State for India in Churchill's war cabinet of 1941-45 and First Lord of the Admiralty and Secretary of State for the Colonies in the 1920s. The young Amery was a Fascist and stayed in Franco's Spain before the war, then went to France and offered his services to the German war propaganda department in October 1942. From then on he addressed his English countrymen in so-called "talks" on German international broadcasting programs, and was also employed to recruit British prisoners of war for the planned "British Legion" in 1943. In 1944 he went on extensive lecture tours throughout German-occupied Europe. Hitler called Amery's broadcasting programs the best propaganda targeted at England that he knew, and he considered inviting Amery to explain his ideas about England to him. Of all the Englishmen in German service (Joyce, Baillie-Stewart, Royston, and others), Amery certainly was the most important and he is no doubt meant here. Based on the sound of the name, the stenographer might have expected a female first name, consequently writing "von der" instead of "von dem." Amery was taken prisoner by Italian partisans at the end of the war. Surprisingly, he confessed his guilt in court, renouncing the quite likely possibility of a successful defense. He was sentenced to death for high treason in England and hanged on December 19, 1945.—*Source: West, p. 211; Nbg.Dok. NG-4537 and NG-4911.*

[495] Kluge had at last urgently demanded a clear-cut objective for the Eastern policy in a letter to the Army Chief of General Staff, and had highlighted the "deepest impression" of Vlasov's propaganda action "on both sides of the front" as well as the risks resulting from a continuation of the hitherto ambiguous policy for the position of the "already indispensable Eastern troops." In his letter he continued as follows, "Out of these considerations, I regard it an indispensable necessity to immediately employ the national committees approved by the Führer. It would, of course, be highly desirable for the implementation of this step to be initiated by the highest political and military leaders. In the event, however, that the necessary political decisions cannot be reached promptly by the Ministry of the East and the Armed Forces High Command, I intend to use a National Committee within the area of Army Group Center at my own discretion ... I ask you to inform me whether decisive measures on the part of the Armed Forces High Command and the Ministry of the East are expected in the very near future. My further decisions will depend on your reply."—*Source: Nbg.Dok NOKW-3521.*

[496] In handwriting after "told," possibly written by Warlimont.

[497] Transcript No. 427/43—Fragment No. 13—Because the surviving shorthand record was heavily charred, the second transcription has large gaps.

[498] Code name for the German offensive near Kursk, which came to a halt after relatively limited but very bloody thrusts into the deep flanks of the Soviet defense area.

[499] The Armed Forces Report of July 25 announced, "During the last fights on the Mius front, the Rhine-Westphalian 16th Panzer Grenadier Division distinguished itself particularly well."

[500] Werner Kempf; born March 9, 1886; 1906 Second Lieutenant, 146th Infantry Regiment; Reichswehr; 1935 Colonel; 1936 Inspector for the Motorization of the Army in the RKM; 1937 Commander 4th Panzer Brigade; 1939 Major General and Commander of 6th Panzer Division; 1940 Lieutenant General; 1941 General of Panzer Troops and Commanding General, XXXVIII Panzer Corps; February 1942 Commander of Army Detachment Kempf; September 30, 1942 to August 18, 1943, Commander-in-Chief, Eighth Army; May to August 1944 Commander of the Armed Forces in Ostland, and at the end of 1944 High Commander in the Vosges Mountains.—*Source, Order of Battle, p. 575; Siegler, pp. 27 and 126; Seemen; Das deutsche Heer, p. 115; Rangliste 1944-45, p. 15; Keilig 211/160.*

[501] He is referring to the disabling of two Russian T 34s by 3.7-cm antitank guns, probably made possible by a temporary deterioration in the Soviet tank material (see also above note 114).

[502] Vollrath Lübbe; born March 4, 1894; 1914 Second Lieutenant, 103rd Infantry Regiment; Reichswehr; 1936 Lieutenant Colonel; 1938 Commander, 13th Cavalry Infantry Regiment; 1939 Colonel; 1941 Commander, 2nd Infantry Brigade; fall 1942 Major General and Commander, 2nd Panzer Division (until February 1, 1944); April 1943 Lieutenant General; April-July 1944 Commander, 81st Infantry Division; and 1945 Commander 443rd Infantry Division.—*Source: Order of Battle, p. 590; Seemen; Das deutsche Heer, p. 565; Rangliste 1944-45, p. 25; Keilig 211/205.*

[503] Reference to the Commander-in-Chief of Army Group Center, Field Marshal v. Kluge.

[504] Josef Harpe; born September 21, 1887; 1911 Lieutenant; taken over to the Reichswehr in the rank of a Captain; 1931 Major; 1935 Commander, 3rd Panzer Regiment; 1937 Colonel; August 1939 Commander, 1st Panzer Brigade; 1940 Major General and Commander, 12th Panzer Division; January 1942 Lieutenant General and Commander (later Commanding General), XXXXI Panzer Corps; late 1942 General of Panzer Troops; November 1943 Commander-in-Chief, Ninth Army; April 1944 Colonel General; June 1944 Commander (later Commander-in-Chief), Army Group North Ukraine (later A); and March/April 1945 Commander-in-Chief, Fifth Panzer Army, after having been relieved as Army Group Commander-in-Chief on January 17, 1945.—*Source: Army High Command Staff Files (Nbg. Dok. NOKW-141); Siegler, p. 122.*

[505] The contradiction between Kluge and Zeitzler which appears here arose from the fact that Army Group Center had been considerably weakened during the attack near Kursk—a position which neither Hitler nor the General Staff of the Army wanted to give up—and now this army group, without sufficient reserves, was facing the far superior Soviet forces in the Orel area.

[506] The Russians had brought their forces in from the north and east against the widely protruding Orel salient on July 11, while the battle to the south of Orel—the northern pincer movement of the German summer campaign against Kursk—was at its height. In view of the overwhelming Russian forces,

the two German Orel armies (the Ninth and the Second Panzer under Colonel General Model) had to withdraw to a line behind a salient east of Briansk. The withdrawal did not begin until July 31, and was successful in spite of heavy Russian pressure. Model carried it out despite a counter-order by Hitler, who had become undecided again literally in the last minute. On August 3, Orel, nothing more than a pile of ruins now, was given up.—*Source: Tippelskirch, p. 382; Görlitz II, p. 208.*

507 Probably a transcription error, as no Lieutenant General Dollmann is known. It's clear that neither the Commander-in-Chief of the Seventh Army, Lieutenant General Friedrich Dollmann, nor Himmler's personal envoy in Italy, SS Standartenführer Dr. Eugen Dollmann, is meant.

508 Soviet field fortified divisions.

509 See below Meeting of July 26, 1943.

510 This planned operation in the area of Army Group Manstein was aimed at holding the rest of the Donets area and eliminating through counterattacks the deep penetrations that the Russians had achieved during their offensive across the Mius and the Donets, which had started on July 17.

511 Field Marshal v. Kluge held only his own point of view and thereby counted on his remaining forces.

512 Meaning "at the least."

513 Not ascertained. It must have been one of the reception battalions for the remaining personnel of the divisions captured in Africa.

514 Incorrect place name (Leghorn).

515 The reference is to the meeting of the "Gran Consiglio del Fascismo" [Grand Council of Fascism]—one of the institutions prescribed by Fascist legislation—whose assignment was to discuss the constitution and political guidelines for the state and party. On July 16, 1943, Mussolini had only reluctantly called a meeting of the Grand Council—which had gathered last on December 7, 1939—for July 24, after unrest had developed among the party ranks because of the country's situation and the irresoluteness shown by the Duce in the face of the looming catastrophe. After a ten-hour meeting, at about 3 a.m. on July 25, the opposition defeated Mussolini's followers. With a vote of 19 to 7, with one abstention (by right-wing extremist Farinacci), the "Ordine del giorno" (Agenda) drafted by Grandi was adopted. This order demanded the reinstatement of the constitutional rights of governmental institutions and the transfer of the military supreme command to the king. Thus, at the time of this situation report, the fate of Fascism had already been sealed for several hours.—*Source: Keesings Archive 1945, p. 19; Rintelen, p. 216; Mussolini, passim.*

516 At that time, the Tiger still suffered from gear problems, which caused many breakdowns. These problems were not resolved until the fall of 1943 when the Tiger II appeared.

517 Reports regarding lost or broken equipment were passed, after completion by the Ib's of the divisions, via the quartermasters or chief quartermasters of the corps, armies, and army groups to the Quartermaster General in the Army High Command, thus providing a control point for the tactical reports.

[518] The number of tanks authorized for the German units in Africa was about 380 around the end of 1942. The real number fluctuated greatly due to the losses (220 German and 120 Italian tanks were lost in 1941 alone, i.e., 85% and 80%, respectively, of the number available) and continual breakdowns, and gave the following picture:

	June 16, 1941	June 20, 1941	Nov. 1941	End of Feb. 1942	March 20, 1942	April 1942	May 25, 1942	June 1, 1942
German	35	136	249	139	161	270	332	124
Italian	-	-	-	63	85	117	252	-

	July 8, 1942	Aug. 1, 1942	Oct. 23, 1942	Oct. 26, 1942	Oct. 27, 1942	Oct. 28, 1942	Oct. 31, 1942	Nov. 2, 1942
German	50	133	230	137	114	66	91	30
Italian	54	-	300	221	206	-	189	-

	Nov. 4, 1942	End of, Nov. 1942	Nov. 28, 1942	Dec. 1, 1942	Dec. 20, 1942	Feb. 10, 1943	March, 1943
German	22	34	54	46	38	129	123
Italian	-	-	42	42	-	-	24

—*Source: Compiled according to Esebeck.*

[519] Adalberto di Savoia, Duke of Bergamo; born March 19, 1898, was a second cousin of the King of Italy. From July 1943 until the surrender he was the nominal commander of the Italian Seventh Army in southern Italy; however, this position did not exclude him from participating in other activities. So, for example, he was attending the funeral of Tsar Boris in Sofia during Italy's surrender, and had to be picked up by Badoglio in a government plane from Budapest. Hitler's characterization of the Dukes of Bergamo and Pistoia, incidentally, does not differ materially from that of the royal cousin of these "weaklings" [i.e., the King of Italy], who used to call them the "due imbecilli di Bergamo e di Pistoia." [Those two idiots of Bergamo and Pistoia]—*Source: Anfuso, p. 238; Ciano, p. 264; Siegler, p. 95.*

[520] The 3,500 km coast of the peninsula—along with, originally, the two big islands—was mostly unprotected; fortifications were located only in the area of the navy ports. The defense—or, more accurately, monitoring—of the coast was the task of the Italian coastal defense divisions, which consisted of older troops equipped with out-of-date weapons. Due to the fact that these men had been standing around on the coast for a year, they had grown tired and lacked the will to resist; most of the fortifications they had built were unusable. The Italian command posts did not deny that these units were unreliable. Roatta's defense plan was thus completely justified and reasonable.—*Source: Rintelen, p. 197; Westphal, pp. 207 and 213.*

[521] Correct: Antifebrin (Acetanilid), today—and already at that time—rarely used as an antipyretic agent; Hitler may have used the term here only because he knew it from World War I.

[522] Italian chemical-pharmaceutical and mining group in Milan; founded in Montecatini in 1888; today one of the largest chemical organizations in the world (Societá Generale per l'Industria Minerale e Chimica), producing in particular sulfur, marble, artificial fertilizers, aluminum, paints, and pharmaceuticals; later became the Montedison company.

[523] Dr. Herbert v. Dirksen, born April 2, 1882; was ambassador in Moscow (from 1928), Tokyo (1933), and London (1938). Dirksen had been employed in the Foreign Office since the beginning of the war.

[524] Despite all precautions, malaria did in fact cause bigger losses in some cases—for the British on Sicily, for example—than the fighting itself.—*Source: Montgomery, p.149.*

[525] Jodl was incorrectly informed, as the Duke of Bergamo was unmarried. His then already deceased mother, however, had been a Wittelsbach (Princess Isabella of Bavaria), and his sister, Princess Bona Margherita, was married to Prince Konrad of Bavaria, while the Duke of Ancona was married to a daughter of the Princess Maria of Bavaria.

[526] Colonel Heinz Heggenrainer—after July 1939 assistant to the military attaché in Rome, after June 1940 Rintelen's and later also Rommel's liaison officer with the Italian Commander-in-Chief in Libya, May 1942 liaison officer for the German armistice commission at Wiesbaden and the Italian armistice commission at Turin—had been liaison officer for the German Commander-in-Chief West (Rundstedt) and the Fourth Italian Army in southern France since the winter of 1942-43. After the Italian surrender (September 8, 1943), Heggenrainer became a German adjutant to the commander of the Italian Ligurian Army, Marshal Graziani.

[527] Admiral Priam Leonardi, the commander of the Augusta naval port, had hastily blown up all the guns when an enemy unit that had landed approached the fortification from the land side. Thus, when the fortification was attacked from the sea, it could no longer open fire effectively (Trizzino even speaks about the occupation of the fortification by two torpedo boats and one landing craft without a fight). Rintelen had visited Mussolini on Hitler's instructions on July 12, in order to express his indignation about this occurrence. Although Mussolini had responded—and had also assured Kesselring—that court-martial procedures had already been initiated against Leonardi, nothing was heard about it in the following days. The fall of Augusta had made a very depressing impression on the Italian public at that time, until, on July 24, the Italian press suddenly sang songs of praise for the "defenders of Augusta and its brave commander"—obviously the last in a series of frequent falsifications initiated by Mussolini, reinterpreting defeats as victories. The Salò Republic, however, convicted Leonardi in absentia for surrender of the fortification without using the available combat forces.—*Source: Rintelen, p. 208; de Belot, p. 228; Kesselring, p. 222; Trizzino, p. 112.*

[528] The "assistance" of the King could hardly have extended to anything more than such pardons, as on June 11, 1940, the day after Italy's entry into war, he proclaimed that he was entrusting Mussolini with the "command over all troops operating on all front lines." The return of the military command to the king was in fact one of the main points of the Agenda approved by the Fascist Grand Council on July 25, 1943. Hitler, however, commented on this issue repeatedly.—*Source: Keesings Archive 1940, p. 4569; Ciano, Diary, pp. 355, 358, and 360.*

[529] Siegfried Westphal; born March 18, 1902; 1922 Second Lieutenant; 1934 Cavalry Captain; 1935-38 in the Operations Branch of the Army General Staff; 1939 Major and Ia, 58th Infantry Division; August 1940 member of the German Armistice Commission; June 1941 Ia German Africa Corps (later: Panzer Group Africa); October 1942 Chief of General Staff, Africa Panzer Army; 1942 Colonel; February 1943 chief of the operations section, Commander-in-Chief, South, and June 1943, Chief of General Staff Commander-in-Chief South; November 21, 1943 to June 5, 1944 Chief of General Staff, Commander-in-Chief, Southwest; April 1944 Lieutenant General; after the beginning of September 1944, Chief of General Staff, Commander-in-Chief, West succeeding Blumentritt (after March 25, 1945: Commander-in-Chief South); and January 1945 General of the Cavalry.—*Source: Westphal, p. 331; Siegler p. 142; Rangliste 1944-45, p. 29; Das deutsche Heer, p. 430; Keilig 211/363.*

[530] The reference is to the Italian XIII Corps, which was in Sicily. The commanding general (the name here was mutilated in German) was General Basso. At that time, the Italians converted the corps staff that had been operating on Sardinia into an Army high command with two corps staffs under it.

[531] The commander of the 90th Panzer Grenadier Division, established on Sardinia from infantry battalions, was Major General (after September 1, 1943: Lieutenant General) Carl Hans Lungershausen. Born July 20, 1896; 1915 Second Lieutenant; Reichswehr, 1936; Commander, 1st Battalion, 8th Cavalry Regiment; 1939 Lieutenant Colonel and IIa, Army Group B; 1940 Colonel; 1941 Commander, 7th Infantry Regiment; 1942 Commander, 7th Infantry Brigade (April) and 164th Light (Africa) Division (August); October 1942 Major General; May 1943 to December 20, 1943 Commander, 90th Panzer Grenadier Division (initially "Sardinia" Division); September 1943 Lieutenant General; and July 1944 (to March 1, 1945) Inspector of the Italian units with the Commander-in-Chief Southwest. Without overestimating their fighting strength, General Lungershausen had created a comradely and comfortable relationship and good cooperation with the Italians on Sardinia; this served him well during the evacuation of the island in September (see note 537).

[532] The *Nembo* was a good Italian parachute division that had received German training in 1942. It was a unit newly formed from the remains of the *Folgore* division from Africa. The *Nembo* stood together with the 90th Panzer Grenadier Division as reserves in the southern central part of the island.

[533] In order not to waste the units that really were of combat strength, the eastern part of Sardinia was given to Italian security divisions that had been deployed

there since the beginning of the war and did not seem to be extremely trust-worthy in terms of conduct and discipline (see above note 520). For the same reason, the northern part of the island had to be left insufficiently safeguarded, but at least moral assistance for the coastal divisions was expected from the strong Italian naval base at La Maddalena. At the time, attention was focused on the Gulf of Cagliari in the south and the Gulf of Oristano in the west, as possible sites for a landing operation.

[534] Meaning the assault brigade RFSS (see below note 537) on Sardinia.

[535] Corsica.

[536] Himmler's guard and escort battalion, expanded into the assault brigade *Reichsführer SS*, was deployed on Corsica at that time, after having been used in Russia until mid-1942. There, as part of the 2nd SS Infantry Brigade (mot.), it had participated in the battles in the north, along the Volkhov and in other regions. In October the brigade was expanded in Slovenia to form the 16th SS Panzer Division *Reichsführer SS.—Source: Schellong, passim; Order of Battle, p. 344.*

[537] Despite this "increase for Sardinia," in view of the much stronger Italian units, the German troops in Corsica and Sardinia (90th Panzer Grenadier Division, assault brigade "RFSS" and smaller units, including Luftwaffe and Navy forces) had no other choice but to evacuate after the surrender of their ally. The German troops withdrew to the north, toward Bastia and Leghorn. On October 4, the evacuation of Corsica had also been completed. With this evacuation, the German troops in Sardinia avoided Italian captivity, with the exception of about 250 men who were held back by the Italians with the alibi of being supply personnel. This was arranged by a gentlemen's agreement between General Basso and General Lungershausen, although the Armed Forces High Command as well as the Commander-in-Chief South demanded the disarmament of the Italian Sardinian army by a German division. After the evacuation, it was not only Lungershausen who had difficulties because of his conduct; Basso was nearly sentenced to death by an Italian military court in Naples.—*Source: Kesselring, pp. 249 and 253; de Belot, p. 239.*

[538] The reference is to General Magli. As the commanding general of the Italian VII Corps, he was the commander of the Italian forces in Corsica. Earlier, as Sotto Capo del Commando Supremo (1941 to February 1943), Magli had maintained good relations with the German Commander-in-Chief South, but in September 1943, following the instructions of his government, Magli fought against his former comrades-in-arms.—*Source: Kesselring, p. 262.*

[539] Probably Porto Vecchio, on the southeastern corner of Corsica. A péniche is a pinnace—a light vessel for guarding the coast.

[540] Of Sicily.

[541] During the night of July 23, the British cruiser *New Foundland* was torpedoed near Syracuse by German submarine *U407*, under Captain Brüller; the ship was only damaged, however.

[542] Reference to the small passenger steamer *Santa Lucia*, which was sunk by a British torpedo bomber near Ventotene Island on July 24.

[543] Boats from the 3rd Motor Torpedo Boat Flotilla.

[544] An operation against the Soviet beachhead at Cape Myshako, near Novorossiisk, carried out by boats from the 1st Motor Torpedo Boat Flotilla.

[545] Attack by a Soviet submarine against a German convoy returning from Sevastopol'.

[546] During this fighter-bomber raid near Messina, the Italian torpedo boat *Partenope* and the corvette *Cigogna* were heavily damaged and sank. The two boats, however, were not a total loss, as they were raised and repaired.

[547] To Crete.

[548] The 265th Infantry Division was newly formed; the 94th Infantry Division was transferred to the Genoa region to protect the coast.—*Source: Order of Battle, pp. 219 and 172.*

[549] The *U199* sank the British passenger steamer *Henzada* (4,161 GRT) south of Rio.

[550] The *U571* was attacked several times by aircraft near the Canary Islands and was heavily damaged.

[551] Probably an American "hunter-killer" group with an escort aircraft carrier, which was operating north of the Azores at the time.

[552] It was in this attack against Trondheim when the *U622* was sunk and the destroyer *Z28* damaged.

[553] This British air raid against Hamburg the previous night (July 24-25, 1943)—the first in a devastating series—can be considered the Stalingrad of the air war. For the first time over Germany, the RAF employed four practices that were decisive in radar-assisted warfare: 1. First large-scale use and first use over German soil of the magnetron that operated on a 9-cm wave; this was an onboard screen device (target as image instead of target as symbol) which depicted the landscape the pilot was flying over, with a radius of 70 km, irrespective of weather and lighting conditions on the screen. (The H²S device was known as the "Rotterdam device" by the Germans, named after the location where they had brought down the first, though somewhat damaged, apparatus of this kind in March 1943.) 2. A secretly established network of jamming stations jammed the Freya devices and thus partly paralyzed the German air warning system. 3. Jamming stations on board the attacking bombers jammed the Würzburg fire control equipment of the anti-aircraft forces and the Liechtenstein devices of the night-fighter aircraft the same way. This was the late but immediately effective result of the English surprise raid on the German Bruneval radar station at Cape d'Antifer on the Channel coast in the night of February 27-28, 1942. Bruneval was equipped with a new Würzburg-C test device, and having taken possession of the main part of the device, the English were able to detect its wavelength and confirm the lack of secret alternate frequencies. 4. Jamming the Würzburg fire control equipment and the night-fight control devices—to the extent of their complete breakdown—by dropping thin aluminum foil slips (dipoles) whose length was half the length of the waves of the attacked devices (ll/2 in this case = 25 cm). The jagged fog ("grass") that this caused in the Braunschen tubes of the devices made it impossible to detect or measure the actual targets. This tactic (the Anglo-Ameri-

cans called these strips "windows," and the Germans called them "Düppel,"
after the Düppel estate near Berlin-Zehlendorf where the first German tests
had taken place) had already been known to both sides for a long time. In Great
Britain, for example, Professor Lindemann had proposed it as early as 1937, but
both sides hesitated to apply it because it could be imitated very easily. Only
when the English no longer feared a new "Blitz" was the use of the "windows"
approved on June 22, 1943. Implementation, delayed to avoid German imitation during the Allied Sicily operation, took place for the first time on July 24-25
against Hamburg. [—] For protection against jamming stations, some initial accessory devices for wave change were secretly in use already, and their production was now increased. It took more than a year, however, before a technically
satisfactory solution emerged with the "Streuwellen-Wismar." To counteract the
dipoles, one fell back on the Doppler Effect, which enabled the distinction between moving and stationary objects—or, like the "windows," those that were
virtually stationary. After just two weeks, the first "Würzlaus" accessory devices,
which were based on the Doppler Effect, were added to the equipment. Nevertheless, insurmountable helplessness in the face of larger quantities of "windows" demanded ongoing tests (K-Laus, Tastlaus) and the application of other
principles (e.g., distinction on the basis of differing metallic compositions:
"Steinhäger"). By the end of the war, however, there was still no completely
satisfactory solution.—*Source: Bley, passi; Hoffmann: Geheimnis Radar, passim; Ewald,
passim; Churchill IV/1, p. 335; Koch: Flak, p. 130; Lusar, p. 113; Feuchter, pp. 233
and 239; Schneider, p. 240; Baumbach, p. 220.*

554 The series of raids against Hamburg during the last week of July 1943 was,
along with the destruction of Dresden in February 1945, one of the most horrible high points of the Allied air war against Germany. Official American records
published in 1945 indicate that during that time Hamburg was attacked six times
at night and twice during the day; more than 50% of the city was destroyed and
12½ square miles were totally burned out. More recent German investigations
provide the following estimates of the bomb loads dropped there: 1,200 aerial
mines, more than 50,000 high-explosive bombs, many hundreds of thousands
of stick-type incendiary bombs, 80,000 phosphorus bombs, and nearly 5,000
phosphorus canisters. The same source mentions 40,000 dead in the city, including more than 5,500 children; 600,000 people lost their homes and 250,000
out of a total of 556,000 apartments were destroyed. Due to the elimination of
the defense forces, the attackers lost fewer than 2% of the aircraft deployed;
Hamburg's three anti-aircraft regiments, for instance, shot down no more than
17 aircraft altogether. In the matter-of-fact language of the Armed Forces High
Command reports, the inferno was reported as follows: July 25, "A strong British bomber unit conducted a terror raid against the city of Hamburg last night,
which caused severe casualties among the population and heavy destruction
of residential areas, cultural institutions and public buildings." [—] July 26:
"Yesterday, Hamburg and Kiel, as well as a few towns along the northern
coast of Germany and in the occupied western regions, were attacked. ...This
again resulted in severe casualties among the population and heavy devasta-

tion in the residential areas of the towns attacked." [—] July 27: "North American bomber units attacked the cities of Hamburg and Hanover yesterday. The population...had casualties" [—] July 28: "Strong hostile bomber units continued their terror raids against the city of Hamburg last night. Further devastation and some large-scale fires resulted in several areas of the city. The population suffered casualties again." [—] July 30: "Enemy bomber units...again carried out a heavy terror attack against Hamburg, which caused further devastation in the city." [—] August 3: "After sporadic thrusts during the day...the British bombed the city of Hamburg and its environs again last night. Again there were casualties among the inhabitants and considerable destruction." [—] As happened again later in Dresden, this last raid followed the bombed-out residents to their alternative shelters on the outskirts of the city.—*Source: Fuller, p. 268; Rumpf, p. 96; Görlitz I, p. 496.*

555 When the war began, only one out of a total of 13 Me 109 groups had tested the "illuminated night fight"—a combat technique operated in conjunction with the searchlight batteries over the searchlight line behind the western border of the Reich, more or less according to the principles of daytime combat. In the winter of 1940-41, the escalating English night raids required—and the advancements in radar technology enabled—the development of "dark" or "directed" night fight in the so-called Himmelbett [tester-bed] process. Each "tester bed," i.e., each ground station, was equipped with a Würzburg or Würzburg-Riese [Würzburg Giant] (see above note 154 and below note 556) to identify the precise location of the hostile unit and to guide the night fighter, as well as a Freya device for the rough location of the units. Depending on the volume of the stream of bombers—because the preparation of each aircraft took 10 to 20 minutes—up to 3 fighters, which waited to be guided by radio beacon, could be deployed per position. The guidance radius was not much more than 30 km when the Würzburg was operated in the normal way. Faced with larger streams of enemy bombers later, the tester-bed process, which could guide individual fighter aircraft only, proved totally insufficient. Thus, directed night fight operations were converted to the Y process (see note 557). The use of the Düppel method during the raids against Hamburg also temporarily revived free night combat operations that were independent of any such technology. (See below note 827.)—*Source: Galland, pp. 203 and 240; Görlitz I, p. 497; Hoffmann: Geheimnis Radar, passim; Baumbach, pp. 226 and 240.*

556 The Freya device was the Luftwaffe's oldest warning and locating device. Its range was 120 km and it operated on a very long wavelength of 240-cm. It had proven its value immediately after the beginning of the war December 18, 1939 when, based in Wangerooge, it located 52 British Wellington bombers flying to Wilhelmshaven, at a distance of 113 km. As a result, 36 aircraft were brought down. The disadvantage of the device, however, was that it provided lateral and distance data but not the height of the measured targets. The latter was measured by the 62/Würzburg apparatus, which was mainly used as anti-aircraft fire control equipment operating on the 50-cm wave, and also the 64/Mannheim and 65/Würzburg-Riese devises. A number of further developments with some

substantial improvements (all-around search, fine adjustment for the enemy-occupied sector, distance accuracy of ± 2.5 m, etc.) either could not be completely implemented or failed because the enemy's jamming tactics could not be sufficiently neutralized. The following table provides the names and, if known, the specifications of the various devices:

	Wavelength in cm	Range in km
A. Fire Control Equipment:		
Anti-Aircraft, etc.		
39 L	–	–
40 L	–	–
62/Würzburg-A/C	50	20-30
65/Würzburg-Giant	50	40-60
63/Mainz	53.6	–
64/Mannheim	53.6	–
77/Marbach V	9	25-35
74/Kulmbach	9	25-35
76/Marbach	9	50
74/76/Egerland	9	–
B. Onboard Locating Equipment		
Liechtenstein	200	8
Berlin (rebuilt Rotterdam)	9	–
C. Air-Raid Warning Devices		
Freya	240	120
Wasserman	–	–
Heavy Wassermann	–	–
Mannheim-Giant	53.6	60-70
Ansbach	53.6	–
Heidelberg	–	398
Elephant	–	300
Mammoth	–	300

—Source: Hoffmann: Geheimnis Radar, passim; Lusar, p. 113.

[557] The Y process and the X process were the standard navigation methods of the German Luftwaffe when attacking ground targets. With the X system, two transmitters located some distance from each other transmitted beams that intersected over the target. The attacking aircraft flew along one of these beams toward the target until the receiver picked up the buzz of the second beam, indicated that the aircraft was over the target. With the Y process, the second beam assisting in distance measurement was replaced by the reflection of the aircraft's guide beam to the ground station. Using a similar system, the "Oboe"

system, the RAF also succeeded in carrying out precision night raids against German cities (the first was against the Krupp factory in Essen on December 21, 1942). On the German side, the Y process was eventually used not only in offensive operations but also increasingly in defensive activities for guiding night fighters (see note 827), where it replaced the tester-bed process guided by the Würzburg.—*Source: Bley, pp. 10 and 15.*

558 Should read: "...recently..." or "... in the last few nights..." The British had last attacked a German town (Aachen) during the night of July 13, and attacked targets in France the following two nights. Since then, only nuisance raiders had entered the Reich territory, and during the last five nights (and also during the days) there hadn't been any enemy intrusions at all.—*Source: Armed Forces High Command reports from July 14-24, 1943.*

559 Dietrich Peltz; born June 9, 1914; 1933 soldier in a motor vehicle detachment, later transferred to the Luftwaffe; 1940 First Lieutenant in a dive bomber wing; 1943 Colonel and Air Commodore in a fighter wing; late 1943 Attack Commander West; and 1944 Lieutenant General and Commanding General, IX Air Corps. Colonel Peltz was awarded the Swords, probably by Hitler himself, on July 23, 1943, two days before this situation conference. Possibly he took this occasion to report on the raids against England and the weather situation there.—*Source: VB of July 25, 1943; Seemen; Order of Battle, p. 604.*

560 This probably refers to the resumption of mining the English waters by aircraft, as had been done in the early stages of the war. The resumption was planned by the Navy but was not carried out in the end, due to a shortage of suitable aircraft. This mine warfare was a clear example of the development war between offensive and defensive weapons. New on the German side after the outbreak of war was the "magnetic mine," which responded to the magnetic field of the ship. But in November 1939, the British had already obtained an intact mine that had fallen into shallow water, and were very quickly able to find efficient countermeasures, such as demagnetizing their ships and, especially, developing suitable sweeping equipment. The next German strike was the installation of timed contacts [*Zählkontakten*], which armed the mine only after several ships had passed over it or after a certain number of days—or even alternated between armed on some days and unarmed on other days. In the fall of 1940, new acoustic mines were added, which responded to the noise of a ship's propeller, although acoustic buoys and other measures were soon available to counter their effects. By late July 1941, the IX Air Corps, which was responsible for the mining, had placed about 8,500 mines in the seas around England and—though probably somewhat optimistically—claimed to have sunk 490 ships of 918,000 GRT. Due to the Russian campaign, however, there were soon no air units available for mine warfare; only a few aircraft continued the operations, and soon they were discontinued completely. [—] When Hitler spoke of a "new mining process" here, he might also have been referring to the use of the pressure box mine, whose deployment, however, was delayed until after the invasion had started (see below note 1202.)—*Source: Baumbach, p. 126; Lusar, p. 143.*

[561] The reference might be to the Trialen bombs, which were first used around the beginning of 1942. Earlier bombs, mines and shells had been filled with Trinitrotoluene (TNT) or Amatol—a mixture of Trinitrotoluene and ammonium nitrate in the ratio of 60:40. Although Trialen also consisted of powder, it was significantly more effective than TNT. It was named after its composition: 70% Trinitrotoluene, 15% aluminum and 15% Hexogen.

[562] The "Oboe" system.

[563] Christian might have been Hitler's de facto adjutant—in his self-selected role—but officially he was a general staff officer or Jodl's adjutant.

[564] Mine sweeping from the air was carried out by aircraft hanging electrically charged cables that formed a horizontal circle above the surface of the water; the magnetic field operated downward and caused the magnetic mines to explode. The Germans used the Ju 52 for this purpose.

[565] In a special report by the Soviet Ministry of Information on the evening of July 24, Radio Moscow announced an Order of the Day by Stalin to Generals Rokossovsky, Vatutin, and Popov, stating the following, "On July 23, after successful battles, our troops have finally smashed the German July offensive in the sector south of Orel and north of Belgorod in the direction of Kursk. On July 5, the Germans started their offensive with strong tank and infantry forces, supported by a large number of aircraft, in the directions of Orel-Kursk and Belgorod. In the Orel-Kursk sector they threw 7 panzer divisions, 2 panzer grenadier divisions and 11 infantry divisions into the battle, while in the area of Belgorod 10 panzer divisions, 1 panzer grenadier division and 7 infantry divisions were deployed. Thus, the Germans initiated the offensive with a total of 17 panzer divisions, 3 panzer grenadier divisions and 18 infantry divisions. The enemy intended to break through our front line, in a narrow front sector, toward Kursk, and to encircle and annihilate our forces. This new German offensive was not unexpected. Our forces were prepared for it. In the Orel-Kursk sector the Germans succeeded in advancing 9 km, with huge casualties. They advanced 15 to 35 km, again with huge casualties, in the Belgorod sector. Our troops exhausted the German elite divisions in bitter combat. During subsequent counterattacks, they not only repelled the Germans and reestablished the front line as it had been on July 5, but also broke through the enemy defense lines in the direction of Orel, advancing by 15 to 25 km. In view of this fact, the German plan represented by this summer attack can be regarded as a complete failure. In the battles of July 5-23, more than 70,000 officers and soldiers fell. At that same time, 2,900 German tanks, 195 assault guns and 844 field guns, as well as 1,392 aircraft and more than 5,000 enemy vehicles, were destroyed or damaged. I congratulate you and the troops under your command on the successful defense against the German summer offensive. I express my gratitude to all soldiers, commanders and political commissars for their outstanding performance. Eternal glory belongs to the heroes who died on the battlefield, fighting for the freedom and honor of our country." The interpretation as expressed by Hitler here is thus not unjustified, but did prove to be deceptive.—*Source: NZZ of July 26, 1943 (morning edition).*

[566] See the OKW report for this day, July 25.

[567] Hans Baur, born June 19, 1897; 1918 in the Luftwaffe; after World War I pilot for the Deutsche Luftpost; 1923 Junkers pilot; 1926 Lufthansa (becoming a captain after having flown 500,000 kilometers); 1921 NSDAP; after 1932 Hitler's senior pilot; and February 1945 SS Gruppenführer. Baur was sentenced to 25 years of hard labor in the Soviet Union and released in October 1955.—*Source: Munzinger Archive.*

[568] This—in principle the normal situation—would mean: 3 infantry regiments with 3 battalions each, 1 artillery regiment with 3 detachments, etc. The first exceptions to the rule were the Jäger [light infantry] divisions built up in late 1940 and reorganized one year later; these had only 2 Jäger regiments each. In the West in 1943, a third division was sometimes formed out of two by removing the third regiment (e.g., the 274th Infantry Division was established this way when the 347th and the 348th Infantry Division gave up 862nd and 865th Infantry Regiments). At the same time, replacement difficulties in the East forced some divisions to disband the third battalions of the infantry regiments and to use their personnel to strengthen the remaining two battalions.

[569] Divisions with numbers above 700 consisted mostly of older personnel and were only poorly armed in terms of heavy weapons. These local defense units were built up as the 15th wave in 1941, and included the following fifteen security divisions:

702nd	Norway
704th	Yugoslavia (spring 1943 renamed the 104th Jäger Division)
707th	East (disbanded in the summer of 1944)
708th	France, temporarily in the East (destroyed in Normandy in August 1944, then reconstituted as the 708th VGD [Volksgrenadier Division])
709th	France (destroyed in Cherbourg in July 1944)
710th	Norway, after December 1944 in Italy
711th	France/Holland
712th	Belgium/Holland, after January 1945 in the East
713th	(Greece) (disbanded in late 1943)
714th	Yugoslavia (spring 1943 renamed the 114th Jäger Division)
715th	Southern France and Italy
716th	Southern France
717th	Yugoslavia (spring 1943 [renamed] 117th Jäger Division)
718th	Yugoslavia (spring 1943 [renamed] 118th Jäger Division)
719th	Holland/Saar

– *Source: Order of Battle, pp. 279 and 316.*

[570] The 271st Infantry Regiment, consisting predominantly of SA volunteers, was given the name *Feldherrnhalle* in August 1942. When this regiment was handed over by the 93rd Infantry Division to the newly formed 60th Panzer Grenadier Division, which had been destroyed in Stalingrad, the latter took over this name. At the end of 1944, the name *Feldherrenhalle* was transferred to a panzer corps that contained—in addition to the 60th Panzer Grenadier Division—the 13th

Panzer Division *Feldherrnhalle*, which was now bearing this name as well. Both divisions were crushed in Budapest in January/February 1945.—*Source: Order of Battle, pp. 172, 294 and 310; Krätschmer, p. 380.*

571 The 13th Waffen SS Mountain Division *Handschar* (Croatian No. 1), for which Bosnian and Herzegovinian Muslims from the independent state of Croatia were recruited, and in some cases actually drafted. The division had been built up in France after the spring of 1943, and also later in Neuhammer (Silesia), and was initially named the BH Division (Bosnian-Herzegovinian); in late 1943 it was moved to Croatia.—*Source: Order of Battle, p. 343; Kiszling, p. 194.*

572 The 11th SS Volunteer Panzer Grenadier Division *Nordland*, consisting of the Panzer Grenadier Regiments *Norge* ["Norway"] and *Danmark* ["Denmark"], was formed in Germany in the summer of 1943 with Norwegians, Danes and ethnic Germans from the Balkans; the *Nordland* Regiment from the *Viking* Division served as the core.—*Source: Order of Battle, p. 342.*

573 The 12th SS Panzer Division *Hitlerjugend* [Hitler Youth] was formed in the summer of 1943 in Belgium, using cadres of the *Leibstandarte* Division—primarily members of the Hitler Youth camps providing physical training for military service.—*Source: Order of Battle, p. 343.*

574 Two divisions that had been virtually destroyed in Stalingrad and then reconstituted in France, and were now being moved to Italy.—*Source: Order of Battle, pp. 164 and 232.*

575 Rommel's Army Group Command B (designated thus after July 14) had been built up in Germany, starting at the end of May 1943, and was standing by for deployment in the Balkans as of July 21; however, due to the developments in Italy, the command was assigned on July 26 to lead the troops in the northern Italian area, and was temporarily transferred to Munich again until August 17. A new Army Group (F) under Field Marshal v. Weichs was established for the proposed operations in the Balkans.—*Source: Siegler, p. 18.*

576 Meaning that if an Allied attack against the Balkans were driven back by German troops, the repercussions could affect other planned landings on other coasts as well.

577 Italians, etc.

578 In Italy.

579 The normal equipment of a Panther detachment included 96 vehicles at the beginning. In the summer of 1943 this number was reduced to 71 Panthers—partly because of the realization that such a strong concentration of these high-quality tanks was not expedient, and partly due to a shortage of tanks.

580 Hans Georg v. Mackensen; born January 26, 1883 (son of the future field marshal); 1902 Second Lieutenant in active service; 1911 transfer to the reserves to study law; 1919 entry into the diplomatic corps (1919 Copenhagen, 1923 Quirinal [Rome], 1926 Brussels, 1931 Madrid); 1933 envoy to Budapest; March 1937 Undersecretary of State in the Foreign Office; and after April 1938 ambassador at the Quirinal [Italy]. Mackensen was called to the Führer Headquarters on August 2, 1943, i.e., one week after this discussion. The following month, due to a difference of opinion with Hitler regarding the Italian issue, he was relieved

from his post, and dismissed in January 1945. Mackensen, who married a daughter of the future Foreign Minister Baron v. Neurath in 1926, died on September 28, 1947.—*Source: Munzinger Archive.*

[581] Göring was supposed to go to Italy for Mussolini's 60th birthday on July 29.

[582] Farinacci was in fact among the initiators of the Grand Council meeting of July 24-25, 1943, but the rebels around Grandi, who had been clever enough to use him as a front, opposed him. The Grandi group wanted to end the war, while Farinacci, on the other hand, wanted to tighten Italy's conduct of war under the Duce and to cooperate more closely with Germany. Farinacci was the first leading Fascist to escape to the Reich in the following days and to report on the incidents that had taken place in Rome. He took an active part in the establishment of the Republic of Salò but was unable to reach the expected leading position because of Mussolini's return. With the title of a state minister without cabinet status, Farinacci returned to Cremona and to the editorial staff of the *Regime Fascista*. After the collapse, he was executed by a partisan firing squad in Lombardy on April 29, 1945.—*Source: Munzinger Archive; Keesings Archive 1945, p. 198; Goebbels Diaries (copy in IfZ archive), pp. 2538, 2556 and 2563.*

[583] Vittorio Emanuele Orlando; born May 19, 1860; 1888 professor of constitutional law in Palermo; 1897 liberal member of parliament; 1903-05 Minister of Education; 1907-09 and 1914-16 Minister of Justice; and 1916-17 Minister of the Interior. In 1919 he was Italy's representative to the Paris Peace Conference and, because he was not able to completely force through Italian claims in the Adriatic, he was ousted in June 1919. Orlando initially established contact with the Fascists, but turned to the opposition in 1925 and retired from parliament in 1928. As Badoglio reported, Orlando was in fact involved in the change of the Italian regime in 1943; he had, for example, assisted in the drafting of the two proclamations by the King and Badoglio. After the war he became a senator and a member of the Constituent Assembly from June 1946 to August 1947. He died on December 1, 1952.—*Source: Badoglio, p. 65; Keesings Archive 1952, p. 3761.*

[584] That Sunday morning (July 25), Mussolini had continued to attend to his daily business in the office as usual, and had received the Japanese ambassador and other persons. At noon he visited, together with Galbiati, the commander of the militia, the areas of Rome that had been bombed during the air raid on July 19. The audience with the King, which had been requested by Mussolini and during which the dictator was deposed and then arrested, did not take place until 4 o'clock in the afternoon.—*Source: Rintelen, p. 219.*

[585] Guido Buffarini-Guidi, a friend of the Petacci family, was Undersecretary of the Interior until the "changing of the guard" on the occasion of Ciano's removal on February 6, 1943. At the meeting of the Grand Council on July 24-25, 1943, Buffarini had voted against Grandi's agenda. In the RSI government of Salò, he served as Minister of the Interior until February 23, 1945. According to statements by SD Führer Wilhelm Höttl, Buffarini was an agent of the Supreme Commander of the SS and Police in Italy, SS Obergruppenführer Karl Wolff, and unconditionally devoted to him. After his release by Mussolini, he was supposedly supported by Wolff, and in April 1945 he allegedly submitted a plan to

the German security police for playing Mussolini, who was becoming uncomfortable, into the hands of the partisans. With the collapse of the regime in northern Italy, Buffarini, like Mussolini, Pavolini, Starace, Farinacci, and others, was summarily executed by the partisans on April 29, 1945. His party comrade Anfuso characterized him as the "last Italian of the Renaissance."—*Source: Keesings Archive 1943, pp. 5823 and 6035, as well as 1945, p. 198; Ciano, passim; Anfuso (It.), p. 106; Mellini, passim; Hagen: Die geheime Front, p. 468.*

[586] During the discussion in Feltre on July 19, 1943, Mussolini had intended—as requested by Ambrosio and others—to point out to Hitler that Italy's military strength had been exhausted and that his country was thus no longer able to continue the war. In Feltre, however, Hitler—as was his custom—delivered a two-hour monologue regarding the necessity of total war and his willingness to conduct warfare without limits. Mussolini returned to Rome without having dared to utter his concerns. But the atmosphere in Feltre was not nearly as warm as it had been during earlier meetings.—*Source: Rintelen, p. 211; Westphal, p. 221.* [NDT: see also Corvaja, *Hitler and Mussolini*, pp. 295-330.]

[587] General of the Infantry Reserves Edmund Glaise v. Horstenau; born February 27, 1882; Austrian officer; during World War I he was, among other things, liaison officer between the Austro-Hungarian and German army commands; 1925 director of the Austrian War Archives; 1936 to 1938 minister without portfolio in the Schuschnigg cabinet; March 1938 to March 1940 Vice Chancellor or Minister of the Interior under Seyss-Inquart; and subsequently in the Armed Forces High Command (inspector of the war graves). From April 12, 1941 to September 7, 1944 Glaise was the German deputy general in Croatia. He was in Rome, perhaps by chance, at the time of the Italian crisis. Glaise committed suicide in the Langwasser camp on July 20, 1946, when he was summoned to Nuremberg as a witness.—*Source: Munzinger Archive; Kiszling, pp. 171, 211 and others.*

[588] Later, Hitler became more suspicious of reconstituted Italian formations, not to mention the fact that there was less and less material available even for the German units. To the indignation of Mussolini and Graziani, his minister of war—who wished to have 25 divisions, including 15 panzer and panzer grenadier divisions—only 4 infantry divisions of the "Republican Fascist Army" and a few battalions of Fascist militia were eventually formed.

[589] After careful preparation, the SD had conducted a large-scale action against the Belgian Communist Party during the past few weeks. Among the functionaries arrested after July 6 were the Secretary General of the Belgian Communist Party, Xavier Relecom; the organization leader of the Belgian Communist Party, Joseph Leemans; the editor-in-chief of the underground newspaper of the Belgian Communist Party, *Drapeau Rouge*, Pierre Joye; and the commander of the Armée Belge des Partisans, Jacques Grippa—who, incidentally, all survived the war. In addition, several members of the technical staff of the Communist underground press were arrested, and typesetting machines and paper stock were confiscated as well. Some non-Communist members of the Front de l'Independence also fell into the hands of the Germans. The SD believed at the

time that it had destroyed the illegal Belgian Communist Party, and called upon the Belgian Communists—in a forged edition of *Drapeau Rouge*—to give up resistance in order to save the lives of their leaders. But the Belgian Communist Party recovered surprisingly quickly, and by August a successor to *Drapeau Rouge* was being published under the name *La lutte continue.*

590 The "Rote Kapelle" ["Red Orchestra"] complex has thus far not been clarified with complete reliability. This designation is understood to refer to Soviet espionage organizations acting before, during and to some degree even after World War II, but it is not clear whether there were any organizational connections between the individual actions of the "R.K.," or whether this was merely an invention of the Reich Security Head Office [RSHA]. In the narrower sense, one also refers to the Schulze-Boysen/Harnack group as "R.K." This was a circle of Communist-minded or only Bolshevik-influenced people of all kinds surrounding the First Lieutenant in the RLM Harro Schulze-Boysen, the representative in the Reich Economics Ministry, Dr. Arvid Harnack, the author Adam Kuckoff, their wives and others. This group (consisting mainly of convinced resistance fighters but in some cases also persons—like the ambassador v. Scheliha—acting out of self interest) delivered information to the USSR via agents and increasingly after June 22, 1941 by radio. At the end of August 1942, the Gestapo struck against the "R.K." The rounding up of the German organization, most of whose members were executed in Plötzensee in late 1942 and early 1943, was successful; however, because of the premature strike, the main organization in the occupied Western regions was warned in time and was able to evade the Gestapo measures.—*Source: Roeder, passim; Flicke, passim; Weisenborn, p. 203; Numerous newspaper and magazine articles from the years 1950-52 in the IfZ archive.*

591 The Interallied Control Commissions established under sections 203-06 of the Versailles Treaty were to control the implementation of the military provisions of the treaty. The three commissions (Army, Navy, and Luftwaffe) conducted numerous inspection visits until they were withdrawn from Germany on January 31, 1927, under the Geneva Protocol of December 12, 1926. The so-called military experts at the Berlin embassies of the Allies, who had been assigned to monitor the implementation of the "remaining points" of Germany's disarmament, left the Reich three years later.—*Source: Schwendemann; Berber; Bretton; Ströhle.*

592 Transcript No. 428/43—Fragment No. 14—The remaining shorthand record was very charred, so the second transcription was possible only with gaps.

593 To Italy.

594 Eliminating the large enemy bridgehead in the area of the Sixth Army and restoring the Mius front. The counterattack started July 30 and was successful. (See also above note 510 and below note 642.)—*Source: Manstein, p. 516.*

595 Here and in the following passages the reference is to Field Marshal v. Kluge and Army Group Center.

596 At that time it was very difficult to convince Hitler to fly in person to any of the headquarters at the front because he regarded himself as irreplaceable. Keitel,

in particular, supported him in this position and warned him not to expose himself to danger. Hitler probably made real visits to the front—to the combat troops—only during the Polish campaign. Until the winter of 1941-42, i.e., during the Western campaign and during the first months of the Eastern campaign, he occasionally visited the army groups and other higher-ranking headquarters, but later, as in this case here, the opposite method was applied—he ordered the front to come to him. So only three visits by Hitler to headquarters at the front are known during the entire final three years of the war: on February 17, 1943, to Army Group South (Manstein) and—after the second stay in Vinnitsa—on March 13, 1943, to Army Group Center (Kluge) and on September 8, 1943, again to Manstein. A visit to Rommel's Army Group B in the West, planned for June 19, 1944, was canceled on short notice.

[597] This took place the following day.

[598] Also an infantry division that was destroyed in Stalingrad and newly reconstituted in Brittany, was now being transferred to Army Group Center's sector.— *Source: Order of Battle, p. 176.*

[599] Meaning 15% troops with combat experience in the East.

[600] From the salient in the Orel region.

[601] Four infantry divisions earmarked exclusively for the West were rearmed with Russian artillery.

[602] Regarding this subject, which was particularly dear to Hitler in those days, see note 694.

[603] From Sicily.

[604] Assembling to the north of Rome.

[605] Reference to the withdrawal of German troops from Sicily. Hitler's opinion, which he repeated several times here (see pp. 212 and 213), is in strange contrast to his position during the evacuation of Stalingrad (see above note 103) or Tunis, and might be the result of a—however temporary—lesson drawn from those two catastrophes. In addition, he probably regarded the units on Sicily, especially the 1st Parachute Division (assessed by the enemy as "one of the best German divisions"—*Order of Battle, p. 323*) and the 1st Panzer Parachute Division *Hermann Göring*, which consisted entirely of volunteers, as high-value divisions whose men were hand-picked and supposedly reflected the "fanatical" National Socialist approach that he considered so necessary. He had heard favorable estimations of these divisions' personnel, and wanted to rescue them at all costs. The following day, however, when the first excitement had calmed down, Hitler's position on this issue was already less strict.

[606] Less than a month later, on August 19, 1943, Jeschonnek committed suicide in desperation over the failure of the Luftwaffe—a failure for which he, as a successful advocate of the theory of a short-term war, was partly responsible.

[607] In southern France.

[608] Rommel had left Wiener Neustadt already at 8 a.m. and was in Salonika at that moment (see below p. 213) to meet Colonel General Löhr, whom he was to replace as Commander-in-Chief of the Southeast, according to a recent decision of Hitler's (see above note 434 and note 575). The upheaval in Italy cre-

ated a new situation, however. Shortly after 11 p.m., Rommel, in Salonika, received a call from the Armed Forces High Command, ordering him immediately to the Führer Headquarters, where he arrived at noon the following day.— *Source: Rommel Papers, p. 431.*

[609] A 34th Panzer Division did not exist; Hitler must have meant either the 24th Panzer Division again or (see below p. 222) the 44th Infantry Division ("Reichs Panzer Grenadier Division Hoch- und Deutschmeister"), which, like the 24th Panzer Division, was transferred from France to northern Italy in August 1943. (See below note 1447.)

[610] The 2nd Parachute Division in southern France.

[611] As a bridgehead near the Straits of Messina.

[612] Dino Grandi; born June 4, 1895; journalist; early Fascist; 1929-32 Foreign Minister, then ambassador in London; 1932 member of the Fascist Grand Council; 1937 given the title of count; July 1939 Minister of Justice; and November 1939 President of the Fasci and Corporations [Parliament]. [—] During this meeting of the Grand Council on July 24-25, 1943, which Hitler described here for the most part correctly, the agenda by Grandi—about whom Mussolini had said only a few hours before, "He is a truly faithful man!"—was adopted by 19 votes to 7. Grandi, who emigrated to South America, was sentenced to death *in absentia* during the proceedings against the members of the Grand Council before a Fascist special court in Verona in January 1944. He was acquitted by the Supreme Court in Rome in another political trial in December 1947.—*Source: Munzinger Archive; Westphal, p. 211.*

[613] Giuseppe Bottai; born September 3, 1895; early Fascist; author of the Fascist labor and economic constitution; 1926 Undersecretary of State in the Ministry of Corporations; 1929-32 Minister of Corporations; 1935 Governor of Rome; and 1936-43 Minister of Education. Bottai voted in favor of the Grandi resolution in the Grand Council, and was also sentenced to death in absentia in Verona in January 1944. Bottai later joined the French Foreign Legion and wrote several volumes of his memoirs before retiring to Rome, where he died in 1959.

[614] This planned action, in which the members of the Badoglio government and the royal family were to be arrested in order to reinstall the Fascist regime, was known by the name operation "Student," after the German parachute Colonel General. Both Kesselring and Rintelen (who were not originally supposed to be let in on the plans for this action) opposed it. Once Rintelen had given Hitler Badoglio's confirmation of loyalty on August 2, Hitler relented somewhat and halted the "Student" action, which was then never implemented.—*Source: Hagen: Unternehmen Bernhard, p. 129; Rintelen, p. 227.*

[615] Code name for the prepared movement of troops to Italy in the event of a defection on the part of the ally. Neither *Alaric* nor similar measures in the Balkan area (*Konstantin*) were implemented, as initially only the Fascist regime was overthrown in Italy while the war continued. In mid-August, when Italy's impending withdrawal from the war became more obvious, planning for the two actions resumed, now under a single code name *Achse.*

616 The following day Goebbels was also summoned to the Führer Headquarters. He and Göring were received by Hitler for a first discussion on July 27 at 10 a.m., as Hitler wanted to "check the situation with his closest assistants." That day Hitler conferred nonstop—with individual midday discussions with Göring, Goebbels, Ribbentrop, Rommel, Dönitz, Speer, Keitel and Bormann, and with as many as 35 persons attending the situation conference in the evening.—*Source: Lochner, pp. 406-416.*

617 In March 1941, after a long hesitation, Prince Regent Paul of Yugoslavia and the Zvetkovic government gave in to German pressure and joined the Tripartite Pact when German troops marched into Bulgaria and Hitler conceded that Yugoslavia would not be obligated to let troop transports pass through its territory. On March 27, two days after the signing of the treaty in Vienna, the former Chief of the General Staff Dusan Simovic revolted against this change in Yugoslavia's policy. King Peter was declared to be of age and ascended the throne, the prince regent fled to Greece, the Zvetkovic government was forced to resign (some members were arrested), and all over the country—except in Croatia—anti-German demonstrations took place. Ten days later Hitler responded with military actions that soon led to the occupation of the country. [—] With the following aside, Keitel probably just wanted to indicate ironically that it was a palace revolution.

618 The Hungarians.

619 The Soviet air force had attacked Budapest on September 6, 1942. While the Soviets spoke of "extensive and continuous destruction of installations critical to the war effort," "a comprehensive bombing attack" and the occurrence of "33 large fires," the Hungarian denial claimed that only a church, a villa and a house on the outskirts of the city had been destroyed by the "random dropping of 17 bombs."—*Source: Macartney, pp. 116 and 262; DNB of Sept. 7, 1942.*

620 Maximilian Baron von Weichs; born November 12, 1881; 1902 Second Lieutenant; 1914 Cavalry Captain; in World War I adjutancy and General Staff positions; Reichswehr; 1923 Major; 1928 Lieutenant Colonel and Commander, 18th Cavalry Regiment; 1930 Colonel; 1933 Infantry Commander III and Major General; December 1933 Commander; 3rd Cavalry Division; 1935 Lieutenant General and Commander, 1st Panzer Division; 1936 General of the Cavalry; 1937 Commanding General, XIII Army Corps, after October 1939 Commander-in-Chief, Second Army in the West, in the Balkans and in the East; 1940 Colonel General; July 1942 Commander-in-Chief, Army Group B in the East, February 1943 Field Marshal, and July 1943 Führer's Reserves. [—] The following month, on August 25, 1943, Weichs (instead of Rommel) took command over the entire Balkan region as Commander-in-Chief Southeast (Army Group F) until March 22, 1945. Weichs was indicted in the Nuremberg trial against the Southeastern generals, but the proceedings were halted because of the state of his health. In November 1948 he was released from prison, and he died on September 27, 1954.—*Source: Army High Command staff files (Nbg. Dok. NOKW-042); Munzinger Archive; Siegler, p. 142.*

[621] Possible correction: "send down to the Balkan" down there, meaning the Balkans.

[622] The issue is again the evacuation of Sicily. Available ship capacity included the French steamers captured in southern France in late 1942 and small German-Italian ships and landing craft.

[623] Possibly a misunderstanding.

[624] The Strait of Messina.

[625] In July 1943 nearly 150,000 Italian workers were still in the Reich.

[626] By the "fellow" Hitler means Leopold III; born November 3, 1901; since February 23, 1934, King of the Belgians. He had surrendered with his army on May 28, 1940, and had been in the hands of the Germans ever since. One of Leopold's sisters, Princess Marie José, had married Italian Crown Prince Umberto on January 8, 1930. [—] The Belgian king had been extremely reserved after his surrender, aside from occasional interventions in favor of his country's population with the German military commander General v. Falkenhausen, and once with Hitler himself on the occasion of a visit to Berchtesgaden. Despite his earlier consent it disturbed Hitler that the king remained in Laeken Castle near Brussels, i.e., in the middle of the country. Perhaps because he was unable to seize "relatives" [of the King], Hitler abandoned, at least for the time being, the idea of "taking this fellow away." It was not until June 6, 1944, that King Leopold was taken to Germany.—*Source: Fabre-Luce, passim; Munzinger Archive.*

[627] When the Austro-Hungarian lands were distributed after World War I, the town of Fiume initially became "independent" during the already bitter border negotiations between Italy and Yugoslavia (Treaty of Rapallo, November 11, 1920)—even though the Italians had raised their claim in a way that could not be ignored (d'Annunzio's coup against Allied-occupied Fiume on September 12, 1919). However, under the agreement concluded by the two neighboring countries on January 27, 1924, it did become part of Italy. The campaign against Yugoslavia in 1941 temporarily provided the Italians with further Dalmatian acquisitions, which greatly angered the Croatians. After Italy's surrender, an administration appointed by Gauleiter Rainer of the Carinthian Gau quarreled with Croatian Undersecretary of State Turina (who had been appointed by the "Poglavnik" Ante Pavelic) over responsibility for the town. Following World War II, not only Fiume (now Rijeka) but also the whole Istrian peninsula up to the city limits of Trieste became part of Yugoslavia.

[628] On Sicily.

[629] Churchill mentions a visit by the King of England to North Africa in June 1943. It is probable that the meeting at the Cairo headquarters, reported to Hitler here, took place at that time.—*Source: Churchill IV/2 p. 456.*

[630] Henry Maitland Wilson (Baron of Libya and Stowlangtoft after 1946), born in 1881; at the beginning of the war, as a lieutenant general, he commanded the rifle brigade in Egypt. He contributed significantly to the conquest of Cyrenaica in 1940 and, in February 1941, became senior commander of the British troops there and military governor of the province. In 1941 he was commander-in-chief in Palestine, Transjordan and Syria, as well as Commander of the 9th Army. In 1942-43 he commanded in Persia and Iraq, and in 1943 he was com-

mander-in-chief in the Middle East. He succeeded Eisenhower as supreme commander of the entire Mediterranean region at Christmas 1943 and commanded—having been promoted to the rank of a field marshal—the Allied landing operations on the southern French coast in August 1944.—*Source: Who's Who 1950, p. 3025.*

631 In southern France.

632 Because the events in Italy were developing much more slowly and did not result in an immediate defection, Kesselring had no cause to implement a voluntary siege like this. On the contrary, he was received—at his urgent request—by the King as well as by Badoglio the next day.—*Source: Kesselring, p. 231.*

633 Meaning large batteries with 6 guns or normal batteries with 4 guns.

634 Recognition for aircraft shot down by the German Luftwaffe required the following evidence: 1. Over hostile territory or sea by day: confirmation by two air witnesses (i.e., usually pilots of other planes); 2. Over hostile territory or sea by night: confirmation by the radio operator or by the radio operator and the mechanic; 3. Over German territory by day: confirmation by two air witnesses (the indication of the location of the wreckage was not absolutely necessary because positioning information during non-guided pursuit was never reliable); 4. Over German territory by night: information about the location of the wreckage according to a targeting arid of where the aircraft was shut down. [—] The commission for aircraft losses decided in questionable cases—for example, in the 4th category, when there were explosions, often only the engine remained, and it might drill itself three or four meters into the ground where it could hardly be distinguished from a bomb crater.

635 Transcript No. 429/43—Fragment No. 15—The preserved shorthand record was heavily charred, so the second transcription was only possible with large gaps.

636 An order that had been prepared previously and had meanwhile been adapted to the new situation in Rome.

637 The suspicions of the German leadership had been particularly aroused in the past few weeks by Roatta's proposal to divide the German forces in Italy into five counterattack reserves, each consisting of two divisions, located in Sicily and Sardinia, and in southern, central and northern Italy, respectively. In actual and strategic terms this move was justified, and had been evaluated quite positively by Rintelen and Zeitzler at the time. Roatta—unlike the head of the *Comando Supremo*, General Ambrosio—was not among the inner circle of the conspirators because (being unaware of the negotiations being conducted at the highest level) he had unsuccessfully established contact with the Allies through General Zanussi in Lisbon. Thus, it seems plausible that he did repeatedly give his sincere denial to Generals Westphal and Toussaint on the night of Italy's armistice declaration, as he confirmed on his word of honor the following night.—*Source: Kesselring, p. 242; Westphal, p. 228.*

638 After the surrender in Tunis, the German general at the *Comando Supremo* was ordered to form three new divisions out of the backlog of units, but only two divisions were actually drawn up. Rintelen was originally supposed to be the

commanding general of this corps, but in the end he remained in his position while General Hube, who had come to Italy recently, went to Sicily in May with his General Command XIV Panzer Corps (Hube group) and essentially served as the head of the operations under the nominal command of the Italian Sixth Army. When he took over this command, Hube was instructed by Hitler not to trust any of the Italian generals and—this was probably meant sarcastically—not to accept any invitations, in order not to be poisoned or otherwise murdered on such an occasion. So Hube was surprised when he realized that the attitude of the Italian generals introduced to him was obviously quite different from that which had been described so clearly to him at the Führer Headquarters. He expressed this in a report—presumably the one quoted here—to the Armed Forces High Command, earning himself a severe rebuke.—*Source: Rintelen, p. 201; Kesselring, p. 224; Tippelskirch, p. 362.*

[639] During the evacuation of Sicily.

[640] The reference is probably to the Allied naval unit off the north coast of Sicily.

[641] Plans to occupy the Vatican, and to kidnap the Pope and bring him under secure German influence, were obvious to the National Socialist mentality, of course, and are mentioned repeatedly in the literature. Gisevius moves them to the spring of 1943, where Oster had heard about the plans and Canaris had thwarted them by giving Rome a hint. Rintelen and Abshagen, on the other hand, move these plans to the months between Mussolini's overthrow and the defection of Italy. Another source indicates that Goebbels and Ribbentrop had torpedoed the plan. Weizäcker gives an even later date. After numerous rumors and press reports, he got a hint from the Vatican as late as October 1943. Despite various efforts and explorations, however, he was unable to get a confirmation or a reliable denial of these rumors until the day the Allies entered Rome.—*Source: Gisevius, p. 470; Abshagen, p. 337; Rintelen, p. 235; Gilbert, p. 71; Weizsäcker, p. 362.*

[642] The reference is to Manstein and his planned relief attack, which is mentioned repeatedly above; "them" refers to the three SS divisions scheduled to be transferred to Italy.

[643] Once Goebbels had arrived at the Führer Headquarters on July 27, he was instructed by Hitler to "take care of the prince" and to keep him away from Italian affairs. The role of the Prince of Hesse did not come to an end until the surrender of his father-in-law.—*Source: Lochner, p. 413.*

[644] Italian fortifications along the passes in the Alps.

[645] Transcript number unknown (presumably 430/43)—Fragment No. 16—Because the preserved shorthand record was heavily charred, the second transcription was possible only with large gaps.

[646] The evacuation of Sicily.

[647] After the first Russian winter, Horthy had appointed Nikolaus v. Kállay the new prime minister on March 10, 1942, under the assumption that he would be the suitable man to "take steps to bring about more friendly relations with the Anglo-Saxons while preserving the foreign relations with Hitler and Germany and without aiding the Soviets." After establishing initial contact through Polish exile circles, Kállay managed to get in direct contact with the English via Turkey in

the summer of 1942. He offered to take active measures against Germany as early as 1943, provided that a way could be found to geographically link the operations of the armed forces of the two countries. On September 9, 1943, a first meeting took place between an official Hungarian representative and the English ambassador in Ankara, Sir Hugh Knatchbull-Hugessen—behind the back of the Hungarian envoy in Turkey, who was unreliable for such purposes. It can be supposed that Hitler was informed about this Hungarian-English entanglement.—*Source: Horthy, p. 251; Kállay, p. 369.*

[648] Himmler, Dönitz and Rommel, like Göring and other high-ranking Nazi personalities, were summoned to Rastenburg to discuss the events in Italy.

[649] Sardinia.

[650] Northern Italy.

[651] In France.

[652] This judgment was also confirmed many times by other unprejudiced parties. Because these divisions consisted of specially selected young people, their attitude is not surprising. This procedure of gathering together an elite in a few privileged divisions also had a negative side. The military was deprived of young conscripts, as these youths were missing when their age groups were called up. A huge number of these boys died as young soldiers; had they survived until they were somewhat older, they would have provided an outstanding new crop of non-commissioned officers and officers for the whole army.

[653] Friedrich Dollmann; born February 2, 1882; 1901 Second Lieutenant; 1914 Captain; Reichswehr; 1930 Colonel; 1931 Commander, 6th Artillery Regiment; 1932 Major General and Artillery Commander, VII; 1933 Lieutenant General; 1934 Commanding General, IV Army Corps; April 1936 General of Artillery; after October 1939 Commander-in-Chief, Seventh Army on the Upper Rhine front and later in northwestern France; and July 1940 Colonel General. On June 27, 1944, during the invasion battles, Dollmann died of heart failure while at his command post.—*Source: VB of July 1, 1944; Seemen; Das deutsche Heer, p. 144; Rangliste 1944-45, p. 14; Keilig 211/67.*

[654] Johannes Blaskowitz; born July 10, 1883; 1902 Second Lieutenant; 1914 Captain; in World War I company commander, battalion commander and General Staff officer; Reichswehr; 1922 Major; 1929 Colonel; 1930 Commander, 14th Infantry Regiment; 1933 inspector of the Arms schools and Lieutenant General; 1935 Commander in Military District [Wehrkreis] II; 1936 General of the Infantry; 1938 Commander-in-Chief, Third Army Group; 1939 Colonel General; in the Polish campaign, Commander-in-Chief, Eighth Army (Kutno, Warsaw); and after October 1939, Commander-in-Chief East. Blaskowitz's memorandum about the excesses of the SS in Poland was taken amiss by Hitler, to the extent that Blaskowitz was given only a reserve command in the French campaign and thus did not receive the marshal's baton. From October 1940 to May 1944 Blaskowitz was inactive as Commander-in-Chief of the First Army in the West; he subsequently became Commander-in-Chief of Army Group G in Southern France, which, however, was disparagingly designated "Armeegruppe" [Army Group] at first. After the retreat from the mouth of the Rhone to the Vosges

mountains, Blaskowitz was—supposedly at the instigation of Himmler, who hadn't forgotten his behavior in Poland, but probably also through Göring's influence—relieved again on September 20, but called back again on December 24. On January 28, 1945, Blaskowitz transferred to the northern wing of the Western front as Commander-in-Chief of Army Group H, and surrendered as Commander-in-Chief Netherlands/Fortress Holland. Blaskowitz, of all people, was accused in the Nuremberg Armed Forces High Command trial; he committed suicide on the way to his first court appearance on February 5, 1948, by jumping into the stairwell.—*Source: Army High Command staff files (Nbg. Dok. NOKW-141); Siegler, p. 113; Munzinger Archive.*

[655] Gerd v. Rundstedt; born December 12, 1875; 1893 Second Lieutenant, 83rd Infantry Regiment; 1909 Captain in the General Staff; in World War I various positions in the General Staff; 1923 Colonel and Commander, 18th Infantry Regiment; 1927 Major General; 1929 Lieutenant General and Commander, 2nd Cavalry Division; 1932 Commander, 3rd Infantry Division and General of Infantry; 1932 to 1938 Commander-in-Chief, First Command Group (Berlin); March 1938 Colonel General; October 31, 1938 left the service; in the Polish campaign, Commander-in-Chief, Army Group South; in France, Commander-in-Chief, Army Group A and also (after October 25, 1940) Commander-in-Chief, West; July 19, 1940 Field Marshal; in the Eastern campaign; Commander-in-Chief, Army Group South until December 3, 1941; from March 1942 to July 3, 1944 and again from early September 1944 to March 10, 1945, Commander-in-Chief West; and (until September 10, 1944) Commander-in-Chief Army Group D. Rundstedt presided over the court of honor that expelled the July assassins from the Armed Forces, and he gave the eulogy at Rommel's "state funeral." He died on February 24, 1953.—*Source: Army High Command staff files (Nbg. Dok. NOKW-141); Munzinger Archive; Blumentritt, passim.*

[656] The reference is probably to the son-in-law of the KZ [concentration camp] organizer Eicke, SS Obersturmbannführer Karl Leiner, who was born June 14, 1905, later commander of the 2nd Heavy Panzer Detachment in the III SS Panzer Corps.

[657] This passing thought did not need to be considered later because the German troops marching through in the days that followed effectively occupied South Tyrol.

[658] Follows as a separate transcript.

[659] Should be "and."

[660] The 1st Parachute Division had just been flown from France to Sicily without its vehicles, etc., earlier in July (air crossing to the island started July 12). The two parachute divisions mentioned several times here were the only ones of that kind at the time. The 1st was established in the spring and the 2nd was still in formation during the summer; six others followed from late 1943 to late 1944, but these soon became triangular Luftwaffe field divisions under different names.—*Source: Order of Battle, p. 322; Kesselring, p. 223.*

[661] Kurt Student; born May 12, 1890; active officer in World War I, pilot with five air victories; Reichswehr; 1933 RLM; 1940 Lieutenant General; jumped over

Holland as the divisional commander of the paratroopers (7th Air Division); initiator and commander of the paratroop action against Crete in May 1941 (XI Air Corps), which involved heavy losses; in September 1943 together with Skorzeny assigned by Hitler to liberate Mussolini; May 1944 Commander-in-Chief, Parachute Army; July 1944 Colonel General; November 1944 to end of January 1945 Commander-in-Chief Army Group H; in the second half of April 1945, Commander-in-Chief, Parachute Army; and, in the last days of the war, Commander-in-Chief Army Group Vistula. In May 1946 Student was sentenced by a British military court in Lüneburg to 5 years of imprisonment.— *Source: Munzinger Archive; Siegler, p. 139; Order of Battle, p. 631; Hove, passim.*

662   During the evacuation of Sicily.

663   After Mussolini accepted German aid for Libya during the Berchtesgaden meeting of January 19-20, 1941, there were, in principle, no difficulties surrounding the transport of German units to Italy. However, the troops had to be reported to the Italians and were subordinated—at least formally—to the *Comando Supremo*, or, after May 1943, to the German Commander-in-Chief South at the *Comando Supremo*. Supposedly because of the expected difficulties, and also to maintain the element of surprise, Ramcke's 2nd Parachute Division, intended for use in Operation *Alaric*, was not transported by land from southern France but was suddenly and surprisingly dropped at the Pratica di Mare airfield near Rome—without even informing Kesselring about it beforehand. This was most likely the result of the situation report at hand. Shortly thereafter, several German divisions marched into Italy by land and occupied the passes in the Alps. Rome was notified of the border crossing only afterward, and the divisions were not subordinated to the Commander-in-Chief South (who was no longer accredited to the *Comando Supremo*) but to Rommel's Army Group B in Munich. The Italians protested in vain. The German march onto the Po plain and the securing of the passes in the Alps were, among other things, issues discussed in the meeting between Ribbentrop and Keitel, and Guariglia and Ambrosio in Tarvisio on August 6, 1943. In addition, there was very nearly a serious incident when the Italian General Gloria gave his men the order to fire on the 44th Infantry Division, which was entering South Tyrol.—*Source: Rintelen, p. 226; Kesselring, p. 234; Rommel Papers, p. 433; Westphal, p. 223.*

664   Due to the Italian news ban, reports about this matter did not trickle through to the international press until July 28. That day in the same issue of the *Neue Zürcher Zeitung* there were two different articles about the former director of the Stefani agency, Senator Morgagni: his resignation was reported from the Italian border, and the Italian press reported his death. Two days later the newspaper published rumors about Morgagni's suicide and that of Virginio Gayda. Giulio Morgagni, born in 1897, had been director of the Stefani agency since 1924 and a senator since 1939. Roberto Suster succeeded him.—*Source: NZZ of July 26 (morning edition), July 28 (evening edition) and July 30 (evening edition), 1943.*

665   Hitler intended to give Rommel the command over all of Italy as soon as the Axis partner went over to the other side. This plan, however, was not implemented—not even when Italy finally renounced Germany on September 3 and

8, 1943. Rather, Rommel had the command in northern Italy only, and even there he led and kept it only until mid-November 1943. Differences between Rommel and Kesselring had already emerged during the African campaign, on one hand due to the opposition between Luftwaffe and Army, which was becoming obvious elsewhere, and on the other because of differing evaluations of the Italian attitude and position. The new division of the command in Italy (army group border line: Elba–Ancona) only brought new conflicts, of course. Because of the relatively favorable developments in the military situation in Italy—developments that had been predicted by Kesselring—Hitler, after much vacillation, decided in favor of Kesselring and his strategic concept (defense south of Rome). Kesselring, as Commander-in-Chief Southwest, was given the supreme command of the Italian theater, effective November 21, 1943.—*Source: Tippelskirch, p. 412; Rommel Papers, p. 425; Kesselring, passim; Westphal, p. 236.*

666 In southern Italy, where they could have made considerable difficulties for the German troops, the war-weary Italian units later simply dispersed. Kesselring, accurately assessing the situation and the Italians' numerical strength, let them go or called for local amicable agreements. In this way, the Carboni corps, hesitantly still in the Rome area, surrendered and was subsequently released. In northern Italy, on the other hand, Rommel—who tried to force Kesselring to take similar measures—interned the Italian units, a practice which drove many of them into the partisan camp.—*Source: Tippelskirch, p. 375; Kesselring, p. 255; Rommel Papers, p. 445; Westphal, pp. 229 and 233.*

667 These somewhat implausible ideas generated in the first hours were never actually implemented. A "Fascist Freedom Army" never existed, but in September, during their first talks after Mussolini's liberation, the two dictators did agree formally on the reconstruction of the "forze armate." In practice, however, the Germans hindered the immediate training and appropriate ideological indoctrination instruction of the half-million military internees they were holding. The operational planning of the Armed Forces High Command—due to not unjustified distrust—also limited the Italian contribution to the defense of the Apennine Peninsula to the deployment of construction battalions and, later, coastal fortification batteries. In 1944, four Fascist divisions (*San Marco, Monterosa, Italia* and *Littoria*) were eventually built up in Germany over the course of the year. They were armed from German arsenals and trained by the German Armed Forces, but the personnel was recruited in Italy—and only a small fraction of them came from the internment camps—as the German authorities (for a variety of reasons, including the labor shortage) continued to forbid voluntary enrollment in Germany. Mussolini had also just inspected these divisions when he arrived at the Führer Headquarters on July 20, 1944, in order to negotiate, among other issues, the transportation and deployment of these units. When the four divisions arrived in northern Italy in October 1944, many of their personnel deserted. The rest were used in the fight against the partisans and made brief contact with Allied forces only in the Garfagnana valley. (See also above note 588.)—*Sources: Anfuso, pp. 249, 254, 273, 295, 301, 310, 323, 328, and 331; Moellhausen, p. 265; Toynbee: Hitler's Europe, p. 325.*

668 Badoglio turned 73 in September 1944. Victor Emmanuel III had reached this age in November 1942.

669 The reference here is either to Leiner again (see above note 656) or Himmler's personal envoy in Italy and rival of Kappler, the regular police attaché there, SS Obersturmbannführer (after November 9, 1943, Standartenführer) Dr. Eugen Dollmann. Dollmann, born August 21, 1900, was originally an art historian, and had made his way as a guide in Italy. He made himself indispensable as an interpreter during Himmler's visit to Libya, then joined the SS and was taken into the German embassy in 1939. The smooth schemer, who became known for his relations with the gilded youth of the Roman aristocracy, had worked against the house of Savoy since 1941 and—as the Italian embassy in Berlin was informed—for Farinacci. During the period of the Republic of Saló, Dollmann was an influential police commander in German-occupied Italy. He is the author of a book, *Roma nazista*, that is full of dubious information.—*Sources: Wiskemann, pp. 157, 285, and 325; Skorzeny, p. 112; Hagen: Unternehmen Bernhard, p. 124.*

670 The division number is incorrect in one of these two cases.

671 The 2nd SS Panzer Division *Das Reich* remained in the East at the time.

672 "Indian" is hardly likely; this was either a misunderstanding or Hitler's ironic term for a unit consisting of foreign personnel.

673 Reconstitution of the General Command IV Army Corps, which had been destroyed in Stalingrad; it remained in the southern sector of the Eastern Front, however.—*Source: Order of Battle, p. 117; Manstein, p. 550 and others.*

674 Badoglio—comrade-in-arms with the French in World War I and certainly against the German alliance from the very beginning—had argued against Italy's joining the war in 1939. This stance was based simply on the knowledge he had acquired in his role as Chief of General Staff of the desperate state of the Italian armed forces and armaments. However, one can hardly speak of a key role for Badoglio, as Hitler wants to know here. Badoglio resigned on December 6, 1940, in connection with the miserable result of the Italian invasion of Greece, and since then he had lived a private life in quiet opposition. (See also above note 410.)—*Source: Ciano; Wiskemann; Cilibrizzi; Badoglio.*

675 Presumably these were Allied naval units operating north of Sicily in support of the Allied troops' advance along the coast.

676 This was the Italian steamer *Viminale*, which was recovered in Palermo on January 3, 1941, after having been damaged by British midget craft, and was towed to Messina. The ship was torpedoed and sunk by the British submarine *Unbending* off Cape Vaticano on July 25, 1943, at 3 a.m.

677 At this point, La Spezia was still a German submarine base, where boats of the 29th Submarine Flotilla anchored.

678 The Germans settled in Italy in the coming weeks, waiting for the Italian defection. They tried at the end of August (with two divisions) to secure La Spezia, where the bulk of the Italian fleet was anchored, saying that this port must have particularly strong protection against a potentially hostile landing. However, the Italians saw through this game and moved other forces to La Spezia, declaring

the protection of this base by their own forces to be an issue of prestige. Thus, the Italian fleet under Admiral Bergamini, fulfilling the armistice conditions, was able to put to sea during the night of September 8 from La Spezia—joined by other minor elements from Genoa, Taranto, Pola, etc.—and follow a zigzag course to Malta for internment, even though it was part of the German *Achse* (or, previously, the *Alarich*) plan to prevent the Italian units from fleeing in case of a collapse. The German command, as well as some of the Italian army officers, obviously including Bergamini himself, were misled by messages about putting to sea for an upcoming decisive battle. All in all, the British were able to intern 5 battleships, 8 cruisers, 31 destroyers and torpedo boats, 40 submarines, and numerous small craft, as well as 170,000 GRT in merchant ships. Some units were sunk by the Germans—for instance, the battleship *Roma* was destroyed by a remote-controlled glider bomb. Four warships were interned in Spain and held there until January 1945. Fifty ships were scuttled in ports under the control of the Germans or the Japanese. Only the popular "Decima MAS" midget craft combat unit—the 10th MAS Flotilla (*motoscafi anti-sommergibili*: motor torpedo boats) under the leadership of Prince Valerio Borghese—remained loyal to Mussolini. Some other shipping was taken over by the Germans, mostly after smaller sabotage actions or sinkings in shallow waters, such as the battleships *Cavour* and *Impero*, 2 aircraft carriers, 2 cruisers, and various torpedo boat and destroyer flotillas in the Ligurian Sea, the upper Adriatic and the Aegean. However, practically without the Italian crews, the smaller units (which only the Germans preferred and which only the Germans put into commission) all had to be manned by German crews. Mussolini at Saló was extremely outraged by this inglorious end to "his" fleet.—*Source: Tippelskirch, p. 368; Ruge: Seekrieg, p. 256; Anfuso, p. 262; Rintelen, p. 248; de Belot, p. 226; Westphal, p. 226; Moellhausen, p. 257; Trizzino, p. 121.*

[679] An attack by the German torpedo squadron (K.G. 26) off the Algerian coast.

[680] The commander of the Eleventh Italian Army in southern Greece was General Vecchiarelli.

[681] During this time, the German side was trying to implement a better—and safer—division of orders in the Balkans. They proposed that the Italians place their Eleventh Army in Greece under the command of the German Commander-in-Chief Southeast/Army Group E (Löhr). In return, the German troops in the region—especially the LXVIII Army Corps (Felmy)—should be placed under the command of this Eleventh Army.

[682] The Adriatic coast of the Balkans as well as the Greek regions along the Ionian Sea, except the Peloponnese, remained occupied by Italian troops. They were not expected to resist an Allied landing very seriously, regardless of where it might take place, but German troops could not replace them before the complete defection of Italy. Thus, the *Konstantin* plan called for German units to move from the hinterland to the coast in preparation. However, the German defense would not have been able to resist a landing either—due to weak forces, the neglect of the coastal fortifications by the Italians, and the constant partisan

warfare. Thus, an Allied invasion through the Balkans toward Central Europe had a very good chance of success, despite the difficult terrain.

[683] It took place one month later.

[684] Hitler's and Göring's assertions were not completely unfounded.

[685] The reason for this conference was probably a letter dated May 7, 1943, from Foreign Secretary Eden to the prime minister of the Yugoslav government-in-exile; the letter was passed on to Mihailović on May 28 and its contents were confirmed on June 1 by the general. In this letter, Eden promised the Četniks increased support, but requested intensified activity against the Axis troops on their part, no further contact with Prime Minister Nedić or the Italians, and an end to the constant friction with the Tito partisans. In London, however, in the next few weeks, the die was cast against Mihailović, and in the course of the year the tone of the British press towards both Yugoslavian rivals began to change as well. Due to constant pressure from Churchill, the Allied support for the Četniks stopped; however, he was not able to get Tito to recognize King Peter. Finally, Teheran and Churchill's speech in the House of Commons on May 24, 1944, brought to light the final consequences of this development.—*Source: Fotitch, p. 223; Matl, p. 99; Churchill V/2, p. 166.*

[686] The "Serbian Volunteer Corps (SDK)," consisting of five battalions, and the "Serbian State Guard," 18,000 men together with the "Serbian Border Guard," were the armed formations created in 1941 or 1942 by the Nedić government.—*Source: Matl, p. 110.*

[687] The relocation of another submarine group into the Mediterranean Sea did not start before September 1943. In July, no submarines came from the Atlantic into the Mediterranean.

[688] On July 23, the *U197* sank a 9,583 GRT Swedish motorized tanker, the *Pegasus*, near Durban.

[689] As a result of the German tonnage war, a British source quotes the following monthly totals of Allied and neutral shipping capacity sunk in 1943:

GRT	January	50	ships	totaling	261,359
GRT	February	73	"	"	403,062
GRT	March	120	"	"	693,389
GRT	April	64	"	"	344,680
GRT	May	58	"	"	299,428
GRT	June	28	"	"	123,825
GRT	July	61	"	"	365,398
GRT	August	25	"	"	119,801
GRT	September	29	"	"	156,419
GRT	October	29	"	"	139,861
GRT	November	29	"	"	144,391
GRT	December	31	"	"	168,524
		597	ships	totaling	3,220,137 GRT

For the losses caused only by submarines in July 1943, an official British source quotes the following figures:

Atlantic/Arctic Ocean   24 ships totaling 136,106 GRT
Indian Ocean   15 ships totaling 82,404 GRT
Mediterranean Sea   5 ships totaling 25,977 GRT

According to a German survey, 50 ships (totaling 248,969 GRT) were sunk by German submarines that month, 38 of them (totaling 213,047 GRT) in the Atlantic. The statement of the 18 submarines lost in that month to date is correct (July 7: *U951*; July 8: *U232*; July 9: *U590*; July 12: *U506*; July 13: *U487*; July 14: *U160*; July 15: *U159*, *U509*, *U135*; July 16: *U67*; July 19: *U513*; July 20: *U558*; July 21: *U662*; July 23: *U527*, *U613*, *U598*; July 24: *U622*; July 26: *U759*); seven others followed.—*Source: Churchill V/1, p. 417; Morison: The Atlantic Battle Won, pp. 365 and 370.*

[690] Here, Dönitz possibly means an acoustically controlled torpedo "Zaunkönig" ["Wren"] (T5) under development for more than 10 years, and first deployed on September 19, 1943. This torpedo used a magnetic-vibration sound receiver that reacted to the destroyers' propeller noise, adjusted itself automatically, and ran toward the destroyer, exploding 3 or 4 meters below the ship (this technique was later improved for the T11 or "Geier" ["vulture"], which no longer reacted to the sonic buoys pulled as decoys by hostile ships). At the same time, the ships were equipped with improved flak and search radar instruments that did not produce detectible signals. [—] But the reference could also be to equipping the boats with a hydraulically extendable aerial mast, the so-called "snorkel," which would make it unnecessary to surface when loading the batteries from the diesel engines—which had became particularly dangerous since the development of the Rotterdam installations. However, the boats were still forced to operate constantly under water, which made them practically immobile due to their low speed. Despite this, the "snorkel" is still part of the equipment in almost all submarines used in special cases.—*Source: Busch, pp. 184 and 287; Görlitz I, p. 561; Assmann, p. 407; Ruge: Seekrieg, p. 234; Lusar, pp. 126 and 136; Bley, p. 25; Hinsley, p. 230.*

[691] In 1943, as long as American four-engine bomber units entered German territory with no (or very little) protection from fighters, Heavy Fighter Wings 26 and 76 were quite successful at shooting down enemy aircraft—the highlight being the air raid against Schweinfurt on October 14, 1943. The new Me 410 (using the frame of the 210 but with different engines)—which was used in addition to the older models, the Me 110 and the faultily constructed Me 210—was better armed, had a greater climbing ability and was about 80 km/h faster than these other types (635 km/h); however, its turning radius was worse, it was more sensitive technically and in combat, and it was difficult for the crew to get out in case of fire. [—] However, the successes did not last very long: with the extension of American long-distance fighter protection over German territory, the destroyers suffered unbearable losses after the end of 1943. When attacking enemy formations, they had to be accompanied by their own fighter protection, and after a short time, they were successful only in cases where there were no enemy escorts. Finally, in the summer of 1944, the destroyer operations stopped

and the two wings were re-equipped with single-engine fighters. [—] Apart from this, the Me 410 was used as a so-called fast bomber in occasional minor "retaliation attacks" against England and as a night fighter against the Mosquitoes. All in all, 900 aircraft of this type were produced (1943: 271, 1944: 629).—*Source: Galland, pp. 260, 271 and 279; Feuchter, pp. 213, 235 and 244; Baumbach, p. 314; Lusar, p. 54.*

692 The Soviets paid special attention to the fighter-bomber intended for direct intervention in ground battle operations. Whereas the Germans preferred the dive-bomber for this purpose, the Western Allies preferred the fighter-bomber, and the Russians had further developed the German armored Junkers "infantry aircraft" (J4) from World War I. In this aircraft type, the engine and crew were housed in a strong armored hull, which protected them from infantry and machine gun projectiles and from the splinters of light anti-aircraft artillery, but which could be penetrated by calibers of more than 2 cm—as stated in the text. Except for this hull, the Russians, due to their lack of light metals, used wood as the primary building material for their fighter IL 2—as well as for all other fighters except the 1944 models LA 7 and LA 9—for the whole rear fuselage, the tail, and the outer parts of the wings. Therefore, the German fighters learned very quickly how to attack the Shturmoviks successfully from above. The German side had also been building an armored fighter-bomber since 1942, the Hs 129.—*Source: Feuchter, pp. 193 and 235; Goudima, p. 119; Hoffmann: Sowjetluftmacht, passim.*

693 Toward the end of the war, a normal panzer regiment had a Panzer IV detachment (which often consisted of—due to the shortage of tanks—an assault gun company) and a Panther division. For the Panther divisions, Hitler's initial wish was to equip each of the four planned companies with 22 tanks (4x5+2 company staff), but due to the existing possibilities they could be equipped only with 17 tanks (3x5+2 company staff).

694 With the new equipment, the panzer division now had only 4x17+3 detachment staff = 71 vehicles.

695 The "Panther" was born under an unlucky star. Intended as a German "T34," the choice between two design options was made in favor of the solution from the MAN factories, which, after a test period of a few weeks, seemed to be successful. However, the 200 Panthers which were supposed to be ready for the summer offensive at the beginning of May 1943 had to be reported as inoperable. They had transmission and engine failures that could not be overcome, despite two modification attempts. Although the defects were resolved after several weeks, this was only the beginning of a series of "teething troubles," which continued until April 1944. The differentials and the optics, for example, were weak points that resulted in many difficulties due to premature use. [—] Here "Ruder" (rudder) is probably a typing error and should mean "Räder" (wheels), which probably meant the gear teeth of the differentials that had to be reinforced. The "membrane" probably meant difficulties related to the fuel pump. As for the "modifications," the reference was to the "aprons," which were fixed

to the Panther and, after February 1943, to the Panzer IV and assault guns: armored sheets loosely fixed at the external walls, which were intended to protect the vertical parts of the hull and the tracks and suspension from armor-piercing infantry ammunition.—*Source: Guderian: Erinnerungen, pp. 258, 271, 279 and 282.*

696 Senior service officer Karl Otto Saur; born June 16, 1902; entered the Todt office in 1937 after twelve years working in industry (Thyssen); after 1940 he worked in the Reich Ministry for Arms and Ammunition (later the Reich Ministry for Armament and War Production); and after 1942 he was head of the technical office there, in March 1944 became head of the "fighter staff" that was not only given special legal powers but was also responsible for the production of fighter-bombers.

697 Lieutenant Colonel (Colonel after August 1, 1944) Friedrich Stollberg, born August 5, 1889, and came from the Armed Forces' periodicals department in the Army Ordnance Office.—*Source: Das deutsche Heer, p. 29; Rangliste 1944-45, p. 234.*

698 Helmuth Stieff; born June 6, 1901; 1917 war volunteer; Reichswehr; 1922 Second Lieutenant; 1934 Captain; 1938 Major in the Senior Quartermaster staff in the 1st Department, Army General Staff; at the beginning of the war he was head of Group III there; in 1941 Ia, Fourth Army; 1942 Colonel; after December 1942 chief of the Organizational Department in the Army General Staff; and January 30, 1944 Major General.—*Source: Munzinger Archive; Keilig 211/328.*

699 Colonel (April 1, 1944, Major General) Werner Marcks, born July 17, 1896; was one of four colonels from the staff of the Inspector General of Panzer Troops who always stayed with the troops to identify and report mistakes, defects, etc.

700 The "Panther" couldn't operate in the Southeast, as the mountainous terrain was not favorable for tank operations.

701 The Hornet (*Hornisse*)—also called "Rhino" (*Nashorn*)—was a 26-ton tank destroyer, a self-propelled 8.8-cm antitank gun on a Panzer IV chassis.

702 French training ground south of Rennes.

703 This was a miscommunication. There never was a Panzer III with an 8-cm long gun.

704 "Assault guns" were developed in 1935-36 to accompany the infantry. They were guns set into tank hulls, which—in contrast to the armored fighting vehicle, and due to the fact that there was no turret—could only operate facing forward within the circle of their pivot range. In the course of the war, despite their minimal speed, these weapons were used as makeshift antitank guns and tank destroyers, and even Panzer detachments had to be partially equipped with assault guns instead of Panzer IVs.

705 Possibly worn-out training equipment.

706 The "Goliath" (BI) was a small, unmanned Panzer, 61 cm high, with a 90.7 kg explosive charge. It was operated by remote control, or—in another version—by a roll-off wire from a 1,000 m distance. The Goliath was used to destroy strongly fortified bases, battery positions, tanks, and bridges, and to find and remove mine fields. Remote control had to take place from a tank in order to

advance as close as possible to the target. Panzer IIIs were usually used, but sometimes—as mentioned here—also assault guns or other tanks. Sometimes this weapon produced good results, but frequent teething troubles with the remote control prevented a final decision on its combat value. Large-scale production was initiated at first, but was practically stopped later. The "Grabenwolf" was a similar remote-controlled mini-tank.—*Source: Schneider, p. 230; Lusar, p. 30.*

[707] 15-cm sIG [heavy infantry gun] 33 L/12 on a Panzer IV chassis (Assault Panzer IV, "Brummbär").—*Source: Wiener: Typen-Numerierung.*

[708] Transcript No. S 142/43—Fragment No. 17—completely preserved.

[709] The first German report about the fall of Mussolini was broadcast the morning of that July 26 during the 7 a.m. news. The announcements regarding the dismissal of the Duce were limited to the following single sentence: "It is assumed that the change in government is due to the state of health of the Duce, who has been ill."—*Source: NZZ of July 26, 1943 (evening edition); DNB of July 26, 1943.*

[710] Since his visit to Italy in May 1938, Hitler had had no illusions about the hostile attitude of many in the Italian upper class toward the alliance with Germany, or their relationship to Fascism. Frequent statements made at the dinner table showed his concern, which continued to increase in the last year of cooperation with this ally: "True Fascism is friendly to Germany, but the Italian court clique is completely hostile toward the German world. In Florence, the Duce told me: My soldiers are decent, well-behaved people, but I cannot trust my officers!...There won't be a positive selection until this upper-class Mafia is abolished...It's not going to get better in Italy unless they produce a pure Führer state!" (Feb. 17, 1942). "...whereby one should take into account that this (Italian royal) court has always made the Duce's work difficult during the long years of Fascism, and even today is still flirting with England." (April 23, 1942). "In the end, Germany owes it to the Duce that Italy is not in the Allies' camp in this war. If we weren't satisfied with the results of the Italian alliance in every respect, it is due to the fact that the king and the court had preserved too many possibilities for intervention in the areas of military and political life." (July 24, 1942). Hitler said to Goebbels on March 20, 1942, that Mussolini was "...the only guarantor of German-Italian collaboration...If here and there German-Italian collaboration doesn't function, that isn't Mussolini's fault but rather because of the lack of military qualities of the Italian people themselves." And one year later, on March 9, 1943, an entry was made in the same Goebbels diary: "The Duce doesn't actually have so much power as it would appear. The aristocracy and the court sabotage all his decisions ... that's the reason why the Führer would like to leave our anti-aircraft in Italy, because he would then have a certain feeling of security as regards Italy." On that same day, Goebbels also mentioned the plan that had been discussed here to draw up 10 to 15 Black Shirt divisions in the Reich and train them in SS methods, in order to provide a "reliable guard" for the Duce "if worst comes to worst." And on April 21, Sepp Dietrich reported that Mussolini had become an old man—

looking ill and frail, and giving a tired and weak impression—and that he was deceived "right, left and center" by his generals.—*Source: Picker, pp. 204, 77 and 121; Lochner, pp. 135, 286, and 339.*

[711] To free the captive Mussolini, the so-called operation "Eiche" ["Oak"] was immediately initiated by Hitler. That same evening of July 26 he selected from among six officers ordered to the Führer Headquarters SS Hauptsturmführer Otto Skorzeny (the head of the sabotage group in Section VI of the RSHA and a former classmate of Kaltenbrunner) and gave him the mission. While Himmler brought together the clairvoyants, astrologists, occultists, etc. (who had been sent to concentration camps after their protector Hess fled to England) in a villa at the Berlin Wannsee to find Mussolini's prison, the German intelligence service in Italy and the Skorzeny team, dressed as paratroopers, actually succeeded in discovering Mussolini's location. The first action against the island of La Maddalena near Sardinia failed on August 26 due to Skorzeny's gross carelessness—the Badoglio authorities were able to transport their prisoner to another location the morning before. But on September 12, Mussolini was successfully freed from a mountain hotel at Campo Imperatore on the Gran Sasso mountain, despite heavy losses due to a risky landing in the rugged Abruzzi Mountains. Nevertheless, the Duce's plane was nearly smashed to pieces on the Abruzzo rocks because of the very short runway and the fact that in this precarious situation Skorzeny had insisted on loading his two hundred kilos into the weak two-seater Storch in order to be able to pose immediately as "Mussolini's liberator."—*Source: Skorzeny, p. 95; Hagen: Unternehmen Bernhard, p. 123.*

[712] The German word "unvesehrt" ("sound") might have been written by mistake; probably "versierte" ("experienced") units were meant instead.

[713] Here it most likely should have been: "These are, first of all, the three armored divisions," meaning—in addition to the 1st *LAH*, the 2nd *Das Reich*, the 3rd *Totenkopf*, or the 5th *Wiking* [Viking]—all those stationed in the Army Group South area at that time. Of these divisions, only the 1st *LAH* was moved to Italy, and it was there only temporarily, until the fall. Hitler left the other two with Army Group South.—*Source: Order of Battle, p. 336; Manstein, p. 518.*

[714] The Orel salient.

[715] In the Orel salient.

[716] Because 25 was the highest German army number—and Hitler would have found a reference to "the XX Army" far too general, and would have questioned it— the 34th Infantry Division must be meant here, which at that time was fighting north of Orel between Voronskii and Iagenovichi.

[717] Strategy expression taken from chess, used to describe a traffic line running behind the front.

[718] Walter Model; born January 24, 1891; Second Lieutenant, 52nd Infantry Regiment; Reichswehr; 1930 Major; 1934 Colonel; 1938 and in the Polish campaign, Chief of General Staff, IV Army Corps as Major General; in the Western campaign, Lieutenant General and Chief of Staff, Sixteenth Army (Busch); November 1940 Commander, 3rd Panzer Division; October 1941 General of the Panzer Troops and Commanding General, XXXXI Panzer Corps; and after January

1942 Commander-in-Chief, Ninth Army and Colonel General. In the withdrawal battles, the "Lion of the Defense" took command at various critical points. In the East in January 1944, he took over command of Army Group North from Küchler, at the end of March he took over command of Army Group North Ukraine from Manstein, and in June he took over command of Army Group Center from Busch. In mid-August he succeeded Kluge as Commander-in-Chief West and took over Army Groups D and B; and he led Army Group B until its surrender in the Ruhr pocket on April 17, 1945. After this finale, Model—who had become field marshal in April 1944 and who had been awarded the Diamonds by Hitler on August 17, 1944—committed suicide in a forest east of Dusseldorf on April 21, 1945.—*Source: Huyssen, passim; Munzinger Archive; Görlitz II, p. 192; Siegler, p. 132; Das deutsche Heer, p. 100; Keilig 211/222.*

[719] Hitler, a bit confused, may have had the picture of a magnet in mind.

[720] The Roman daily, *Il Messaggero*, had been edited by the former minister of education, Pavolini, who, like Gayda at the *Giornale d'Italia* and the other Fascist editors, was dismissed from his post. So the *Messaggero* was no exception; all other Italian newspapers cheered the fall of the regime as well.—*Source: NZZ of July 28 (evening edition) and July 29 (morning edition), 1943.*

[721] The improvement of the "Hagen Line, i.e., the Dnieper Line, had just begun that summer, although Zeitzler had recommended the construction of such a reserve position shortly after Stalingrad. Hitler rejected the idea, fearing that his generals would be tempted to retreat to it if they knew there was a solid line behind them. But now Hitler needed forces for Italy and thus demanded a shortening of the front. Kluge, however, thought it necessary to continue operating east of the Dnieper until the improvements to the Hagen Line were completed; according to his plans, the position would not have been occupied until the beginning of the winter, after a slow retreat in several stages. The withdrawal movement, initially to the east of Briansk, now began on July 31 and progressed as planned despite strong Russian pressure.—*Source: Wilmot, p. 149; Tippelskirch, p. 382; Gilbert, p. 60.*

[722] As the mayor of the Lokot' District, 80 km southeast of Briansk, an engineer Kaminskii, a native resident full of Social-Fascist ideas—with support from Second Panzer Army AOK 2 (General Rudolf Schmidt) stationed in Orel—established a militia, as was done in many other places, to fight against partisan attacks. The militia, later called "Volkswehr" (Narodnaia Strasha) was intended as a real farmers' resistance. In his district, which he extended with other districts to form the "autonomous district of Lokot'," he commanded a well-functioning administrative apparatus and an armed force to be reckoned with, the so-called RONA (*Russkaia Osvoboditel'naia Narodnaia Armiia*—Russian People's Liberation Army). In the fall of 1943, "Brigadier General" Kaminski (this rank had been "awarded" to him by the Second Panzer Army) had to move to the west with his units—which had been equipped with heavy guns and T 34s in the meantime—along with the majority of the civilian population. The brigade was settled in the Lepel' District by the Belarussian Commissioner General v. Gottberg, where it was used to fight against the partisans

in the rear (as it would be again later, after another retreat). During these missions, however, the Kaminski brigade (Kaminski had in the meantime been awarded the uniform of an SS Oberführer) became increasingly demoralized, until even the SS leaders lost control of the brigade. The men carried out baseless and excessive plundering during the suppression of the Warsaw insurrection in the summer of 1944, when they worked together with the notorious Dirlewanger Probationary [Penal] Unit. In his flight through the Carpathian Mountains, Kaminski was captured by the SS—in a way that is not quite clear—and killed; the blood of animals was used to fake a robbery. According to statements by Reinefarth, the leader of the Warsaw action, Kaminski was "executed" because he was unwilling or unable to prevent his brigade from plundering, slaughtering, and committing other atrocities, despite an order forbidding these actions. His remaining troops were absorbed in November by the 1st Vlasov Division (the 600th Infantry Division).—*Source: Thorwald: Wen sie…, pp. 80, 316, 435 and 439; Aufzeichnungen von Dr. Fritz Rudolf Arlt und von Maximilian Preuss [Records/Notes of Dr. Fritz Rudolf Arlt and Maximilian Preuss] (Thorwald material in the IfZ); Fischer, p. 42.*

[723] Fighting against partisans in the East was the task of the SS (except in the operational areas) according to Führer Directive 46, dated August 18, 1942, and the preceding agreement between Himmler and the Armed Forces High Command, announced in an SS order dated July 28, 1942.—*Source: Nbg. Dok. NO-1666 and NO-1662.*

[724] Manstein.

[725] The evacuation of the projecting [Viaz'ma] salient between Iukhnov and Rzhev in February 1943.

[726] See above note 713.

[727] Sepp Dietrich was famous for wanting to collect all attainable units and weapons he could get his hands on.

[728] At that time it would probably still have been Colonel Henning von Tresckow, who was known as a leader of the military resistance against Hitler, and who took a two-month leave at the end of July to coordinate the resistance circles at the front and in the Reserve Army, and to prepare the coup d'état. Otherwise, the reference could have been to his successor, Colonel v. d. Groeben.—*Source: Zeller, p. 142; Schlabrendorff, p. 125; Ritter: Carl Goerdeler, p. 527.*

[729] In consideration of Finland, Hitler did not believe it wise to give up on Leningrad, although the Russians had already broken up the encirclement around the city on January 18, 1943.

[730] At the Kuban bridgehead.

[731] Ewald v. Kleist; born August 8, 1881; 1901 Second Lieutenant; during World War I, a cavalry captain mostly in General Staff positions; 1922 Major; 1929 Colonel; 1931 Commander, 9th Infantry Regiment; 1932 Commander, 2nd Cavalry Division and Major General; 1933 Lieutenant General; 1934 Commanding General, VIII Army Corps; 1936 General of the Cavalry; left the service in February 1938; reactivated at the beginning of the war; during the Polish cam-

paign, Commanding General, XXII Army Corps; in the Western campaign, a commander in Panzer Group Kleist, later First Panzer Group; 1940 Colonel General; November 1940 to November 1942 Commander-in-Chief, First Panzer Army; and Commander-in-Chief Army Group A. On March 30, 1944, Kleist, together with Manstein, was removed from his command. After the war, in 1948 in Yugoslavia, he was sentenced to 15 years in prison; he was extradited to the USSR where he died in early November 1954.—*Source: Army High Command staff files (Nbg. Dok. NOKW-141); Munzinger Archive; Siegler, p. 126.*

[732] Transcript number unknown—Fragment No. 52—Preliminary remarks by the stenographer at the time of the second transcription in May 1945: "These are the remainders of both shorthand records of a short evening situation report, which probably took place in February 1944 in the "Wolfsschanze" compound. Both shorthand records have serious fire damage. The burned edges run in such a way that on the individual pages, less than half of each line was preserved. Thus, larger, interconnected statements cannot be deciphered. In general, the shorthand records consist of reports of the daily military events, given by Colonel General Zeitzler, Colonel General Jodl, and Colonel v. Below. The passages that might have a more far-reaching interest have been excerpted in the following text." Contrary to the date given by the stenographer, this record was most probably dated October 3, 1943, as this was the day the Spanish request for the return of the "Blue Division" was received (excerpt 1), a new Armed Forces High Command order on organizing combat in Italy was prepared (excerpt 4), and the more detailed reports on the Leuthen group were available (excerpt 3).

[733] In August 1943, the British ambassador in Madrid requested the return of the Blue Division from the Eastern Front, and at the beginning of October, Franco could no longer resist this pressure. On October 3, a corresponding Spanish request was received at the Führer Headquarters; the transport was to be carried out in November. Upon his departure on October 12, 1943, Lieutenant General Esteban-Infantes, who was the commander of the division at that time and the successor of Muños Grandes, was awarded the Knight's Cross. Because of Esteban-Infantes' trip to Rastenburg to receive the award, the departure of the 13,700 Spaniards was delayed somewhat, and the last of the "Division Azul" was not unloaded in Valladolid until December 22. To sweeten the pill a bit, Franco had ordered that a regiment-strength legion, consisting of volunteers, should remain in Russia. However, as the Allied pressure continued, and as Hitler was somewhat annoyed at Franco, this Spanish legion—whose "voluntariness" consisted primarily of troops commanded to fulfill this order—was withdrawn already in January 1944. Only 200 to 300 Spaniards, who stayed as real volunteers without the permission of the Spanish general staff, remained in the Waffen SS. In an agreement with the Western powers, the Spanish government declared on May 2, 1944, that all units of the Blue Division and the Blue Squadron had returned home, with the exception of some injured persons and administrative agencies.—*Source: NZZ of Dec. 22, 1943 (evening edition); Times of May 3, 1944; Hoare, pp. 335, 363, 366, 422, and 424.*

[734] In his notorious "commando order" dated October 18, 1942, Hitler, on the basis of alleged violations of international law by British sabotage troops (commandos) ordered: "From now on during all commando actions in Europe or in Africa, all enemies stopped by German troops—even if externally they appear to be soldiers in military uniforms, or demolition troops with or without weapons—regardless if they are fighting or fleeing, should be killed, down to the last man. It does not matter whether they arrived by ship or plane, or jumped by parachute. Even if these subjects, when discovered, seem to wish to offer themselves as captives, no pardon should be given." As late as June 24, 1944, the Armed Forces Operations Staff explicitly ordered that these regulations were to be "completely maintained"; however, the direct landing area in Normandy, as a major landing zone, was excepted under section 5 of the commando order.— *Source: Nbg. Dok. 498-PS, 532-PS and 551-PS.*

[735] This reference is to attacks on the convoys ON 202 and ONS 18 by the "Leuthen" group. During this operation, the Zaunkönig [Wren] torpedo (see above note 690) was used for the first time. According to the submarine reports, 12 destroyers were sunk and torpedoed; in fact, only 3 escort vessels were sunk and another damaged. The exaggerations were due to the fact that—for technical reasons—the boats were not able to watch their hits optically. Instead, they had to dive down quickly to depth, so as not to be hit by their own torpedoes. When they heard a detonation, they were not able to determine exactly whether it was a hit or a final detonation.

[736] Meaning the German Luftwaffe in the Mediterranean area.

[737] The enemy.

[738] Transcript number unknown—Fragment 37—One of the two original shorthand records was completely destroyed, and the other was charred in such a way that the first half could not be deciphered at all, and the other half only with major gaps. The first transcription consisted of 47 typewritten pages (instead of the 15 reproduced here).

[739] One of the three German-Croatian Legion divisions set up within the framework of the German Army by the "Poglavnik" [Ante Pavelic], consisting of Croatian personnel with German cadres. At the time of this meeting, two of these units already existed: the 369th Infantry Division (*Teufelsdivision* ["Devil's Division"]) established in 1942, and the 372nd Infantry Division (*Tigerdivision* ["Tiger Division"], established in 1943; the number according to Kiszling, Schmidt-Richberg, the *Order of Battle* and Keilig: 373rd). At the end of 1943, the 392nd Infantry Division *Plava* followed. (See also below note 1077.)—*Source: Kiszling, pp. 187, 188, 195 and 207; Order of Battle, pp. 250, 251 and 256.*

[740] Probably meaning Mihailović. After the British government halted military and material support for the Četniks during the summer, the tone of the British press changed accordingly.—*Source: Matl, p. 111.*

[741] The 264th [Infantry Division] was formed in Belgium; the 181st: [Infantry Division] previously in Norway; the 1st Cossack [Division] formed in Poland; all were now being moved to Yugoslavia (the 181st to the coast of the lower Adriatic, the other two to Croatia).—*Source: Order of Battle, pp. 219, 195 and 285.*

742 Naples was evacuated three days before, on October 1, as Kesselring wrote, "after the supplies had been moved out," which probably included all the motor vehicles on hand as well.—*Source: Kesselring, p. 258.*

743 To Lower Silesia.

744 The 242nd Infantry Division moved from Belgium to southern France; the 356th went from there to Italy.

745 From France to Italy and Slovenia.

746 During this operation, from September 12 to October 4, 1943, the *U 410* (Lieutenant Fenski) sank for sure—according to documents available thus far—three ships with a total of 18,031 GRT. The torpedoing of two additional steamers has not been confirmed.

747 The evacuation of Corsica was completed the night before. In the early morning hours of October 4, General von Senger und Etterlin, previously Armed Forces Commander in Sardinia and Corsica, landed in Leghorn with the last of the island occupation forces.

748 On October 3 in the Gulf of Genoa, the submarine chaser *UJ2208* used depth charges to sink the British submarine *Usurper*.

749 The evacuation of the Kuban bridgehead, finished five days later on October 9.—*Source: Tippelskirch, p. 391.*

750 During the night, a battle took place in the western part of the Channel, between the 4th Torpedo Boat Flotilla with *T22, T23, T25, T26,* and *T27,* and British destroyers; one destroyer was damaged by a torpedo, and other British boats were hit by artillery shells.

751 The Republic P47 "Thunderbolt" was an American single-engine single-seat fighter, an improvement on the P35 design (1938), and was used for the first time in the fall of 1943 (highest speed nearly 700 km/h, 12,000 m altitude, 4 hours flying time, 8 heavy machine guns). The "Thunderbolt" was mainly used as a long-range fighter, but also as a fighter-bomber, with six rocket shells or two 450-kg bombs.—*Source: Feuchter, pp. 230, 234 and 275; Hébrard, p. 268.*

752 The Hawker "Typhoon" was an English single-engine single-seat fighter (fighter-bomber). The first flight by the prototype was on February 24, 1940, and the first deployment was in the summer of 1942. The "Typhoon" was armed with twelve machine guns or four 2-cm guns, and carried two 225-kg bombs.—*Source: Feuchter, p. 214; Hébrard, p. 262.*

753 The Armed Forces High Command report dated October 4, 1943, reported on this matter: "Last night enemy bombers attacked Kassel. The damage, primarily in the old town center, is serious. There were losses among the population. During these attacks, air defense forces destroyed 44 enemy aircraft."

754 This probably refers to the landing of the British XIII Army Corps on October 3, on the Adriatic near Termoli, behind the German Biferno front. Although the breakthrough was avoided by bringing the 16th Panzer Division over in forced marches from the right wing of the army, the front had to be pulled back to the Trigno.—*Source: Kesselring, p. 259; Tippelskirch, p. 411.*

755 Aircraft taken over from the Italians, probably the three-engine Savoia S 79, or S 84.—*Source: Feuchter, p. 87.*

[756] The Me 323 "Gigant" ["Giant"], a six-engine transport plane with a wingspan of 55 meters and a service load of 19 tons. From 1942 to 1944, a total of 200 planes were produced.—*Source: Baumbach, p. 316; Lusar, p. 54 (here mistakenly: Me 321); VB of Nov. 25, 1943.*

[757] Luftwaffe Chief of the General Staff; see List of Participants.

[758] Hitler meant little trees or dummy trees, which were erected at the "Wolfsschanze" on the grass in front of the Führer's bunker.

[759] Hitler's German Shepherd dog.

[760] Yosuke Yogu Matsuoka, born March 1880, Christian religion, studied legal and political science in the United States, entered the Japanese foreign service at the age of 25, attended the Paris peace conference as a secretary. After he left the diplomatic service he took a position with the South Manchurian Railway; later he became its president. In 1932 he was Japan's chief delegate to the League of Nations, and the following year he announced the withdrawal of his country from that organization. As an opponent of parliamentarism, he soon left parliament and—again while employed as a senior executive in the South Manchurian Railway—worked on a reform program to strengthen the throne and build up a uniform national organization. In August 1940, this Army liaison officer and supporter of close cooperation with Germany was appointed Minister of Foreign Affairs by Prince Konoye, and in this position he signed the Tri-Partite Pact shortly thereafter. Just five months before Japan entered the war, on July 16, 1941, Matsuoka was expelled from the Konoye cabinet for his sharp attitude toward the United States. In later cabinets he served as Minister of Justice. In November 1945 the American occupation forces arrested him, but he died of tuberculosis of the lungs on June 24, 1946, before the opening of the war crimes trial. [—] The later Foreign Minister Togo also confirms that in the summer of 1941 Matsuoka supported an attack against the USSR, and that in July he was forced out because (apart from Konoye's personal antipathies) under his leadership the Foreign Ministry negotiations with the United States did not seem to be progressing in a promising manner—although his demand to wage war against the USSR did contribute to his downfall. In addition, he seemed to have made himself unpopular because of his close familiarity with the German ambassador. [—] The attitude of the Japanese Navy command and the fear of an American oil embargo are represented correctly.—*Source: Frankfurter Zeitung of March 12 and 21, 1943; Tansill, p. 680; Keesings Archive, 1941 p. 5121, 1945 p. 530 and 1946-47 p. 832; Langer/Gleason, passim (esp. pp. 4 and 639); Togo, p. 72; Toynbee: The Initial Triumph, pp. 610 and 651.*

[761] On October 3, the Dodecanese island of Kos was snatched from the British, who had occupied it after the Italian capitulation.

[762] On October 4, Germany changed from daylight saving time to standard time (CET), i.e., the clocks were set back by one hour at 3 a.m. Daylight saving time, which made better use of daylight and therefore saved power, was introduced in 1916 in most of the European countries—usually in effect from the end of

April to the beginning of October. After the war it was retained in most of Western Europe, while in Germany it was abolished in 1919 due to protests from agricultural circles. It was not reintroduced in Germany until World War II, and was maintained afterward on Allied orders until 1949.

763 The connection is not clear. In any case, there are no oil fields in Finland—at most there is oil shale, as in Estonia and Sweden, but only in minor quantities. Possibly it should be "ore region."

764 Paul Pleiger; born September 28, 1899; son of a miner; mechanic; mechanical engineering college; engineer; 1925 machinist; 1932 NSDAP; 1933 economic consultant for the South Westphalia Gau; 1937 to 1945 in various key positions at the Reichswerke [Reich factories] Hermann Göring; 1941 to 1945 head of the Reich Coal Association; 1941 Administrative Council of the Mines and Metallurgical plants in the East; 1942 Reich Coal Commissioner in the Occupied Territories, Prussian State Council, and Wehrwirtschaftsführer [Head of Defense Economy]. At the Wilhelmstrasse trial, Pleiger was sentenced to 15 years in prison (later reduced to 9 years).—*Source: Trials XI I, p. 19.*

765 Hitler attached special importance to Nikopol' because of the manganese ore mines east of the town (total resources: 522 million tons), the ownership of which he saw as absolutely necessary for the war economy. Thus, Nikopol'—as a bridgehead protruding far to the southeast over the Dnieper River—was held until February 8, 1944.—*Source: Manstein, pp. 549, 554 and 581; Tippelskirch, p. 510.*

766 On Hitler's orders, a beachhead was maintained east of the Dnieper in front of Zaporozh'e, so that the dam and power station remained in German hands. The Russians attacked this bridgehead, at first in vain. Later, however, on October 14, they forced the defenders back over the river (blowing up the railway bridge, which had just been repaired, and the dam crossing).—*Source: Manstein, pp. 537 and 547; Tippelskirch, p. 394.*

767 Transcript No. 627/43—Fragment No. 44—The transcript was charred on the edges.

768 The reference is probably to Manstein.

769 The I Cavalry Corps, just established at that time, consisted of the 3rd and 4th Cavalry Brigades (later 3rd and 4th Cavalry Divisions); apart from the XV Cossack Cavalry Corps (see below note 1417), it was the only one of its kind. The commanding general was Lieutenant General (later General of Cavalry) Gustav Harteneck.—*Source: Rangliste 1944-45, p. 324; Keilig 11/70.*

770 The 50th Infantry Division—which was supposed to be moved from the Kerch Peninsula to the Melitopol' front, but then had to be pulled in with the other forces to defend the isthmus of Perikop after the Soviet breakthrough—was never an "assault division." At that time, there was only one unit of this kind: the 78th Assault Division located in Army Group Center's sector. Its assignment was the tactical testing of new weapons and combat organizations, so its armaments were significantly superior to those of the normal infantry divisions; among other things, it had additional antitank equipment, engineer companies, an assault gun detachment, and a heavy mortar battalion.—*Source: Keilig 15/24.*

[771] The first airborne units were established in the Red Army as early as 1930. In 1932, there were four such battalions, which later developed into regiments and brigades. The Soviet Stavka employed them massively during the Battle of Moscow (February-March 1942) and once again along the Dnieper River in September 1943, but the operations turned out to be costly failures. Throughout the remaining three years of the war, the Soviets employed airborne divisions mainly as elite forces in the ground campaign.—*Sources: Glantz, A History of Soviet Airborne Forces (London: Frank Cass,1994) and Hoffmann: Sowjetluftmacht, 1st Forts. Heft 6 [Vol. 1 No. 6]; Lee, p. 96.*

[772] The previous month, on September 11, Russian Naval troops had arrived by sea and landed at the Kuban beachhead behind Novorossiisk. After some of the landed enemy troops were destroyed by German counterattacks, the Russians seized the town four days later, in heavy street fighting. On the Crimea itself, on October 21 (five days before this meeting), a landing attempt near Cape Illy, by a commando (airborne) unit of 500 men, had failed; ten days later the Soviets landed northeast of Kerch near Enikale and south of the town near El'tingen. While German and Romanian troops were able to destroy the latter beachhead between December 4 and 12, the first could only be sealed off. [—] The assumptions expressed here did not come true: The Russians landed neither near Feodosiia nor Yalta, but instead took their time and did not attack the remotely situated Crimea for nearly six months. Not until April 8 did the Soviets open the access route in the north, coming from the Perekop Isthmus, where they were able to form a small beachhead south of the Putrid Sea (Sivash' Sea). The beachhead, which was regarded by the Germans as not too dangerous because of the swampy land, was built by the civilian population at night by connecting a dam (the upper edge of which was just under the surface of the water, so it could not be detected by German air reconnaissance) with the mainland. After the fall of Sevastopol' three days before, the last units of the Seventeenth Army surrendered on May 12. The Soviet Armed Forces report spoke of 100,000 dead and captured; the Germans calculated that 96,800 of 128,500 Germans and 40,200 of 96,800 Romanians had been transported across to the mainland after the beginning of the Russian attack on April 8—so, according to these figures, 31,700 Germans and 25,800 Romanians would have died or been captured.—*Source: Tippelskirch, pp. 391 and 436; Pickert, p. 126; Weitershausen, passim; Meister, p. 272.*

[773] Meaning supply lines or connections. A common term in the general staff jargon.

[774] On the way back from Italy.

[775] On October 14, 1943, Hitler sent a personal letter to the Finnish president Ryti, in which he warned against excessive compliance in dealing with the increasingly vocal opposition. He also complained about the impolite tone of the Finnish press, and remonstrated that the Finnish government had not yet granted diplomatic recognition to the [new] Mussolini regime. Ryti's answer, which was handed over in Berlin on October 26 (the day of this situation report), justified the attitude of his government toward the opposition (based on democratic traditions and the parliamentarian system), promised to take measures against

clear mistakes by the press, and avoided the Mussolini issue. Although this answer did not satisfy Hitler, of course, the German-Finnish relationship relaxed a bit in the next few months—partly due to the intransigence of the Soviets—and the impending break was postponed for the moment.—*Source: Erfurth: Der finnische Krieg, p. 217; Blücher, p. 342.*

776 After the Soviet-Finnish winter war of 1939-1940 and the Russian occupation of the Baltic States, Finland was constantly fearful of further Soviet desires and had been forced closer and closer to Germany in the search for effective protection. When Hitler, after Molotov's visit to Berlin, finally made up his mind concerning the long-planned armed confrontation with the Soviet Union, contact between the German and Finnish General Staff was initiated by Germany after January 1941, and soon led to closer cooperation. Although Finland never agreed to a formal link, the dispatch of the "Liaison Staff North" on June 13, the Finnish mobilization on June 17, and the joint German-Finnish assembly of troops at the Russian border left no room for doubt concerning the attitude of the country. Soviet air attacks provided the excuse for Finland to join the war on June 25, 1941. The Finns, however, conducted the war with restricted aims (for example, they did not allow themselves to be persuaded to attack the Murmansk railway), and always refused to sign an alliance agreement. Instead, they viewed their "third war of liberation" more as a sequel to the winter war ("continuation war"), independent from the war of the Great Powers. In this way, Finland managed to maintain its—continually loosening—relations with the United States until June 30, 1944. The United States, like Sweden, made several attempts, starting in August 1941, to get Finland out of the war. The Finnish attitude toward these temptations changed according to the military situation in the East. So a change in attitude was noticeable, particularly after the fall of 1942. After Stalingrad, President Ryti and Field Marshal Mannerheim agreed on February 3, 1943, to pull out of the war at the first opportunity. In March 1943 the pro-German Rangell cabinet was replaced by Linkomies' "free hand cabinet," and in the fall of that year the Finnish parliament acknowledged [the government's] peace resolution. The tone of the press, at least in some instances, became quite anti-German for a time.—*Source: Erfurth: Der finnische Krieg, pp. 17 and 191; Wuorinnen, p. 91; Horn, passim; Hölter, passim; Mannerheim, p. 420; Blücher, p. 191.*

777 These "fine declarations"—probably meaning the Finnish press comments—concerned the Allied foreign minister conference, which had been convening in Moscow since October 19. The developments of these meetings, and the increasingly obvious strength of the Soviet position, gave Finland great cause for alarm—alarm that was heightened by the extent of the German retreat in the East. Characteristic of Finnish public opinion in those days was a remark by the rightwing *Uusi Suomi* on October 25, which said that the military successes of the Russians and the mere thought of the possibility of a separate peace between the Germans and the Soviets might provide such effective thumbscrews against the Western Allies that the smaller neighbors of the Soviet Union had every reason to be afraid of the presumed result of this conference. In addition,

the resurfacing of the old Soviet demand for satisfactory "strategic borders" brought back bad memories for the Finns.—*Source: NZZ of Oct. 26 (midday edition) and 27 (morning and midday edition), 1943.*

778 The reference is to two units that were supposed to be reconstituted in the rear area of the Crimea, using battered divisions coming from other sectors of the Eastern Front.

779 See above note 466.

780 The "A4" (Aggregate 4) was the liquid-fuel rocket (in contrast to the powder rocket used in smoke-shell mortars, multiple-rocket launchers, bazookas, etc.) of the Peenemünde Army Research Institute. The "A4" would later become famous under the name of "V2." As early as 1929 the German military had started testing this type of rocket propulsion for military purposes, and in 1932 development work began on the first liquid-fuel rocket "A1," driven with oxygen and alcohol. Construction of the "A4"—a rocket intended for practical deployment, which had to carry heavy loads over long distances with accuracy—began in the summer of 1936, but further development was soon postponed (due to engine problems) in favor of the new "A5"experimental rocket. By the fall of 1939, the newly gained experience could have been used to improve the A4, but Hitler's elimination of all rocket weapons from the "urgency list" further delayed the development. Not until October 3, 1942, was the first A4 launched, and in July 1943 it was finally possible to get Hitler interested—who had a generally positive attitude toward the development of the V-weapons [rockets]—in the rocket program, to the point that Peenemünde moved to the top of the urgency list of. [—] In contrast to the A4, the V1 (the Fi 103 model from the Fieseler factory), developed by the Luftwaffe only after 1942, was a winged projectile—an aerial torpedo that was catapulted in the firing direction from a concrete runway. The V1 was much cheaper (3,500 RM compared with 38,000 RM per A4), easier to handle, had a smaller consumption of less valuable fuel, and needed only 280 man-hours to produce; however, it required stationary launching locations, and because the firing direction was fixed, the V1 was relatively easily shot down by fighters and antiaircraft artillery. In addition, the sound announced the rocket's arrival in advance, allowing the enemy to sound the alarm in time. The V2, on the other hand, allowed a free range of fire from a mobile firing position. Its position could be changed quickly, it could be steered even in the air by an electric beam of light, and it had the very low dispersion rate of only 1.5%. Defense and diversion were impossible with the means available at the time. The impact occurred without warning, and its effectiveness was significantly increased by the 192 million meter kg (with 25,000 kgp thrust and 650,000 hp) force of impact, caused by the high speed. But the V2 was more expensive and it demanded sensitive and extensive supply arrangements; moreover, its high consumption (3,965 kg of 75% alcohol and 4,970 kg of liquid oxygen) permitted only 30 launches per day, as each of the 35 oxygen-production plants available in Germany was able to produce only enough for a single launch. [—] Data for both weapons:

	Length (m)	Weight (t)	Explosive charge (kg)	Speed (m/sec.)	Altitude (km)	Flight path like	Propellant fuel	Range (km)
V 1	8	2.2	800	166	3	Small airplane	Propellant oil + oxygen from the air	300-370
V 2	14	12.6	1,000	1,520	90	Projectile	Ethyl alcohol + liquid oxygen	320-400

	1st Deployment	Highest Monthly Production	Engine
V 1	June 15, 1944	2,000	Ramjet engine (Ramjet, Schmidt-Argus barrel)
V 2	September 8, 1944	nearly 800	Rocket engine

Statements concerning the number of launches vary considerably, though they are generally very detailed, so a more precise citation makes little sense. In general, the following figures should be fairly accurate:

V1	against England	more than 9,000
V1	against Belgium and the southern Netherlands	more than 10,000
V2	against England	between 1,100 and 1,500
V2	against Belgium and the southern Netherlands	more than 2,000

—*Source: Dornberger, passim; Schneider, p. 236; Görlitz I, p. 461; Baumbach, p. 261; Lusar, p. 95; Hébard, p. 433; Kaiser, passim; Heilmann: Rakete, passim.*

[781] On October 19, Reichsorganisationsleiter [the Reich organization leader] Dr. Ley spoke in the new assembly hall at the University of Berlin during the Reich labor meeting of the foreign and Gau liaison men of the DAF. The part of the speech mentioned here was not published, at least not by DNB-Inland.

[782] For the first time in World War II, from October 17 to 20, 1943, there had been an exchange of German and Western Allied—English and Canadian, primarily—disabled or seriously ill prisoners. The exchange had been mediated by Switzerland as a mutual protective power. Two hospital ships and six trains with 4,340 English and other prisoners were brought to Sweden from Germany, while two hospital ships with 835 Germans were brought from England (the unequal number was caused by the fact that the exchange was carried out according to categories rather than headcount). In Götheborg, where the Swedish Red Cross was responsible for organizing the exchange, the transfer from ship to ship and from the trains took place via the passenger steamer *Drottninholm*. The Swedish

crown princess and four representatives of the International Red Cross observed the exchange. [—] Another exchange, which had been proposed by Sweden a year earlier, did not take place. Altogether, there were three operations of
this kind.—*Source: NZZ of Oct. 19, 1943 (midday edition).*

[783] On November 3, 1923, Crown Prince Gustav Adolf of Sweden—future King
Gustav VI Adolf—married (it was his second marriage) Lady Louise
Mountbatten, a daughter of Prince Ludwig von Battenberg, First Marquess of
Milford Haven. The crown princess—who, until her 17th year, had been raised
in Darmstadt—was politically very cautious, as the Swedish constitution did not
allow any other attitude, and could hardly be called hostile to the Germans or a
"driving force." [—] German-Swedish relations had worsened throughout the
year in 1943, caused on the one hand by changing fortunes of war and on the
other by the toughening of the German occupation policies in Denmark and
Norway. Although the Swedish government did not abandon its policy of neutrality until the end of war, its attitude—as well as public opinion—stiffened
considerably against Germany. In addition to the various sharp exchanges due to
border violations, abuse of the air courier traffic, sinking of ships and other incidents of this sort, a good example of the changed atmosphere was, in particular,
the termination on August 6, 1943, of the "transit traffic" that had existed since
the summer of 1940, i.e., the German Armed Forces furlough traffic through
Sweden to Norway. The Swedish government also had to bear additional press
attacks in the following months because of a one-time transit permission that
had been granted at the beginning of the Eastern campaign to a German division marching through to Finland.—*Source: Jahrbuch der Weltpolitik 1944, p. 370.*

[784] The reference is probably to a field gun.

[785] The 17th and 18th on the French Channel coast, the 16th and 19th in the Netherlands.

[786] Several lines are missing here.

[787] After the occupation of Czechoslovakia in March 1939, the production of heavy
field howitzers by Skoda was halted.

[788] To determine the effectiveness of the Russian 15.2-cm heavy field howitzer,
Hitler had ordered an experimental shelling of small steel bunkers, which were
used at that time for installations in fortified field positions. To save ammunition
and time, the shelling had been carried out by the Armaments Ministry in such
a way as to fire from a very short distance (so that every single shot had to be a
hit), with the propelling charge reduced so as to make the force of impact against
the target equivalent to the force of impact of a shell fired from 3,000 m with
normal propelling charge. This reduced propelling charge is referred to here as
"reduced loading" by Buhle, and he rejects the test conditions because the results were unrealistic due to the different angles of impact.

[789] Transcript number unknown—Fragment No. 21—Because the preserved shorthand record was partially charred, the second transcription was possible only
with gaps.

[790] Meaning the supply locations for the German submarines, which were supplied
by submarine tankers in the areas around the Azores, the Canaries and the Cape

Verde islands. On numerous occasions, the submarines were observed and attacked by airplanes from American escort aircraft carriers during supply. It has not been established, however, that the Allies deployed submarines against these supply points.

791 Railway junction 30 km southwest of Cherkassy with connections to Zvenigorodka–Uman'/Vinnitsa, Belaia Tserkov'–Fastov–Kiev/Zhitomir, Cherkassy, Kirovograd/Krivoi Rog and Voznesensk–Odessa. The last rail line on the lower Dnieper ran east of the Bug via Rovno–Berdichev–Fastov/Zvenigorodka–Smela, i.e., without touching Romanian territory at the time. The Smela Station occupied a key position for the whole railroad system between the Dnieper and the Bug.

792 The Soviet summer offensive in 1943 threw the southern wing of the German front back from the Danube to the Dnieper. At the beginning of October, the front ran along the Dniepr bend projecting far to the east between Kiev and Zaporozh'e. In the south, the German troops still held a bridgehead on the left bank at Zaporozh'e; however, the Russians had managed to create a large bridgehead on the right bank of the Dnieper bend southeast of Kiev. On October 7, the major Soviet fall offensive began, which between October 17 and 24 managed to tear open the German Dnieper defense between Kremenchug and Dnepropetrovsk, while at the beginning of November—also in the Kiev area—the 1st Ukrainian Front advanced across the river and far to the west. On November 20, the day after this meeting, the Russians finally attacked the German positions around Cherkassy as well—the remaining piece of the old German Dnieper Line above Nikopol'.—*Source: Tippelskirch, p. 392.*

793 Presumably Zhitomir.

794 The antitank gun equipment of the Soviet units had improved again significantly after the great losses in 1941-42. In addition, the normal Russian field gun (7.62 cm) could, with armor-piercing shells, be used quite effectively as an antitank gun.

795 Again referring to losses due to technical problems in the first production runs.

796 Ernst Busch: born July 6, 1904; Second Lieutenant, 13th Infantry Regiment; in World War I battalion commander; Reichswehr; 1932 Commander, 9th Infantry Regiment and Colonel; 1935 Major General and Commander, 23rd Division; 1938 General of the Infantry and Commanding General, VIII Army Corps in the French campaign and in Russia (Lake Il'men'); until October 1943 Commander-in-Chief; Sixteenth Army; 1940 Colonel General; and February 1, 1943 Field Marshal. Busch was Commander-in-Chief, Army Group Center from October 12, 1943, until the end of July 1944. He was Commander-in-Chief Northwest during the final weeks of the war, and was then taken into English captivity, where he died on July 17, 1945.—*Source: Munzinger Archive; Das deutsche Heer, p. 135; Siegler, p. 115; Keilig 211/51.*

797 General Ilia Steflea was Chief of General Staff of the Romanian Army from March 1942 to August 1944.

798 Allusion to the death of the Bulgarian Tsar Boris, who had died 3 months before on August 28, 1943. Rumors and allegations by political opponents sur-

faced immediately afterward, claiming that the king had inhaled a delayed-action poison when, on his flight back from Hitler's headquarters, in a German airplane, he had to use an oxygen mask while flying across the Carpathians. This visit, however, had taken place 8 days before his sudden illness and 13 days before his death. So although the death of the tsar is still an unsolved mystery, the reason cited above was toxicologically impossible.

799 Paul Giesler; born June 15, 1895; architect; after 1924 SA Führer; 1933 MdR [member of the Reichstag]; 1938 Führer SA Group Alpenland; 1941 South Wesphalia Gauleiter; and June 26, 1942 assigned deputy leadership of the businesses of the Munich-Upper Bavaria Gauleiter. After the death of Ludwig Siebert and Adolf Wagner, Giesler became Bavarian minister president and State Minister of Internal Affairs as well as Gauleiter of Munich-Upper Bavaria. He committed suicide on May 2, 1945.

800 Alfred Jacob; born April 1, 1883; 1904 Second Lieutenant; Reichswehr; 1929 Commander, 7th Engineer Battalion; 1931 Department Head (Waffen [Weapons Testing] 5) in the Army Weapons Office; 1933 Colonel; 1935 Senior Engineer Commander at Group Command 1 (Berlin); 1936 Major General and Inspector of the Eastern Fortifications; March 1938 Lieutenant General; after December 1, 1938 Inspector of the Engineers, Railway Engineers and Fortifications in the Army High Command; October 1939 General of Engineers and Fortifications in the Army High Command; June 1940 General of Engineers; and 1944 General of Engineers and Fortifications also in the Armed Forces High Command.

801 Because of the defects mentioned several times before, Hitler had toyed with the idea of entrenching the "Panther" as a small tank fortification along defensive fronts, rather than using it as a mobile weapon. Here the discussion concerned strengthening the western defense with armor-piercing weapons that could not be deployed in the East or that had been replaced there by newly produced weapons. In addition to guns (7.5-cm Kwk [combat vehicle gun], 8.8-cm anti-aircraft artillery), these weapons included the "Panthers" from the first series (A-C), whose turrets were designed to pivot hydraulically, powered by the main engine—now unavailable. Beginning with series "D," a DKW motor was installed in the "Panther" as an auxiliary motor for the turret pivot. [—] The plans for such a deployment of the "Panther" were never implemented.

802 There never was a 1st Panzer Grenadier Division; it must have been: "...the 16th Panzer Division..."

803 The discussion here concerns a special production of tank turrets to be installed in fortified positions. To make his thoughts clear to less-informed listeners, Hitler often took pencil and paper and sketched out his ideas. His technical predisposition caused him to concern himself with many details of weapon technology. In all fairness, one must admit that many of his ideas were usable, and in some cases even pioneering. For example, it was Hitler in the end who insisted on equipping the tanks with long guns, in opposition to the opinion of many experts. On the other hand, he also made wrong decisions with far-reaching effects on critical questions of armament production

(misjudging the significance of sufficient vehicle production, delaying the fighter deployment of the Me 262, etc.).

[804] The 16th Panzer Division was moved from Italy (Sangro) to Russia (Bobruisk) at that time, and the 44th Infantry Division (Reich Infantry Division Hoch- und Deutschmeister) from Slovenia to Italy. The mention of the 2nd Panzer Division might have been a transcription error; that division was stationed and remained in the East at the time.—*Source: Order of Battle, p. 295, 153 and 286.*

[805] Probably the mountain artilleryman Lieutenant Colonel Baron Peter von le Fort.—*Source: Rangliste 1944-45, p. 116.*

[806] Probably "between Drina and Spreèa" in eastern Bosnia, where in the fall of 1943 the hardest battles took place against strong partisan forces moving from western Bosnia to Serbia. Tuzla is also in this area.—*Source: Kiszling, p. 200.*

[807] He probably meant the Njegoš in Montenegro. "German area" probably means "German offensive sector." The name of the commander of this operation could not be verified; from the sound of the name alone, it could have been Colonel Gevers, an artillerist.

[808] This "Karst Training Battalion" of the Reichsführer SS later became (in the fall of 1944) a complete division: the 24th Waffen SS Mountain Karst Light Infantry Division. This unit was one product of Himmler's strange thought processes. Himmler, as is well known, found no idea too far-fetched, no plan too implausible, and no invention too outrageous to commence experimentation. In this case, a Karst specialist had convinced him that this unique geographical formation, with all its peculiarities, required specially equipped and trained troops. In the military circles of the Waffen SS, this project was regarded as a joke.

[809] Probably the German-Croatian 392nd Infantry Division.

[810] Probably the Chief of General Staff of the Commander-in-Chief Southeast, Lieutenant General Hermann Foertsch.

[811] These incidents in the Dodecanese (though receiving little notice because of the events in the "main" theaters of war) led to one of the last German successes in World War II—a success gained by the last major deployment of the German paratroopers, which had fallen into disgrace after the Crete operation. After the capitulation of Italy, the Italian occupation forces were ready to hand the islands over to the Americans—if they could only come in time. Due to an operation in Burma, the planned action against the main island of Rhodes had to be cancelled for the time being. But Hitler—against the counsel of the Army and Navy, justifiably concerned about the attitude of Turkey—decided to remain on Crete and the Dodecanese. German troops took the islands of Rhodes and Karpanthos; an English surprise strike on Rhodes on September 9 came too late and failed. Between September 8 and 18 the English were able to occupy Kos, Leros, Samos and four additional islands, but American concerns regarding the preparations for "Overlord" (the invasion), the needs of the Indian-Malayan theater, and finally the German decision to defend Rome, prevented effective support. Thus, German paratroops and landing forces were able to snatch Kos from the English on October 3, and Leros—which was fiercely defended by three elite battalions—between

November 12 and 15. Samos and the smaller islands were then evacuated without a fight.—*Source: Churchill V/I, p. 237; Ruge: Seekrieg, p. 257; de Belot, p. 240; Metzsch, p. 56.*

[812] Could not be identified with certainty. The reference is probably not to Lieutenant General (after May 1944 General of the Artillery) Dr. Georg Pfeiffer, who fell on June 28, 1944, or to Major General (after June 1944 Lieutenant General) Hellmuth Pfeifer, who died the following year. At this time, the former was leading the 94th Infantry Division in Italy and the latter had been with Army Group South in the East until August 1943 and then took over the 65th Infantry Division in Italy on December 1. It is not very likely that he would have had a short-term command in the Balkans in the meantime.—*Source: Rangliste 1944-45, pp. 21 and 38; Order of Battle, p. 605; Seemen; Keilig 211/249.*

[813] The "Ustashe" [Ustaša] had been founded as a Croatian revolutionary organization on January 7, 1929, by Dr. Ante Pavelic, the future "Poglavnik," and built up initially from clubs of town youth and students in Agram. Shortly thereafter Pavelic was forced into exile, and the military-like Ustashe movement also continued to exist primarily among Croatian emigrants in Italy. As a result of the murder of the Yugoslavian King Alexander in Marseilles on October 9, 1934, this Croatian nationalist and anti-Yugoslav movement became more widely known for the first time. When, after the breakup of Yugoslavia, the Axis forces founded a Croatian satellite state in April 1941, they fell back upon—according to Italian wishes—Pavelic and his Ustashe, while the German foreign office still supported the Farmers' Party of the Croatian opposition leader Maček at the beginning of April. As a result of its terror measures, however, the regime of the Ustashe emigrants quickly made itself hated. The Ustashe participated in the partisan war, in particular, with even more cruelty than was typical in the Balkans. The victorious Tito units got their revenge by 1945 and butchered the Ustashe in droves, while the members of the Ustashe government succeeded in escaping from the country in time. Pavelic lived in Argentina until the fall of Peron as many like-minded persons; he died in Madrid on December 28, 1959.—*Source: Ustascha-Bewegung, passim; Matl: Jugoslawien..., pp. 102, 105 and 209; Bauer, passim; Anfuso (It.), p. 184.*

[814] The 4th Volunteer Panzer Grenadier Brigade *Nederland* was established in the fall of 1943 in Germany, primarily with Dutch troops. It was deployed temporarily in Yugoslavia in November 1943 (Podbereszhye region), before being moved to the Eastern Front in December 1943. When Keitel speaks here of a "battalion," it could be a—perhaps not unintentional—indication of the strength of the brigade at the time, if he was not referring to an individual formation. The unit is not to be confused with the *Landstorm Nederland*, which was established a year later as a kind of a Home Army in preparation for the invasion defense, and which was euphemistically renamed the "34th SS Volunteer Infantry Division" in 1945.—*Source: Order of Battle, p. 350.*

[815] Units of this kind probably did not appear until the summer of 1944 during the final battles in Yugoslavia and, as far as is known, were significantly weaker than this.

816 Hungary and Romania had tried since the summer of 1942 and the beginning of 1943, respectively, to get in touch with the Western Allies in order to escape the sinking ship of the Axis. These contacts were initiated in several neutral countries. Key locations of negotiations included Ankara, Bern and Stockholm in the case of Hungary, and Ankara and Stockholm in the case of Romania. Some lines also ran through Lisbon as well, which caused Hitler in April 1943 to demand the recall of the Romanian envoy in Lisbon. But nothing decisive seems to have taken place in Lisbon, nor is a joint action between Hungary and Romania very probable, considering the historic and never resolved disagreements between the two countries (for example, Transylvania), a fact that Hitler also points out here.—*Source: Hillgruber, p. 167; Kállay, pp. 369 and 388.*

817 As in all occupied countries, a resistance movement had formed in Denmark, which took action against the German occupation forces—and especially against Danish collaborators—through sabotage and assassinations. The number of such actions increased steadily, especially after the elimination of the Danish government and the removal of the last elements of sovereignty on August 29, 1943. The "other procedure" Hitler mentions here as an alternative to sentencing by German occupation courts was implemented in the new year. In a meeting with Best, Hanneken and the Supreme SS and Police Commander, SS Obergruppenführer Pancke, Hitler prohibited further legal measures against Danish saboteurs on December 30, 1943, and gave the definitive order for counter-terror after the Armed Forces High Command had already given an equivalent order to Hanneken in mid-November. From that point on, the "Peter Group" of the security police responded to each case of sabotage or assassination with a corresponding German action—usually murder or bomb attacks—against persons with Danish nationalist attitudes or against their property. Altogether 225 such acts of counter-terror were proven in the 1948 trial against Best, Hanneken, Pancke and the Sipo [Sicherheitspolizei—security police] chief Bovensiepen for the time period from January 10, 1944, to April 21, 1945.—*Source: Urteil des Gerichts in Kopenhagen gg. Best u.a. [Sentence of the court in Copenhagen against Best and others], Sept. 20, 1948 (NG-5887) as well as additional Nbg. Dok. [Nuremberg documents]: NG-4007, NG-4756, NG-5089, NG-5176, NG-5419, NG-5888 and various sabotage reports.*

818 Dr. Werner Best; born July 10, 1903; administrative lawyer; after 1928, judge. In 1931 he was released from the civil service for authoring the so-called Boxheimer documents, which revealed the anti-constitutional efforts of the NSDAP, and was accused of high treason before the Reich court (proceedings were halted in the fall of 1932); 1933 chief of the Hessian police, November 1933 Führer SD Oa. Southwest, 1934 Führer SD Oa South, January 1935 to 1940 head of Dept. I (Administration) in the Gestapo office RSHA) from 1936-39), 1940 Head of War Administration for the Military Commander France, after November 5, 1942 envoy and Reichsbevollmächtigter (authorized agent of the Reich) in Denmark. Best had become a member of the NSDAP in 1930, a MdL [member of the Landtag] in Hesse in 1931, and a member of the SS in 1931; in 1942 he became Gruppenführer in Hesse and in

1944 Obergruppenführer. The city court in Copenhagen sentenced him to death
in September 1948 (this sentence was reduced to 5 years' imprisonment on appeal in 1949, and in 1950 it was increased again by the Obersten Gerichtshof
[supreme court] to 12 years); in August 1951 he was released on the condition
that he leave Denmark.—*Source: Munzinger Archive; Urteil des Gerichts in Kopenhagen
gg. Best u.a. [Sentence of the court in Copenhagen against Best and others] (NG-5887).*

819 Hermann v. Hanneken; born January 5, 1890; 1909 Second Lieutenant;
Reichswehr; 1935 Colonel; 1936-37 Chief of Staff Army Weapons Office; 1937
Deputy General for Iron and Steel Management/Rationing; 1938 Major General and head of Main Department II in the Reich Economics Ministry; thereafter April 1939 Undersecretary of State; 1940 Lieutenant General; December
1941 General of the Infantry; and September 1942 Armed Forces Commander
in Denmark. Hanneken was arrested in January 1945, demoted, and sentenced
to 8 years in prison for black marketeering. In 1948 in Denmark he was also
sentenced in the first court case to 8 years for alleged war crimes; in 1949 he was
acquitted in the second court case on appeal.—*Source: Munzinger Archive; Urteil
des Gerichts in Kopenhagen gg. Best u.a. [Sentence of the court in Copenhagen against Best
and others] (NG-5887); Keilig 211/119.*

820 The reference is to operations by the Schill 1, 2, and 3 groups against the convoys MKS30 and SL139; only *U238* was successful, by torpedoing the British
sloop *Chanticleer*. In addition, *U648* and *U618* each shot down a British airplane
with anti-aircraft artillery.

821 Assmann's strikingly detailed presentation, touching on even very minor incidents, is explained by the fact that at this low point in the submarine war any
detail could be of some significance and could help point the way to the not yet
fully understood reasons for this decline. Because of new developments in Allied
radar technology—the details of which were not clear to the German Navy leadership—and the constant increase in deployment of enemy air forces, the German submarine forces had suffered several serious reversals (see above note 152)
since the first deployment in March 1943 of the British Rotterdam devices (see
above note 553). Certain technical developments enabling the Germans to counteract enemy locating methods did not emerge until later—and were insufficient
even then. For a considerable length of time, for example, the primitive "Naxos"
was the only defensive measure: a detector-receiver with a small finger antenna,
which the radar operator had to hold with an outstretched arm while standing
on the boat's conning tower…and continuously rotating around his own axis. The
device covered a radius of 9 km, which, at best, enabled it to report the approaching aircraft about one minute before the attack—while the submarine's diving
maneuver required 30 to 40 seconds. Thus, due to extremely strong defense and
heavy losses, the German submarines' main battlefield, the north Atlantic, had
to be temporarily abandoned in 1943. The immense increase in new Allied ship
construction, which by the beginning of the year had already surpassed the
number of ships sunk, offered the final proof that the hopes set on the submarine war (as a result of the experiences in World War I) would never be fulfilled.
A diagram published by Assmann shows this development very clearly:

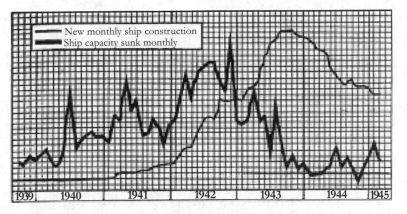

Allied and neutral ship capacity destroyed by submarines (A) in the Atlantic/ Arctic Ocean and (B) in the Mediterranean Sea, as well as (C) total losses from all enemy actions on all seas, according to Morison:

	A		B		C	
	Ships	GRT	Ships	GRT	Ships	GRT
May 1943	41	211,929	1	5,979	72	328,931
June	7	37,825	6	23,720	44	157,976
July	24	136,106	5	25,977	75	389,222
August	4	27,941	5	20,673	38	176,423
September	8	46,892	6	32,478	43	178,845
October	11	53,886	3	17,688	53	168,339
November	6	29,917	3	7,481	56	184,913
December	7	47,785	1	8,009	47	209,864
January 1944	5	36,065	0	0	51	184,732
February	2	7,048	6	21,706	46	167,402
March	8	41,562	4	33,724	56	198,264
April	7	47,763	2	14,386	39	160,772
May	3	17,277	1	7,147	12	40,427
June	8	38,556	(none after		46	123,800
July	7	33,175	May 1944)		28	102,803
August	8	40,944			44	154,232
September	6	37,698			34	87,652
October	0	0			22	40,944
November	5	15,567			28	67,935
December	8	51,338			44	166,160
January 1945	11	56,988			37	120,866
February	14	58,057			36	112,952
March	13	65,077			44	142,758
April	13	72,957			33	136,765
May	3	10,022			9	23,919

—Source: Busch, p. 287; Assmann, pp. 339, 404 and 405; Churchill V/1, p. 417; Wilmot, p. 127; Morison: The Battle of the Atlantic, p. 410; Morison: The Atlantic Battle Won, p. 365; Bley, p. 24.

[822]	The Finns had laid small mine barriers (Saipa 1 and 2) around the Russian Seiskari Islands—which remained in Soviet hands the whole time—near the Björko heights and the mouth of the Luga.—*Source: Meister, p. 64*

[823]	Prisoners taken during the operations against Leros and Kos (see above note 811) were brought to Piräus in boats from the 9th Torpedo Boat Flotilla and the 21st Submarine-Chaser Flotilla.

[824]	The USAAF attacked Schweinfurth and its strategic ball-bearing industry during two daytime attacks on August 17 and October 14, 1943. Although these attacks caused heavy damage and caused a temporary reduction of up to 50% of production, both operations could be considered among the few successes of the German air defense. Here, shortly before the appearance of the American long-distance fighter escort, the air defense shot down 60 aircraft from each of the two approaching formations of 376 and 226 four-engine bombers, and damaged another 100 and 140, respectively. The city and its critical industry also suffered many air attacks in the following year—for example, on February 24-25 (combined American day and English night attacks with 266 and 734 aircraft, respectively), on April 13 and 26-27, July 19 and 21, and October 9, 1944—but by that time the German ball-bearing industry had largely been decentralized by the armaments ministry.—*Source: Rumpf, p. 103; Galland, pp. 256 and 261; Churchill V/2, p. 237.*

[825]	Hitler was probably alluding to an airplane accident presumably experienced in 1943 by Josef Terboven (born May 23, 1898, after 1928 in Essen first district leader; later Gauleiter, after 1936 Senior President of the Rhine province; after 1940 Reich Commissioner for the occupied Norwegian territories). When Terboven blew himself up at the end of war—during the night of May 8, 1945—in his bunker in Oslo, a fractured arm that he had suffered in an accident not long before enabled the identification of the few parts of his body that could be found.

[826]	The Armed Forces High Command bulletin for this day (November 19, 1943) reported the following: "Enemy air units attacked Norwegian territory yesterday and numerous cities in western and northern Germany last night, including the capital of the Reich. Serious damage was reported from Mannheim. The population suffered limited losses. According to the reports received thus far, air defense forces destroyed 46 British and North American bombers."

[827]	Guided night interception using the Y process. Better known is the free night interception, called the *Wilde Sau* ["Wild Sow"], which reached its highpoint during this time. Although searchlights again became necessary after the jamming of the radar devices, the searchlight barriers had in the meantime been broken up and the batteries moved to vulnerable points to support the guns there (in particular, to equip southern Germany, which had been completely dark until that time). This transfer, as well as the tactical predominance that the more flexible pursuit had gained over the barrage theory, now forced the night fighters over the target. But this practice soon indicated that the effectiveness of the twin-engine aircraft—the only ones deployed for (guided) night interception—was hampered too much by anti-aircraft artillery, and several times air-

craft ran into friendly fire. Because of this problem, in the summer of 1943 Major Hajo Herrmann initiated the so-called *Wilde Sau,* meaning the target night interception, supported by searchlights, anti-aircraft signal rockets, and bonfires at the target (*Leichentuch* ["Shroud"]) by single-engine aircraft not equipped with on-board search radar. These aircraft, because of their smaller size, were less vulnerable to the anti-aircraft artillery and were also usually able to climb up out of anti-aircraft range—above 6,000 m—which the twin-engine aircraft were generally too slow to do. Night interception by single-engine aircraft of the 30th Fighter Division failed, however, because the demand for replacement crews for the three squadrons (301st, 302nd, 303rd) was too high and also, most importantly, because of excessive losses in bad weather. At the end of their flight time, which was restricted to 30 minutes by their fuel supply, these aircraft were simply helpless. Without adequate navigation aids, the pilot was often unable to find an airfield in the dark, and very often simply "jumped out" when he ran out of fuel. The *Wilde Sau* was therefore suspended again in 1944, before reemerging once more in the final battle for Berlin.— *Source: Galland, pp. 240 and 254; Bley, p. 17.*

828 A reinforcement of the fighter cover for southern Germany was urgently needed in the fall of 1943 because of the increasingly threatening air attacks on the area—now also from the south, after the loss of the Italian airfields. In southern Germany at that time, there were only the staff and the III Group of the 3rd Fighter Wing, along with the 76th Heavy Fighter Wing. The discussion here concerns a group from this heavy fighter wing.

829 In the tester-bed process, 4 to 6 "night intercept radar stations" were soon brought together into one "night intercept area" to facilitate central command, thus enabling more extensive night-fighting operations. However, these area commanders had by this time—i.e., after the introduction of the "Düppel" method by the English—already lost their relevance and were being scattered throughout the main combat areas in the West. Despite all evasive measures, the tester-bed method was, for all practical purposes, finished where attacking bomber formations were concerned; deployments were possible only against the enemy's return flights, which usually did not employ the "Düppel" method. The night interception stations maintained at least some of their relevance as long as they were able to deliver data to the Luftwaffe concerning the situation in the air.— *Source: Galland, p. 204.*

830 Electric submarines with an underwater speed of 15 knots had already been built in England during World War I, but the immense weight of the batteries needed for electric propulsion, as well as other obstacles, stood in the way of the complete development of such pure underwater boats. Professor Helmut Walter from Kiel had drawn up plans for a fast submarine that was to take the oxygen required for its gas turbines from hydrogen peroxide carried along on board. These plans had also existed already before World War II, but worries about the chemical activity of the H_2O_2 had delayed further development until the situation became urgent. Thus, by the end of the war, only a life-size wooden model of the 845-ton Walter boat, model XXVI, had been built. The develop-

ment of the 1,485-ton Walter model XVIII also remained unfinished. Only four boats of the 236-ton model XVII (*U792* to *795*) and one 655-ton boat (*U791*) reached the test stage, and scuttled themselves at the end of war. [—] Apart from these efforts, the submarine department of the Naval Vessel Construction Office—when developments in enemy radar techniques caused an urgent need for a fast submarine—developed an electric submarine equipped with powerful batteries. Two different models of this submarine were built (1,600 t XXI and 250 t XXIII). It was called an "electric boat" because the power of the two electric engines was greater than that of the diesel one: in the XXI 2,510 hp each compared with 2,000 hp, and in the XXIII 620 hp each compared with 560 hp. The maximum speed under water—which could be maintained by the Walter boat for only a few hours, depending on the amount of H_2O_2 on board, and by the electric boats for only about 2 hours but with at least the possibility of reloading—reached 12.5 knots in model XXIII, 17.5 knots in model XXI, and 23 to 28 knots in the Walter boats. Top speed for standard submarines, on the other hand, was only about 7 knots—and in the (usually necessary) "stealth mode" only 1 to 2 knots. The first boat of the XXI model was launched in April 1944, and 120 boats were delivered altogether; however, as a result of numerous teething troubles, the first boat (*U2511*) would not actually be put into action until shortly before the end of the war. During the capitulation process, this boat had to be stopped and ordered to return to Norway. Of the 61 XXIII model boats delivered, 5 were put into action off the east coast of England in 1945.—*Source: Ruge: Seekrieg, p. 234; Busch, p. 295; Lusar, p. 127.*

[831] Franz Hofer; born November 27, 1902; radio merchant; 1931 NSDAP; 1932 deputy Gauleiter of Tyrol; 1933 sentenced to two years' imprisonment for illegal activity (freed by his supporters); May 1938 Gauleiter of Tyrol; and after April 1940 Gauleiter and Reich governor. Hofer escaped on a transport from Dachau to Munich in October 1948 and was never found again.—*Source: Munzinger Archive.*

[832] Transcript number unknown—Fragment No. 35—A first transcription that was heavily burned along the tops of the pages, especially at the beginning. In May 1945 the stenographers filled in some of the missing parts, according to their knowledge of the content and the manner of speaking of the meeting participants. These additions are in parentheses. At that time an attempt was also made to guess the date of the meeting ("very likely December 20, 1943"). Contradicting this statement—assuming it's not a transcription error—is a remark by Zeitzler on p. 436 concerning the intervention that was to take place "probably on the 20th." It is not possible to ascertain the exact date; also the movements of the divisions mentioned, when compared with the following discussions, do not give a clue as to the precise day. [—] One dotted line corresponds in this fragment to 3-4 destroyed lines.

[833] At that time Commander-in-Chief of the First Panzer Army. [—] So a Russian corps is meant here.

[834] Hans Reinhardt; born March 1, 1887; 1908 Second Lieutenant, 107th Infantry Regiment; 1916 Captain; Reichswehr; 1927 Major in the RWM; 1931 Lieuten-

ant Colonel and Commander, 3rd Battalion 10th Infantry Regiment; 1934 Colonel; 1935 Chief of 4th Department in the Army General Staff; 1937 Major General and Commander, 1st Infantry Brigade; 1938 Commander, 4th Panzer Division; 1939 Lieutenant General; 1940 Commanding General, XXXXI Army Corps and General of Panzer Troops; October 1941 to August 16, 1944 Commander, Third Panzer Group or (after January 1, 1942) Commander-in-Chief, Third Panzer Army; January 1, 1942 Colonel General; and August 16, 1944 to January 26, 1945 Commander, Army Group Center. At the Nuremberg trial, Reinhardt was sentenced to 15 years in prison; he was released on July 17, 1952.—*Source: Army High Command staff files (Nbg. Dok. NOKW-141); Munzinger Archive; Siegler, p. 134.*

835 Beginning on December 18, the remains of the 197th Infantry Division, the Panzer Grenadier Division *Feldherrenhalle* and the below-mentioned 5th Jäger [Light Infantry] Division of the Third Panzer Army were led toward Vitebsk. The following assembled: the 197th Infantry Division as an army reserve northeast of Vitebsk until December 24, the *Feldherrenhalle* as an army group reserve northwest of Vitebsk until December 21, and the 5th Jäger Division northeast of Polotsk until December 26.—*Source: Heidkämper, p. 77*

836 For training reasons the 60th Panzer Grenadier Division *Feldherrenhalle* was not considered completely ready for action. Like the remains of the 20th Panzer Division and the 87th Infantry Division, it was positioned west of Vitebsk.— *Source: Heidkämper, p. 84 and others.*

837 Meaning General Jaenecke, the Commander-in-Chief of the Seventeenth Army on the Crimea. Regarding Stefflea, see above.

838 This refers to a Romanian design proposal for a light assault gun with a high-power weapon. Antonescu set great store in it and had informed Hitler about it. On the German side, however, there were some serious doubts concerning the usability of the design. The Romanians were provided the necessary armoring to produce a few test models, but the project probably never got beyond the construction of these models.

839 What Hitler means here by "13-tonner" is difficult to determine. In principle, the normal assault guns, such as the Panzer III and IV, had a weight of 24 t.

840 Could not be identified; probably a misunderstanding or transcription error.

841 The Russians lined up against the Third Panzer Army on December 13 to attack southward from the penetration area near Nevel', which had been occupied since October, and on December 15 managed to cut off the 87th Infantry Division on the north wing of the army. That division then succeeded the following day in breaking out of the encirclement and pushing through to the German lines with 4,750 men, including 1,000 wounded. All heavy weapons, however, as well as most vehicles, had to be left behind.—*Source: Tippelskirch, p. 401; Heidkämper, p. 69.*

842 Baron Mauritz von Strachwitz und Gross-Zauche; born December 12, 1898; 1917 Second Lieutenant, 4th Hussar Regiment; 4, Reichswehr; 1938 1a, 18th Division; 1939 Lieutenant Colonel and (November) Ia, VIII Army Corps; October 1940 Ia, Eighteenth Army; January 1942 Colonel and Chief of the Gen-

eral Staff, X Army Corps; after November 20, 1943 Commander, 87th Infantry Division; and 1944 Major General (February) and Lieutenant General (August). Strachwitz died on December 10, 1953, in Soviet captivity. Hitler confuses him here with Lieutenant General of the Reserves Hyacinth Count Strachwitz v. Gross-Zauche und Camminetz, who was five years older and in the panzer troops—and a future recipient of the Diamonds award.—*Source: Order of Battle, p. 631; Rangliste 1944-45, p. 41; Seemen; Keilig 211/330.*

[843] The Eighteenth Army, positioned outside Leningrad since September 1941, had never managed to eliminate the Soviet bridgehead near Oranienbaum to the west of Leningrad; the bridgehead was supported by the island fortress of Kronstadt and by Russian warships deployed as floating batteries. On January 14, 1944, as Hitler had feared, the Soviets attacked out of the Oranienbaum bridgehead, in addition to their attack from the east; this pincer operation led, on January 19, to the complete break-up of the former siege ring around Leningrad. The following day the Oranienbaum bridgehead achieved the connection with the main Soviet front line.—*Source: Tippelskirch, p.441.*

[844] Presumably reports on the conferences in Teheran and Cairo. In Teheran (November 28 to December 1, 1943) the "Big Three" had definitely and conclusively set the plans for the Allied invasion in 1944: Operation "Overlord" (landing in northwestern France) was to be initiated in May in conjunction with a landing operation on the French Mediterranean coast. Plans for an additional landing in the eastern Mediterranean, which Churchill had repeatedly advocated, were finally dropped. Nevertheless, Roosevelt and Churchill met with Turkish president Ismet Inönü from December 4 to 6 in Cairo, to try to persuade Turkey to enter the war. Churchill had already contacted the Turks in Adana after the conference of Casablanca, and Eden had met foreign minister Menemencioglu in Cairo three weeks before Teheran. By this time, however, the German intelligence service had probably informed Hitler that the Anglo-Saxons did not intend to force Turkish participation in the war.—*Source: Churchill V/2, pp. 27, 99; Wilmot (Engl.), p. 140; Sherwood, pp. 637, 650 and 653; Kordt, p. 381.*

[845] Hitler's concerns about a landing in Norway had surfaced repeatedly, at almost regular intervals, since the time of the German occupation, though, aside from a few ship movements in the distant approaches to the Norwegian coast and occasional commando operations near the coast, there had never been any sign of Allied attack plans. Hitler, however, had always insisted on reinforcing the defense along the Norwegian coast with an ever-greater number of coastal batteries, and had also had an enormous ground services organization established for the Luftwaffe. Until the beginning of 1944, despite the urgent need for forces in all the other theaters of war, the only reduction allowed in the Army units stationed there (12 infantry divisions and one panzer division) was the removal of one panzer division in the summer of 1943. But the forces there were also never reinforced, in spite of Hitler's recurring concerns. He left matters at the planning stage for reinforcement in the event of a landing attack, as was the case here. On the other hand, Hitler, who considered Norway a "zone

of destiny" for the war, had, after 1942, assembled almost all the remaining surface vessels off the Norwegian coast.—*Source: Hinsley, p. 195.*

[846] It was a particular preference of Hitler's to busy himself with technical improvisations that were intended to be as surprising as they were effective. Such designs, which also interested Rommel, were actually deployed in great number and variety against the danger of an invasion in the West (underwater obstacles of various kinds with explosive charges, fields of stakes to prevent airborne landings, etc.). Often these measures failed to have a stronger effect only because they had been given away by enemy agents or because troops were not present to defend the obstacles in time. The deployment of the flame-thrower as a close-combat weapon was a particular pet project of Hitler's. Mass production for the infantry had been pushed through against the wishes of the Inspector of the Engineers, who considered the flame-thrower a special weapon of *his* forces.

[847] The reference is to the DZ 44, which had a pressure and pull igniter that caused the mine to detonate when picked up, i.e., during sweeping.—*Source: Leeb, p. 37.*

[848] Meaning the Commander-in-Chief of the Navy, Grand Admiral Dönitz.

[849] British steel production did indeed decline somewhat at this time, due to increasing difficulties in meeting manpower needs. A few numbers indicate the decrease (in thousands of tons):

	1942	1943	1944
Iron ore mined	19,540	18,487	15,496
Pig iron production	7,604	7,187	6,760
Scrap	7,688	7,782	7,349
Raw steel production	12,764	13,031	12,116
Finished steel released	11,386	11,006	10,270

The same applied to British coal, the production of which (in millions of tons) had been decreasing since the beginning of the war:

Winter	1939-40	115.7
Summer	1940	112.5
Winter	1940-41	100.3
Summer	1941	103.4
Winter	941-42	102.7
Summer	1942	100.6
Winter	1942-43	101
Summer	1943	95.8
Winter	1943-44	93.1
Summer	1944	91.2

Hitler was fundamentally wrong, however, in his assessment of the American deliveries—as, overall, he fell victim to his own propaganda regarding the economic capabilities of the United States. With regard to war material alone, the United States provided the following percentages of the total English supply (in parenthesis the percentage relation of the American deliveries to Britain's own production, excluding the dominions): tanks 47 (104), infantry weapons 21 (36), vehicles 17 (39), aircraft excluding transport planes 18 (24), infantry-weapon ammunition 28 (67).—*Source: Postan, pp. 216, 247 and others; Court, p. 388; Hurstfield, pp. 449 and 473.*

850 In the 4th secret protocol of February 24, 1940, and in a supplementary proto-col dated March 13, 1940, Germany was committed to deliver 1 million tons of coal to Italy every month; later, 1,040,000 tons were agreed upon. But this amount was achieved in one month only; the rest of the time the deliveries were less than 900,000 tons, even as low as 700,000 tons. So Mussolini probably calcu-lated a little more generously when, in his defense speech before the Fascist Grand Council on July 24, 1943, he spoke about the total of 40 million tons of coal that Italy had received from Germany between 1940 and mid-1943.—*Source: Documents on German Foreign Policy VIII, pp. 809 and 904; Rintelen, p. 218.*

851 Jodl probably meant the V-rocket attack on England, which, however, was then delayed until June 15-16.

852 Hitler's obvious confidence in Germany's ability to repel the invasion was not shared by many senior officers at headquarters or at the front, due to the rela-tion of forces in the West and the successful Allied landing attacks that had taken place thus far on the Mediterranean and in the Far East. Everyone knew, however, that gaining freedom in the West was Germany's only chance of fend-ing off the Soviet superiority in the East. Moreover, at headquarters an inner circle also knew Hitler's often-repeated words: "If the invasion is *not* driven back, the war will be lost for us." Maintaining and demonstrating confidence became more than ever a precondition for the prospects—though these were still uncertain—of a successful defense.

853 Meaning the building sites of the launch bases for the V1. [—] The Fi 103 ("Kirschkern," ["Cherry Pit"], V1) had been offered to the technical office of the Luftwaffe by the Fieseler factory on June 5, 1942. Mass production, which began in the fall of 1943, initially at the Fallersleben VW plant, had to be stopped again because testing had revealed the need for major changes. At the beginning of 1944, Hitler, who had demanded the provision of 3,000 units before the first launch, gave the order for deployment of the V1 on February 15, though at that time the production had just been started up again. In the meantime, the con-struction of launching platforms in the Netherlands and northern France had been underway since August 1943; in 1944 these had to be lengthened, which caused further delay. The numerous French workers employed there, as well as agent reports, awakened the interest of the Allies, who, after December 5, 1943, deployed 1,300 heavy bombers against the platforms. By the end of the month, 57% of all construction sites had been attacked, with 10% destroyed completely, 10% severely damaged and 10% moderately damaged. By the end of the five-week attack series, 73 out of 96 building sites were damaged so severely that repairs were no longer worthwhile. Thus, out of necessity, the principle of dis-location—which was recommended from the beginning by, for example, the General of Anti-Aircraft Armaments, among others—won out over the idea of large-scale bunkering attributed to Hitler (though this text seems to imply some-

thing else). After one test (which did not go beyond 10 rounds of harassment fire) during the night of June 12, the main deployment of the V1 began on June 15, 1944, at 11:40 p.m. This was 10 days after the beginning of the invasion; the deployment was unable to affect the preparation or implementation of the invasion. A few weeks later the launching bases fell into enemy hands. Of the approximately 8,000 projectiles that had been fired exclusively onto London by that time, only 29% (only 9% at the end of the offensive, as a result of the improved English defense) reached the target area; 25% went astray, and 24% fell victim to British fighters, 17% to anti-aircraft artillery and 5% to balloon barrages. The V1 was subsequently dropped on London by the He 111.—*Source: Baumbach, p. 256; Görlitz I, p. 465; Wilmot, pp. 158 and 332; Schramm (W.), p. 61.*

854 The standard models of the German light anti-aircraft artillery weapon were the 2 cm and the 3.7 cm, which were usually deployed as double-barreled or four-barreled (in the case of the 2 cm) guns. For the submarines the Navy had also developed a 3-cm double-barreled gun because the 3.7 double-barreled was too heavy for the boats and too difficult to handle. This new weapon was intended for, among other things, the new model XXI submarines, which were supposed to receive two double-barreled guns each. Production of the 3-cm anti-aircraft gun began in the winter of 1943-44, but until the end of war it was not possible to produce a sufficient number for deployment at the front.

855 This was Hitler's wish—to concentrate a greater number of submarines along the west coast of Norway in order to have them available in case of an Allied landing. The formation of such submarine groups did not occur until the spring of 1944 because the Submarine Command was not able to pull the boats away from the battle in the Atlantic before then.

856 The reference is probably to the 274th Infantry Division (home), which was established in the summer through transfers from two Western divisions and was moved to Norway in the fall. In any case, it definitely did not originate in Romania; that must have been a misunderstanding or a transcription error. The 295th Infantry Division—likewise home—which was destroyed at Stalingrad, was also reconstituted in Norway at the end of 1943. On the other hand, the 181st Infantry Division, with the exception of one regiment, had been pulled out and transferred to Yugoslavia.—*Source: Order of Battle, pp. 223, 230 and 195.*

857 A so-called "Panzer Division Norway" had been established there temporarily, but this unit was disbanded again even before the formation was completed. In addition to staff (former staff of the 21st Panzer Brigade), the unit was made up of an artillery detachment, an engineer and intelligence company consisting of only one tank destroyer detachment, one partly motorized armored infantry regiment on bicycles, and a tank detachment.—*Source: Order of Battle, p. 305; Koch: Gliederung und Stärke, 3rd Forts., H. 1/58, p. 16.*

858 Before the war, the attention of the airplane designers—always keen on an increase in speed—had already been turned toward jet propulsion, because propeller drive and piston engines were approaching their economical limit perfor-

mance level peaked at 775 km/h). Thus, in 1935, the Luftwaffe had demanded
jet engines in its technology research and development in addition to the (later
abandoned by German military aviation) turbo-prop engines (units on crank-
shafts). But the world's first rocket-propelled airplanes had also flown as early as
1939: Heinkel's He 176 as well as a design by Lippisch. The Lippisch design was
later purchased by Messerschmitt for 400,000 RM; it was further developed and
eventually became known as the Me 163 "Komet" ["Comet"] ("Kraftei" ["Power
Egg"]). These planes burned—as did the later V2—fuel with oxygen brought
along (here, as with most Walter drives, using highly concentrated H_2O_2 as an
oxygen carrier). Turbine-jet propulsion that worked with oxygen in the air was
17 times more economical as to fuel, but unusable either in the stratosphere or
under water. The world's first jet, which flew on August 27, 1939, was the He
178 equipped with this turbine-jet propulsion. Heinkel had designed it without a
contract, and it was further developed only as far as the twin-engine jet fighter
He 280, which was abandoned after 16 trial models. The most successful development of this kind, far ahead of its time, was the Me262. Having flown already
in 1941, it had been sufficiently tested by May 1943 to be mass-produced—
though it was later neglected. Its major advantages were the high speed of about
900 km/h (200 km/h faster than the fastest propeller fighter of the time), the
lighter weight, and the more aerodynamic construction its lighter weight made
possible. The aircraft also had a lighter and simpler undercarriage and the possibility of using less-valuable diesel-like oil instead of high-octane knock-proof
aircraft fuel. But the consumption of fuel per hp was higher for jet propulsion.
Mass production was delayed by Hitler, even though the Me 262 had received
the high-urgency number 0 as early as 1942. At the beginning of December
1943, shortly before this meeting took place, Hitler, considering enemy preparations for the invasion, recognized—as a result of a casual remark by Messerschmitt
on the occasion of a presentation in Insterburg—the Me 262 as the urgently
needed *Blitzbomber* [lightning bomber] (as, indeed, the model had originally been
announced), although at this time two announced jet bombers (Ju 287 and Ar
234) were already in development. Although the Luftwaffe was able to delay the
change of program for a short time, Hitler gave the explicit order to equip the
Me 262 exclusively as a high-speed bomber. Even the 120 aircraft that had already been delivered up to that point had to be re-equipped. Nevertheless, the
bomber deployment, which finally took place in August 1944, did not achieve
any important successes because the accuracy was insufficient under the available technology of the time. Not until the end of October was it possible, with
the support of Himmler and Speer, to again consider deploying the Me 262 as a
fighter; by November, the first German jet-fighter wing, the 7th Fighter Wing,
(Major Weissenberger) had been established. In 1945 followed the inexpensive *Volksjäger* ["People's Fighter"] He 162, which was demanded by the Armaments Ministry and built in a great hurry (the design was presented, the
order was placed, a model was constructed and the production was begun—
all in September 1944). This aircraft was supposed to be taken over by the
Fighter Wing. [—] Production numbers for the jet and rocket aircraft were as

follows (while assessing them, however, one has to consider that the Commander-in-Chief of the Reich Air Fleet never had more than 82 Me 262s available—in various locations—and ready for action):

	1944	1945	Total
Ar 234	150	64	214
Me 262	564	730	1,294
He 162	—	116	116
Me 163	327	37	364
Total	1,041	947	1,988

Technical data:

	Speed (km/h)	Armaments	Range (km)	Thrust per Engine (kgp)	Number of Engines
Ar 234	875	2 2-cm guns	2,000	810	4
Ar 234	870	4 3-cm guns	1,050	810	2
(in parentheses: A2 *Sturmvogel*)	(920)	or 24 rockets	(1,365)	(1,200)	
He 162	840	2 3-cm guns	1,000	810	1
Me 163	1,004 max.	2 3-cm guns	80	1,500	1

—Source: Lusar, pp. 45, 49 and 62; Baumbach, pp. 92, 242 and 315; Galland, p. 340; Bartz, p. 208; Heilmann: Gebt uns…, passim; Heilmann, Rakete, passim; Feuchter, p. 274; Hébrard, p. 440.

[859] At La Rochelle.

[860] Here Hitler, annoyed by Buhle's remark, probably wants to appeal to Zeitzler to confirm the correctness of his decisions. Moreover, Zeitzler had no other choice but to continually ask for more units for the East.

[861] On November 7, 1944, Franklin D. Roosevelt won, though not by as much as before and not by a landslide as he had believed he would: 24.25 million voters voted for him, and 21.2 million gave their votes to the Republican opposition candidate, Thomas Dewey. In the Electoral College, however, the actual results looked different: Roosevelt had 432 electoral votes and his opponent only 127.—*Source: VB of Nov. 11-12, 1944; Sherwood, p. 793.*

[862] By the beginning of the war in 1939, the income tax in Germany had been raised by 50% and the consumption tax had also effectively been raised. Thus, the portion of war expenses covered by taxes was far higher than, for example, in 1914-18; however, Hitler also financed his war to a great extent through national debt. From 1934 until the day the war broke out, armaments already accounted for 59% of total Reich expenses—or 60 billion RM. Only about half of this could be covered by income from regular (taxes, duties, etc.) and other (Reich railway, Reich postal service, etc.) sources and budget cuts, while the rest was raised by short-term and long-term credits, by the famous "Mefo" bills [bonds], delivery bonds, and tax coupons. During the war, total Reich expendi-

tures amounted to 683 billion RM. Of this figure, there were 453 billion RM for pure Armed Forces expenses and family support and 240 billion RM for civil expenses. One must keep in mind, however, that a large share of the expenses booked for the civilian departments were in fact war expenses. These measures were covered at 33% by domestic income (in 1939 still 42%, in 1944 only 19%), 12% by the occupied territories and 55% by debt. So the Reich debt (excluding Länder and communities) rose during the period of the Third Reich from 8.5 billion RM at the beginning of 1933 to 47.3 billion (Lütge: 30.8 billion) at the outbreak of war and 387 billion at the end of the war. The latter figure consisted of 143 billion RM in long- or medium-term credits, 235 billion RM in short-term credits, 8 billion RM in Mefo bills [bonds] and 1.7 billion RM in tax coupons, etc. In contrast to World War I, the Reich's indebtedness did not take place on the free capital market; instead, to avoid the so-called "financial referendum," the money was silently collected at capital collecting points (banks, saving banks, insurance companies, etc.), which then had to take on treasury bonds and debentures. After the summer of 1944, with the fading trust in the mark and the run on credit institutions by refugees and those suffering from bomb damage, the system collapsed and inflation, which had been kept under control until then, increased. [—] The pure currency circulation rose from 10.4 billion RM on January 1, 1939, to 56.4 billion RM at the end of the war.—*Source: Schwerin-Krosigk, passim; Aufz. dess.: Die Kriegsfinanzierung seit 1939 (Nbg. Dok. NG-3057); Lütge, p. 252.*

[863] During the Allied landings in North Africa at the end of 1942, the British had left the supreme command to the Americans, while the later action starting from England against the continent was to be led by an Englishman. Originally, the chief of the British Imperial General Staff, General Sir Alan Brooke (later Lord Alanbrooke) had been designated commander-in-chief for the invasion. As a result of the growing American predominance, however, and the Americans' increasing share in the invasion due to the expanding plans for Overlord, Churchill offered—as he reported—a shift in the supreme command which satisfied President Roosevelt. (Originally a 1:1 ratio of forces had been planned, but it was later discovered that while the British had just enough men for an equal share at the time of the landing, the entire burden of the expansion of the theater of war had to be carried by the Americans, which led to a final ratio of 3:1.) On August 17, 1943, in Quebec, Churchill suggested that an American should command the invasion, while the command over the secondary Mediterranean theater of war would shift from Eisenhower to an Englishman. In the last 24 hours, however—to universal surprise and against the objections of his political advisors and the requests of his allies—Roosevelt had changed his previous decision. On December 6, 1943, instead of the previously designated General George C. Marshall, he appointed General Dwight D. Eisenhower as commander-in-chief of Overlord, despite his political blunders in the Mediterranean, and gave him the order: "You will enter the continent of Europe and, in conjunction with other Allied Nations, undertake operations aimed at the heart of Germany and the destruction of her armed forces." The delay in the appointment of an Allied

commander-in-chief, and thus in the coordination of the plans, had significant negative consequences, including the postponement of the invasion to June and the consequent inability to take advantage of the excellent May weather. The British general Sir Henry Maitland Wilson became Eisenhower's successor in the Mediterranean.—*Source: Churchill V/1, p. 101, V/2, pp. 68, 114 and 121; Wilmot (Engl.), pp. 142, 172 and 462; Sherwood, pp. 620 and 654.*

864 Henri-Honoré Giraud; born January 8, 1879; St. Cyr Military School; served in Tunisia; Captain in World War I; after 1922 Lieutenant Colonel in Morocco (Rif War against Abd el-Krim); 1930 General and commander of French Forces in southern Morocco; 1936 Commanding General in Metz; and 1939 member of the Supreme War Council and Commander-in-Chief, Seventh Army. After his capture on May 19, 1940, and his escape from the Königstein fortress on April 17, 1942, he went to North Africa on November 9, 1942, to take over the supreme command of the Free French forces that had landed there and those that had joined the Allies. In February 1943 he became supreme civilian and military commander in North Africa. In May of the same year, together with de Gaulle, he became co-president of the French Committee of National Liberation [CFLN]; and he resigned from all these posts in 1944, and in 1946 he became a representative in the Constituent Assembly. General Giraud died on March 11, 1949.—*Source: Munzinger Archive; Nycop, p. 50.*

865 This comparison between the combat experience of enemy assault troops and German occupation forces did not correspond to reality, as few German divisions in the West had combat-experienced cadre. The 700-series fortress divisions on the coast, in particular, had neither combat experience nor adequate cadre with combat experience. In fact, at the time of the Allied landings there, there was not a single first-class infantry division in the West, and of the six German infantry divisions in the Normandy landing area (91st, 243rd, 709th, 352nd, 716th, 711th), only the 352nd had cadre from the former 268th and 321st Infantry Division, which had experience in the East.

866 In the early morning hours of August 19, 1942 (after two postponements on July 4 and 8, due to unfavorable weather conditions), as a major exercise for the invasion of the continent—and also as psychological substitute for the suspended operation "Sledgehammer"—the Canadian 2nd Division, reinforced by smaller Allied units (in addition to 4,963 Canadians, approximately 1,075 English, 50 Americans, and 15 French), landed at the northern French seaport of Dieppe, 80 km northeast of the mouth of the Seine. They landed with the order to occupy the city and to destroy the harbor installations and all the vessels lying there (operation "Jubilee"). Although the English intelligence service had identified only lower-quality German defense forces in the area, and although the mission itself—despite a general fear of landings—had remained totally secret to the enemy, the operation failed with considerable losses and without requiring the Germans to deploy significant reserves. The landing directly in front of the city progressed smoothly after surprising two 15-cm batteries outside of Dieppe, but some of the tanks got stuck in the shore gravel and the few that reached the shore road failed to advance past the brick walls along the access

roads to the city. By 2 p.m. the attack had already been driven back. Only 2,211 of the Canadians who landed returned; 806 fell (with an additional 101 dead among the prisoners and those who returned) and 1,946 were captured. Total losses, including wounded, were 3,542 men on the Allied side and 591 on the German side. The outcome of this operation led on the German side to a fatal underestimation of the chances of success for a possible enemy landing, and on the Allied side to an enlargement of the invasion base.—*Source: Stacey, p. 325; Churchill IV/2, p. 115; Wilmot, p. 195; Tippelskirch, p. 466; Ruge: Seekrieg, p. 207.*

[867] Here Buhle means the use of flame-throwers by the enemy. Hitler jumps to German flame-thrower equipment in the following statements.

[868] Hitler's judgment of the flame-thrower as a defensive weapon is undoubtedly correct—provided that this close-combat weapon is in the hands of a very experienced close-combat fighter. In any case, German flame-thrower production was increased significantly in the last few months before the invasion, in order to strengthen the Western defense. In addition, several thousand captured Russian flame-throwers had been set up in the West. These were stationary—combined in batteries—and could be ignited electrically.

[869] Transcript No. 742/43—Fragment No. 53—The date was determined from the transcript number of the midday situation report on December 22, 1943 (743/43); the text also points to this connection. Only the last page (p. 19) of the original transcript was preserved. The rest of the transcript was destroyed, as were both original shorthand records.

[870] Presumably the discussion concerns the planned reprisals for the judgment in the Khar'kov war criminal case.

[871] Unclear; possibly also: "…was hit."

[872] Transcript No. 743/43—Fragment No. 34—This is the first transcription, of which pages 1-28 were burned on the lower half. The missing parts of those pages are indicated by dotted lines. The text of the final page (page 29) was preserved completely, as the page was only half full.

[873] Southeast of Kirovograd, in the area of the XXXX Panzer Corps, which was engaged in a relief attack. The Armed Forces High Command report recorded on December 22 that the corps had brought in 1,300 prisoners and captured or destroyed 274 tanks and 306 guns since December 5.—*Source: VB of Dec. 23, 1943; Manstein, p. 562.*

[874] To the Crimea.

[875] In October, the 336th Infantry Division was transferred from the Melitopol' front to the Crimea in place of the 50th Infantry Division (see above note 770), when the movements of both divisions were thwarted by the Soviet offensive at Melitopol' and the advance on Perikop, and the units were torn apart. Contrary to their original orders, both divisions were now assigned to the Crimea. In the case of the 50th, the already relocated units were sent back by air and sea, while in the case of the 336th, the units that had been left behind were sent on to join the rest of the division.

[876] The Soviet offensive started here two days later.

[877] The 18th Artillery Division had been established in the area of Army Group South. It was an attempt to concentrate the Army artillery more tightly, and also to have a suitable fire control system available for massed employment. The 18th Artillery Division seems to have remained the only unit of this kind.— *Source: Manstein, p. 565.*

[878] In the attack against the 14th Infantry Division, the enemy offensive had also crossed over to the front east of Vitebsk on December 19. The division had been pushed back 3 to 5 km along a width of about 12 km, when the Russians suddenly stopped their attacks for a day (December 22, the day of this meeting).—*Source: Heidkämper, p. 78.*

[879] Probably Polotsk–Vitebsk.

[880] The 12th Infantry Division and the 12th Panzer Division were both located in the area of Army Group Center at that time, so the reference here could be to the 12th Luftwaffe Field Division, which was located in the area outside Leningrad.

[881] On the morning of December 19, 1943, three Germans (Wilhelm Langheld, Reinhardt Retzlaw and Hans Ritz) who had fallen into Soviet hands were hanged in public in Khar'kov, together with a Russian collaborator, the chauffeur Bulanov, in front of 40,000 spectators. The day before, they had been sentenced to death as war criminals by a military court in Khar'kov after a brief trial. Ritz was doubtless a junior SS commander, and probably a member of Sortie Group D. The reports about the military affiliation of Retzlaw and Langheld stated that one of them held the rank of an officer, the other was a non-commissioned officer or a rank and file soldier. According to official Soviet reports, both belonged to the Secret Field Police; according to another report, one was an Army administration officer. This Khar'kov trial—the first war crimes trial of World War II—was an initial result of the resolution passed by the Allies in Moscow regarding the prosecution of war criminals, and caused some surprise in the West because of its suddenness. Immediately after recapturing Khar'kov, the Soviets had set up a National Commission (to which the Metropolitan of Kiev also belonged) to examine the "German Fascist crimes" committed there. Altogether, nine members of the German Armed Forces and SS were found guilty of the "executions of tens of thousands of Soviet people,". In addition to these executed men, the following were sentenced in absentia: SS Obergruppenführer Sepp Dietrich; the commander of the *Totenkopf* Division, SS Gruppenführer Simon; the chief of the Khar'kov Special Command, SS Sturmbannführer Hannebitter; Police Commissioner Kirchen; the chief of the 560th Group of the Secret Field Police, Moritz; and the deputy police chief of Khar'kov, Wulf.—*Source: NZZ of Dec. 14 (evening edition), 20 (morning and evening edition), 22 (morning edition) and 25, 1943.*

[882] The paper presented here was read at the foreign press conference on December 22 as an official German announcement that same day, and concluded with the threat: "The German military courts will therefore in the near future have to deal with the English and American prisoners who have been accused of severe violations of international law without thus far having been brought to trial."

For some time the German leadership—for whom the first public discussion (in the Khar'kov trial) of the notorious gas wagons of the SD Einsatzgruppen had been quite unpleasant—considered countermeasures against the Anglo-American commando members and "air gangsters," since Soviet prisoners of war had been viewed and treated from the very beginning as outside the law and having no rights, and therefore were not appropriate for reprisals. However, only a propaganda action was carried out, as the possible cases had for the most part already been "settled" quietly.—*Source: NZZ of Dec. 23, 1943 (morning edition); Armed Forces High Command file on the Khar'kov show trial (excerpts in Nbg. Dok. 1487-PS).*

[883] Jodl's strategic analysis was incorrect, for the most part. But because of the Germans' limited reconnaissance capabilities at that time, they could not determine that the enemy reorganization on the Adriatic coast was a deception, which would be followed a month later, on January 22, by the landing at Anzio-Nettuno in the rear of the southern wing of the German front.

[884] Could not be identified. A Major v. Schulenburg was said to have been with the 1st Parachute Division.

[885] Although raised a Catholic, Jodl displayed an absolutely anti-clerical attitude— thus his participation in Hitler's derision.

[886] The discussion concerns using concrete to strengthen and improve the rear positions.

[887] This remark is not very clear. Because Hitler also deals with the same subject in the following passage, the reference here could be to King Peter II of Yugoslavia. Peter married Princess Alexandra of Greece on March 20, 1944, and it is not impossible that reports—true or false—regarding a split between the engaged couple could have reached Hitler at that time. But Alexander Bogomoloff had been the accredited Soviet envoy to the Yugoslav government-in-exile for some time already, after diplomatic relations between the two governments were temporarily suspended by the Soviets on May 12, 1941, in the vain hope of calming Hitler.—*Source: Fotitch, pp. 113 and 169.*

[888] On December 21 the radio station of Tito's Yugoslavian Liberation Army had transmitted a report that made clear the longstanding rivalry between Tito and Mihailović. Sharply critical of King Peter, the report said: "The people of Yugoslavia oppose all adherents of the traitorous fugitive Yugoslav government abroad; from now on, the only Yugoslavian government is that of General Tito…The king and the monarchy have become the last refuge of reactionary, anti-national elements. Under the flag of the monarchy, the most terrible crimes and betrayals are committed…King Peter is the commander-in-chief of the traitorous Četnik gangs, which form an integral part of the occupation forces against which the National Liberation Army is leading a life-and-death struggle." And on the 23rd, one day after this meeting, the same radio station reported that the "Anti-Fascist National Counsel for the Liberation of Yugoslavia" had decided in its second session to deprive the Yugoslav government-in-exile of all rights and to forbid King Peter to return to Yugoslavia. The main headline of the *Völkischer Beobachter* announced happily that same day: "Tito's Banishment of

Peter."—*Source: NZZ of Dec. 21 (evening edition) and 23 (midday edition), 1943; VB of Dec. 23, 1943.*

889 Probably a special commando (10a) of Einsatzgruppe D of the Chief of the Security Police and the SD. The reference here is probably to Hans Ritz, who was executed in Khar'kov.

890 Milan Nedic; born 1882 (1877?); Serbian officer; after 1908 in the General Staff; professor of strategy at the Military Academy after the Balkan Wars and World War I, in which he distinguished himself; 1930 commanding general; 1939-40 Yugoslavian War Minister in the Zvetkovic cabinet. In the hope of using his authority to prevent his countrymen from taking action against the occupation forces, thus protecting them from German reprisals, General Nedic established, on order of the German military commander in Serbia, a Serbian government on August 30, 1941, and relieved the previous interim leadership in occupied Serbia." From the very beginning he supported the Četniks' Draza Mihailović, to the point that it even came to a formal agreement in September 1944 regarding the joining of forces into a combined anti-Communist front. Nedic considered himself, as he explicitly stated in a message to King Peter in 1943, as governor only until the return of the monarch and his legal government, a position, however, which did not prevent him from collaborating with the occupation forces. Nedic left the country with the German army in October 1944, but rejected all calls to establish a government-in-exile and lived as a private citizen in Austria. Handed over to Tito by the Allies in September 1945, he died the evening before his trial, on February 6, 1946, from a mysterious fall from the window of the OSNA building in Belgrade. Officially, it was considered a suicide, but a public discussion of the German-Communist collaboration in Yugoslavia prior to June 22, 1941, would hardly have been in the interest of the Tito regime.—*Source: Matl: Jugoslawien..., p. 109; Fotitch, p. 140.*

891 Because of his political balancing acts in 1932-33, General Schleicher had gained among the National Socialists a reputation as a schemer. It seemed to the general's negotiating partners that—because of the many threads he was trying to pull—he sometimes didn't know what he had said to whom. Hitler's party, in particular, felt betrayed by him in the fall of 1932.

892 Channel coast.

893 The Belgian "Reduit National,"[National Redoubt] the territory along the Dutch border north of the Schelde River bend between Ghent and Antwerp, had already played a significant role for the Belgian army in 1914, as it was able to threaten the German right wing from there. During the Western campaign, in order to take this region quickly and without losses, Hitler wanted the paratroopers and airborne troops not used in Poland—i.e., the 7th Air Division and the 22nd Parachute Division—to land there at the beginning of the attack (operation "G"). Hitler first expressed his intention to Lieutenant General Student on October 27, 1939—at a time when the original plan to occupy also Holland militarily had been set aside by the Army High Command for the time being. Operation "G" was finally canceled on January 14, 1940, in favor of mass action against "Fortress Holland." The abandonment of the operation was due more

to resistance from the Luftwaffe and the Army—because the deployment area was too far from the ground troops' combat area—than to the reason Hitler gives here. In addition, the "Reduit" had lost some of its operational significance with the re-involvement of the Netherlands, which had been achieved in the meantime through pressure from the Luftwaffe—although the rear defense of the border could have been replaced partly by the mouth of the Schelde.— *Source: Jacobsen: Fall Gelb, p. 154.*

[894] On January 10, 1940, Major Hellmuth Reinberger left the 220th Air Command— a supply station for the only German parachute division at that time (the 7th Air Division)—in his Me 108 to attend a meeting in Cologne with Major Hoenmanns, the air base commander at Loddenheide near Munster. Reinberger carried "secret command matters" (instructions and orders for the Second Air Fleet and the 7th Air Division for the attack planned for one week later) across Germany's western border. The plane lost its way in deteriorating visibility, and engine trouble led to a forced landing in Belgium near Mechelen on the Meuse. For the most part, Reinberger succeeded in burning the documents before his capture, but the Belgians were able to confirm the planned German attack, which they already knew about, from the charred remains, and also obtained details about planned individual operations by German parachute and airborne units against Belgium. As a result of the Belgian "alert" (which, of course, was only partly caused by the Mechelen affair) and unfavorable weather forecasts, Hitler postponed the attack. But the significant transfer of the main focal point—to the southern wing of Army Group A, pushing in the direction of the Meuse and lower Somme—did not take place until February; Mechelen had no effect on that.—*Source: Jacobsen: 10. Januar 1940, passim; Vanwelkenhuyzen, passim.*

[895] Heinrich Müller; born April 28, 1900; 1914 aircraft mechanic; 1917 war volunteer; 1919 assistant in the police administration in Munich; 1929 police secretary; member of the Bavarian Political Police and close to the Bavarian Volkspartei [People's Party]; 1933 Criminal investigator; April 1934 as Untersturmführer taken into the SS and transferred to the Berlin Secret State Police office; 1935 Senior crime investigator and Sturmbannführer; 1937 SS Standartenführer and member of the Government High Council and Crime Council in the main office of the Security Police; 1938 NSDAP; 1939 Oberführer; after the establishment of the Reich Security Main Office [RSHA] in the fall of 1939, Chef Amt IV [Office IV] [Gestapo]; 1940 Brigadeführer [Brigade commander]; and 1941 Gruppenführer [Group commander]. Müller disappeared from the Führer's bunker after Hitler's death and did not reappear. Rumors suggested that the Soviets had taken the capable (as well as unscrupulous and unprincipled) head of the Gestapo into their service, as he had been in contact with them already since 1944 through the so-called radio games (passing on the radio connections of enemy agents).—*Source: SS staff files (BDC); Hagen: Die geheime Front, p. 72; Crankshaw, p. 96.*

[896] Mussolini, who in Salò retreated more and more to the political ideas of his youth, had initiated an extensive socialization program, to which the mostly Communist northern Italian workers responded with strikes, according to their

Party program. Thus, the situation in northern Italy was very chaotic. In addition to the strikes, partisan actions and the countermeasures that resulted—such as hostage shootings, declarations of a state of emergency, etc.—caused emotions to run high. At this time, around December 22, the center of interest was the assassination of the Fascist provincial secretary of Milan, Aldo Resega, the reprisals that followed, and the incidents at his funeral.—*Source: Anfuso, p. 294; NZZ of Dec. 22 (morning and evening edition) and Dec. 23, 1943 (morning and evening edition).*

897   The outpost patrols were the *Sylt, Borkum, Föhr,* and *Amrun* groups, which had been set up in the area between Ireland and Newfoundland at that time.

898   A mine barrier to extend the "Atlantic Wall" was laid out by the destroyer *Hans Lody,* the torpedo boat *T28* and a mine layer.

899   The submarines south of Bear Island were part of the *Eisenbart* outpost patrol against convoy JW 55.

900   Meaning the French submarine *Casabianca,* which was operating under British command.

901   On the northwestern coast of the Crimea.

902   The Armed Forces High Command report of December 22, 1943—in the year of the first enemy thousand-bomber attack—considered even those miserable four-engine aircraft worth mentioning: "German aircraft led nuisance raids against southeast England during the night of December 22."

903   The Supermarine "Spitfire" was the standard English single-engine, single-seat fighter. This aircraft had been used already before the war, and it appeared during the war (to a certain degree as the British counterpart to the Me 109) with continual improvements—more powerful engines, in particular—in numerous models, designated with Roman numerals up to XXII. The armaments usually consisted of 2 canons and 2-4 machine guns or 4 canons with 230 kg bomb weight; the maximum speed reached 720 km/h. The Me 109, which was originally at least as good as the Spitfire, failed in the development contest between the two standard models because the Spitfire had a much larger airframe, enabling the aircraft to carry more powerful engines and larger amounts of fuel. The fact that the German Messerschmitt aircraft were designed at the outer limits of stability, and that they were ahead of the British in this respect, was useless.—*Source: Hébrard, p. 262; Feuchter, pp. 214 and 247; Royal Air Force III, p. 407.*

904   Transcript number unknown—Fragment No. 7. Because the shorthand record was partly burned, the second transcription was possible only with numerous gaps.

905   South. The reference is to attacks north of Kirovograd.

906   Zeitzler corrects him here because there was no 529th Division.

907   The reference is probably to the 17th Panzer Division, which had been pulled out of the Sixth Army—for the time being remaining under the command of Army Group South—on the lower Dnieper and sent to the Fourth Army on the threatened north flank of Army Group South. This movement was the beginning of the castling to the left wing, which Manstein had ordered by telex from the Führer headquarters. The 17th Infantry Division was also located on the

lower Dnieper, near Nikopol', but no major movements of that division were recorded during this period.—*Source: Manstein, p. 566.*

[908] The 16th Panzer Division, together with the 4th Mountain Division (see the following discussion), the 1st Infantry Division and the General Command [Headquarters] XXXXVI Panzer Corps of Army Group South, was supposed to be made available to the threatened Fourth Panzer Army.—*Source: Manstein, p. 567.*

[909] On Christmas day the *Feldherrnhalle* Panzer Grenadier Division had deployed southeast of Vitebsk to defend against a Russian attack that threatened the Vitebsk–Orsha road.—*Source: Heidkämper, p. 86.*

[910] The reference may be to a Russian unit, as the only German division with this number—the 29th Panzer Grenadier Division—was in Italy. Confusion with the 329th Infantry Division cannot be excluded, but this division was already fighting in the front sector of Army Group North.

[911] Meaning the evacuation of the tip of the position west of Nevel', which could no longer be held.

[912] On December 24 Vatutin's 1st Ukrainian Front conducted a major offensive against the German Fourth Army west of Kiev to smash the northern flank of Army Group South's front line, which projected far to the east by the lower Dnieper, further back to the west. The Russians created an 80 km wide and 40 km deep gap in the German front near Radomysl' and captured that town as well as Brusilov. This, of course, strengthened the argument for a quick and timely evacuation of the front salient in the Dnieper bend north of the Black Sea. That is why Manstein, in his evaluation of the situation, expressed the opinion that "the time for trying to master the situation on the north wing of the army group through individual measures, such as the addition of single divisions, is over." Within the next few weeks, in the region of Korosten'–Zhitomir–Berdichev–Vinnitsa the decision would be made as to whether the south wing of the Eastern Army would be cut off from its rear connections and finally pushed aside. To avoid that, Manstein called for the abandonment of the eastern part of the Dnieper bend and the withdrawal of the front to a new line in Dnieper bend west of Nikopol' and Krivoi Rog. Six of the 12 divisions that would be saved by shortening the front were to be shifted to the northern wing of the army group, together with First Panzer Army headquarters, and deployed from the east against the enemy penetration spearhead at Zhitomir. The rest of the divisions were to remain with the Sixth Army along the lower Dnieper. With further additional forces that the Army High Command was to bring in, the redeployed First Panzer Army forces were to line up from the west against the Soviet penetration spearhead after blocking the encircling movement that threatened the north wing of the Fourth Panzer Army. [—] Hitler refused to evacuate the eastern Dnieper bend and the Nikopol' bridgehead at this time (and also again in January), based on the doubtful attitude of Turkey if the Crimea were to be lost. Later, on December 31, he did approve the transfer of the First Panzer Army to the northwest (which had been ordered by the army group), but this could only be carried out with weaker forces than suggested, due to the

continuing efforts to hold the Dnieper bend.—*Source: Tippelskirch, p. 428; Manstein, p. 566.*

913 The double-track main line from Fastov via Belaia Tserkov' and Smela to Cherkassy or into the industrial area. The two branch lines mentioned further below: from Berdichev via Kazatin as well as from Vinnitsa to Zvenigorodka-Smela.

914 Could not be identified.

915 The Romanians administered part of the occupied Soviet territory: the area between the Dnestr and the Bug, including the harbor city of Odessa. Because the satellites in the southeast were usually extremely mindful to maintain their sovereignty rights, the use of their facilities frequently required lengthy initial discussions and then still often resulted in difficulties.

916 From the term introduced by the quartermaster general for the road connection between Lemberg [L'vov]–Ternopol'–Vinnitsa–Kirovograd–Krivoi Rog–Dnepropetrovsk–Stalino–Rostov (the route in the sector mentioned here: Vinnitsa–Gaissin–Uman'–Novo Archangel'sk–Novo Ukrainka–Kirovograd). There were a few large East–West connections of this type (e.g., the D V: Brest Litovsk–Khar'kov), which didn't necessarily follow main roads but also included secondary roads that were especially maintained by the road construction authorities. These connections were crossed by the North–South connection PK [PC] (Petersburg–Crimea). [—] Perhaps this mention reminded Hitler of his Eastern colonization plans, in which the D IV had played a role. German settlement bases were to have been established along this route to connect the "Gotengau" (Crimea and Cherson area)—which was to have been totally colonized by Germany—with the German settlement area. [See also H. Trevor-Roper, Ed., *Hitler's Table Talk 1941-1944*, Enigma 2000, pp. 339, 577, 578.]

917 Regarding the 4th Mountain Division, see above note 908.

918 During their attacks against the German Dnieper front, the Soviets concentrated against Kiev on November 3, tore apart the German front on the 6th and broke through to the town of Fastov, 60 km southwest of Kiev, on the 7th. The German salient, projecting far to the east along the lower Dnieper, began at Fastov. To make sense, the passage here should probably read: "...and *not* carried out the Fastov action...," because the reference is likely to the German counterattack in mid-November.—*Source: Tippelskirch, p. 396.*

919 Hitler agrees here not to Manstein's suggestion, but only to a minor regrouping, due to which—as is stated below—one division will be set free: the 4th Mountain Division. Zeitzler also argues for the larger evacuation, as can be seen clearly from the discussion that follows.

920 In pursuit of his favorite plan for an operation (even though limited) in southeastern Europe, Churchill also spoke with the Turks in early December 1943 in Cairo, following Teheran, regarding preparations for Operation "Saturn." After the completion of Turkish air bases with Allied help, Allied air forces were to land in Turkey during the first half of February to enable operations in the Aegean Sea, and Salonika. Because of "Cicero" those preparations were well known to the Germans, but they expected, as the result of some error, a sudden

occupation of the Turkish airfields on February 15 instead of *by* February 15. "Saturn" did not materialize, however, because the Turks were not ready yet at this stage of the war to participate, and also because neither the Americans nor the Russians showed much interest in this plan. The Turks therefore were able to make excuses, with reference to their insufficient supply and equipment, until the British military delegations (including Air Marshal Linnell, who was in charge of preparations for the Aegean mission), left Turkey in disgust on February 3, 1944.—*Source: Churchill V/2, p. 111; Papen, pp. 584, 588 and 592.*

[921] Probably meaning by the English in Turkey, as long as German troops still stood in the Crimea and on the lower Dnieper.

[922] But it actually was the beginning of the winter battle.

[923] In the Dnieper bend.

[924] Erich Koch was Gauleiter of East Prussia from 1928 to 1945. Fritz Sauckel was Gauleiter of Thuringia from 1927 to 1945. Robert Ley, however, was never Gauleiter of Mecklenburg; he was Gauleiter of the Rhineland (see above the mention of Cologne) from 1925 to 1931. The Gauleiter of Mecklenburg-Lübeck was Friedrich Hildebrandt from 1925 to 1945.

[925] Karl Weinrich, born December 2, 1887, after September 1, 1927 Gauleiter of Kurhessen. Weinrich failed during the heavy air attack on Kassel, the capital of his Gau, on the night of October 22, 1943. He had taken part in a social evening outside Kassel during the attack and returned to the burning town only after the all-clear signal—not to head up damage control but to rescue his furniture. Because, in addition, he had not evacuated Kassel thoroughly, had not driven the bunker construction energetically enough, and had established only a limited number of fire ponds, he was blamed for the "desolate conditions" in the town and for the disproportionately high number of 5,000 to 6,000 dead, including 1,000 children. When Goebbels visited the destroyed town on November 6, he thus decided to report Weinrich's wretched role to Hitler and to demand his immediate dismissal. After Bormann agreed two days later, Karl Gerland was given the command of the Kurhessen Gau and was finally named Gauleiter at the beginning of January 1945. Weinrich was interned by the Allies after the war, until the end of October 1950.—*Source: Lochner, pp. 496, 497, and 502; Oven, p. 147; VB of Jan. 5, 1945.*

[926] The reference is to Karl Kaufmann; born October 10, 1900; 1921 member of the NSDAP; 1925 to 1928 Gauleiter of Rhineland North (after 1926: Ruhr Gau); and after 1929 Gauleiter of Hamburg.

[927] Nevel', the boundary position between Army Groups North and Middle, was taken by the Russians on October 7, 1943. Since then, because of the salient pointing at Dünaburg [Daugavpils], Vitebsk was under threat from the north. As a result, Hitler had insisted for more than two months that Nevel' be taken back and the front straightened—which caused further heavy losses. Hitler saw the egotism of the army group commanders in the fact that they (partly because their forces were constantly tied down in other dangerous locations on their front lines) failed to gather enough forces for the attack against Nevel' at the same time. The reproach made by Hitler here is also made by the other side.— *Source: Tippelskirch, p. 400; Heidkämper, p. 40.*

[928] Meaning the Crimea. The Seventeenth Army, then with five German and seven Romanian divisions, as well as individual coastal defense units, was still in the Crimea when the German front fell behind the Dnester in April of the following year, and in fact suffered Stalingrad's fate to a great extent. The rear units of the divisions, the main body of the army following, and the majority of the Romanians were successfully transported out of Sevastopol', but most of the army's combat units were captured (exactly one year before the end of the war) after a three-week occupation of the fortress. The transportation was delayed too long, and in the end there was a shortage of small ship capacity to assist in the embarkation, as the transporters stood ready in open water outside the range of the Russian artillery.—*Source: Weitershausen, passim; Pickert, passim.*

[929] In the Crimea at that time, in addition to three German divisions—the 98th Infantry Division near Kerch and the 50th and 336th Infantry Divisions in the north—there were seven Romanian divisions. Later two additional German divisions were brought over to the Crimea: the 73rd Infantry Division (Kerch) and the 111th Infantry Division (Army reserves, later in the north), while the Romanian forces decreased and were evacuated first in the final partial evacuation of the Crimea. However, the reason for this was not only consideration for Antonescu, but primarily the unreliability of those troops. In the end, the troops could not be used at the front anymore, as they rightly doubted the sense of those battles at a point in time when their homeland was already seriously threatened. The Romanian formations involved were the 1 Mountain Army Corps with three mountain divisions, two cavalry divisions and two infantry divisions.— *Source: Pickert, p. 142; Weitershausen, passim.*

[930] The 16th Panzer Division had been reconstituted in France in the spring of 1943 after its destruction in Stalingrad, and had been used since then in Italy, until the fall. It had recently been relocated to the Eastern front and put under the command of Army Group Center. Now, according to the following considerations, it was to be deployed in the area of Kiev, which, of course, meant further weakening of Army Group Center.—*Source: Order of Battle, p. 295.*

[931] Here the reference is already to the retreat from the Volkhov River and Lake Il'men' to the Narva–Lake Peipus line, i.e., on the old Estonian border (see also the meeting that took place two or three days later between Hitler and Zeitzler and Küchler, on December 29 or 30, 1943.). This retreat was then forced by the Soviet winter offensive in January and February 1944.—*Source: Tippelskirch, p. 441.*

[932] As Hitler correctly assumed, the Red Army attacked Vitebsk fiercely starting in January. In February the German front had to be pulled back to the so-called Outskirt [Stadtrand] position. But Hitler combined the permission for that with the statement that Vitebsk must be "held at all cost as the last major Russian city, for reasons of prestige." In fact the Soviets did not succeed in taking the city until the end of June 1944.—*Source: Tippelskirch, pp. 446 and 535; for details on the battle of Vitebsk: Heidkämper, passim.*

[933] The first closed volunteer unit of the Waffen SS was the "SS Flander's Legion," whose members were recruited primarily from the DeVlag organization Staf de Clerq. It had been deployed since the winter of 1941-42 in the East, first within

the scope of the 2nd SS Infantry Brigade (mot.) in the Svir offensive in the area of Leningrad, and after mid-March 1943 under the command of the SS Police Division. The legion had been expanded to the 6th SS Volunteer Assault Brigade *Langemarck* in the fall of 1943, but Hitler's remark here hints at the size of the unit at that time. In the fall of 1944 it was expanded and renamed the 27th SS Volunteer Panzer Grenadier Division *Langemarck*, but it was not deployed collectively anymore. [—] Previously there was a *Langemarck* Regiment, the original 4th *Totenkopf* Regiment, which, like the Flander's Legion, had been deployed with the 2nd SS Infantry Brigade (mot.) in the winter of 1941-42, but it was pulled out later and replaced by the *Netherlands* Legion. In the early summer of 1942, this *Langemarck* Regiment was then added as a mobile regiment to the SS *Reich* Division, which had been reorganized as a panzer division in France. The Flemish members of this unit were placed under the command of the SS Assault Brigade *Langemarck*, which took over the tradition of the Flander's Legion, as well as that of the SS *Langemarck* Regiment, in the fall of 1943.—*Source: Order of Battle, pp. 337 and 348; Schellong, passim; Hausser, p. 69; Himmler's Order of the Day for March 27, 1943 and Entwurf [Draft] RFSS/Pers. Stab betr. SS Assault Brigade "Langemarck" o.D. (Himmler files in IfZ 2/11/7).*

[934] Friedrich (Fritz) Fromm; born October 8, 1888; 1908 Second Lieutenant; Reichswehr; 1933 Colonel; 1934 Head of the General Army Office; 1935 Major General; 1939 General of Artillery and Commander of the Replacement Army [Ersatzheer] and chief of Army armaments; and July 1940 Colonel General. Later, Fromm played a not entirely clear role in the events of July 20, 1944. Although he refused direct participation and was confined by the conspirators to his private rooms (on word of honor), he gave Colonel General Beck the opportunity to commit suicide after his liberation by Remer's men, and had Olbricht, Stauffenberg and others shot in Bendlerstrasse without orders. Because of this, Fromm was taken into custody on word of honor that same night and relieved by Himmler as Commander of the Replacement Army the following day. He was executed for cowardice on March 12, 1945.—*Source: Munzinger Archive; Zeller, passim; Keilig 211/92; Das deutsche Heer, p. 22.*

[935] Transcript number unknown—Fragment No. 10. Almost completely preserved.

[936] Manstein's evaluation of the situation (already discussed with Zeitzler earlier) and his suggestion to significantly shorten the Army Group South positions along the Dnieper bend. One week later, on January 4, 1944, Manstein presented his wishes personally at the Führer Headquarters, but with no more success. [—] Jodl had probably not been at the headquarters during the last few days—perhaps over Christmas—and was just now hearing about Manstein's request (for which the Armed Forces Operations Staff was not in principle responsible). The discussion regarding the deployment of the *Langemarck* Assault Brigade indicates that the date is correct and that this meeting really did take place one day after the meeting between Hitler and Zeitzler (Fragment No. 7). Zeitzler had spoken about it with Himmler in the meantime.

[937] Should probably be: "*that he tries* via Kirovograd or Krivoi Rog..."

938   Nikopol' was economically important as the center of the largest European manganese ore deposits, which provided for a third of the requirements of the German steel industry. Krivoi Rog was a center of the iron and steel industry. Both towns were strategically important to the extent that Hitler still believed that the connection with the cut-off Crimea could be restored from this position on the lower Dnieper. Nikopol' was lost on February 8, and Krivoi Rog at the end of February.

939   Manstein pressed for a decision on the request he had submitted by telegram on December 25, but he received from Zeitzler only the prospect of adding three divisions, which had been agreed to the day before.—*Source: Manstein, p. 567.*

940   Thirty-five km southwest of Vinnitsa, beyond the Bug and so already in Transnistria. The double-track Ternopol'-Odessa line also ran via Zhmerinka.

941   Marshal Antonescu.

942   This is an ironic repetition of the assumptions imputed to Manstein. The contrast between "these" and "these" or "here" and "here" means in most cases "Dnieper bend" vs. "Northern flank in the area of Zhitomir-Berdichev-Kazatin." Here it probably means "Germans" and "Russians."

943   The 25th Panzer Division was established in Norway at the beginning of 1942 and was held in reserve until the summer of 1943, when it was first relocated to northern France, and then in October to the southern sector of the Eastern Front, in the Kiev area. There the division was immediately engaged in heavy combat, for which it was not prepared, due to a lack of experience. But Hitler also had a sharp eye on the division because the former commander, Lieutenant General v. Schell, had provoked his displeasure in his previous position as deputy general of the motor transport service.—*Source: Order of Battle, p. 301.*

944   Beginning with the Norwegian campaign in 1940, Hitler had shifted command of the Army directly to the Armed Forces High Command (OKW) in individual theaters, eliminating the Army High Command (OKH). In the end, the Army High Command (OKH) commanded only in the East. As a result of this extremely significant separation of responsibility, Zeitzler, as Army Chief of General Staff, became Hitler's only advisor for the East, while Jodl took over the same assignment for all other theaters of war, and Hitler alone overviewed the general situation. Only the exceptionally difficult situation on the southern wing of the Eastern Front and the possible need to withdraw forces from the Southeast, South or West (as demanded by Manstein), led Hitler to discuss Manstein's request also with Jodl that evening.

945   The mobilization and new activation of infantry divisions took place in so-called waves. The active divisions of the Peacetime army had formed the 1st wave, and another three waves had been planned in the original mobilization plan. The activation of the six (seven, including the 274th Fortress Division, which had already existed since the summer) divisions of the 22nd wave—from remnants of destroyed units—began in December 1943 (second activation of the 271st, 272nd, 275th [this one for the first time], 276th, 277th, and 278th Infantry Divisions). [—] The wave designation indicated personnel strength, organization and equipment, and therefore also to some degree the combat value of the

relevant divisions. The following year, the divisions of the 32nd wave already received an externally differentiated designation: the "Volksgrenadierdivisionen" ["People's grenadier divisions"].—*Source: Mueller-Hillebrand I, p. 68 and II, p. 161; Order of Battle, p. 222; Keilig 100/3.*

946 To the West; however, the "Hermann Göring" and the 90th Panzer Grenadier Division ultimately remained in Italy.

947 Hermann Hoth; born April 12, 1885; 1905 Second Lieutenant; 1914 Captain in the Great General Staff; Reichswehr; 1924 Major; 1929 Lieutenant Colonel and Commander, 1st Battalion, 4th Infantry Regiment; 1932 Colonel and Commander, 17th Infantry Regiment; 1943 Major General and Infantry Commander III; 1935 Commander, 18th Division; 1936 Lieutenant General; 1938 General of Infantry and Commanding General, XV Army Corps (Jena; in the Western campaign Panzer Group Hoth); July 1940 Colonel General; November 1940 Commander, Third Panzer Group; October 1941 Commander-in-Chief, Seventeenth Army in southern Ukraine; and after May 1942 Commander-in-Chief, Fourth Panzer Army. In December 1942 Hoth led the unsuccessful relief attack on the Stalingrad pocket. In early September 1943, after the failure of the offensive near Belgorod against the southern flank of the Kursk salient, his army was operationally penetrated by the Soviet counteroffensive and could no longer establish a continuous front even in retreat. He was barely able to withdraw the army across the Dnieper River north and south of Kiev. As a result, Hoth was removed from his command (as of December 10) and was not reemployed again until shortly before the end of the war, as "Commander Erzgebirge." In the Armed Forces High Command trial he was sentenced to 15 years of imprisonment. He was released on parole in 1954.—*Source: Army High Command staff files (Nbg. Dok. NOKW-141); Munzinger Archive; Tippelskirch, p. 383; Siegler, p. 124.*

948 Manstein had received two of these five panzer divisions in October, and the other three (1st, 25th, and 1st SS) in mid-November for the defense against the Soviet attacks in the large Dnieper bend, directed at Krivoi Rog. In November the field marshal, whose attention was always directed toward the northern wing and the danger of getting cutting off there, then received permission to deploy the three later arrivals in the area of Kiev with the Fourth Panzer Army. The 14th and the 24th Panzer Divisions remained with the First Panzer Army in the Dnieper bend.—*Source: Manstein, pp. 549 and 555.*

949 This was a baseless allegation by Hitler. Manstein's troops were not at all "demoralized," but only very worn out due to Hitler's own unrealistic demands. In this discussion of Manstein's presentation, Hitler's ill feeling and dissatisfaction are evident. The field marshal was relieved of his command on April 2, 1944, after the Soviet successes in March.

950 This date is probably not accurate; neither division came to the East until the fall (probably October).—*Source: Order of Battle, pp. 295 and 300; Grams, p. 125.*

951 The Commander-in-Chief of Army Group South shifted his headquarters to Proskurov at the end of the year, then to Kamenets-Podolsk in early March 1944, and then later to L'vov [Lemberg].—*Source: Manstein, pp. 575 and 595.*

[952] Manstein writes about Hoth's departure: "Unfortunately, the initial rapid shift of the Fourth Panzer Army corps to the south or the west caused Hitler to think that the command of this army should be placed in different hands. Despite my protest that it was not errors by the army's command, but the superiority of the enemy and the weakness of our exhausted divisions that finally led to the loss of the Dnieper front, Hitler believed that Colonel General Hoth needed a rest after the excessive stress of the last few years. Hoth was transferred to the Führer's reserves. I was very sorry to see him relieved, but at least received the promise that he would get an army in the West after his leave."—*Source: Manstein, p. 557.*

[953] Manstein's perspective: "He [Hitler] always argued in response to suggestions of shortening the front that enemy forces would be freed up as well. That, of course, could not be denied. What Hitler studiously overlooked, though, was the following. An attacker may wear himself out if faced with a sufficiently strong defensive front. But when a front cannot be occupied beyond the level of a kind of security line, the attempt to hold it will cause excessive losses among the inadequate defensive forces—if the enemy fails to simply overrun them."— *Source: Manstein, p. 563.*

[954] Manstein based this assumption on the condition of the railway system on both sides of the Dnieper, which had been severely damaged or would be further destroyed before the German retreat.—*Source: Manstein, p. 571.*

[955] Hitler saw great significance in this, as it was his own former "Wehrwolf" headquarters on the road from Vinnitsa to Zhitomir, which he had used from July 13 (Greiner: July 16) to November 1, 1942, and from February 18 to March 12, 1943. Manstein had moved into the former Führer Headquarters at the beginning of October.—*Source: Manstein, p. 546.*

[956] Balta is located north of Transnistria on the Kodyma River. Balti is located 130 km west of this in northern Bessarabia on the Radausti [Rautul] River.

[957] In a letter dated October 25, 1943, Hitler himself had, among other things, suggested to Marshal Antonescu that the railway system command in Romanian-occupied Transnistria be handed over to the Germans. In his November 15 reply, Antonescu asked that this suggestion about the transfer of the railways be reconsidered, as they had worked well under Romanian direction. In order not to offend the Romanians, Hitler, for better or for worse, had to agree in the end.—*Source: Hillgruber, p. 176.*

[958] In the area of the Fourth Panzer Army, Soviet forces succeeded in creating a wide penetration to the southwest, in the direction of Vinnitsa, on the day of this meeting. However, the Russians did not reach the area east of the town until January 16, 1944, and, in the course of the battles, the area became a German salient in front of the retreating lines. It was held until March 20.—*Source: Manstein, p. 568; Tippelskirch, pp. 428 and 432.*

[959] Read: weak.

[960] Probably the Zaporozh'e dam, and therefore the following: "this" means the area between Zaporozh'e and Nikopol', "here" this means the area downriver of Nikopol'.

[961] Gerhard Count v. Schwerin; born June 23, 1899; B. [Berlin] Lichterfelde Cadet Institute; 1915 Second Lieutenant; 1920 left the service; 1922 Reichswehr (1st and 17th Infantry Regiments among others); 1936 Major, 1938 in the 3rd Department of the Army General Staff; 1939 Lieutenant Colonel and Commander, 1st Battalion, *Grossdeutschland* Infantry Regiment; 1941 Colonel and Commander, 200th Regiment (seconded for special duty) and (July) 76th Infantry Regiment; fall 1942 Major General and Commander, 16th Panzer Grenadier Division; June 1943 Lieutenant General; May 1944 Commander, 116th Panzer Division; December 1944 Commander, 90th Panzer Grenadier Division; and April 1945 General of Panzer Troops and Commanding General, LXXVI Panzer Corps. Schwerin had received the Swords award the previous month (November 4, 1943).—*Source: DNB of Nov. 6, 1943; Order of Battle, p. 625; Seemen; Das deutsche Heer, p. 15; Rangliste 1944-45, p. 25; Keilig 211/313.*

[962] The position on both sides of Melitopol', which protected the northern (land) entrance to the Crimea, had collapsed before the Soviet assault on October 23, 1943. This operation formed a part of the Russian offensive against the lower Dnieper.

[963] Code name for the evacuation of the Viaz'ma bend between Iukhnov and Rzhev in February 1943.

[964] The 21st wave, which was formed starting in October 1943, consisted of the 349th, 352nd, 353rd, 357th, 359th, 361st, 362nd, 363rd, 364th, and 367th Infantry Divisions, of which the 357th, 359th, 363rd, and 364th Infantry Divisions were in the Polish area (according to Keilig the 355th and 356th Infantry Divisions may also have been part of the 21st wave; according to *Order of Battle* they belonged to the 19th wave, which Keilig doesn't exclude.)—*Source: Order of Battle, p. 245; Keilig 100/3.*

[965] Actions against the partisans in the East and Southeast were frequently given such idyllic code names as "Frühlingsfest" ["Spring Festival"], "Hasenjagd" ["Hare Hunt"], "Sternenlauf" ["Star Run"], "Winterzauber" ["Winter Magic"], "Pfingstausflug ["Whitsun Trip"], "Regenschauer" ["Rain Shower"], and so on.

[966] Meaning, "It's still led there with the Commander-in-Chief Southwest [new name for the Commander-in-Chief South, as of November 21, 1943], where it was earlier." The 371st Infantry Division had been relocated from Brittany to northern Italy in November and then to Croatia in December. In January the division would be thrown into the southern sector of the Eastern front as result of these considerations.—*Source: Order of Battle, p. 251.*

[967] Into the West.

[968] In Italy.

[969] The 5th Luftwaffe Field Division. The discussion concerns the lower course of the Dnieper.

[970] There was no doubt in the minds of the National Socialist leadership about the ultimate aim of incorporating the Netherlands as well as Belgium into the Reich; however, they regarded a premature "solution to the problem" during the war as inopportune, as they understood quite clearly that at least 95% of the involved population opposed such plans. The military commander in Belgium, General v.

Falkenhausen, received the order to leave all possibilities open, while the SS and above all the SS Main Office, responsible for the "Germanic work," had already arranged the division of Belgium into the two Gaus of Wallonia and Flanders under the designated Gauleiters Leon Degrelle and Jef van de Wiele, with the aim of later annexing both areas into the Reich. Under "Reich" the Main Office understood citizens of the Grossdeutsche Reich in a narrower sense, rather than those of the yet to be established "Grossgermanische Reich." So Berger's office in Belgium, with his DEVLAG (Deutsch-Flämische Arbeitsgemeinschaft [German-Flemish Working Group] under van de Wiele), fought under cover but successfully against the "Grossdietschen" endeavors of the VNV (Vlaamsch Nationaal Verbond under Staf de Clerq, and later Dr. Elias). The VNV supported Mussert's idea of a merger between the Netherlanders and Flanders to establish a "Grossdietschland" inside the "Grossgermanische" Reich of Adolf Hitler, thus creating a new crystallization point on Germany's northwestern border. Berger called the "Grossdietsche" demands or the desire for cultural autonomy "enormously presumptuous and arrogant" with respect to the Führer, who would himself determine one day "how he would lead the individual Germanic tribes into this, his Reich" (speech at the DEVLAG conference in Brussels on August 29, 1943). The separate deployment of Flemish and Walloon units, as demanded by Himmler here, can perhaps also be explained by this tendency toward fragmentation in the effort to achieve better integration at an appropriate time. The classification of the Walloons as Germanic—mandatory for political purposes, despite previous scornful perceptions—was reflected in Himmler's summer 1943 guidelines, which were expressed as follows in a letter from the Volkspolitisches Amt [People's Political Office] of the DAF on June 28, 1943: "The Walloons are to be regarded as a core Germanic people. Today's scientific investigations [sic] have concluded that the Walloons, like the Flemish, have 80% Germanic blood. Unlike the Flemish, however, they do not originate from Fälisch-Saxon-Frisian but from Frankish stock."—*Source: Nbg. Dok. NG-1636, NG-2258, NG-2381, NG-2800, NG-3481, NG-5078, NG-5430, NG-5495, NO-617, NO-623, NO-624, NO-857, NO-953, NO-1106, NO-1659 and NO-1844; Toynbee: Hitler's Europe, p. 483.*

[971] The Netherland's [*Nederland*] Legion was "new" in that it was appearing now for the first time on the Eastern Front after rehabilitation and reorganization as the 4th SS Volunteer Panzer Greandier Brigade *Nederland*, and after a temporarily partisan deployment in Yugoslavia. This legion was the second Dutch volunteer formation and was deployed in the winter of 1941-42—like the Flander's Legion, within the scope of the 2nd SS Infantry Brigade (mot.). Without any combat experience, they were thrown onto the southern edge of the Soviet Volkhov penetration and sustained heavy losses right from the beginning. They also appeared later on the Volkhov, until summer, when they were transferred to the Reich for rehabilitation and reorganization.—*Source: Schellong, passim; Nbg. Dok. NO-1604 and NO-1607.*

[972] Regarding the 5th Jäger [Light Infantry] Division, see above. This excellent division (the former regular 5th Division) made no substantial progress in its coun-

terattacks against the Russians, who had advanced northwest of Vitebsk across the road between Sirotino and Vitebsk to the Polotsk-Vitebsk railway line during the last few days (December 26-27).—*Source: Heidkämper, p. 88.*

973 Meaning perhaps Trikraty, about 20 km north of Voznesensk. The town was on the rail line from Cherkassy and Kirovograd, but the bridge over the Bug was situated—at least originally—at Voznesensk.

974 Transcript number unknown—Fragment No. 11. Completely preserved.

975 Might mean "Zug" (train) calculations.

976 Vitebsk-Polotsk. This rail line was temporarily interrupted on December 26, first through artillery fire and then through a blast from advancing hostile forces.—*Source: Heidkämper, p. 89.*

977 Outside Vitebsk in the Third Panzer Army sector. Also the 12th Panzer Division, mentioned further below, was newly supplied to this army.—*Source: Heidkämper, p. 93.*

978 Northwest of Vitebsk, along the endangered railway to Polotsk.

979 For a renewed German counterattack against the south flank of the Russians, who had broken through.

980 This withdrawal contributed significantly to the breakdown of Army Group North, as the Soviets initiated an attack there as well on January 14, 1944. The German front was thrown back to the Luga River and finally to Lake Peipus [Lake Chud].

981 Regarding Hube, see other mentions above. It was then ordered that Hube's First Panzer Army must hand over its sector by January 1 to Hollidt's Sixth Army, in order to take over (by January 3 at the latest) the command over the front sector from the Dnieper to approximately 45 km southeast of Berdichev, previously belonging to the Fourth Panzer Army. "Send up" means in this case into the huge Dnieper bend; "up above" means on the north flank between the Dnieper and Berdichev].—*Source: Manstein, p. 567.*

982 Ferdinand Schörner; born June 12, 1892; originally intended career: teacher; 1911 one-year volunteer; 1914 Second Lieutenant in the Reserves; 1917 activated as reserve officer (Pour le mérite); Reichswehr; 1934 Major; 1937 Lieutenant Colonel and Commander, 98th Mountain Jäger [Light Infantry] Regiment; 1940 Colonel and Commander, 6th Mountain Division; August 1940 Major General; January 1942 Lieutenant General and Commanding General, Mountain Corps Norway (XIX Mountain Army Corps); June 1942 General of Mountain Troops; November 1943 Commander, XXXX Panzer Corps at the Nikopol' bridgehead; March 15, 1944 chief of NS operations staff in the Army High Command; March 31, 1944 Colonel General; Commander or Commander-in-Chief, Army Group South Ukraine after March 31, 1944; Army Group North after July 23, 1944; and Army Group Center after January 17, 1945, until the capitulation. Schörner, promoted to field marshal on April 5, 1945, was named Commander-in-Chief of the Army in Hitler's will. While his troops continued fighting in Bohemia after the official capitulation (on his orders), Schörner fled in civilian clothes to the Americans, who sent him to the USSR. Schörner was released from there in January 1955 and returned to the Federal Republic,

where he became the defendant in a supply conflict and lawsuit (4½ years in prison, 1957-58).—*Source: Army High Command staff files (Nbg. Dok. NOKW-141); Munzinger Archive; Siegler, p.137.*

983 Manstein.

984 Transcript number unknown—Fragment No. 12—completely preserved.

985 West of Kiev.

986 Meaning enemy units. The discussion again refers to the area northwest of Vitebsk and the Vitebsk–Polotsk railway line. The forest mentioned by Hitler below was along this rail line to the northeast at Savias'e, about 10 km further east of the former blast area and still about 20 km outside Vitebsk.

987 Meaning his attack.

988 The 5th Jäger Division.

989 To pull back the front.

990 This passage is unclear. Part of the "Rollbaun [Highway] Position" ran a bit to the east, and part ran directly along the Leningrad-Khodovov sector of the Leningrad–Moscow rail line. It meant giving up the Eighteenth Army's salients to the northeast. This position, however, as Küchler's other explanations also indicate, was not yet ready to be defended and was not entered until mid-January 1944. Possibly this discussion deals with a smaller section of the position.

991 Main Battle Line (HKL) is synonymous with Main Line of Resistance (MLR) in English usage.

992 The Lake Peipus [Lake Chud] position. Connecting with Army Group Center to the south, the "Panther" position (Line) continued along a line running from east of Nevel' to northeast of Surazh to Babinovichi. The order to scout it had already been given at the end of August, and most of the improvements should have been completed by November 1. As a result of enemy pressure, however, this front sector had to be occupied as early as mid-September or early October (evacuation of Smolensk).—*Source: Heidkämper, pp. 18 and 21.*

993 The freezing of the lake was imminent, after which it would no longer be an obstacle.

994 Curt v. Gottberg; born February 11, 1896; 1933 SS Untersturmführer; 1937 Standartenführer and head of the Settlement Office in the RuSHA; 1939 Oberführer; 1940 head of the Registration Office in the SSHA; 1942 Brigadeführer and SS and Police Commander Belorussia; September 1943 successor to Commissar General Kube there; 1944 Supreme SS and Police Commander Russia-Center; and SS Obergruppenführer. Later he temporarily led the fight against partisans in France and was Commanding General, XII SS Corps. Gottberg supposedly died in May 1945 in Berlin.—*Source: SS staff files (Ngg. Dok. NO-1732) as well as NO-1861 and others; Krätschmer, p. 319.*

995 Friedrich Jäckeln; born February 2, 1895; 1930 SS Sturmbannführer; 1933 Gruppenführer; 1934 Führer SS Oberabschnitt Northwest (Braunschweig); renamed "Center" in 1936); 1936 Obergruppenführer; summer 1941 Supreme SS and Police Commander Russia-South; after mid-December 1941 in exchange with Prützmann Führer, SS Oberabschnitt Ostland and Supreme SS and Police Commander Russia-North; and February 1945 Commanding General, V SS

Corps. Jäckeln was sentenced to death on February 3, 1946, by a Soviet court in Riga and was hanged that same day in the city's former ghetto.—*Source: Reitlinger: Endlösung, p. 585; SS Dienstalterlisten; Nbg. Dok. NO-2042 and others.*

[996] The establishment of Latvian and Estonian units began, initially on a voluntary basis, as early as 1941. While the province administrations [*landeseigenen Verwaltungen*] tended to create their own armies out of those security troops [*Schutzmannschaften*] ("Schuma" battalions), the SS administrative detachments responsible for the military registration of these people proceeded to establish more and larger units within the scope of the Waffen SS. In order to fill the units, the men of these occupied territories were drafted by age group under violation of international law. At the time of this meeting, the age groups 1915 to 1924 were involved in both countries. The original "legions" continued to expand, and in the end there were (in addition to replacement, home, and smaller units) one Estonian and two Latvian SS Divisions.—*Source: Nbg. Dok. NO-766, NO-2271, NO-3300, NO-3302, NO-3303, NO-3379 and NO-4479.*

[997] Indication on the map. The command staffs at the front complained occasionally about the "rigid" fixing of their borders. Different points of view, as can be seen in the following discussion, played a role, of course. Usually the objectionable cases were traffic routes, which, running at a sharp angle to the front, led to a city behind the lines of unit X but crossed the front in the sector of neighboring unit Y. If the enemy pressed against this intersection, the flank of Y naturally went back in the direction of its own unit, leaving the traffic route in the back of X uncovered and exposed.

[998] At Nevel'.

[999] Per division. Sufficient for a quiet front in those geographic conditions, but inadequate for a combat focal point.

[1000] The Soviet offensive that started on January 14 against Army Group North made these considerations irrelevant, although at least the preparations—transporting away of ammunition, equipment, heavy artillery, etc.—could have been carried out if permission had been granted for the withdrawal movement. However, Zeitzler had to report to Army Group North on January 5 that his efforts had failed and that Hitler had refused to approve the withdrawal to the "Panther" Line

[1001] The following statements reveal the troops' reluctance to leave positions they had become accustomed to. Lindemann, who had a very close relationship with his soldiers, was more open to such considerations than the commander-in-chief of the army group or the Army High Command.

[1002] Küchler had commanded the I Army Corps (1st Military District [Wehrkreis I]) in East Prussia from April 1, 1937, until the beginning of the war. This unit was formed in 1934 from the old 1st Division of the Reichswehr. The three infantry divisions of the corps were the 1st, 11th, and 21st. On his return to Pleskau [Pskov], Küchler received the order to give the 1st Infantry Division to Army Group South.

1944

[1003] *Hitlers Lagebesprechungen, die Protokollfragmente seiner militärischen Konferenzen 1942-1945*, Quellen und Darstellungen zur Zeitgeschichte, Vol. 10, Stuttgart 1962.

[1004] Loc. cit., pp. 252-68.

[1005] The film is on National Archives Microcopy T-120, Container 2621, Serial 5489, pp. E 381869-99.

[1006] See Waldemar Besson, "Zur Geschichte des Nationalsozialistischen Führungsoffiziers (NSFO)," in this journal 9 (1961), pp. 76-116. A large number of the documents published by Besson appeared, with some additions, in the collection of the party chancellery: *Verfügungen, Anordnungen, Bekanntgaben*, Vol. VI (1944, Part I), Munich 1944, pp. 251-80.

[1007] Text in Besson loc. cit., p. 94; *Verfügungen*, p. 257.

[1008] *Verfügungen*, p. 256. The publication of the transcript of January 7, 1944, refutes the thesis of an arbitrary act on the part of Bormann, which was suggested as a possibility by Besson (p. 79, note 4).

[1009] Order 6/44 of January 7, 1944, in *Vefügungen*, pp. 258-59.

[1010] Text in Max Domarus (ed.), *Hitler, Reden und Proklamationen, 1932- 1945*, Vol. II, Würzburg 1963, p. 2078.

[1011] One such meeting (on January 27, 1944) is described by Erich von Manstein, *Verlorene Siege*, Bonn 1955, p. 579.

[1012] See note 1010.

[1013] The publication of a new magazine, *Offiziere des Führers, Die Nationalsozialistische Monatszeitschrift der Wehrmacht für Politik, Weltanschauung, Geschichte und Kultur* (edited by the NS Leadership Staff of the Armed Forces High Command, for use only within the Armed Forces), apparently also dates to this time. See in particular the articles by General Reinecke and General Walter Scherff in the first issue, 1944.

[1014] See note 1004.

[1015] Besson loc. cit., p. 80.

[1016] See note 1004.

[1017] Besson loc. cit., pp. 104-12; *Verfügungen*, pp. 267-79. See also Hassell loc. cit., pp. 341-42 (entry from February 23, 1944).

[1018] For this time period, all we have of Hitler's *Tischgespräche* [Table Talk] is Bormann's report regarding the night of January 27-28, 1944, in Oron J. Hale, "Hitler and the Post-War German Birthrate," *Journal of Central European Affairs* 17 (1957), pp. 166-73; See also Bormann's remarks in the letter to his wife dated January 27, 1944, in: Hugh R. Trevor-Roper (ed.), *The Bormann Letters*, London 1954, p. 45.

[1019] Finally, it must be pointed out that, as in the case of the documents published here, the possibility of finding additional transcripts in the preserved files of Reich and party agencies does not appear impossible.

[1020] The present work of the author has been supported by a grant from the Horace R. Rackham School of Graduate Studies at the University of Michigan.

[1021] Reinecke's name is consistently reproduced in the transcript as "Reinicke." This spelling mistake was corrected; the rest of the document is printed verbatim.

[1022] On the first page of this document, Martin Bormann made the following handwritten notes: "1) Pg Klopfer z.K. [zur Kenntnis—FYI] 2) Pg Friedrichs z.K. 3) II Pg Ruder B. (ormann) Jan. 24, 1944. *Secret Reich matter*, only to be given confidentially from hand to hand! B. 24/1." Undersecretary of State Dr. Gerhard Klopfer and Helmuth Friedrichs, both senior employees of the party chancellery, initialled the transcript on January 29, 1944. Willy Ruder's initials have the date of February 1, 1944.

[1023] Martin Bormann, Secretary of the Führer, Head of the Party Chancellery.

[1024] Field Marshal General Wilhelm Keitel, Chief of the Armed Forces High Command.

[1025] Lieutenant General Rudolf Schmundt, Chief, Adjutant of the Armed Forces at the Führer Headquarters.

[1026] Major General Walter Scherff, [Representative] for the Recording of Military History.

[1027] Lieutenant Colonel Heinrich Borgmann, Adjutant of the Army at the Führer Headquarters.

[1028] Probably meaning Keitel's order of February 6, 1944 (*Verfügungen*, p. 259) and Reinecke's Implementing Regulations of February 9 (loc. cit., pp. 261-67).

[1029] So the official channel was presented accurately to Hitler; see Besson loc. cit., p. 79.

[1030] The reference is to Alfred Rosenberg's office as representative of the Führer for the supervision of the entire intellectual and ideological training and education of the NSDAP. Regarding the cooperation of this office with the Armed Forces, see the unpublished dissertation of Herbert P. Rothfeder, "A Study of Alfred Rosenberg's Organization for National Socialist Ideology," Ann Arbor, University of Michigan, 1963, pp. 309-24.

[1031] See Ernst Deuerlein, "Hitlers Eintritt in die Politik und die Reichswehr," in this journal *Vierteljahrshefte für Zeitgeschichte* 7 (1959), pp. 177-227.

[1032] On December 10, 1943, Hitler had relieved Colonel General Hermann Hoth from command of the Fourth Panzer Army.

[1033] See also the characteristic remark of the Hauptbereichsleiter Ruder in a memorandum of December 30, 1943 (published in Besson loc. cit., p. 101): "In the selection of NS operations officers, the attempt must be made to win more and more active officers, so that the troops won't have the impression that the NS operations officers are 'outside forces' commissars!), but that they belong to the National Socialist Armed Forces."

[1034] General of Infantry Kurt Zeitzler, Chief of the Army General Staff.

[1035] The reference here is probably to Hitler's speech to a large number of officer candidates in Breslau on November 20, 1943; see Domarus, Vol. II, pp. 2060-62.

[1036] See Domarus loc.cit., pp. 2078, note 17.

[1037] See note 1011.

[1038] See Rothfeder loc.cit., pp. 316-24.

[1039] Lieutenant Colonel Walter Nicolai was Chief of Department IIIb with the Chief of General Staff of the Field Army during World War I. His memoirs appeared under the title *Nachrichtendienst, Presse und Volksstimmung im Weltkrieg*, Berlin 1920.

[1040] The reference here is probably to Hitler's servant Junge, toward whom Hitler was obviously well disposed; he was sent to the front and perished in August 1944. See also Hugh R. Trevor-Roper, *Hitler's Table-Talk, 1941-44*, London 1953, Jan. 24-25, 1942, pp. 244-45; Martin Bormann to Gerda Bormann, Aug. 22, 1944, *Bormann Letters*, p. 85; Gerhard L. Weinberg (ed.), "Hitler's Private Testament of May 2, 1938," *Journal of Modern History* 27 (1955), p. 418. Hitler's secretary Junge was the servant's wife.

[1041] Meaning Keitel.

[1042] Reinecke means the deputy commanders in the military districts [Wehrkreisen].

[1043] This may refer to a meeting arranged by the Chief of the Armed Forces High Command on October 19, 1943; Hitler spoke to the participants at the end (see Domarus, Vol. II, p. 2047).

[1044] See note 1022.

[1045] The reference here is to the German Officers' Union [Bund], established in the fall of 1943. The commanding general of the LI Army Corps, General of Artillery Walter von Seydlitz-Kurzbach, who was captured in Stalingrad, was one of the founders. See Heiber loc. cit., pp. 124-31.

[1046] Marshal of the Soviet Union Mikhail Nikolaevich Tukhachevsky, Deputy People's Commissar of Defense of the USSR, was executed in 1937 after a secret trial.

[1047] The "German salute" wasn't actually introduced until the day after July 20, 1944; see "Bekanntmachung Görings im Namen der Oberbefehlshaber aller drei Wehrmachtsteile," in Domarus, Vol. II, p. 2131.

[1048] Colonel General Werner Baron von Fritsch, Commander-in-Chief of the Army, 1934-38.

[1049] Underlined by hand.

[1050] Grand Admiral Karl Dönitz, Commander-in-Chief of the Navy.

[1051] Keitel returns here to the question of the NSFO.

[1052] General of Mountain Troops Ferdinand Schörner became Chief of the NS Operations Staff in the Army High Command for a short time in March 1944.

[1053] Transcript number unknown—Fragment No. 36—Only about one-third of the shorthand record was preserved, so the second transcription was possible only with large gaps. The date has been reconstructed (see, for example, note 1085). As Manstein (p. 579) reports, Hitler had ordered all the commanders-in-chief on the Eastern Front and a large number of additional senior officers to the Führer Headquarters on January 27. This occasion would explain the participation of Model (and possibly that of other front generals not mentioned) in this meeting.—*Source: Manstein, p. 579.*

[1054] General Buhle, for example, also participated in this meeting.

[1055] By the spring of 1944, the Russians had several times—but, in general, still infrequently—used tank decoys to deceive the enemy. On the German side, the best-known example is Rommel's successful use of tank decoys during his first thrust into the desert in the spring of 1941.

[1056] Meaning perhaps Tarasovka, 10 km northeast of Zvenigorodka.

[1057] The Armed Forces High Command report for this date, January 28, reported that 115 enemy tanks had been destroyed southwest of Shashkov and Pogrebishche.

[1058] Manstein wanted to throw the III Panzer Corps with the 16th Panzer Division, 17th Panzer Division, the 1st SS Panzer Division and the Baeke's heavy panzer regiment into the new crisis spot; the 1st Panzer Division was to follow as quickly as possible.—*Source: Manstein, p. 583.*

[1059] Referring to the German counterthrust (see above preliminary remark for January 28, 1944).

[1060] In the wide gap between Army Groups Center and South, which, in Pripiat' Marsh area, now reached nearly 300 km deep and almost as wide, only the weak and isolated LIX Army Corps fought its way back to Rovno, which, until shortly before, had been the seat of the "Reich Commissioner Ukraine," the notorious Gauleiter Erich Koch.—*Source: Manstein, p. 575; Tippelskirch, p. 428.*

[1061] Karadzha is a small village on the western tip of the Crimea. What was meant here is probably Tarashcha, 40 km southeast of Belaia Tserkov'.

[1062] The Third Panzer Army gave the 87th Infantry Division away on 5 February. Its sector northwest of Vitebsk was taken over by the 20th Panzer Division, which was reintegrated into that army between January 31 and February 3.— *Source: Heidkämper, p. 109.*

[1063] Theodor Busse; born December 15, 1897; 1917 Second Lieutenant, 12th Infantry Regiment; Reichswehr; 1933 Cavalry Captain in RWM; 1937 Ia [operationa officer] 22nd Infantry Division; 1939 Lieutenant Colonel in the 4th Department of the Army General Staff; 1940 Ia, Eleventh Army (after November 1942 Army Group Don, after February 1943 Army Group South); 1941 Colonel; March 1943 Major General and Chief of Staff, Army Group South; and September 1943 Lieutenant General. Busse became Commander of the 121st Infantry Division in July 1944; in September Commander, (after November General of Infantry and Commanding General), I Army Corps; and after January 19, 1945, Commander, Ninth Army.—*Source: Army High Command staff files (Nbg. Dok. NOKW-141).*

[1064] Manstein (see above p. 442).

[1065] Field Marshal v. Küchler (see above note 101) was relieved as commander of Army Group North on January 29, 1944, and replaced by the "Lion of the Defense," Colonel General Model (see above note 718). Model was to bring the retreating front of the army group to a halt. The front had been pushed back from the Volkhov River and Lake Il'men' during the period of the Soviet winter offensive, which began on January 14.

[1066] Meaning target designators. Some fighter wings had a target designation squadron.

[1067] On the Anzio–Nettuno beachhead. On January 22, 1944, at 2 a.m., the American VI Army Corps began landing at Anzio and Nettuno on the Tyrrhenian

Sea—*hic et nunc* completely surprising the Germans. The two panzer grenadier divisions (the 29th and 90th under the control of the XI Air Corps), which, with difficulty, had been saved to defend against what was, in reality of course, an expected landing operation, only shortly before had been committed in support of the wavering 94th Infantry Division along the lower Garigliano River, where the British X Army Corps had been attacking since January 17-18 with superior forces. Although nearly unavoidable, this employment was obviously a mistake because the attack along the Garigliano River only served to divert and contain the German reserves. Kesselring claimed that he had relied too much on a report from the defense chief Canaris, who—whether despite better knowledge remains unclear—had denied the existence of immediately threatening enemy landing preparations. Other than a few stationary coastal barriers, there were initially just two battalions to oppose the Americans, and only the hesitant advance of the enemy made it possible for the German leadership to eventually erect a defensive front.—*Source: Tippelskirch, p. 420; Kesselring, p. 268.*

[1068] A heavy attack by the American VI Corps, according to Kesselring on January 25 and then again on January 31.—*Source: Kesselring, p. 271.*

[1069] February.

[1070] Since the 3rd Panzer Division was never in Italy, this was probably the 3rd Panzer Grenadier Division. The 715th Infantry Division (originally a fortress division, now just expanded to a full division and partly motorized) had been given up by the Commander-in-Chief West and came from the French Mediterranean coast (see also below p. 451).—*Source: Kesselring, p. 271; Order of Battle, pp. 287, 305 and 283.*

[1071] Probably meaning the 71st Infantry Division, being brought in at that time from Slovenia, since the 371st Infantry Division was transferred during that month from Croatia to the Eastern Front.—*Source: Order of Battle, p. 162 and 251.*

[1072] According to Kesselring this refers—probably correctly—to the 1027th and 1028th Panzer Grenadier Regiments, brought in at that time from Germany.—*Source: Kesselring, p. 271.*

[1073] Meaning the south-facing main front in Italy.

[1074] On the "southern front."

[1075] There had been two Slovakian brigades fighting in the East for quite some time, but after the change in the military situation they no longer proved valuable. One of them was moved as a construction brigade to Italy, and the other was then destroyed in the Crimea.

[1076] The 114th Jäger [Light Infantry] Division was on the march from the Balkans to Italy, in order to release forces there for the West.

[1077] In Croatia three German-Croatian infantry divisions (see above note 739), established with German help and strongly permeated with German personnel, were formed, and also (with a smaller German quota) eight Croatian Jäger (light infantry) and mountain brigades. All these units were intended only for partisan warfare in their own country. In addition, during the first years of the Eastern campaign, there was the Croatian 100th Infantry Regiment, which was then destroyed at Stalingrad (see above note 29). Without German participa-

tion, the Croatian government maintained the paramilitary "Ustashe" formations (see above note 813). Regarding the Croatian SS formations, see below
note 1078.

[1078] The experiences with the foreign units were, as also seen here, not entirely
pleasant. In addition, the foreign units were constantly changing. They were
drawn up, then dissolved again or renamed and reorganized as the next higher
formation, etc. In the Army there were, finally, the Croatian units (see above
note 1077), the Eastern battalions (see above note 482) and the 845th Arabian
Battalion. The Waffen SS had a number of legions, freikorps [free corps],
regiments, etc., but also smaller units, such as, for example, a Finnish battalion
(see below note 1499) or a Swiss company. According to a Führer order dated
January 30, 1945, most of these units were expanded to division status. However, it must be born in mind that the divisions marked with an asterisk below
were, for all practical purposes, only formation staffs, whose units did not
exceed regimental or at most brigade strength. The following consisted partly
of Germanic volunteers:

5th SS Panzer Division "Viking" ["Wiking"]
6th SS Mountain Division "North" ["Nord"] (only to a small degree)
11th SS Volunteer Panzer Grenadier Division "Northland" ["Nordland"]

Except for the personnel cadre and the non-infantry units, the following consisted of forign peoples [Fremdvölkische]:

13th Waffen SS Mountain Division "Handschar" (Croatian No. 1)
14th Waffen SS Infantry Division (Galician No.1)
15th Waffen SS Infantry Division (Latvian No. 1)
19th Waffen SS Infantry Division (Latvian No.2)
20th Waffen SS Infantry Division (Estonian No.1)
*   21st Waffen SS Mountain Division "Skanderbeg" (Albanian No.1)
22nd Volunteer Cavalry Division ("Maria Theresia"); partly Hungarian ethnic Germans)
*   23rd Waffen SS Mountain Division "Kama" (Croatian No. 2)
25th Waffen SS Infantry Division "Hunyadi"(Hungarian No.1)
26th Waffen SS Infantry Division (Hungarian No.2)
*   27th SS Volunteer Infantry Division "Langemarck"
*   28th SS Volunteer Infantry Division "Wallonien"
*   29th Waffen SS Infantry Division (Russian No. 1); turned over to Vlasov;
after April 1945: Italian No.1)
30th Waffen SS Infantry Division (Russian No. 2)
*   31st SS Volunteer Infantry Division "Bohemia-Moravia" ["Böhmen-Mähren"]
(see below note 1450)
*   33rd Waffen SS Infantry Division "Charlemagne" (French No. 1)
*   34th SS Volunteer Infantry Division "Landstorm Nederland"
*   37th SS Volunteer Cavalry Division
1st Cossack Cavalry Division
2nd Cossack Cavalry Division/(see below note 1417)

as well as:

East Turkish Waffen SS Unit
Caucasian Waffen SS Unit
Serbian SS Volunteer Corps
Indian SS Volunteer Legion
Waffen SS Infantry Regiment (Romanian No.1)
Waffen SS Infantry Regiment (Romanian No.2)
Waffen SS Infantry Regiment (Bulgarian No.1)
British Free Corps (SS)

—*Source: Letter from Berger to Himmler on Feb. 10, 1943 (Nbg. Dok. NO-1486); Edition RFSS/Adj. of Aug. 1, 1944 (NO-1728); Edition SSFHA of Mar. 26, 1945 (NO-175).*

[1079] On January 27, 1944, a communiqué was published regarding the just-concluded two-day session of the Sobranje, which said that, "all the delegates who spoke approved of the course of the government, which had led to the fulfillment of the national ideals and rights of Bulgaria." At the same time, all the speakers emphasized that the Bulgarian border territories, including Thrace and Macedonia, must be defended with the entire strength of the nation.—*Source: NZZ of Jan. 28, 1944 (morning edition); VB of Jan. 29, 1944.*

[1080] During the war, basic training in the German Army normally lasted three months, but in 1944 it sometimes lasted only two months.

[1081] See also above note 482 and below note 1200.

[1082] OT [Todt Organization] Chief Construction Manager Karl Weis; born March 2, 1897; originally construction official in the Bavarian interior ministry; 1938 brought by Todt into the OT; and after 1942, deputy head of the OT under Dorsch (see below note 1084). In 1940 he was entrusted with the erection of heavy coastal batteries in France for Operation "Sea Lion" [Seelöwe], and was later influentially involved in the construction of the "Atlantic Wall."

[1083] See also below pp. 575 and following.

[1084] Xaver Dorsch; born December 24, 1899; in November 1933 brought from the Munich construction company Sager & Woerner by Todt—as ministerial counselor and department head—into the general inspectorate of the German road network system; rose by means of his success with the Western Wall construction after the general exclusion of the Armed Forces on May 16, 1938; and was after 1940 head of the OT headquarters, i.e., the staff of the OT under Todt or Speer. In April 1944, Ministerial Director Dr. of Engineering Dorsch was made head of the Unified Construction/Todt Organization Office in the Reich Ministry for Armaments and War Production, a member of the Hunter Staff [Jägerstab] and a deputy of Speer.

[1085] The English had attacked Berlin on the evening of January 27, 1944; the Armed Forces High Command report for January 28 stated the following about the attack: "British terror pilots used the favorable weather conditions yesterday evening for a renewed terror attack against the Reich capital. With low, closed cloud cover, numerous enemy aircraft flew over the area of Greater Berlin and dropped mine, high explosive, incendiary and incendiary phosphorous bombs on various city districts. Damage resulted, especially in densely populated residential districts and cultural areas. The population suffered losses. Despite difficult defense conditions, 23 enemy bombers were shot down, according to reports received thus far." The here-mentioned correction of the report appeared then in the Armed Forces report of the following day, January 29: "The number of enemy aircraft brought down during the night of January 27 increased to 32."

1086 The 17th Patrol Boat Flotilla had to be withdrawn from the Skagerrak to the Gulf of Finland.

1087 The 4th Destroyer Flotilla lay in Kristiansan [note different spelling in the text] and Oslo at this time.

1088 This was an ONS convoy, a slow England–America convoy, against which the "Hinein" group was launched, without the submarines obtaining any success.

1089 On January 25, 1944, U 532 sank the 7,176 GRT American steamer *Walter Camp* in 10 N/71-48 E.

1090 Referring to the expected invasion in the West.

1091 The operation against St. Nazaire on March 28, 1942, was the largest-scale British commando operation of World War II. The attack unit consisted of 18 large motorboats as well as the *Campbeltown*, which was loaded with three tons of high explosives. The *Campbeltown*, one of fifty old destroyers supplied by the U.S., entered the mouth of the Loire unrecognized around 2 a.m. It's assignment was to blow up the huge "Normandy" lock in the St. Nazaire harbor (the only Atlantic repair-shipyard in German hands that was suitable for battleships) and also, if possible, to destroy the middle lock of the harbor, which was used as a submarine base. The unit was spotted during its 8-km trip inland and was fired upon, but the *Campbeltown* managed to reach the huge floodgate and ram into it at full power. Further operations against the middle lock and the shipyard equipment—by a landing group that had been dropped nearby—failed because of the German defense. As a result of a time-fuse failure, the *Campbeltown* didn't blow up until eight hours later, but nevertheless destroyed the outer floodgate. A number of German soldiers and technicians, who had been inspecting the ship that was wedged into the gate, also died. However, the "Normandy" lock was closed only temporarily, and not rendered unusable after all. Of the English boats, only four returned home.—*Source: Ruge: Sekrieg, p. 206; Churchill IV/1, p.147; Heydel, passim.*

1092 This probably refers to a USA-Gibraltar convoy.

1093 The transport was carried out by the 9th T [Torpedo Boat] Flotilla.

1094 The cooperation between the naval forces available to the Badoglio government—5 battleships, 9 cruisers, 11 destroyers, 40 torpedo boats, 37 submarines and 30 M.A.S. motor torpedo boats—and the Allied forces had begun on local initiative immediately after the ceasefire announcement on September 12. After the declaration of war on Germany and the Allied recognition of the Italian "participation in warfare" on October 13, all vessels in the Italian fleet, with the temporary exception of the battleships, joined the operations. When, at the end of the year, the Soviets then pressed for their share of the Italian spoils, which had been allotted to them in Teheran (1 battleship, 1 cruiser, 8 destroyers and 4 submarines), the Anglo-Americans advised against approaching the Italians about this, in the interest of preserving the prestige of the Badoglio government. Instead, the Russians were provided with comparable English ships for the duration of war, until a transfer of the Italian units could be arranged after the conclusion of the war.—*Source: Badoglio, pp. 129 and 224; de Belot, p. 229; Churchill V/2, pp. 86 and 158.*

[1095] In fact the following were available for the invasion on June 6, 1944: 233 LSTs (landing-ship tank, i.e., landing ships for up to 30 tanks) and 835 LCTs (landing-craft tank, i.e., landing craft for approximately 6 to 10 tanks). Of these, 188 were American LSTs and 279 American LCTs, out of a total American supply of 409 LSTs and 687 LCTs. The relatively limited American participation was due to a preference for strong concentrations in the Pacific, where, for example, small landings against a single Japanese division were carried out with 87 LSTs; this was an ongoing point of contention with the British. Thus, the Americans had granted, out of a total of 31,123 available to them on May 1, 1944, not more than 2,493 landing craft to Operation "Overlord," and even those were offered only reluctantly. The American fear of being left alone with the Japanese opponent after a joint victory over Hitler, and the resulting jealous safeguarding of and preferential treatment for the needs of the Pacific theater (for which the U.S. alone was responsible), led to several failed plans and disagreements among the Western forces.—*Source: Wilmot, pp. 184 and 188; Eisenhower, p. 76.*

[1096] Here there are already signs of the surprising unawareness of the technique of amphibious operations and the grotesque misjudgment of the enemy situation that would later have disastrous consequences. In reality, the Allied landing potential hardly reached a third of German assumptions. In addition, the Allied landing forces were overestimated to almost the same degree—due in large part to the "ghost divisions" invented in 1943 by the General Staff. These ghost divisions were originally used only to make the severity of the situation clear to Hitler, but had taken on a more and more solid form over the course of the months. Thus, while at the beginning of the invasion there were fewer than 50 British and American divisions in England, of which only 37 were available for Overlord (another 10 divisions were to land in the Mediterranean, and more than 40 were to be brought in directly from the U.S. only after the occupation of the French overseas harbors), the Germans assumed 94 to 98 divisions. Both factors, supported by the successful deception operation "Fortitude" (see below note 1175), led the German leadership to believe, almost until the fall of Paris, that the landing in Normandy (which took place with a landing capacity of 6 divisions) as only a secondary partial action, while they continued to wait for the main attack still to come in the Strait of Dover [Pas de Calais]. On July 26, the situation and the estimate of the situation by the German leadership were approximately as follows:

	In the beachhead	Still standing by in Great Britain	Of which, immediately available for landing operations
De facto	25 (+5 armored brigades)	21	15
German estimate of the situation	27-31	67	57

As a result, on this day—the day of the loss of Cherbourg—just as many German divisions were waiting between the Seine and the Schelde Rivers for a landing of the nonexistent ghost divisions as were fighting in Normandy against the Allied bridgehead (see also below note 1196).—*Source: Wilmot, pp. 262, 348 and 475.*

[1097] See also above note 1085. The next attack then hit Berlin during the early morning hours of January 29. The third heavy attack of this series, which was obviously intended as a contribution to the "Seizure of Power Day" celebrations, followed on the evening of January 30.

[1098] Experimental installation of firing tubes for the 21-cm smoke-shell mortars (powder rockets). Rocket projectiles were used by German fighters during aerial combat against enemy bombers for the first time on January 11, 1944. Now fighters and fighter-bombers were increasingly being equipped with rockets.—*Source: Feuchter, p. 248.*

[1099] The Armed Forces High Command report of January 28 said: "The Luftwaffe continued the attacks against the enemy landing fleet by day and night. They damaged 6 transporters totaling 34,000 GRT—some seriously—and sank one landing craft of 1,000 GRT."

[1100] The Armed Forces High Command report of the following day, January 29, 1944, stated: "Near Anzio, German fighter-bombers fought the enemy transport fleet as well as further enemy unloading activities. Four freighters totaling 14,000 GRT and three larger landing craft were damaged, some seriously. Direct hits were achieved on the harbor installations and on landing-boat assemblies."

[1101] Recalling the German considerations and problems during the time of the landing plans against England during the summer and fall of 1940, as the Army demanded that the landing take place on as wide an area as possible, while the Navy believed it could only adequately secure an operation limited to a small sector.

[1102] Meaning the upcoming presidential elections to be held in November 1944, which actually were not without influence on the invasion (see above note 861).

[1103] Anzio–Nettuno.

[1104] Regarding the He 177, see above note 231.

[1105] Hitler is probably speaking about the latest German air raid against London, about which the Armed Forces High Command report of January 22 had said: "Strong German Luftwaffe units attacked London during the night of January 21 in several waves. Numerous large fires were observed." This was, excluding the activity of nuisance raiders, the first German attack against England after a long interruption. A further attack followed on the evening of January 29, then nine in February, eight in March, nine in April, and three attacks still in May. At first only heavy fighters and high-speed bombers were employed; after mid-February, with the use of the window [Düppel] and pathfinder [Pfadfinder] methods, attacks by at least 100 bombers could be flown. Soon, however, the units had to be mixed again. All types of aircraft had to be scraped together, as sufficient bombers could not be provided even for such small units. On May 29 the last German attack was flown, followed by the invasion and V-weapon [rocket] employment.—*Source: Feuchter, p. 258.*

[1106] Transcript number unknown—Fragment No. 18. The preserved shorthand record was partly charred, so the second transcription was possible only with gaps.

[1107] Despite the formation of strong salients, forced by strong enemy pressure in the east as well as, and especially, in the northwest, the First Panzer Army and the Eighth Army had not been able to return to their boundary position. Their joined forces now formed a corridor stretching far northward to the Dnieper River at Kanev; Hitler hoped, by operating out of this corridor, to be able to retake the lost large Dnieper River bend lying to the east (this was likely also what was meant on p. 546: "…the whole operation is lost"). Therefore, the left wing of the Eighth Army, consisting of the XI Army Corps, and the right wing of the First Panzer Army, made up of the XXXXII Army Corps, to a certain degree, fought back to back: the XXXXII Army Corps with its front facing to the northwest, the XI Army Corps with its front facing to the east. With the breakthrough of Soviet tanks from both sides and their meeting at Zvenigorodka, both corps were cut off; this "Cherkassy pocket" [called by the Soviets Korsun'-Shevchenkovskii] was now dependent on costly air supply by the Ju 52. A relief attack, initiated on February 4, failed 13 km from the pocket as a result of the weather and had to be halted on February 15. Not until then did the two corps, which were now pressed together in a narrow area around Korsun' (45 by 15 km), receive permission to break out to the south. The breakout succeeded during the night of February 16 to 17: Abandoning most of the heavy weapons as well the seriously wounded and huge amounts of materiel, 30,000 to 32,000 men were still able to fight their way through to the German lines (the strength of both corps totaled 54,000 men, but some of the rear units were not encircled).—*Source: Manstein, pp. 574 and 582; Tippelskirch, p. 429; Vormann, passim (according to Vormann only 20,000 to 25,000 out of 50,000 men were able to fight through to the staging area north of Uman').*

[1108] Presumably meaning on the Dnieper between Kanev and Cherkassy.

[1109] Most likely Shpola, 35 km southeast of Zvenigorodka.

[1110] In the end, the Russians pushed no less than 26 rifle divisions and 7 to 9 tank, mechanized and cavalry corps into this area, so Manstein employed two panzer corps in the relief attack for the Cherkassy pocket. From the First Panzer Army he employed the III Panzer Corps with the already mentioned 17th Panzer Division, as well as the 16th Panzer Division and the 1st SS Panzer Division; from the Eighth Army he employed the XXXXVII Panzer Corps, also with three divisions.—*Source: Manstein, p. 583.*

[1111] Transcript number unknown—Fragment No. 51—Very heavily charred remains of a shorthand record, which, for this reason, and as they concerned only purely military matters, were not transcribed a second time by the stenographers at all, with the exception of the following lines from page 48.

[1112] Transcript number unknown—Fragment No. 40. A first transcription with heavy damage, which becomes less severe on successive pages. The damage begins in the upper right-hand corner, so from the first pages only the lower left corner was preserved, and from the last everything except the upper right-hand corner. The missing parts are indicated with dotted lines; line beginnings without context were, as an exception, omitted if they had no relevant meaning.

[1113] The attack against the Crimea began then two days later, on April 8. The armies of the 4th Ukrainian Front attacked out of the bridgehead at Kerch, as well as across the Perekop [Landengen] Isthmus on the northern edge of the peninsula, where they succeeded in crossing over the island-dotted Sivash Sea [Putrid Sea]— a western branch of the Sea of Azov. (See above note 772 and note 928.)— *Source: Tippelskirch, p. 436.*

[1114] The First Panzer Army was brought in to close the gap stretching from Mogilev to Ternopol' when the overextended front of the Fourth Panzer Army was penetrated on March 23 in the Ternopol'-Proskurov area. They arrived too late, however, and were outflanked north of the upper Dnestr River on both flanks, and were encircled in the Kamenets-Podol'sk-Shkala area. Supplied by air, the encircled army was able to hold, and it tied down so many enemy forces that Zhukov's advance to the south lost considerable strength. Newly brought-in forces attacking from the west were able to free them from the encirclement. Regarding the relief attack, which succeeded after 14 days of fighting, the Armed Forces report announced on April 9, probably still formulated under the sign of Stalingrad, that the German forces under General Hube had "defeated the encirclement attempt."—*Source: Tippelskirch, pp. 432 and 435; VB of April 11, 1944.*

[1115] After Marshal Vatutin was mortally wounded, Marshal Georgi K. Zhukov assumed command of the 1st Ukrainian Front at the beginning of March 1944, shortly before the major offensive began. Zhukov, born December 2, 1896, had distinguished himself in 1939 as an army commander in the Russian-Japanese battles Khalkhin Gol (see above note 319); in 1940 he was commander of the Kiev Special Military District; at the beginning of 1941 he was Deputy People's Commissar of Defense and also Chief of the Red Army General Staff. During the fall of 1941 he commanded the Soviet Western Front during the Battle of Moscow; and in late 1942 commanded the Kalinin and Western Front during the aborted Operation Mars againnst German Army Group Center's Rzhev salient. He served as Stavka representative and front commander during 1943 and 1944, finally commanding the 1st Belorusssian Front in 1945 during the capture of Berlin. After war's end, he served as Soviet representative in the Allied Control Commission until March 1946, when Stalin "exiled" him to military district command. After Stalin's death in the spring of 1953 he became Deputy Defense Minister, then from February 1955 until his removal in October 1957 Defense Minister of the USSR.—*Source: Tippelskirch, p. 431; Munzinger Archive; Nycop, p. 111.*

[1116] Brought in from the West (see also below note 1302).

[1117] East of Lemberg [L'vov].

[1118] Helmut Friebe; born November 4, 1894; 1914 Second Lieutenant; Reichswehr; 1935 Major and Commander, 3rd Battalion, 2nd Infantry Regiment; 1938 Lieutenant Colonel; 1939 Commander, 1st Infantry Replacement Regiment; 1940 Commander, 164th Infantry Regiment; 1941 Colonel; April 1942 Commander, 419th Infantry Regiment; after the end of December 1942, Commander, 125th Infantry Division; March 1943 Major General; and September 1943 Lieutenant General. In March 1944 Friebe became commander of the well-known 22nd Infantry Division (Parachute Division) on Crete and, in April 1945, Commander of the LXIV Army Corps—*Source: Order of Battle, p. 551; Das deutsche Heer, p. 250; Seemen; Rangliste 1944-45, p. 26; Keilig 211/90.*

[1119] At the end of January, the Russians could only be stopped partially in improved positions on the Enge Isthmus between Lake Peipus [Lake Chud] and the Gulf of Finland, because they had succeeded in advancing to the west in the dense wooded terrain north of the lake, across the Narva River, and digging in south of the Reval-Narva highway. From this point, the Russians intended, by turning in to the north, to push forward in the direction of the Gulf of Finland and encircle the German units at Narva, supported by an attack by amphibious landed forces from the opposite direction. The amphibious landing attempt was crushed by the German troops, but the Soviets, coming from the south, succeeded in pushing across the Reval-Narva highway to the north in two places. One of the resulting spearheads, the "Western pocket," was destroyed at the end of March in concentric attacks by the German forces that had originally belonged to the Eighteenth Army and were now (for more effective command and control) combined together with Army Group Narva under General Friessner. On this day, April 6, the corresponding operation against the "Eastern pocket" began, which was concluded successfully after three days. This freed the Reval–Narva highway again and eliminated the threat to the north flank of being cut off.

[1120] See above note 1114.

[1121] The evacuation of Odessa was underway at that time. After destroying the militarily important installations, the last German troops then left the city on April 9. The Red Army marched in the following day, welcomed by 10,000 partisans who had hidden in the catacombs of the city.—*Source: Tippelskirch, p. 435.*

[1122] The attempts to free Ternopol', which had been encircled for weeks, failed. The city fell on April 15 after desperate resistance on the part of the occupying forces and fierce street combat. Units that broke out to the west were still able to reach the German lines.—*Source: Tippelskirch, p. 435; VB of April 15-18, 1944.*

[1123] Kovel' was one of the very infrequent cases where an encircled city, left behind as a fortified place behind the Soviet front lines during the Soviet advance, was successfully liberated. The battles, lasting from March 27 to April 5 in the Pripiat' region, which was already softening as the muddy period began, were extremely difficult. Success was most likely only achieved because the Russians had not set any extensive goals for themselves in this area and at this point in time. The Armed Forces High Command report of April 6 stated: "The occupation forces of the city of Kovel', encircled since March 17, withstood the weeks-long storm of far superior hostile forces with exemplary courage under the leadership of SS Gruppenführer and Lieutenant General of the Waffen SS Gille. After days of hard attacking combat through the Pripiat' Marshes in unusually difficult terrain, Army and Waffen SS units, under the overall command of Colonel General Weiss and under the command of Generals of Infantry Hossbach and Mattenklott, broke open the enemy ring around Kovel' and freed their comrades from the encirclement."—*Source: Tippelskirch, p. 449; VB of April 8, 1944; Zantke, passim.*

[1124] Doubtless this sentence would have continued along the lines of: "... fighters on the one hand and Russian ... on the other." Or instead of "German" or "Finnish" it must have been "Russian," because clashes between German and Finnish troops were never reported and almost certainly did not occur before Finland's change of sides in early 1944.

[1125] This apparently means pressure on the Finnish government concerning a separate peace (see also note 776), which is evident from the preceding mention of the name "Tanner" on a page that is totally charred up to the beginning of that line.

[1126] Regarding the German-Swedish relationship, see above note 783. [—] This possibly refers to the effects of the mobilization (on a trial basis) of the entire Swedish territorial defense force, which was ordered on January 2, 1944. Or perhaps it was a routine calling up of new reservists. This took place frequently, as Sweden was in a state of peace and could not keep the same individuals armed indefinitely. Hitler was concerned each time by these drafts, as he feared an Anglo-American invasion in Norway (see above note 845) and linked to that a Swedish attack from behind. In reality, the Swedes had not strengthened their army substantially, as, since 1943, they no longer needed to fear a German invasion.

[1127] The "interesting reference to the Aaland Islands" possibly means a rumor circulating in Stockholm and reported to Berlin by the German military attaché in Stockholm, saying that the well-known Swedish military publicist Colonel Gyllenbrok was named Commander of the Finnish Aaland Islands, which enabled one to make certain inferences about Finland's attitude. The rumor about employing Gyllenbrok—who was well known in Germany for a book about the Western campaign and had visited, on German invitation, troops and military installations within the Reich—soon proved groundless. Hitler was very interested in the Aaland Islands, and, to secure continued German control in the northern Baltic Sea, the following February he ordered that the islands be occupied if Finland left the war.

[1128] The Nettuno beachhead.

[1129] The mention of "Tomahawk" is surprising, as it is an American Curtiss fighter that was used only occasionally within the first years of war and was quite outdated. By 1941 only a few squadrons in the Middle East Command of the RAF were supplied with this model, and in the list of the Anglo-American Air Force, the Tomahawk did not appear at all after 1943. Even the two other Curtiss models, "Kittyhawk" and "Warhawk," were employed only in the Mediterranean that year.—*Source: Royal Air Force I, p. 411 and II, p. 382; Feuchter, pp. 97 and 208.*

1130 Hitler—as mentioned already (see above p. 305 and note 816)—was aware of Hungary's attempts to make contact with the Allies and the Kállay government's readiness to capitulate. When he did not succeed in forcing Kállay's resignation in Budapest, he sent for State Administrator Horthy. At Klessheim on March 18, Hitler informed Horthy of Hungary's occupation by German troops (Operation "Margarete"), which had begun that same hour. Horthy then agreed to the German demand that he remain in his position, and on March 23, after rejecting a new Imrédy cabinet, appointed a pro-German government under the previous Hungarian envoy to Berlin, General Döme Sztójay. But in reality the new envoy and Reich Deputy Dr. Edmund Veesemeyer governed from now on in Budapest. The Hungarian Armed Forces had participated in the fight against Bolshevism with only a few weak security divisions in the rear area after the collapse of the Second Hungarian Army in the winter of 1942-3. Hungary had held back the majority of its forces because of a supposed fear of a Romanian invasion, but was now being prepared for new action against the Soviets.—*Source: Horthy, p. 261; Various records of the AA [German Foreign Ministry], AA [German Foreign Ministry] telegram exchange; German Legation Budapest from Mar. 19-27, 1944, in the Nbg. Dok. NG-1543, NG-2602, NG-2947, NG-5520, NG-5521, NG-5522, NG-5524, NG-5525, NG-5658, NG 5765; also: NG-5575, NG-5580 and NG-5683.*

1131 The Romanians and Hungarians.

1132 At the end of March 1944, on Hitler's orders, the Panzer Training Division was withdrawn from the West to occupy Hungary, weakening the West's already limited defenses even further. The Commander-in-Chief West, supported by the Armed Forces Chief of Staff, insisted that the division be sent back to the West in light of the daily threat of invasion. Hitler, on the other hand, wanted the division to remain in Hungary in case of further uprising there. In May the division was finally sent back to France, to the area of Orléans.

1133 Meaning the preparations for invasion.

1134 In February civilian travel between the United Kingdom and Ireland had been stopped, and now in April a 10-mile-wide coastal strip along the southern and southeastern coast of England as well as on both sides of the Firth of Forth was off-limits to all visitors. In addition, foreign diplomats and couriers were not allowed to leave the country and their mail was censored.—*Source: Wilmot, p. 210.*

1135 Wendell Willkie, born February 18, 1892, Republican presidential candidate in 1940, and leader of the left wing of the Republican Party. Willkie withdrew his candidacy for the presidential election of 1944 after being defeated by the Governor of New York (1942-54), Thomas E. Dewey, when Wisconsin chose its

Republican delegates for the June convention—which was considered decisive for the Midwest's attitude. Hitler refers to these elections. Dewey (born
March 24, 1902) was then nominated Republican candidate for president on
June 28. Willkie died October 8, 1944, even before the election. Hopkins'
biographer, Sherwood, says that Roosevelt would not have exposed himself to
the strains of a fourth presidential election and would have refused another
candidacy if the Republicans had again nominated Willkie in 1944.—*Source:
Hagedorn/Sherwood, pp. 659 and 677; Keesings Archives 1944, p. 6344; Munzinger
Archive.*

[1136] Korten probably means the English acoustic buoys, which were used against
torpedoes (see above note 690).

[1137] This is, despite many contrary claims, the remarkable confession that their own
intelligence service and reconnaissance had failed to detect all of the landings
made thus far by the Allies (North Africa, Sicily, Salerno, Anzio-Nettuno).

[1138] This comment refers to a wild miners' strike, particularly in Yorkshire, where
two-thirds of all miners had laid down their work. The strike, which officials
claimed was based on the actions of Trotskyite spies, had smoldered for some
time already but now grown to such a size that the trade union movement let out
impassioned appeals and the British government had to threaten the miners
with lawful punishment. Although only 10 to 15 percent of all British coalmines
were on strike and a war-production shutdown was not feared for the time being, the quotas for gas- and waterworks did have to be reduced by 20 percent.
The above-mentioned appeal spoke about a feared "serious national catastrophe," and even about an "endangerment of the Allies' victory" and a "stab in
the back of our comrades in arms."—*Source: NZZ of April 5 (evening edition),
April 8 (morning edition) and April 9, 1944.*

[1139] Meaning the area along the coast of Normandy. Hitler had already guessed the
later invasion area at this time—either with the help of his reawakened "strategic intuition" or as a result of private reports not yet made known to others.
Even in the final hours he quickly tried to strengthen the security of those poorly
defended coasts. But the necessary forces were lacking even more than usual,
particularly since divisions and materiel had repeatedly been pulled out and sent
to the East, to Italy, and to occupy Hungary.

[1140] Out of the East for the West (see above note 181).

[1141] Meaning that the exhausted core should be extracted from "over there" in the
East, placed back "here" in the West, and replenished to create a full division,
which indeed happened.

[1142] The 12th SS Panzer Division *Hitlerjugend* ["Hitler Youth"] (see above note 573).

[1143] The 1st SS Panzer Division had been with the First Panzer Army in the Skala
pocket, which had just linked up with the main German front (see above note
1114). The division was later relocated to Belgium for rehabilitation.

[1144] Out of Hungary.

[1145] Perhaps the XXII Mountain Army Corps of General of Mountain Troops Hubert
Lanz, which was located in the Balkans. Major General Joachim-Friedrich Lang

and Lieutenant General Viktor Lang led only divisions (the 5th Infantry Division and 218th Infantry Division, respectively).—*Source: Keilig 211/190.*

1146 Units of the Bulgarian occupying forces in Serbia (see above note 445).

1147 Meaning the 13th Waffen SS Mountain Division "Handschar" (see above note 574).

1148 Two days earlier, on April 4, the *Völkischer Beobachter* had run under the title, "German Care for Cultural Assets," the following report from Salonika: "During excavations in Salonika, a valuable antique robed statue from the time of Constantine the Great was found. The statue was exposed carefully by the German soldiers and recovered in good condition. With the greatest care and protection, the valuable discovery was transported and secured, for the time being, by a propaganda company. Naturally, the statue, like all other cultural treasures and documents found by the German Armed Forces, remains in the possession of the Greek State." Hitler obviously did not find this "natural" at all.

1149 Rear Admiral a.D. Hermann Lorey, born September 25, 1877, had been director of the Naval Museum since 1924 and also, since 1934, director of the Berlin Armory. His special field was—in addition to naval war history—the history of weaponry.—*Source: Degeners, p. 997; Lohmann/Hildebrand 291/213.*

1150 The background of this affair: The German embassy in Madrid had received a telegram from Ambassador Ritter (the liaison between the Foreign Office and the Armed Forces High Command) saying that the Führer planned to give 24 Spanish gun barrels from the 17th/18th Centuries, captured at Schneider-Creusot, as a present to the head of state, Franco. The embassy wanted to clarify if Franco accepted the present, and to convey the answer and the location of the handover to the Commander-in-Chief West as soon as possible. By order of the ambassador, after having received no reply after three days, the military attaché informed War Minister Asensio and insisted on an answer. Thereupon Asensio transmitted within 12 hours Franco's grateful acceptance. After conveying the information by telegram to the Commander-in-Chief West, the military attaché received the amazing reply that the handover of the Spanish barrels would be possible only if Spain offered an equivalent amount of nonferrous metal in return. The German representation in Madrid, of course, refused to raise this issue with the Spanish government, so the military attaché demanded from the Commander-in-Chief West an immediate decision by the Armed Forces High Command regarding the "Führer gift." He was informed by telegram that the matter was being passed on to the Armed Forces High Command. The present situation conference should be dated around this point in time, where Hitler's astonished expressions could relate to an extracurricular activity of some Foreign Office or Armed Forces High Command personnel. The German military attaché in Madrid received the answer from the Armed Forces High Command that any "Führer gift" was out of the question, and the subject was not raised with the Spanish again. It was understandable that Spain also let the matter drop, as Franco could not have been eager to experience the embarrassment that would result from receiving a late gift from Hitler out of the store of the obviously victorious Allies.

[1151] The bust of the ancient Egyptian Queen Nefertiti was discovered in 1912 by the well-known German-Jewish archeologist Dr. H. C. Ludwig Borchardt during the German Oriental Society's excavations in Tel Amarna, the residence—established around 1370 B.C.—of King Echnaton (1375-1357 B.C.). Borchardt had found the bust of Nefertiti, the main wife of this king, in the studio of the contemporary sculptor Thutmosis. According to the contractual division of all discoveries, the bust went to Berlin. Either its extraordinary value wasn't known or—more likely—it was purposely concealed by German excavators. When the bust was exhibited after World War I and quickly became very popular, the Egyptians considered themselves cheated and offered objects of equal value in exchange for the return of Nefertiti. For years the experts in Berlin were undecided; only after Hitler came to power did the Egyptians receive a final rejection.—*Source: Die Büste der Königin Nofretete, passim; Degeners, p. 167; Der Spiegel, 10th Jg. [Vol.?] 1956, No. 35.*

[1152] Hitler and Göring were significant "art collectors" in the areas occupied by German troops, and their representatives bought or confiscated whatever they could get. While Hitler mostly "collected" for the museum that he wished to have built in Linz, Göring was primarily busy with the tasteful furnishing of his numerous apartments and country homes, especially the planned gallery for Karinhall. The endeavors of both marauders began first in Austria, then continued in the Czech Republic, and after that in the thorough plundering of Poland, where many treasures—such as the Veit-Stoss Altar of Krakow—were "returned to their place of origin." The two made their biggest raids among the "ownerless" Jewish property confiscated in France. They also exchanged valuable objects for "degenerate art." The occupation of Italy offered a chance for profitable purchases, and the evacuation of the occupied Eastern territories provided the occasion for one last catch. Rosenberg's operational headquarters was extensively involved as well, partly on behalf of Hitler and Göring, and partly in its own name as well, for the planned "Hohe Schule" at the Chiemsee.—*Source: IMT, passim.*

[1153] Tito's headquarters were relocated 100 km westward from Jajce to Drvar at the end of December 1943, under pressure from a major German action. Only after the German paratroop operation "Rösselsprung" against Drvar on May 25, 1944, did Tito—who had escaped very narrowly—draw back by air over Bari in Italy toward the above-mentioned Dalmatian island of Vis (Lissa), located far into the Adriatic. Later, he was followed by his scattered staff from Drvar and also by the National Committee. Pag, the island located 175 km northwest of Vis and directly off the Croatian coast, is nowhere listed as a command center, therefore, it was not possible to confirm this report.—*Source: Dedijer, pp. 201 and 209; Kiszling, p. 201.*

[1154] Meaning the renewed laying out of the large submarine net used in 1943, between Reval and Porkalla, which blockaded the Finnish Bay (see below note 1465).

[1155] Kola coast (Jakonsk).

[1156] It must probably be Salerno.

1157 The German Luftwaffe had already used 2-kg bombs (SD 2) for attacks against living targets (marching troops, heavily packed airfields, etc.) in the first campaigns of the war. So the idea itself wasn't that absurd, but using small bombs to bombard large areas as Hitler wished would not have been very successful, according to Luftwaffe experts. Munitions depots could hardly be brought to explosion that way—at most a few open tanks could be destroyed. Indeed, in the last years of the war such small bombs were produced by the General-luftzeugmeister again at Hitler's suggestion. They were dropped from multi-bomb containers holding 38 bombs each.

1158 Referring to the British submarine *Ultor*.

1159 That was done on Hitler's orders, as he wanted to establish a center of defense against enemy airborne landings in Normandy, and there were not enough light anti-aircraft guns available.

1160 As those in charge of German armament production did not (from the beginning) trust the ability of French industry to produce usable war materiel, it was the principle under Todt—later expanded by Speer—to strengthen the defense industry within the Reich and to call on French capacity for the production of consumer goods for Germany. So in the air armaments sector, only a training aircraft was produced in France—and also, in Paris, new production of the indestructible Ju 52, which was no longer built in the Reich. All other production—including production at the above-mentioned Heinkel and Junkers factories in Toulouse—belonged to a relatively unimportant [subcontracting] feeder industry.

1161 The Armed Forces High Command report of the same day said: "During a daytime advance of North American bombers into the Ploesti area, 53 four-engine aircraft were brought down by German and Romanian air defense forces. This destroyed at least one-third of the attacking enemy force." Any additional attack on Bucharest that day was not reported.

1162 Martin Fiebig; born May 7, 1891; 1910 entered the service; 1920 discharged; 1934 joined the Luftwaffe; 1939 as Oberst Kommodore, 4th Bomber Wing; August 1940 Chief of Air Security in RLM [Reichs Air Ministry]; April 1941 Major General and Nahkampfführer [Dog-fight Leader] in the IV Air Corps (June 1941 in the II Air Corps, November 1941 in the VIII Air Corps); April 1942 Lieutenant General and Commander, 1st Air Division; July 1942 Commanding General, VIII Air Corps; 1943 General of Aviation (March); (May) Commander-in-Chief, Luftwaffe Command Southeast; and January 1945 Commanding General, II Air Corps. Fiebig was turned over by the English to Yugoslavia after the war and was executed there in November 1947.

1163 Regarding this attack, the Armed Forces report of April 5 said, "A daytime attack by North American bomber units against the city of Bucharest caused damage and losses among the population. Forty-four enemy aircraft were destroyed by German, Romanian, and Bulgarian air defense forces. Romanian fighters had a special part in this success." The attacks on those two days (see above note 1161) were the beginning of the Allied air offensive against the Romanian petroleum fields.—*Source: Hillgruber, p. 189.*

[1164] Regarding this attack, the Armed Forces High Command report of March 31, 1944, said, "Last night our air defense forces had their biggest success so far in the defense against British terror attacks at Nuremberg. They prevented the implementation of a combined attack and destroyed 132 four-engine bombers. In the municipal area of Nuremberg and in other places in southern Germany damages and loss among the population occurred." By the next day, the number of destroyed enemy bombers had already been increased to 141. The English first admitted to losing 96 aircraft and then later reduced the number to 94. This would remain the biggest success of the German air defense. Much of the success was due to the night fighters, which under favorable conditions were able to fly in a concentrated formation against the 795 approaching bombers.— *Source: Galland, p. 294; NZZ of April 1 (morning edition), April 2 and April 5 (morning edition), 1944.*

[1165] A gas mask.

[1166] Like the people's gas mask.

[1167] Transcript number unknown—Fragment No. 45—Probably a first transcription. The lower parts of pages 1-12 were destroyed; the missing portions are indicated by dotted lines. The final page (page 13) was preserved completely, though it was hardly written on.

[1168] The French Expeditionary Corps broke through north of Formia in the Petrella Range. This attack destabilized the German defensive position. Kesselring, as Commander-in-Chief Southwest at that time, blamed the 94th Infantry Division for not placing its reserves on the left wing of the Petrella Range as expressly ordered, instead of positioning them on the coastal strip.—*Source: Kesselring, p. 284.*

[1169] Meaning a previously encountered enemy group in the area of Naples.

[1170] Kesselring observes that he had no fear of further landings after the first few days of attack. The attack of the American VI Army Corps from the Nettuno bridgehead started May 23.—*Source: Kesselring, pp. 283 and 285.*

[1171] Friedrich-Wilhelm Hauck; born January 10, 1897; war volunteer; 1917 Reserve Lieutenant; 1918 activated; Reichswehr; 1935 Major; 1938 Ia [operations officer], V Army Corps; 1939 Lieutenant Colonel; 1940 Chief of General Staff, XXXVII Army Corps and Colonel; 1941 Quartermaster, Eleventh Army; December 1942 Commander, 186th Infantry Regiment; after March 1943, Commander, 305th Infantry Division; June 1943 Major General; March 1944 Lieutenant General; March 1945 Commanding General, LI Army Corps; and April General of Artillery. Here Hauck leads the 305th Infantry Division, the 334th Infantry Division and the 114th Jäger Division—added to the Hauck Corps Group—on the left northeast wing of the Tenth Army.—*Source: Das deutsche Heer, p. 110; Rangliste 1944-45, p. 28; Order of Battle, p. 562; Keilig 211/123; Kesselring, p. 277.*

[1172] The successful operation of the American Fifth Army against the Thyrrenian (southwest) wing of the Tenth Army threatened the rear of the Fourteenth Army, which encircled the Anzio-Nettuno bridgehead. That is why first, in the Adriatic (northeast) wing of the Tenth Army, the 334th and the 305th Infantry Divisions were replaced by the 278th Infantry Division from Istria and sent to reinforce the worn-out 71st and 94th Infantry Divisions on the Thyrrenian coast; and second, from the reserves, the 26th Panzer Division and later (against the objections of the Fourteenth Army) the 29th Panzer Grenadier Divisions were called in as well. But despite these efforts, the Americans with their VI Army Corps could not be prevented from making contact at the bridgehead, which sealed Rome's fate.—*Source: Kesselring, pp. 218 and 284.*

1173 To be completed: "...division in Denmark." Of the 21 Luftwaffe field divisions (see above note 227) activated at the end of 1942 and the beginning of 1943, the following units still existed at the time of this discussion: in the East the 4th, 6th, 12th and 21st; in the West the 16th, 17th, 18th and 19th (the latter was relocated to Italy in June); in Greece the 11th; in Norway the 14th and in Denmark the 20th (relocated to Italy in May). During the following months of war further disbanding occurred; only 5 Luftwaffe field divisions existed on March 1, 1945: the 11th, 12th, 14th, 20th and 21st.—*Source: Order of Battle, p. 326; Nbg. Dok. 1795-PS.*

1174 Probably those actions belong to the establishment of the 116th Panzer Division, which during that time was built up from the 179th Reserve Panzer Division (Panzer Lehr Regiment), located in northwest France since the end of 1943, and the rest of the 16th Panzer Grenadier Division, relocated from the Dnieper River to France that May. The new 116th Panzer Division then remained in the West.—*Source: Order of Battle, pp. 194, 307 and 302.*

1175 The Anglo-Americans were at that time interested in the German coastal obstructions and mine fields in the coastal approaches below the high-water level, which they had discovered through the explosion of a bomb in coastal waters during an attack on a coastal battery. The actual reconnaissance of the planned invasion area had already been completed one or two days before; as a result of this mission, on May 17 Eisenhower fixed the date of June 5 for the planned invasion (which was ultimately postponed for one day because of bad weather). The reconnaissance efforts reported here no doubt belonged to the so-called Operation "Fortitude," which was to simulate (for the benefit of the German leadership) the Straits of Calais as the intended invasion area: all missions, reconnaissance, bombardments, etc. were then directed to the area around Pas de Calais in a minimum ratio of 2:1. Nevertheless, Hitler, with his correct intuition, believed already at the beginning of April (in opposition to the opinion of Rundstedt in particular, but also that of Rommel) that the invasion would be centered in Normandy .—*Source: Wilmot (Engl.), pp. 195, 199, 205 and 220.*

1176 Meaning in Italy.

1177 This judgment of Hitler's was meant seriously and refers to General Juins' divisions in Italy. The French Expeditionary Corps fighting at the Garigliano (next to the American II Army Corps established on the coast) consisted of an armored brigade as well as a motorized division (1st), two Moroccan divisions (2nd and 4th) and an Algerian (3rd) division. For the Polish it was the Polish II Army Corps with two divisions (3rd and 5th) and an armored brigade, positioned north of Cassino (between the French and the Polish there was the British XIII Army Corps at the Liri and outside Cassino).—*Source: Kesselring, p. 277.*

[1178] Hitler probably meant the battles in the Baltic region after World War I, where—in his opinion—the "best people" were concetrated in the Freikorps and in the case of their successful assertion against the "Marxist" Germany of the Weimar Republic, would have "come forward." The connection with the previous thought was that after a defeat it's always the best who do not acknowledge the defeat and who come together in Freikorps outside their homeland and oppose even their own "traitor" government.

[1179] In Hungary.

[1180] The 18th SS Volunteer Panzer Grenadier Division "Horst Wessel" and the 8th SS Cavalry Division "Florian Geyer." The first division developed from the 1st SS Infantry Brigade (motorized), which was pulled from the Eastern Front; the second was formed in the fall of 1942 from the SS cavalry brigade and was put into action in the East until being relocated to Yugoslavia (in the area of Brod) at the end of 1943 and now to Hungary.—*Source: Order of Battle, pp. 341 and 345.*

[1181] Probably the 22nd Volunteer Cavalry Division of the SS, while the term "Volks-deutsche" is likely to have a broader meaning (see above note 1078).

[1182] The Armed Forces High Command report of the following day said, "North American bombers led terror attacks against several towns in southeastern Europe yesterday. Damage and losses among the population were especially severe in the towns of Belgrade and Ploesti. Thirty-five enemy aircraft were shot down by German and Romanian air defense forces as well as by Navy anti-aircraft artillery."

[1183] Because of the continuing Allied attacks on the oil fields after April 4 and 5, Antonescu asked the Armed Forces High Command on April 26 for increased support from the German air defense forces in Romania. At the beginning of May, two fighter units were brought in from Hungary and Italy, and the number of night fighters was increased. The Reich also delivered to the Romanians (beyond its contractual duties) 40 fighters and 17 flak batteries. But the government in Bucharest was apparently not satisfied by these measures, as it sent a call for help directly to the German government after the appeal to the Armed Forces High Command.—*Source: Hillgruber, p. 189; Armed Forces Operations Staff War Diary, 1944, 2nd appendix: Romania (Nbg. Dok. 1800-PS), p. 37.*

[1184] Following analogously: "We will answer to the Romanians: 1. …, 2. The current situation and the enemy advance into the allied countries is solely and entirely attributed to those…"

[1185] The 29th Panzer Grenadier Division. This probably means the reserves still available on the Italian front (see above note 1172).

[1186] The 1st Parachute Division had defended Monte Cassino grimly as well as successfully and they literally had to be driven out of their positions by Kesselring in person—an action made necessary by unfavorable developments on the other side of the Liri. On May 18 the headquarters of General Alexander reported the capture of more than 4,500 prisoners since the beginning of the Allied offensive against the "Gustav line."—*Source: Kesselring, p. 284; NZZ of May 19, 1944 (morning edition).*

[1187] Probably referring to shelters made of steel (see above p. 417).

[1188] Code name for the last German offensive, mentioned above several times, in the summer of 1943 (July 5) against the Soviet salient around Kursk in the central sector of the Eastern Front.

[1189] Transcript No. 325/44—Fragment No. 20—The pages of both original sets of shorthand notes were only half intact, so the second transcription has many gaps, both major and minor. Large gaps are indicated with dotted lines. Location names were written down the way they sounded to the stenographers (as usual for transcripts that were preserved only in shorthand form), so mistakes are possible. [—] Hitler had just returned from France that day, where he had met the day before with Field Marshals Rundstedt and Rommel fro 9 a.m. to 4 p.m. at the Margival headquarters near Soisson (built for him during the Western campaign in 1944, but never used). Although Hitler, under pressure from Rommel, had announced that he would be at his headquarters in La Roche-Guyon the following day, he returned to Berchtesgarden during the night. The reason for this surprising change of plans, according to Speidel—but denied by Hitler's former military colleagues—was that a V1, whose gyroscopic controls had failed, struck the headquarters right after the departure of both field marshals.—*Source: Speidel, p. 112.*

[1190] On the morning of June 18, the American 9th Division was successful in breaking through from its landing area "Utah," north of Carentan on the eastern coast of the Cotentin Peninsula, to the peninsula's western coast near Barneville. Cherbourg was thus sealed off.—*Source: Wilmot (Engl.), p. 328.*

[1191] This refers to the V1 launches that began two days earlier (see above note 780 and note 853). But the 169 launches reported here (each with 800 kg dynamite) within 22½ hours were, of course, not enough for a really massive employment, but Hitler nevertheless expected a big effect on morale.

[1192] The "Paradedivision," which had been practically destroyed in May 1943 in Tunis, had been rehabilitated in France during the summer. Before the enemy landing, the division had been located between Caen and Falaise; the members of the division were among the first German troops to be involved in the fighting. Since then, the division had defended Caen and earned the name "Devil's Division" (see also below note 1613). Major Hans-Ulrich v. Luck (born July 15, 1911) led the 125th Panzer Grenadier Regiment, which belonged to the 21st Panzer Division.—*Source: Wilmot, passim; Order of Battle, pp. 298 and 385; Seemen, p. 172; DNB of Aug. 21, 1944.*

[1193] He probably meant Quinéville on the eastern coast of the Cotentin Peninsula, which fell that day.—*Source: Wilmot, p. 337.*

[1194] The enemy.

[1195] In the direction of Cherbourg and to the south.

[1196] The invasion forces were continuously strengthened from England and later directly from the USA. After the earlier airborne landing of 3 divisions, the actual invasion was carried out with 5½ divisions and 3 brigades in the first wave, and 7½ divisions and 3 brigades for the second wave. The original plan of the Allied chiefs of staff in Quebec had called for only 5 divisions and 2 airborne brigades. Employed were:

  a) for the air landing
      1. in the Orne Valley: British 6th Airborne Division
      2. at Cotentin: American 82nd and 101st Airborne Divisions
  b) in the first wave, sea landing
      1. Sword Beach: British 3rd Infantry Division and 27th Armored Brigade
      2. Juno Beach: Canadian 3rd Infantry Division and 2nd Armored Brigade
      3. Gold Beach: British 50th Infantry Division and 8th Armored Brigade
      4. Omaha Beach: American 1st Infantry Division and parts of the 29th Infantry Division
      5. Utah Beach: American 4th Infantry Division
  c) in the second wave
      1. Sword: British 51st Highland Division, 4th Armored Brigade and 1st Special Brigade
      2. Juno: British 4th Special Brigade
      3. Gold: British 7th Armored Division and 49th Infantry Division
      4. Omaha: American 29th Infantry Division (remainder) and 2nd Infantry Division
      5. Utah: American 90th, 9th and 79th Infantry Divisions

On the German side, the forces in the West were distributed as follows:

  1. in Normandy
      6 infantry divisions (the 243rd, 709th, 91st, 352nd, 716th, and 711th) 3 panzer divisions (the 21st and 12thSS), also south of Chartes the Panzer Training Division
  2. in Brittany
      9 divisions (the 275th Infantry, 5th Parachute, 265th Infantry, 2nd Parachute, 343rd Infantry, 353rd Infantry, 3rd Parachute, and 266th and 77th Infantry)
  3. on the Channel Islands
      1 infantry division (the 319th)
  4. between the Seine and the Somme
      3 infantry divisions (the 346th, 348th and 245th)
      1 panzer division (the 116th)
  5. in the Atlantic, south of the Loire
      2 infantry divisions (the 276th and 708th)
      3 divisions in training (the 189th, 159th and 158th)
      1 panzer grenadier division (the 17th SS)
      2 panzer divisions (the 11th and 2nd SS)
  6. in northern France, north of the Somme
      8 infantry divisions (the 344th, 85th, 49th, 17th Luftwaffe Field, 326th, 84th, 47th and 331st)
      1 division in training (1the 82nd)
      1 panzer division (the 2nd)

7. in Belgium and Holland

6 infantry divisions (the 18th Luftwaffe Field, 48th, 712th, 719th, 16th Luftwaffe Field, and 347th)

1 division in training (the 165th)

2 panzer divisions (the 1st SS and 19th)

8. in the Mediterranean

6 infantry divisions (the 272nd, 277th, 271st, 338th, 244th and 242nd)

2 divisions in training (149th and 157th)

1 panzer division (the 9th)

Thus, on June 6, 1944, in the entire Western area, there were:

48 infantry, etc. divisions, 7 of them in training

1 panzer grenadier division

10 panzer divisions (of which the 19th was not operational)

In addition to the 8 divisions located in Normandy at the beginning of the invasion, the German leadership put (along with the Panzer Training Division and 3 combat groups) only 4 further divisions into action on the day of invasion: the 2nd SS Panzer Division, 17th SS Panzer Division, the 77th Infantry Division and the 3rd Parachute Division. During the following 7 weeks, 15 divisions were added, but further reinforcement was made difficult by the situation in the East, the threat of the Maquis [French underground], and especially the apparent existence of more than 40 "ghost divisions" in England (see above note 1096). During that same time, the Allies landed 36 divisions as well as many auxiliary troops and air force units. On June 18, the Western powers had 20 divisions available, which were faced by only 18 German divisions (and which had the fighting strength of only 14 divisions).—*Source: Wilmot, pp. 138, 209, 217, 224, 227, 320, 331, 406 and 409.*

[1197] Meaning that they would become units fit for action.

[1198] Field Marshal v. Rundstedt (see above note 655), the most senior of the German field marshals, was appointed Commander-in-Chief West (Army Group D) on March 1, 1942—after Hitler had relieved him as Commander-in-Chief of Army Group South in the East (at the beginning of December 1941) because of disagreements over the evacuation of Rostov. Rommel's Army Group Command B was relocated to the Channel coast in early December 1943 after the unification of command in Italy (see above note 665), and was put under the Commander-in-Chief West. There Rommel was in charge of the LXXXVIII Army Corps in Holland, the Fifteenth Army between Antwerp and the Orne, and the Seventh Army between the Orne and the Loire. The First Army on the Bay of Biscay and the Nineteenth Army on the Mediterranean were directly under the Commander-in-Chief West until Army Group G under Colonel General Blaskowitz was put in between on May 8, 1944. The fragmentation of German command between Rundstedt and Rommel on the invasion front contributed to the German failure.—*Source: Speidel, p. 49; Wilmot (Engl.), p. 188; Siegler, p. 48; Assmann, p. 419.*

[1199] Even Rundstedt, if he had had a free hand, would have (following Rommel's advice) brought in the 319th Infantry Division—uselessly located on the heavily fortified Channel Islands—for the battle in Normandy. Rundstedt knew, though, that Hitler would not agree to this move, and so he rejected Rommel's proposal. It remains unclear whether or not this was the best way to behave toward Hitler. Even Jodl obviously adjusted his style of presentation to the wishes of his "Supreme Commander" without any second thoughts.

[1200] Because of partially real and partially alleged unreliability, Hitler had ordered the withdrawal of the Eastern units (see note 482) from the Eastern Front and recommendedtheir relocation to Armed Forces High Command theaters—to the Balkans, to Italy and especially to the West. Thus, 72 Eastern battalions reached France in early 1944, but, on order of the Armed Forces High Command, they were not allowed to take part as independent units in the divisional arrangements [Divisionsrahmen], but instead had to be brought into German regiments as third or fourth battalions. To coordinate them, Major General v. Wartenberg, until then commander of the Eastern Troops 703, was named "Commander of the Volunteer Units under the Commander-in-Chief West." Eastern units continued to arrive in France through May. The first battalions (numbered 439th, 441st and 642nd) were already involved in fighting on the morning of invasion. Generally the Eastern troops fought well, although there were exceptions—such as the mutiny and disarming of the 797th Georgian Battalion. With the weakening of the German opposition, their reliability naturally diminished.—*Source: Thorwald: Wenn sie…, pp. 294, 297, 319 and 349; Walther Hansen: als Ia beim Kdr. D. Freiwilligenverbände beim Ob.West, 3rd part (Thorwald Material in the IfZ).*

[1201] Meaning the German rank badges or insignia. This question was of practical importance as it concerned the equalization of Eastern ranks with the equivalent German ranks, eliminating a form of discrimination that had caused much annoyance among the Russian officers. Nevertheless, this belated equalization could not eliminate the negative feelings, as Russian General Malyschkin reported on July 10 to General v. Niedermayer (Wartenberg's successor as of the middle of June) after a trip to the front.—*Source: Hansen (same as preceding note).*

[1202] Pressure-box mines were ground mines with a new type of ignition mechanism, which were developed using the principle of water pressure and which could not cleared by the methods available at that time. The explosion was caused by the decrease in water pressure that developed when a ship passed over the mine location. The Luftwaffe had wished to use the mines in offensive blockades of enemy harbors even before the invasion. However, the naval warfare leadership, whose position Hitler agreed with, had prevented the use of the new mines along the English and French coasts out of fear that the enemy mght copy the new ignition mechanism and employ the mines in the Baltic. So pressure-box mines were not dropped until three nights after the invasion, in the Seine Bay, where, despite all precaution, some intact samples had already fallen into enemy hands by June 10. Tests conducted by the British admiralty soon showed that the ignition mechanism would not function if a ship was moving slowly and the consequent change in water pressure was gradual. [—] Because of the delay in employing these new mines, only the following mine protection existed in water and on land at the beginning of the invasion:

1. Defensive blockades a specific distance from the French coast. These blockades, however, dated from 1942 and were considered scarcely functional. The planned new blockade system—which Rommel opposed—was to be erected only in the case of real signs of an enemy landing. This proved to be too late then, as the mines could not be brought in time because of Allied air attacks against the French railway system.

2. Coastal mines in beach obstacles. Delivery had been delayed because of production difficulties, and placement in the Seine Bay was especially delayed. There were no coastal mines placed in the strip of coast that was actually attacked.

3. Land mines. Of 50 million planned land mines only 4 million had been placed.

—*Source: Assmann, p. 426; Wilmot, pp. 240 and 330; Lusar, p. 143.*

[1203] Here again is the concern about the second landing between the Schelde Estuary and the mouth of the Seine River (near Le Havre)—which is why the Fifteenth Army, located there and closest to the battlefield in Normandy, remained inactive on the coast with 12 of its original 17 large units (see above note 1096 and note 1196).

[1204] He probably meant Radicofani.

[1205] The Commander-in-Chief Southwest, Field Marshal Kesselring.

[1206] On the Island of Elba, the Anglo-Americans had landed in the early hours of June 17. Although the German occupation troops succeeded at first in pushing the enemy back into the sea at some positions in the north and the southeast, the German troops were finally forced together into the northeastern part of the island and had to be withdrawn to the mainland during the night of June 20.— *Source: Armed Forces High Command reports of June 17-20, 1944.*

[1207] The enemy.

[1208] The Armed Forces High Command had earlier ordered that the Orbetello–Spoleto–Civitanova line be held, but the enemy had already crossed this line in places when the order reached the troops. Most likely it is the position in front of the Trasimenian Sea that is meant here.—*Source: Tippelskirch, p. 456.*

[1209] If Kesselring's statement is correct there is a misunderstanding here, because he indicates as the "Albert" Position a line before Orvieto that had already been crossed. Wherever the error may lie, the reference is certainly to one of the intermediate positions between the Trasimenian Lake and the planned final "Green" Position in the Apennines north of the Pesaro–Urbino–Florence–Pisa Line. This "Green" Position cannot be what is referred to here (despite the mention of the "Green Line"), because, firstly, Hitler knew very well that work was being done on that position (and had been since the fall of 1943), and secondly, Kesseling was so dissatisfied with the status of the line's development that he tried to extend the resistance of the intermediate positions for as long as possible.—*Source: Kesselring, pp. 266, 292 and 297.*

[1210] On Elba.

[1211] Meaning further back, corresponding to the withdrawal proposed by the Commander-in-Chief Southwest.

[1212] Probably meaning the Gulf of Genoa and the Riviera.

[1213] The four divisions of the 26th wave, built up from replacement troops in May 1944, had no numbers, but names. They were used—as in this case—for filling out destroyed divisions.—*Source: Keilig 100/4.*

[1214] See above note 569 and note 1070.

[1215] The Armed Forces High Command report of the following day said, "A North American bomber group flew into northwestern Germany and carried out terror attacks against several towns. Damage and personal loss were especially severe in the residential areas of Hamburg, Bremen, Hannover, and Wesermünde. Sixteen enemy aircraft were destroyed by Luftwaffe and Navy anti-aircraft artillery."

[1216] This refers to the Stülcken shipyard in Hamburg, diagonally opposite the St. Pauli piers on the southern shore of the (northen) Elbe River.

[1217] Meaning between 50 and 80 percent cloud coverage at 500 m cloud height.

[1218] Rudolf Meister; born August 1, 1897; 1915 Lieutenant; Reichswehr; 1931 Captain; 1933 transferred to Luftwaffe; 1935 Major; 1937 Lieutenant Colonel; 1938 tactics instructor at the Luftwaffe War Academy; January 1940 Colonel and Chief of Staff, I Air Corps; October 1940 Chief of Staff, VIII Air Corps; March 1942 Chief, 1st Department Luftwaffe General Staff; September 1942 Major General; March 1943 Lieutenant General; June Chief of Luftwaffe Operational Staff; September 1943 Commanding General, IV Air Corps; January 1944 Commanding General Replacement Staff East; June 1944 again Commanding General, IV Air Corps; September 1944 General of Aviation; October 1944 Commanding General of German Luftwaffe in Denmark; and December 1944 Chief of Luftwaffe Personnel Office. Meister died on September 11, 1958.

[1219] Buhle here resists using the captured Russian guns, as there was no ammunition available for them and it could not be produced without delaying the production of existing ammunition types. Furthermore, he judged the performance of some of the guns to be insufficient.

[1220] At the start of a new ammunition production process, all cartridges have to be newly produced for some time; later one can expect a certain return of used cartridges.

[1221] After the end of the battles that had been going on since May 12, and which finally led to Rome's surrender on June 4.

[1222] Hitler's claims about the Czech captured guns of 1939 are considered untenable by military experts of the time. The following can be established: The very good Czech heavy field howitzer had been stockpiled and was distributed in large numbers at the front during the war. The production of the Czech 21-cm gun continued after the occupation, as the foreign order from Sweden (mentioned above) was still being processed until 1943. When Hitler, as happened quite often, placed a "huge order" that was not fulfilled, the reason was that the production capabilities were not available. Furthermore, a significant share of the captured Czech materiel had been stored in German ordinance depots, and at the end of 1939 the 5th and 6th wave of infantry divisions were equipped with those supplies. This setup would not have been possible with German equipment at that time.

1223 This transcript is not from the Berchtesgaden collection, but was made available to the Institute of Contemporary History by the State Institute for War Documentation in Amsterdam. According to the State Insitute, it belongs to the Himmler archives, which had initially been stored in the Berlin Document Center after the war. It was found in the file N 101 (N = Persönlicher Stab RFSS). It is probably this copy which is now found in the Dept. Rec. Br. Alexandria (EAP 13m/10-1). The record has the diary number S 121/44 of the Stenographic Service at the Führer Headquarters, and was dictated by the stenographers Krieger and Dr. Reynitz in the usual manner. It is complete. A printed excerpt can be found in Baumbach: *Zu spät?*, p. 211.

1224 Meaning the combat troops —the fighting troops.

1225 He no doubt means "if."

1226 After the loss of France, the success rate of the German submarine war in the Atlantic in fact decreased to zero in the month of October, but increased again slightly during the last months of war (see above note 821).

1227 Tungsten is important for steel production (tools and magnetic steel) and for electrical engineering (filaments and cathodes). The most important European deposits are in Portugal and Spain, with France following at some distance. The French tungsten output was capable of significant development, as was proven by the 56-fold increase from 1938 to 1954 (from 10 tons to 560, while Portugal increased from 1,831 to 2,508 tons during that same time span).

1228 Hitler is constantly criticized by his former military colleagues for his habit of counting the theoretical number of dvisions without regard to their mobility or readiness for action. This method of counting (which Hitler himself criticizes here) is seen as one of his cardinal faults. If this is justified (which can hardly be doubted, considering the multitude of statements), then this passage proves the presence of occasional lucid intervals in the mania and delusions of grandeur that have been so reliably testified to.

1229 This happened some months later in the Ardennes offensive and eventually during Operation "Bodenplatte" against enemy airfields in Belgium and northern France on January 1, 1945 (see below note 1473).

1230 Hitler is referring to the July 20 attempt on his life.

1231 The Communications Inspector, General Fellgiebel (see above noe 393), and the Army Quartermaster General, General Wagner (see above note 346 and below note 1313), belonged to the circle of the July conspiracy.

1232 Possibly Hitler meant "intelligence" also in a different sense. The military Abwehr [Intelligence Service] (Foreign Intelligence Offce of the Armed Forces High Command/Armed Forces Operations Staff) under Admiral Canaris had already been abolished by Hitler's order (on February 12, 1944) regarding the establishment of a unified reporting service under the Reichsführer SS. The Intelligence Sections I and II, namely espionage and sabotage, were first formed as an independent Military Section in the RSHA, and the Intelligence Section

III was integrated into its Section IV (Gestapo). Now, after July 20, the Military Section was integrated more and more into Section VI (Foreign Security Division).

1233 With his next sentence Hitler already limits the claim again. It is, of course, totally absurd to blame the development and outcome of the war on the information given here and there to the enemy by convinced opponents of the regime. However one wishes to judge such behavior, it has been factually established that the extent and success of those actions could not have been sufficient to justify even a weak connection.

1234 By the spring of 1943, a substantial portion of the military conspiracy against Hitler had already been uncovered. The Customs Investigation Office in Prague had arrested two employees of the Munich Inteligence Intelligence Office [Abwehrstelle] on account of totally private foreign exchange affairs. In the hope of clearing themselves, they gave statements regarding an anti-Nazi conspiracy in Intelligence Central [Abwehrzentrale]. On April 4, 1943, the Gestapo arrested Reich legal counsel v. Dohnányi, the closest colleague of Major General Oster, the head of the Central Section in the Foreign Intelligence Office. Oster himself, who imprudently tried to cover for Dohnányi and remove incriminating papers during a search of his office, was suspended immediately. He was removed from office at the end of the year and lived from then on under supervision in a suburb of Leipzig. Two relatives of Dohnányi, pastor Dietrich Bonhoeffer and Justus Delbrück, and the Munich lawyer Dr. Josef Müller were also involved in this affair and arrested. The investigations extended until July 20, 1944—on the one hand because of delaying tactics by Admiral Canaris and chief judge Dr. Sack, but on the other hand because of remarkable caution, apparent blind confidence, and a conspicuous lack of interest on the part of Himmler and his Gestapo chief Müller. To this day it remains unclear just how far into the circle of conspiracy Himmler and his people were able to follow the threads—which had fallen into their hands by accident—by July 20. It is widely acknowledged that Himmler's behavior toward the entire military conspiracy was not unequivocal.—*Source: Gisevius II, p. 277; Abshagen, p. 356; Ritter: Goerdeler, p. 352; Zeller, pp. 24 and 142.*

1235 It is correct that German tanks and assault guns had been drastically improved during the war, but it is a pure untruth when Hitler speculates that the quality of the Russians' materiel had decreased. The amount of American materiel alone that wnt to the Soviet Union within the last few years makes this claim absurd.

1236 Regarding the attitude of Turkey, see note 448, note 844, note 920 and note 1494; regarding the attitude of Finland, note 776, note 1391 and note 1502.

1237 Turkey broke off diplomatic relations two days later, on August 2.

1238 Regarding the attitude of Bulgaria, see below note 1386.

1239 Hungary leads Europe in the output of bauxite; the resources are located in the Bakony Forest, in the Vértes Mountains, and in the area south of Pecs [Fünfkirchen]. Manganese resources are mined in the Bakony Forest.

1240 The "coup d'état against Mr. Horthy" was initiated on October 15, 1944, but failed due to German preventive measures (see above note 1130 and below note 1453).

1241 See below note 1491. Regarding Hitler's fears concerning an enemy landing in the eastern Mediterranean, see above note 158 and note 366.

242 He probably meant at the Strait of Dover [Pas de Calais]; Hitler moves to the West now. Regarding the fears expressed concerning further landings, see note 1096.

1243 Italy.

1244 Carl Heinrich v. Stülpnagel; born January 2, 1886; 1906 Second Lieutenant, 115th Infantry Regiment; 1918 Captain in the General Staff; 1932 Colonel and Section head in the Reichswehr Ministry; 1935 Major General and division commander; 1937 Lieutenant General; 1938 Senior Quartermaster II in the Army General Staff; 1939 General of Infantry and (October) Senior Quartermaster I; June 21, 1940 Chairman of the German Armistice Commission for France; February to November 1941 Commander-in-Chief, Seventeenth Army; and February 1942 successor to his distant cousin Otto v. Stülpnagel as Military Commander in France. Stülpnagel had been taking part in the putsch plans since 1938, and became one of the most active members of the military opposition against Hitler. During the night of July 21, 1944, he successfully carried out an overthrow in Paris, eliminating the SD. After the failure of the putsch in Berlin and the refusal of the Commander-in-Chief West v. Kluge to support the mission, he had to withdraw his orders. Stülpnagel was ordered to the Führer Headquarters immediately. He attempted suicide on the way there, at Verdun; however, he only lost his eyesight. He was sentenced to death by the People's Court on August 30, 1944, and was executed that same day.—*Source: Zeller, pp. 22, 301 and 424; Ritter: Goerdeler, pp. 245, 274 and 398; Schramm (W.), passim; Munzinger Archive; Keilig 211/333.*

1245 Somme–Marne–Saône–Jura. This position [Defense Line] had already been reconnoitered by the Commander-in-Chief West in December 1943 on an order from the Armed Forces High Command or Hitler (see below p. 463). Hitler issued the written construction order for the establishment of the field positions on August 2. The speed of the Allied advance in France made all efforts useless.

1246 This was in fact Montgomery's plan. Eisenhower's, in contrast, called for regular attacks along a wide front, without establishing any centers, in order to "reach the Rhine along its entire run" before attacking inner Germany. The final decision was made when Eisenhower took over the immediate leadership of the ground operation on September 1, after Montgomery had explained his opinion again on August 23—now directly, but again without effect. (See also below note 1418.)—*Source: Wilmot, p. 486.*

1247 This idea of a "Special Staff" had already been implemented by Hitler during the Norwegian campaign. Now, in 1944, Jodl was able to prevent the threatened restriction of his authority by establishing a special working group within the Armed Forces Operations Staff for this assignment. Stationed in the Führer

Headquarters, this group consisted of a single officer, Lieutenant Colonel Kleyser, and was a pure farce.

1248 See also below p. 450. In the Black Forest, the relevant location was probably the "Tannenburg" headquarters at the Kniebis, west of Freudenstadt. The "Tannenburg" had been used from June 27 until July 1940. Like the "Felsennest" near Münstereifel in the Eifel region (which was occupied from May 10 to June 8, 1940), it was built for the Western campaign. Because of Hitler's state of health and the development of the situation in the East, the Führer Headquarters were not relocated into the West in the summer of 1944. Not until November did Hitler travel to Berlin, from where he moved on December 10 (for about a month) into the West, in order to lead his plannd offensive more effectively. This time, however, he was further to the rear—toward Ziegenberg near Bad Nauheim ("Adlerhorst").

1249 The establishment of the Führer Headquarters was the responsibility of Hitler's adjutancy.

1250 Hitler left behind several harbors as "fortresses" in advance of the weakening front, some of which were able to hold out until the end of the war (see note 1485). In fact, the Allies suffered considerable supply difficulties when their armies advanced into Belgium and eastern France, because all of their supplies still had to be transported via Bayeux and Cherbourg. In October, after they had taken Dieppe and Ostende without a fight, and the "Fortresses" of Le Havre, Boulogne and Calais had been conquered, the desperate supply situation slowly improved. However, the Allies still had to deal with the lack of big dock cranes, which would have been able to unload the heavy equipment arriving directly from the United States. German troops had rendered the cranes in Cherbourg and Le Havre inoperable before the evacuation. The equipment was available only in the Antwerp harbor, which fell into English hands almost intact on September 4, but it could not be used until the end of November because of German blockades across the mouth of the Schelde (see below note 1513 and note 1514).—*Source: Wilmot, pp. 501 and 578.*

1251 Kluge had taken over from Rundstedt as Commander-in-Chief West (Army Group D) on July 3, and had also taken charge of Army Group B after Rommel's departure on July 17, as a takeover by SS General Hausser (suggested by Schmundt) was feared. This joint staff arrangement, which Jodl justly attacks here, remained until September. Kluge led from the headquarters of Army Group B in La Roche-Guyon, while the connection to the headquarters of the Commander-in-Chief West in St. Germain, 65 km away, was maintained by telephone calls and trips by staff officers. Model, who initially replaced Kluge on August 18 in both positions, also had to adopt this leadership technique. At the insistence of the staff, and with Model's agreement, Rundstedt returned as Commander-in-Chief West on September 5—this time to Arnberg, near Koblenz.— *Source: Blumentritt, p. 240; Siegler, pp. 16 and 18; Speidel, p. 142.*

1252 See above note 1245.

1253 Hitler had already declared on July 23 that he agreed that preparations for a possible reuse of the Western Wall should be initiated.

1254 See below p. 592.

1255 These captured Russian guns were also used in the fall to help build up the antitank defense of the Western Wall. But they were not remodeled into split-trail carriages (as happened earlier, since the old box-trail carriages of those guns had too limited traversing capability). Instead, they now received a specially constructed stationary makeshift carriage with a wider traversing capability. Authorities at that time doubted that there were 1,200-2,000 such captured guns still available and in a functional state.

1256 This headquarters was one of the newer facilities. Huge complexes were also built at the Zobten in Silesia and in Ohrdruf. Like Diedenhofen, these had never been used.

1257 See below note 1725.

1258 Fegelein combines the names "Hofacker" and "Rahtgens" (see below note 1289 and note 1314). He meant Lieutenant Colonel of the Reserves Dr. Caesar v. Hofacker; born March 11, 1896; war volunteer; 1918 First Lieutenant and Squadron Captain; 1921-1925 studied law, various industry positions; after 1936 company secretary [Prokurist] of the United Steelworks; 1940 Luftwaffe Wing Commander; 1941 official in charge of the iron and steel industry in the military administration of France; after October 1943 on Stülpnagel's staff (although he was an officer seconded for special duty and not Chief of Staff—here he is mixed up by Fegelein again, this time with Colonel v. Linstow). Hofacker, who was a cousin of Stauffenberg, provided the connection between the Paris group of the military conspiracy and the Berlin headquarters. He stayed in Berlin for the last time from July 10 to 17, to inform Beck and Stauffenberg about his report to Rommel on July 9. The field marshal had judged the military situation in the West to be very dark, and had emphasized the necessity of concluding an immediate peace treaty detaining Hitler through an action at a central position. Hitler had returned to Rastenburg from Berchtesgaden on July 14, and it is not impossible that Hofacker was also there on that occasion. Hofacker was arrested on July 24, sentenced to death by the People's Court [Volksgerichtshof] on August 30, and executed on December 20.—*Source: Leber, p. 259; Zeller, pp. 190, 222, 233, and others; Wheeler-Bennett, pp. 684, 706 and 761; Speidel, p. 133.; Schramm (W.), passim.*

1259 Hitler either means the large Jobourg Peninsula (Cap de la Hague) northwest of Cherbourg, where the last German bases were located until July 1, or the Cap Lévi Peninsula in front of the harbor in the east—the former location of the "Hamburg" naval battery. Furthermore, it was primarily his fault that Cherbourg was lost sooner than necessary. Although the fall of the fortress was just a question of time after the blockade of the Cotentin Peninsula (considering the increasing enemy superiority and the inadequate fortification on the land side), Hitler repeatedly ordered various advance lines to stop, making it impossible to man the fortifications adequately and in time, and thus hastening the loss of the city.—*Source: Wilmot, p. 338; Hayn, pp. 41 and 59.*

1260 Hitler is obviously referring to the breakthrough at Avranches in Brittany, which was practically complete already. There the Americans spread out from the town (which had fallen on the evening of July 30) and won a bridgehead over the Selune at Pountaubault. The next day, Army Group B received the following order from the Führer Headquarters: "The enemy must under no circumstances be allowed to operate in the open. Army Group B prepares a counterattack together with all panzer units, to break through up to Avranches, to cut off the enemy penetration and to destroy it. All available panzer units are to be pulled from their current employment without replacements...The outcome of the campaign in France depends on this attack." When Warlimont arrived at Kluge's headquarters on August 2 (see below note 1267) and was received by the field marshal in the early hours of the following morning, he did not in fact deliver—as Wilmot said—"the order from the Führer that the front must be reestablished." At the time of Warlimont's departure from Rastenburg and thus at the time of the present conference, the temporary closure of the breach near Avranches was expected (this passage confirms that) and the staff of the Führer Headquarters were of the opinion that the war in France would continue for the time being with slowly retreating fronts—as had been the case thus far in Normandy.—*Source: Speidel, p. 151; Wilmot, pp. 416 and 423.*

[1261] Analogously: "...which could fall into the enemy's hands in the case of a breakthrough..."

[1262] The commander at Cherbourg had been Lieutenant General Karl Wilhelm v. Schlieben, who, in the usual obituary in the German press, was described as the "brave defender of Cherbourg." According to a German report about those battles, Schlieben was not captured until June 26, during the house-to-house fighting in the inner city. He was captured in his subterranean bunker after having fought for many hours alongside his staff, with infantry weapons, at various bunker exits. Of course, something else was obviously stated in the foreign radio service reports, which Hitler received and to which he no doubt refers here. The foreign press reported on an order of the day from Schlieben, which the Americans had intercepted on June 24, stating that anyone who did not continue the resistance until the end would be shot. The capture of the German commander was described in a June 27 UP report as follows: "[v. Schlieben and Rear Admiral Hennecke, the Navy Commander in Normandy,] were captured when the Americans stormed the entrance of an underground fort. A German lieutenant suddenly appeared in front of the fort, waving a white flag. The officer arrived at the Allies' line and declared that v. Schlieben and Hennecke were inside the fort and were ready to surrender, together with the rest of the occupying forces. A few minutes later the lieutenant returned to the fort, and both officers came out with hands raised, leading a line of more than 300 soldiers. Lieutenant General v. Schlieben, who, in an order of the day a few days before had ordered the garrison to resist until the last, was imprisoned."—*Source: Hayn, p. 63; Wilmot, p. 346; NZZ of June 26 (morning edition) and June 28 (midday edition), 1944.*

[1263] Remer (see below note 1869).

1264 See above note 523.

1265 At Avranches, where the enemy's strategic breakthrough had not been discovered yet (see above note 1260).

1266 In 1806 the Prussian fortresses were—following the strategic considerations of those times—neglected, as they were assigned to officers who had become unfit for military field service through age or illness. Not until after the Battle at Jena was the order given to arm the fortresses—and by that time the enemy was already advancing. The moral strength of the commanders collapsed under the impact of the rapid sequence of events. Erfurt, Stettin, Küstrin, Hameln, Neinburg, Plessenburg, Spandau, Magdeburg and Danzig capitulated practically without a fight. In Silesia, Schweidnitz fell after only four days, Breslau and Glogau—heavily armed—capitulated after only 20 days, and the totally neglected Brieg fell as well. The handover of Glatz and Silberberg did not take place because of the peace treaty. Neisse was overwhelmed after 36 days of brave defense. Only three fortresses—Kosel, Graudenz and Kolberg—held up against the enemy until the end of the campaign.—*Source: Alten, p. 541.*

1267 In Kluge's headquarters. Warlimont's trip was actually the unofficial reason for the present conference. His visit to Normandy (where so far, since the beginning of the invasion, only junior officers of the Armed Forces Operations Staff—up to major—had looked around), had originally been planned for the days immediately after July 20 and therefore had to be postponed. But now such a project had to be taken on with care. The matter had to be raised delicately with Hitler, as he feared that such journeys brought a defeatist influence to the front. This meeting was therefore planned by Jodl—his manner of speaking shows this—to get Hitler to give Warlimont a general overview of the situation and his opinion, and to a certain extent an oral agreement wih Kluge for the discussion of the possible—as was still assumed at this hour—case of an enemy breakout from Normandy. The actual reason, the trip to the West, was then included casually in the discussion. The next day, Hitler toyed with the idea of recalling Warlimont, who was on his way through Germany. Jodl made a note in his personal diay on August 1: "The Führer has concerns about sending Warlimont into the West. I offered to fly there myself, but the Führer does not want me to. He lets Warlimont travel ahead based on my argument that calling him back would attract attention." As Jodl reported after the end of the war, Hitler had suspected that Warlimont could discuss a new attempt on his life with Kluge. This was probably meant as a joke, since both suspects were hardly suited to revolution. (See also above note 1260.)

1268 General Carl Heinrich v. Stülpnagel (see above note 1244).

1269 Otto Abetz; born March 26, 1903; 1927 art teacher; 1930 founder of the "Sohlberg Circle" (German-French youth meetings); 1933 France Adviser of the Reich Youth Leadership; 1943 French expert for Ribbentrop's office; July 1939 residence prohibition in France; 1940 deputy for the Foreign Office at the Military Commander France; anf from August 1940, German ambassador based in Paris. [—] Despite numerous disagreements regarding the treatment of France and despite the judgment given here by Hitler, Abetz was not relieved until the middle of November 1944 from his position as German representative at the French government-in-exile in Sigmaringen. In 1949 he was sentenced to 20 years of forced labor by a French military tribunal, but was released in April 1954. Abetz died in an accident on May 5, 1958.—*Source: Abetz, passim; Munzinger Archive.*

[1270] Ludwig Beck; born June 29, 1880; 1899 Second Lieutenant; after 1913 and in World War I in the General Staff; transferred into the Reichswehr as Major; 1931 Major General; 1932 Lieutenant General; October 1933 chief of the Trop Office [Truppenamt] at the Army Command; and 1935 General of Artillery and Army Chief of General Staff. In this position Beck became more and more opposed to Hitler's military policy and pursued, before the Sudetenland mission, a collective step of the generals against Hitler, but he was abandoned by Brauchitsch at the decisive moment. As a consequence, Beck handed in his resignation in August 1938 (effective October 31, 1938, with reassignment to the post of Colonel General in the reserve). He then became a central figure in the conspiracy against Hitler, which reached its climax with the July assassination attempt. After the mission's failure, General Fromm forced him to suicide, which had to be concluded by a coup de grâce.—*Source: Beck, passim; Foerster, passim; Keilig 211/18.*

[1271] Maurice Gamelin; born September 20, 1872; colleague of Joffre in World War I as chief of the Operations Department in the primary French headquarters; 1925-1929 Commander-in-Chief in Syria as Weygand's successor; 1931 Army Chief of General Staff; and 1935 Army Inspector General, Vice President of the Supreme War Council, and thereby also Generalissimo in the event of war. After the French failures in the German Western campaign, Gamelin was relieved by Weygand on May 19, 1940, whose replacement so far had failed due to Daladier's resistance. Vichy France put him—without issuing a verdict—before the National Law Court in Riom. He was held by the French until April 1943, and was then in German custody afterward. In May 1945 he was freed by American troops in Germany. Gamelin died on April 18, 1958.—*Source: Munzinger Archive.*

[1272] Beck had been in Paris from June 16 to 20, 1937, officially as a guest of his personal friend, the military attaché Lieutenant General Kühlenthal, and as visitor to the World Fair, and he naturally also took this opportunity to pay a courtesy visit to the leaders of the French army. In reality, however, Beck had four quite extensive talks with Gamelin during those days, and he characterized Gamelin in his official travel report as follows: "After my repeated meetings with General Gamelin, I must say that he gives me an unusually fresh, youthful impression. He is clear, military and highly educated. He says little and keeps his word. His outward behavior is also excellent." Therefore, it is correct that Gamelin impressed Beck. However, Hitler could have known of his supposed enthusiasm only second hand, as the Chief of General Staff had not given him a report on his visit to Paris.—*Source: Beck, p. 295; Foerster, p. 63.*

[1273] Hitler (or his source) probably exaggerated a bit here, but back then even Kesselring was not satisfied with the development. He had visited the Apennine position at the beginning of July and had noticed some progress and satisfactory results, but considered other parts—in particular the focal point patrols [Schwerpunktstreifen]—to be "far behind."—*Source: Kesselring, p. 297.*

[1274] He most likely meant General Förster, who was followed by Hitler with almost pathological aversion (see above p. 66 and below p. 594).

[1275] Regarding General Kitzinger, 1941 Armed Forces Commander Ukraine, see below note 1647.

[1276] In his *Verlorenen Siegen*, Manstein states that the Dnieper Line had initially been improved against Hitler's will, but was later described by him with great exaggeration as the "Eastern Wall." Manstein also described as a "Developed Position" the Melitopol'–Zaporozh'e Line mentioned here. The Sixth Army had withdrawn to this line at the end of September 1943, and, after a Soviet breakthrough at the end of October, the line was "taken back surprisingly quickly toward the West." When Manstein establishes this in his usual careful phrasing, one can easily imagine Hitler's indignation and his search for the guilty parties.—*Source: Manstein, pp. 537, 544 and 550.*

[1277] Regarding Jaco, see above note 800; regarding Dorsch, note 1084.

[1278] Because there were practically no steel ties in the East, the problem of a suitable rail cutter was not that urgent until the beginning of the retreat from France. Furthermore, no special equipment was needed for steel ties, as they could be ripped out using a standard steel cable wound around the end of the tie. From the 35 possible models that were shown to Hitler in September 1943 in Arys, a reconstruction of a Soviet type was finally selected. It was mass-produced by Schwarzkopf as a "track wolf" for wooden ties.

[1279] A presentation of the Armed Forces Operations Staff on July 28 regarding the "combat procedure in the event of an enemy breakthrough in Normandy," which suggested to Hitler a retreat from the coastal front.

[1280] The 8th SS Cavalry Division "Florian Geyer" (see above note 1180) and the 22nd SS Volunteer Cavalry Division (which had just been built up using parts of the 8th SS Division).—*Source: Order of Battle, pp. 341 and 347.*

[1281] Damage to both eardrums and an irritation of the auditory canal were the worst effects on Hitler's health resulting from the July 20 bomb explosion. Only after a lengthy period of bed rest did those injuries heal. He also had burns on his leg, a wound on his right elbow, and a bruise on his back from a collapsed ceiling beam.—*Source: Bullock, pp. 746 and 767; Görlitz/Quint, pp. 605 and 613.*

[1282] Hitler had received the attendees of a meeting of "the men responsible for armaments and war production," called by Speer, and had spoken to them. The text of this speech was published by DNB on July 5. According to the recollection of a participant, this meeting had already taken place on June 26 in the Platterhof at the Obersalzberg. The attendees—about 100 armament experts—had been brought by special train from their meeting point at Linz to Freiburg/Berchtesgaden. Hitler had obviously given several other speeches around that time as well, which are also possibilities—for example, a speech before the generals and officers on June 22, also at the Platterhof.

[1283] The reference here is probably to Sonnleithner, who had joined the meeting in the meantime, though he is not included in the List of Participants. Sonnleithner had taken part in the situation report on July 20, when Stauffenberg made the assassination attempt.

[1284] Today, physicians assume that Hitler's severe nerve problem was *paralysis agitans*, or Parkinson's Disease (not to be confused with the progressive paralyis of syphilitic origin), a degenerative disease of certain brain parts, which manifests itself in serious organic nerve damage and also influences the mental and emotional life, often leading to paranoid and manic delusions. The illness first appeared—probably as a result of the stress of the first Russian winter—at the beginning of 1942, with heavy dizzy spells. At the same time, the stomach problems he had complained about for a long time worsened. That same year, or in early 1943 at the latest, he also began to suffer from a shaking of the limbs on the left side of his body (first the arm, later also the leg), which steadily worsened—apart from the temporary improvement mentioned here, which was obviously the result of the shock from the attempted assassination. Hitler's physician, Dr. Morell, treated him with 28 different medications, both pills and injections. These medications however, did not prevent his illness from worsening toward the end of the war, to the point where he usually had to use a cane for walking, and he attempted to use his right extremities to keep the left ones as still as possible. Physically, Hitler was a sick man after 1943, in the fall of 1944 (September to November), and again even severely ill in April 1945.—*Surce: Bullock, pp. 720 and 767; Zoller, pp. 64 and 70; Trevor-Roper: Hitlers letzte Tage, p. 62; Görlitz/Quint, p. 579; Guderian: Erinnerungen, p. 402.*

[1285] See above note 529.

[1286] See List of Participants. Krebs, General of Infantry as of August 1, 1944, became Chief of General Staff of Army Group B in the West, as the successor to Speidel, at the beginning of September.

[1287] Record number unknown—Fragment No. 46—A first transcription, of which the lower third was destroyed on the first 15 pages.

[1288] Since 1942, Kluge (see above note 267)—then Commander-in-Chief of Army Group Middle in the East—had been wooed constantly by the conspirators, who thought they needed an active field marshal with troop command to start their actions. The Ia [operations officer] of the army group, Colonel v. Tresckow, who belonged to the resistance group, had meaningful personal influence on Kluge, but was unable to get more from him than an assent in the case of Hitler's death. Kluge stepped down in October 1943 after an accident, and did not receive a new front command for three-quaters of a year. On July 3, 1944, he took over from Rundstedt as Commander-in-Chief West, and then on July 18 also took over from the wounded Rommel as Commander-in-Chief of Army Group B. In these positions he maintained his wait-and-see attitude toward the conspiracy, and gave his final rejection to Stülpnagel only on the evening of July 20, after Hitler's survival had been confirmed. Throughout the course of the following weeks, news filtered into the Führer Headquarers about the ambiguous attitude of the field marshal, who was also incriminated by involuntary or forced statements from those who had been arrested. The statements made by Hitler here indicate that Kluge was finally pulled into the assassination investigation only on August 30—that is, 11 days after his suicide (see also below note 1318). Another issue in his removal had obviously been the suspicion that Kluge was flirting with the idea of a separate peace in the West (see below note 1320), as well as Hitler's anger over the Americans breaking out of their beachhead and the encirclement of the Seventh Army at Falaise. But in a file note from Bormann, dated August 17, 1944, regarding Kluge's discharge, it was already stated that he has been "the commander-in-chief over Tresckow and other traitors." The note said: "Field Marshal Kluge's behavior is not entirely acceptable; according to investigations conducted thus far, Kluge must have known about individual thoughts and ideas of individual traitors. He did not report these." Because Hitler no longer trusted him completely, he could not remain commander-in-chief. Without prior announcement, Kluge was replaced by Field Marshal Model on August 17 and was ordered to report to headquarters immediately. Kluge wrote a letter to Hitler—in which he emphasized the necessity of signing a peace treaty soon, but which was at the same time a panegyric to Hitler's greatness (see Wilmot, p. 779)—and got into his car for the trip home on the morning of August 19. Between Clemont-en-Argonnes and Domnâsle he pulled off the road and poisoned himself.—*Source: Bormann's file note of August 17, 1944 (Archive IfZ, Fa 116, Bl.13); Wheeler; Bennett, pp. 551, 609, 650, 684 and 693; Wilmot (Engl.), p. 420; Zeller, passim; Schramm (W.), pp. 65, 335 and others.*

1289 The People's Court trial concluded on August 30. Accused were the Military Commander in France, General of Infantry Heinrich v. Stülpnagel (see above note 1244), his Chief of Staff Colonel v. Linstow, Kluge's Senior Quartermaster, Colonel Finckh (see below note 1258), as well as the Lieutenant Colonels v. Hofacker (see above note 1311), Rahtgens and Smend. All the accused were sentenced to death and executed that same day, except v. Hofacker (December 20, 1944) and Smend (September 8, 1944).—*Source: Zeller, p. 427; Pechel, p. 335; Wheeler-Bennett, p. 759.*

1290 Kluge was without connection to his headquarters for more than twelve hours on August 15, after he left at 9:30 a.m. for a trip into the Falaise pocket. After his return, he reported that he had spent most of the day in a trench because of heavy artillery fire and a fighter-bomber attack. His staff officers considered this claim to be true, and it is supported by Hitler's accusations here, which the Allied side has not yet confirmed. In any case, nothing is known about a released German officer who was supposed to get in touch with Kluge. Despite Schramm's repeated explanation of the escort officer Tangermann, the behavior of the field marshal remains peculiar that day. At this critical moment, the Commander-in-Chief West goes to a front area—which, as no one could know better than he, was made practically impassable by the swarms of enemy fighter-bombers—to seek death on the battlefield, but then, facing death, chose rather to spend the afternoon sleeping in a shelter (see also below p. 478). When the message arrived at the Führer Headquarters on July 16 around 6 o'clock that Kluge had established contact again, Hitler had already called Model back from Russia a few hours before and ordered him to immediately take over of both of Kluge's commands. [—] The field marshal's son, Lieutenant Colonel in the General Staff v. Kluge, had been appointed by his father as head of the Eberbach group, which was located inside the pocket.— *Source: Wilmot, p. 444; Liddell Hart: The German Generals, p. 246; Schramm (W.), p. 353.*

[1291] Hitler's reproaches against the staff of the Seventh Army were probably based mostly on his aversion to the long-time commnder-in-chief of this army, Colonel General Dollmann (see above note 653), who died of a heart attack during the battle in Normandy on June 27 (29?). On August 31, General of Panzer Troops Eberbach had just been replaced by General of Panzer Troops Brandenberger as commander of this army (see above note 34).

[1292] The Seventh Army, together with the Fifteenth Army, had been under Field Marshal Rommel until his car accident during the fighter-bomber attack on the afternoon of July 17. It cannot be stated for certain whether Hitler already knew at this point about Rommel's involvement in the July 20 assassination attempt (which forced Rommel to commit suicide on October 14), as the following text suggests. But it can be assumed that this whole complex was initiated by the proceedings against Stülpnagel and his officers at the end of August. Zeller points out that Rommel's house in Herrlingen, near Ulm, had been under observation by Bormann's representatives long before October 14. Also, his Chief of General Staff, Speidel, had been recalled without explanation on September 5 and arrested September 7—one week after this meeting—and taken into the cellar at Prinz Albrecht Street.—*Source: Speidel, pp. 170 and 175; Zeller, p. 309.*

[1293] Hitler meant the Italian theater of war (see above note 665), because it had never been considered for the West.— Regarding Rommel's "pessimism," see also p. 45.

[1294] That was Hitler's opinion, but it was less justified after the reserves coming over the Mediterranean failed.

[1295] Obviously, Hitler has the picture of the retreat movement in mind, since it should be "on the right side." He is referring to the western Egyptian Qattâra depression, a sand-drift desert of about 20,000 square kilometers, 134 meters below sea level at its lowest point, sprinkled with numerous salt lakes and impassable for motor vehicles. South of El Alamein, the Qattâra comes closest to the coast—within 65 km.

[1296] Hitler's claim is a bit bold. On the evening of October 23, 1942, the English prepared to attack the German-Italian Alameinposition, after the Axis troops that had reached the Alamein line on June 30 had failed to break through to the Nile 70 km away. The massed Allied forces and English air superiority put such heavy pressure on the German-Italian units (which were suffering from lack of supplies) that on the evening of November 2, Rommel asked the Armed Forces High Command and the *Comando Supremo* for permission to retreat—an action he had already initiated. This report from Rommel is the one referred to by Hitler here. It had in fact been presented to him late due to a mistake by the Armed Forces Operations Staff officer in charge. It arrived on November 3 at 3 a.m., but did not reach Hitler until about 10. (The officer in charge was demoted

and put into a penal punishment unit, and General Warlimont fell out of favor
for some time.) In response, Hitler, not understanding the seriousness of the
situation, ordered Rommel to hold the position and not to give up a single
meter of territory: "It would not be the first time in history that the stronger will
has ruled over the stronger battalion. You can only show your troops the way to
victory or death." Rommel initially obeyed and reversed the retreat movement,
under considerable difficulty. But the following day, the English—in addition to
breaking through the German lines—were able to create a 20-km-wide hole in
the front after the destruction of the Italian XX Corps. Rommel had no more
reserves to fight back the danger, and he ordered a retreat to the Fuka Position
on the early afternoon of November 4. This retreat, however, took on an ava-
lanche-like character and really only ended on May 7-12 in Tunis. Hitler agreed
to this November 4 retreat command the next day, via radio message. That
first order from the Führer, on November 3, actually did reach Rommel belatedly (1:30 p.m.), which resulted in more difficulties, especially in relocating the
Italian troops. However, Rommel would have been defeated by the English the
following day in any case—after a quiet night.—*Source: Tippelskirch, p. 334; Westphal,
p. 186; Rommel Papers, p. 317; Rintelen, p. 176.*

[1297] He is probably referring to Rommel's demands to end the war, which the field
marshal had presented to Hitler during his visit to the West on June 17 and
again during his report in Berchtesgaden on June 29. Otherwise (see above
note 1292), Hitler could already be speaking about Rommel's contacts with
the July men, which militarily could hardly have happened yet as long as men
like Speidel, for example, were still at large.—*Source: Speidel, pp. 118 and 127;
Blumentritt, p. 233.*

[1298] In fact, Hitler would rather have avoided war against the "Germanic brother
nation" and was never able to understand why England refsed to give him
continental supremacy. When he speaks here of "renouncing everything," he
means only *English* territory and *English* reparations, of course. A renunciation
of his conquests so far would never have been considered. The remark about
the year 1936 means the appointment of Ribbentrop as German ambassador to
London, who was given the explicit command to probe the possibility of a
German-English understanding. "Ribbentrop, bring me the English union!" are
said to have been Hitler's words of farewell. Further above, Hitler speaks of the
"offer" that he made to the English ambassador Henderson on August 25, 1939:
He would agree to the British Empire and was willing to commit himself
personally to its existence—as well as, if necessary, to use the strength of Germany for its defense—under the preconditions that a) the Danzig corridor problem would be "solved," b) the colonial demands of Germany would be met, and
c) his obligations toward Italy and the Soviet Union would not be touched. After
the French campaign, Hitler—without mentioning any details—made an "appeal to reason" during his Reichstag speech on July 19, 1940: He had never
planned to "destroy or even damage" the British Empire and therefore did not
see any reason for the continuation of the war.—*Source: Hofer, p. 94; VB of July
20, 1940; Ribbentrop, p. 91.*

[1299] Robert Gilbert Vansittart; born June 25, 1881 and after 1941 Baron of Denham, had entered the British diplomatic service in 1902 and held office from 1928 to 1930 as Assistant Under-Secretary of State for Foreign Affairs; 1930-37 as Permanent Under-Secretary also in the Foreign Office; and 1938-41 as Chief Diplomatic Advisor to the Foreign Secretary. Vansittart was used by Goebbels as a symbol of anti-German behavior and was constantly attacked. He died on February 14, 1957.—*Source: Who is Who 1950, p. 2856; Vansittart, passim.*

[1300] Model (see above note 718) had taken over the command of Army Group Center on June 28, 1944, from Field Marshal Busch, whose entire front had been torn open by the Soviet attack that started June 22.—*Source: Tippelskirch, p. 530; Siegler, p. 132.*

[1301] Here Hitler is probably repeating Rommel's statements, which were made during the meeting between Hitler, Rundstedt and Romme on June 17, 1944, near Soissons. (Compare here Speidel, p. 112, where the above-mentioned points are not discussed.)

[1302] Hitler himself had ordered the transportation of both SS panzer divisions into the East on March 25, 1944; they had been employed in front of Ternopol' (see above note 1116). Furthermore, he had been notified several times about materiel and personnel shortages among most of the Western units. In fact, the 700-series of divisions located on the so-called Atlantic Wall were in no shape for a major battle—neither with respect to personnel nor equipment. They were immobile fortress divisions with, in many cases, older age groups, and equipped with captured French, Czech and Russian weapons. All other divisions were only present in the West temporarily—either for initial formation or for rehabilitation before being sent back into the East or to Italy. The latter was true also for the panzer divisions, with the exception of the 21st Panzer Divison. This division had been set up 1943 in the West and equipped laboriously with captured French vehicles, but, like the 700-series divisions, it had no battle experience.

[1303] Of the possible Schulenburgs, the one probably meant here is Friedrich Werner Graf v. d. Schulenburg, born in 1875. Schulenburg, who succeeded Nadolny as ambassador in Moscow from October 1934 until June 1941, had welcomed the German-Soviet rapprochement of 1939 as a resumption of Bismarck's traditional orientation toward the East, and was disturbed by Hitler's attack on the Soviet Union in 1941. After Stalingrad, he joined the conspirators and competed with Ulrich v. Hassell as Stauffenberg's candidate for Foreign Minister in a possible Goerdeler cabinet, as he had asked for an immediate peace with Russia, provided that contact could be made with Stalin. Even though Ritter in his Goerdeler book in no way characterizes Schulenburg as a blind adherent of an "Eastern Solution," his political concept of Hitler's situation at the time is likely presented correctly here. Schulenburg was executed on November 10, 1944.—*Source: Goerdeler, pp. 364, 379, 534, 542 and 602; Zeller, pp. 391 and 432; Wheeler-Bennett, pp. 352, 637 and 764.*

[1304] With those remarkable words, Hitler judges his own policy during the final years of the war. If he considered it so "stupid" to play the Russians off against the

English, his expansion of the war toward Stalingrad and Tunis, and at least up to Avranches, could have the single purpose of lengthening his life and the lifespan of his regime at the expense of the German people—while his propaganda slogans trumpeted that the cause must be more important than anything else, and that even the last German must be willing to give himself up.

1305 It is correct that Hitler lived in his headquarters in dangerously unrealistic isolation—in an atmosphere that Jodl in Nuremberg called a cross between a monastery and a concentration camp—and that he gave up all private life. The time span mentioned here is to be taken with a grain of salt, however, as Hitler's isolation was not that intense in the first years of war, and was of quite limited duration. It was not until partway through the war, for instance, that he finally gave up his habit of watching films after dinner.—*Source: IMT XV, p. 325; Bullock, p. 723.*

1306 Rudolf Gercke; born August 17, 1884; 1904 Second Lieutenant; Reichswehr; 1923 left the service as brevet Major; 1933 re-entering as Major and detachment leader in RWM; 1937 Colonel and Chief of the Transportation Department in the Army General Staff; 1939 Major General and head of the Armed Forces Trnsportation System (in both positions until the end of the war); 1940 Lieutenant General; and 1942 General of Infantry. Gercke died in 1947 in American captivity.—*Source: Keilig 211/98; Seemen, p. 285; Order of Battle, p. 553; Das deutsche Heer, p. 11; Rangliste 1944-45, p. 16.*

1307 Wit the July 20 events.

1308 Here he refers to Army Group Center in the East, where, in Hitler's opinion, the collapse of June 1944 was accelerated by the fact that the Soviets used captured German officers to cross back over the line (made possible by the total breakdown of the front), rejoin the command system, and cause confusion. No evidence came to light after the war that could support this claim; the only certain thing is that several of the German generals and officers captured during this Soviet offensive did immediately step over to the side of the National Committee and offer themselves to the Russians.

1309 Only in Paris did the conspirators—led by the Military Commander in France, General Carl Heinrich v. Stülpnagel—experience a brief triumph on July 20, despite the first indecisive then negative attitude of the Commander-in-Chief West. At 11 p.m., when everything was already over in Berlin, they had rounded up the senior SS and police commanders in France, including Gruppenführer Oberg and the men from his headquarters on Avenue Foch, and, within half an hour, had secured the vast majority of the 2,000 men (Schramm: 1,200) in the Parisian SS and SD forces, and had put them out of action. At dawn on July 21, the captured men had to be set free again, in consideration of the hopeless general situation and Kluge's attitude.—*Source: Wheeler-Bennett, p. 683; Schramm (W.), passim.*

1310 Günther Blumentritt; born February 10, 1892; 1912 Second Lieutenant; Reichswehr; 1933 Major; 1938 Colonel and Chief, 4th Section in the Army General Staff; 1940 Chief of Staff, Fourth Army; 1941 Major General; January 1942 Senior Quartermaster I in the Army High Command; September 1942 Chief of

Staff, Army Group D and Lieutenant General; and April 1944 General of Infantry. After this meeting, Blumentritt was replaced by Westphal during the first few days of September. In October 1944 he became Commander, XII SS Corps; January 1945 Commander, Twenty-Fifth Army; end of March Commander, 1st Parachute Army; and after April 15, Commander-in-Chief, Blumentritt Army. Hitler's opinion about Blumentritt was also shared by his commander-in-chief, Rundstedt, who wrote in his assessment on September 9, 1944: "He deserves special mention for his clear position and his firm measures surrounding the events of July 20, 1944, in the area of the Commander-in-Chief West."—*Source: Army High Command staff files; (Nbg. Dok. NOKW-141); Order of Battle, p. 530; Siegler, p. 113.*

[1311] Eberhard Finckh; born November 7, 1899; came from the 41st Artillery Regiment; 1934 Captain, War Academy; 1938 assigned to the 10th Section of the Army General Staff; November 1942 Colonel in the General Staff Senior Quartermaster for Army Group Don/South; and after April 1944, Senior Quartermaster for the Commander-in-Chief West. On August 30, 1944, as a participant in the July conspiracy, Finckh was sentenced by the People's Court to death by hanging and was executed that same day. (See also above note 1291.)—*Source: DNB of May 11, 1944; Das deutsche Heer, p. 12; Manstein, p. 326.*

[1312] See above note 346. Wagner, who had been close to Beck and who already agreed with his attitude toward Hitler before the war, had been a participant in the July 20 conspiracy and had committed suicide on July 23 (22?), 1944.—*Source: Wheeler-Bennett, pp. 481 and 765.*

[1313] Neither Kluge's promotions nor his decorations were particularly unusual. He had been Colonel General for only nine months when he received the marshal's baton during the great field marshal promotion on July 19, 1940. At that time, however, when ranks were even skipped, this quick success was nothing out of the ordinary. The highest award he received was the Schwerter [swords], while Hitler had already awarded the Brillianten [diamonds] to four Army generals (Rommel, Hube, Model and Balck) that same day. But Kluge—like all generals from the army commander rank upward—had, in addition to his field marshal salary of 36,000 Reich Marks [RM] (gross), received special tax-free bonuses from Hitler's private funds. He also received a check from Hitler for more than 250,000 RM for his 60th birthday on October 30, 1942, as well as a building permit for his property in Brandenburg worth about half of that sum. Kluge had accepted the check as well as the building permit.—*Source: Wheeler-Bennett, p. 552; Schlabrendorff, p. 61.*

[1314] See above note 1289. Karl Ernst Rahtgens, Lieutenant Colonel in the General Staff, was a relative of Kluge, as his mother was born a v. Kluge—probably a cousin of the field marshal.

[1315] Roland Freisler; born October 30, 1893; law studies; Communist; from Russian war imprisonment Bolshevik commissioner; after his return lawyer in Kassel; after 1925 member of the NSDAP; 1932 Landtag member in Prussia; March 1933 as Ministerial Director head of the Personnel Department in the Prussian Ministry of Justice; that same year Under-Secretary of State (after the unfication of the Reich Ministry of Justice); and Prussian State Council and member of the Reichstag. As Thierack's successor, Freisler became president of the People's Court in August 1942, and tried to compensate for this demotion and his politically dubious past by carrying out his duties with extraordinary enthusiasm and an excess of toughness and cruelty. Freisler died during an air raid on Berlin on February 3, 1945, in the cellar of his office building.—*Source: Reichstags-Handbücher; Munzinger Archive; Schlabrendorff, p. 213.*

1316 Stieff (see above note 698) had contacted the conspirators via Tresckow and was one of the actors in the July 20 assassination attempt. In the main trial, the "smallest and youngest Armed Forces general" was sentenced to death by hanging on August 8, 1944, and executed two hours later.

1317 Erich Höppner; born September 14, 1886; 1906 Second Lieutenant; Reichswehr; 1933 Colonel; 1936 Major General; 1938 Lieutenant General and Commander, 1st Mobile Division; November 1938 Commanding General, XVI Army Corps (Berlin); 1939 General of Cavalry; with his corps in Poland and France; July 1940 Colonel General; and in the Eastern campaign Commander, Fourth Panzer Group (October 1941 renamed Fourth Panzer Army). On January 8, 1942, Hoepner received his dishonorable discharge from the Army, "for cowardice and disobedience," because he had carried out unauthorized retreat movements and because he had spoken disparagingly—which had reached Hitler's ears—about the "non-professional leadership." At the end of 1943, Hoepner was introduced to the revolt plans by Olbricht, his neighbor in Dahlem, and was tapped for the role of commander-in-chief of the Replacement Army. He was also sentenced to death by hanging by the People's Court on August 8, 1944, and executed that same day.—*Source: Munzinger Archive; Siegler, p. 124; Keilig 211/139; Zeller, passim; and others.*

1318 At that time (since the end of December 1941) Commander-in-Chief of Army Group Center, to which Hoepner's Fourth Panzer Army belonged.

1319 It is not quite clear what Hitler meant here. He, at least, was certainly not silent "back then."

1320 Kluge's death was not made public; on short notice Hitler prohibited the planned burial ceremony on his [Kluge's] Böhne estate in Altmark. According to Blumentritt's statement, a state funeral was originally planned as well, but was cancelled after the poison was discovered during an examination of the corpse (ordered by Keitel); at first, only a heart attack had been discussed. After the field marshal's corpse had been stored in the Böhne church for nearly two weeks, and tumult was increasing among the population, the propaganda department emphasized via verbal propaganda that Kluge had died of a heart attack. Keitel informed the military district commanders of the death on August 31, and requested that the generals be informed in a "suitable way." This text said: "From a letter Kluge left behind, we read that he obviously acted under the impression that he bore heavy responsibility for the outcome of the battle in Normandy." And, in conclusion: "There will be no further discussion of these events." The discussion began, though, at least abroad, since the Allies captured this order at the end of December 1944.—*Source: RdSchr.*

Parteikanzlei 219/22 gRs.; Report RpropAmt Dessau Sept. 5, 1944 and others (Archive IfZ, Fa 116, Bl. 18); Files of the Propaganda Department in the German central archives in Potsdam, Bd. 863; Schramm (W.), p. 376; NZZ Dec. 29, 1944 (midday edition).

[1321] Record number unknown—Fragment No. 43—A first transcription, the majority of which was destroyed. The damage, starting in the lower left-hand corner, became worse with each successive page, and on the last four of the 85 pages there was not a single completely legible sentence.

[1322] After Manstein's and Kleist's retirement on March 30, 1944, Army Group South was renamed North Ukraine (Model, and after June 28 Harpe) and Army Group A became South Ukraine (Schörner, and after July 25 Friesser). On September 20, both staffs were renamed again, keeping their commanders-in-chief, but now vice versa: North Ukraine became "A," and South Ukraine became South. South remained under Wöhler (after December 23) and Rendulic (after April 7, 1945) until the capitulation. "A" (after January 17 Schörner) was renamed again as Center on January 25, 1945, while the Army Group Center, which had existed since 1941, was renamed North and the previous Army Group North was renamed Courland that same day. So the resulting arrangement of the German army groups is as follows:

April 1, 1941	North (ex. C)	Center (ex. B)	South (ex. A)	
May 1942				A (New Homeland)
July 15, 1942			B	
Nov. 22, 1942				Don (ex. 11th Army
Feb. 14, 1943			disbanded	South
Mar. 30, 1944				North South
				Ukraine Ukraine
Sept. 20, 1944				A South
Jan. 25, 1945	Courland	North Vistula	Center	
April 2, 1945		disbanded		
Capitulation				

—Source: According to Siegler, p. 18.

[1323] Hermann Winkler; born August 11, 1888; 1919 Second Lieutenant, 102nd Infantry Regiment; Reichswehr; 1934 Colonel; 1937 Commander of the Psychological Testing Office II; 1941 Major General and Commander, Dept. of Aptitude Tests XI; June 1942 Field Commander of Nikolaev; and after September 1944, Commander, 153rd Field Training Division in Romania, April 1945 Lieutenant General. Winkler was executed in Nikolaev in 1946.—*Source: Keilig 211/ 366; Order of Battle, p. 643.*

[1324] Friedrich Mieth; born June 4, 1888; 1907 Second Lieutenant, 2nd Jäger [Light Infantry] Battalion; Reichswehr; 1935 Colonel; 1936 Commander, 27th Infantry Regiment; 1938 Major General and Chief of General Staff, XII Army Corps; 1939 Chief of Staff, First Army; spring 1940 Senior Quartermaster I in the Army High Command and Lieutenant General; December 1940 Commander, 112th Infantry Division; April 1943 General of Infantry and Commanding General, Corps Mieth; and after July 1943, Commanding General, IV Army

Corps. Mieth had especially distinguished himself on the bridgehead at Nikopol' at the end of 1943. The news of his death turned out to be true and was officially acknowledged the next day.—*Source: Siegler, p. 132; VB March 5 and Oct. 3, 1944; Das deutsche Heer, p. 164; Rangliste 1944-45, p. 17; Keilig 211/221.*

[1325] On August 23 a political revolution took place in Romania, after rival armistice contacts had already been made at the end of 1943: by the two Antonescus with the Soviets (Mme. Kollontai) in Stockholm, and by the Democrats under the Farmers' Party leader Maniu with the Anglo-Americans in Cairo. The major Soviet offensive of August 20 helped speed things up. The hesitant Antonescus gave their Stockholm negotiators authority to arrange official armistice discussions, and, as a result, the Maniu group advanced their coup—originally planned for August 26—by 3 days. With the help of the king, the regime was overthrown, the Antonescus arrested, and the cessation of hostilities announced. That same day, the new Romanian government offered free retreat to the German troops, as long as they refrained from any kind of hostility. But the next day, August 24, the first skirmishes took place between German and Romanian troops, along with German air attacks on Bucharest. Consequently, Romania declared war on the Reich on August 25—an action that had been planned for later anyway. Nevertheless, the Western powers gave Maniu the cold shoulder and pointed to Moscow, which continued the war as if nothing had happened and agreed to sign an armistice declaration only on September 12, after occupying all of the country except for Transylvania [Siebenburgen]. Romania then had to agree to take part in the war against Germany with at least 12 infantry divisions. In the meantime, Romanian units had already taken up the fight against the Germans and Hungarians in Transylvania—a fact which did not prevent 130,000 Romanian soldiers from being taken captive by the Soviets before September 12. All in all, the change of fronts went fairly smoothly. In Transylvania, as later in Hungary and Slovakia, the Romanian armies (5th, 4th and 1st with 21 infantry and five cavalry divisions, as well as a tank division—altogether 386,000 men) fought against the German and Hungarian forces and suffered severe losses (approximately 78,000 dead with 90,000 wounded).—*Source: Bretholz, p. 93; Hillgruber, pp. 209 and 229; Toynbee: Hitler's Europe, p. 625; Seton-Watson, p. 87; Friessner, p. 85.*

[1326] Hitler speaks of Bulgaria, whose northern border was reached by the Red Army in the Dobrudja and along the Danube River. The Regentcy Council under Prince Kyrill had reigned there since the death of Tsar Boris III on August 28, 1943 (see above note 799) on behalf of Boris's underage son, Simeon. In a letter to Hitler, Prince Kyrill had mentioned his wish that Bulgaria would not need to take part in the war. (See also below note 1386.)—*Source: Ausarbeitung WFSt/ Kriegstagebuch über Rumänien, p. 69 (Nbg. Dok. 1806-PS).*

[1327] During 1944 a Maquis [resistance], consisting primarily of deserters, had formed in the Tatra Mountains and in the western Beskydy. The group's command, the Slovakian National Council, in expectation of the advancing Red Army and in agreeent with the Soviet Union and the Czechoslovakian government-in-exile, ended the uprising on July 27. At the beginning of August—about at the same time as the Warsaw uprising—separate partisan group actions began, which soon forced the Slovakian government to declare a state of siege. On August 25, the actual revolt was started, and most of the Slovakian troops allied themselves with the partisans. The most important cities in central Slovakia were occupied and the entire country was practically at war; because the government was unable to get the rebels in the higher Waag and Gran valleys under control, the Germans marched in on the 29th to occupy the country and disarmed the rest of the troops that had remained loyal to the government. On September 1, SS Obergruppenführer Berger took over the command as German General in Slovakia. The overthrow of the rebels, to which belonged War Minister Čatlos and into whose hands the gold and currency holdings of the National Bank were played by the Slovakian economic dictator Karvaš, still needed some time, however. Not until October 27—two days before the Red Army crossed the Slovakian border—did the Germans conquer the uprising centers of Banska Bystrica (Neusohl) and Zvolen (Altsohl). The riot leaders were executed, but individual guerrilla battles continued.—*Source: Toynbee: Hitler's Europe, p. 602; Seton-Watson, p. 146; Frantis, passim; Brügel, passim; Jilemnicky, passim; Die Vertreibung der deutschen Bevölkerung aus der Tschechoslowakai, p. 158; Mikus, p. 185.*

[1328] Commander-in-Chief of Army Group North Ukraine (see above note 504 and note 1322).

[1329] Wilhelm Berlin; born April 28, 1889; 1910 Second Lieutenant; Reichswehr; 1936 Colonel; 1937 Commander, 33rd Artillery Regiment; 1939 commander, 101st Artillery Command [Arko]; 1940 Major General and Commander, Jüterbog Artillery School; 1942 Lieutenant General; 1943 Commander, 227th Infantry Division; May 1944 Commander, XXVI Army Corps; and after July 21, 1944 General of Artillery in the Armed Forces High Command.—*Source: Keilig 211/24; Das deutsche Heer, p. 500.*

[1330] The 1st Ski-Jäger-Division, a special unit set up as the 1st Ski Brigade in October 1943 (Division after the summer of 1944), was set up in the Vistula River bend in September 1944 and was relocated later to Slovakia.—*Source: Order of Battle, p. 313.*

[1331] The German troops had unsuccessfully attacked the three Soviet bridgeheads west of the Vistula during the month of August. The Russian positions on the west shore, established in July/August, were located:

1. Near Magnuszew on the mouth of the Pilica River, about 50 km south of Warsaw;
2. 60 km further upstream, near Pulawy, on the easternmost point of the Vistula bend; and
3. Near Sandomierz and Baranow, between the mouth of the Wisloka and the San Rivers, 80 to 100 km further upstream.

The Russians were able to hold and extend these bridgeheads; from there they began their attack toward the Oder River on January 12 and 13, 1945. (See also below note 1688.)—*Source: Tippelskirch, pp. 546, 556 and 612.*

1332 The SS "Totenkopf" ["Deaths Head"] Division was set up in October 1939 from the 1st, 2nd, and 3rd "Totenkopf" Regiments (6,500 men out of 14,000 men total in the "Totenkopf" units), used for the KL, plus police reinforcement under the command of the KL and TV inspector Theodor Eicke. The division, which was reorganized as the 3rd SS Panzer Division "Totenkopf" in late fall 1942, was employed in the Warsaw area during the fall of 1944.—*Source: Hausser, p. 15; Order of Battle, p. 338; Nbg. Dok. NG-5792 and NO-1995.*

1333 When the armies of Rokossovsky's 1st Belorussian Front were advancing inexorably toward the Polish capital at the end of July, the Western-oriented Polish underground movement [the Home Army] claimed that the hour for revolt had arrived. On July 30, the canon thunder from the front could be clearly heard, and the German civilians had left the city. Two days later, the uprising of the Home Army of 40,000 men and more than 4,000 women broke out. The uprising was directed against the German occupation as well as the Soviet-oriented Lublin Committee and its "People's Army," which the Soviet government had organized. Two-thirds of Warsaw was controlled by the rebels, the railway stations were occupied, most of the German offices in the city were cut off from the outside, and all through roads were blocked off. The Russian offensive continued, however, and the Soviets made it difficult to supply the city by air from the West, due to landing prohibitions for the aircraft, etc. Thus, the Germans succeeded in regaining control over their encircled offices and the railway stations, and pushing the rebels together into individual districts, although they still lacked the strength for a total clearance. On September 5, a repeated German demand for capitulation was rejected by the Polish general Bor-Komorowski, in expectation of the Red Army attack against the Vistula bridgehead east of Warsaw, which would begin five days later. On September 13-14, Rokossovsky took the Praga suburb, located on the eastern shore of the Vistula, but did not cross the river or help the rebels for several days. Facing the employment of strong SS and police forces under the command of SS Obergruppenführer von dem Bach-Zelewski (see above note 72), the Poles could do nothing but capitulate at last. After taking over several rebel districts in the last few days of September, the capitulation agreement was signed in Ozarow on October 2. Six Polish generals and 12,000 members of the Home Army—15,000 members had been killed during the fighting—were imprisoned by the Germans; the German side had 10,000 dead and 7,000 missing.—*Source: Toynbee: Realignment (Auth. Sidney Lowery), p. 166; Tippelskirch, p. 545; VB of Oct. 3-7/8, 1944; Korbonski, p. 350; Bor-Komorowski, passim.*

1334 See below note 1335.

1335 Fegelein is probably understating. The Warsaw ghetto had been already partly destroyed by the Luftwaffe in the month-long fighting that began on April 19, 1943, and continued until May 16. On June 11, Himmler repeated his not-yet-fulfilled order of February 16, 1943, "that the city area of the former ghetto be totally flattened, and every cellar and every sewer be filled up. After completing this work, topsoil will be placed over the area and a large park will be laid out."

The work started July 19, 1943, during a great labor shortage; on October 9, a third of the area was reported destroyed. When the advance of the Red Army finally forced the work to stop on July 29, 1944, the ordered destruction was practically completed, but the leveling out was not finished and Himmler's park had not been laid out.—*Source: Nbg. Dok. NO-2496, NO-2514/16; Reitlinger: Endlösung, p. 315.*

[1336] Philip Kleffel; born December 9, 1887; 1907 Second Lieutenant; Reichswehr; 1929 Major; 1935 Colonel; 1936 Commander, 14th Cavalry Regiment; 1938 Senior Cavalry Officer 4; 1939 Major General and Deputy Chief of Staff, XI Army Corps; 1940 Commander, 1st Infantry Division; 1941 Lieutenant General; 1942 General of Cavalry and Commanding General, L Army Corps; January 1944 Commander, Military District IX (Kassel); July 1944 Commanding General with General Command Kleffel (from November 1944 on XVI Army Corps); and March/April 1945 Commander, Twenty-Fifth Army.—*Source: Army High Command staff files (Nbg. Dok. NOKW-141); Order of Battle, p. 377; Siegler, p. 126; Keilig 211/165.*

[1337] In the Tukkum area, the Russians were indeed unable to advance up to the Gulf of Riga again. The second and final cutting off of Army Group North took place at the beginning of October in Lithuania and was completed on the 10th near Polangen, north of Memel.—*Source: Tippelskirch, p. 562.*

[1338] Then Commander-in-Chief of Army Group North (see above note 981).

[1339] Probably the panzer grenadier Colonel Karl Mellwig, who had received the Knight's Cross from Hitler the day before.

[1340] Meaning in the rear of the enemy facing the Third Panzer Army and especially Group Kleffel. Hitler and Guderian had already considered the idea of attacking the enemy's flank during the successful German advance to the Gulf of Riga. This operation, an attack near Bauske, proved impossible in view of the balance of forces.—*Source: Tippelskirch, p. 547.*

[1341] Meinrad v. Lauchert; born August 29, 1905; 1924 Corporal; 1931 Second Lieutenant, 5th Cavalry Regiment; 1937 Captain in 5th Antitank Defense Detachment; 1938 Captain and Commander, 2nd Battalion, 35th Panzer Regiment; 1941 Major; in the summer of 1943 Commander, 51st Panzer Detachment, the first German panzer detachment (see above 255) employed at Kursk; August 1943 Lieutenant Colonel and Commander, 15th Panze Regiment, 11th Panzer Division; 1944 Colonel and (December) Commander, 2nd Panzer Division; and March 1945 Major Geneal.—*Source: Order of Battle, p. 586; Das deutsche Heer, p. 609; Rangliste 1944-45, p. 83; DNB Feb. 25, 1944; Keilig 211/192.*

[1342] The ideas developed by Hitler regarding the tactical use of tank weapons were shared by the tank people. Guderian repeated his well-known principle: "Big groups, not small ones" ["Klotzen, nicht kleckern!"]

[1343] The reference here is to the river combat group of Rear Admiral (Ing.) Zieb. While the German Black Sea Fleet relocated to Varna and was finally scuttled off the Bulgarian coast, the head of the Senior Shipyard Staff in Constanza built up a river combat group—after blowing up the coastal weapons, the shipyards and other such facilities—which, beginning on 24 August, fought its way upstream from Braila. This group was enlarged from time to time by ships that had escaped or by German ships on the Danube that had already been seized by the Romanians and freed again. These ships, which ultimately numbered more than 100—artillery tenders, flat-bottomed lighters, barge, mine sweepers, assault boats and other small ships—had found considerable support along the Bulgarian shore. On the morning of September 1, after a last artillery duel during the night with Romanian 12.5-cm weapons in the Calafat bunker positions, they had gone to the Serbian Danube town of Prahovo. This was the last stop of the combat group, as the Iron Gate fell into Soviet hands immediately afterward and could not be won back. First, the wounded people, women and children were transported to Nish by train, while the men who were still able to fight were forced to dig themselves in after the army group ordered a stop to the sinking of the ships, which was already in progress. Zieb's strong calls at Belgrade then obtained approval for the clearance of Prahovo, but the combat group had to be "picked up" by the Brandenburg Regiment and had to start back to Belgrade on foot, as the railway to Nish had already been broken up by the partisans. The scuttling of the ships impeded the continually strengthening enemy influence from the Romanian shore.—*Source: Kuhlmann, passim; Friessner, p. 96; Conrady, p. 75.*

1344 When preparations for withdrawing Army Group North back to the Narva–Lake Peipus–Pskov [Pleskau] line were being made in the fall of 1943, it became necessary to set up a strong Lake Peipus flotilla (the Soviet flotilla, consisting of, among other things, two motor torpedo boats, had been destroyed during engagements in 1941). By June 1944 approximately 24 Navy artillery lighters (180 tons; weapons: two 7.5- or 8.8-cm antitank guns or flak, six 2-cm, one mortar; speed 8 knots) from the 4th AT Flotilla had been brought over land to Dorpat [Tartu] and assembled there. In addition, there were four small mine layers and a number of other boats of various kinds—tugs, motorized punt boats and Siebelfähren. After reaching the lake, the Russians transported motor torpedo boats and flat-bottomed gunboats (the lake is at most 17 m deep!), but remained quite passive. Stronger Soviet landing attempts—which Hitler feared—or coastal shootings did not take place. While the mine layers (two had been destroyed in the meantime, but were replaced by others) were successfully evacuated by train on August 23, just before the fall of Dorpat [Tartu], the MAL, which was primarily responsible for coastal shooting, fell victim to Russian air attacks in late August/early September.—*Source: Meister, p. 205.*

1345 As long as Shlissel'burg—at the southwestern corner of Lake Ladoga—was in German hands, i.e., from September 8, 1941 to 19 January 1943 with a break in the fall of 1942, Leningrad was dependent upon supply via Lake Ladoga. Underestimating the Russians' ability to improvise, the full significance of this opportunity was not recognized by the German command when the attack on Leningrad was halted in the fall of 1941, as there were no major harbors on the southeastern or eastern shore, nor did major railway lines lead there. The blockade attempt in 1942 was a complete failure. The Russians were said to have transported 800,000 people, 16,000 head of cattle and 1 million tons of food, fuel and ammunition over the lake during the siege of Leningrad. Not only did they succeed in supplying the city and the troops, but they also supplied Leningrad industries with raw materials on a fairly large scale. The German Luftwaffe was unable to interrupt the steady stream of ships crossing the lake during the summer months, and was equally unable to prevent the construction of a railway over the frozen lake in the winter. The German and Finnish air forces were not entirely unsuccessful, however. They sank—according to their own reports—22 vessels in 1941 and 27 in 1942, including a torpedo boat and at least four steamers of more that 1,000 GRT.—*Source: Rieker, p. 44; Meister, p. 190.*

[1346] This report from Dönitz probably refers to the American air attack on Kiel two days earlier, on the afternoon of August 30.

[1347] During this withdrawal, the majority of all seaworthy mine sweepers and patrol boats, as well as individual torpedo boats and mine sweepers, were withdrawn though the straits to the east without significant losses.

[1348] Here and in the following statements the discussion concerns the "coastal fortresses" that had to be left behind in front of the lines—on Hitler's orders—during the German retreat in the West. (See also below note 1485.)

[1349] Probably an odd-sized French caliber.

[1350] Meaning the German Navy coastal battery Ile de Cézembre (a fortified island off of St. Malo), which—after the city's citadel had fallen on August 17, 1944, following eleven days of heavy fighting—still resisted despite continuous enemy fire, including from a battleship. The battery, under Lieutenant Colonel (MA.) of the Reserves Richard Seuss, was mentioned several times in the Armed Forces report. The battery blocked the entrance to the harbor of St. Malo until succumbing to the enemy's superior strength on September 2, after five weeks of battle. Seuss received Oak Leaves in addition to the Knight's Cross, which had been awarded to him in the middle of August.—*Source: Armed Forces High Command reports from Aug. to Sept. 4, 1944.*

[1351] The following statements apparently refer to northern Jutland. A landing in Denmark had, however—as far as can be determined—never seriously been considered on the Allied side.

[1352] Devices for preventing or impeding the clearance of blockades. Such devices included, for example, explosive buoys, which were designed to destroy mine-clearing equipment.

[1353] During the final phase of the war, the Navy developed a number of so-called midget craft, which were employed in particular during the landing operations in Italy and France. The following weapons were included in this category:

Marder [Marten]: A sharp torpedo attached to a torpedo without explosive charge or warhead, manned by a torpedo commander looking through a glass dome installed in the center. The "Marder" could thus be steered toward a target and fired. It could make short dives (before the improvement that brought the diving capability, it was known as "Nigger," as it was only usable at night due to its low speed). Production: about 500 units.

Biber [Beaver]: Single-man submarine of 6.3 t, 8.7 m long, speed of 6 nautical miles [per hour], 30 m diving depth, Opel-Kapitän engine, radius of action 80 nautical miles (200 nautical miles with additional tanks), armed with two electric torpedoes hung outside along the hull. Production: about 325 units.

Molch [Newt or Salamander]: enlarged "Biber" ["Beaver"], 11 t, 10.8 m long, speed of 4 nautical miles [per hour], 13-hp electric engine. The "Molch" was a developmental failure. Huge losses occurred due to diving problems and gas development in the interior. From the mission presumably referred to here, in the mouth of the Schelde, only 8 percent of the employed "Molche" returned. Production: about 395 units.

Other mini-submarines employed in the following months were the not combat-ready "Hecht" ["Pike"] (11.8 t) and the improved, very reliable "Seehund" ["Seal"] (15 t). —*Source: Lusar, p. 139; Lusar: Seehunde…, passim.*

1354 Meaning the northern part of Jutland.

1355 Stuttgart.

1356 The Nineteenth Army's divisions retreating from the Mediterranean Sea up the Rhône Valley, some of whose rearguards were then fighting near Valence at the mouth of the Isère River.

1357 Then Commander-in-Chief of Army [Armeegruppe] Group "G" (after September 10, 1944: Army Group [Heeresgruppe] "G;" see above note 654.

1358 Must be "Lucht." Walther Lucht; born February 26, 1882; 1902 Second Lieutenant; 1925 Major; 1932 left the service as brevet Colonel; 1936 Training Commander, Karlsruhe; 1937 reentered the service; 1938 Colonel; 1939 Training Commander, Heilbronn; 1940 Major General and Commander, 44th Artillery Command [Arko]; 1941 Commander, 87th Infantry Division; January 1942 Commander, 310th High Artillery Command [Harko]; March 1942 Commander, 336th Infantry Division; November 1942 Lieutenant General; July 1943 Commander, Kerch Strait; and end of 1943 General of Artillery and Commanding General, LXVI Reserve Corps (later Army Corps) on the French Mediterranean coast and during the retreat. In April 1945 Lucht became Commander of the Eleventh Army.—*Source: Army High Command staff files (Nbg. Dok. NOKW-141); Siegler, p. 130; Order of Battle, p. 590.*

1359 Plateau de Langres. The remains of the First Army retreated over the plateau from the Bay of Biscay and from southwest France, worn out from fighting the French resistance movement. So to a certain degree, there was a projection of the German lines—to the extent that they can be considered lines at all—between the Allied forces coming from the Channel and from the Mediterranean. Under the command of Fifth Panzer Army, released from the front, the German forces wanted—according to the Rastenburg plans—to lead an attack northward against the southern flank of the American Third Army, which was advancing toward Metz. But even before enough forces could be brought together, the northern sector of the salient was thrown back over the Moselle River, and an enemy push via Nancy to Lunéville tore a gap in the German positions. Thus, the forces of the Fifth Panzer Army were now desperately needed for defense.—*Source: Tippelskirch, p. 518.*

[1360] The Western Wall had been totally dismantled since the winter of 1940-41. Only in the summer of 1944 was armament and occupation by local personnel started again. Because of the speed of the Allied movement, however, this could only be done in an improvised manner.

[1361] 8.8 cm was the largest antitank gun caliber.

[1362] Guderian had taken over the preparation of trench positions behind the Eastern Front. These were equipped with security guards to prevent the troops from simply running across the lines during retreat. All possible sorts of men and materials had been collected for this project. The fortress antitank gun detachments mentioned here also belonged to the units—which, of course, were anything but high quality—originally set up for this purpose.

[1363] Probably meaning the Metz Infantry School, as the preceding text fragments indicate.

[1364] The 501st and 504th Antitank Gun Detachments were not among those somewhat doubtful fortress antitank gun units; they were good motorized and towed Army troops.

[1365] From here on (page 34 of the transcription) the lower parts of the typewritten pages are missing entirely, as nothing useful could be deciphered from the totally charred remains.

[1366] Walter Schroth; born June 3, 1882; 1903 Second Lieutenant, 46th Infantry Regiment; Reichswehr; 1931 Colonel; 1933 Commander of an infantry school; 1934 Major General; 1935 Commander, 1st Infantry Division; 1936 Lieutenant General; 1938 General of Infantry and Commanding General, XII Army Corps; May 1942 Commander, Military District IV; and after May 1943, Commander, Military District XII (Wiesbaden). Schroth was killed in an accident on October 6, 1944. Hitler's praise back then did not hinder Schroth from leading the generals' seniority roll with a date of rank of February 1, 1938.—*Source: Siegler, p. 138; Rangliste 1944-45, p. 15; Keilig 211/307.*

[1367] Military District XIII: Nuremberg (Franken, Upper Palatinate, western Sudetenland); Military District V: Stuttgart (Württemberg, Baden, Alsace).

[1368] The improved Tiger model (special motor vehicle 182), which became known by the enemy name "Königstiger" ["King Tiger"] had five instead of four outer wheels and rounded, sloping surfaces, one gun with caliber length L 71 (barrel length 6.25 m compared to 3.97 m for Tiger I), and increased mobility.—*Source: Von der Panzerattrappe..., p. 27; Lusar, p. 30; Senger-Etterlin, p. 27.*

[1369] Before the war, the upper Rhine had been fortified to a limited depth—in association with the Western Wall—by concret combat positions, which, in consideration of flood danger, had to be built not under water but above the ground, and which were easily neutralized by methods known in 1944. The necessary field improvements to the upper Rhine positions had been made at the beginning of the war, but those positions had mostly collapsed again over the course of the years.

[1370] This refers to the transfer of trucks from the Luftwaffe to the Army). By this time, relations between Hitler and Göring had already cooled significantly; just half a year earlier Hitler probably wouldn't have made such a decision without consulting Göring.

1371 Hitler's remark about the Commander-in-Chief of the Armed Forces as a "Reich Defense General Staff" is a fantasy that even he could not really have believed in anymore. The former Reich War Minister v. Blomberg had established the position of Commander-in-Chief of the Armed Forces, the highest command authority over the branches of the Armed Forces, as early as 1933, but it had never gotten off the ground. The Army General Staff, as well as the Commanders-in-Chief of the Navy and the Luftwaffe, had taken care right from the beginning to maintain their independence. Their resistance, after Blomberg's departure in February 1938, was not directed against Hitler, who, from this point on, held not only the representative but also the actual command over the entire Armed Forces as head of the Armed Forces High Command; rather, they fought against the coordinating activities of a superior operations staff. Hitler himself further weakened the Armed Forces High Command when he did not name a successor to Blomberg, but was satisfied with the weak personality of Keitel as—in effect—"Chief of Staff of the Armed Forces High Command" (abbreviated "Chief Armed Forces High Command"). Even if one claims that this German arrangement of the top military leadership represented a barely functional solution at the beginning of the war, its basic concept was upset in 1940 already by the establishment of the so-called Armed Forces High Command war theaters. From that time on, there were essentially two Chiefs of Geeral Staff. So when the highest command began to interfere more and more in the operational command of the various branches of the Armed Forces, and even in their tactical command (Hitler as Commander-in-Chief of the Army), severe tensions were unavoidable. In addition, the unequal influence of the personalities also played a role. The efforts by the Commanders-in-Chief of the Navy and the Luftwaffe to maintain independence made an actual Armed Forces command possible only through the person of the "Führer and Commander-in-Chief," while the relatively weak personalities of the Chief of the Armed Forces High Command and the Chief of the Armed Forces Operations Staff could never prevail against him. The influence of the Armed Forces High Command in all armament matters—in any case not significant—was taken away by Speer, to some degree as early as 1940, and then completely in the summer of 1942. And with the change of the Chief of General Staff of the Army in September 1942, the Chief of the Armed Forces Operations Staff was finally and also officially excluded from the Armed Forces command. From that point on, the Armed Forces Operations Staff was left only with its name, and it was in fact no longer Hitler's military staff for the entire conduct of the war, but instead an incomplete operations staff for those parts of the Army employed in the Armed Forces High Command theaters of war in the North, West and South—with virtually no influence on the Navy and Luftwaffe. The entire command was still led only by the "Führer and Commander-in-Chief." There was no Chief of Staff to coordinate the three branches of the Armed Forces, or even operations with allies. There was hardly any strategic plan anymore, and the operational suggestions from the Chiefs were notably one-sided. Another consequence of these splintering tendencies was the 1944 transfer of the Information and Intelligence Service [Nachrichten- und Abwehrdienst] to the Reich Security Chief's Office of the SS. Zeitzler, Manstein and others, incidentally, had already tried long before to convince Hitler of the necessity of organizing the Armed Forces command differently. (See also above note 944).

[1372] Meaning guns with Lafette carriages and chassis (special trailers)—so, on the one hand, without the concrete pedestals (stationary), but also without tractors (motorized). On September 1, 1944, the mobility of the available Luftwaffe anti-aircraft batteries was as follows:

	Motorized	Partially Motorized	Mobile	Stationary
Light and medium	128	31	510	452
Heavy	228	44	612	1175

– *Source: Koch: Flak, p. 177.*

[1373] Julius Schaub; born August 20, 1898; pharmacist; 1917-20 soldier; then constant companion of Hitler; together with him in Landsberg (verdict: 1 year, 3 months); end of 1924 Hitler's adjutant; after 1933 as personal adjutant also in the Reich Chancellery and later in the Führer Headquarters; and 1936 Member of the Reichstag.—*Source: Reichstagshandbücher; Munzinger Archive.*

[1374] To the Western Wall or to Metz.

[1375] 8.8-cm antitank gun on a Panther chassis; see below note 1616.

[1376] In this emergency situation, Hitler, on August 19, 1944, ordered the Replacement Army to build up these 25 divisions out of nothing. For the most part, he did reach his goal by combing through industry and commerce once again, by reorganizing the Armed Forces (smaller division size, reconstitution instead of replacement, and so on), and by exerting extreme pressure on armaments. The reference here is to the so-called "Volksgrenadierdivisionen" [Volsgrenadier Divisions] "People's infantry divisions," with a significantly reduced size of about 10,000 men. As a rule, these divisions were to consist 50% of soldiers with combat experience and 50% of exemptions from the restriction and shutting down measures [for factories] of August 24, 1944. Two more Volksgrenadier divisions were formed during the last months of the war. In March 1945 the usually reliable American intelligence service identified about 50 of these units: 9th, 12th, 16th, 18th, 19th, 26th, 35th, 36th, 45th, 47th, 56th, 62nd, 78th, 79th, 95th, 167th, 183rd, 212th, 246th, 251st, 256th, 257th, 271st, 272nd, 275th , 276th, 277th, 299th, 320th, 326th, 340th, 349th, 352nd, 361st, 363rd, 541st, 542nd, 544th, 545th, 547th, 548th, 549th, 551st, 552nd, 553rd, 558th, 563rd and 708th, including the reorganization of already existing divisions. The officers' corps for these Volksgrenadier divisions— and also for the 15 "Volkswerferbrigaden" [Volksmortar brigades—"people's mortar brigades"] and 13 "Volksartilleriekorps" [Volksartillery Corps—"people's artillery corps"] (see below note 1377)—was handpicked by the Army Personnel Office. The officers were not allowed to transfer to other units, since they were regarded as the nucleus of the National Socialist "Volksheer" [Volks Army—"People's Army"] which Hitler intended to establish after the war. (See also below note 1407.)—*Source: Order of Battle, p. 140; Görlitz II, p. 369; Wilmot, p. 509.*

1377 With this objection, Buhle wanted to prevent Hitler from taking guns—as often happened—for which plans had already been made. The reference here is to the Volksartillerie [People's Artillery] Corps that were being developed at that time, and which, like the Volksgrenadier divisions, were intended to form the core of a National Socialist Volks Army (see also note 1376). These formations were being built up, first of all, in response to the American and Russian model of concentrated artillery employment, and, second, because of the loss of practically all the artillery located in France. The Volksartillerie Corps, which were equivalent to artillery brigades, were equipped with 7.5-cm antitank guns, 10.5-cm, 15-cm and 17-cm guns, as well as 21-cm heavy howitzers. The numbers of the twelve Volksartillerie Corps: 388, 401, 402, 403, 404, 405, 407, 408, 409, 410, 766 and 1095 (according to Keilig also 406, but not 1095).—*Source: Order of Battle, pp. 39 and 435; Görlitz II, p. 369; Fritz Lucke: Deutsche Volksartillerie; in: VB of Feb. 19, 1945; Guderian: Erinnerungen, p. 328; Keilig 112/9.*

1378 Commander of the Replacement Army, i.e., since the July assassination attempt, Himmler.

1379 See above note 1359.

1380 From Brest (see above note 137).

1381 See above note 1356.

1382 Guderian rightfully criticizes the confusing mess of conflicting and overlapping areas of authority, which was typical of the Third Reich and which Hitler constantly and intentionally created in all areas.

1383 In the Apennines.

1384 At that time, all the Po River bridges had fallen victim to hostile air raids. All attempts to repair the bridges proved useless because of the overall air supremacy of the enemy.

1385 The events taking place in Romania and soon also in Bulgaria made the evacuation of the German positions in Greece urgently necessary, although Hitler had forbidden such preparations just days before. On the day of this meeting, September 1, the Commander-in-Chief of Army Group "E," who had been ordered to Rastenburg, received permission for the "abandonment" of Greece. During the evacuation operation, all men and as much equipment and supplies as possible were to be brought back. On the following day, September 2, the transports from Crete and the Aegean Islands began—first from Rhodes and Kos. The excellent 22nd Infantry Division, which was located on these islands (see below note 1835), was brought by air transport to the mainland without all of its heavy equipment, as it was the task of this unit to secure the withdrawal routes and railways from Salonika–Skopje–Belgrade to the east. Because a complete evacuation of the island could not be guaranteed due to the tense air transport situation, the decision was made around September 20 to leave behind occupation forces (which could defend themselves) on the most important islands—besides Crete, the islands designated were Rhodes, Leros, Kos, Milos, Piskopi and Simi. These Aegean islands, except for Simi and Piskopi (see below note 1933), held until the capitulation.—*Source: Schmidt-Richberg, pp. 34 and 38; Metzsch, p. 62.*

[1386] Meaning the Bulgarians. In fact, the following day would bring not only the defection of Finland, but also Bulgaria. Bulgaria withdrew from the war on September 2, following armistice talks that the government had been holding in Ankara and Cairo since the middle of January. Those talks failed because of the Allied demand for unconditional surrender, which was technically impossible, since there were no Western troops located near the Bulgarian border and the country was not at war with the Soviet Union—it even still had diplomatic relations with the USSR. When the Red Army reached the Bulgarian border on September 2, a new government was established under the commander of the right wing of the opposition Farmers' Party, Muraviev in Sofia. The new government immediately declared the neutrality of Bulgaria; however, Soviet machinations prevented the originally intended declaration of war against Germany at the same time. On September 5, the USSR took the hesitation, provoked by them, as an excuse for the Soviet declaration of war—which was necessary for the occupation of the country, and which could no longer be influenced by the belated Bulgarian declaration of war against Germany on September 8. On September 9, the coup d'état by the "Väterlichen Front" ["Patriotic Front"]—instigated by the Communists and the professional revolutionary Zveno League—finally gave the country into Soviet hands.—*Source: Bretholz, p. 53; Toynbee: Hitler's Europe, p. 627; Seton-Watson, p. 96.*

[1387] Hitler meant the tanks that Germany had delivered to Bulgaria. As Guderian reports in his memoirs, until September 1944 Hitler did not believe the gloomy reports of officers who were located in Bulgaria. Instead, he continued the German deliveries of weapons to Bulgaria until the end (see above note 392).—*Source: Guderian: Erinnerungen, p. 331.*

[1388] As the main traffic route between Salonika and Belgrade, the railway and the road along the Vardar River and the Morava River via Skopje and Nish seemed suitable for the retreat of Army Group "E" to Serbia. A side route, branching off in Skopje, also went through Kosovska Mitrovica and Kraljevo to the north. Both routes were frequently damaged by demolition and air raids, etc., and were at times interrupted. It is not known when the main route through Nish (the town itself was lost on October 14)was cut off; however, the Russians finally cut both routes to Belgrade southeast of the capital on October 10, so that only the route over the mountains and the Drina to Bosnia remained.—*Source: Schmidt-Richberg, p. 40; Metzsch, p. 65.*

[1389] Transcript number unknown—Fragment No. 42—A first transcription, of which approximately half was destroyed. The lower part of pages 1-45 was missing; the gaps are indicated with dotted lines. Pages 46-53 were preserved with only small gaps.

1390 Here and in other places (see the evening situation report on January 9, 1945), the situation is presented by Lieutenant Colonel Waizenegger, Jodl's Army adjutant. It had become the rule toward the end of the war that Jodl was represented by someone else—either entirely or at least for the report—in the second meeting around midnight, during which only the changes of the last few hours were discussed.

1391 The 7th Mountain Division, which had been in Finland since the spring of 1942, covered the German retreat to Norway. On August 25, after various preliminary talks, Finland had finally asked to initiate peace negotiations in Moscow. As a precondition, the Soviets demanded an immediate break with Germany and the withdrawal of the German troops in Finland by September 15. On September 2, the Finnish parliament accepted these demands and broke off relations with the Reich. On the morning of September 4, Finnish troops stopped fighting; the Russians did so as well after a delay of 24 hours. The removal of the German troops and agencies from southern Finland went smoothly from September 7 to September 13. However, the Twentieth Mountain Army under Rendulic, located in Lapland, finally received Hitler's decision on September 5—due to economic interests (Petsamo nickel)—not to withdraw to northern Norway but to move into the Ivalo position on Finnish territory. Because of this decision—and, in addition, after the German forces had made an unsuccessful surprise attack on the island of Suursaari (Hogland) in the Gulf of Finland on September 14 and 15—combat between German and Finnish troops still occurred in Lapland in September. The fighting became increasingly fierce because of the German destruction tactics. So the Finns had been fighting the Twentieth Mountain Army since the end of September—supported by Soviet forces—although they did not officially declare war on the Reich until March 1, 1945. It took until the end of April until the last German troops left Finnish ground, although Petsamo had already been in the possession of the Soviets since October 15, 1944, and the nickel mine in Kolosjoki since October 21.—*Source: Mannerheim, p. 525; Erfurth: Der finnische Krieg, pp. 270 and 287; Blücher, p. 397; Toynbee: The Realignment, p. 261; Meister: Die letzte Landungsoperation, passim.*

1392 Combat Group "Nord" ["North"], which had been in Oslo and Bergen since 1940 and which consisted of two reinforced "Totenkopf" regiments, was reorganized as the 6th SS Mountain Division "Nord" ["North"] in the early summer of 1941, after the transfer to Finland in April/May. This division had been in action on the Finnish front throughout the entire year, and was now withdrawing into Lapland with the Twentieth Mountain Army. The evacuation of its positions, which had pushed forward the furthest toward the east, had initiated the German retreat during the night of September 8; during the next night the Seventh Mountain Army followed. Both divisions belonged, together with Division Group "K," to the southern wing of the XVII Mountain Corps, which formed the Lapland Army.—*Source: Order of Battle, p. 340; Rendulic: Gekämpft..., p. 291.*

1393 The LVII Panzer Corps was located on the new Maros front, which had been occupied after the evacuation of the Szekely salient from September 7 to September 13; the Frankish-Sudeten German 46th Infantry Division was on its left wing in the eastern Carpathians.—*Source: Friessner, pp. 112 and 116.*

[1394] In order to relieve the struggling Sixteenth Army south of Riga, the German panzer forces that had advanced up to the Gulf of Riga (see above p. 484) had resumed their attacks west of Elgava [Mitau] again.—*Source: Tippelskirch, p. 548.*

[1395] Probably the Cyklades island of Thira (Santorini).

[1396] See above note 1325.

[1397] Could not be identified with certainty. Because Temeschburg is located near the Serbian border, and because the 4th SS Police Panzer Grenadier Division—probably the only major German unit (see Rendulic, pp. 129 and 259)—had just been transferred from Yugoslavia into that area, Dr. Hermann Behrends is likely the officer referred to here. Behrends was born May 11, 1907; 1926-30 studied law; 1930 junior lawyer; 1932 SS; 1933 Untersturmführer;1934 Obersturmbann-führer; 1936 government assessor; 1937 SS Oberführer and Stabsführer of the Volksdeutsche Mittelstelle head office; 1941 Brigade Commander; 1943-44 Hauptsturmführer or Sturmbannführer of the Reserves in various Waffen SS units (lastly with the 13th SS Volunteer Mountain Division "Handschar"); March 1944 High SS and Police Commander in Serbia; August 1944 Gruppenführer and Lieutenant General of the Police; and November 1944 Führer Reserves. It can be assumed that Behrends participated in the defense of Serbia and the Banat as reserve commander of the Waffen SS together with an alarm unit consisting of members from various SS offices.—*Source: SS staff files (Nbg. Dok. NO-4066); SS Dienstalterslisten.*

[1398] This most likely refers to the disarming of the Bulgarian 15th Infantry Division in the area of Prilep (until then southern Serbia, occupied by Bulgaria). The last units of the 4th SS Police Panzer Grenadier Division—which were on their way to Belgrade and then further to the area of Temeschburg—participated in this action.—*Source: Schmidt-Richberg, p. 36.*

[1399] The following section discusses the Anglo-American airborne operations between Neerpelt and Arnhem. Montgomery had planned at the beginning of September to drive a corridor northward from his position along the Meuse-Schelde Canal to Arnhem, in order to advance to the Zuider Zee from there, and also to encircle the Ruhr area in the north. To achieve this goal, it was necessary to seize the bridges located between the English Neerpelt bridgehead on the Meuse-Schelde Canal and Arnhem. These bridges were:

1. at Zon over the Wilhelmina Canal
2. at Vechel over the Zuid Willems Vaart
3. at Grave over the Meuse
4. at Nijmegen over the Waal and
5. at Arnhem over the Rhine

At noon on September 17 (the day of this meeting), the following divisions jumped to begin the capture of the five bridges:

the American 101st Airborne Division between Eindhoven and Vechel
the American 82nd Airborne Division between Grave and Nijmegen
the British 1st Airborne Division northwest of Arnhem

At the same time, English armored forces (X Corps) advanced northward from the Neerpelt bridgehead to establish the connection with the airborne troops and extend the corridor. The attackers immediately took the bridges near Vechel and Grave, while the bridge near Zon had already been blown up by German troops. The Nijmegen and Arnhem bridges remained in German possession. During the course of the operations, which were disadvantaged by unfavorable weather conditions, the link-up with the 101st Airborne Division was established on September 18 and with the 82nd Airborne Division on September 19. On September 20, Nijmegen and its bridge, which had remained undamaged due to a German mistake, fell into the hands of the Anglo-Americans. However, the 1st Airborne Division near Arnhem failed, with heavy losses. Thus, the operational goal of the entire mission remained unfulfilled. Out of a division that had landed with about 10,000 men, only 2,163 were withdrawn to the southern bank of the lower Rhine during the night of September 25; 6,450 men were captured and 1,130 killed.—*Source: Wilmot, p. 530; Tippelskirch, p. 523.*

[1400] Karl Maria Demelhuber; born May 27, 1896; 1935 transferred from the Bavarian State Police to the SS as Obersturmbannführer; 1936 Regimental Commander and Commander SS Regiment "Germania"; 1939-40 Commander, SS Regiment "Germania" in Poland and France; end of 1940 Commander of the Waffen SS in the General Government (Poland) and brigade commander; May 1941 Commander, SS Mountain Division "Nord" ["North"]; May 1942 Commander of the Waffen SS in the Netherlands; and June 1944 SS Obergruppenführer. In October, Demelhuber was appointed an Inspector General of the Waffen SS in the SS Chief Command Office, after his previous position was eliminated when the replacement troops were withdrawn into the Reich.—*Source: SS Dienstalterslisten.*

[1401] Meaning enemy transport gliders.

[1402] Originally a division headquarters for the reserve units of Military District VI (Münster), it was thrown into the Arnhem area with alarm unit activations.— *Source: Order of Battle, p. 259.*

[1403] The bazooka, i.e., the 8.8-cm antitank rocket launcher 44 "Panzerschreck," was the most important antitank close-combat weapon at that time. It was a 1.64 m long tube with a gun shield (weight: 9.2 kg), out of which an 8.8-cm caliber rocket with an electrically ignited hollow-charge shell was shot from the shoulder. The maximum range of this weapon, which could be operated by one man, was 400 meters. The most effective range was 100 to 150 meters. An antitank rocket launcher had already been produced in February 1942; however, it was perfected only after the Americans used their bazooka—a smaller one—in North Africa. The "Panzerschreck," which was practically an imitation of the American bazooka, with a larger caliber, reached the troops in the fall of 1943. By the end of the war there was also a 2 m long model with a 10 cm caliber, but it is uncertain whether this weapon was ever used.—*Source: Schneider, p. 236; Lusar, p. 37; Elser, p. 39.*

[1404] On September 4, Colonel General Student (see above note 661)—with his First Parachute Army headquarters, which had been functioning as a training and maintenance organization in Italy, Germany and France up to that time—took over the front along the Albert Canal between Antwerp and Maastricht and closed the gap in northern Belgium. The core of his army consisted of initially six parachute regiments, which, in this emergency situation, Göring had surprisingly offered the Army, together with the promise of additional formations. (See also below pp. 514 and 657)—*Source: Wilmot, p. 509; Siegler, p. 30.*

[1405] An 18-ton armored patrol car did not exist. The "8-ton" is probably meant here, meaning the heavy patrol car of 8.3 t, armed with the 5-cm or 7.5-cm gun.

[1406] Military District X: Hamburg (Schleswig-Holstein, Oldenburg, East Friesland], northwestern Lower Saxony); Military District XI: Hanover (Lower Saxony, Braunschweig], Magdeburg, Anhalt).

[1407] The 363rd VGD [Volksgrenadier Division]—a reconstitution of the old unit which had been destroyed at Falaise—and other divisions of this kind were indeed used against the English airborne troops near Arnhem. These Volksgrenadier divisions of the 32nd wave, whose formation had been ordered less than a month before, were employed prematurely (see above note 1376). The first official announcement about these last-minute emergency measures said wistfully: "The Volksgrenadier divisions are among the troops that have been employed in the last few weeks and which have already helped to catch the Anglo-American armies outside the western border of the Reich." They were formed by Reichsführer SS Himmler in his capacity as Commander of the Replacement Army. The men of this division are, on average, 18 to 20 years old, have completed a thorough training, and a commander of one of those divisions characterized them as follows: 'These soldiers are like young lions who want to compete with a strong enemy. If necessary, they will fight against tanks with 'only a simple gun.' ... These units of the Volksgrenadier divisions consist half of young, well-trained soldiers, but who do not have combat experience. The others, especially the junior commanders and the officers, are battle-hardened soldiers from the East, South and West ... The new Volksgrenadier divisions are therefore an excellent mixture of young, inexperienced men and older, experienced soldiers and commanders. After occasionally being used as blocking units, they passed their critical test defending against the air attack on the Netherlands, and additional divisions have bloodily driven back numerous North American attacks on the Eifel front and on the Moselle."—*Order of Battle, p. 249; VB of Oct. 11, 1944.*

[1408] Already before the beginning of the invasion, the Germans had considered the possibility of dropping the V1 from aircraft. It was determined that the V1, released from an] He 111—for example, from a height of 200 m—could reach an approach height of 3,500 m with its own propulsion. The practical application of the method was first attempted on September 17, the day of this meeting, after the destruction of the northern French launching ramps (see above note 853)—which had been cut off from supply by the hostile advance on Antwerp—finally had to be halted on September 5. The He 111 started with its cargo in Oldenburg, flew to a certain point over the Dutch islands, and then released its load. The English fighter defense, however, caused such heavy aircraft losses that the systematic employment had to be discontinued after a certain time. In total, about 1,200 V1s (another source claims—probably wrongly—only 150) were released in this way, aimed at London; only about 80 reached the urban area. (See also above note 780 and below note 1605.)— *Source: Baumbach, p. 260; Lusar, p. 97; Armed Forces High Command reports from Sept. 2, 5 and 17, 1944.*

1409 See below note 1583.

1410 Near Stolberg.

1411 A town halfway between Metz and Nancy—unless it was written incorrectly and Nomexy, 15 kilometers north of Epinal, was meant.

1412 Halfway between Epinal and Vesoul. Jussey lies about 40 km west-southwest of Fougerolles.

1413 It is unclear whether the reference is to Rundstedt or Blaskowitz.

1414 The 16th Infantry Division had sustained heavy losses in the last few days in the area around Nancy, and, with the addition of numerous local units, had to be practically reconstituted as the 16th Volksgrenadier Division of the 32nd wave. However, the First Army may actually have been meant here, since the Ninetenth Army—which was moving up the Rhône Valley from the French Mediterranean coast and which was finally put into action in Upper Alsace—was located considerably further south.—*Source: Order of Battle, p. 144.*

1415 From central and southern France.

1416 Meaning the Russians.

1417 The 1st Cossack Cavalry Division, under the command of Lieutenant General Helmuth v. Pannwitz (see below note 1839), which had been established during the first half of 1943 in Mielau, had been involved in the partisan operations in Yugoslavia (see above note 484 and note 741) since September 1943. When Pannwitz faced materiel difficulties in the summer of the following year, during the enlargement—at his request—of his division into a corps under the Army High Command, he established connections with the SS in July and interested them in his Cossacks. On August 26 he spoke with Himmler and defined the essential elements of the takeover by the SS and the enlargement to the XV (SS) Cossack Cavalry Corps: insignia and uniforms were to remain unchanged "initially," but the Cossacks would be educated about the SS and its spirit. In addition, Pannwitz was promised the unified command of the Cossacks who were located in the area ruled by Germany, including the units then trekking to the Adriatic coast after their hasty flight through Russia. The Cossacks mentioned here in connection with the Western Front were probably the reserve units that had been located in France and which consisted of several thousand men. (See also below note 1452)—*Source: Aktennotiz RFSS from Aug. 26, 1944 (Nbg. Dok. NO-2423); Thorwald: Wen sie..., pp. 249, 311 and 345; Aufzeichnungen von Constantin Wagner und Artur Timm (Thorwald Material in the IfZ).*

1418 In 1940, while breaking through the Maginot Line. [—] Hitler's assumptions about the hostile attack plan were wrong, though in principle operationally correct. The Allies proceeded differently at that time, to the great annoyance of Montgomery. While he was demanding the bulk of forces and supply, in order to—just as Hitler assumed here—invade the northern German lowlands via Belgium and the Ruhr area, Eisenhower was not ready to decide on that. Instead, he left it in the hands of Bradley's American army group to advance on southern Germany, with the result that both army groups remained stuck at the beginning of winter in the area of the Western Wall. (See also above note 1246.)— *Source: Wilmot (Engl.), pp. 460 and 562.*

1419   In East Prussia. The 349th Infantry Division was replenished in August/September after heavy losses during the Soviet summer offensive, and was also reorganized into a Volksgrenadier division. The division was based in East Prussia (Military District I) and was also located there at the time of this meeting.— *Source: Order of Battle, p. 245.*

1420   The Führer-Grenadier Brigade was established as an independent Army unit at the beginning of 1944. It consisted of two panzer grenadier battalions, one panzer detachment, one assault gun detachment and one anti-aircraft detachment. The brigade, which was well equipped with staff and materiel, was located in Rastenburg in order to secure the Führer Headquarters—until it took part in the Ardennes offensive in December with the Fifth Panzer Army. Afterward it was pulled out of the Western Front once again and filled up to form a division, then employed in the East with Army Group Vistula—first in Pomerania, and then in Kottbus during the final weeks of the war. (See also below note 1809.)—*Source: Order of Battle, p. 86; Tippelskirch, p. 603.*

1421   The reference is to an airborne landing in the area of the Führer Headquarters in East Prussia.

1422   With their special trains, Göring ("Asien" ["Asia"]), Himmler ("Heinrich") and Ribbentrop ("Westfalen" ["Westphalia"]) usually remained near Rastenburg in order not to lose contact with the "court."

1423   To the West. The 25th Panzer Grenadier Division had suffered severe losses during the summer in the area of Minsk, and was located at that time in Grafenwöhr for replenishment. The division would now be thrown into the Lorraine front.—*Source: Order of Battle, p. 309.*

1424   Not ascertained. The former Commander, X Expeditionary Headquarters, Major General Georg-Thilo Baron v. Werthern, could hardly be meant here.

1425   The employment of the Replacement Army against airborne landings, labor unrest among foreign workers, etc. had been restructured by Colonel General Fromm at the end of 1943. The new system defined, for example, how an operational battalion should be formed out of a replacement regiment and how it should be employed. These new orders were released with the code name "Valkyrie," which the Bendler Strasse people tried to use during the failed mobilization of the Replacement Army against the SS and the party on July 20, 1944. When Himmler became Commander of the Replacement Army, he formed units for the front using the "Valkyrie" system. It is these units that are referred to here.

1426   Stationary artillery detachments, equipped partly with German—but mostly captured—weapons, activated in France in late summer because of the heavy artillery losses.—*Source: Order of Battle, p. 39.*

[1427] An English military mission had already been with the Tito troops since May 1943. Jodl's claim that the English had also been identified with the "nationalist partisans" is probably based on a mix-up with the Americans. At the end of May 1944, the British government recalled its representative to the Četniks, who had been there since October 1941. An American mission under Colonel McDowell, on the other had, stayed until November 15, 1944, with the Mihailović units, which were on their way from liberated Serbia—now ruled by Tito—to Bosnia, etc.—*Source: Churchill V/2, p. 169; Dedijer, pp. 189 and 203; Fotitch, pp. 202, 268, 277 and 282; Lazitch, p. 63.*

[1428] The DNB reported the morning of September 17 from Madrid: "'*Informaciones*' reports from Buenos Aires that the news coming from the Brazilian-Uruguayan border speaks of serious events in Brazil. Although the strict Brazilian press censorship did not allow any news to come through, it is known that all telephone and telegraph connections have been disconnected for the last 48 hours. People speak of a military movement and the arrest of numerous generals and leading Brazilian personalities. The troops were in their garrisons, and the military parade that had been planned for the Brazilian national holiday was canceled." No further reports followed.—*Source: DNB of Sept. 17, 1944.*

[1429] According to a report published that day, General Eisenhower had ordered that a proclamation, signed by him, be posted in all German towns occupied by the Allies. The proclamation contained the following statements: "We come to you as victors, but not as oppressors. We will extinguish National Socialism in all its forms; all racial laws—and all laws in general, which were passed under the ideology of the Nazis—will immediately be repealed." The proclamation also named thirty state and party organizations that had been disbanded. The following day Eisenhower announced the establishment of the Allied Military Government for Germany. Nothing is known about a German counter-proclamation.—*Source: NZZ of Sept. 17 and 19, 1944 (morning edition).*

[1430] See above note 429.

[1431] Siegfried Kasche; born June 18, 1903; cadet institute; 1918 participant in the Spartakiad competitions; 1919 Baltic Freikorps; various positions in industry; 1926 NSDAP; 1928 to 1931 deputy Gauleiter Ostmark, 1930 MdR [member of the Reichstag], 1932 Commander SA group Ostmark; 1934 SA group Lower Saxony; 1937and SA group Hansa and SA Obergruppenführer. On April 20, 1941, Kasche was named one of five "SA diplomats" to be sent to the Southeast to the German legation in Agram. In contrast to the German authorized representative, General Glaise-Horstenau, who had in the meantime been replaced by Lieutenant General Juppe at the beginning of September 1944 and later (in December) by SS Obergruppenführer Prützmann, he was unconditionally on the side of Pavelic and significantly overestimated the unstable Ustashe regime. On June 7, 1947, in the trial of Kvaternik and others, Kasche was sentenced by the Supreme Court of VR [the Free Republic of] Croatia to be hanged.— *Source: VB of April 21, 1941; Illustrierter Beobachter of Aug. 14, 1941; Matl: Jugoslawien, p. 106; Keesings Archive 1946-47, p. 1109; Kiszling, pp. 171 and others.*

[1432] Dr. Ante Pavelic, the Croatian "Poglavnik," held a speech at a Ustashe meeting on September 7. Among other things, the following was explained: "Even if the enemy is achieving some success at the moment, and even if certain statesmen become weak, I personally believe in our victory and the victory of our allies. We want to work and fight, and the victory will be ours. We will endure it together with our allies and we will win together with our allies. The Croatian people will not betray themselves or their allies." At that time, Pavelic had just reorganized his government; he had excluded the former Minister of the Interior Lorkovic, the War Minister Vokic and others from the Ustashe, and had ordered their arrest.—*Source: Keesings Archive 1944, p. 6516.*

[1433] The "Danish National Council" in London had called upon its people to strike—from noon on September 16 until September 18—in protest against the transportation of about 190 Danish political prisoners out of the concentration camp in Froeslev to Germany. The transfer of the prisoners into the Reich was thought to be a reprisal in response to increased Danish sabotage action, and had already caused spontaneous strikes the day before in the area of Froeslev, in northern Schleswig. The strike order, which had been spread by flyers, was followed, despite the German threat of drastic countermeasures. The strike mostly affected the traffic system, which was paralyzed in places, so the German military occupied several railway stations and German railway workers took over the western routes. Because the strike threatened to become a general strike, the High SS and Police Commander Denmark, SS Obergruppenführer Pancke, declared—on Hitler's orders—a police state of emergency on the morning of September 19, and ordered the Danish police disarmed. In most of the cities, this measure brought about a two-day general strike. There was also shooting in front of the castle in Copenhagen when the royal guards thought they would be disarmed as well. The incident cost 8 lives and was only settled when the Danish king stepped in. There had also been a general strike in Copenhagen on June 30, 1944, protesting 8 death sentences against Danes accused of sabotage; in mid-August a smaller strike had broken out in Jutland.—*Source: NZZ of Sept. 18, 1944 (midday edition); Nbg. Dok. NG-5812 and NG-5244; Toynbee: Hitler's Europe, p. 532; Ausarbeitung WFSt/KTB [Armed Forces Operations Staff/War Diary] "Der nördliche Kriegesschauplatz, II. Teil" (Nbg. Dok. 1795-PS).*

[1434] Wipert v. Blücher; born July 14, 1893; since 1911 in the foreign service; 1931 envoy in Teheran; and envoy in Helsinki from May 1935 until the breaking off of diplomatic relations on September 2, 1944.—*Source: Degeners Wer ist's, p. 140; Blücher, passim.*

[1435] Antti Hackzell; born September 20, 1881; before World War I lawyer in St. Petersburg; after the war a long-time Finnish envoy in Moscow; 1932 to 1936 Foreign Minister in the Kivimäki cabinet; one of the leaders of the Sammlungspartei [Unity Party]; and chairman of the Finnish employer associations. Hackzell was named Prime Minister on August 8, 1944, after the presidential change and the resignation of the Linkomy cabinet (see above note 776), and led the delegation to Moscow for armistice negotiations in September. On September 14, the first day of the conference there, he suffered a cerebral

stroke, which ended his political career. On Saturday, September 16, the following medical bulletin was published in Moscow: "During the last 24 hours, the
condition of the Finnish Prime Minister Hackzell has worsened considerably as
a result of an inflammation of the lower part of the right lung. The patient is
gradually losing consciousness. The paralysis has not changed. This state of the
patient remains serious." The Hackzell cabinet resigned after the negotiations
concluded on September 22.—*Source: Blücher, pp. 18, 58 and 390; Mannerheim,
pp. 524 and 531; NZZ of Sept. 17, 1944.*

1436 Hermann Neubacher; born June 24, 1893; 1912 Vienna College of Agricultural
Sciences; 1919 forestry engineer; 1920 Dr. of Agricultural Science; until 1934 in
the Public Economy Housing and Building Material Institute (finally as Director General); 1925 founder of the Austrian-German Volksbund [People's Union];
December 1934 NS country leader for Austria; 1935 imprisoned for membership in the illegal NSDAP and Anschluss [Union] Movement; March 1938 mayor
of Vienna; 1939 SA Gruppenführer (1944 Obergruppenführer); January 1940
with the German legation in Bucharest as special envoy for economic issues,
and later authorized representative for oil matters in the Southeast; October
1942 special representative of the Reich for economic and financial issues in
Greece, and after August 1943, special deputy representative of the Foreign
Office for the Southeast, responsible for the coordination of German policy in
Serbia, Montenegro, Greece and—soon after—Albania, and also for the unified
leadership of the fight against Communism in the Southeast. This assignment
explicitly included the authority to organize the national anti-Communist forces
in the individual countries and to negotiate with the "partisan band leaders."
Neubacher's appointment, for all practical purposes, initiated a new German
policy of cooperation with the national resistance groups in the Southeast that
were threatened by advancing Bolshevism. In August 1951, Neubacher was sentenced by the military court in Belgrade to 20 years in prison; however, he was
released in November 1952. He then became an economic advisor and city
planner in Addis Ababa, and, later, was active in the administration of various
state institutions in Austria.—*Source: Nbg. Dok. NG-2861 (SA staff files) and NG-
3439; Munzinger Archive; Matl: Jugoslawien, p. 108; Neubacher, passim; Süddeutsche
Zeitung of Jan. 19, 1959.*

1437 Meaning to go over to the other side. Tito had guaranteed every Croatian who
joined the "People's Liberation Army" by September 15, 1944 would go unpun-
ished. This led to the break up of almost all regular Croatian units. The hated
Ustashe, of course, could not count on any pardon.—*Source: Matl: Jugoslawien, p. 108.*

1438 See above note 587. See also note 1431.

1439 Lothar Rendulic; born November 23, 1887; 1910 Second Lieutenant k.u.k.,
99th Infantry Regiment; after World War I Austrian Federal Army; studied law
(Dr. of Law); 1933 Colonel and Austrian military attaché in Paris; 1938 Armed
Forces, Chief of Staff, XVII Army Corps; 1939 Major General; 1940 Commander, 14th Infantry Division; after October, commander, 52nd Infantry Division; 1941 Lieutenant General; end of 1942 Commanding General, XXXV
Army Corps and General of Infantry; April 1943 Commander-in-Chief, Second

Panzer Army (Southeast); April 1944 Colonel General; June 1944 Commander-in-Chief, Twentieth Mountain Army in northern Finland and Norway; January 1945 Commander-in-Chief, Army Group North; March 1945 Commander-in-Chief, Army Group Courland; and (March 25) Commander-in-Chief, Army Group South. In Nuremberg in 1948, Rendulic was sentenced to 20 years in prison; he was released in December 1951.—*Source: Rendulic, passim; Munzinger Archive; Siegler, p. 134; Keilig 211/267.*

[1440] Glaise-Horstenau and Rendulic, as well as Neubacher and Sonnleithner, were from Austria.

[1441] Artur Phleps; born November 29, 1881 in Transylvania; cadet school in Pressburg [Bratislava]; Austrian officer; 1918-19 Chief of Staff of a Transylvanian division; transferred to the Romanian Army and promoted to division general; 1941 released at his own request and joined the Waffen SS as volunteer; SS brigade commander and commander of a combat group in the Ukraine; 1942 commander of the newly established 7th SS Volunteer Mountain Division "Prince Eugen"; and summer 1943 as Obergruppenführer and Commanding General, V SS Mountain Corps. Phleps flew to Transylvania in September 1944 in order to help with the defense of his homeland, and was supposedly killed in action there on September 21, i.e., four days after this meeting. The circumstances of his death, however, have not been completely clarified. He was supposedly shot after his capture by a Soviet officer, to prevent his escape during a German air attack; however, it was also said—although it is probably sheer speculation—that Phleps was killed on Himmler's order.—*Source: Krätschmer, p. 202; Hausser, p. 106; SS Dienstaltersliste 1942; Reitlinger: The SS, p. 200; Kern, p. 160.*

[1442] See above p. 513 and note 1433.

[1443] The medium armored personnel carrier Sd.Kfz. [Special Motor Vehicle] 251—originally (251/1) equipped with two machine guns—was armed in the 251/9 version with the 7.5-cm StuK [assault gun] L/24, in the 251/21 version with a 2-cm or 1.5-cm three-barreled anti-aircraft gun, and in the 251/17 version with a 2-cm anti-aircraft gun.—*Source: Senger-Etterlin, p. 48.*

[1444] Transcript No. 567/44—Fragments No. 2 and 3—Completely preserved.

[1445] Szolnok had been lost on November 4.—*Source: Friessner, p. 171.*

[1446] The panzer advance against the Russian flank just outside Budapest had come from the northeast, starting in the Pils area and moving in the direction of Ujhartyan. The enemy then retreated from the penetration area on the southeast edge of Budapest back behind the Taksony–Monor line on November 6, the day of this meeting.—*Source: Friessner, p. 168.*

[1447] The 44th Infantry Division, after May 1943 the German Infantry Division *Hoch- und Deutschmeister*, was established in 1938 from the Viennese 4th Regiment "Hoch- und Deutschmeister" and had been employed in the Polish and French campaigns as well as in the suthern sector of the Eastern Front. The division was destroyed in the Stalingrad pocket, but was newly formed in France in April 1943 and was employed in Italy after August 1943 (see above note 609).—*Source: Order of Battle, p.153; Rönnefarth, passim.*

1448 After each situation report, a brief summary of the important results was made for the officers in the Armed Forces Operations Staff. The preserved abstract for the present meeting (Jodl made a note every day) says: "The Führer orders the transfer of the 44th Infantry Division to the command of the Army General Staff. There the division will be employed on the far-right wing of Army Group South, to ensure a tight connection between the northern wing of Army Group "F" and Army Group South on the Danube." (See also below pp. 530 and 532.)—*Source: Nbg. Dok. 1787-PS.*

1449 Jodl's obvious uncertainty led to the following order to his staff on November 6, 1944: "When reporting the strength of the different divisions (represented in colored columns), from now on the ration strength, etc., must be reported."— *Source: Nbg. Dok. 1787-PS.*

1450 The 31st Waffen SS Infantry Division was formed for the first time in September 1944 (regarding the second formation, see also note 532) and consisted of—as Fegelein corrects himself on p. 686—Hungarians, except for cadre personnel. At this point, he obviously confuses it with the 600th Infantry Division (Russian), which was then being formed at the Münsingen troop training grounds as the 1st Vlasov Division, incorporating the remains of the Kaminski Brigade (see also note 722) and parts of the Belorussian 30th SS Armed Infantry Division (Siegling)—which had been decimated on the way back from France. As a matter of fact, there was little chance for confusion here, but in his head many things were muddled. Perhaps Fegelein had just heard about this re-formation and was throwing together random bits of knowledge to give at least some sort of answer.—*Source: Thorwald: Wen sie..., pp. 434 and 457; Order of Battle, p. 349.*

1451 Hans Siegling, who was born on December 24, 1912, was—from August 14, 1944, SS Obersturmbannführer and Lieutenant Colonel in the municipal police—commander of the Belorussian 30th SS Waffen Grenadier Division, which, for all practical purposes, consisted of only one regiment. This division was renamed in March 1945 as the "Waffen SS Infantry Brigade (Belorussian)." See also below note 1995.—*Source: SS Dienstaltersliste 1944; Order of Battle, p. 626.*

1452 Because of the missing map indications, it is impossible to establish with any degree of certainty what is meant by "here." At this time, the real Cossack corps (see above note 1417) was in Slavonia between Save and Drau, and in April/May 1945 it was dragged into the retreat of Army Group "E." The two divisions reached—although the second one suffered heavy casualties—the English lines in Carinthia, where they were interned on May 12 and handed over to the Soviets on May 27-28—which led to many desperate acts. (See also below note 1839.)—*Source: Thorwald: Wen sie..., pp. 312 and 564.*

1453 After the secret initialing of an armistice agreement in Moscow four days before, the Hungarian State Deputy v. Horthy announced the cessation of hostilities by the Honved in a proclamation to the people of Hungary on October 15. Although the situation in Budapest was cleared up in only a few hours—Operation "Panzerfaust" had been prepared in advance—and although Horthy was led away to Germany and a new government was established under Szàlasi, the leader of the Fascist Movement, signs of disintegration in the three Hungarian armies nevertheless increased. The Commander-in-Chief of the First Army, Colonel General Miklós, deserted with a few of his troops; the Commander-in-Chief of the Second Army, Colonel General Verres, gave the order to retreat and had to be arrested; and in the Third Army, an extensive purge was carried out in agreement with the Commander-in-Chief, Colonel General Hoszlenyi. However, most of the Hungarian units remained, although unreliable and war-weary. This discussion here concerns several penetrations of the Hungarian IX Army Corps lines, which eventually led to the loss of the upper Theiss as well.—*Source: Macartney II, p. 391, especially p. 415; Friessner, pp. 141 and 172; Horthy, p. 281; Kállay, p. 458.*

[1454] The 18th SS Volunteer Panzer Grenadier Division *Horst Wessel* was set up in Hungary in the spring of 1944, by expanding the 1st SS Infantry Brigade (motorized). The division was employed in October to put down the Slovakian revolt.—*Source: Order of Battle, p. 345.*

[1455] Meaning a frontal attack instead of a push into the flank or the rear.

[1456] District town on the middle Wisloka River. Wenck is mistaken. This area was not one of the focal points of the Russian offensive in January.

[1457] Most likely meaning, "…if it does not need to go to the bridgehead…" or something similar. The 25th Panzer Division had come back to the Eastern Front in the fall from Denmark, where it had gone in April for replenishment after experiencing heavy losses during the retreat from the Ukraine.—*Source: Order of Battle, p. 301.*

[1458] The 3rd SS Panzer Division *Totenkopf.* See also note 1332.

[1459] Regarding Soviet artillery, see below note 1602. In the Armed Forces report of November 6 it says: "The city of Goldap in East Prussia has been freed from the Bolshevists. In three day of bitter combat, the trapped Soviet regiments were for the most part destroyed, and the survivors were arrested. Fifty-nine tanks and assault guns, 134 guns of all kinds, and countless heavy and light weapons fell into our hands. Many dead Bolshevists covered the battlefield."

[1460] The Russians had learned quite quickly to use the wide expanse of their territory—mostly at night, of course—to escape encirclement, while on the German side, the expansive territory and decreasing troop strength made it more and more difficult to encircle the areas properly. In addition, there was the toughness of the Russian flanks and the utter contempt for death that the Soviet soldiers demonstrated under the eyes of their commissars.

[1461] See below p. 530. Hitler probably means—correct in the long term—the great bend in the Vistula River.

[1462] After heavy artillery and fighter-bomber preparation southeast of Libau [Liepaia] and in the area of Autz, the Soviets lined up for a major attack against Army Group North on October 27, which was cut off in Courland [Kurland]. The attempted breakthrough failed. On the following day, November 7, a decrease in Russian pressure to the southeast of Libau was reported, and the Armed Forces High Command report of the 8th said: "The force of the Bolshevik attacks against our Northern front decreased also in the area of Autz yesterday... With that, the Russians' attempted breakthrough in Courland failed. In a bitter twelve-day defensive battle, our divisions withstood the onslaught of the superior Bolshevik forces and destroyed a major part of the Soviet assault units, particularly the tank corps. Between October 26 and November 7, 602 enemy tanks were destroyed and 239 Soviet aircraft were shot down over the battle-field, 110 of them by Luftwaffe anti-aircraft artillery."—*Source: Armed Forces High Command reports from Oct. 28 to Nov. 11, 1944.*

[1463] In the course of the Estonian conquest, the Soviets had landed on Dagö Island on October 2 and on Ösel Island on October 5. Dagö had to be evacuated on October 3; on Ösel the defenders slowly retreated to the southern Sworbe Pen-insula until October 7, where they managed to hold on until November 24—toward the end with intense fighting.—*Source: Armed Forces High Command reports from Oct. 10 to Nov. 25, 1944.*

[1464] This refers to the approximately 25-km distance between the Führer Headquar-ters at Rastenburg and the Armed Forces High Command headquarters outside Angerburg. The danger from low-flying aircraft [hedge-hoppers] had increased in East Prussia.

[1465] After the capitulation of Finland and the Soviet breakthrough to the Gulf of Riga, the Baltic Sea came back into the operational area of the Soviet fleet units. Until then, the inner Gulf of Finland [Gulf of Bothnia] had been closed off completely from the Baltic Sea by a double net barrier "Walross" ["Walrus"], which reached almost to the ground, between Nargön and Porkkala. Before the first nets had been laid in the spring of 1943, a few Soviet submarines, just above the ground, had broken through the barriers—which at that time were formed only with mines—and had operated with modest success in the Baltic Sea (sunk in 1941: 1 boat with 3,724 GRT; 1942: 25 boats with 50,664 GRT). Now again, after the re-opening brought about by events in the East, only mo-tor torpedo boats and 22 Russian submarines fanned out into the Baltic Sea, while the larger units were held back in the Gulf of Finland.—*Source: Ruge: Seekrieg, pp. 221 and 296; Rohwer: Die sowjetische U-Bootwaffe, passim; Meister, p. 9.*

[1466] The reference here is to *U1199*, which on October 21 sank a steamer of 8,000 GRT.

[1467] After this meeting, because the Navy wanted to have a free hand and because political considerations played a less important role after Sweden had given in to Allied pressure and practically halted trade with Germany, the German Navy High Command expanded the operation area—which had been limited to the Gulf of Finland since February 10, 1942—into the Baltic Sea. The Germans warned against travel in the operational area, which included by now the entire sea territory east of the line from Rügenwalde to the southern tip of the island of Oeland, except for Swedish territorial waters and the area between the Swed-ish mainland and the island of Gotland. Sweden, which saw these measures primarily as a German strike against its connections with renegade Finland, pro-tested vehemently.—*Source: NZZ of Nov. 13, 1944 (morning edition).*

[1468] The Armed Forces High Command report of November 6 reported on the enemy air attacks: "Anglo-American bomber units and low-flying craft continue with their terror attacks against the western, southwestern and southern Reich territory. The urban area of Vienna was hit extremely hard. Air-defense units shot down 48 enemy airplanes, primarily four-engine bombers." The air attack, which was carried out with 1,200 "Fortress" ["Flying Fortresses"] and "Liberator" aircraft as well as 650 fighters against Frankfurt, Karlsruhe and Ludwigshafen, was reported as follows by the Americans: "The German flak was extremely intense, especially above Ludwigshafen....30 American bombers and 23 fighters have not returned to their British bases. There is reason to believe, however, that some aircraft, including at least 6 fighters, were able to make an emergency landing on Allied territory."—*Source: NZZ of June 11, 1944 (midday edition).*

1469 The Lockheed P 38 "Lightning" was an American twin-engine double-fusilage single-seater, which was employed as a reconnaissance plane in 1942 and as a fighter and long-range fighter after 1943. As a fighter, the "Lightning" was armed with a 2.3-cm gun and four machine guns when loaded with two 450-kg bombs; the fighter had a speed of more than 600 km/h, a 12,000 m cruising altitude and a 1,600 km range. [—] Here the correct phrase is probably "with heavy bombs," which would probably mean only one heavier bomb per plane. Regarding the well-known and partially successful British attack on the dams between the Rhine and the Weser in 1943, see above note 384.—*Source: Hébrard, p. 268; Feuchter, pp. 214 and 234.*

1470 Albert Hoffmann; born October 24, 1907; tobacconist until 1933; after 1922 member of the NS movement; 1933 district propaganda leader for Bremen; 1934 party chancellery; and 1938 as Reich department leader he was censorship commissioner for clubs, organizations and associations in Austria, as well as later in the Sudetenland and in the protectorate, and was therefore substantially involved in the Gleichschaltung in these areas. February 1941 Deputy Gauleiter of Upper Silesia, February 1943 engaged as Giesler's successor as m.W.d.G. of the Gauleiter of southern Westphalia and employed as Reich Defense Commissioner, after June 19, 1943 Gauleiter. Hoffman was member of the Reichstag after 1941 as well as SS Gruppenführer. He was accused before an Allied court in Arnsberg of mistreating shot-down "Terrorflieger," and was acquitted in September 1946.—*Source: Der Grossdeutsche Reichstag, 1943; Munzinger Archive.*

1471 It was Bormann's ambition, with the help of the party's news and information-gathering network, to inform Hitler about air raids on the Reich territory sooner and more comprehensively than the Luftwaffe could via its official channels. Hitler appreciated this rivalry—as he always did—while Göring deliberately overlooked this competing civilian reporting system.

1472 Albert Bormann; born September 2, 1902; younger brother of Martin Bormann; bank functionary; after 1931 in Hitler's private chancellery and its leader since 1933; NSKK Gruppenführer; Hitler's personal adjutant.—*Source: Der Grossdeutsche Reichstag, 1943.*

1473 The Luftwaffe was preparing at this time the so-called "big strike" against the stream of Anglo-American bombers. All commodores and commanders in the I Fighter Corps in Treuenbrietzen were brought together to plan theoretical maneuvers. With an employment of 3,000 fighters, 400 to 500 enemy bombers were supposed to be shot down, from which lasting efects on the Allied air strategy were expected. On November 12, six days after this meeting, Galland was able to report the whole fighter force ready for action, with a never-before-seen strength of 18 squadrons with 3,700 aircraft. More than 3,000 of them— perhaps the 3,100 mentioned here by Hitler—were supposed to be employed in the "big strike." However, this strike never took place, because in mid-November Hitler—perhaps because of the calculations he made here (p. 527)—designated this Reich defense force, which had been built up with such difficulty, for employment in the Ardennes offensive. There, without appropriate training, it received its death knell. The definitive end was Operation "Bodenplatte," flown against the Allied airfields in Belgium and northern France in the late-morning hours of January 1, 1945; this operation did not result in the intended spectacular success.—*Source: Galland, p. 331; Wilmot, p. 596; Heilmann: Bodenplatte, passim; Feuchter, p. 290.*

[1474] On November 3 the Armed Forces report had said: "During the day, Anglo-American terror bombers with strong fighter cover attacked central German territory as well as the cities of Bielefeld, Duisburg and Trier. Eighty-two aircraft were shot down in bitter aerial combat and by anti-aircraft guns. Last night, night fighters and anti-aircraft artillery achieved another defensive success by shooting down 52 four-engine bombers during the British attacks on Düsseldorf. Altogether, the enemy has lost 134 aircraft, including 108 four-engine bombers, over the Reich territory in the last 24 hours."

[1475] The assault fighters—or, more precisely, the assault squadrons or assault groups— originated out of the need to enable the German airmen to employ the classic fighter attack from behind also against the heavily armed four-engine bombers. In the meantime, the German fighters had avoided the frontal attack, in which a lack of heavy weapons could be deadly for them, but in which chances for success were minimal due to the shorter shooting time when flying toward each other. For this reason, the FW 190s of some squadrons (or later groups) were given heavier arms, were armor-plated at the nose, and were employed as Sturmstaffeln [assault squadrons] against the four-engine bombers in the classic attack. The first of these units went into action at the beginning of November 1943. The disadvantage was that the aircraft became so slow as a result of the added weight that they were unable to engage in aerial combat with the enemy escort fighters anymore. Thus, the Sturmjäger [assault fighters] were moved deeper into the Reich, and in the end they flew their attacks only in the Geschwaderverband [wing unit], which positioned the Sturmjäger [assault fighters] in the middle and provided fighter cover. One should not confuse these Sturmstaffeln [assault squadrons] with different later efforts to draw up volunteer ramming or self-sacrifice [suicide] employment—modeled after the Japanese kamikazes—such as the "manned V1" launches. These plans were carried out only occasionally (for example, in operation "Werwolf" on April 7, 1945).— *Source: Galland, p. 281; Baumbach, p. 268; Reitsch, p. 280.*

[1476] If one considers how Göring spent the war until the end—Karinhall, Rominten, Obersalzberg, shopping trips to France, holiday trips to Italy, visits at his

Veldenstein and Mauterndorf castles, and in between "official" inspections of his units to express great discontent—his cluelessness can't be much of a surprise. This discussion is representative of the attitude in the Führer Headquarters, where Göring's reputation had sunk to zero.—*Source: Lange, passim.*

1477 "Failed-to-land reports" were the missing-person reports within the relevant daily mission intelligence reports, as opposed to observed and confirmed total losses. Some of these missing persons had gone down in other places and were later found. An astonishingly high number of aircraft and crew, however, disappeared without a trace—with no indication even to this day of where they might have gone down (see note 1975). Approximately 50% of the "failed-to-land reports" were resolved later, with 35-40% of these confirmed as losses. Thus, 85-90% of these "failed-to-land reports" could be considered as total losses.

1478 Hans-Jürgen Stumpff; born June 15, 1889; 1908 Second Lieutenant; in World War I, primarily in General Staff positions; Reichswehr; 1928 Troop Office; 1933 head of the Luftwaffe's Personnel Department; 1936 Major General; June 1937 to January 1939 Luftwaffe Chief of Staff; January 1940 Senior-Major; May 1, 1940 to November 1943 Commander-in-Chief, Fifth Air Fleet in Norway and Finland; after July 1940 Colonel General; and January 1944 Luftwaffe Commander, Center (February 1944 renamed Commander-in-Chief, Air Force Reich). In October 1947, a British military court acquitted Stumpff of the charge of passing on the "terror flight order."—*Source: Munzinger Archive; Siegler, p. 140.*

1479 Adolf Galland; born March 19, 1912; 1932 commercial aircraft training; 1934 joined the 10th Infantry Regiment; 1935 transferred to the Luftwaffe; 1937-38 in Spain as (among other things) a squadron leader; 1939 Captain; 1940-41, one of the most successful German fighters on the Channel coast and, finally, Lieutenant Colonel and Commander, 26th Fighter Wing "Schlageter"; after the death of von Mölders on November 22, 1941 appointed his successor as "General of Fighter Pilots; December 1941 Colonel, honored with "Diamonds" on January 28, 1942 for 94 air victories; November 1942 Major General; November 1944 Lieutenant General; and January 1945 relieved as General of Fighter Pilots and Commander, 44th Jet Fighter Unit. From the end of 1948 to the end of 1954, Galland was an advisor to the Argentine Air Force.—*Source: VB of Jan. 29, 1942; Munzinger Archive; Galland, passim.*

1480 It is correct that models such as the Me 109 were still being produced without consideration of the fact that they were already obsolete and were competitive only in the East (the Me 109, for example, with the record production of 12,807 units in 1944!), and was to a certain degree the prerequisite for the production records that were established by the Fighter Staff beginning in 1944—at first only under consultation with Speer's staff, then from August 1 under their own exclusive responsibility. On the other hand, it was Hitler who cosiderably hindered the development of new technical possibilities (see above note 858); these had a limit as well: the production number of jet aircraft, for example, was totally dependent on the limited production capacity for jet engines.

[1481] See also above note 1450. When Fegelein says here, "There is almost nothing left of the Russian personnel," this is only supposed to hide his ignorance, which was demonstrated just a few minutes before. No Russians had ever been in this division.

[1482] The name is probably spelled incorrectly (Kammler?; see below note 1941) or it is referring to a combat group rather than a division. There was a Friedrich Kammerer, but at this time he was only an SS Sturmbannführer and was at the Rasse- und Siedlungshauptamt SS [SS Head Office for Race and Settlement].

[1483] In the Warsaw area, the SS Panzer Division *Viking*—weakened but still combat-ready—was supposed to be pulled out for replenishment and for later use in Hungary. To keep the front from losing this division's fighting strength, the *Viking* was supposed to transfer some forces to the 3rd SS Panzer Division "Totenkopf," which was still fighting in the Warsaw area—perhaps 2,000 men, if the junior officer staff of the Totenkopf was numerous enough. (See also pp. 522 and 643.)

[1484] Regarding the V1 shelling of London by He 111s, see above note 1408.

[1485] The following coastal fortresses were maintained on Hitler's order behind the retreating German front in France. Hitler wanted to contain enemy forces and restrict the Allied possibilities for landing. (The fortresses are listed in geographical order, with the day of eventual capitulation in parentheses.)

Gironde South (April 20, 1945)	Channel Islands (May 9, 1945)
Gironde North (April 19, 1945)	Le Havre (September 12, 1944)
La Rochelle (May 7, 1945)	Boulogne (September 24, 1944)
St. Nazaire (May 8/9, 1945)	Cap Gris Nez (October 1, 1944)
Lorient (May 8, 1945)	Calais (October 2, 1944)
Brest (September 18, 1944)	Dünkirchen [Dunkirk] (May 5, 1945)
St. Malo (August 17, 1944)	

—*Source: Armed Forces High Command reports; NZZ of May 11, 1945 (morning edition).*

[1486] Hitler—who, despite sometimes knowing better (see above p. 616), always expected differences in the enemy's camps—found this report particularly interesting because it indicated that the Russians were touching on the most sensitive issue in the Russian-British relationship. It could not be determined whether this news was ever confirmed or not; in any case, it had no significant consequences.

[1487] Sonnleithner is asked here by Hitler to comment on this purely military question, as he was not a born Viennese (born 1905 in Salzburg), but had studied in Vienna and had been working there for many years at the Austrian federal police headquarters and in the federal chancellery.—*Source: Berlin–Rome–Tokyo, Vol. 5, No. 4, April 4, 1943.*

[1488] The reference here is to the only road still open (or threatened only by partisans) for the retreat to Bosnia—if Kraljevo (Rankoviçevo today) could not be held against the Russians. The street went through the former "Sandzhak" from Kosovska Mitrovica or Raška via Novipazar-Prijepolje to Višegrad at the Drina and further to Sarajevo. This "Sandzhak Street" was severely damaged, as were the bridges at Prijepolje, Priboj, Rudo, Višegard, etc. The first serious hold-ups had occurred during the battle for Prijepolje. The Četnik units were also causing a disturbance, as they tried to win the Adriatic and thereby cut through the German movement—as they had also done during the retreat from the victorious Communist troops. The combat group under General Scheuerlen, which had successfully fought for the Sandzhak road, reached the Drina near Dobrunje on November 9. The following day connection was established with the Müller group, which had cleared the above-mentioned road from Kraljevo via Uzice to Višegard.—*Source: Schmidt-Richberg, p.54.*

[1489] At this time, the Commander-in-Chief Southeast was the Commander-in-Chief of Army Group "F," Field Marshal v. Weichs; before the formation of this army group on August 26, 1943, and again after it was disbanded on March 25, 1945, the Commander-in-Chief Southeast was the Commander-in-Chief of Army Group "E," Colonel General Löhr.—*Source: Siegler, pp. 19 and 37.*

[1490] At the request of Army Group "E," the Commander-in-Chief Southeast had ordered the V SS Corps in Sarajevo to send one field replacement battalion to meet the advance guard of Army Group "E" at Višegrad, to start the restoration of the road bridge there. Increased support from the north was not to be expected. The battalion reached Višegrad, but was immediately encircled by partisans and was only freed when the advance guard of Army Group "E" arrived.—*Source: Schmidt-Richberg, p. 56.*

[1491] The Moscow agreements mentioned here were preceded by British attempts—since the spring of 1944—to negotiate with the Soviets' spheres of interest in southeastern Europe, in order to curb the Communist infiltration that threatened there as well as in Italy. Churchill was especially interested in "taking over the responsibility for Greece," in exchange for giving Russia the same rights in Romania. Moscow was willing to reach clear agreements, but these attempts failed because of the Americans' horror of anything that sounded like colonialism and because of Roosevelt's illusions concerning lasting harmony between the Allies. When visiting Moscow on October 10, 1944, the British prime minister had informally divided up southeastern Europe on a piece of notepaper, checked off by Stalin. In commercial percentage calculations, the proportions of influence looked like this (according to the statements of Churchill; in parentheses American information):

	Soviets	Anglo-Americans
Romania	90% (75-80)	10% (20-25)
Greece	10% (–)	90% (100)
Yugoslavia	50% (50)	50% (50)
Hungary	50% (75-80)	50% (20-25)
Bulgaria	75% (75-80)	25% (20-25)

—*Source: Churchill VI/1, pp.95 and 268; Dedijer, p.211; Zilliacus, p. 167; Hull II, p. 1451; Stettinius, p.10.*

[1492] The statement of Prime Minister Papandreu about the Communist militias had been published on November 6, the day of this meeting. The statement included the following: "When the government returned to Greece, the gendarmerie [police force] had ceased to exist almost everywhere; it was replaced by the militia "EAM-ELAS." To restore order, the following resolutions have been passed unanimously:

1. The national militia "EAM-ELAS" will be subordinate to the government. This measure does not apply to Athens, the Piräus, and their suburbs, where the police are still on duty and a militia does not exist.

2. The gendarmerie is to be called "National Home Army."

3. Until the "National Home Army" is organized, its functions will be carried out by a temporary "local brigade" [Ortswehr]. For this purpose, the 19-25 age group will be called up from each province, and will start serving on December 1, commanded by army officers..."

Because the Communists did not allow themselves to be easily eliminated, arguments developed into regular fights between the government troops and the ELAS units. Even military communiqués from the Allied headquarters in the Mediterranean reported on the course of these fights.—*Source: NZZ of Nov. 11, 1944 (evening edition).*

[1493] A transfer of English air combat forces to the Balkans or to Hungary obviously did not take place at this time.—*Source: Royal Air Force III, p. 245.*

[1494] Meaning the Russian. This paragraph probably concerns the English control of northern Greece. Since October 4, British troops had landed in Greece and had succeeded the German troops who evacuated the country that same month—although in practice the British had to share power with the Communist EAM partisan movement. The British had advanced to the western border of Turkish Eastern Thrace, while the Russians had been standing at the northern border since the occupation of Bulgaria in September. The Russians not only remembered with anger the Turkish refusal to participate in war, but they had also focused on the Straits for centuries. The Montreux Convention of July 20, 1936, was in effect by that time, which guaranteed the Black Sea powers access to the Mediterranean, but which, in the case of war, closed the straits to military vessels of all nations at war—as long as Turkey was not involved. During negotiations with the Turks in 1939 as well as in 1940 in Berlin, the Soviets had tried in vain to reach an agreement on shared defense of the straits. In Teheran, Stalin had again raised the issue of the Straits on November 30, 1943, and at Yalta he demanded on February 10, 1945, the revision of the Straits Convention and the removal o the Turkish "hand on the Russian throat." Here, Hitler seems to expect a direct Russian action in the near future.—*Source: Churchill VI/1, p. 331; Bechtoldt, passim; Kirk, p. 411.*

[1495] Sir Harold Alexander (of Tunis, 1946 Viscount of Errigal); born December 10, 1891; graduated from Sandhurst; participated in World War I; 1936-37 adjutant to the King; 1937 Major General; 1940, Lieutenant General and Commanding General, I Corps' 1940-42 Commander-in-Chief, Southern Command; 1942 General; 1942-43 Commander-in-Chief, Burma, then the Middle East; 1943 Commander-in-Chief, Eighteenth Army Group in North Africa; 1943-44 Commander-in-Chief of the Allied Forces in Italy (Fifteenth Army Group); and

1944 Field Marshal and Supreme Allied Commander in the Mediterranean. Alexander wrote a report about the campaign in Italy, which was published on November 2.—*Source: Who's Who 1950, p. 31; NZZ of Nov. 3, 1944 (morning edition).*

[1496] The Allied front in Italy.

[1497] In the Balkans.

[1498] In the November 6 edition, the VB—in contrast to the DNB Commentary No. 39 from November 5—had failed to distinguish clearly between the people of Finland and the "small group of traitors," and to show Finnish resistance against the "orders from Moscow." The VB corrected this mistake the following day, and the Stockholm correspondent K.A., who shared part of the responsibility, also delivered the missing facts two days later on November 8, in a report on the disbanding of Finnish units. This example of National Socialist press manipulation is instructive enough to include at length.

DNB had stated on November 5:

"The Finnish people feel the consequences of their betrayal. [—] The decisive standard Soviet interpretation. [—] Artful misrepresentations by the Finnish Minister of the Interior.

DNB Berlin, November 5. Although the Finnish newspapers, after their sudden change of mind, are trying to keep their people clueless about the severity of the diktat and to make all the reports about its consequences as short and insignificant as possible—while, on the other hand, bringing out the advantages of Bolshevism to the greatest degree possible—the deep concern of the Finnish people about the way they have been led by dishonorable traitors cannot be suppressed any longer. Not the least part of this awaking is due to rumors about the increasing severity of the diktat according to the Soviet practice of interpreting it. The Stockholm correspondent of the Swiss newspaper *Die Tat* also points out the fact that the control commission interprets the original conditions in a way that makes them much more oppressive in Finland. In addition to the increased tribute, Finland's participation in the processes against the forces of the fight for freedom is supposed to be carried out in a way that cannot possibly be reconciled with the independence of the country. Also, the members of the Swedish local delegation who were in Helsinki have reported that the Bolshevists interpret the agreements very freely and arbitrarily. [—] Because of this, Minister of the Interior Hillilä felt compelled to admit his people's concerns about these further developments in a radio speech. In this speech, Hillilä made some statements that cannot remain uncontested. That applies especially to the remark that Finland has lost the war. As a matter of fact, no Bolshevik soldier was on Finnish territory, and there was no cause at all for capitulation. For the people of Finland, it would have been much better if Finland had defended its honor, freedom and independence with the same persistence that is now to be applied to the fulfillment of the Moscow diktat, as Hillilä announces. If Hillilä here thinks he can make outrageous reproaches against the German Armed Forces because of the things happening in Lapland, then these reproaches will fall back on the group that prepared this cowardly policy of surrender and betrayal and willingly misled the German leadership about its treacherous activi-

ties. The Finnish government has broken its repeated promises—not to have any special meetings with the Soviets and to continue the fight—in the most underhanded way. The government knew that an evacuation of northern Finland would take months. If they nevertheless promised something different to the Bolshevists, they could not expect the German Armed Forces to drink the betrayal by its former brothers-in-arms down to the dregs. [—] In his speech, Hillilä could not totally avoid discussing the disagreements about the interpretation of the diktat. He had to admit that all incidents of increasing Bolshevization of public life in Finland directly support the conditions of the diktat, because the Finnish government agrees with the Moscow interpretation every time and has totally given up expressing a different opinion. The traitors who have in the basest way besmirched the honorable coat of arms of the Finnish Army squirm today to keep the truth away from the people, who have nothing in common with this betrayal. They will not stop the terrible awakening that is spreading among the people of Finland and opening their eyes to the horrible process of destruction into which a very small group of unprincipled rogues has thrown them."
In contrast, the next day the VB published the following—as Dietrich says—"self-made" text:

"Finnish government is helpless. [—] The Minister of the Interior must agree to Soviet measures. K.A. Stockholm, November 5. The Finnish Minister of the Interior Hillilä held a radio speech the day before yesterday, in which he tried to counter the bitterness and helplessness that have taken hold of the people of Finland after the recent incidents. The minister had no other comfort to offer than to admit that Finland had lost the war and is therefore forced to fulfill the armistice conditions. Hillilä called it self-evident that certain recent incidents had led to a worsening mood among the Finns, but at the same time called this development unfounded. What had happened thus far was based on the armistice contract and on the interpretation the Soviets had given to each section. [—] No one can doubt that the humiliating incidents that are happening in Finland now are nothing but the consequences of capitulation and betrayal. What comfort one was supposed to find in this remained the secret of Hillilä. The minister proved a true henchman of the Soviets by explaining that the round-ups organized by the commissioners were a measure the Finnish government agreed with in order to keep the honorable shield of the Army clean, and by trivializing the high value of the disbanded protection corps organization. The Soviets could not ask for more from a leading Finnish minister. It could not be more clear that Mannerheim and his Soviet-enslaved cabinet are nothing but the willing tools of the Soviets, whose job is to defend the Moscow dictatorship to the people."
And a postscript from November 7:
"Excuses of a traitor. VB Berlin, November 6. As we reported already, the Minister of the Interior of the Finnish capitulation government, Hillilä, has tried in a radio speech to give comfort—a hopeless task, considering the terrible reality—to the people of Finland, who have been deceived by a cowardly group and betrayed to the deadly Bolshevik enemy. One could not expect such a man,

who was one of the first to help betray his people, to even try to cling to the truth. [—] So Hillilä started with the impudent lie—with the statement that the war had been lost for Finland, and one now has the duty to fulfill the Bolshevik diktat tenaciously and conscientiously. It would have been better and more beneficial for the future of the people of Finland, if the capitulation group had used their "tenaciousness and conscientiousness"—which they are now using to bring the people of Finland under the law of Moscow—to strengthen the brave Finnish northern front, instead of stabbing it in the back. [—] Hillilä was, as everyone knows, the first member of the government to defend the betrayal of his own people and the German comrades-in-arms after the subjection to Moscow and—in the case of a careful implementation of the capitulation conditions—announcing the preservation of freedom and life for the Finnish people. How it looks now, only two month later, is very obvious. Hillilä's appeal for blind fulfillment and slave-like obedience to the Soviets gives a particular impression. It was born in the cowardice of capitulation."

And the correction of the Stockholm correspondent K.A. from November 8: "…this White Guard's position has brought back the Minister of the Interior of the Finnish capitulation government, Hillilä, who had just declared in a radio speech, with doglike submissiveness, that his government would do anything to fulfill the armistice diktat. Faced with indignation from Finland's nationalist and honorable circles, he sent another appeal to the Finnish public and again asked them to submit to the shameful Moscow diktat. It is remarkable, the *Daily Mail* notes, that the appeal has not had much of an effect until now, which shows that the number of people willing to defend themselves against the shameful betrayal of a small group of dishonorable politicians—Hillilä being their main actor—is getting bigger and bigger. The Bolshevists do everything they can to let the Finnish people feel the knout of Moscow…"

[1499] Between Sibenik on the Adriatic Sea and Knin at the base of the Dinarian Alps.

[1500] Istead of "Varanger Fjord" it should probably be "Porsanger Fjord." That is where the central group of the Twentieth Mountain Army, consisting of the XXXVI Mountain Corps and the 169th Infantry Division, retreated (the southern group was on the Finnish-Swedish border road, and the northern on the Norwegian National Route 50), followed by the Finns, after having fortunately passed the straits of Ivalo three days before, on November 3. The Varanger Fjord was in enemy hands by this time, and the rear guards of the northern march group (XIX Mountain Corps) had already reached the Tana Fjord.— *Source: Rendulic, p. 301, especially p. 308; Aufz. WFSt/KTB [Armed Forces Operations Staff, War Diary] "Der nördliche Kriegsschauplatz," part II, p.76 (Nbg. Dok. 1795-PS).*

[1501] In the daily reports—initialed by Jodl—communicating the results of the situation reports, the November 6 account said, "In correlation with the resistance that is now forming in Finland, it is to be reported, through the Armed Forces Press and Propaganda Department and Twentieth Mountain Army, which measures have been prepared to support this Finnish freedom movement and to bring in more of the Finnish troops under Russian command. In particular, strong subversive propaganda must be prepared in case the Finns are forced to attack the Vitdal Position. In connection with our own counterattacks, great successes may be attained.—*Source: Nbg. Dok. 1787-PS*

1502 Already before the start of the Eastern campaign—beginning in March 1941— Himmler had enlisted volunteers in Finland for his Germanic *Viking* Dvision. Although the two-year commitment was not yet fulfilled, it was evident that only a few of the 500 members left from the original 1,000 members of the "Finnish Volunteer Battalions of the Waffen SS" planned to extend their commitment, so the battalion had to be dismissed and sent home by the end of June 1943. Berger, the leader of the SS Head Office, suggested another enlistment effort in Finland, giving the new unit the name 27th SS Motorcycle Regiment "Finnish Jägers [Light Infantry]" to add the incentive of the continuation of the 27th Jägers tradition (in World War I, nearly 2,000 Finnish deserters and prisoners formed a Jäger battalion that was extremely well trained and proved itself on the Eastern Front; it was called the 27th Royal Prussian Jäger Battalion, and, after its return to Finland in February 1918, was a core group in the fight for freedom). Despite toleration by the Finnish government, the plan failed due to resistance from Marshal Mannerheim. In June 1944 Ribbentrop had suggested collecting 1,000 determined Finns for a pro-German putsch, and returned to this idea after the breaking off of relations at the beginning of September. At the same time, on September 5, Hitler approved a suggestion of Army Group North to set up a Finnish 27th Jäger Battalion for Finnish soldiers unwilling to capitulate. The Twentieth Mountain Army tried during these weeks to collect *frondierende* [soldiers who in the confusion of battle become lost and wander around behind and ahead of the front lines searching for their units] Finnish soldiers, and Himmler finally considered new recruitment campaigns. All of these projects failed, however, because an overwhelming majority—even within the Finnish Armed Forces—agreed with the peace policy of Mannerheim; enlistment in the German Armed Forces happened only as an exception.—*Source: Mannerheim, pp. 163, 186 and 496; Erfurth: Der finnische Krieg, p. 279; Blücher, pp. 291, 369 and 406; Nbg. Dok. NG-1579, NO-630. NO-632 and NO 1486; Aaltonen, passim.*

1503 The retreat of the German troops from Finland, in the case of an independent Finnish withdrawal from the war, had been prepared as early as November 1943. Even Hitler had agreed to a planned evacuation, though he had originally demanded that the Germans occupy the Aaland Islands (see above note 1127) and also remain in the valuable nickel region near Petsama in northern Finland— both of which proved impracticable. Thanks to the thorough preparations, the road building, the construction of camps of all kinds and extensive transports under the most difficult terrain, sea and weather conditions, the evacuation was a complete success, although the Finns—fulfilling their armistice contract with the Russians, which called for the expulsion or internment of all German troops still on Finnish territory after September 15—tried to hasten the German retreat by force of arms. [—] It is not clear whether the mention of Narvik is a mistake, or if perhaps instead of the 6th Mountain Division the 6th SS

Mountain Division "North" was meant. From Rendulic's records one can see (and the former commander confirms it), that the 6th Mountain Division stood further north at this time, while the 6th SS Mountain Division—having reached Norway as the first unit of the Lapland Army—might have been here on their march to Oslo, with the motorized units leading and the rest following on foot. In mid-October, Rendulic received the news that he would have to send this division to the Western Front; it was employed on the Western Front at the end of December. Similarly, the majority of the Finland (Twentieth Mountain) Army was sent to other theaters of war, while some of the German troops took up their position for final defense at the above-mentioned Lyngen Fjord.—*Source: Rendulic, pp. 257, 302, 309, 315 and 324; Erfurth: Der finnische Krieg, p. 310.*

[1504] Hitler was especially interested in these divisions—the 2nd Mountain Division, the 163rd Infantry Division, the 169th Infantry Division and the above-mentioned (intended) 6th SS Mountain Division—because they were scheduled for departure to the Western and Eastern Fronts (the 169th for the East; the 2nd Mountain, the 163rd and the 6th SS Mountain for the West. The 560th Volksgrenadier Division also went to the Western Front, from southern Norway via Denmark.—*Source: Rendulic, p. 309; Order of Battle, pp. 189, 191, 275, 319 and 340.*

[1505] The *Tirpitz* was a battleship of officially 35,000 tons (really 42,000 t), 30-31 sm [knots] speed, and with eight 38-cm and twelve 15-cm guns. Construction had begun in 1936, and the ship was launched in April 1939 and employed in February 1942. At the beginning of 1942, the *Tirpitz* operated out of Norway in and around the Arctic Ocean, until it was put out of action for half a year on September 22, 1943, in its net cage in the Alta Fjord by small British submarines. Ready for action again after April 3, 1944, the *Tirpitz* was—almost immediately—severely damaged in its superstructure by air attacks. The enemy continued attacking the ship, concluding with 28 four-engine Lancasters carrying 6-ton bombs on September 15, 1944. For this purpose, the 9th and 617th Wings of the R.A.F., having become known for their dam attack in May 1943 (see above note 384), were moved to the Archangel'sk area in northern Russia in order to get the Alta Fjord within the range of the Lancaster. One of these "tallboys" destroyed the forecastle of *Tirpitz* so badly that the ship was barely in running condition. Because no repair capacity remained in Germany, the ship was brought into shallow water in a fjord around Tromsö (Sandesund) as a floating battery at a depth of 50 feet, which again brought it into the range of the R.A.F. special squadrons. Even before the ship was firmly secured, the *Tirpitz* was ripped open on its port side by numerous direct hits in a November 12 surprise attack by the English (six days after this situation report), who did not know about the irreparable condition of the ship. The ship capsized from the suction of additional 6-ton bombs. Despite the immediate vicinity of the coast, 1,204 dead were reported (Lohmann: 902), as only the keel and parts of the starboard side reached above of the water. Eight hundred and six men were able to save themselves, and an additional 82 members of the crew were cut out from the lower rooms of the steel coffin.—*Source: Ruge: Seekrieg, pp. 24,*

208, 215, 218 and 310; Rendulic, p. 319; Brickhill, p. 221; Brennecke, passim; Lohmann/ Hildebrand, 52/3.

1506 From Stockholm it was reported on November 6: "After German military patrols crossed the Swedish border on several occasions last week to get hay in Sweden, a severe violation of Swedish territory happened on Saturday afternoon (November 4). Six German soldiers crossed the Swedish border in pursuit of three fleeing Norwegians, including a seven-year-old girl, into the province of Värmland. The soldiers continued pursuing them for 4 km on Swedish sovereign territory, and in the course of the pursuit they shot several times. The Norwegians were able to save themselves, and the Germans had to return to Norway without having achieved anything—after forcing a Swedish forestry worker to show them their way back through the forest. The Swedish press appeals to the government to strengthen the border guards..." The following day it was reported that the German legation apologized to the Swedish government for border violations by German patrols that had occurred recently at the northern and western borders of Sweden. [—] Because the Swedish-Norwegian border leads through empty territory, border violations took place on both sides from time to time, and were always settled in the appropriate diplomatic way. (See also below note 1510.)—*Source: NZZ of Nov. 11, 1944 (evening edition).*

1507 There were negotiations underway at this time in Stockholm, between the Foreign Minister and Minister of Justice in the Norwegian government-in-exile on one hand and the Swedish government on the other hand, and the communiqués also mentioned the Norwegian police forces that had been set up in Sweden. This concerned—as was announced—about 11,000 Norwegians who had received arms training in Sweden to "support liberation and the maintenance of public order in their homeland." The first group of this unit was now supposed to be moving into the northern Norwegian regions being evacuated by the Germans, after Sweden and Norway had agreed to a step-by-step employment of these forces as Norway was liberated. The existence of this police troop, which had at first been denied by the Swedish Foreign Ministry when the Germans inquired, made Hitler quite nervous, as he always feared that Sweden would attack him from behind in Norway (see above note 1126).—*Source: NZZ of Nov. 3, 1944 (midday edition).*

1508 Meaning at the Twentieth Mountain Army.

1509 Experts doubt that the Swedes were searching for a reason to move troops into the north, as their strongest military base, the Boden Fortress, had been in this region for a long time.

1510 During a foreign press conference on November 14, a spokesman of the Foreign Office gave a somewhat veiled statement concerning this issue, which was printed also by the national press. In the VB of November 15, 1944, for example, one could read under the headline "Swedish press polemicize against Germany": "The Swedish press these days have taken alleged border incidents with German soldiers at the Swedish-Finnish or Swedish-Norwegian border as a reason for engaging in inflammatory polemics against Germany, without waiting for a clarification of the facts from official German agencies. During the foreign press conference, after the German statement in regard to the Swedish campaign, a spokesman of the Foreign Office declared the following: "From the Swedish press and the Swedish Foreign Ministry, the Foreign Office has learned about assertions concerning some German soldiers reportedly violating the Swedish border. In one case, German soldiers are said to have pursued a Norwegian onto Swedish territory; in another case, it is said that German soldiers took hay from Swedish barns during hay harvest. Considering the very strict orders the German troops have concerning respect for the Swedish border, one must look at these assertions of the Swedish press with a healthy dose of skepticism [sic!]. On the German side, an investigation has been initiated. These are the facts. If one remembers that, at most—and this hasn't even been confirmed yet—a couple of German soldiers ran past the boundary stones along a very complicated border route in the deserted northern Scandinavian region, and they didn't even throw hand grenades or bombs, and didn't shoot with machine guns or undertake any military actions—no, they mixed up a Swedish barn with a Norwegian barn and pursued a Norwegian man, accused of a crime, a few hundred meters onto deserted territory in the high North—then one has to wonder about the press campaign that the Swedish newspapers have started regarding these incidents. In addition, the Swedish government has thus far not confirmed a single border violation by German soldiers along the very long Swedish-Norwegian border. On the other hand, it is a well-known fact that Swedish soldiers in uniform have repeatedly crossed the border into Norway without the German press writing a single line about it. Local military offices have settled these cases to everyone's satisfaction. Also, it is widely known: that in Sweden thousands of fugitive Norwegians are being trained for the so-called police service and—violating the neutrality agreement—are being prepared for employment in occupied Norway; that Anglo-American bombers use Sweden as an assembly point on their terror flights against German cities and repeatedly—not by mistake—violate the Swedish airspace to cut short their attack routes to Germany; that Soviet bombers have dropped bombs on residential areas of Stockholm, Bolshevik agents print their leaflets against the Reich government and against the German front soldiers on Swedish presses and employ them in illegal ways, etc. But what did the Swedish press write about all of this? They found excuses for the bomb attacks by Soviet aircraft against Stockholm. The methodical violation of Swedish neutrality by English-American terror airplanes is noted—if at all—with a minimum of formal protest. The meddling in Norwegian affairs is proclaimed as a self-evident right. The "violated" Swedish barn and the "jumped-over border stream" are blown out of proportion as a danger to Swedish sovereignty and integrity, with angry attacks against the Reich. From the German side, one cannot imagine that this indignation is real. We don't know what the real reason for this storm of bitterness might be. I have heard about several rumors making their way around the diplomatic circles of Stockholm. It is not my assignment to talk about rumors here. In any case, the Germans can note again with great indignation that the Swedish press has made all effort—as usual, without waiting for the facts to be explained—to create an atmosphere of hostility between the people of Germany and Sweden.—*Source: VB of Nov. 15, 1944; NZZ of Nov. 16, 1944.*

[1511] Presumably the counterattack at Stolberg, mentioned in greater detail below (p. 543), is meant here. The Armed Forces report of November 6 wrote regarding this counterattack: "In the penetration area southeast of Stolberg, our fighting troops, coming from south and east, made quite good progress on their counterattack and cut off enemy forces." See also below note 1515. The commander Schmidt, mentioned immediately afterward, could not be identified with certainty; it is probably the commander of the 275th Infantry Division, Lieutenant General Hans Schmidt, who was confirmed as fighting in the region of Aachen in September. Schmidt was born March 14, 1895, 1915; Second Lieutenant, Bavarian 7th Infantry Regiment; 1935 Major and Commander, 3rd Battalion, 41st Infantry Regiment; 1938 Lieutenant Colonel; 1940 Commander, 245th Infantry Regiment and Colonel; 1943 Major General and Commander, 68th Infantry Division; and, from the end of 1943, Lieutenant General (October) and Commander, 275th Infantry Division.—*Source: Keilig 211/299; Seemen; Das deutsche Heer, p. 293; Rangliste 1944-45, p. 27.*

[1512] The following units are, for the most part, units that participated in the Ardennes offensive.

[1513] On October 1, the Canadian First Army had begun to fight for the mouth of the Schelde River, so that the important harbor of Antwerp, which had by luck been taken almost intact, could finally be used (Cherbourg, Le Havre and also Marseilles proved inadequate, as their value was either reduced due to destruction or they were too far away from the operational bases). After stubborn resistance, the German troops were finally driven from the southern bank on November 2. In the meantime, the R.A.F. had, in several air attacks—following an idea of Canadian Lieutenant General Simonds—destroyed the dams on Walcheren Island, which formed the northern bank of the mouth of the Schelde. Three-quarters of the island was flooded with seawater, crowding the inhabitants and occupation forces together in a few coastal areas and the three cities. After Vlissingen and Westkapelle had fallen, an amphibious English unit pushed into flooded Middelburg—mentioned here—on November 6. There, German Lieutenant General Daser, Commander of the 70th Infantry Division, surrendered the German troops—already crowded together in the upper floors of the houses—to the British lieutenant. Hitler for the Ardennes offensive used the time gained by defending the mouth of the Schelde.—*Source: Wilmot, p. 582; Tippelskirch, p. 589.*

[1514] Clearing the mines from the mouth of the Schelde—by no fewer than 100 minesweepers—cost the Allies three more valuable weeks. The first convoy could not enter the harbor of Antwerp until November 28, and it took another month before the leader of the American Transportation Corps, Major General Cross, could announce that the harbor was "in full working order."—*Source: Wilmot, p. 584; NZZ of Jan. 10, 1945 (evening edition).*

[1515] These are towns in the area of Stolberg. The Armed Forces reports for the two following days reported the destruction of the American group that was cut off southeast of Stolberg, and the recapturing of Kommerscheidt. The battles in Hürtgen Forest near Vossenack continued into December.—*Source: Armed Forces High Command reports from Nov. 8 and 9, Dec. 6, 10 and 14, 1944.*

[1516] The following discussion concerns the area Hitler intended to use for the winter offensive. Since the establishment of this front line in September, the front sector between the Ruhr and the Moselle Rivers had been calm, providing a replenishment area for units of the Bradley's American Army Group, which were organized according to their attack plans and operational goals. So in the north there were 16 divisions on the approximately 65 km front line between Geilenkirchen and Monschau, in the south 10 divisions on the 95 km Saar front, and 5 divisions along the whole 160 km in between. Two of these divisions were lying in the north between Monschau and Butgenbach (2nd and 99th) and two or three (106th after the beginning of December, 28th and 4th) and an inexperienced armored division (9th) between Butgenbach and the Moselle (the American 8th Division, also mentioned here, was—at least at the time of the German attack—further north near the Ruhr dams). North of Monschau, the 78th Division joined in, and was also attacked later by the Germans. On the German side, the following troops lined up (from north to south):

1. from the Fifteenth Army, parts of the 272nd Volksgrenadier Division;
2. the Sixth SS Panzer Army (246th Volksgrenadier Division (VGD), 326th VGD, 277th VGD, 3rd Parachute Division, 12th VGD, 12th SS Panzer Division, 1st SS Panzer Division, and 150th Panzer Brigade);
3. the Fifth Panzer Army (18th VGD, 560th VGD, 116th Panzer Division, 2nd Panzer Division, 26th VGD, and Panzer Lehr-Division); and
4. from the Seventh Army (5th Parachute Division, 352nd VGD, 276th VGD, and 212th VGD.

—*Source: Wilmot, pp. 608 and 621.*

[1517] The attack against Diedenhofen and Metz began on the morning of November 8 in the area south of Metz, and continued the following day also north of town.—*Source: Armed Forces High Command reports from Nov. 8 and 10, 1944.*

[1518] On a trip through Savoy, General de Gaulle had announced at a rally in Annecy on November 4 that the war was still not over. To win, one had to cross the Rhine and then finally dictate the law of freedom.—*Source: NZZ of Nov. 6, 1944 (morning edition).*

[1519] Franco, in an interview with a United Press representative on November 4, had declared that Spain had never been Fascist or National Socialist, and had never been allied with the Axis powers—neither in secret nor in any other way. In any case, Spain could never ally with Germany or any other country that was not led by the principles of Catholicism. The Spanish regime would not hinder cooperation with the Allied forces—including Russia. The presence of Spanish volunteers in the Soviet Union was certainly not the result of a hostile design against any country, and the Spanish government had taken the necessary steps to arrange for the return of these volunteers to Spain when the government learned "that the presence of these volunteers might have an influence on the relationship with the Allied countries with which Spain had friendly relations." In a short note, the German press also brought out the tenor of this Franco interview on November 9 (see also below note 1529).—*Source: NZZ of Nov. 6, 1944 (midday edition); VB of Nov. 9, 1944.*

1520 Hitler is speaking here about the Spanish agreement to the attack on Gibraltar, which had been planned four years earlier. On December 11, 1940, Operation "Felix"—scheduled for January 10, 1941—was delayed by Franco's refusal when Canaris asked him on behalf of Hitler for his final agreement. Until then, Spain had agreed half-heartedly, though their continual excuses must have shown that they were not particularly enthusiastic about the whole affair, and they tried to deflect Hitler's urging whenever possible. Franco's arguments on the one hand concerned Spain's poor supply situation with regard to food and other necessary goods, and on the other hand he declared his worries about the fate of the Canary Islands and other overseas properties in the face of the superior strength of the British Navy. The territorial demands of the Caudillo, however—one cannot say if they were serious or if they were simply designed to create artificial obstacles at a time when Franco's belief in Hitler's immediate victory had already been shattered—included French Morocco and Oran, in addition to Gibraltar. Although Hitler was in principle not opposed to the idea, he shied away from an open and binding agreement because of the French colonial armies, some of which were fighting against the English. If it is an exaggeration to call the result of the Montoire and Hendaye discussions "Hitler's option on France," he at least thought to reduce Franco's demands in Africa for the moment, so that even two years later the Spanish ambassador Vidal, in a discussion with State Secrtary Weizsäcker, was able to place the responsibility for the aborted joint Gibraltar operation on the Reich's deliberate sparing of French interests in Africa. So there is certainly a partial truth to Hitler's assertions. [—] The agreement with Pétain mentioned here could be the protocol concerning the situation in Africa, printed by Abetz. Point four says: "The Führer showed the French head of state that after the defeat of England and after the return of the German colonies by the peace treaty, a general revision of the property situation on the African continent must take place. Considering mutual interests, this reallocation must take into account the political necessities and economic demands of the participating European nations. For this redistribution, Germany, Italy, France and Spain will be considered first. If the revision in Africa necessitates a change in the actual French colonial properties, the Axis powers will compensate France territorially through the peace agreement with England, so that the future colonial property in Africa will be just as valuable as the current one."—*Source: Abetz, p. 158; Trevor-Roper: Hitler und Franco, passim; Girard, passim; Aron, p. 293; Greiner, p. 152; Seraphim, passim; Tippelskirch, p. 135; Nbg. Dok. NG-3026.*

1521 Regarding the revolt in Slovakia, see above note 1327.

1522 The 167th Volksgrenadier Division was the reactivation of an infantry division that had been surrounded and practically destroyed in the Korsun' (Cherkassy) pocket during the previous winter. It came to Slovakia for training and relieved the 708th Volksgrenadier Division, which was the reactivation of a division that had been destroyed in Normandy and which was moved to the Alsatian front in the West.—*Source: Order of Battle, pp. 190 and 281.*

1523 The 11th SS Volunteer Panzer Grenadier Division "Nordland" was placed under the III (German) SS Panzer Corps and fought on the northern section of the front after January 1944, now in Courland. The 23rd SS Panzer Grenadier Regiment "Norge" ["Norway"] (Norwegian No. 1) and the SS Panzer Grenadier Regiment "Danmark" ["Denmark"] (Danish No. 1) belonged to this division.—*Source: Order of Battle, pp. 334 and 342; Aufstellung SSFHA from March 26, 1945 (Nbg. Dok. NO-175).*

1524 "Bruno" was the name of a type of railway gun—old 28-cm Navy barrels that had been taken over by the Army in 1936 and set onto railway mounts by Krupp. "Bruno N." might mean a special version of this gun; the only parameters known are the lengths of the barrels and the different v_0 [initial velocity] and ranges of the various types: kz. (short, barrel length 1,120 cm), lg. (long, 1,260cm) and s. (heavy, 1,400 cm) as well as "Theodor-Bruno" (840 cm), with a caliber of 24 cm (ranges: 29.5 km, 37 km, 36 km and 26.5 km, respectively).—*Source: Schirmer, p. 111.*

1525 "Siegfried" railway gun, 38-cm caliber, barrel length 1,976 cm, range: 54.8 km.—*Source: Schirmer, p.111.*

1526 "K 5" was a Krupp railway gun, caliber 28 cm, barrel length 2,128 cm (L/76). The number 5 means that the original range of this gun was about 50 km (accordingly, the names K 3, K 12 and so on show the range, divided by 10). "K 5" was a first-class, very modern railway gun, whose range could be increased to 150 km with sabot projectiles.—*Source: Schirmer, p. 111.*

1527 A railway gun with a 32-cm caliber is not known. Either the reference is to the Czech 30.5-cm Skoda howitzers or—in a transposition of the numbers—the (also Czech) 23-cm guns on the 30.5 howitzer mounts, which, with electric motor propulsion, could also run on rails. The reference could also be to the nine 31-cm coastal guns, built from Rhine metal, that were originally intended for Turkey—for defense of the straits—but were never delivered because of the war.

1528 Buhle probably means the Krupp gun of Sevastopol'—the 60-cm mortar "Thor." It weighed 120 tons and, from a barrel of only 5½ meters length, shot 2,200- and 2,500-kg shells to distances of 2.5 to 6.4 km. There were 3 or 4 guns of this type, which were all blown up or scrapped after bomb hits.—*Source: Lusar, p. 20.*

1529 The English press had rejected Franco's statements (see above note 1519)—as at least the VB registered with malicious joy on November 9—as impudent, ridiculous and fantastic, and had called the Caudillo a usurper and an enemy of democracy.

1530 A corresponding notice appeared, for example, in the VB on November 7, under the headline: "Soviet-enslaved newspapers in Finland." It said: "As *Nya Dag* (a Swedish newspaper) has reported, the Finnish Communist newspaper *Vapaa Sana* appeared for the first time on November 6. Also the radically left-wing pro-Soviet Social Democratic opposition has created itself a new mouthpiece with the weekly magazine called *Vapaa Pohjola*. The Helsinki correspondents of the Stockholm press emphasize that these publications are providing further impetus for Communist and radically left-wing propaganda in Finland. In addition to *Vapaa Sana*, the Communists are planning to publish another weekly magazine, called *Kommunisti*, which will have the character of a Communist/Marxist magazine. Also, the association in support of the rapprochement between Finland and the Soviet Union is planning 'a new mouthpiece.' All these papers will promote Bolshevism."

1531 After British and American oil companies had been negotiating with Iran since the fall of 1943 regarding concessions in the south of the country, the Soviet Union also demanded, in September 1944, a concession for a region of about 200,000 square km in northern Iran. The Iranian government decided not to give any concessions at all for the duration of the war, and not to start negotiations before the Allied troops had departed. After this, the Soviets mobilized the Iranian "Freedom Front," especially the pro-Communist Tudeh Party, and directed massive diplomatic attacks against the government of Mohammed Saed. The government was accused of mantaining a pro-Fascist attitude as well as tolerating hostile action against the Soviet reinforcement lines. Street demonstrations and attacks by the Iranian left-wing press joined in as well. On November 9, the Sad government resigned, but the Soviets were unable to reach their aims with the successors either. Hitler must have followed these incidents in Iran with special interest, because here the contrast between the Allies of World War II appeared first and was initially the harshest. On November 6, the date of this meeting, TASS brought up new accusations against the Saed cabinet, while AP expressed the surprise of American government circles regarding the Soviet action, after *Isvestiia* had severely attacked the government of Iran the day before.—*Source: Kirk, p. 474; VB of Nov. 5, 7, 8 and 10, 1944; NZZ of Nov. 6, 1944 (evenin edition)*.

1532 According to the VB of the following day, the report from Tokyo sounded a little more modest. According to this report, a submarine sank an aircraft carrier east of the Philippines during the night of November 3, while on November 5 a Kamikaze special attack corps sank a carrier west of the Philippines and damaged another one, as well as heavily damaging another carrier east of the Philipines. The Kamikaze "death corps"—in English, "divine wind"—were new Japanese special units of "suicide fighters." The Kamikaze airmen, understanding the desperate situation of their fatherland, threw themselves with their cargo of bombs onto American ships to try to turn back the disaster that threatened their country—in a similar manner to the mythological "divine wind" that was said to have destroyed the invading fleet of Kublai Khan in the Middle Ages. The first non-spontaneous (see above note 215), planned and scheduled sacrifice attack with an undamaged aircraft had been flown by Rear Admiral Arima on October 15, 1944, in the battle over Leyte. This provided the impetus needed to set up the long-discussed units, and, on October 25, the first 10 Kamikazes threw themselves onto a group of American aircraft carriers; one of them sank, and four were severely damaged. The American leadership was deeply concerned about the Kamikazes.—*Source: Ruge: Entscheidung, p. 286*.

[1533] Probably the reference here is to the Republican presidential candidate Dewey (see above note 1135), who, in the last days before the election on November 7, had held several speeches.

[1534] On November 5, the previously latent Finnish governmental crisis had worsened dangerously as a result of the splitting up of the Social Democratic party in view of the new pro-Soviet direction. The opposition against Tanner had increased, and the Social Democrat Fagerholm and the union leader Wuori threatened to relinquish their offices as ministers if serious changes in the government did not take place. On November 8, Social Minister Fagerholm and Labor Minister Wuori resigned, after an expansion of the government to the left had failed; on November 11 the whole Castrén cabinet resigned. The disbanding of the "Defense Corps," a militia organization, and the demobilization led to further tensions. Organizations promoting a stronger relationship with the Soviet Union and branches of the Communist Party sprang up everywhere.— *Source: NZZ of Nov. 6 (evening edition), Nov. 9 (evening edition) and Nov. 12, 1944.*

[1535] The Soviet Union had literally at the very last minute refused to participate in the international aviation conference in Chicago, which started on November 1, 1944, even though the Soviet delegation had already reached Canada. The refusal was based on the participation of Spain, Portugal and Switzerland—none of which had diplomatic relations with the USSR, and which had pursued anti-Soviet policies for years. In Washington and London this reasoning aroused amusement and surprise, and one guessed that the Russians were trying to maintain the unrestricted sovereignty of their airspace.—*Source: NZZ of Nov.1 (evening edition), Nov. 2 (midday edition), Nov. 3. (evening edition) and Nov. 6 (morning edition); DNB of Nov. 7, 1944; VB of Nov. 8 and Dec. 2/3, 1944.*

[1536] The conference revealed a discrepancy between the North American and British interpretations, which was symptomatic of the rising concerns about postwar competition between the national economies. While the English argued for an international organization that would have the authority to assign national traffic shares and establish transport taxes, etc., the Americans favored free competition between the airlines and were only willing to agree to the issuing of international orders regarding technical questions. So instead of a real international flight authority, only a corporation of consultative character would be established. |—| Dietrich worked quickly, and, following Hitler's directions, had the following DNB report about this "aviation affair" released that same evening: "At the so-called international civil aviation conference currently taking place in Chicago, the Americans made an instructive suggestion reflecting Roosevelt's goal of extending the U.S.-American predominance into the civil aviation sector. This American suggestion calls for the election of an 'executive aviation committee,' composed of a number of permanent members, in which only the bigger states are to have seats and again the biggest states are to have a double vote. The Americans regard themselves and the Soviet Union—which is not even represented, as Stalin refused participation—as states that should be given the double vote. The British Commonwealth would not have a joint representation, but would be represented by the individual dominions. Now, obviously based on English suggestion, the representatives of the South American republics have issued a joint statement in which they reject the American suggestion and demand an organization in which every nation would have a seat and an equal vote. The British Reuters office stated that, in view of the joint opposition to the U.S. idea by the South American republics, the conference might experience 'drastic changes.'"—*Source: McNeill, p. 514; NZZ of Nov. 1-6, 1944; DNB of Nov. 6, 1944, No. 63.*

1537 A number of rumors were circulating in the English press at that time, claiming that Hitler had been driven out as head of state—at least de facto—by Himmler. There were various suggestions that Hitler had succumbed to illness, nervous breakdown, exhaustion, flight, death or imprisonment.—*Source: NZZ of Nov. 14, 1944 (morning edition).*

1538 The Ardennes offensive.

1539 Transcript number unknown—Fragment No. 28—During the second transcription in May 1945, the stenographer remarked: "In preparation for the Ardennes offensive starting on December 16, 1944, Hitler spoke on December 11 and 12 to about 20-30 senior officers—army leaders, commanding generals, and division commanders with their staff officers. These officers had been called to the 'Adlerhorst' headquarters for an introduction to their assignments during the attack. This fragment contains the first part—about half—of the speech held on December 12. Hitler spoke without a script; the machine transcription is only a fragment and was made from the stenographic record with only minor stylistic changes. The stenographers who had been responsible for recording the original meeting deciphered the fragment—very poorly preserved, especially the severely burned upper portion of the pages. The parts in parentheses were added based on the meaning and on Hitler's mode of expression." Hitler had arrived at the "Adlerhorst" command post—fitted out for him in Ziegenberg at Bad Nauheim—with a small operations staff on December 10.—*Source: Westphal, p. 279.*

1540 A gap of about three lines; the gaps below are generally smaller.

1541 A speech of a similar kind had preceded this, on December 11 (see above note 1539).

1542 Hitler tries to justify initiating the war (also below on p. 594) and the moment chosen to initiate it. This means admitting responsibility for a preventative war, which was denied at this time in the official propaganda.

1543 This memorandum was printed as document 052-L in the "Blauen Reihe" ["Blue Series"] *Der Prozess gegen die Hauptkriegsverbrecher vor dem Internationalen Militärgerichtshof* [The war Crimes Trial before the International Military Tribunal], vol. XXXVII, pp. 466. It is dated October 9, 1939, and is directed to the commanders-in-chief of the Armed Forces branches and the Chief of the Armed Forces High Command, under the title *Denkschrift und Richtlinien über die Führung des Krieges im Westen.* ["Memorandum and Guidelines for the Conduct of War in the West"] Here Hitler had written quite clear-sightedly on page 7: "Time—in this war, as in the course of all historical events—is not a factor that has inherent value in and of itself, but one which has to be evaluated. In the current situation, under these conditions, time can be seen as an ally of the Western forces rather than an ally of ours." And further below, on page 16 and following, under the headline, "The Dangers of the German Situation": "The first danger for Germany is that in a long war, some states might be drawn to the opposite side, either because of their economic necessity or because special interests have arisen. The second danger is that a long war could alarm states that might in principle wish to join Germany's side—they might remember the last war and take it as a warning, and therefore refrain from joining us. The third danger in a long war is the difficulty of securing nourishment for the people, based on the restricted food and raw-material base, and getting the means to conduct war. Also, the mental attitude of the people will at least be burdened by it."

[1544] Already in his speech before the Reichstag on September 1, 1939, Hitler had stated that he had spent "more than 90 billion for the building up of our Armed Forces." This number is in contrast to the statements of Schwerin-Krosigks, who calculated 60 billion Reichsmark for Armed Forces and armament costs between January 1, 1934, and August 1, 1939 (see above note 862). This figure is validated by all the documents available today. Hitler might have included all costs that contributed to armament even indirectly—such as railway, canal, and street construction, and similar investments—and he probably rounded up to achieve the desired propaganda effect. That Hitler's statements are not quite correct is evident from the fact that in the time span mentioned, total Reich expenditures were 101.5 billion RM.

[1545] The KV I was a heavy tank of 43.5 tons, and the famous T 34 a medium tank of initially 26.3 tons (after 1944 T 34-85 of 30 tons), both armed with a 7.62-cm KwK L/30.5 (T 34-85: 8.5-cm KwK L/53). At first, they dominated everything the German attacking armies could bring up and hindered their mobile warfare. A KV II is unknown; Hitler probably meant the KV I S with the 7.62-cm KwK L/41.5.—*Source: Senger-Etterlin, pp. 120 and 240.*

[1546] Here Hitler is fantasizing freely. Although Britain did start arming in 1936 as a result of the Ethiopian War and the German conscription measures, neither universal conscription nor a two-billion-pound credit was introduced. On the contrary, after one year, on January 6, 1937, the British Minister of Defense, Sir Thomas Inskip, explicitly declared that the government was not thinking—despite problems with replacements—of introducing universal conscription. The armament credits were 119 million pounds in the fiscal year 1935-36 and 188 million pounds in the fiscal year 1936-37. Not until a white paper was published on February 16, 1937, did the government demand 1.5 billion pounds for armament purposes, to be spent over the next 5 years. Because 400 million of this sum was to be covered by a loan granted on February 18, this meant an increase in the defense budget of only about 220 million pounds per year over the following five years. Perhaps Hitler confused pounds and marks, in which case it would be correct that the English defense budget surpassed 2 billion RM in 1936 for the first time.—*Source: Keesings Archive 1935-37; Times from Jan. 7, Feb. 17, and Feb. 19, 1937.*

1547 In this famous, disastrous term—here supplemented by a strange concept of "territorial armament"—Hitler's policy of war lies *in nuce*. Today it seems unbelievable how widely accepted an axiom could have become back then, when—even just considering the unavoidable and significant overlapping of claims—it could only have been valid for a small minority of desperados.

1548 Here Hitler was talking about the "war in sight" crisis of 1875, but he confused the facts for his own purposes. It is true that the Prussian General Staff under Moltke had been rattling swords quite heavily and had approved a preventative war because Moltke thought—which later proved to be wrong—that France would not be able to support its armament weight much longer and would have to free itself of it soon through war (the origin of this crisis was a new French Army organization law, which was quite overrated in Germany at this time). But the plans for this preventative war did not fail, as Hitler pretends here, because of the "internal German parliamentary situation," but because of Bismarck's dislike for preventative war, at least after 1870—which has been substantiated, even if the chancellor was using the threat of war to further his political chess game at that time. Also, this crisis—in which Bismarck tried to halt the French rearmament program through intimidation and bluffing—was the first time, as a prelude to later alliances, that England and Russia took France's side.—*Source: Ritter: Staatskunst, p. 289; Eyck: Bismarck III, p. 149; Herzfeld, p. 222; Meyer, A.O., p. 513; Oncken I, p. 145; Jeismann, p. 91.*

1549 See above note 154, note 553, and note 821.

1550 See above note 830.

1551 This is, of course, just the opposite of reality: The allies dropped out when an offensive war was no longer possible. Hitler expanded on this thought in his daily order to the Armed Forces on January 1, which included the following: "If in this immense struggle—which is fought not only for Germany, but for the future of Europe—we have had to bear setbacks, the responsibility does not lie with the German people and its Armed Forces, but with our European allies. From the breakdown of the Romanian-Italian-Hungarian front along the Don and the subsequent total dispersal due to sabotage of our joint warfare, to the Italian royalty, to the putsch against the Fascist Italy of the Duce who was on our side, it is a straight line of betrayal. It has continued with the dreadful capitulation of the Finnish state leaders, with the breach of faith by the Romanian King and his circle, with the self-abandonment of Bulgaria, and with the disgraceful conduct of the former Hungarian State Administrator. These betrayals had serious effects on the political and military warfare."—*Source: VB of Jan. 2, 1945.*

1552 This passage is not clear, as there are no known memoranda or files from the year 1917 to which Hitler's statements could apply. Perhaps he is referring to the peace resolution of the majority parties, which demanded a compromise peace and the explicit renunciation of annexations; the Reichstag accepted the resolution on July 19, 1917 by a margin of 212 votes to 126.

1553 Compare above on p. 477 the completely opposite statements Hitler made to a smaller circle.

[1554] The decision to take offensive action in the West had developed in Hitler's mind as early as during the Polish campaign, where the extent of German military successes brought up this possibility in answer to the unexpected entry of the Western forces into the war. Hitler's ideas had met with immense resistance, especially among Army General Staff. The resistance was based on various reasons: a general reluctance to engage in war, concerns about violating the neutrality of Belgium and the Netherlands, objections against the winter date initially suggested by Hitler, and other issues. The decisive factor was undoubtedly the fact that the leaders of the Army High Command obviously did not have the necessary strategic genius, which was soon found in Hitler and the Chief of General Staff of Army Group "A," Lieutenant General v. Manstein. Only later did the General Staff accept the plan for the attack internally and then—apart from the usual exactness of the composition—expanded the plan significantly . (See also below note 1601.)—*Source: Jacobsen: Fall Gelb, passim, especially p. 145.*

[1555] Regarding these statements by Hitler, see below p. 566 and note 1605.

[1556] In the European and North African theater, American deaths totaled 174,000 in World War II. Even if Hitler here—as was common practice—used the term "losses" to include wounded and imprisoned as well as deaths, his number seems very high for a period of only three weeks.

[1557] Transcript number unknown—Fragment No. 41—The stenographer made the following introductory remark during the second transcription in May 1945: "This was a meeting that took place in preparation for the last German offensive in lower Alsace and the Saar, with the Commander-in-Chief of Army Group "G" and the Commander-in-Chief West. Following almost directly after this meeting was Hitler's speech to the participating division commanders, etc. (see fragment No. 27). The upper half of the typed fragment of the individual pages is almost totally burned."

[1558] See below note 1919.

[1559] While the Ardennes offensive was grinding to a halt, Hitler believed he could take advantage of the fact that the American reserves were tied up in the Ardennes region and conduct an operation in lower Alsace (Operation "Nordwind" ["North Wind"]). He wanted to retain the initiative in the West at all costs, and prevent the Anglo-Americans from making a simultaneous attack in conjunction with the expected Soviet winter offensive. On New Year's Eve the eight divisions mentioned here—from the Saar region and the area around Bitsch—attacked during the night in the direction of the Zabern valley. After initial local successes and small penetrations into the Maginot Line, the attack was stopped by an advance northward from the Colmar bridgehead in upper Alsace, in the direction of Strasbourg. Eisenhower, who in fact did not have any more reserves in this area, considered a temporary evacuation of Strasbourg and a complete retreat to the Vosges, but was initially hindered by French pride. Soon it became evident that the strength of the German attack was waning, well before the defense of Strasbourg became necessary. The outcome of Operation "Nordwind" ["North Wind"] was little more than the forward movement of the front line between Bitsch and the Rhine, which gained some ground in front of the Western Wall in this area and allowed for the building of a useless new small bridgehead on the left bank of the Rhine, north of Strasbourg.—*Source: Tippelskirch, p. 610; Görlitz II, p. 445; Wilmot, p. 650; Supplements to the KTB/ WFSt [War Diary of the Armed Forces Operations Staff] from Jan. 3 and 4, 1945 (Nbg. Dok. 1797-PS).*

1560 At the site of penetration in the Ardennes.

1561 This reference is also to the Ardennes offensive.

1562 In contrast to the Ardennes offensive (see below note 1589), this attack did not take the Americans by surprise.—*Source: Wilmot, p. 650.*

1563 Hitler probably feared that the Americans—as turned out to be true—would pull back to the south into the region of Strasbourg, and would thereby escape the planned encirclement and destruction. The original plan was obviously to conduct this pincer movement only from the Palatinate or the Saar against American forces in the northeastern corner of Alsace. Hitler obviously did not yet have great faith in the chances of success for Himmler's attacks from the south and the newly built bridgehead north of Strasbourg—an operation that Hitler, against Rundstedt's resistance, would later turn into a main focus.

1564 At the climax of the crisis in the West, when their armies were falling back hastily onto the Reich's borders, the German leadership faced the problem of occupying the Western Wall and the upper Rhine—at least in a makeshift manner—in time to take in the stream of returning units there. As regards the manning of the actual Western Wall, there were several fortress battalions and fortress tank destroyer detachments, etc., while for the upper Rhine there were no troops at all except from some training battalions from Military District V. In this situation, Hitler named the Reichsführer SS and Commander-in-Chief of the Replacement Army as Commander-in-Chief, Upper Rhine. He did so, as he once said himself, based on the following thoughts: "Himmler always has reserves of police or SS units that no one knows about and which he does not give away. If he is responsible for the front along the upper Rhein, he will be forced to bring together everything that he can get a hold of." And Hitler was right. So for Himmler's first employment as a military leader, it was not his military leadership qualities that were decisive. (See also below note 1759.)

1565 The extremely heavy 653rd Tank Destroyer Detachment was the first and only "Jägdtiger" ["Hunter-Tiger"] unit. This Tank Destroyer VI was armed with a 12.8-cm antitank gun 44 L/55 and was the only German armored vehicle with a long weapon of this caliber, which penetrated 202 mm tanks from a distance of 1 km. The speed of 12-15 km/h mentioned in the following discussion can only be correct for certain difficult terrain conditions, as the highest speed of this Hunter-Tiger was 35km/h, although it was said to be rather difficult to move. When 250 mm armor is mentioned here, it could only be referring to the turret shield, because the armor on the nose was 100 mm at a 40° angle (driver's front 150 mm), and the sides and rear were armored with 80 mm plating at a 60° angle (the real strength of these armor plates measured vertically to the surface was accordingly lower). In spite of the fragmentary character of these statements by Hitler, and in spite of the contradictions in his statements, one can exclude the possibility that at a certain point he was talking about his 180-ton monster tank "Maus," which was also supposed to be armed with a 12.8-cm gun. For the "Maus," the construction design had actually called for 250 mm armor plating; this was achieved if the measurements were taken horizontally (actual armor strength on the nose, measured vertically to the surface: 200 mm). Two "Mäuse" were built, one of sheet metal and one with armor plating, both of which fell into the hands of the Russians.—*Source: Senger-Etterlin, p. 192.*

[1566] Hitler's assessment of the Maginot Line was probably correct; critical parts such as electrical installations, etc., had been dismantled.

[1567] The combat weight of the "Hunter-Tiger" according to Senger-Etterlin: 70.6 tons.

[1568] Himmler had already taken control of the border police—whose responsibility was to supervise the German border traffic—in 1937, and in September 1944 he also incorporated the customs border guard into the Amt IV/RSHA, i.e., into the Gestapo. The job of the border guards, who until then had reported to the Reich Ministry of Finance, was to safeguard the financial security of the Reich through border protection measures. The staff was about 55,000 men at that time, but shortly thereafter 10,000 were given to the Waffen SS. It seems, however, that the incorporation into the RSHA had not been fully completed. A few days before the end of the war, the whole organization was moved back into the Reich financial administration.—*Source: IMT I, p. 297, XI, p. 343. and XXII, p. 578; Nbg. Dok. Gestapo (A) 31.*

[1569] A "decree from the Führer regarding the concentration of armaments and war production," dated June 19, 1944, published in the "News from the Reich Minister for Armaments and War Production", No. 41, says under section II/2 concerning the Armed Forces: "The capacities of the forces employed in the ordnance offices of the Armed Forces branches, and the specialists of all kinds, who until now have been working in business—including businesses owned by the Armed Forces and responsible for new developments for the Armed Forces branches—can be employed by the Reich Minister for Armaments and War Production in the pursuit of revolutionary new developments, as determined by me, without regard to these persons' former obligations to the Armed Forces branches, so that these new developments will come to fruition as soon as possible." As in this case concerning the specialists, Speer probably later obtained authorization concerning the raw materials stored by the Armed Forces. This is quite likely, as it was Speer's usual method of operation to get "Führer orders" for everything possible—even for such things as the confiscation of streetcars in Brussels.

[1570] August Frank; born April 5, 1898; commercial apprenticeship; participant in World War I after 1916; 1920-1930 in the Bavarian police service (lastly as police secretary); merchant; after 1933 SS administration; 1935 Sturmbannführer and Hauptabeilungsleiter Haushalt in the SS administration office; 1938 Oberführer and Stabsführer for the head of SS administration; and 1939-42 head of the SS

Administrative Offfice and permanent deputy of the chief of the Head Office, Pohl. In addition, after 1940 head of war direction for the Waffen SS, 1943 Gruppenführer and chief of economic administration in the head office of the Ordnungspolizei order police, after August 1944, chief of Army Administration in the Army High Command, and October 1944, Obergruppenführer. At the Nuremberg Pohl trial, he was sentenced on November 3, 1947, to life imprisonment; in 1951 the sentence was reduced to 15 years.—*Source: SS staff files (Nbg. Dok. NO-1592); Aff. Frank from Jan. 17, 1947 (NO-1576).*

1571 This 38-ton, known as the "Hetzer" ["Hustler"], was a very low—and difficult to locate in open terrain—16-ton tank destroyer (see below note 1617) with a 7.5-cm antitank gun 39 L/48 and 1 machine gun, and a speed of 38 km/h.[Check this—there are two weapons mentioned] The 38-ton was originally a Czech tank, whose production was discontinued in 1942. To use the unexploited production capacity, especially in the Bohemian and Moravian Machine Factory, the model was redesigned as an assault gun or tank destroyer. The prototype was presented in January 1944 in Rastenburg, and on April 20, 1944, the first 16 38-ton vehicles were ready for action and participated in a tank parade in Klessheim. In July 1944, 83 units were built, and by the end of the year the monthly production had risen to 400 units. Even in the first quarter of 1945, 1,138 pieces were built—all in the protectorate. The very unusual (for the time) increase in production indicates the perceived importance of this weapon. Speer's Führer Protocol of November 29, 1944 (No. 30) says the following about the 38-ton: "The Führer points out again the especially high value of the 38-ton and urges that everything be done to reach the target production rate in the shortest possible time. He considers this vehicle one of the biggest successes of this war in terms of weapons technology and therefore expects that its further production—especially the new type with the air-cooled Tatra diesel engine—will receive every imaginable support." In April 1945, the prototype of a significant improvement in weapons technology was completed: the 38-ton with a recoilless gun (providing more room for ammunition, crew, etc).—*Source: Die deutsche Industrie, p. 115; Lusar, p. 34; Senger-Etterlin, p. 192.*

1572 This relates to the fact mentioned above, that the 38-ton was built very low (height: 220 cm, compared with Panzer III: 244, Panzer IV: 268, Panzer V: 310 and Panzer VI: 288 cm). On the other hand, however, the rather weak armoring of the 38-ton (nose 60 mm, sides 20 mm, rear 8 mm) argued against the dug-in employment demanded by Hitler.—*Source: Senger-Etterlin, p. 192.*

1573 Surprisingly, on December 22, the British government had ordered the conscription of an additional 250,000 men to "strengthen our armies on the front." For the most part, these were men who had turned 18 since the last regular conscription, as well as men released from the armaments industry; some were also transfers from the Navy and RAF to the Army. At that time, it must have been explicitly stated that these conscriptions were in no way related to the significant worsening of the situation in the West, but were to be interpreted as a reflection of the decision to continue the war with all possible means.—*Source: NZZ of Dec. 24, 1944.*

[1574] Here even Himmler tries—though in vain—to pour cold water on Hitler's ideas. Even in these fragments, one can clearly see how Hitler loses himself more and more in flimsy arguments, blowing the enemy's minimal difficulties out of proportion and resorting more and more to unfounded wishful thinking.

[1575] Transcript number unknown—Fragment No. 27—The following introductory remark was made by the stenographer during the second transcription in May 1945: "The speech was held prior to the German offensive in lower Alsace, which was to begin January 1, 1945, at 12 a.m. The attendees were 20 to 30 senior officers—commanding generals and divisional commanders with their staff officers—who had been called to the Führer Headquarters for instructions regarding their assignments during the operation. Hitler spoke, as he always did for these speeches, without a script. The transcript, typed afterward from the stenographic records, communicates Hitler's words with only a few minor stylistic changes. The edges of the pages that were charred have been filled in."

[1576] Before the House of Commons on December 15, 1944, Churchill had explained: "If Poland gives up Lemberg and the surrounding areas in the south, according to the border designated as Curzon Line A…, if Poland makes this concession and these countries are united with the Ukraine, it will gain in the north all of East Prussia to the west and south of the Königsberg fortress, including the large city Danzig with its harbor—one of the most beautiful cities and one of the most beautiful harbors in the world, which has been known for centuries as a major trading point for the Baltic Sea and even for the world. All this will belong to Poland…I can't imagine that Poland would turn down such an offer. A population exchange in the north and east would certainly follow. The resettlement of several million people should be organized from the east to the west or north, as should the expulsion of the Germans—because that was suggested: total expulsion of the Germans from all territories that Poland gains in the north and west. Because this expulsion, to the extent that we are in a position to oversee it, would be the most satisfactory and lasting measure."—*Source: Rhode/Wagner, p.123; VB of Dec. 18, 1944.*

[1577] In Greece, the Civil War—the revolt of the Communist EAM and its ELAS units—had started on December 3. After that time, there had been heavy clashes on the streets, especially in Athens, in which English troops were also involved on the side of the government. The main point of contention was the return of King George, which was demanded by the English government. The British agencies in Greece saw the inopportuneness of such a measure at that moment, and pleaded for regency by the archbishop Damaskinos, who, because of his sympathies for the left, refused to support King George in London. To gain a clearer picture of the situation, Churchill had flown to Greece with Eden on Christmas night and had brought the representatives of the conflicting parties together around one table on December 26 and 27, under the chairmanship of the archbishop. Churchill returned to London on the 29th, and the agents' reports and press reports released at that time showed—as Hitler notes triumphantly—no signs of agreement. Civil War continued in Athens and an assassination attempt was even made at Churchill's hotel. In reality, however, this spectacular interlude was more of an anticlimax in the course of Greek events. A significant result of this Christmas visit was the British government's decision to support Damaskinos from that point on. Accordingly, pressure was placed on King George until he declared on the night of December 29—after a long conference with Churchill and Eden—that he was ready to support the archbishop.—*Source: Churchill VI/1, pp. 336 and 357; VB of Dec. 28 and 29, 1944; Woodhouse, p. 223.*

[1578] This comparison of population numbers was quite irrelevant, of course, in the age of cabinet wars and mercenary armies.

[1579] Against the German Ardennes offensive.

[1580] While the American losses during the Ardennes offensive are definite, there are two completely contrary estimates of the German losses. The following table shows:
a) Losses of the American First and Third Army in the Ardennes according to the SHAEF [Supreme Headquarters Allied Expeditionary Forces Europe] report, as recorded by Wilmot, and in general corresponding to Eisenhower's estimates;
b) German losses according to German assessments and estimates from Rundstedt's circle (as recorded by Wilmot and Eisenhower);
c) German losses according to Westphal.

	Dead	Wounded	Missing	Total
a)	8,407	46,170	20,905	75,482
b)	12,652	120,000		
c)	6,000	25,000		

—*Source: Eisenhower: Kreuzzug, pp. 423 and 562; Wilmot, p. 715; Westphal, p. 284.*

[1581] Hitler's ideas about the drastic results his Ardennes offensive would have on the American plans are generally correct. The Americans were in fact totally surprised by the German attack, and panicky results reached all the way to the area around Paris. On December 18 Bradley was forced to cancel the offensive—scheduled for the 21st—by the American Third Army against the Saar region, because Patton was to lead a strong strike against the south flank of the German spearhead in the Ardennes instead. The lack of reserves necessitated time-consuming reorganizations. But one must also recognize the price that was paid on the German side for this operation. The Eastern Front was exposed by the removal of all reserves, immensely easing the push of the Red Army into the heart of the Reich in January. The stubborn resistance in the Ardennes awakened in the Western powers exaggerated worries about German strength. These worries were taken to Yalta by the American statesmen in early February. But the influence of the Ardennes offensive on Yalta should not be overrated. Important decisions, such as those concerning the German occupation zones, had already been made before the offensive, and the weakness of the Anglo-American position vis-à-vis Stalin was much more conditioned by President Roosevelt's conceptions of "Uncle Joe" and honest Communism, by American anti-colonialism—which almost bred an anti-English complex during these months—

and by the American attempts to make the Russians join the fight against Japan, whose strength was overestimated by Roosevelt and King at the time.—*Source: Wilmot, pp. 629 and 674; Montgomery, p. 249; Eisenhower: Kreuzzug, p. 398; Churchill VI/1, pp. 319 and VI/2, p. 7; Sherwood, p. 689; Stettinius, passim; Byrnes, p. 37.*

[1582] Stocked supplies.

[1583] When the first attack on Aachen, in mid-September, did not succeed in advancing past the industrial areas outside the town, the rapid progress of the Anglo-Americans through Western Europe was temporarily halted . The American VII and XIX Corps then resumed the attack against Germany's westernmost city on October 2. Because Goebbels made this battle a beacon for the Fatherland and declared it an example of the German people's unshaken will to fight, while the Americans were just as stubborn in their attempt to conquer this first German town, a sizeable materiel battle developed around Aachen in the following weeks. The VB wrote about the "immense masses of steel" the Americans had thrown into the conflict and reported 8,700 salvos against German bases in 24 hours. Gradually Aachen was encircled, except for a narrow corridor to the east, and on October 13 this last connection was also severed. American sources reported that the city had to be cleared house-by-house and block-by-block, with heavy artillery employment. Not until October 21 did the last German occupation forces capitulate among the smoking rubble.—*Source: Wilmot, pp. 527 and 576; Tippelskirch, p. 592; Gilbert, p. 162; VB of Oct. 19 and 23, 1944.*

[1584] The commander of the 17th SS Division, Standartenführer Hans Lingner, said the following about this Saar offensive when he was later imprisoned: "We obviously underestimated the Allied strength, because we were extremely surprised by the number of divisions that still [i.e., in spite of the movements to the north to block of the Ardennes offensive] faced us."—*Source: Shulman, p. 469.*

[1585] See Hitler's hints on pp. 558, 561, 566, 568 and 577. According to Wilmot, Hitler planned to take up the offensive against the Meuse again after the operation on the Saar front; the remarks on p. 561 ("…then, above all, we will get the iron situation in order again"), p. 566 ("…this threat to our left flank [i.e., in the Ardennes] will stop") and, similarly, p. 568 argue rather for an operation in the Lorraine, as had been planned initially.—*Source: Wilmot, p. 649.*

[1586] Here and in the following discussion the reference is to the Ardennes.

[1587] The 6th SS Mountain Division "Nord" ["North"]; see above note 1503 and note 1504.

[1588] The Allied commanders—some more, others less—had believed in the possibility of a German attack, but they were surprised by the location as much as by the strength of the Ardennes offensive. As late as December 12, the head of the intelligence detachment of the American Twelfth Army Group had reported the following regarding the enemy situation: "The breakdown could come rapidly and without announcing itself." And in an order from Montgomery, the day before the offensive, one could read: "His [the enemy's] situation is such that he can't initiate major offensive operations." Eisenhower himself wrote, looking back: "The enemy had clearly managed to surprise us in two ways—first concerning the date of attack. Considering the terrible destructive strikes we had conducted against him in the late summer and fall, and the extreme measures he had been forced to take to mobilize fresh forces, we did not believe that he would be able to mount a major attack so soon. We were also surprised by the strength of his attack." On the German side, every effort had been made to disguise the extensive preparations (in the end, there were approximately 100 additional trains arriving in the West each day with troops and supplies) in spite of the absolute air superiority of the enemy. For example, all initiated officers, on Hitler's order, had to sign a declaration stating that they understood that they had forfeited their lives if they were the least bit careless in matters pertaining to disguising the operation. (See also below note 1620).—*Source: Wilmot, p. 629; Eisenhower: Kreuzzug, p. 402; Westphal, p. 278.*

[1589] This is not quite correct, of course. It's true that the enemy was able to collect enough information before the major German campaigns in Poland in 1939, in Norway and France in 1940, and in the Southeast and Russia in 1941 to expect a German attack. The same was true of most individual operations. However, the element of surprise was achieved in most cases, both tactically and with regard to the direction of the operation.

[1590] At this time the Russians were progressing rapidly in Hungary. They had crossed the Danube River and had pushed the German forces back to the Lake Balaton–Lake Velencze line. In the last week, the Soviet troops had broken through north of Lake Valencze and were already operating in the Bakony Forest. Budapest had been encircled since December 24, and on the 27th the Armed Forces report had to recount the first battles in that city. On the day of this meeting, December 28, the report said in somber words: "In Hungary, the battle taking place between Plattensee [Lake Balaton] and the southern border of Slovakia increased in scope and strength. With strengthened forces, the enemy turned to the west from the area of Stuhlweissenburg [Szekesferhervar]-Felsögalla and northward, and attacked Budapest aggressively from the west, southeast and northeast. The German-Hungarian occupation forces resisted the attacking Bolshevists fiercely along the inner defense circle."

[1591] Meaning the above-mentioned (see note 858) jet aircraft Me 262, Ar 234 and later He 162.

[1592] The caliber of the usual heavy mortar was 8.1 cm, in contrast to the light 5-cm mortar (production halted in 1940). The Russians had made extensive and successful use of this infantry weapon, and had brought together 12-cm mortars in separate detachments. These extremely heavy mortars were copied afterward in Germany, and in 1942 the Germans also drew up heavy mortar battalions consisting of 3 companies with twelve 12-cm mortars Model 42 each. In addition, during the last months of the war the Skoda 21-cm mortar (initially called "Wurfmörser [Throwing Mortar] Model 69") mentioned here also gained importance. This mortar, developed in 1943-44, was presented to Hitler in the fall of 1944; however, apparently as a result of insufficient testing, it did not quite meet expectations when employed by the troops. There were also a number of trial designs, such as the—never employed—30.5-cm mortar and 42-cm mortar with fin-stabilized shells (both were Skoda designs as well, and were originally "Wurfmörser"["throwing mortars"]). Only one model of the latter was completed, on the chassis of a "Tiger," right at the end of the war.—*Source: Schneider, p. 227; Order of Battle, p. 29; Lusar, p. 89; Speer's Führer Protocol of Dec. 3, 1944 (Nbg. Dok. 124-R); Leeb, p. 40; Elser, vol. 1956, p. 136.*

[1593] Here even Hitler says what was, in principle, obvious: Even in the best case they could only hope to "halfway manage to clear it out." Herein lay his inconsistency and his betrayal of the German people and the German soldiers. Before the invasion, he had said in an intimate circle that the attack in the West would decide the war. He had also explained at that time that Germany would never be able to obtain the means to withstand long materiel battles against the well-equipped Western forces. Now, however, the struggle was nevertheless continued with increasingly insufficient means, as Hitler had blocked every exit to ending the war.

[1594] If Hitler blames, to a certain extent, the poor roads and blown-up bridges for the lack of progress in the Ardennes offensive, one can say that the goals and timetable were already unrealistic and could never have been met even in the very best circumstances, due to the misjudgment of the effective balance of forces. In addition, it is the responsibility of the leadership to take blown-up bridges into consideration, as well as the fact that the roads might be in worse condition in December than they would be in May.

[1595] See below note 1655.

[1596] The marching speed of a panzer division in peacetime was approximately 6:1 in comparison with a non-motorized infantry division. One calculated a daily march of 25-30 km for a non-motorized infantry division and 150 km for a panzer division.

[1597] During the Western campaign, the 1st Mountain Division, which belonged to the Twelfth Army (to the Sixth Army after June 2, 1940), had marched behind Guderian's panzer corps—which became involved in traffic jams—to the Meuse River. There, after crossing the river without a fight on May 16, they were employed along the Oise–Aisne Canal before the Chemin des Dames as flank protection for the German spearhead to the English Channel. The division was here from May 21 until June 5, when it lined up for an attack across the Channel and the Chemin des Dames. The following afternoon the division reached the Aisne River at Soissons.—*Source: Gebirgsjäger, p. 74; Buchner, passim.*

[1598] Meaning that the engine is left running at night.

[1599] The German offensives of 1918 were supposed to defeat the English decisively at the English Channel. The Michael offensive, from March 21 to April 5—on both sides of St. Quentin in the Somme River bend, directed toward Amiens—had led to the "big battle in France." However, although the advance, which was focused on the boundary between the Allies, led to some successes, it did not achieve the desired breakthrough. The next attack, on April 9, was aimed at the English forces' northern flank on the Lys River (the Battle of Armentières). Here the German forces finally tired as well, after immense sacrifices in the course of conquering Mont Kemmel on April 25. The German Army leaders continued to cling to their operational aim against the British Army, but needed stronger forces than before to do so. To maintain the initiative during the period required to bring these forces up, and to try to remove the French reserves from the British front, the Germans launched holding attacks and diversionary assaults against the French. Because German forces were inadequate to the task, the time interval between these offensives—between the Aisne operation and the Battle of the Marne (May 27 to June 3), the engagement at Noyon (June 9 to 13) and the fighting on both sides of Rheims (The Second Battle of the Marne on July 15-17)—was so great that the holding and diversionary efforts failed. Instead of continuing to press the British as a follow-up to the spring offensive, the Germans became involved in extensive battles with wholly intact French armies. When the French launched their counteroffensive at Soissons on July 18, the plan for a new (Hagen) offensive in the north became irrelevant, and the final defeat was assured.—*Source: Stegemann IV, p. 532; Kuhl II, p. 302; Der Weltkrieg 1914-1918 XIV, passim.*

[1600] Here Hitler is speaking about the battle between the Aisne and the Marne from May 27 to June 3, 1918 (see above note 1599), where the German attack was directed via the Chemin des Dames and the Aisne River to the Marne River in front of Château Thierry. Hitler had participated in this offensive with the List Regiment. The left wing of the German Somme offensive had come to a halt outside Compiègne by the end of March.—*Source: Meyer (Adolf), p. 82; Görlitz/ Quint, p. 94.*

[1601] During the final days of September 1939, Hitler communicated his decision to undertake offensive action in the West (see above note 1554) with the commanders-in-chief of the Armed Forces branches. Führer Order No. 6, which concerned the attack across the western border, was dated October 9. November 12 had been scheduled since the end of October as the earliest possible attack date, and after the initially positive weather forecast the corresponding troop movements were also initiated. The date was first delayed for three days, followed by 12 more delays of the D-Day—until January 20, 1940, when the harsh winter forced the final postponement of the attack until spring. The official cause for these delays was always the weather; however, it was probably the unwillingness of the Army generals to attack France (for a variety of reasons) that was, in the end, decisive.—*Source: Lossberg, p. 45; Tippelskirch, p. 34; Jacobsen: Fall Gelb, passim, especially p. 141.*

[1602] Experts consider Hitler's statements here regarding German and Russian ammunition consumption to be totally erroneous. While German ammunition usage in the West was without doubt considerably lower than that of the enemy, the "general opinion" Hitler refers to was quite correct. On the German Eastern Front, one must understand that the Russians had up to three times as much artillery available at this time (their Army artillery was, in contrast to the divisional artillery, far superior), and they were able to employ even ten to twenty times as much ammunition in their main attack sectors than their German adversary. The German ammunition situation was so desperate by the fall of

1943 that even identified Soviet concentration could not be engaged and broken up as they should have been. Particularly after the losses in France, a noticeable shortage of gun materiel existed, which led in part to the immense strain on the gun barrels of German artillery in the East. So Hitler is interweaving truth and untruth. His statement might be correct for this point in time if calculated on the basis of individual guns. However, with regard to the overall situation, it reflected the exact opposite of real conditions, since Soviet ammunition consumption at that time was estimated to be twice the German consumption.

[1603] See also above note 1585.

[1604] Technically this calculation is correct, because in May 1940 Hitler had 136 divisions deployed along the western German border, which faced 137 enemy divisions, including 91 French, 12 British, 23 Belgian and 11 Dutch. By the end of 1944, however, Hitler had 76 divisions at least nominally available in the West, while Eisenhower had 78 divisions to employ against them at that time. But this does not take into consideration the German divisions' numerical weakness (many of the divisions were scarcely the size of brigades), their largely quite dreadful personnel composition, or their inferiority in terms of materiel. Nor does it take into account the Allies' air superiority or the life-threatening danger on the Eastern Front that Hitler accepted in order to carry out his offensive in the West.—*Source: Wilmot, pp. 667 and 668 notes; Tippelskirch, p. 78; Jacobsen: Fall Gelb, p. 244.*

[1605] Nothing is known about the V-weapons [rockets] being copied during the war, much less a planned employment of these copies by the Allies. It is also rather improbable, because for them these makeshift means (this is indeed what they were, considering the stage of development at the time) would not have been useful at all due to their unlimited air superiority. When Hitler pretends here that the enemy could almost totally demolish the Ruhr area with a mass barrage of V1s, he is envisioning the effects of the V-weapons with wholly calculated optimism. In reality, all of the 5,622—or even, according to another source, 8,698 V1s and 1,982 V2s—that were fired against the later primary target of Antwerp caused no more damage than a moderately heavy "conventional" aerial attack (3,470 deaths among the civilian population, but targets that were militarily important were hardly damaged). The damage caused by the V1 in England, according to the British government, amounted to 23,000 totally destroyed and 750,000 damaged buildings, 5,649 (or 6,184) dead and 16,196 (17,981) injured. The V2 killed 2,724 people in England and injured 6,467. [—] Regarding the V2, it is also known that the Americans (who were lagging in rocket research) had the German specialists who were captured in "Operation Paperclip" introduce them to the captured weapons—and this did not take place until after the German surrender. After war's end, the V1 and V2 were further developed in the USSR and in the USA.—*Source: Wilmot, p. 711; Lusar, pp. 97 and 100.*

[1606] Concerning this issue, three somewhat different-sounding statements by Hitler: "I am totally cold here as well. If the German people aren't willing to engage themselves for their own survival, fine. Then they should disappear!" (On January 27, 1942, while dining.)

"If the German people should be defeated in this struggle, then it would be because they were too weak to endure this test of history and were only worthy of destruction!" (August 1944 at a Gauleiter meeting.)

"If the war is lost, this nation will disappear as well. It is unavoidable. That's why it would be more sensible to destroy all these things ourselves [meaning production plants, traffic systems, etc.], because these people have proven the weaker ones and the future belongs to the stronger nation in the East. Besides, the ones who will survive the battle will be the inferior ones, because the good ones have fallen." (In April 1945 to Speer.)—*Source: Hitlers Tischgespräche, p. 202; Trevor-Roper, p. 54; Musmanno, p. 164.*

1607 What Hitler might have in mind here when he says "always" is not immediately clear. As far as military incidents on New Year's Eve are concerned, there was really only Blücher's famous Rhine River crossing at Kaub in 1814.

1608 What could be announced on New Year's Day was not overwhelming and had to be reduced to these two sentences in the middle of the Armed Forces High Command report: "In Alsace-Lorraine our troops are conducting several thrusts against the American front, which has now been borne by stronger forces. On both sides of Bitsch, along a broad front, they attacked the enemy's combat outpost positions and threw him back onto the main fighting line." Altogether the German troops advanced about 20 km, but did not even reach their first target: the Zabern valley. As a highpoint, the Armed Forces High Command reported on January 5—underlined heavily in the newspapers: "The front between Saargemünd and the Rhine is in motion. In spite of the counterattacks by enemy units that have now been brought in closer, our troops are continuing to advance, particularly in the lower Vosges. In addition to numerous towns in Lorraine, the city of Weissenburg in Alsace was liberated, and the Lauter was crossed in a southerly direction."

1609 This is a repetition of the "Fundamental Order" of the so-called "Führer Order" No. 1, which Hitler issued after the Mecheln affair in January 1940 (see above note 894), and which occasionally led to grotesque situations. The order said that anyone who did not really need to know about a secret matter was not supposed to learn anything, and that no one should learn anything more—or sooner—than necessary to carry out his assignment. Hitler had given this order verbally before, using almost the same wording (for example, in the meeting with the commanders-in-chief of the Armed Forces branches and other officers on May 23, 1939).—*Source: Nbg. Dok. Gestapo Exh. 25 and 079-L.*

1610 Transcript No. S 200/44—Fragment No. 30—Completely preserved. Hitler liked listening to General Thomale because he knew his numbers well and occasionally still had inactive reserves to offer.

1611 Here, as in similar cases, it was actually the following day that was meant (here: December 30), because the stenographers' cycle was also calibrated to Hitler's division of the day.

1612 With regard to the imminent offensive on the upper Rhine.

1613 Edgar Feuchtinger; born November 9, 1894; Second Lieutenant; Reichswehr; 1937 Major and Commander, 3rd Battalion, 26th Artillery Regiment; 1938 Lieutenant Colonel; 1939-1942 Commander, 227th Artillery Regiment; 1941 Colonel, after May 1943 Commander, 21st Panzer Division; August 1943 Major General; and August 1944 Lieutenant General. With regard to the 21st Panzer Division, see above note 1192. The division had been employed in the Saar and in northern Alsace since September 1944.—*Source: Keilig 211/83; Das deutsche Heer, p. 486; Seemen; Rangliste 1944-45, p. 37; Order of Battle, pp. 547 and 298.*

1614 Arnold Burmeister; born February 28, 1899; 1916 war volunteer; 1920 discharged as a brevet lieutenant; 1922 rejoined the Reichswehr; 1924 Second Lieutenant; 1936 Major and Commander, 2nd Battalion, 14th Cavalry Regiment; 1939 Commander, 2nd Battalion, 6th Panzer Regiment; 1940 Lieutenant Colonel; 1942 Colonel and Commander, 23rd Panzer Regiment (later 26th Panzer Regiment; 1943 Commander, 10th Panzer Brigade; April 1944 with the Inspector General of Panzer Troops; after September 1944, Commander, 25th Panzer Grenadier Division; January 1, 1945 Major General; and April 1945 Lieutenant General. The 25th Panzer Grenadier Division—reorganized from the 25th Infantry Division in August 1940—had been employed in the East until a few months before. It had suffered such severe losses already in the summer of 1943 in the Kursk offensive, and then again in the following summer east of Minsk, that it had to be withdrawn from the front for rehabilitation. It had returned to the Western Front in the fall and was employed in the area around Bitsch in December.—*Source: Keilig 211/51; Das deutsche Heer, p. 431; Seemen; Rangliste 1944-45, p. 58; Order of Battle, pp. 535 and 309.*

1615 The 17th SS Panzer Grenadier Division *Götz von Berlichingen* had been formed in October 1943 in western France and was composed of, among others, Romanian Volksdeutsche [ethnic Germans from Romania]. In June 1944 the division had suffered severe losses in Normandy. Now in December this unit was in the Saar. The training regiment mentioned several times below was probably the 16th Panzer Grenadier Training Regiment.—*Source: Order of Battle, p. 345.*

1616 The SS Command Headquarters (SSFHA) was formed at the beginning of war from the Inspectorate of the SS Supply Troops. Subordinate to this were the field group units of the Waffen SS—except when they were subordinate to the Army with regard to operational and tactical employment and supply—and the parts of the training and reserve troops, schools, garrisons and affiliated command authorities that were involved with the reserve system of the field troops. The responsibilities of the SSFHA were primarily formation, organization, and training; it was not responsible for the recruiting system (the SS Hauptamt [main office]), the justice system (the SS Hauptamt [main court]), the supply system (the main economy and administration office, except when tactically subordinated to the Army) and the Führerpersonalien [commanders' personal data] (the SS Personalhauptamt [main personnel office]).

1617 Panzerjäger [self-propelled antitank guns] and tank destroyers were antitank guns on tank chassis. They were developed because of initial combat experiences where towed antitank guns proved inferior to tanks because of their immobility, and could achieve success only in special situations (lack of evasion capabilities, slowly advancing tank attacks). As an immediate solution, antitank guns were placed on tank chassis and were provided with light armor protection, particularly at the front. Later the weapon was improved, but these vehicles were called upon more and more frequently to substitute for the missing armored combat vehicles rather than to carry out their own intended assignment. There were the following models (regarding the 38 t, see also above note 1571):

| | Weapons | Armor (mm) | | Weight (tons) | Speed (km/h) |
		Front	Side		
Tank Destroyer IV	7.5-cm antitank gun	75-80	30	26	32-35
Tank Destroyer V ("Panther" Destroyer)	8.8-cm antitank gun 1 machine gun	80	40-45	51.5	35
Tank Destroyer VI ("Tiger" Destroyer)	12.8-cm antitank gun 1 machine gun	100	80	70	35
Tank Destroyer "Elefant" (initially "Ferdinand")	8.8-cm antitank gun 1 machine gun	102-200	82	727	20
Self-propelled anti-tank gun "Marder"	7.5-cm antitank gun	10-35	10-15	116	40
Self-propelled anti-tank gun "Nashorn" (or "Hornisse")	8.8-cm antitank gun	10-30	10-22	26.3	40

In construction—disregarding the gun and the varying tactical employment—these tank destroyers were identical to the assault guns: they were tanks without the rotating turrets and, thus, had restricted lateral movement for their weapons. None of these constructions, however, fulfilled the most important requirement: to be faster than the tanks and to be able to pursue and catch them. In the end, they all were less-than-ideal solutions born out of the production bottleneck. The Allies did not have these problems because they could afford to produce more tanks.—*Source: Guderian: Panzer, Marsch!, pp. 117 and 234; Lusar, pp. 23 and 33; Senger-Etterlin, p. 190.*

[1618] Toward the end of the war, because the panzer divisions often had more trained crews than tanks, the motorized units had more drivers than vehicles. The unit commanders couldn't let these people just sit and watch, so they often were employed for infantry purposes when the battle started. This caused immense losses of qualified personnel who would be needed again later. But this was a dilemma that was almost unavoidable.

[1619] Motorization was an ongoing problem for the Armed Forces in the last war. The force logistical trains, in particular, mentioned here, had always been poorly equipped. While the average infantry division entered the Polish campaign with three motorized and three horse-drawn supply convoys, this ratio worsened to 2:4 during the French campaign and even 1:5 during the Eastern campaign.

[1620] To keep the planned Ardennes offensive and the assembled troop concentrations secret (see above note 1588), the participating units had been forbidden to use their radios before the offensive began. These radio camouflage efforts were obviously prerequisites for every offensive.

[1621] The armored personnel carrier was an armored half-tracked vehicle that served to transport the men in the panzer units. Experimentation with armored vehicles for the purpose of crew transportation had already halted before the war, and another solution had been adopted: adding an armored body to the chassis of the 1- and 3-ton tractors. Of the two makeshift solutions, the larger one— the medium armored personnel carrier, which had already been employed in several units at the beginning of war—did not prove successful, as it was rather sensitive to mud because of its relatively low engine power, and it failed on steep slopes. On the other hand, the troops had positive experiences with the light armored personnel carrier, which was not introduced in larger numbers until 1942. Technical data for the light armored personnel carrier: 5.7 t combat weight, 6-man crew, 60 km/h on flat road; correspondingly, for the medium armored personnel carrier: 8.5 t, 12 men, 50 km/h. The armaments of both models varied based on intended use and consisted either of two machine guns, one 3.7-cm antitank gun, one 2-cm anti-aircraft gun, one 1.5- or 2-cm anti-aircraft Drilling [three-barreled gun], an 8-cm mortar, a 7.5 cm assault gun L/24 or—on the medium armored personnel carrier only—a frame for six 28-cm Wurfminen [mine projection] or a 15-cm mortar with 10 barrels.—*Source: Senger-Etterlin, pp. 45 and 193; Senger-Etterlin: Die Entwicklung der SPW, passim; Lusar, p. 27.*

[1622] "Vomag" was the internal term for an assault gun produced by the Voigtländische Maschinenfabrik A.G., probably on a Panzer IV chassis (according to other sources: on a Panzer III chassis) with a long 7.5-cm gun (L 48).

[1623] Training area east of Magdeburg, occupied with the organizational staff of the assault gun school in the Burg at Magdeburg, which was responsible for forming new and rehabilitating worn-out assault gun units.—*Source: The German Replacement Army, pp. 181, 387 and 394.*

[1624] Hasso v. Manteuffel; born January 14, 1897; 1916 Second Lieutenant, 3rd Hussar Regiment; Reichswehr; 1933 Cavalry Captain; 1936 Major; 1939 chief instructor in the Cavalry School; 1941 Colonel and Commander, 6th Infantry Regiment; 1942 Commander, 7th Panzer Grenadier Brigade; 1943 Major General and Commander, 7th Panzer Division; January 1944 Commander, Panzer Grenadier Division *Grossdeutschland* and (February) Lieutenant General; September 1944 General of Panzer Troops] and Commander (January 1945 Commander-in-Chief), Fifth Panzer Army; and March 1945 Commander-in-Chief, Third Panzer Army. As a representative of the FDP [Freie Demokratische Partie—Free Democratic Party] (after 1956, the FVP [Freiheitliche Volkspartei—The Freedom

Peoples Party]) Manteuffel was a member of the 2nd German Bundestag.— *Source: Army High Command staff files (Nbg, Dok. NOKW-141); Munzinger Archive.*

[1625] See also above note 1565. The 653rd Tank Destroyer Detachment had been scheduled to participate in the Ardennes offensive but could not been employed because of its delayed arrival. The heavy weight of its vehicles considerably reduced its mobility on the battlefield (bridges, slopes, etc.) however, the Germans employed about 80 Hunter-Tigers [Jagdtiger] in 1945.

[1626] Chief of Staff, Commander-in-Chief West (see above note 529).

[1627] The light Panzer II was used for reconnaissance in the panzer regiments and detachments. The number 220 was certainly transcribed or heard incorrectly. It was probably 22 reconnaissance tanks.

[1628] Field Marshal Model, the Commander-in-Chief of Army Group "B," urged the Führer Headquarters to give up the planned offensive along the upper Rhine and to instead employ these forces in the penetration area in the Ardennes in order to exploit the success there at least by clearing enemy forces out of the salient in the Aachen area, after the original aim of the Ardennes offensive (Antwerp) proved unrealistic.—*Source: Wilmot, p. 644*

[1629] During late 1944, 1,199 assault guns were produced in November and 1,764 armored combat vehicles were produced from September to November. However, only 1,371 of these reached the Armed Forces. In December, production reached its highest level ever, with a total of 1,838 armored vehicles leaving the production plants. By mid-1944, Speer had succeeded in increasing the armament production level to three times what it was at the beginning of 1942, and even five times what it was at the beginning of 1941 (see above note 342). The production in 1944 alone would have been enough to equip completely 225 infantry divisions and form 45 panzer divisions. As a whole, German war materiel production reached its highest level ever in July 1944. By radically reducing production for the civilian sector, the output of weapons and ammunition was, for the most part, maintained or even increased until the fall. However, Allied air attacks destroyed much of this equipment before it reached the Armed Forces, or it was rendered unserviceable because of technical problems caused by often chaotic production conditions. A few key items such as infantry weapons, anti-aircraft ammunition and 38-t tank destroyers were still developed, but the production of heavy weapons and tanks decreased rapidly in the New Year. The Allied air attacks, in particular, led to a number of desperate substitutes, although some amazing successes had been achieved in repairing attack damage: materials were consumed as they arrived, some assembly took place right off the production line without entering storage, drastic rationalization measures were introduced, etc. The production of German tanks and assault guns developed as follows:

	1940	1941	1942	1943	1944
Light tanks	800	2,300	3,600	7,900	10,000
Medium tanks	1,400	2,900	5,600	9,400	12,100
Heavy tanks	–	–	100	2,500	5,200

The monthly production rose from 1942 to 1944 as follows:

	Beginning of 1942	Mid-1944
Armored combat vehicles	350	800
Assault guns	50	600
Tank destroyers	–	200

The table below illustrates how the production of assault guns and tank destroyers overtook the production of actual tanks. This is clearly shown by the movement of the index numbers (January/February 1942=100):

	Armored vehicles in total	Armored combat vehicles	Assault guns Assault tanks Tank destroyers
January 1943	154	105	289
July 1943	367	247	680
January 1944	438	324	884
July 1944	589	402	1,849
October 1944	516	258	2,287
January 1945	557	210	2,813

The futility of the German efforts, however, can be seen from the following table, which indicates the value of the armaments produced by the Great Powers in 1941 and 1943, in billions of dollars:

	1941	1943
USA	4.5	37.5
Great Britain	6.5	11.1
USSR	8.4	13.9
Total	19.5	62.5
Germany	6.0	13.8
Japan	2.0	4.5
Total	8.0	18.3

—*Source: Wilmot, pp. 151, 406 and 592; Die deutsche Industrie, pp. 66, 70, 87, 113, 178 and 182.*

[1630] The tensions becoming visible here between the production experts in the armaments ministry and the accepting agencies in the Armed Forces, which led to personal enmities that were said to outlast the war. The armaments managers accused the military of coming too late and being hindered too long by incapable generals, while the military spoke about the armaments ministry's obsession with numbers and about weapons being produced that often lacked important parts and were thus unusable, and which cost the leaders the self-confidence of the German soldiers. The truth was probably somewhere in the middle. On one hand, it cannot be denied that the team of managers put together by

Speer (who wasn't personally accused by the generals) achieved production successes that—observed purely as a technical phenomenon—seem unbelievable within the context of the collapsing Reich and that would have been unthinkable under the direction of the bureaucratic technical generals. On the other hand, it also cannot be denied that some worthless products did leave the factories, some materiel was unusable because of missing components, and the production of spare parts was severely neglected. In addition, real successes were sometimes manipulated by—in this situation rather macabre—juggling production numbers. One must also consider that there would naturally be variations between the production and acceptance reports for the weapons because, for example, of losses due to air attacks after the completion of the actual production process. Another source of errors was the always-controversial question of including repairs.

[1631] See also above note 1585.

[1632] This should probably say: "But even if I only receive…" Regarding the medium armored personnel carriers, see above note 1621.

[1633] This should probably be: "…for the Commander-in-Chief Southwest…"

[1634] The medium armored personnel carrier was equipped with the 7.5-cm antitank gun 48 by the end of the war. The information in Senger-Etterlin's *Taschenbuch der Panzer 1943-1954* (pp. 48 and 193) is incomplete.

[1635] See also above note 377. In addition to the actual range of 35 m, one must also add the heat wave of approximately the same range, which brings the radius of action to about 70 m.

[1636] For the tactical employment of the flame-throwing tanks, the plan was to employ them in the second or third wave. They were supposed to follow the regular armored combat vehicles in order to—after these had smashed the heavy fortifications—"burn and smoke out" the remaining isolated nests. Here Hitler requested heavy armor for the flame-throwing tanks to enable them to attack alone instead of only following the other tanks.

[1637] Meaning transferring the personnel from the Tiger I tanks to the new Tiger II (King Tiger) tanks. With the remaining Tiger Is, the turrets could be removed or they could be exchanged for vehicles with damaged turrets, which could then be employed as flame-thrower tanks.

[1638] Tiger I tanks were also used as radio command tanks when teething problems made them unsuitable for regular employment. With this heavy vehicle they could drive closer to the hostile positions and better coordinate the Goliaths (see above note 706). In some of these heavy panzer detachments, the radio-controlled Panzer B IV was also employed. At its bow, it had a 450-kg explosive charge that could be released via radio control. This tank was fast and flexible and was used to destroy or blind strong field fortifications, remove obstacles, and clear mines. In contrast to this method—driving up via remote control, dropping the charge, and returning to the command tank—the Goliath blew up at the target with all its charge.—*Source: Senger-Etterlin, p. 65.*

[1639] This must have been a test model. The common flame-thrower tanks had the above-mentioned range.

[1640] This figure must be a transcription error, as such a distance—as can be seen from the preceding information—is completely unrealistic. Hitler, who was certainly not conservative in his requirements, had always demanded the production of a flame-thrower with a range of 200 meters, but even this requirement could not quite be met.

[1641] "Thomale's man" was Colonel Dr. Hermann Oehmichen, who held the official position (established at the end of July 1944) of "General der Panzerabwehr aller Waffen beim Generalinspekteur der Panzertruppen" ["General of Panzer Defense of all Weapons under the Inspector General of Panzer Troops"]. At Guderian's order, Oehmichen had examined the possibility of installing the 7.5-cm gun into the 3.7-cm gun emplacements (with concrete mounts for each gun) of the Western Wall, as ordered by Hitler. There were, first of all, technical difficulties hindering the installation, including the size of the emplacements, the size of the muzzle recoil, and other factors that probably would have been manageable. But there were also two important tactical counter-arguments:

1. The emplacements had been built based on now-obsolete views about suitable and unsuitable terrain for tanks, at a time when tank defense was largely a matter of theoretical discussion.
2. The emplacements were built for a network of many mutually supporting weapons, and only a small fraction of them could be equipped with the 7.5-cm gun. When installed in the bunkers, the range of traverse of these guns was restricted by a relatively narrow space, isolating them and preventing them from effectively supporting and complementing one another.

The General of Panzer Defense therefore argued that the 7.5-cm and the 8.8-cm guns should be positioned on open ground to take advantage of the weapons' effective radius.

[1642] The M 4 "General Sherman" was an American tank that appeared after 1942 in various related forms. It had the following data: 30.5–34-ton battle weight, 37–46 km/h, 7.5-cm or 7.62-cm gun, 51–105-mm front plating and 40-mm side plating.—*Source: Senger-Etterlin, pp. 147 and 213.*

[1643] Within the context of employing these 8.8-cm guns on the Western Wall, they discussed using a number of gun barrels that were originally made for the tank destroyer. These weapons were available because the production of guns had outpaced the production of tanks. For the above-mentioned employment along the Western Wall, the Speer ministry constructed a temporary mount with a rather large range of traverse.

[1644] Hitler's marginalia on Oehmichen's presentation was: "What ass wrote this?" The controversy, however, became irrelevant once the Allied forces rolled up the Western Wall.

[1645] Hitler's argument, that freestanding antitank guns would be destroyed by preceding air strikes or by artillery, is certainly legitimate. The tank defense specialists had thus suggested orienting the field emplacements toward the bunkers—the gun would deploy well camouflaged in the open field, but the crew could use the nearby bunker while bombs were falling or hostile artillery was firing.

[1646] The so-called "Remise antitank-gun" was a subterranean antitank-gun bunker that was considered very useful by the former Inspector of Engineering and Fortifications, General Förster (see above note 220). It was not intended as a firing emplacement, but instead as a type of garage for an antitank gun. The dugout had a concrete, sloping exit toward the rear, through which the gun was to be pulled when a hostile tank approached, in order to conduct the defensive fight in the open field between the fortifications. Hitler criticized these installations, as he remembered the extent of the artillery barrages during World War I.

[1647] Karl Kitzinger, born April 18, 1886, was originally an Army engineer recruited by Göring in 1937 out of In 5/OKH and appointed Commander of Air Defense Zone West. After 1939 he was an Air General and, after September 1941, Armed Forces Commander, Ukraine. After the assassination attempt of July 1944, he was named successor to Stülpnagel as Military Commander in France with orders to build up a defensive position all across France along the Abbeville–Amiens–Soissons–Epernay–Chalons–St. Dizier–Plateau de Langres–Besancon line ("The Kitzinger Line")—from which the men in Hitler's circle promised themselves wonders. The project failed, not only because of a shortage of labor and materiel, but also because of the speed of the American advance, which did not stop at the Seine River as expected. Kitzinger also played an unlucky role in other situations—in his orders to isolated field headquarters to hold out, and in his orders to defend Paris.—*Source: Siegler, p.126; Order of Battle, p. 576; Görlitz II, pp. 349 and 357.*

[1648] Regarding General Förster, see above note 220. Förster could not remember ever having had a confrontation with Hitler about flame-throwers and Fort Douaumont. At the point of time indicated by Hitler—1939—it would not have been possible anyway, since Förster had already left the position of Inspector of Engineering and Fortifications in October 1938, and was Commanding General in Münster in 1939. The occasion for Förster's fall from grace with Hitler was not the flame-throwers from Douaumont, but the Western Wall fortifications that had been constructed by that time. Hitler considered them to be inadequate and criticized them very harshly in an informal meeting at the Berghof on May 16, 1938. From then on, he employed the OT [Todt Organization] (Dorsch) to perform much of the construction on the Western Wall. In the case of the flame-thrower discussion, Hitler probably confused Förster with his successor, General Alfred Jacob (see above note 800). However, since a corresponding remark of Hitler had already been recorded in mid-1938 (see below note 1649), and the stated year could therefore be wrong, Hitler's opponent on the side of the "senior engineering officers" cannot be confidently pinpointed. (For Hitler's attitude toward the flame-thrower, see also above pp. 319-321.)

[1649] The Germans captured Fort Douaumont, the northeastern corner post of Verdun's outer fortifications, on February 25, 1916, in a raid by the 24th Infantry Regiment from Brandenburg. The cause of the explosion in the early morning hours of May 8, 1916—over which Hitler claimed to have had a quarrel with General Förster—could not be accurately determined. According to investigations published in the official Great War documentation of the Reich archive, hand grenades were supposedly ignited through carelessness on the lowest floor of the fort, reaching the flame-throwers and then spreading to a store of French 15-cm shells, which exploded. Since the fortification was staffed with eight companies, one regiment staff and four battalion staffs, and the hospital was overflowing with wounded, the misfortune claimed 29 officers and at least 650 men. [—] Hitler's argument for the flame-thrower, including his quarrel with General Förster about Douaumont, can also be found in his "Memorandum on the Question of our Fortifications" of July 1, 1938, where he wrote, "I consider the flame-thrower one of the most effective defensive weapons. It will demonstrate its value as a defensive weapon in the future, because it does not need to be carried to the enemy. Instead, it awaits him and comes into action— as the final and most morale-affecting defensive instrument—in that moment when the enemy has tediously approached to within hand-grenade distance. The question of the endangerment of our own men by flame-throwers has been argued many times during the war, and the examination of these dangers has never led to any other result than the affirmation of the flame-thrower. The possibility of injury to the weapon bearer always exists; there are diverse and considerable dangers associated with nearly every weapon. The reference to the highly explosive nature of the flame-thrower oil is a criticism that can also be made about every other explosive material. That bodily harm may be caused by the use of the flame-thrower can no less be denied than the possibility of gun barrel detonations in the artillery. And during the war, although poor-quality ammunition caused them to suffer gun barrel detonations after only a few thousand rounds per gun, no one argued against the further use of artillery. Furthermore, the evidence I received from a senior engineering officer about the explosion in Fort Douaumont is not conclusive. As far as could be determined afterward, soldiers had tried to make coffee using flame-thrower oil. During this experiment, signal flare ammunition and hand grenades lying nearby started to burn and then exploded. That led to the well-known catastrophe. I believe it is necessary to store flame-throwers and oil in very small concrete safety rooms. The crews of these zones should be instructed in the basic handling of the flame-thrower. For that purpose, asbestos suits should, when necessary, also be placed in the relevant bunkers. The flame-thrower can also have success against tanks."—*Source: Der Weltkrieg 1914 to 1918 X, p.161; Nbg.Dok.1801-PS and 1802-PS.*

[1650] Here Hitler contradicts himself to some extent within a few minutes, obviously because he expressed on the one hand his later and on the other hand his earlier opinion. The underground Maginot Line installations were indeed quite extensive, but the apparatus described here by Hitler is clearly exaggerated, as certain devices could never be avoided within the subterranean facility. While the army engineers also accepted this principle in 1938, at that time, Hitler argued for stronger construction of surface buildings—as did General Kitzinger. In 1944 he had obviously revised his view somewhat. What Hitler mentions here in this second passage was also the basic principle of his above-mentioned "Memorandum on the Question of our Fortifications" of July 1, 1938: "It is not the purpose of a fortified installation to ensure, under all circumstances, the preservation of the lives of a certain number of troops; its purpose is to maintain their fighting effectiveness. That alone shall be preserved to the greatest extent possible. Consequently, any installation must be called wrong that hinders the limited number of defenders from completely utilizing and stretching their greatest weapon employment, and instead just simply enables them to do it. Fortifications should not be a shelter for non-fighters, but must secure the preservation of the fighter for the fight—meaning securing his use of weapons ... But it is unsustainable to erect a huge infantry fortification for 70, 100 or 140 men whose whole defensive effectiveness lies, in the end, in two machine guns. Because the third machine gun, intended to protect the entrance of the facility, cannot be considered a defensive weapon. Because the purpose of the facility is not to prevent the men from suffering an invasion by the enemy, but to prevent a breakthrough of the enemy through their own defensive activities. But it is impossible to fulfill such an assignment if you do not give the defense effective weapons. All men who find themselves in such a subterranean fortification system and who linger in barracks or in connecting passages, etc., fail as enemy-harming forces. Thus, such facilities do not lead to an increase, but to a decrease of the defensive power ... But if such a front is ripped open for the first time and a stream of hostile forces passes through it, then it is completely irrelevant what is still going on in the intermediate sections underground—if there are still so-called fighters, if you can get at them or if you cannot get at them. The decisive factor is that they cannot get out anymore, and that their weapons will not threaten the invading enemy any longer. But in that way the purpose of such a fortification will be turned around. Instead of being a support for heroic fighters, these 'fortifications' will serve only to protect non-fighters, for whom surrender, sooner or later, is the only option."—*Source: Nbg.Dok. 1801-PS and 1802-PS.*

[1651] Already during the erection of the Western Wall, Hitler expressed the principle that would lead to high losses: "Not an inch of German ground is to be given up," while the responsible specialists of In 5 carried out the extension of deeply staggered defense zones. On Hitler's instructions, the fortification builders had to bring forward their installations to the river Saar, so they built the first defensive positions immediately on the shore of the Saar, in order to fight the enemy effectively at its weakest moment—while crossing the river. That is what Hitler's words "...remained down in the valley" refer to.

[1652] See above note 1270.

[1653] Franz Halder; born June 30, 1884; 1904 Second Lieutenant Bavarian 3rd Field Artillery Regiment; accepted into the Reichswehr as a Captain; 1931 Colonel and Chief of Staff, 6th Infantry Division; 1933 Artillery Commander VII; 1934 Major General; 1935 Commander, 7th Infantry Division; 1936 Lieutenant General and Senior Quartermaster II in the Army General Staff; February 1938 General of Artillery and (March) Senior Quartermaster I; August 27, 1938 Army Chief of General Staff as successor to Beck; and 1940 Colonel General. Halder was relieved on September 24, 1942 and dismissed from the Armed Forces on January 31, 1945. He was imprisoned in various concentration camps and taken into American custody after the war.—*Source: Army High Command Staff Files (Nbg.Dok.NOKW-141); Munzinger Archive; Keilig 211/ 117.*

[1654] See above note1570.

[1655] Regarding the reorganization then underway, see below note 1657. For the conditions in the West at that time, where operational opportunities were minimal, the panzer units' motor vehicle equipment was no doubt excessive, and it often became a burden. In the East, however, this was not the case. If the panzer divisions, in their organization and strength at that time, were seen as improperly configured for the future, it could not be ignored. If they are improperly configured today, then it is likely due to other causes (the effects of atomic weapons!) rather than the reason mentioned by Hitler.

[1656] The German panzer divisions were named somewhat inaccurately, because the majority of their fighters were not armored (of the generally two panzer grenadier regiments in a panzer division, only one battalion was designated as a "Panzer Grenadier Battalion (gp)" or an "Armored Infantry Carrier Battalion"—(equipped with armored personnel carriers). The Americans, on the other hand, did have fully armored divisions. [—] Hitler's demand for increased mobility in these months led to consideration of a change to full-tracked armored personnel carriers on a 38-ton chassis.—*Source: Senger-Etterlin: Die Entwicklung des SPW, passim; Order of Battle, p.31.*

[1657] The longer the war lasted and the more human lives were lost, the fewer qualified leaders were left—and the more inadequately trained leaders were promoted. In contrary to this lack of leadership development, however, stood the tendency of the unit leaders—within the Waffen SS in particular, and there especially Sepp Dietrich—to regularly add new units and new vehicle types to augment their units continuously. Because the baggage transport [logistical trains] increased enormously, overwhelming their own combat units (in the end, the trains required more supplies than the fighting troops), a reorganization of the panzer units was begun in 1943-44. First, they removed maintenance companies from various divisions and removed the panzer maintenance companes from the panzer regiments, and finally moved the logistical trains to the corps level. This led, for the first time in the history of the German Army, to the creation of tight corps relations instead of the previous general command staff system with often-changing divisions. This development resulted in the creation by the end of the war of five new-type panzer corps, including *Grossdeutschland, Hermann Göring* and *Leibstandarte Adolf Hitler.* Furthermore, the divisions were reduced in size—to increase mobility—by withdrawing one of the two panzer greandier regiments; they now consisted of only one panzer grenadier regiment and one panzer regiment.

[1658] See above note 1621.

[1659] That means the 7.5-cm combat-vehicle guns of the twelve motorized platoons (i.e., platoons with armored personnel carriers); the third companies of the tank destroyer detachment were to be placed on 38-ton self-propelled guns (see above note 1571), which would free up twelve armored personnel carriers (see above note 1621).

1660 Transcript number unknown—Fragment No. 31—The first transcription consisted of 141 typed pages. The gaps indicated are up to two typed lines long. Regarding the date: In the Armed Forces Operations Staff war diary, the Soviet 1st Guards Mechanized Corps was first mentioned as being newly brought in on January 10, 1945; the present transcript is therefore probably from January 9.

1661 General of Artillery Wilhelm Berlin was General of the Artillery in the Army High Command (OKH). He had nothing to do with communications matters or—as artillery advisor only to the Chief of the Army General Staff—with the Chief of the Army High Command. Thus, the notation, General of Signal Troops, provided by the stenographer in brackets behind the name, could be correct—but there must have been a mix-up with the name itself. Presumably, the reference is to Fellgiebel's successor, General of Signal Troops Albert Praun, then Chief of Army Communications in the Army High Command and Chief of Armed Forces Communication Links in the Armed Forces High Command (OKW). Praun reported weekly to Keitel. Praun was born December 11, 1894; 1914 Second Lieutenant; Reichswehr; 1935 Major and Commander, 38th Communications Detachment; 1939 Colonel and Commander, 696th Communications Regiment; 1940 chief of communications in various staffs, lastly in the Second Panzer Army; 1942 Major General and Commander, 129th Infantry Division; 1943 Lieutenant General and (October) chief of communications in Army Group Center; April 1944 Commander 277th Infantry Division; after August 1944 in above-named position; and October 1944 General of Signal Troops.—*Source: Keilig 211/ 256.*

1662 Luftwaffe communications units were made available by the evacuation of France and the transfer from other fronts. Göring had made these units available to Sepp Dietrich to assist his panzer army in the Ardennes offensive, but since Dietrich had not been trained to control an army using radio communications, there was a great deal of improvisation. As a result, the Army Communications chief of the Sixth SS Panzer Army was quite dissatisfied.

1663 Although German communications links managed to satisfy expectations while the fronts were stretched farthest in 1942, complaints increased after the retreat from France in 1944. There were shortages of communications personnel and equipment, both of which had been lost on a large scale. At the end of 1944, the Army Signal Corps consisted of approximately 200,000 men, while that of the Luftwaffe had 400,000 men. (The members of both the Signal Corps and the more numerous signal troops personnel were called "radio operators.") Where—as was the case in Italy ("with Kesselring")—the front remained intact in slowly developing defensive battles, the communication links remained intact. During the hasty mass engagement of the Sixth SS Panzer Army in the Ardennes ("with Sepp Dietrich"), however, there were numerous communications failures due to broken telephone and radio operations links. As a result of the enemy's superiority—particularly in the air—the wire communications lines along the roads were very difficult to maintain. Radio links also suffered under the crowded conditions and the frequently insufficient training of the leaders of such large units.

[1664] To Jodl.

[1665] This refers to the second transfer of Luftwaffe personnel to the Army in the fall of 1944. A first transfer of 100,000 men had already taken place before, after the Army discovered that Göring had not called up redundant staff out of his quota, but had put them into the defense industry instead. In October and November of 1944, after the catastrophes in Russia, France and Romania, the Army had a shortage of 350,000 to 400,000 men. Hitler agreed to a new transfer of 500,000 men from the substantially reduced Luftwaffe. It cannot be doubted that such extensive staff reorganizations did result in breakdowns—which Jodl exploits here to exact revenge.

[1666] Commander-in-Chief of Army Group South in Hungary.

[1667] Herbert Gille; born March 8, 1897; Main Cadet Institute; 1915 Second Lieutenant; 1919 left the service; agricultural administrator; 1931 SS; 1937 Sturmbannführer, leading participant in the creation of the Waffen SS (SS Standarte *Germania*); 1939 Commander, 5th SS Artillery Regiment (*Viking* Division); 1942 Brigadeführer and Commander, 5th SS Panzer Division *Viking*; 1943 SS Gruppenführer; April 1944 awarded Diamonds for performance at Cherkassy pocket); Commanding General, IV SS Armored Corps; and November 1944 SS Obergruppenführer.—*Source: Munzinger Archive; Krätschmer, p. 129; Seemen; Order of Battle, p. 554; SS Dienstalterlisten.*

[1668] The report from the informant "Whisky" was by and large correct. That was the greatest disaster the rocket attacks on Antwerp caused. The "Rex" cinema in the Avenue de Keuzer was—while filled to capacity with 1,200 persons—when it was struck on December 16 (not 17), 1944, at 3:30 p.m., completely destroyed. The cleanup effort, which took hours, uncovered 567 dead (including 296 soldiers), and of the 291 who were seriously injured (including 194 soldiers), approximately half later died of their wounds.—*Source: Franssen, p. 50.*

[1669] There is no clue as to how Hitler reached this assumption. The Lend-Lease Act came into operation in March 1941 for a period of two years; it was renewed for another year in the spring of 1943 and again in 1944. At the end of 1944, for Great Britain, only a few raw materials and products were excluded; on the other hand, practically all export prohibitions combined with the Lend-Lease assistance under this category. The Americans had tedious quarrels with the Soviets because of Moscow's attempts to use Lend-Lease goods to invest in the reconstruction of Soviet industries. Possibly this reference concerns rumors and speculations connected with President Roosevelt's budget presentation to Congress on January 9, 1945. Lend-Lease assistance was also discussed in this context, while Roosevelt's message to Congress on January 6 had explained the general situation and key aspects of American post-war policies. That the United States would have suggested the structuring of Europe into different "spheres of influence"—whether in the context of Lend-Lease assistance or in some other way—seems improbable. The Americans, with their practically unrivaled economic power, feared that such plans would restrict free competition, which was beneficial to them and which they promoted in the post-war economy.— *Source: McNeill, pp. 241, 444, 513 and 784; NZZ of Aug. 1 (morning edition) and Oct. 1 (noon edition), 1945.*

[1670] Presumably the reference is to two of the five squadrons that were converted to jets on October 18, 1944 (with Me 262s: KG [Bomber Wing] 6, 27 and 54; with Ar 234s: KG 30 and 55).

[1671] Hitler probably meant here the area of Nikopol'–Krivoi Rog on the lower Dnieper River. Reading these lines might give the impression that Hitler had only withdrawn from Russia on the advice of certain generals, while, in fact, he had done so of his own free will. One must bear in mind this kind of reinterpretation in the assessment of these excursions after the fact.

[1672] Domestic nickel production amounted to 7 percent of German demand in 1938. Consumption totaled 845 tons per month in 1939, sank to 625 tons in 1942, then rose again to 794 tons at the beginning of 1944. The reserves were 10,900 tons at the end of 1939, 8,600 tons at the end of 1943, and 7,900 tons at the end of 1944, meaning that at the latter date they still had enough to cover demand for 10 months.—*Source: Die Deutsche Industrie, pp. 18, 110, 165 and 169.*

[1673] Tempering steel via electrochemical means belongs in principle to the usual procedures (see, for example, the mention in the context of the Donets basin). In this case, however, the reference is to a method invented in 1944, which used a special electrochemical process to further harden material that had already been tempered. With this procedure, it was possible to obtain a much higher degree of hardness than could be achieved through normal processing—which was of considerable significance for highly stressed weapon parts such as gun-barrel locks.

[1674] After the invasion (the traffic system in the north of France was destroyed before it began), the Allied air attacks were—in addition to the terror bombings— concentrated against the German hydrogenation factories and the railway network. The following example shows to what degree, despite feverish repair work, the paralysis of the traffic network was achieved: the number of railway cars removing coal from the Ruhr area, which was important for the entire German industry, dropped from 21,400 in January 1944 to 12,000 in December and finally to 9,000 in January 1945. The Allies' post-war assessment of the successes of their air attacks on the German railway system (in the Western zones only) lists the following as having been destroyed: 3,428 km of tracks, 14 tunnels, 2,395 railway bridges, 10,111 locomotives, 11,281 freight cars, 16,425 passenger cars, 4,632 signals, 50,929 signal boxes and 12,890 switches.—*Source: Tippelskirch, p. 585; Görlitz I, p. 519.*

[1675] Refers to the summer 1938 memorandum by the former Army Chief of the General Staff, Colonel General Beck. This memorandum, which was approved by the Commander-in-Chief of the Army, warned Hitler during the Sudeten crisis against violently pursuing his political aims because a new World War would be catastrophic for the German Reich.

[1676] Hitler expressed a similarly positive view of Wallenstein on April 12, 1942, at a dinner: "Wallenstein was right when he rejected the training of an army of

5,000 men with the observation that he could only build an army of 50,000 men. It would be pure madness to spend a single Pfennig on an army that is not strong enough to fight if necessary and to win."—*Source: Hitlers Tischgespräche, p. 141.*

[1677] Regarding the confusion about the Me 262, see above.

[1678] Dr. of Engineering Albert Ganzenmüller; born February 25, 1905; participant in the November 1923 putsch as member of the "Reich War Flag" ["Reichskriegsflagge"] organization; 1931 NSDAP; employee in the Main Technical Office [Hauptamt für Technik]; since 1932 at the Reich railway; after university studies, Reich railway advisor in Munich; later department president in Innsbruck; October 1941 chief of the Main Railroad Administration East [Haupteisenbahndirektion Ost] in Poltava; February 1942 General commissioner of the Railway [Eisenbahngeneralkommissar] for the occupied Eastern territories; and after May 27, 1942 Kleinmann's successor as Undersecretary of State in the Reich Transport Ministry [Reichsverkehrsministerium]. Ganzenmüller reportedly moved to Argentina after the war.—*Source: VB of May 28, 1942; Wiener Library Bulletin, vol. X 1956, H. 3/4.*

[1679] Transcript number unknown—Fragment No. 9—Size of destroyed passages: up to two lines.

[1680] Presumably Güdingen/Saar, between Saarbrücken and Saargemünd.

[1681] There is no town called Lambach on the Palatinate border, but—on the Lorraine side—there is a Lembach and a Dambach. Lemberg, mentioned further below, lies 10 km west of Dambach.

[1682] Presumably he meant Rittershofen and Surburg. Also the following Alsatian town names seemed to be reproduced incorrectly, and some are unidentifiable— for example: Forstfeld, Rohrweiler, Häussern, Herbsheim (Herbitzheim?), Rossfeld (Rosteig?), and so on.

[1683] Main battle line [Hauptkampflinie] is the same as main line of resistance [MRL] in western armies.

[1684] Hermann Breith; born May 7, 1892; 1911 Second Lieutenant, 60th Infantry Regiment; Reichswehr; 1936 Lieutenant Colonel; 1938 Commander, 36th Panzer Regiment; 1939 Colonel; 1940 Commander, 5th Panzer Brigade; 1941 Major General and Commander, 3rd Panzer Division; 1942 Lieutenant General; and February 1943 Commanding General, III Panzer Corps and (March) General of Panzer Troops. The III Panzer Corps fought in Hungary after the fall of 1944.—*Source: Keilig 211/45; Order of Battle, pp. 533 and 117; Seemen.*

[1685] The "Panzerfaust" (antitank grenade launcher, which was similar to the American bazooka) served the individual fighter in close combat with tanks. It consisted initially of a barrel 103 cm long (later 115 cm to increase the range) with a diameter of 4.5 or 5 and, in the end, 6 cm. Using rocket propulsion, it fired a shell with a hollow-charge warhead. Its range reached 150 m in the end, but the greatest accuracy was achieved at 25 m. The hollow-charge projectile of the panzerfaust—despite its low impact velocity of 40 m/sec.—penetrated all existing tank armor, regardless of the angle of impact. It was a very useful short-range weapon against tanks, and was very successful in 1945—as long as the men had adequate experience operating the weapon.—*Source: Lusar, p. 36 (2nd edition, p. 51, with substantial corrections); Elser 1957, p. 39.*

[1686] Meaning 8 trains per day, i.e., quite slow.

[1687] Formed in the fall of 1943 as the 1st Ski Brigade; expanded to the 1st (and only) Ski Jäger Division with the addition of parts of the 86th Infantry Division in the summer of 1944. Employed first in the area of Army Group Center, then after 1944 in Slovakia and in southern Poland.—*Source: Order of Battle, p. 313.*

[1688] Soviet troops had seized three bridgeheads on the western bank of the Vistula: near Magnuszew at the mouth of the Pilica River, at Pulawy, east of Radom, and at Baranow–Sandomierz north of the confluence of the Vistula and San Rivers. For its winter offensive, the Soviet concentrated the following within the bridgeheads: at Baranow, Koniev's 1st Ukrainian Front with 60 rifle divisions, eight tank corps, eight other tanks units and a cavalry corps; at Pulawy and Magnuszew, Zhukov's 1st Belorussian Front with 31 rifle divisions, five tank corps and three other tank units; and at the Narew bridgehead at Pultusk, Rokossovsky's 2nd Belorussian Front and, in eastern East Prussia, Cherniakhovsky's 3rd Belorussian Front each with 54 rifle divisions, two tank corps and nine other tank units. On January 12, three days after this meeting, Koniev's forces broke out of the Baranow bridgehead, with Zhukov and Cherniakhovsky following on the 13th and Rokossovsky on the 15th.—*Source: Tippelskirch, p. 614.*

[1689] This report was confirmed the following day, with discussion of even stronger artillery concentrations. With his simplistic calculations, Hitler is obviously trying to take the threatening concentration of Russian artillery to absurd extremes. These figures could, of course, hold true only for a few focal points.

[1690] Transcript No. 19/45—Fragment No. 33—Both sets of shorthand notes were available, but two-thirds destroyed, so only a small part of the second transcription was possible. The designation "midday situation report" was maintained, even though the meetings usually did not take place until late afternoon during these final months.

[1691] Bodo Zimmermann; born November 26, 1886; Cadet; 1907 Second Lieutenant, 145th Infantry Regiment; 1914 First Lieutenant; during World War I, company commander, adjutant and General Staff officer; 1916 Captain; 1920 departed service as Brevet Major; publishing industry (founder and head of the military publishing house "Offene Worte"); 1939 Reserve Major and Ia F First Army; after 1940 Ia [operations officer] Army Group "D" (Commander-in-Chief West); 1941 Lieutenant Colonel; 1942 Colonel; fall 1944 Chief of the Operations Section, Commander-in-Chief West and (December) Major General; and May 1945 Lieutenant General. Zimmerman gives the situation report for the West because Hitler was at the Western Front and, therefore, was accessible.

[1692] The "Meillerwagen" [Meiller truck], named after the Munich-based Meiller Trailer Factory [Kippanhangerfabrik], was the transport vehicle for the V2 with a hydraulic lift arm. While the "Vidal-Wagen" [Vidal truck] was used for longer road transport, the "Meiller" truck was intended for immediate troop use, i.e., transporting the rocket to the launching platform and raising it into a vertical shooting position. The presentation regarding the "leak" of an obviously secret measure, or something similar—which prompted Göring's remarks here—could not be identified.—*Source: Dornberger, pp.111 and 139 (illustration on p. 144).*

[1693] Rundstedt.

[1694] Here the reference is to so-called combat groups [kampfgruppen], meaning the increasingly common practice—dictated by the current tactical situation—of abolishing the normal hierarchical relationships between units and establishing instead ad hoc organizations according to the current conditions at the front. What proves useful in exceptional situations and emergencies, can, of course, easily become an obsession.

[1695] As the attack of the Sixth SS Panzer Army, and with it the Ardennes offensive, came to a halt in front of Monschau, a combat group containing parts of the 1st SS Panzer Division *Leibstandarte Adolf Hitler*—under the command of the commander of the 1st SS Panzer Regiment, SS Obersturmbannführer Joachim Peiper (born January 30, 1915)—managed to advance to La Gleize. There, however, after a six-day battle, the combat group had to blow up its vehicles during the night of December 23 because of a lack of fuel. They then had to fight their way through to the German line on foot. This operation—for which Peiper received the Iron Cross with Swords on February 16, 1945—supposedly involved terror measures against the civilian population and the murder of prisoners-of-war. Peiper and 72 other members of the *Leibstandarte* were accused in an American military court in the Dachau "Malmedy Trial" of having killed 142 American prisoners-of-war and a number of Belgian civilians. Of these charges, it was only proven that 71 American soldiers had been killed by a panzer advance guard of the Combat Group Peiper on December 17 at an intersection southeast of Malmedy. To what extent this was a combat engagement and to what extent it involved genuine flight and illegal shooting, remained unclear, despite the preliminary inquiry and trial that concluded on July 16, 1946, with 43 death sentences, 22 life sentences and 8 imprisonment sentences. In any case, it is significant that none of the death sentences were carried out. The men condemned in the Malmedy trial were meanwhile released from Landsberg.—*Source: First Army report of Jan. 27, 1945 (Nbg. Dok. 1634-PS); Ziemssen, passim; Krätschmer, p. 182; Görlitz II, p. 439.*

[1696] Regarding the dotted lines, see below.

[1697] The 6th Mountain Division, established during the winter of 1939-40 in Klagenfurt, was employed during the campaign in France and also distinguished itself in Greece, near Salonika, and during the Crete operation. During the summer of 1941, the division was transferred to Finland, where it was positioned in the far north on the Arctic front, until the fall of 1944 when the battles of withdrawal into northern Norway began. At that time, the Führer Headquarters regretted that this brilliant division had been—as they called it—"on ice" in northern Finland for so long.—*Source: Order of Battle, p. 321; Rendulic, p. 257.*

[1698] The close combat antitank groups [Panzernahkampftrupps], equipped with "stove pipes' [Ofenrohren] and Panzerfausts [antitank grenade launchers], became mobile with bicycles and trucks. These types of fighter commandos [Jägdkommandos], which were usually placed directly under the local commanding officer, were created for the first time in France during the summer of 1944, as armored Anglo-American advance guards threatened the area far behind the retreating front. Such commands were often assembled from training schools, field commands, etc., and their value varied accordingly. In the East, during the final months of the war, there were also tank destroyer companies that were permanent units; these had also been formed from disbanded rear services— the Jüterbog Artillery School, for example.

[1699] It was probably only the staff of the 553rd Volksgrenadier Division that was assigned to such tasks—first in the Karlsruhe region and then across the Rhine River from Strasbourg. The units of that division had suffered heavy losses in November in the Vosges Mountains, and the remaining troops were largely taken over into the 361st Infantry Division. Jodl's mild criticism of Hitler's praise for Himmler is noteworthy here.—*Source: Order of Battle, p. 273.*

[1700] The self-propelled gun "Nashorn" ["Rhinoceros"] was an improved "Hornisse" ["Hornet"], i.e., an 8.8-cm antitank gun 43 L/71 on a special Panzer IV chassis.—*Source: Lusar, p.24.*

[1701] Alimnia, a small island about 10 km off the west coast of Rhodes; Calchi— where in November 1944 a landing attempt was driven back—is 5 km southeast of Rhodes.

[1702] Ludwig Steyrer; born May 12, 1888; 1910 Second Lieutenant, Bavarian 4th Field Artillery Regiment; 1920 left the service; 1936 rejoined as Major (E); 1938 activated as Lieutenant Colonel, Commander, 1st Battalion, 114th Artillery Regiment; 1940 Commander, 209th Artillery Regiment; 88th Artillery Regiment, and (December to June 1942), 107th Artillery Regiment; 1941 Colonel; 1942 Commander, Reception Center for Officer Candidates VII; and after September 1943, (October 1944 Major General), 422nd Artillery Command [Arko 422] on the staff of the XXII Mountain Army Corps. While this corps was withdrawing from Epirus via Veles to Skopje, Steyer marched with his combat group—formed from seven fortress brigades and security brigades at Lake Ohrid—to Albania and formed the rear guard of the XXI Mountain Army Corps, which fought from there back to Montenegro. The 22nd Infantry Division, which had protected the withdrawal of Army Group "E" through Macedonia and Kosovo was sent from Prijepolje at the end of November to link up with the XXI Mountain Corps, in order to clear the road. The division made the link-up 15 km south of Mojkovaè and secured the route while the Albanian Corps marched through.— *Source: Order of Battle, p. 630; Rangliste 1944-45, p. 47; Schmidt-Richberg, pp. 23 and 62; Metzsch, p. 74; Keilig 211/328.*

[1703] In the East.

[1704] A White Paper by the Swedish foreign minister, from around the end of 1957, stated that, during the final months of the war, the Norwegian and Swedish governments-in-exile actually did try repeatedly to instigate an armed Swedish intervention against Germany.

[1705] According to the stenographers, the Navy report followed; however, it could not be reconstructed from either shorthand report.

[1706] After the Russians had advanced from the southeast in early November 1944 to reach the defensive ring around the city, Budapest was cut off from the last connection to the West on December 24. In addition to Hungarian troops and Hungarian Volkssturm [militia], the Budapest defense force included 50,000 German soldiers—among them the 8th SS Cavalry Division *Florian Geyer*, the 22nd SS Volunteer Cavalry Division, the 13th Panzer Division *Feldherrnhalle*, the 60th Panzer Grenadier Division *Feldherrnhalle*, and a Volksgrenadier division. The commanding officer of the fortress, however, was not a soldier but a police officer: SS Obergruppenführer Pfeffer-Wildenbruch, who was the commanding general of the IX SS Corps. Two relief attacks undertaken on Hitler's orders, the first beginning on January 1 and the second on January 18, 1945, failed to reach the city, despite additional reinforcements from other fronts—East Prussia, for example, which was also severely threatened. After several areas of the city were lost, the battle for the downtown core began on January 15. But this last part of Pest was held only for a short time; during the night of January 18, the defenders had to withdraw to Ofen, blowing up the bridges over the Danube. After three more days, only the southwestern part of the city and Margaret Island remained in the hands of the occupying forces; at the end of the month they held only the castle, the Citadel, and the area between. After February 12, Budapest was not mentioned in the Armed Forces report again until the report about the breakout of the occupying forces on February 15. Of the 26,750 remaining soldiers, including 10,000 wounded, only 785 reached the German lines. "Budapest cannot be considered important, either politically or militarily, in its present condition," reported a correspondent of the VB on February 19. "One can hardly call it a city anymore."—*Source: Tippelskirch, p.572 ; Görlitz II, p. 484; Krätschmer, p. 380; VB of Jan. 16, 1945 to Feb. 19, 1945.*

[1707] Because the previous field staff of the OKH had not moved with the Führer Headquarters to Ziegenburg near Bad Nauheim (Adlerhorst) at the beginning of the Ardennes offensive, Guderian could only report on the situation on the Eastern Front if he had just driven from Berlin to Ziegenburg for a visit. Usually one of his officers, who maintained communications between the Army High Command and higher field commands, made this report. Here, Lieutenant Colonel Hermani spoke in this capacity.

[1708] The OKW report of January 12 reported the capture of Zamoly.

[1709] The Russians reported daily on the blocks of houses captured in Budapest. These figures (Jan. 1: 200, Jan. 2: 295, Jan. 3: 167, Jan. 4: 277, Jan. 5: 233, Jan. 6: 173, Jan. 7: 116, Jan. 8: 130) added together (1,591) do not quite match Jodl's number. On January 8 it was reported that around 2,000 out of about 4,500 blocks were in Russian hands.—*Source: NZZ of January 2 to 9, 1945.*

[1710] It must be either 1:250,000, or—if this is the city map mentioned previously—Keitel must have said, "Ten centimeters equal 3 (more exactly, 2½) kilometers."

[1711] Guderian had visited General Wöhler, General Balck and SS General Gille during the last few days (January 5 to 8) in Hungary, to inform himself about why the relief attacks on Budapest had been unable to move forward.—*Source: Guderian, p. 349.*

[1712] The principle of the "piggy-back plane" ["Huckepackflugzeug"]—also known as "Mistel," "Beethoven," or, after the figures of the then well-known cartoonist O. E. Plauen, "Father and Son"—consisted of a large pilotless plane (in the 1944 plans for suicide missions, this one was also manned), which was filled with explosives and flown to the target by a smaller plane attached to the larger one. Immediately after arriving over the target, the pilot released his plane, started his engine and returned to base. The joining of two aircraft for special purposes had also been practiced before the war; in December 1941, the Junkers test pilot Holzbauer had the idea of using this concept for bombers. The Luftwaffe High Command delayed the construction for a year and a half because this develop-ment—to use the old expression—was not *Kriegsentscheidend* [decisive for the outcome of the war], and would come at the expense of the overall production. The "Mistel" tests began in 1943. A FW 190 (first a Me 109) was used with a Ju 88 (training for the suicide missions used the Me 328, which was not employed anywhere else, on a Do 217), whose cockpit consisted of a maximum 3.8-ton high-explosive hollow-cone charge that could penetrate 1 meter of steel armor plating or 18 meters of reinforced concrete. The "Mistel" had a speed of 380 km/h and 2,000 km range because only the motors of the carrier plane were used for the approach. Originally they were to be used against the Ural power stations (Operation "Eisenhammer" ["Iron Hammer"]), but using it became impossible after the Eastern Front moved westward. The first 12 "Mistel" were finally used in a mission against the invasion fleet (sinking the battleship *Courbet*) and later in the attacks against the Remagen bridge and the Vistula and Oder bridges. A planned major offensive against the British Home Fleet in Scapa Flow remained unexecuted. In their few opportunities to prove them-selves, the "Mistel" produced quite good results in terms of effectiveness and accuracy.—*Source: Lusar, pp. 76 and 54; Bartz, p. 227; Baumbach, p. 97; Reitsch, p. 280; Feuchter, p. 292.*

[1713] The term used for the Armed Forces transportation method for transporting the highest priority materials. Transport was to be nonstop from the loading station to the destination at the front, while all other trains were removed from the route. It was primarily used for urgent transports of ammunition, tanks, etc. for planned attacks or for blocking enemy penetrations.

[1714] The 31st Volksgrenadier Division was withdrawn from Courland and joined the new Army Group Center (still "A" at that point). In the first months of 1945, 10 out of the 26 divisions in Courland were evacuated by sea to assist in the de-fense of the Reich.—*Source: Order of Battle, p. 150; Tippelskirch, p. 564.*

[1715] A new kind of anti-aircraft ammunition with the following improvements: 1. Instead of the normal filling of iron fragments, the iron pieces were stamped in jagged patterns so as to tear into the especially vulnerable aircraft fuel tanks, creating holes that would not re-close with the leather and rubber layer of the cover, as they did when hit by the old filling or small splinters. 2. Shrapnel effect instead of shell effect, which meant concentrated, massed effect in front—di-rectional. Thus, in principle, this type of ammunition had to be fired somewhat shorter than the old type; this could be achieved through an adjustment in the fire control predictor. 3. Increased incendiary effect when the shell was filled with phosphorus incendiary materials. This type of ammunition was ordered as part of a new development program in 1942, and was developed in 1943. The date "February 1944" could mean that this presentation was a progress report on the initial employment of the ammunition that month. At that time, the German air defense had experienced considerable success in one week—primarily during attacks on southern Germany—which could be partly explained by this incendiary shrapnel ammunition. (The OKW reports provided the following number of aircraft victories: 83 on February 20, 49 on the 21st, 33 on the 22nd, 119 on the 23rd, 45 on the 24th, 166 on the 25th, and 106 on the 26th).

[1716] "Smoke trails" on departing aircraft could be attributed to engine or other fires, or they could be fuel trails, when fuel ran out of the leaking tank and sprayed in the air. An American Air Force mission intelligence report from the final year of the war indicated that 24 percent of the aircraft employed return to their home base with dead or wounded on board and with heavy damage, which required extensive repairs.

[1717] The number given here—10,000 rounds of anti-aircraft fire to bring down one aircraft—could include barrage fire, because in World War I, 12,000 flak rounds were needed for one aircraft victory, and with directed fire at the beginning of World War II, 8,000 rounds were needed for one aircraft victory. After 1943, the number fell to only 4,100 rounds. The above-mentioned 205 rounds of incendiary shrapnel ammunition required to bring down a single aircraft must have taken place during a particularly fortunate exercise, as even the excellent Rotring ammunition introduced toward the end of the war—with double fuses (time and impact)—still required 800 to 850 rounds per aerial victory.

[1718] The Boeing B29 "Super Fortress," was a long-distance bomber whose prototype was first flown on September 21, 1942, and which was mass-produced after January 1944. The B29 was used against Japan after June 15, 1944, but did not appear in the European skies.—*Source: Feuchter, p. 276; Hébrard, p. 198.*

[1719] Regarding the He 177, see above. The unfortunate diving capability requirements, which necessitated, for example, the troublesome tandem arrangement of the engines, came from Jeschonnek. It can no longer be determined with certainty whether Göring knew that or not. Like Hitler here, he complained in September 1942, "It is sheer idiocy to demand that a plane with four engines dive. If someone had told me about it, I would have answered immediately, 'What nonsense! Aircraft with four engines don't need to dive...' To demand that a four-engine plane be able to dive is terrible nonsense. Now we have this problem!" The leading Luftwaffe generals deny this; they claim that Göring had known about the diving requirements for a long time.—*Source: Baumbach, p. 153; Bartz, p. 84.*

[1720] The dive-bomber technique was brought from the U.S. by Udet, and, after 1935, developed further by the Luftwaffe. The future Chief of the General Staff, Jeschonnek, was particularly impressed by this kind of attack, which supposedly led to very damaging exaggerations in the end. The first dive-bomber was the He 50. At the beginning of the war, two types were used. One of them, the

Hs 123, was already out of date by this time and was used only in individual cases or as a fighter-bomber. The other type was the famous Ju 87, with its characteristic folded wings, which proved itself during the first years of the war and was still being used successfully at the end of the war in the East. Because of the substandard airfields there, durable aircraft were required, and the Fourth Air Fleet rejected the sensitive FW 190—thus production of the already discontinued Ju 87 was once again increased. The Ju 88 twin-engine bomber could also make diving attacks, but this aircraft was not completed until the end of 1941, when the dive-bombing attack no longer played the same tactical role. The mistake on the German side was, on one hand, that these attacks were made compulsory and that diving capability was demanded of aircraft that were much too heavy, and, on the other, that they did not draw the correct conclusions when defensive developments led to heavy losses—the diving attack should have been replaced by the low-flying fighter-bomber attack. In the end, the Ju 87 was more and more frequently chased away by the increasingly powerful Anglo-American fighters in the West. At the beginning of the war, the Luftwaffe had nine dive-bomber groups with a total of 336 Ju 87s and a group with 40 Hs 123s. The production of the Ju 87 developed as follows:

1939	1940	1941	1942	1943	1944	1945	Total
134	603	500	960	1,672	1,012	–	4,881

—*Source: Baumbach, pp. 85, 87 and 315; Feuchter, pp. 124 and 335.*

[1721] Hitler's demand, which he had made since the fall of 1943, that the 5-cm combat-vehicle gun L42 be installed in the fighter, was in principle completely legitimate. The massed appearance of the heavily armed and armored Anglo-American four-engine bomber showed that a larger caliber was absolutely necessary to shoot from a longer range and still achieve deadly effect with a hit. The 5-cm gun was rebuilt as an automatic weapon, with about 15 shells in the magazine and a rate of fire of one round per second. The weapon was installed in the Me 410s of two destroyer groups (2nd Squadron, 76th Heavy Fighter Wing) and 2s Squadron, 26th Heavy Fighter Wing). In addition to jammed loading mechanisms, which emerged as unavoidable teething troubles, there were difficulties arising from the limited carrying capacity of the aircraft themselves: after the installation, the units could not fly above 7,000 meters. Thus, the streams of enemy bombers could fly over them unopposed. In addition, attempts were made to install the 7.5-cm field gun in the Ju 88, but this weapon was clearly too heavy. Another attempt at using the 8.8-cm anti-aircraft gun as an aircraft weapon failed because the propeller cracked. Another solution to the problem of arming fighters against heavy bombers was provided by a weapon that had already been in use for a year (since January 11, 1944): the rocket launcher.—*Source: Bartz, p. 219; Lusar, p. 54; Feuchter, p. 248; Galland, p. 247.*

[1722] The Consolidated B 24 "Liberator" and the Boeing B 17 "Flying Fortress," in various forms, were the standard aircraft of the American air war against the Reich. The "Fortress" flew its first attack in Europe against Rouen on August 17, 1942, and the "Liberator" against Lille and Romilly-sur-Seine on December

20, 1942. After that, both aircraft were in continuous employment over Europe. The "Liberator" (spring 1940 prototype) had the following specifications: crew 9 men, bomb load 2,270 kg, range 2,575 km, speed 450 km/h, altitude 9,000 m. While the USAAF (Army Air Force) had only 18 four-engine bombers at the time of the Japanese attack on Pearl Harbor, American aviation industry quickly reached the following production numbers: 1941: 317; 1942: 2,615; 1943: 9,615; 1944: 16,331; 1945: 6,865. In the same time period in Germany, 263 heavy bombers were produced. An overall comparison of the aviation industry output in both countries clearly shows the hopeless German inferiority:

	1939	1940	1941	1942	1943	1944	1945	Total
US bombers	–	–	4,115	12,627	29,355	35,003	16,492	97,592
GR bombers	737	2,852	3,373	4,337	4,649	2,287	–	18,235
US fighters	–	–	4,416	10,769	23,988	38,873	21,696	99,742
GR fighters	605	2,746	3,744	5,515	10,898	25,285	4,936	53,729
US total aircraft	–	–	19,433	47,836	85,898	96,316	47,714	297,199
GR total aircraft	2,518	10,247	15,409	15,409	24,807	40,593	7,540	113,515

—*Source: Hébrard, p. 198; Feuchter, p. 210; Baumbach, p. 313; Bartz, p. 152.*

[1723] Meaning "like Bormann said about Mecklenburg."

[1724] Here the stenographer who made the second transcription made a note: "A dotted line entered here means a gap of at least 1 to 1½ typewritten pages in the original copy." Whether this also applies to preceding dotted lines is uncertain.

[1725] The enemy did not really have 18-ton bombs, but on March 14, 1945, British bombs of 10 tons (22,000 lbs.) were used for the first time, against viaducts in Bielefeld and Ansberg. The following table shows the first employments of Anglo-American high-explosive bombs over Germany (the effective weight shows a minor variation because of the conversion to the metric system):

0.9-ton high-explosive bomb	July 1-2, 1940
1.8-ton high-explosive bomb	March 3, 1941
3.6-ton high-explosive bomb	April 10, 1942
5.4-ton high-explosive bomb	September 15, 1943
10-ton high-explosive bomb ("Grand Slam")	March 14, 1945

In addition, since the fall of 1944, the Americans had given their 5.4-ton bombs streamlined contours, which significantly improved the ballistic properties. In early 1945, they dropped an armor-piercing bomb for the first time, which had additional rocket propulsion and reached a diving speed of 360 m/sec. The introduction of the new "Pent" explosive also improved the effectiveness of the enemy bombs at this time. But even more than increasing the weight and effectiveness of their bombs, the Anglo-Americans increased the number of bombs dropped. The table shows the contrast between (a) the number of bombs the Anglo-Americans dropped over Germany and the occupied territories and (b) the bomb load the Luftwaffe dropped over England (in tons):

	1940	1941	1942	1943	1944	1945	Total
a	14,631	35,509	53,755	226,513	1,188,577	477,051	1,996,036
b	36,844	21,858	3,260	2,298	9,151	761	74,172

—*Source: Feuchter, pp. 217, 236, 276 and 299; Brickhill, pp. 47, 117, 166 and 249.*

[1726] Karl Witzell; born October 18, 1884; 1902 entered the Imperial Navy; in World War I on the cruiser *Elbing* at the Skagerrak battle among others; 1920 accepted into the Reich Navy as Lieutenant Commander; Administrator in the weapons department of the Navy Administration and later head of this department; 1934 Chief of the Navy Armaments Office and president of the New Construction Committee in the Navy High Command; 1937 Admiral; 1939 until end of August 1942, Chief of the Navy Armaments Head Office; and member of the Presidential Council of the Reich Research Council and Armaments Council. Witzell was released from Soviet captivity in October 1955.—*Source: Munzinger Archive; Seemen; Siegler, p. 143.*

[1727] Hitler made this comment in response to an objection by Göring, who presumably had pointed out—in face of all the heavy reproaches—his exoneration in the development of the V1 by the Luftwaffe. Hitler had never believed that the V1 could decide the war either.

[1728] The "Liberator" reached an altitude of 9,000 m with a 2¼-ton bomb load; the "Fortress" had an optimal altitude of 7,000-8,000 m.—*Source: Hébrard, pp. 198 and 200.*

[1729] A device for shooting lower-caliber ammunition in guns of the next higher caliber, designed to achieve a greater propelling charge by increasing the v_0 (initial velocity) and with it the range. The "Treibspiegel" was a ring that fit around the shell, which filled up the caliber and fell to ground at the firing position after the shot. In this manner, a 10.5-cm shell could be shot in a 12.8-cm gun and an 8.8-cm shell in the 10.5-cm gun (known as "Pfeilgeschoss" ["arrow shells"]).—*Source: Koch: Flak, p. 210.*

[1730] The reference is probably to the Japanese ramming missions.

[1731] This probably concerned an order that Speer received from Hitler on November 4, 1944, regarding the forced production of anti-aircraft guns. The betrayal mentioned here was perhaps carried out by an agent introduced by the British into the Luftwaffe Central office telephone exchange in Utrecht, who then quickly sent various Luftwaffe [internal communications] to Great Britain.

[1732] Transcript number unknown—Fragment Nos. 24 and 25—completely preserved. On January 16 Hitler arrived in Berlin again, and, after some hesitation, finally decided to desist from his adventurous plans of attack in the West—based on the extent of the Russian offensive that had been rolling forward since January 12. From January 17 on, reports from the Eastern Front came first in the OKW report.

[1733] The plan to break up the ice on the Oder was soon abandoned, as the exhausted Corps v. Saucken did not manage to destroy the Russian bridgehead at Steinau. Koniev had been along the Oder since January 23. In the end, the whole Oder line between Oppeln and the mouth of the Görlitzer Neisse was lost; the front stopped only at the edge of the Sudeten Mountain range. Supported by statements from witnesses, Thorwald reported on another downstream attempt to cut the ice—which resisted all explosives—from the Oder with power saws. But the cut blocks froze immediately, before they could be removed from the river. Strangely enough, in the same period of time—only a few days later—events took place (for example, the withdrawal of Corps v. Saucken to the left Oder bank at Steinau with a pontoon bridge, which was then floated down the Oder) and recollections (for example, General Nehring: a German military doctor from Russian-occupied Upper Silesia drifted down the river bound on a raft)—that would have required a free-flowing Oder. Interviews have also indicated that in Silesia (in contrast to East Prussia, mentioned above) it may not have been excessively cold in those days.

[1734] The reference must be to the attack reported in the Armed Forces High Command report of the same day, between the Lake Velencze and Vali sector to the north during the night of January 26. On the following day, heavy enemy attacks were reported in the same area.—*Source: OKW reports from Jan. 27-28, 1945*

[1735] The Soviet *Cavalry-Mechanized Group*, which together with the *6th Guards Tank Army*, had led the thrust in the Ipel salient in December 1944.—*Source: Friessner, pp. 176, 186 and 192.*

[1736] The 20th Panzer Division was thrown back to Upper Silesia.

[1737] Such a realization, however, did not prevent Hitler himself from making this mistake, repeatedly and with disastrous results.

[1738] Although 20,000 men were left on the islands (the complete evacuation would take several more weeks), the retreat from Greece required two full months (September 2 to November 2, 1944).

[1739] Probably "the least."

[1740] Meaning the enemy in Hungary.

[1741] Herman Balck; born December 7, 1893; 1914 Second Lieutenant; 1935 Major; 1937 Commander, 1st Bicycle Detachment; 1939 Commander, 1st Infantry Regiment; 1940 Colonel; May 1941 Commander, 2nd Panzer Brigade; November 1941 General of Mobile Troops in the Army High Command; 1942 Major General and Commander, 11th Panzer Division; 1943 Lieutenant General and Commander, Panzer Grenadier Division *Grossdeutschland*; November 1943 General of Panzer Troops and Commander (after February 1, 1944, Commanding General), XXXXVIII Panzer Corps; August 1944 Commander (after September 1 Commander-in-Chief) Fourth Panzer Army; August 31, 1944 awarded Diamonds; September 21, 1944 Commander-in-Chief, Army Group "G"; and December 23, 1944 until the surrender, Commander-in-Chief, Army Group Fretter-Pico

(Sixth Army). In 1948 in Stuttgart, Balck was sentenced to 3 years' imprisonment on a manslaughter charge (the shooting of a regimental commander without a court martial in November 1944). In 1950 the Paris military court sentenced him in absentia to 20 years of forced labor, for destroying the city of Gérardmer.—*Source: OKW staff files (Nbg. Dok. NOKW-141); Munzinger Archive; Siegler, p. 112.*

1742 Meaning that the small combat groups in this composition would work together to reach tactical short-term goals, instead of teamwork among the relevant weapons within the scope of the division, with operational goals.

1743 Side armor in mm/°: Panzer III, Assault Gun III, Panzer IV: 30/90; Tank Destroyer IV: 40/60; Panzer V, Tank Destroyer V: 50/55; Panzer VI/1: 80/90, Panzer VI/2, Tank Destroyer VI: 80/60.—*Source: Senger-Etterlin, p. 191.*

1744 In the direction of Budapest.

1745 Szekesferhervar [Stuhlweissenburg] was recaptured during the night of January 22, in the course of the failed second relief offensive against Budapest.—*Source: OKW report from January 23, 1945.*

1746 With encircled Budapest.

1747 Previously Army Group "A"; renamed two days earlier and now under the new Commander-in-Chief Schörner.

1748 This reference is probably to the Sagan–Liegnitz–Breslau railway line.

1749 The battle for the Upper Silesian industrial area commenced at the beginning of the third week in January. Koniev's 1st Ukrainian Front attacked from the north, while Petrov's 4th Ukrainian Front pushed in—for the most part held off by the First Panzer Army—from the east. The Seventeenth Army under General of Infantry Friedrich Schulz defended the last intact German industrial district. While the last coal trains rolled toward the West, and work continued by day, the Russian soldiers advanced step by step. On January 26 the OKW had to report the enemy's ominous "local territorial gain" on the northern edge, and on the 27th the loss of Gleiwitz (the city where Hitler had started the war); on the 28th Beuthen and Kattowitz were also reported as lost.—*Source: OKW reports; Tippelskirch, p. 620.*

1750 Code name for newly activated units from the Replacement Army.

1751 Unidentifiable.

1752 Unidentifiable.

1753 Cities west of the Oder between Glogau and Steinau. Köben lies on the west bank of the river and Steinau is 15 km upstream.

1754 Friedrich Kirchner; born March 26, 1885; Second Lieutenant, 107th Infantry Regiment; Reichswehr; 1932 Lieutenant Colonel; 1933 Commander, 11th Cavalry Regiment; 1934 Colonel and Commander, 1st Infantry Regiment; 1938 Major General and Commander, 1st Infantry Brigade; 1939 Commander, 1st Panzer Division; 1940 Lieutenant General, after November 1941, Commanding General, LVII Panzer Corps; and 1942 General of Panzer Troops. The day before this meeting, Kirchner had received the award of Swords for his role in the withdrawal from Romania and the battles for Budapest. At this time, as Commanding General, LVII Panzer Corps, he was situated on the western bank of the Oder, south of the Russian Steinau bridgehead.—*Source: DNB of Feb. 24, 1944, and Jan. 29, 1945; Das deutsche Heer, p. 190; Order of Battle, p. 576; Seemen-Keilig 211/163.*

1755 The staff of the 16th Panzer Division under Major General Dietrich v. Müller had, along with the headquarters of the XXIV Army Corps, left the pocket east of the Oder, in which the divisions of the Panzer Corps *Grossdeutschland* (v. Saucken) and the XXIV Army Corps (Nehring) were located, to take command of the Oder defense in the area of Glogau. Here he led an attack against the Russian Steinau bridgehead on the left bank of the Oder. The attack failed, as did the subsequent attack by Group v. Saucken on the right bank.

1756 Dietrich von Saucken; born May 16, 1892; 1912 Second Lieutenant; Reichswehr; 1934 Major; 1937 Commander, 2nd Cavalry Regiment; 1939 Colonel; 1940 Commander, 4th Infantry Brigade; 1942 Major General and commander of the Krampnitz School for Mobile troops; 1943 Lieutenant General and Commander, 4th Panzer Division; June 1944 Commander, III Panzer Corps; August 1944 General of Panzer Troops and Commanding General, XXXIX Panzer Corps; December 1944 Commanding General, Panzer Corps *Grossdeutschland*; and March 1945 Commander, Second Army. On the day of capitulation, v. Saucken became the last (27th) recipient of the Diamonds award from the Armed Forces, and fell into Russian captivity as Commander, of the Army in East Prussia; in October 1955 he was released.—*Source: Army High Command staff files (Nbg. Dok. NOKW-141); Seemen; Siegler, p.136.*

1757 Georg Jauer; born June 25, 1896; war volunteer; 1916 Second Lieutenant, 15th Reserve Foot Artillery Regiment; Reichswehr; 1934 Army Personnel Office advisor, (later head of department); 1939 Lieutenant Colonel; 1940 Colonel; 1941 Commander, 29th Artillery Regiment; 1942 Commander, *Grossdeutschland* Artillery Regiment; and after January 1943 (Major General in April, Lieutenant General in October), Commander, 20th Panzer Grenadier Division. With the XXIV Panzer Corps of General Nehring, he had fought back out of the Baranow pocket, but at the Warthe [Warta] River, his division was placed under the command of *Grossdeutschland.* That Jauer was named in the same breath with v. Saucken here—i.e., a division commander being used to support the position of his commanding general—is unusual, but can perhaps be explained by the fact that Jauer had just recently come from Nehring to v. Saucken, and thus wasn't quite yet considered "part of" the group. On March 12, Jauer became Commanding General of the Panzer Corps *Grossdeutschland* as successor to v. Saucken (after March 15 General of Panzer Troops).—*Source: Rangliste 1944-45, pp. 27 and 332; Order of Battle, p. 571; Walther Nehring: Die Kämpfe im Raum von Glogau (Thorwald Material in the IfZ); DNB of May 24, 1944.*

1758 Panzer Corps *Grossdeutschland*—established from the *Brandenburg* Panzer Grenadier Division (see below note 1764), the 1st Parachute Panzer Division *Hermann Göring* and the 20th Panzer Grenadier Division—under General v. Saucken was ordered to destroy the Russian Oder bridgehead at Steinau; it was to remain on the eastern side of the Oder, turn to the south, and attack the enemy from behind. The troops were extremely exhausted, however, since v. Saucken, with his headquarters and the *Brandenburg* and *Hermann Göring* Divisions, had just been transferred from East Prussia to Lodz. There, while unloading, the divisions had been fired upon immediately by Russian artillery that had broken through. Due to this weakness, and the usual heavy Russian flank protection, the plan failed. On the enemy-occupied east bank, v. Saucken was unable to advance to Steinau. When his attack ground to a halt after about 6 to 10 km, he was thrown against the river between Glogau and Steinau, where his units were finally able to reach the west bank in early February, via a pontoon bridge provided by Army Group Schörner after a long delay. This type of action against the Russian bridgehead was blamed on Hitler, and occasionally also Schörner, by the generals (Tippelskirch, p. 621; Nehring notes: "… a typical Hitler order, issued arbitrarily, without understanding the situation at the front, inspired by a misunderstood reading of Clausewitz—as happened so often!"). This passage and the verbal exchange between Guderian and Hitler on page 629, however, show clearly that Hitler—if one doesn't wish to imply that he couldn't read situational maps—was first informed about this mission after it had already begun, and then agreed with it. The spiritual father of the operation was likely Schörner, who also took an enthusiastic attitude toward it. However, the Army General Staff obviously did not raise any objections either. *Source: Tippelskirch, pp. 616 and 621; Görlitz II, pp. 471 and 480; Walther Nehring: Die Kämpfe im Raum von Glogau (Thorwald Material in the IfZ); Guderian: Erinnerungen, pp. 355 and 361.*

[1759] On January 24 Hitler created Army Group "Vistula" under the former Commander-in-Chief Upper Rhine, Reichsführer SS Himmler, in order to combine the German forces (chaotically splintered by the Russian attacks) between the Vistula River at Thorn and the Oder River east of Frankfurt. The remains of the Ninth and Second Armies were in this area, along with the alarm units raised by the Stettin Military District along the eastern Pomeranian border. Guderian initially suggested Baron v. Weichs for the position of commander-in-chief, but both Hitler and Jodl rejected him (Hitler thought Weichs was too tired and Jodl thought he was too Catholic). Guderian apparently attempted to make the exising staff of Army Group Weichs ("F" in the Southeast) available to Himmler, but Hitler rejected that as well. Himmler then chose as chief the outgoing commander of the 2nd SS Panzer Division, SS Brigadeführer Lammerding. Himmler, of course, failed to defend the Obra-Warta fortifications against the Russian thrust to the middle Oder, just as he was later unable to hold the Netze line against the attack on the mouth of the Oder; however, this failure was due more to the impossible nature of the task than to the "inexperienced and confused leadership" of which he was—certainly not unjustly—accused. The suspicion that Bormann was not uninvolved in the naming of his rival cannot be dismissed.—*Source: Tippelskirch, p. 623; Görlitz II, p. 478; Guderian: Erinnerungen, p. 366; Thorwald: Es began…, p. 272.*

[1760] Walther Nehring; born August 15, 1892; 1913 Second Lieutenant; 1926 Captain in the General Staff; 1934 Lieutenant Colonel (Inspector of the Motor Transport Troops); 1937 Colonel and Commander, 5th Panzer Regiment; 1939 Chief of Staff, XIX Army Corps; 1940 Major General and Commander, 18th Panzer

Division; 1942 Lieutenant General, after February 27, 1942, Commander (July 1, 1942 General of Panzer Troops and Commanding General) German Africa Corps; July 1943 Commanding General, XXIV Panzer Corps; June 1944 temporary commander, Fourth Panzer Army (for Harpe); and August 1944 again Commanding General, XXIV Panzer Corps. One week earlier, on January 22, 1945, Nehring had received the award of Swords for his withdrawal from the Vistula River. After March 20, 1945, he was Commander of the First Panzer Army.—*Source: Army High Command staff files (Nbg. Dok. NOKW-141); Munzinger Archive; VB of Jan. 27, 1945.*

[1761] After the collapse of the Vistula front on both sides of Nehring's XXIV Panzer Corps, the corps broke through to the rear as a "roving pocket" ["Wandernder Kessel"] and linked up with the assembling *Grossdeutschland* Corps at Warta on January 22, 1945. Nehring's divisions were then placed under that headquarters, which had taken over the overall command of the pocket. The XXIV Panzer Corps headquarters was pulled out, along with a few tanks and the staff from the shattered 16th Panzer Division, in order to conduct the defense of the Steinau sector on the Oder (except for Glogau–Neusalz). Afterward, his [Nehring's] units absorbed the still valuable 20th Panzer Grenadier Division, except for the *Grossdeutschland* Panzer Corps: primarily—as can be read here—the 19th Panzer Division, which had not belonged to the corps before, as well as the remnants of the 16th and 17th Panzer Divisions and the XXXXII Army Corps, which had been destroyed in the Vistula salient and whose remnants had joined Nehring.

[1762] When the Eastern Front reached closer to the East Prussian border in the summer of 1944, the military district commanders in the Reich were gradually subordinated to the returning armies; however, at the time of this decision, a tug-of-war had developed between the organizations involved, and subordination sometimes came too late for the interests of the front troops (see Keitel's remark below). [—] Regarding the Tirschtiegel position, Himmler had issued the following order two days before, on January 25: "Upon receipt of this telegram, SS Obergruppenführer Krüger will take over the command of all units in the Tirschtiegel Position, including currently present and arriving units of the Army and the Waffen SS, as well as the anti-aircraft units being brought in. SS Obergruppenführer Krüger will inform all commanders and officers that the Tirschtiegel Position is the furthest west position that we want to occupy. No one must leave the position alive under enemy pressure. The necessary Volkssturm battalions should be deployed into the position immediately; this will release Army battalions, which are to push forward aggressively—as much and as rapidly as possible—to develop an additional position further to the east. The unshakeable goal must be the Colmar-Posen-Glogau position. The thought that we might abandon the German city of Posen and its occupation forces is unthinkable and unbearable. I expect the troops to fight in this spirit. Long live the Führer!" [—] The commander of Military District III, however, was primarily concerned with the defense of his military district, and, in view of the threat to his flanks, stopped the troops that were marching east to the Warthegau River.— *Source: Telegram from Himmler to Fegelein on Jan. 25, 1945 (Nbg. Dok. 1781-PS).*

[1763] The 1st Parachute Panzer Division *Hermann Göring*—the designation "parachute" was only an honorary name—was formed as a brigade from the *General Göring* Regiment in the summer of 1942 and expanded into a panzer division at the end of 1942. Part of the division was destroyed in Tunis. The division, which consisted only of volunteers after its refitting, fought in Italy until July 1944, and was then transferred to the Warsaw sector on the Eastern Front and in October to East Prussia. There, at the end of 1944, the 2nd Parachute Panzer Division *Hermann Göring* was formed from its cadres. Then in mid-January, the regular division was added to the *Grossdeutschland* headquarters as a replacement for the *Grossdeutschland* Panzer Division—which remained in East Prussia—and was transferred to the Lodz area.—*Source: Order of Battle, pp. 304 and 312.*

[1764] After it had officially lost its special assignments following the formation of the SS Jäger units, the *Brandenburg* Division was reorganized as a panzer grenadier division in October 1944 in Vienna, and was initially placed directly under the OKH (Army High Command). When the *Grossdeutschland* Panzer Corps was formed in East Prussia in mid-December, it [the "Brandenburg"]—after employment in Yugoslavia and Hungary—joined this headquarters with the *Grossdeutschland* Panzer Division. In mid-January it [the *Brandenburg*] was transferred with the corps staff and the 1st *Hermann Göring* into the Lodz area to help defend against the Russian penetration, while the *Grossdeutschland* Panzer Division remained in East Prussia and joined the XX Army Corps.—*Source: Order of Battle, p. 312; Kriegsheim, p. 314.*

[1765] Jodl's objection was perfectly justifiable and Guderian's reply somewhat captious. At this time, the 19th Panzer Division under Lieutenant General Hans Källner was actually still in Gostyn, protecting the north wing of the geographically (if not de facto) surrounded *Grossdeutschland* Panzer Corps; however, the division was taken away from the corps in the days that followed and was thus no longer available for the attack on Steinau. Instead, the division pushed—withdrawing westward—toward Nehring's XXIV Panzer Corps in the Glogau area.

[1766] The Berlin War Academy had almost reached the end of a 135-year tradition. Because its qualified instructors were needed in the Army field forces, the academy had already been closed once at the beginning of World War II, and its participants introduced as General Staff candidates in their mobilization positions. But when it became apparent that the war would last longer, two so-called General Staff courses were introduced as substitute training. From January 1940 to spring 1941, the 12-week courses were held in Dresden and Berlin. The first Russian winter intensified the need for officers, so four new 9- to 10-week courses (for around 60 officers each) were offered until February 1943. After the course size had been significantly increased (to 150 to 250 candidates, through the generous release of young line officers), and after extending the theoretical education to six months during the winter of 1942-43, the courses were renamed "War Academy" in March 1943. The increasing air attacks early in August forced the transfer of the academy away from Berlin—first to Bad Salzbrunn in Silesia, and two months later finally to Hirschberg. After the premature discontinuation of the ongoing courses, as mentioned here (due to the situation at the front and the emergency deployment that apparently followed), the academy was evacuated to Bad Kissingen until the surrender and—after March—to Lenggries (Upper Bavaria).—*Source: Erfurth: Generalstab, p. 221.*

[1767] The Berlin Guard regiment [Wachregiment] had been responsible for all guard duty for the capital since the time of the Reichswehr. At that time, it consisted of rotating infantry troop units (three infantry companies, three machine-gun companies and one infantry-gun company), which were assigned to this duty for a quarter of a year. With the introduction of universal conscription, and the expansion of the troop training operations that were required as a result, the regiment received a fixed organization and grew, eventually,—without a battalion structure—to a strength of eight companies. On June 14, 1939, it was renamed Infantry Regiment *Grossdeutschland*. The regiment entered field service with this name and was later expanded to a division, while a "Guard Regiment" remained in Berlin for ongoing guard duty as a base and replacement unit [for its parent division]. [—] After the union of Germany and Austria, there had also been a "Vienna Guard Battalion."

[1768] The 8th SS Cavalry Division *Florian Geyer* (established in the fall of 1942 from the SS Cavalry Brigade, and after that employed in Yugoslavia and later in Hungary) and the 22nd SS Volunteer Calvary Division (established in the summer of 1944 in Hungary from units handed over by the 8th) were among the encircled units in Budapest. Their commanders, SS Brigadeführer Joachim Rumohr and SS Brigadeführer August Zehender, were awarded the Oak Leaves on February 4, for preferring death to captivity in Budapest.—*Source: Order of Battle, pp. 341 and 347; VB of Feb. 5, 1945.*

[1769] Posen, which Hitler, as usual, defined as a fortress (in this case actually with some legitimacy)—and whose Gauleiter had already departed on January 20—had been surrounded since January 25 by the Soviet armies that had begun streaming past the city on the 22nd, moving toward the Oder along a wide front. The core of the occupying forces, which were a motley grouping of local militia [*Landesschützen*], escaped soldiers, and Luftwaffe members, was formed by 2,000 young officers from Infantry Ensign School No. 5 under the "Blood Order" recipient, Major General Gonell. On the day of this meeting, January 27, the Russians succeeded—with a single attack—in breaking through into the city. By early February most of Posen was lost, and the occupation forces were divided into two parts. On February 16, the units, which were crowded together in a narrow area on the eastern bank of the Warta River, received permission from Gonell to break out—against the orders of Army Group Himmler. The effort remained undiscovered initially, and many succeeded in escaping. In the meantime, the OKW report announced on February 15 that the enemy had broken into the interior of the fortress. On the 21st there were reports of battles in the central fortified area. When the Soviets threatened to shoot the wounded soldiers who had fallen into their hands, the commander, Major General Mattern (previously commander of the Warthe Training Area), capitulated on February 23. The capitulation was not announced until March 1 in the OKW report. The day before the surrender, Gonell had committed suicide on a Reich battleflag; some of the defenders remained hidden for several weeks in the casemates of the fortress.—*Source: Tippelskirch, p. 622; OKW reports; Thorwald: Es began..., p. 87.*

1770 Schneidemühl was mentioned for the first time in the Armed Forces High Command report on January 27. On February 12 it was reported that the enemy had broken into the interior of the "fortress." Two days later, the city was mentioned for the last time. That same day, the fortress commander, Major General Heinrich Remlinger, received the Knight's Cross. Remlinger was previously commander of the Armed Forces' Torgau prison. He was executed in 1946 in Russia.—*Source: Armed Forces High Command reports from Jan. 27 to Feb. 14, 1945; Seemen, p. 210; Rangliste 1944-45, p. 34.*

1771 According to Tippelskirch (p. 623) Himmler should already have arrived with an improvised staff in the Ordensburg Crössinsee at Falkenburg in eastern Pomerania on January 24. According to Guderian (p. 368), Görlitz (II, p. 478) and Thorwald (*Weichsel*, pp. 274 and 280), however, Himmler stopped first with his staff in Deutsch Krone in Grenzmark, 45 km southeast of Crössinsee, and was not driven away to the Ordensburg by Zhukov and his advancing troops until the day of this meeting, January 27.

1772 The 15th Waffen SS Infantry Division (Latvian No. 1), which was moved from Riga to Gdingen [Gdynia] in August 1944. Latvian labor-service age groups 1925-26 had filled up the division, which was in training in eastern Pomerania when it was alerted and committed through Konitz on the Netze River. After capturing Nakel, the Latvians then had to withdraw to the northwest through Flatow to Jastrow, since, in the meantime, the Soviets had captured Bromberg. The sister division, the 19th Waffen SS Infantry Division (Latvian No. 2), was fighting in Courland at the time (in the VI Latvian SS Corps), where in early December serious mutinies developed, although the Latvian units generally performed quite well.—*Source: Steiner, p. 311; Nbg. Dok. NO-777 and NO-1717.*

1773 The 337th Volksgrenadier Division under Lieutenant General Kinzel received a telegram from Himmler on the evening of January 26: "The division is to advance against the enemy pushed up on the west bank of the Vistula, and to throw [him] out. The Vistula–Netze position must be cleared and held. General Kinzel, I expect the supreme effort from you and your division. The German people can demand this from us. We have the opportunity to attack the enemy—who has pushed forward into Germany—in the foreseeable future and to destroy him. Be sure that the conditions for that are achieved. Long live the Führer!"—*Source: Telegram from Himmler to the 337th VGD on Jan. 26, 1945, 10 p.m. (Nbg. Dok. 1787-PS).*

1774 In his *Erinnerungen* (p. 368), Guderian claimed that Himmler had ordered the evacuation of Thorn, Kulm and Marienwerder from his headquarters, "without the permission of the Army High Command."

1775 Graudenz was also first mentioned in the Armed Forces report on January 27, but the Nogat–Vistula front up to this city continued to hold for some time against the Soviet spearhead, which had reached Elbing. On February 18

Graudenz was finally encircled, but held—strengthened by ongoing Courbière propaganda—until March 5. The commander was Major General Ludwig Fricke.—*Source: Tippelskirch, p. 627; OKW reports from Jan. 27 to Mar. 8, 1945.*

[1776] On the morning of January 27, at 2:45 a.m., the new army group commander-in-chief, Himmler, gave the commander-in-chief of the Second Army the following directives by telegram, with regard to the Vistula front. These instructions are very useful in the assessment of Himmler's guest performance as a general. "1. The Marienburg–Elbing front must held at all cost. It protects the very important Danzig and Gotenhafen harbors, as well as the starting point for the next operations, which must establish a solid rail and land connection with the Reichs Gau of East Prussia and Army Group North. [—] 2. The Vistula front, with its Graudenz and Kulm bridgeheads, must be stabilized in the next 3-4 days through the efforts of all forces, despite the troops' exhaustion. The necessary foxholes must be blasted, the artillery positions built, barrage fire areas established, wooden bunkers built by the Volkssturm and the local population, and tunnels blasted, so that the troops will be in a position—in terms of defense through their weapons and in terms of strength through rest for body and mind—to withstand the next enemy attack with complete success. The Volkssturm battalions of the West Prussian Gau will be integrated into the divisions. Even the refitting of the troops must be accomplished in these positions. The fire brigades must build up assault guns for an enemy who could potentially cross at any point. This defense form applies in particular to the Vistula front north of Kulm. [—] 3. The endangered corner south of Kulm, as well as the Netze sector, particulary up to Bromberg, must be fought free by exerting the last strength of the troops; then the troops must occupy positions. [—] 4. I will endeavor to bring the 2-cm anti-aircraft gun to the whole Vistula front as quickly as possible, and heavy anti-aircraft batteries at endangered points—and along the entire front medium mortars, which will be brought together in mortar battalions by the Volkssturm. [—] 5. The Thorn fortress must engage in active fighting. Only then will it fulfill its purpose. It must disturb the supply routes of the enemy to Kulm, in the Weichsel bend and south of the Vistula as much as possible through continuous combat patrols and sallies and well-timed and prudent firing with heavy weapons. A runway must be built in one of the streets in Thorn as quickly as possible. Every aircraft that lands in Thorn must carry out the wounded, as well as—first German, later Polish—women and children."—*Source: Nbg. Dok. 1787-PS.*

[1777] The division came from Courland.

[1778] The reference is probably to the situation in the western part of East Prussia.

[1779] The tank destroyer companies were the 10th, but sometimes also the 14th Companies of the Volksgrenadier Divisions—equipped with "Panzerschreck" and "Panzerfaust" [antitank grenade launchers]. In addition, outside the divisional framework, there were individual "Panzerzerstörer" [tank destroyer] battalions. These were generally numbered in the four-hundred-series (e.g., the 471st-479th Tank Destroyer Battalions).—*Source: Order of Battle, pp. 23, 29, and 425.*

1780 The 302nd Higher Artillery Commander (Harko 302), belonging to the Fourth Army, then Lieutenant General Herbert Wagner. Here several emergency units, probably improvised, were placed under this staff.—*Source: Keilig 112/4.*

1781 Hans-Egon v. Einem; born September 26, 1907; 1928 Reichswehr (3rd Cavalry Regiment); 1934 First Lieutenant; 1939 Captain and squadron chief, 3rd Cavalry Regiment; 1942 Major; 1944 Lieutenant Colonel and commander of a panzer regiment (24th Panzer Division); and January 1, 1945 Colonel. Einem died on May 8, 1945, when the Russians entered Freiberg.—*Source: Das deutsche Heer, p. 422; Rangliste 1944-45, p. 140.*

1782 Guderian meant the 18th Panzer Grenadier Division, which had been fighting since the fall of 1944 in East Prussia. The 18th Panzer Division had been disbanded after suffering heavy losses in the German counterattack near Kiev in the fall of 1943.—*Source: Order of Battle, pp. 297 and 308.*

1783 The reference here is to the *Grossdeutschland* Panzer Division, which remained in East Prussia when the corps was transferred southward to Lodz. As a meeting participant remembered clearly, the indication that this well-known division would be thrown in to the focal point was enough to improve Hitler's mood, although Guderian had just noted that there was no fuel for the unit at the moment. A change of mood like this, based on next to nothing, was typical for Hitler in these final months.

1784 Colonel General Reinhardt handed over the command of Army Group North (formerly Center) to Colonel General Rendulic that same afternoon. Rendulic had just taken over Army Group Courland the day before and was now relieved in a great rush. Hitler accused Reinhard—and the army commander-in-chief, General Hossbach—of withdrawing the Fourth Army to the west and giving up the Lötzen Fortress without authorization. Hossbach had decided after the choking of East Prussia on January 22 to save his Fourth Army before the encirclement; he turned around and broke through westward to the Second Army behind the Vistula. [—] The "circumstances" mentioned here were then discussed the next day by the new Commander-in-Chief of Army Group North with the Commander-in-Chief of the Third Panzer Army. In Samland, Russian troops had pushed forward along the Kurischen Haff to east of Cranz. It was now a matter of holding the area around Cranz and the southern end of the Kurischen Spit on the Samland coast, and keeping the withdrawal route clear for the XXVIII Army Corps—surrounded in Memel—via the spit to Samland.—*Source: Rendulic, pp. 338 and 340; Guderian, p. 362; Tippelskirch, p. 618.*

1785 Otto Lasch; born June 25, 1893; 1914 Second Lieutenant, 2nd Jäger Battalion; 1920 State Police [Landespolizei]; 1935 returned to the Army as Major; 1936 Commander, 3rd Battalion, 3rd Infantry Regiment; 1937 Lieutenant Colonel; 1939 Colonel and Commander, 43rd Infantry Regiment; 1942 Major General and Commander, 217th Infantry Division; 1943 Lieutenant General and Commander, 349th Infantry Division; September 1944 Commanding General, LXIV Army Corps; and after November 1944, General of the Infantry and Commander, Military District I (Königsberg). Lasch, with command over 3½ fractured divisions, was commander of the Königsberg Fortress, which, for all practical purposes, had been surrounded since January 31, 1945. But the Russians didn't begin their major offensive until April 6, after eliminating the Fourth Army pocket at Heiligenbeil. When the enemy entered the city and all the ammunition was expended, Lasch capitulated with the permission of his divisional commanders. In the Armed Forces report of April 13, Hitler had the following announced: "General of the Infantry Lasch was sentenced by the War Court to death by hanging, for cowardly surrender to the enemy. His family will be held liable." Indeed, his wife and daughters were arrested; he himself returned from Russian captivity at the end of October 1955.—*Source: Munzinger Archive; Aufzeichnungen von Bruno Kerwin, Dr. Hans Twiehaus und Martin Wegener (Thorwald Material in the IfZ): Thorwald: Es began..., p. 185; Seemen; Rangliste 1944-45, pp. 25 and 332; Keilig 211/192.*

[1786] Regarding Koch, see above. Koch left Königsberg, the threatened capital of his Gau, in time and in mid-January 1945 reached safety in Pillau, from where he traveled on February 6 to the Neutief auf der Frischen Spit. It was only by a matter of hours that the Reich Defense Commissar reached his capital in the "Storch," while at least one ship had been kept under steam for him since early April. On the 23rd (27th) he embarked with his staff in the open-sea icebreaker *Ostpreussen* and "disappeared" via Hela, Rügen and Copenhagen to Flensburg, where he went underground. As farm laborer "Rolf Berger" he was arrested in Hamburg in late May 1949 and was handed over to Poland in January 1950. There he was sentenced to death by the Warsaw court in March 1959, after several months of legal proceedings.—*Source: Munzinger Archive; Aufzeichnungen von Martin Wegener und Kerschies (Thorwald Material in the IfZ); Thorwald: Es began..., p. 167.*

[1787] Army troops. These were equal in firing power to the old assault gun detachments (which, for all practical purposes, had only company strength at that time), and were probably named this to raise morale. The punctuation of the original is unclear; perhaps—and the following text supports this—it could also be: "the 278th Mortar Brigade, assault gun brigade."—*Source: Order of Battle, pp. 39 and 456.*

[1788] This refers to the Stalag Luft III [prisoner-of-war camp], which became famous for the execution of 50 Allied—mostly British—pilots in March and April 1944. These were participants in an escape effort by 76 Allied pilots during the night of March 24, 1944, and the whole affair was intended as a deterrent against the Western Allied prisoners' increasingly frequent escape attempts. The evacuation of the camp discussed here led to an evacuation march at war's end with inadequate transportation and provisions, causing a high death toll.—*Source: IMT I, p. 57; Regarding the so-called "Sagan Case" see among others the summary judgements in the following document numbers: NG-2318, NG-3496, NG-3901, NG-5844 and NOKW-998.*

[1789] Himmler. This report obviously brought Göring much pleasure.

[1790] In the main Nuremberg trial, Major Büchs declared it improbable that Göring had said this; it could have come from Fegelein. The stenographers had to write what they heard without looking up, so such mistakes were possible, particularly since four to six people would frequently speak at the same time. But however well intended this statement by Büchs in defense of his accused former commander-in-chief was, the remark in question is "genuine Göring" (see the "Kristallnacht conference" of November 12, 1938) and doesn't fit at all with the colorless Fegelein.—*Source: IMT XV, p. 645.*

[1791] Here the reference is probably to the Vernehmungsprotokolle transcripts regarding members of the Vlasov Army after clashes with the Germans. At the end of October 1944, the order was issued to form two Russian divisions. Beginning on November 10, at the Münsing Training Area, the 1st Vlasov Division—officially the 600th Infantry Division (Russian)—was established under Colonel Buniatshchenko, and, after the end of January 1945, the 2nd Vlasov Division (the 650th Infantry Division) under Colonel Sveriew was formed at the Heuberg Training Area. Vlasov himself received the rank of army commander-in-chief and formed a staff together with Major Colonel Truchin as chief of staff and Colonel Nerianin as Ia [operations officer]. At the end of January, the formation of the 1st Division ended, and in the middle of the following month, the first tank destroyer commands left for the Oder front. On March 6 the division—armed with assault guns, among other things—began marching toward Army Group Vistula and was engaged during the night of April 12 in an unsuccessful attack against a small Soviet bridgehead south of Frankfurt am Oder. Then the division, which was gradually pulling out of the German chain of command, headed southwest and traveled slowly through Saxony to Bohemia. There, in early in May, the division—by now more than 20,000 strong—actively attacked German forces in Prague. After this intervention on behalf of the Czech Nationalists on May 7 and 8, the Americans captured Buniatshchenko. In the meantime, the 2nd Division—now also in Münsing, as was the officers' school established there under Colonel Meandrov—marched out on April 19 toward Linz, in advance of the approaching Americans. They reached the Budweis area, where they were captured by the Russians; the officers' school and the Vlasov army staff successfully crossed over to the American side. A few days later, however, the Americans handed all Vlasov members over to the Russians, who moved everyone who was not massacred there to the East. Andrei Andreevich Vlasov and eleven of his generals and colonels were hanged on August 2, 1946, in Red Square in Moscow.—*Source: Thorwald: Wen sie..., p. 434; Fischer, p. 94.*

[1792] The numerous suicides by members of the Vlasov troops before the arrival of the Red Army demonstrate, as did their ultimate fate, that there was little real risk that Vlasov's forces in the East would desert to the Soviet Army, although, of course, this did happen in isolated instances and when infiltrated agents withdrew. In the West, on the other hand, where the hopes of the Russian Liberation Army were pinned toward the end of the war, such fears were more justified. In late 1944, for example, on the Dutch island of Texel, a Georgian battalion—which did not really belong to the actual Vlasov Army—mutinied, killed the German staff, and set themselves up defensively while waiting in vain for the British to arrive.—*Source: Thorwald: Wen sie..., pp. 463 and others.*

1793 National Socialist fanatics tried, with every means of defamation and threat—and later even with open terror—to hinder the rebuilding of a German civilian administration in the enemy-occupied western German areas. The most striking example was the longest-occupied city, Aachen. One week after the city was taken by the Americans, the German papers reported triumphantly: "They can find no traitor! The Anglo-Americans search in vain for a new mayor for Aachen." But when, despite the agitation, responsible citizens were found to start the vital administration in spite of Hitler's destructive mania, an example was set in this city. During the night of March 27 (24?), 1945, Mayor Franz Oppenhoff was killed by "German freedom fighters." This murder of the "dishonorable mercenary of the nation's enemy" was the signal for the failed "Werwolf" Operation, which was proclaimed four days later—on Easter Sunday, April 1—with the motto: "Hate is our prayer and revenge our field cry."—*Source: Poll, p. 268; Kuby, p. 96; VB of Oct. 31, 1944, Mar. 31, 1945 and April 3, 1945.*

1794 Hans Jüttner; born March 2, 1894; high school; 1913 bank apprenticeship; 1914 war volunteer; 1915 Second Lieutenant; after 1917 in Turkey; 1920 discharged as First Lieutenant; businessman (1929 independent); 1931 SA and NSDAP; 1933 leader SA High School Office Breslau and military sports instructor; 1934 staff leader in the state administration consultant VII of the training system in Munich; May 1, 1935 Hauptsturmführer with the SS supply troops; 1936 Sturmbannführer and at the Inspectorate of the Supply Troops; 1939 Standartenführer and Inspector of the Replacement Troops for the SS Supply Division (1940 renamed Commandant for SS Supply Troops); August 1940 Chief of Staff SS Führungshauptamt (SSFHA) [SS command headquarters]; 1941 Gruppenführer; 1943 Chief SSFHA (January) and SS Obergruppenführer (June); and after July 21, 1944, permanent representative for Himmler as Commander of the Replacement Army and head of Army armaments. In 1948 Jüttner was sentenced in a court to 10 years in a labor camp (1949 reduced to 4 years).—*Source: Munzinger Archive; SS Dienstalterslisten; Aff. Fütner of May 3, 1948 (Nbg. Dok. NG-5216); SS staff files (NO-271/79 and NO-327/29).*

1795 Richard Glücks; born April 22, 1898; 1933 SS Untersturmführer; 1939 Standartenführer at SS TV/KL; 1937 Oberführer, at the beginning of the war part of the Concentration Camp Inspectorate as the representative for Eicke (who was sent into the field with the Totenkopf units) and later successor to Eicke; 1941 Brigadeführer, after leaving the Concentration Camp Inspectorate as Amt VI/SSFHA and being placed under the Economic Administration Headquarters; after March 16, 1942 chief of Office Group D/WVHA [Economic Administration Headquarters]; 1943 SS Gruppenführer. Glücks went underground during the I.R.K. proceedings in April 1945 and remained missing.—*Source: SS Dienstalterslisten; Nbg. Dok. NO-019, NO-719 and NO-3169; Reitlinger: Endlösung, p. 583.*

1796 Hans-Ulrich Rudel; born July 2, 1916; 1936 joined the Luftwaffe as an Airman First Class; Legion Condor, in the Polish and French campaigns, a navigator in a reconnaissance group; and after December 1940 in a dive-bomber wing. Rudel distinguished himself in the East as a combat pilot in the fight against Russian naval targets and especially tanks. At the end of war he was colonel and commodore of the 2nd Ground Attack Wing "Immelmann," where he had previously led the 9th Squadron and after 1943 the III Group. On January 1, 1945, he became the only recipient of the Golden Oak Leaves award. Rudel moved to Argentina in 1948; after the fall of Perón he escaped to Paraguay.—*Source: Rudel, passim; Munzinger Archive; Seemen; Frankfurter Neue Presse of Dec. 31, 1955.*

[1797] See also Rudel, p. 222.

[1798] Eduard Hauser; born June 22, 1895; 1915 Second Lieutenant; Reichswehr; 1938 Lieutenant Colonel in the staff of Army Group Command 5; 1939 XIX Army Corps staff; 1940 Commander, 18th (4th) Panzer Regiment; 1941 Colonel and Commander, 25th Panzer Regiment; 1943 Commander 13th Panzer Division and Major General; and after June 1944, Lieutenant General and Commander, Combat Group Hauser.—*Source: Keilig 211/124; Das deutsche Heer, p. 73; Seemen.*

[1799] East Prussia.

[1800] As of this day, January 27, Commander-and-Chief of Army Group North, the former Army Group Center.

[1801] Oldwig v. Natzmer; born June 29, 1904; 1925 Corporal; 1928 Second Lieutenant, 9th Cavalry Regiment; 1938 Army General Staff, 1941 Ia [operations officer] 161st Infantry Division and (July) XXXIX Panzer Corps; 1942 Lieutenant Colonel and Chief of Staff, Panzer Grenadier Division *Grossdeutschland*; and 1943 Colonel. As Major General, Natzmer was Chief of Staff of Army Group North (now Army Group Courland) under Schörner from July 19, 1944 to January 26, 1945. On January 27 he took over responsibility of the Chief of Staff for the new Army Group North (the former Army Group Center) under Rendulic until February 16 when he became Chief of Staff for Schörner again (then Army Group Center). Natzmer remained in this position—as Lieutenant General after March 15, 1945—until the capitulation.—*Source: Order of Battle, p. 599; Siegler, p. 132; Rangliste 1944-45, p. 75; Seemen; Keilig 211/231.*

[1802] See also Guderian: *Erinnerungen*, p. 369. The 1928 age group was used as Luftwaffe assistants in the flak batteries from the beginning of 1944 to early March 1945. The men were—in some cases after participating in a military training camp—conscripted that same month to the RAD. At this time (March 15 to April 3, 1945), the 1929 age group was already registered in the personnel roster and during the last weeks of the war these men were employed in whatever uniforms were available.—*Source: VB of Mar. 12, 1945; Kuby, p. 135.*

[1803] Military Districts.

I:	Königsberg (East Prussia, Southeast Prussia, Bialystok)
XX:	Danzig (Danzig-West Prussia)
XXI:	Posen (Wartheland)
VI:	Münster (Westphalia, Northern Rhineland)
XII:	Wiesbaden (Southern Rhineland, Palatinate, Lorraine)
VIII:	Breslau (Silesia, East Upper Silesia, eastern Sudetenland)
II:	Stettin (Mecklenburg, Pomerania, Grenzmark)
III:	Berlin (Brandenburg)

[1804] It is probably an automatic rifle that is meant here (previous designation: Machine Pistol 44). The call for an automatic gun was old, but the development had been delayed by the demand that standard gun ammunition be used (considering that with the significant recoil caused by the large powder charge, the weapon would become too heavy). An Army Weapons Office development of 7.9 mm short cartridges (i.e., bullets like a carbine 98 k) was thus rejected by the Armed Forces leadership in the spring of 1943, although the development had demonstrated its worth in the Kholm pocket (as "Machine Carbine 42") and the Russians had had success with similar weapons. An introduction of two types of ammunition for infantry small arms seemed impossible. The production, which began slowly nevertheless, was halted in the summer of 1943. Not until the fall of that year did the front officers convince Hitler to introduce an automatic rifle. It came as an improved version of the MP-44, and reached the troops in large quantities in late summer 1944. The weight of the gun was 5.4 kg and the maximum accuracy range was around 600 m. The magazine could carry 28 to 32 rounds, and the fastest rate of fire during sustained fire was 60-90 rounds per minute.—*Source: Leeb, p. 34; Elser 1956, p. 113; Lusar, p. 15.*

[1805] A simplified standard gun with a cartridge 98, whose mass production was easier (seven instead of twelve man-hours). The introduction was suggested by the Army Weapons Office in November 1944; at the time of this meeting a production of 70,000 units was proposed. A "Volksgewehr" ["people's gun"] obviously did not reach the Army in any quantity worth mentioning.—*Source: Leeb, p. 35.*

[1806] Regarding Gille, see above. According to a schedule for mid-October 1944, the 1st and 23rd Panzer Divisions—in addition to the 13th—were already under the headquarters of the III Panzer Corps (Breith) west of Debrecen; at the end of December the 1st and the 23rd (between Plattensee [Lake Balaton] and Velenczsee [Lake Velencze]) belonged to that corps.—*Source: Friessner, p. 260.*

[1807] To Hungary.

[1808] Meaning the Russians in Hungary.

[1809] Regarding the Führer Grenadier Brigade, see above. The Führer Escort Brigade was formed during the second half of 1944, after the former Führer Escort Battalion was strengthened by the addition of the 928th and 929th Reserve Infantry Battalions. The brigade was under the command of Colonel (later Major General) Remer and included three panzer greandier battalions, an anti-aircraft detachment, a panzer regiment, an artillery detachment and a reconnaissance detachment. The Führer Escort Brigade also participated in the Ardennes offensive, and was finally—like the Führer Grenadier Brigade, with which it formed a panzer corps—thrown into the Eastern front. There, in the last months of the war, it was designated the "Führer Escort Division," probably based on an order from Hitler (dated January 30, 1945) that all independent units be named "divisions." In addition to these two brigades, there was also the Führer Intelligence Detachment and the Führer Air Intelligence Detachment.—*Source: Order of Battle, p. 85.*

1810 A town of Ottilienberg did not exist, nor did the below-mentioned Nevenbach, etc. If the reference was not to Weiler or something similar, the names were obviously garbled in the second transcription.

1811 Meaning the enemy. This likely refers to the insignificant German attacks in Alsace, at Bitsch and Hagenau, which started on January 25. At that time several calming statements were issued in the Allied capitals and headquarters, indicating a certain—if unfounded—nervousness in the Western Allied public. Since the initial surprising success of the Ardennes offensive, people in the West had been sensitive concerning German counterattacks.

1812 A German report on January 30 spoke of 100,000 dead and wounded Americans and 26,438 captured since December 16. In America they announced the transfer of 85,000 Air Force members and other units to the infantry, which Hitler was probably referring to. "Lost" must again be understood here in a wider context. In World War I the Americans lost a total of 68,000 dead, and in World War II 229,000 soldiers (174,000 of them in the North African/European theater and 55,000 in the East Asian theater).—*Source: NZZ of Jan. 30 (evening edition) and Jan. 31 (morning edition), 1944; Arntz, passim.*

1813 In the southeastern corner of Luxemburg. A city called Schlossberg does not exist.

1814 Left tributary of the Rhône, on which Hagenau lies.

1815 The Colmar bridgehead had been under attack by the French First Army since January 21. At first the Nineteenth Army was able to hold off these attacks, but when a four-division American corps reinforced the French, the bridgehead splintered. On February 3 Colmar fell, and by February 9 no part of the left-Rhine area above Strasbourg remained in German hands.—*Source: Tippelskirch, p. 633.*

1816 In Jodl's notes the following statement was made regarding this situation report: "The Führer indicates with all emphasis the necessity of correcting the enemy penetration at Nineteenth Army in the direction of Breisach. He ordered that the possibility of transferring the 6th SS Mountain Division into this area be investigated, in order to attack with the 2nd Mountain Division in the general northwest direction of Rappoltweiler."—*Source: Nbg. Dok. 1787-PS.*

1817 Student led in the West: from September 4 to January 18, 1944, the Parachute Army and then—partially overlapping—after October 27, 1944, Army Group "H," renamed Army Group Student on November 7, 1944, finally in the Netherlands and on the lower Rhine. Student was now actually relieved by Colonel General Blaskowitz, the former Commander-in-Chief of Army Group "G," who had been replaced by Hausser. In April, however—as Göring correctly predicted here—Student was called upon again. He again led the Parachute Army from April 10/16 to April 28, 1945, and took over Army Group Vistula during the last days of the war.—*Source: Siegler, p. 139.*

1818 In the Western campaign, in May 1940, Student led the following operations: The capture of Eben Emael Fortress, the cornerstone of the Belgian border defense, with transport gliders; seizing numerous bridges over the Albert Canal with transport gliders and paratroopers; capturing the bridges in Rotterdam and at Moerdyk (critical for the north-south movements; and, in the same manner, seizing the Hague from the air. In Italy in the summer of 1943, Student was involved decisively with his parachute division in preventive measures against the defection of Italy and in control of the operation to free Mussolini.

[1819] Paul Hausser; born October 7, 1880; Cadet Corps; 1913 Captain in the General Staff; after the armistice, a major in Grenzschutz Ost [the eastern border guards]; Reichswehr, 1930 Infantry Commander IV (Magdeburg); January 31, 1932 left the service as a brevet Lieutenant General; Stahlhelm-Landesführer Berlin-Brandenburg; after the takeover of the Steel Helmets, SA Standartenführer; 1934 transferred to the SS leader of the SS Junker [Officer] School in Braunschweig; 1936 Brigadeführer and inspector SS VT [supply troops]; 1939 SS Gruppenführer on the staff of Panzer Division Kempf (Polish campaign); in France, Yugoslavia and in the East as Commander SS Support Division (later *Das Reich*); 1941 Obergruppenführer; 1942 Commanding General, first SS headquarters (later, headquarters, II SS Panzer Corps); June 1944 (as successor to Dollmann) Commander-in-Chief, Seventh Army until being wounded while breaking out of Falaise on August 21, and, in the same month, SS Oberstgruppenführer and recipient of the Swords award. On January 23, 1945, Hausser took over Army Group Upper Rhine (Nineteenth Army under the Twenty-fourth Army), formerly led by Himmler, which, on January 28, joined Army Group "G" (the First and Seventh Army, until then Blaskowitz) on the Saar (Army Group G with the First Army and the Nineteenth Army under the Twenty-Fourth; the Seventh Army joined Army Group "B"). These five days in which Hausser led Army Group Upper Rhine are presumably the reason he was described as being "familiar with" the situation. Hausser remained then until April 2 as Commander-in-Chief Army Group "G."—*Source: Munzinger Archive; Siegler, pp. 49 and 122; Seemen; Krätschmer, p. 37.*

[1820] A few days before, Himmler was moved from the upper Rhine to Pomerania. The tone in which Hitler's brother-in-law Fegelein talked about his "Reichsführer" was remarkable. It becomes clear in the following text, however, that Fegelein was no longer quite in favor, and his heroic nonsense got on his future brother-in-law's nerves. His surprising end three months later thus becomes more plausible.

[1821] Army Group "G" and Commander-in-Chief Upper Rhine.

[1822] The flooding in the Netherlands had been prepared for a long time and was carried out by Student as the local commander. And only incomplete measures were involved, since Eisenhower had requested at the end of April and beginning of May 1945 that Blaskowitz refrain from opening other dikes.—*Source: Eisenhower: Kreuzzug, p. 477.*

[1823] Friedrich Christiansen; born December 12, 1879; navigation school; 1900 officer in the merchant marine; 1904 captain; 1913 flight training; Navy pilot in World War I (Lieutenant at the end); 1921-29 captain in the merchant marine; 1930-33 pilot with Dornier; commander of a flying boat *Do X* among others; March 1933 with the "Reich Commissioner for the Luftwaffe" or RLM; corps leader NSFK; 1939 Air General; from May 29, 1940 to the capitulation Armed Forces Commander Netherlands, and from November 10, 1944 until January

28, 1945 also Commander-in-Chief, Twenty-Fifth Army. Christiansen was sentenced by the Dutch Special Court in Arnhem to 12 years' imprisonment; he was released at the end of 1955.—*Source: Munzinger Archive; Siegler, p. 115; Deutsches Führerlexikon.*

[1824] The reference is apparently to Himmler's old staff from the upper Rhine, now taken over by Hausser. Because the General Staff had limited trust in Himmler's leadership qualities, General Wenck, head of the operations group in the Army High Command, was later ordered to Army Group Vistula from time to time; on one of these trips he was involved in a serious car accident.

[1825] Jodl's order protocol regarding the situation report of January 27, 1945, said the following: "At the suggestion of the Chief of the Armed Forces Operations Staff, the Führer approves following command structure in the West:

Army Group "H" with Twenty-Fifth Army and First Parachute Army: Colonel General Blaskowitz,

Army Group "B" with Fifteenth Army, Fift Panzer Army, and Seventh Army: Field Marshal Model,

Army Group "G" with First Army and Nineteenth Army: Oberstgruppenführer Hausser."

—*Source: Nbg. Dok. 1787-PS.*

[1826] Apparently Hausser.

[1827] Hitler was referring to the spring battle of La Bassée–Arras, which began with a powerful artillery duel on May 9, 1915. Hitler's "List" Regiment and the 6th Bavarian Field Artillery Regiment—whose 2nd Detachment was commanded by Major Joseph v. Parseval—both belonged to the 6th Bavarian Reserve Division that was under attack.—*Source: Das Bayernbuch I, pp. 64, 170 and 175.*

[1828] While the Americans were very confident, the British were actually somewhat concerned about Russian successes in eastern Germany. It was not only for this reason that they opposed Eisenhower's planned campaign over the Rhine with multiple main attacks. They feared that the Russians would sweep across the Oder and the Elbe to the North Sea while the British and Americans were clearing out the Rhineland, and argued instead for a single massive thrust over the lower Rhine in the direction of the German naval bases. Curiously, it was only because of the British-American disagreement that such fears about the Russian advance could emerge. In the Allied European Advisory Commission (EAC), the British suggestion about the division of the German occupation zones—which established the borders of the Soviet zone and the status of Berlin, corresponding to the later arrangement—had already been accepted by the Soviets in February 1944. Only the British-American quarrel about which of the two was to get the economically valuable northwest zone and who was to get the southern zone delayed the official commitment. In Quebec that September, when the Americans agreed to take over the now somewhat larger southern German zone, there were further difficulties between the Anglo-Americans regarding the position of Bremen and its access routes. Thus, the final zone agreement signed by the EAC on November 14 was ratified only by the British government. The Russians, as usual, waited for the agreement of both Allies, while the Americans, without thinking politically, continued to haggle over privileges for Bremen. The U.S. government did not provide its consent until February 1, 1945, and then on February 6 the Soviet government—which had never made any attempt to extend its zone—followed, bringing into effect the legally binding three-power agreement regarding the occupation zones.—*Source: Moseley, passim; Wilmot, p. 715.*

1829 On October 8, 1941, in Soviet Camp 58, a first "conference of German anti-Fascist prisoners of war" was held, and passed a resolution against the Hitler regime. These efforts did not increase, however, until after the capitulation of the Sixth Army in Stalingrad. At a second meeting in Krasnogarsk on July 12-13, 1943, the "National Committee for a Free Germany" [NCFG] was founded, with the emigrant poet Erich Weinert as president and a Major Hetz and Bismarck's grandson Heinrich Graf v. Einsiedel as vice presidents. This NCFG was strengthened by the "German Officers' Union," founded two months later under General v. Seydlitz (Commanding General, LI Army Corps) and Lieutenant General v. Daniels (Commander, 376th Infantry Division) that joined it; they were now both vice presidents of the NCFG as well. The committee was based in Lunovo, but most of the emigrants stayed in Moscow, where they could have more control. Created as a mixture of Communist functionaries and German national officers from circles that had supported an "Eastern orientation" since the emergence of Prussia, the NCFG was used by the Russians for propaganda work aimed at the German Armed Forces, particularly on the Eastern Front. The organization used a variety of media to disseminate its messages, including leaflets, the black-, white- and red-bordered weekly newspaper *Freies Deutschland*, loudspeakers, and radio. Although the Soviets gave them a relatively free hand, and at least did not reject the possibility of a later pact with a German army that would overthrow Hitler, the success was virtually nil. When the NCFG—which Field Marshal Paulus also joined (on Witzleben's execution day), and whose summons in December 1944 brought in a field marshal, a colonel general, six generals, 13 lieutenant generals and 29 major generals—failed completely in its assignment to prepare the Cherkassy pocket and later the Courland Army for capitulation, the Russians lost what remaining interest they had, which in any case had decreased significantly after the strengthening of the Allies' cohesiveness in Teheran. After the occupation of Germany, there were no further assignments for the NCFG members and on November 2, 1945, the NCFG and German Officers' Union disbanded. Not until 1948 did a few former committee members move into leadership positions in the Soviet zone.—*Source: Paetel, passim; Puttkamer, passim; Einsiedel, passim; Hahn, passim; Gollwitzer, passim; Winzer, p. 200; Bohn, passim.*

1830 United Press reported on January 24 from Ankara: "According to a report that arrived here from Sofia, 50 German prisoners in Russia, including numerous generals, held a meeting under the leadership of General Paulus and resolved to establish a 'provisional German military government' that will begin to function immediately after the occupation of Königsberg by the Red Army...At the head of the new German government, it says, will be General Paulus...After the establishment of a new German government, a new 'free German army' will also be created, which will participate with the Russians in the war against National Socialist Germany." As Hitler predicted, in London ten days later Vansittart spoke fiercely against this project: the NCFG people were "evil people," and the Russians would see through them. Vansittart said, "The Russians are completely capable of looking after these areas [that they have occupied] without any such useless support or obtrusiveness." This difference of opinion showed that the Russians were entering Germany with a firm political concept, while the Western Allies—aside from some vague crusade ideas—thought only in antiquated occupation terms.—*Source: NZZ of Jan. 25 (evening edition) and Feb. 5 (midday edition), 1945.*

[1831] The formation of a police unit or a three-division "Paulus Army" was actually discussed in NCFG circles (see, for example, the previous note), as a means of saving the substance of the German army; however, the Russians brusquely rejected any such suggestions.

[1832] The monitoring intelligence reports from Göring's "Luftwaffe Research Department," printed on brown paper, were known as the "Braune Blätter [Brown Pages]." These reports came mostly from diplomatic communications. This institution was Göring's private intelligence service, which monitored telegraph and telephone communication in particular, especially from foreigners.—*Source: IMT IX, pp. 325 and 490, XII, p. 219.*

[1833] Here the reference is to the combat elements of this infantry division, which was being transported to the East.—*Source: War Diary of the Armed Forces Operations Staff from Jan. 27, 1945 (Nbg. Dok. 1797-PS).*

[1834] Such hypnosis treatments were the customary and usually exclusive content of the "trusting and cordial discussions" between Hitler and his satellite chiefs. As a result of this "hypnosis," the following was officially announced the next day: "The Führer received the Norwegian Prime Minister Vidkun Quisling in his headquarters for a trusting and cordial discussion. In the discussion of all questions of mutual interest to Germany and Norway, total agreement and sincere understanding were reached. The Führer again confirmed his decision, publicly announced in September 1943 by the Norwegian Reich Commissioner Terboven, that after the victorious end of the European battle of destiny, Norway will be restored to total freedom and independence while taking on the commitments that arose for the Norwegian state during the joint efforts to safeguard the security of the "European community of peoples." [—] What really happened was reported by the chief of the SS head office, Obergruppenführer Berger, to Reichsführer Himmler on February 6, 1945, "Prime Minister Quisling originally intended, based on the results of the Norwegian ministerial conference discussions, to present the following: 1. Peace agreement between the Greater German Reich and Norway. 2. Quisling, as 'Riksforstander,' takes over all government power in Norway. 3. The Reich Commissariat will end, and the Greater German Reich will be represented by an embassy in Norway. 4. Germany agrees to officially recognize the freedom, independence, indivisibility and inalienability of Norway. [—] Of these four wishes, Quisling was able to gain acceptance of only the final point during his last visit. In view of the immense burden placed on the Führer by the unfortunate situation, he had not dared to bring up points 2 and 3 after the first point failed on the objection of the Reich Foreign Minister. Remarkably, this time Reich Minister Lammers also agreed with the Reich Foreign Minister." Hitler was speaking ironically: Quisling needed one more day to end the state of war between Germany and Norway—this was a request that Quisling had repeated several times in the past. (See also below p. 867.)—*Source: DNB of Jan. 28, 1945; Schreiben Bergers an Himmler [Letter from Berger to Himmler?] dated Feb. 6, 1945 (Nbg. Dok. NG-4643).*

[1835] The 22nd Infantry Division was the well-known parachute division from the Dutch campaign in 1940. The division had fought in 1941-42 in southern Ukraine and in the Crimea (Sevastopol') and was on Crete as a security division from October 1942 to August 1944. Since then it had covered the withdrawal route of the northward marching Army Group "E". After Prijepolje was given up on January 10 it also reached the Drina River at Višegrad. There a bridgehead was held, which initially reached to Mokragora and then to Dobrunje, and finally narrowed to the hills around the city itself.—*Source: Metzsch, passim; Order of Battle, p. 146; Schmidt-Richberg, p. 87.*

[1836] Meaning attacks against the Russians in Hungary on both sides of Plattensee [Lake Balaton]; Army Group "E" was to support these attacks with an attack over the Drava River from the south. This operation, which had been planned by Hitler in January, was put off several times and did not begin until March 6, and did not get beyond building bridgeheads on the north bank of the Drava. Because the Plattensee [Lake Balaton] offensive remained stuck at the beginning as well, the Drava bridgeheads were evacuated again between March 15 and 22.—*Source: Schmidt-Richberg, p. 98.*

[1837] Adolf Fischer; born July 23, 1893; 1914 war volunteer; 1915 Second Lieutenant in the Reserves; 1920 discharged as First Lieutenant; 1921 police; 1935 transferred to the Army as a Major; 1936 Commander, 1st Battalion, 88th Infantry Regiment; 1938 Lieutenant Colonel; 1940 Commander, 459th Infantry Regiment; 1941 Colonel; May 1944 Commander, 367th Infantry Division; July 1944 Major General; and September 1944 Commander, Combat Group Southeast. General Fischer had defended Kragujevac and Kraljevo with his group in October and November 1944 and had then taken over the command of the 104th Jäger Division, which was then on the Drava, upriver from Esseg.—*Source: Keilig 211/84; Schmidt-Richberg, pp. 50, 52 and 69.*

[1838] This reference was probably to an operation against the Papuk mountains, which were dominated by partisans, to the rear of the Drava front. The operation began on February 6. In addition to the Cossacks, Group Fischer, the 297th Infantry Division and the 7th SS Mountain Division *Prinz Eugen* participated. These mopping-up actions served to secure the Drava front.—*Source: Schmidt-Richberg, p. 95.*

[1839] Helmuth v. Pannwitz; born October 14, 1898 in Upper Silesia; war volunteer; 1915 Second Lieutenant; 1920 left the service; 1935 reactivated as Cavalry Captain; 1938 Major and Commander, 2nd Battalion, 11th Cavalry Regiment; in the Polish, French and Eastern campaigns as Lieutenant Colonel (1940) and Commander, 45th Divisional Reconnaissance Detachment; November 1941 Army High Command; 1942 Colonel and Commander, Combat Group (Cavalry Unit v. Pannwitz); June 1943 Major General and named by Stauffenberg as Commander, 1st Cossack Cavalry Division; with this unit in partisan action in Yugoslavia after fall 1943; April 1944 Lieutenant General; and early 1945 taken over with his units into the Waffen SS as Commanding General XV SS Cossack Cavalry Corps with the intention of becoming Hetman [chief] of all Cossacks. At the surrender, Pannwitz succeeded in withdrawing to Carinthia to British captivity, but was handed over to the Soviets on May 27, 1945, and hanged by them on January 16, 1947.—*Source: Aufzeichnungen von Constantin Wagner, Siegfried Ungermann und Artur Timm (Thorwald Material in the IfZ); Thorwald: Wen sie…, pp. 249, 309 and 564; Seemen; Das deutsche Heer, p. 429; Rangliste 1944-45, p. 29; DNB of Jan. 5, 1943; Der deutsche Soldat, 22nd Jg., p. 55; Keilig 211/245.*

[1840] Bruno v. Uthmann; born April 17, 1891; 1912 Second Lieutenant, 1st Guard Infantry Regiment; 1918 First Lieutenant; Reichswehr; 1929 instructor at the War Academy; 1932 Major; 1934-35 Battalion Commander; 1936 Colonel and instructor at the War Academy again; after 1938 military attaché in Stockholm, Oslo and Copenhagen (after 1940 only in Stockholm) based in Stockholm; 1939 Major General; and 1941 Lieutenant General.

[1841] This probably refers to an incident with the Swedish newspaper *Socialdemokraten*. After returning from a reception, Uthmann received a telephone call in the middle of the night from the editorial staff of the paper, requesting a photo for an article about the Stockholm military attaché. Put out by the time of the call, Uthmann gave an unfriendly response, for which the *Socialdemokraten* took revenge some days later with a notice saying that according to information in their hands, the military attaché would be the next member of the German diplomatic and consular corps in Sweden to leave his position and request asylum (there had already been two cases up to that point).

[1842] Dr. Hans Thomsen; born September 14, 1891; Universities of Heidelberg and Bonn; 1913 Dr of Law; 1915 junior lawyer; 1913 Army service (at the end, Second Lieutenant in the Reserves); 1917 appointed to the German legation in Oslo; 1919 entry into diplomatic service; 1921-23 vice consul in Milan and Naples; 1924 in the Foreign Office; 1926 legation council; 1932 senior legation council (1933 Ministerial Council) in the Reich Chancellery and foreign affairs councilor; 1936 Embassy Council in Washington, chargé d'affaires there from November 1938 to December 1941; from January 1943 until the capitulation, envoy in Stockholm.—*Source: Who's Who in Germany… II, p. 166; Degeners Wer ist's?, p. 1607.*

[1843] Here Hitler seems to be mixing up two different announcements. On this date, January 27, DNB reported from Geneva with the headline, "The Cry for Truth: New complaints about the dishonesty of the Anglo-American war news": 'The Western Front means hell for our troops, but we are forbidden to write about it.' That is one of many accusations made by war correspondent David Walker in a lengthy article in the *Daily Mirror*, against the news provided by the Allied military authorities. Both press and radio in the U.S. and Britain received war news that was in most cases edited by the headquarters. Sometimes it was 'only' a wrong interpretation of the facts, but mostly it was 'pure lies.' Walker speaks then of 'misinterpreting the real war situation' and 'concealing' the unpleasant things." [—] And the next day, under the title, "American Acknowledgment of the Superiority of the German Panzers: the front knows it, only the American people don't hear the truth," the following was reported from Stockholm: "The American magazine *Time* explains the crazy idea of the Americans, who have always considered themselves the most competent men on earth and so always expect to have the best things. The article cites a report by the *New York Times'* military contributor, Hannson Baldwin, regarding the German Panzer force, which proved superior during battles in the Ardennes. The German Panzers, writes Baldwin, are better than any of the Anglo-American tanks. Their armor and the penetrating power of their guns are stronger, and they are able to drive through any kind of debris. This reality, *Time* continues, is well known by the fighting men at the front. But the Americans—who consider it only natural that their sons should have the best equipment in the world and the best weapons— are, of course, surprised by German superiority, because the truth was withheld from them."—*Source: DNB of Jan. 27, 1945, No. 2, and Jan. 28, 1945, No. 17.*

[1844] Meaning in Hungary. Hungary had a minor oilfield at Lispe, 30 km southwest of Plattensee [Lake Balaton], which was connected by a pipeline to a refinery in Csepel, directly south of Budapest. The output of oil-importing Hungary is so small, however, that it is not even mentioned in the statistics. But western Hungary also protected the lower Austrian field of Zistersdorf, which, although it had supplied less than a fifth of the old Reich's production in 1939 (145,000 t per year out of 741,000 t), Hitler had in the meantime improved it to the point where it was producing more than 100,000 tons per month. However, Tippelskirch was not entirely incorrect when he claimed that the western Hungarian area had become an obsession for Hitler (also confirmed, for example, by Guderian). He would soon attempt to motivate the protection of the last remaining oil sources with exclusively foreign-policy arguments, although the primary reason lay more in the fact that Hitler felt closer to Vienna (despite the love-hate relationship) and his whole Austrian homeland than to the other German districts.—*Source: Stat. Jahrbuch 1941-42, p. 62*; Tippelskirch, p. 575; Guderian: Erinnerungen, p. 379.*

[1845] An enemy tank named "Boxer" could not be identified. This was also the only report at the time, which was not confirmed by any further sightings. On the German side, rumors of an American 100-ton tank—of which there were supposedly pictures—were discussed at that time. However, this incident was either a false report or concerned only test models. In any case, this tank did not appear in greater numbers.

[1846] L/... refers to the so-called caliber length, i.e., the barrel length in the caliber or the ratio of the barrel length to the caliber, which influences the v_0 [initial velocity] and thus the range and penetrating power of the projectile.

[1847] v. Senger-Etterlin called the Hunter Panther [*Jägdpanther*] the best German tank destroyer and praised its excellent firepower and ideal design accompanied by completely adequate mobility, which is lacking in the Hunter Tiger [*Jägdtiger*]. Other tank drivers shared this opinion as well. On a larger scale, though, this kind of assessment is a question of the terrain, as the Hunter Tiger, for example, was clearly much too heavy for mountainous areas.—*Source: Senger-Etterlin, pp. 33 and 35.*

[1848] Meaning again in the terrain.

[1849] After a number of reports were published in the foreign press in the preceding days regarding the supposed escaped inventor of the "V 4," the Berlin *Diplomatische Information* reported to representatives of the foreign press on January 27: "The Swedish press are publishing reports about a scientist allegedly acquainted with the problems of the V-weapons, who supposedly flew out of Germany and is now speaking out about details of the V-weapons. This man is, according to these reports, a professor Hartmann. It has been determined by the appropriate German authorities that such a person, who was involved with the V-weapons, does not exist at all and is a fabrication."—*Source: NZZ of Jan. 19, 1945 (morning edition).*

[1850] Shortly after the beginning of the war, the international exchange of weather reports was halted, as this information had now become secret. The naval operations in the north Atlantic and Artic, however, were particularly dependent on reliable weather forecasts. Thus, in September 1940, the Germans began sending out weather observation ships, of which only the *Sachsen* (sunk in early 1943) had success on a few voyages. Later, in November 1944, the *Wuppertal* reached the edge of the ice but then disappeared in January 1945. Because of the uncertainty of these ship actions, the trend after the fall of 1941 was to drop off meteorological detachments with equipment in isolated positions in the polar area. These troops would periodically radio their observations until the ice broke up the following summer, when—if they hadn't already been discovered and taken captive—they would be picked up by a submarine or aircraft. There were 10 of these operations altogether (five times to Spitzbergen, twice to Greenland, twice to Hope, and once to Franz Josef Land; two Greenland attempts failed in 1944 due to American defense), two of which took place during the winter of 1944-45: "Haudegen" on the Nordostland (Rijpfjord) of Spitzbergen (dropped off by the steamboat *Busch* and *U507* in September 1944, picked up in September 1945) and "Polarwolf" on the island of Hope southwest of Spitzbergen (dropped off by *U636* in October 1944, also not picked up until after the end of the war). The Bäreninseln [Bear Islands] mentioned here lie directly south of Spitzbergen and thus about 350 km from Hope, but it could be this "Polarwolf" mission that was under discussion.—*Source: Ruge: Seekrieg, p. 219; Chevalier, passim.*

[1851] Along the Norwegian coast, the following were transferred to the West: *Z 31, Z 33, Z 34* and *Z 38* under Captain Baron v. Wangenheim.

[1852] See also above note 1504.

[1853] Convoys from Gotenhafen [Gdynia] via Danzig to Libau.

[1854] The refugee route across the Baltic became enormously significant after January 23 when East Prussia was cut off by the Russian thrust to Elbing. At the end of

1944, of the 1¾ million people still in East Prussia after the preceding occupation of the eastern districts and the quiet migration, 450,000 were transported
across the sea from Pillau, while 900,000 succeeded in arriving west of the Vistula
River on foot, via the Frische Haff [Bay] and the Frische Nehrung [Spit], where,
however, about half then ended up in the second refugee movement or were
overrun by the Russians. The evacuation by sea from Pillau had begun two days
before, on January 25; by February 15, 204,000 refugees had already been transported out by ship. On March 8 the transport from Pillau was halted for three
weeks, as all ship capacity was needed for the evacuation of the threatened
harbors of Danzig and Gdingen. The ship traffic then recommenced at the end
of the month and continued until April 20 when the five-day battle over Pillau
began. Evacuations by sea also had to be made—as already mentioned—when,
on March 1, as a result of the loss of Köslin, West Prussia and eastern East
Pomerania were practically cut off, followed by western Pomerania two days
later when the Russians appeared on the Oder at Stettin.—*Source: Die Vertreibung
(Oder-Neisse) I/1, pp. 16E and 33E.*

[1855] The 14,600-ton cruiser *Prinz Eugen* (launched in August 1937) was completed in
the spring of 1941 and immediately thereafter accompanied the *Bismarck* on its
death tour—itself escaping to Brest. In February 1942 it took part in the successful channel breakthrough of the Atlantic battleship squadron and was then
employed in the Artic. After the opening of the Gulf of Finland in the fall of
1944 the ship was assigned to defend the German supply and evacuation lines in
the Baltic against the Soviet naval forces, and to hold the Baltic harbors as long
as possible. At the end of war, the *Prinz Eugen* was, in addition to the light cruiser
Nürnberg, the last large German ship still in running order. It was delivered and
sunk as an experimental ship during an American atomic bomb test on November 15, 1947, off the coral island Kwajelain, one of the Marshal Islands 350 km
southeast of Bikini.—*Source: Ruge: Seekrieg, pp. 131, 203, 208, 297, 300 and 311;
Tippelskirch, p. 628; Gröner, p. 8.*

[1856] The line ships *Schleswig-Holstein* and *Schlesien*, launched in 1906, were Germany's
last large ships remaining after World War I. In 1939—while the modern ships
sailed against the British in the North Sea—these two ships, along with minesweeping units, conducted the naval war against Poland in the Baltic. There, the
Schleswig-Holstein in particular became known for the bombardment of the
Westerplatte and the Hela Peninsula. The two "old ships" were then used as
training ships in the Baltic, mostly in Gdingen, where the *Schleswig-Holstein* was
sunk by a bomb in shallow water on December 18, 1944; later, on March 21,
1945, the ship was blown up. The *Schlesien* was transferred into the western Baltic; it sank outside Swinemünde after hitting a mine on May 4, 1945.— *Source:
Ruge: Seekrieg, pp. 34 and 300; Gröner, p. 26.*

[1857] From Budapest.

[1858] Hitler was mistaken; the Allied "Big Three" met from February 4-11 in Yalta.

[1859] The Prussian general Guillaume René Baron de l'Homme de Courbière, from a
refugee family, born February 23, 1733, had, as governor, successfully defended

the Graudenz Fortress against the French in 1806-07 and was afterward promoted to field marshal and named governor general of West Prussia.

[1860] The subject broached here was already under consideration by the Army personnel office in 1944. At that time they had solicited the opinion of various commanders regarding the question of whether or not officers who had been promoted very quickly because of bravery, fortunate circumstances, etc. could be reduced in rank if it turned out afterward that they didn't have the qualifications corresponding to the responsibilities of their rank. None of these plans was realized, however.

[1861] Goebbels was named Reich plenipotentiary for all military employment on July 25, 1944.

[1862] Rhön.

[1863] A famous parallel: Colonel T. E. Lawrence.

[1864] In England, appointment to a new duty position was automatically accompanied by promotion to the corresponding rank. The bestowal of this rank was also automatically reversed, however, upon leaving the appointment and taking over a lower command. But in England, an officer was also unable to lose the rank earned through the normal "slow grind." So except for the somewhat misleading expression "regularly promoted," the description by Göring was correct.

[1865] This remark is characteristic of the standards of Hitler's future brother-in-law: There was apparently no difference between Britain and America as far as he was concerned! If Christian had been in America once, he certainly must have a good understanding of the British circumstances.

[1866] With six ranks, Tolsdorf probably held the promotion record. He started as a first lieutenant at the beginning of the war and was a lieutenant general by the end of the war.

[1867] The reference must be to Major Anton Baron v. Tuboeuf (born June 28, 1870), who led the List Regiment from April 1917 to July 1918 and recommended Hitler for the the Iron Cross I class.

[1868] In World War I promotion depended on the authorized posts from the last peacetime budget. It gave only the company commander, etc., raises as financial compensation or reward of rank. The promotion prospects for the lower ranks were better (because of losses) than in peacetime, but the many new formations were not taken into account, so at the end of war a regiment was usually being led by a major or lieutenant colonel. Sometimes a lieutenant who had led a company at the front continuously since August 1914 wasn't even promoted to first lieutenant until the end of the war. In World War II, in contrast, someone who held a given position would usually be promoted to the corresponding rank after a six-month probation period. In 1943-44 this practice was made a formal principle by Schmundt: anyone who held a position for half a year automatically received the corresponding rank. This discussion concerns, to a certain degree, the attempt to use this Schmundt principle in reverse—downward—as an enormous number of officers were available without relevant appointments after the extensive withdrawals (see Burgdorf's comments).

[1869] Otto Ernst Remer; born August 18, 1912; 1933 Corporal; 1935 Second Lieutenant, 4th Infantry Regiment; 1939 chief, 15th Company, 89th Infantry Regiment and 13th Company, 479th Infantry Regiment; 1940 chief, 701st Infantry Gun Company; 1941 Captain; 1942 Commander, 1st Battalion, 10th Infantry Regiment, and (April) 4th Battalion, Panzer Grenadier Division *Grossdeutschland*; 1943 Major; and May 1944 Commander, Berlin Guard Regiment. In this capacity he did not carry out the arrest of propaganda minister Göbbels on July 20 as ordered; instead, he suppressed the plot on Hitler's behalf. As a result, Hitler promoted Remer to colonel out of turn, and a half year later to major general (Function: Commander Führer Escort Brigade or, after January 31, 1945, Führer Escort Division). Hitler's description of the reaction in the officer corps is probably accurate.—*Source: Munzinger Archive; Keilig 211/267.*

[1870] In the provisional Reichswehr, the old insignia of rank were eliminated by decrees of the Reich government on January 19 and May 5, 1919, and replaced with stripes on the upper arm for non-commissioned officers or with (one to six) blue cords on the forearm for officers. These were derided from the right as "water-level marks" and were soon changed to silver braids, then to silver cords on the shoulders and finally to the old silver shoulder loops. The motive behind this measure, however, was an attempt to democratize the Army and not a surplus of officers. On the other hand, that same year, in the Erhardt brigade, there actually were officers of the old army in closed officers' companies performing the duties of privates in privates' uniforms. It seems out of the question, however, that there were similar cases in the provisional Reichswehr (Ebert supposedly had at his disposal an officers' company that performed guard duty, etc. in privates' uniforms). Thus, Keitel's remark could refer to the first mobilization planning of the Reichswehr around 1930, which, in the case of mobilization, called for a trebling of the current divisions (from 7 to 21) and the use of many retired and reserve officers from the Great War. At that time, the command positions were designed with corresponding pay—standard pay with an increase based on the duty position—but without rank. Insignia of rank were thus discontinued, as the position of the relevant platoon, company, battalion, etc. commander was to be indicated by stars on the collar.—*Source: Maerchker, p. 82; Benoist-Méchin, p. 128; Freksa, p. 94.*

[1871] Foreigners could obtain German citizenship either by application or automatically through appointment as a government official. Because the Austrian Hitler had always refused to make such an application—as he was of the opinion (which cannot be entirely dismissed) that this should not be necessary after four years of frontline service in the German Army—the National Socialists took the other route. The first opportunity presented itself with Frick's entry into the Thuringian interior ministry: In July 1930 Hitler was to be named temporarily as Police Commissioner in Hildburghausen, but this plan failed because of opposition from the rest of the State Ministery. The issue became urgent when Hitler decided in February 1932 to become a candidate in the Reich presidential election—which only Reich Germans could do. The action now shifted to the State of Braunschweig, where the National Socialist Klagges was First Minister in the

State Ministry and where National Socialists and National Germans formed the ruling coalition. The first thought was to name Hitler as, among other things, professor at the Technical College, assigned to teach political pedagogy. Because the opponents from the Hildburghausen case protested against the illegal false appointment, an inaugural lecture was even considered. The coalition partner caused this project to fail, but on February 25 Hitler was named Government Councilor in the Brunswick legation in Berlin with the assignment to "safeguard the interests of the Brunswick economy." The following day Hitler took the oath in front of the Brunswick envoy Boden and generously renounced his stipend immediately. It can hardly be assumed that Hitler entered "his" legation frequently, as he was immediately placed on leave.—*Source: FZ of Feb. 4 and 23-26, 1932; Goebbels: Kaiserhof, pp. 39 and 51; Görlitz/Quint, p. 335; Bracher, p. 461.*

1872 The report was not published, so apparently it did not prove true.

1873 Transcript No. 119/45—Fragment No. 6—Completely preserved. The following preliminary remark was made by the stenographer at the time of the second transcription in May 1945: "This is a shorthand record from a daily nighttime situation report which—in the final months—usually only lasted half an hour. If there were no particular events to report, there would only be a brief presentation by a representative of the Army General Staff and Hitler's adjutants, regarding the changes in the military situation since the afternoon meeting."

1874 During their encirclement attacks against Budapest in December 1944, the Russians had advanced in numerous places across the Gran [Hron] (Slovakian tributary of the Danube that flows into the Danube some 30 kilometers above the big bend), but were pushed back in some locations. They were, however, able to hold a bridgehead in the Párkány area west of the mouth of the Gran, from where they lined up for the attack against Komarom [Komorn] and Neuhäusel in the then Hungarian South Slovakia on January 16. They were pushed back here, too, but were able to hold an area of some 250 square kilometers west of the Gran as an assembly area. Units of the German Eighth Army marched against this bridgehead on February 17 from the north and across the Danube from the south, and succeeded in encircling the Soviet troops. The OKW report for February 25 (the day just now dawning) announced the mentioned destruction of this remaining enemy bridgehead on the west bank. The report for the following day spoke of 700 dead on the Soviet side and 4,000 prisoners, as well as the destruction or capture of 90 tanks and 304 guns.—*Source: Tippelskirch p. 576; VB of Feb. 24-27, 1945.*

1875 Karl Hanke; born August 24, 1903; German Müllers School in Dippoldiswalde; 1928 Gewerbelehrer commercial instructor in Berlin and joined the NSDAP; 1931 dismissed from the educational system because of political activity; 1932 Member of the Reichstag and Member of the Landtag in Prussia; private secretary and personal Secretary to Goebbels; 1933 to 1939-41 in the Propaganda Ministry; in April 1937 Ministerial Director there; in November 1937 State Secretary as successor to Funk; 1938 Vice President of the Reich Culture Board; head of the the Main Office in the Reich Propaganda Ministry; 1938 he became known for his affair with Magda Goebbels; August 1939 joined the Armed Forces as volunteer; after the partition of Silesia, Gauleiter and High President of Upper Silesia after January 27, 1941; and 1944 SS Obergruppenführer. In 1945 Hanke led the defense of Breslau with rigorous means and in Hitler's will of April 29 he was named Reichsführer SS and chief of the German police. Under this pretext he left Breslau on May 5 in a "Storch." He then landed in Hirschberg and presumably attempted—initially in the uniform of a Waffen SS Unterführer—to get through the Sudetenland to the west. During that attempt he was supposedly shot and killed in June at Neudorf, between Komotau and Brüx, by Czech guards.—*Source: Munzinger Archive; Reichstags-Handbücher; BBZ of Nov. 27, 1937 and Jan. 28, 1941; Der Angriff of Jan. 20, 1938.*

[1876] After February 1 the fighting had shifted to the territory outside Breslau. On the 13th-14th the Russians managed to encircle the city. The encirclement was broken open again along the Freiburger railway line on the 15th, but was then final after the 16th. Under the fanatical Gauleiter Hanke and the commanding officer Major General v. Ahlfen (after March 6, Lieutenant General Niehoff), 15,000 men from the Volkssturm and 30,000 regular troops fought for the city. In addition, approximately 250,000 civilians remained in Breslau. The continuous hope of relief was nurtured by the fact that the front between Strehlen and Striegau remained stable—Zobten, which was visible with the naked eye, was in German hands until the very end—and that the rumbling of the guns was heard with increasing strength. Aside from loud propaganda and a very few reinforcements that were flown in, the city could not be helped from the outside. After the occupation forces had survived hard attacks and artillery and aerial bombardment—especially during the days around Easter—Breslau surrendered on May 6. The capitulation was preceded by an intervention of the clergy of both confessions and Hanke's escape.—*Source: Tippelskirch p. 622; Thorwald: Es began..., pp. 114 and 126; Thorwald: Das Ende..., p. 314; Görlitz II, p. 480; Aufzeichnungen von Hans v. Ahlfen (Thorwald material in the IfZ); Konrad, passim; Various newspaper articles.*

[1877] Meaning the former Breslau civilian airport of Gandau (near which Mölders crashed in 1941). Because the military airfield of Schöngarten had already fallen, and the city was dependent on air supply, the successful defense of Gandau proved to be of vital importance. This airport could not be used during the day because it was so close to the front line—the Soviets carried out their main attacks from the west and also from the south—and the runways were also too short for many of the tactical aircraft used for supply, so they couldn't even fly in by night. Thus, another substitute airfield was being built east of the city on the island of Scheitning in the Friesenwiese area. Further into the city, Hanke had civilians pull down a residential area around the Kaiserstrasse on the Scheitniger Stern to make space for another makeshift airfield after the beginning of March.—*Source: Thorwald: Es began..., pp. 127, 132 and 135; Aufzeichnungen von Hans v. Ahlfen und Dr. K. D. Staemmler (Thorwald material in the IfZ); Various newspaper articles.*

[1878] Probably meaning Triebel in the Niederlausitz.

[1879] Waffen SS Infantry Brigade *Charlemagne*, established in November and December 1944 by joining the regiment-strength "French Volunteer Assault Brigade," which had existed since July 1944, with the reinforced 638th French Infantry Regiment, which had been taken over by the Army. In March the brigade was renamed the 33rd Waffen SS Infantry Division *Charlemagne* (French No. 1).— *Source: Order of Battle, p. 350; Nbg. Dok. NO-175.*

1880 Should read: "...is unmistakable."

1881 Near Heiligenbeil. Seerappen, which is mentioned further below, is near Königsberg. There is no town called Ragitten (Ragnit on the Memel could hardly be meant by this point).

1882 The MG 15 was an aircraft weapon that—modified as a drum magazine—was also used by Luftwaffe ground units. The MG 34 was the light machine gun used most frequently by the Army in the first years of the war (until the introduction of the MG 42).

1883 Name probably incorrect.

1884 Chief of General Staff of Army Group "B." General Westphal, mentioned in the following text, was Chief of Staff for the Commander-in-Chief West.

1885 Since the end of November 1944, the American Ninth Army had remained in front of the Ruhr. The forces were trapped in place not so much by the German defensive lines but by the seven German-controlled dams on the upper reaches of the Ruhr and its upper tributaries (best known: the Urft and the Ruhr or Schwammenauel dams) and the ever-present danger of flooding in the case of bomb attacks during an offensive. Two attacks against the dam area in November had failed, as had attempts by the R.A.F. to eliminate the threat by destroying the dams with its heaviest bombs. A further attempt with stronger forces in mid-December had to be broken off because of the Ardennes offensive. Now, the major Anglo-American offensive against the Rhine had been moving forward since February 8. When some of the American forces reached the dams, however, the Germans were able to blast the Urft and Ruhr dams in time. The Americans were forced to draw back again because of the flooding, leaving the Canadians and British on their own for two weeks in the northern sector. Not until the previous morning (February 23) did six divisions of the American Ninth and First Armies begin to cross the Ruhr, which was still flooded. The attack, which was surprising for this reason, was successful at the first attempt; at the time of this situation conference (i.e., the evening of the second day) the American engineers had already built 19 bridges, including seven tank bridges.— *Source: Wilmot (Engl.), pp. 569, 582, 612, and 672; Tippelskirch, p. 635; Armed Forces High Command report of Feb. 12, 1945.*

1886 These numbers given by Burgdorf don't make much sense. The two big dams, the Schwammenauel and the Urft, held 100 million and 45 million cubic meters of water, respectively. It is therefore unlikely that Burgdorf's numbers could refer to *millions* of cubic meters. The Armed Forces Operations Staff war diary entry for that same day says a further bombing of the Ruhr dam "would bring down 4 million cubic meters of water within six days."—*Source: Nbg. Dok. 1797-PS.*

1887 Probably Wittringen, some 10 km up the Saar from Saargemünd; Klein-Bittersdorf is downriver from this city, already in German territory. Waxweiler and Nieder-Pierscheid are between Prüm and Neuerburg; Oberbillig, Wasserbillig and Könen are in the Moselle area on the Luxembourg border; there is no town called Neuhaus.

[1888] The OKW report of February 25 reported: "Anglo-American terror-pilots attacked cities in western, northwestern and southeastern Germany yesterday. Bomb attacks on residential areas and attacks by low-flying aircraft with aircraft armaments caused losses amongst the civilian population. Last night the British bombed several towns in the Rhine–Westphalia area, and also the Reich capital. Air defense forces brought down 22 enemy aircraft."

[1889] It is not quite clear what type of device was under discussion here—possibly an ultrasound locator for use on escort vessels, although that principle was already known before the war.

[1890] Transcript number unknown—Fragment No. 26—Only a few individual pages of the shorthand record were preserved. Regarding the date: fighting for the Erft took place from February 28 to March 5. Kempen, which is mentioned in this text, fell into enemy hands—temporarily at first—on March 3. The Americans reached the Rhine in that front sector on March 2, south of Düsseldorf (Wilmot, p. 725). Thus, the fragment must date from the 1st or—at the latest—2nd of March. But if the beginning of the sentence, "In Cologne the last bridge..." was to be completed with "...blown up," or something similar, this fragment No. 26 would have to be dated March 6, on which day, at 11 a.m., the Hohenzollern bridge in Cologne—the last bridge on this section of the Rhine—was blown up. The engagements mentioned in the Erft sector, however, argue against such a later date; thus, the report on the Cologne bridge is likely connected with a note in the war diary of the Armed Forces Operations Staff, which says under March 2: "In Cologne one of the bridges collapsed" (Nbg. Dok. 1797-PS). Because neither Burgdorf nor apparently Göring are present—both participants in the meetings recorded in Fragments 49, 1a and 1b—and the following mention of Burgdorf in connection with the supreme command on the upper Rhine is likely to have been made prior to his remark, this fragment No. 26 would more likely be from March 1, which is confirmed by the above-mentioned "takeover of the 7th Army."

[1891] On the upper Rhine front.

[1892] In the Netherlands.

[1893] He probably meant Konradsheim, near Lechenich, on the west bank of the Erft. The town called Plate, which is mentioned next, does not exist either; the reference could be to Vlatten between the Ruhr dam and Euskirchen, or else further south, to Platten above Wittlich.

[1894] The following was reported from Eisenhower's headquarters on March 1: "The Erft was crossed in the three places by strong units of the American First Army. One of the bridges was taken intact and is now allowing the deployment of heavy armored forces in the western suburbs of Cologne."—*Source: NZZ of March 1, 1945 (midday edition).*

[1895] Named divisions were first employed in May 1944 when four divisions of the 26th wave were created from replacement units (used to replenish shattered front units), and again in the final months of the war when some units were scraped together using personnel from the Replacement Army, division remnants, schools, RAD and Luftwaffe ground personnel.—*Source: Keilig 100/4.*

[1896] In the situation book of the Armed Forces Operations Staff, it says under March 2, 1945: "This morning Army Group "G" will take over the command of the Seventh and First Armies. The front on the upper Rhine goes immediately under the command of the Commander-in-Chief West."—*Source: Nbg. Dok. 1797-PS.*

[1897] Transcript number unknown—Fragment No. 1a—Regarding the date: the fighting over Dramburg, which is mentioned in the text, took place on March 2-3. The Meuse River was last mentioned in an OKW report on March 2; the war diary of the Armed Forces Operations Staff says under the same date that it had become necessary to withdraw from the Meuse. This fragment here could therefore be from March 2, and—because it was recorded by the same stenographer as No. 1b—was presumably, like No. 49, part of the midday situation conference on March 2, 1945.

[1898] Referring to the upper Rhine front.

[1899] Heinz Reinefarth; born December 26, 1903; Freikorps; law study at Jena; 1927 junior lawyer; 1930 Assessor [civil servant]; 1932 lawyer; August 1932 NSDAP and SA; December 1932 transfer to the SS; 1934 Untersturmführer; 1937 Hauptsturmführer; 1939 drafted; 1940 Second Lieutenant; 1942 discharged from the Armed Forces because of frostbite, entered the legal office of the Ordnungspolizei; April 1942 Brigadeführer; after July administrative legal advisor in Prague; after mid-1943 with the title "Inspector general for administration with the deputy Reich protector;" October 1943 head of legal office in Orpo; January 1944 Supreme SS and Police Commander and Commander of the Warthe; in summer and fall 1944 as commander of a combat group participated in the suppression of the Warsaw revolt and in operation "Panzerfaust" against the Horthy government; August 1944 SS Gruppenführer; November 1944 assigned to deploy the XVIII SS Corps in Army Group Upper Rhine and named lieutenant general of the Waffen SS; mid-January 1945 Reception Staff, Frankfurt/Oder; and, after early February, commanding officer at Küstrin. On March 30 he broke out with 800 men, against specific orders, and was arrested and imprisoned in the Armed Forces detention center at Torgau until April 20, then he was turned over to the Reich War Court. In 1957 Reinefarth was mayor of Westerland (Sylt) and Member of the Landtag of Schleswig-Holstein. Regarding Bach-Zelewski, see note above.—*Source: SS staff files (Berlin Doc. Center); SS Dienstalterslisten; Nbg. Dok. NO-1402 and NO-2042; Order of Battle, p. 609; Seemen; Krätschmer, p. 361.*

[1900] Otto Skorzeny; born June 12, 1908; 1926 technical college in Vienna (mechanical engineering); 1931 Dr. of Engineering; 1932 NSDAP; 1932-33 College for World Trade in Vienna; 1939 Luftwaffe; March 1940 joined the Waffen SS as Unterscharführer (*Reich* Division); 1940 Untersturmführer and engineering officer; May 1943 as Hauptsturmführer assigned to form the 502nd SS Jäger Battalion (RSHA VI/S); with this unit freed Mussolini from Gran Sasso on September 12, 1943, and carried out operation "Panzerfaust" against the Horthy government in Budapest in October 1944 under Bach and Reinefarth; end of 1944 Obersturmbannführer and Commander, 502nd SS Jägdverbände (expansion of the 502nd Jägd Battalion); in the Ardennes offensive, intended as Commander of the 150th Panzer Brigade, which was to occupy the Meuse bridges wearing American uniforms (operation "Greif"); and February 1945 commanding officer of the Schwedt/Oder bridgehead. Skorzeny was captured by the Americans in May 1945 and was acquitted in 1947 by a military court in Dachau.— *Source: Skorzeny, passim; Munzinger Archive; Nbg. Dok. NO-1425, NO-1426, NO-1632, NO-1633, NO-1636, NO-1688, NO-1689, NO-1776, NO-2224, NO-2254 and No-2738.*

[1901] v. d. Bach-Zelewski.

[1902] SS Obergruppenführer Karl Pfeffer-Wildenbruch, born June 12, 1888, and in Budapest for quite some time as Commanding General IX SS Mountain Corps and Commander of the Waffen SS in Hungary, where he had been taken prisoner in the meantime. It does not seem very likely that he would have been commanding temporarily on the upper Rhine. However, the only person by the same name among the Army generals, the commanding general of the former IV Army Corps, General of Artillery Max Pfeffer, had been in Russian captivity since Stalingrad.—*Source: Order of Battle, p. 605; Seemen; Rangliste 1944-45, p. 397.*

[1903] Meaning Bach-Zelewski again.

[1904] As a result of the numerous changes, the command structure was somewhat complicated. When Himmler was commander-in-chief on the upper Rhine, he brought Bach-Zelewski and Reinefarth in as commanding generals. So when the New Year began, Bach was Commanding General, XIV SS Corps in the Strasbourg area and Reinefahrt was Commanding General, XVIII SS Corps in the Mühlhausen area. In the second half of January, Bach was then commanding the SS X Corps, formed from his old staff "head of the [Partisan] Band Warfare Units," but was replaced in mid-February by General Krappe. Bach— who, as Guderian mentioned here, "wasn't quite well for a while"—then took over the Oder Corps based on the fact that "this corps has a sector in which defense is predominant and pressure from the enemy is not so strong." Burgdorf's remark that Bach was commanding the X SS Corps *now*, is therefore puzzling; it also contradicts the previous statements by Guderian and Göring and is therefore likely to have been misunderstood or misinterpreted by the stenographer. (Although in Görlitz' book the X SS Corps is called the "Oder Corps," which is contradictory to documentary evidence from February 1945. If such a renaming had actually taken place in the second half of the month, that would explain the disagreements appearing here. In any case, the organizational chaos of the final weeks seems to have caused confusion even in the leading circles.)—*Source: Order of Battle, p. 336; Aktenvermerke SSPHA of Jan. 29 and Feb. 17, 1945 (Nbg. Dok. NO-2042); Görlitz II, p. 487.*

[1905] Both imprisoned generals, Feuchtinger and v. Hanneken, were accused of having enriched themselves personally through their appointments.

1906 Manstein, who is referred to here, wrote the following: "Hitler had given the order that the Zaporozh'e, Dnepropetrovsk, Kremenchug, and Kiev bridgeheads should be held during the retreat—an order against which there could have been no objection if the army group had had enough forces for their defense. Because this was not the case, the commander-in-chief of the army group had planned to evacuate the bridgeheads after completing the river crossing, which Hitler tacitly accepted for the three mentioned last. On the other hand, he had insisted with specific orders that the bridgehead at Zaporozh'e be enlarged and be held despite all protests. Aside from the necessity of holding the large Dnieper dam with its power station, he had argued that the enemy would not dare to advance against the Melitopol' front of the Sixth Army as long as we held the bridgehead. The latter point of view was worth considering from an operational perspective, but Hitler was again pursuing too many goals at once. In any case, the result of this order to hold Zaporozh'e was that the First Panzer Army was unable to relieve the XXXX Panzer Corps in time. That eliminated the possibility of counterattacking and destroying the enemy, who had crossed the river halfway between Dnepropetrovsk and Kremenchug, before he became strong enough to hold a large bridgehead south of the river." Strong enemy attacks at the beginning of October were still pushed back at first, but on October 14, faced with an assault by ten divisions and strong armored troops, the bridgehead had to be evacuated. Three days later the German Dnieper line was torn apart at Kremenchug and a week later on both sides of Dnepropetrovsk. "In any case, the attempt—forced by Hitler—to hold Zaporozh'e had cost us too much," said Manstein.—*Source: Manstein, pp. 545 and 547; Tippelskirch, p. 395.*

1907 The "Organization Consul" (OC), active since the spring of 1921, was an illegal follow-up organization to the "Ehrhardt Brigade," which was disbanded after the Kapp Putsch, but there were also members of other Freikorps in their ranks. The head office was in Munich, where Captain Hermann Ehrhardt—the "Consul"—had fled, and operated there under the cover of a "Bavarian Society for the use of Wood" while enjoying the support of the Munich police chief Pöhner. The goals of this secret organization were military physical training and education, the cultivation of nationalistic thinking, and fighting against everything anti-national or international, against Judaism, social democracy and left radicalism—in short, against the Weimar Republic. The OC people became notorious for this fight in particular, because they were responsible for most of the 354 "people's justice" and "lynch-law" killings committed between 1919 and June 1922. The two best-known of these deeds—the murder of Erzberger on August 26, 1921, and the murder of Rathenau on June 24, 1922—were carried out by OC members. When the Law for the Protection of the Republic was passed after the killing of Rathenau, the OC was past its peak. Between October 22 and 25, 1924, 26 OC members, including v. Killinger and Hoffmann, were sentenced at the State Court in Leipzig, along with 20 defendants—for membership in illegal secret societies—to ridiculous prison terms of up to 8 months.—*Source: Waite, p. 313; Augsburger Postzeitung of Oct. 23-26, 1924; Schulthess 1924, p. 101.*

[1908] The German Navy had been friendlier toward the Freikorps than the Army.

[1909] Horst v. Petersdorf; born December 30, 1892; severely wounded in World War I in 1914; 1917-18 commander of a detachment in Syria; 1919 as First Lieutenant drew up the Petersdorf Freikorps (employed in Berlin, Upper Silesia and in the Baltic area, first in the "Eisernen Division [Iron Division]"; actions included the attack on Essern, freeing Mitsau and Riga, summer 1919 going over to the radical "Baltic National Defense;" 1922 NSDAP; 1923 SA; at the end Brigadeführer in the SA group Berlin-Brandenburg (departed 1932); 1939 Captain and battalion commander, 180th Infantry Regiment 180; 1940 Major and severely wounded again; 1942 Commander, 1st Reserve Mountain Regiment; 1943 head of the German industrial commission in Hungary and Slovakia; 1944 Colonel; and arrested after July 20, acquitted by the People's Court.—*Source: Oertzen, p.34; Salomon, p. 129 and others; VB of Jan. 30, 1942.*

[1910] Franz v. Pfeffer (von Salomon); born February 19, 1888; junior lawyer; officer on the Western Front and in the General Staff; January 1919 established the "Westphalian Volunteer Battalion Münster" (later "Westphalian Freikorps Pfeffer"); actions in Münster, against Spartakus Mannheim, in Upper Silesia, in the Baltic area (Libau coup of April 16, 1919), and on the Ruhr (action by General Watter in March 1920); sentenced to death by an Allied court; 1923 action against Wesel (hijacking of 200 train cars); 1924 placed under the command of the NSDAP; SA Führer and Gauleiter for Westphalia; 1926 SA Führer and Gauleiter in the Ruhr; November 1926 to August 1930, Oberster SA Führer (OSAF), and then SA Obergruppenführer; 1932-41 Member of the Reichstag, both after the seizure of power; and after July 20 arrested for several months. Pfeffer is not to be confused with Fritz Pfeffer von Salomon (the "von Salomon" was not used by either member of the Pfeffer von Salomon family, for obvious reasons) who was SA Gruppenführer, president of the Kassel police and later DP [Deutsche Partei—German Party] functionary in Hesse. Hitler said the following about his former "OSAF" during a dinner conversation on June 28, 1942: "Our nobility are famous for the fact that so many ancestors did this and that. 'Von Pfeffer' traces his family back to Charlemagne. These feudal generations left so much waste that he'd be better called 'caraway'." And on February 17, 1942: "I've learned from experience with people like von Pfeffer: if some people take on a mentality, then it becomes their flesh and blood. The moral ethos, the idealism, sinks into a calculated idealism, in which the border between idealism and egoism is blurred."—*Source: ZS Pfeffer in the IfZ archive; Reichstags-Handbücher; Waite, p. 113; Oertzen, p. 61, 400 and 423; Salomon, pp. 17, 85, 128, 395 and 431; Schmidt-Pauli, p. 361; Hitlers Tischgespräche, pp. 171 and 204; Degeners Wer ist's? p. 1204.*

[1911] The idea that Petersdorf and Pfeffer were never at the front is nonsense, of course.

[1912] Most likely meaning Pfeffer again.

[1913] Petersdorf clashed with Guderian in 1940 at the time of the capture of Château Thierry.

[1914] Heinrich Kirchheim; born April 6, 1882; 1900 Second Lieutenant; participated in the Herero and Hottentot [African tribes] battles with the defense forces in Southwest Africa; 1914 Captain; 1918 awarded Pour le mérite; January 1919 established the "Hanovarian Volunteer Jäger Battalion, Kirchheim from the remains of his battalions and other units ("Goslarer Jäger"; employed on the Eastern Front—Obra, Rawitsch—disbanded fall 1919)' recruited by the Reichswehr as a company commander; 1923 Major; 1930 Commanding officer of Glatz; 1931 Colonel; 1932 left the Army; 1939 Commander, 276th Infantry Regiment and (Dec.) Commander, 169th Infantry Division as a brevet Major General; 1940 Major General; 1941 Commander, Special Agency, Libya or Commander, Special Staff, Tropics in the Army High Command; 1942 Lieutenant General; 1943 Commander, Special Staff "C" in the Army High Command; and October 1944 to March 1945, Inspector in the Armed Forces Recruiting and Replacement Inspectorate in Berlin.—*Source: Keilig 211/163; Geschichte der Ritter...I, p. 571; Salomon, pp. 215 and 227; Das deutsche Heer, p. 936; Rangliste 1944-45, p. 21.*

[1915] It must actually have been the Second British Army, which was fighting in the Meuse sector. The Americans mentioned subsequently would most likely be the American Ninth Army in the Ruhr sector, if not the Canadian First Army on the Meuse River and the lower Rhine. Although there were still German troops left—already outflanked—between the Meuse and the lower Rhine during those first days of March, Allied troops had already reached the German Rhine in various places on March 2.—*Source: Wilmot (Engl.), p. 671.*

[1916] Meaning the enemy.

[1917] Still Rundstedt until March 10; he was then relieved by Kesselring. Model was Commander-in-Chief Army Group "B."

[1918] In January, Hitler had thrown the Sixth SS Panzer Army under Sepp Dietrich into Hungary, after the failure of the Ardennes offensive.

[1919] Hans v. Obstfelder, born September 6, 1886; 1906 Second Lieutenant; 1915 Captain; Reichswehr; 1933 Colonel; 1936 Major General and Commander, 28th Infantry Division; 1938 Lieutenant General; 1940 General of Infantry and Commanding General, XXIX Army Corps; August 1943 Commanding General, LXXXVI Army Corps; December 1944 Commander, First Army; and after March 1, 1945, Commander, Nineteenth Army in exchange with Foertsch. From March 26 until the capitulation Obstfelder, commanded the Seventh Army.—*Source: Army High Command staff files (Nbg. Dok. NOKW -141); Siegler, p. 133; Seemen; Order of Battle, p. 601.*

[1920] Herrmann Foertsch; born April 4, 1895; 1914 Second Lieutenant, 175th Infantry Regiment; Freikorps Hindenburg; taken into the Reichswehr as a First Lieutenant; 1932 Major and head of the press office in the RWM; 1936 Lieutenant Colonel and Commander, 1st Battalion, 4th Infantry Regiment; 1937 tactics instructor at the War Academy; 1938 Colonel; 1939 Chief of General Staff, XXVI Army Corps; 1940 Commander of General Staff training courses; May 1941 Chief of Staff, Armed Forces Commander Southeast (Twelveth Army); 1942 Major General and Chief of Staff, Commander-in-Chief Southeast (Army

Group "E," after August 1943 Army Group "F"); 1943 Lieutenant General; March 1944 Commander, 21st Infantry Division; September 1944 Commanding General, X Army Corps; November 1944 General of Infantry; February 15-28, 1945, Deputy Commander, Nineteenth Army; and March 1945 until the capitulation, Commander, First Army. Foertsch was acquitted in 1948 in the trial of the Southeastern generals. He is the author of *Kriegskunst heute und morgen, Schuld und Verhängnis,* and other writings.—*Source: Keilig 211/87; Munzinger Archive; Siegler, p. 118; Order of Battle, p. 549; Deutsche Soldatenzeitung, April 1955.*

[1921] Hitler expressed himself even more crassly in a meeting at the beginning of the Eastern campaign (July 16, 1941), when the filling of positions in the Eastern areas was discussed. Bormann noted: "Rosenberg stated that he wanted to use Captain v. Petersdorf because of his merits; general horror, general refusal. The Führer and the Reichsmarshal emphasized that v. Petersdorf was without doubt mentally ill." —*Source: Nbg. Dok. 221-L.*

[1922] Transcript number unknown—Fragment No. 49—Only two pages of the shorthand record were preserved. Regarding the date: because the fifth Courland battle had apparently ended by this time but the new Soviet attack had not yet started, and because Guderian reported in March still on a comment by Hitler against the Geneva Convention, this fragment must be dated between March 1 and 4. Because it is a shorthand record by the same stenographers who recorded fragments 1a and 1b, it is likely a fragment from the same transcript.

[1923] In the area of Army Group Courland. There, on February 28, the Russians halted their attempts to break through to Libau, ending the fifth Courland battle. Four days later, they resumed their attack, this time with the main focus on the Frauenburg area, but again without decisive success.—*Source: Armed Forces High Command reports of Mar. 1, 1945 and following.*

[1924] Goebbels—according to statements by Speer and Göring at Nuremberg—had proposed to Hitler since the beginning of February that Germany abandon the 1927 Geneva Convention on prisoners of war, and possibly also other international agreements such as the Hague Land War Regulations. Hitler seems not to have seriously considered this idea until later in March when—during the Anglo-American offensive in the Rhineland, which had begun February 8—more and more German troops showed themselves unwilling to fight and surrendered. In any case, Hitler definitely mentioned such an intention on February 17, and again in the situation conference on the 19th, with regard to the Anglo-American air attacks (Dresden). After a discussion with Hitler, Dönitz, in conversation with Jodl, Ambassador Hewel and Admiral Wagner, made a statement against such plans, calling them inexpedient; Jodl and Hewel agreed. Also the following day, in an extensive notation by Jodl, the disadvantages of termination were described as too serious and the advantages seemed predominant. Guderian reported a further statement by Hitler in March: "On the Eastern Front, the men fight much better. The reason they capitulate so quickly in the West is all because of that stupid Geneva Convention, which assures them that they will be treated gently after being captured. We have to abandon this stupid convention!" Presumably these were Hitler's comments in the situation conference presented here.—*Source: IMT IX, p. 434, XIII, p. 517, XVI, p. 542, XVIII, p. 397, XXXIV, p. 644 (Dok. 158-C), XXXV, p. 181 (Dok. 606-D); Guderian: Erinnerungen, p. 387.*

[1925] The magnitude of the numbers mentioned here is correct for the first days of March. On this particular morning (March 2), for example, Eisenhower's headquarters reported that the First Army had taken 20,000 prisoners in one week; on March 1 it had been announced that on the previous day more than 7,000 prisoners had been brought in. Regarding German resistance, it was said to be poor in those days, and one could hardly speak of an organized defense anymore.—*Source: NZZ of Mar. 2 (morning and midday editions), Feb. 27 (morning edition), and Feb. 28 (midday issue), 1945.*

[1926] Note by the stenographer: Pomerania.

[1927] Regarding Italy. There may be a larger gap before Jodl's first remark.

[1928] Since February 18 the chief of the Operations Group in the Army High Command (see List of Participants).

[1929] Transcript number unknown—Fragment No. 1b—The date was not preserved, but it can be determined without a doubt by: 1. the situation in the air, 2. the landing on Piskopi, 3. the receipt of the radio message from *U1064*. The Commander-in-Chief of Army Group "E" in the Southeast, Colonel General Löhr, participated in this meeting as well; Löhr's presence at the Führer Headquarters on March 2, 1945, is documented by the Armed Forces Operations Staff entry in the situation book for that day (Nbg. Dok. 1797-PS). Initially, in connection with the last German offensive in Hungary, the attacks taking place at the same time across the Drava, especially at Valpovo, were discussed.

[1930] The attack on both sides of the Plattensee [Lake Balaton], to which the following remarks refer, began on March 9, one week after this meeting. In the south, the Second Panzer Army soon came to a halt; in the north, the Sixth Panzer Army was more successful, despite the fact that the ground had softened with the beginning of spring. The army—consisting of the I and the II SS Panzer Corps with the 1st, 2nd, 9th and 12th SS Panzer Divisions—had fought in the West until the end of January (Ardennes offensive), had been quickly replenished in the Reich in February, and by March 3 had been moved train by train to Hungary. The attack made good progress via Szekesferhervar [Stuhlweissenburg] and almost reached the Danube River; there, however, the SS troops were at the end of their strength. Tanks and other vehicles sank in the mud, and anyone who retreated later went on foot. Despite the army's report, that retreat was necessary due to the worsening ground conditions [and the beginning of a massive new Soviet offensive west of Budapest], Hitler ordered the continuation of the offensive—in vain, of course. In his extreme disappointment, he took the sleeve insignia off his *Leibstandarte*. The situation conference on March 24 discusses this setback.—*Source: Tippelskirch, p. 577; Hausser, p. 206; Siegler, p. 32.*

[1931] Maximilian de Angelis; born October 2, 1889 in Budapest; 1910 Second Lieutenant; Mödling Technical Military Academy; 1916 General Staff; 1918 in Italian captivity as captain; 1920 recruited into the Austrian Army; 1926 Major; 1927 Army school; 1934 at the disarmament conference in Geneva as colonel; March 3, 1938 State Secretary for National Defense; April 1938 Major General in Fifth Army Group Command; November 1938 Artillery Commander XV; 1939 Commander, 76th Infantry Division; 1940 Lieutenant General; 1942 General of Artillery and Commanding General, XXXXIV Army Corps; November-December 1943 and April-July 1944, Commander, Sixth Army; and July 1944 until the capitulation, Commander (after September, Commander-in-Chief), Second Panzer Army in the Balkans and, after November 1944, in Hungary. In 1946 the Americans extradited Angelis to Yugoslavia, where he was sentenced in 1947 and handed over to the USSR in 1948.—*Source: Army High Command staff files (Nbg. Dok. NOKW-141); DNB of Nov. 16, 1943; Siegler, p. 112; Order of Battle, p. 522.*

1932 The Plattensee [Lake Balaton] operation was to be supported by an attack by Army Group "E" across the Drava River (Operation "Waldteufel" ["Forest Devil"]), which had begun already on March 6. The plans called for the river to be bridged at Valpovo and at Donji Miholjac, but success was achieved only at the first location. The goal of the 11th Luftwaffe Field Division, crossing at Valpovo, and the 104th Jäger Division and 297th Infantry Division, attacking Miholjac—exploited by the Cossack units of General v. Pannwitz—was the seizure of the Danube River crossings at Batina and Mohács, as the final goal of the entire operation was the recapture of Budapest.—*Source: Schmidt-Richberg, p. 98; KTB [War Diary] of the Armed Forces Operations Staff from Mar. 6, 1945 (Nbg. Dok. 1797-PS).*

1933 Rhodes and some other separate islands in the Aegean Sea were, at that time, still occupied by German troops who could not be transported out. With regard to the landing on Piskopi, the Armed Forces report of March 4 says: "The occupation forces on the small island of Piskopi, northwest of Rhodes, have tied up a considerable number of enemy naval forces for four months. Now, after having driven back numerous enemy attacks, the company was overpowered by a superior enemy." As early as October 31, 1944, there had already been enemy forces—although weaker—on Piskopi, on the small island of Calchi west of Rhodes, and on the Cyclades island of Milos, which was also occupied by a German unit that had been left behind. At that time all three islands (Piskopi: November 1, Calchi: November 3, Milos: November 8) were then cleared of enemy troops again.—*Source: Armed Forces High Command reports of Oct. 31, 1944, Nov. 2, 1944, Nov. 4, 1944, Nov. 9, 1944, and Mar. 4, 1945; KTB [War Diary] of the Armed Forces Operations Staff for Mar. 2, 1945 (1797-PS).*

1934 When Great Britain gave an ultimatum on February 20, saying that participation in the founding of the United Nations in San Francisco would only be possible if war was declared against Germany by March 9 at the latest, Turkey decided on the 24th to declare war, effective March 1. On March 2 the "Declaration of the United Nations" was also signed by the Turks. The reception of this declaration of war *in extremis* on the side of the Allies was admittedly cool, however; a handing over of Rhodes was certainly not to be considered.

[1935] Hitler was probably referring to his trip to Memel on the destroyer *Deutschland*, during which he had been quite seasick. As an inlander he had no natural relation to the sea. A statement made in conversation with Raeder is typical of his attitude and self-assessment: "On land I am a hero, but on the sea I am a coward." This aversion didn't stop him from promoting the interests of the Navy and thereby feeling to a certain degree like a descendant of Wilhelm II.—*Source: Martienssen, p. 2.*

[1936] The Heiligenbeil.

[1937] There were approximately three million Germans living between the lower reaches of the Vistula and the Oder at that time, plus about half a million refugees from East Prussia and the northern Warthegau, who had not moved any further. Of these, around 900,000 fugitives were transported by ship to the West from the Gulf of Danzig and the harbors of East Pomerania, while only 200,000 to 300,000 escaped from eastern Pomerania via land routes. The transport out of Danzig began at the end of January after the arrival of the first East Prussian migrations. On March 25 the harbor installations of Danzig and Gdingen [Gdynia] were blown up and shipping was halted. From the Hela Peninsula— where people came until the very end on small boats, ferries and lighters from the last German bases of Pillau, Oxhöft and Weichselmündung-Schiewenhorst— 387,000 civilians and soldiers were moved out in April; the last ships left Hela on May 6. In Pomerania, in the meantime, Stolpmünde harbor fell on March 8, the following day Leba, and finally, on March 18, after eleven days of siege—during which 70,000 of the 80,000 people in the city were transported out by sea— Kolberg fell as well. At least 1½ million refugees altogether, as well as four complete Courland divisions, were transported out by sea from Courland, East Prussia, West Prussia and Pomerania.—*Source: Die Vertreibung (Oder-Neisse) I/1, p. 41E; Ruge: Seekrieg, p. 299.*

[1938] *U 1064* (Lieutenant Commander Schneidewind), operating in the Northern Channel and the Irish Sea, had reported sinking 25,000 GRT in a radio message that came in on March 2, 1945.

[1939] The "Auster" was a light plane in the U.S. Army Air Force, equivalent to the "Storch." It was used for courier flights, tactical reconnaissance and artillery observation.—*Source: Royal Air Force III, p. 222.*

[1940] The British single-seat fighter, the Hawker "Tempest," was a relatively new model, used in Europe since 1943. It was armed with 12 machine guns, 4 guns or 8 rocket projectiles, and could carry a 450-kg bomb load at a maximum speed of more than 700 km/h.—*Source: Royal Air Force III, p. 407; Feuchter, p. 234.*

[1941] Dr. of Engineering Hans Kammler, born August 26, 1901; until the end of 1941 Government construction director in the Luftwaffe; then SS Oberführer and head of Office Group C (buildings) in the newly established Main Economic Administration Office (Kammler had already been a Führer [commander] in the Allgemeine [general] SS since 1938) and therefore responsible for concentration camp buildings, among others; 1942 Brigadeführer; 1944 Gruppenführer and Chief "Kammler Special Action"; August 1944 assigned by

Himmler to prepare for the V2 employments; and September 1944 Commander, Reserve Division; December 1944 Commanding General, Army Corps z.b.V. Special Purposes Army Corps (previously LXV Army Corps) and commander of the V2 employment. Kammler supposedly fell as divisional commander during the Battle for Berlin.—*Source: SS Dienstalterslisten; Dornberger, pp. 225 and 254; Reitlinger: The SS, p. 510; Nbg. Dok. NO-1571, NO-2144 and NO-2335.*

[1942] The Armed Forces High Command report for March 2 stated: "Yesterday during their terror attacks in southern, southwestern and southeastern Germany, North American bomber units again destroyed primarily residential dwellings. There was particularly heavy damage in the urban areas of Ulm, Ingolstadt and Reutlingen. British terror attacks were again directed against Mannheim-Ludwigshafen and other towns in Westphalia. In the evening hours, British aircraft dropped bombs on the capital of the Reich. 27 Anglo-American low-flying airplanes were shot down over the western Reich territory, in heavy aerial combat and by anti-aircraft artillery."

[1943] The Allied forces, on the contrary, reported "a new low" in their bomber losses that day: "The German defense appeared very weak again." Of 2,800 bombers and 500 fighters operating over southwestern Germany on March 1, only 12 bombers and 5 fighters were lost, according to Allied reports.—*Source: NZZ of Mar. 2, 1945 (midday edition).*

[1944] Meaning the Moosbierbaum Factory of Donauchemie A.G. in Heiligeneich in lower Austria, between St. Pölten and Tulln. At that time the factory belonged to the I.G. Farben Group and produced petroleum-based products, superphosphates and sulfuric acid, and in the early stages also light metals.

[1945] Probably meaning supplying Breslau.

[1946] For the *Panzerfaust* [antitank grenade launcher] (see note above).

[1947] The 7.5 cm were captured guns that now had to be used in this time of need. The production of suitable ammunition had to be initiated as well, and the manufacture of brass Hülsen shell cases played a significant role because of the limited amount of copper. To shorten the long return of the shell cases back to the factories and thereby reduce the great quantity of initial production required, the Army Weapons Office conducted experiments on reusing the shell cases on site. The range of the guns—corresponding to the usual artillery methods—was to be increased by supplemental powder loads; however, the powder bottleneck also imposed limits here. Putting the Geschoss bullet in the cartridge this way just before firing was a common procedure, especially with medium and heavy artillery, but the captured gun tested here had originally fired shell cartridges.

[1948] The 10-cm gun and the 15-cm howitzer were bored from the same blocks. The discussion here concerns the production ratios of the two weapons. Hitler wanted the same quantity of both guns to be produced as a general rule, while the troops wanted more of the 15-cm howitzer than the 10-cm gun.

[1949] The "Hunter Tiger" [Jägdtiger] usually carried a 12.8-cm antitank gun, but because the production and delivery of these guns was insufficient at the time, existing 8.8 cm guns were now supposed to be installed. This project was never realized, however, as the interruption in the gun production was over before the necessary design changes could be made for the installation of the 8.8 cm.

[1950] Transcript number unknown—Fragment No. 19a—Only individual, heavily charred shorthand pages were preserved, without indication as to their order. Regarding the date, it could only be determined (during the second transcription in May 1945) that these pages were from the end of February or mid-March 1945. The date here was derived from information provided by the city administration of Datteln i. Westfalen [Datteln in Westphalia], indicating that the air attack against the junction of the Dortmund Ems Canal with the Lippe (canal basin of the Datteln harbor), which is mentioned at the beginning of the text, took place on March 9, 1945, at 2 p.m. The mention of the German air attacks against the Rhine bridge at Remagen confirms this dating.

[1951] The Ar(ado) 234 was the German jet bomber whose prototype was first flown in December 1943. It was a single-seater and was used as a reconnaissance plane as well. 150 were built in 1944 and 64 in 1945. Technical data: two 2-cm guns, 500-kg bomb capacity for a normal takeoff (1,000 kg if using rocket-assisted takeoff equipment), 810-900 km/h (depending on equipment and turbines), 1,450-2,000 km range depending on the model. It should probably say: "and three Arado 234s," as the situation book of the Armed Forces Operations Staff for March 10, 1945, says the following about these attacks: "We flew 32 sorties against the Remagen bridge, achieving two hits. The traffic continues, however."—*Source: Lusar, p. 62; Hébrard, p. 449; Baumbach, p. 315; Nbg. Dok. 1798-PS.*

[1952] The North American P51 "Mustang," a much-used American fighter-bomber and reconnaissance plane employed since 1942 in various models; it was also used as a long-range fighter after the end of 1943. Technical data: eight machine guns, four 2-cm guns or six rocket projectiles, two 450-kg bombs, 650 km/h, 1,900 km range, 12,000 m altitude. *–Source: Hébrard, pp. 200 and 266; Feuchter, pp. 214, 230, 234 and 275.*

[1953] The telephone exchange room in the Reich chancellery. The following conversation is part of an attempt on the part of Hitler's associates—after the heavy bombing strikes on Berlin (with hits on the Reich Chancellery since February 3)—to compel him to change his quarters, even if only temporarily, to the "Reich" Luftwaffe bunker at Wannsee or the "Zeppelin" camp near Zossen.

[1954] Probably meaning the Luftwaffe High Command headquarters in Potsdam-Wildpark.

[1955] Probably to be filled in with: "...could provide replacement engines for..." To avoid a delay in the mass production, the changes to the Me 262 that became necessary after production had started were not made on the assembly line, but after the aircraft had been completed with follow-up equipment. Previously, these continual improvements had been a considerable burden to the manufacturing process.

[1956] According to the recollection of the original stenographer, the discussion that followed concerned the use of horses in place of motor vehicles and also for feeding the population.

[1957] Center of the large nickel deposit in northern Finland. Regarding the supply of nickel for German industry.

[1958] The transfer of the German armaments industry underground had begun in 1942, but the project was initiated on a large scale in the spring of 1944. The first focus was on the Motoren- und Triebwerkfertigung [engine production] for the Luftwaffe, as well as individual components of Panzers, weapons, V-weapons [rockets], etc. The "Sonderauftrag Kammler [Kammler Special Mission]" was known as a major action, and was carried out by concentration camp prisoners under the leadership of SS Gruppenführer Kammler, the Office Group Chief C (buildings) in the WVHA. After July 1944, Junkers were transferred from Magdeburg to the tunnels at Niedersachswerfen (South Harz) and to an underground facility at Wolffsleben. For gasoline production/synthesis and the refinement of crude oil, there was an underground building program for seven large and numerous small plants. By the end of 1945, the monthly underground production of petroleum products was to have reached 300,000 tons; in March 1945 a production of 52,000 tons was achieved. On the whole, one can conclude that after the fall of 1944, bomb attacks could no longer cause serious problems for armaments production, aside from the gasoline sector and the transport problem.—*Source: Aff. Oswald Pohl of Mar. 21, 1947 (Nbg. Dok. NO-2570); Görlitz I, p. 516; Die deutsche Industrie, p. 106.*

[1959] Transcript number unknown—Fragments No. 22 and 23—Completely preserved.

[1960] The 8th Parachute Division was mistaken, and even the army group's 15th Panzer Grenadier Division could not help much: the landing of the "company" on March 23 at Rees between Emmerich and Wesel was the preparatory phase for Montgomery's Twenty-First Army Group airborne drop over the lower Rhine—which would take place during this night—for the final strike against the German armies in northern Germany. An hour later the next landing had already taken place at Wesel; 250,000 tons of ammunition, provisions and bridge-building equipment lay on the west bank in preparation for this action. During the night the 51st Highland Division and the Scottish 15th Division stormed across the river, and a bit further upriver at Rheinberg the American 30th and 79th Infantry Divisions followed at around 3 a.m. The action was supported the following morning by the landing of the British 6th and 17th Airborne Divisions. By the evening of the 24th, the Anglo-Americans were already 10 km east of the Rhine; on the 26th the two bridgeheads were linked up and 12 pontoon bridges were in use. 20 divisions with 1,500 tanks were on the east bank one week after the crossing.—*Source: Wilmot, p. 736; Tippelskirch, p. 644; Görlitz II, p. 520.*

[1961] Immediately after their advance to the Rhine, the Americans were able to build a bridgehead on the right side of the river at Remagen, since the Ludendorff railway bridge had fallen intact into the hands of their 9th Armored Division on March 7. Motorized advance detachments reached the bridge just before 4 p.m., when the blasting was scheduled. The defenders managed to trigger some explosive charges, and although the bridge shook it did not collapse, as the fuse on the main charge failed. Before nightfall the Americans already had a first narrow bridgehead on the right side of the Rhine firmly under control. Ten days later, on March 17, when the damaged supports finally collapsed after attacks from the air and fire from long-range artillery, the Americans had already built a substitute bridge. At the time of this meeting, the bridgehead reached north up to the Sieg and extended to the south out across the Wied. German occupation forces continued to defend in the eastern part of Neuwied.—*Source: Wilmot, p. 726; Tippelskirch, p. 638; Armed Forces High Command reports of Mar. 22-24, 1945.*

[1962] Meaning over the Rhine at the American Oppenheim bridgehead. When the Remagen bridge fell into American hands in the north, Patton's Third Army stormed through the Palatinate in the direction of the middle Rhine; engineers with assault boats and bridge equipment followed immediately behind the tanks. In the evening hours of March 22, as a result of these preparations, six battalions of the American 5th Infantry Division succeeded—*before* the long-planned crossing by Montgomery—in capturing the right bank of the Rhine across from Oppenheim (west of Darmstadt) in a surprise attack and building a temporary bridge. The surprise was complete, and the total losses in the attack were eight dead and 20 wounded. On the evening of the 23rd, at the time of this situation report, tanks were already rolling along the right bank of the Rhine, and the infantry held a bridgehead that was 11 km wide and 10 km deep. (See also Hitler's remarks on pp. 705 and 706.)—*Source: Wilmot, p. 730; Tippelskirch, p. 645; Görlitz II, p. 519.*

[1963] Fighters with gasoline engines as opposed to jet aircraft.

[1964] Successor to Rundstedt as Commander-in-Chief West, since March 11 (see note 136).

[1965] Presumably the former (1938-39) adjutant of the Defense District Command, Oschatz draft registration office Grimma, Lieutenant Colonel Walter Löffler, born February 13, 1895.—*Source: Das deutsche Heer, p. 912; Rangliste 1944-45, p. 251.*

[1966] The American Third Army had reported bringing in 20,000 German prisoners on March 19 and 14,000 on March 20. On March 23 the Allied Supreme Command announced that in the last eight days alone, more than 100,000 German soldiers had turned in their arms.—*Source: NZZ of Mar. 21-23, 1945.*

[1967] Meaning a line.

[1968] Regarding the German offensive at the Plattensee [Lake Balaton], see above note. In the meantime, the attack had been driven back. On March 16, the Armed Forces High Command report spoke for the first time of "successful defense" and "counterattacks" at the Plattensee [Lake Balaton?]. On March 19 it was already "bitter defense." On March 24—during the first hours of which the present meeting took place—the Armed Forces report said that "north of the Plattensee [Lake Balaton], the Bolshevists' forward attack groups had been brought to a standstill on both sides of Veszprém and north of Zirez after heavy enemy losses." On the 30th (Good Friday) it finally had to be announced that the German troops had been thrown back to the border of the Reich (i.e., the Austrian border). At that point an evacuation panic developed in Graz, but the front held at the border almost until the capitulation.

[1969] The reference is probably to Balatonfüred, whose "stubborn resistance" was mentioned in the Armed Forces report of March 26.

[1970] The Plattensee [Lake Balaton].

[1971] Hans-Günther (Czeppan) v. Rost; born November 15, 1894; 1914 Second Lieutenant, 10th Field Artillery Regiment; Reichswehr; 1937 Lieutenant Colonel; 1938 adjutant, 5th Army Group Command; 1939 Colonel and Commander, 13th Artillery Regiment; 1942 in various staffs; March 1943 Major General and Deputy Chief of Staff, III Army Corps; May 1944 Lieutenant General and (June) Commander, 3rd Panzer Grenadier Division; and after June 25, 1944 Commander, 44th German Infantry Division Hoch- und Deutschmeister. v. Rost fell on March 23, 1945, at Szekesferhervar [Stuhlenweissenburg].—*Source: Keilig 211/278; Order of Battle, p. 613; Rangliste 1944-45 p. 29.*

[1972] The Küstrin Fortress on the right bank of the Oder remained in German hands when the Russians reached the lower reaches of the Oder at the beginning of March. The only road to the west, however, was seriously threatened by two Soviet bridgeheads on the left bank of the Oder on either side of the Oder bridge. Both sides now tried to clear up the situation; at this time, a final German attempt to throw the Russians back over the Oder and to free the rear of the almost-encircled fortress had just failed. On March 30, SS General Reinefarth then evacuated Küstrin. The town Klessin mentioned next is north of Lebus on the west bank of the Oder.—*Source: Tippelskirch, pp. 654 and 656.*

[1973] Walter Weiss; born September 5, 1890; cadet corps; 1909 Second Lieutenant; in the Great War as adjutant and company commander and as Captain in the eastern border guards; accepted in the Reichswehr; 1921 German-Polish Border Determination Commission; 1922 liaison officer to the A.A.; 1931 Major; 1934 Infantry Commander II (Schwerin); 1937 Colonel; 1938 Commander, 1st Infantry Regiment; 1939 Chief of Staff, I Army Corps; 1940 Major General and Commander, 97th Infantry Division; 1941 Commander, 26th Infantry Division; 1942 General of Infantry and Commanding General, XXVII Army Corps; February 1943 Commander-in-Chief, Second Army; 1944 Colonel General; and from March 12, 1945 until April 2, 1945, Commander, Army Group North in East Prussia.—*Source: Army High Command staff files (Nbg. Dok. NOKW-141).*

[1974] Meaning aircraft.

[1975] Hitler's suspicion that planes were deserting to the enemy was unfounded. Of course, at this time, when the lines of communication were breaking down and there were daily attacks against the military airfields, the so-called missing-plane reports increased considerably. Aircraft crashing above waterways or in lakes or wooded areas were either not found at all or found only weeks later. With the increasing strain on the air defense forces, there was often no time the following day to investigate the losses of the day before. Furthermore, when a four-engine plane with heavy aircraft armaments suffered a direct hit, the whole plane would often break up; the only thing that remained intact was the engine block, which often drilled into the earth three or four meters deep, and nothing more would remain of the whole aircraft than a crater—which would only differ from a "normal" bomb crater in that a few pieces of metal might be lying around. At most only a very few individual planes could have flown over to the enemy; otherwise, it would have been made known after the war. Also, this would not have been an easy thing to do, as the risk of being shot down was quite high.

[1976] The OKW report of March 24 reported: "Yesterday the enemy air activity over the Reich area was again primarily directed against the Rhine-Westphalia area near the front, where especially in several places in the Ruhr area there were again personal losses and heavy damage to residential areas. Other units attacked cities in northern, central and southeastern Germany. In the night only weak forces flew into the Reich. 29 Anglo-American aircraft were shot down."

[1977] In 1944 Speer's ministry made substantial efforts to increase the German production of synthetic fuel by 20% and thereby become largely independent of the endangered Romanian oil (in 1943 6 million tons of synthetic gasoline were produced, and 2 million tons crude oil were imported from Romania and Hungary). But in reality the production sank to 25% by the end of the year, and even to 8% by February 1945. Even more disastrous was the high-quality aircraft fuel situation. There was even a "zero-production day" in the summer of 1944, when not a single drop of fuel was produced; only with extreme effort was the production increased again after that—on individual days even up to 60%. This collapse was the result of the Anglo-American "gasoline-offensive." Starting in May 1944 (first major attack on May 30), approximately 80 German fuel-production targets were systematically attacked—first by the Americans, then after mid-June also by the R.A.F. After September the oil targets were the absolute center of the Allied bomb offensive; from December 1944 to March 1945 they shared priority with the railway targets and were only pushed into third place in April. In February 1945 there were heavy daytime attacks on Gelsenkirchen and Kamen, as well as two night attacks each against Pölitz, Wanne-Eickel and Böhlen b. Leipzig. Leuna was brought to a standstill after 6,552 bombers dropped 18,328 tons of bombs on it in 22 attacks. Speer's "Special Staff Geilenberg," with 350,000 mostly foreign workers, tried in vain to repair the damages immediately and to rebuild smaller, more scattered plants. In total, after 1940, 2 million tons of Allied bombs fell on Europe, 1.2 million tons of which (or 60%) were dropped after July 1944; nearly half of these 1.2 million tons fell on traffic installations and on the oil industry. A few informative tables clarify the development of this most important and most endangered sector of the German supply:

A. Total Greater German production of petroleum (in millions of tons):

1941	1942	1943
4.8	5.6	6.6

B. Consumption of fuel (excluding lubricating oil) in Greater Germany (in 1,000 t):

	Total	of this, by the Armed Forces
1940	5,856	3,005
1941	7,305	4,567
1942	6,483	4,410
1943	6,971	4,762

C. Composition of the German petroleum supply in the 1st quarter of 1944 (in 1,000 t):

	Aircraft fuel	Vehicle fuel	Diesel	Heating oil	Lubricating oil	Other	Total
Synthesis	503	315	200	222	14	228	1482
Domestic crude oil refinement	1	43	111	9	211	137	512
Import of petroleum [mineral oil] products	42	271	185	47	40	165	750
From all sources	546	629	496	278	265	530	2744

D. Production of important types of petroleum industry and bomb loads dropped on petroleum plants:

	Production in 1,000 t			Bomb loads in short tons
	Aircraft fuel	Vehicle fuel	Diesel oil	
January 1944	159	118	117	114
March 1944	181	134	100	–
May 1944	156	94	74	5,146
August 1944	17	59	69	26,320
December 1944	26	50	66	13,900
February 1945	1	50	77	22,635
March 1945	–	39	39	30,937

E. Fuel supply proportions (German supply in mid-1944=100)

	Mid-1944	Early 1945
Germany	100	31
Enemy forces	2,920	3,117

—Source: Die Deutsche Industrie, pp. 52, 55, 92, 104, 110 and 127; Royal Air Force III, pp. 260, 266 and 268; Feuchter, p. 277; Görlitz I, p. 506; Tippelskirch, p. 585; Bartz, p. 237; Galland, pp. 297, 308 and 312.

[1978] As reports about the final Battle for Berlin indicate, the east-west axis between the Siegessäule [Victory Column] and the Brandenburg Gate actually was used as a runway for both taking off and landing, and in the last days it provided the encircled inner city with the only possible remaining connection to the outside. The cutting down of the Tiergarten embankment, which Hitler forbade here, seems not to have taken place later either, according to eyewitness reports. His concern for a few hundred trees, however (which seems absurd in this situation and in the face of his ruthlessness in every other regard), was in vain. During the winters that followed, not only these strips along the edge but the entire Tiergarten—whatever had survived the heavy combat for the last German bases, the Reich Chancellery and zoo bunker—went into the ovens of the city of millions, which was freezing and stripped of almost all necessities of existence.

1979 The Siegessäule on the Grossen Stern [Great Roundabout] survived the war and post-war period.

1980 Willy Langkeit; born June 2, 1907; 1924 Reichswehr; 1934 Second Lieutenant, 1st Motor Vehicle Detachment (Coburg), later the 1st Antitank Defense Detachment; 1938 Captain and Chief, 8th Company, 36th Panzer Regiment (Schweinfurt); beginning of 1942, Major and battalion commander in the 36th Panzer Regiment; September 1942 Commander, 36th Panzer Regiment and (December) Lieutenant Colonel; December 1943 Colonel; March 1944 Commander, *Grossdeutschland* Panzer Regiment; November 1944 Commander *Grossdeutschland* Replacement Brigade; after January 23, 1945, Commander, Panzer Division *Kurmark*, and April 20, 1945, Major General. Langkeit (after 1951 Federal Border Guards, was actually not from upper Bavaria, but instead was born in East Prussia, although he had served for a long time in Frankish units. Thus, it is not impossible that there was a mix-up or a misunderstanding or transcription error, especially since it was not Colonel Langkeit but Colonel Langhaeuser who temporarily took over the command of the 12th Infantry Division (until the beginning of March) from Major General Engel, who had been severely wounded on December 29, 1944.—*Source: Order of Battle, p. 585; DNB of December 11, 1943; Das deutsche Heer, p. 610; Seemen; Rangliste 1944-45, p. 81; Keilig 211/191.*

1981 Here the discussion concerns the replacement of Guderian as Chief of Army General Staff. Guderian truly had a heart disease—he then spent the remaining weeks of the war at the Ebenhausen sanatorium near Munich—but primarily Hitler wanted to get rid of him. On March 21 Hitler had already told him, "I see that your heart disease has gotten worse. You must take a four-week leave immediately." Guderian countered this attack by pointing out that there was no replacement for him on hand. The chief of the operations group in the Army High Command, General Wenck, had had an accident on the Berlin–Stettin Autobahn on February 17, returning from a situation conference to Himmler's Army Group Vistula, with which he had been leading an attack in the Arnswalde area for the past two days. On this day, however, Guderian had promised to look for a suitable replacement. One week later, on March 28, there was a final break over the heavy accusations Hitler made against General Busse because of the failed relief of Küstrin: "Colonel General Guderian! Your health requires an immediate leave of six weeks!" General Krebs, Wenck's previous [temporary replacement], became Guderian's replacement and the last Chief of Army General Staff (like Guderian, only temporary). Wenck had recovered adequately by April 12 to be able to take over the Twelfth Army, which became famous for its attempted relief of Berlin.—*Source: Guderian: Erinnerungen, pp. 375 and 386; Tippelskirch, p. 654.*

[1982] The Obersalzberg actually was attacked by 318 four-engine R.A.F. "Lancasters" on the morning of April 25. Hitler's tea house was obscured by clouds and blended in with the snowy landscape. The Berghof and the barracks of the *Leibstandarte*, however, could be seen clearly and were bombed with direct visibility. The only person of major importance in the Third Reich who was at the Obersalzberg at the time was Göring—in SS custody. The "mountain" looked—as the SD leader Frank reported from Berchtesgarden—like a lunar landscape after the attack: the houses of Göring and Bormann, for example, were completely destroyed, and the SS barracks and the Berghof heavily damaged.— *Source: Koller, p. 48; Royal Air Force III, p. 277; Brickhill, p. 258.*

[1983] The headquarters of the Army High Command in Zossen, near Berlin, had been bombed for 45 minutes at midday on March 15. Because of the advance warning, there were minimal casualties. Only a few employees of the operations department were injured, including General Krebs, who was unable to work for several days.—*Source: Guderian: Erinnerungen, p. 386.*

[1984] Should most likely be "under."

[1985] This statement by v. Below is partially incorrect, as the bunker had already been built for the Reich Air-raid Protection School at the request of the air-raid protection inspector at that time, and the work had already begun during peacetime. At the beginning of February 1944, when the staff of the Luftwaffe Commander Center was expanded into Air Force Reich, the command post was still located in a small bunker on the Reich sports ground, which also housed the staff of the 30th Fighter Division. The search for more spacious quarters led to the Air-raid Protection School bunker on Grossen Wannsee, and the parts of the school that were still accommodated there were asked to move out. The command apparatus still had to be installed—for example, the communication lines and the large air-situation frosted-glass panel, behind which the units were marked by Luftwaffe assistants posted on three floors.

[1986] Under the Reich Chancellery.

[1987] In Zossen.

[1988] De facto correct, but formally and more accurately Chief of the Operations Group (see List of Participants).

[1989] In the conference room.

[1990] This "Danube Shadow Division" could not be identified. Geographical terms, such as "Danube" here, were attached to some makeshift divisions that were drawn up at the end of the war. The term "shadow Division" [*Schattendivision*] was likely only used to indicate that it wasn't a real division, but only a thrown-together mass from the Replacement Army. Brudermüller's suggestion of using this "shadow division" to fill up worn-out units points in the same direction.

[1991] Military District XI: Hannover (southern Lower Saxony, northern province of Saxony, Braunschweig, Anhalt);
IX: Kassel (Kurhessen, Thuringia);
VII: Munich (Upper Bavaria, Lower Bavaria, Swabia).

[1992] De Maizière's correction is accurate: the 19th Waffen SS Infantry Division was the Latvian No. 2, while the 20th was the Estonian No. 1. Both divisions owed their considerable strength to the draft of those subject to military service, initiated by the German occupation authorities in 1943. The 19th had emerged from the 2nd Latvian SS Volunteer Brigade in the spring of 1943 and had since been employed in Army Group North—now in Courland. The 20th was an expansion of the Estonian SS Brigade and was employed in the area of Narva in the spring of 1944. After the evacuation of Estonia, however, it was transferred first to Germany, then to Poland.—*Source: Order of Battle, p. 346; Numerous Nbg. Dok. of the NO series.*

1993 The formation of the "Indian Legion," which remained pro forma a part of Bose's Indian National Army administered in trust until the end, had already begun in 1941. There were initially eight Indians who followed the call of the nationalist leader in Germany; by 1945 the strength of the legion then grew to more than 2,000 men (see also Göhler's figure, which was probably somewhat high), almost all of them former prisoners of war from the North African or Italian theaters. The legion, which was considered ineffective in combat and was primarily important for propagandistic purposes, had been at the Bay of Biscay until being dragged into the retreat from France in 1944. The unit, which had previously belonged to the Army, then became the "Indian Legion of the Waffen SS" and had to give up its heavy weapons after the artillery debacle in France. SS Oberführer Heinz Bertling, a lecturing counsel of legation from the Foreign Office, became commander of the legion. The fact that he didn't concern himself much with his unit and soon had to be relieved again becomes somewhat more understandable considering Hitler's following description.—*Source: Anlage "Die Indische Legion der Waffen-SS"series 69 RLD (Reichsleiterdienst) of Dec. 5, 1944 (Nbg. Dok. NO-1863); Draft by Berger of a letter from Himmler to Bertling dated Nov. 1944 (NO-2052); v. Trott to SS Hauptsturmbannführer Grothmann on Aug. 21, 1942 (NG-3638).*

1994 Subhas Chandra Bose; born January 23, 1897 to an old Bengali family; studied in Calcutta and Cambridge; 1921 turned to nationalism and worked with the nationalist leader Das and founded the Independence Party; 1929 vice president of the Pan-Indian Congress; 1938 president of the Independence Movement, but pushed out of the Congress by the Ghandi-Nehru school of passive resistance; spring 1941 voyage to Germany and Italy via the USSR; February 28, 1942 first appeal over German radio; June 1943 to Japan in a submarine; July 4, 1943 founded the "Provisional Government of a Free India" in Singapore; president of the Indian Independence League and "Nethaji" (leader); October 25, 1943 declaration of war against the United States and Great Britain; and after February 1944, fought with the Indian National Liberation Army on the Burmese-Indian border. One week after the Japanese capitulation, Bose died, while flying back to Japan, in an airplane crash over Formosa on August 18, 1945.—*Source: Nbg. Dok. NG-3493, NG-3868, NG-5465 and others; Keesing's Archive 1942: pp. 5414 and 5512, 1943: pp. 5982, 5999, 6028 and 6150, 1944: p. 6279; Munzinger Archive.*

1995 Regarding this confusion about the Galician and the Ukrainian division it must first be pointed out that Galicians are also Ukrainians—from the eastern

Galician region around Lemberg [L'vov], which had previously belonged to Poland, was a part of the General Government [Poland] during the time of the German occupation, and then the USSR and after 1991, of Ukraine. The 14th Waffen SS Infantry Division that was recruited there was initially named "Galician No. 1." The division was formed in the spring of 1943 and was employed after March 1944, first in the central sector of the Eastern Front, later in southern Poland (Brody). On a RFSS adjutancy list from August 1, 1944, it is still designated "Galician No. 1," while in a SSFHA schedule from March 1, 1945, the name is "Ukrainian No. 1." The 30th Waffen SS Infantry Division ("division" meaning nothing more than a better regiment here), which was probably formed from auxiliary police battalions in France in the summer of 1944, or transferred from Poland to France, first had the name "Russian No. 2." Later, in the list from March 1945, it was "Belorussian No. 1"; in the end, it was renamed Waffen Infantry Brigade. This division was considered unreliable. Why Göhler calls it "Galician" here is unexplainable. Perhaps it was another one of those cases where a quick answer was intended to conceal a lack of knowledge.— *Source: Order of Battle, pp. 344 and 349; Aufz. Adj. RFSS of Aug. 1, 1944 (Nbg. Dok. NO-1728); Aufstellung SSFHA of March 26, 1945, according to the state on March 1, 1945 (NO-175).*

[1996] The 18th SS Volunteer Panzer Grenadier Division *Horst Wessel*, established in March 1944 by expanding the 1st SS Infantry Brigade (motorized).—*Source: Order of Battle, p. 345.*

[1997] Developmental version of the automatic rifle.

[1998] Should most likely be SPWs [Schützenpanzerwagen—armored personnel carriers]—that is, armored vehicles employed to transport infantry.

[1999] Could not be identified with certainty. These could have been armored vehicles for the transport of ammunition, half-tracked vehicles (Sd.Kfz. [Special Vehicle] 252) adapted from the light armored personnel carriers for this special use. However, the reference could also be to "Mannschafts-Kübelwagen" [a vehicle made by Volkswagen]. This latter option would make sense insofar as these Kübelwagen—armed with two superheavy machine guns—have been confirmed in the same connection in weapons equipment lists of other SS units. The Waffen SS had taken these vehicles over from the Luftwaffe.

[2000] Eastern caterpillar tractors.

[2001] Reference to the presentation.

[2002] Training area north of Paderborn.

[2003] The discussion again concerns the superheavy 653rd Tank Destroyer Detachment, which has been mentioned several times previously. The commander who was relieved—an Austrian decorated with the golden medal of honor received by wounded—apparently hadn't shown himself capable of dealing with the difficult situation.

[2004] Meaning the Inspector General of Panzer Troops, Colonel General Guderian. Five days later, however, on March 28, 1945, he was "placed on leave" in this function, as he was in his capacity as Chief of the General Staff as well.—*Source: Guderian: Erinnerungen, p. 260; Siegler, p. 121.*

[2005] Albert Forster; born July 26, 1902; High school; business apprenticeship, transferred into the banking profession; 1923 SA and NSDAP; 1924 dismissed for
political activity; traveler; Ortsgruppenleiter of Fürth and employee of the *Stürmer*;
1930 Member of the Reichstag; October 1930 Gauleiter of Danzig; May 1933
leader of the German Union of White-Collar Workers; Prussian State Council;
SS Gruppenführer (1941 Obergruppenführer); August 24, 1939 Chief of State
of the free city of Danzig; and October 1939 Gauleiter and Reich Governor of
Danzig-West Prussia. Forster was found in an English prison camp in July 1946
and extradited to Poland in August 1947. There he was sentenced to death at the
beginning of May 1948; his execution is not completely certain, however.—
Source: Reichstags-Handbücher; SS Dienstalterslisten; Munzinger Archive.

[2006] Ernst Kaltenbrunner; born October 4; 1903, lawyer; 1932 (Austrian) SS; 1937
Führer of the Austrian SS after serving a prison sentence for participation in
subversive activities against the government; March 1938 SS Brigadeführer;
Führer of the Danube section and State Secretary for Security; September 1938
SS Gruppenführer; January 1943 Heydrich's successor as chief of the Reich
Security Service's Head Office (RSHA); and June 1943 SS Obergruppenführer.
Kaltenbrunner was sentenced to death in the main trial in Nuremberg and hanged
on October 16, 1946.—*Source: Munzinger Archive.*

[2007] The "Do 335" was a new multi-purpose aircraft (originally night fighter and
daytime destroyer) with 4½ hours' flight time, two tandem engines of 1830 hp
each, armed with five machine guns, and a maximum speed of 750 km/h. The
revolutionary feature was the engine arrangement: one at the nose of the fuselage and one at the tail behind the pilot's seat (for pulling and thrust). That gave
the plane the power of a twin-engine aircraft but the aerodynamic advantages
of a single-engine aircraft, as it eliminated the unfavorable air resistance caused
by engines mounted on the wings. In total, eleven units were produced and
employed (seven in 1944 and four in 1945). This aircraft was modified after the
war to serve as a model for the American twin-engine "Mustang" F 82.—*Source:
Lusar, p. 64; Baumbach, p. 317.*

[2008] Meaning that the production of both German standard gasoline-engine fighters, the Me 109 and FW 190, should be stopped (in 1945 there were still 2,969
Me 109s produced, 2,798 of them fighters, and 2,734 FW 190s, 1,630 of them
fighters). The fighter-bomber 152 mentioned as a replacement here was a development of the Focke-Wulf chief designer Prof. Tank (thus the name "Tank
fighter" further below): the Ta 152, a redesign of the FW 190 with a pressurized
cabin and much stronger engine. It was intended at first as a high-altitude fighter,
bomber, and reconnaissance plane; 34 units were produced in 1944 (17 employed) and 33 in 1945 (22 employed). The construction of another model, the
twin-engine wood-construction night fighter Ta 154, the German "Mosquito,"
was halted in 1944 after the production of eight units (employed: one). Prof.
Tank was also the creator of most of the FW planes; the practice of naming
the FW models after the designer began in 1943.—*Source: Lusar, p. 76; Baumbach,
p. 314; Conrady, p. 219 and 368.*

[2009] Here the reference is to the Do 335 again—as it is approximately five lines below as well: "those things."

[2010] Josef Kammhuber; born August 19, 1896; war volunteer; 1917 Second Lieutenant (infantry); Reichswehr; 1926-29 General Staff officer training; 1930 Captain in the operations section of the Army General Staff; 1933 Group leader in the organization section of the RLM; 1936 Commander of a fighter group; end of 1937 Chief of the Organizational Section of the RLM; 1939 Chief of Staff, Second Air Fleet; 1940 Air Commander, 51st Bomber Group 51 and temporarily in French captivity; mid-1940 assigned the organization of night fighters; October 27, 1940 Commander, Night Fighter Division; August 1941 reorganized as XII Air Corps (Night Combat); 1941 Lieutenant General; January 1943 Air General; November 1943 to October 1944 Commander-in-Chief, Fifth air Fleet in Finland/Norway; and February 1945 Special Commissioner to fight the four-engine aircraft. As Lieutenant General, Kammhuber became chief of Department VI (Luftwaffe) in the Ministry of Defense in the Federal Republic of Germany in June 1956 (1957: Luftwaffe Inspector).—*Source: Munzinger Archive; Siegler, p. 125; Seemen; Order of Battle, p. 573.*

[2011] Gerhard Degenkolb, born June 26, 1892, director of the Demag Company, Duisburg. In 1940 he was called into the Munitions Ministry under the motto "Selbstverantwortung der Industrie" [Industrial Self-Reliance], and was first ordered to boost the critical production of the iron mills (needed to produce iron ammunition propulsion rings). In March 1942 he became head of the "Special Committee for Locomotives," as well as head of the "Special Committee A 4" (V2) after mid-1943.—*Source: Dornberger, p. 84; Wer leitet?, p. 144.*

[2012] Willy Messerschmitt; born June 26, 1898; 1918-23 Munich Technical College] (Dr. of Engineering); 1923 founded his own aircraft-construction enterprise; 1928 Interressengemeinschaft [community of interests] with the Bavarian aircraft plants; 1930 teaching assignment for aircraft construction and honorary professor at Munich Technical College; 1933 chairman of the board of directors of the Bavarian aircraft plants; 1938 National award winner, Honorary Dr. of Engineering, Munich Technical College; and 1941 NSFK Brigadeführer. After the war Messerschmitt opened a factory for sewing machines and bubble cars and after 1956 became interested in building aircraft again.—*Source: Spruchkammerakten; Munzinger Archive.*

[2013] SS Obergruppenführer Felix Steiner did not carry out Hitler's order to intervene in the Battle of Berlin with "Group Steiner."

[2014] General Walther von Seydlitz was vice president of the Communist "National Committee for a Free Germany" [Nationalkomitee Freies Deutschland] established by the Soviets in July 1943 in the Krasnogorsk prison camp.

[2015] In March 1945 Colonel General Heinrich von Vietinghoff was made Commander-in-Chief Southwest, succeeding Field Marshal Albert Kesselring.

[2016] Lloyd George, British Prime Minister from 1916 to 1922, visited Hitler in September 1936 in Berchtesgaden.

[2017] After the death of Franklin D. Roosevelt on April 12, 1945, Vice President Harry S. Truman became the new U.S. president.

[2018] Field Marshal General Ferdinand Schörner was, since January 1945, Commander-in-Chief of Army Group Center, fighting in Czechoslovakia.

[2019] Lieutenant General Rudolf Holste was, as of April 20, 1945, Commanding General of the XXXXIX Army Corps.

[2020] Alfred Hugenberg was leader of the extreme right German National Peoples' Party [Deutschnationalen Volkspartei], and belonged to Hitler's government as Reich Economic Minister from January to June 1933. General Schleicher was Hitler's predecessor as Reich Chancellor, from December 1932 to January 1933.

[2021] Field Marshal General Werner von Blomberg was Reich War Minister from 1933 to 1938.

BIBLIOGRAPHY

Aaltonen, B.X., Das finnische Freiwilligenbataillon der Waffen-SS, in: Waffenbruder Finnland. Ein Buch die deutschen Soldaten in Finnland, hrsg. Von Hptm. Dr. Ruppert, Leipzig u. Berlin 1942

Abetz, Otto, Das offene Problem, Köln 1951

Abshagen, Karl Heinz, Canaris. Patriot und Weltbürger, 9.-11. Tsd., Stuttgart 1950

Alfieri, Dino, Deux dictateurs face à face, Paris 1948

v. Alten, Georg, Handbuch für Heer und Flotte, Bd. 9, Berlin 1912

Anfuso, Filippo, Roma-Berlino-Salò, o.O. 1950

Anfuso, Filippo, Rom-Berlin im diplomatischen Spiegel, München 1951

Arntz, Prof. Dr. Helmut, Die Menschenverluste der Beiden Weltkriege, in: Universitas, 8 Jg. (1953).

Aron, Robert, Histoire de Vichy 1940-1944, Paris 1954

Assmann, Kurt, Deutsche Schicksalsjahre, Wiesbaden 1950

Badoglio, Pietro, Italien im 2. Weltkrieg, München 1947 [L'Italia nella seconda guerra mondiale]

Bartz, Karl, Als der Himmel brannte, Hannover 1955

Bauer, Ernest, Italien und Kroatien 1938-1945, in: Zeitschrift für Geopolitik, 26, Jg. (1955)

Baumbach, Werner, Zu spat? München 1949

Baumont, Maurice, Gloires et tragédies de la IIIᵉ République, Paris 1956

Das Bayernbuch vom Weltkriege 1914-1918, 2 Bde., Stuttgart 1930

Bechtoldt, Heinrich, Moskau und die Meerengen, in: Aussenpolitik, 4. Jg. (1953)

Beck, Ludwig, Studien, hrsg. Von Hans Speidel, Stuttgart 1930

de Belot, Raymond, The Struggle for the Mediterrenean 1939-1945, Princeton 1951

Benoist-Méchin, J., Geschichte des Deutschen Heeres seit dem Waffenstillstand, Berlin 1939 [Histoire de l'armée allemande]

Berber, Fritz, Das Diktat von Versailles, Essen 1939

Berger, Gottlob, Zum Ausbau der Waffen-SS, in: Nation Europa, 3. Jg. (1953)

Bertram, Hptm., Das Regiment General Göring, in: Jahrbuch der deutschen Luftwaffe 1940, Leipzig 1940

v. Bethmann Hollweg, Th., Betrachtungen zum Weltkrieg, 2 Tle., Berlin 1919 u. 1921

Beyer, Hans, Der Plan einer Balkaninvasion, in: Südostdeutsche Heimatblätter, 4. Jg. (1955)

Bilanz des Zweiten Weltkrieges, Oldenburg u. Hamburg 1953

Blahut, Theodor, Die Entwicklung des Rassengedankens im Faschismus, in: Italien-Jahrbuch 1938, Essen 1939

Bley, Dr. Curt, Geheimnis Radar, Hamburg 1949

v. Blücher, Wipert, Gesandter zwischen Diktatur und Demokratie, Wiesbaden 1951

Blumentritt, Günther, von Rundstedt, London 1952

Bohn, Helmut, Die patriotische Karte der sowjetischen Deutschland-Politik, in: Ost-Probleme, 7. Jg. (1955)

Bor-Komorowski, T., The Secret Army, New York 1951

Bossi Fedrigotti, Anto Graf, Bersaglieri paradieren im Laufschritt, in: Der Frontsoldat erzählt, 19. Jg. (1955), Nr. 10

Bracher, Karl Dietrich, Die Auflösung der Weimarer Republik, 2. Aufl., Stuffgart u. Düsseldorf 1957

Brennecke, Jochen, Schlachtachiff "Tirpitz." Das Drama der "Einsamen Königin des Nordena," Hamm 1953

Bretholz, Wolfgang, Ich sah sie stürzen, München 1955

Bretton Henry L., Stresemann and the Revision of Versailles, Stanford 1953

Brickhill, Paul, The Dam Busters, London 1951

Brügel, J. W., Vor zehn Jahren in der Slowakei, in: Die Zukunft, Jg. 1954

Buchner, Alex, Angriff über einen Fluss, in: Wehrkunde, 4. Jg. (1955)

Die Büste der Königin Nofretete, Berlin 1954

Bullock, Alan, Hitler. A Study in Tyranny, London 1952

Busch, Harald, So war der U-Boot-Krieg, Bielefeld 1952

Byrnes, J. F., In aller Offenheit, Frankfurt/M. o. J.

Chevalier, A., Die deutschen meteorologischen Unternehmungen in der Arktis während des Krieges 1939-1945, in: Marine-Rundschau, 50. Jg. (1953) (übernommen aus: La Revue Maritime Nr. 78, Oktober 1952)

Churchill, Winston Spencer, Der Zweite Weltkrieg, 6 Bde., Bern 1949-1954

Ciano, Galeazzo, Diario, 2 Bde., o.O. 1946

Ciano, Galeazzo Graf, Tagebücher 1939-1943, 2. Aufl., Bern 1947

Cilibrizzi, Saverio, Pietro Badoglio. Rispetto a Mussolini e di fronte alla storia, Napoli o. J.

The Conferences at Malta and Yalta 1945 (Foreign Relations of the United States Diplomatic Papers), Washington 1955

Conradis, Heinz, Nerven, Harz und Rechenschieber, Göttingen 1955

v. Conrady, D.H.D., Die Kriegsmarine im Schwarzen Meer 1941 bis 1944, in: Marine-Rundschau, 53. Jg. (1956)

v. Conrady, Heinz Detrich, Quer durch Europa. Die Geschichte zweier Überführungen, in: Marine-Rundschau, 54. Jg. (1957)

Court, W.H.B., Coal (History of the Second World War), London 1951

Crankshaw, Edward, Gestapo, London 1956

Dallin, Alexander, German Rule in Russia 1941-1945. A Study of Occupation Policies, London 1957

Deane, John R., Ein seltsames Bündnis, Wien 1946

Dedijer, Vladimir, Tito, Berlin 1953

Degeners Wer ist's? 1935

Denzel, E., Die 21. LW.-Felddivision (Adler-Division) und ihr Weg, in: Luftwaffenring, Jg. 1957

Das deutsche Führerlexikon 1934/35, Berlin 1934

Das deutsche Heer 1939, hrsg. von H. H. Podzun, Bad Nauheim 1953

Die deutsche Industrie im Kriege 1939-1945, Berlin 1954

Dienstaltersliste der Schutzstaffel der NSDAP. Bearbeitet von der SS-Personalkanzlei, Berlin 1934, 1936, 1938, 1942, 1944

Documents on British Foreign Policy 1919-1939, hrsg. von E. L. Woodward und Rohan Butler, 3. Serie, Bd. VII, London 1954

Documents on German Foreign Policy 1918-1945, Series D (1937-1945), Vol. VIII: The War Years, Washington 1945

Dornberger, Dr. Walter, V2—Der Schuss ins Weltall, Esslingen 1952

Einsiedel, Heinrich, Graf, Tagebuch einer Versuchung, Stuttgart 1950

Eisenhower, Dwight D., Kreuzzug in Europa, Amsterdam 1948

Elser, Gerhard, Die Bewaffnung der Deutschen Infanterie 1939-1945, in: Feldgrau, 4. Jg. (1956)

Erfurth, Waldemar, Der finnische Krieg 1941-1944, Wiesbaden 1950

Erfurth, Waldemar, Die Geschichte des deutschen Generalstabs von 1918 bis 1945, Göttingen 1957

v. Esebeck, Hanns Gert, Afrikanische Schicksalsjahre, Wiesbaden 1949

Ewald, Gustav, Die Schaffung des Luftlagebildes, in: Luftwaffenring, 2. Jg. (1953)

Eyck, Erich, Bismarck, 3 Bde., Erlenbach u. Zürich 1941/44

Eyck, Erich, Das persönliche Regiment Wilhelms II., Erlenbach u. Zürich 1948

Fabre-Luce, Alfred, Une tragédie royale. L'affaire Léopold III., Paris 1948

Feis, Herbert, The Road to Pearl Harbor, Princeton (New Jersey) 1950

Feuchter, Georg W., Geschichte des Luftkriegs, Bonn 1954

Fischer, George, Soviet Opposition to Stalin, Cambridge (Mass.) 1952

Flicke, W. F., Die Rote Kapelle, Hilden 1949

Foerster, Wolfgang, Generaloberst Ludwig Beck. Sein Kampf gegen den Krieg, München 1953

Fotitch, Constantin, The War We Lost, New York 1948

Franssen, Theo. La bataille d'Anvers, Antwerpen 1945

Frantis, Dr. Kurt, Der Aufstand von Banska Bystrica, in: Der europäische Osten, Jg. 1954/55

Freksa, Friedrich, Kapitän Erhardt, Berlin 1924

Friessner, Hans, Verratene Schlachten. Die Tragödie der deutschen Wehrmacht in Rumänien und Ungarn, Hamburg 1956

Fuller, J.F.C., Der zweite Weltkrieg 1939-1945, Wien 1950

Galai, N., Geschichte der sowjetischen Panzerwaffe, in: Ost-Probleme, 7. Jg. (1955)

Galland, Adolf, Die Ersten und die Letzten, Darmstadt 1953

Gebirgsjäger, Die 1. Gebirgsdivision 1935-1945, Bad Nauheim 1954

The German Replacement Army (Ersatzheer) February 1945, hrsg. von der Militery Intelligence Division, War Department, Washington (1945)

Die Geschichte des Panzerregiments 2, Kleve 1953

Feschichte der Ritter des Ordens "pour le mérite" im Weltkrieg, 2 Bde., hrsg. von Hans Möller, Berlin 1935

Gilbert, Felix, Hitler Directs His War, New York 1950

Girard, Louis-Dominique, Montoire—Verdun diplomatique, Paris 1948

Gisevius, Hans Bernd, Bis zum bittern Ende, 2. Bd.: Vom Münchner Abkommen zum 20. Juli 1944, 2. Aufl., Zürich 1946

Goebbels, Joseph, Vom Kaiserhof zur Reichskanzlei, 38. Aufl., München 1942

Goebbels-Tagebücher, als z. T. ungeddrucktes Manuskript im Archiv IfZ

Görlitz, Walter, Der Zweite Weltkrieg, 2 Gde., Stuttgart 1951

Görlitz, Walter und Herbert A. Quint, Adolf Hitler, Stuttgart 1951

Gollwitzer, Helmut, Und Führen, wohin Du nicht willst, München 1951

Goudima, Robert, L'Armée Rouge dans la paix et la guerre, Paris 1947

Grams, Rold, Die 14. Panzer-Division 1940-1945, Bad Nauheim 1957

Greiner, Helmuth, Die Oberste Wehrmachtführung 1939-1943, Wiesbaden 1951

Gröner, Erich, Die Schiffe der deutschen Kriegsmarine und Luftwaffe 1939-45 und ihr Verbleib, München 1954

Der Grossdeutsche Reichstag, IV. Wahlperiode, Berlin 1938, 1943

Guderian, Heinz, Erinnerungen eines Soldaten, Heidelberg 1951

Guderian, Heinz, Panzer—Marsch! München 1956

Hadeler, Wilhelm un Erich Gröner, "Yamato" und "Musashi" der japanischen Marine, die grössten Schlachtschiffe der Welt, in: Marine-Rundschau, 52. Jg (1955)

Hagedorn, H., Americans, New York 1946

Hagen, Walter, Die Geheime Front, Linz u. Wien 1950

Hagen, Walter, Unternehmen Bernhard, Wels 1955

Hahn, Assi, Ich spreche die Wahrheit, Esslingen 1951

Haupt, Werner, Die Flieger der "Esquadrón Azúl," in: Der deutsche Soldat, 22. Jg. (1958)

Hausser, Paul, Waffen-SS im Einsatz, Göttingen 1953

Hayn, Friedrich, Die Invasion. Von Cotentin bis Falaise, Heidelberg 1954

Hébrard, J., Vingt-cinq années d'aviation militaire, Bd. II, Paris 1947

Heidkämper, Otto, Witebsk. Kampf und Untergang der 3. Panzerarmee, Heidelberg 1954

Heilmann, Will, Gebt uns endlich die Me 262! in: Der Frontsoldat erzählt, 19. Jg. (1955)

Heilmann, Will, "Bodenplatte" kostete das Rückgrat, in: Der Frontsoldat erzählt, 19. Jg. (1955)

Heilmann, Will, Rakete mit 10000 Stundenkilometern, in: Der Frontsoldat erzählt, 19, Jg. (1955)

Herhudt v. Rohden, Hans-Detlef, Die Luftwaffe ringt um Stalingrad, Wiesbaden 1950

Herzfeld, Hans, Die moderne Welt, Teil I, Braunschweig o. J.

Heydel, Hugo, Der englische Handstreich auf St. Nazaire, in: Marine-Rundschau, 50. Jg. (1953)

Hillgruber, Andreas, Hitler, König Carol und Marschall Antonescu, Wiesbaden 1954

Hinsley, F. H., Hitler's Strategy, Cambridge 1951

Hitler, Adolf, Mein Kampf, 145.-146. Aufl., München 1935

Hitler's Europe (Survey of International Affairs 1939/46), hrsg. von Arnold Toynbee, Oxford 1954

Hitlers Tischgespräche, hrsg. von Henry Picker, Bonn 1951

Hoare, Sir Samuel, Gesandter in besonderer Mission, Hamburg 1949

Hölter, H., Die Probleme des deutsch-finnishcen Koalitionskampfes, in: Wehrkunde, 2. Jg. (1953)

Hofer, Walther, Die Entfesselung des Zweiten Welfkriegs, Stuttgart 1954

Hoffmann, Karl Otto, Das Geheimnis Radar, in: Der Frontsoldat erzählt, 18. Jg. (1954)

Horn, Walter, Finnland, Russland und Deutschland, in: Aussenpolitik, 5. Jg. (1954)

v. Horthy, Nikolaus, Ein Leben für Ungarn, Bonn1963

v. Hove, Alkmar, Achtung Fallschirmjäger! Leoni 1954

Hurstfield, J., The Control of Raw Materials (History of the Second World War), London 1953

Huyssen, Hans, Wie starb Generalfeldmarschall Model? in: Der Frontsoldat erzählt, 16. Jg. (1952)

The Initial Triumph of the Axis (Survey of International Affairs 1939-1946), hrsg. von Arnold und Veronica M. Toynbee, Oxford 1958

Internationales biographisches Archiv (Munzinger-Archiv), Ravensburg

Italien-Jahrbuch 1938, Essen 1939

Italien-Jahrbuch 1939, Essen 1940

Jacobsen, Hans-Adolf, Fall Gelb. Der Kampf um den deutschen Operationsplan zur Westoffensive 1940 (Veröffentlichungen des Instituts für europäische Geschichte Mainz, Bd. 16), Wiesbaden 1957

Jacobsen, Hans-Adolf, 10. Januar 1940—Die Affäre Mecheln, in: Wehrwissenschaftliche Rundschau, 4. Jg. (1954)

Jahrbuch der deutschen Akademie der Luftfahrtforschung 1938/39

Jahrbuch der deutschen Luftwaffe 1940, Leipzig 1940

Jahrbuch der Weltpolitik 1944, Berlin 1944

Jeismann, Karl-Ernst, Das Problem des Präventivkrieges, Freiburg u. München 1957

Jilemnicky, Peter, Der Wind dreht sich, Berlin 1952

Jones, F. C., Japan's New Order in East Asia. Its Rise and Fall 1937-1945, London 1954

Jones, F. C., Hugh Borton und B. R. Pearn, The Far East 1942-1946 (Survey of International Affairs 1939-1946), London 1955

Jürgens, Hans, Die Flakartillerie von 1935-1945, in: Feldgrau, 1. Jg. (1953) u. 2. Jg. (1954)

Jugoslawien, Osteuropa-Handbuch, Köln u. Graz 1954

Kaiser, Hans, K., Vom "Wasserfall" zum "Feuervogel," in: Der Frontsoldat erzählt, 19. Jg. (1955)

Kalinow, Kyrill D., Sowjetmarschälle haben das Wort, Hamburg 1950

Kállay, Nicholas, Hungarian Premier, New York 1954

Kammerer, Albert, La passion de la flotte Française, Paris 1951

Keesings Archiv der Gegenwart, Wien

Keilig, Wolf, Das deutsche Heer 1939-1945, Bad Nauheim, Loseblasssammlung 1957

Kern, Erich, Der gross Rausch, Zürich 1948

Kesselring, Albert, Soldat bis zum letzten Tag, Bonn 1953

Kesselring, Albert, Die deutsche Luftwaffe, in: Bilanz des Zweiten Weltkrieges, Oldenburg u. Hamburg 1953

Kirk, Geore, The Middle East in the War (Survey of International Affairs 1939-1946), Oxford 1952

Kiszling, Rudolf, Die Kroaten. Der Schicksalsweg eines Südslawenvolkes, Graz u. Köln 1956

Koch, Horst-Adalbert, Flak, Bad Nauheim 1954

Koch, Horst-Adalbert, Gliederung und Stärke des deutschen Heeres im Herbst 1943, in: Feldgrau, 5 Jg. (1957)

Koch, Horst-Adalbert, Die organisatorische Entwicklung des Regiments General Göring, in: Feldgrau, 3. Jg. (1955)

Koch, Horst-Adalbert, Division Brandenburg, in: Feldgrau, 5. Jg. (1957)

Koller, Karl, Der letzte Monat, Mannheim 1949

Komarnicki, Titus, Rebirth of the Polish Republic. A Study in the Diplomatic History of Europe, 1914-1920, London 1957

Konrad, Joachim, Das Ende von Breslau, in: Vierteljahrshefte für Zeitgeschichte, 4. Jg. (1956)

Korbonski, Stefan, Fighting Warsaw. The Story of the Polish Underground State 1939-1945, London 1956

Kordt, Erich, Wahn und Wirklichkeit, 26. bis 50. Tsd., Stuttgart 1948

Krätschmer, Ernst-Günther, Die Ritterkreuzträger der Waffen-SS, Göttingen 1955

Kriegsheim, Herbert, Getarnt, Getäuscht und doch Getreu. Die Geheimnisvollen "Brandenburger," Berlin 1958

Kuby, Erich, Das Ende des Schreckens, München 1955

v. Kuhl, Hermann, Der Weltkrieg 1914-1918, Bd. II, Berlin 1929

Kuhlmann, Arthur, Donaurückmarsch durch den Feind, in: Der deutsche Soldat, 22. Jg. (1958)

Lange, Eitel, Der Reichsmarschall im Kriege, Stuttgart 1950

Langer, William L. und S. Everett Gleason, The Undeclared War 1940-1941, New York 1953

Lazitch, Branko, La tragédie du general Draja Mihailovitch, o. O. 1946

Leber, Annedore, Das Gewissen entscheidet, Berlin u. Frankfurt/Main 1957

Lee, Asher, The Soviet Air Force, London 1950

Leeb, Emil, Aus der Rüstung des Dritten Reiches (Das Heereswaffenamt 1938-1945) (Beih. 4, Wehrtechnische Monatshefte), Frankfurt, Mai 1958

Liddel Hart, B. H., The German Generals Talk, New York 1948

Lochner, Louis P., Goebbels Tagebücher, Zürich 1948

Lodewyckx, Dr. A., Das Deutschtum in Austalien, Taschenbuch des Grenz- und Auslanddeutschtums H. 40, Berlin o. J.

Lohmann, Walter und Hans H. Hildebrand, Die deutsche Kriegsmarine 1939-1945, Bad Nauheim, Loseblattsammlung 1956

v. Lossberg, Bernhard, Im Wehrmachtführungsstab, Hamburg 1949

Ludendorff, Erich, Meine Kriegserinnerungen 1914-1918, Berlin 1919

Lütge, Friedrich, Die Deutsche Kriegsfinanzierung im ersten und zweiten Weltkrieg, in: Beiträge zur Finanzeissenschaft und zur Geldtheorie, Festschrift für Rudolf Stucken, S. 243ff., Göttingen 1953

Der Luftschutz im Weltkrieg, Berlin 1941

Lusar, Rudolf, Seehunde, Molche und Hechte, in: Der Frontsoldat erzählt, 16. Jg. (1952)

Lusar, Rudolf, Die Deutschen Waffen und Geheimwaffen des 2. Weltkrieges und ihre Weiterentwicklung, München 1956

Macartney, C. A., October Fifteenth. A History of Modern Hungary 1929-1945, 2 Bde., Edinburgh 1956/57

McNeill, William Hardy, America, Britain and Russia (Survey of International Affairs 1939-1946), Oxford 1953

Maerchker, Vom Kaiserheer zur Reichswehr, Leipzig 1922

Mannerheim, G., Erinnerungen, Zürich 1952

v. Manstein, Erich, Verlorene Siege, Bonn 1955

Martienssen, Anthony, Hitler and His Admirals, New York 1949

Martin, Carl E., Kurze Zusammenstellung über die italienische Armee und die faschistische Nationalmiliz, Berlin 1933

Matl, Josef, Die Emigranten aus Jugoslawien, in: Jugoslawien. Osteuropa-Handbuch, Köln u. Graz 1954

Matl, Josef, Jugoslawien im Zweiten Weltkrieg, in: Jugoslawien. Osteuropa-Handbuch, Köln u. Graz 1954

Meister, Jürg, Der Seekrieg in den osteuropäischen Gewässern 1941-1945, München 1958

Meister, Jürg, Die letzte Landungsoperation im Osten. Das misslungene Unternehmen gegen die Insel Suursaari, in: Der deutsche Soldat, 21. Jg. (1957)

Mellini Ponce de Leon, Alberto, Guerra diplomatica a Salò, Bologna 1950

The Memoirs of Cordell Hull, New York 1948

Mensch un Staat in Recht und Geschichte. Festschrift für Herbert Kraus, Kitzingen 1954

Messe, Giovanni, La Guerra al fronte russo, Milano 1947

v. Metzsch, Friedrich-August, Die Geschichte der 22. Infanterie-Division 1939-1945, Kiel 1952

Meyer, A. O., Bismarck, Stuttgart

Meyer, Adolf, Mit Adolf Hitler im Bayr. Res.-Inf.-Rgt. 16 List, Neustadt/Aisch 1934

Michaux, Theo, Rohstoffe aus Ostasien, in: Wehrwissenschaftliche Rundschau, 5. Jg. (1955)

Mikus, Joseph A., La Slovaquie dans le drame de l'Europe, Paris 1955

Moellhausen, Eitel Friedrich, Die gebrochene Achse, Alfield 1949

Montgomery, Von El Alamein zum Sangro, Hamburg 1949

Mordal, Jacques, Die französische Marine im Zweiten Weltkrieg, in: Marine-Rundschau, 53. Jg. (1956)

Morison, Samuel Eliot, The Struggle for Guadalcanal August 1942-February 1943 (History of the United States Naval Operations in World War II, vol. V), Boston 1950

Morison, Samuel Eliot, The Battle of the Atlantic (dass. Vol. I), Boston 1950

Morison, Samuel Eliot, The Atlantic Battle Won (dass. Vol. X), London 1956

Moseley, Philip E., The Occupation of Germany, in: Foreign Affairs, 28. Jg. (1949/50)

Mueller-Hillebrand, Burkhart, Das Heer 1933-1945, Bd. I: Das Heer bis zum Kriegsbeginn, Bd. II: Die Blitzfeldzüge 1939-1941, Darmstadt 1954 u. 1956

Musmanno, Michael A., In zehn Tagen kommt der Tod, München o. J.

Mussolini, Benito, Storia di un anno, Milano 1944

Neubacher, Hermann, Sonderauftrag Südost 1940-1945, Göttingen 1956

Nowack, Wilhelm, Australien. Kontinent der Gegensätze, Leipzig 1938

Nycop, Carl-Adam, Die grossen Zürich 1944

v. Oertzen, F. W., Die deutschen Freikorps 1918-1923, München 1936

Oncken, Hermann, Das Deutsche Reich und die Vorgeschichte des Welfkrieges, 1. Bd., Leipzig 1933

Order of Battle of the German Army March 1945, hrsg. von der Military Intelligence Division, War Department, Washington (1945)

v. Oven, Wilfried, Mit Goebbles bis zum Ende, 2 Bde., Buenos Aires 1949

Paetel, Karl O., Das Nationalkomitee Freies Deutschland, in: Politische Studien, 6. Jg. (1955/56)

v. Papen, Franz, Der Wahrheit eine Gasse, München 1952

Pattee, R. und A. M. Rothbauer, Spanien, Graz 1954

Pechel, Rudolf, Deutscher Widerstand, Erlenbach u. Zürich 1947

Personalakten des OKH, im Auszug in: Nürnberger Dokument NOKW-141

Picker, Henry, Hitlers Tischgespräche, Bonn 1951

Pickert, Wolfgang, Vom Kuban-Brückenkopf bis Sewastopol, Heidelberg 1955

Pini, Giorgio, Geschichte des Faschismus, Berlin 1941

Playfair, I. S. O., The Mediterranean and Middle East, vol. 1: The Early Successes against Italy, London 1954

Poll, Bernhard, Das Schicksal Aachens im Herbst 1944, Aachen 1955

Postan, M. M., British War Production (History of the Second World War), London 1952

Der Prozess gegen die Hauptkriegsverbrecher vor dem Internationalen Militärgerichtshof Nürnberg, 14. November 1945- 1. Oktober 1946 (Blaue Reihe), 42 Bde., Nürnberg 1949

v. Puttkamer, Jesco, Irrtum und Schuld, Neuwied 1948

Rangliste des deutschen Heeres 1944/45, hrsg. von Wolf Keilig, Bad Nauheim 1955

The Realignment of Europe (Survey of International Affairs 1939-1946), hrsg. von Arnold und Veronica M. Toynbee, Oxford 1955

Reichstags-Handbuch, Berlin 1920 (I. Wahlperiode), 1924 (II. Wahlperiode), 1924 (III Wahlperiode), 1928 (IV. Wahlperiode), 1930 (V. Wahlperiode), 1932 (VI. Wahlperiode), 1933 (VIII. Wahlperiode), 1933 (IX. Wahlperiode)

Reitlinger, Gerald, The SS, Alibi of a Nation, London 1956

Reitsch, Hanna, Fliegen—mein Leben, Stuttgart 1951

Rendulic, Lothar Gekämpft—gesiegt—geschlagen, Wels u. Heidelberg 1952

Rendulic, Lothar, Der Partisanenkrieg, in: Bilanz des zweiten Weltkrieges, Oldenburg u. Hamburg 1953

Rhode, Gotthold und Wolfgang Wagner, Quellen zur Entstehung der Oder-Neisse-Linie, Stuttgart 1956

v. Ribbentrop, Joachim, Zwischen London und Moskau, Leoni 1953

Richards, Denis, The Fight at Odds (Royal Air Force 1939-45, vol. I), London 1953

Richards, Denis, und Hilary St. George Saunders, The Fight Avails (Royal Air Force 1939, vol. II), London 1954

Rieckhoff, H. J., Trumpf oder Bluff? Genf 1945

Rieker, Karlheinrich, Ein Mann verliert einen Weltkrieg, Frankfurt/M. 1955

v. Rintelen, Enno, Mussolini als Bundesgenosse, Tübingen u. Stuttgart 1951

Ritter, Gerhard, Carl Goerdeler und die deutsche Widerstandsbewegung, Stuttgart 1954

Ritter, Gerhard, Staatskunst und Kriegshandwerk, München 1954

Roeder, Manfred, Die Rote Kapelle, Hamburg 1952

Roehrbein, Erich, Die Familie im faschistischen Recht, in: Italien-Hahrbuch 1939, Essen 1940

Rönnefarth, Helmuth K. G., Reichs-Grenadier-Division "Hoch- und Deutschmeister" 1938-1945, in: Feldgrau, 4. Jg. (1956)

Rohwer, Jürgen, Die japanische Ubootswaffe im 2. Weltkrieg, in: Marine-Rundschau, 50. Jg. (1953)

Rohwer, Jürgen, Zum 15. Jahrestag von Pearl Harbor, in: Wehrkunde, 5. Jg. (1956)

Rohwer, Jürgen, Die sowjetische U-Bootswaffe in der Ostsee 1939-45, in: Wehrwissenschaftliche Rundschau, 6. Jg. (1956)

The Rommel Papers, hrsg. von B. H. Liddell Hart, London 1953

Royal Air Force 1939-1945, 3 Bde., London 1953/54

Rudel, Hans-Ulrich, Trotzdem, Waiblingen/Wttbg. O. J.

Ruge, Friedrich, Entscheidung im Pazifik, Hamburg 1951

Ruge, Friedrich, Der Seekrieg 1939-1945, Stuttgart 1954

Rumpf, Hans, Der hochrote Hahn, Darmstadt 1952

v. Salomon, Ernst, Das Buch vom deutschen Freikorpskämpfer, Berlin 1938

Sava, George, The Četniks, London o. J.

Schellong, Conrad, Langemarck, in: Nation Europa, 5. Jg (1955)

Schellong, Conrad, Langemarck, in: Wiking-Ruf, 3. Jg. (1954)

Schirmer, Friedrich, Die deutsche Artillerie 1939-1945, in: Feldgrau, 6. Jg. (1958)

v. Schlabrendorff, Fabian, Offiziere gegen Hitler, 3. Aufl., Zürich o. J.

v. Schmidt-Pauli, Edgar, Geschichte der Freikorps 1918-1924, Stuttgart 1936

Schmidt-Richberg, Erich, Der Endkampf auf dem Balkan. Die Operationen der Heeresgruppe E von Griechenland bis zu den Alpen, Heidelberg 1955

Schneider, Erich, Technik und Waffenentwicklung im Kriege, in: Bilanz des Zweiten Weltkrieges, Oldenburg u. Hamburg 1953

Schramm, Percy Ernst, Die Treibstoff-Frage vom Herbst 1943 bis Juni 1944, in: Mensch un Staat in Recht und Geschichte. Festschrift für Herbert Kraus, Kitzingen 1954

Schramm, Wilhelm Ritter von, Der 20. Juli in Paris Wörishofen 1953

Schröter, Heinz, Stalingrad, Osnabrück o. J.

Schulthess' Europäischer Geschichtskalender, München

Schwendemann, Karl, Versailles nach 15 Jahren, Berlin 1935

Schwerin v. Krosigk, Lutz Graf, Wie wurde der Zweite Weltkrieg finanziert? in: Bilanz des Zweiten Weltkrieges, Oldenburg u. Hamburg 1953

v. Seemen, Gerhard, Die Ritterkreuzträger 1939-45, Bad Naueheim 1955

v. Senger und Etterlin, Dr. F., Taschenbuch der Panzer 1943-1954, München 1954

v. Senger und Etterlin, Dr. F. M., Die Entwicklung des Schützenpanzerwagens, in: Wehrkunde, 3. Jg. (1954)

Seraphim, Hans-Günther, "Felix" und "Isabella," in: Die Welt als Geschichte, 15. Jg. (1955)

Seton-Watson, Hugh, The East-European Revolution, London 1950

Sherwood, Robert E., Roosevelt and Hopkins, New York 1950

Shulman, Milton, Die Niederlage im Westen, Gütersloh 1949

v. Siegler, Fritz Frhr., Die höheren Dienststellen der deutschen Wehrmacht 1933-1945, München 1953

Skorzeny, Otto, Geheimkommando Skorzeny, Hamburg 1950

Die Sondereinheiten in der früheren deutschen Wehrmacht, Kornelimünster 1952

Speidel, Hans, Invasion 1944, Tübingen u. Stuttgart o. J.

Stacey, C. P., Six Years of War, Ottawa 1955

Statistisches Jahrbuch für das Deutsche Reich, 59. Jg. 1941/42 u. a., hrsg. vom Statistischen Reichsamt, Berlin 1942

Stegemann, Hermann, Geschichte des Krieges, Bd. IV, Stuttgart u. Berlin 1921

Steiner, Felix, Die Freiwilligen. Idee und Opfergang, Göttingen 1958

Stettinius Jr., Edward R., Roosevelt and the Russians, New York 1949

St. George Saunders, Hilary, The Fight is Won (Royal Air Force 1939-1945, vol. III)

Ströhle, Albert, Von Versailles bis zur Gegenwart, Berlin 1928

Tansill, Charles Callan, Die Hintertür zum Kriege, 3. Aufl., Düsseldorf 1957

Teske, Hermann, Die silbernen Spiegel, Heidelberg 1952

Thorwald, Jügen, Es began an der Weichsel, Stuttgart 1950

Thorwald, Jügen, Das Ende an der Elbe, Stuttgart 1950

Thorwald, Jügen, Wen sie verderben wollen, Stuttgart 1952

v. Tippelskirch, Kurt, Geschichte des zweiten Weltkriegs, Bonn 1951

Togo, Shigenori, Japan im Zweiten Weltkrieg. Erinnerungen des japanischen Aussenministers 1941-42 und 1945, Bonn 1958

Trevor-Roper, H. R., Hitlers letzte Tage, Zürich 1946

Trevor-Roper, Hugh, Hitler und Franco, in: Der Monat, 5. Jg (1953)

Trials of War Criminals before the Nuernberg Military Tribunals, 15 Bde. (Grüne Reihe), Washington o. J.

Trizzino, Antonino, Die verratene Flotte. Tragödie der Afrikakämpfer, Bonn 1957

Ustascha-Bewegung, Zagreb 1943

Vansittart. Lord, The Mist Procession, London 1958

Vanwelkenhuyzen, Jan, Die Krise vom Januar 1940, in: Wehrwissenschaftliche Rundschau, 5. Jg. (1955)

Die Vertreibung der deutschen Bevölkerung aus den Gebieten östlich der Oder-Neisse (Dokumentation der Vertreibung der Deutschen aus Ost-Mitteleuropa, Bd. I/1), hrsg. von Theodor Schieder, Gross-Denkte o. J.

Die Vertreibung der deutschen Bevölkerung aus Tschechoslowakei (dass. Bd. IV/1), Bonn 1957

Von der Panzerattrappe zum Patton-Panzer, in: Der Frontsoldat erzählt, 17. Jg. (1953)

v. Vormann, Nikolaus, Tscherkassy, Heidelberg 1954

Wagenführ, Horst, Italien, Leipzig 1943

Wagner, Fritz, Geschichte und Zeitgeschichte. Pearl Harbor im Kreuzfeuer der Forschung, in: Historische Zeitschrift, Bd. 183 (1957)

Waite, Robert G. L., Vanguard of Nazism, Cambridge (Mass.) 1952

Weidermann, Alfred, Der rechte Mann am rechten Platz, in: Bilanz des Zweiten Weltkrieges, Oldenburg u. Hamburg 1953

Weisenborn, Günther, Der lautlose Aufstand, Hamburg 1953

v. Weitershausen, Die Verteidigung und Räumung von Sewastopol im Mai 1944, in: Wehrwissenschaftliche Rundschau, 4 Jg. (1954)

v. Weizsäcker, Ernst, Erinnerungen, München 1950

Der Weltkrieg 1914-1918, Bd. 10: Die Operation des Jahres 1916, Berlin 1936

Der Weltkrieg 1914-1918, Bd. 14: Die Kriegführung an der Westfront im Jahre 1918, hrsg. von der Kriegsgeschichtlichen Forschungsanstalt des Heeres (Bundesarchiv), Berlin 1944 (Koblenz 1956)

Wer leitet? Die Männer der Wirtschaft und der einschlägigen Verwaltung 1940, Berlin 1940

West, Rebecca, The Meaning of Treason, New York 1947

Westphal, Siegfried, Heer in Fesseln, Bonn 1950

Wheeler-Bennett, John W., Die Nemesis der Macht, Düsseldorf 1954

Who is Who 1950, London 1950

Who's Who in Germany and Austria, London (1945)

Wiener, Fritz, Die deutsche Panzertruppe 1939-1945, in: Feldgrau, 5. Jg. (1957)

Wiener, Fritz, Die Typen-Numerierung der Kraftfahzeuge der Deutschen Wehrmacht 1933-1945, in: Feldgrau, 6. Jg. (1958)

Wilmot, Chester, The Struggle for Europe, London 1952

Wilmot, Chester, Der Kampf um Europa, Frankfurt/M. 1954

Winzer, Otto, 12 Jahre Kampf gegen Faschismus und Krieg, Berlin 1955

Wiskemann, Elizabeth, The Rome-Berlin Axis, New York, London 1949

Woodhouse, C. M., Apple of Discord. London 1948

Wuorinen, John H., Finland and World War II 1939-1945, New York 1948

Yuorichitch, Evgueniyé, Le process Tito—Mihailovitch, Paris 1950

Zantke, Siegfried, Wir halfen Kowel durchhalten, in: Der Frontsoldat erzählt, 18. Jg. (1954)

Zeller, Eberhard, Geist der Freiheit, 3.Aufl., München 1956

Ziemssen, Dietrich, Der Malmedy-Prozess, Brackenheim 1952 (z. T. abgedruckt bei: Hausser, Paul, Waffen-SS im Einsatz, Göttingen 1953)

Zilliacus, K., Tito of Yugoslavia, London 1952

Zoller, Albert, Hitler privat, Düsseldorf 1949

INDEX

A

Aaltonen, B. X. 1025, 1128
Abetz, Otto 458, 770, 797, 979–80, 1128, 1031
Abraham, Erich 9, 40, 766
Abshagen, Karl Heinz 882, 974, 1128
Absolon, Rudolf 756
Adalberto di Savoia, Duke of Bergamo 175–76, 862–63
Adam, Wilhelm 800
Adler, G. 858
Ahlfen, Hans von 1102
Ahr', von xxix
Albrecht, Eric 761
Alexander, Sir Harold 522, 966, 1021–022
Alexander I [Emperor of Russia] iii
Alexander I [King of Yugoslavia] 910
Alexandra, Princess of Greece 928
Alfieri, Dino 826, 1128
Allen, George R. iv, ix, xi, xxiii–xxv, 760–61
Alten, Georg 979, 1128
Ambrosio, Vittorio 103, 826, 875, 881, 885
Amery, John 859
Amery, Leopold Stennett 859
Amsberg, Erik von 444, 492, 499, 505, 740
Anfuso, Filippo 802, 829, 842–43, 845, 851, 862, 875, 886, 888, 910, 931, 1128
Angelis, Maximilian de 685–86, 1111–112
Antonescu, Ion xiv, 44, 310, 781, 830, 917, 935, 937, 939, 991, 1132
Arima, Masafumi 1033
Arlt, Fritz Rudolf 896
Arnim, Hans-Jürgen von 770, 815

Arrese, José Luis de 815
Arntz, Helmut 1089, 1128
Aron, Robert 797, 1031, 1128
Asensio Carlos [Franco's War Minister] 961
Assmann, Heinz 300–01, 401, 411–13, 425, 428–29, 619, 653–54, 687–89, 744
Assmann, Kurt 890, 912–13, 969, 971, 1128
Auchinleck, Claude 811
Axmann, Arthur 727, 734
Axthelm, Walther von 756, 789

B

Bach-Zelewski, Erich von dem 17, 678, 773–74, 993, 1105–106
Backe, Herbert 158–59, 855
Badoglio, Pietro 201, 203–04, 206–07, 213–14, 218, 234, 240–41, 252, 266, 802, 826, 838, 842–43, 862, 874, 878, 881, 887, 894, 952–53, 1128–129
Balbo, Italo 788
Balck, Hermann 623, 988, 1068, 1074–075
Baldwin, Hannson 1096
Balfour, Arthur James 840
Bartz, Karl 807, 923, 1069–072, 1120, 1128
Basso, Antonio 864–65
Bastianini, Giuseppe 138, 841
Bastico, Ettore 770, 845
Battenberg, Ludwig von 906
Bauer, Ernest 910, 1128
Baumbach, Werner 806–07, 849, 867–68, 870, 891, 900, 905, 921, 923, 973, 1007, 1017, 1069–072, 1115, 1125, 1128

Baumont, Maurice 773, 1128
Baur, Hans 189, 872
Bechtoldt, Heinrich 1021, 1128
Beck, Ludwig 458–59, 581, 588, 936, 977, 980, 988, 1059, 1063, 1128, 1130
Becker, Karl 60, 799
Becker, Sybille 758
Behrends, Hermann 494, 1004
Beisswänger, Hugo 756
Belot, Raymond de 788, 863, 865, 888, 910, 953, 1128
Below, Nicolaus von 63, 70, 267, 282, 401, 437, 444, 451, 454, 640, 543, 618, 647, 649, 652, 672, 694–95, 697–99, 703, 705–10, 716, 727, 729, 735, 738, 740, 754, 797, 897, 1122
Bennecke, Götz 746, 977, 983, 986–88
Benoist-Méchin, J. 1100, 1128
Berber, Fritz 876, 1128
Berg, Karl 744
Bergamini, Alberto 888
Berger, Gottlob 756, 784, 951, 992, 1025, 1128
Berger, Heinrich xvi–xvii, xxiv, xxvi, 795
Berlin, Wilhelm 471, 586, 992, 1061
Bernardi, Tullio 838
Berndt, Alfred Ingemar 156, 853
Bertram, Hptm. 789, 1128
Besson, Waldemar 945–46
Best, Werner 300, 330, 911–12
Bethmann-Hollweg, Theobald von 157, 854, 1128
Beyer, Hans 791, 1128
Biroli, Pirzio 129, 835, 842
Bismarck, Otto von 534, 986, 1037, 1092, 1114, 1130, 1134
Blahut, Theodor 828, 1128
Blaskowitz, Johannes 221, 481, 487, 543–46, 548–49, 552, 644–46, 763, 883–84, 969, 1007, 1089–091
Bley, Curt 790, 867, 870, 890, 913, 915, 1128
Blomberg, Werner von 736, 999, 1127
Blücher von Wahlstatt, Gebhard 655, 1025, 1049

Blücher, Wipert 502, 903, 1003, 1010–011, 1129
Blume, Walter 756
Blumentritt, Günther 467, 756, 884, 976, 985, 987–89, 1129
Boden, Friedrich 1027, 1101
Bodenschatz, Karl 5, 14, 29, 32, 144, 149–51, 153, 205–07, 209, 211, 216–17, 269, 750
Boehm-Tettelbach, Karl 744
Bogomoloff, Alexander 928
Böhme, Hermann 756
Bohn, Helmut 1092, 1129
Boldt, Gerhard 760
Bona Margherita, Princess of Bergamo 863
Bonhoeffer, Dietrich 974
Bonin, Bogislaw von 746
Bor-Komorowski, Tadeusz 993, 1129
Borchardt, Ludwig 962
Borghese, Prince Valerio 888
Borgmann, Heinrich 332, 346, 348, 351–52, 354–55, 364, 375, 387, 401, 432, 437, 596, 667, 697, 712, 714–15, 739, 946
Boris III [Bulgarian Tsar] 830, 862, 907, 991
Bormann, Albert 1016
Bormann, Gerda 947
Bormann, Martin xiv–xvii, xx, xxii, 386, 387, 388, 392–96, 398, 514, 612, 754, 854, 879, 934, 945, 946, 947, 983, 984, 1016, 1072, 1077, 1110, 1122
Borton, Hugh 1132
Bose, Subhas Chandra 712, 1123
Bossi, Ferdigotti 815, 1129
Bottai, Giuseppe 878
Bovensiepen, Otto 911
Bracher, Karl Dietrich 1101, 1129
Bradley, Omar 1008, 1030
Brandenberger, Erich 7, 764
Brauchitsch, Bernd von xxxiii, 596, 618, 749
Braun, Eva 738

Bräuer, Bruno 132, 837
Breith, Hermann 593, 638, 1064, 1088
Brennecke, Jochen 1027, 1129
Bretholz, Wolfgang 991, 1002, 1129
Bretton Henry L. 876, 1129
Brickhill, Paul 835, 1027, 1073, 1122, 1129
Brügel, J. W. 1129
Brooke, Alan 924
Brudermüller, Hermann 697–99, 700, 705, 710–11, 714–15, 742
Brügel J. W. 992, 1129
Brüller, Captain 865
Buchholz, Heinz xi, xvi, xx, xxii, xxiv–xxv
Buchner, Alex 1046, 1129
Büchs, Herbert 293, 302–04, 314, 322, 326, 331, 401, 406, 414, 421–22, 430–31, 437, 441, 444, 469, 476–77, 492, 495–96, 500–02, 504, 507, 513–18, 596, 605, 618, 639–40, 654, 689–91, 694–95, 743, 1084–085
Buffarini-Guidi, Guido 195–96, 874–75
Buhle, Walter xii, 11, 17–19, 32, 38–9, 51, 64, 68, 89, 103, 119–21, 123–32, 144–45, 173–74, 178–79, 193–95, 201, 203–06, 208–09, 218, 226, 240, 249–51, 269, 278, 280, 282–84, 287–88, 292–93, 295–96, 302, 310, 315–17, 319–22, 437, 440, 442, 469, 481, 486–87, 492, 495–96, 498–500, 505, 507, 530, 534–35, 571–72, 574, 576–79, 581–83, 587, 596, 599, 610, 618, 626, 637–38, 651–52, 692–93, 707, 714, 744, 756, 768, 774, 906, 923, 926, 947, 972, 1001, 1032
Bulanov [Russian collaborator] 927
Bullock, Alan 759, 981–82, 987, 1129
Buniatshchenko, Sergei 1085
Burgdorf, Wilhelm xxix, 469, 492, 499, 597, 618, 636, 650, 655–57, 659–60, 662–65, 667–68, 672–73, 675, 678, 680–82, 697, 703, 705–11,

715–18, 739, 748, 787, 1099, 1103–104, 1106
Burmeister, Arnold 568, 570, 1050
Busch, Ernst 288–89, 292, 325, 372, 790, 800, 894–95, 907, 986
Busch, Harald 890, 913, 916, 1129
Busse, Theodor 405, 720, 727, 729–30, 733, 735, 948, 1121
Buttlar-Brandefels, Horst von, Baron Treusch 401, 743, 851
Byrnes, J. F. 1044, 1129

C
Canaris, Wilhelm 815, 882, 949, 973–74, 1031, 1128
Cartellieri, Wolfgang 756
Cass, Frank 902
Čatlos, Ferdinand 992
Cavallero, Ugo 63, 802, 826, 845
Charlemagne [King of the Franks] 1108
Cherniakhovsky, Ivan 1065
Chevalier, A. 1097, 1129
Chevallerie, Botho von 7
Chevallerie, Helmuth von der 7
Chevallerie, Kurt von der 7, 41, 763
Chiang Kai-shek 852–53
Chiappe, Jean 772
Christ, Torsten 756
Christian, Eckhard 27, 29, 41, 51, 53–5, 63, 67, 72, 78–82, 93, 95–9, 106, 114–16, 144, 149–53, 180–81, 184–90, 202, 205, 208–09, 211–15, 235, 237–38, 246–47, 271–75, 507, 514–17, 521–22, 529, 532, 607–08, 616, 646, 657, 676, 684, 688, 691–92, 694–96, 742, 750
Christian X [King of Denmark] 397
Christiansen, Friedrich 1090–091
Churchill, Winston Spencer 94, 245, 466, 534, 555, 790–92, 802, 811, 813, 816, 847, 859, 867, 880, 889, 891–92, 911, 920, 924–25, 930, 933–34, 942, 952–53, 1009, 1020–021, 1042–044, 1129

Ciano, Edda 141, 842
Ciano, Galeazzo 141, 203, 206–07, 785–86, 829, 840–43, 845, 847, 851, 862, 864, 874–75, 887, 1129
Cilibrizzi, Saverio 887, 1129
Clausewitz, Karl von 722, 1077
Clerq, Staf de 935
Conrady, D.H.D. von 762, 1125 1129
Conrady, Heinz 762, 995, 1129
Conrath, Paul 131, 756, 836
Corvaja, Santi 851, 875
Crankshaw, Edward 930, 1129
Cross, General 1029

D
Daladier, Edouard 772–73, 980
Dallin, Alexander 852–54, 856–58, 1129
Daniels, General von 1092
D'Annunzio, Gabriele 880
Darges, Fritz 189, 207, 332, 345–46, 367, 401, 437, 740
Daser, Wilhelm 1029
De Courbière Guillaume, René von 1098
De Felice, Renzo 828, 842
De Gaulle, Charles 528, 925
Deane, John R. 782, 1129
Decker [Labor Leader] 734
Dedijer, Vladimir 792, 962, 1009, 1020, 1129
Degenkolb, Gerhard 716, 1126
Degrelle, Leon 801, 941
Deichmann, Paul 756
Delbrück, Justus 974
Demany, Fernand 756
Demelhuber, Karl Maria 494, 1005
Denzel, E. 805, 1129
Dessloch, Otto 824
Deuerlein, Ernst 946
Dewey, Thomas E. 424, 923, 959–60, 1034
Dieckhoff, Hans-Heinrich 428–29, 819–20
Dietrich, Joseph (Sepp) xiv, 40, 126, 146, 245, 261, 437, 507, 522–23,

573, 582, 586, 701, 783, 834, 845, 893, 896, 927, 1060–061, 1109
Dietrich, Otto 754
Dimitrescu, Joan 801, 826
Dirksen, Herbert von 863
Dirlewanger, Oskar 896
Djuršic, Pavle 142, 501, 843
Dohnányi, von [Reich legal counsel] 974
Dollmann, Eugen 861, 887
Dollmann, Friedrich 169, 221, 861, 883, 887, 1090
Domarus, Max ix, 945–47
Dönitz, Karl viii, 227–28, 235–38, 246, 469, 478–80, 485, 733, 737, 751, 812, 879, 883, 890, 919, 947, 996, 1110
Dornberger, Walter 799, 905, 1066, 1114, 1126, 1130
Dörr, Fritz xvi
Dörr, Hans 756
Dorsch, Xaver 411, 460, 716, 951, 981
Dreyfus, Alfred 772
Duce, see Mussolini, Benito
Dumitrache, Joan 801

E
Eberbach, General 464, 984
Ebert, Friedrich 1100
Echnaton [Egyptian Pharaoh] 962
Eden, Anthony 721, 811, 889, 918, 1042–043
Ehrhardt, Hermann 1107
Eicke, Theodor 884, 993, 1086
Einem, Hans-Egon von 632, 1083
Einem, Kurt von 756
Einsiedel, Heinrich von 1092, 1130
Eisenhower, Dwight D. 3, 318, 436, 501, 881, 924–25, 953, 965, 975, 1008–009, 1038, 1043–045, 1048, 1090–091, 1104, 1111, 1130
Elias, Hendrik 941
Elser, Gerhard 1005, 1046, 1065, 1088, 1130
Encioglu, Menem 802
Engel, Gerhard 60–1, 739, 756, 795, 1121
Erzberger, Matthias 104, 828, 1107

Erdmenger, Hans 812
Eremenko, Andrei 767
Erfurth, Waldemar 801, 830, 903, 1003, 1025–026, 1130
Esebeck, Hanns Gert von 862, 1130
Esser, Willi 756
Esteban-Infantes, Emilio 897
Etzdorf Hasso von 821
Ewald, Gustav 867, 896, 1130
Eyck, Erich 772, 1037, 1130

F
Fabre-Luce, Alfred 880, 1130
Fagerholm, Karl-August 1034
Falkenhausen, Alexander von 880, 941
Falkenhayn, Erich 854
Farinacci, Roberto 105, 195–96, 203, 231, 253, 828, 861, 874–75, 887
Fegelein, Hermann 401, 403, 426–27, 429, 444, 455, 461–62, 469, 472–73, 486, 507, 509, 511, 517–18, 530–31, 618, 628–29, 632, 634–36, 645–47, 657, 660, 663, 665–66, 678, 700, 718–19, 752, 977, 993, 1013, 1019, 1078, 1084–085, 1090
Feis, Herbert 822–23, 1130
Fellgiebel, Erich 132, 836, 973, 1061
Felmy, Helmuth 73, 810–11
Fenski, Horst-Arno 899
Feuchter, Georg W. 794, 808, 847–49, 867, 891, 899, 923, 931, 954–55, 959, 1016–017, 1069–073, 1113, 1115, 1120, 1130
Feuchtinger, Edgar 568, 572, 678, 680, 1049, 1106
Fiebig, Heinz 9, 766
Fiebig, Martin 431, 963
Finckh, Eberhard 467, 983, 988
Fischer, Adolf 650, 1094
Fischer, George iv–v, ix, 851–53, 856–58, 896, 1085, 1094, 1130
Flicke, W. F. 876, 1130
Focke, Wulf 807, 1125, 1130
Foerster, Wolfgang 980, 1130
Foertsch, Hermann 909, 1109–110

Forster, Albert 715, 1125
Förster Otto 66, 580, 756, 772, 803–04, 981, 1057, 1058
Forstner, Baron von 772
Förtsch, Herrmann 682, 1109
Fotitch, Constantin 792, 844, 847, 889, 928–29, 1009, 1130
Franco, Francisco 427, 528, 531, 897, 961, 1030–032, 1138
Frank, August 551, 581, 1040
Frank, Bernhard 1122
Frank, Hans xxii, xxix
Franssen, Theo 1062, 1130
Frantis, Kurt 992, 1130
Franz Joseph I, Emperor of Austria 844
Frederick II [King of Prussia] 397, 468, 539, 555, 583, 655, 723
Frederick Wilhelm I [King of Prussia] 655
Freisler, Roland 468, 988–89
Freksa, Friedrich 1100, 1130
Frenz [photographer] xviii
Freyend, Ernst John von 401, 469, 596, 618, 742, 757
Freytag von Loringhoven, Bernd 469, 618, 638
Frick, Wilhelm 1100
Fricke, Ludwig 1082
Friebe, Helmut 420, 957
Friedrichs, Helmuth 946
Friessner, Hans 756, 827, 957, 991, 995, 1004, 1012, 1014, 1074, 1088, 1130
Fritsch, Werner von 398, 947
Fromm, Friedrich (Fritz) 346, 936, 980, 1008
Frot, Eugène 772–73
Fuller, J.F.C. 868, 1130
Funk, Walter 1101

G
Galai, N. 782, 1130
Galbiati, Enzo 874
Galland, Adolf 516, 611, 808–09, 813, 835, 868, 891, 914–15, 923, 964, 1017–018, 1071, 1120, 1130

Gambara, Gastone 144, 845
Gamelin, Maurice 458–59, 980
Ganzenmüller, Albert 590, 1064
Gariboldi, Italo 761
Gayda, Virginio 885, 895
Gehlen, Reinhard 852
Geilenberg, Edmund 1119
George VI [King of England] 1042–043
Gercke, Rudolf 467, 987
Gerland, Karl 934
Gevers, Colonel 297, 909
Giesler, Paul 292, 908
Gilbert, Felix iv, ix, xii, xxvi, 786, 792, 882, 895, 1131
Gille, Herbert 587, 638, 958, 1062, 1068, 1088
Girard, Louis-Dominique 59, 318, 797, 925, 1131
Giraud, Henri-Honoré 925
Gisevius, Hans Bernd 882, 974, 1131
Glaise-Horstenau, Edmund 196, 503, 875, 1009, 1012
Glantz, David M. 902
Gleason, Everett 822–23, 900, 1133
Gloria, Alessandro 885
Glücks, Richard 636, 1086
Goebbels, Joseph xxvii–xxix, 278, 393, 395–96, 656, 706–07, 721–727, 730–32, 735, 793, 814, 874, 879, 882, 893, 934, 986, 1044, 1099, 1101, 1110, 1131, 1134–135
Goebbels, Magda 1101
Goerdeler, Carl 896, 974–75, 986, 1136
Göerlitz, Walter 1001
Göhler, Johannes 596, 619, 697, 700–01, 711–14, 753, 1123–124
Gollwitzer, Helmut 1092, 1131
Gonell, General 1080–081
Göring, Hermann xv, xvii, xxi, xxvii, 50, 68, 73, 109, 124, 130–31, 137, 151, 172–73, 203, 206, 217, 220–25, 228–32, 234–41, 244–47, 263, 352, 365, 428, 433, 484, 495, 586, 589–90, 596, 599, 604, 606–11,

613–19, 622, 626, 629–30, 632, 634–37, 639–41, 643–46, 648–49, 651–53, 655–65, 678, 684, 691, 695–96, 717, 748, 750, 768, 785, 787, 789, 794, 801, 805–06, 808, 824–25, 836, 840–41, 844, 854, 858, 874, 877, 879, 883–84, 889, 901, 938, 947, 962, 998–99, 1006, 1008, 1016–018, 1057, 1060–062, 1066, 1070, 1073, 1076, 1079, 1084–085, 1089, 1093, 1099, 1104, 1106, 1110, 1122, 1128, 1133
Görlitz, Walter 768, 782, 784, 825, 846, 861, 868, 890, 895, 905, 921, 981–82, 1039, 1047, 1057, 1063, 1068, 1074, 1077, 1081, 1101–102, 1106, 1116–117, 1120, 1131
Gottberg, Curt von 378, 895, 943
Goudima, Robert 782, 891, 1131
Grabmann, Walter 756
Grams, Rold 938, 1131
Grandi, Dino 874, 878
Graziani, Rodolfo 838, 845, 863, 875
Greim, Robert Ritter von 98, 749, 800, 804, 824
Greiner, Helmuth ix–x, 759, 1031, 1131
Grippa, Jacques 875
Groeben, Peter von 896
Gröner, Erich 1098, 1131
Groos, Otto 76, 813
Groza, Peter 801
Guariglia, Raffaele 885
Guderian, Heinz vii–viii, 128, 218, 252, 287, 293, 469–76, 481–91, 498, 586–90, 592, 607, 618, 621–39, 645–48, 650–52, 664–65, 678–80, 683–86, 688, 708, 745, 748, 768–69, 784, 803, 829, 834–35, 892, 982, 994, 998, 1001–002, 1046, 1051, 1056, 1068, 1077, 1079, 1081, 1083, 1087, 1096, 1106, 1108, 1110–111, 1121–122, 1124
Günsche, Otto 132, 137–38, 208, 437, 469, 485, 492, 498, 504, 507, 596, 619, 697, 741

Guss [Soviet reporter] 726
Gustav VI, Adolf [King of Sweden] 906
Gyllenbrok, Colonel 958

H
Haagen, Kurt xv–xvi, xxi–xxiv, 385, 760–61
Hacker, Oskar 782
Hackzell, Antti 502, 1010–011
Hadeler, Wilhelm 821, 1131
Hagedorn, H. 960, 1131
Hagen, Walter 839, 875, 878, 887, 894, 930, 1131
Hahn, Assi 1092, 1131
Halder, Franz xii, xxxiii, 581, 1059
Hale, Oron J. 9, 945
Halm xxix
Hammerstein, General 732
Hanke, Karl 668, 672, 703, 713, 1101–102
Hannebitter, SS Sturmbannführer 927
Hanneken, Hermann von 300, 330, 678, 680, 911–12, 1106
Hannibal [Carthaginian General] 615, 636
Hansen, Walther 970
Hansen–Nootbaar, Jan-Heinrich 469, 751
Harnack, Arvid 876
Harpe, Josef 168, 470, 860
Harteneck, Gustav 901
Hartmann, Alexander von 67, 652, 804
Hassell, Ulrich von 945, 986
Hauck, Friedrich Wilhelm 433, 964
Haupt, Werner 815, 1131
Hauser, Eduard 636, 1087
Hausser, Paul 593, 645–46, 660, 756, 764, 775, 795–96, 832, 834, 846, 936, 976, 993, 1012, 1089–091, 1111, 1131, 1139
Hayn, Friedrich 977–78, 1131
Hébrard J. 808, 847–49, 899, 905, 923, 931, 1016, 1070, 1072–073, 1115, 1131
Heggenrainer, Heinz 176–77, 863

Heiber, Helmut iv–vi, ix, xi, 385, 758, 947
Heidkämper, Otto 756, 917, 927, 932, 934–35, 942–43, 948, 1131
Heilmann, Will 905, 923, 1017, 1131
Heim, Heinrich xv
Heinkel, Ernst 69, 415, 430, 611, 807, 922, 963
Heinz-Heinrich, Wilhelm ix
Heitz, Walther 67, 804
Helling, Hans xi, xv, xviii, xix–xxi
Hellmich, Heinz 853
Henderson, Sir Neville 985
Hennecke, Walter 978
Henschel [German industrialist] 271, 782, 834
Herman, August 747
Hermani, Lieutenant Colonel 596, 605–10, 1068
Herre, Heinz Danko 756, 851–52
Herrgesell, Gerhard xi, xvii, xxi–xxv, 760
Herrmann, Hajo 915
Herzfeld, Hans 1037, 1131
Hess, Rudolf 894
Hetz, Karl 1092
Heusinger, Adolf 23, 25–6, 28, 31–4, 39–40, 43, 45, 106–07, 288, 292, 322–26, 401, 403, 405, 745–46
Hewel, Walther 74, 92–5, 132, 136, 138, 141, 148, 154, 172, 176, 195–96, 198, 204, 207–08, 211, 215–17, 230, 232, 234, 267, 274, 401, 408, 416, 507, 513, 519, 528, 532, 591, 596, 604, 618, 651–53, 655–57, 666–67, 697, 706, 708, 753, 1110
Heydel, Hugo 952, 1131
Heygendorff, Ralph von 858
Hildebrand, Hans H. 755–56, 813, 838, 961, 1027, 1134
Hildebrandt, Friedrich 934
Hillgruber, Andreas 827, 911, 939, 963, 966, 991, 1132
Hillilä, Kaarlo Henrik 1022–024

Himmler, Heinrich xxi, 13, 196, 219–
25, 230–32, 234, 237, 243–44, 543,
547, 550–53, 601–02, 636, 643,
683, 726, 752, 773, 779, 832, 838,
857, 861, 865, 883–84, 887, 894,
896, 909, 922, 936, 941, 951, 973–
74, 993–94, 1001, 1006–008, 1012,
1025, 1035, 1039–040, 1042, 1067,
1077–078, 1080–082, 1084, 1086,
1090–091, 1093–094, 1106, 1114,
1121, 1123
Hindenburg, Paul von xxix, 732
Hinsley, F. H. 833, 890, 919, 1132
Hoare, Sir Samuel 897, 1132
Hoenmanns, Major 930
Hoepner, Erich 803, 989
Hofacker, Caesar von 977, 983
Hofer, Franz 306, 841, 916, 985
Hofer, Walther 1132
Hoffmann, Albert 514, 1016
Hoffmann, Albrecht 627, 1107
Hoffmann, Karl Otto 627, 790, 867–
69, 891, 902, 1132
Hollidt, Karl 10, 43, 103, 374, 767, 776–
78, 785, 796
Holste, Rudolf 722, 727–29, 1127
Hölter, H. 903, 1132
Holzbauer [Junkers test pilot] 1069
Hopkins, Harry 960, 1137
Höppner, Erich 468, 989
Horn, Walter 903, 1132
Hörnlein, Walter 6, 8, 763
Horthy, Nikolaus 448, 830, 882–83, 959,
975, 1013–014, 1132
Hossbach, Friedrich 958, 1083
Hoszlenyi, Vitéz-Josef 1014
Hoth, Hermann 18, 56, 353, 355, 390,
776–77, 779, 784, 938–39, 946
Höttl, Wilhelm 874
Hove, Alkmar 786, 885, 1132
Hube, Hans 214, 215, 307, 374, 730,
798, 882, 942, 956, 988
Hugenberg, Alfred 732, 1127
Hull, Cordell 822, 1020, 1134

Humboldt Dachroeden, Hubertus von
667–71, 728, 747
Hurstfield, J. 920, 1132
Huyssen, Hans 895, 1132

I
Imrédy, Adalbert 959
Inönü, Ismet 802, 847, 918
Inskip, Sir Thomas 1036
Isabella, Princess of Bavaria 863

J
Jäckeln, Friedrich 378, 943
Jacob, Alfred 292, 321, 410, 460, 757,
908, 981, 1057
Jacobsen, Hans-Adolf 930, 1038, 1047–
048, 1132
Jaenecke, Erwin 62–3, 310, 801, 917
Jaschke, Erich 8, 765
Jauer, Georg 757, 1076
Jedlicka, Ludwig 757
Jeismann, Karl-Ernst 1037, 1132
Jeschonnek, Hans 64, 66, 68–70, 202,
205, 219, 228–30, 238–41, 742,
749–50, 806, 877, 1070
Jilemnicky, Peter 992, 1132
Jodl, Alfred xii–xiv, xxvi, xxxiii, 4–7,
11–4, 16, 19–20, 25–6, 29–33, 35,
37, 39, 46, 48–55, 64–8, 72–7, 85–
7, 90–6, 100, 102–03, 105–06, 108–
09, 114, 116–17, 170, 172–79, 181–
82, 190–93, 196, 200–24, 227–35,
238–39, 241, 267–69, 272, 274,
278–82, 311–12, 314–16, 322,
326–30, 346–54, 358, 363–66, 368,
370, 401, 407–12, 416, 432–44,
449–54, 457–62, 469, 480–83, 488,
490–91, 493, 495, 497–505, 507–
08, 517–30, 532, 543, 547, 586–87,
590, 596, 599–604, 607–08, 610,
617–18, 628, 638–43, 645–650,
661–63, 666, 675–77, 679–87, 694,
698, 722, 733, 742, 762, 764, 770–
71, 773, 802, 817, 863, 871, 897,
920, 928, 936–37, 970, 975–76,

979, 987, 1003, 1009, 1013, 1024,
  1062, 1067–068, 1077, 1079, 1089,
  1091, 1110–111
Joffre, Joseph 980
Johannmeyer, Willy 543, 667, 674, 697,
  707, 710, 715, 740
Jones, F. C. 823, 853, 1132
Jonuschat, Hans xvi, xxiii
Joyce, William 859
Joye, Pierre 875
Junge, Wolf 113, 174, 176, 179–81,
  183–85, 187, 235–37, 245–46, 394,
  396, 596, 744, 947
Juppe, General 1009
Jürgens, Hans 789, 1132
Jüttner, Hans 636–37, 1086

K
Kaether, Ernst 718–20
Kaiser, Hans K. 905, 1132
Kalinow, Kyrill D. 782, 1133
Kállay, Nikolaus von 882–83, 911, 959,
  1014, 1133
Källner, Hans 1079
Kaltenbrunner, Ernst 716, 1125
Kaminski, Bronislav 259, 509, 895, 896,
  1013
Kammerer, Albert 517, 788, 1133
Kammerer, Friedrich 1019
Kammhuber, Josef 716, 1126
Kammler, Hans 691, 1113–114, 1116
Kappler, Herbert 887
Kärcher F. W. 757
Karvaš, Emmerich 992
Kasche, Siegfried 502–04, 1009
Kaufmann, Karl 934
Keilig, Wolf von 755, 763–67, 780, 784,
  787, 797–98, 801, 803–04, 814,
  829–31, 833, 836, 857, 860, 864,
  883, 892, 895, 898, 901, 907, 910,
  912, 918, 936, 938, 940, 957, 961,
  964, 972, 975, 980, 987, 989–92,
  994, 998, 1001, 1012, 1029, 1050,
  1060–061, 1064, 1067, 1076, 1083–

084, 1087, 1094–095, 1100, 1105,
  1109–110, 1118, 1121, 1133, 1135
Keitel, Wilhelm xii, xiii, xxvi, 7, 14, 17,
  65, 67, 69, 116–17, 119–32, 135–
  44, 148, 154–59, 163–68, 171, 173,
  177–78, 181–82, 184–85, 194–95,
  197, 200–02, 204–12, 215–23, 229,
  234, 238, 241, 248–51, 253–54,
  260, 282, 284, 294–300, 310, 313,
  315, 319, 321, 328, 346, 387–90,
  392, 395–99, 401, 411, 415, 420,
  422–29, 432, 464, 466–67, 469,
  481–82, 484, 486, 488, 492–94,
  496, 498–99, 503, 507–08, 519,
  528, 530, 543, 545, 548, 550–52,
  554, 586, 596, 599–601, 606, 610,
  614, 617–18, 622, 637, 639–41,
  645–46, 652, 657, 660–62, 664,
  675, 677–78, 680, 684, 692, 717–
  18, 722, 727, 733, 741, 759, 771,
  783, 841, 845, 851, 858, 876, 879,
  885, 910, 946–47, 989, 999, 1061,
  1068, 1078, 1100
Kempf, Werner 167, 860
Kennes, Werner 757
Kerensky, Alexander iii, 158
Kern, Erich 1012, 1133
Kersten, Heinz 697, 741
Kerwin, Bruno von 1084
Kesselring, Albert xii, 46, 48,–50, 63–
  4, 72–3, 75, 135, 137, 214, 219, 223,
  231, 238, 241, 269, 295, 327, 365,
  465, 585, 699–700, 705, 770–71,
  786–88, 802, 806, 809, 838–39,
  841, 844, 863, 865, 878, 881–82,
  884–86, 899, 949, 964–67, 971,
  980–81, 1061, 1109, 1126, 1133
Killinger, Manfred von 1107
Kimura, Masanori 818
King, Ernest 1044
Kinzel, Eberhard 1081
Kirchen [Police Commissioner] 927
Kirchheim, Heinrich 680, 1109
Kirchner, Friedrich 627, 1075
Kirk, George 1021, 1033, 1133

Kiszling, Rudolf 792, 844, 873, 875, 898, 909, 962, 1009, 1133
Kitzinger, Karl 580, 981, 1057–058
Klagges, Dietrich 1100
Klatt, Paul 8, 765
Kleffel, Philip 473, 994
Kleikamp, Helmut 757
Kleinmann, Wilhelm 1064
Kleist, Ewald von 264, 363, 367, 369, 796, 800, 896–97, 990
Kleyser, Colonel 976
Klopfer, Gerhard 946
Kluge, Günter von 80, 84, 115, 157, 160, 165, 171, 199, 225, 252–60, 262– 65, 453, 457, 464, 468, 781, 814, 852, 856, 859–61, 876–77, 895, 975–76, 978–79, 982–84, 987–89
Knatchbull-Hugessen, Sir Hugh 883
Koch, Erich 158–60, 340, 633, 774, 789, 809, 846, 849, 854, 867, 921, 934, 948
Koch, Horst-Adalbert 1000, 1073, 1084, 1133
Koga, Yneichi 801
Koller, Karl 618, 636, 716, 750, 1122, 1133
Kollontai, Alexandra 991
Komarnicki, Titus 853–54, 1133
Koniev, Ivan 418–19, 506, 717, 1065, 1074–075
Konoye, Prince Fumimaro 900
Konrad, Joachim 1102, 1104, 1133
Konrad, Prince of Bavaria 863
Korbonski, Stefan 993, 1133
Kordt, Erich 918, 1133
Korten, Günther 273, 289, 291, 302– 06, 401, 411–13, 415–16, 420, 425, 429–31, 749, 793
Köstring, Ernst 852–53, 858
Krancke, Theodor 12–4, 19, 28, 49–50, 52, 751
Krappe, Günter 1106
Krätschmer, Ernst-Günther 783, 846, 873, 943, 1062, 1066, 1068, 1090, 1105, 1133

Kraus, Herbert 1134, 1137
Krebs, Hans 464–65, 468, 673, 685, 709, 717–19, 722, 727–29, 733–35, 737, 746–47, 982, 1121–122
Kreipe, Werner 469, 473, 477, 484, 488, 489, 499, 749
Krieger, Ludwig xi, xvi–xvii, xxv, 385, 759–60, 973, 1133
Kriegsheim, Herbert 846, 1079, 1133
Krüger, Friedrich-Wilhelm 1078
Krupp, von 870, 1032
Kube, Wilhelm 943
Kublai Khan 1033
Kuby, Erich 1086–087, 1133
Küchler, Georg von 27, 37, 85, 160, 291, 374–75, 377–84, 406, 757, 780, 796, 834, 856, 895, 943–44, 948
Kuckoff, Adam 876
Kuhl, Hermann 1047, 1133
Kühlenthal, Erich 980
Kuhlmann, Arthur 995, 1133
Kurzbach 62
Kurusu, Saburo 821–22
Kvaternik, Slavko 1009
Kyrill [Bulgarian Prince] 991

L
Lahousen, Erwin 815
La Marmora, Alfonso 815
Lakatos, Edler 801
Lammerding, Heinz 1077
Lammers, Hans-Heinrich 160, 165, 652, 1094
Lammineur, Robert 757
Lang, Hubert 427
Lang, Joachim-Friedrich 960
Lang, Viktor 961
Lange, Eitel 1018, 1133
Langemann, Heinz 132
Langer, William L. 822–23, 837, 900, 1133
Langhaeuser, Rudolf 1121
Langheld, Wilhelm 927
Langkeit, Willy 1121
Lanz, Hubert 960

Lascar, Mihai 62, 801, 826
Lasch, Otto 633, 1083–084
Lauchert, Meinrad von 476, 994
Laval, Pierre 78, 830
Lawrence, T. E. 1099
Lazitch, Branko 792, 1009, 1133
Le Fort, Peter von 909
Leber, Annedore 977, 1133
Lee, Asher 902, 1133
Leeb, Emil 802, 919, 1046, 1088, 1133
Leeb, Wilhelm Ritter von 780, 799
Leemans, Joseph 875
Leiner, Karl 884, 887
Lenin, Vladimir 158
Leonardi, Priam 176, 863
Leopold III [King of the Belgians] 880,
    1130
Levetzow, Admiral 732
Lewinski, Erich von, see Manstein, Erich
    von
Ley, Robert 281, 341, 396, 905, 934
Liddel Hart, Sir Basil 984, 1133
Lindemann, Georg 162–63, 383, 857,
    867, 944
Linge, Heinz 225, 741
Lingner, Hans 1044
Linkomies, Edwin 903
Linnarz, Viktor 507, 748
Linnell, Francis 934
Linstow, Hans von 977, 983
Lippisch 922
List, Wilhelm xii
Lloyd George, D. 725, 1126
Lochner, Louis P. xxvii, 814, 879, 882,
    894, 934, 1134
Lodewyckx, A. 820, 1134
Löffler, Walter 699, 1117
Lohmann, Walter 755, 813, 838, 961,
    1026–027, 1134
Löhr, Alexander 132, 139–40, 143, 242,
    244, 685–86, 836–37, 877, 888,
    1020, 1111
Lorenz, Heinz 596, 667, 754
Lorey, Hermann 427, 961

Loringhoven von Bernd, Baron Freytag
    746
Lorkovic, Mladen 1010
Lossberg, Bernhard 1047, 1134
Louise Mountbatten, Lady 906
Lousse, Emile 757
Lübbe, Vollrath 168, 860
Lucht, Walter 997
Luck, Hans-Ulrich von 437, 481, 967
Lucke, Fritz 1001
Ludendorff, Erich 157, 161, 854, 1134
Ludwig von Battenberg, Prince 906
Lungershausen, Carl Hans 757, 836,
    864–65
Lusar, Rudolf 757, 768–69, 790, 807,
    818, 826, 834, 849, 867, 869–70,
    890–91, 893, 900, 905, 916, 923,
    971, 997–98, 1005, 1007, 1032,
    1041, 1046, 1048, 1051–052, 1065,
    1067, 1069, 1071, 1088, 1115,
    1125, 1134
Lütge, Friedrich 924, 1134

M
Maass, Bruno 757
MacArthur, Douglas 818
Macartney, C. A. 879, 1014, 1134
Maček, Vladko 911
Mackensen, Frau 208
Mackensen, Hans Georg von 195–96,
    202, 204, 208, 216, 234, 844, 873–
    74
Maèek, Croatian politician 910
Maerchker 1100, 1134
Mafalda, Princess of Savoy 141, 842–43
Magirus [German industrialist] 783
Magli, Giovanni 865
Maisel, Ernst 748, 787
Maizière, Ulrich de 697, 700–04, 709,
    711–12, 747, 1122
Malyschkin, Vassily 970
Maniu, Julius 991
Mannerheim, Carl Gustav 801, 903,
    1003, 1011, 1023, 1025, 1134
Mansergh 811

Manstein, Erich von 9, 18, 22, 30, 33, 42–3, 57–8, 100, 107–08, 110, 115, 171, 198, 225, 260–61, 286, 335, 338, 340–42, 346, 348, 352, 355, 357, 361, 363, 368, 371, 374, 403, 679, 682, 757, 766, 775–77, 779–80, 784–85, 795–98, 800–01, 813, 827, 831–32, 861, 876, 877, 882, 887, 894–97, 901, 926–27, 931–33, 936–39, 942–43, 945, 947–48, 955, 981, 988, 990, 1000, 1038, 1107, 1134

Manteuffel, Hasso von 573, 1052–053

Marcks, Werner 249, 892

Maria, Princess of Bavaria 863

Marie José, Princess of Savoy 880

Marshall, George C. 924

Martienssen, Anthony 1113, 1134

Martin, Carl E. 779, 1134

Marx, Colonel, see Marcks, Werner

Massow, General 177–78

Matl, Josef 792, 889, 898, 910, 929, 1134

Matsuoka, Yosuke Yogu 274, 822–23, 900

Mattenklott, General 958

Mattern, Ernst 1080

Matteotti, Giacomo 829

McDowell, Colonel 1009

McNeill, William Hardy 1035, 1063, 1134

Meandrov, Mikhail 1085

Meier-Welcker, Hans 757

Meister, Jürg 902, 914, 972, 995–96, 1003, 1015, 1134

Meister, Rudolf 750, 972

Mellini, Ponce de Leon 875, 1134

Mellwig, Karl 994

Mende, Gerhard von 774, 856

Menemencioglu 918

Messe, Giovanni 762, 1134

Messerschmitt, Willy 716, 922, 1126

Metzsch, Friedrich-August 1002, 1067, 1094, 1134

Meyer, Adolf 1037, 1047, 1134

Meyer-Detring, Wilhelm 543, 743

Michael I [King of Romania] 1037

Michaux, Theo 812, 824, 1134

Mieth, Friedrich 469, 990–91

Mihailović Draza 129, 245, 504, 791–92, 844, 889, 898, 928–29, 1009, 1133

Miklós, Vitez 1014

Mikus, Joseph A. 992, 1135

Milch, Erhard 99, 757, 824–25

Model, Walter 247, 255, 259, 262, 401, 410, 415, 436, 466, 468, 575, 597, 643, 681, 800, 814, 861, 894–95, 947–48, 976, 983, 986, 988, 990, 1053, 1091, 1109

Moellhausen, Eitel Friedrich 886, 888, 1135

Mohnke, Wilhelm 727, 731–32, 734, 737–38

Mölders, Werner 1018, 1102

Molotov, Vyacheslav 721, 723–24, 903

Moltke, Helmuth von xxix, xxxi, 537, 655, 818, 820, 1037

Montgomery, Bernard Law 3, 18, 674, 785, 791, 863, 975, 1004, 1007, 1044, 1116 117, 1135

Mordal, Jacques 788, 1135

Morell, Theodor xxxiii, 982

Morgagni, Giulio 885

Morison, Samuel Eliot 803, 819, 890, 913, 1135

Moritz 927

Moseley, Philip E. 1092, 1135

Moseley, Ray 842

Mueller-Hillebrand, Burkhart 799, 938, 1135

Müller, Dietrich von xxii, 843, 974, 1076

Müller, Friedrich Wilhelm 1101

Müller, Hans 1020

Müller, Heinrich 330, 930

Müller, Josef 974

Muraviev, Konstantin 1002

Muñoz-Grandes, Augustin 801, 897

Musmanno, Michael A. 1049, 1135

Mussert, Anton 941

Mussolini, Benito 46, 50, 76, 103–05, 119, 135–36, 138, 140–42, 147, 153–54, 195–96, 201–04, 206, 213, 221–22, 227, 241, 252–53, 255, 644, 761, 770, 779, 781, 785, 802, 815, 827–30, 835–36, 838–45, 847, 850–51, 861, 863–64, 874–75, 878, 882, 885–86, 888, 893–94, 902–03, 920, 930, 1037, 1090, 1106, 1129, 1135–136
Mussolini, Edda, *see* Ciano, Edda

N
Nadolny, Rudolf 986
Napoleon iii, 459
Natzmer, Oldwig von 636, 1087
Navarini, Enea 144, 845
Nebel, Rudolf 826
Nedic Milan 328, 792, 889, 929
Nefertiti [wife of Egyptian Pharaoh] 962
Nehring, Walther 627, 634, 1074, 1076–079
Nerianin, Colonel 1085
Neubacher, Hermann 502–04, 1011–012, 1135
Neurath, Constantin Alexander von 92, 132–37, 820, 838–39, 874
Nicholas II [Emperor of Russia] iii
Nicolai, Walter 393, 947
Niedermayer, Oskar Ritter von 163–64, 857–58, 970
Nikita, *see* Nikolaus, King of Montenegro
Nikolai Nikolievitch, Grand Prince of Yugoslavia 844
Nikolaus [King of Montenegro] 142, 844
Nomura, Kichisaburo 822
Nowack, Wilhelm 820, 1135
Nycop, Carl-Adam 925, 957, 1135

O
Oberländer, Theodor 775
Obstfelder, Hans von 543, 1109
Oehmichen, Hermann 1056

Oertzen, F. W. von 1108, 1135
Olbricht, Friedrich 936, 989
Oncken, Hermann 1037, 1135
Oppenhoff, Franz 1086
Orlando, Vittorio Emanuele 874
Osborne, Francis 839
Oshima, Hirosho 821
Oster, Hans 882, 974
Oven, Wilfried 934, 1135

P
Paetel, Karl O. 1092, 1135
Paillole, Paul 833
Palmer, Captain 761
Pancke, Günter 911, 1010
Pannwitz, Helmuth von 650, 775, 1007, 1094–095, 1112
Papen, Franz 63, 802, 847, 934, 1135
Parseval, Joseph von 648, 1091
Pattee, R. 815, 1135
Patton, General 533, 697, 1043, 1117
Paul, Prince Regent of Yugoslavia 879
Paulus, Friedrich xii, 56, 59–60, 62, 65–6, 785, 797–801, 803, 827, 1092–093
Pavelic, Ante 830, 880, 898, 910, 1009–010
Pavolini, Alessandro 875, 895
Pearn, B. R. 1132
Pechel, Rudolf 836, 983, 1135
Peiper, Joachim 597, 1066
Peltz, Dietrich 185, 716, 870
Pemsel, Max-Josef 757
Perón, Juan Domingo 1087
Peschel, Kurt xi, xv–xvii, xxi–xxii, xxiv–xxv, 759–61
Petacci family 874
Pétain, Philippe 528, 1031
Peter I [King of Serbia] 844
Peter II, King of Serbia 791, 879, 889, 928–29
Petersdorf, Horst von 679, 680, 682, 757, 1108, 1110
Petrov, Ivan 1075
Pfeffer, Max 678–80, 682, 1106

Pfeffer, Fritz von Salomon 1108
Pfeffer, Franz von Salomon 1108
Pfeffer-Wildenbruch, Karl 1068, 1106
Pfeiffer, Hellmuth 287, 298, 375
Pfeiffer, Georg 910
Pfeiffer, Hans 741
Philip, Prince of Hesse 141, 154, 174,
    177, 204, 217, 842–43, 850, 882
Phleps, Artur 504, 846, 1012
Picker, Henry 839, 894, 902, 935, 1135
Pickert, Wolfgang 902, 935, 1135
Pilsudski, Jozef 853
Pini, Giorgio 828, 1135
Plauen, O. E. 1069
Playfair, I. S. O. 811, 1135
Pleiger, Paul 275, 858, 901
Pöhner, Ernst 1107
Pokrowsky, J. W. 773
Poll, Bernhard 1086, 1135
Popov, General 871
Porsche, Ferdinand 126, 782, 834
Postan, M. M. 920, 1135
Prange, Gordon W. 822
Praun, Albert 757, 1061
Pressler, Gustav 98, 824
Preuss, Maximilian 896
Prützmann, Hans 943, 1009
Puttkamer, Karl-Jesko von 61–2, 87,
    315, 317, 401, 432, 437, 591, 596,
    618, 654, 667, 672–74, 680, 740,
    800–01, 1092, 1135

Q
Quint, Herbert A. 981–82, 1047, 1101,
    1131
Quisling, Vidkun 649, 652, 830, 1093–
    094

R
Rackham, Horace R. 945
Raeder, Erich xxxiii, 751
Rahtgens, Karl Ernst 977, 983, 988
Rainer, Gauleiter 880
Ramcke, Bernhard 46, 488, 786–87

Rangell [Finnish Minister] 903
Rathenau, Walther 1107
Rattenhuber, Hans 843
Reichenau, Walter von 827, 834
Reinberger, Hellmuth 930
Reinecke, Hermann 386–99, 945–47
Reinefarth, Heinz 678, 726, 896, 1105–
    006
Reinhardt, Hans 473, 633, 916–17, 927,
    1083
Reitlinger, Gerald 1086, 1114, 1136
Reitsch, Hanna 1017, 1069, 1136
Relecom, Xavier 875
Remer, Otto Ernst 659, 978, 1088, 1100
Remlinger, Heinrich 1081
Rendulic, Lothar 503, 504, 636, 792,
    990, 1003–004, 1011–012, 1024,
    1026–027, 1066, 1083, 1087, 1136
Resega, Aldo 931
Retzlaw, Reinhardt 927
Reuter, von 772
Reynitz, Ewald xi, xvi, 760, 973
Rhode, Gotthold 1042, 1136
Ribbentrop, Joachim von xiv, 96, 466,
    741, 753, 838, 840–41, 879, 882,
    885, 979, 985, 1008, 1025, 1136
Richards, Denis 1136
Richthofen, Wolfram von 110, 114, 214,
    425, 429, 800, 803, 829
Rieckhoff, H. J. 806, 1136
Rieker, Karlheinrich 996, 1136
Rintelen, Enno von 135, 140, 762, 771,
    757, 779, 802, 829, 836, 838–40,
    842–43, 861–63, 874–75, 878,
    881–82, 885, 888, 920, 985, 1136
Ritter, Gerhard 896, 961, 974–75, 986,
    1136–037, 1109
Ritz, Hans 927, 929
Roatta, Mario 132, 134–37, 213, 838,
    862, 881
Röchling, Hermann 808
Rodenburg, Carl 757
Roeder, Manfred 876, 1136
Roehrbein, Erich 828, 1136

Rohden, Herhurdt von 794
Röhm, Ernst xxviii, 783
Rohden, Herhudt von 794, 1131
Rohwer, Jürgen 756, 819, 822, 1015, 1136
Rokossovsky, Konstantin 767, 798, 871,
    993, 1065
Rommel, Erwin xix, 3–4, 46–8, 56, 63,
    71–2, 74, 86, 99, 132, 136–38, 143–
    44, 153, 173–74, 191, 202, 207–08,
    218, 230–31, 234, 242–45, 296,
    321, 465–66, 770–71, 785–88, 809,
    815, 838–39, 841, 844–45, 854,
    863, 873, 877–79, 883–86, 919,
    948, 965, 967, 969–71, 976–77,
    982, 984–86, 988, 1136
Rönnefarth, Helmuth K. G. 1012, 1136
Roosevelt, Franklin D. 245, 317–18,
    415, 424, 726, 791, 822, 918, 923–
    24, 960, 1020, 1034, 1043–044,
    1062, 1126, 1137
Rosenberg, Alfred xxvii, 20, 155–56,
    158–59, 161, 165, 389, 393, 529,
    852, 854, 946, 962, 1110
Rost, Hans-Günther (Czeppan) von
    700, 1118
Rothbauer, A. M. 1135
Rothfeder, Herbert P. 946–47
Rudel, Hans-Ulrich 636, 1086–087,
    1136
Ruder, Willy 386, 946
Ruge, Friedrich 134, 762, 816–17, 819,
    822, 838, 888, 890, 910, 916, 926,
    1015–026, 1097–098, 1113, 1136
Rumohr, Joachim 1080
Rumpf, Hans 793, 808–09, 813, 868,
    914, 1136
Rundstedt, Gerd von viii, 221–22, 453,
    467, 543–50, 552, 568, 803, 850,
    863, 884, 965, 967, 969–70, 976,
    982, 986, 988, 1007, 1039, 1066,
    1109, 1117, 1129
Ruoff, Joachim, 757
Ruppert, Dr. 1128
Ryti, Risto 902–03

S
Sack, Carl 974
Saed, Mohammed 1033
Sager [German industrialist] 951
Salomon, Ernst von 1108–109, 1136
Saracoglu, Sükrü 802
Sauckel, Fritz 104, 136, 259, 341, 770,
    827, 934
Saucken, Dietrich von 627, 628, 651,
    757, 1074, 1076–077
Saur, Karl Otto 248, 320–21, 575, 577–
    78, 611, 617, 652, 693, 699, 716,
    757, 892
Sava, George 792, 1136
Schaub, Julius 485, 1000
Scheele, Hans-Karl von 115, 831
Scheidt, Wilhelm 507, 745, 761
Scheliha, Rudolf von 876
Schell, Adolf von 937
Schellong, Conrad 865, 936, 941, 1136
Scherer, Theodor 784
Scherff, Walter iv, xix–xx, xxii, 132, 155,
    223–24, 252, 332, 348, 375, 387,
    398, 401, 432, 437, 543, 596, 618,
    744, 760, 837, 945–46
Scheuerlen, Heinz 1020
Schieder, Theodor von 1020, 1138
Schirmer, Friedrich 1032, 1136
Schlabrendorff, Fabian 896, 988–89,
    1137
Schleicher, Kurt von 329, 732, 929, 1127
Schlieben, Karl Wilhelm von 978
Schlicffcn, Alfred von xxix, 655
Schmidt, Arthur 9, 59, 62, 65–6, 525,
    785, 797
Schmidt, Hans 1029
Schmidt, Rudolf 895
Schmidt-Pauli, Edgar 1108, 1137
Schmidt-Richberg, Erich 898, 1002,
    1004, 1020, 1067, 1094, 1112, 1137
Schmundt, Rudolf xxix, 27, 76, 132, 138,
    155, 162–63, 165, 346, 358, 375,
    386–88, 390–92, 395–99, 401, 437,
    438, 608, 739, 851, 946, 976, 1099

Schneider, Erich 757, 768, 799, 807, 818, 867, 893, 905, 961, 1005, 1046, 1137
Schneider, Karl 114, 831
Schörner, Ferdinand 374, 399, 474, 530, 626, 628–29, 636, 647, 655, 727, 734–35, 800, 942, 947, 990, 1075, 1077, 1087, 1127
Schramm, Percy Ernst 765, 1137
Schramm, Wilhelm Ritter von 921, 975, 977, 983–84, 987, 990, 1137
Schröter, Heinz 763, 767, 777, 785, 794, 797–801, 804, 827, 1137
Schroth, Walter 482, 998
Schulenburg, Friedrich Werner von 326, 466, 928, 986
Schulte 24, 26, 30, 32, 40–1, 779
Schulz, Friedrich 828, 1075
Schulze, Richard 507, 740
Schulze-Boysen, Harro 876
Schuschnigg, Kurt 875
Schuster, Oskar 619, 620, 750
Schwartzkopf [German, industrialist] 981
Schweitzer, Colonel 763
Schwendemann, Karl 876, 1137
Schwerin, Gerhard von 940
Schwerin von Krosigk, Lutz Graf xviii–xix, xxi–xxii, 757, 924, 1137
Seeckt, von 635
Seemen, Gerhard von 763–66, 769, 781, 783–84, 786, 798, 801, 803, 824, 829, 831, 837, 860, 870, 883, 910, 918, 940, 957, 967, 987, 1029, 1050, 1062, 1064, 1073, 1076, 1081, 1084, 1087, 1090, 1095, 1105–106, 1109, 1121, 1126, 1137
Senger-Etterlin, Ferdinand 757, 769, 899, 998, 1012, 1036, 1040–041, 1051–052, 1055–056, 1060, 1075, 1097, 1137
Senger-Etterlin, Fridolin von 757
Seraphim, Hans-Günther 1031, 1137
Seton-Watson, Hugh 991–92, 1002, 1137
Seuss, Richard 996

Seydlitz-Kurzbach, Walter von 59–60, 62, 65–6, 396–97, 719, 797–98, 803, 947, 1092, 1126
Seyss-Inquart, Artur 875
Sherwood, Robert E. 918, 923, 925, 960, 1044, 1137
Shulman, Milton 1044, 1137
Siebert, Ludwig 908
Siegler, Fritz 764, 771, 783–84, 786–87, 793–94, 802, 804, 811, 813–14, 824–27, 829, 837–38, 857, 860, 862, 864, 873, 879, 884–85, 895, 897, 907, 917, 938, 943, 969, 976, 986, 988–91, 994, 997–98, 1006, 1012, 1018, 1020, 1057, 1073, 1075–076, 1087, 1089, 1090–091, 1109–112, 1124, 1126, 1137
Siegling, Hans 509, 1013
Simon, Max 927
Simonds, G. 1029
Simovic, Dusan 879
Skoropadsky, Paul 854
Skorzeny, Otto 678, 839, 885, 887, 894, 1105–106, 1137
Smend, Günther 746, 983
Sonnleithner, Franz von 469, 492, 501–04, 507, 519, 753, 757, 981, 1012, 1019
Speer, Albert viii, x, xiv, xxi, 11, 89, 283, 319, 437, 442, 461, 615–17, 709, 716, 753, 768, 796, 879, 922, 951, 963, 981, 999, 1018, 1040, 1046, 1049, 1053, 1055–056, 1073, 1110, 1119
Speidel, Hans 838, 967, 969, 976–78, 982, 984–86, 1128, 1137
Sperrle, Hugo 824
Stacey, C. P. 926, 1137
Staemmler, K. D. 1102
Stalin, Joseph iii, v–vi, ix, 20, 94, 96, 188, 245, 501, 587, 720, 723, 725, 730, 735, 771, 871, 956, 986, 1020–021, 1034, 1043
Starace, Achille 875

Stauffenberg, Schenk von 977, 982, 986
Stavisky, Alexandre 772–73
Steflea, Ilia 291, 310, 907
Stegemann, Hermann 1047, 1137
Stegmann 1075
Steiner, Felix 718–19, 729, 734, 1020, 1081, 1126, 1137
Stettinius Jr., Edward R. 1020, 1044, 1137
Steyrer, Ludwig 782–83, 1067
Stieff, Helmuth 249, 468, 892, 989
Stollberg, Friedrich 248, 892
Strachwitz von Gross-Zauche Hyacinth 918
Strachwitz, Mauritz, Baron 917
Strecker, Karl 65, 797, 803
Ströhle, Albert 876, 1137
Stucken, Rudolf 1134
Student, Kurt 228, 230, 234, 238–39, 241, 495, 643–46, 676, 884–85, 929, 1005, 1089, 1090
Stülpnagel, Carl Heinrich von 450, 975, 977, 979, 982–84, 987
Stülpnagel, Otto von 975
Stumpff, Hans-Jürgen 516, 757, 1018
Sun Yat-sen 853
Sündermann, Helmut 697, 754
Suster, Roberto 885
Sveriew, Colonel 1085
Szàlasi, Franz 1013
Szombathelyi, Ferenc 143, 844
Sztójay, Döme 959

T
Tangermann, Albrecht 983
Tanner, Väinö 958, 1034
Tansill, Charles Callan 822, 1137
Teodorini, Cornello 801
Terboven, Josef 914, 1093
Teske, Hermann 801, 1137
Thierack, Otto 989
Thomale, Wolfgang 11, 224, 226, 248–51, 469, 482–90, 569–78, 581–83, 588, 609, 699, 714–15, 748, 757, 768, 1049, 1056

Thomsen, Hans 651, 757, 1095
Thorwald, Jügen 775, 852–53, 856–58, 896, 970, 1007, 1013, 1074, 1076, 1077, 1081, 1084–085, 1095, 1102, 1137
Thöt, Karl xv–xvi, 760
Thutmosis [Egyptian sculptor] 962
Tiemann, Otto 7, 9, 764
Tillessen, Heinrich 828
Timm, Artur 1007, 1095
Tippelskirch, Kurt von 758, 762, 767, 774, 777, 781, 785, 796, 804, 813, 819, 861, 882, 886, 888, 895, 899, 901–02, 907, 917–18, 926, 933–35, 938–39, 948–49, 955–58, 971, 985–86, 992–94, 997, 1004–005, 1008, 1029, 1031, 1039, 1044, 1047–048, 1063, 1065, 1068–069, 1075, 1077, 1081–083, 1089, 1096–097, 1099, 1102–104, 1108, 1112, 1117–120, 1122–123, 1137
Tippelskirch, Werner von 757, 851
Tiso, Josef 830
Tito (Josip Broz) vii, 245, 269, 503, 520, 830, 889, 910, 928–29, 962, 1009, 1011, 1129, 1139
Todt, Fritz 799, 892, 951, 963
Togo, Shigenori 821, 900, 1137
Tolsdorff, Theodor 1099
Toppe, Alfred 757
Toussaint, Rudolf 839, 881
Toynbee, Arnold 811, 886, 900, 941, 991–93, 1002–003, 1010, 1132, 1136
Toynbee Veronica M. 811, 886, 900, 1010, 1132, 1136
Tresckow, Henning von 896, 982–83, 989
Trevor-Roper, Hugh R. 933, 945, 947, 982, 1031, 1049, 1138
Trizzino, Antonino 810, 863, 888, 1138
Troost, Paul Ludwig 754
Trott, von 1123
Truchin, Fedor 1085
Truman, Harry S. 1126

Tschücke, Colonel 9
Tuboeuf, Anton von 1099
Tukhachevsky, Mikhail 397, 947
Twiehaus, Hans 1084
Tzschöckell, Paul 9, 766

U
Ueberschar, Gerd R. x
Umberto of Savoy, Prince of Piedmont 838, 880
Ungermann, Siegfried 1095
Uthmann, Bruno von 651, 757, 1095

V
Vansittart, Rober Gilbert 466, 986, 1093, 1138
Vanwelkenhuyzen, Jan 930, 1138
Vatutin, Nikolai 871, 932, 956
Vecchiarelli, Carlo 888
Veesemeyer, Edmund 959
Vercellino, Mario 813
Verres, Lajos Dàlnoki 1014
Victor Emmanuel III [King of Italy] 843–44, 887
Vietinghoff, Heinrich von 1126
Vlasov, Andrei ix, 155, 161–65, 635, 852, 857–59, 896, 950, 1013, 1085
Vogel, Winfri x
Vokic, Ante 1010
Vormann, Nikolaus 955, 1138
Voss, Hans-Erich 152–53, 267, 277–78, 285, 301, 305, 312–16, 319, 322, 330, 437, 439, 441, 469, 478, 492, 507, 513, 524, 596, 618, 727, 729–30, 733, 735, 752

W
Wagenführ, Horst 828, 1138
Wagner, Adolf 108, 467, 469, 822, 908, 973, 988, 1042, 1095, 1110
Wagner, Constantin 1007
Wagner, Eduard 829
Wagner, Fritz 1138
Wagner, Gerhard 751
Wagner, Herbert 1083

Wagner, Wolfgang 1136
Waite, Robert G. L. 1108, 1138
Waizenegger, Heinz xviii, 205, 275, 285, 432, 435, 437, 444, 469, 492–95, 507, 591, 593–96, 618, 742–43, 1003
Walker, David 1095–096
Wallenstein, Albrecht von 589, 1063
Walter, Helmut 915–16, 922
Walter, Paul 858
Wang Ching-wei 853
Wangenheim, Hubert von 1097
Warlimont, Walter xii, 38, 119–22, 123, 125, 127, 130–32, 134–41, 144, 146–49, 154, 176, 178–79, 181–83, 188, 192, 242–45, 422–28, 444, 458, 469, 743, 755–56, 845, 851, 859, 978–79, 985
Wartenberg, Bodo von 970
Watter, Oscar 1108
Wecke, Walter 789
Wcgc, General 173
Wegener, Martin 1084
Weichs, Maximilian von 800, 837, 873, 879, 1020
Weidermann, Alfred 828, 1138
Weidling, Helmuth 717, 720, 726–27, 736–38
Weinberg, Gerhard L. i, ix, 385–86, 947
Weinrich, Karl 934
Weis, Karl 951
Weise, Hubert 790
Weisenborn, Günther , 876, 1138
Weiss, Rudolf 596, 598, 608, 704, 748, 958
Weiss, Walter 1118
Weissenberger, Theodor 922
Weitershausen von 902, 935, 1138
Weizsäcker, Ernst 821, 882, 1031, 1138
Wenck, Walter 469, 476, 472, 499, 507–13, 607, 610, 636, 708, 717–18, 720, 722, 727–30, 733, 735, 746–47, 757, 1091, 1121
Werthern, Georg-Thilo von 499, 1008
West, Rebecca 859, 1138

Westphal, Siegfried 464, 467, 469, 490,
    543, 549–51, 573–74, 673, 757,
    771, 838–39, 845, 862, 864, 875,
    878, 881, 885–86, 888, 901, 985,
    988, 1035, 1043, 1045, 1103, 1138
Wever, Walter 806
Weygand, Maxime 980
Wheeler-Bennett, John W.,   836, 977,
    983, 986–88, 1138
Wiele, Jef van de 941
Wiener, Fritz 768–69, 787, 834, 877,
    893, 1138
Wilhelm II [Kaiser] 772, 816, 842, 1113,
    1130
Willkie, Wendell 424, 959, 960, 959
Wilmot, Chester 768, 791, 842, 895, 913,
    918, 921, 925–26, 953–54, 959,
    965, 967, 969, 971, 975–78, 983–
    84, 1001, 1005–006, 1008, 1017,
    1029–030, 1039, 1043–045, 1048,
    1053–054, 1092, 1103–104, 1109,
    1116–117, 1138
Wilson, Henry Maitland 210, 880, 925
Winkler, Hermann 469, 990
Winter, August 596, 618, 622, 638, 640,
    743, 757
Winzer, Otto 1092, 1139
Wiskemann, Elizabeth 829, 841, 851,
    887, 1139
Witzell, Karl 615, 1073
Witzig, Rudolf 12, 769
Woerner [German industrialist] 951
Wöhler, Otto 41, 586–87, 590, 623, 758,
    784, 990, 1068
Wolff, Karl 752, 874
Woodhouse, C. M. 1043, 1139
Wulf [deputy police chief of Khar'kov]
    927
Wuori, Eero Aarne 1034
Wuorinen, John H. 903, 1139

Y
Yamamoto, Isoroku 801, 822
Yourichitch, Evgueniyé 792, 847, 1139

Z
Zander, Wilhelm 619, 697, 700, 706–
    07, 754
Zantke, Siegfried 958, 1139
Zanussi, Giacomo 881
Zehender, August 1080
Zeitzler, Kurt xxvi–xxvii, 7–10, 18–45,
    57–63, 78–82, 84–6, 89, 100–04,
    106–17, 121, 128, 131, 144–46,
    148, 154–55, 158, 160–73, 176–77,
    198–201, 203, 225–27, 233–34,
    240, 252–67, 276–78, 280, 285–93,
    296, 307, 313–16, 318, 323, 338,
    349–63, 365–68, 372–84, 391,
    401–07, 417–22, 424, 745, 758,
    764, 778, 795, 814, 825, 829, 835,
    851–52, 860, 881, 895, 897, 916,
    923, 931, 933, 935–37, 944, 946,
    1000
Zeller, Eberhard 896, 936, 974–75, 977,
    983–84, 986, 989, 1139
Zhukov, Georgi 418, 420, 441, 618, 674,
    717, 852, 956, 1065, 1081
Zieb, Paul Willy 994–95
Ziemssen, Dietrich 1066, 1139
Zilliacus, K. 792, 1020, 1139
Zimmermann, Bodo 596–600, 602,
    1065
Zitzewitz, Coelestin von 61, 800
Zoller, Albert 982, 1139
Zvetkovic [Yugoslavian politician] 879,
    929

ACKNOWLEDGEMENTS

The publisher wishes to extend a special thanks to David Kahn for his initial suggestion that Enigma Books publish this English-language edition and to Dr. Gerhard L. Weinberg for his expert advice and introduction. We also wish to thank Mr. Jean-Paul Dop for his help in the field of aeronautics history and attorney Walker Mang for his expertise in German military terminology. The arduous task of translating and editing this document belongs to a Berlin team directed by Roland Winter, with Krista Smith and Mary Beth Friedrich. The publisher wishes to thank them all. In New York we thank Jay Wynshaw, Asya Kunik and Todd Bludeau for their excellent work on the final English text.